PUBLIC ADMINISTRATION

Concepts and Cases

SEVENTH EDITION

Richard J. Stillman II
University of Colorado

Houghton Mifflin Company   Boston   New York

For my wife, Kathleen
my daughter, Shannon Marie
my son, Richard J. III

Editor in Chief: Jean L. Woy
Sponsoring Editor: Melissa Mashburn
Editorial Associate: Vikram Mukhija
Project Editor: Tracy Patruno
Assistant Manufacturing Coordinator: Andrea Wagner
Senior Marketing Manager: Sandra McGuire

Cover design: Walter Kopec
Cover image: Bill Horsman/Stock, Boston

Photos on pages 48, 220 and 442: Bill Horsman/Stock, Boston

Printed in the U.S.A.

Library of Congress Catalog Card Number: 99-71937

ISBN: 0-395-90606-7

23456789—CRS—03 02 01 00

Contents

Topic Correlation Chart　　*ix*

Preface　　*xix*

1　The Search for the Scope and Purpose of Public Administration　　*1*

Reading 1.1: Introduction　　*1*
The Study of Administration　　*6*
　　Woodrow Wilson

Reading 1.2: Introduction　　*16*
The Study of Public Administration in the United States　　*17*
　　Richard J. Stillman

Case Study 1: Introduction　　*30*
The Blast in Centralia No. 5: A Mine Disaster No One Stopped　　*31*
　　John Bartlow Martin

PART ONE

The Pattern of Public Administration in America: Its Environment, Structure, and People　　*48*

2　The Formal Structure: The Concept of Bureaucracy　　*50*

Reading 2: Introduction　　*50*
Bureaucracy　　*54*
　　Max Weber

Case Study 2: Introduction　　*63*
How Kristin Died　　*64*
　　George Lardner, Jr.

3　The General Environment: The Concept of Ecology　　*80*

Reading 3: Introduction　　*80*
The Ecology of Public Administration　　*82*
　　John M. Gaus

Case Study 3: Introduction   *87*

Dumping $2.6 Million on Bakersfield (Or How *Not* to Build a Migratory Farm
Workers' Clinic)   *88*
    Michael Aron

A Retrospective: Weedpatch Revisited   *96*
    B. J. Moore

**4   The Political Environment: The Concept of Administrative
Power**   *101*

Reading 4: Introduction   *101*

Power and Administration   *103*
    Norton E. Long

Case Study 4: Introduction   *109*

The Last Flight of the Space Shuttle *Challenger*   *110*
    Michael T. Charles

**5   Intergovernmental Relations (IGR): The Concept of IGR as
Interdependence, Complexity, and Bargaining**   *125*

Reading 5: Introduction   *125*

American Intergovernmental Relations: An Overview   *127*
    Laurence J. O'Toole, Jr.

Case Study 5: Introduction   *146*

Wichita Confronts Contamination   *147*
    Susan Rosegrant

**6   Internal Dynamics: The Concept of the
Informal Group**   *156*

Reading 6: Introduction   *156*

Hawthorne and the Western Electric Company   *160*
    Elton Mayo

Case Study 6: Introduction   *169*

Uniforms in the Closet   *170*
    Jennifer Egan

**7   Key Decision Makers Inside Public Administration: The
Concept of Competing Bureaucratic Subsystems**   *182*

Reading 7: Introduction   *182*

Inside Public Bureaucracy   *183*
    Richard J. Stillman II

Case Study 7: Introduction   *207*

The Decision to Bomb the Serbs   *208*
    Elaine Sciolino and Ethan Bronner

PART TWO

The Multiple Functions of Public Administrators: Their Major Activities, Responsibilities, and Roles   *220*

8 Decision Making: The Concept of Incremental Choice   *222*

Reading 8: Introduction   *222*

The Science of "Muddling Through"   *225*
    Charles E. Lindblom

Case Study 8: Introduction   *236*

The MOVE Disaster   *238*
    Jack H. Nagel

9 Administrative Communication: The Concept of its Professional Centrality   *257*

Reading 9: Introduction   *257*

Administrative Communication (Or How to Make All the Rest Work): The Concept of its Professional Centrality   *260*
    James L. Garnett

Case Study 9: Introduction   *277*

Waco   *279*
    William J. Vizzard

10 Executive Management: The Concept of Effective Public Organizations   *296*

Reading 10: Introduction   *296*

Galloping Elephants: Developing Elements of a Theory of Effective Government Organizations   *299*
    Hal G. Rainey and Paula Steinbauer

Case Study 10: Introduction   *321*

The Lessons of ValuJet 592   *322*
    William Langewiesche

11 Public Personnel Motivation: The Concept of the Public Service Culture *340*

Reading 11: Introduction   *340*

The Public Service Culture   *342*
   Lois Recascino Wise

Case Study 11: Introduction   *353*

Admiral Boorda's War   *354*
   Peter J. Boyer

12 Public Budgeting: The Concept of Budgeting as Political Choice *374*

Reading 12: Introduction   *374*

The Politics of Public Budgets   *376*
   Irene S. Rubin

Case Study 12: Introduction   *392*

County Prison Overtime   *393*
   Tom Mills

13 Implementation: The Concept of An Ambiguity-Conflict Model *403*

Reading 13: Introduction   *403*

Synthesizing the Implementation Literature: The Ambiguity-Conflict Model of Policy Implementation   *407*
   Richard E. Matland

Case Study 13: Introduction   *426*

The Political Paradox of Rationing: The Case of the Oregon Health Plan   *427*
   Lawrence R. Jacobs, Theodore Marmor, and Jonathan Oberlander

PART THREE:

Enduring and Unresolved Relationships: Central Value Questions, Issues, and Dilemmas of Contemporary Public Administration *442*

14 The Relationship Between Politics and Administration: The Concept of Issue Networks *444*

Reading 14: Introduction   *444*

Issue Networks and the Executive Establishment   *447*
   Hugh Heclo

Case Study 14: Introduction   *456*

Reinventing School Lunch: Transforming a Food Policy into a
Nutrition Policy   *457*
   Laura S. Sims

15 **The Relationship Between Bureaucracy and the
Public Interest: The Concept of Public Sector
Deregulation**   *473*

Reading 15: Introduction   *473*

Bureaucracy and the Public Interest   *476*
   James Q. Wilson

Case Study 15: Introduction   *485*

But No Cigar: How a Rescue Mission Failed, Just Barely,
In Orange County   *486*
   Laura Jereski

Epilogue   *490*
   Alan Saltzstein

16 **The Relationship Between Ethics and Public
Administration: The Concept of Competing Ethical
Obligations**   *498*

Reading 16: Introduction   *498*

Public Administration and Ethics: A Prologue to a Preface   *501*
   Dwight Waldo

Case Study 16: Introduction   *512*

Madonna's *Sex*   *513*
   Douglas F. Morgan

Index   *526*

Topic Correlation Chart

Budget and Finance

Reading 1.2: The Study of Public Administration in the United States   *17*

Case Study 3: Dumping $2.6 Million on Bakersfield (Or How *Not* to Build a Migratory Farm Workers' Clinic)   *88*

Case Study 4: The Last Flight of Space Shuttle *Challenger*   *110*

Reading 5: American Intergovernmental Relations: An Overview   *127*

Case Study 5: Wichita Confronts Contamination   *147*

Reading 12: The Politics of Public Budgets   *376*

Case Study 12: County Prison Overtime   *393*

Case Study 13: The Political Paradox of Rationing: The Case of the Oregon Health Plan   *427*

Reading 14: Issue Networks and the Executive Establishment   *447*

Case Study 14: Reinventing School Lunch: Transforming a Food Policy into a Nutrition Policy   *457*

Reading 15: Bureaucracy and the Public Interest   *476*

Case Study 15: But No Cigar: How a Rescue Mission Failed, Just Barely, in Orange County   *486*

Bureaucracy

Reading 1.1: The Study of Administration   *6*

Reading 1.2: The Study of Public Administration in the United States   *17*

Case Study 1: The Blast in Centralia No. 5: A Mine Disaster No One Stopped   *31*

Reading 2: Bureaucracy   *54*

Case Study 2: How Kristin Died   *64*

Case Study 4: The Last Flight of Space Shuttle *Challenger*   *110*

Reading 5: American Intergovernmental Relations: An Overview   *127*

Case Study 5: Wichita Confronts Contamination   *147*

Case Study 6: Uniforms in the Closet   *170*

Reading 7: Inside Public Bureaucracy   *183*

Case Study 7: The Decision to Bomb the Serbs   *208*

Reading 8: The Science of "Muddling Through"   *225*

Case Study 8: The MOVE Disaster   *238*

Reading 9: Administrative Communication (Or How to Make All the Rest Work): The Concept of its Professional Centrality   *260*

Case Study 9: Waco   *279*

Reading 10: Galloping Elephants: Developing Elements of a Theory of Effective Government Organizations   *299*

Case Study 10: The Lessons of ValuJet 592   *322*

Reading 11: The Public Service Culture   *342*

Case Study 11: Admiral Boorda's War   *354*

Reading 13: Synthesizing the Implementation Literature: The Ambiguity-Conflict Model of Policy Implementation   *407*

Case Study 13: The Political Paradox of Rationing: The Case of the Oregon Health Plan   *427*

Reading 14: Issue Networks and the Executive Establishment   *447*

Case Study 14: Reinventing School Lunch: Transforming a Food Policy into a Nutrition Policy   *457*

Reading 15: Bureaucracy and the Public Interest   *476*

Case Study 15: But No Cigar: How a Rescue Mission Failed, Just Barely, in Orange County   *486*
Reading 16: Public Administration and Ethics: A Prologue to a Preface   *501*
Case Study 16: Madonna's *Sex*   *513*

Citizen's Rights and Participation

Case Study 1: The Blast in Centralia No. 5: A Mine Disaster No One Stopped   *31*
Case Study 2: How Kristin Died   *64*
Case Study 3: Dumping $2.6 Million on Bakersfield (Or How *Not* to Build a Migratory Farm Workers' Clinic)   *88*
Reading 5: American Intergovernmental Relations: An Overview   *127*
Case Study 5: Wichita Confronts Contamination   *147*
Reading 6: Hawthorne and Western Electric Company   *160*
Case Study 6: Uniforms in the Closet   *170*
Case Study 8: The MOVE Disaster   *238*
Case Study 9: Waco   *279*
Case Study 11: Admiral Boorda's War   *354*
Case Study 13: The Political Paradox of Rationing: The Case of the Oregon Health Plan   *427*
Reading 14: Issue Networks and the Executive Establishment   *447*
Case Study 14: Reinventing School Lunch: Transforming a Food Policy into a Nutrition Policy   *457*
Reading 15: Bureaucracy and the Public Interest   *476*
Reading 16: Public Administration and Ethics: A Prologue to a Preface   *501*
Case Study 16: Madonna's *Sex*   *513*

Communications in Administration

Case Study 1: The Blast in Centralia No. 5: A Mine Disaster No One Stopped   *31*
Case Study 2: How Kristin Died   *64*
Case Study 3: Dumping $2.6 Million on Bakersfield (Or How *Not* to Build a Migratory Farm Workers' Clinic)   *88*
Reading 4: Power and Administration   *103*
Case Study 4: The Last Flight of Space Shuttle *Challenger*   *110*
Reading 5: American Intergovernmental Relations: An Overview   *127*
Reading 6: Hawthorne and Western Electric Company   *160*
Case Study 6: Uniforms in the Closet   *170*
Reading 7: Inside Public Bureaucracy   *183*
Case Study 7: The Decision to Bomb the Serbs   *208*
Reading 8: The Science of "Muddling Through"   *225*
Case Study 8: The MOVE Disaster   *238*
Reading 9: Administrative Communication (Or How to Make All the Rest Work): The Concept of its Professional Centrality   *260*
Case Study 9: Waco   *279*
Case Study 10: The Lessons of ValuJet 592   *322*
Reading 11: The Public Service Culture   *342*
Reading 13: Synthesizing the Implementation Literature: The Ambiguity-Conflict Model of Policy Implementation   *407*
Case Study 13: The Political Paradox of Rationing: The Case of the Oregon Health Plan   *427*
Reading 14: Issues Network and the Executive Establishment   *447*
Case Study 14: Reinventing School Lunch: Transforming a Food Policy into a Nutrition Policy   *457*

Congress, State Legislatures, County Boards, or City Councils

Case Study 1: The Blast in Centralia No. 5: A Mine Disaster No One Stopped   *31*

Case Study 3: Dumping $2.6 Million on Bakersfield (Or How *Not* to Build a Migratory Farm Workers' Clinic)   *88*

Reading 4: Power and Administration   *103*

Case Study 4: The Last Flight of Space Shuttle *Challenger*   *110*

Reading 5: American Intergovernmental Relations: An Overview   *127*

Reading 7: Inside Public Bureaucracy   *183*

Case Study 7: The Decision to Bomb the Serbs   *208*

Case Study 9: Waco   *279*

Reading 12: The Politics of Public Budgets   *376*

Case Study 12: County Prison Overtime   *393*

Case Study 13: The Political Paradox of Rationing: The Case of the Oregon Health Plan   *427*

Reading 14: Issue Networks and the Executive Establishment   *447*

Case Study 14: Reinventing School Lunch: Transforming a Food Policy into a Nutrition Policy   *457*

Reading 15: Bureaucracy and the Public Interest   *476*

Case Study 15: But No Cigar: How a Rescue Mission Failed, Just Barely, in Orange County   *486*

Decision Making

Case Study 3: Dumping $2.6 Million on Bakersfield (Or How *Not* to Build a Migratory Farm Workers' Clinic)   *88*

Case Study 4: The Last Flight of Space Shuttle *Challenger*   *110*

Reading 5: American Intergovernmental Relations: An Overview   *127*

Case Study 5: Wichita Confronts Contamination   *147*

Case Study 6: Uniforms in the Closet   *170*

Case Study 7: The Decision to Bomb the Serbs   *208*

Reading 8: The Science of "Muddling Through"   *225*

Case Study 8: The MOVE Disaster   *238*

Reading 9: Administrative Communication (Or How to Make All the Rest Work): The Concept of its Professional Centrality   *260*

Case Study 9: Waco   *279*

Reading 10: Galloping Elephants: Developing Elements of a Theory of Effective Government Organizations   *299*

Case Study 10: The Lessons of ValuJet 592   *322*

Reading 11: The Public Service Culture   *342*

Case Study 11: Admiral Boorda's War   *354*

Reading 12: The Politics of Public Budgets   *376*

Case Study 12: County Prison Overtime   *393*

Reading 14: Issue Networks and the Executive Establishment   *447*

Case Study 14: Reinventing School Lunch: Transforming a Food Policy into a Nutrition Policy   *457*

Reading 15: Bureaucracy and the Public Interest   *476*

Case Study 15: But No Cigar: How a Rescue Mission Failed, Just Barely, in Orange County   *486*

Reading 16: Public Administration and Ethics: A Prologue to a Preface   *501*

Case Study 16: Madonna's *Sex*   *513*

Ethical and Moral Issues of Public Administration

Case Study 1: The Blast in Centralia No. 5: A Mine Disaster No One Stopped   *31*
Case Study 2: How Kristin Died   *64*
Case Study 3: Dumping $2.6 Million on Bakersfield (Or How *Not* to Build a Migratory Farm
    Workers' Clinic)   *88*
Reading 4: Power and Administration   *103*
Case Study 4: The Last Flight of Space Shuttle *Challenger*   *110*
Case Study 5: Wichita Confronts Contamination   *147*
Case Study 6: Uniforms in the Closet   *170*
Case Study 7: The Decision to Bomb the Serbs   *208*
Case Study 8: The MOVE Disaster   *238*
Reading 9: Administrative Communication (Or How to Make All the Rest Work): The Con-
    cept of its Professional Centrality   *260*
Case Study 9: Waco   *279*
Case Study 10: The Lessons of ValuJet 592   *322*
Reading 11: The Public Service Culture   *342*
Case Study 11: Admiral Boorda's War   *354*
Reading 15: Bureaucracy and the Public Interest   *476*
Reading 16: Public Administration and Ethics: A Prologue to a Preface   *501*
Case Study 16: Madonna's *Sex*   *513*

Health and Human Services

Case Study 1: The Blast in Centralia No. 5: A Mine Disaster No One Stopped   *31*
Case Study 2: How Kristin Died   *64*
Case Study 3: Dumping $2.6 Million on Bakersfield (Or How *Not* to Build a Migratory Farm
    Workers' Clinic)   *88*
Case Study 5: Wichita Confronts Contamination   *147*
Reading 6: Hawthorne and Western Electric Company   *160*
Case Study 6: Uniforms in the Closet   *170*
Case Study 9: Waco   *279*
Reading 11: The Public Service Culture   *342*
Case Study 11: Admiral Boorda's War   *354*
Case Study 13: The Political Paradox of Rationing: The Case of the Oregon Health
    Plan   *427*
Case Study 14: Reinventing School Lunch: Transforming a Food Policy into a Nutrition Pol-
    icy   *457*
Reading 15: Bureaucracy and the Public Interest   *476*

Implementation

Case Study 1: The Blast in Centralia No. 5: A Mine Disaster No One Stopped   *31*
Case Study 3: Dumping $2.6 Million on Bakersfield (Or How *Not* to Build a Migratory Farm
    Workers' Clinic)   *88*
Case Study 4: The Last Flight of Space Shuttle *Challenger*   *110*
Case Study 5: Wichita Confronts Contamination   *147*
Reading 7: Inside Public Bureaucracy   *183*
Case Study 7: The Decision to Bomb the Serbs   *208*
Case Study 8: The MOVE Disaster   *238*
Case Study 9: Waco   *279*
Reading 13: Synthesizing the Implementation Literature: The Ambiguity-Conflict Model of
    Policy Implementation   *407*

Case Study 13: The Political Paradox of Rationing: The Case of the Oregon Health Plan   *427*

Case Study 14: Reinventing School Lunch: Transforming a Food Policy into a Nutrition Policy   *457*

Reading 15: Bureaucracy and the Public Interest   *476*

Case Study 15: But No Cigar: How a Rescue Mission Failed, Just Barely, in Orange County   *486*

Intergovernmental Programs and Policies

Case Study 1: The Blast in Centralia No. 5: A Mine Disaster No One Stopped   *31*

Case Study 3: Dumping $2.6 Million on Bakersfield (Or How *Not* to Build a Migratory Farm Workers' Clinic)   *88*

Reading 5: American Intergovernmental Relations: An Overview   *127*

Case Study 5: Wichita Confronts Contamination   *147*

Reading 10: Galloping Elephants: Developing Elements of a Theory of Effective Government Organizations   *299*

Reading 12: The Politics of Public Budgets   *376*

Reading 13: Synthesizing the Implementation Literature: The Ambiguity-Conflict Model of Policy Implementation   *407*

Case Study 13: The Political Paradox of Rationing: The Case of the Oregon Health Plan   *427*

Reading 14: Issue Networks and the Executive Establishment   *447*

Case Study 14: Reinventing School Lunch: Transforming a Food Policy into a Nutrition Policy   *457*

National Defense and International Relations

Case Study 6: Uniforms in the Closet   *170*

Reading 7: Inside Public Bureaucracy   *183*

Case Study 7: The Decision to Bomb the Serbs   *208*

Case Study 11: Admiral Boorda's War   *354*

Reading 14: Issue Networks and the Executive Establishment   *447*

Organizational Behavior

Case Study 1: The Blast in Centralia No. 5: A Mine Disaster No One Stopped   *31*

Reading 2: Bureaucracy   *54*

Case Study 2: How Kristin Died   *64*

Case Study 3: Dumping $2.6 Million on Bakersfield (Or How *Not* to Build a Migratory Farm Workers' Clinic)   *88*

Case Study 4: The Last Flight of Space Shuttle *Challenger*   *110*

Case Study 5: Wichita Confronts Contamination   *147*

Reading 6: Hawthorne and Western Electric Company   *160*

Case Study 6: Uniforms in the Closet   *170*

Reading 7: Inside Public Bureaucracy   *183*

Case Study 8: The MOVE Disaster   *238*

Reading 9: Administrative Communication (Or How to Make All the Rest Work): The Concept of its Professional Centrality   *260*

Case Study 9: Waco   *279*

Case Study 10: The Lessons of ValuJet 592   *322*

Reading 11: The Public Service Culture   *342*

Case Study 11: Admiral Boorda's War   *354*

Case Study 12: County Prison Overtime   *393*
Reading 14: Issue Networks and the Executive Establishment   *447*
Case Study 14: Reinventing School Lunch: Transforming a Food Policy into a Nutrition
   Policy   *457*
Reading 15: Bureaucracy and the Public Interest   *476*
Case Study 15: But No Cigar: How a Rescue Mission Failed, Just Barely, in Orange
   County   *486*
Reading 16: Public Administration and Ethics: A Prologue to a Preface   *501*
Case Study 16: Madonna's *Sex*   *513*

Organization and Management

Reading 1.1: The Study of Administration   *6*
Reading 1.2: The Study of Public Administration in the United States   *17*
Case Study 1: The Blast in Centralia No. 5: A Mine Disaster No One Stopped   *31*
Reading 2: Bureaucracy   *54*
Case Study 2: How Kristin Died   *64*
Case Study 3: Dumping $2.6 Million on Bakersfield (Or How *Not* to Build a Migratory Farm
   Workers' Clinic)   *88*
Reading 4: Power and Administration   *103*
Case Study 4: The Last Flight of Space Shuttle *Challenger*   *110*
Reading 5: American Intergovernmental Relations: An Overview   *127*
Case Study 5: Wichita Confronts Contamination   *147*
Case Study 6: Uniforms in the Closet   *170*
Reading 7: Inside Public Bureaucracy   *183*
Reading 10: Galloping Elephants: Developing Elements of a Theory of Effective Govern-
   ment Organizations   *299*
Case Study 10: The Lessons of ValuJet 592   *322*
Reading 11: The Public Service Culture   *342*
Reading 13: Synthesizing the Implementation Literature: The Ambiguity-Conflict Model of
   Policy Implementation   *407*
Case Study 13: The Political Paradox of Rationing: The Case of the Oregon Health
   Plan   *427*
Reading 15: Bureaucracy and the Public Interest   *476*
Case Study 15: But No Cigar: How a Rescue Mission Failed, Just Barely, in Orange
   County   *486*

Personnel and Civil Service

Reading 1.1: The Study of Administration   *6*
Case Study 1: The Blast in Centralia No. 5: A Mine Disaster No One Stopped   *31*
Reading 2: Bureaucracy   *54*
Case Study 2: How Kristin Died   *64*
Case Study 3: Dumping $2.6 Million on Bakersfield (Or How *Not* to Build a Migratory Farm
   Workers' Clinic)   *88*
Reading 4: Power and Administration   *103*
Reading 5: American Intergovernmental Relations: An Overview   *127*
Reading 6: Hawthorne and Western Electric Company   *160*
Case Study 6: Uniforms in the Closet   *170*
Reading 7: Inside Public Bureaucracy   *183*
Case Study 8: The MOVE Disaster   *238*
Reading 10: Galloping Elephants: Developing Elements of a Theory of Effective
   Government Organizations   *299*

Reading 11: The Public Service Culture   *342*
Case Study 11: Admiral Boorda's War   *354*
Reading 14: Issue Networks and the Executive Establishment   *447*
Case Study 14: Reinventing School Lunch: Transforming a Food Policy into a Nutrition
  Policy   *457*
Reading 15: Bureaucracy and the Public Interest   *476*
Reading 16: Public Administration and Ethics: A Prologue to a Preface   *501*
Case Study 16: Madonna's *Sex*   *513*

Planning and Policy Development

Reading 3: The Ecology of Public Administration   *82*
Case Study 3: Dumping $2.6 Million on Bakersfield (Or How *Not* to Build a Migratory Farm
  Workers' Clinic)   *88*
Reading 4: Power and Administration   *103*
Case Study 4: The Last Flight of Space Shuttle *Challenger*   *110*
Reading 5: American Intergovernmental Relations: An Overview   *127*
Case Study 5: Wichita Confronts Contamination   *147*
Case Study 6: Uniforms in the Closet   *170*
Reading 7: Inside Public Bureaucracy   *183*
Case Study 7: The Decision to Bomb the Serbs   *208*
Reading 8: The Science of "Muddling Through"   *225*
Case Study 8: The MOVE Disaster   *238*
Reading 9: Administrative Communication (Or How to Make All the Rest Work): The Con-
  cept of its Professional Centrality   *260*
Case Study 9: Waco   *279*
Reading 10: Galloping Elephants: Developing Elements of a Theory of Effective Govern-
  ment Organizations   *299*
Case Study 10: The Lessons of ValuJet 592   *322*
Reading 12: The Politics of Public Budgets   *376*
Case Study 12: County Prison Overtime   *393*
Reading 13: Synthesizing the Implementation Literature: The Ambiguity-Conflict Model of
  Policy Implementation   *407*
Case Study 13: The Political Paradox of Rationing: The Case of the Oregon Health
  Plan   *427*
Reading 14: Issue Networks and the Executive Establishment   *447*
Case Study 14: Reinventing School Lunch: Transforming a Food Policy into a Nutrition Pol-
  icy   *457*
Reading 15: Bureaucracy and the Public Interest   *476*
Case Study 15: But No Cigar: How a Rescue Mission Failed, Just Barely, in Orange County
  486
Case Study 16: Madonna's *Sex*   *513*

Power and Politics in Administration

Case Study 1: The Blast in Centralia No. 5: A Mine Disaster No One Stopped   *31*
Reading 2: Bureaucracy   *54*
Case Study 3: Dumping $2.6 Million on Bakersfield (Or How *Not* to Build a Migratory Farm
  Workers' Clinic)   *88*
Reading 4: Power and Administration   *103*
Case Study 4: The Last Flight of Space Shuttle *Challenger*   *110*
Reading 5: American Intergovernmental Relations: An Overview   *127*
Case Study 5: Wichita Confronts Contamination   *147*

Case Study 6: Uniforms in the Closet   *170*
Reading 7: Inside Public Bureaucracy   *183*
Case Study 7: The Decision to Bomb the Serbs   *208*
Case Study 8: The MOVE Disaster   *238*
Case Study 9: Waco   *279*
Reading 11: The Public Service Culture   *342*
Case Study 11: Admiral Boorda's War   *354*
Reading 12: The Politics of Public Budgets   *376*
Case Study 12: County Prison Overtime   *393*
Case Study 13: The Political Paradox of Rationing: The Case of the Oregon Health
    Plan   *427*
Reading 14: Issues Networks and the Executive Establishment   *447*
Case Study 14: Reinventing School Lunch: Transforming a Food Policy into a Nutrition
    Policy   *457*
Reading 15: Bureaucracy and the Public Interest   *476*
Case Study 15: But No Cigar: How a Rescue Mission Failed, Just Barely, in Orange
    County   *486*
Case Study 16: Madonna's *Sex*   *513*

The Presidency, Governorship, Mayors, or County Commissioners

Case Study 1: The Blast in Centralia No. 5: A Mine Disaster No One Stopped   *31*
Reading 4: Power and Administration   *103*
Reading 5: American Intergovernmental Relations: An Overview   *127*
Case Study 7: The Decision to Bomb the Serbs   *208*
Case Study 8: The MOVE Disaster   *238*
Reading 12: The Politics of Public Budgets   *376*
Case Study 12: County Prison Overtime   *393*
Reading 14: Issue Networks and the Executive Establishment   *447*
Reading 15: Bureaucracy and the Public Interest   *476*
Case Study 15: But No Cigar: How a Rescue Mission Failed, Just Barely, in Orange
    County   *486*

Regulation, Rule Enforcement, and Law Enforcement

Reading 1.1: The Study of Administration   *6*
Case Study 1: The Blast in Centralia No. 5: A Mine Disaster No One Stopped   *31*
Reading 2: Bureaucracy   *54*
Case Study 2: How Kristin Died   *64*
Case Study 4: The Last Flight of Space Shuttle *Challenger*   *110*
Case Study 5: Wichita Confronts Contamination   *147*
Case Study 6: Uniforms in the Closet   *170*
Case Study 8: The MOVE Disaster   *238*
Case Study 9: Waco   *279*
Case Study 10: The Lessons of ValuJet 592   *322*
Case Study 11: Admiral Boorda's War   *354*
Case Study 13: The Political Paradox of Rationing: The Case of the Oregon
    Health Plan   *427*
Reading 15: Bureaucracy and the Public Interest   *476*
Case Study 16: Madonna's *Sex*   *513*

State and Local Government

Case Study 1: The Blast in Centralia No. 5: A Mine Disaster No One Stopped   *31*
Case Study 2: How Kristin Died   *64*
Reading 3: The Ecology of Public Administration   *82*
Case Study 3: Dumping $2.6 Million on Bakersfield (Or How *Not* to Build a Migratory Farm Workers' Clinic)   *88*
Reading 5: American Intergovernmental Relations: An Overview   *127*
Case Study 5: Wichita Confronts Contamination   *147*
Reading 7: Inside Public Bureaucracy   *183*
Case Study 8: The MOVE Disaster   *238*
Reading 9: Administrative Communication (Or How to Make All the Rest Work): The Concept of its Professional Centrality   *260*
Case Study 9: Waco   *279*
Reading 10: Galloping Elephants: Developing Elements of a Theory of Effective Government Organizations   *299*
Case Study 10: The Lessons of ValuJet 592   *322*
Reading 11: The Public Service Culture   *342*
Case Study 12: County Prison Overtime   *393*
Reading 13: Synthesizing the Implementation Literature: The Ambiguity-Conflict Model of Policy Implementation   *407*
Case Study 13: The Political Paradox of Rationing: The Case of the Oregon Health Plan   *427*
Reading 15: Bureaucracy and the Public Interest   *476*
Case Study 15: But No Cigar: How a Rescue Mission Failed, Just Barely, in Orange County   *486*
Case Study 16: Madonna's *Sex*   *513*

The Study of Public Administration as a Discipline

Reading 1.1: The Study of Administration   *6*
Reading 1.2: The Study of Public Administration in the United States   *17*
Reading 2: Bureaucracy   *54*
Reading 3: The Ecology of Public Administration   *82*
Reading 4: Power and Administration   *103*
Reading 5: American Intergovernmental Relations: An Overview   *127*
Reading 6: Hawthorne and Western Electric Company   *160*
Reading 7: Inside Public Bureaucracy   *183*
Reading 10: Galloping Elephants: Developing Elements of a Theory of Effective Government Organizations   *299*
Reading 11: The Public Service Culture   *342*
Reading 13: Synthesizing the Implementation Literature: The Ambiguity-Conflict Model of Policy Implementation   *407*
Reading 14: Issue Networks and the Executive Establishment   *447*
Reading 15: Bureaucracy and the Public Interest   *476*

Third-Party Government

Case Study 4: The Last Flight of Space Shuttle *Challenger*   *110*
Reading 5: American Intergovernmental Relations: An Overview   *127*
Case Study 5: Wichita Confronts Contamination   *147*
Reading 7: Inside Public Bureaucracy   *183*

Case Study 10: The Lessons of ValuJet 592   *322*
Reading 13: Synthesizing the Implementation Literature: The Ambiguity-Conflict Model of
    Policy Implementation   *407*
Case Study 14: Reinventing School Lunch: Transforming a Food Policy into a Nutrition
    Policy   *457*
Reading 15: Bureaucracy and the Public Interest   *476*
Case Study 15: But No Cigar: How a Rescue Mission Failed, Just Barely, in Orange
    County   *486*

Women, Minority, and Gay Issues

Case Study 2: How Kristin Died   *64*
Case Study 3: Dumping $2.6 Million on Bakersfield (Or How *Not* to Build a Migratory Farm
    Workers' Clinic)   *88*
Case Study 6: Uniforms in the Closet   *170*
Case Study 8: The MOVE Disaster   *238*
Case Study 11: Admiral Boorda's War   *354*
Case Study 14: Reinventing School Lunch: Transforming a Food Policy into a Nutrition
    Policy   *457*

Preface

The publication of this seventh edition marks the twenty-fifth anniversary of this text's first appearance in print. When the first edition was published, I hoped that this text would offer an improved way to teach the "basics" of public administration that would be both exciting and challenging for students. Over the intervening two and a half decades, it has succeeded more than I could have imagined. I hope that readers of this seventh edition will find that this edition continues to meet their needs for a different and better way of introducing the field of public administration to both new students and "old hands."

Format and Approach

The methodological format and design of the first six editions remain intact in the seventh edition. The approach seeks to interrelate many of the authoritative conceptual works in public administration with contemporary case studies.

By pairing a reading with a case study in each chapter, the text serves four important purposes:

1. The concept-case study method permits students to read firsthand the work of leading administrative theorists who have shaped the modern study of public administration. This method aims at developing in students a critical appreciation of the classic administrative ideas that are the basis of modern public administration.
2. The text encourages a careful examination of practical administrative problems through the presentation of contemporary cases—often involving major national events—that demonstrate the complexity, the centrality, and the challenge of the current administrative processes of public organizations.
3. The book seeks to promote a deeper understanding of the relationship between the theory and practice of public administration by allowing readers to test for themselves the validity of major ideas about public administration in the context of actual situations.
4. Finally, the concept-case method develops a keener appreciation of the eclectic breadth and interdisciplinary dimensions of public administration by presenting articles—both conceptual and case writings—from a wide variety of sources, using many materials not available in the average library.

The immense quantity of literature in the field has always made selecting the writings a challenge. My final choice of writings is based on affirmative answers to the following four central questions:

1. Do the writings focus on the central issues confronting public administrators?
2. Do the writings, individually and collectively, give a realistic view of the contemporary practice of public administration?
3. Do the individual conceptual readings and case studies relate logically to one another?

4. Are the writings interesting and long enough to convey the true sense and spirit intended by the authors?

The arrangement of the selections follows an order of topics used by many instructors in the field, moving from a definition of public administration to increasingly specific issues and problems. Many subjects (such as headquarters-field
relationships, position classification, enforcement, government regulation, productivity, and personnel recruitment), though not treated separately, are discussed within
various chapters under other headings (refer to the topic index for additional cross-
references).

This diagram may help readers to understand the design of the book more clearly.

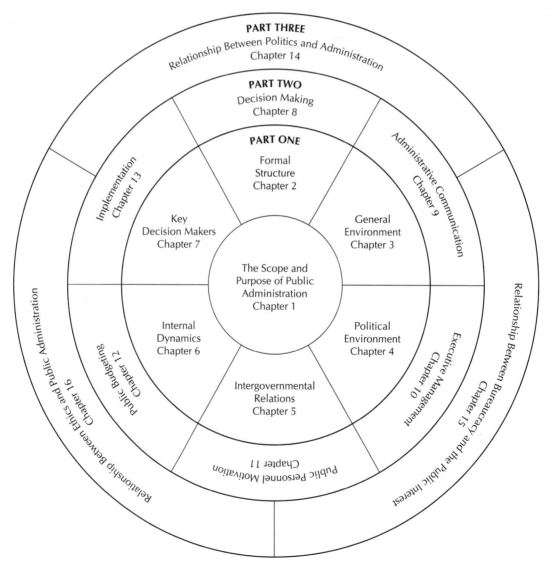

At the center of this schematic figure is Chapter 1, which discusses "The Scope and Purpose of Public Administration," perhaps the most difficult, central intellectual problem in public administration today. The first ring outward is Part One, "The Pattern of Public Administration in America." These six chapters present concepts and cases pertaining to the broad environment surrounding public administration and the work of public administrators. The second ring is Part Two, "The Multiple Functions of Public Administrators." These six chapters focus on the major activities, roles, and responsibilities of practicing administrators in the public sector. The exterior ring is Part Three; these three chapters discuss "Enduring and Unresolved Relationships" in public administration, ones especially critical during the last decade of the 20th century for the field as a whole.

New Material in the Seventh Edition

Readings and cases have been carefully selected with an eye to readability and contemporary appeal to ensure that the text stays current and continues to reflect the ideas and events shaping public administration today. In this edition, special attention has been paid to ensuring the accessibility of writings for students: contemporary topics and issues that students want and need to know about make up nearly half of the new selections.

Six new readings appear in this edition:

Reading 1.2: The Study of Public Administration in the United States (Richard J. Stillman II)

Reading 5: American Intergovernmental Relations: An Overview (Laurence J. O'Toole, Jr.)

Reading 9: Administrative Communication (Or How to Make All the Rest Work): The Concept of its Professional Centrality (James L. Garnett)

Reading 10: Galloping Elephants: Developing Elements of a Theory of Effective Government Organizations (Hal G. Rainey and Paula Steinbauer)

Reading 11: The Public Service Culture (Lois Recascino Wise)

Reading 13: Synthesizing the Implementation Literature: The Ambiguity-Conflict Model of Policy Implementation (Richard Matland)

Seven case studies are also new to this edition:

Case Study 6: Uniforms in the Closet (Jennifer Egan)

Case Study 7: The Decision to Bomb the Serbs (Elaine Sciolino and Ethan Bronner)

Case Study 9: Waco (William J. Vizzard)

Case Study 10: The Lessons of ValuJet 592 (William Langewiesche)

Case Study 11: Admiral Boorda's War (Peter J. Boyer)

Case Study 13: The Political Paradox of Rationing: The Case of the Oregon Health Plan (Lawrence R. Jacobs, Theodore Marmor, and Jonathan Oberlander)

Case Study 14: Reinventing School Lunch: Transforming a Food Policy into a Nutrition Policy (Laura S. Sims)

Revised and expanded introductions, alerting students to the main ideas that follow, open each selection. Also updated are the review questions, key terms, and suggestions for further reading that conclude each chapter, as well as the subject index and topic correlation chart. Epilogues have also been added to several cases to provide students with updates on the aftermath of events.

The Instructor's Guide

The *Instructor's Guide* complements the text by offering insights, practical suggestions, and resources for teaching introductory and graduate students. The guide is organized as a set of memoranda from myself to the instructor. Each memo addresses a separate important topic, such as "How to use case studies in the classroom." The guide also includes sample quizzes, exams, and course evaluation forms. Appendices include the Federalist Papers, nos. 10 and 51, the Declaration of Independence, and the Constitution.

Acknowledgments

Various people have contributed to this book either by helping to shape its focus in the early stages or by reviewing the finished manuscript. Special thanks are due:

Anne C. Cowden, California State University, Sacramento

William A. Diaz, University of Minnesota, Minneapolis

Don Frazier, Shippensburg University

Michael Frazier, Howard University

William C. Garriott, Jr., Centre College

Frank McKenna, Bowling Green State University

James Pfiffner, George Mason University

John Pope, Embry-Riddle Aeronautical University

Thanks must also go to my editors at Houghton Mifflin for their generous support and enthusiastic encouragement throughout this difficult writing and editing assignment, particularly Jean Woy, Melissa Mashburn, Vikram Mukhija, Tracy Patruno, Charline Lake, and Sandra McGuire. Nancy Howe and Carolynne White, both graduate students at the Graduate School of Public Affairs, University of Colorado, Denver have shaped this text in more ways than I can calculate—or thank them for: To these and many others, I owe a debt of gratitude for their assistance.

R.J.S. II

CHAPTER 1

The Search for the Scope and Purpose of Public Administration

*O*ur own politics must be the touchstone for all theories. The principles on which to base a science of administration for America must be principles which have democratic policy very much at heart.

Woodrow Wilson

Introduction

A definition of the parameters of a field of study, that is, the boundaries, landmarks, and terrain that distinguish it from other scientific and humanistic disciplines, is normally considered a good place to begin any academic subject. Unfortunately, as yet, no one has produced a simple definition of the study of public administration—at least one on which most practitioners and scholars agree. Attempting to define the core values and focus of twentieth-century public administration provides lively debates and even deep divisions among students of the field.

A major difficulty in arriving at a precise and universally acceptable definition arises in part from the rapid growth in the twentieth century of public administration, which today seems to be all-encompassing. Public administrators are engaged in technical, although not necessarily mundane details: they prepare budgets for a city government, classify jobs in a post office, have potholes patched and mail delivered, or evaluate the performance of a city's drug treatment centers. At the same time, they are also concerned with the major goals of society and with the development of resources for achieving those goals within the context of a rapidly changing political environment. For instance, if an engineering staff of a state agency proposes to build a highway, this decision appears at first glance to be a purely administrative activity. However, it involves a wide range of social values related to pressing concerns such as community land-use patterns, energy consumption, pollution control, and mass transit planning. Race relations, the general economic well-being of a community, and the allocation of scarce physical and human resources affect even simple administrative decisions about highway construction.

Public administration does not operate in a vacuum but is deeply intertwined with the critical dilemmas confronting an entire society. The issue then becomes: How can a theorist reasonably and concisely define a field so interrelated with all of society?

The rapidly increasing number and scope of activities involving public administration have led theorists to develop a variety of definitions. Consider twelve offered during the past two decades by leading textbook writers:

> Public Administration is the production of goods and services designed to serve the needs of citizens-consumers.
>
> Marshall Dimock, Gladys Dimock, and Douglas Fox,
> *Public Administration* (Fifth Edition, 1983)

> We suggest a new conceptual framework that emphasizes the perception of public administration as *design,* with attendant emphasis on participative decision making and learning, purpose and action, innovation, imagination and creativity, and social interaction and "coproduction."
>
> Jong S. Jun,
> *Public Administration* (1986)

> In ordinary usage, public administration is a generic expression for the entire bundle of activities that are involved in the establishment and implementation of public policies.
>
> Cole Blease Graham, Jr., and
> Steven W. Hays,
> *Managing the Public Organization* (1986)

> Public administration:
> 1. is a cooperative group effort in a public setting.
> 2. covers all three branches—executive, legislative, and judicial—and their interrelationships.
> 3. has an important role in the formulation of public policy, and is thus part of the political process.
> 4. is different in significant ways from private administration.
> 5. is closely associated with numerous private groups and individuals in providing services to the community.
>
> Felix A. Nigro and Lloyd G. Nigro,
> *Modern Public Administration* (Seventh Edition, 1989)

> . . . Public administration is centrally concerned with the organization of government policies and programs as well as the behavior of officials (usually nonelected) formally responsible for their conduct.
>
> Charles H. Levine, B. Guy Peters, and Frank J. Thompson,
> *Public Administration: Challenges, Choices, Consequences* (1990)

> The practice of public administration involves the dynamic reconciliation of various forces in government's efforts to manage public policies and programs.
>
> Melvin J. Dubnick and Barbara S. Romzek,
> *American Public Administration: Politics and the Management of*
> *Expectations* (1991)

Public administration is concerned with the management of public programs.

Robert B. Denhardt,
Public Administration: An Action Orientation (1995)

Public administration may be defined as all processes, organizations, and individuals (the latter acting in official positions and roles) associated with carrying out laws and other rules adopted or issued by legislatures, executives, and courts.

George J. Gordon and Michael E. Milakovich,
Public Administration in America (1995).

Public Administration in all modern nations is identified with the executive branch.

James W. Fesler and Donald F. Kettl
The Politics of the Administrative Process (Second edition, 1996)

Public Administration can be portrayed as a wheel of relationships focused on the implementation of public policy.

William C. Johnson
Public Administration: Policy, Politics and Practice (Second Edition, 1996)

Public administration is the use of managerial, political, and legal theories and processes to fulfill legislative, executive, and judicial governmental mandates for the provision of regulatory and service functions for the society as a whole or for some segments of it.

David H. Rosenbloom and Deborah D. Goldman,
*Public Administration: Understanding Management, Politics, and Law in
the Public Sector* (Fourth Edition, 1997)

Traditionally, public administration is thought of as the accomplishing side of government. It is supposed to comprise all those activities involved in carrying out the policies of elected officials and some activities associated with the development of those policies. Public administration is . . . all that comes after the last campaign promise and election-night cheer.

Grover Starling,
Managing the Public Sector (Fifth Edition, 1997)

Generally, these attempts at defining public administration seem to identify it with the following: (1) the executive branch of government (yet it is related in important ways to the legislative and judicial branches); (2) the formulation and implementation of public policies; (3) the involvement in a considerable range of problems concerning human behavior and cooperative human effort; (4) a field that can be differentiated in several ways from private administration; (5) the production of public goods and services; and (6) rooted in the law as well as concerned with carrying out laws. However, trying to pin down public administration in more specific detail becomes, according to specialists such as Harold Stein, a fruitless endeavor. The many variables and complexities of public administration make almost every administrative situation a unique event, eluding any highly systematic categorization. As Harold Stein writes:

"public administration is a field in which every man is his own codifier and categorizer and the categories adopted must be looked on as relatively evanescent."[1]

For some writers like Frederick C. Mosher, the elusiveness of a disciplinary core for public administration gives the subject its strength and fascination, for students must draw upon many fields and disciplines, as well as their own resources, to solve a particular administrative problem. As Mosher writes: "Perhaps it is best that it [public administration] not be defined. It is more an area of interest than a discipline, more a focus than a separate science. . . . It is necessarily cross-disciplinary. The overlapping and vague boundaries should be viewed as a resource, even though they are irritating to some with orderly minds."[2]

But for others like Robert S. Parker, the frustrations of dealing with such a disorderly discipline mitigate against its being a mature, rewarding academic field of study. "There is really no such subject as 'public administration,'" writes Parker. "No science or art can be identified by this title, least of all any single skill or coherent intellectual discipline. The term has no relation to the world of systematic thought. . . . It does not, in itself, offer any promising opportunity to widen or make more precise any single aspect of scientific knowledge."[3]

Despite Parker's pessimistic assessment of the present and future status of public administration, the search for a commonly accepted definition of the field, both in its academic and professional applications, continues by many scholars.

Indeed, defining public administration—its boundaries, scope, and purpose—has become, in recent decades, a preoccupation and difficulty confronting public administration theorists. The field's "identity crisis," as Dwight Waldo once labeled the dilemma, has now become especially acute because a plethora of models, approaches, and theories now purport to define what public administration is all about.

To help us understand public administration today, it is useful to study the rationale for creating this field, as outlined in an essay written in 1887 by Woodrow Wilson, a young political scientist at the time. Wilson (1856–1924) is better known as the twenty-eighth President of the United States (1913–1921), father of the League of Nations, Commander-in-Chief during World War I, and author of much of the "New Freedom" progressive reform legislation. Wilson is also credited by scholars with writing the first essay on public administration in the United States and therefore is considered by many as its American founder. His short but distinguished essay, "The Study of Administration," was published a century after the U.S. Constitution's birth. Wilson had just begun his academic career, teaching political science at Bryn Mawr College in Pennsylvania, after earning his Ph.D. at Johns Hopkins University. The editor of a new journal *(Political Science Quarterly)* asked Wilson to contribute an essay on this developing subject. At that time, public administration had been a well-established discipline in Europe, but was largely unknown in America.

Geographic isolation, agrarian self-sufficiency, the absence of threats to national security, and limited demands for public services, among other things, had allowed the

---

[1]Harold Stein, Public Administration and Policy Development: A Case Book (New York: Harcourt Brace Jovanovich, 1952), p. xxv.

[2]Frederick C. Mosher, "Research in Public Administration," Public Administration Review, 16 (Summer 1956), p. 177.

[3]Robert S. Parker, "The End of Public Administration," Public Administration, 34 (June 1965), p. 99.

United States to get along reasonably well during its first century of existence without the self-conscious study of public administration. However, many events were forcing Americans to take notice of the need for public administration. By the late nineteenth century, technologic innovations such as the automobile, telephone, and light bulb and growing international involvement in the Spanish-American War, combined with increasing public participation in a democratic government, created urgent needs for expanded, effective administrative services. As a consequence, we also required an established field of administrative study. Wilson wrote his essay at the time when civil service reform had been instituted in the federal government (the Civil Service Act or "the Pendleton Act," named for its legislative sponsor, had been passed in 1883). Much of Wilson's centennial essay was, not surprisingly, a plea for recognizing the central importance of administrative machinery, especially a well-trained civil service based on merit, rather than politics, to operate a modern democratic government.

Just as the *Federalist Papers,* authored by James Madison, Alexander Hamilton, and John Jay had a century before advocated the passage of the U.S. Constitution, Wilson called in 1887 for the necessity of this new field "to run a constitution" during its second century. His essay strived to encourage the development of public administration and to underscore the importance of effective administration for the Constitution's survival in the future.

But how could Americans graft public administration into their Constitution, which had not mentioned this subject? For Wilson—and modern students of the field—this was the critical issue. In developing public administration—both practically and academically—Wilson's basic difficulty was to reconcile the notions of constitutional democracy with inherent concerns for popular control and participation with theories of efficient, professional administration, and their stress on systematic rules and internal procedures as distinct from democratic oversight and influence. For Wilson, this inevitable conflict could be settled by dividing government into two spheres—"politics," in which choices regarding what government should do are determined by a majority of elected representatives, and "administration," which serves to carry out the dictates of the populace through efficient procedures relatively free from political meddling.

Although modern administrative scholars generally reject the possibility or desirability of drawing any hard-or-fast line between politics and administration, or what most call "the politics-administration dichotomy," the issues Wilson raised are enduring and important. Read the essay for yourself and see how you judge the validity of Wilson's arguments.

How did Wilson define public administration and why did he believe it was so critical to the future of the United States? Are his arguments for its basic rationale and value still valid?

Why did Wilson distinguish between "politics" and "administration" as important terms for creating public administration? In your opinion, is such a "politics-administration dichotomy" practical and workable? What are the advantages and disadvantages of using such a dichotomy today as a way to advance this field of study?

What sources did Wilson believe the U.S. should draw on in developing this new field? And what sources should Americans avoid in shaping their administrative enterprise? And why?

What issues and challenges did Wilson pose for administrative study and practice? Are these still priorities today?

The Study of Administration

WOODROW WILSON

I suppose that no practical science is ever studied where there is no need to know it. The very fact, therefore, that the eminently practical science of administration is finding its way into college courses in this country would prove that this country needs to know more about administration, were such proof of the fact required to make out a case. It need not be said, however, that we do not look into college programmes for proof of this fact. It is a thing almost taken for granted among us, that the present movement called civil service reform must, after the accomplishment of its first purpose, expand into efforts to improve, not the *personnel* only, but also the organization and methods of our government offices: because it is plain that their organization and methods need improvement only less than their *personnel.* It is the object of administrative study to discover, first, what government can properly and successfully do, and, secondly, how it can do these proper things with the utmost possible efficiency and at the least possible cost either of money or of energy. On both these points there is obviously much need of light among us; and only careful study can supply that light.

Before entering on that study, however, it is needful:

I. To take some account of what others have done in the same line; that is to say, of the history of the study.

II. To ascertain just what is its subject-matter.

Reprinted with permission from *Political Science Quarterly,* 2 (June 1887): 197–222.

III. To determine just what are the best methods by which to develop it, and the most clarifying political conceptions to carry with us into it.

Unless we know and settle these things, we shall set out without chart or compass.

I.

The science of administration is the latest fruit of that study of the science of politics which was begun some twenty-two hundred years ago. It is a birth of our own century, almost of our own generation.

Why was it so late in coming? Why did it wait till this too busy century of ours to demand attention for itself? Administration is the most obvious part of government; it is government in action; it is the executive, the operative, the most visible side of government, and is of course as old as government itself. It is government in action, and one might very naturally expect to find that government in action had arrested the attention and provoked the scrutiny of writers of politics very early in the history of systematic thought.

But such was not the case. No one wrote systematically of administration as a branch of the science of government until the present century had passed its first youth and had begun to put forth its characteristic flower of systematic knowledge. Up to our own day all the political writers whom we now read had thought, argued, dogmatized only about the *constitution* of government;

about the nature of the state, the essence and seat of sovereignty, popular power and kingly prerogative; about the greatest meanings lying at the heart of government, and the high ends set before the purpose of government by man's nature and man's aims. The central field of controversy was that great field of theory in which monarchy rode tilt against democracy, in which oligarchy would have built for itself strongholds of privilege, and in which tyranny sought opportunity to make good its claim to receive submission from all competitors. Amidst this high warfare of principles, administration could command no pause for its own consideration. The question was always: Who shall make law, and what shall that law be? The other question, how law should be administered with enlightenment, with equity, with speed, and without friction, was put aside as "practical detail" which clerks could arrange after doctors had agreed upon principles.

That political philosophy took this direction was of course no accident, no chance preference or perverse whim of political philosophers. The philosophy of any time is, as Hegel says, "nothing but the spirit of that time expressed in abstract thought"; and political philosophy, like philosophy of every other kind, has only held up the mirror to contemporary affairs. The trouble in early times was almost altogether about the constitution of government; and consequently that was what engrossed men's thoughts. There was little or no trouble about administration,—at least little that was heeded by administrators. The functions of government were simple, because life itself was simple. Government went about imperatively and compelled men, without thought of consulting their wishes. There was no complex system of public revenues and public debts to puzzle financiers; there were, consequently, no financiers to be puzzled. No one who possessed power was long at a loss how to use it. The great and only question was: Who shall possess it? Populations were of manageable numbers; property was of simple sorts. There were plenty of farms, but no stocks and bonds; more cattle than vested interests.

• • •

There is scarcely a single duty of government which was once simple which is not now complex; government once had but a few masters; it now has scores of masters. Majorities formerly only underwent government; they now conduct government. Where government once might follow the whims of a court, it must now follow the views of a nation.

And those views are steadily widening to new conceptions of state duty; so that, at the same time that the functions of government are every day becoming more complex and difficult, they are also vastly multiplying in number. Administration is everywhere putting its hands to new undertakings. The utility, cheapness, and success of the government's postal service, for instance, point towards the early establishment of governmental control of the telegraph system. Or, even if our government is not to follow the lead of the governments of Europe in buying or building both telegraph and railroad lines, no one can doubt that in some way it must make itself master of masterful corporations. The creation of national commissioners of railroads, in addition to the older state commissions, involves a very important and delicate extension of administrative functions. Whatever hold of authority state or federal governments are to take upon corporations, there must follow cares and responsibilities which will require not a little wisdom, knowledge, and experience. Such things must be studied in order to be well done. And these, as I have said, are only a few of the doors which are being opened to offices of government. The idea of the state and the consequent ideal of its duty are undergoing noteworthy change; and "the idea of the state is the conscience of administration." Seeing every day new things which the state ought to do, the next thing is to see clearly how it ought to do them.

This is why there should be a science of administration which shall seek to straighten the paths of government, to make its business less unbusinesslike; to strengthen and purify its organization, and to crown its duties with dutifulness. This is one reason why there is such a science.

But where has this science grown up? Surely not on this side of the sea. Not much impartial scientific method is to be discerned in our administrative practices. The poisonous atmosphere of city government, the crooked secrets of state administration, the confusion, sinecurism, and corruption ever and again discovered in the bureaus at Washington forbid us to believe that any clear conceptions of what constitutes good administration are as yet very widely current in the United States. No; American writers have hitherto taken no very important part in the advancement of this science. It has found its doctors in Europe. It is not of our making; it is a foreign science, speaking very little of the language of English or American principle. It employs only foreign tongues; it utters none but what are to our minds alien ideas. Its aims, its examples, its conditions, are almost exclusively grounded in the histories of foreign races, in the precedents of foreign systems, in the lessons of foreign revolutions. It has been developed by French and German professors, and is consequently in all parts adapted to the needs of a compact state, and made to fit highly centralized forms of government; whereas, to answer our purposes, it must be adapted, not to a simple and compact, but to a complex and multiform state, and made to fit highly decentralized forms of government. If we would employ it, we must Americanize it, and that not formally, in language merely, but radically, in thought, principle, and aim as well. It must learn our constitutions by heart; must get the bureaucratic fever out of its veins; must inhale much free American air.

If an explanation be sought why a science manifestly so susceptible of being made useful to all governments alike should have received attention first in Europe, where government has long been a monopoly, rather than in England or the United States, where government has long been a common franchise, the reason will doubtless be found to be twofold: first, that in Europe, just because government was independent of popular assent, there was more governing to be done; and, second, that the desire to keep government a monopoly made the monopolists interested in discovering the least irritating means of governing. They were, besides, few enough to adopt means promptly.

• • •

The English race . . . has long and successfully studied the art of curbing executive power to the constant neglect of the art of perfecting executive methods. It has exercised itself much more in controlling than in energizing government. It has been more concerned to render government just and moderate than to make it facile, well-ordered, and effective. English and American political history has been a history, not of administrative development, but of legislative oversight,—not of progress in governmental organization, but of advance in law-making and political criticism. Consequently, we have reached a time when administrative study and creation are imperatively necessary to the well-being of our governments saddled with the habits of a long period of constitution-making. That period has practically closed, so far as the establishment of essential principles is concerned, but we cannot shake off its atmosphere. We go on criticizing when we ought to be creating. We have reached the third of the periods I have mentioned,—the period, namely, when the people have to develop administration in accordance with the constitutions they won for themselves in a previous period of struggle with absolute power; but we are not prepared for the tasks of the new period.

Such an explanation seems to afford the only escape from blank astonishment at the fact that, in spite of our vast advantages in point of political liberty, and above all in point of practical political skill and sagacity, so many nations are ahead of us in administrative organization and administrative skill. Why, for instance, have we but just begun purifying a civil service which was rotten full fifty years ago? To say that slavery diverted us is but to repeat what I have said—that flaws in our Constitution delayed us.

Of course all reasonable preference would declare for this English and American course of politics rather than for that of any European country. We should not like to have had Prussia's history for the sake of having Prussia's administrative skill; and Prussia's particular system of administration would quite suffocate us. It is better to be untrained and free than to be servile and systematic. Still there is no denying that it would be better yet to be both free in spirit and proficient in practice. It is this even more reasonable preference which impels us to discover what there may be to hinder or delay us in naturalizing this much-to-be desired science of administration.

What, then, is there to prevent?

Well, principally, popular sovereignty. It is harder for democracy to organize administration than for monarchy. The very completeness of our most cherished political successes in the past embarrasses us. We have enthroned public opinion; and it is forbidden us to hope during its reign for any quick schooling of the sovereign in executive expertness or in the conditions of perfect functional balance in government. The very fact that we have realized popular rule in its fullness has made the task of *organizing* that rule just so much the more difficult. In order to make any advance at all we must instruct and persuade a multitudinous monarch called public opinion,—a much less feasible undertaking than to influence a single monarch called a king. An individual sovereign will adopt a simple plan and carry it out directly; he will have but one opinion, and he will embody that one opinion in one command. But this other sovereign, the people, will have a score of differing opinions. They can agree upon nothing simple: advance must be made through compromise, by a compounding of differences, by a trimming of plans and a suppression of too straightforward principles. There will be a succession of resolves running through a course of years, a dropping fire of commands running through a whole gamut of modifications.

In government, as in virtue, the hardest of hard things is to make progress. Formerly the reason for this was that the single person who was sovereign was generally either selfish, ignorant, timid, or a fool,—albeit there was now and again one who was wise. Nowadays the reason is that the many, the people, who are sovereign have no single ear which one can approach, and are selfish, ignorant, timid, stubborn, or foolish with the selfishnesses, the ignorances, the stubbornnesses, the timidities, or the follies of several thousand persons,—albeit there are hundreds who are wise. Once the advantage of the reformer was that the sovereign's mind had a definite locality, that it was contained in one man's head, and that consequently it could be gotten at; though it was his disadvantage that that mind learned only reluctantly or only in small quantities, or was under the influence of someone who let it learn only the wrong things. Now, on the contrary, the reformer is bewildered by the fact that the sovereign's mind has no definite locality, but is contained in a voting majority of several million heads; and embarrassed by the fact that the mind of this sovereign also is under the influence of favorites, who are none the less favorites in a good old-fashioned sense of the word because they are not persons but preconceived opinions; *i.e.*, prejudices which are not to be reasoned with because they are not the children of reason.

Wherever regard for public opinion is a first principle of government, practical reform must be slow and all reform must be full of compromises. For wherever public opinion exists it must rule. This is now an axiom half the world over, and will presently come to be believed even in Russia. Whoever would effect a change in a modern constitutional government must first educate his fellow-citizens to want *some* change. That done, he must persuade them to want the particular change he wants. He must first make public opinion willing to listen and then see to it that it listen to the right things. He must stir it up to search for an opinion, and then manage to put the right opinion in its way.

The first step is not less difficult than the second. With opinions, possession is more than nine points of the law. It is next to impossible to dislodge them. Institutions which one generation regards as only a makeshift approximation to the realization of a principle, the next generation honors as the nearest possible approximation to that principle, and the next worships as the principle itself. It takes scarcely three generations for the apotheosis. The grandson accepts his grandfather's hesitating experiment as an integral part of the fixed constitution of nature.

Even if we had clear insight into all the political past, and could form out of perfectly instructed

heads a few steady, infallible, placidly wise maxims of government into which all sound political
doctrine would be ultimately resolvable, *would the
country act on them?* That is the question. The
bulk of mankind is rigidly unphilosophical, and
nowadays the bulk of mankind votes. A truth must
become not only plain but also commonplace before it will be seen by the people who go to their
work very early in the morning; and not to act upon
it must involve great and pinching inconveniences
before these same people will make up their minds
to act upon it.

And where is this unphilosophical bulk of
mankind more multifarious in its composition than
in the United States? To know the public mind of
this country, one must know the mind, not of
Americans of the older stocks only, but also of
Irishmen, of Germans, of Negroes. In order to get
a footing for new doctrine, one must influence
minds cast in every mould of race, minds inherit-
ing every bias of environment, warped by the histories of a score of different nations, warmed or
chilled, closed or expanded by almost every climate of the globe.

• • •

II.

The field of administration is a field of business.
It is removed from the hurry and strife of politics;
it at most points stands apart even from the debatable ground of constitutional study. It is a part of
political life only as the methods of the counting-
house are a part of the life of society; only as machinery is part of the manufactured product. But it
is, at the same time, raised very far above the dull
level of mere technical detail by the fact that
through its greater principles it is directly connected with the lasting maxims of political wisdom, the permanent truths of political progress.

The object of administrative study is to rescue
executive methods from the confusion and costliness of empirical experiment and set them upon
foundations laid deep in stable principle.

It is for this reason that we must regard civil service reform in its present stages as but a prelude to a
fuller administrative reform. We are now rectifying
methods of appointment; we must go on to adjust
executive functions more fitly and to prescribe better methods of executive organization and action.
Civil service reform is thus but a moral preparation
for what is to follow. It is clearing the moral atmosphere of official life by establishing the sanctity
of public office as a public trust, and, by making the
service unpartisan, it is opening the way for making
it businesslike. By sweetening its motives it is rendering it capable of improving its methods of work.

Let me expand a little what I have said of the
province of administration. Most important to be
observed is the truth already so much and so fortunately insisted upon by our civil service reformers; namely, that administration lies outside the
proper sphere of *politics*. Administrative questions
are not political questions. Although politics sets
the tasks for administration, it should not be suffered to manipulate its offices.

This is distinction of high authority; eminent German writers insist upon it as of course. Bluntschli,
for instance, bids us separate administration alike
from politics and from law. Politics, he says, is state
activity "in things great and universal," while "administration, on the other hand," is "the activity of
the state in individual and small things. Politics is
thus the special province of the statesman, administration of the technical official." "Policy does
nothing without the aid of administration"; but administration is not therefore politics. But we do not
require German authority for this position; this discrimination between administration and politics is
now, happily, too obvious to need further discussion.

There is another distinction which must be
worked into all our conclusions, which, though but
another side of that between administration and
politics, is not quite so easy to keep sight of; I
mean the distinction between *constitutional* and
administrative questions, between those governmental adjustments which are essential to constitutional principle and those which are merely
instrumental to the possibly changing purposes of
a wisely adapting convenience.

One cannot easily make clear to every one just where administration resides in the various departments of any practicable government without entering upon particulars so numerous as to confuse and distinctions so minute as to distract. No lines of demarcation, setting apart administrative from non-administrative functions, can be run between this and that department of government without being run up hill and down dale, over dizzy heights of distinction and through dense jungles of statutory enactment, hither and thither around "its" and "buts," "whens" and "howevers," until they become altogether lost to the common eye not accustomed to this sort of surveying, and consequently not acquainted with the use of the theodolite of logical discernment. A great deal of administration goes about *incognito* to most of the world, being confounded now with political "management," and again with constitutional principle.

Perhaps this case of confusion may explain such utterances as that of Niebuhr's: "Liberty," he says, "depends incomparably more upon administration than upon constitution." At first sight this appears to be largely true. Apparently facility in the actual exercise of liberty does depend more upon administrative arrangements than upon constitutional guarantees; although constitutional guarantees alone secure the existence of liberty. But—upon second thought—is even so much as this true? Liberty no more consists in easy functional movement than intelligence consists in the ease and vigor with which the limbs of a strong man move. The principles that rule within the man, or the constitution, are the vital springs of liberty or servitude. Because dependence and subjection are without chains, are lightened by every easy-working device of considerate, paternal government, they are not thereby transformed into liberty. Liberty cannot live apart from constitutional principle; and no administration, however perfect and liberal its methods, can give men more than a poor counterfeit of liberty if it rest upon illiberal principles of government.

A clear view of the difference between the province of constitutional law and the province of administrative function ought to leave no room for misconception; and it is possible to name some roughly definite criteria upon which such a view can be built. Public administration is detailed and systematic execution of public law. Every particular application of general law is an act of administration. The assessment and raising of taxes, for instance, the hanging of a criminal, the transportation and delivery of the mails, the equipment and recruiting of the army and navy, etc., are all obviously acts of administration; but the general laws which direct these things to be done are as obviously outside of and above administration. The broad plans of governmental action are not administrative; the detailed execution of such plans is administrative. Constitutions, therefore, properly concern themselves only with those instrumentalities of government which are to control general law. Our federal Constitution observes this principle in saying nothing of even the greatest of the purely executive offices, and speaking only of that President of the Union who was to share the legislative and policy-making functions of government, only of those judges of highest jurisdiction who were to interpret and guard its principles, and not of those who were merely to give utterance to them.

This is not quite the distinction between Will and answering Deed, because the administrator should have and does have a will of his own in the choice of means for accomplishing his work. He is not and ought not to be a mere passive instrument. The distinction is between general plans and special means.

There is, indeed, one point at which administrative studies trench on constitutional ground—or at least upon what seems constitutional ground. The study of administration, philosophically viewed, is closely connected with the study of the proper distribution of constitutional authority. To be efficient it must discover the simplest arrangements by which responsibility can be unmistakably fixed upon officials; the best way of dividing authority without hampering it, and responsibility without obscuring it. And this question of the distribution of authority, when taken into the sphere of the higher, the originating functions of government, is obviously a central constitutional question.

If administrative study can discover the best principles upon which to base such distributions, it will have done constitutional study an invaluable service. Montesquieu did not, I am convinced, say the last word on this head.

To discover the best principle for the distribution of authority is of greater importance, possibly, under a democratic system, where officials serve many matters, than under others where they serve but a few. All sovereigns are suspicious of their servants, and the sovereign people is no exception to the rule; but how is its suspicion to be allayed by *knowledge*? If that suspicion could but be clarified into wise vigilance, it would be altogether salutary; if that vigilance could be aided by the unmistakable placing of responsibility, it would be altogether beneficent. Suspicion in itself is never healthful either in the private or in the public mind. *Trust is strength* in all relations of life; and, as it is the office of the constitutional reformer to create conditions of trustfulness, so it is the office of the administrative organizer to fit administration with conditions of clear-cut responsibility which shall insure trustworthiness.

And let me say that large powers and unhampered discretion seem to me the indispensable conditions of responsibility. Public attention must be easily directed, in each case of good or bad administration, to just the man deserving of praise or blame. There is no danger in power, if only it be not irresponsible. If it be divided, dealt only in shares to many, it is obscured; and if it be obscured, it is made irresponsible. But if it be centred in heads of the service and in heads of branches of the service, it is easily watched and brought to book. If to keep his office a man must achieve open and honest success, and if at the same time he feels himself entrusted with large freedom of discretion, the greater his power the less likely is he to abuse it, the more is he nerved and sobered and elevated by it. The less his power, the more safely obscure and unnoticed does he feel his position to be, and the more readily does he relapse into remissness.

Just here we manifestly emerge upon the field of that still larger question,—the proper relations between public opinion and administration.

To whom is official trustworthiness to be dis-

closed, and by whom is it to be rewarded? Is the official to look to the public for his meed of praise and his push of promotion, or only to his superior in office? Are the people to be called in to settle administrative discipline as they are called in to settle constitutional principles? These questions evidently find their root in what is undoubtedly the fundamental problem of this whole study. That problem is: What part shall public opinion take in the conduct of administration?

The right answer seems to be, that public opinion shall play the part of authoritative critic.

But the *method* by which its authority shall be made to tell? Our peculiar American difficulty in organizing administration is not the danger of losing liberty, but the danger of not being able or willing to separate its essentials from its accidents. Our success is made doubtful by that besetting error of ours, the error of trying to do too much by vote. Self-government does not consist in having a hand in everything, any more than housekeeping consists necessarily in cooking dinner with one's own hands. The cook must be trusted with a large discretion as to the management of the fires and the ovens.

In those countries in which public opinion has yet to be instructed in its privileges, yet to be accustomed to having its own way, this question as to the province of public opinion is much more readily soluble than in this country, where public opinion is wide awake and quite intent upon having its own way anyhow. It is pathetic to see a whole book written by a German professor of political science for the purpose of saying to his countrymen, "Please try to have an opinion about national affairs"; but a public which is so modest may at least be expected to be very docile and acquiescent in learning what things it has *not* a right to think and speak about imperatively. It may be sluggish, but it will not be meddlesome. It will submit to be instructed before it tries to instruct. Its political education will come before its political activity. In trying to instruct our own public opinion, we are dealing with a pupil apt to think itself quite sufficiently instructed beforehand.

The problem is to make public opinion efficient without suffering it to be meddlesome. Directly exercised, in the oversight of the daily details and in the choice of the daily means of government, public criticism is of course a clumsy nuisance, a rustic handling delicate machinery. But as superintending the greater forces of formative policy alike in politics and administration, public criticism is altogether safe and beneficent, altogether indispensable. Let administrative study find the best means for giving public criticism this control and for shutting it out from all other interference.

But is the whole duty of administrative study done when it has taught the people what sort of administration to desire and demand, and how to get what they demand? Ought it not to go on to drill candidates for the public service?

There is an admirable movement towards universal political education now afoot in this country. The time will soon come when no college of respectability can afford to do without a well-filled chair of political science. But the education thus imparted will go but a certain length. It will multiply the number of intelligent critics of government, but it will create no competent body of administrators. It will prepare the way for the development of a sure-footed understanding of the general principles of government, but it will not necessarily foster skill in conducting government. It is an education which will equip legislators, perhaps, but not executive officials. If we are to improve public opinion, which is the motive power of government, we must prepare better officials as the *apparatus* of government. If we are to put in new boilers and to mend the fires which drive our governmental machinery, we must not leave the old wheels and joints and valves and bands to creak and buzz and clatter on as the best they may at bidding of the new force. We must put in new running parts wherever there is the least lack of strength or adjustment. It will be necessary to organize democracy by sending up to the competitive examinations for the civil service men definitely prepared for standing liberal tests as to technical knowledge. A technically schooled civil service will presently have become indispensable.

I know that a corps of civil servants prepared by a special schooling and drilled, after appointment, into a perfected organization, with appropriate hierarchy and characteristic discipline, seems to a great many very thoughtful persons to contain elements which might combine to make an offensive official class,—a distinct, semi-corporate body with sympathies divorced from those of a progressive, free-spirited people, and with hearts narrowed to the meanness of a bigoted officialism. Certainly such a class would be altogether hateful and harmful in the United States. Any measures calculated to produce it would for us be measures of reaction and of folly.

But to fear the creation of a domineering, illiberal officialism as a result of the studies I am here proposing is to miss altogether the principle upon which I wish most to insist. That principle is, that administration in the United States must be at all points sensitive to public opinion. A body of thoroughly trained officials serving during good behavior we must have in any case: that is a plain business necessity. But the apprehension that such a body will be anything un-American clears away the moment it is asked, What is to constitute good behavior? For that question obviously carries its own answer on its face. Steady, hearty allegiance to the policy of the government they serve will constitute good behavior. That *policy* will have no taint of officialism about it. It will not be the creation of permanent officials, but of statesmen whose responsibility to public opinion will be direct and inevitable. Bureaucracy can exist only where the whole service of the state is removed from the common political life of the people, its chiefs as well as its rank and file. Its motives, its objects, its policy, its standards, must be bureaucratic. It would be difficult to point out any examples of impudent exclusiveness and arbitrariness on the part of officials doing service under a chief of department who really served the people, as all our chiefs of departments must be made to do.

• • •

The ideal for us is a civil service cultured and self-sufficient enough to act with sense and vigor, and yet so intimately connected with the popular thought, by means of elections and constant public counsel, as to find arbitrariness or class spirit quite out of the question.

III.

Having thus viewed in some sort the subject-matter and the objects of this study of administration, what are we to conclude as to the methods best suited to it—the points of view most advantageous for it?

Government is so near us, as much a thing of our daily familiar handling, that we can with difficulty see the need of any philosophical study of it, or the exact point of such study, should it be undertaken. We have been on our feet too long to study now the art of walking. We are a practical people, made so apt, so adept in self-government by centuries of experimental drill that we are scarcely any longer capable of perceiving the awkwardness of the particular system we may be using, just because it is so easy for us to use any system. We do not study the art of governing: we govern. But mere unschooled genius for affairs will not save us from sad blunders in administration. Though democrats by long inheritance and repeated choice, we are still rather crude democrats. Old as democracy is, its organization on a basis of modern ideas and conditions is still an unaccomplished work. The democratic state has yet to be equipped for carrying those enormous burdens of administration which the needs of this industrial and trading age are so fast accumulating. Without comparative studies in government we cannot rid ourselves of the misconception that administration stands upon an essentially different basis in a democratic state from that on which it stands in a non-democratic state.

After such study we could grant democracy the sufficient honor of ultimately determining by debate all essential questions affecting the public weal, of basing all structures of policy upon the major will; but we would have found but one rule of good administration for all governments alike. So far as administrative functions are concerned, all governments have a strong structural likeness; more than that, if they are to be uniformly useful and efficient, they *must* have a strong structural likeness. A free man has the same bodily organs, the same executive parts, as the slave, however different may be his motives, his services, his energies. Monarchies and democracies, radically different as they are in other respects, have in reality much the same business to look to.

It is abundantly safe nowadays to insist upon this actual likeness of all governments, because these are days when abuses of power are easily exposed and arrested, in countries like our own, by a bold, alert, inquisitive, detective public thought and a sturdy popular self-dependence such as never existed before. We are slow to appreciate this; but it is easy to appreciate it. Try to imagine personal government in the United States. It is like trying to imagine a national worship of Zeus. Our imaginations are too modern for the feat.

But, besides being safe, it is necessary to see that for all governments alike the legitimate ends of administration are the same, in order not to be frightened at the idea of looking into foreign systems of administration for instruction and suggestion; in order to get rid of the apprehension that we might perchance blindly borrow something incompatible with our principles. That man is blindly astray who denounces attempts to transplant foreign systems into this country. It is impossible: they simply would not grow here. But why should we not use such parts of foreign contrivances as we want, if they be in any way serviceable? We are in no danger of using them in a foreign way. We borrowed rice, but we do not eat it with chopsticks. We borrowed our whole political language from England, but we leave the words "king" and "lords" out of it. What did we ever originate, except the action of the federal government upon individuals and some of the functions of the federal supreme court?

We can borrow the science of administration with safety and profit if only we read all fundamental differences of condition into its essential tenets. We have only to filter it through our constitutions, only to put it over a slow fire of criticism and distill away its foreign gases.

• • •

Let it be noted that it is the distinction, already drawn, between administration and politics which makes the comparative method so safe in the field of administration. When we study the administrative systems of France and Germany, knowing that we are not in search of *political* principles, we need not care a peppercorn for the constitutional or political reasons which Frenchmen or Germans give for their practices when explaining them to us. If I see a murderous fellow sharpening a knife cleverly, I can borrow his way of sharpening the knife without borrowing his probable intention to commit murder with it; and so, if I see a monarchist dyed in the wool managing a public bureau well, I can learn his business methods without changing one of my republican spots. He may serve his king; I will continue to serve the people; but I should like to serve my sovereign as well as he serves his. By keeping this distinction in view,—that is, by studying administration as a means of putting our own politics into convenient practice, as a means of making what is democratically politic towards all administratively possible towards each,—we are on perfectly safe ground, and can learn without error what foreign systems have to teach us. We thus devise an adjusted weight for our comparative method of study. We can thus scrutinize the anatomy of foreign governments without fear of getting any of their diseases into our veins; dissect alien systems without apprehension of blood-poisoning.

Our own politics must be the touchstone for all theories. The principles on which to base a science of administration for America must be principles which have democratic policy very much at heart. And, to suit American habit, all general theories must, as theories, keep modestly in the background, not in open argument only, but even in our own minds,—lest opinions satisfactory only to the standards of the library should be dogmatically used, as if they must be quite as satisfactory to the standards of practical politics as well. Doctrinaire devices must be postponed to tested practices. Arrangements not only sanctioned by conclusive experience elsewhere but also congenial to Amer-

ican habit must be preferred without hesitation to theoretical perfection. In a word, steady, practical statesmanship must come first, closet doctrine second. The cosmopolitan what-to-do must always be commanded by the American how-to-do-it.

Our duty is, to supply the best possible life to a *federal* organization, to systems within systems; to make town, city, county, state, and federal governments live with a like strength and an equally assured healthfulness, keeping each unquestionably its own master and yet making all interdependent and cooperative, combining independence with mutual helpfulness. The task is great and important enough to attract the best minds.

This interlacing of local self-government with federal self-government is quite a modern conception. It is not like the arrangements of imperial federation in Germany. There local government is not yet, fully, local *self*-government. The bureaucrat is everywhere busy. His efficiency springs out of *esprit de corps,* out of care to make ingratiating obeisance to the authority of a superior, or, at best, out of the soil of a sensitive conscience. He serves, not the public, but an irresponsible minister. The question for us is, how shall our series of governments within governments be so administered that it shall always be to the interest of the public officer to serve, not his superior alone but the community also, with the best efforts of his talents and the soberest service of his conscience? How shall such service be made to his commonest interest by contributing abundantly to his sustenance, to his dearest interest by furthering his ambition, and to his highest interest by advancing his honor and establishing his character? And how shall this be done alike for the local part and for the national whole?

If we solve this problem we shall again pilot the world. There is a tendency—is there not?—a tendency as yet dim, but already steadily impulsive and clearly destined to prevail, towards, first the confederation of parts of empires like the British, and finally of great states themselves. Instead of centralization of power, there is to be wide union with tolerated divisions of prerogative. This is a tendency towards the American type—

of governments joined with governments for the pursuit of common purposes, in honorary equality and honorable subordination. Like principles of civil liberty are everywhere fostering like methods of government; and if comparative studies of the ways and means of government should enable us to offer suggestions which will practically combine openness and vigor in the administration of such governments with ready docility to all serious, well-sustained public criticism, they will have approved themselves worthy to be ranked among the highest and most fruitful of the great departments of political study. That they will issue in such suggestions I confidently hope.

READING 1.2

Introduction

Before going on to the case study, as normally happens in this text's concept-case methodology, which pairs concepts with cases throughout this book, let's look at one more conceptual overview that attempts to define what is the nature and substance of the study of public administration (as opposed to its practice). Unlike the Wilson essay, which is an argument for its development in 1887, the following piece by the author of this textbook tries to sketch the academic study of public administration from the vantage point of its broad historical evolution in America. He argues that public administration as a field of study is a product of a unique political tradition that he labels as "antistatist." This "antistatist" tradition permitted America to ignore this field until the late nineteenth century, but it arose as a response to the rapidly changing socio-political-economic environment throughout the twentieth century.

Because much of the following essay attempts to define the field of American Public Administration by arguing that its outlook and values were—and still are—pervasively dominated by anti-statism, it is worth briefly defining "statism" and "anti-statism" as an introduction to this essay. What do those two terms mean?

As one leading expert on this topic recently defined "state":

> A state is any set of relatively differentiated organizations that claims sovereignty and coercive control over a territory and its population, defending and perhaps extending that claim in competition with other states. The core organizations that make up a state include administrative, judicial, and policing organizations that collect and dispense revenues, enforce the constitutive rules of the state and society, and maintain some modicum of domestic order, especially to protect the state's own claims and activities.[1]

"Statism" therefore is doctrines and ideas that advocate strengthening the role and sovereignty of the state institutions in society. "Anti-statism" is the opposite, namely ideas and doctrines expressly hostile to these central governing institutions in society, which argue for reducing, limiting, even eliminating their role(s) and activities.

[1]Theda Skocpol, *Protecting Soldiers and Mothers: The Political Origins of Social Policy in the United States* (Cambridge, MA: Harvard University Press), p. 43. Skocpol's conceptualization of "state," as she indicates in a footnote, draws heavily from the writings of Max Weber and Otto Hintz.

As you read this "dragnet overview" of the study of Public Administration, you might ask yourself these questions:

How does the field define itself today in contrast with Wilson's 1887 perspective? What are its basic values and outlooks?

What are the central problems Public Administration is trying to address now in comparison to Wilson's era?

How does the field today view the problem of relating politics and administration, by contrast to Wilson's essay?

Do you agree that "The Refounding Movement" is the correct label for what happened within Public Administration in the 1990s? If so, what are the implications for the *practice* of public administration?

The Study of Public Administration in the United States: "The Eminently Practical Science"

RICHARD J. STILLMAN II

The study of Public Administration[1] in the United States, unlike other nations, can be understood only within the context of a radically antistatist political tradition. The U.S. Constitution, the core framing document, says nothing about civil service, budgets, executive departments, planning, and yes, public administration, all essential to promoting effective government performance. Rather, the Great Charter of 1787 places a tangle of limits upon government action by means of federalism, separation of powers, periodic elections, enumerated powers, a bill of rights, and so forth—all aimed at negating public power, not enhancing it, in order to secure, in Thomas Jefferson's ringing words of the Declaration of Independence, "life, liberty and the pursuit of happiness."

The Founders, to paraphrase Louis Hartz, were "locked into John Locke" (Hartz 1955). They

framed the American Constitution premised on erecting a "night watchman"–style government by means of a strict "social contract" with the people to provide for only defense, courts, foreign affairs, trade relations, coin money, and little else.

In turn, this new governing edifice was firmly founded upon a rock-hard Calvinism that viewed human nature as sinful due Adam's fall, so that no one can be trusted with power for very long. Or in Madison's apt phrase coined to support the separation of powers in *Federalist No. 51,* "Ambition must be made to counteract ambition" (Hamilton, Madison, and Jay 1961).

An eighteenth-century enlightenment-inspired Constitution, based upon seventeenth-century Lockean politics and sixteenth-century Calvinist religion, made it hard to accommodate twentieth-century "positive" administrative action or thought. Indeed, the framers sought to stamp out anything that smelled of the slightest whiff of European-style statism, for their opponents, the antifederalists, were even more rabid on that subject—and they nearly won!

America's belief in antistatism was further soundly reinforced over more than three centuries

[1]Note: This essay was written especially for this volume. Because the English language does not differentiate between administrative institutional practice versus theory, the author follows Dwight Waldo's approach throughout this essay by capitalizing "Public Administration" when referring to ideas or theory of the study of this field, as opposed to lowercase for describing its practice and institutions.

by waves of immigrants fleeing all sorts of oppressive regimes, from the Puritans in 1620 to this century's escapees from fascism, communism, and numerous other varieties of "isms," all carrying a peculiarly virulent hostility towards statism. There were no stout advocates of Machiavelli's "Prince," Bodin's "divine right of kings," or Hobbes's "Leviathan." If there were any British Tories, the Revolutionary War chased them off to Canada or back to England for good in 1776!

Quite by accident and no thanks to Adam Smith, the first century of American national life conspired to underscore the notion that "state" was not only "evil" but unnecessary. Geographic isolation, a largely self-supporting rural populace, the absence of significant external threats, little need for sizable armed forces or social services, the frontier mentality, and the lack of an industrial revolution created a unique hothouse environment where antistatism flourished with little challenge as the political norm. Perhaps Harvard sociologist Theda Skocpol most aptly characterized this odd situation: just as Prussia in the eighteenth century was less a state with an army than an army with a state, the early United States was "not so much a country with a post office, as a post office that gave popular reality to a fledging nation" (Skocpol 1996). During the 1830s and 1840s, three-quarters of all federal employees were postal workers, and until the Civil War, 85 percent of growth in the entire federal government occurred within that single department.

The Uniqueness of American Public Administration Thought

What does all this unrelenting antistatism have to do with the study of Public Administration in America? First, it explains why this academic field arrived so late on this side of the Atlantic. Without much necessity for public administration or its institutions and practices, why bother with Public Administration or its study and ideas? It took a century *after* the Constitution was written—in 1887, to be precise—for the first essay that merely

advocated its study: Woodrow Wilson's now famous centennial essay, "The Study of Administration." It took another nearly four decades for the first American textbook to appear: Leonard White's *An Introduction to the Study of Public Administration* (1926). Indeed, the growth of public administrative research and training did not appear until the 1930s and 1940s more than a century after the subject had been well established on the European continent.

Contextual forces in the late nineteenth and early twentieth century forced Americans to build an administrative enterprise, like it or not, in response to the closing of the frontier, massive migration from abroad, rapid technological as well as industrial change with concomitant jarring "economic booms and busts," clashes between management and labor as well as the drive for international markets abroad. Only then did the development of a professional civil service, military, and diplomatic corps become urgent new priorities.

Suddenly a prophetic phrase in Wilson's 1887 essay became meaningful: "It is getting harder to run a Constitution than frame one." Up to roughly the dawn of the new century, even well into the 1920s, Americans studied government as law, proper constitutional design, and political philosophy, largely salted with Lockean-Calvinistic-Jeffersonian-antistatism. Thus, its second unique quality: U.S. Public Administration appeared well after the U.S. administrative state became an established reality and "running the Constitution" a necessity. Most scholars date the building of the American State between 1877 and 1920 (Skowronek 1982), and administrative ideas gelled only later. Again by stark contrast to continental Europe, where the development of both state and administrative sciences preceded democratic constitution-making, intense antistatism reversed the process in America and so, as a result, first its constitution, next its state and *then* its study emerged.

Third, unlike Europe's Public Administration, where top-down state-building fostered top-down, rational administrative sciences, American Public Administration, "bubbled up" quietly and haphazardly from grassroots reforms, imbued with protestant "moral uplift" and "democratic idealism." It evolved in bits and pieces through the experimentation by a variety of local reform groups such as the National Civil Service League, National Municipal League, New York Bureau of Municipal Research, and more generally across the nation through the "bureau movement." To this day, American Public Administration Thought remains considerably more experimental, fragmented, inductive, applied, and reformist in caste and character compared with other countries. Again missing a sense of state, indeed vigorously opposed to it, any kind of top-down, rationalized administrative way of thinking would, for Americans, be out of the question, even inconceivable. Thus *both* U.S. public administration as well as its Public Administration literally had to be built from the ground up by adding a civil service system here, an executive budget there, a council-manager plan over there, moving upward to the federal levels *and* toward a unique way of administrative thought that gelled under a label that today is called Public Administration.

Fourth, unlike many nations, where the positive law tradition became the basic methodology for teaching and research, particularly to create and expand welfare states on the Continent during the nineteenth century (Rutgers and Raadschelders unpublished), Americans, rooted in a common law tradition as well as in the fundamental law of its Constitution that largely negated public power, had to look elsewhere to find the substance and scope of, not to mention legitimacy for, its administrative ideas. Rather, the field of management along with scientific methods founded upon a sharp differentiation between politics and administration became its unique intellectual early framework and identity, as well as its "meat and potatoes" content.

The two most important writings that so profoundly influenced early students, akin to Old and New Testaments for field, were Frank Goodnow's *Politics and Administration* (1900). As its title denotes, it offered up the rationale for just such a clear-cut dichotomy. Frederick W. Taylor's *The*

Principles of Scientific Management (1911), also as its title emphasizes, gave the emerging field both rational managerial methodology as well as solid scientific legitimacy to "do good" public administration, buttressed neatly by the popularity of business symbols during the progressive reform era.

Again without a sense of state, Americans had little choice but to advance a clear dichotomy that would free up "clean" administration from messy and corrupt "machine politics" while at the same time press for "respectable" business and scientific methods. While Goodnow and Taylor's ideas may seem quaint, even far-fetched, today, they in fact provided necessary answers to very real, complex empirical issues of the times. As Frederick C. Mosher astutely observed: the developments that created "the management movement were in a considerable degree, *a response* [author's emphasis] to the conditions . . . [of] fragmentation of responsibilities; lack of unified leadership; political corruption and spoils. They were spawned in an era of reform, of progressivism, of growing professionalism and occupational specialization and faith in rationality and applied sciences" (Mosher 1976).

Finally, public administration as well as Public Administration's origins and growth after the dawn of the twentieth century were directly related to the rapid expansion of democracy in all phases of public life. The twentieth century saw successful progressive challenges to "boss rule" and machine politics, with the passage of women's suffrage, direct election of senators, initiative, referendum and recall measures, combined with the rising public demands for government regulation of business, social services, and the like. In turn, these democratic forces only heightened existing issues of governance. In the words of historian Robert Wiebe, America became a "distended society" (Wiebe 1968) that, in response, demanded more, not less, administrative thought, research, and training in order to knit together an increasingly fragmented or segmented society.

Whether these administrative ideas worked all that well, let alone efficiently and effectively, is another matter, but again unlike other countries,

American Public Administration Thought became—and remains—a handmaiden of constitutional and democratic values. For without a preexisting stable state, its administrative ideas and institutions always had to be open for adjustment as well as to immediate shifting interests of the public, who was ultimately in charge. Therefore, U.S. administrative thought has never been—nor can ever be—defined as a fixed doctrine or set of doctrines but instead stays in flux, always chasing the shifting constitutional-democratic priorities of each new American generation. Thus too, Public Administration seems to transform itself into a new intellectual construct every generation, or every twenty years, often through highly innovative and creative methods, in order to respond to the pressing demands of the moment. Four eras of Public Administration, in retrospect, are apparent during the twentieth century, each with its distinct doctrines, ideals, theories, frameworks, methodologies, and agendas, largely shaped by the particular generational needs of that era: 1926–46, 1947–67, 1968–88, and 1989 to the present.

POSDCORB Orthodoxy, 1926–1946

Nineteen twenty-six can be considered as the precise date for the intellectual birthing of American Public Administration. In that year, the first American textbook appeared: Leonard White's *Introduction to the Study of Public Administration* (1926). To be sure, after the turn of the century numerous basic texts were published on various functional fields such as city management, military administration, school administration, and business, but White's book stands out as a remarkable achievement. Here was the earliest volume offering Americans a subject labeled Public Administration. White's book succeeded as no other had at gluing together various functional specializations as well as disparate ideas of Taylorism, Goodnow's dichotomy, and other administrative innovations under the rubric that we term today Public Administration.

At the heart of White's theoretical synthesis was a POSDCORB-way of thought that Luther Gulick, a decade later, most forcefully and fully articulated in *The Papers on the Science of Administration* (1937). The acronym stood for a logical sequence of steps for practicing "good" administration, ideally in the order in which they should be accomplished, namely, planning, organizing, staffing, direction, coordinating, reporting, and budgeting. In many aspects, it reflected an efficient military model of "good management" that White applied universally throughout American civilian government.

POSDCORB certainly arrived at the right moment. Not only were the first graduate M.P.A. programs emerging and needing a basic text, beginning at the The Maxwell School, Syracuse University (1924) and University of Southern California (1928), but far more important, POSDCORB addressed as well as any alternative the twin crises of that era, the Great Depression and World War II. In the most turbulent period of the twentieth century, the nation confronted its worst economic and military conflicts back-to-back. How to plan, organize, staff, and so on, in order to cope with these unprecedented emergencies was indeed very real, and POSDCORB orthodoxy was near at hand for "the cure." Of course, what POSDCORB provided was a pretty stiff cure based upon a sharp separation of politics and administration, a no-nonsense Taylorism, applied in lockstep military fashion, raised to the highest levels of government, for reorganizing the Presidency, thanks to the Brownlow Report on The President's Committee on Administration Management in 1937 (Karl 1963). Because Public Administration reached such visibility and prominence at the top levels of public life to deal successfully with the most pressing problems of these times, some later would envision it as "the golden age" for the field (Newland 1984).

Perhaps an exaggeration, though on a deeper level, POSDCORB indeed did knit together a respectable intellectual framework for the new academic field. It also gave a common outlook and cause for a small but creative and committed band of academics who founded such key institutions as the Public Administration Clearing House (1930), the American Society for Public Administration (1939), and the *Public Administration Review* (1940), which significantly advanced research and teaching agendas for the field. POSDCORB further provided a cohesive and comprehensive academic rationale for setting up graduate programs advancing research as well as its applications throughout all levels of government, federal, state, local. In short, POSDCORB, as both an idea and a practice for doing "good" administration, allowed the field to begin, grow, and even flourish in national prominence in a manner that it never quite has achieved since. Yet, to the next generation of students, POSDCORB hardly seemed heroic, but rather full of contradictions—unscientific, value-laden, time-bound, and rigid, as well as hardly the best means to meet the needs of the postwar era. Of course, there were some persistent critics of the POSDCORB orthodoxy during the 1930s, such as Chester Barnard, Mary Parker Follett, Elton Mayo, Fritz Roethisberger, Ordway Tead, W. W. Willoughby, and "The Brookings Group." Yet, they remained distinct "outsiders" who were only later "discovered" in the postwar era, by Public Administration Scholarship.

Social Science Heterodoxy, 1947–1967

Having won dual victories over the Great Depression and fascism, the United States by default became the postwar free world leader and over the next four decades engaged in a fierce Cold War with communism, at times turning into hot flashpoints in Korea, Vietnam, and elsewhere. In James Fesler's fitting aphorism, "America rapidly shifted its concern from the Fascist Axis to the Communist Nexus" (Fesler 1975).

In retrospect, it is hard to overestimate the profound influence of the Cold War in shaping American society as a whole as well as its public administration and its Administrative Sciences in particular. Just as the ancient Egyptian pyramids were products of slave labor harnessed for the greater glory of the Pharaoh's "hereafter," likewise fearful demons from abroad, fanned by popular press and political paranoia, drove postwar Americans into a self-protectionist frenzy of administrative state-building. Not only did a massive military-industrial complex emerge, as symbolized by the Pentagon, but a host of domestic administrative activities were justified by national security needs such as the space program, educational assistance, scientific research, and even the largest public work's project in the nation's history, the National Defense Highway Act (1955)— all in the name of beating the Russians!

American Administrative Sciences became the direct beneficiary of public largess through the new necessities for government training programs to staff the civil service at all levels, as well by expanded funding for scientific and applied administrative research. American universities, driven by exploding enrollment of returning veterans, opened their doors to talented young professors, themselves often fresh from New Deal and wartime work, to teach, research, and rethink the field. Thus teaching and research opportunities grew rapidly in higher education, particularly with the wider range of demands for international scholarship. For many administrative academics, especially those who had experienced public administration firsthand during the Great Depression and World War II, and now were confronted with entirely different administrative challenges in the postwar world, prewar POSDCORB orthodoxy suddenly seemed ill-equipped to grasp the new administrative "realities" and deal with their "essentials."

In 1947 a young Yale political scientist, Robert Dahl, wrote a seminal *Public Administration Review* essay that perceptively and prophetically pointed out three central intellectual problems of prewar orthodoxy (Dahl 1947). In "The Science of Public Administration: Three Problems," Dahl challenged Public Administration, first, to rethink its normative assumptions that had been based on the sharp dichotomy between politics and administration; second, to expand its conception of human behavior, beyond a view of a narrow, technical "rational man," in order to comprehend "the whole man" and thus explain more realistically how humans act within organizations; third, to embrace broader historical, economic, and social conditions, not merely techniques or technicians, as influential factors that affect administrative results. Dahl's orientation, or rather reorientation, of the field, by contrast to prewar orthodox values, stressed values of "realism," "behavioralism," and "scientific rigor."

Herbert Simon's book *Administrative Behavior: A Study of Decision-Making Process in Administrative Organization,* also published in the same year (1947), made, however, the most profound and original theoretical impact on postwar administrative sciences in the United States (Simon 1947). For Simon, drawing upon logical-positivist continental analytic philosophy, POSDCORB failed to live up to "true scientific methodology." His first chapter began with a slashing, if not dramatic, attack on POSDCORB principles, which he concluded were little more than "folk wisdom" or "proverbs" that confused "facts with values." Simon then set out ambitiously to refound the entire field on an entirely new interdisciplinary decision-making model, one he called "bounded rationality," to explain, as the book's title indicates, "administrative behavior." POSDCORB orthodoxy, as a result, would never look quite the same to anyone who read Simon's text.

Under the withering intellectual crossfire of Dahl, Simon, and others of that generation, Dwight Waldo, Norton Long, James Fesler, Carl Friedrich, and Herman Finer, POSDCORB rapidly faded as the commonly accepted orthodoxy and soon became simply "posdcorb," or one among many competing ideas to explain the field. By the 1950s the rich infusion of a new variety of social sciences into Public Administration, from economics, political sciences, psychology, comparative studies, decision-sciences, business, and elsewhere had turned the field into a dizzying array of heterodoxies in order to *both* comprehend and to cope with enormous administrative challenges at home and overseas. In the process, American Public Ad-

ministration became far broader, less parochial, more theoretical, even academically more "respectable" and enriched with multiple doctrines, methodologies, ideas, and vast new data, as well as with factual information. The field also gravitated increasingly into formal university settings, especially within the social sciences, as opposed to prewar dominance by practitioners, or academics with mostly applied backgrounds. Furthermore, its way of thinking and its dominant values became more dynamic and process oriented, again emphasizing "realism," "behavioralism," and "science," by comparison to its prewar values, with more stable, Newtonian-like application of fixed POSD-CORB Principles for understanding *and* doing "good" public administration. Indeed, what was "good" public administration turned out to be less certain, more problematic, and relative, no longer confined to promoting only twin *E*s of economy and efficiency. "Effectiveness," at best a slippery value, found favor at the core of many heterodoxies, either as part of a new trilogy of *E*s that combined the old *E*s and a new *E,* or as a standalone value orientation. One does not have to dig very deeply into the writings of several of the leading scholars during this period—Frederick Mosher, Paul Appleby, Don Price, and others—to find their value emphasis on "institutional effectiveness," not to mention "realism," "behavioralism," and "rigor." Likewise, the basic texts in the 1950s, such as those by John Pfiffner or Felix Nigro, or even Leonard White's textbook, then in its fourth edition, echoed such thinking and were popular no doubt because they spoke forcefully and thoughtfully to the continuing administrative demands of state-building during the Cold War.

The Reassertion of Democratic Idealism, 1968–1988

As this essay underscored from the outset, rejection of statism has deep roots in American soil, yet no era during the twentieth century of U.S. Public Administration witnessed a more intense outpouring of antistatism literature than from the late

1960s to the late 1980s. The reasons for the outbreak of rabid antistatism during that generation remain unclear even today. Perhaps it was caused by a backlash to perceived administrative misdeeds in Vietnam or Watergate—or later, Irangate? Was it due to the popularity of the counterculture? The widespread media criticisms of government? Growth of the civil rights, environmental, consumer, feminist, and gay movements? Assassinations of charismatic figures like President John F. Kennedy and the Reverend Martin Luther King Jr.? Dashed hopes from program failures in the New Frontier and the Great Society? Or Presidents Jimmy Carter and Ronald Reagan waging successful campaigns against Washington, D.C. and Big Government?

Whatever the causes, Herbert Kaufman characterized this period by the title of a lead essay in the *Public Administration Review,* "Fear of Bureaucracy: A Raging Pandemic" (Kaufman 1981). Or in the words of Samuel P. Huntington, the 1960s and early 1970s inaugurated "a democratic surge" that was similar to the eras of Jefferson-Jacksonian democracy and Progressive Reform, in which "there was a vital reassertion of democratic idealism in all phases of American public life" (Huntington 1974).

The 1968 Minnowbrook Conference best symbolized the starting point of this shift toward democratic idealism within Public Administration. It was named for Syracuse University's Minnowbrook Conference Center, where the meeting took place during the warm summer of 1968, ironically not too distant from Woodstock, an even more noteworthy symbol of a generational gathering of that era. Minnowbrook involved mostly under-thirty-year-old academics, largely from political science. Their conference papers that were later published argued for the field to adopt fresh intellectual perspectives, or for a "new public administration," based on ideals of participation, consensus-building, sharing ideas, mutual trust, and even "love of mankind" (Marini 1971). These "young turks" exhibited particular hostility toward traditional public administration aimed at state-building and toward enhancing administrative ef-

ficiency, economy, and effectiveness as embodied in POSDCORB, as well as newer rational techniques such as operations research, decision sciences, systems theory, PPBS, MBO, or other techoprofessional "inventions" stressing "rationality," "science," "behaviorism," "realism," or any sort of "hard" empirical quantitative methodologies. Unlike the "young turks" in the late 1940s, Dahl, Simon, and others, who had revolted against POSDCORB precisely because they saw it had failed to accurately describe postwar administration sciences and deal with what they believed were new postwar administrative priorities, these late-1960s "young turks" (few of whom had worked in or even had held degrees in public administration) saw POSDCORB as all *too* real, *too* powerful, *too* much the embodiment of *the* establishment and therefore fundamentally detrimental to egalitarian, democratic, humane values.

If the New Public Administration challenged the prior generational way of thinking from the left, public choice economics did so even more fiercely and profoundly from the right. In the same year as Minnowbrook, Indiana University professor Vincent Ostrom of Alabama began writing *The Intellectual Crisis in American Public Administration* (Ostrom 1973). More than any other single book, Ostrom introduced and advanced public choice doctrines throughout the field. Much like the Minnowbrookers, but using a far different vocabulary and scientific paradigm, Ostrom frontally assaulted older state-building ideas that he labeled as "The Wilson-Weber Paradigm" with its "single-centered administration," "hierarchical structures," and "sharp separation of politics and administration." Based on his reading, or rather rereading, of *The Federalist Papers,* Alexis de Tocqueville's *Democracy in America* and the growing literature in a new economic subfield of public choice, Ostrom advocated a radically antistatist alternative, one he called "the Democratic Administrative Paradigm." Here was the very reverse of "Wilson-Weber" featuring "diverse decision-making centers," "popular participation," and "fragmented, overlapping, decentralized authority." In brief, Ostrom sought to enhance "public choice"—or read it as "individual choice"—using economic language and economic methods applied with fierce anti-governmental zeal.

So if Minnowbrook and Ostrom best symbolized the "democratic temper of the times"—or is it distemper?—what distinctive marks did such literature leave on the field? Briefly, seven legacies come to mind:

1. *Clashing moral absolutes:* No longer did science, realism and behaviorism hold the dominant intellectual center, but new ideological stridency appeared throughout Public Administration thought as epitomized by the clashing moral absolutes of democratic ideals inherent in Minnowbrook and Public Choice thinking.

2. *The new two Es and one L:* If the two prior generations had promoted economy, efficiency and effectiveness, new key values emerged as dominant, mainly aimed to limit or control bureaucratic discretion and broaden democratic participation. Thus, "ethical," "legal," and "economizing" constraints on government due to "fear of bureaucracy" became paramount concerns and spawned a new infusion of "ethics," "law," and "economics" classes and texts throughout Public Administration Education.

3. *A cry for relevancy:* Both *Minnowbrook* and *The Intellectual Crisis* began by attacking the old orthodoxies as irrelevant for addressing the pressing problem of the late 1960s and early 1970s. Public Administration, its label and content, suddenly appeared old-fashioned and out of touch for many in this new generation. Alternative labels, often with far different connotations and implications, grew increasingly into favor—for example, "public management," "public affairs," "public policy," and "implementation", under which "bread and butter" Administration Sciences came to be taught.

4. *The fragmentation—or decline?—of generalist Public Administration:* Concomitant with the rise of more specialized approaches

often emphasizing policy implementation and management, generalist Public Administration education and research declined in academic status, especially at major universities that had been longtime leaders, like Harvard, Berkeley, or Chicago. They shifted to becoming "policy schools" with their own professional associations and journals. Generalist associations, like the American Society for Public Administration, that had served as the focus for academic-practitioner exchange since 1940, no longer were dominant or were active at the forefront of the field. ASPA increasingly seemed to be displaced by narrower, more specialized groups dealing with aspects of Public Administration, such as the National Academy of Public Administration, or the National Association of Schools of Public Administration.

5. *The proliferation of subfields and techniques:* As specialization grew, new subfields and sub-subfields emerged as important to teach and train public administrators, often under functional fields like criminal justice, health, or public works. Techniques such as ZBB, MBO, or OD were popularized and proliferated into a vast hodgepodge of often faddish, unrelated techniques with problematic aims.

6. *A field in intellectual crisis?* Ostrom's book title perhaps most succinctly captured the mood of the times (and it's no doubt why, in large part, it became such a popular text), for indeed many academics felt that the field was on the verge of "flying apart" and experiencing "a profound intellectual crisis." With the combination of declining status, increasing specialization, and faddishness, what was unique about "public administration," even what defined "public" or the study of government, became more problematic, a murky enigma, at least to many old hands, not to mention those new to the field.

7. *A widening gap between theory and practice:* If the pre- and post-World War II eras

mingled and mixed administrative academics and practitioners with relative ease, due to a degree of shared purposes between both, this era by contrast, 1968 to 1988, saw a much sharper differentiation. As the academic enterprise grew larger, more diverse, and more predicated on "publish or perish," with little or no common concerns for public service or for the advancement of the public interest, "the academy" became more remote, often devoting itself more to theory, with limited exposure to practice and the immediate needs of practitioners. This widening gap served to enrich theory as well as various specializations, yet it also created vexing distances, divisions, and debates over just what is Public Administration: a field or focus? theory or practice? art or science? craft or profession? or what?

The Refounding Movement, 1989 to the Present Day

As the twenty-first century was about to dawn, once more the socio-political-economic-military landscape of the United States, indeed the world, dramatically changed. The fall of the Berlin Wall in 1989 signaled the end of the Cold War and the collapse of communism. America suddenly assumed the unique role as the last global superpower, with far-flung security responsibilities. Along with the U.S. hegemony, or possibly because of it, a borderless, global economy prospered, along with the explosion of new information technologies, while serious environmental threats involving air, water, solid waste also appeared on a worldwide, at times life-threatening scale. The lengthy list of such changes profoundly reshapes America's complexities and challenges of government. Certainly public administration, and its people, processes, and institutions, stand at the heart of helping *or* hindering the nation's present capacity to govern and to deal with this new policy agenda effectively.

In response, Public Administration likewise seems to be entering a new era of refounding its basics. During the last decade or so, several clusters of academics have emerged to rethink fundamental questions such as, What is Public Administration? What is the meaning of the "good life" and "good society"? Who should govern, and how? What are the criteria for proper administrative actions—and what defines improper or unethical action? Should public administration be centralized and/or decentralized? What is its proper size and scope within society? Should public administrators behave as servants of the people, or as free-wheeling entrepreneurs? Indeed how can old concepts like the "public interest," "accountability," "responsibility," and "public welfare" be reframed and recast to respond to twenty-first–century needs?

Right now the field seems to be in the midst of a yesty debate over these and other seminal administrative questions. While the answers remain unclear, six identifiable clusters or schools of thought with shared perspectives—frequently expressed through their own publications, associations and leading academics—are evident and influential today:

1. *The Reinventors:* During the early 1990s clearly the first and most significant group to suggest fundamental alternatives was that associated with the ideas put forward by David Osborne and Ted Gaebler's *Reinventing Government* (1992). Their book, which became a popular best-seller and a major part of President Bill Clinton's plan to reform the federal government, advocated "a third way" or a challenge to what was referred to as "old-style big bureaucracy" and "free-market methods" for doing the "public's business." Rather, the authors suggest building the "entrepreneurial spirit" throughout government as their "answer." While the enthusiasm for "reinventing" has markedly declined by the late 1990s for various reasons, it nonetheless has had profound effects on the size, scope, methods, *and way of thinking* about public administration at all levels of government.

2. *The communitarians:* Communitarian ideas also became popular and influential in many quarters during the 1990s, largely due to the writings of academic sociologists such as Amatai Etzioni, William Galston, David Chrislip, and Philip Selznick. Unlike the "reinventors," made up mostly of consultants and practitioners focused on advancing pragmatic administrative reforms to enhance "efficient, entrepreneurial" government operations for "customers," communitarians wrestle with larger issues of rebuilding "community" and "citizenship." While they touch on few explicit administrative "reforms," most of their voluminous writings do implicitly suggest administrative arrangements to nurture moral ties of family, strengthen bonds in neighborhoods and in the workplace, and encourage wider citizen participation as well as public service.

3. *The VPI refounders:* By contrast to the two aforementioned schools, the Virginia Polytechnic Institution (VPI) refounders are largely composed of senior scholars who have been closely associated throughout their careers with American Administrative Sciences: Gary L. Wamsley, Robert N. Bacher, Charles T. Goodsell, Philip S. Kronenberg, John A. Rohr, Camilla M Stivers, Orion F. White, and James F. Wolf. Their twin multiauthored books *Refounding Public Administration* (1990) and *Refounding Democratic Public Administration* (1996), while containing often contradictory and complex themes, seek nothing less than a fundamental philosophical, institutional, and theoretical refounding of the entire field (as both titles stress). Or in the words of Gary L. Wamsley, they sought to develop "a new normative theory of American public administration and . . . a theory of the American state . . ." (1990, p.4). The authors provoke and challenge stereotypes as well as advance ambitious agenda for the entire field, but by no means do they offer clear-cut convincing strategies or alternative doctrines necessary to resolve deep issues of

legitimacy or securing a stable place for public administration within the context of an antistatist society, at least so far.

4. *The interpretivists:* As direct heirs of the New Public Administration movement, interpretivists are oriented toward phenomenology, or "subjective-intersubjective relations, which they see undergirding the social constructions of reality." As their name suggests, they explore and interpret values, assumptions, and ideas concerning the very nature of being or human existence—that is, the study of ontology. Unquestionably these administrative theorists probe some of the deepest and most profound questions confronting the field. They also have some of the liveliest and most interesting debates over these questions, as represented in several important scholarly books, such as Henry Kass and Byard Catron's (eds.) *Images and Identities in Public Administration* (1990); or within the pages of their peer-reviewed journal, *Administrative Theory and Praxis;* or as reflected in their well-attended annual PAT-NET conferences; or as found in their impressive, Sage book series, "Advances in Public Administration." While probing and provoking, more than any other cluster of current administrative scholars, Interpretists remain the most removed from the mainline day-to-day world of practitioners.

5. *The tools-makers:* Technologists and technology have played major roles in shaping the field from its origins, as discussed before in this essay with Taylorism. Though due to the rise of implementation theory and policy studies, newer "hard" quantitative, analytical methodologies have appeared and have been applied throughout Public Administration research and training in recent years to better understand theoretically, and to better run practically, government programs. One of the most innovative examples of this line of thinking was the creative product of several policy analysts, mainly associated with the Urban Institute, *Beyond Privatization*

(1989), edited by Lester Salamon. The authors offer a "new analytical framework" for understanding and evaluating government programs. Chapter by chapter, this book analyzes various "tools of service delivery" by government. These authors advance new "analytic methods" with no right or wrong answers, only methods for weighing the costs and benefits, of various alternatives.

6. *New bureaucratic analysts:* Finally a rich vibrant stream of ideas and literature continues to advance Public Administration, largely from the pens of political scientists, on a broad range of political and policy issues associated with public bureaucracy, such as public accountability, oversight, control, power, institutional performance, and responsiveness to democracy and to interest groups. Prominent names of this "cluster" of contributors today include James Q. Wilson, Louis Gawthrop, Paul Light, Martha Derthick, James Pfiffner, Lois Wise, Robert Durant, Don Kettl, and Hal Rainey. These and numerous other junior and senior scholars thoughtfully continue to influence the field just as the young political scientist Woodrow Wilson once did beginning in 1887 with the very first American essay advocating the study of Public Administration. Their writings individually and collectively tend to address the broadest and most profound political issues of the field: What is the relationship between politics and administration? What is the role of ethics in administration? How are good and correct policies made? Is the policy process for dealing with the pressing issues of today meeting "public needs" and securing "the public interest?"

Conclusion: Public Administration As "The Eminently Practical Science"

What will the future hold for American Administration Sciences? If the past is any guide to the present—and to the future—U.S. Public Administration, unlike Public Administration elsewhere, will remain dominated by its own unique brand of inductive, experimental, reformist mindset, closely interconnected to the practicalities of coping with the immediate needs of democratic governance. Or in the best sense of Woodrow Wilson's opening lines of his famous 1887 essay, it will remain "the eminently practical science." Within a radically antistatist culture, U.S. Administrative Sciences have no alternative but to steadfastly persist at being open to change, elusive in form, pragmatic in content, a servant of democracy, and above all, keep a low profile. Born without a sense of state, as this essay repeatedly stressed, Americans only reluctantly bought into administrative state-building—and Administrative Sciences—roughly a century *after* the U.S. Constitution was written. Thus, neither its administrative institutions nor academic enterprise seems quite legitimate, even today. Their deep-seated *positive* government prescriptions never fit well—or at all—with the *negative* government values embedded at the core of the Great Charter of 1787.

Debates still rage in the serious literature about whether Public Administration as a field of study exists and what "it" is. Of course it exists, but with a sort of protean cast and character, as Table 1 summarizes, that seems to transform itself into new shapes and purposes every generation, or on twenty-year cycles, to respond to the particular needs of the times. This unobtrusive adaptability to deal with the immediate public demands of the moment may well be U.S. Public Administration's greatest strength. Administrative study must always chase—and cope with—the elusive, shifting yet low-keyed, as catch-as-catch-can public priorities. Whether it "catches" up and then copes successfully, or at all adequately with the pressing issues of society, is another matter, but certainly today in the present period of the Refounding Movement, it continues to try.

And so here within its very strength, one finds also the chief downside of the field readily apparent: its very elusiveness and adaptability makes it a questionable, indeed suspect, academic

Table 1   Four Eras of U.S. Public Administration Thought

Eras and Dates	POSDCORB Orthodoxy 1926–46	Social Science Heterodoxy 1947–67	Reassertion of Democratic Idealism 1968–88	Refounding Movement 1989 to Present
Key Shaping Events	Depression & World War II	Cold War abroad; prosperity at home	Vietnam, Watergate, "fear of bureaucracy"	America as last global superpower, end of cold war and fall of Berlin Wall
Intellecual Benchmark Event and Date	Leonard White's textbook (1926)	Dahl's essay and Simon's book (1947)	Minnowbrook & Ostrom's (1968)	First "refounding books" published (1989)
Framing Administrative Idea	POSDCORB	Social sciences heterodoxy	Democratic idealism	Refounding movement
Leading Administrative Theorist(s)	Leonard White and Luther Gulick	Robert Dahl, Herbert Simon, Dwight Waldo, Frederick Mosher, and Don Price	New PA and public choice scholars	Multiple "refounding" schools
Major Institution(s) Promoting Ideas within Public Administration	"The Chicago School," PACH, ASPA, PAR, White's text	The Maxwell School, USC, and other "generalist" programs	"Policy schools" at Harvard or Berkeley, and "think tanks" at Heritage, AEI and CATO	Professional associations such as NASPAA, ASPA, APSA, APPAM or PAT-NET
Central Values of the Field	POSDCORB Principles rooted in "economy and efficiency," as well as politics-administration dichotomy	Applied "realistic and rigorous," interdisciplinary perspectives promoting institutional effectiveness	"Two Es and One L"	In search of new legitimacy, conceptual framework and values
Main Orientation of Administrative Sciences	Dealing with depression and wartime issues	National/international issues of the Cold War	Ethical, economic, legal, oversight/control issues of bureaucracy	In search of a new overall orientation
Key Theoretical Question	How to build and apply Administrative Sciences?	What is Public Administration?	Where is Public Administration?	What will be the field's new identity?
Education Methods	Learning generalist management functions of POSDCORB	Applying ideas from economics, politics, history, and social sciences	Training in numerous administrative techniques, concepts and technologies	"All depends" on a particular school's perspective and theories
Lasting Contributions	Birth of field; highest visibility; creation of key institutions like ASPA and PAR	Rich infusion of social sciences; global influence; expanded views and ideas about the field	New ideas of law, economics, implementation; analytical methods; rapid growth of size of field	Fundamental rethinking of "basics" like PA's legitimacy, purposes, etc.

enterprise, one that continues to defy, even at the dawn of the twenty-first century, authoritative definition or a settled place within higher education. Is it part of political science? Part of business? A separate field? Or what? One can certainly hear the refrains of all these value accents and methodological emphases from earlier eras in the current refounding movement: the business values apparent within the reinventors; Taylorite themes within the tools-makers; New Public Administration idealism within the interpretists, or political science within the new bureaucratic analysts. Within each school, new administrative concepts are therefore emerging and then gelling, while old ones are declining or disappearing according to contemporary and quickly shifting societal needs—much like a bubbling brew where some bubbles rise whereas others fall seemingly at random. Possibly the various levels of external necessities (state-building needs of society) determine the internal intensity of the boiling bubbles (concept-creation by the academy)? In essence, the field's potential genius may well be that it is continuously "bubbling up" with multiple new perspectives for understanding, defining, and dealing with salient public issues of the here-and-now by means of its own brand of interdisciplinary hands-on conceptual creativity, while frequently being maligned as a marginal, unscientific academic player within contemporary American higher education.

References

Dahl, R.A. 1947. "The Science of Public Administration: Three Problems." *Public Administration Review* 7:1.

Fesler, J.W. 1975. "Public Administration and the Social Sciences: 1946 to 1960." p.98 in *American Public Administration: Past, Present, Futures,* ed. F.C. Mosher. Tuscaloosa, Ala.: University of Alabama Press.

Goodnow, F.J. 1900. *Politics and Administration.* New York: Macmillan.

Gulick, L. 1937. "Notes on the Theory of Organization." p.13 in *Paper on the Source of Administration,* ed. L. Gulick, and L. Urwick.

New York: Institute of Public Administration.

Hamilton, A., J. Madison, and J. John. 1961. *The Federalist Papers.* New York: Mentor.

Hartz, L. 1955. *The Liberal Tradition in America.* New York: Harcourt, Brace.

Huntington, S.P. 1975. "The United States." pp. 74–75 in *The Crisis of Democracy,* ed. M. Crozier et. al. New York: New York University Press.

Karl, B.D. 1963. *Executive Reorganization and Reform in the New Deal.* Chicago: University of Chicago Press.

Kass, H.D., and B.L. Catron, eds. 1990. *Images and Identities in Public Administration.* Newbury Park, Calif.: Sage.

Kaufman, H. 1981. "Fear of Bureaucracy: A Raging Pandemic." *Public Administration Review* 41(1): 1–9.

Marini, F., ed. 1971. *Toward a New Public Administration: The Minnowbrook Perspective.* Scanton, Penn.: Chandler.

Mosher, F.C. 1956. *"Research in Public Administration." Public Administration Review* 16 (Summer) 16: 177.

————, ed. 1976. *Basic Documents of American Public Administration, 1776–1950.* New York: Holmes & Meier.

Newland, C.A. 1984. *Public Administration and Community: Realism in the Practice of Ideals.* McLean, VA.: Public Administration Service.

Osborne, T., and T. Gaebler. 1992. *Reinventing Government: How the Entreprenuerial Spirit Is Transforming the Public Sector from the Schoolhouse to Statehouse, City Hall to the Pentagon.* Reading, Mass.: Addison-Wesley.

Ostrom, V. 1973. *The Intellectual Crisis in American Public Administration.* Tuscaloosa, Ala.: University of Alabama Press.

Raadschelders, J.C.N., and M.R. Rutgers. 2000. "The Waxing and Waning of the State and Its Study," in *The Modern State and Its Study*, ed. W. J. M. Kickert and R. Stillman. London: Edward Elgar, Chapter 2.

Salamon, L.M., ed. 1989. *Beyond Privatization:*

The Tools of Government Action. Washington, D.C.: Urban Institute Press.

Simon, H.A. 1947. *Administrative Behavior: A Study of Decision-Making Process in Administrative Organization.* New York: Macmillan.

Skocpol, T. 1996. "Presidential Address for the Annual Meeting of Social Science History Association, unpublished manuscript, p. 10."

Skowronek, S. 1982. *Building a New American State: The Expansion of National Administrative Capacities, 1877–1920.* Cambridge: Cambridge University Press.

Taylor, F.W. 1911. *The Principles of Scientific Management.* New York: W.W. Norton.

Waldo, O. 1948. *The Administrative State: A Study of the Political Theory of American Public Administration.* New York: Ronald Press.

Wamsley, G. et. al. 1990. *Refounding Public Administration.* Newbury Park, Calif.: Sage.

Wamsley, G. et al. 1996. *Refounding Democratic Public Administration.* Newbury Park, Calif.: Sage.

White, L.O. 1926. *Introduction to the Study of Public Administration.* New York: Macmillan.

Wiebe, R.H. 1967. *The Search for Order, 1877–1920.* New York: Hill and Wang.

Wilson, W. 1887. "The Study of Administration." *Political Science Quarterly* 2 (June): 197–222.

☐ CASE STUDY 1

Introduction

The following story may shed some further insight into the role of public administration in modern society. The story, "The Blast in Centralia No. 5: A Mine Disaster No One Stopped," is an excellent account of a mine disaster that occurred two generations ago in Centralia, Illinois, killing 111 miners. This article is an unusual case study in public administration; not only does the author, John Bartlow Martin, carefully recount the facts of the catastrophe, but he also attempts to understand the reasons behind the disaster. In his search for clues, the writer reveals much about the inner complexities of the administrative framework of our modern society—a coal company sensitive only to profit incentives; state regulatory agencies inadequately enforcing mine safety legislation; federal officials and mine unions complacent about a growing problem; and the miners incapable of protecting themselves against the impending disaster.

This is an example of administrative reality that, for some, will only confirm their suspicions about the inherent corruption of modern administrative enterprises. The victims died, they might argue, because the mine owners were only interested in profits, not in human lives. But is this the correct interpretation? Martin does not blame any one individual or even a group of individuals but stresses the ineffectiveness of the administrative structure on which all the disaster victims were dependent for survival.

After reading this story you will probably be struck by how much modern society depends on the proper functioning of unseen administrative arrangements—for safeguarding our environment; for protecting the purity of our food; for transporting us safely by road, rail, or air; for sending us our mail; or for negotiating an arms limitations agreement at some distant diplomatic conference. All of us, like the miners in Centralia No. 5, rely throughout our lives on the immovable juggernaut of impersonal administrative systems. A functioning, ordered public administration, as this story illustrates, is an inescapable necessity for maintaining the requisites of a civilized modern society.

As you read this selection, keep the following questions in mind:

What does this case study tell us are the central problems and issues facing public administrators in their work? Why is government administration such a complex and difficult task according to this study?

Given the themes and problems in this case study, how would you frame a suitable definition of the field of public administration? Does it "square" with Woodrow Wilson's or any of the more recent theories put forth in Stillman's prior essay?

What does the case say about the special *public* obligations of public administrators compared to the obligations of those engaged in private administration?

Finally, if you had actually been one of the leading administrative officials in the case—Driscoll O. Scanlan, Dwight Green, or Robert Medill—what would have been your view of public administration, and how might such a perspective on administration have helped to shape the outcome of the story?

The Blast in Centralia No. 5: A Mine Disaster No One Stopped

JOHN BARTLOW MARTIN

Already the crowd had gathered. Cars clogged the short, black rock road from the highway to the mine, cars bearing curious spectators and relatives and friends of the men entombed. State troopers and deputy sheriffs and the prosecuting attorney came, and officials from the company, the Federal Bureau of Mines, the Illinois Department of Mines and Minerals. Ambulances arrived, and doctors and nurses and Red Cross workers and soldiers with stretchers from Scott Field. Mine rescue teams came, and a federal rescue unit, experts burdened with masks and oxygen tanks and other awkward paraphernalia of disaster. . . .

One hundred and eleven men were killed in that explosion. Killed needlessly, for almost everybody concerned had known for months, even years, that the mine was dangerous. Yet nobody had done any-

thing effective about it. Why not? Let us examine the background of the explosion. Let us study the mine and the miners, Joe Bryant and Bill Rowekamp and some others, and also the numerous people who might have saved the miners' lives but did not. The miners had appealed in various directions for help but got none, not from their state government nor their federal government nor their employer nor their own union. (In threading the maze of officialdom we must bear in mind four agencies in authority: The State of Illinois, the United States Government, the Centralia Coal Company, and the United Mine Workers of America, that is, the UMWA of John L. Lewis.) Let us seek to fix responsibility for the disaster. . . .

The Centralia Mine No. 5 was opened two miles south of Centralia in 1907. Because of its age, its maze of underground workings is extensive, covering perhaps six square miles, but it is regarded as a medium-small mine since it employs but 250 men and produces but 2,000 tons of coal daily. It was owned by the Centralia Coal Company, an appendage of the Bell & Zoller empire, one of the Big

Six among Illinois coal operators. . . . The Bell & Zoller home office was in Chicago (most of the big coal operators' home offices are in Chicago or St. Louis); no Bell & Zoller officers or directors lived at Centralia.

There are in coal mines two main explosion hazards—coal dust and gas. Coal dust is unhealthy to breathe and highly explosive. Some of the dust raised by machines in cutting and loading coal stays in suspension in the air. Some subsides to the floor and walls of the tunnels, and a local explosion will kick it back into the air where it will explode and, in turn, throw more dust into the air, which will explode; and as this chain reaction continues the explosion will propagate throughout the mine or until it reaches something that will stop it.

The best method of stopping it, a method in use for some twenty-five years, is rock dusting. Rock dusting is simply applying pulverized stone to the walls and roof of the passageways; when a local explosion occurs it will throw a cloud of rock dust into the air along with the coal dust, and since rock dust is incombustible the explosion will die. Rock dusting will not prevent an explosion but it will localize one. Illinois law requires rock dusting in a dangerously dusty mine. Authorities disagreed as to whether the Centralia mine was gassy but everyone agreed it was exceedingly dry and dusty. The men who worked in it had been complaining about the dust for a long time—one recalls "the dust was over your shoetops," another that "I used to cough up chunks of coal dust like walnuts after work"—and indeed by 1944, more than two years before the disaster, so widespread had dissatisfaction become that William Rowekamp, as recording secretary of Local Union 52, prepared an official complaint. But even earlier, both state and federal inspectors had recognized the danger.

Let us trace the history of these warnings of disaster to come. For in the end it was this dust which did explode and kill one hundred and eleven men, and seldom has a major catastrophe of any kind been blueprinted so accurately so far in advance.

Driscoll O. Scanlan (who led the rescue work after the disaster) went to work in a mine near Centralia when he was 16, studied engineering at night school, and worked 13 years as a mine examiner for a coal company until, in 1941, he was appointed one of 16 Illinois state mine inspectors by Governor

Green upon recommendation of the state representative from Scanlan's district. Speaking broadly, the job of a state inspector is to police the mine operators—to see that they comply with the state mining law, including its numerous safety provisions. But an inspector's job is a political patronage job. Coal has always been deeply enmeshed in Illinois politics.

Dwight H. Green, running for Governor the preceding fall, had promised the miners that he would enforce the mining laws "to the letter of the law," and however far below this lofty aim his administration fell (as we shall see), Scanlan apparently took the promise literally. Scanlan is a stubborn, righteous, zealous man of fierce integrity. Other inspectors, arriving to inspect a mine, would go into the office and chat with the company officials. Not Scanlan; he waited outside, and down in the mine he talked with the miners, not the bosses. Other inspectors, emerging, would write their reports in the company office at the company typewriter. Not Scanlan; he wrote on a portable in his car. Widespread rumor had it that some inspectors spent most of their inspection visits drinking amiably with company officials in the hotel in town. Not Scanlan. Other inspectors wrote the briefest reports possible, making few recommendations and enumerating only major violations of the mining law. Scanlan's reports were longer than any others (owing in part to a prolix prose style), he listed every violation however minor, and he made numerous recommendations for improvements even though they were not explicitly required by law.

Scanlan came to consider the Centralia No. 5 mine the worst in his district. In his first report on it he made numerous recommendations, including these: "That haulage roads be cleaned and sprinkled. . . . That tamping of shots with coal dust be discontinued and that clay be used. . . ." Remember those criticisms, for they were made February 7, 1942, more than five years before the mine blew up as a result (at least in part) of those very malpractices.

Every three months throughout 1942, 1943, and 1944 Scanlan inspected the mine and repeated his recommendations, adding new ones: "That the mine be sufficiently rock dusted." And what became of his reports? He mailed them to the Department of Mines and Minerals at Springfield, the agency which supervises coal mines and miners. Springfield is dominated by the Statehouse, an ancient structure of spires and towers and balconies, of colonnades and domes; on its broad front steps Lincoln stands in stone. Inside all is gloom and shabby gilt. The Department of Mines and Minerals occupies three high-ceilinged rooms in a back corner of the second floor. The Director of the Department uses the small, comfortable, innermost office, its windows brushed by the leaves of trees on the Statehouse lawn, and here too the Mining Board meets. In theory, the Mining Board makes policy to implement the mining law, the Director executes its dictates; in practice, the Director possesses considerable discretionary power of his own.

In 1941 Governor Green appointed as Director Robert M. Medill, a genial, paunchy, red-faced man of about sixty-five. Medill had gone to work in a mine at sixteen; he rose rapidly in management. He had a talent for making money and he enjoyed spending it. He entered Republican politics in 1920, served a few years as director of the Department of Mines and Minerals, then returned to business (mostly managing mines); and then, after working for Green's election in 1940, was rewarded once more with the directorship. Green reappointed him in 1944 with, says Medill, the approval of "a multitude of bankers and business men all over the state. And miners. I had the endorsement of all four factions." By this he means the United Mine Workers and its smaller rival, the Progressive Mine Workers, and the two associations of big and little operators; to obtain the endorsement of all four of these jealous, power-seeking groups is no small feat. As Director, Medill received $6,000 a year (since raised to $8,000) plus expenses of $300 or $400 a month. He lived in a sizable country house at Lake Springfield, with spacious grounds and a tree-lined driveway.

To Medill's department, then, came Driscoll Scanlan's inspection reports on Centralia Mine No. 5. Medill, however, did not see the first thirteen reports (1942–44); they were handled as "routine" by Robert Weir, an unimaginative, harassed little man who had come up through the ranks of the miners' union and on recommendation of the union had been appointed Assistant Director of the Department by Green (at $4,000 a year, now $5,200). When the mail brought an inspector's report, it went first to Medill's secretary who shared the office next to Medill's with Weir. She stamped the report [with date of receipt] . . . and put it on Weir's desk. Sometimes, but by no means always, Weir read the report. He gave it to one of a half-dozen girl typists in the large outer office. She edited the inspector's recommendations for errors in grammar and spelling, and incorporated them into a form letter to the owner of the mine, closing:

"The Department endorses the recommendations made by Inspector Scanlan and requests that you comply with same.

"Will you please advise the Department upon the completion of the recommendations set forth above?

"Thanking you . . ."

When the typist placed this letter upon his desk, Weir signed it and it was mailed to the mine operator.

But the Centralia company did not comply with the major recommendations Scanlan made. In fact, it did not even bother to answer Weir's thirteen letters based on Scanlan's reports. And Weir did nothing about this. Once, early in the game, Weir considered the dusty condition of the mine so serious that he requested the company to correct it within ten days; but there is no evidence that the company even replied.

This continued for nearly three years. And during the same period the federal government entered the picture. In 1941 Congress authorized the U.S. Bureau of Mines to make periodic inspections of coal mines. But the federal government had no enforcement power whatever; the inspections served only research. The first federal inspection of Centralia Mine No. 5 was made in September of 1942. In general, the federal recommendations duplicated Scanlan's—rock dusting, improving ventilation, wetting the coal to reduce dust—and the federal inspectors noted that "coal dust . . . at this mine is highly explosive, and would readily propagate an explosion." In all, they made 106 recommendations, including 33 "major" ones (a government official has defined a "major" hazard as one that "could . . . result in a disaster"). Four months passed before a copy of this report filtered through the administrative machinery at Washington and reached the Illinois Department at Springfield, but this mattered little: the Department did nothing anyway. Subsequent federal reports in 1943 and 1944 showed that the "major" recommendations had not been complied with. The federal bureau lacked the power to force compliance;

the Illinois Department possessed the power but failed to act.

What of the men working in the mine during these three years? On November 4, 1944, on instructions from Local 52 at Centralia, William Rowekamp, the recording secretary, composed a letter to Medill: "At the present the condition of those roadways are very dirty and dusty . . . they are getting dangerous. . . . But the Coal Co. has ignored [Scanlan's recommendations]. And we beg your prompt action on this matter."

The Department received this letter November 6, and four days later Weir sent Inspector Scanlan to investigate. Scanlan reported immediately:

"The haulage roads in this mine are awful dusty, and much dust is kept in suspension all day. . . . The miners have complained to me . . . and I have wrote it up pretty strong on my inspection reports. . . . But to date they have not done any adequate sprinkling. . . . Today . . . [Superintendent Norman] Prudent said he would fix the water tank and sprinkle the roads within a week, said that he would have had this work done sooner, but that they have 20 to 30 men absent each day." (This last is a claim by the company that its cleanup efforts were handicapped by a wartime manpower shortage. This is controversial. Men of fifty-nine—the average wartime age at the mine—do not feel like spending weekends removing coal dust or rock dusting, a disagreeable task; winter colds caused absenteeism and miners are always laying off anyway. On the other hand, the company was interested in production and profits: as Mine Manager Brown has said, "In the winter you can sell all the coal you can get out. So you want top production, you don't want to stop to rock dust.")

At any rate, Rowekamp's complaint got results. On December 2, 1944, he wrote Scanlan: "Well I am proud to tell you that they have sprinkled the 18th North Entry & 21st So. Entry and the main haulage road. . . . Myself and the Members of Local Union #52 appreciate it very much what you have done for us." It is apparent from this first direct move by Local 52 that Scanlan was working pretty closely with the Local to get something done.

But by the end of that month, December 1944, the mine once more had become so dirty that Scanlan ended his regular inspection report, ". . . if necessary the mine should discontinue hoisting coal for a few days until the [cleanup] work can be done."

But all Weir said to the company was the routine "The Department endorses. . . ."

Early in 1945 it appeared that something might be accomplished. Scanlan, emerging from his regular inspection, took the unusual step of telephoning Medill at Springfield. Medill told him to write him a letter so Scanlan did:

"The haulage roads in this mine are in a terrible condition. If a person did not see it he would not believe. . . . Two months ago . . . the local officers [of Local Union 52] told me that . . . if [the mine manager] did not clean the mine up they were going to prefer charges against him before the mining board and have his certificate canceled. I talked them out of it and told them I thought we could get them to clean up the mine. But on this inspection I find that practically nothing has been done. . . . The mine should discontinue hoisting coal . . . until the mine is placed in a safe condition. . . . The coal dust in this mine is highly explosive. . . ."

This stiff letter was duly stamped "Received" at Springfield on February 23, 1945. A few days earlier a bad report had come in from Federal Inspector Perz. And now at last Medill himself entered the picture. What did he do? The Superintendent at Centralia had told Scanlan that, in order to clean up the mine, he would have to stop producing coal, a step he was not empowered to take. So Medill bypassed him, forwarding Scanlan's letter and report to William P. Young, Bell & Zoller's operating vice-president at Chicago: "Dear Bill. . . . Please let me have any comments you wish to make. . . . Very kindest personal regards." From his quiet, well-furnished office near the top of the Bell Building overlooking Michigan Avenue, Young replied immediately to "Dear Bob" [Medill]: "As you know we have been working under a very severe handicap for the past months. The war demand for coal . . . we are short of men. . . . I am hopeful that the urgent demand of coal will ease up in another month so that we may have available both the time and labor to give proper attention to the recommendations of Inspector Scanlan. With kindest personal regards. . . ."

A week later, on March 7, 1945, Medill forwarded copies of this correspondence to Scanlan, adding: "I also talked with Mr. Young on the phone, and I feel quite sure that he is ready and willing. . . . I would suggest that you ask the mine committee [of

Local 52] to be patient a little longer, inasmuch as the coal is badly needed at this time."

The miners told Scanlan they'd wait till the first of April but no longer. On March 14 Medill was to attend a safety meeting in Belleville. Scanlan went there to discuss Centralia No. 5 with him. According to Scanlan, "When I went up to his room he was surrounded with coal operators . . . all having whiskey, drinking, having a good time, and I couldn't talk to him then, and we attended the safety meeting [then] went . . . down to Otis Miller's saloon, and I stayed in the background drinking a few cokes and waited until the crowd thinned out, and went back up to his hotel room with him. . . . I told him that the mine was in such condition that if the dust became ignited that it would sweep from one end of the mine to the other and probably kill every man in the mine, and his reply to me was, 'We will just have to take that chance.' " (Medill has denied these words but not the meeting.)

On the first of April the president of Local Union 52 asked Scanlan to attend the Local's meeting on April 4. The miners complained that the company had not cleaned up the mine and, further, that one of the face bosses, or foreman, had fired explosive charges while the entire shift of men was in the mine. There can be little doubt that to fire explosives on-shift in a mine so dusty was to invite trouble—in fact, this turned out to be what later caused the disaster—and now in April 1945 the union filed charges against Mine Manager Brown, asking the State Mining Board to revoke his certificate of competency (this would cost him his job and prevent his getting another in Illinois as a mine manager). Rowekamp wrote up the charges: ". . . And being the Mine is so dry and dusty it could of caused an explosion. . . ."

Weir went to Centralia on April 17, 1945, but only to investigate the charges against Brown, not to inquire into the condition of the mine. He told the miners they should have taken their charges to the state's attorney. Nearly a month passed before, on May 11, Weir wrote a memorandum to the Mining Board saying that the company's superintendent had admitted the shots had been fired on-shift but that this was done "in an emergency" and it wouldn't happen again; and the Board refused to revoke Manager Brown's certificate.

Meanwhile, on April 12 and 13, Scanlan had made his regular inspection and found conditions worse than in February. He told the Superintendent: "Now, Norman, you claim Chicago won't give you the time to shut your mine down and clean it up. Now, I am going to get you some time," and he gave him the choice of shutting the mine down completely or spending three days a week cleaning up. The Superintendent, he said, replied that he didn't know, he'd have to "contact Chicago," but Scanlan replied: "I can't possibly wait for you to contact Chicago. It is about time that you fellows who operate the mines get big enough to operate your mines without contacting Chicago." So on Scanlan's recommendation the mine produced coal only four days a week and spent the remaining days cleaning up. For a time Scanlan was well satisfied with the results, but by June 25 he was again reporting excessive dust and Federal Inspector Perz was concurring: "No means are used to allay the dust." Following his October inspection Scanlan once more was moved to write a letter to Medill; but the only result was another routine letter from Weir to the company, unanswered.

Now, one must understand that, to be effective, both rock dusting and cleanup work must be maintained continuously. They were not at Centralia No. 5. By December of 1945 matters again came to a head. Scanlan wrote to Medill, saying that Local 52 wanted a sprinkling system installed to wet the coal, that Mine Manager Brown had said he could not order so "unusual" an expenditure, and that Brown's superior, Superintendent Prudent, "would not talk to me about it, walked away and left me standing." And Local 52 again attempted to take matters into its own hands. At a special meeting on December 12 the membership voted to prefer charges against both Mine Manager Brown and Superintendent Prudent. Rowekamp's official charge, typed on stationery of the Local, was followed next day by a letter, written in longhand on two sheets of dime-store notepaper, and signed by 28 miners. . . . At Springfield this communication too was duly stamped "Received." And another Scanlan report arrived.

Confronted with so many documents, Medill called a meeting of the Mining Board on December 21. Moreover, he called Scanlan to Springfield and told him to go early to the Leland Hotel, the gathering place of Republican politicians, and see Ben H. Schull, a coal operator and one of the operators' two men on the Mining Board. In his hotel room, Schull (according to Scanlan) said he wanted to discuss privately Scanlan's report on Centralia No. 5, tried to persuade him to withdraw his recommendation of a sprinkling system, and, when Scanlan refused, told him, "you can come before the board." But when the Mining Board met in Medill's inner office, Scanlan was not called before it though he waited all day, and after the meeting he was told that the Board was appointing a special commission to go to Centralia and investigate.

On this commission were Weir, two state inspectors, and two members of the Mining Board itself, Schull and Murrell Reak. Reak, a miner himself, represented the United Mine Workers of America on the Mining Board. And Weir, too, owed his job to the UMWA but, oddly, he had worked for Bell & Zoller for twenty years before joining the Department, the last three as a boss, so his position was rather ambiguous. In fact, so unanimous were the rulings of the Mining Board that one cannot discern any management-labor cleavage at all but only what would be called in party politics bipartisan deals.

The commission had before it a letter from Superintendent Prudent and Manager Brown setting forth in detail the company's "absentee experience" and concluding with a veiled suggestion that the mine might be forced to close for good (once before, according to an inspector, the same company had abandoned a mine rather than go to the expense entailed in an inspector's safety recommendation). Weir wrote to Prudent, notifying him that the commission would visit Centralia on December 28 to investigate the charges against him and Brown; Medill wrote to the company's vice-president, Young, at Chicago ("You are being notified of this date so that you will have an opportunity to be present or designate some member of your staff to be present"); but Medill only told Rowekamp, "The committee has been appointed and after the investigation you will be advised of their findings and the action of the board"—he did not tell the Local when the commission would visit Centralia nor offer it opportunity to prove its charges.

Rowekamp, a motorman, recalls how he first learned of the special commission's visit. He was working in the mine and "Prudent told me to set out an empty and I did and they rode out." Prudent—remember, the commission was investigating charges against Prudent—led the commission through the mine. Rowekamp says, "They didn't see nothing.

They didn't get back in the buggy runs where the dust was the worst; they stayed on the mainline." Even there they rode, they did not walk through the dust. Riding in a mine car, one must keep one's head down. In the washhouse that afternoon the men were angry. They waited a week or two, then wrote to Medill asking what had been done. On January 22, 1946, Medill replied: the Mining Board, adopting the views of the special commission, had found "insufficient evidence" to revoke the certificates of Prudent and Brown.

He did not elaborate. Next day, however, he sent to Scanlan a copy of the commission's report. It listed several important violations of the mining law: inadequate rock dusting, illegal practice in opening rooms, insufficient or improperly placed telephones, more than a hundred men working on a single split, or current, of air. In fact, the commission generally concurred with Scanlan, except that it did not emphasize dust nor recommend a sprinkling system. Thus in effect it overruled Scanlan on his sprinkling recommendation, a point to remember. It did find that the law was being violated yet it refused to revoke the certificates of the Superintendent and the Mine Manager, another point to remember. Weir has explained that the board felt that improvements requiring construction, such as splitting the airstream, would be made and that anyway "conditions there were no different than at most mines in the state." And this is a refrain that the company and the Department repeated in extenuation after the disaster. But actually could anything be more damning? The mine was no worse than most others; the mine blew up; therefore any might blow up!

The miners at Centralia were not satisfied. "It come up at the meeting," Rowekamp recalls. Local 52 met two Wednesday nights a month in its bare upstairs hall. The officers sat at a big heavy table up front; the members faced them, sitting on folding chairs which the Local had bought second-hand from an undertaker. Attendance was heavier now than usual, the men were aroused, some were even telling their wives that the mine was dangerous. They wanted to do something. But what? The state had rebuffed them. Well, why did they not go now to the higher officials of their own union, the UMWA? Why not to John L. Lewis himself?

One of them has said, "You have to go through the real procedure to get to the right man, you got to start at the bottom and start climbing up, you see? If we write to Lewis, he'll refer us right back to Spud White." Spud White is Hugh White, the thick-necked president of the UMWA in Illinois (District 12), appointed by Lewis. Now, Lewis had suspended District 12's right to elect its own officers during the bloody strife of the early 1930s, when the members, disgusted with what they called his "dictator" methods and complaining of secret payrolls, expulsions, missing funds, stolen ballots, and leaders who turned up on operators' payrolls, had rebelled; in the end the Progressive Mine Workers was formed and Lewis retained tight control of the UMWA. A decade later the Illinois officers of UMWA demanded that he restore their self-government, but Lewis managed to replace them with his own men, including Spud White. By 1946 President White, a coal miner from the South, was consulting at high levels with Lewis, he was receiving $10,000 a year plus expenses (which usually equal salary), and he was maintaining a spacious house on a winding lane in the finest residential suburb of Springfield, a white house reached by a circular drive through weeping willows and evergreens.

Evidently the perplexed miners at Centralia already had appealed to District 12 for help, that is to White. Certainly Murrell Reak, the UMWA's man on the Mining Board and a close associate of White's, had asked Weir to furnish him with a copy of the findings of the special commission: "I want them so I may show the district UMWA. So they in turn may write Local Union down there, and show them that their charges are unfounded or rather not of a nature as to warrant the revocation of mine mgr. Certificate. . . ." Jack Ripon, the bulky vice-president of District 12 and White's right-hand man, said recently, "We heard there'd been complaints but we couldn't do a thing about it; it was up to the Mining Department to take care of it."

And yet in the past the UMWA has stepped in when the state failed to act. One unionist has said, "White could have closed that mine in twenty-four hours. All he'd have had to do was call up Medill and tell him he was going to pull every miner in the state if they didn't clean it up. It's the union's basic responsibility—if you don't protect your own wife and daughter, your neighbor down the street's not going to do it."

Perhaps the miners of Local 52 knew they must go it alone. They continued to address their official complaints to the State of Illinois. On February 26

Rowekamp wrote once more to Medill: "Dear Sir: At our regular meeting of Local Union 52. Motion made and second which carried for rec. secy. write you that the members of local union 52 are dissatisfied with the report of the special investigation commission. . . ." No answer. And so the members of Local 52 instructed Rowekamp to write to higher authority, to their Governor, Dwight H. Green.

It took him a long time. Elmer Moss kept asking if he'd finished it and Rowekamp recalls, "I'd tell him, Elmer, I can't do that fast, that's a serious letter, that'll take me a while." He wrote it out first in pencil and showed it to a couple of the boys and they thought it sounded fine. Then, sitting big and awkward at his cluttered little oak desk in the living room of his home outside town, he typed it, slowly and carefully—"anything important as that I take my time so I don't make mistakes, it looks too sloppified." He used the official stationery of the Local, bearing in one corner the device of the union—crossed shovels and picks—and in the other "Our Motto—Justice for One and All." He impressed upon it the official seal—"I can write a letter on my own hook but I dassen't use the seal without it's official"—and in the washhouse the Local officers signed it. Rowekamp made a special trip to the post office to mail it. It was a two-page letter saying, in part:

Dear Governor Green:
  We, the officers of Local Union No. 52, U. M. W. of A., have been instructed by the members . . . to write a letter to you in protest against the negligence and unfair practices of your department of mines and minerals . . . we want you to know that this is not a protest against Mr. Driscoll Scanlan . . . the best inspector that ever came to our mine. . . . But your mining board will not let him enforce the law or take the necessary action to protect our lives and health. This protest is against the men above Mr. Scanlan in your department of mines and minerals. In fact, Governor Green this is a plea to you, to please save our lives, to please make the department of mines and minerals enforce the laws at the No. 5 mine of the Centralia Coal Co. . . . before we have a dust explosion at this mine like just happened in Kentucky and West Virginia. For the last couple of years the policy of the department of mines and minerals toward us has been one of ignoring us. [The letter then recited the story of the useless

special commission.] We are writing you, Governor Green, because we believe you want to give the people an honest administration and that you do not know how unfair your mining department is toward the men in this mine. Several years ago after a disaster at Gillespie we seen your pictures in the papers going down in the mine to make a personal investigation of the accident. We are giving you a chance to correct the conditions at this time that may cause a much worse disaster. . . . We will appreciate an early personal reply from you, stating your position in regard to the above and the enforcement of the state mining laws.

The letter closed "Very respectfully yours" and was signed by Jake Schmidt, president; Rowekamp, recording secretary; and Thomas Bush and Elmer Moss, mine committee. Today, of these, only Rowekamp is alive; all the others were killed in the disaster they foretold.

And now let us trace the remarkable course of this letter at Springfield. It was stamped in red ink "Received March 9, 1946, Governor's Office." In his ornate thick-carpeted offices, Governor Green has three male secretaries (each of whom in turn has a secretary) and it was one of these, John William Chapman, that the "save our lives" letter, as it came to be called, was routed. Two days later Chapman dictated a memorandum to Medill: ". . . it is my opinion that the Governor may be subjected to very severe criticism in the event that the facts complained of are true and that as a result of this condition some serious accident occurs at the mine. Will you kindly have this complaint carefully investigated so I can call the report of the investigation to the Governor's attention at the same time I show him this letter?" Chapman fastened this small yellow memo to the miners' letter and sent both to Medill. Although Medill's office is only about sixty yards from the Governor's, the message consumed two days in traversing the distance.

The messenger arrived at the Department of Mines and Minerals at 9:00 a.m. on March 13 and handed the "save our lives" letter and Chapman's memorandum to Medill's secretary. She duly stamped both "Received" and handed them to Medill. He and Weir discussed the matter, then Medill sent the original letter back to the Governor's office and dictated his reply to Chapman, blaming

the war, recounting the activities of the special commission, saying: "The complaint sounds a good deal worse than it really is. The present condition at the mine is not any different than it has been during the past ten or fifteen years. . . . I would suggest the Governor advise Local Union No. 52, U. M. W. of A., that he is calling the matter to the attention of the State Mining Board with instructions that it be given full and complete consideration at their next meeting."

This apparently satisfied Chapman for, in the Governor's name, he dictated a letter to Rowekamp and Schmidt: "I [i.e., Governor Green] am calling your letter to the attention of the Director of the Department of Mines and Minerals with the request that he see that your complaint is taken up at the next meeting of the State Mining Board. . . ." This was signed with Governor Green's name but it is probable that Green himself never saw the "save our lives" letter until after the disaster more than a year later. Nor is there any evidence that the Mining Board ever considered the letter. In fact, nothing further came of it.

One of the most remarkable aspects of the whole affair was this: An aggrieved party (the miners) accused a second party (Medill's department) of acting wrongfully, and the higher authority to which it addressed its grievance simply, in effect, asked the accused if he were guilty and, when he replied he was not, dropped the matter. A logic, the logic of the administrative mind, attaches to Chapman's sending the complaint to the Department—the administrative mind has a pigeonhole for everything, matters which relate to law go to the Attorney General, matters which relate to mines go to the Department of Mines and Minerals, and that is that—but it is scarcely a useful logic when one of the agencies is itself accused of malfunction. Apparently it did not occur to Chapman to consult Inspector Scanlan or to make any other independent investigation.

And Jack Ripon, Spud White's second-in-command at the District UMWA, said recently, "If I get a letter here I turn it over to the department that's supposed to take care of it, and the same with Governor Green—he got some damn bad publicity he shouldn't have had, he can't know everything that's going on." Ripon's sympathy with Green is understandable—he must have known how Green felt, for he and Spud White received a copy of the same letter. Ripon says, "Oh, we got a copy of it. But it wasn't none of ours, it didn't tell us to do anything. So our hands was tied. What'd we do with it? I think we gave it to Reak." Perhaps Murrell Reak, the UMWA's man on the Mining Board, felt he already had dealt with this matter (it was Reak who, to Scanlan's astonishment, had joined the other members of the special commission in upholding the Superintendent and Mine Manager in their violations of the law and then had been so anxious to help White convince the members of Local 52 "that their charges are unfounded"). At any rate, Reak apparently did not call the Board's attention to the "save our lives" letter, even though it was a local of his own union which felt itself aggrieved. And White took no action either.

As for Medill, on the day he received the letter he called Scanlan to Springfield and, says Scanlan, "severely reprimanded" him. According to Scanlan, Medill "ordered me to cut down the size of my inspection report," because Medill thought that such long reports might alarm the miners, "those damn hunks" who couldn't read English (Medill denied the phrase); but Scanlan took this order to mean that Medill wanted him to "go easy" on the operators— "it is the same thing as ordering you to pass up certain things." And one day during this long controversy, Medill buttonholed Scanlan's political sponsor in a corridor of the Statehouse and said he intended to fire Scanlan; Scanlan's sponsor refused to sanction it and but for this, Scanlan was convinced, he would surely have lost his job.

But now hundreds of miles away larger events were occurring which were to affect the fate of the miners at Centralia. In Washington, D.C., John L. Lewis and the nation's bituminous coal operators failed to reach an agreement and the miners struck, and on May 21, 1946, President Truman ordered the mines seized for government operation. Eight days later Lewis and Julius A. Krug, Secretary of the Interior, signed the famous Krug-Lewis Agreement. Despite strenuous protests by the operators, this agreement included a federal safety code. It was drawn up by the Bureau of Mines (a part of the U.S. Department of the Interior). And now for the first time in history the federal government could exercise police power over coal mine safety.

Thus far the efforts of the miners of Local 52 to thread the administrative maze in their own state had produced nothing but a snowfall of memoranda, reports, letters, and special findings. Let us now observe this new federal machinery in action. We shall learn nothing about how to prevent a disaster but we may learn a good deal about the administrative process.

"Government operation of the mines" meant simply that the operators bossed their own mines for their own profit as usual but the UMWA had a work contract with the government, not the operators. To keep the 2,500 mines running, Secretary Krug created a new agency, the Coal Mines Administration. CMA was staffed with only 245 persons, nearly all naval personnel ignorant of coal mining. Theirs was paper work. For technical advice they relied upon the Bureau of Mines plus a handful of outside experts. More than two months passed before the code was put into effect, on July 29, 1946, and not until November 4 did Federal Inspector Perz reach Centralia to make his first enforceable inspection of Centralia No. 5. Observe, now, the results.

After three days at the mine, Perz went home and wrote out a "preliminary report" on a mimeographed form, listing 13 "major violations" of the safety code. He mailed this to the regional office of the Bureau of Mines at Vincennes, Indiana. There it was corrected for grammar, spelling, etc., and typed; copies then were mailed out to the Superintendent of the mine (to be posted on the bulletin board), the CMA in Washington, the CMA's regional office at Chicago, the District 12 office of the UMWA at Springfield, the UMWA international headquarters at Washington, the Bureau of Mines in Washington, and the Illinois Department at Springfield. While all this was going on, Perz was at home, preparing his final report, a lengthy document listing 57 violations of the safety code, 21 of them major and 36 minor. This handwritten final report likewise went to the Bureau at Vincennes where it was corrected, typed, and forwarded to the Bureau's office in College Park, Maryland. Here the report was "reviewed," then sent to the Director of the Bureau at Washington. He made any changes he deemed necessary, approved it, and ordered it processed. Copies were then distributed to the same seven places that had received the preliminary report, except that the UMWA at Springfield received two copies so that it could forward one to Local 52. (All this was so complicated that the Bureau devised a "flow sheet" to keep track of the report's passage from hand to hand.)

We must not lose sight of the fact that in the end everybody involved was apprised of Perz's findings:

that the Centralia Company was violating the safety code and that hazards resulted. The company, the state, and the union had known this all along and done nothing, but what action now did the new enforcing agency take, the CMA?

Naval Captain N. H. Collison, the Coal Mines Administrator, said that the copy of the inspector's preliminary report was received at his office in Washington "by the head of the Production and Operations Department of my headquarters staff . . . Lieutenant Commander Stull. . . . Lieutenant Commander Stull would review such a report, discuss the matter with the Bureau of Mines as to the importance of the findings, and then . . . await the final report"— unless the preliminary report showed that "imminent danger" existed, in which case he would go immediately to Captain Collison and, presumably, take "immediate action." And during all this activity in Washington, out in Chicago at the CMA's area office a Captain Yates also "would receive a copy of the report. His duty would be to acquaint himself with the findings there. If there was a red check mark indicating it fell within one of the three categories which I shall discuss later, he would detail a man immediately to the mine. If it indicated imminent danger . . . he would move immediately." The three categories deemed sufficiently important to be marked with "a red check mark" were all major hazards but the one which killed 111 men at Centralia No. 5 was not among them.

These, of course, were only CMA's first moves as it bestirred itself. But to encompass all its procedures is almost beyond the mind of man. Let us skip a few and see what actually resulted. The CMA in Washington received Perz's preliminary report November 14. Eleven days later it wrote to the company ordering it to correct one of the 13 major violations Perz found (why it said nothing about the others is not clear). On November 26 the CMA received Perz's final report and on November 29 it again wrote to the company, ordering it to correct promptly all violations and sending copies of the directive to the Bureau of Mines and the UMWA. Almost simultaneously it received from Superintendent Niermann a reply to its first order (Niermann had replaced Prudent, who had left the company's employ): "Dear Sir: In answer to your CMA8-gz of November 25, 1946, work has been started to correct the violation of article 5, section 3c, of the Federal Mine Safety Code, but has been discontinued,

due to . . . a strike. . . ." This of course did not answer the CMA's second letter ordering correction of all 57 violations, nor was any answer forthcoming, but not until two months later, on January 29, 1947, did the CMA repeat its order and tell the company to report its progress by February 14.

This brought a reply from the company official who had been designated "operating manager" during the period of government operation, H. F. McDonald. McDonald, whose office was in Chicago, had risen to the presidency of the Centralia Coal Company and of the Bell & Zoller Coal Company through the sales department; after the Centralia disaster he told a reporter, "Hell, I don't know anything about a coal mine." Now he reported to CMA that "a substantial number of reported violations have been corrected and others are receiving our attention and should be corrected as materials and manpower become available." For obvious reasons, CMA considered this reply inadequate and on February 21 told McDonald to supply detailed information. Three days later McDonald replied ("Re file CMA81-swr"): He submitted a detailed report—he got it from Vice-President Young, who got it from the new General Superintendent, Walter J. Johnson—but McDonald told the CMA that this report was a couple of weeks old and he promised to furnish further details as soon as he could get them. The CMA on March 7 acknowledged this promise but before any other correspondence arrived to enrich file CMA81-swr, the mine blew up.

Now, the Krug-Lewis Agreement set up two methods of circumventing this cumbersome administrative machinery. If Inspector Perz had found what the legalese of the Agreement called "imminent danger," he could have ordered the men removed from the mine immediately (this power was weakened since it was also vested in the Coal Mines Administrator, the same division of authority that hobbled the state enforcers). But Perz did not report "imminent danger." And indeed how could he? The same hazardous conditions had obtained for perhaps twenty years and the mine hadn't blown up. The phrase is stultifying.

In addition, the Krug-Lewis Agreement provided for a safety committee of miners, selected by each local union and empowered to inspect the mine, to make safety recommendations to the management, and, again in case of "an immediate danger," to order the men out of the mine (subject to CMA review). But at Centralia No. 5 several months elapsed before Local 52 so much as appointed a safety committee, and even after the disaster the only surviving member of the committee didn't know what his powers were. The UMWA District officers at Springfield had failed to instruct their Locals in the rights which had been won for them. And confusion was compounded because two separate sets of safety rules were in use—the federal and the state—and in some instances one was the more stringent, in other instances, the other.

Meanwhile another faraway event laid another burden upon the men in the mine. John L. Lewis' combat with Secretary Krug. It ended, as everyone knows, in a federal injunction sought at President Truman's order and upheld by the U.S. Supreme Court, which forbade Lewis to order his miners to strike while the government was operating the mines. (Subsequently Lewis and the UMWA were fined heavily.) The members of Local 52 thought, correctly or not, that the injunction deprived them of their last weapon in their fight to get the mine cleaned up—a wildcat strike. A leader of Local 52 has said, "Sure we could've wildcatted it—and we'd have had the Supreme Court and the government and the whole public down on our necks."

The miners tried the state once more: Medill received a letter December 10, 1946, from an individual miner who charged that the company's mine examiner (a safety man) was not doing what the law required. Earlier Medill had ignored Scanlan's complaint about this but now he sent a department investigator, who reported that the charges were true and that Mine Manager Brown knew it, that Superintendent Niermann promised to consult Vice-President Young in Chicago, that other hazards existed, including dust. Weir wrote a routine letter and this time Niermann replied: The examiner would do his job properly. He said nothing about dust. This letter and one other about the same time, plus Young's earlier equivocal response to Medill's direct appeal, are the only company compliance letters on record.

There was yet time for the miners to make one more try. On February 24, 1947, the safety committee, composed of three miners, wrote a short letter to the Chicago area office of the Coal Mines Administration: "The biggest grievance is dust. . . ." It was written in longhand by Paul Compers (or so it is believed: Compers and one of the two other committee members were killed in the disaster a month

later) and Compers handed it to Mine Manager Brown on February 27. But Brown did not forward it to the CMA; in fact he did nothing at all about it.

And now almost at the last moment, only six days before the mine blew up, some wholly new facts transpired. Throughout this whole history one thing has seemed inexplicable: the weakness of the pressure put on the company by Medill's Department of Mines and Minerals. On March 19, 1947, the St. Louis *Post-Dispatch* broke a story that seemed to throw some light upon it. An Illinois coal operator had been told by the state inspector who inspected his mine that Medill had instructed him to solicit money for the Republican Chicago mayoralty campaign. And soon more facts became known about this political shakedown.

Governor Dwight H. Green, a handsome, likeable politician, had first made his reputation as the young man who prosecuted Al Capone. By 1940 he looked like the white hope of Illinois Republicans. Campaigning for the governorship, Green promised to rid the state of the Democratic machine ("there will never be a Green machine"). He polled more votes in Illinois than Roosevelt; national Republican leaders began to watch him. Forthwith he set about building one of the most formidable machines in the nation. This task, together with the concomitant plans of Colonel Robert R. McCormick of the Chicago *Tribune* and others to make him President or Vice-President, has kept him occupied ever since. He has governed but little, permitting subordinates to run things. Reelected in 1944, he reached the peak of his power in 1946 when his machine succeeded in reducing the control of the Democratic machine over Chicago. Jubilant, Governor Green handpicked a ward leader to run for mayor in April of 1947 and backed him hard.

And it was only natural that Green's henchmen helped. Among these was Medill. "Somebody," says Medill, told him he was expected to raise "$15,000 or $20,000." On January 31, 1947, he called all his mine inspectors to the state mine rescue station in Springfield (at state expense), and told them—according to Inspector Scanlan who was present—that the money must be raised among the coal operators "and that he had called up four operators the previous day and two of them had already come through with a thousand dollars . . . and that he was going to contact the major companies, and we was to contact the independent companies and the small companies." Medill's version varied slightly: he said he told the inspectors that, as a republican, he was interested in defeating the Democrats in Washington and Chicago, that if they found anybody of like mind it would be all right to tell them where to send their money, that all contributions must be voluntary.

After the meeting Scanlan felt like resigning but he thought perhaps Governor Green did not know about the plan and he recalled that once he had received a letter from Green (as did all state employees) asking his aid in giving the people an honest administration: Scanlan had replied to the Governor "that I had always been opposed to corrupt, grafting politicians and that I wasn't going to be one myself; and I received a nice acknowledgement . . . the Governor . . . told me that it was such letters as mine that gave him courage to carry on. . . ." Scanlan solicited no contributions from the coal operators.

But other inspectors did, and so did a party leader in Chicago. So did Medill: he says that his old friend David H. Devonald, operating vice-president of the huge Peabody Coal Company, gave him $1,000 and John E. Jones, a leading safety engineer, contributed $50 (Jones works for another of the Big Six operators and of him more later). No accounting ever has been made of the total collected. The shakedown did not last long. According to Medill, another of Governor Green's "close advisers" told Medill that the coal operators were complaining that he and his inspectors were putting pressure on them for donations and if so he'd better stop it. He did, at another conference of the inspectors on March 7.

Since no Illinois law forbids a company or an individual to contribute secretly to a political campaign, we are dealing with a question of political morality, not legality. The Department of Mines and Minerals long has been a political agency. An inspector is a political appointee and during campaigns he is expected to contribute personally, tack up candidates' posters, and haul voters to the polls. Should he refuse, his local political boss would have him fired. (Soliciting money from the coal operators, however, apparently was something new for inspectors.) Today sympathetic Springfield politicians say: "Medill was just doing what every other department was doing and always has done, but he got a tough break." But one must point out that Medill's inspectors were charged with safeguarding lives, a more serious duty than that of most state employees,

and that in order to perform this duty they had to police the coal operators, and that it was from these very operators that Medill suggested they might obtain money. A United States Senator who investigated the affair termed it "reprehensible."

What bearing, now, did this have on the Centralia disaster? Nobody, probably, collected from the Centralia Coal Company. But the shakedown is one more proof—stronger than most—that Governor Green's department had reason to stay on friendly terms with the coal operators when, as their policemen, it should have been aloof. As a miner at Centralia said recently: "If a coal company gives you a thousand dollars, they're gonna expect something in return."

Here lies Green's responsibility—not that, through a secretary's fumble, he failed to act on the miners' appeal to "save our lives" but rather that, while the kingmakers were shunting him around the nation making speeches, back home his loyal followers were busier building a rich political machine for him than in administering the state for him. Moreover, enriching the Green machine dovetailed nicely with the personal ambitions of Medill and others, and Green did not restrain them. By getting along with his old friends, the wealthy operators, Medill enhanced his personal standing. Evidence exists that Bell & Zoller had had a hand in getting him appointed Director, and remember, Weir had worked as a Bell & Zoller boss. By nature Medill was no zealous enforcer of laws. As for the inspectors, few of them went out of their way to look for trouble; some inspectors after leaving the Department have obtained good jobs as coal company executives. Anyway, as one inspector has said, "If you tried to ride 'em, they'd laugh at you and say, 'Go ahead, I'll just call up Springfield.' " As one man has said, "It was a cozy combination that worked for everybody's benefit, everybody except the miners." And the miners' man on the Board, Murrell Reak of the UMWA, did not oppose the combination. Nor did Green question it.

As the Chicago campaign ground to a close, down at Centralia on March 18 Federal Inspector Perz was making another routine inspection. General Superintendent Johnson told him the company had ordered pipe for a sprinkler system months earlier but it hadn't arrived, "that there would be a large expenditure involved there . . . they had no definite arrangements just yet . . . but he would take it up with the higher officials of the company" in Chicago. Scanlan and Superintendent Niermann were there too; they stayed in the bare little mine office, with its rickety furniture and torn window shades, till 7:30 that night. No rock dusting had been done for nearly a year but now the company had a carload of rock dust underground and Scanlan got the impression it would be applied over the next weekend. (It wasn't.) Perz, too, thought Johnson "very conscientious . . . very competent." Scanlan typed out his report—he had resorted wearily to listing a few major recommendations and adding that previous recommendations "should be complied with"—and mailed it to Springfield. Perz went home and wrote out his own report, acknowledging that 17 hazards had been corrected but making 52 recommendations most of which he had made in November (the company and the CMA were still corresponding over that November report). Perz finished writing on Saturday morning and mailed the report to the Vincennes office, which presumably began processing it Monday.

The wheels had been turning at Springfield, too, and on Tuesday, March 25, Weir signed a form letter to Brown setting forth Scanlan's latest recommendations: "The Department endorses. . . ." But that day, at 3:26 p.m., before the outgoing-mail box in the Department was emptied, Centralia Mine No. 5 blew up. . . .

The last of the bodies was recovered at 5:30 a.m. on the fifth day after the explosion. On "Black Monday" the flag on the new city hall flew at half staff and all the businesses in town closed. Already the funerals had begun, 111 of them. John L. Lewis cried that the 111 were "murdered by the criminal negligence" of Secretary Krug and declared a national six-day "mourning period" during this Holy Week, and though some said he was only achieving by subterfuge what the courts had forbidden him—a strike and defiance of Krug—nonetheless he made the point that in the entire nation only two soft coal mines had been complying with the safety code; and so Krug closed the mines.

Six separate investigations began, two to determine what had happened, and four to find out why. Federal and state experts agreed, in general, that the ignition probably had occurred at the extreme end, or face, of the First West Entry, that it was strictly a coal-dust explosion, that the dust probably was ig-

nited by an explosive charge which had been tamped and fired in a dangerous manner—fired by an openflame fuse, tamped with coal dust—and that the resulting local explosion was propagated by coal dust throughout four working sections of the mine, subsiding when it reached rock-dusted areas. . . .

And what resulted from all the investigations into the Centralia disaster? The Washington County Grand Jury returned no-bills—that is, refused to indict Inspector Scanlan and five company officials ranging upward in authority through Brown, Niermann, Johnson, Young, and McDonald. The Grand Jury did indict the Centralia Coal Company, as a corporation, on two counts of "willful neglect" to comply with the mining law—failing to rock dust and working more than 100 men on a single split of air—and it also indicted Medill and Weir for "palpable omission of duty." The company pleaded nolo contendere—it did not wish to dispute the charge—and was fined the maximum: $300 on each count, a total of $1,000 (or less than $10 per miner's life lost). The law also provides a jail sentence of up to six months but of course you can't put a corporation in jail.

At this writing the indictments against Medill and Weir are still pending, and amid interesting circumstances. Bail for Medill was provided by Charles E. Jones, John W. Spence, G. C. Curtis, and H. B. Thompson; and all of these men, oddly enough, are connected with the oil and gas division of the Department from which Medill was fired. And one of them is also one of Medill's defense attorneys. But this is not all. Medill and Weir filed a petition for a change of venue, supported by numerous affidavits of Washington County residents that prejudice existed. These affidavits were collected by three inspectors for the oil and gas division. They succeeded in getting the trial transferred to Wayne County, which is dominated by a segment of Governor Green's political organization led locally by one of these men, Spence. Not in recent memory in Illinois has the conviction of a Department head on a similar charge been sustained, and there is little reason to suppose that Medill or Weir will be convicted. Medill performed an act of great political loyalty when he shouldered most of the blame at Centralia, in effect stopping the investigation before it reached others above him, and this may be his reward.

Why did nobody close the Centralia mine before it exploded? A difficult question. Medill's position (and some investigators') was that Inspector Scanlan could have closed it. And, legally, this is true: The mining law expressly provided that an inspector could close a mine which persisted in violating the law. But inspectors have done so very rarely, only in exceptional circumstances, and almost always in consultation with the Department. Scanlan felt that had he closed the Centralia mine Medill simply would have fired him and appointed a more tractable inspector. Moreover, the power to close was not his exclusively: it also belonged to the Mining Board. (And is not this divided authority one of the chief factors that produced the disaster?) Robert Weir has said, "We honestly didn't think the mine was dangerous enough to close." This seems fantastic, yet one must credit it. For if Scanlan really had thought so, surely he would have closed it, even though a more pliable inspector reopened it. So would the federal authorities, Medill, or the company itself. And surely the miners would not have gone to work in it.

Governor Green's own fact-finding committee laid blame for the disaster upon the Department, Scanlan, and the company. The Democrats in the Illinois joint legislative committee submitted a minority report blaming the company, Medill, Weir, and Green's administration for "the industrial and political crime . . ."; the Republican majority confessed itself unable to fix blame. After a tremendous pulling and hauling by every special interest, some new state legislation was passed as a result of the accident, but nothing to put teeth into the laws: violations still are misdemeanors (except campaign solicitation by inspectors, a felony); it is scarcely a serious blow to a million-dollar corporation to be fined $1,000. Nor does the law yet charge specific officers of the companies—rather than the abstract corporations—with legal responsibility, so it is still easy for a company official to hide behind a nebulous chain of command reaching up to the stratosphere of corporate finance in Chicago or St. Louis. It is hard to believe that compliance with any law can be enforced unless violators can be jailed.

As for the Congress of the United States, it did next to nothing. The Senate subcommittee recommended that Congress raise safety standards and give the federal government power to enforce that standard—"Immediate and affirmative action is impera-

tive." But Congress only ordered the Bureau of Mines to report next session on whether mine operators were complying voluntarily with federal inspectors' recommendations. . . .

After the Centralia disaster each man responsible had his private hell, and to escape it each found his private scapegoat—the wartime manpower shortage, the material shortage, another official, the miners, or, in the most pitiable cases, "human frailty." Surely a strange destiny took Dwight Green from a federal courtroom where, a young crusader, he overthrew Capone to a hotel in Centralia where, fifteen years older, he came face to face with William Rowekamp, who wanted to know why Green had done nothing about the miners' plea to "save our lives." But actually responsibility here transcends individuals. The miners at Centralia, seeking somebody who would heed their conviction that their lives were in danger, found themselves confronted with officialdom, a huge organism scarcely mortal. The State Inspector, the Federal Inspector, the State Board, the Federal CMA, the company officials—all these forever invoked "higher authority," they forever passed from hand to hand a stream of memoranda and letters, decisions and laws and rulings, and they lost their own identities. As one strives to fix responsibility for the disaster, again and again one is confronted, as were the miners, not with any individual but with a host of individuals fused into a vast, unapproachable, insensate organism. Perhaps this immovable juggernaut is the true villain in the piece. Certainly all those in authority were too remote from the persons whose lives they controlled. And this is only to confess once more that in making our society complex we have made it unmanageable.

Author's Epilogue

Illinois Governor Dwight Green was ruined politically by the Centralia disaster. He had been mentioned as a possible Republican vice-presidential candidate in 1948 and had all the makings of a successful national political figure, but in 1948 he even lost his bid for reelection to the governorship. One of the issues that his opponent, Adlai Stevenson, raised during the campaign was mine safety. Governor Stevenson eventually became a national political figure, running twice—unsuccessfully—for U.S. president in 1952 and 1956.

Robert M. Medill, director of the Illinois Bureau of Mines and Minerals, was asked to resign his post and did so, April 1, 1947. His assistant, Robert Weir, though indicted, remained in his post until his retirement.

The mine owners, Bell and Zoller Coal Company, paid the fine of $1000, but none of the company's officers were indicted or imprisoned.

Despite the six separate investigations of the disaster that were undertaken by various state and federal authorities, neither the state of Illinois nor the federal government changed its mine safety laws or enforcement policies. Only after the 1952 West Frankfurt, Kentucky, coal mine disaster was a stricter federal mine safety code enacted and enforcement procedures improved.

The Centralia blast created 99 widows and 76 fatherless children under the age of 18, which prompted the United Mine Workers Union to change its welfare death benefits from lump sum payouts to monthly stipends. The union used the disaster to press for higher wages and benefits for miners elsewhere.

The Centralia Mine was sold to the Peabody Coal Company and reopened on July 21, 1947, with sixty miners, including many of the survivors, but was closed in two years due to the high costs of production. The mine was abandoned and sealed with concrete. In 1980 a solid waste disposal company bought the property, bulldozed the remaining buildings and plans someday to grind up solid waste and deposit it in the mine shafts. Today coal fragments and slate can be found around the grounds, along with foundations of the old mine and rusting equipment overgrown with weeds. In the nearby Centralia Foundation Park and in the Village of Wamac, plaques recently were dedicated to the miners who lost their lives in Centralia.

Chapter 1 Review Questions

1. How did Woodrow Wilson justify the creation of the new field of public administration? Why does he view public administration as being so critical to the future of the United States? Do you agree? What does Wilson conclude are the best ways to develop this new field? Are these ideas still valid? By contrast, based on your reading of Stillman's essay, how is the field evolving today? Is it evolving along the lines Wilson's essay envisioned?

2. Why does Wilson stress throughout his essay the importance of finding the appropriate relationship between democracy and public administration? What does he mean by that? For example? According to Stillman's essay, how does the field now deal with this issue?

3. Did the case, "The Blast in Centralia No. 5," help you to formulate your own view of what the scope and purpose of the field are or should be today? Does the case contradict or support the conclusions about the importance of this field made in the Wilson essay? Or in Stillman's essay?

4. Based on your reading of the case, what do you see as the central causes of the tragedy in "The Blast in Centralia No. 5"? Why did these problems develop?

5. What reforms would you recommend to prevent the tragedy from reoccurring elsewhere? How could such reforms be implemented?

6. Based on your analysis of "The Blast in Centralia No. 5," can you generalize about the importance of public administration for society? Can you list some of the pros *and* cons of having a strong and effective administrative system to perform essential services in society?

Key Terms

public administration
politics-administration dichotomy
Reinventing Minnowbrook
communitarians
the refounding movement
democratic idealism

POSDCORB
social sciences heterodoxy
VPI refounders
tools approach
antistatism
public choice theory

Suggestions for Further Reading

The seminal book on the origins and growth of public administration in America remains Dwight Waldo, *The Administrative State: A Study of the Political Theory of American Public Administration* (New York: Ronald Press, 1948), which was reissued in 1984, with a new preface, by Holmes and Meier Publishers. For other writings by Waldo, see "The Administrative State Revisited," *Public Administration Review,* 25 (March 1965), pp. 5–37, and *The Enterprise of Public Administration: A Summary View* (Novato, Calif.: Chandler and Sharp Publishers, 1980). For a helpful commentary on Waldo's ideas and career, see Brack Brown and Richard J. Stillman II, *A Search for Public Administration* (College Station: Texas A&M University Press, 1986). Also for insightful review of Dwight Waldo's contributions, read Frank Marini, "Leaders in the Field: Dwight Waldo," *Public Administration Review,* 53 (Sept./Oct. 1993), pp. 409–18. For two excellent reassessments of Woodrow Wilson and his influence on the field, read Paul P. Van Riper, ed., *The Wilson Influence on Public Administration: From Theory to Practice* (Washington, D.C.: American Society for Public Administration, 1990); and Daniel W. Martin, "The Fading Legacy of Woodrow Wilson," *Public Administration Review* (March/April 1988), pp. 631–636.

Much can be learned from the writings of important contributors to the field, like Woodrow Wilson, Frederick Taylor, Luther Gulick, Louis Brownlow, Herbert Simon, and Charles Lindblom. For an excellent collection of many of those classic writings with insightful commentary, see Frederick C. Mosher, ed., *Basic Literature of American Public Administration 1787–1950* (New York: Holmes and Meier, 1981), and for a recent selection of key theorists, read Frederick S. Lane, ed., *Current Issues in Public Administration,* 5th ed. (New York: St. Martin's Press, 1993). Equally valuable is the four-volume history of public administration prior to 1900 by Leonard D. White: *The Federalists* (1948); *The Jeffersonians* (1951); *The Jacksonians* (1954); and *The Republican Era* (1958), all published by Macmillan. Michael W. Spicer, *The Founders, the Constitution, and Public Administration: A Conflict in World Views* (Washington, D.C.: Georgetown Press, 1995), offers a recent study of the constitutional origins of the field. Some of the important books that document the rise of public administration in the twentieth century are Jane Dahlberg, *The New York Bureau of Municipal Research* (New York: New York University Press, 1966); Robert H. Wiebe, *The Search for Order, 1877–1920* (New York: Hill & Wang, 1967); Don K. Price, *America's Unwritten Constitution* (Baton Rouge, La.: Louisiana State University Press, 1983); John A. Rohr, *To Run a Constitution: The Legitimacy of the Administrative State* (Lawrence: University of Kansas Press, 1986); Barry Karl, *Executive Reorganization and Reform in the New Deal* (Cambridge, Mass.: Harvard University Press, 1963); and Stephen Skowronek, *Building a New American State: The Expansion of National Administrative Capacities, 1877–1920* (New York: Cambridge University Press, 1982). Any thorough understanding of how American Public Administration since the early 1970s was decidedly shaped by Minnowbrook and Public Choice theory ideas and requires reading both Frank Marini (ed.) *Toward a New Public Administration: The Minnowbrook Perspective* (Scranton, PA: Chandler Publishing, 1971) and Vincent Ostrom, *The Intellectual Crisis in American Public Administration,* 2d ed. (University: The University of Alabama Press, 1973, revised ed., 1974)

Because Frederick Taylor was so critical to the early development of the field, a noteworthy biography of his life and work is Hindy Lauer Schachter, *Frederick Taylor and the Public Administration Community: A Reevaluation* (Albany, N.Y.: State University of New York Press, 1989). For a broader biographical treatment of the field's major figures, see Brian R. Fry, *Mastering Public Administration: From Max Weber to Dwight Waldo* (Chatham, N.Y.: Chatham House, 1989).

In addition, several other impressive retrospectives on key founders of the field have appeared in recent years: James A. Stever, "Marshall Dimock: An Intellectual Portrait," *Public Administration Review,* 50 (Nov./Dec. 1990), pp. 615–622; Lyle C. Fitch, "Luther Gulick," *Public Administration Review,* 50 (November/December 1990), pp. 604–638; Max O. Stephenson, Jr., and Jeremy F. Plant, "The Legacy of Frederick C. Mosher," *Public Administration Review,* 51 (March/April 1991), pp. 97–113; L. R. Jones, "Aaron Wildavsky: A Man and Scholar for All Seasons," *Public Administration Review,* 55, (January/February 1995), pp. 3–16, as well as the entire issue of the *Public Administration Quarterly* (Fall 1988) devoted to an appraisal of Herbert Simon's work. For excellent insights into Simon's life and work, read his autobiography: Herbert A. Simon, *Models of My Life* (New York: Basic Books, 1991).

Numerous shorter interpretive essays on the development of the field include Herbert Kaufman, "Emerging Conflicts in the Doctrines of Public Administration," *American Political Science Review* (December 1956), pp. 1057–1073; David H. Rosenbloom, "Public Administration Theory and the Separation of Powers," *Public Administration Review,* 43 (May/June 1983), pp. 213–227; Luther H. Gulick, "Reflections on Public Administration, Past and Present," *Public Administration*

Review, 50 (November/December 1990), and Laurence J. O'Toole, Jr., "Harry F. Byrd, Sr. and the New York Bureau of Municipal Research: Lessons from an Ironic Alliance," *Public Administration Review,* 46 (March/April 1986), pp. 113–123.

The past decade has witnessed an outpouring of new, rich, and diverse perspectives on what public administration is and ought to be. Among the recent, more challenging points of view, which attempt to "reformulate the basics" of the field, are: James A. Stever, *The End of Public Administration* (Ardley-on-the-Hudson, N.Y.: Transnational Publishers, 1988); Lester M. Salamon (ed.), *Beyond Privatization* (Washington, D.C.: The Urban Institute Press, 1989); Gary L. Wamsley et al., *Refounding Public Administration* (Newberry Park, Calif.: Sage, 1990) as well as *Refounding Democratic Public Administration* (Sage, 1996); Henry D. Kass and Bayard L. Catron, eds., *Images and Identities in Public Administration* (Newberry Park, Calif.: Sage, 1990); Richard J. Stillman II, *Preface to Public Administration: A Search for Themes and Direction* 2d ed., (Burke, VA: Chatelaine Press, 1998), Camilla Stivers, *Gender Images in Public Administration: Legitimacy and the Administrative State* (Newbury Park, Calif.: Sage, 1993); Charles J. Fox and Hugh T. Miller, *Postmodern Public Administration: Toward a Discourse* (Newbury Park, Calif.: Sage, 1995); Jong S. Jun, *Philosophy of Administration* (Seoul, Korea: Daeyoung Moonhwa International, 1994); Jay D. White and Guy B. Adams, eds., *Research in Public Administration* (Newbury Park, Calif.: Sage, 1994); and O.C. McSuite, *Legitimacy in Public Administration: A Discourse Analysis* (Thousand Oaks, Calif.: Sage, 1997). For the most useful comprehensive guide to public administration literature, see Daniel W. Martin, *The Guide to the Foundations of Public Administration* (New York: Marcel Dekker, 1989); and for a comparative view of European and American administrative thinking, see Walter J. M. Kickert and Richard Stillman (eds.), *The Modern State and Its Study* (London: Elgar, 2000). The three best journals that cover administrative theory today are the *Public Review, Administrative Theory and Praxis,* and *Administration and Society.*

PART ONE

The Pattern of Public Administration in America: Its Environment, Structure, and People

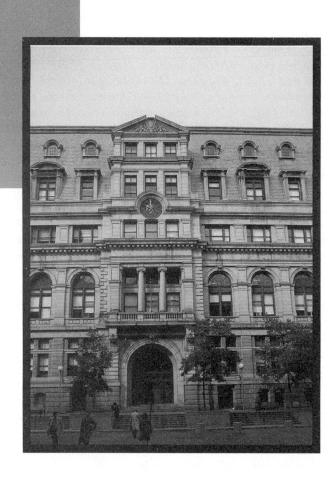

P ublic administrators are surrounded by multiple environments that serve to shape decisively what they do and how well (or how poorly) they do it. Part One discusses the major conceptual ideas about the key environmental factors that profoundly influence the nature, scope, and direction of contemporary public administration. Each reading in Part One outlines one of these important environmental concepts, and each case study illustrates that concept. The significant environmental concepts featured in Part One include:

CHAPTER 2
The Formal Structure: *The Concept of Bureaucracy* What are the formal elements of the bureaucratic structure that serve as core building blocks in the administrative processes?

CHAPTER 3
The General Environment: *The Concept of Ecology* How does the general administrative environment significantly influence the formulation, implementation, and outcomes of public programs?

CHAPTER 4
The Political Environment: *The Concept of Administrative Power* What is the nature of the political landscape in which public agencies operate, and why is administrative power key to their survival, growth, or demise?

CHAPTER 5
Intergovernmental Relations (IGR): *The Concept of IGR as Interdependence, Complexity, and Bargaining* Why do intergovernmental relationships create complex problems for modern American public administrators? What is the structure of these relationships at the dawn of the 21st century?

CHAPTER 6
Internal Dynamics: *The Concept of the Informal Group* How does the internal environment of organizations affect the "outcomes" of the administrative processes? Can administrators identify them and then cope with "internal groups"?

CHAPTER 7
Key Decision Makers Inside Public Administration: *The Concept of Competing Bureaucratic Subsystems* Who are the key decision makers in public agencies today? Why are they so vital to shaping public policy?

CHAPTER 2

The Formal Structure: The Concept of Bureaucracy

*U nder normal conditions, the power position of a fully developed bureau-
cracy is always overtowering. The "political master" finds himself in the
position of the "dilettante" who stands opposite the "expert." . . .*

Max Weber

READING 2

Introduction

To most Americans, "bureaucracy" is a fighting word. Few things are more disliked
than bureaucracy, few occupations held in lower esteem than the bureaucrat. Both are
subjected to repeated criticism in the press and damned regularly by political soap box
orators and ordinary citizens. "Inefficiency," "red tape," "stupidity," "secrecy," "smug-
ness," "aggressiveness," and "self-interest" are only a few of the emotionally charged
words used to castigate bureaucrats.

There may be considerable truth to our dim view of bureaucrats. We also may be
justified in venting our spleens occasionally at the irritating aspects of bureaucracy
that arise almost daily—we may even experience a healthy catharsis in the process.
But this understandably testy outlook should not prevent us from grasping the central importance and meaning of this phenomenon of bureaucracy.

From the standpoint of public administration and social science literature in general, "bureaucracy" means much more than the various bothersome characteristics of
modern organizations. The term in serious administrative literature denotes the general, formal structural elements of a type of human organization, particularly a governmental organization. In this sense bureaucracy has both good *and* bad qualities; it
is a neutral term rather than one referring to only the negative traits of organizations.
It is a lens through which we may dispassionately view what Carl Friedrich has appropriately tagged "the core of modern government."

The German social scientist, Max Weber (1864–1920), is generally acknowledged
to have developed the most comprehensive, classic formulation of the characteristics
of bureaucracy. Weber not only pioneered ideas about bureaucracy but ranged across
a whole spectrum of historical, political, economic, and social thought. As Reinhard

Bendix observed, Weber was "like a man of the Renaissance who took in all humanity for his province." In his study of Hindu religion, Old Testament theology, ancient Roman land surveying, Junker politics, medieval trading companies, and the Chinese civil service, he sought to analyze objectively the nature of human institutions and to show how ideas are linked with the evolution of political, economic, and social systems. One of his best works, *The Protestant Ethic and the Spirit of Capitalism,* established the critical intellectual ties between the rise of Protestantism and capitalism in the sixteenth and seventeenth centuries. He constantly pressed for answers to enormously complex problems. What is the interplay between ideas and institutions? What distinguishes the Western culture and its ideas? Why has a particular society evolved the way it has?

We cannot summarize here the numerous ideas formulated by Max Weber's fertile mind, but we can examine a few aspects of his thought that bear directly on his conception of bureaucracy. Weber believed that civilization evolved from the primitive and mystical to the rational and complex. He thought that human nature progressed slowly from primitive religions and mythologies to an increasing theoretical and technical sophistication. World evolution was a one-way street in Weber's nineteenth-century view: he visualized a progressive "demystification" of humanity and humanity's ideas about the surrounding environment.

In keeping with his demystification view of progress, Weber describes three "ideal-types" of authority that explain why individuals throughout history have obeyed their rulers. One of the earliest, the "traditional" authority of primitive societies, rested on the established belief in the sanctity of tradition. Because a family of rulers has always ruled, people judge them to be just and right and obey them. Time, precedent, and tradition gave rulers their legitimacy in the eyes of the ruled.

A second ideal-type of authority, according to Weber, is "charismatic" authority, which is based on the personal qualities and the attractiveness of leaders. Charismatic figures are self-appointed leaders who inspire belief because of their extraordinary, almost superhuman, qualifications. Military leaders, warrior chiefs, popular party leaders, and founders of religions are examples of individuals whose heroic feats or miracles attract followers.

Weber postulated a third ideal-type of authority that is the foundation of modern civilizations, namely, "legal-rational" authority. It is based on "a belief in the legitimacy of the pattern of normative rules and the rights of those elevated to authority under such rules to issue commands." Obedience is owed to a legally established, impersonal set of rules, rather than to a personal ruler. Legal-rational authority vests power in the office rather than in the person who occupies the office; thus anyone can rule as long as he or she comes to office "according to the rules."

This third type of authority forms the basis for Weber's concept of bureaucracy. According to Weber, bureaucracy is the normal way that "legal-rational" authority appears in institutional form; it holds a central role in ordering and controlling modern societies. "It is," says Weber, "superior to any other form in precision, in stability, in stringency of its discipline, and in its reliability. It thus makes possible a particularly high degree of calculability of results for the heads of organizations and for those acting in relation to it." It is finally superior in its operational efficiency and "is formally capable of application to all kinds of administrative tasks." For Weber, bureaucracy is indispensable to maintaining civilization in modern society. In his view, "however much people may complain about the evils of bureaucracy it would be sheer illusion to think for a moment that continuous administrative work can be carried out in any field except by means of officials working in offices."

A great deal of Weber's analysis of bureaucracy dealt with its historical development. According to Weber, modern bureaucracy in the Western world arose during the Middle Ages when royal domains grew and required bodies of officials to oversee them. Out of necessity, princes devised rational administrative techniques to extend their authority, frequently borrowing ideas from the church, whose territories at that time encompassed most of Europe. "The proper soil for bureaucratization of administration," writes Weber, "has always been the development of administrative tasks." Bureaucracy grew because society needed to do things—to build roads, to educate students, to collect taxes, to fight battles, and to dispense justice. Work was divided and specialized to achieve the goals of a society.

Weber also identified a monied economy as an important ingredient for the development of bureaucracy. "Bureaucracy as a permanent structure is knit to the presupposition of a constant income for maintenancy. . . . A stable system of taxation is the precondition for the permanent existence of bureaucratic administration." Other cultural factors contributing to the rise of highly structured bureaucracies were the growth of education, the development of higher religions, and the burgeoning of science and rationality.

Weber listed in a detailed fashion the major elements of the formal structure of bureaucracy. Three of the most important attributes in his concept of bureaucracy were the division of labor, hierarchical order, and impersonal rules—keystones to any functioning bureaucracy. The first, specialization of labor, meant that all work in a bureaucracy is rationally divided into units that can be undertaken by an individual or group of individuals competent to perform those tasks. Unlike traditional rulers, workers do not *own* their offices in bureaucracy but enjoy tenure based on their abilities to perform the work assigned. Second, the hierarchical order of bureaucracy separates superiors from subordinates; on the basis of this hierarchy, remuneration for work is dispensed, authority recognized, privileges allotted, and promotions awarded. Finally, impersonal rules form the life-blood of the bureaucratic world. Bureaucrats, according to Weber, are not free to act in any way they please because their choices are confined to prescribed patterns of conduct imposed by legal rules. In contrast to "traditional" or "charismatic" authority, bureaucratic rules provide for the systematic control of subordinates by superiors, thus limiting the opportunities for arbitrariness and personal favoritism.

Weber theorized that the only way for a modern society to operate effectively was by organizing expertly trained, functional specialists in bureaucracies. Although Max Weber saw bureaucracy as permanent and indispensable in the modern world, he was horrified by what he believed was an irreversible trend toward loss of human freedom and dignity:

> It is horrible to think that the world could one day be filled with nothing but those little cogs, little men clinging to little jobs and striving towards bigger ones—a state of affairs which is to be seen once more, as in the Egyptian records, playing an

ever-increasing part in the spirit of our present administrative system and especially of its offspring, the students. This passion for bureaucracy . . . is enough to drive one to despair.[1]

And although he despaired over the increasing trend toward bureaucratization in the modern world, Weber also observed the leveling or democratizing effect of bureaucracy on society. As Reinhard Bendix wrote of Weber's idea: "The development of bureaucracy does away with . . . plutocratic privileges, replacing unpaid, avocational administration by notables with paid, full-time administration by professionals, regardless of their social and economic position. . . . Authority is exercised in accordance with rules, and everyone subject to that authority is legally equal."[2]

Over the last fifty years, certain elements in Max Weber's conception of bureaucracy have fueled repeated academic debate and scholarly criticism.[3] There are those social scientists who criticize his "ideal-type" formulations as misleading. They contend that it offers neither a desirable state *nor* an empirical reality. Others suggest that he overemphasizes the *formal* elements of bureaucracy—i.e., specialization, hierarchy, rules, division of labor, etc.—and does not appreciate the *informal* dimensions—such as human relationships, leadership, communication networks, etc.—as equally, if not more important, for influencing bureaucratic performance and efficiency. Still others say that Weber neglects the deficiencies of large-scale bureaucracies that can encourage alienation of workers and citizens alike, in contrast to the stimulating creativity that small, fluid networks of specialists can enhance. Some scholars charge Weber's concept as being both time-bound and culture-bound to the late nineteenth and early twentieth century German "scientific" heritage. They say he idealized the German bureaucratic state that dominated that era. This list of social science criticisms could go on, and they are all to some degree telling criticisms.

Nevertheless, the main outline of Weber's classic formulation is generally accepted as true and significant. For students of public administration, his concept forms one of the essential intellectual building blocks in our understanding of the formal institutional structure of public administration.

As you read this selection, keep the following questions in mind:

Where can you see evidence of Weber's concept of bureaucracy within familiar organizations?

In what respects does Weber's characterization of bureaucracy as a theoretical

---

[1]As quoted in Reinhard Bendix, *Max Weber: An Intellectual Portrait* (New York: Doubleday and Co., 1960), p. 464.

[2]Ibid., p. 429.

[3]For an excellent discussion of general academic criticism and revision of Weber's ideas, read either Alfred Diamant, "The Bureaucratic Model: Max Weber Rejected, Rediscovered, Reformed," in Ferrel Heady and Sybil L. Stokes, *Papers in Comparative Public Administration* (Ann Arbor, Mich.: Institute of Public Administration, 1962), or Peter M. Blau and Marshall W. Meyer, *Bureaucracy in Modern Society* (New York: Random House, 1971). For a recent bold and different interpretation of Weber, see the essay on Weber by Robert Leivesley, Adrian Carr, and Alexander Kauzmin, in Ali Farazmand, ed., *Handbook of Bureaucracy* (New York: Marcel Dekker, 1994).

"ideal-type" miss the mark in describing the practical reality? In what respects is it on target?

How is Weber's bureaucratic model relevant to the previous case, "The Blast in Centralia No. 5"? On the basis of that case as well as your own observations, can you describe some positive and negative features of modern bureaucracy?

Bureaucracy[1]

MAX WEBER

1. Characteristics of Bureaucracy

Modern officialdom functions in the following specific manner:

I. There is the principle of fixed and official jurisdictional areas, which are generally ordered by rules, that is, by laws or administrative regulations.

1. The regular activities required for the purposes of the bureaucratically governed structure are distributed in a fixed way as official duties.
2. The authority to give the commands required for the discharge of these duties is distributed in a stable way and is strictly delimited by rules concerning the coercive means, physical, sacerdotal, or otherwise, which may be placed at the disposal of officials.
3. Methodical provision is made for the regular and continuous fulfilment of these duties and for the execution of the corresponding rights; only persons who have the generally regulated qualifications to serve are employed.

In public and lawful government these three elements constitute "bureaucratic authority." In private economic domination, they constitute bureaucratic "management." Bureaucracy, thus understood, is fully developed in political and ecclesiastical communities only in the modern state, and, in the private economy, only in the most advanced institutions of capitalism. Permanent and public office authority, with fixed jurisdiction, is not the historical rule but rather the exception. This is so even in large political structures such as those of the ancient Orient, the Germanic and Mongolian empires of conquest, or of many feudal structures of state. In all these cases, the ruler executes the most important measures through personal trustees, table-companions, or court-servants. Their commissions and authority are not precisely delimited and are temporarily called into being for each case.

II. The principles of office hierarchy and of levels of graded authority mean a firmly ordered system of super- and subordination in which there is a supervision of the lower offices by the higher ones. Such a system offers the governed the possibility of appealing the decision of a lower office to its higher authority, in a definitely regulated manner. With the full development of the bureaucratic type, the office hierarchy is monocratically organized. The principle of hierarchical office authority is found in all bureaucratic structures: in state and ecclesiastical structures as well as in large party organizations and private enterprises. It does

Bureaucracy, pp. 196–233, from Max Weber: Essays in Sociology by Max Weber, edited and translated by H. H. Gerth & C. Wright Mills. Translation copyright 1946, 1958 by H. H. Gerth and C. Wright Mills. Renewed copyright 1943 by Hans H. Gerth. Used by permission of Oxford University Press, Inc.

[1]*Wirtschaft und Gesellschaft,* part III, chap. 6, pp. 650–78.

not matter for the character of bureaucracy whether its authority is called "private" or "public."

When the principle of jurisdictional "competency" is fully carried through, hierarchical subordination—at least in public office—does not mean that the "higher" authority is simply authorized to take over the business of the "lower." Indeed, the opposite is the rule. Once established and having fulfilled its task, an office tends to continue in existence and be held by another incumbent.

III. The management of the modern office is based upon written documents ("the files"), which are preserved in their original or draught form. There is, therefore, a staff of subaltern officials and scribes of all sorts. The body of officials actively engaged in a "public" office, along with the respective apparatus of material implements and the files, make up a "bureau." In private enterprise, "the bureau" is often called "the office."

In principle, the modern organization of the civil service separates the bureau from the private domicile of the official, and, in general, bureaucracy segregates official activity as something distinct from the sphere of private life. Public monies and equipment are divorced from the private property of the official. This condition is everywhere the product of a long development. Nowadays, it is found in public as well as in private enterprises; in the latter, the principle extends even to the leading entrepreneur. In principle, the executive office is separated from the household, business from private correspondence, and business assets from private fortunes. The more consistently the modern type of business management has been carried through the more are these separations the case. The beginnings of this process are to be found as early as the Middle Ages.

It is the peculiarity of the modern entrepreneur that he conducts himself as the "first official" of his enterprise, in the very same way in which the ruler of a specifically modern bureaucratic state spoke of himself as "the first servant" of the state. The idea that the bureau activities of the state are intrinsically different in character from the management of private economic offices is a continental European notion and, by way of contrast, is totally foreign to the American way.

IV. Office management, at least all specialized office management—and such management is distinctly modern—usually presupposes thorough and expert training. This increasingly holds for the modern executive and employee of private enterprises, in the same manner as it holds for the state official.

V. When the office is fully developed, official activity demands the full working capacity of the official, irrespective of the fact that his obligatory time in the bureau may be firmly delimited. In the normal case, this is only the product of a long development, in the public as well as in the private office. Formerly, in all cases, the normal state of affairs was reversed: official business was discharged as a secondary activity.

VI. The management of the office follows general rules, which are more or less stable, more or less exhaustive, and which can be learned. Knowledge of these rules represents a special technical learning which the officials possess. It involves jurisprudence, or administrative or business management.

The reduction of modern office management to rules is deeply embedded in its very nature. The theory of modern public administration, for instance, assumes that the authority to order certain matters by decree—which has been legally granted to public authorities—does not entitle the bureau to regulate the matter by commands given for each case, but only to regulate the matter abstractly. This stands in extreme contrast to the regulation of all relationships through individual privileges and bestowals of favor, which is absolutely dominant in patrimonialism, at least in so far as such relationships are not fixed by sacred tradition.

2. The Position of the Official

All this results in the following for the internal and external position of the official:

I. Office holding is a "vocation." This is shown, first, in the requirement of a firmly prescribed course of training, which demands the entire capacity for work for a long period of time, and in the generally prescribed and special examinations which are prerequisites of employment. Furthermore, the position of the official is in the nature of a duty. This determines the internal structure of his relations, in the following manner: Legally and actually, office holding is not considered a source to be exploited for rents or emoluments, as was normally the case during the Middle Ages and frequently up to the threshold of recent times. Nor is office holding considered a usual exchange of services for equivalents, as is the case with free labor contracts. Entrance into an office, including one in the private economy, is considered an acceptance of a specific obligation of faithful management in return for a secure existence. It is decisive for the specific nature of modern loyalty to an office that, in the pure type, it does not establish a relationship to a *person,* like the vassal"s or disciple's faith in feudal or in patrimonial relations of authority. Modern loyalty is devoted to impersonal and functional purposes. Behind the functional purposes, of course, "ideas of culture-values" usually stand. These are *ersatz* for the earthly or supra-mundane personal master: ideas such as "state," "church," "community," "party," or "enterprise" are thought of as being realized in a community; they provide an ideological halo for the master.

The political official—at least in the fully developed modern state—is not considered the personal servant of a ruler. Today, the bishop, the priest, and the preacher are in fact no longer, as in early Christian times, holders of purely personal charisma. The supra-mundane and sacred values which they offer are given to everybody who seems to be worthy of them and who asks for them. In former times, such leaders acted upon the personal command of their master; in principle, they were responsible only to him. Nowadays, in spite of the partial survival of the old theory, such religious leaders are officials in the service of a functional purpose, which in the present-day "church" has become routinized and, in turn, ideologically hallowed.

II. The personal position of the official is patterned in the following way:

1. Whether he is in a private office or a public bureau, the modern official always strives and usually enjoys a distinct *social esteem* as compared with the governed. His social position is guaranteed by the prescriptive rules of rank order and, for the political official, by special definitions of the criminal code against "insults of officials" and "contempt" of state and church authorities.

   The actual social position of the official is normally highest where, as in old civilized countries, the following conditions prevail: a strong demand for administration by trained experts; a strong and stable social differentiation, where the official predominantly derives from socially and economically privileged strata because of the social distribution of power; or where the costliness of the required training and status conventions are binding upon him. The possession of educational certificates—to be discussed elsewhere—are usually linked with qualification for office. Naturally, such certificates or patents enhance the "status element" in the social position of the official. For the rest this status factor in individual cases is explicitly and impassively acknowledged; for example, in the prescription that the acceptance or rejection of an aspirant to an official career depends upon the consent ("election") of the members of the official body. This is the case in the German army with the officer corps. Similar phenomena, which promote this guild-like closure of officialdom, are typically found in patrimonial and, particularly, in prebendal officialdoms of the past. The desire to resurrect such phenomena in changed forms is by no means infrequent among modern bureaucrats. For instance, they have played a role among the demands of the quite proletarian and expert officials (the *tretyj* element) during the Russian revolution.

   Usually the social esteem of the officials

as such is especially low where the demand for expert administration and the dominance of status conventions are weak. This is especially the case in the United States; it is often the case in new settlements by virtue of their wide fields for profitmaking and the great instability of their social stratification.

2. The pure type of bureaucratic official is *appointed* by a superior authority. An official elected by the governed is not a purely bureaucratic figure. Of course, the formal existence of an election does not by itself mean that no appointment hides behind the election—in the state, especially, appointment by party chiefs. Whether or not this is the case does not depend upon legal statutes but upon the way in which the party mechanism functions. Once firmly organized, the parties can turn a formally free election into the mere acclamation of a candidate designated by the party chief. As a rule, however, a formally free election is turned into a fight, conducted according to definite rules, for votes in favor of one of two designated candidates.

In all circumstances, the designation of officials by means of an election among the governed modifies the strictness of hierarchical subordination. In principle, an official who is so elected has an autonomous position opposite the superordinate official. The elected official does not derive his position "from above" but "from below," or at least not from a superior authority of the official hierarchy but from powerful party men ("bosses"), who also determine his further career. The career of the elected official is not, or at least not primarily, dependent upon his chief in the administration. The official who is not elected but appointed by a chief normally functions more exactly, from a technical point of view, because, all other circumstances being equal, it is more likely that purely functional points of consideration and qualities will determine his selection and career. As laymen, the governed can become acquainted with the extent to which a candidate is expertly qualified for office only in terms of experience, and hence only after his service. Moreover, in every sort of selection of officials by election, parties quite naturally give decisive weight not to expert considerations but to the services a follower renders to the party boss. This holds for all kinds of procurement of officials by elections, for the designation of formally free, elected officials by party bosses when they determine the slate of candidates, or the free appointment by a chief who has himself been elected. The contrast, however, is relative: Substantially similar conditions hold where legitimate monarchs and their subordinates appoint officials, except that the influence of the followings are then less controllable.

Where the demand for administration by trained experts is considerable, and the party followings have to recognize an intellectually developed, educated, and freely moving "public opinion," the use of unqualified officials falls back upon the party in power at the next election. Naturally, this is more likely to happen when the officials are appointed by the chief. The demand for a trained administration now exists in the United States, but in the large cities, where immigrant votes are "corraled," there is, of course, no educated public opinion. Therefore, popular elections of the administrative chief and also of his subordinate officials usually endanger the expert qualification of the official as well as the precise functioning of the bureaucratic mechanism. It also weakens the dependence of the officials upon the hierarchy. This holds at least for the large administrative bodies that are difficult to supervise. The superior qualification and integrity of federal judges, appointed by the President, as over against elected judges in the United States is well known, although both types of officials have been selected primarily in terms of party considerations. The great changes in American metropolitan administrations demanded by reformers have proceeded essentially from elected mayors working with an apparatus of officials who were appointed by them. These reforms have thus come about in a "Caesarist" fashion. Viewed technically, as an organized form of authority, the efficiency of "Caesarism," which often grows out of democracy, rests in general upon the position of the "Caesar" as a free trustee of the masses (of the army or of the citizenry), who is unfettered by tradition. The "Caesar" is thus the unrestrained master of a body of highly qualified military officers and officials whom he selects freely and personally without regard to tradition or to any other considerations. This "rule of the personal genius," however, stands in contradiction to the formally "democratic" principle of a universally elected officialdom.

3. Normally, the position of the official is held for life, at least in public bureaucracies; and this is increasingly the case for all similar structures. As a factual rule, *tenure for life* is presupposed, even where the giving of notice or periodic reappointment occurs. In contrast to the worker in a private enterprise, the official normally holds tenure. Legal or actual life-tenure, however, is not recognized as the official"s right to the possession of office, as was the case with many structures of authority in the past. Where legal guarantees against arbitrary dismissal or transfer are developed, they merely serve to guarantee a strictly objective discharge of specific office duties free from all personal considerations. In Germany, this is the case for all juridical and, increasingly, for all administrative officials.

Within the bureaucracy, therefore, the measure of "independence," legally guaranteed by tenure, is not always a source of increased status for the official whose position is thus secured. Indeed, often the reverse holds, especially in old cultures and communities that are highly differentiated. In such communities, the stricter the subordination under the arbitrary rule of the master, the more it guarantees the maintenance of the conventional seigneurial style of living for the official. Because of the very absence of these legal guarantees of tenure, the conventional esteem for the official may rise in the same way as, during the Middle Ages, the esteem of the nobility of office rose at the expense of esteem for the freemen, and as the king's judge surpassed that of the people's judge. In Germany, the military officer or the administrative official can be removed from office at any time, or at least far more readily than the "independent judge," who never pays with loss of his office for even the grossest offense against the "code of honor" or against social conventions of the salon. For this very reason, if other things are equal, in the eyes of the master stratum the judge is considered less qualified for social intercourse than are officers and administrative officials, whose greater dependence on the master is a greater guarantee of their conformity with status conventions. Of course, the average official strives for a civil-service law, which would materially secure his old age and provide increased guarantees against his arbitrary removal from office. This striving, however, has its limits. A very strong development of the "right to the office" naturally makes it more difficult to staff them with regard to technical efficiency, for such a development decreases the career-opportunities of ambitious candidates for office. This makes for the fact that officials, on the whole, do not feel their dependency upon those at the top. This lack of a feeling of dependency, however, rests primarily upon the inclination to depend upon one's equals rather than upon the socially inferior and governed strata. The present conservative movement among the Badenia clergy, occasioned by the anxiety of a presumably threatening separation of church and state, has been expressly determined by the desire not to be turned "from a master into a servant of the parish."

4. The official receives the regular *pecuniary* compensation of a normally fixed *salary* and the old age security provided by a pension. The salary is not measured like a wage in

terms of work done, but according to "status," that is, according to the kind of function (the "rank") and, in addition, possibly, according to the length of service. The relatively great security of the official's income, as well as the rewards of social esteem, make the office a sought-after position, especially in countries which no longer provide opportunities for colonial profits. In such countries, this situation permits relatively low salaries for officials.

5. The official is set for a *"career"* within the hierarchical order of the public service. He moves from the lower, less important, and lower paid to the higher positions. The average official naturally desires a mechanical fixing of the conditions of promotion: if not of the offices, at least of the salary levels. He wants these conditions fixed in terms of "seniority," or possibly according to grades achieved in a developed system of expert examinations. Here and there, such examinations actually form a character *indelebilis* of the official and have lifelong effects on his career. To this is joined the desire to qualify the right to office and the increasing tendency toward status group closure and economic security. All of this makes for a tendency to consider the offices as "prebends" of those who are qualified by educational certificates. The necessity of taking general personal and intellectual qualifications into consideration, irrespective of the often subaltern character of the educational certificate, has led to a condition in which the highest political offices, especially the positions of "ministers," are principally filled without reference to such certificates. . . . [pp. 202–204]

6. Technical Advantages of Bureaucratic Organization

The decisive reason for the advance of bureaucratic organization has always been its purely technical superiority over any other form of organization. The fully developed bureaucratic mechanism compares with other organizations exactly as does the machine with the nonmechanical modes of production.

Precision, speed, unambiguity, knowledge of the files, continuity, discretion, unity, strict subordination, reduction of friction and of material and personal costs—these are raised to the optimum point in the strictly bureaucratic administration, and especially in its monocratic form. As compared with all collegiate, honorific, and avocational forms of administration, trained bureaucracy is superior on all these points. And as far as complicated tasks are concerned, paid bureaucratic work is not only more precise but, in the last analysis, it is often cheaper than even formally unremunerated honorific service.

Honorific arrangements make administrative work an avocation and, for this reason alone, honorific service normally functions more slowly; being less bound to schemata and being more formless. Hence it is less precise and less unified than bureaucratic work because it is less dependent upon superiors and because the establishment and exploitation of the apparatus of subordinate officials and filing services are almost unavoidably less economical. Honorific service is less continuous than bureaucratic and frequently quite expensive. This is especially the case if one thinks not only of the money costs to the public treasury—costs which bureaucratic administration, in comparison with administration by notables, usually substantially increases—but also of the frequent economic losses of the governed caused by delays and lack of precision. The possibility of administration by notables normally and permanently exists only where official management can be satisfactorily discharged as an avocation. With the qualitative increase of tasks the administration has to face, administration by notables reaches its limits—today, even in England. Work organized by collegiate bodies causes friction and delay and requires compromises between colliding interests and views. The administration, therefore, runs less precisely and is more independent of superiors; hence, it is less unified and slower. All advances of the Prussian administrative organization have been and will in the future be advances of the bureaucratic, and especially of the monocratic, principle.

Today, it is primarily the capitalist market economy which demands that the official business of the administration be discharged precisely, unambiguously, continuously, and with as much speed as possible. Normally, the very large, modern capitalist enterprises are themselves unequalled models of strict bureaucratic organization. Business management throughout rests on increasing precision, steadiness, and, above all, the speed of operations. This, in turn, is determined by the peculiar nature of the modern means of communication, including, among other things, the news service of the press. The extraordinary increase in the speed by which public announcements, as well as economic and political facts, are transmitted exerts a steady and sharp pressure in the direction of speeding up the tempo of administrative reaction towards various situations. The optimum of such reaction time is normally attained only by a strictly bureaucratic organization.[2]

Bureaucratization offers above all the optimum possibility for carrying through the principle of specializing administrative functions according to purely objective considerations. Individual performances are allocated to functionaries who have specialized training and who by constant practice learn more and more. The "objective" discharge of business primarily means a discharge of business according to *calculable rules* and "without regard for persons."

"Without regard for persons" is also the watchword of the "market" and, in general, of all pursuits of naked economic interests. A consistent execution of bureaucratic domination means the leveling of status "honor." Hence, if the principle of the free-market is not at the same time restricted, it means the universal domination of the "class situation." That this consequence of bureaucratic domination has not set in everywhere, parallel to the extent of bureaucratization, is due to the differences among possible principles by which polities may meet their demands.

The second element mentioned, "calculable rules," also is of paramount importance for modern bureaucracy. The peculiarity of modern culture, and specifically of its technical and economic basis, demands this very "calculability" of results. When fully developed, bureaucracy also stands, in a specific sense, under the principle of *sine ira ac studio*. Its specific nature, which is welcomed by capitalism, develops the more perfectly the more the bureaucracy is "dehumanized," the more completely it succeeds in eliminating from official business love, hatred, and all purely personal, irrational, and emotional elements which escape calculation. This is the specific nature of bureaucracy and it is appraised as its special virtue.

The more complicated and specialized modern culture becomes, the more its external supporting apparatus demands the personally detached and strictly "objective" *expert,* in lieu of the master of older social structures, who was moved by personal sympathy and favor, by grace and gratitude. Bureaucracy offers the attitudes demanded by the external apparatus of modern culture in the most favorable combination. As a rule, only bureaucracy has established the foundation for the administration of a rational law conceptually systematized on the basis of such enactments as the latter Roman imperial period first created with a high degree of technical perfection. During the Middle Ages, this law was received along with the bureaucratization of legal administration, that is to say, with the displacement of the old trial procedure which was bound to tradition or to irrational presuppositions, by the rationally trained and specialized expert. . . . [pp. 214–216]

10. The Permanent Character of the Bureaucratic Machine

Once it is fully established, bureaucracy is among those social structures which are the hardest to destroy. Bureaucracy is *the* means of carrying "community action" over into rationally ordered

---

[2]Here we cannot discuss in detail how the bureaucratic apparatus may, and actually does, produce definite obstacles to the discharge of business in a manner suitable for the single case.

"societal action." Therefore, as an instrument for "societalizing" relations of power, bureaucracy has been and is a power instrument of the first order—for the one who controls the bureaucratic apparatus.

Under otherwise equal conditions, a "societal action," which is methodically ordered and led, is superior to every resistance of "mass" or even of "communal action." And where the bureaucratization of administration has been completely carried through, a form of power relation is established that is practically unshatterable.

The individual bureaucrat cannot squirm out of the apparatus in which he is harnessed. In contrast to the honorific or avocational "notable," the professional bureaucrat is chained to his activity by his entire material and ideal existence. In the great majority of cases, he is only a single cog in an ever-moving mechanism which prescribes to him an essentially fixed route of march. The official is entrusted with specialized tasks and normally the mechanism cannot be put into motion or arrested by him, but only from the very top. The individual bureaucrat is thus forged to the community of all the functionaries who are integrated into the mechanism. They have a common interest in seeing that the mechanism continues its functions and that the societally exercised authority carries on.

The ruled, for their part, cannot dispense with or replace the bureaucratic apparatus of authority once it exists. For this bureaucracy rests upon expert training, a functional specialization of work, and an attitude set for habitual and virtuoso-like mastery of single yet methodically integrated functions. If the official stops working, or if his work is forcefully interrupted, chaos results, and it is difficult to improvise replacements from among the governed who are fit to master such chaos. This holds for public administration as well as for private economic management. More and more the material fate of the masses depends upon the steady and correct functioning of the increasingly bureaucratic organizations of private capitalism. The idea of eliminating these organizations becomes more and more utopian.

The discipline of officialdom refers to the attitude-set of the official for precise obedience within his *habitual* activity, in public as well as in private organizations. This discipline increasingly becomes the basis of all order, however great the practical importance of administration on the basis of the filed documents may be. The naive idea of Bakuninism of destroying the basis of "acquired rights" and "domination" by destroying public documents overlooks the settled orientation of *man* for keeping to the habitual rules and regulations that continue to exist independently of the documents. Every reorganization of beaten or dissolved troops, as well as the restoration of administrative orders destroyed by revolt, panic, or other catastrophes, is realized by appealing to the trained orientation of obedient compliance to such orders. Such compliance has been conditioned into the officials, on the one hand, and, on the other hand, into the governed. If such an appeal is successful it brings, as it were, the disturbed mechanism into gear again.

The objective indispensability of the once-existing apparatus, with its peculiar, "impersonal" character, means that the mechanism—in contrast to feudal orders based upon personal piety—is easily made to work for anybody who knows how to gain control over it. A rationally ordered system of officials continues to function smoothly after the enemy has occupied the area; he merely needs to change the top officials. This body of officials continues to operate because it is to the vital interest of everyone concerned, including above all the enemy.

During the course of his long years in power, Bismarck brought his ministerial colleagues into unconditional bureaucratic dependence by eliminating all independent statesmen. Upon his retirement, he saw to his surprise that they continued to manage their offices unconcerned and undismayed, as if he had not been the master mind and creator of these creatures, but rather as if some single figure had been exchanged for some other figure in the bureaucratic machine. With all the changes of masters in France since the time of the First Empire, the power machine has remained essentially the same. Such a machine makes "revolution," in the sense of the forceful creation of entirely new formations of authority, technically more and more impossible, especially when the apparatus controls the modern means of communication (telegraph, et cetera) and also by virtue of its internal rationalized structure. In classic fashion, France has demonstrated how this process has substituted *coups d'état* for "revolutions": all successful transformations in France have amounted to *coups d'état*.

11. Economic and Social Consequences of Bureaucracy

It is clear that the bureaucratic organization of a social structure, and especially of a political one, can and regularly does have far-reaching economic consequences. But what sort of consequences? Of course in any individual case it depends upon the distribution of economic and social power, and especially upon the sphere that is occupied by the emerging bureaucratic mechanism. The consequences of bureaucracy depend therefore upon the direction which the powers using the apparatus give to it. And very frequently a crypto-plutocratic distribution of power has been the result.

In England, but especially in the United States, party donors regularly stand behind the bureaucratic party organizations. They have financed these parties and have been able to influence them to a large extent. The breweries in England, the so-called "heavy industry," and in Germany the Hansa League with their voting funds are well enough known as political donors to parties. In modern times bureaucratization and social leveling within political, and particularly within state organizations in connection with the destruction of feudal and local privileges, have very frequently benefited the interests of capitalism. Often bureaucratization has been carried out in direct alliance with capitalist interests, for example, the great historical alliance of the power of the absolute prince with capitalist interests. In general, a legal leveling and destruction of firmly established local structures ruled by notables has usually made for a wider range of capitalist activity. Yet one may expect as an effect of bureaucratization, a policy that meets

the petty bourgeois interest in a secured traditional "subsistence," or even a state socialist policy that strangles opportunities for private profit. This has occurred in several cases of historical and far-reaching importance, specifically during antiquity; it is undoubtedly to be expected as a future development. Perhaps it will occur in Germany.

The very different effects of political organizations which were, at least in principle, quite similar—in Egypt under the Pharaohs and in Hellenic and Roman times—show the very different economic significances of bureaucratization which are possible according to the direction of other factors. The mere fact of bureaucratic organization does not unambiguously tell us about the concrete direction of its economic effects, which are always in some manner present. At least it does not tell us as much as can be told about its relatively leveling effect socially. In this respect, one has to remember that bureaucracy as such is a precision instrument which can put itself at the disposal of quite varied—purely political as well as purely economic, or any other sort—of interests in domination. Therefore, the measure of its parallelism with democratization must not be exaggerated, however typical it may be. Under certain conditions, strata of feudal lords have also put bureaucracy into their service. There is also the possibility—and often it has become a fact, for instance, in the Roman principate and in some forms of absolutist state structures—that a bureaucratization of administration is deliberately connected with the formation of *estates,* or is entangled with them by the force of the existing groupings of social power. The express reservation of offices for certain status groups is very frequent, and actual reservations are even more frequent. The democratization of society in its totality, and in the *modern* sense of the term, whether actual or perhaps merely formal, is an especially favorable basis of bureaucratization, but by no means the only possible one. After all, bureaucracy strives merely to level those powers that stand in its way and in those areas that, in the individual case, it seeks to occupy. We must remember this fact—which we have encountered several times and which we shall have to discuss repeatedly: that "democracy" as such is opposed to the "rule" of bureaucracy, in spite and perhaps because of its unavoidable yet unintended promotion of bureaucratization. Under certain conditions, democracy creates obvious ruptures and blockages to bureaucratic organization. Hence, in every individual historical case, one must observe in what special direction bureaucratization has developed.

12. The Power Position of Bureaucracy

Everywhere the modern state is undergoing bureaucratization. But whether the *power* of bureaucracy within the polity is universally increasing must here remain an open question.

The fact that bureaucratic organization is technically the most highly developed means of power in the hands of the man who controls it does not determine the weight that bureaucracy as such is capable of having in a particular social structure. The ever-increasing "indispensability" of the officialdom, swollen to millions, is no more decisive for this question than is the view of some representatives of the proletarian movement that the economic indispensability of the proletarians is decisive for the measure of their social and political power position. If "indispensability" were decisive, then where slave labor prevailed and where freemen usually abhor work as a dishonor, the "indispensable" slaves ought to have held the positions of power, for they were at least as indispensable as officials and proletarians are today. Whether the power of bureaucracy as such increases cannot be decided *a priori* from such reasons. The drawing in of economic interest groups or other non-official experts, or the drawing in of non-expert lay representatives, the establishment of local, inter-local, or central parliamentary or other representative bodies, or of occupational associations—these *seem* to run directly against the bureaucratic tendency. How far this appearance is the truth must be discussed in another chapter rather than in this purely formal and typological discussion. In general, only the following can be said here:

Under normal conditions, the power position of a fully developed bureaucracy is always overtowering. The "political master" finds himself in the position of the "dilettante" who stands opposite the "expert," facing the trained official who stands within the management of administration. This holds whether the "master" whom the bureaucracy serves is a "people," equipped with the weapons of "legislative initiative," the "referendum," and the right to remove officials, or a parliament, elected on a more aristocratic or more "democratic" basis and equipped with the right to vote a lack of confidence, or with the actual authority to vote it. It holds whether the master is an aristocratic, collegiate body, legally or actually based on self-recruitment, or whether he is a popularly elected president, a hereditary and "absolute" or a "constitutional" monarch. . . . [pp. 228–233]

⌐⎯⎯⎤ **CASE STUDY 2**

Introduction

At first glance, the following story may seem out of place—or odd—to follow such a highly abstract and theoretical essay by Max Weber. It is a personal story told by a father, George Lardner, who recounts the details of the shooting death of his 21-year-old daughter Kristin on May 30, 1992. She had been raised in Washington, D.C. and was living in Boston, studying in a fine arts program, jointly sponsored by the Museum of Fine

Arts and Tufts University. For two and a half months she had been dating 22-year-old Michael Cartier, a local nightclub bouncer, but had broken up with him on April 16. That night he became violent, beating her up a few blocks from her apartment. Increasingly he became obsessed by her rejection of him.

What follows is a sorry tale of Kristin's attempts to rely on the bureaucratic system and the subsequent breakdown of that system to protect her from a brutal "stalker." Although it is about the worst nightmares of women—and their parents and friends—the study dispassionately probes the background of Cartier and the reasons why "the system" left him "on the street," which ultimately led to Kristin's death as well as Cartier's. In the process of recounting the events surrounding this tragedy, the author, perhaps unconsciously, underscores the importance of a well-functioning, effective bureaucracy, one containing many of the key elements outlined in the foregoing essay by Max Weber, in order to protect the lives and safety of all of us.

As you read this selection, try to reflect on the following:

What were the chief elements in the overall bureaucratic system that failed to protect Kristin?

What caused their breakdown?

How does Weber's conceptualization of bureaucracy help us to understand bureaucracy, its role in society and sources of failure—as well as strengths?

Does this story "square" with Weber's conception of bureaucracy and the vital role he believed it fulfilled in modern society?

Do Weber's generalizations fit or fail to fit the American experience as portrayed by this case? The basic design of bureaucracy? Its formal scope and powers? Its informal influence on our lives? Sources of problems of modern bureaucracy?

How Kristin Died

GEORGE LARDNER, JR.

The phone was ringing insistently, hurrying me back to my desk. My daughter Helen was on the line, sobbing so hard she could barely catch her breath. "Dad," she shouted. "Come home! Right away!"

I was stunned. I had never heard her like this before. "What's wrong?" I asked. "What happened?"

"It's—it's Kristin. She's been shot . . . and killed."

Kristin? My Kristin? Our Kristin? I'd talked to her the afternoon before. Her last words to me were, "I love you Dad." Suddenly I had trouble breathing myself.

It was 7:30 p.m. on Saturday, May 30. In Boston, where Kristin Lardner was an art student, police were cordoning off an apartment building a couple of blocks from the busy, sunlit sidewalk where she'd been killed 90 minutes earlier. She had been shot in the head and face by an ex-boyfriend who was under court order to stay away from her. When police burst into his apartment, they found him sprawled on his bed, dead from a final act of self-pity.

This was a crime that could and should have been prevented. I write about it as a sort of cautionary tale, in anger at a system of justice that failed to protect my daughter, a system that is addicted to looking the other way, especially at the evil done to women.

But first let me tell you about my daughter.

She was, at 21, the youngest of our five children, born in Washington, D.C., and educated in the city's public schools, where not much harm befell her unless you count her taste for rock music, lots of jewelry, and funky clothes from Value Village. She loved books, went trick-or-treating dressed as Greta Garbo, played one of the witches in "Macbeth" and had a grand time in tap-dancing class even in her sneakers. She made life sparkle.

When she was small, she always got up in time for Saturday morning cartoons at the Chevy Chase library, and she took cheerful care of a succession of cats, mice, gerbils, hamsters and guinea pigs. Her biggest fault may have been that she took too long in the shower—and you never knew what color her hair was going to be when she emerged. She was compassionate, and strong-minded too; when a boy from high school dropped his pants in front of her, Kristin knocked out one of his front teeth.

"She didn't back down from anything," said Amber Lynch, a close friend from Boston University. "You could tell that basically from her art, the way she dressed, the opinions she had. If you said something stupid, she'd tell you."

Midway through high school, Kristin began thinking of becoming an artist. She'd been taking art and photography classes each summer at the Corcoran School of Art and was encouraged when an art teacher at Wilson High decided two of her paintings were good enough to go on display at a little gallery there. She began studies at Boston University's art school and transferred after two years to a fine arts program run jointly by the School of the Museum of Fine Arts and Tufts University. She particularly liked to sculpt and make jewelry and, in the words of one faculty member, "showed great promise and was extremely talented."

In her apartment were scattered signs of that talent. Three wide-banded silver and brass rings, one filigreed with what looked like barbed wire. Some striking sculptures of bound figures. A Madonna,

painstakingly gilded. A nude self-portrait in angry reds, oranges and yellows, showing a large leg bruise her ex-boyfriend had given her on their last date in April.

"It felt as though she was telling all her secrets to the world," she wrote of her art in an essay she left behind. "Why would anyone want to know them anyway? But making things was all she wanted to do. . . . She always had questions, but never any answers, just frustration and confusion, and a need to get out whatever lay inside of her, hoping to be meaningful."

Kristin wrote that essay last November for a course at Tufts taught by Ross Ellenhorn, who also happens to be a counselor at Emerge, an educational program for abusive men. He had once mentioned this to his students. He would hear from my daughter in April, after she met Michael Cartier.

By then, Kristin had been dating Cartier, a 22-year-old bouncer, for about two and a half months. She broke off with him on the early morning of April 16. On that night, a few blocks from her apartment, he beat her up.

They "became involved in an argument and he knocked her to the ground and started kicking her over and over," reads a Brookline, Mass., police report. "She remembers him saying, 'Get up or I'll kill you.' She staggered to her feet, a car stopped and two men assisted her home.

"Since that night," the report continues, "she has refused to see him, but he repeatedly calls her, sometimes 10 or 11 times a day. He has told her that if she reports him to the police, he might have to do six months in jail, but she better not be around when he gets out.

"She also stated the injuries she suffered were hematomas to her legs and recurring headaches from the kicks."

Kristin didn't call the police right away. But she did call Ellenhorn in hopes of getting Cartier into Emerge. "I made clear to her that Emerge isn't a panacea, that there was still a chance of him abusing her," Ellenhorn says. "I told her that he could kill her . . . because she was leaving him and that's when things get dangerous."

Cartier showed up at Emerge's offices in Cambridge, around April 28 by Ellenhorn's calculations. Ellenhorn, on duty that night, realized who Cartier was when he wrote down Kristin's name under victim on the intake form.

"I said, 'Are you on probation?' " Ellenhorn remembers. "He said yes. I said, 'I'm going to need the name of the probation officer.' He said, '[Expletive] this. No way.' "

With that, Cartier ripped up the contract he was required to sign, ripped up the intake form, put the tattered papers in his pocket and walked out.

"He knew," Ellenhorn says. "He knew what kind of connection would be made." Michael Cartier was, of course, on probation for attacking another woman.

Cartier preyed on women. Clearly disturbed, he once talked of killing his mother. When he was 5 or 6, he dismembered a pet rabbit. When he was 21, he tortured and killed a kitten. In a bizarre 1989 incident at an Andover restaurant, he injected a syringe of blood into a ketchup bottle. To his girlfriends, he could be appallingly brutal.

Rose Ryan could tell you that. When Kristin's murder was reported on TV—the newscaster described the killing as "another case of domestic violence"—she said to a friend, "That sounds like Mike." It was. Hearing the newscaster say his name, she recalls, "I almost dropped."

When Ryan met Cartier at a party in Boston in the late summer of 1990, she was an honors graduate of Lynn East High School, preparing to attend Suffolk University. She was 17, a lovely, courageous girl with brown hair and brown eyes like Kristin's.

"He was really my first boyfriend," she told me. "I was supposed to work that summer and save my money, but I got caught up with the scene in Boston and hanging out with all the kids. . . . At first, everything was fine."

Cartier was a familiar face on the Boston Common, thanks to his career as a freelance nightclub bouncer. He had scraped up enough money to share a Commonwealth Avenue apartment with a Museum School student named Kara Boettger. They dated a few times, then settled down into a sort of strained coexistence.

"He didn't like me very much," Boettger said. "He liked music loud. I'd tell him to turn it down."

Rose Ryan liked him better. She thought he was handsome—blue eyes, black hair, a tall and muscular frame—with a vulnerability that belied his strength. To make him happy, she quit work and postponed the college education it was going to pay for. "He had me thinking that he'd had a bad deal his whole life," she said, "that nobody loved him and I was the only one who could help him."

Cartier also knew how to behave when he was supposed to. Ryan said he made a good first impression on her parents. As with Kristin, it took just about two months before Cartier beat Ryan up. She got angry with him for "kidding around" and dumping her into a barrel on the Common. When she walked away, he punched her in the head; when she kept going, he punched her again.

"I'd never been hit by any man before and I was just shocked," she said. But what aggravated her the most, and still does, is that "every time something happened, it was in public, and nobody stopped to help."

Cartier ended the scene with "his usual thing," breaking into tears and telling her, "'Oh, why do I always hurt the people I love? What can I do? My mother didn't love me. I need your help.' "

Shortly after they started dating, Ryan spent a few days at the Cartier-Boettger apartment. He presented her with a gray kitten, then left it alone all day without a litter box. The kitten did what it needed to do on Cartier's jacket.

"He threw the kitten in the shower and turned the hot water on and kept it there under the hot water," Ryan remembers in a dull monotone. "And he shaved all its hair off with a man's shaving razor."

The kitten spent most of its wretched life hiding under a bed. On the night of Oct. 4, 1990, Cartier began drinking with two friends and went on a rampage. He took a sledgehammer and smashed through his bedroom wall into a neighbor's apartment. And he killed the kitten, hurling it out a fourth-floor window.

"I'd left the apartment without telling them," Ryan said. "When I came back, the police were in the hallway. . . . They said, 'Get out. This guy's crazy.' They were taking him out in handcuffs."

Three months later, Cartier, already on probation, plea-bargained his way to probation again—pleading guilty to malicious destruction. Charges of burglary and cruelty to animals were dismissed; the court saw nothing wrong with putting him back on the street.

"I thought he was going to jail because he violated probation," Kara Boettger said. So did Cartier.

"[But after the January hearing] he told me . . . 'Oh yeah, nothing happened. They slapped my wrist.' "

When Michael Cartier was born in Newburyport, Mass., his mother was 17. Her husband, then 19, left them six months later; Gene Cartier has since remarried twice. Her son, Penny Cartier says, was a problem from the first.

"He'd take a bottle away from his [step]sister. He'd light matches behind a gas stove. He was born that way," Penny Cartier asserted. "When he was five or six, he had a rabbit. He ripped its legs out of its sockets."

"None of this," she added in loud tones, "had anything to do with what he did to Kristin. . . . Michael's childhood had nothing to do with anything."

Life with mother, in any case, ended at age 7, when she sent him to the New England Home for Little Wanderers, a state-supported residential treatment center for troubled children. Staff there remember him—although Penny Cartier denies this—as a child abused at an early age. "That's the worst childhood I've ever seen," agrees Rich DeAngelis, one of Cartier's probation officers. "This didn't just happen in the last couple of years."

Cartier stayed at the New England Home until he was 12. In October 1982, he was put in the Harbor School in Amesbury, a treatment center for disturbed teenagers. He stayed there for almost four years and was turned over to his father, a facilities maintenance mechanic in Lawrence.

Michael Cartier was bitter about his mother. "I just know he hated her," Kara Boettger said. "He said he wanted to get a tattoo, I think maybe on his arm, of her hanging from a tree with animals ripping at her body."

Penny Cartier didn't seem surprised when I told her this. In fact, she added, after he turned 18, "he asked my daughter if she wanted him to kill me."

Cartier entered Lawrence High School but dropped out after a couple of years. "He was just getting frustrated. He couldn't keep up," said his father. By his second semester, he was facing the first of nearly 20 criminal charges that he piled up in courthouses from Lawrence to Brighton over a four-year period.

Along the way, he enjoyed brief notoriety as a self-avowed skinhead, sauntering into the newsroom of the Lawrence Eagle-Tribune with his bald friends in June 1989 to complain of the bad press and "neo-Nazi" labels skinheads usually got. "The state supported me all my life, with free doctors and dentists and everything," Cartier told columnist Kathie Neff. "My parents never had anything to do with that because they got rid of me. This is like my way of saying thanks [to them]."

Neff said Cartier cut an especially striking figure, walking on crutches and wearing a patch on one eye. He had just survived a serious car accident that produced what seems to have been a magic purse for him. He told friends he had a big insurance settlement coming and would get periodic advances on it from his lawyer. Gene Cartier said his son got a final payment late last year of $17,000 and "went through $14,000" of it before he murdered Kristin.

The high-ceilinged main courtroom in Brighton has a huge, wide-barred cell built into a wall. On busy days, it is a page from Dickens, crowded with yelling, cursing prisoners waiting for their cases to be called.

Cartier turned up in the cage April 29, 1991, finally arrested for violating probation. Ten days earlier, when Rose Ryan was coming home from a friend's house on the "T," Boston's trolley train and subway system, Cartier followed her—and accosted her at the Government Center station with a pair of scissors. She ducked the scissors and Cartier punched her in the mouth.

Even before that, Ryan and her older sister Tina had become alarmed. After a party in December, Cartier got annoyed with Rose for not wanting to eat pizza he'd just bought. She began walking back to the party when he back-handed her in the face so hard she fell down. "And I'm lying on the ground, screaming, and then he finally stopped kicking me after I don't know how long, and then he said, 'You better get up or I'll kill you.' "

The same words he would use with Kristin. And how many other young women?

Rose Ryan said Cartier threatened to kill her several times after they broke up in December and, in a chance encounter in March, told her he had a gun. The Ryan sisters called his probation officer in Brighton, Tom Casey. He told Rose to get a restraining order and, on March 28, he obtained a warrant for Cartier's arrest. It took a month for police to pick him up even though Cartier had, in between, attacked

Rose in the subway and been arraigned on charges for that assault in Boston Municipal Court.

"Probation warrants have to be served by the police, who don't take them seriously enough," said another probation officer. "Probationers know . . . they can skip court appearances with impunity."

When Cartier turned up in Brighton, "he was very quiet. Sullen and withdrawn," Casey said. "It was obvious he had problems, deeper than I could ever get to." Yet a court psychiatrist, Dr. Mike Annunziata, filed a report stating that Cartier had "no acute mental disorder, no suicidal or homicidal ideas, plans or intents." The April 29, 1991, report noted that Cartier was being treated by the Tri-City Mental Health and Retardation Center in Malden and was taking 300 milligrams of lithium a day to control depression.

Cartier, the report said, had also spent four days in January 1991 at the Massachusetts Mental Health Center in Boston. He was brought there on a "Section 12," a law providing for emergency restraint of dangerous persons, because of "suicidal ideation" and an overdose of some sort. On April 2, 1991, he was admitted to the Center on another "Section 12," this time for talking about killing Rose Ryan with a gun "within two weeks." He denied making the threats and was released the next day.

Tom Casey wanted to get him off the streets this time, and a like-minded visiting magistrate ordered Cartier held on bail for a full hearing in Brighton later in the week. When the Ryan sisters arrived in court, they found themselves five feet away from Cartier in the cell. "Soon as he saw me," Tina Ryan said, "he said, 'I know who you are, I'm going to kill you too,' all these filthy words, calling me everything he could. . . ."

After listening to what the Ryans had to say, the judge sent Cartier to jail on Deer Island for three months for violating probation. The next month, he was given a year for the subway attack, but was committed for only six months.

That didn't stop the harassment. Cartier began making collect calls to Ryan from prison and he enlisted other inmates to write obscene letters. The district attorney's office advised the Ryans to keep a record of the calls so they could be used against Cartier later.

Despite all that, Cartier was released early, on Nov. 5, 1991. "'He's been a very good prisoner and we're overcrowded,'" the Ryans say they were told.

Authorities in Essex County didn't want to see him out on the streets even if officials in Boston didn't care. As soon as he was released from Deer Island, Cartier was picked up for violating his probation on the ketchup-bottle incident and sentenced to 59 days in the Essex County jail. But a six-month suspended sentence that was hanging over him for a 1988 burglary—which would have meant at least three months in jail—was wiped off the books.

"That's amazing," said another probation officer who looked at the record. "They dropped the more serious charges."

Cartier was released after serving 49 of the 59 days.

Ryan had already been taking precautions. She carried Mace in her pocketbook, put a baseball bat in her car and laid out a bunch of knives next to her bed each night before going to sleep. "I always thought that he would come back and try to get me," she said.

Kristin loved to go out with friends until all hours of the morning, but she didn't have many steady boyfriends. Most men, she said more than once, "are dogs" because of the way they treated girls she knew.

She was always ready for adventure, hopping on the back of brother Charles's motorcycle for rides; curling up with Circe, a pet ball-python she kept in her room; and flying down for a few weeks almost every August to Jekyll Island, Ga., to be with her family, a tradition started when she was less than a week old. Last year she caught a small shark from the drawbridge over the Jekyll River.

"I think she'd give anything a go," said Jason Corkin, the young man she dated the longest, before he returned last year to his native New Zealand. "When she set her mind to something, she wouldn't give it up for anything."

She could also become easily depressed, especially about what she was going to do after graduation. As she once wrote, her favorite pastime was "morbid self-reflection." Despite that, laughter came easily and she was always ready for a conversation about art, religion, philosophy, music. "I don't really remember any time we were together that we didn't have a good time," said Bekky Elstad, a close friend from Boston University.

Left in her bedroom at her death was a turntable with Stravinsky's "Rites of Spring" on it and a tape player with a punk tune by Suicidal Tendencies. Her books, paperbacks mostly, included Alice Walker's "The Color Purple" and Margaret Atwood's "The Handmaid's Tale," along with favorites by Sinclair Lewis, Dickens and E.B. White and a book about upper- and middle-caste women in Hindu families in Calcutta.

Her essays for school, lucid and well-written, showed a great deal of thought about art, religion and the relationship between men and women. She saw her art as an expression of parts of her hidden deep inside, waiting to be pulled out, but still to be guarded closely: "Art could be such a selfish thing. Everything she made, she made for herself and not one bit of it could she bear to be parted with. Whether she loved it, despised it or was painfully ashamed of it . . . she couldn't stand the thought of these little parts of her being taken away and put into someone else's possession."

Buddhism appealed to her, and once she wrote this: "Pain only comes when you try to hang on to what is impermanent. So all life need not be suffering. You can enjoy life if you do not expect anything from it."

She met Cartier last Jan. 30 at a Boston nightclub called Axis, having gone there with Lauren Mace, Kristin's roommate and best friend, and Lauren's boyfriend. At Axis, Kristin recognized Cartier as someone she'd seen at Bunratty's, a hard-rock club where Cartier had been a bouncer. Cartier was easily recognizable; he had a large tattoo of a castle on his neck.

What did she see in him? It's a question her parents keep asking themselves. But some things are fairly obvious. He reminded her of Jason, her friend from New Zealand. He could be charming. "People felt a great deal of empathy for him," said Octavia Ossola, director of the child care center at the home where Cartier grew up, "because it was reasonably easy to want things to be better for him." At the Harbor School, said executive director Art DiMauro, "he was quite endearing. The staff felt warmly about Michael."

So, at first, did Kristin. "She called me up, really excited and happy," said Christian Dupre, a friend since childhood. "She said 'I met this good guy, he's really nice.' "

Kristin told her oldest sister, Helen, and her youngest brother, Charlie, too. But Helen paused when Kristin told her that Cartier was a bouncer at Bunratty's and had a tattoo.

"Well, ah, is he nice?" Helen asked.

"Well, he's nice to me," Kristin said.

Charlie, who had just entered college after a few years of blue-collar jobs, was not impressed. "Get rid of him," he advised his sister. "He's a zero."

Her friends say they got along well at first. He told Kristin he'd been in jail for hitting a girlfriend, but called it a bum rap. She did not know he'd attacked Rose Ryan with scissors, that he had a rap sheet three pages long.

Kristin, friends say, often made excuses for his behavior. But they soon started to argue. Cartier was irrationally jealous, accusing her of going out with men who stopped by just to talk. During one argument, apparently over her art, Cartier hit her, then did his "usual thing" and started crying.

Cartier, meanwhile, was still bothering Ryan. A warrant for violating probation had been issued out of Boston Municipal Court on Dec. 19, in part for trying to contact her by mail while he was in jail. But when he finally turned up in court, a few days before he met Kristin, he got kid-glove treatment. Rather than being sentenced to complete the one-year term he'd gotten for the scissors attack, he was ordered instead to attend a once-a-week class at the courthouse for six weeks called "Alternatives to Violence."

"It's not a therapy program, it's more educational," said John Tobin, chief probation officer at Boston Municipal Court. "It's for people who react to stress in violent ways, not just for batterers. Cartier . . . showed up each time. You don't send probationers away when they do what they're supposed to do."

What Tobin didn't mention was that Cartier had actually dropped out of his Alternatives to Violence course—and, incredibly, was allowed to sign up for it again. According to a chronology I obtained elsewhere, Cartier attended the first meeting of the group on Feb. 5 and skipped the class Feb. 12. His probation was revoked two days later. But instead of sending him back to jail, the court allowed him to start the course over, beginning April 1.

Cartier's probation officer, Diane Barrett Moeller, a "certified batterer specialist" who helps run the program, declined to talk to me, citing "legal limitations" that she did not spell out. Her boss, Tobin, said she was "a ferocious probation officer."

"We tend to be a punitive department," Tobin asserted. "We are not a bunch of social rehabilitators."

However that may be, it is a department that seems to operate in a vacuum. Cartier's record of psychiatric problems, his admissions to the Boston mental health center in January and April 1991 and his reliance on a drug to control manic-depression should have disqualified him from the court-run violence program.

"If we had information that he had a prior history of mental illness, or that he was treated in a clinic or that he had been hospitalized, then what we probably would have done is recommend that a full-scale psychological evaluation be done for him," Tobin told the Boston Herald last June following Kristin's murder. "We didn't know about it."

Probation officer Tom Casey in Brighton knew. All Tobin's office had to do was pick up the phone to find out what a menace Cartier was. Meanwhile, in Salem, where she had moved to work with her sister at a family-run business, Rose Ryan remained fearful. But she had a new boyfriend, Sean Casey, 23, and, as Rose puts it, "I think he intimidated Mike because he had more tattoos. Mike knew Sean from before."

Around March 1, Sean went to Boston to tell Cartier to leave Rose alone. As they were talking, Kristin walked by. Sean didn't know who she was, but recognized her later, from newspaper photos.

Cartier nodded at Kristin as she passed. "He said, 'I don't need Rose any more,' " Casey recalled. " 'I have my own girlfriend.' "

Cartier was a frequent visitor at the six-room flat Kristin shared with Lauren Mace and another BU student, Matt Newton, but he didn't have much to say to them or the other students who were always stopping by. He told Kristin they "intimidated" him because they were college-educated.

As the weeks wore on, they started to argue. When he hit her the first time, probably in early March, Kristin told friends about it, but not Lauren. She was

probably too embarrassed. She had always been outspoken in her disdain for men who hit women.

"He hit her once. She freaked out on that . . . ," Bekky Elstad said. "She wanted him to get counseling. . . . He told her he was sorry. He was all broken up. She wanted to believe him."

Kristin came home to Washington in mid-March, outwardly bright and cheerful. She was more enthusiastic than ever about her art. She was "really getting it together," she said. She had yet to tell her parents that she had a boyfriend, much less a boyfriend who hit her.

When she got back to Boston, Cartier tried to make up with her. He gave her a kitten. "It was really cute—black with a little white triangle on its nose," Amber Lynch said. "It was teeny. It just wobbled around."

It didn't last long. Over Kristin's protests, Cartier put the kitten on top of a door jamb. It fell off, landing on its head. She had to have it destroyed.

Devastated, Kristin called home in tears and told her parents, for the first time, about her new boyfriend. Part of her conversation with her mother was picked up by a malfunctioning answering machine.

Rosemary: What does Mike do?

Kristin: Well, he does the same thing Jason did actually. He works at Bunratty's.

Rosemary: He does what?

Kristin: He works at Bunratty's.

Rosemary: Oh. Is he an artist also?

Kristin: No.

Rosemary: Well, that's what I was asking. What does he—? Is he a student?

Kristin: No. He just—he works. He's a bouncer.

"Oh," Rosemary said, asking after a long pause why she was going out with a boy with no education. Kristin told her that she wanted to have a boyfriend "just like everyone else does."

When I came home, Rosemary said, "Call your daughter." When I did, Kristin began crying again as she told me about the kitten. She was also upset because she had given Cartier a piece of jewelry she wanted to use for her annual evaluation at the Museum School. He told her he'd lost it.

Gently, perhaps too gently, I said I didn't think she should be wasting her time going out with a boy who did such stupid things. We talked about school and classes for a few minutes more and said goodnight.

She went out with him for the last time on April 16, the day after one of his Alternatives to Violence classes. He pushed her down onto the sidewalk in front of a fast-food place, cutting her hand. She told him several times to "go home and leave me alone," but he kept following her to a side street in Allston.

"Kristin said something like, 'Get away from me, I never want to see you again,'" Bekky Elstad remembers. But when Kristin tried to run, he caught up with her, threw her down and kicked her repeatedly in the head and legs. She was crying hysterically when she got home with the help of a passing motorist. She refused to see him again.

But Cartier kept trying to get her on the phone. He warned her not to go to the police and, for a while, she didn't. She felt sorry for him. She even agreed to take a once-a-week phone call from him the day he went to his Alternatives to Violence class.

He was rated somewhat passive at the meetings, but he got through the course on May 6 without more truancy. The next day, he walked into Gay's Flowers and Gifts on Commonwealth Avenue and bought a dozen red roses for Kristin. He brought in a card to be delivered with them.

Leslie North, a dark-haired, puffy-faced woman who had known Cartier for years, had helped him fill it out in advance. "He always called me when he had a fight with his girlfriends," she said. "He said that he was trying to change, that he needed help, that he wanted to be a better person. He said, 'I'm trying to get back with her.'"

Flower shop proprietor Alan Najarian made the delivery to Kristin's flat. "One of her roommates took them," Najarian remembers. "He was kind of reluctant. . . . I think he must have known who they were from."

Police think Cartier may have gotten his gun the day of the murder, but Leslie North remembers his showing it to her "shortly after [he and Kristin] broke up," probably in early May.

Why did he get the gun? "He said, 'Ah, just to have one,'" North says. "I asked him, 'What do you need a gun for?' He said, 'You never know.' I didn't realize you're not supposed to get a gun if you've been in jail. I didn't tell anyone he had it."

"He told me he paid $750 for it," she continues. "I showed him just a little bit of safety . . . how to hold it when you shoot. . . . It looked kind of old to me."

The gun found in Cartier's apartment after he killed Kristin and himself was 61 years old, a Colt .38 Super, serial number 13645, one of about a 100 million handguns loose in the United States. It was shipped brand new on Jan. 12, 1932, to a hardware store in Knoxville, Tenn., where all traces of it disappeared.

North remembered something else she says Cartier told her after he got the gun. "He goes, 'If I kill Kristin, are you going to tell anyone?'

"I said, 'Of course, I'm going to tell.' I didn't take him seriously. . . . He said that once or twice to me."

On May 7, the same day Cartier sent flowers to Kristin, he told her that he was going to cheat her out of the $1,000 Nordic Flex machine she'd let him charge to her Discover card. When she told him over the phone that she expected him to return the device, he laughed and said, "I guess you're out the $1,000."

Kristin was furious. She promptly called Cartier's probation officer, Diane Barrett Moeller, and gave her an earful: the exercise machine, the beating.

Kristin's call for help was another of the probation office's secrets. Tobin said nothing about it to the Boston press in the days after Kristin's murder, when it grew clear that there was something desperately wrong with the criminal justice system. Tobin told me only after I found out about it from Kristin's friends.

"Your daughter was concerned," Tobin said. "She put a lot of emphasis on the weight machine. Mrs. Moeller said, 'Get your priorities straight. You should not be worrying about the weight machine. You should be worrying about your safety. . . . Get to Brookline court, seek an assault complaint, a larceny complaint, whatever it takes . . . and get a restraining order.'"

According to Tobin, Kristin wouldn't give her name even though Moeller asked for it twice. "We can't revoke someone's probation on an anonymous phone call," he said. Kristin, he added, "did say she didn't want this man arrested and put behind bars."

Tobin also claimed that his office could have taken no action because Kristin was "not the woman in the case we were supervising," which is like saying that probationers in Boston Municipal Court should only take care not to rob the same bank twice.

The next day, Friday, May 8, instead of moving

to revoke Cartier's probation, Moeller called Cartier and, in effect, told him what was up. Tobin recalled the conversation. "She told him to get the exercise machine back to her. She told him she didn't want to hear about it anymore. And she ordered a full-scale psychiatric evaluation of him. She also ordered him to report to her every week until the evaluation is completed."

Cartier did all that while planning Kristin's murder.

When Cartier called Kristin again, she told him that if he didn't return the exercise machine, she was going to take court action. "He called back 10 minutes later from a pay phone," remembers Brian Fazekas, Lauren's boyfriend. "He said, 'Okay, okay, I'll return the stupid machine.' "

Kristin was skeptical about that. And she was worried about more violence. The warnings of her friends, her brother Charlie, her teacher Ross Ellenhorn and now Cartier's probation officer rang in her ears. Her art reflected her anguish. She had painted her own self-portrait, showing some of the ugly bruises Cartier had left. Hanging sculptures showed a male, arms flexed and fists clenched. The female hung defensively, arms protecting her head.

By Monday, May 11, she had made up her mind. She was going to rely on the system. She decided to ask the courts for help. She talked about it afterwards with her big sister, Helen, a lawyer and her lifelong best friend. Kristin told her, sparingly, about the beating and, angrily, about the exercise machine. Helen kept the news to herself, as Kristin requested. "She said she found out what a loser he was. She said, 'He's even been taking drugs behind my back,' " Helen recalls. He was snorting heroin, confirms Leslie North—it helped him stay calm, she remembers him saying.

Late in the day, Kristin went to the Brookline police station, Lauren Mace and Brian Fazekas beside her.

"The courts were closed by the time we got there. We waited outside," Lauren said. "An officer showed her [Cartier's] arrest record. When she came out, she said, 'You won't believe the size of this guy's police record. He's killed cats. He's beat up ex-girlfriends. Breaking and enterings.' The officer just sort

of flashed the length of it at her and said, 'Look at what you're dealing with.' "

Brookline police sergeant Robert G. Simmons found Kristin "very intelligent, very articulate"—and scared. Simmons asked if she wanted to press charges, and she replied that she wanted to think about that. Simmons, afraid she might not come back, made out an "application for complaint" himself and got a judge on night duty to approve issuance of a one-day emergency restraining order over the phone. The next day, Kristin had to appear before Brookline District Judge Lawrence Shubow to ask for a temporary order—one that would last a week.

Other paperwork that Simmons sent over to the courthouse, right next door to the police station, called for a complaint charging Cartier with assault and battery, larceny, intimidation of a witness and violation of the domestic abuse law. It was signed by Lt. George Finnegan, the police liaison officer on duty at the courthouse that day, and turned over to clerk-magistrate John Connors for issuance of a summons.

The summons was never issued. Inexcusably, the application for it was still sitting on a desk in the clerk's office the day Kristin was killed, almost three weeks later.

Other officials I spoke with were amazed by the lapse. Connors shrugged it off. "We don't have the help," he said. "It was waiting to be typed."

Shubow was unaware of the criminal charges hanging over Cartier's head at the May 12 hearing. And Shubow didn't bother to ask about his criminal record. Restraining orders in Massachusetts, as in other states, have been treated for years by most judges as distasteful "civil matters." Until Kristin was killed, any thug in the Commonwealth accused under the domestic abuse law of beating up his wife or girlfriend or ex-wife or ex-girlfriend could walk into court without much fear that his criminal record would catch up with him. Shubow later told The Boston Globe, "If there is one lesson I learned from this case, it was to ask myself whether this is a case where I should review his record. In a case that has an immediate level of danger, I could press for a warrant and immediate arrest."

Instead, Shubow treated Docket No. 92-RO-060 as a routine matter. He issued a temporary restraining order telling Cartier to stay away from Kristin's school, her apartment and her place of work for a week, until another hearing could be held by another judge on a permanent order, good for a year.

"The system failed her completely," Shubow told me after Kristin's death. "There is no such thing as a routine case. I don't live that, but I believe that. All bureaucrats should be reminded of that."

Downtown, in Boston Municipal Court, chief probation officer Tobin said that "if we had found out about the restraining order, we would have moved immediately." But Tobin's office made no effort to find out. Cartier's probation officer knew that the anonymous female caller lived in Brookline; a call to officials there would have made clear that Cartier had once again violated probation by beating up an ex-girlfriend. No such call was made.

Apparently, the probation officer didn't ask Cartier for the details either. According to a state official who asked not to be identified, Diane Moeller met with Cartier on May 14, just eight days after he completed her Alternatives to Violence course and three days after Kristin obtained her first restraining order. Moeller did nothing to get him off the streets.

"She was concerned about getting additional assistance for this guy," the state official said of the May 14 meeting. "No charges were filed."

In Brookline, Lt. Finnegan said he sensed something was wrong. He walked up to Kristin outside the courthouse on May 12. "I had this gut feeling," he said. "I asked her, 'Are you really afraid of him?' She said, 'Yeah.' I asked her if he had a gun. She said, 'He may.'"

Finnegan told her to call the police if she saw Cartier hanging around.

The phone rang at the Brookline Police Station shortly after midnight on May 19; Kristin's request for a permanent restraining order was coming up for a hearing that morning. Now, in plain violation of the May 12 order, Cartier had called around midnight, got Kristin on the line and asked her not to go back to court. She called the cops.

Sgt. Simmons, on duty that night as shift commander, advised Kristin to file a complaint and sent officer Kevin Mealy to talk to her; Mealy arrived at her apartment at 1:10 a.m. "Ms. Lardner said that Mr. Cartier attempted to persuade her not to file for an extension of the order," Mealy wrote in his report, which he filed as soon as he got back to the station house. "A criminal complaint application

has been made out against Mr. Cartier for violating the existing restraining order."

Sgt. Simmons says, "I told Kevin, 'They've got a hearing in the morning.' The documents went over there. But who reads them?"

Kristin arrived at the courthouse around 11:30 a.m. May 19, accompanied by Lauren Mace and Amber Lynch.

"He [Cartier] was out in front of the courthouse when we got there," Lynch said. "We all just walked in quickly. We waited a long time. He kept walking in and out of the courtroom. I think he was staring at her."

There was no one in the courtroom from the Norfolk County D.A.'s office to advise Kristin. Brookline probation officials didn't talk to her either. They had no idea Cartier was on probation for beating up another woman.

Neither did District Judge Paul McGill, a visiting magistrate from Roxbury. Like Shubow, he didn't check Cartier's criminal record. Unlike Shubow, it didn't trouble him. To him, it was a routine hearing. Kristin was looking for protection. She was processed like a slice of cheese.

"She thought he was going to be arrested," Lauren said. Brian Fazekas said, "It was her understanding that as soon as he got the permanent restraining order, he was going to be surrendered" for violating probation.

"What he [Cartier] did on the 19th was a crime," David Lowy, legal adviser to Gov. William Weld and a former prosecutor, said of the midnight call. "He should have been placed under arrest right then and there."

The hearing lasted five minutes. It would have been shorter except for a typical bit of arrogance from Cartier, trying to stay in control in the face of his third restraining order in 18 months. He agreed not to contact Kristin for a year and to stay away from her apartment and school. But he said he had a problem staying away from Marty's Liquors, where Kristin had just started working as a cashier. "I happen to live right around the corner from there," Cartier complained, according to a tape of the hearing.

The judge told him to patronize some other liquor store, but not before more argument from Cartier about how he would have to "walk further down the street" and about how close it was to Bunratty's, only half a block away. McGill ended the hearing by ordering Cartier to avoid any contact with Kristin, to stay at least 200 yards away from her and not to talk to her if he had to come closer when entering his home or the nightclub.

And with that, Cartier walked out scot-free. Yet, Massachusetts law, enacted in 1990, provides for mandatory arrest of anyone a law enforcement officer has probable cause to believe violated a temporary or permanent restraining order. In addition, a state law making "stalking" a crime, especially in violation of a restraining order, had been signed by Gov. Weld just the day before, May 18, effective immediately.

McGill later said that if he'd known Cartier had violated his restraining order by calling Kristin that morning, he would have turned the hearing into a criminal session.

The application for a complaint charging Cartier with violating the order was moldering in clerk John Connors's offices. Like the earlier complaint accusing him of assault and battery, it was still there the day Kristin was killed.

"Kristin could have said something [in court], I suppose," Lauren said. "But she just figured that after that, he would be out of her life. She said, 'Let's go home.' She felt very relieved that she had this restraining order."

Kristin, who now had 11 days to live, talked enthusiastically about going to Europe after graduation, only a year away. After that she was hoping to go to graduate school. She had lost interest in boys, wanting to concentrate on her art.

"I spoke to her the night before [she was killed]," Chris Dupre said. "She was like the most optimistic and happiest she'd been in months. She knew what she wanted to do with herself, with her art."

She even had a new kitten, named Stubby because its tail was broken in two places. She was working part-time in the liquor store and hoping for more hours as summer approached. But she liked to stay home and paint or just hang out with friends now that classes were over.

Cartier was still skulking about, even after issuance of the permanent restraining order. One afternoon, Kristin stepped out of the liquor store to take a break. She saw Cartier staring at her from the doorway of Bunratty's.

On the afternoon of May 28, she and Robert Hyde, a friend who had just graduated from BU, decided to get something to eat after playing Scrabble (Kristin won) and chess (Robert won) at Kristin's flat. The two hopped on the back of his Yamaha and were off. First stop was the Bay Bank branch on Commonwealth Avenue, two doors from Marty's Liquors. As they turned a corner, Kristin saw Cartier looking in Marty's window. "Did you see that?" she asked Hyde moments later as they got off the bike. "Mike was peeking in the window. What a weirdo!"

Hyde didn't think that Cartier saw them, but later that night, after taking Kristin home, he went over to Bunratty's to play pinball. Cartier was there, and he began an awkward conversation to find out where Hyde lived.

"I thought it was kind of weird, but I didn't think too much of it," Hyde said. He shuddered about it after the shooting.

Cartier had always been disturbingly jealous—and unpredictable. "He'd get under pressure, he'd start breathing heavy and start talking all wild," a longtime friend, Timothy McKernan, told the Lawrence Eagle-Tribune.

He couldn't handle rejection either. Cartier "told his friends that she broke up with him because she wanted to see other people," Bekky Elstad said. "That's not true. But that's why he killed her, I think. If he couldn't have her, no one else was going to."

If Kristin was bothered by the stalking incident that Thursday, she seemed to put it out of her mind. The usual stream of friends moved through the flat all day. She called me that afternoon in an upbeat mood. We talked about summer school, her Museum School evaluation and a half dozen other things, including the next month's check from home. I assured her it was in the mail. She had a big smile in her voice. All I knew about Cartier was that she had gotten rid of the creep. When I made some grumpy reference to boyfriends in general, she laughed and said, "That's because you're my dad."

Cartier called his father that day, too.

Gene Cartier knew about Kristin and about the restraining order. "I asked him what happened," the older Cartier said. "He said, 'Well, me and my girlfriend had a fight.' I figured they argued. . . . He loved animals, he loved children. He wouldn't hurt a fly."

A man with a persistent drinking problem, Gene

Cartier at times seemed to confuse Kristin with other girlfriends his son had, but his son's last call about her stuck firmly in his mind. "He said, 'She's busting my balls again,'" Cartier recalled. "I think she was seeing another guy—in front of Michael—to get him jealous. . . . He was obsessed with her."

Kristin went to bed that night with a smile. It had been Lauren's last day at Marty's and some of the students who worked there stopped by the flat. "We were having a really, really good time," Lauren Mace said. "I remember, I said, 'Good night, Kristin.' I gave her a hug. The next morning, I saw her taking her bike down the street, on the way to work. I did not see her again."

Saturday, May 30, was a beautiful spring day in Boston, a light breeze rustling the trees on Winchester Street below the flat. Kristin was looking forward to a full day's work; Lauren was supposed to meet her at 6, when she was done at Marty's. Lauren had just graduated from BU; they were going to buy a keg for a big going-away party at the flat on Sunday.

One of the managers at the liquor store, David Bergman, was having lunch across the street at the Inbound Pizza when Kristin walked in. He waved her over to his table. She had a slice of Sicilian pizza and then, as he remembers, two more. "We talked for half an hour," Bergman said. "She was going to travel to Europe with her friend, Lauren. She had all these plans laid on."

After lunch, the day turned sour. Leslie North walked into Marty's with another girl. So, clerks say, did a man in his thirties with rotting teeth and thinning hair—North's boyfriend. He got in Kristin's checkout line and started cursing at her.

Not long after North and her friend left Marty's, J.D. Crump, the manager at Bunratty's, walked in for a sandwich from the deli counter. He'd known Kristin since she had dated Jason. "She said she was having a tough day," he told the Globe. "The customers were being mean. I told her it would get better."

When Crump spoke with Kristin on May 30, it was about 4:30. Cartier, meanwhile, was at a noisy show at the Rathskellar on Kenmore Square. Friends told the Lawrence Eagle-Tribune that he was acting strangely, greeting people with long hugs instead of the usual punch in the arm or a handshake.

"He wasn't the hugging type," Timothy McKernan told the Eagle-Tribune. "I think he knew what he was going to do." Cartier left suddenly, running out the door.

Kristin was scheduled to work until 6, but at 5 p.m., she was told, to her chagrin, to leave early, losing an hour's pay. "We had other cashiers coming in," the manager explained. Instead of hanging around to wait for Lauren, Kristin decided to go to Bekky Elstad's apartment and return at 6. It was a decision that seems to have cost her her life.

Lauren had come by around 5:40 p.m., and left when told Kristin had already gone. Kristin was still at Bekky's, keeping her eye on the clock and by now recounting how this "disgusting . . . slimy person" had been cursing at her at the cash register.

"She was laughing about how gross he was and then his being with these two girls—friends of Michael's—who were so gross," Bekky Elstad said. "She seemed pretty much in a good mood."

It was getting close to 6. By now, Cartier was back in the neighborhood, looking for a crowbar. He first asked for one at the Reading Room, a smoke shop about a block away, "maybe 20 minutes before it happened," said the proprietor. "I asked him why he wanted a crowbar. He said he had to go help somebody." Then he went over to Bunratty's, in a fruitless search for the same thing.

At one minute to 6, Kristin was heading down Commonwealth Avenue toward Marty's. Cartier, approaching from the other direction, stopped at a Store 24 convenience shop on the other side of Harvard Avenue. J.D. Crump was there, buying a pack of cigarettes. According to the police report: "Crump stated that while in Store 24 . . . he saw Michael and asked him [whether] he was going to work that night. Mike said that he was but had [to] shoot someone first. Crump stated that he did not take him seriously and walked away from him."

The shots rang out seconds later. Mike Dillon, a clerk at Marty's who clocked out at 6, had just stepped onto the sidewalk when he heard the first shattering noise.

"It was very loud," he said. "I looked up immediately. I saw Kristin fall."

Dressed all in black, she dropped instantly to the

pavement outside the Soap-A-Rama, a combination laundromat, tanning salon and video rental store four doors from Marty's.

"She was lying on her right side, curled up in kind of a fetal position," Mike Dillon said. "I kind of froze dead in my tracks."

Cartier must have seen her and hid in a doorway or alley until she passed by him. Witnesses said he came at her from behind and shot into the rear of her head from a distance of 15 or 20 feet. Then he ran into a nearby alley.

Al Silva, a restaurant worker, started to walk towards Kristin to see if he could help when Cartier darted back out of the alley, rushed past Silva, and leaned down over her.

"He shot her twice more in the left side of the head," Mike Dillon said. "Then I saw him run down the alley again. . . . I was still in shock. I didn't know what to do. I took one of her hands for a second or so, I don't know why. Then I ran back to call the police, but I saw a woman in the flower shop. She was already on the phone."

Chris Toher, the proprietor at Soap-A-Rama, heard the first shot from the back of his store and hurried up to the doorway. "I saw him fire the final shots," Toher said. "It happened so fast she never had a chance. She was completely unconscious at the point he ran up to her. Her eyes were shut."

A brave young woman was dead.

The killer fled down the alley, which took him to Glenville Avenue where he lived in a red brick apartment building. Back on Commonwealth Avenue, police and an ambulance arrived within minutes. But the ambulance was no longer necessary.

Police questioned Crump at the Soap-A-Rama and learned where Cartier lived. Brooke Mezo, a clerk from Marty's who witnessed the interrogation, heard Crump say "that Michael had spoken to him in the past couple of weeks and said he couldn't live without her, that he was going to kill her. And he talked about where to get a gun."

That made at least two people who knew Cartier had or wanted a gun and was talking about killing Kristin. How many others should have known she was in grave danger?

Police quickly sealed off the area around Cartier's apartment. "He had apparently made statements to several people that he hated policemen and had no reservations about shooting a cop," homicide detective Billy Dwyer said in his report. "He stated that he would never go to prison again."

A police operations team entered Cartier's apartment at 8:30 p.m. He was dead, lying on his bed with the gun he used to kill Kristin in his right hand. He had put it to his head and fired once. Police recovered the spent bullet from the bedroom wall. They found three other shell casings in the area where he murdered Kristin.

Later that night, Leslie North walked into Bunratty's, looking for Cartier. "I said, 'He shot Kristin,' " said J.D. Crump. "She didn't look surprised. I said, 'Then he went and shot himself.' At that point, she lost it. She started screaming, 'What a waste! What a waste! He's dead!' "

Crump later said, "I've had to live the past couple of weeks feeling I could have stopped him. I should have called his probation officer."

It's doubtful that would have done any good. The system is so mindless that when the dead Cartier failed to show up in Boston Municipal Court as scheduled on June 19, a warrant was issued for his arrest.

It is still outstanding.

Author's Epilogue

Starting in 1994, Congress passed a series of laws collectively known as the Violence Against Women Act (VAWA). These laws make certain behaviors a crime and set up the punishment for some offenses. Some states have moved to improve their methods for tracking abusers. Massachusetts, where Kristin was killed, now has a computerized, statewide domestic-violence registry that judges are required to consult. Although Massachusetts is still the only state to require this, almost half of the states now have, or are in the process of setting up, similar registries. Also, the FBI recently started a nationwide system that should eventually allow officials to access data from all those states at once.

Very few prosecutions under VAWA's criminal provisions have been undertaken over the last three years. A major reason why is the difficulty in getting states to cooperate effectively to enforce a provision of VAWA in which a woman who obtains a protective order in one state should receive the same protection in any other state.

There seems to be legal questions as well. In one example from Washington D.C., a woman named Deborah Fulton has been to court more than twenty times since she first got a protection order in February 1995. Her estranged husband lives across the state line and continues to harass her. When he was finally locked up, he was charged with misdemeanors for assault and violating the D.C. protective order. Even though at the time of his arrest he was awaiting trial in a D.C. court on an earlier charge of violating the same order, federal officials say it is unclear whether they can move the case up to federal court.

Another problem is that women seeking protection also face continued resistance by judges unwilling to take these cases seriously. Many judges give the benefit of the doubt to men and blame female victims for instigating or causing violence against them. Some judges exclude evidence of past behaviors. By the time most batterers come before them, they generally are not first-time offenders.

Finally, it remains uncertain what policies work best to protect female victims. Some thwarted abusers simply direct their wrath elsewhere, and therefore many experts say protective orders could be strengthened to deal with these men. Other experts believe violators should get automatic jail time. Some believe "permanent" orders should be truly permanent and available in more than just a few states. Still others also suggest treatment programs should last longer. According to Andrew Klein, the chief probation officer for the Quincy, Massachusetts, District Court, "A lot of guys can hold anything together for six months, but this is chronic behavior."

Despite these problems, experts generally agree that in most cases a protective order is a woman's best defense—when properly crafted and enforced. Protective orders succeed in keeping many abusive men away from their victims, and according to a 1994 study, make more than 80 percent of women feel safer.

Chapter 2 Review Questions

1. What are the formal elements of Weber's model of bureaucracy? Based on your reading of the case or your own experiences with public bureaucracies, did Weber fail to mention any attributes of bureaucracy in his description?
2. What were Kristin's reasons for relying on public bureaucracy for protection? Why did the system fail to protect her?
3. Does this case in your view support or contradict Weber's arguments about the monolithic power position of bureaucracy in society? About the nature of bureaucratic rationality? Its hierarchy? Specialization? Narrow latitude of bureaucratic rule enforcement? High degree of efficiency?
4. After reading the foregoing case study, where would you modify Weber's model to account more accurately for the pattern and the characteristics of America's bureaucracy?
5. According to the case, what are the sources of bureaucratic failure? What do you recommend to remedy the problems outlined in this case? Are there comparisons with the previous case, "The Blast in Centralia No. 5," in response to this failure?
6. Think about the case and what it says about the value of bureaucracy in modern society. Why are bureaucracies important? And yet so disliked? In your view, can anything be done about the fundamental public hostility toward bureaucracy particularly to strengthen bureaucratic effectiveness and responsiveness in serving the public?

Key Terms

ideal-types
traditional authority
charismatic authority
legal-rational authority
bureaucratic hierarchy
tenure in office

objective experts
bureaucratic rules
monied economy
bureaucratic power
bureaucratic secrecy

Suggestions for Further Reading

For a thoughtful understanding of Weber's background, his intellectual development, and continuing influence, read the introduction of H. H. Gerth and C. Wright Mills, eds., *From Max Weber: Essays in Sociology* (New York: Oxford University Press, 1946); Reinhard Bendix, *Max Weber: An Intellectual Portrait* (New York: Doubleday, 1960); and Marianne Weber, *Max Weber: A Biography* (New York: John Wiley, 1975). For a short but insightful piece, see Alfred Diamant, "The Bureaucratic Model: Max Weber Rejected, Rediscovered, and Reformed," in *Papers in Comparative Administration,* edited by Ferrel Heady and Sybil L. Stokes (Ann Arbor, Mich.: The University of Michigan Press, 1962).

The current literature on bureaucracy is vast but uneven and should be read selectively. Some of the better introductions include Graham Allison, *Essence of Decision: Explaining the Cuban Missile Crisis* (Boston: Little, Brown, 1971); Peter M. Blau and Marshall W. Meyer, *Bureaucracy in Modern Society,* 2d ed. (New York: Random House, 1971); Francis E. Rourke, *Bureaucracy, Politics and Public Policy,* 3d ed. (Boston: Little, Brown, 1984); Peter Woll, *American Bureaucracy,* 2d ed. (New York: W. W. Norton, 1977); Kenneth J. Meier, *Politics and the Bureaucracy: Policy Making in the Fourth Branch of Government,* 2d ed. (North Scituate, Mass.: Duxbury Press, 1987); Douglas Yates, *Bureaucratic Democracy: The Search for Democracy and Efficiency in American Government* (Cambridge, Mass.: Harvard University Press, 1982);

Harold Seidman and Robert Gilmour, *Politics, Position, and Power,* 4th ed. (New York: Oxford University Press, 1997); Gary C. Bryner, *Bureaucratic Discretion* (New York: Pergamon Press, 1987); Richard J. Stillman II, *The American Bureaucracy,* 2d ed. (Chicago: Nelson-Hall, 1996); James Q. Wilson, *Bureaucracy: What Government Agencies Do and Why They Do It* (New York: Basic Books, 1989); and Maureen Hogan Casamayou, *Bureaucracy in Crisis* (Boulder, Colo.: Westview Press, 1993). Francis E. Rourke's *Bureaucratic Power in National Politics,* 4th ed. (Boston: Little, Brown, 1986), is a balanced, thorough collection of various excerpts from seminal writings on this subject as well as Ali Farazmand, ed., *Handbook of Bureaucracy* (New York: Marcel Dekker, 1994); and Larry B. Hill, ed., *The State of Public Bureaucracy* (New York: M. E. Sharpe, 1992).

For three historic treatments of the rise of bureaucratic institutions, see the two volumes of E. N. Gladden, *A History of Public Administration* (London: Frank Cass, 1972); Ernest Barker, *The Development of Public Services in Western Europe, 1660–1930* (New York: Oxford University Press, 1944); and Frederick C. Mosher, *Democracy and the Public Service,* 2d ed. (New York: Oxford University Press, 1982). Leonard D. White's four-volume history of American public administration up to 1900 (cited in the previous chapter's "Suggestions for Further Reading") is certainly valuable reading on this topic. Martin Albrow, *Bureaucracy* (New York: Praeger,

1970); Stephen Skowronek, *Building a New American State: The Expansion of National Administrative Capacities, 1877–1920* (New York: Cambridge University Press, 1982); Don K. Price, *America's Unwritten Constitution* (Baton Rouge, La.: Louisiana University Press, 1983); Martin J. Schiesl, *The Politics of Efficiency* (Berkeley, Calif.: University of California Press, 1977); Guy Benveniste, *The Politics of Expertise,* 2d ed. (San Francisco: Boyd & Fraser, 1977); Thomas K. McCraw, *Prophets of Regulation* (Cambridge, Mass.: Harvard University Press, 1984); Richard J. Stillman II, *Creating the American State* (University: University of Alabama Press, 1998); Frederick C. Mosher, *A Tale of Two Agencies* (Baton Rouge, La.: Louisiana University Press, 1984); Theda Skocpol, *Protecting Soldiers and Mothers* (Cambridge, Mass.: Harvard University Press, 1992); Jerry Mitchell, *The American Experiment in Government Corporation* (Armouk, NY: M.E. Sharpe, 1998); and Mathew Crenson, *The Federal Machine* (Baltimore: Johns Hopkins University Press, 1975) offer unique and highly original conceptual and historical perspectives, as well as James Q. Wilson's essay, "The Rise of the Bureaucratic State," in *The Public Interest* (Fall 1975).

Serious students of bureaucracy should examine primary materials—executive orders, legislative acts, and official reports. Many key materials are contained in Frederick C. Mosher, ed., *Basic Documents of American Public Administration, 1776–1950* (New York: Holmes and Meier, 1976), and Richard J. Stillman II, ed., *Basic Documents of American Public Administration Since 1950* (New York: Holmes and Meier, 1982).

Three books that depict very different contemporary views of this topic today are Gerald Gavey, *Facing the Bureaucracy* (San Francisco: Jossey-Bass, 1993); B. Dan Wood and Richard W. Waterman, *Bureaucratic Dynamics* (Boulder, Colo.: Westview Press, 1994); and Charles T. Goodsell, *The Case for Bureaucracy,* 3d ed. (Chatham, N.J.: Chatham House, 1993).

Works that attempt to view bureaucracy from a comparative perspective are Joel D. Aberbach, Robert D. Putnam, and Bert Rockman, *Bureaucrats and Politicians in Western Democracies* (Cambridge, Mass.: Harvard University Press, 1981); Metin Heper, ed., *The State and Public Bureaucracy* (New York: Greenwood, 1987); B. Guy Peters, *The Politics of Bureaucracy,* Fourth Edition (White Plains, N.Y.: Longman, 1995); and Ali Farazmand, ed., *Handbook of Comparative and Development Public Administration* (New York: Marcel Dekker, 1991); and Ferrel Heady, *Public Administration: A Comparative Perspective,* 5th ed. (New York: Marcel Detter, 1996)

For a helpful up-to-date, comprehensive guide through the history of this vast literature, see Jos C. N. Roadschelders, *Handbook of Administrative History* (Brunswick, N.J.: Transaction Books, 1998). Also, journals covering public bureaucracy include: *Public Administration Review, The Bureaucrat, Admininstration and Society,* and *The American Review of Public Administration.*

CHAPTER 3

The General Environment: The Concept of Ecology

*A*n ecological approach to public administration builds, then, quite literally
from the ground up. . . .

John M. Gaus

READING 3

Introduction

Ecology entered the lexicon of social science and public administration literature
long before it became popular in the media and on college campuses in the 1970s as
a word synonymous with protecting the natural beauty of the landscape. Originally,
the term was derived from the ancient Greek word *oikos,* meaning "living place," and
was used extensively by nineteenth-century Darwinian botanists and zoologists to describe how organisms live and adapt to their environments. Sociologists during the
1920s borrowed the ideas of plant and animal ecology and applied the concept to
human life; they emphasized the *interdependence* of human life within an increasingly
complex organic system and the tendency of living systems to move toward an *equilibrium,* or stabilization of life forms in relation to the surrounding environment.

Ecology was introduced into the public administration vocabulary primarily
through the writings of the late Harvard Professor John M. Gaus (1894–1969), one
of the early pioneers of public administration; he elaborated on ecology in a series of
famous lectures at the University of Alabama in 1945, later published as *Reflections
on Public Administration.*

In this work, as well as in his other writings, Gaus was particularly adept at weav-
ing the patterns and ideas of public administration into the total fabric of the issues
and events of modern American society. Better than most observers, he showed how
public administration, its development, and its activities were influenced by its setting, or its ecology. In his words, ecology "deals with all interrelationships of living
organisms and their environment." Thus, "an ecological approach to public administration builds . . . quite literally from the ground up; from the elements of a place—
soils, climate, location, for example—to the people who live there—their numbers and

ages and knowledge, and the ways of physical and social technology by which from the place and in relationships with one another, they get their living." For Gaus, administrative systems were inextricably intertwined with the fabric of society. In particular, he delineated several important elements that he found useful "for explaining the ebb and flow of the functions of government: people, place, physical technology, social technology, wishes and ideas, catastrophe, and personality." He addressed himself to the importance of these ecological factors in the following selection abridged from his *Reflections on Public Administration.*

Gaus began teaching political science shortly after World War I (prior to Harvard, he taught at the University of Wisconsin) with an early interest in public administration. He interspersed teaching with numerous state and national administrative assignments, and he brought these practical experiences to his classes. Throughout his career, Gaus was fascinated by the interplay of forces between public administration and the larger society.

Gaus shared much in common with Frederick Jackson Turner, an early twentieth-century American historian who poured over maps, soil samples, statistical data of regions, and voting records in his empirical study of the growth of the American nation. Similarly, Gaus asked students of public administration to observe the environment of administration so as to understand how the characteristics of its ecology influence the development of administrative institutions. For Gaus, the term *ecology* was relevant not only to cloistered scholars of administration at work on universal theories of the administrative process, but also to on-the-line practitioners of administration. A conscious awareness of ecological factors permits administrators to respond more wisely to the demands and challenges of the external environment of their organizations. Thus, in the hands of the practitioner, ecology can become a diagnostic tool; it can help in visualizing the major elements in the administrative processes and provide a yardstick for measuring their impact on an organization. However, Gaus was aware that prediction would not be simple: "The task of predicting the consequences of contemporary action, of providing the requisite adjustment, is immensely difficult with the individual or in family life. The difficulty increases with the size and complexity of the unit and expansion and range of variables."

Gaus's concern with ecology of administration was prompted by a special concern with "change." He was a member of the generation rocked by the hardships of a catastrophic economic depression in the 1930s, and he saw the American landscape rapidly being transformed in myriad ways. As he observed, "Change which we have found to be so characteristic of American life, change that has disrupted neighborhoods, that has destroyed cultural stabilities, that has reflected the sweep across the continent, the restless migration to city and back to farm, from one job to another, has brought widely hailed merits. Its merits have been so spectacular, indeed, that we speak of it as progress. . . . Its costs are also becoming clearer, registered in the great dramatic collapses of the depression, more subtly in the defeat, disintegration and frustration of individuals. . . ." Gaus looked to public administration "to find some new source of content, of opportunity for the individual to assert some influence on the situation in which he finds himself." In one essay, "American Society and Public Administration," he stated: "My thesis is that through public instruments some new institutional bases which will enable the individual to find development and satisfaction can be created and some sense of purpose may flower again."[1]

Gaus was both pessimistic and optimistic about the condition of human society. His pessimism welled up when he saw change destroying the patterns of existence familiar to his generation, breaking down the stabilizing institutional arrangements, and confronting individuals with serious economic and personal hardships. Yet Gaus perceived a bright hope in applied social science: through an ecological approach to public administration he believed that new and renewed institutional patterns could be devised for individuals living in an age of change. Ecology in public administration became for Gaus a vital instrument for comprehending, directing, and modulating the forceful shocks of change in contemporary life. In the more than 40 years that have passed since Gaus's studies of ecology were published, younger scholars in the field, such as Fred Riggs, have been active in the wider application of the ecological approach, especially in the newer areas of developmental and comparative public administration.

As you read this selection, keep the following questions in mind:

Why does Gaus argue that knowledge of the general environment is so critical for administrators?

If you were to revise this essay for today's readers, what other environmental factors that affect modern public administration might you add to Gaus's list? (You might include, for example, computers or ethnic and racial problems or media factors.)

In what ways can administrators recognize changes in the general environment?

What might be the price paid for the failure of organizations to respond swiftly and correctly to external environmental change?

As you read Gaus's essay, reflect on its relevance to Case Study 1, "The Blast in Centralia No. 5." How did ecological factors influence the outcome of that case?

The Ecology of Public Administration

JOHN M. GAUS

The study of public administration must include its ecology. "Ecology," states the Webster Dictionary, "is the mutual relations, collectively, between or-

[1]John Gaus, "American Society and Public Administration," in John M. Gaus, Leonard D. White, and Marshall E. Dimock, *The Frontiers of Public Administration* (Chicago: University of Chicago Press, 1936).

Abridged from *Reflections on Public Administration* by John M. Gaus, pp. 6–19. Copyright © 1947 by The University of Alabama Press. Reprinted by permission of the Estate of Janette Gaus.

ganisms and their environment." J. W. Bews points out that "the word itself is derived from the Greek *oikos,* a house or home, the same root word as occurs in economy and economics. Economics is a subject with which ecology has much in common, but ecology is much wider. It deals with all the interrelationships of living organisms and their environment."[1] Some social scientists have been returning to the use of the term, chiefly employed by the biologist and botanist, especially under the stimulus of studies of anthropologists, sociologists, and pioneers who defy easy classification, such as the late Sir Patrick Geddes in Britain. In the lecture of Frankfurter's already quoted, the linkage between physical area, population, transport and government is concretely indicated. More recently, Charles A. Beard formulated some axioms of government in which environmental change is linked with resulting public administration. "I present," he stated, "for what it is worth, and may prove to be worth, the following bill of axioms or aphorisms on public administration, as fitting this important occasion.

1. The continuous and fairly efficient discharge of certain functions by government, central and local, is a necessary condition for the existence of any great society.
2. As a society becomes more complicated, as its division of labor ramifies more widely, as its commerce extends, as technology takes the place of handicrafts and local self-sufficiency, the functions of government increase in number and in their vital relationships to the fortunes of society and individuals.
3. Any government in such a complicated society, consequently any such society itself, is strong in proportion to its capacity to administer the functions that are brought into being.
4. Legislation respecting these functions, difficult as it is, is relatively easy as compared with the enforcement of legislation, that is, the effective discharge of these functions in their most minute ramifications and for the public welfare.
5. When a form of government, such as ours, provides for legal changes, by the process of discussion and open decision, to fit social changes, the effective and wise administration becomes the central prerequisite for the perdurance of government and society—to use a metaphor, becomes a foundation of government as a going concern.
6. Unless the members of an administrative system are drawn from various classes and regions, unless careers are open in it to talents, unless the way is prepared by an appropriate scheme of general education, unless public officials are subjected to internal and external criticism of a constructive nature, then the public personnel will become a bureaucracy dangerous to society and to popular government.
7. Unless, as David Lilienthal has recently pointed out in an address on the Tennessee Valley Authority, an administrative system is so constructed and operated as to keep alive local and individual responsibilities, it is likely to destroy the basic well-springs of activity, hope, and enthusiasm necessary to popular government and to the following of a democratic civilization."[2]

An ecological approach to public administration builds, then, quite literally from the ground up; from the elements of a place—soils, climate, location, for example—to the people who live there—their numbers and ages and knowledge, and the ways of physical and social technology by which from the place and in relationships with one another, they get their living. It is within this setting that their instruments and practices of public housekeeping should be studied so that they may better understand what they are doing, and appraise reasonably how they are doing it. Such an approach is of particular interest to us as students seeking to cooperate in our studies; for it invites—indeed is dependent upon—careful observation by many people in different environments of the roots of government functions, civic attitudes, and operating problems.

With no claim to originality, therefore, and indeed with every emphasis on the collaborative nature of the task, I put before you a list of the factors which I have found useful as explaining the ebb and flow of the functions of government. They are: people, place, physical technology, social technology, wishes and ideas, catastrophe, and personality. I have over many years built up a kind of flexible textbook in a collection of clippings, articles and books illustrative of each, as any one can do for himself. Such illustrations of the "raw material of politics" and hence administration are in themselves the raw material of a science of administration, of that part of the science which describes and interprets why particular activities are undertaken through government and the problems of policy, organization and management generally that result from such origins.[3]

By illustrating concretely the relation of these environmental factors, a cooperative testing of the theory will be facilitated. The changes in the distribution of the people of a governmental unit by time, age and place throw light on the origins of public policy and administration. At our first census, we were a people 80 per cent of whom lived on farms; at our last census, one hundred and fifty years later, 80 per cent of us did not live on farms. Over a third are now living in a relatively few metropolitan areas; but the growth of these areas is not in the core or mother city; it is in the surrounding suburbs, separate political entities, frequently also separate economic-status and cultural entities, yet sharing with the mother city, which is often absolutely declining in population, the public housekeeping problems of a metropolitan organism for which no—or no adequate—political organization exists. Our population is increasingly one with a larger proportion distributed among the older age classes. These raw facts—too little known and appreciated by citizens, which should be at once placed before them in discussing many of our public questions—in themselves explain much about our functions of government. Coupled with factors of place and technology, they clarify many an issue that is usually expressed in sterile conflicts. For example, the old people in the more frequent large family on a farm of a century ago, where more goods and services were provided on the farm, had a function still to perform and a more meaningful place in the lives of younger generations of the family. In a more pecuniary economy, separated from the family-subsistence economy, ignored in the allocation of the work and rewards of an industrial society, the demand for pensions became irresistible.

The movement of people (by characteristic age and income groups) from the mother city to sub-urbs (as guided by factors of time-space and cost in the journey to work, the dispersal of shopping centers, the search of industry for land space for straight-line production facilitated by paved roads, trucks and distribution of power by wires, and other technological changes, and changes in what we wish for in residential environment) produces its repercussion in the values of land and buildings, in the tax basis for public services already existent in older areas and demanded in the new, in the differential requirements and capacities-to-pay of people for housing (including the site and neighborhood equipment) and in the adjustment of transport and utility requirements for the ever-changing metropolitan organism.

Thus the factors of people and place are inextricably interwoven. And not merely in crowded urban centers. I have watched the same process of change in sparsely settled areas of farm and forest, and its potent effect on government.

Where there are extensive cut-over areas in the Lake States, where the older farm lands of New England or New York are no longer profitable to agriculture and reforestation is too recent to yield timber crops, in the Great Plains where lands best suited to grazing and with limited rainfall have been subjected to the plough, in the cut-over and eroded lands of the Southern Piedmont, or in the anthracite region of Pennsylvania, physical conditions—the exhaustion of the resource which originally brought settlement—have produced a chain of institutional consequences. Land values and tax payments decline, tax delinquent land reverts to county or state, public schools, roads and other services can no longer be locally financed. Immediate relief through state financial aids or state administered services in turn are inadequate when widespread catastrophic economic depression undermines state revenues. Efforts aimed at restoring a source of production, such as encouragement of cropping timber through favoring taxation or the building up of public forests adequate for permanent wood-using industries, or the restoration of soil, will require a long period of time for efficacy, and equally require an atmosphere in which political leadership, the careful integration of national, state, local, and individual and corporate policies, and skilled technical personnel can be established and supported steadily. Such an atmosphere, however, is not likely to be present among the frustrate population of such areas, or the better-provided populations of other areas called upon to tax themselves for local units of government in areas which they have never seen or whose problems they do not understand. Thus changes in place, or the use of the resources and products of a place, are coercive in their effect upon public administration.[4]

My own generation has had a great lesson in the importance of change in physical technology in witnessing the adoption of the automobile and the role it has come to play. It may be noted that its widespread use was made possible by the development of paved highways provided necessarily as a public service. Highway expansion and design have been affected by the coercion of political forces created by the physical invention. Groups of automobile users, manufacturers, hotel proprietors, road builders, road machinery and materials suppliers, persons seeking jobs in highway construction and administration and many others, have contended with those using horses, carriage and harness makers and persons opposed to the increased taxation that paved roads would require. The original causes—a combination of physical inventions such as the internal combustion engine and the vulcanization of rubber—get obscured in the ultimate disputes over taxation, jurisdiction, requirement of liability insurance and examination for drivers' licenses, or over the merits or defects of systems of traffic control or the financing of overhead crossings or express highways. The citizen blames "bureaucrats" and "politicians" because the basic ecological causes have not been clarified for him. This process of public function adoption may also be reversed by other changes—as we see, for example, in the abandonment of many publicly financed and constructed canals, when new technologies of transport rendered them obsolete.

Changes in physical technology, however slowly their institutional influences may spread, are more obvious even to the point of being dramatic, to the citizen. But he sometimes forgets the importance of the invention of social institutions or devices, and their continuing influences which coerce us. Thus the pooling and application of the savings of many through the invention of the corporation has set new forces to ripple through the social order, disarranging human relationships and creating new possibilities of large scale enterprise financially capable of utilizing extensive equipment and personnel and creating new relationships between buyer and seller, employer and employee—from which coercions for a new balance of forces, through consumer, labor and investor standards, have resulted.

You will have noted how interrelated all of these factors are in their operation. Perhaps the subtlest one is that for which I have difficulty in finding a satisfactory term. I have used the words "wishes and ideas." What you don't know, it is said, won't hurt you. I wonder whether this is true. If you do know that some new drug, or method of treatment of disease, will prevent the illness or perhaps death of those dear to you, you will have a new imperative for action, even if that action requires a public program. If you know or think you know that a combination of legislative and administrative measures will safeguard your bank deposit or insurance from destruction, that idea will have a coercive effect upon your political action. If you think that public officials are corrupt, that a tariff act or a regulation of a trade is a "racket," that too will influence the political decisions of your time. If you value material well-being, and if that desire takes so definite a form as a house and yard and garden, there are inevitable consequences in standards of public services that will facilitate the realization of your desire. Down that long road one will find the public insurance of mortgages to achieve lower interest rates and longer-term financing and zoning ordinances.

The originators of ideas and of social as well as physical invention are persons. We students of public administration will do well to study the elements in the influences which Bentham, the Webbs, the city planner Burnham, the health officer Biggs, the pioneers in the New York Bureau of Municipal Research and its Training School for Public Service have wielded. Relevant preparation, longevity, personal or institutional resources for research, sympathetic disciples, frequently some catastrophic situation in which prevailing attitudes were sufficiently blasted to permit the new ideas to be applied, channels of publication and of communication generally, as well as inner qualities of industry and integrity all, or nearly all in some combination, will be found. We each will have touched some one of this kind, perhaps, in our own community; if not a pioneer in original invention, an enlightened civic interpreter, agitator, or organizer. Thus the late Governor Alfred E. Smith had a genius for relating his sense of people's needs, his experience in party and legislative processes and his position as Governor to a political and administrative program in which the special knowledge of many persons was most effectively used in the service of the State of New York.

Catastrophe, especially when leadership and knowledge are prepared with long-time programs into which the immediate hurried relief action can be fitted, has its place in the ecology of administration. It not only is destructive, so that relief and repair are required on a scale so large that collective action is necessary, but it also disrupts, jostles or challenges views and attitudes, and affords to the inner self as well as to others a respectable and face-saving reason for changing one's views as to policy. The atomic bomb gave to many, perhaps, a determining reason for a change of attitude toward international organization. But I incline to the view that the effects of catastrophe on our thinking are relatively short-lived, and confined to relatively smaller institutional changes, and that older forces flood back with great strength to cancel most of the first reaction. A frightened and frustrated society is not one in which really significant changes will take root, unless careful preparation and wise administration of the relief period are available.

The night club fire in Boston in recent years in which so many service men from various parts of the country were killed is a tragic example of one role of catastrophe. In the lurid glare of that fire, weaknesses in building codes and the administration of them were revealed. So many vested interests of materials, construction and crafts center in building codes that they are difficult to keep in tune with invention and changing social needs. The fact that many in the fire were from remote places, and were men in the armed services, gave unusually wide reporting of the tragedy for some days, especially as many victims lingered on in hospitals. One result of the shock of the catastrophe was therefore action in cities throughout the world to inspect their places of public amusement and survey their fire-prevention legislation and administration. On a vaster scale, the catastrophe of economic world depression led to a varied array of responses through collective action in which there was much similarity despite regional and ideological differences among the various states of the world, since there were also like ecological factors, common to modern power industry and the price system. World wars illustrate the extent to which a large area of collective action is necessarily adopted under modern conditions of total war— and equally illustrate the tremendous pull of older customary views at the close, when the pressure to remove the controls rises, and individuals in office are held responsible for the frustrations once borne as a patriotic offering. Wise and fortunate indeed is that community that has so analyzed its problems and needs, and has so prepared to make use of catastrophe should it come by plans for carrying out programs of improvements, that the aftermath of tragedy finds its victims as well cared for as humanly possible and in addition some tangible new advance in the equipment and life of the community. I have seen some communities which, because they had equipped themselves with personnel capable of fresh thinking, had obtained from depression work-relief programs recreation facilities that were their first amenities.

Such an approach as this to our study of public administration is difficult, in that it makes demands upon our powers to observe, upon a sensitive awareness of changes and maladjustment and upon our willingness to face the political—that is, the public-housekeeping—basis of administration. These factors—you may improve upon my selection—in various combinations lie behind a public agency. In their combination will be found the reasons for its existence, and the reasons for attack upon it as well. Only in so far as we can find some essentially public core in the combination can we hope to have an agency free from spoils or abuse of power. The process of growth and formulation of a public policy out of these environmental materials links environment and administration. We may be too responsive to change, or we may fail to achieve our best selves by ignoring what we might do to advantage ourselves by collective action, if we perform this task of politics badly.

"When I pay taxes," wrote Justice Holmes to his friend Sir Frederick Pollock, "I buy civilization." It is no easy task of the citizen in this complicated world to get fair value in what he buys. That task is one of discovery of the causes of problems, of the communication of possible remedies, of the organizing of citizens, of the formulation of law. It is the task, in short, of politics. The task will be more fruitfully performed if the citizen, and his agents in public offices, understand the ecology of government.

Notes

1. J. W. Bews, *Human Ecology* (London: Oxford University Press, 1935), p. 1.
2. From "Administration, A Foundation of Government," by Charles A. Beard, in *American Political Science Review,* XXXIV, No. 2 (April, 1940), p. 232. Reprinted by permission of the American Political Science Association.
3. The methods as well as the substantive interpretations of Frederick Jackson Turner should be familiar to students of public administration so far as the printed page permits. It was a rich experience to be present as he worked over maps and statistical data of a county, state or region, putting geology, soils, land values, origins of residents, and voting records together for light on the resulting social action.
4. A reverse picture is the sudden demand on the use of ores in the Adirondack region during the world war because of changes in the conditions of ocean shipment. In one remote village a public housing project, to take care of the expanded work force, was a consequence, again, of the catastrophe of war.

☐ CASE STUDY 3

Introduction

The concept *ecology of administration* can be well illustrated by most case studies on public administration, for it would be a rare public administrator who was *not* influenced by at least a few of the major ecological factors that John Gaus outlined in the preceding essay. The theme of ecology runs throughout administrative activities, serving to shape and reshape the course and direction of public policy. The following case study, "Dumping $2.6 Million on Bakersfield," is a good example of how ecological factors can affect public administration and what can happen to administrators who fail to take these external factors into account before initiating a public program.

Michael Aron, a California-based journalist, writes an interesting account of the planning and implementation of a federal program sponsored by the U.S. Department of Health, Education, and Welfare (HEW) to build health clinics for migratory farm workers near the small central California town of Bakersfield. Formulated with good intentions, the program sounded ideal in the initial planning stage, but it nearly failed because inadequate attention was paid to the surrounding social ecology of administration. Aron ably details the ensuing intense struggle between various local forces for control of the health program—the black community, Mexican-American groups, local politicians, and established medical groups. HEW's Washington office and its regional San Francisco office soon became caught in the middle of a conflict that they neither wanted, nor had anticipated.

When reading this selection, keep the following questions in mind:

If you had been the administrator at HEW responsible for the planning of this migratory health program, how would you have assessed the local administrative ecology and better adapted your program to suit its characteristics?

Who were the key interest groups or "stakeholders", and what were their individual points of view?

In what ways did HEW's own actions in implementing the program intensify the conflict among the major interest groups? In particular, what environmental factors did they fail to recognize in designing and implementing this program?

What were the various viewpoints of the Bakersfield situation *within* HEW? How did these conflicting forces, in turn, influence the course of development of HEW's program?

Do Gaus's ideas on the ecology of administration need adjusting to conform more closely to the current demands and problems confronting modern public administrators, such as those outlined in the case study? If so, specifically in what ways?

Dumping $2.6 Million on Bakersfield (Or How *Not* to Build a Migratory Farm Workers' Clinic)

MICHAEL ARON

Like the coming of the railroad, the arrival of big federal money in a small, out-of-the-way California town causes a certain amount of uproar, especially when it is dumped in a bundle by an agency that has to get rid of it quick. In this case, the money comes from the Department of Health, Education, and Wel-

From "Dumping $2.6 Million on Bakersfield (Or How *Not* to Build a Migratory Farm Workers' Clinic)" by Michael Aron, *The Washington Monthly* (October 1972), pp. 23–32. Reprinted by permission of The Washington Monthly Company.

fare, for one of its 131 migrant health programs, and the town that has to fight over the grant is Bakersfield.

But it could just as well have been one of the other 130 migrant health programs, or any federal effort where the bureaucrat is mandated both to spend money fast and also to insure that local people control their own destinies. Controlling your own destiny, in these days of decentralization and revenue sharing, really means that the locals can help decide how to divvy up federal money among themselves. Bakersfield is a consequence of the whole idea of community participation in federal projects, but in this instance, the town only began participating after the money was pumped in—for very obvious reasons and with some very disruptive results.

Our story begins in Washington, D.C., in March, 1970, with the passage by Congress of the Migrant Health Act. Senator Walter Mondale's Migratory Labor subcommittee drafted the legislation, authorizing an $11-million appropriation for migrant programs in fiscal 1970, and it was Mondale, personally, who pressed for insertion of an amendment providing that "persons broadly representative of all elements of the population to be served [be] given an opportunity to participate in the implementation of such programs."

Since this was the time the Nixon Administration was striving to decentralize the "vast" federal bureaucracy, it fell to the regional offices of HEW to implement the legislation. Region IX, headquartered in San Francisco, and responsible for seven Western states (it has since lost Oregon and Washington), proposed four areas with heavy migrant "homebase" populations as possible locations for health projects. Three were in rural California counties, the fourth in the state of Washington. One was Bakersfield, Kern County, California.

HEW's plan was to find a chicano community group in each area to become its delegate agency for day-to-day administration of a project, in the same way that local anti-poverty groups became delegate agencies of the Office of Economic Opportunity. But there was a time problem: the legislation had been passed relatively late in the fiscal year, giving HEW only a few months in which to spend the money or else forfeit it back to Treasury. Compounding the problem was the fact that Bakersfield seemed to have no chicano community groups—20,000 chicanos, but no groups.

With the end of the fiscal year only six weeks away, anxious rural health officials turned their attention to a black group, the Kern County Liberation Movement (KCLM). Born six months earlier in the waning hours of a poor people's workshop and designated a consumers' auxiliary of the local anti-poverty agency, KCLM was little more than a collection of low-income citizens. As its first official act, KCLM had applied to HEW for a $70,000 planning grant to assay the health needs of Bakersfield's black ghetto; that application was still in the pipeline when regional HEW asked KCLM if it would accept

$2.6 million to immediately establish a health center.

KCLM responded enthusiastically: certainly they would accept a grant—who wouldn't? In late May, 1970, an official from the Rural Health Office of the Community Health Service of the Health Services and Mental Health Administration (HSMHA) of the Public Health Service of the regional office of HEW flew to Bakersfield to help KCLM prepare a formal application. All this was done very quietly, without fanfare. Final contracts were signed in June, three weeks before the end of the fiscal year.

It wasn't until July that Kern County's health establishment got wind of the news—and when they did, all hell broke loose. The entire roster of local health agencies—the county medical society, the dental society, Kern General Hospital, the county health department, the board of supervisors, the state health department, the California Medical Association; and the congressionally mandated regional planning bodies, Comprehensive Health Planning and Regional Medical Programs—vented their spleen because none had been consulted prior to the awarding of the grant. The medical society had a special reason for bitterness: it had been operating its own federally-funded migrant clinic for years in two old trailers outside of town, and HEW was cutting the budget on that program at the same time it was handing $2.6 million to a bunch of poor people with no experience whatsoever in the administration or delivery of health care.

Creative Fumbling

For five days the flap over the award commanded headlines in the *Bakersfield Californian* (in sky-blue ink, no less); the paper also editorialized against the grant ("More Fumbling and Bumbling") and even ran a two-part feature on the medical society's "wonderful clinic." Bakersfield's two Republican state assemblymen called press conferences to denounce the award. Congressman Robert Mathias sent an angry telegram to HEW Secretary Elliot Richardson questioning how the department could possibly sanction such behavior on the part of its regional office. "Is this what the Administration means by 'creative federalism'?" Mathias asked. For the next three weeks the Bakersfield health establishment would virtually convulse in an effort to get the grant canceled.

On July 14, Dr. James Cavanaugh, deputy assistant secretary for health, announced a "full review" of the conditions surrounding the awarding of the grant, intimating that the contract would be canceled "if irregularities are detected."

On July 15, Cavanaugh flew from Washington to the regional office in San Francisco. In what is reported to have been a rather stormy session, Cavanaugh and regional officials rewrote the guidelines on community health grants so as to insure consultation with all appropriate state and local agencies. In Washington, meanwhile, Mathias' staff had done some checking and discovered that the Kern County Liberation Movement was not registered with OEO as an official delegate arm of the local anti-poverty agency. Mathias called Cavanaugh to ask if this were sufficiently "irregular" to warrant cancellation of the contract. When Cavanaugh said he didn't think so, Mathias asked if the contract could possibly be renegotiated under the new guidelines just promulgated. Cavanaugh said he doubted it. A Mathias press release the next day called HEW's action "inexcusable" and fixed the blame on "middle-level bureaucrats [who] ignored the letter of the law" (a reference to their failure to consult the congressionally mandated regional planning bodies).

While Mathias was busy reverse pork-barreling in Washington, physicians and politicians in Bakersfield were writing letters to anyone they could think of who might be able to reverse the decision. Let me quote from some of these letters:

Kern General Hospital Administrator Dr. Owen Hatley, to Dr. Vernon Wilson, an HEW official in Rockville, Maryland:

> When an independent, unbiased consulting firm, experienced in developing health delivery systems, presents a program for Kern County, then and only then will I support any sponsoring agency in any of these endeavors. Reputable, experienced consulting firms are available, in contrast to falsefront organizations [KCLM] created to obtain desired answers to fuzzy-minded hypotheses conjured up by some social planners.

Congressman Barry Goldwater, Jr. (representing a neighboring district) to Secretary Richardson:

> This group [KCLM] has absolutely no experience that would even remotely qualify them for a grant of this magnitude. . . . I request that you immediately investigate this matter and withdraw the grant.

State Assemblyman William Ketchum to HEW Undersecretary John Veneman, his former colleague in the California legislature:

> I object to the "cart before the horse" manner in which this has been handled and request that you immediately stop funding . . . [HEW's] "better to spend now than undertake planning" philosophy is a classic symptom of the whole OEO syndrome.

On July 27, KCLM held a press conference to refute the "numerous unfounded charges leveled against us in recent days." Considering the group's relative inexperience, it was an artful performance. One moment they were militant: "The low income community of Kern County wants to see a migrant health center that will meet their needs and they want to see it not after a two- or three-year planning study. Frankly we are *tired* of being studied. We want direct medical services now." The next moment, conciliatory: "Naturally we welcome the cooperation and support of any agencies interested in meeting the common goal of comprehensive health care for the entire community."

In San Francisco, meanwhile, regional HEW was kept busy trying to explain its actions to HEW officials in Washington. An assistant regional director recalls: "Washington was not terribly happy with us, and that's the understatement of the year. Of course, we knew what we were doing all along. We were going to get funding into that area no matter who it upset, and not by the traditional route of currying favor with conservative county medical societies. To get things done, you go do them and fight the political battles after—especially in this Administration. We like to think of ourselves as 'bureaucratic guerrillas' fighting for what we believe in."

By July 29, it was compromise time. Cavanaugh and Mathias flew to Bakersfield together to announce that HEW was suspending project funds for 90 days pending a "restructuring" of the KCLM board of directors. The suspension, Cavanaugh told a press conference, would be lifted only when the board, then made up entirely of "consumers," added professional health-care "providers" to its membership. Cavanaugh's, too, was an artful performance (which may help explain why he is now on the White House staff). He seemed genuinely pained by "this unfortunate misunderstanding." He urged the Bakersfield health establishment to play an "activist" role on the consumer-provider board, and assured his good friends that "this sort of thing will not happen again." Privately, he told Mathias that HEW would consider canceling the grant if KCLM should fail in any way to execute its provisions. And when the man from HEW left town that night, KCLM was still the beneficiary of the potential $2.6 million.

Although project funds were technically suspended, regional HEW began sending "emergency" funds to KCLM to keep it on its feet. The grant had called for expenditures of $391,000 in the first year—$248,000 for staff salaries and the rest for clinic facilities and supplies. (And when they tell you they're putting X million dollars into programs for poor people, remember: professionals, clericals, and private businesses get the money; the poor get services.) Before any of this money could be spent, however, it would be necessary to hire a project director, preferably one who could court the favor of the health establishment and orchestrate a restructuring of the board.

Regional HEW proposed that a young dental school graduate from San Francisco become interim project director until a permanent director could be found. KCLM agreed, and Robert Isman, D.D.S., assumed his duties in August.

Through the fall months Isman worked hard to win the cooperation of local health agencies, but two things were working against him: his longish hair and what they call in Bakersfield "ultraliberal leanings." City officials, whose own budgets only added up to something like $12 million, simply could not understand why HEW would select such a character to supervise a $2.6-million project. He had no experience, either dental or administrative. He showed up for meetings with bankers and lawyers wearing cutoff jeans and thongs. To this day, people talk about Isman as if his eight months in Bakersfield had been profitably spent dealing hashish on the side.

It took much persuasion and several trips to Bakersfield by regional HEW officials, but in November the KCLM board was restructured to include 10 professional health providers representing various agencies in the county, including the medical society, which put its migrant clinic director on the board but instructed him not to vote. (The argument is sometimes advanced that the medical society joined only to sabotage the project, because free health care for the poor takes money out of the pockets of local physicians and the county hospital; but there's too much conspiracy theory there, or at least not enough money involved to make it credible.)

That the consumers still outnumbered the providers 25 to 10 irked some people, however. Mathias' local aide called the restructuring "a token effort to appease the community." Assemblyman Stacey branded it "a sham and a fraud" and joined the ranks of the countless politicians who at one time or another have accused HEW of "strong-arm tactics."

With the board restructured, everyone expected funding to resume, but HEW suddenly attached new conditions to the lifting of the suspension. KCLM either had to demonstrate broad-based community support, or hire a permanent project director.

In the meantime, forces were still at work trying to get the grant canceled. In December, the medical society applied to HEW for $325,645, ostensibly to expand its existing clinic program, in effect proposing itself as an alternative to KCLM. In Washington, Mathias continued to warn HEW that the project was "doomed to failure" unless local agencies were brought into the fold and given more say in board policy. Quietly, Mathias also asked the Government Accounting Office for a full investigation of the activities of the local anti-poverty umbrella agency, the Kern County Economic Opportunities Corporation.

Three months went by with no progress made toward filling the project director's job and mounting hostility towards Isman from the establishment. Then in April, 1971, HEW decided to step in and temporarily take over the project itself. Vincent Garza, a Mexican-American public health officer stationed at headquarters, was dispatched to replace Isman as interim project director for 90 days. To complement this action, regional HEW abruptly canceled the dental component of the project, thus insuring Isman's complete removal from the scene. Both sides in Bakersfield welcomed the two moves—the health establishment because Garza was a professional like themselves; KCLM because it meant immediate resumption of funding.

From this point on, the struggle ceases to be one pitting organized medicine and its friends against poor people. As you will see, it evolves into a struggle pitting poor people of one race against poor people of another. There are no Machiavellian plots here, no designs by the establishment to divide and conquer. That's just the way it happens.

Dude Ranch Junket

Most of the farm workers of Kern County are Mexican-Americans; maybe 20 per cent are Mexican nationals who came north to follow the softfruit season (legally or illegally) and managed to linger longer.

For years, these people have lived in shacks and camps or slept unsheltered on the banks of irrigation canals. Their general health is not good. They get skin diseases from working in fields sprayed with pesticides; they suffer high incidences of venereal disease, eye defects, heart trouble, and nervous disorders; obesity, hypertension, and diabetes are so prevalent that local health authorities believe these conditions to be hereditary in Mexicans; 90 percent of the children have serious dental problems. "They're learning that an unhealthy body produces nothing," one official said, adding as an afterthought, "They've certainly learned it the hard way." It used to be that when someone got sick, he worked it off or waited it out—unless he got real sick, in which case his family piled him into a car and drove the 20 miles to Kern General Hospital where they would wait for hours in the emergency room hoping that the next intake nurse spoke Spanish. Of course, there was also the medical society's migrant clinic in trailers in Lamont, but it operated only during "the season" (May to September; the actual season is eight to 10 months), and then only three nights a week from 6 p.m. to 10 p.m. At regional HEW the clinic is still referred to as a "band-aid station."

The first thing on Garza's agenda when he arrived in Bakersfield was to find a suitable location for a health center. For several days he, an architect, and Mathias' local aide drove around the Lamont-Arvin-Weedpatch area looking for a site—and immediately a conflict arose. KCLM thought they ought to be looking in the Lakeview district, where blacks live. Garza explained that these were *migrant* funds and that it had been HEW's intention all along to put

a health center someplace where the campesinos would have easy access to it. But this had not been KCLM's understanding at all; they had been led to believe, they said, that the center would be located in a black neighborhood and that campesinos from all over the county would be encouraged to use it and think of it as their own.

KCLM felt suddenly betrayed. After fighting off the encroachments of the health establishment for almost a year, they now learned that HEW wanted to put the health center in a part of the county where less than one percent of the population is black. A bitter pill; several KCLM board members chose to resign rather than swallow it.

To sweeten it, perhaps, Garza organized a weekend outing for KCLM board members at a ranch-retreat 80 miles north of Bakersfield and invited the HEW regional director to come along and to bring some of his staff. A good time was presumably had by all, and the regional director soothed ruffled feathers by promising that no matter what happened in the future, KCLM's efforts would not go unrewarded; but folks in Bakersfield took a different view of the outing. Garza returned to Bakersfield on a Monday morning to find himself being blasted on the front page of the *Californian* for his $2,500 dude ranch junket financed by "the taxpayers." (The story was written by the son of the county health superintendent, which says something about small cities.) Three weeks later, Garza left Bakersfield and the Public Health Service and went to Yale on a fellowship.

Garza was replaced in July, 1971, by Charles Pineda, a Mexican-American native of Kern County, the son of a fruit picker and holder of a master's degree in social work. Pineda continued the search for a clinic site and also began to think about recruiting a medical staff.

Hmm . . . Federal Funding

In September, 15 months after the awarding of the grant, a makeshift clinic was finally opened in Lamont. Pineda had found a young doctor from Los Angeles to become clinic physician ($25,000), had lured an aging South American from a hospital in the Bronx to become medical director ($27,500), and the three of them had talked the medical society into renting its trailers to KCLM until a permanent location could be found ($1,600, which has never been paid). As soon as the medical society clinic shut down for the "winter," KCLM occupied the trailers and began treating its first farmworker patients. Pineda, meanwhile, found an old grocery store in Weedpatch, leased it, and gradually moved the project into it over the next three months.

The clinic in Weedpatch is a shock when you first see it. Somehow the term "migrant health center" leads you to expect a depressing storefront, partitioned in half, and dimly lit, with maybe a purple curtain separating the waiting room from the examining room, and a wizened old doctor inside waiting to grab you in his palsied, age-blotched hands. You walk into the clinic in Weedpatch, however, and your first thought is "hmmm . . . federal funding." The clinic is partitioned all right, but partitioned into a large reception room, two intake offices, five examining rooms, a treatment room, a laboratory, a records library, staff offices, and a lounge. The staff numbers about 25. The equipment is brand new, ultra-modern, and *clean.* When you open your mouth to say "aaahh . . ." in this clinic, you're opening it to an electronic implement coming out of a wall console.

To the campesinos and their families, the clinic is a godsend. It heals them, soothes them, educates them, trains them, employs a few of them—all free of charge, for the time being. HEW wants the clinic to become self-sufficient, so patient billings will begin in the near future; but treatment will still be "free" (sort of) for the 90 percent who belong to the union's "Robert F. Kennedy Farm Workers' Medical Plan" (for which a small premium is deducted from their paychecks). At last count, the clinic had given treatment to 6,000 patients from 1,200 families, and thanks to the imperatives of bureaucracy, each one now has a detailed record of his medical history, probably for the first time in his life. Ask the campesinos whom they thank for all this, and you get a surprising—no, not surprising—answer. Senator Kennedy, of course. The young one.

Chicanos in the Wings

But don't get the idea that just because the clinic opened, the infighting ceased. On the contrary, now there was something tangible to fight over.

An interesting bit of correspondence circulated around Bakersfield at this time, copies of an exchange between HEW Secretary Richardson and Senators Walter Mondale and Adlai Stevenson III, past and present chairmen of the Migratory Labor subcommittee. Richardson's letter to the subcommittee requested "clarification of congressional intent" regarding the consumer-participation amendment to the Migrant Health Act. Mondale wrote back: "I was shocked to learn that there is still substantial doubt as to your Department's implementation of an amendment which became effective in March of 1970." Stevenson wrote: "I am extremely concerned that Migratory Health Program relations and guidelines provide the basis for 'meaningful' farm-worker participation, rather than a degree of 'tokenism.' This, of course, requires a policy-making function for the farm-worker participants rather than merely an advisory role."

It was regional HEW that flooded Bakersfield with copies of the exchange. And for a reason. KCLM was still the delegate agency administering the project, but it no longer could be said to represent the true "consumers." Now that the clinic had opened in Weedpatch, the consumers were campesinos. It was *they* who should be doing the community-participating.

This was fine with project director Pineda, a chicano whose father was still out in the fields; it was fine, as well, with the clinic staff, half of whom were Mexican, and others who had to have been sympathetic to the plight of farm workers in the first place in order to have accepted a job in a town as Godforsaken as Weedpatch. KCLM, on the other hand, was naturally upset: first, they had "lost" the clinic itself; now they were faced with possible loss of control over it and forfeiture of their status as a bona fide government delegate agency.

Acting on their own authority, but with behind-the-scenes encouragement from regional HEW, Pineda and several clinic staff members appointed five reasonably intelligent, but non-English-speaking, campesinos to a "campesino board," a kind of shadow cabinet that would wait in the wings ready to take over at the earliest signal from HEW. That they were non-English-speaking meant that they had to rely on people like Pineda to tell them what was going on. This was in October.

On December 14, KCLM voted to fire Pineda. The official reasons are not worth going into—

basically they questioned Pineda's competence. The actual reason was that Pineda had been attempting to serve two masters at once, KCLM and the campesinos, and his allegiance to the former seemed to be flagging. Informed of the dismissal, regional HEW immediately ordered him reinstated, saying that KCLM no longer had legal authority to make such a decision (because it no longer represented "consumers").

At its next regular meeting, on December 22, KCLM voted to change its name to the Kern County Health Committee (KCHC). This is not insignificant. It represents a conscious grab at respectability and tacitly acknowledges its new position in the battle configuration. How can you call yourself a liberation movement when you're fighting to preserve a vested interest?

Culturally Unfit

Two things of consequence happened in January. First, elections for a new campesino board were held in Lamont-Arvin-Weedpatch; four of the five men who had been appointed by Pineda in October won election to the board. (The fifth would have won, too, had he chosen to run.) The board then incorporated itself as Clinica De Los Campesinos, Inc. (CDLC). Second, the clinic's South American medical director failed his state medical board examination, meaning he was without a license to practice in California.

In February, the roof caves in.

On February 14, 24 hours before KCHC was supposed to transfer authority to CDLC, the KCHC board notifies Pineda of his dismissal in a memo listing eight specific grievances, one claiming he hired the South American medical director without consulting the board and another charging him with "loading" the clinic staff with Mexican-Americans.

On February 15: KCHC, citing election "irregularities," rejects the legitimacy of the CDLC board and refuses to transfer control of the project.

On February 16: 200 chicano demonstrators mass in front of the clinic, Pineda and two clinic staff members among them, carrying picket signs and threatening to "shut it down" (in Spanish). The black chairman of KCHC wades into the angry mob and fires the two staff members on the spot. Half of the demonstrators move down the highway to the

KCHC administrative office in Lamont. The demonstrations last until midnight without serious incident.

February 17: The clinic has been splattered with paint during the night. There are bullet holes in the plate glass window. KCHC's black chairman appoints himself "acting project director." Regional HEW officials fly down from San Francisco in the hope of restoring order; they put the KCHC chairman on notice that his assumption of the project directorship constitutes a flagrant conflict of interest. Two-thirds of the clinic staff send individual letters to HEW declaring their allegiance to CDLC.

February 18: A provider member of the KCHC board calls the executive secretary of the medical society at midnight and, on behalf of KCHC, pleads for help. The executive secretary calls his 30-year-old assistant, Riley McWilliams, at 2:30 a.m. and orders him to report to KCHC the next day to become interim project director.

February 23: Telegram to KCHC from regional HEW states: actions of KCHC in direct contradiction to agreements; therefore, project funds would be suspended indefinitely and funding to KCHC would terminate on April 15, 1972.

February 24: Local aide sends confidential memo to Mathias in Washington warning of black-brown racial conflict that could engulf the county; says black community promises reprisals if any harm comes to KCHC chairman; surmises that United Farm Workers are involved in demonstrations.

February 26: CDLC writes to Secretary Richardson—letter begins, "Honorable Sire"; informs that Riley McWilliams made project director without HEW approval; ends with veiled threat to close clinic down as "last resort."

February 28: Medical society applies to HEW for $155,891 grant to expand its own clinic; application states, "basic to this proposal is removal of the existing clinic."

February 29: KCHC chairman reports alleged threats to his person.

March 10: CDLC submits application to HEW to take over administration of project; application actually written by four clinic staff members.

March 17: Twelve clinic staff draft joint letter to HEW threatening to resign if CDLC not made delegate agency; claim Riley McWilliams culturally unfit to be project director.

Bent in the Fields

April 15, the date HEW said it would terminate the project funding to KCHC, came and went, with no word from San Francisco. Three weeks later, the regional director sent letters to KCHC and CDLC proposing a joint luncheon meeting on May 10 at the posh (for Bakersfield) Casa Royale motel. He also sent a letter to the medical society announcing an award of $67,000 to continue their clinic-on-wheels, providing they move it to Buttonwillow, in the southwest part of the county. (Buttonwillow's one physician raised a stink, but that is another story.)

The regional director, the black project officer, and the chicano Public Health Service officer from Los Angeles arrived in Bakersfield the morning of the 10th. At noon they joined the KCHC board for lunch. The CDLC board had been invited to come at 1 p.m., but the hour passed 2 p.m. and the five campesinos had yet to show. Someone suggested that they might have gotten lost, since surely they had never been to the Casa Royale before. Someone else was delegated to go look for them. He found them in their customary positions for that hour, bent over in the fields in 95-degree heat. They said they had not been notified of the meeting. There was reason to think that one of their advisors on the clinic staff had intercepted the letter for reasons she believed to be in their best interests. The meeting proceeded without them. A radical Lutheran minister acted as their unofficial spokesman.

When it was over, an elaborate compromise had been drawn up: 1) the CDLC board would be absorbed into the KCHC board; 2) four providers mutually agreed upon by KCHC and CDLC would join the five campesinos, together to constitute a separate board-within-a-board; 3) the mini-board would serve in a "policy-recommending" capacity and receive the benefit of "whatever training and experience is available"; 4) on or before January 1, 1973, KCHC would transfer administrative control of the project to CDLC, retaining for itself only the role of fiscal intermediary. A fifth provision went unstated, but was well understood nonetheless: in return for its great efforts and considerable sacrifice, KCHC would become HEW's "umbrella agency" for all future projects in the county.

HEW and KCHC signed the compromise that afternoon. In the evening the five campesinos met with their supporters in the basement of the Lutheran Church in Lamont. Heated debate lasted past midnight, but the campesinos finally decided to sign the compromise. "It was not a victory, it was not a defeat," said CDLC chairman, Natividad Arreolo, weary perhaps in the knowledge that he was due out in the fields again at 4 a.m.

If Weedpatch Had Movies

That should be the end of the story. You know it's not. In the months since, there have been controversial hirings and firings, protest resignations, accusations of petty theft, and at least one false rumor of a sexual nature deliberately planted to discredit a potential project director. Dr. Garcia, the South American medical director, took his state boards again in June, and the delay in reporting his grade leads to speculation that it is being deliberately held up in channels for political reasons. As of September 1, the young medical society executive was still project director, a fact from which few but the medical society derive any comfort, and yet he is there.

The question remains as to whether KCHC will cede its little fiefdom to the campesinos by January 1, as agreed. HEW says it is committed to seeing the campesinos take over on schedule, and it is hard to imagine what KCHC could possibly gain by holding out. One also can't help but wonder whether the campesinos really are capable of running the project.

The real problem with this project, and, one suspects, with others as well, has been the ease with which political considerations were able to obscure the stated objective, namely, comprehensive health care for farm workers—combined with the fact that HEW would seem to have subordinated the stated objective to an unstated, or at least secondary one, namely, Mexican-American community organization. Thus, it took 15 months of sparring and jockeying before a single patient was seen. And once opened, the clinic had to shorten its hours anytime HEW felt it necessary to suspend funds in order to reprimand this faction or that. The community of 20,000 is still without a dentist because of an essentially political decision.

The medical society seems to think that because doctors can save lives on a surgical table, their expertise necessarily embraces all facets of medicine, including how it should be delivered to people whom the doctors barely understand, can't talk to, and don't especially like—and the medical society fights to preserve the integrity of that idea. The poor people, black and brown, want better medical care than they are accustomed to receiving, but they also want power and respectability and anything else that might foster the illusion that they are swimming into the mainstream, and if a government health project is the only game in town, they'll jump at the chance to play it, and they'll play it as fiercely and seriously as they imagine it to be played elsewhere, and so what if the brothers and sisters have to wait a little longer for something they have never had anyway. And the whites on the clinic staff and the others lurking in the background all the time probably wouldn't be so eager to stir up the waters if only Weedpatch had a movie theater.

The government, through all this, has been like a ship captain steering the project towards shores the crew can't see yet. For the crowd in San Francisco, the project has been, and continues to be, "an interesting social experiment" (an assistant regional director's words), originally conceived to meet a singular need, but taking on added dimensions as it unfolds. Can blacks and browns work together? Are illiterate campesinos capable of self-administration? What adjustments can we make to keep the community from blowing apart? "I would say we've basically been more interested in using the clinic as an instrument of long-range social change than in meeting the short-run health needs of the target community," one HEW official admitted, fully aware that this is the kind of statement bureaucrats get roasted for every day.

To date $400,000 has been spent on the project, a mere fraction of the $13 billion HEW spends every year on health programs. One shudders at the thought of KCLMs and medical societies and campesino-equivalents plotting and maneuvering against each other and intramurally in every community where federal grants have been won; and yet, that is probably what happens, and is happening, all over the country at this moment.

"Kern County?" a project officer asked rhetorically. "Oh, it's not so bad there. These things are usually much worse in urban areas."

A Retrospective: Weedpatch Revisited

B. J. MOORE

Michael Aron's article chronicled the actions and problems associated with implementing the Community Health Clinic Act in Weedpatch, California during the 1970s. Local control and direct participation of citizens and service users were a distinctive feature of this Act, as it was in many other Great Society programs. The *Clinica de los Campesinos* case was portrayed as an implementation failure—the inability of public administrators to understand the limitations of the local context and the inability of citizens to manage cooperatively, as well as financially and strategically run, a health care organization.

Where Is The Clinic Today?

Clinica de los Campesinos, renamed *Clinica Sierra Vista* in 1972, is now a nonprofit organization with a 22 million-dollar budget, over four hundred employees, and eleven clinic facilities throughout the southern San Joaquin Valley. Its health care priority is still to provide access to primary health care and preventive health care education for underserved

B. J. Moore is on Assistant Professor in the Department of Policy and Public Administration, School of Business and Public Administration, at the California State University—Bakersfield and a board member of *Clinica Sierra Vista.*

She prepared this "retrospective" especially for this volume.

populations. However, the concept of underserved has evolved locally and nationally from a focus on farm workers in the early 1970s to now include the aged, mothers, children, those with HIV/AIDS, a variety of ethnic groups, the homeless, and pregnant and parenting teens. Nevertheless, over 60 percent of services currently provided through *Clinica* are to Hispanics, and the majority are children and women of childbearing age. In fiscal year 1998 the organization served more than 52,000 individuals, who accounted for over 350,000 visits.

In January 1973, with a reformed board and a stronger funding source, *Clinica* hired a program director and began providing services from a storefront warehouse in Weedpatch. Its strategy included taking a low profile in the political and medical communities and focusing on acquiring new leadership on the board and better management within various organizational levels. A permanent facility was constructed in 1975 in Lamont, just down the road from Weedpatch, and a designation as a Health Manpower Shortage Area also allowed physicians and mid-level medical practitioners to satisfy their National Health Service Corp obligations at *Clinica.* By the late 1970s, funding from the Women, Infants and Children Program (WIC), as well as the Maternal Child Outreach Program (MCOP), permitted opening a dental program and the construction of a dental clinic. The first satellite clinic began in 1978. Since then, *Clinica* has had a consistent supply of both staff and financial resources to permit an ongoing expansion of its services throughout the region.

Challenges met by *Clinica* over the years resulted recently in national recognition as a multiinstitutional model for rural health care delivery. A success locally, *Clinica,* like other publicly funded health programs, faces a difficult contemporary health care environment. Nonetheless, the continuous process of adjustment, change, and compromise allowed this organization to adapt and flourish during the last twenty-five years, especially by means of four strategies: (1) continually branching out, (2) developing an effective management team; (3) adopting the local cultural values, and (4) taking risks at the top.

Continually Branching Out

Throughout the 1980s and early 1990s the organization continued to expand geographically in both rural and urban locations. Its leadership particularly took advantage of available funding opportunities. Currently *Clinica* supports itself by a patchwork of thirty grants and contracts—various combinations of federal, state, local, and private funding and partnerships. Low-interest mortgage construction grants and renovations created a network of free-standing clinics, conveniently located and aesthetically attractive.

Clinica aggressively sought to branch out to other underserved populations in various locales and with numerous needs. *Clinica* now provides dental services in several rural communities, in addition to expanded services for family-planning, counseling for pregnant and parenting teens, a mobile van for reaching the homeless, a school-based health clinic, and soon a program for homeless individuals following their hospitalization.

Developing an Effective Management Team

The challenges today—as in the past—center on development of scarce organizational resources, especially fiscal, human, and information strategies to position the clinic to better deliver services for the underserved. The Executive Director, Steve Schilling, many of the management team, and a number of board members have been together since the early 1970s. Long-term and strategic planning is thus facilitated by such lengthy tenure. Financially the organization is now asset secure but still scrambles for grants and contracts to sustain adequate "cash flows."

Adopting the Local Cultural Values

Cultural values of the Kern County region also supported the clinic's continual expansion over the last twenty-five years. The legacy of the immigrants from Oklahoma who preceded Hispanic immigrants to Weedpatch gave Kern County residents a fierce sense of self-determination. This rugged individualism of the immigrants from Oklahoma and western pioneers in general was bequeathed to the *Campesinos* and continues to influence *Clinica* leaders today, specifically through their own opportunistic use of whatever federal funding is available. The Oklahoma immigrants took advantage of federal funding during the Great Depression, especially for education, water, and farm development; the Hispanic migrants use funding in much the same way today, in this case for health care. *Clinica* administrators effectively "work" the legislative agenda at the federal or state levels. This entrepreneurial strategy has been crucial to organizational survival and growth throughout its entire history.

Taking Risks at the Top

Finally, and perhaps most important, is the strong, sustained leadership by the CEO, Steve Schilling, who continues to take innovative risks to expand and enhance programs. For example, as part of an initiative from the Federal Bureau of Primary Health Care, *Clinica* applied for and was selected to receive financial assistance with its accreditation process. In 1998 *Clinica Sierra Vista* was accredited by the Joint Commission for the Accreditation of Health Care Organizations. In addition, the organization has converted to a computer-based financial system and now is able to analyze service delivery patterns, as well as better track and evaluate its overall program effectiveness.

Chapter 3 Review Questions

1. What were the chief elements in the administrative ecology that HEW planners failed to take into account prior to developing the migratory farm workers' health clinic in Bakersfield? If you had been in charge of the project at HEW Regional Headquarters in San Francisco, what would you have done to ensure that the project began properly?

2. What was the role of the local press, politicians, and special interest groups in affecting the start-up of this federally supported program? Can you generalize about the impact of such special interest groups on national programs?

3. Can you distinguish between the institutional factors (such as the budgetary process) and the personnel leadership factors (such as the various persons assigned by HEW to administer the program at the local level) that prevented effective initial comprehensive planning for this local public program? What reforms would you recommend to enhance better program planning in the future?

4. Compare Case Study 1, "The Blast in Centralia No. 5," with this case. How did the geographical distances in both cases influence the administrative decisions that were made? Can you generalize about the difficulties of effective administrative actions as the *distances* between the administrator and the "administered" expand?

5. Why were there various points of view about the purposes of this program *within* HEW? What were these competing viewpoints? Can you generalize about the difficulties of effective administrative actions as the *levels of bureaucracy* between the administrative and the "administered" expand? How did this case compare with Case Study 2, "How Kristen Died," in terms of these sorts of factors or problems affecting the administrative outcomes?

6. After reviewing this case study, would you modify Gaus's ideas about the nature of modern administrative ecology? In your view, for instance, does he adequately cover the problems of ethnic differences? Class differences? Media

influence? Leadership factors? Fragmented government oversight? Particularly after reviewing the epilogue, what factors would you amend to Gaus's List that promoted the clinic's survival and growth during the last two decades?

Key Terms

administrative ecology
physical technology
social technology

general environment
wishes and ideas
catastrophe

Suggestions for Further Reading

Gaus spent much of his life thinking about the ecology of public administration; therefore you would do well to begin by reading the entire book from which the reading in this chapter was reprinted, *Reflections on Public Administration* (University, Ala.: University of Alabama Press, 1947). In recent years comparative administrative scholars are perhaps the ablest group carrying on Gaus's investigations in this area; see Fred Riggs, *The Ecology of Administration* (New York: Asia Publishing House, 1967), as well as Ferrel Heady, *Public Administration: A Comparative Perspective,* 5th ed. (New York: Marcel Dekker, 1996). For an insightful retrospective on the comparative movement, read Ferrel Heady, *One Time Around* (Albuquerque: School of Public Administration, University of New Mexico, 1999).

Biographies and autobiographies offer some of the finest observations on the interplay between social forces and public administration, and the most outstanding ones are Louis Brownlow, *A Passion for Anonymity* (Chicago: University of Chicago Press, 1958); Robert Caro, *The Power Broker: Robert Moses and the Fall of New York City* (New York: Random House, 1974); Leroy F. Harlow, *Without Fear or Favor: Odyssey of a City Manager* (Provo, Utah: Brigham Young University Press, 1977); Thomas K. McCraw, *Prophets of Regulation* (Cambridge, Mass.: Harvard University Press, 1984); David Stockman, *The Triumph of Politics: The Inside Story of the Reagan Revolution* (New York: Harper & Row, 1986); Deborah Shapley,

Promise and Power: The Life and Times of Robert McNamara (Boston: Little, Brown, 1993); as well as several biographies in Jameson W. Doig and Erwin C. Hargrove, eds., *Leadership and Innovation* (Baltimore: Johns Hopkins University Press, 1987). There are several classic social science studies of this subject, including Philip Selznick, *TVA and the Grass Roots: A Study of the Sociology of Formal Organization* (Berkeley: University of California Press, 1949); Herbert Kaufman, *The Forest Ranger—A Study in Administrative Behavior* (Baltimore: Johns Hopkins University Press, 1960); Arthur Maass, *The Army Engineers and the Nation's Rivers* (Cambridge, Mass.: Harvard University Press, 1951); Milton D. Morris, *Immigration: The Beleaguered Bureaucracy* (Washington, D.C.: Brookings Institute, 1985); and Paul Light, *Artful Work: The Politics of Social Security Reform* (New York: Random House, 1985). For an excellent set of current cases at the local level, read James H. Svárá and associates, *Facilitative Leadership in Local Government* (San Francisco: Jossey-Bass, 1994).

You should not overlook the rich case studies available through the Inter-University Case Program (P.O. Box 229, Syracuse, N.Y. 13210) as well as the John F. Kennedy School of Government Case Program (Kennedy School of Government, Case Program, Harvard University, 79 JFK Street, Cambridge, Mass. 02138), most of which explore and highlight various dimensions of administrative ecology. The first ICP case book, Harold Stein, ed.,

Public Administration and Policy Development: A Casebook (New York: Harcourt Brace Jovanovich, 1952), contains an especially good introduction by Stein focusing on this topic.

Two short but useful pieces that should be read as well are Herbert G. Wilcox, "The Culture Trait of Hierarchy in Middle Class Children," *Public Administration Review* (March/April 1968), pp. 222–232, and F. E. Emery and E. L. Trist, "The Causal Texture of Organizational Environments," *Human Relations,* 18 (February 1965), pp. 21–32.

Certainly *must* reading for comprehending the whole cultural-social milieu within which American public administration operates remains the two volumes of Alexis de Tocqueville, *Democracy in America* (New York: Vintage, 1945), or for that matter, several of the other historical treatments of the American Experience: James Bryce, *The American Commonwealth,* 2 volumes (New York: Macmillan, 1888); Richard Hofstadter, *The American Political Tradition* (New York: Vintage Book, 1948); Michael Kammen, *People of Paradox* (New York: Vintage Books, 1972); Henry Steele Commanger, *The Empire of Reason* (New York: Doubleday, 1977); and Samuel P. Huntington, *American Politics; The Promise of Disharmony* (Cambridge, Mass.: Harvard University Press, 1981).

CHAPTER 4

The Political Environment: The Concept of Administrative Power

The lifeblood of administration is power.

Norton E. Long

Introduction

While John Gaus stressed the broad evolutionary perspective of administrative ecology, Norton E. Long (1910–1994), a distinguished American political scientist and former New Deal civil servant, zeroes in on the immediate environment of public administration, namely, that of administrative power. In his classic essay, "Power and Administration," Long argues that administrative institutions—public agencies, departments, bureaus, and field offices—are engaged in a continual battle for political survival. In this fierce administrative contest bureaucrats contend for limited power resources from clientele and constituent groups, the legislative and executive branches, and the general public to sustain their organizations. As he writes, "The lifeblood of administration is power. Its attainment, maintenance, increase, and losses are subjects the practitioner and student can ill afford to neglect." And yet, "it is the most overlooked in theory and the most dangerous to overlook in practice."

For Long, the concept of power cannot be bottled in a jar and kept safely tucked away for future use; nor can its nature be revealed by simply examining the U.S. Constitution, the legislative mandates, or the formal hierarchy of an organizational chart. It is, rather, an ephemeral substance that is part of the disorderly, fragmented, decentralized landscape of American public administration—a landscape reminiscent more of tenth-century warring medieval fiefs than of twentieth-century modern government. Power in this chaotic terrain is everywhere, flowing "in from the sides of an organization, as it were; it also flows up the organization to the center from the constituent parts."

This fluid situation arises partly, in Long's view, from the failure of the American party system to protect administrators from political pressures and to provide adequate direction and support for government bureaus and agencies. The American party system "fails to develop a consensus on a leadership and a program that makes possible administration on the basis of acceptable decisional premises." Left to their own devices and discretion, public agencies are forced to enter the "business of building, maintaining and increasing their political support."

Administrators seek to build strong public relations and mobilize political support by developing a "wide range of activities designed to secure enough 'customer' acceptance to survive and, if fortunate, develop a consensus adequate to program formulation and execution." If public servants are to succeed, they must understand the political environment in which they operate and the political resources at their disposal. On this point, Long has direct relevance to some of the central political problems faced by administrators in Case Study 1, "The Blast in Centralia No. 5," and in Case Study 3, "Dumping $2.6 Million on Bakersfield."

How can Long's disorderly array of narrow interests weld itself together to develop an overall scheme of the national purpose? Rational schemes of coordination always run counter to "the self-centered demands of primary groups for funds and personnel." Again Long visualizes the power factor as significant in any reorganization plan for government. Improved coordination through any governmental reorganization plan will "require a political power at least as great as that which tamed the earlier feudalism." "Attempts to solve administrative reorganization in isolation from the structure of power and purpose in the polity are bound to prove illusory" and have "the academic air of South American Constitution-making."

In his perceptive essay, Long raises another important issue, namely, that because the decentralized nature of the American political system puts administrators in the midst of numerous competing interest groups, they are plagued with the continual problem, "To whom is one loyal—unit, section, branch, division, bureau, department, administration, government, country, people, world history, or what?" A precise consensus on what should be done and who should be obeyed rarely exists and will not so long as the American system fails to establish organized, disciplined political parties or so long as presidents are unable to find firm and continuing majorities in Congress for their legislative programs. Unlike the Parliamentary system, according to Long, each agency in the American executive branch must fend for itself in the political arena, grasping for its own share of political resources to sustain its programs. Therefore, Long advises American administrators to read Machiavelli, La Rochefoucauld, Duc de Saint Simon, or Madison on the reality of power rather than the classic texts on public administration that often only stress the formal components of public organizations.

The following excerpt from Long's essay, "Power and Administration," is based on his perceptive understanding, his training in classical political philosophy, as well as his practical administrative experiences while working at the local, state, and national levels during the Depression, World War II, and the postwar period, particularly his experience at the National Housing Administration in New York City and the Office of Price Administration in Washington. Long's perspectives on power were also significantly shaped by the "new realism" of such insightful students of governmental administration during the 1930s and 1940s as E. Pendleton Herring, Paul Appleby, and Herbert Simon who, like Long, were sober realists about the nature and substance of administrative power. For some traditionalists, Long may seem uncomfortably iconoclastic and politically cynical in his thinking, offering few simple answers to the questions he poses. Nevertheless, his essay raises several perplexing problems that are still critical in public administration today.

As you read this selection, keep the following questions in mind:

How does Long define administrative power? Why is it important? Are there any differences between political power and administrative power? How is administrative power attained and maintained?

What are the appropriate "ends" or "purposes" of the contest for power in administration?

Will the administrative struggle necessarily, if left unchecked, produce a coordinated, effective, and responsible public policy?

How can better planning and rationality be incorporated into the administrative system?

How does Long's approach differ from Weber's or Gaus's approach?

Power and Administration

NORTON E. LONG

There is no more forlorn spectacle in the administrative world than an agency and a program possessed of statutory life, armed with executive orders, sustained in the courts, yet stricken with paralysis and deprived of power. An object of contempt to its enemies and of despair to its friends.

The lifeblood of administration is power. Its attainment, maintenance, increase, dissipation, and loss are subjects the practitioner and student can ill afford to neglect. Loss of realism and failure are almost certain consequences. This is not to deny that important parts of public administration are so deeply entrenched in the habits of the community, so firmly supported by the public, or so clearly necessary as to be able to take their power base for

granted and concentrate on the purely professional side of their problems. But even these islands of the blessed are not immune from the plague of politics. . . . To stay healthy one needs to recognize that health is a fruit, not a birthright. Power is only one of the considerations that must be weighed in administration, but of all it is the most overlooked in theory and the most dangerous to overlook in practice.

The power resources of an administrator or an agency are not disclosed by a legal search of titles and court decisions or by examining appropriations or budgetary allotments. Legal authority and a treasury balance are necessary but politically insufficient bases of administration. Administrative rationality requires a critical evaluation of the whole range of complex and shifting forces on whose support, acquiescence, or temporary impotence the power to act depends.

Analysis of the sources from which power is

derived and the limitations they impose is as much a dictate of prudent administration as sound budgetary procedure. The bankruptcy that comes from an unbalanced power budget has consequences far more disastrous than the necessity of seeking a deficiency appropriation. The budgeting of power is a basic subject matter of a realistic science of administration.

It may be urged that for all but the top hierarchy of the administrative structure the question of power is irrelevant. Legislative authority and administrative orders suffice. Power adequate to the function to be performed flows down the chain of command. Neither statute nor executive order, however, confers more than legal authority to act. Whether Congress or President can impart the substance of power as well as the form depends upon the line-up of forces in the particular case. A price control law wrung from a reluctant Congress by an amorphous and unstable combination of consumer and labor groups is formally the same as a law enacting a support price program for agriculture backed by the disciplined organizations of farmers and their Congressmen. The differences for the scope and effectiveness of administration are obvious. The presidency, like Congress, responds to and translates the pressures that play upon it. The real mandate contained in an executive order varies with the political strength of the group demand embodied in it, and in the context of other group demands.

Both Congress and President do focus the general political energies of the community and so are considerably more than mere means for transmitting organized pressures. Yet power is not concentrated by the structure of government or politics into the hands of a leadership with a capacity to budget it among a diverse set of administrative activities. A picture of the presidency as a reservoir of authority from which the lower echelons of administration draw life and vigor is an idealized distortion of reality.

A similar criticism applies to any like claim for an agency head in his agency. Only in varying degrees can the powers of subordinate officials be explained as resulting from the chain of command. Rarely is such an explanation a satisfactory account of the sources of power.

To deny that power is derived exclusively from superiors in the hierarchy is to assert that subordinates stand in a feudal relation in which to a degree they fend for themselves and acquire support peculiarly their own. A structure of interests friendly or hostile, vague and general or compact and well-defined, encloses each significant center of administrative discretion. This structure is an important determinant of the scope of possible action. As a source of power and authority it is a competitor of the formal hierarchy.

Not only does political power flow in from the sides of an organization, as it were; it also flows up the organization to the center from the constituent parts. When the staff of the Office of War Mobilization and Reconversion advised a hard-pressed agency to go out and get itself some popular support so that the President could afford to support it, their action reflected the realities of power rather than political cynicism.

It is clear that the American system of politics does not generate enough power at any focal point of leadership to provide the conditions for an even partially successful divorce of politics from administration. Subordinates cannot depend on the formal chain of command to deliver enough political power to permit them to do their jobs. Accordingly they must supplement the resources available through the hierarchy with those they can muster on their own, or accept the consequences in frustration—a course itself not without danger. Administrative rationality demands that objectives be determined and sights set in conformity with a realistic appraisal of power position and potential. . . .

The theory of administration has neglected the problem of the sources and adequacy of power, in all probability because of a distaste for the disorderliness of American political life and a belief that this disorderliness is transitory. An idealized picture of the British parliamentary system as a Platonic form to be realized or approximated has exerted a baneful fascination in the field. The majority party with a mandate at the polls and a firmly seated leadership in the cabinets seems to solve adequately the problem of the supply of power necessary to permit administration to concentrate on the fulfillment of accepted objectives. It is a commonplace that the American party system provides neither a mandate for a platform nor a mandate for a leadership.

Accordingly, the election over, its political meaning must be explored by the diverse leaders in the executive and legislative branches. Since the parties have failed to discuss issues, mobilize majorities in their terms, and create a working political consensus on measures to be carried out, the task is left for others—most prominently the agencies concerned. Legislation passed and powers granted are frequently politically premature. Thus the Council of Economic Advisors was given legislative birth before political acceptance of its functions existed. The agencies to which tasks are assigned must devote themselves to the creation of an adequate consensus to permit administration. The mandate that the parties do not supply must be attained through public relations and the mobilization of group support. Pendleton Herring and others have shown just how vital this support is for agency action.

The theory that agencies should confine themselves to communicating policy suggestions to executive and legislature, and refrain from appealing to their clientele and the public, neglects the failure of the parties to provide either a clear-cut decision as to what they should do or an adequately mobilized political support for a course of action. The bureaucracy under the American political system has a large share of responsibility for the public promotion of policy and even more in organizing the political basis for its survival and growth. It is generally recognized that the agencies have a special competence in the technical aspects of their fields which of necessity gives them a rightful policy initiative. In addition, they have or develop a shrewd understanding of the politically feasible in the group structure within which they work. Above all, in the eyes of their supporters and their enemies they represent the institutionalized embodiment of policy, an enduring organization actually or potentially capable of mobilizing power behind policy. The survival interests and creative drives of administrative organizations combine with clientele pressures to compel such mobilization. The party system provides no enduring institutional representation for group interest at all comparable to that of the bureaus of the Department of Agriculture. Even the subject matter committees of Congress function in the shadow of agency permanency.

The bureaucracy is recognized by all interested groups as a major channel of representation to such an extent that Congress rightly feels the competition of a rival. The weakness in party structure both permits and makes necessary the present dimensions of the political activities of the administrative branch—permits because it fails to protect administration from pressures and fails to provide adequate direction and support, makes necessary because it fails to develop a consensus on a leadership and a program that makes possible administration on the basis of accepted decisional premises.

Agencies and bureaus more or less perforce are in the business of building, maintaining, and increasing their political support. They lead and in large part are led by the diverse groups whose influence sustains them. Frequently they lead and are themselves led in conflicting directions. This is not due to a dull-witted incapacity to see the contradictions in their behavior but is an almost inevitable result of the contradictory nature of their support.

Herbert Simon has shown that administrative rationality depends on the establishment of uniform value premises in the decisional centers of organization. Unfortunately, the value premises of those forming vital elements of political support are often far from uniform. These elements are in Barnard's and Simon's sense "customers" of the organization and therefore parts of the organization whose wishes are clothed with a very real authority.

A major and most time-consuming aspect of administration consists of the wide range of activities designed to secure enough "customer" acceptance to survive and, if fortunate, develop a consensus adequate to program formulation and execution.

To varying degrees, dependent on the breadth of acceptance of their programs, officials at every level of significant discretion must make their estimates of the situation, take stock of their resources, and plan accordingly. A keen appreciation of the real components of their organization is the beginning of wisdom. These components will be found to stretch far beyond the government payroll. Within the government they will encompass Congress, Congressmen, committees, courts, other agencies, presidential advisors, and the President. The Aristotelian analysis of constitutions is equally applicable and equally necessary to an understanding of administrative organization.

The broad alliance of conflicting groups that makes up presidential majorities scarcely coheres about any definite pattern of objectives, nor has it by the alchemy of the party system had its collective power concentrated in an accepted leadership with a personal mandate. The conciliation and maintenance of this support is a necessary condition of the attainment and retention of office involving, as Madison so well saw, "the spirit of party and faction in the necessary and ordinary operations of government." The President must in large part be, if not all things to all men, at least many things to many men. As a consequence, the contradictions in his power base invade administration. The often criticized apparent cross-purposes of the Roosevelt regime cannot be put down to inept administration until the political facts are weighed. Were these apparently self-defeating measures reasonably related to the general maintenance of the composite majority of the administration? The first objective—ultimate patriotism apart—of the administrator is the attainment and retention of the power on which his tenure of office depends. This is the necessary pre-condition for the accomplishment of all other objectives.

The same ambiguities that arouse the scorn of the naive in the electoral campaigns of the parties are equally inevitable in administration and for the same reasons. Victory at the polls does not yield either a clear-cut grant of power or a unified majority support for a coherent program. The task of the presidency lies in feeling out the alternatives of policy which are consistent with the retention and increase of the group support on which the administration rests. The lack of a budgetary theory (so frequently deplored) is not due to any incapacity to apply rational analysis to the comparative contribution of the various activities of government to a determinate hierarchy of purposes. It more probably stems from a fastidious distaste for the frank recognition of the budget as a politically expedient allocation of resources. Appraisal in terms of their political contribution to the administration provides almost a sole common denominator between the Forest Service and the Bureau of Engraving.

Integration of the administrative structure through an overall purpose in terms of which tasks and priorities can be established is an emergency phenomenon. Its realization, only partial at best, has been limited to war and the extremity of depression. Even in wartime the Farm Bureau Federation, the American Federation of Labor, the Congress of Industrial Organizations, the National Association of Manufacturers, the Chamber of Commerce, and a host of lesser interests resisted coordination of themselves and the agencies concerned with their interests. A presidency temporarily empowered by intense mass popular support acting in behalf of a generally accepted and simplified purpose can, with great difficulty, bribe, cajole, and coerce a real measure of joint action. . . . Only in crises are the powers of the executive nearly adequate to impose a common plan of action on the executive branch, let alone the economy.

In ordinary times the manifold pressures of our pluralistic society work themselves out in accordance with the balance of forces prevailing in Congress and the agencies. Only to a limited degree is the process subject to responsible direction or review by President or party leadership. . . .

The difficulty of coordinating government agencies lies not only in the fact that bureaucratic organizations are institutions having survival interests which may conflict with their rational adaptation to overall purpose, but even more in their having roots in society. Coordination of the varied activities of a modern government almost of necessity involves a substantial degree of coordination of the economy. Coordination of government agencies involves far more than changing the behavior and offices of officials in Washington and the field. It involves the publics that are implicated in their normal functioning. To coordinate fiscal policy, agricultural policy, labor policy, foreign policy, and military policy, to name a few major areas, moves beyond the range of government charts and the habitat of the bureaucrats to the marketplace and to where the people live and work. This suggests that the reason why government reorganization is so difficult is that far more than government in the formal sense is involved in reorganization. One could overlook this in the limited government of the nineteenth century but the multi-billion dollar government of the mid-twentieth permits no facile dichotomy between government and economy. Economy and efficiency are the two objectives a laissez faire society can prescribe in peacetime as over-all government objectives. Their inadequacy either as motivation or standards has long been obvious. A planned economy clearly requires a planned government. But, if one can afford an unplanned economy, apart from gross extravagance, there seems no compelling and therefore, perhaps, no sufficiently powerful reason for a planned government.

Basic to the problem of administrative rationality is that of organizational identification and point of view. To whom is one loyal—unit, section, branch, division, bureau, department, administration, government, country, people, world history, or what? Administrative analysis frequently assumes that organizational identification should occur in such a way as to merge primary organization loyalty in a larger synthesis.

The good of the part is to give way to the reasoned good of the whole. This is most frequently illustrated in the rationalizations used to counter self-centered demands of primary groups for funds and personnel. Actually the competition between governmental power centers, rather than the rationalizations, is the effective instrument of coordination.

Where there is a clear common product on whose successful production the subgroups depend for the attainment of their own satisfaction, it is possible to demonstrate to almost all participants the desirability of cooperation. The shoe factory produces shoes, or else, for all concerned. But the government as a whole and many of its component parts have no such identifiable common product on which all depend. Like the proverbial Heinz, there are fifty-seven or more varieties unified, if at all, by a common political profit and loss account.

Administration is faced by somewhat the same dilemma as economics. There are propositions about the behavior pattern conducive to full employment—welfare economics. On the other hand, there are propositions about the economics of the individual firm—the counsel of the business schools. It is possible to show with considerable persuasiveness that sound considerations for the individual firm may lead to a depression if generally adopted, a result desired by none of the participants. However, no single firm can afford by itself to adopt the course of collective wisdom; in the absence of a common power capable of enforcing decisions premised on the supremacy of the collective interest, *sauve qui peut* is common sense.

The position of administrative organizations is not unlike the position of particular firms. Just as the decisions of the firms could be coordinated by the imposition of a planned economy so could those of the component parts of the government. But just as it is possible to operate a formally unplanned economy by the loose coordination of the market, in the same fashion it is possible to operate a government by the loose coordination of the play of political forces through its institutions.

The unseen hand of Adam Smith may be little in evidence in either case. One need not believe in a doctrine of social or administrative harmony to believe that formal centralized planning—while perhaps desirable and in some cases necessary—is not a must. The complicated logistics of supplying the city of New York runs smoothly down the grooves of millions of well adapted habits projected from a distant past. It seems naive on the one hand to believe in the possibility of a vast, intricate, and delicate economy operating with a minimum of formal overall direction, and on the other to doubt that a relatively simple mechanism such as the government can be controlled largely by the same play of forces. . . .

It is highly appropriate to consider how administrators should behave to meet the test of efficiency in a planned polity; but in the absence of such a polity and while, if we like, struggling to get it, a realistic science of administration will teach administrative behavior appropriate to the existing political system.

A close examination of the presidential system may well bring one to conclude that administrative rationality in it is a different matter from that applicable to the British ideal. The American presidency is an office that has significant monarchical characteristics despite its limited term and elective nature. The literature on court and palace has many an insight applicable to the White House. Access to the President, reigning favorites, even the court jester, are topics that show the continuity of institutions. The maxims of La Rochefoucauld and the memoirs of the Duc de Saint Simon have a refreshing realism for the operator on the Potomac.

The problem of rival factions in the President's family is as old as the famous struggle between Jefferson and Hamilton. . . . Experience seems to show that this personal and factional struggle for the President's favor is a vital part of the process of representation. The vanity, personal ambition, or patriotism of the contestants soon clothes itself

in the generalities of principle and the clique aligns itself with groups beyond the capital. Subordinate rivalry is tolerated if not encouraged by so many able executives that it can scarcely be attributed to administrative ineptitude. The wrangling tests opinion, uncovers information that would otherwise never rise to the top, and provides effective opportunity for decision rather than mere ratification of prearranged plans. Like most judges, the executive needs to hear argument for his own instruction. The alternatives presented by subordinates in large part determine the freedom and the creative opportunity of their superiors. The danger of becoming a Merovingian is a powerful incentive to the maintenance of fluidity in the structure of power.

The fixed character of presidential tenure makes it necessary that subordinates be politically expendable. The President's men must be willing to accept the blame for failures not their own. Machiavelli's teaching on how princes must keep the faith bears rereading. Collective responsibility is incompatible with a fixed term of office. As it tests the currents of public opinion, the situation on the Hill, and the varying strength of the organized pressures, the White House alters and adapts the complexion of the administration. Loyalties to programs or to groups and personal pride and interest frequently conflict with whole-souled devotion to the presidency. In fact, since such devotion is not made mandatory by custom, institutions, or the facts of power, the problem is perpetually perplexing to those who must choose.

The balance of power between executive and legislature is constantly subject to the shifts of public and group support. The latent tendency of the American Congress is to follow the age-old parliamentary precedents and to try to reduce the President to the role of constitutional monarch. Against this threat and to secure his own initiative, the President's resources are primarily demagogic, with the weaknesses and strengths that dependence on mass popular appeal implies. The unanswered question of American government—"who is boss?"—constantly plagues administration.

Introduction

In the foregoing essay, Norton Long discusses how critically important it is for public administrators at all levels of government to understand the dynamics and realities of administrative power—its sources, influence, and impacts on their programs and themselves, as well as the methods for enhancing and maintaining their power bases. He argues that "power" is the most frequently overlooked or ignored aspect of public administration. Recall his opening lines: "There is no more forlorn spectacle in the administrative world than an agency and a program possessed of statutory life, armed with executive orders, sustained in the courts, yet stricken with paralysis and deprived of power." Long's realism about the central importance and nature of administrative power for practicing public administrators is underscored poignantly throughout his writings.

Yet Long's essay was written almost a half century ago, and so is today's problem of relating politics and administration the same? Or, as some suggest, is it indeed the reverse of what Long's essay outlines? Rather than neglecting "power," do contemporary public administrators suffer from "too much political involvement" or too much "micromanagement" by their political superiors that prevents them from fulfilling their responsibilities effectively—or at all?

The following case, "The Last Flight of Space Shuttle Challenger," by Michael T. Charles, a professor at Illinois State University, describes the events leading up to the worst disaster ever experienced by America's space program. It caused the deaths of the seven-member crew of the *Challenger* on January 28, 1986, which included a teacher, Christa McAuliffe. The flight of the *Challenger* began at 11:38 a.m. and ended 73 seconds later. Before a worldwide television audience of an estimated eighty million people, the *Challenger* exploded in a fireball of hydrogen and oxygen propellents, destroying the rocket and the space shuttle and killing all of the crew members. The immediate cause of the accident, in the words of the Presidential Commission on the Space Shuttle Accident (the Rogers Report): "The Commission concluded that the cause of the accident was the failure of the pressure seal in the aft field joint of the solid rocket motor. The failure was due to a faulty design unacceptably sensitive to a number of factors. These factors were the effects of temperature, physical dimensions, the character of the materials, the effects of reusability processing and the reaction of the joint to dynamic loading." In plain language, a small washer-like seal in the rocket, called an O-ring, failed to function correctly in the extreme cold weather and was the immediate cause of the accident.

Or was the O-ring responsible for the *Challenger* disaster?

Professor Charles probes the causes behind the disaster and according to him, rather than focusing on the technical flaw of the O-ring that caused the accident, or what he calls, "the technical fix," he argues that it is far more important "to develop an appreciation of the human side of the management and its influence on the Shuttle Disaster." In elaborating on the details of this terrible event, what the author reveals at the end is how the enormous external political pressures placed upon NASA led to a chain of flawed decisions to launch the shuttle. Top NASA officials and managers at Morton Thiokol, the prime contractor responsible for building the *Challenger's* rocket booster, agreed to the launch in order to maintain congressional funding as well as "the can-do" PR image of NASA. They ignored or suppressed the repeated warnings of professional engineers who were close to the O-ring problem. As Charles concludes, "engineers not having management responsibilities viewed the data regarding the O-ring performance at cold temperatures quite differently than did management personnel."

As you read this case, you might reflect on several issues:

Where did the political pressure come from for launching the *Challenger,* according to Charles?

Why were the views of the engineers who were close to the O-ring problem not fully considered or ignored entirely?

Do you agree with the author that the "appreciation of the human side of management" is more important than focusing on "the technical fix"?

Does this case support or contradict, in your view, Long's central thesis that it is dangerous for administrators to neglect power and politics?

The Last Flight of Space Shuttle Challenger

MICHAEL T. CHARLES

Public Affairs Officer: Coming up on the 90-second point in our countdown. Ninety seconds and counting. The 51-L Mission ready to go. . . .

T minus 10, 9, 8, 7, 6, we have main engine start, 4, 3, 2, 1. And liftoff. Liftoff of the 25th space shuttle mission and it has cleared the tower. . . .

Mission Control: Challenger, go with throttle up.

Francis R. Scobee, Challenger Commander: Roger, go with throttle up.

Public Affairs Officer: One minute 15 seconds, velocity 2,900 feet per second, altitude 9 nautical miles, down range distance 7 nautical miles. [Long pause.]

Flight controllers here looking very carefully at the situation. [Pause.]

Obviously a major malfunction. We have no

downlink [communications from Challenger]. [Long pause.]

We have a report from the flight dynamics officer that the vehicle has exploded.[1]

After being postponed four times and delayed several hours, Space Shuttle Challenger, Mission 51-L, lifted off from pad 39B at Kennedy Space Center, Merritt Island, Florida. The lift-off was on Tuesday January 28, 1986, at approximately 11:38 Eastern Standard Time (EST). This was to be the tenth mission of the Challenger Orbiter and the 25th mission of the Space Transportation System (STS) program. The flight appeared normal until Mission Control lost its signal from the Shuttle, 73 seconds into the flight. A bright flash was observed almost immediately after the last radio signal from the Challenger was received by Mission Control. The massive explosion resulted in the total destruction of the Orbiter and its external fuel tank (see Figure 4.1). The left and right Solid Rocket Boosters were blown clear by the initial explosion, but were destroyed some 30 seconds later by the Air Force range safety officer, as the boosters began to fly aimlessly toward populated areas.

Michael T. Charles, "The Last Flight of Space Shuttle Challenger," in Uriel Rosenthal, Michael T. Charles, Paul T. Hart, *Coping with Crises: The Management of Disaster, Riots and Terrorism* 1989. Courtesy of Charles C. Thomas, Publisher, Springfield, Illinois.

This was the worst disaster ever experienced in the United States space program, with all seven crew members lost, including the "First Teacher in Space," Christa McAuliffe.[2] In financial terms it would cost in excess of $2 billion to replace the lost STS. The disaster was a heart wrenching experience for a nation and a shock for the world. The catastrophe shook America's trust in the National Aeronautics and Space Administration (NASA), and it was the beginning of a long and difficult investigation designed to determine the cause of the disaster.

In the end the Presidential Commission on the Space Shuttle Challenger Accident concluded that the disaster was caused by:

> In the view of the findings, the Commission concluded that the cause of the Challenger accident was the failure of the pressure seal in the aft field joint of the right Solid Rocket Motor. The failure was due to a faulty design unacceptably sensitive to a number of factors. These factors were the effects of temperature, physical dimensions, the character of materials, the effects of reusability, processing, and the reaction of the joint to dynamic loading.[3]

While it was extremely important for the Presidential Commission to discover and reveal the technical fault that caused the Challenger disaster, serendipitously, the Commission found that a faulty decision-making process was to blame for the launch of flight 51-L and the ultimate catastrophe. In fact, the Commission referred to the tragedy as "An Accident Rooted in History." It is to this end, i.e., elucidating the historical errors in decision making, that the author focuses attention in this case. Interestingly, there is strong evidence that many an "accident" is rooted in "management" history. . . .

Intriguingly, the decision making and judgmental errors made in the launch of STS 51-L appear to have been easily avoidable; however:

> Although it is flattering to believe that we would have known all along what we could only know in hindsight, that belief hardly affords us a fair appraisal of the extent to which surprises and failures are inevitable. It is both unfair and self-

defeating to castigate decision makers who have erred in fallible systems, rather than admitting to that fallibility and doing something to improve the system.[4]

Consequently, the reader must put him/herself into the environment of the shuttle program at the time decisions were made, and under the conditions in which they were decided. It is far less difficult to discern the errors made and to develop seemingly simplistic organizational remedies to overcome shortfalls in the system, than it is to truly understand the subtle side of human nature; the interaction between co-workers; the interpretations afforded policy documents by various individuals; non-verbal communication; the impact of statements made by important corporate executives and government officials on organizational members; and individual judgmental discretion, in a real life setting. However, to develop an appreciation of the human side of management and its influence on the Shuttle disaster, a chronology of events, dating as far back as the early seventies when Thiokol was awarded the contract by NASA to design and build the Solid Rocket Motor Boosters, must be understood.

The purpose of this case study, therefore, is: First, to demonstrate the organizational failings that resulted in the Challenger catastrophe. These failings included such phenomena as an environment of pressured decision making, lucrative contracts, Congressional funding, and bureau-political infighting within NASA and among NASA, the military, and other governmental agencies competing for space dollars. The second function is to provide an analysis of the organizational failings. This analysis will present several reasons, from a social-psychological perspective, on how an agency such as NASA, with its excellent reputation for management, technology, and safety, could produce such a catastrophic event. The particular significance of this case is the fact that "well managed," complex, and tightly coupled industries, i.e., organizations where ". . . different parts of the system can be quite dependent on one another . . .",[5] will have normal or system accidents. Simply stated, "The odd term normal accident is meant to signal that, given the system characteristics, multiple and unexpected interactions of failures are inevitable."[6]

The Challenger Crisis

Background: The Public and Private Sectors

The National Aeronautics and Space Administration is that governmental agency responsible for the development and management of the Space Shuttle Program. However, NASA has awarded several private firms contracts to develop and design the STS, and to assist in the launch process. Those private corporations included such major contractors as: (1) Rockwell International Corporation's Space Transportation Systems Division. They were responsible for the design and development of the Shuttle Orbiter. (2) Martin Marietta Denver Aerospace secured the contract from NASA for the development and fabrication of the Shuttle's external tank. (3) The Mor-

ton Thiokol Corporation won the contract to build the Solid Rocket Boosters, which are used to help launch the Shuttle. It was the right Solid Rocket Booster on STS 51-L that failed, causing the destruction of the vehicle. And, (4) Rocketdyne, a division of Rockwell, was chosen to design the main engines for the Orbiter.

Managing STS

Managerial responsibility for the shuttle program was divided by NASA into three field areas. Management of the Orbiter was the responsibility of the Johnson Space Center in Houston, Texas. Marshall Space Flight Center Huntsville, Alabama, assumed managerial responsibility for the Solid Rocket Boosters, the Orbiter's main engines, and the External Tank. Finally, the job of assembling the Shuttle components,

Figure 4.1 NASA Private Contractors Responsible for Shuttle Development

testing them, and conducting launches was the job of Kennedy Space Center, Merritt Island Florida.

NASA built a total of five space shuttles for their use. The first Orbiter built was the Enterprise, which while a full size vehicle, and used in early Shuttle testing, was constructed without engines and other systems needed for space flight. The vehicle was used to test aerodynamic and flight control characteristics of the Shuttle in atmospheric flight. The remaining Shuttles capable of space flight included: Columbia, Challenger, Discovery, and Atlantis. It was with these four reusable shuttles that the ambitious, if not unrealistic, 1986 and 1987 flight schedule of 17 missions each year, and the 24 scheduled missions in 1988, were to be accomplished.

After the first four test flights of the Space Transportation System were completed by Columbia in June of 1982, NASA declared the STS program "Operational," and then proceeded with the now "Routine" task of space flight. This philosophy and resulting attitude together created an atmosphere conducive to overconfidence, carelessness, and inattention to detail among many NASA officials and contractor personnel. A condition that played an important role in the decision to fly the STS 51-L on that cold morning in January.

The Decision-Making Process: Pre-Launch Meetings

Meeting One. After three postponements in the launch of STS 51-L, which was originally scheduled for lift-off in July 1985, and a scrubbed mission because of high winds at Kennedy Space Center on January 27, 1986, the Challenger was rescheduled for launch on January 28, 1986. During the short meeting following the Mission Management team's decision to scrub the January 27 lift-off, no mention of the Solid Rocket Boosters, or the earlier O-ring erosion found on previous shuttle flights launched in cold weather was made, even though temperatures were expected to drop into the low twenties overnight.

Meeting Two. The second meeting of the Mission Management Team on January 27 began at approximately 14:00 EST. Discussion at this meeting concentrated on the effect the expected cold weather

would have on such things as eye wash and shower water, water drains, the fire suppression system, and the overpressure water trays. At this meeting it was decided that the Orbiter heaters should be activated, but again there was no mention of the Solid Rocket Booster O-rings.

Meeting Three. It was not until approximately 14:30 EST that Robert Ebeling (see Figure 4.2) (Manager, Ignition System and Final Assembly, Solid Rocket Motor Project, at Thiokol's Wasatch, Utah plant) after hearing about the cold weather forecast, convened a meeting of several engineers at the Wasatch facility. At the close of that meeting sufficient concerns regarding the low temperature forecasted for Kennedy Space Center were voiced that Mr. Ebeling phoned Allan McDonald (Director, Solid Rocket Motor Project, Morton Thiokol) who was staying at the home of a Morton Thiokol colleague near Kennedy Space Center while preparing for the upcoming launch. During this phone conversation Mr. Ebeling expressed his and the other engineers' misgivings regarding the performance of the O-rings in the Solid Rocket Booster field joints at cold temperatures. This conversation resulted in Mr. McDonald contacting the Kennedy Space Center launch operations center to collect temperature data for Mr. Ebeling to review.

Meeting Four. The fourth meeting was conducted via teleconference and began at 17:45 EST. This meeting included project managers from the Marshall Space Flight Center as well as numerous people from Kennedy Space Center and the Thiokol-Wasatch facility. At this meeting Thiokol representatives voiced their concerns about the performance of the Solid Rocket Booster O-rings at cold temperatures, and they presented what O-ring failure data related to temperature they were able to collect and organize prior to the hastily called meeting. In reviewing the Commission transcripts on this meeting, it appears that Thiokol recommended that the launch should be delayed until noon or later when the temperature was higher. However, some members of the teleconference such as Mr. Stanley R. Reinartz (Manager, Shuttle Projects Office, Marshall Space Flight Center) testified before the Commission that, "I did not perceive it that way. I perceived that they were raising some questions and issues which required looking into by all the right parties, but I did not perceive it as a recommendation delay."[7]

Despite the conflicting opinions regarding Thiokol's position at this meeting, participants of the conference agreed to hold yet another teleconference. Additional Thiokol and NASA representatives were to be contacted for the follow-up meeting, so that a complete and thorough discussion of the O-ring problem could be held. In addition, it was also recommended by Dr. Judson A. Lovingood (Deputy Manager, Shuttle Projects Office, Marshall Space Flight Center) that, "I said that I thought we ought to have an inter-center meeting involving Dr. Lucas [Director, Marshall Space Flight Center] and Mr. Kingsbury [Director, Science and Engineering, Marshall Space Flight Center] and then plan to go on up to level II and level I."[8] In fact, at the close of the teleconference Dr. Lovingood telephoned Stanley Reinartz and told him that he should alert Mr. Arnold D. Aldrich (Manager, National Space Transportation Systems Program Office-level II, Johnson Space Center) to the possibility that levels II and I needed to consider the O-ring problem. However, Mr. Reinartz did not contact Mr. Aldrich, nor did he effectively relay, although he was in contact with Mr. Lucas and Mr. Kingsbury prior to the fifth meeting, the grave concerns some members of the teleconference had regarding the launch, or the invitation for them to join in the scheduled 20:15 EST teleconference.

Meeting Five. The penultimate meeting preceding the Challenger accident began at approximately 20:45 EST. Prior to the meeting several charts were telefaxed from Thiokol-Wasatch to both Kennedy Space Center and Marshall Space Flight Center. The charts included information regarding: (1) A history of O-ring blow-by and erosion in the Solid Rocket Booster joints of previous flights; and (2) the results of subscale testing and static tests on the O-rings.

Mr. Roger Boisjoly (Senior Scientist and member Seal Task Force, Thiokol-Wasatch) presented most of the data Thiokol personnel had quickly assembled for the teleconference. He was also the most vocal opponent of a January 28 launch, which would

---

> **Stanley R. Reinartz, Manager, Shuttle Projects Office, Marshall Space Flight Center**
>
> **Judson A. Lovingood, Deputy Manager, Shuttle Projects Office, Marshall Space Flight Center**
>
> **Dr. Lucus, Director, Marshall Space Flight Center**
>
> **Mr. Kingsbury, Director, Science and Engineering, Marshall Space Flight Center**
>
> **Arnold D. Aldrich, Manager, National Space Transportation Systems Program Office, Johnson Space Center**
>
> **Roger Boisjoly, Senior Scientist and Member Seal Task Force, Thiokol-Wasatch**
>
> **Robert K. Lund, Vice President, Engineering, Thiokol-Wasatch**
>
> **George B. Hardy, Deputy Director, Science and Engineering, Marshall Space Flight Center**
>
> **Lawrence B. Mulloy, Manager, Solid Rocket Booster Projects Office, Marshall Space Flight Center**
>
> **Joe Kilminster, Vice President, Space Booster Programs, Thiokol-Wasatch**
>
> **Allen J. McDonald, Director, Solid Rocket Motor Project, Thiokol-Wasatch**
>
> **Jerald Mason, Senior Vice President, Thiokol-Wasatch**
>
> **Calvin Wiggins, Vice President and General Manager, Space Division, Thiokol-Wasatch**
>
> **Cecil Houston, Marshall Space Flight Center, Resident Manager at Kennedy Space Center**
>
> **Dr. Rocco Petrone, President, Rockwell Space Transportation Systems Division, Downey, California**
>
> **Robert Glaysher, assistant to Dr. Petrone at Kennedy Space Center**
>
> **Martin Cloffoletti, assistant to Dr. Petrone at Kennedy Space Center**

Figure 4.2 NASA, Thiokol, and Rockwell personnel responsible for the safety and development of STS.

occur outside the data base that Thiokol had at the present time. The three major reasons presented by

Mr. Boisjoly supporting a no-launch decision were as follows.

First, If there was erosion of the primary O-ring seal there would be a high probability that the secondary O-ring seal would be incapable of seating properly.

Originally the Solid Rocket Boosters were designed with two O-ring seals, the primary and secondary seals. This was done because if hot gases and flame were to blow-by and erode the primary seal because of its inability to seat quickly enough, the secondary seal would seat and contain the hot gasses and flames until the boosters burned out and were jettisoned from the vehicle. Redundancy, i.e., having two pieces of equipment designed to perform a similar function, was incorporated in the Solid Rocket Booster joints, because failure of a joint would result in the loss of human life and the vehicle. Consequently, the Solid Rocket Booster joints were originally classified on the Critical Items List, November 24, 1980, as Criticality 1R. This meant that NASA believed the secondary O-ring would seal in the event that the primary O-ring failed. More will be said of the O-ring criticality issue at a later point.

Second, bench tests of the O-rings indicated that during the initial phase of launch, from 0–170 milliseconds after the boosters were fired, there was capability for the primary O-ring to seal. However, Mr. Boisjoly based this conclusion on what he referred to before the Commission as, ". . . normal circumstances, normal being within the data base we had."[9]

Given the weather forecast for the morning of January 28 (low 20s Fahrenheit), the launch would not be conducted under "normal circumstances." The lowest temperature that the shuttle had been launched previously was 53 degrees Fahrenheit. The thrust of Mr. Boisjoly's argument, therefore, was that there would be a change in the O-ring timing function. The time it takes for the O-ring to expand and seal the Solid Rocket Booster joint might be slowed because of a decrease in resiliency due to cold temperature. If the cold temperature were to slow the O-ring resiliency to the extent that it took more than 170 milliseconds to seat, the possibility of joint failure was increased considerably. The analogy used by Mr. Boisjoly before the Commission to explain this phenomenon was, ". . . it would

be likened to trying to shove a brick into a crack versus a sponge."[10]

Third, it was also pointed out by Mr. Boisjoly that there had been evidence of blow-by found in the Solid Rocket Motor joints on previous shuttle flights. Of particular importance to Mr. Boisjoly's contention that cold weather slowed O-ring resiliency was flight 51-C, Orbiter Discovery, which flew in January of 1985. Shuttle 51-C lifted-off from Kennedy Space Center with an O-ring temperature of 53 degrees Fahrenheit. In a post flight check of the field joints both Solid Rocket Boosters were found to have black grease between the O-rings, which meant that the integrity of the joint had been breached. This blow-by condition was considered quite serious by Thiokol. And, in the opinion of Mr. Boisjoly, and other engineers at Thiokol, it was sufficient evidence that cold temperatures affected O-ring resiliency and thus indicated the need to delay the Challenger launch.

During the discussion, however, it was pointed out that flight 61-A, another Orbiter Challenger mission, was launched in October of 1985 with an O-ring temperature of 75 degrees Fahrenheit, and that this flight had soot blow-by as well. The counter argument obviously being made was that the temperature of the O-rings was not an important factor. In addition, Mr. Boisjoly was asked to support his claim of slowed O-ring resiliency in quantitative terms. Mr. Boisjoly was unable to provide analytical data beyond that which he had already presented because, although he and Mr. Arnold Aldrich had tried to obtain this data since October of 1985, they had not as yet received it. Mr. Boisjoly did, however, point out to the members of the teleconference that by far the worst blow-by to occur in the Shuttle's history was on flight 51-C, and that this was an indication that temperature was a factor of O-ring resilience.

Other Thiokol-Wasatch personnel presented additional charts and their concerns regarding the effect of cold temperature on the O-rings. The final recommendation by Thiokol at this time was presented by Mr. Robert K. Lund (Vice President, Engineering, Thiokol-Wasatch). The recommendation was that STS 51-L should not be launched until the O-ring temperature reached 53 degrees Fahrenheit. This was the lowest temperature of any previous flight.

Shortly following Thiokol's no-fly recommendation, Mr. George B. Hardy (Deputy Director, Science and Engineering, Marshall Space Flight Center) was asked by Mr. Stanley R. Reinartz to comment on the Thiokol recommendation. Mr. Hardy stated that he was "appalled" by Thiokol's recommendation, but that he would not go against the contractor's no-launch recommendation. In addition, while Commission transcripts were unclear as to exactly what Mr. Lawrence B. Mulloy (Manager, Solid Rocket Booster Projects Office, Marshall Space Flight Center) said, it is clear that he did indicate that there were currently no-launch commitment criteria for temperature, and that Thiokol was trying to set new launch commitment criteria on the eve of the launch. Mr. Mulloy reportedly concluded by saying, "My God, Thiokol, when do you want me to launch, next April?"[11]

Mr. Mulloy and Mr. Hardy, two NASA administrators, were of the opinion that based on the Thiokol data presented, they had an effective simplex seal on STS 51-C, Orbiter Discovery, as was indicated in the 1982 Critical Items List. They were, therefore, not convinced that the cold weather would result in a slowed O-ring, blow-by, or ultimate disaster of the Challenger.

The Thiokol-Wasatch Caucus. Shortly after Mr. Mulloy's and Mr. Hardy's striking comments, Mr. Joe Kilminster (Vice President, Space Booster Programs, Thiokol-Wasatch) asked for a five-minute recess from the teleconference so that Wasatch personnel could caucus and discuss the concerns presented and review the data once again. However, before leaving the net to caucus, Mr. Allen J. McDonald (Director, Solid Rocket Motor Project, Thiokol, at Kennedy Space Center) who was representing Thiokol at Kennedy Space Center at the time, asked Mr. Kilminster to consider that the secondary O-ring would be ". . . in the proper position to seal if blow-by of the primary O-ring occurred."[12] Interestingly, while many members of the teleconference perceived Mr. McDonald's comment as a supporting statement for a launch go ahead, Mr. McDonald did not intend to communicate that message. In fact, even Mr. Roger Boisjoly was momentarily confused by McDonald's comment. Mr. McDonald merely wanted Thiokol-Wasatch to review this issue. In fact,

Mr. McDonald was totally opposed to a launch at such cold temperatures.

The caucus began with Mr. Jerald Mason (Senior Vice President, Wasatch Operations) ". . . saying that a management decision was required."[13] During the caucus the Thiokol engineers and management people continued to discuss the issues presented during the teleconference. However, one additional piece of data was brought to the attention of the group. It was pointed out that in an earlier test, engineers had cut an O-ring 125 thousandths of an inch, and it still seated properly. This had no effect on either Mr. Boisjoly, or Mr. Arnold R. Thompson (Supervisor, Rocket Motor Cases). They both continued to argue vigorously against the launch because of the cold temperature. In addition, while Mr. Boisjoly and Mr. Thompson were the most vocal participants of the caucus opposing the launch of 51-L, not one engineer in a non-management position made any positive statement supporting a launch. In fact, Mr. Boisjoly stopped arguing only ". . . when it was apparent that I couldn't get anybody to listen."[14]

After some discussion Mr. Jerald Mason said, ". . . we have to make a management decision."[15] Mr. Mason then asked Mr. Robert Lund ". . . to take off his engineering hat and put on his management hat."[16] At that point a final "management" review was conducted among executives at Thiokol-Wasatch. Those managers involved in the management discussion included, in addition to Mr. Mason and Mr. Lund, Mr. Joe Kilminster and Mr. Calvin Wiggins (Vice President and General Manager, Space Division, Thiokol-Wasatch).

The Teleconference Continues. The final management decision was presented to all members of the teleconference by Mr. Kilminster when the meeting resumed at approximately 23:00 EST. Mr. Kilminster recommended that the STS 51-L launch proceed on January 28, 1986. This new recommendation was supported by Thiokol management in the following manner: (1) the temperature data was not conclusive in predicting primary O-ring blow-by; (2) the demonstrated sealing threshold of the O-ring was 0.038, which was three times greater than the erosion experienced on STS 51-C; and (3) if the primary seal fails to seat the secondary seal will.

The teleconference ended with Mr. Stanley R. Reinartz asking for any final comments from anyone on the net. No concerns were voiced at this time; even though none of the engineers at Thiokol-Wasatch supported the launch decision. Mr. Kilminster was then asked by Mr. Mulloy to send a copy of his flight readiness rational and recommendation, via telefax, to Marshall Space Flight Center and to Kennedy Space Flight Center.

At this point in the meeting Mr. Allen McDonald informed NASA officials at Kennedy Space Center that ". . . I felt that I was the one who was going to have to sign it [the Thiokol flight readiness recommendation], because I was at the Cape; and I said I wouldn't sign it. I couldn't; it would have to come from the plant."[17]

McDonald's Doubts. Once the conference had ended, Mr. McDonald and NASA officials waited for the flight recommendation telefax from Thiokol-Wasatch. While waiting, Mr. McDonald presented his final concerns to NASA officials at Kennedy Space Center. Mr. McDonald pointed out that although he himself did not believe that the shuttle motor and all its elements had been qualified at 40 degrees Fahrenheit; although many NASA and Thiokol people did, he could not understand how either NASA or Thiokol could accept a launch recommendation when the predicted temperature was as low as 26 degrees Fahrenheit.

Mr. McDonald went so far as to say, "I told them I sure wouldn't want to be the person that had to stand in front of a board of inquiry to explain why we launched this outside of the qualification of the solid rocket motor or any shuttle system."[18] Mr. McDonald went on to present three reasons why the launch should be canceled: (1) the concern for cold O-rings; (2) the booster recovery ships were in a survival mode, with seas as high as 30 feet and winds of 50 knots and gusts of 70 knots. Recovery ships were heading for shore. Under those conditions it would be highly unlikely that the Solid Rocket Booster parachutes or the thrustums would be recovered; and (3) the formation of ice on the launch pad.

When Mr. McDonald left the room to retrieve the telefax from Wasatch, Mr. Mulloy and Mr. Reinartz telephoned Mr. Arnold D. Aldrich and relayed Mr. McDonald's concerns about icing on the launch pad and high seas at the Solid Rocket Booster

recovery sight. Mr. Aldrich did not feel that the launch should be scrubbed because of high seas. The loss of parachutes and thrustums was acceptable, and it was felt that the Solid Rocket Boosters would not be put in undue jeopardy. At the end of this conversation everyone left Kennedy Space Center for the evening.

Final Phase: Indecision at Rockwell. During the late night of January 27, and the early morning of January 28, the ice problem at Kennedy Space Center was causing concern for NASA and Rockwell representatives. Due to the imminent launch of 51-L it was decided that water should be left running through the water pipes to prevent their freezing. This caused considerable ice accumulation to form below the 240 foot level of the Shuttle's fixed service structure. The ice accumulation was discovered at approximately 02:00 on January 28, and was assessed periodically throughout the morning. A Mission Management Team meeting was called for 09:00 at Kennedy Space Center, and Rockwell was to provide its assessment of the ice condition relative to the safety of the launch.

Prior to the Mission Management Team meeting Dr. Rocco Petrone (President, Rockwell Space Transportation Systems Division, Downey, California facility) informed his two assistants, Mr. Robert Glaysher and Mr. Martin Cioffoletti, who were on site at Kennedy Space Center for the launch that:

> . . . we could not recommend launching from here [Downey, California], from what we see. We think the tiles would be endangered, and we had a very short conversation. We had a meeting to go through [the Mission Management Team Meeting], and I said let's make sure that NASA understands that Rockwell feels it is not safe to launch. . . .[19]

At the 09:00 meeting both Mr. Glaysher and Mr. Cioffoletti indicated Rockwell's position, or did they? Mr. Glaysher testified before the Commission that they informed the Mission Management Team that Rockwell could not say it was 100% safe to fly under the ice conditions. Perhaps Mr. Glaysher best described how the Rockwell no-fly decision was communicated. "[M]y exact quote—and it comes in two parts. The first one was, Rockwell could not 100 percent assure that it is safe to fly which I quickly changed to Rockwell cannot assure that it is safe to fly . . ."[20]

Unfortunately, this non-committal communication from Rockwell representatives was not perceived by NASA officials to be a no-launch recommendation. Horrace Lambarth (Director, Shuttle Engineering, NASA) reported to Commission investigators at Kennedy Space Center that the language used by Rockwell, "we can't give you 100 percent assurance," did not mean to him that the shuttle should not fly the morning of January 28.

Finally, it was quite clear from Commission testimony that crucial information did not reach important decision makers. Had top decision makers known that none of the Thiokol-Wasatch engineers supported the launch of 51-L, it is unlikely that the launch would have taken place.

The Challenger Disaster: Analysis

A variety of organizational phenomena impacting the decision-making process of the Challenger flight have been presented above; however, attempting to understand how these errors, blunders, and mistakes could occur in an organization as highly regarded for its management and professionalism as NASA, is extremely important. It is only through understanding of these phenomena that efforts to improve the decision-making process can occur.

The following analysis provides a review of the decision-making process: First, the political context of the space shuttle project is outlined; second, it is shown how the politics of space travel affected NASA management; and third, with this background it is possible to understand the operational decision-making process concerning the O-ring problem. Without reviewing the political and managerial context in which the shuttle program existed, it is impossible to develop a true understanding of the disaster scenario. A major failing of the Presidential Commission was their focus on what Kouzmin and Jarman call the "technical fix,"[21] e.g., emphasizing only the O-ring problem

and the flawed operational decision-making process in the narrowest sense. An attempt is made here to move beyond the limits of "technocratic thinking" to a more comprehensive, contingent understanding of the organizational and political factors influencing decision making in high technological environments. . . .

I. NASA: Politics, Contracts, and Business Interests

The original selection of a contractor to design and build the boosters for the STS system was a political battle in which the winner would receive a lucrative cost-plus-fee contract. Thiokol won the contract from NASA with the help of the chairman of the Senate Aeronautics and Space Science Committee, Democratic Senator Frank Moss, and the NASA administrator Dr. James Fletcher, both of whom were part of the Utah political hierarchy.[22] Thiokol's victory was not, however, won without difficulty and protests from other unsuccessful bidders.[23] These protests, combined with lobbying efforts in Congress, resulted in Congressional pressure being placed on NASA to again open the bidding process for the production of solid rocket boosters. This decision put Thiokol, for the first time in thirteen years, in the position of losing a one-billion-dollar contract. Thiokol had been in serious negotiations with NASA for this contract through January of 1986. In fact a teleconference was scheduled for January 28, after the Challenger lift-off, between Thiokol representatives and NASA to discuss this very contract. The impact of this factor on Thiokol managers during Meeting Five when Mr. Stanley Reinartz stated that he was "appalled" by Thiokol's recommendation, or the equally disquieting comment of Mr. Lawrence B. Mulloy, "My God, Thiokol, when do you want me to launch, next April?" may never be fully known. However, immediately following these comments, Mr. Joe Kilminster (who was well aware of the contract negotiations between Thiokol and NASA) immediately requested an off net caucus for Thiokol. This caucus, which culminated in a "management decision," reversed Thiokol's earlier recommendation to NASA officials, and was contrary to the collective opinion of those engineers attending the caucus. Upon rejoining the teleconference thirty minutes later, Thiokol management recommended launch and provided "engineering" criteria to substantiate their decision.[24]

The High Politics of NASA. Equally difficult to discern is the impact of political infighting between Congress, NASA, Commerce, Transportation, and the military regarding the funding of the NASA space program. The Pentagon, which even at present has a budget three times NASA's budget for space projects, pushed hard for Congressional leaders to support military projects at the expense of the NASA budget.[25] If NASA could not (and can not) demonstrate that the shuttle program was in fact "Operational," and that they could meet an aggressive and pressure ladened launch schedule, NASA funding could, and most probably would, be diverted to the military so that they might increase their rocket fleet to place satellites in space.

NASA was aware of the importance of public and Congressional support for the continued flow of massive funding into NASA. Their selection of Utah Republican Jake Garn, who was chair of the Senate committee overseeing NASA's budget, to ride the shuttle in April 1985, was done for more than altruistic reasons. Equally, the teacher in space program was a public relations effort that not only demonstrated the President's support of education, but it put NASA in the limelight, and it furthered the image that shuttle flight was as safe and common as airline travel. In fact, the President was expected to mention the Challenger mission and the teacher in space program during his State of the Union address on January 28. While there is conflicting evidence regarding the impact of these factors on NASA officials,[26] it is difficult to believe that these real or perceived threats to the financial security of the space program did not affect the position of NASA officials, albeit we may never know to what extent, on the evening of January 27, during Meeting Five.

While it is uncertain to what degree each of these system pressures individually or collectively influenced decisions at Thiokol or NASA, or in what way these same pressures dominated the casual response of Thiokol management to the O-ring problem, they were a part of the decision process. Perhaps Otto Lerbinger provides a partial answer when he states, "People make convenient assumptions because they want to move on. They note risks involved, but forget their assumptions and forget the risks they originally recognized. . . ."[27]

II. Managing NASA: Victims of Success

It is not surprising that a Commission composed almost solely of individuals with scientific and engineering backgrounds serendipitously stumbled on the flawed managerial process at NASA. Equally predictable is the fact that although the Commission was able to describe some of the flaws in the formal organization, they were unable to explain how these flaws came about from a social scientific viewpoint. In addition, the Commission was misleading when they gave the impression in their recommendations that changes in the formal structure of the agency would resolve the problems at NASA. The "formal" structure was not "the" problem. The major problem was the informal or shadow organization that had developed. The Commission only scratched the surface regarding the problems at NASA leading up to the Challenger disaster. Consider, as Romzek and Dubnick suggest, that there has been a shift in NASA from a system of professional accountability, which emphasizes ". . . deference to expertise within the agency,"[28] to a management system incorporating bureaucratic accountability, which emphasizes ". . . an organized and legitimate relationship between a superior and a subordinate in which the need to follow 'orders' is unquestioned; and close supervision or a surrogate system of standard operating procedures or clearly stated rules and regulations"[29] exists. For example, there is no better evidence of the autocratic management style and leadership tone at Marshall Space Flight Center than that presented in a letter simply signed "Apocalypse." The now famous Apocalypse letter was sent to Marshall's Inspector General two months after the Challenger disaster. Within this letter Apocalypse graphically condemns Marshall Director William Lucas,

> It has been apparent for some time that the Flight Readiness Review process developed by Lucas and other senior NASA managers simply was not doing the job. It was not determining flight readiness. Rather, it established a political situation within NASA in which no center could come to a review and say that it was "not ready." To do so would invite the question "If you are not ready, then why are you not doing your job? It is your job to be ready." At each Flight Readiness Review, every center and every contractor

are asked to vote on readiness. It is a "no win" situation. For someone to get up and say that they are not ready is an indictment that they are not doing their job. As a consequence, each center gets up and basically "snows" Headquarters with highly technical rationales that no one but the immediate experts involved can completely judge. Lucas made it known that, under no circumstances, is the Marshall Center to be the cause for delaying a launch. . . . [30]

In addition, Romzek and Dubnick suggest that superimposed on the bureaucratic model is the political accountability system, which requires the administrator to be responsive to various constituencies of his agency, be they Congress, the President, tax payers, or patrons of their service. Perhaps Michael Brody best represents the results of the dual bureaucratic-political accountability system proposed by Romzek and Dubnick:

The agency's leaders have been preoccupied with raising money for NASA from Congress. To win over the politicians, they have set goals for the shuttle program totally out of sync with the resources at their command. Organizational components that were supposed to work closely together—the Marshall, Kennedy, and Johnson space centers—have behaved like quasi-independent baronies, uncommunicative with one another and with the top. Watching the agency's fortunes decline, employees have tended to act like cowed bureaucrats. The result: an organization in which the flow of vital information up and down was as flawed as the now notorious O-rings. . . .[31]

Certainly, government agencies have to be responsive to the needs and demands of their constituents in democratic countries, but while NASA's ". . . emphasis on political and bureaucratic accountability was a relevant response to changing institutional expectations in NASA's environment, . . . they were inappropriate for the technical tasks at hand."[32] Consequently, both the formal and informal structure of NASA began taking on an organizational ambiance that supported compliance to administrative needs, which were a response to both internal and external pressures. This environment produced directive agents[33] within the administrative ranks that imposed formal and informal constraints on the discovery and free flow of information that would "slow" the progress of space flight. Within this atmosphere it was possible for administrators to wittingly or unwittingly avoid or rationalize away scientific data that suggested needed time consuming and/or expensive design changes. While NASA maintained the external image of a highly efficient and safety conscious agency, over time they slowly became increasingly closed due to overconfidence and susceptibility to external and subsequently internal pressures.

III. The O-Ring Problem Revisited: Managerial Influence

The O-ring problem did not first come to light during the January 27 meeting. There had been blow-by and erosion on seven previous shuttle missions; in fact, concern for the integrity of the Solid Rocket Booster joints was severe enough that a special task force had been instituted by Thiokol at the request of NASA, to study the O-ring problem.

The O-rings were designed under the assumption that hot gasses would not come into contact with the seals. However, early tests and flight experience demonstrated that the O-rings not only could and did come into contact with hot gasses, but they were damaged as a result. The NASA and Thiokol response to these design flaws was to minimize the problem in briefings and to begin defining, however poorly, acceptable erosion depth. Considering the fact that it was known that a failure in the Solid Rocket Joints would result in catastrophe, a fact supported by the criticality 1R and later criticality 1 designation assigned to the O-rings on the Critical Items List, it seems folly that design changes were not instituted immediately.[34]

There are several reasons available to explain the NASA response to the O-rings. First, since the O-rings were similar to the O-rings used in the Titan design, which was the most successful rocket produced by NASA, it appears that there was an overconfidence in the similar O-ring design used in STS. Interestingly, however, there were five major design differences between the Booster joint design of the Titan and Challenger joints. These differences were conveniently overlooked by both Thiokol and NASA personnel;[35] consequently, by ignoring the differences between the two designs they were able to support the desired belief that the joints were safe. Second, one of the major considerations used by NASA in selecting Thiokol to produce the O-ring was the low budget they were able to submit. NASA had been quite concerned about maintaining and increasing Congressional funding for some years. NASA needed to produce success stories to impress Congress and thus encourage funding. NASA did not want delays or large budget deficits caused by redesign. Third, over the years NASA had become famous for its gung ho, we-can-do-anything attitude. While this attitude had served them well in making the United States number one in the space race, it also encouraged unnecessary risk taking and over confidence, especially in recent years.

Certainly, the fact that there had already been 24 successful shuttle missions, and that the O-rings had always held in the past, influenced their decision to fly. It must be remembered that NASA was in an "operational" mode. As far as most members of the teleconference were concerned, as well as others, there was no O-ring problem. The O-ring was well within the erosion parameters established. It must be remembered, however, that these parameters were established after it was discovered that the O-rings were experiencing erosion for which they were not designed to tolerate. Perhaps Dr. Richard Feynman; Presidential Commission member, and physicist; best summarized this attitude:

> a kind of Russian roulette. . . . [The Shuttle] flies [with O-ring erosion] and nothing happens. Then it is suggested, therefore, that the risk is no longer so high for the next flights. We can lower our standards a little bit because we got away with it last time. . . . You got away with it, but it shouldn't be done over and over again like that.[36]

NASA and ultimately its contractors had left the traditionally conservative design, development, and testing stage behind. The result was that they began to rationalize away, they failed to communicate, they improperly analyzed data, and generally became somewhat sloppy in their work and overconfident of their successes due to their past shuttle flights. . . .

Notes

1. "From the Beginning to the End," *The New York Times,* January 29, 1986, p. A 1.
2. The only other astronauts to lose their lives were Virgil I. Grissom, Edward H. White, and Roger B. Chaffee. They perished on January 27, 1967, when their Apollo spacecraft caught fire on the launch pad. See "Doubts and Changes After Past Disasters," *The New York Times* January 29, 1986, p. A 10.
3. *Report of the Presidential Commission on the Space Shuttle Challenger Accident,* Washington, D.C.: Government Printing Office, 1986, vol. I, p. 72. The facts concerning the Challenger disaster can be found in the five volume series prepared by the Presidential Commission. The overall summary of the Commissions findings can be found in volume one; consequently, references are provided only when direct quotations were incorporated into the text, or when other sources were used.
4. B. Fischhoff, S. Lichtenstein, P. Derby, L. Stephen, and R. Keeney, *Acceptable Risk* (New York: Cambridge University Press, 1981), p. 42.
5. C. Perrow: *Normal Accidents* (New York: Basic Books, 1984), p. 8.
6. Ibid., p. 5.
7. *Report of the Presidential Commission on the Space Shuttle Challenger Accident,* vol. I, p. 87.
8. Ibid.
9. Ibid., p. 88.
10. Ibid., p. 89.
11. Ibid., p. 96.
12. Ibid., p. 99.
13. M. McConnell, *Challenger: A Major Malfunction* (Garden City, New York: Doubleday, 1987), p. 199.
14. Ibid.
15. *Report of the Presidential Commission on the Space Shuttle Challenger Accident,* vol. I, p. 93.
16. Ibid.
17. *Report of the Presidential Commission on the Space Shuttle Challenger Accident,* Washington, D.C.: Government Printing Office, 1986, vol. IV, p. 725.

18. Ibid., p. 726.

19. *Report of the Presidential Commission on the Space Shuttle Challenger Accident,* vol. I, pp. 114–115.

20. Ibid.

21. Alan Jarman and Alexander Kouzmin, "Decision Pathways From Crisis: A Contingency-Theory Simulation Heuristic for the Challenger Shuttle Disaster (1983–88)." Paper presented at the International Conference of the European Group of Public Administration, Leuven, Belgium. September 7–10, 1988 (mimeographed).

22. McConnell, p. 7.

23. Ibid., pp. 44–61.

24. *Report of the Presidential Commission on the Space Shuttle Challenger Accident,* vol. I, p. 104.

25. M. Beck and M. Hager, "Why Are We Up There?" *Newsweek* (October 10, 1988), pp. 36–38.

26. T.E. Bell and K. Esch, "The Fatal Flaw in Flight 51L" *IEEE Spectrum* (February, 1987).

27. Ibid., p. 50.

28. B.S. Romzek and M.J. Dubnick, "Accountability in the Public Sector: Lessons from the Challenger Tragedy," *Public Administration Review* (47), 1987, p. 229.

29. Ibid., p. 228. Cited from A. Gouldner, *Patterns of Industrial Bureaucracy* (New York: The Free Press, 1954), pp. 159–162.

30. McConnell, p. 109.

31. M. Brody, "NASA's Challenge: Ending Isolation at the Top," *Fortune* (May 12, 1986), p. 26.

32. Romzek and Dubnick, p. 235. See also W.H. Starbuck and F.J. Milliken, "Challenger: Fine-Tuning the Odds Until Something Breaks," *Journal of Management Studies* (25:4) (July, 1988), pp. 319–340.

33. I.L. Janis and L. Mann, *Decision Making: A Psychological Analysis of Conflict, Choice, and Commitment* (New York: The Free Press, 1977), p. 256.

34. For safety reasons shuttle components were assigned criticality categories. The categories included: criticality 1—loss of life or vehicle if the component failed; criticality 2—loss of mission if the component failed; criticality 3—all others; criticality 1R—redundant components, the failure of both could cause loss of life or vehicle; criticality 2R—redundant components, the failure of both could cause loss of mission.

35. Bell and Esch, p. 42.

36. *Report of the Presidential Commission on the Space Shuttle Challenger Accident,* vol. I, p. 148. See also Starbuck and Milliken, pp. 321–322.

Author's Epilogue

The most thorough (nearly six hundred pages) recent scholarly treatment of the Challenger launch decision is found in Diane Vaughan's *The Challenger Launch Decision: Risky Technology, Culture and Deviance at NASA* (Chicago: University of Chicago Press, 1996). The author concludes:

"Possibly the most significant lesson from the Challenger case is how environmental and organizational contigencies create prerational forces that shape worldview, normalizing signals of potential danger, resulting in mistakes with harmful human consequences. The explanation of the Challenger launch is a story of how people who worked together developed patterns that blinded them to the consequences of their actions. It is not only about the development of norms but the incremental expansion of normative boundaries: how small changes—new behaviors that were slight deviations from the normal course of events—gradually become the norm, providing a basis for accepting additional deviance. No rules were violated; there was no intent to do harm. Yet, harm was done. Astronauts died." (pp. 409–410)

Chapter 4 Review Questions

1. On the basis of your reading of the Long essay and the case study, how would you define the term *administrative power*? Can it be measured? If so, how?

2. Based on the case study, how did the political environment influence the deci-

sion to launch the space shuttle *Challenger*? Particularly who was involved and who was not?

3. What were the sources of these political pressures? Their points of view?

4. In your view, who was most responsible for the decision to launch the shuttle? How can one determine "responsible" or "irresponsible" use of administrative power? *And* ensure its "responsible" use? Especially to prevent, as the Author's Epilogue points up, "the incremental expansion of normative boundaries"?

5. Can you list the reasons why "the political dimensions" are repeatedly overlooked or ignored? Was this true in this case study? Or also in case's No.1 and No. 2?

6. On the basis of Long's essay and your analysis of the case study, can you generalize about the most significant problems facing public administrators today in relating politics and administration? Does the Wilson essay in Chapter 1 offer any useful advice on this problem?

Key Terms

interest groups   coordination of government
organizational fragmentation   sources of conflict
administrative rationality   sources of cohesion
balance of power   maintaining political support

Suggestions for Further Reading

The classic works on interest groups and their influence on the governmental process are Arthur F. Bentley, *The Process of Government* (Cambridge, Mass.: Harvard University Press, 1908); E. Pendleton Herring, *Public Administration and the Public Interest* (New York: Russell and Russell, 1936); and David Truman, *The Governmental Process* (New York: Alfred A. Knopf, 1951). The influence of politics on public administration and the general power politics within administrative processes were especially emphasized and popularized by the "new postwar realism" of authors such as Paul H. Appleby, *Big Democracy* (New York: Alfred A. Knopf, 1945) and *Policy and Administration* (University, Ala.: University of Alabama Press, 1949); Robert A. Dahl and Charles E. Lindblom, *Politics, Economics, and Welfare* (New York: Harper and Brothers, 1953); and Herbert Simon et al., *Public Administration* (New York: Alfred A. Knopf, 1950). Of course, Long's numerous essays did

much to explore as well as contribute to this topic and they are available in a single volume, *The Polity* (Chicago: Rand McNally and Co., 1962).

The last three decades have witnessed an enormous outpouring of books and articles on this subject. Perhaps some of the very best contemporary analyses of the aspects of power influencing administrative actions are found in Harold Seidman, *Politics, Position, and Power,* 5th ed. (New York: Oxford University Press, 1997); Allan J. Cigler and Bardett A. Loomis, *Interest Group Politics,* 4th ed. (Washington, D.C.: Congressional Quarterly Press, 1998); Jeffery Berry, *Interest Group Society,* 3d ed. (Reading, MA: Addison-Wesley, 1997); Francis E. Rourke, *Bureaucracy, Politics and Public Policy,* 3d ed. (Boston: Little, Brown, 1984); as well as Rourke's excellent edited collection entitled *Bureaucratic Power in National Policy Making,* 4th ed. (Boston: Little, Brown, 1986). Particularly good treatments of congressional oversight of administrative agencies are found in Joel D. Aberbach, *Keeping a Watchful Eye: The Politics of Congressional Oversight* (Washington, D.C.: The Brookings Institution, 1990); Morris P. Fiorina, *Congress: Keystone of the Washington Establishment,* 2d ed. (New Haven: Yale University Press, 1989); and Christopher H. Foreman, Jr., *Signals from the Hill* (New Haven: Yale University Press, 1988). The rise of the power of "think tanks" in shaping policy agendas is well described by David M. Ricci, *The Transformation of American Politics: The New Washington and the Rise of Think Tanks* (New Haven: Yale University Press, 1993).

For "overviews" of national political power, see Hedrick Smith, *The Power Game: How Washington Works* (New York: Random House, 1988); Bradley H. Patterson, Jr., *Rings of Power: The White House Staff and Its Expanding Role in Government* (New York: Basic Books, 1988); and at the local level, both Robert J. Waste, *Ecology of City Policy Making* (New York: Oxford University Press,

1989); and James H. Svara, *Official Leadership in the City: Patterns of Conflict and Cooperation* (New York: Oxford University Press, 1990). For an excellent general review of academic literature pertaining to this topic, see Chapter 3, "The Impact of Political Power and Public Policy," in Hal Rainey, *Understanding and Managing Public Organizations*, 2d ed. (San Francisco: Jossey-Bass, 1996).

You should not overlook biographies and autobiographies as offering worthwhile insights, particularly Joseph A. Califano, Jr., *Governing America* (New York: Simon and Schuster, 1981); William Manchester, *American Caesar: Douglas MacArthur, 1880–1964* (Boston: Little, Brown, 1978); Norman Polmar and Thomas B. Allen, *Rickover: A Biography* (New York: Simon and Schuster, 1982); Robert Caro, *The Power Broker,* cited in Chapter 3; David Stockman, *The Triumph of Politics,* cited in Chapter 3; Deborah Shapley, *Promise and Power,* cited in Chapter 3; and Jameson W. Doig and Erwin C. Hargrove, *Leadership and Innovation,* cited in Chapter 3.

CHAPTER 5

Intergovernmental Relations (IGR): The Concept of IGR as Interdependence, Complexity, and Bargaining

*T**he problems and tensions in the modern (intergovernmental) system are not primarily the product of ill will or ignorance, nor can they be traced to one level of government. Rather, the American intergovernmental system was founded on ambivalent principles and built to establish arenas for conflict and controversy.*

Laurence J. O'Toole, Jr.

READING 5

Introduction

In some countries, the subject of intergovernmental relations (IGR) is not a frequent topic of conversation. Unitary forms of government, found in communist societies, Third World or developing nations, and even modernized traditional Western state regimes, allow for little or no semiautonomous local units of government. Within these unitary models, power flows from the top downward, and no competition with national sovereignty is tolerated from governmental subunits. Local autonomy is simply unknown.

By contrast, the central framing idea of the U.S. government was federalism. The federal structure, as designed by the U.S. Constitution, distributes authority among the various levels of federal, state, and local government. In part, federalism was a pragmatic requirement in 1787. The founders were faced with the difficult necessity of winning state support for ratification, and thus adopting a unitary form that would abolish or severely restrict state authority was clearly out of the question. However, ideological considerations were also important in opting for federalism. The founders had vivid memories of the dangers from top-down unitary government of George III's monarchy as well as the loose, extreme decentralization of the Articles of Confederation (in reality the U.S.'s first constitution). Neither had produced satisfactory government and so the founders chose a mixture of both, the novel federal format. Though it is and remains the central framing idea in the U.S. Constitution, the Constitution on the specifics of this subject, as in many others, was imprecise and unclear. The details of the wheres and whys of how the various functions of government would be parceled out among the levels and units are not addressed in the U.S. Constitution beyond the items listed in Article I, Section 8.

In the United States, public administrators, thus, work within an unusual, complex framework in which authority over agency and program activities is frequently shared by various levels, jurisdictions, and units of government. Because of this "scattering" of authority, administrative problems arise, leading in turn to the important study of IGR, which involves comprehending the complexities of the federal system based on mutual interdependence, shared functions, and intertwined influence. Morton Grodzins once aptly showed the confusion for public administrators who operate under this system. In the case of a county health officer, called "a sanitarian" in a rural county:

> The sanitarian is appointed by the state under merit standards established by the federal government. His base salary comes jointly from state and federal funds, the county provides him with an office and office amenities and pays a portion of his expenses, and the largest city in the county also contributes to his salary and office by virtue of his appointment as a city plumbing inspector. It is impossible from moment to moment to tell under which governmental hat the sanitarian operates. His work of inspecting the purity of food is carried out under federal standards; but he is enforcing state laws when inspecting commodities that have not been in interstate commerce; and somewhat perversely, he also acts under state authority when inspecting milk coming into the county from producing areas across the state border. He is a federal officer when impounding impure drugs shipped from a neighboring state; a federal-state officer when distributing typhoid immunization serum; a state officer when enforcing standards of industrial hygiene; a state-local officer when inspecting the city's water supply; and (to complete the circle) a local officer when insisting that the city butchers adopt more hygienic methods of handling their garbage. But he cannot and does not think of himself as acting in these separate capacities. All business in the county that concerns public health and sanitation he considers his business. Paid largely from federal funds, he does not find it strange to attend meetings of the city council to give expert advice on matters ranging from rotten apples to rabies control. He is even deputized as a member of both the city and county police forces.[1]

Morton Grodzins's example of the county health officer may be extreme, but it is not uncommon to find public administrators wearing several "governmental hats." Federalism confounds and confuses public administrators' roles and responsibilities to an extreme degree in the United States. Who's the boss? The federal government? State? Locals? Or . . . ? For many administrators, the answer, as that of the county health officer cited by Grozdins, is the ambiguous: "It all depends."

Laurence J. O'Toole, Jr. (1948–), a professor of political science at the University of Georgia and author of numerous works on intergovernmental relations, federalism, and public administration, explores the current dimensions of IGR. This newly revised

[1]Morton Grodzins, "The Federal System," in The American Assembly, *Goals for Americans* (N.J.: Prentice-Hall, Inc., 1960), p. 265.

essay serves as an introduction to his own third-edition volume on the subject and provides readers with a unique broad-brush 200-year overview of the topic. In particular, O'Toole's study begins by carefully differentiating "federalism" from "intergovernmental relations" and demonstrates how these concepts are rooted in the framework of the U.S. Constitution. The author shows how the idea of "dual federalism" of the nineteenth century evolved into more complex interrelationships in the twentieth century. The essay outlines the diverse factors that have resulted in fundamentally changed IGR dynamics and how particularly in recent decades various presidents have advanced different reforms to cope with the apparent dilemmas and issues of the intergovernmental system. O'Toole's thesis is: Despite the subsequent repeated reform initiatives by presidents, the modern pattern of IGR since the 1960s has been marked by three persisting characteristics: interdependence, complexity, and bargaining.

As you read O'Toole's insightful article, you might reflect on:

What does O'Toole mean by those three terms, "interdependence," "complexity," and "bargaining"?

How did this IGR pattern emerge and why does it persist today, according to O'Toole?

What does this concept of IGR mean for practicing public administrators and how should they train themselves to deal with these problems (think about the prior case study, "Dumping $2.6 Million on Bakersfield," in order to help you draw some conclusions)?

What were the various reform agendas proposed by presidents to improve and strengthen IGR, and why is it so difficult to change this intergovernmental system?

How does "federalism" differ from "IGR," according to O'Toole?

American Intergovernmental Relations: An Overview

LAURENCE J. O'TOOLE, JR.

Who should determine the provisions of public policy regarding health, including support for health care for those who cannot afford it? Which authorities should act as the front line of defense in protecting the nation's environment? What does it mean when welfare is "reformed"? Who decides where the "safety net" is placed, and under whom?

American Intergovernmental Relations, 3d ed. Laurence J. O'-Toole, Jr. (Washington, D.C.: CQ Press, 1999), 1-31. Reprinted by permission of the publisher.

Should state governments be able to force localities to initiate new activities without providing the cash to cover expenses? How about Washington doing the same to the states themselves? Should the nation adopt a common and upgraded school curriculum in an effort to improve education and, as a consequence, economic competitiveness with other nations? Or should local districts be permitted, even encouraged, to make their own decisions and create their own innovations?

Should states and the national government be involved in encouraging, or restricting, the economic development efforts of American cities? In creating or limiting the instruments available to them to advance themselves—such as development authorities or municipal debt? When counties and states allow or encourage the construction of megamalls and superhighways that contribute to sprawl, congestion, and the degradation of air quality and natural resources, should the national authorities have any influence? How much? What is the best way for the federal government to be strongly involved in the enforcement of such important policies as ensuring citizens' civil rights and encouraging equal employment opportunity? And how can local police and fire departments be protected against micromanagement from Washington?

How should the people handle problems that confront one part of the United States but surpass that region's ability to cope? When a huge oil spill devastates parts of the precious Alaskan wilderness, who should take action, and how? When a reform of national tax law creates unintended negative effects on the finances of the states, what should be done? When acid rain from industrial air pollution contributes to the deterioration of natural resources a thousand miles away, who should take responsibility? All these and many more are topics of intergovernmental relations.

Intergovernmental relations is the subject of how our many and varied American governments deal with each other and what their relative roles, responsibilities, and levels of influence are and should be. This subject is no flash-in-the-pan concern; it has generated longstanding interest—indeed constant and pervasive controversy—throughout American political and administrative history.

In fact, the establishment of the United States was itself a sort of experiment in intergovernmental relations, since an effort to create a federal system like this one had never before been attempted. Nearly every major matter of domestic policy debated and decided throughout the nation's existence has been imbued with important intergovernmental aspects. Intergovernmental issues have contributed to such significant events in American history as the Civil War, the establishment of the social welfare state during the New Deal era, the at-

tack on poverty in the 1960s, the attempt to shift responsibilities to the states during the Reagan years, and the enactment of "welfare reform" in the 1990s.

But the subject is more than a collection of isolated issues. Indeed, it would be difficult to make sense of the many policy disputes without first understanding the intergovernmental system—its historical development as well as its current structure. To prepare for an exploration of current issues and disputes and to provide a context for the readings that follow, this chapter offers a brief overview of the intergovernmental system in the United States, with an emphasis on the federal government's role in the system's development.

Federalism, as the term is understood today, means a system of authority constitutionally apportioned between central and regional governments.[1] In the American system, the central, or national, government is often called the federal government; the regional governments are the states. The federal-state relationship is interdependent: neither can abolish the other and each must deal with the other. Intergovernmental relations is the more comprehensive term, including the full range of federal-state-local relations.

As the new century dawns, there are approximately 85,000 American governments—one national, fifty state, and the rest local. The last-mentioned consist of several distinct types. *Counties,* numbering some 3,000 units, are general-purpose governments originally created throughout most of the country to administer state services at the local level. Today, counties are genuine local governments providing an array of services to their citizens, and many—especially the larger, more urban ones—are increasingly involved in complex intergovernmental arrangements with other local jurisdictions, states, and the national government. *Municipalities,* numbering about 19,000, are local governments established to serve people within an area of concentrated population. The nation's largest cities and smallest villages alike are municipalities, although the types of powers they have and the services they offer may vary considerably. Municipalities are created to serve explicitly the interests of the local community. Through much of American history, municipalities have had extensive and often highly conflicting relationships with their "parent" states—relationships sometimes made all the more challenging from the point of view of the municipalities since they are not granted constitutionally independent status by the states, as are the states in the U.S. framework. Since the New Deal era in the 1930s and the rapid expansion of the intergovernmental system in the 1960s, municipalities—especially large cities—have dealt directly with Washington on many matters. And as federal cutbacks to these governments took hold in certain important policy sectors in the 1980s and beyond, municipalities have often developed defensive and somewhat conflictual relations with both state and national authorities—as they have also sought to develop additional revenue sources and less one-sided dependence on the other levels.

Additional local governments include:

- Townships (approximately 17,000), which are usually subdivisions of rural counties and are relatively unimportant except in some parts of New England and the mid-Atlantic states.
- School districts (more than 14,000), which are separate governments established in many parts of the country to direct public school systems.
- Special districts (numbering 31,555 in a recent count), which are limited-purpose governments set up to handle one or perhaps a few public functions over a specially designated area.[2]

Special districts are currently responsible for managing public housing; building and maintaining bridges, tunnels, and roads; supplying water and sewage services to residents; assessing and regulating air quality; and caring for the district's mass transit needs. The creation of many of these districts over the years has been directly or indirectly encouraged by other governments—such as the states and Washington—which sought coordinated local action on one or another policy problem.

If given a chance to view their handiwork today,

it is likely that the founders of the United States would find much to surprise them in the operations of American politics and government, especially in the intergovernmental workings. Yet intergovernmental developments over the past couple of centuries have been affected greatly by some fundamental choices consciously made by those early Americans.

The Founding and the Framework

The framers of the U.S. Constitution sought a way to combine the several states into a structure that would minimize "instability, injustice, and confusion," in the words of James Madison.[3] The founders were familiar with the arguments of earlier political thinkers who claimed that government protection of individual rights would have to be small-scale and cover a geographically limited jurisdiction. Yet their own experience suggested problems with such an arrangement. Under the Articles of Confederation, enacted after the Revolution, the thirteen American states had agreed on a formal arrangement that is now called a *confederation*.[4] The states were loosely joined for certain purposes, but their association fell far short of a real nation. The states retained almost all power, and the "united states" under the Articles found it virtually impossible to act with dispatch on matters of importance.

To solve this problem, the "federalists" of that period proposed to organize a nation able to act in a unified and central fashion for certain purposes. They argued that large republics, not small ones, were more likely to be able to prevent internal tyranny. They also suggested, however, that the states themselves remain independent governments with correspondingly independent jurisdictions. As a matter of fact, state autonomy was a political necessity at the time if widespread support of a new constitutional order were to be elicited. In the absence of any such historical arrangement, the new experiment in intergovernmental relations would have to develop out of the American experience.

The founders' construction of the new system virtually ensured continuing controversy about the respective roles of the national and state governments by creating sufficient ambiguity to leave many of the most important questions unresolved. As a result, later years were to see major changes in American intergovernmental relations under the influence of various political, economic, and social forces, while the basic framework remained in place.[5]

What does that framework actually stipulate? The Constitution seems to divide responsibilities between the two levels of government according to subject. Certain functions (for example, interstate commerce and national defense) are assigned to the national authorities, while many others (such as selection of presidential electors) are left to the states. Furthermore, the Tenth Amendment in the Bill of Rights asserts that "the powers not delegated to the United States by the Constitution, nor prohibited by it to the States, are reserved to the States respectively, or to the people." The states appear to have been given an advantage.

Yet the explanation cannot end here, for the same Constitution provides conflicting cues, authorizing the national Congress to "provide for the . . . general Welfare" and to "make all Laws which shall be necessary and proper" for executing this and the other powers given to the legislature. What constitutes the "general welfare" and which laws are necessary and proper are inherently political questions. Thus, it should be no surprise that the answers adopted by different people and at different times have not been consistent. The founders established a framework in which American governments would have separate but not completely independent spheres. The different levels would find it both useful and necessary to engage in conflict and cooperation; neither would be willing or able to ignore the other.

The Idea of Dual Federalism

Even in the earliest decades of the nation's existence, this tension was evident between the idea of

dual federalism (that is, each of the two levels of government operating independently within its separate jurisdiction without relying on the other for assistance or authorization) on the one hand and ambiguous overlap on the other.

The notion of dual federalism influenced the decisions of the Supreme Court at least until the early decades of the twentieth century. Furthermore, during the 1800s various presidents sometimes vetoed legislation that would have created a federal presence in policy fields such as public works construction on the grounds that the Constitution simply did not permit such national involvement in arenas reserved for the states.[6] In a number of fields, like education and social policy, dual federalism was the predominant view of federal-state intergovernmental relations.

Conflict and Cooperation in Earlier Times

Yet neither sphere was completely independent, even in the early years. Throughout the nineteenth century, the national government and the states often disagreed about the limits of their own authority. The Civil War is perhaps the prime example, but conflict occurred on other matters as well, such as policy on labor, social welfare, and economic regulation. To resolve jurisdictional disputes, therefore, the federal and state governments found it necessary to recognize their interdependence.

Conflict was not the only stimulus, however, for interaction. As various policy problems captured the attention of the nation's officials and citizenry, federal and state governments were sometimes able to piece together intergovernmental mechanisms to address immediate concerns. For instance, if some early national and state leaders viewed direct federal aid for internal improvements (for example, road and canal construction) as a violation of constitutional restrictions on intergovernmental arrangements, the governments *were* able to agree to cooperate in the formation of *joint stock companies,* part public and part private entities created to surmount the restrictions on direct participation by the national government. (Governments and private businesses could buy stock in a company and appoint members to its board of directors, thus indirectly supporting and influencing its operations.)[7]

Another mechanism for cooperation during the nineteenth century, before the dramatically increased intergovernmental interdependence of recent years, was the *land grant*. Through this device, the federal government would offer some of its land (it owned plenty) to the states for specified purposes. The recipient government would be obliged to abide by certain federal requirements, but direct involvement by the national government was minimal. Land grants were intended to help achieve goals in the fields of education (thus the origins of today's nationwide set of land-grant colleges and universities), economic development, and (on a very limited scale) social welfare.

Other forms of intergovernmental cooperation, such as technical assistance from federal to state governments and informal exchanges and loans of personnel during peak or crisis periods, were relatively common occurrences even during the nation's first century. Nevertheless, it was not until the twentieth century that the dual federal perspective declined appreciably in significance and American intergovernmental relations developed into a system with sustained high levels of *interdependence* and consequent *complexity*. Several political, economic, and social events and trends fueled these developments.

Developments in the Early Twentieth Century

From early in the twentieth century until recent years, federal involvement, especially financial involvement, in intergovernmental relations escalated. The Progressive Era at the turn of the century brought an expanded role for government in general, as reformers argued that the society and the economy could not tolerate laissez-faire (that is, a completely unregulated free market). The concentration of power in large corporations, the reluctance of some state governments to enact regulatory and other social welfare legislation (although other states were leaders in enacting farsighted and sometimes tough policy on such subjects), and the dawning recognition that the nation's natural resources were limited and would have to be conserved encouraged an expanded domestic policy role for Washington. This shift was also encouraged in many cases by the newly developing and professionalizing state bureaucracies, which saw in federal involvement opportunities for upgrading and for expanded funding, and by some interest groups that had been pushing at the state level for public attention to one problem or another. (Then, as now, organized interests—whether concerned with expanded highway construction or social services—have recognized that it is usually easier and more effective to deal with one central government on such matters than with scores of divergent ones throughout the states.)

The growing national will to attempt action in new arenas was followed by the central government's acquiring the practical wherewithal for action. The resources needed were money and clear authority; by the 1920s both had been generated.

Federal Financial Aid

In 1913 the U.S. Constitution was amended to permit the enactment of a federal income tax. Previously the national government had provided some limited financial support to the states, but the intergovernmental fiscal ties were few and far between. Until very recently the passage of the Sixteenth Amendment enabled the national government to raise revenue more easily than the subnational ones. The income tax, which was elastic (that is, its receipts increased faster than the economy during periods of growth), has been a more politically palatable revenue source than other sources typically emphasized by the states and by local governments.

This situation has changed in recent years. First, the income tax increased its bite in individuals' paychecks during the period of rapid inflation in the 1970s, resulting in a decline in its popularity and the enactment of an indexing provision to control the effects of inflation. Second, federal legislative changes during the 1980s reduced the progressiveness of the tax, that is, the extent to which it draws revenue from the affluent. Additional tax cuts in the 1990s created more tax breaks for the middle class and above, and other federal taxes, especially Social Security, began to assume a larger burden. Third, most states and even some local governments enacted income taxes of their own, with formulas tied in complicated ways to various provisions of the federal tax code. The development of intergovernmental finances in recent decades therefore documents one way in which the system has been linked via complexity. Thus, with the income tax the federal government created a source of money that could be tapped repeatedly to fill needs that had not yet received the states' wholehearted attention.

The obvious mechanism of intergovernmental cooperation in many such cases was the *grant-in-aid.* By 1920 there were eleven grants-in-aid operating in the United States. Land grants and other varieties of intergovernmental assistance were never again to outstrip cash grants in importance. In light of the significance of grants-in-aid since the early twentieth century, it would be useful to explain at this point some of the basic implications of this kind of program.

A grant-in-aid is a transfer of funds from one government to another for some specified purpose. Typically the recipient government is asked by the donor to abide by certain terms as conditions of the assistance.[8] These usually include a requirement that the recipient unit match the donor's financial contribution with one of its own, as well as a series of "strings," or stipulations, as to how the funds will be used, how the program will be managed, and how the recipient government will report to the donor.

Starting on a small scale early in the twentieth century, and then expanding rapidly during certain periods—especially the New Deal and Great Society eras—grants-in-aid from the federal government to the states and eventually local governments became extremely important features of the intergovernmental system in the United States. States, too, have provided financial support to their local governments. (In 1994 total state aid to other governments amounted to $225 billion. This total includes some federal aid passed to the local units through the states.)[9] But federal aid, because of its size, relative newness, and capacity to produce large-scale alterations in the intergovernmental system, may be considered an especially significant feature of America's fiscal federalism (see Table 1).

Validation of Grants-in-Aid

As the national government began to exercise influence through the use of grants-in-aid in the early 1900s, some observers wondered if the grant mechanism was an unconstitutional federal intrusion into the affairs of the states. Armed with the doctrine of dual federalism, critics of federal grants argued that Washington's offers were actually coercive inducements and violated the notion of separate spheres for these two levels of government. In a pair of landmark decisions in 1923 the Supreme Court paved the way for major expansions in the grant system—and for tremendously increased interdependence and complexity among levels of government—in succeeding years. The Court asserted that grants were voluntary arrangements and the federal government was therefore not violating the constitutionally established separation of functions in the federal system.[10] As the years elapsed, the grant framework became a dominant feature of the American intergovernmental network; it tied thousands of governments intricately together, for better or worse.

Basic Types of Assistance

Grants have offered the opportunity for substantially expanded federal influence over state and local governments, and a number of important political and administrative consequences flow from this fact. Yet it is essential to recognize that while grants create opportunities for national involve-

Table 1   Federal Aid to State and Local Governments, Selected Years

Year	Amount (Billions)[a]	Amount in Constant 1992 Dollars (Billions)	Number of Grants
1902	0.028		5
1912	—		7
1913	0.039		—
1920	—		11
1922	0.242		—
1932	0.593		12
1934	2.4		—
1937	—		26
1940	0.87	9.9	—
1946	0.82	6.9	28
1952	2.4	14.0	38
1960	7.0	33.4	132
1964	10.2	45.8	—
1967	15.2	64.8	379
1975	49.8	126.6	442
1978	77.9	159.5	—
1981	94.7	146.4	539
1982	88.1	127.4	441
1984	97.6	129.5	405
1987	108.4	130.4	435
1990	135.3	144.7	—
1992	178.1	178.1	—
1995	225.0	208.5	—
1998	246.1	215.2	—
2001 (est.)	300.7	246.7	—

[a]1961 dollars through 1937; otherwise, current dollars.

SOURCES: U.S. Advisory Commission on Intergovernmental Relations, *The Federal Role in the Federal System: The Dynamics of Growth—A Crisis of Confidence and Competence* (Washington, D.C.: ACIR, July 1980), 120–121; *Significant Features of Fiscal Federalism, 1990,* vol. 2, *Revenues and Expenditures* (Washington, D.C.: ACIR, August 1990), 42; American Council on Intergovernmental Relations, *Significant Features of Fiscal Federalism 1995,* vol. 2, *Revenues and Expenditures* (Albany, N.Y.: Nelson A. Rockefeller Institute of Government, February 1998), 38; and *Historical Tables, Budget of the United States Government, Fiscal Year 2000* (Washington, D.C.: Government Printing Office, 1999), Table 12.1, 203–204.

ment, they do not vitiate the pluralism of the intergovernmental system—at least not necessarily. Grants have developed as the prime instruments used to promote bargaining and jockeying for advantage among governments; they have frequently stimulated both cooperation and conflict among donor and recipient governments. It should therefore surprise no one that the system of aid employed in the United States has elicited ambivalent evaluations from participants and citizens alike.

Grants come in many shapes and sizes. The donor government may structure the purpose quite narrowly, offering aid for the construction of certain kinds of highways within a state. Such *categorical grants* were typical in the early 1900s. The donor may also design an intergovernmental program for a variety of purposes within a broad field such as education, community development, or social services. This type of aid, called a *block grant,* gained some prominence in more recent decades. In the early 1970s a new form of aid, *revenue sharing,* was created to enable one government to offer financial aid to another with virtually no restrictions on its use.[11]

When enacted, all of these types of intergovernmental assistance required some rules and regulations regarding the method of distributing the aid. How is a unit selected to receive assistance and how much is it entitled to? Some grants, including all federal block grants, specify a precise formula in the legislation creating the program. Such *formula grants* include quantifiable elements, such as size of population, amount of tax effort, proportion of population unemployed or below poverty level, density of housing, or rate of infant mortality. The specified formula is a rule that tells potential recipient governments precisely how they can calculate the quantity of aid to which they are entitled under the provisions of the law, as long as the recipient qualifies for such assistance under the other stipulations of the program. Usually, the elements in a formula are chosen to reflect characteristics related to the purpose of the aid (number of school-age children for an education grant, age and/or density of residential housing for housing assistance). Some factors in the formula are also likely to have political significance since there is no such thing as a neutral formula—all formulas reward some states or localities more than others, depending on their relative standing given the formula specified.

However, another method of distributing aid is available. *Project grants* allocate funding on a competitive basis, and potential recipients have no advance knowledge about the size of the grant. Instead, the authorizing legislation typically indicates the sorts of jurisdictions that are eligible to apply for aid and the criteria that will be employed to judge the merit of a government's application. Whether or not a government then receives funding depends on how strong a case it can make in its own behalf. Bureaucrats in the federal departments that supply aid determine the relative worthiness of different proposals and different jurisdictions, often by means of a detailed decision-making and evaluation system.

Why bother to make these distinctions among types of aid? The answer is that different types of grants have tended to produce different types of relationships between and among the participating governments. Much of the intergovernmental system in the twentieth century can be rendered intelligible by analyzing the consequences of different types of aid, one of the subjects treated in the remainder of this chapter.

The Legacy of the New Deal

Most of the grant-in-aid programs developed by the national government in the early decades of the 1900s were relatively limited. They assisted other governments primarily in fields that commanded strong political support, such as agriculture and road construction. Federal assistance, and thus national influence, was directed almost entirely toward the states rather than local governments. During this period, and until the 1960s, the system of intergovernmental aid was dominated by categorical formula grants. For the first part of the century, these were accompanied by relatively few strings, required considerable matching on the part of the recipients, and were rare enough that they did not seem to impose much of an administrative or political burden on the states.

With the New Deal in the 1930s the federal government under the leadership of President Franklin D. Roosevelt tackled the challenging economic and social problems of the Depression era. Although it would have been technically possible to establish new national-level programs to cope with the difficulties of the period, the more politically palatable method of the grant-in-aid was repeatedly used instead. Thus, while the national government's role expanded, the states and local governments retained significant leverage. Within a two-year period, categorical grants were established in such a variety of fields—free school lunches, aid to dependent children, emergency work relief, and so on—that they became the foundation for the social welfare state in America. The first real forms of assistance to some of the nation's local governments, the cities, were initiated during this period as well. For the states and some of their local governments, then, national authorities were no longer distant or sporadically communicating entities. Instead, in many areas of domestic policy, two or three levels of government were tied together in intricate patterns of intergovernmental relations—more like a marble cake, than the layer cake of dual federalism.[12]

Thus, the New Deal period witnessed a permanent increase in the density and importance of intergovernmental relationships in the United States, and during the next couple of decades—even during the administration of Republican president Dwight D. Eisenhower—the number of federal programs and quantity of federal aid continued to grow. Eisenhower himself was uncomfortable with the apparently prominent role of the national government in domestic policy matters, and he established the Commission on Intergovernmental Relations with the explicit charge to identify areas of federal involvement that could feasibly be "returned" to the states. But even the very modest suggestions of this commission went unimplemented. During the 1950s it seemed, as it often has since then, that the idea of separating functions by level of government was supported in the abstract but was exceedingly difficult to execute. Concerted efforts to reduce the levels of interdependence and complexity in the intergovernmental system have been, for the most part, singularly unsuccessful. In later decades, occasional efforts to simplify had some limited impacts; yet even these were not without costs, and they introduced complicating changes as well, such as increased intergovernmental mandating in place of the grant mechanism in policy sectors from transportation to the environment. Mandates, in turn, have been a major issue during the most recent decade.

The difficulty experienced by American governments when they try to reduce their reliance on one another is not surprising. Since the New Deal, citizens and public officials have tried to harness the national government's tremendous resources in order to attack pressing problems and redress inequities. They have attempted at the same time to retain diversity and innovation through vital state and local governments wherever possible. Shifting to some form of dual federalism, with a much less intense pattern of relationships and dependencies, could affect federal commitments in a multitude of important policy areas, like environmental protection, civil rights, income security, and education. Furthermore, such a change might entail radical

shifts in the nation's tax system. And even the most carefully considered plans would have to face bewildering dilemmas about how to reduce intergovernmental interdependence without inflicting serious inequities on some states and localities.

These days, when, as in the 1950s, one hears proposals to limit the federal role in the intergovernmental system and simplify the pattern of American governments, such caveats are useful to keep in mind. While many of the states are assuming newly resurgent roles in many policy sectors at the end of the century, Washington is certain to play a crucial part for the foreseeable future. It may even be asserted that creating a radically simplified intergovernmental arrangement by moving the national government out of a direct role in many important policy arenas is not a practical or responsible option. Why, then, the clamorous call for reform? Why have so many policy makers and intergovernmental experts complained about the "overloaded" pattern?[13] Later in this book, the considerable validity of a number of the criticisms will become clear. Focusing on the major developments affecting the intergovernmental system since the 1960s will be useful in understanding this controversy.

Creative Federalism and Its Implications

With Lyndon Johnson's presidency and the election of a heavily Democratic and activist Congress in 1964, a several-year period of tremendously expanded intergovernmental activities and initiatives began. Johnson proposed a "creative federalism" that would signify multiple new national commitments to assist states, localities, and private individuals and organizations in their efforts to solve many of the domestic difficulties of American society. These efforts of the Johnson era were directed primarily at problems of racial discrimination, poverty, and urban and rural development. The president and the Congress responded not just with rhetoric but with hundreds of intergovernmental programs.

Indeed, the number of federal programs of grant-in-aid tripled from the beginning of the 1960s to 1975 (Table 1). Almost all of the new programs from Washington were categorical grants, and—unlike earlier times—most of them were project grants. By the late 1960s most of the available grants were project grants, although many of these were relatively small and in toto constituted a minority of the aid dollars. In addition, the amount of support offered directly to local governments rose sharply. Many localities (especially the nation's older, larger, more fiscally strapped cities) came to consider the federal government more of an ally than their own state governments and became increasingly reliant on federal largesse. The results of these and other massive changes in the intergovernmental system enacted in such a compressed period were, as might be expected, mixed.

Intergovernmental Activism

In many respects the consequences of this major increase in intergovernmental activity were impressive. Although hampered by fiscal constraints, especially as the war in Southeast Asia drained its resources, the nation made measurable progress on a number of troubling problems.[14] The dramatic increase in federal support was especially welcome to many state and local governments, which had difficulty obtaining the resources to fund programs demanded by their citizenry; also, the emphasis on a variety of project grants meant that potential recipients could find appropriately targeted programs.

The explosion in the grant system had the further effect of encouraging or mandating the professionalization of personnel and the use of up-to-date financial procedures in the administrative agencies handling the programs in the recipient governments. Intergovernmental programs became increasingly influenced by functional specialists at all levels of government. The requirements attached to many of the new grants also forced states and localities to devote renewed attention to public problems they may have overlooked in the past.

Another trend fueled by creative federalism was the growth of interest groups in the nation's capital, especially intergovernmental groups. Those concerned with specific intergovernmental programs, whether on environmental pollution or juvenile delinquency, increasingly looked to Washington as they tried to influence legislation and the implementation of regulations, to monitor the actions of the federal agency involved, and to maintain contact with other interested parties. The tremendous expansion of the grant system in the 1960s was both a result of and a stimulus for a burgeoning number of interest groups operating at the national level in intergovernmental politics. These changes, too, contributed to the growing complexity of intergovernmental policy making and have served, since then, as a brake on any substantial efforts to disentangle the system.

These sorts of interest groups were not the only ones to achieve a heightened national presence. As the grants became ever more important and the system increasingly more complex, officials of state and local governments found it crucial to acquire information about the decision-making process in Washington. Furthermore, state and local officials began to realize that their own interests might deserve representation in the policy process at the national level. Accordingly, several groups of state or local general-purpose officials organized for the first time, moved their operations to Washington, or upgraded their staff and expanded their activities. These groups, including entities like the National Governors' Association, the Council of State Governments, the National Association of Counties, and the U.S. Conference of Mayors, refer to themselves as public interest groups, or *PIGs* (really). By the 1960s they became increasingly recognized as leaders in the representation of state and local interests in national policy making. In addition to the individual state and local governments as well as associations of governments that began to locate offices and representatives in Washington, other more functionally specialized groups of state and local officials, such as highway officials, budget officers, and social workers, have organized into national groups and participate in the policy process. Nowadays, even in the midst of the financial constraints influencing intergovernmental decisions quite directly, any discussion of an intergovernmental issue in Congress or an administrative agency is likely to elicit concern, participation, lobbying, and debate involving many such organizations.

Thus, the Johnson era encouraged several salutary developments in intergovernmental relations and further elaborated other interesting trends. Yet, as might be expected when such massive changes are effected, difficulties and tensions also arose.

Emergent Frustrations and Tensions

Because the choices made available to state and local officials as a result of the tremendous increase in intergovernmental programs were almost limitless, potential recipients could afford to shop around and bargain for the most favorable deal. As a result of the interagency competition for clients, federal requirements would sometimes be loosely enforced. Recipients were more and more able to evade federal intent while absorbing federal dollars.

Conversely, the system, which now had huge numbers of partially overlapping (and often duplicating) grants, created vexing difficulties for officials at state and local levels. With several related programs available to assist a city in such tasks as rebuilding its sewers, a great deal of time, effort, and information went into deciding which program or programs to pursue. Grants established ostensibly for the same purpose might be housed in different federal agencies, require entirely different application and approval processes, stipulate very different matching requirements, and be implemented with conflicting schedules. Furthermore, as potential recipients of project grants scrambled to complete detailed applications for scores of grant requests on short notice, the winners were not necessarily the most competent or the most needy jurisdictions. Instead, the one who packaged proposals in the most salable fashion (exercising

what came to be called grantsmanship), was often rewarded.

The systemic changes generated another set of tensions for state and local governments. With the multitude of programs, many of which were now funded by grants constructed with high matching ratios (that is, Washington would pay for most of the total expenses incurred under the program), state and local governments were finding it increasingly difficult either to abstain from commitments to federal aid or to make such commitments wholeheartedly. A program that can be subsidized by grant money becomes cheaper and therefore more attractive to the recipient government. However, a mushrooming number of appealing programs can significantly distort the recipient's budgeting process. Instead of spending its locally generated revenue on the public services judged most important by its own officials and citizens, a city can be encouraged to use its money as matching funds for programs that are, in essence, national priorities. The expansion of the aid system in the 1960s prompted complaints on this score from uneasy mayors, governors, and others who were concerned about their apparently declining ability to maintain some independence.

Such general-purpose officials had other concerns as well. Many of them believed the expanded system of categorical grants was composed of unduly narrow programs that were not readily adaptable to the needs in their own jurisdictions. Furthermore, the pattern, taken as a whole, had become so complex that it was all but impenetrable to generalists. These officials had a difficult time even figuring out how much aid was being received from federal sources. And many of the important, detailed decisions that are made as part of an intergovernmental grant bargain—for instance, determining the eligibility of clients for programs or establishing goals—were made far from the general-purpose officials. Increasingly important in the intergovernmental policy process was a great number of specialists across governmental levels—especially in administrative agencies charged with executing the program, legislative committees with responsibility for the substantive area, and pressure groups with a strong interest in the program. Intergovernmental experts, particularly those concerned about the decreasing ability of general officials to oversee and direct activities in this maze, dubbed these policy networks *vertical functional autocracies.*

In these chains of influence, it became increasingly difficult for anyone, even major officials like governors or mayors or presidents, to decipher just *who* was causing *what* to happen intergovernmentally. When responsibility is so diffused, the mechanisms of democratic government cannot readily ensure that policy reflects the will of the people or their representatives. In other words, another possible cost of such an arrangement is a decline in political responsiveness.

In short, then, the era of creative federalism brought energy and inventiveness to intergovernmental questions; but the massive changes in the system meant a significant escalation in costs and frustrations as well. It should not be surprising, therefore, that interdependence and complexity emerged as major political features during the decades following the Johnson era. Despite manifold differences in emphasis, approach, and impact, intergovernmental actors during the most recent period have grappled with a structure exhibiting common characteristics and daunting demands. The following pages first characterize the modern intergovernmental pattern in general terms and then explore important events and efforts during several recent national administrations.

Interdependence, Complexity, and Intergovernmental Bargaining

In the pattern that emerged from the explosive growth of creative federalism it became difficult for actors in the system to make rational decisions to benefit the individuals or activities for which they held responsibility. It was also difficult to design any coherent change in the system itself. These problems stemmed directly from the dominant characteristics of the intergovernmental system: its interdependence and related complexity.

It would be helpful to define these two concepts more precisely here. *Interdependence* means that power is shared among branches and layers of government, even within policy sectors. Instead of one level consistently controlling decisions about policy, nearly any change requires mutual accommodation among several levels of government. No one is in control of the system itself, and unanticipated consequences are a fact of life. Complexity accompanies such interdependence. *Complexity* means that the intergovernmental network is large and differentiated; no one participating government can consistently possess enough information about its components and dynamics to make rational decisions on its own or to operate in isolation from the rest.

Especially since the era of creative federalism, but also as a consequence of the framework established by the founders, many participants in the intergovernmental system have plenty of opportunities to exercise influence—particularly to delay or frustrate action to which they are opposed. It is much more difficult, however, to generate and systematically execute *positive* action in a straightforwardly rational manner.

An important result of the system's grounding in interdependence and complexity (one that became obvious in the 1960s and endures in altered form) is that the typical style of decision making in the American intergovernmental system is one of bargaining under conditions of partial conflict among the participants. The actors in the system, including the various governments involved, have different interests to serve and objectives to seek; yet they cannot succeed by acting unilaterally. They may join together into one or more loose coalitions aimed at achieving some intergovernmental objective.[15] But they must perforce negotiate as a nearly ceaseless activity if they are to have any chance of defending themselves or achieving even some of their goals.

Of course, bargaining under conditions of partial conflict is a very abstract notion and encompasses many different types of situations. The bargaining between governments in a project grant structure differs in predictable and important ways from the bargaining activity likely with a formula grant: the former setting typically provides more influence to bureaucratic actors associated with the donor government, those who write the rules and evaluate the competitive applications from potential recipients. The fact of bargaining and its pervasiveness throughout the system, however, is important to keep in mind. Bargaining is typical even today, a time when many grant programs have not grown at nearly the pace of earlier periods and when other ties, ostensibly more controlling, unilateral, or regulatory ties have become prominent between levels. As readings in this book document, recent years have brought unfunded mandates (rather than grants) that have become increasingly used as a mechanism of coordination across governments. Yet these shifts do not unambiguously signify a new centralization. In some ways, also documented later in this volume, the states are now able to initiate more action, or to resist more, than in earlier periods. And federal officials may have fewer levers to enforce their own efforts at intergovernmental influence when the grant mechanism is absent from, or less prominent in, the bargaining arena. It may be concluded, therefore, that the shifts of the last two decades or more have altered the *types* of bargaining and the issues subject to negotiation. The fact of bargaining nevertheless remains crucial to an understanding of American intergovernmental dynamics.

Some of the tensions inherent in such an interdependent and complex system became visible in the 1960s and have escalated since. Red tape, which is the continuation of intergovernmental negotiation and conflict by other means, is one manifestation. The federal government has usually viewed the requirements it imposes on its grants as essential to ensure a program's integrity. Yet recipient units claim that the burdens have become excessive. (Localities also blame the states in part for their red-tape burden.) Federally created intergovernmental mandates have escalated sharply since 1975 and in the 1990s became the bête noire of state and local officials.

Two general points emerge. First, the problems and tensions in the modern system are not primarily the product of ill will or ignorance, nor can they be traced primarily to one level of government.

Rather, the American intergovernmental system was founded on ambivalent principles and built to establish arenas for conflict and controversy. Second, changing the particular pattern of intergovernmental relationships or reforming certain aspects of the system—for example, through the enactment of spending and policy shifts like those the Republican congressional majority sought during the late 1990s—would have important consequences but could hardly resolve the value conflicts of a complex and interdependent system. At this point, accordingly, we should examine some of the developments in the American intergovernmental system since the period of creative federalism. Many of these are made comprehensible by an awareness of the difficulties just surveyed, and many, in turn, presage some of the topics of current interest and controversy.

Nixon's New Federalism

Richard Nixon reacted to the tensions in the changing system by proposing reforms ostensibly aimed at increasing the influence of general-purpose (especially elected) officials at all levels, shifting power away from Washington and toward federal field offices and state and local governments, reducing the control exercised by functional specialists, and trimming intergovernmental red tape. (This direction was maintained, though with somewhat diminished effort and effectiveness, by his successor, Gerald Ford.)

Of what, exactly, did Nixon's "new federalism" consist? He proposed a series of initiatives:

1. *Revenue sharing.* One of Nixon's most ambitious initiatives was to establish a program of revenue sharing from the federal level to state and local governments. Revenue sharing (also called general revenue sharing) seemed to meet the demands of state and local governments for more discretion, was attractive to the most financially hard-pressed jurisdictions, and could shift some influence to the general-purpose elected officials. In 1972 the State and Local Fiscal

Assistance Act was passed with the support of much of the Democratic leadership in Congress as well as of the major PIGs of state and local officials. This law established a revenue-sharing program of approximately $6 billion per year for five years. All state governments and general-purpose local governments were eligible for aid, which was to be allocated on the basis of complicated formulas. The program was extended, with modifications, in 1976, and again in 1980. In 1984 revenue sharing was reenacted for localities alone, as the federal budget tightened. And in 1986, the program was ended because Congress found itself facing an increasingly severe national deficit. During its tenure, revenue sharing helped many governments. But even at its peak, it constituted only a small fraction of total federal assistance for the larger recipient governments.

2. *Block grants.* These began during the Johnson administration, but the idea is most closely identified with Nixon, who proposed a set of enactments in six policy fields along with the elimination of a series of closely related categorical grants. Defenders of these latter programs, including members of the vertical functional autocracies, resisted; their concerns would have no statutory protection once a block grant was put into place. Further, the Nixon proposals would have reduced the overall level of intergovernmental funding. Ultimately, only three of the additional block grants emerged from this period: in employment, social services, and community development. Yet some of these programs have had a major impact on intergovernmental affairs, and they were followed by additional block grants enacted during the Reagan years.

3. *Administrative initiatives.* Nixon encouraged the implementation of administrative reforms by supporting a series of efforts to simplify and expedite the grant application and review process.

Despite all these changes, the intergovernmental system was not radically altered. The more traditional categorical grant was by no means disused. Indeed, such programs and the amount of aid going to support them increased even through the Nixon years. And administrative and regulatory difficulties in the system proved to be more tenacious than many had anticipated. Impressively complex and interdependent, the system continued to face criticism from virtually all directions.

The Carter Period

President Jimmy Carter was not the activist in intergovernmental matters that Nixon was—or, for that matter, that his successor would be. But, as a former governor familiar with the concerns of general political executives and of state and local units, Carter worked at developing communication links with the PIGs and with state and local governments, tried to advance some administrative reforms, and paid special attention to economic problems facing the cities.

Yet Carter proposed no overall plan for reform of the system, nor did he recommend any major changes in the pattern of intergovernmental aid. Two developments during the late 1970s exacerbated some of the difficulties faced by policy makers and managers. First, a combination of sour economic conditions, federal budget difficulties, and Carter's fundamentally conservative fiscal instincts placed stringent limits on any efforts to increase federal aid. Federal spending increases slowed and in 1978 reversed direction: aid was being limited at a time when many units of government had come to depend on it. Second, during this period the federal government, especially Congress, did not easily loosen its hold on other units of government. Instead, Washington sought to accomplish its intergovernmental goals via direct requirements, frequently including some that were mandated across many different programs.

Reagan's Attempted Revolution

The first part of Ronald Reagan's time as president saw perhaps the most systematic, if not the most sustained, effort to remake the American intergovernmental system since the New Deal. Reagan ardently believed that the United States had been created as a system in which national powers and jurisdiction were severely limited, and in which the states had the strongest, most vital governments, with the broadest jurisdiction over domestic matters. Accordingly, he sought to reshape the intergovernmental pattern in a manner consistent with this understanding. Since his other priorities included tax reductions and significant defense spending increases, a related consequence was a renewed vulnerability of intergovernmental aid to sizable cuts. Since pressures by citizens and interest groups to address a whole set of policy issues at state and local levels did not abate, the stage was set for higher levels of tension and conflict in the system.

Reagan's major proposals, for which he adopted Nixon's term, the new federalism, were as follows:

1. *An additional series of block grants.* Reagan quickly proposed that more than 100 categoricals be combined into a handful of broadly based block grants with very few regulations. Congress complied with several of these initiatives.

2. *A dramatic simplification of the system of intergovernmental aid.* Program responsibilities were to be shifted to single levels of government and away from the "marble cake" configurations. Congress made no move to approve this plan, and Reagan's attention was diverted from this contentious issue.

3. *A devolution of responsibilities for many policies from the national level to the states.* Reagan suggested that scores of programs involving federal participation, including most of the remaining expensive ones, be turned over to the states in their entirety and that an appropriate quantity of revenue be shifted to the states as well. No action was taken on this proposal. Yet several years after Reagan had left office, some of the intent behind this idea was being fulfilled. By the 1990s new policy initiatives that might involve substantial new expenditures from Washington had become nearly impossible to enact in the political and budgetary climate of the time. Meanwhile, many states, which were being pressed by interest groups and the citizenry to address daunting problems like health care, infrastructure financing, education, and economic development, had become centers of more policy activism than had been seen in years outside of the nation's capital.

4. *Administrative simplification.* The president worked to trim red tape and lighten the putative burden of federal mandates. In this regard, Reagan scored his "successes," as did his predecessors. Yet many complained about the abdication of federal responsibility for important national goals, and others felt the reforms did not go nearly far enough. Several years after Reagan's departure from the White House, the evidence accumulated that mandates from Washington had increased overall.

Reagan's efforts to restructure the intergovernmental system were challenged by many. By the second half of his first term, the most ambitious proposals had been set aside in favor of further grouping of categorical programs into block grants. Even these suggestions encountered hostility or indifference in Congress.

Nevertheless, the Reagan administration's efforts, and the complicated responses they stimulated, presaged a series of changes in the intergovernmental system as the century drew to a close.

Crosscurrents at Century's End: Struggles for Reform, Pressures toward Globalization

The administration of President George Bush did not signal a major departure from the intergovernmental trends of Reagan's second term, nor did President Bill Clinton seek to grab center stage with dramatic attempts to recraft the nature of the system. But by the middle of the 1990s events and influences from elsewhere had combined to place the American intergovernmental network in the midst of a variety of consequential forces. Most of the issues receiving attention during the Reagan years remained on the agenda, but shifts in political fortunes, economic conditions, and federalism jurisprudence combined during the 1990s to amplify the turbulence in the system. By the dawn of the twenty-first century the resolution of these influences is still uncertain, with forces pushing actively in quite different directions. But it is clear that a number of these recent developments will continue to be felt well into the new millennium. And it is equally clear that the prime characteristics of the system, complexity and interdependence, will continue to shape the details of intergovernmental bargaining and frustrate the efforts of reformers to impose or craft a clear and coherent design.

For instance, and perhaps most prominently, by 1995 the Republican leadership in Congress had swept to victory. They had touted a "Contract with America" that offered a governmental future in which Washington would retreat from policy activism and leadership, taxes would be cut, and subnational governments would be freed from the shackles of irksome and expensive unfunded mandates imposed by the center. Meaningful steps were taken to convert the Contract into a reality. The Republicans in Congress sought to impose tight budgetary discipline, even to cut many programs dramatically, and passed an Unfunded Mandates Reform Act (UMRA) during their first year in power. But with resistance from the Democratic president Clinton, as well as the unpopularity

of the apparent game of chicken between the branches culminating in the "shutdown" of government offices during 1995 and 1996, it became clear to the leadership in each branch that some accommodation with their counterpart institution would be necessary.

One result was a continuation, indeed increase, in intergovernmental assistance (see Table 1), even as politicians like Clinton announced that the era of big government was over. Leaders of both parties could find agreement on such aid useful as a means of acquiescing to the continuing realities of interdependence while also energizing and devolving discretion to other governments. The continuing appeal of block grants in this regard was obvious, with political leaders of both parties supporting these in principle even while disagreeing on many details. Significantly for the longer term, an important block grant, the program of Temporary Assistance to Needy Families, or TANF, was enacted in 1996, as part of the Personal Responsibility and Work Opportunity Reconciliation Act. This initiative ended the nationally supported Aid to Families with Dependent Children (AFDC) program, which had been the intergovernmental assistance effort at the core of the nation's social welfare protection for many of its poorest people.

AFDC as a categorical grant program had come to symbolize welfare, a program much maligned even if much less expensive than many had supposed. While Clinton and the Republican congressional leadership sought to glean advantage from the situation, they did agree to enact this major change in the nation's welfare policy—and major shift in responsibility "downward" to the states. TANF put an end to long-term welfare assistance, a frequent occurrence under the older program, and was designed to encourage welfare recipients to move permanently into the work force. The initiative also increased greatly the flexibility of states to shape their own approach—and their responsibility to fund the choices they made.

TANF symbolized, in a sense, one of the major currents in the turbulent intergovernmental maelstrom of the time: increased state discretion and innovation amid continuing intergovernmental ties.

While some observers continue to worry that states will use their energies to benefit the most privileged interests, and that enhanced state fiscal responsibilities inevitably signal less redistribution and social protection in many of the nation's poorest states, others see this shift as emblematic of a healthy recognition that state governments have become more professional, competent, and energetic, and that the states are better equipped to meet the challenges of the new century than is Washington.

Furthermore, with fiscal pressures mounting in expensive policy sectors like health, Republican policy makers in particular advocated replicating the TANF action with block grants to replace costly intergovernmental programs like Medicaid. Here the politics, the stakes, and the concern on the part of PIGs that they not be buried under huge and escalating costs made taking radical action much more difficult. Stalemate characterized much of the intergovernmental debate on health policy during the 1990s.

More generally, as well, the 1990s produced evidence aplenty, amidst the partisanship and turbulence in Washington, that simple and dramatic shifts in the intergovernmental system would be unlikely—even as substantial efforts were mounted to make things happen in a big way. The complexity and interdependence of the system— and the fact of the public's mixed and ambivalent attitudes toward such major changes—continued to produce nuanced and complicated results, even for all the attempts at systematization and "revolution."

A prime example has been the quixotic efforts at mandate reform. No one approves of unfunded mandates in principle, and yet their appearance escalated throughout the 1980s and into the 1990s. The Republican Contract with America called for their elimination. Meanwhile, the Democratic White House had initiated an administrative overhaul of the national government under the direction of Vice President Al Gore, the National Performance Review (NPR). NPR too called for a rationalizing of the nation's approach to intergovernmental relations; and, while avoiding the radical rhetoric of the

Contract, the NPR trumpeted the need for an end to unfunded mandates imposed on the states and localities. The UMRA had been enacted quickly, and yet years later it became clear that, while not completely ineffective, the act has been unsuccessful in legislating an end to the kinds of nationally initiated regulatory ties that stimulated its passage. As Paul Posner shows (reading no. 25 in this book), *both* political parties find reasons to support mandating, even if the mandates and policy sectors vary. And using legislation as a way of trying to prevent the intergovernmental regulation and associated (often acrimonious) bargaining does not address the more fundamental sources of these ties in the first place.

In the meantime, the UMRA also required the U.S. Advisory Commission on Intergovernmental Relations, a respected governmentally established forum for analysis and improvement of the system active since the 1950s, to undertake an examination of the nation's mandates with a view toward recommending the elimination of the most onerous. The requirement resulted in a staff-produced, strongly argued critique of national mandates with several specific suggestions for mandate reduction. These proposals in turn ignited a firestorm of protest, as coalitions of groups mobilized to protect the national standards and regulations they had worked so hard to see enacted, on policy matters ranging from the rights of the disabled to emissions controls under the Clean Air Act. The Clinton administration, which had expressed general support for controlling mandates, was nonetheless responsive to this pressure from parts of its core constituencies and resisted the ACIR staff's recommendations. The full commission rejected its own staff's recommendation as this long-standing intergovernmental body was caught in the crossfire, and shortly thereafter the ACIR was defunded. The commission has ceased to function.

The death of the ACIR is a prime example of the perils of today's American intergovernmental relations: while virtually everyone favors "reform" and "simplification," at least as general principles, the reality is that the complexity and interdependence endemic in the system are no accidents. They have emerged as products of a long series of function-specific demands and political supports for cost sharing, standard setting, and cross-governmental bargaining. Remaking the system on behalf of goals like allocating functions to "appropriate" levels of government, clarifying the often obscure mechanisms of intergovernmental influence and administration, and reducing fiscal pressures imposed from Washington can be expected to run afoul of intense support for problem solving and bargaining in adaptation to the crosscurrents of policy change. The general desire for "reform," coupled with the considerable difficulty in building a coalition supportive of concrete and significant steps in that direction, is not confined to one political party or another, nor is the tendency unique to the environment of Washington, D.C. The states, for instance, are themselves heavy imposers of mandates on their own local governments. Rather, the tension between pragmatic problem solving for concrete and pressing issues, on the one hand, and worthy but rather abstract desires for systemwide reform, on the other, has been a hallmark of intergovernmental relations throughout the past several decades. This uncomfortable tension is likely to continue.

Meanwhile, neither the jurisprudence of federalism nor economic developments are likely to catalyze an easy reform or simplification of the system. Although both spheres witnessed important events during the 1990s, the impacts overall have been complicated and somewhat uncertain.

The Supreme Court, for instance, stirred the waters with potentially important decisions aimed, in part, at protecting or reclaiming some distinctive policy space for subnational authorities. Perhaps most significantly, the Court voided a national law in *United States v. Lopez* (1995) on the grounds that Washington had enacted a policy with no connection to interstate commerce. This limitation on national authority was the first since the 1930s decided on these grounds, and some observers have become hopeful—or fearful—that the federal judiciary might begin to establish national-state boundaries limiting the reach and interdependence in the system. The pattern nonetheless remains uncertain, with other precedents during the last two decades suggesting support for national author-

ity.[16] Evidence on both tendencies is examined in some of the readings in this book.

Similarly, economic developments in recent years have had important effects on the system but have not constituted a force for reform or simplification. During his administration, for instance, President Clinton was not an ardent advocate for subnational governments—thus disappointing some who had hoped his experience as governor of Arkansas would make him especially sensitive to the needs and potential of the states, in particular. But this period did see significant increases in intergovernmental aid, as discussed above, despite a budget politics in Washington focused primarily on issues like tax reductions and "saving" Social Security. This more supportive fiscal development was a trend often neglected in the much more visible war over mandates.

Even this tendency, however, was complex. The growth in federal aid was concentrated in a few sectors and devoted primarily to big increases in spending for transfer payments. In many other spheres, the purse strings remained remarkably tight. And local governments have scrambled to replace national funding for some of their programs with state aid and alternative sources. The PIGs, which in earlier decades had organized into nationally important forces with the onset of large-scale federal assistance, struggled to define new roles of comparable influence in the lingering era of budgetary constraint. And the federal government continued to seek day-to-day influence through the channels of the hundreds of existing programs and the scattering of new ones enacted in recent years. All these participants continue to jockey for influence in the interdependent, complex, and fiscally strained system.

And as if this intricate pattern were not complex enough, increasing economic pressures toward globalization have now added another set of actors and considerations to the constraints and opportunities in the intergovernmental system. Business and market connections around the world—and, importantly, national governmental commitments to international agreements in a multitude of policy sectors—have pulled city managers, state economic development experts, local and state education specialists, and national environmental policy makers, among many others, into the ambit of forces and constraints emanating from abroad. In these crosscurrents of (primarily economic) influence, the bargaining has begun to include more parties and more options, for at least some of the decision makers. The overall system is, furthermore, even less transparent to citizens—with potential implications for responsiveness and the quality of democratic life. And potent pressures to extend and concentrate national influence to deal effectively with global forces have begun to penetrate domestic intergovernmental decision making.

The dizzying transformations at the end of the century, then, have resulted in an intergovernmental arrangement buffeted by a variety of shifts and shocks. Certainly the system differs in key respects from the one in place at the dawn of the Reagan period, for instance. And yet any vision of radical simplification—like that articulated by Reagan or, for that matter, by the congressional leadership during the 1990s—can be seen as chimerical. The notion of a dual federalism that could meet the challenges of the new century, of the nation's needs and aspirations in an increasingly interdependent world, seems increasingly remote, for all the apparent agreement on the attractiveness of reform and rationality. Despite the crosscurrents, regardless of the multiple developments of the last several years, the most fundamental aspects of American intergovernmental relations, including the strengths, weaknesses, frustrations, and dilemmas of the pattern, have remained prominent.

There is no denying that the form of the system has changed considerably since the nation's founding. Political, economic, and social forces have stimulated major changes in the overall scope of governmental activity, in the mix of values that intergovernmental arrangements are meant to serve, in the relative influence of the different governments, and in their degree of reliance on one another. Far from preserving a simple, stratified pattern, the choices made centuries ago created opportunities for dramatic shifts toward new forms of interdependence and complexity in the intergovernmental network.

Notes

1. Thus the term *federal* has two meanings in contemporary usage. One refers to a system of governance that employs a constitutional partitioning of authority between central and regional units. The other is as a synonym for the national government. Both notions are employed in this chapter and in various readings throughout the book. The meaning should be clear from the context.

2. U.S. Bureau of the Census, *1992 Census of Governments,* vol. 1, no. 1, *Governmental Organization* (Washington, D.C.: U.S. Government Printing Office, 1994), v.

3. Federalist No. 10, *The Federalist Papers,* ed. Clinton Rossiter (New York: New American Library, 1961), 77.

4. At the time, the term *federation* had a meaning close to that of *confederation* today. See Martin Diamond's essay in this book (no. 2). The meaning changed after the initiation of the American experiment in federated government.

5. The concepts of federalism (in the first sense mentioned in note 1) and intergovernmental relations are linked but not identical. The former refers to certain aspects of the dealings between national and regional governments, while the latter is meant to encompass relations among all governments within a nation. Intergovernmental relations are considerably affected but not completely determined by federalism. This book examines federalism but focuses broadly on intergovernmental relations. Nevertheless, interstate and interlocal relations receive relatively less attention because of space limitations.

6. One example is Madison's veto of a bill to authorize construction of roads and canals in the states. See Daniel J. Elazar, *The American Partnership: Intergovernmental Cooperation in the Nineteenth Century* (Chicago: University of Chicago Press, 1962), 15.

7. Ibid.

8. The terms *recipient* and *donor* are borrowed from Jeffrey L. Pressman, *Federal Programs and City Politics* (Berkeley: University of California Press, 1975).

9. American Council on Intergovernmental Relations, *Significant Features of Fiscal Federalism 1995,* vol. 2, *Revenues and Expenditures* (Albany, N.Y.: Nelson A. Rockefeller Institute of Government, February 1998), 9.

10. The cases were *Massachusetts v. Mellon* and *Frothingham v. Mellon,* 262 U.S. 447 (1923).

11. As explained later in this chapter, this experiment proved temporary. Federal financial constraints during the Carter and Reagan administrations persuaded Congress to follow presidential recommendations; the program was ended for state and then local governments, respectively.

12. See Morton Grodzins's classic essay in Part I of this volume (no. 3).

13. For example, David B. Walker, *Toward a Functioning Federalism* (Cambridge, Mass.: Winthrop, 1981); and see Deil S. Wright, *Understanding Intergovernmental Relations,* 3d ed. (Pacific Grove, Calif.: Brooks/Cole, 1988), 94.

14. See Norman Furniss and Timothy Tilton, *The Case for the Welfare State: From Social Security to Social Equality* (Bloomington: Indiana University Press, 1977); and John E. Schwarz, *America's Hidden Success: A Reassessment of Twenty Years of Public Policy* (New York: Norton, 1988).

15. Thomas Anton, *American Federalism and Public Policy: How the System Work* (Philadelphia: Temple University Press 1989).

16. *United States v. Lopez,* 115 S.Ct. 142 (1995).

☐ CASE STUDY 5

Introduction

In the foregoing essay, Professor O'Toole clearly and concisely presents an overview of the development of American intergovernmental relations as an important aspect of American government. He stresses that the contemporary nature of IGR particularly entails three characteristics: interdependency, complexity and bargaining among officials. How do these major features of IGR influence the practice of modern public administration? Shape the work of local government officials? Affect the outcomes of what they do?

The following case, "Wichita Confronts Contamination," by Susan Rosegrant of Harvard's John F. Kennedy School of Government, illustrates well several of the themes discussed in O'Toole's essay. In the summer of 1990, the Kansas Department of Health and Environment (KDHE), acting on behalf of the federal Environmental Protection Agency (EPA), reported that Wichita, Kansas, was sitting on a vast underground polluted lake of various commercial and industrial chemicals. It was located beneath the central downtown business district, called the Gilbert-Mosley site, and the hazardous chemicals were known to cause cancer and other health problems. The report said the contamination was spreading about a foot a day, and it was feared that serious community health problems and water quality deterioration would result if this underground pollution went unchecked. Besides the very vocal public outcry for government to "do something about the problem," the report also triggered an immediate reaction from the banking community which stopped making loans to downtown residential and commercial owners in the Gilbert-Mosley area, thereby causing serious economic repercussions. What should the city do to protect its environment and economy—indeed the very health of its citizens?

In the following case, the city manager, Chris Cherches, who is faced with the responsibility of drafting a plan of action to deal with this crisis, must work with various intergovernmental bodies such as the KDHE and EPA to frame options and devise a strategy to clean up the affected site. In the process, Cherches achieves a workable plan, but one that very much develops within—and depends on—an IGR framework, as described in the O'Toole essay.

As you read this case, try to think about:

How did IGR entities help to identify the problem, then frame the options for the city manager, and finally help him create a workable plan of action for the affected site?

Why were the environmental problems—*and* the IGR problems—so complex in this case?

Can you identify the negotiations among the various IGR actors in this story that occurred. Why were these negotiations so critical to dealing with Wichita's contamination?

In general what does this case tell us about the importance of IGR to the work of public administrators in the 1990s? And the IGR features of interdependency, complexity, and political bargaining?

Wichita Confronts Contamination

SUSAN ROSEGRANT

In the summer of 1990, the central business district of Wichita, Kansas, faced familiar problems of urban decline, along with the prospect of revitalization.

This case was written by Susan Rosegrant for Professor Alan Altshuler, director of the Taubman Center for State and Local Government at the John F. Kennedy School of Government, for use at the Program on Innovation in State and Local Government "CEO Symposium," September 24–26, 1992. Funding provided by the Ford Foundation. (1292)

Source: Case Program, John F. Kennedy School of Government, Harvard University, Parts A & B C16-92-1157.0 & C16-92-1158.0

The downturn in the regional oil and gas industry had exacerbated the nationwide real estate slump, leaving downtown Wichita stagnant. At the same time, local business leaders were pursuing a common formula for renewal: a project relying on substantial public improvements to leverage new private investment, a $375 million undertaking in all.

In downtown Wichita, however, a special problem was brewing. Hazardous chemicals known to cause cancer and other health problems had been detected in some private and industrial wells in Wichita's core area. Banks were growing more careful about requiring site inspections, and even soil and water sampling, before they would grant loans. And in June, local manufacturer Coleman Co., Inc., the venerable maker of camp stoves and other outdoor equipment, approached the city's legal department for advice about a contamination problem it had first discovered during routine tests in the fall of 1988.

In late August, the calm was shattered as the pieces of bad news suddenly fit together to form a frightening whole. The Kansas Department of Health and Environment (KDHE), acting on behalf of the Environmental Protection Agency (EPA), reported that Wichita was sitting on an underground lake polluted by a variety of commercial and industrial chemicals. The area of contamination—dubbed the Gilbert and Mosley site after a street intersection near its center—was extensive, covering a plot about four miles long and one-and-one-half miles wide. Moreover, the polluted aquifer lay squarely beneath the city's central business district. The 8,000 parcels affected had an assessed value of about $86 million. Major banks, hotels, industrial headquarters, and homes all lay in the six-square-mile area. The worst pollution, consisting of high concentrations of trichloroethene, a chemical degreaser used to clean metal parts before painting, was found at Coleman's headquarters at the north end of the site.

Although KDHE had completed a preliminary study on Gilbert-Mosley the previous November, the August 1990 Listing Site Investigation was the first comprehensive contamination report that City Manager Chris Cherches had seen. According to his office's quick estimates, to clean the aquifer could cost as much as $20 million and take as long as 20 years. KDHE offered just two options in its report recommendations: either the companies responsible for the contamination could band together to clean up the area, or the state would rank the site for National Priority Listing, the first step toward activating Superfund.[1]

Contamination Fallout

The Wichita community did not view Gilbert-Mosley as a serious health risk. Although the contamination was moving south at the rate of about a foot a day, the polluted aquifer lay 15 feet below the surface and was not used for drinking water. "Kansas is not that concerned about water quality," explained William Cather, chair of the Sierra Club's

small Kansas chapter. "We are concerned about water quantity."

But the potential economic impact of the contamination had the community up in arms. KDHE's report identified 508 area businesses as Potentially Responsible Parties (PRPs) under Superfund law. If Gilbert-Mosley became a Superfund site, all of these businesses would be potentially liable for cleanup costs regardless of whether they had contributed to the contamination. In the days following release of the Listing Site Investigation, KDHE received a barrage of phone calls from business owners anxious to understand the implications of their PRP status.

Even more threatening, however, was the response of the financial community. Just a few months earlier, in *US vs. Fleet Factors Corp.*, the US 11th Circuit Court in Atlanta had ruled that a lender may incur Superfund liability "by participating in financial management to a degree indicating a capacity to influence the corporation's treatment of hazardous wastes."[2]

Simply put, the ruling opened lenders to Superfund liability. Not only that, because of their relatively "deep pockets," financial institutions made ideal targets for Superfund cleanup cost recovery.

In the wake of the dramatic report, Wichita bankers took abrupt action, halting virtually all lending activity in Gilbert-Mosley, the heart of the city. "I don't think you could have hit a banker over the head with a two-by-four and gotten him to make a loan then," declared J.V. Lentell, chairman of the Kansas State Bank and Trust Co. "We already knew property values were plummeting in the downtown area. Downtown was drying up. It was the last thing we needed."

The banks' redlining had an immediate impact on both commercial and residential property owners. David C. Burk, for example, an architect turned developer, had formed an investment company to de-

---

[1]Congress created Superfund, the Comprehensive Environmental Response, Compensation and Liability Act of 1980 (CERCLA), to give EPA the resources to clean up hazardous waste sites nationwide. Six years later, Congress passed the Superfund Amendments and Reauthorization Act of 1986 in an attempt to improve what critics had characterized as a sluggish and ineffective program.

[2]David R. Tripp, "Wichita Strikes Back at the Blob," *Toxics Law Reporter*, June 25, 1991.

velop restaurant, retail, apartment, and office space in a few blocks of abandoned brick warehouses near Coleman's headquarters. Although he had drilled 20 test holes without finding contamination before launching his ill-timed venture, all three buildings he had contracts on, as well as those he had options to buy, fell within the contaminated zone. "As soon as Gilbert-Mosley came in, we lost our investors," he reported grimly. Residents were similarly affected, as they found it suddenly impossible to sell their homes. "There were hundreds of tragedies wrapped up here," declared Mayor Bob Knight. "I started getting calls from sons and daughters, trying to make provisions for a parent who was left alone and aged, who were unable to liquidate property."

As city government struggled in the days following the report's release to understand and respond to the crisis, it became clear that the twin threats of uncertain liability and the bank-imposed real estate freeze posed a substantial hazard to the city's tax base. Properties in the area had generated more than $12 million of the $203 million in local property taxes the previous year, but already, the county appraiser's office was receiving requests for reduced valuations. If all Gilbert-Mosley properties lost substantial value, or were frozen for months, or even years, not only would the redevelopment plan die, but the entire core area would be threatened. "When the groundwater problem came along," recalled city attorney Thomas R. Powell, "it looked like it was going to be the death knell."

The City Weighs Its Options

City Manager Cherches, who faced the immediate responsibility for drafting a plan, enlisted a cadre of staffers to study KDHE's two recommended options. In evaluating the possibilities, Cherches stressed that two priorities remained uppermost: to begin cleaning up the aquifer as soon as possible, and to preserve property values. The only way to do that: convince the banks to resume lending in the area.

1) *Let Companies Responsible for Contamination Clean Up the Site*

The first impulse on the part of some of Cherches's staff was to encourage Coleman and other polluters

to take charge of the Gilbert-Mosley site. "In the very early stages, it was viewed as a business problem," recalled Mark Glaser, special assistant to the manager for management research. "The businesses contributed to the contamination. The businesses are basically responsible for cleaning up the contamination." Added city attorney Powell, "Our hope was that somehow Coleman would solve the problem."

But history argued strongly against this choice. Gilbert-Mosley was not the city's first experience with contaminated sites. Three years earlier, groundwater contamination had been discovered at a smaller site about two miles north of Gilbert-Mosley, known as 29th and Mead. There, also, the banks had stopped lending, and the county appraiser had lowered property values 40 percent. A group of about 100 potentially responsible parties at the site, including both the city and Coleman, had formed a PRP group to strike an agreement on how to pay for the initial EPA-required Remedial Investigation and Feasibility Study (RI/FS), which would identify sources and types of contamination along with remediation methods. But group negotiations had become divisive, then stalled, and the state had already placed the site on the National Priorities List (NPL). If the group fared no better in determining ultimate cleanup liability, it would face full implementation of Superfund and many years of real estate paralysis.

Given this experience, it seemed highly unlikely that the more than 500 PRPs at Gilbert-Mosley would be able to reach a timely agreement on liability. In addition, it was questionable whether Coleman would cooperate. Although the company had been a lead party at 29th and Mead, it had not pushed for a speedy resolution. Moreover, while Coleman acknowledged that it had found some pollution at its Gilbert-Mosley site, it was already discounting its responsibility for the overall contamination. Remarked city attorney Powell, "When they said they were going to pay for what they were responsible for, I didn't know if we would ever *agree* on what they were responsible for." If a PRP group at Gilbert-Mosley fared no better than the one at 29th and Mead, there would be no quick cleanup in sight, and no incentive for banks to resume lending until the threat of contamination had been removed.

2) *Rank the Site for Possible Superfund Status*

As unproductive as forming a PRP group might appear, Cherches and his staff soon concluded that KDHE's second option—to allow the site to be ranked for Superfund—was far less appealing.

If EPA became directly involved, Cherches learned, the cost of cleaning up Gilbert-Mosley would increase dramatically. The agency typically hired an oversight contractor, for example, to watch over the work of the regular contractor—a step that automatically added up to 40 percent to the cleanup bill. In addition, possible polluters faced the prospect of paying for the administrative oversight of EPA itself; the Superfund law called on EPA staffers to charge their time to the private firms. Moreover, EPA was allowed to overcharge as a means of replenishing its cleanup fund and punishing noncomplying businesses.

The threat of prolonged multi-party litigation was an even bigger deterrent to reliance on Superfund. Because any business in a contaminated area could be held responsible for cleanup costs, regardless of its contribution, lawyers played a major part in any Superfund resolution, as polluters sought to spread the blame, and faultless property owners struggled to avoid liability. In fact, Superfund law spread potential liability to such a broad number of parties, many of whom were wholly innocent, that any hope of quick resolution became mired in stalling tactics and litigation. This legal wrangling, along with third party lawsuits against polluters seeking damages due to contamination-related declines in property values, had given rise to Superfund's nickname as "The Lawyers' Full Employment Act of 1980." One city that Cherches talked to reported that its $30 million cleanup had sparked an estimated $700 million in civil law suits. A study commissioned by the American Insurance Association estimated that cleaning up 1,800 Superfund sites would generate $8 billion in legal fees.[3]

Finally, both litigation, and the oversight and administrative steps that EPA requires, add years to a typical Superfund cleanup. Of the average 10 years taken to clean up a site, seven are spent on study and assessment, legal proceedings, and crafting a remedy before the actual cleanup begins.[4] Judging from this track record, if Gilbert-Mosley became a Superfund site, it would be years before cleanup could even start.

According to Mayor Knight, who consulted a number of other mayors about Gilbert-Mosley, cities with major contamination problems faced a bleak prognosis. "I couldn't find any successful models," he recalled. "The only thing we found was failure: division, frustration, assigning blame, financial ruin, and, ultimately, the very worst thing that can happen to people who love cities, decline."

Special Assistant Glaser also placed successive phone calls in a desperate bid to find a new alternative:

> What we kept hearing was, "I can't tell you what to do, but do something. Don't let it go Superfund. Once it goes Superfund, you're in trouble." We knew we had to do something, but nobody knew what that something would be.

A Third Option

Cherches rejected both of KDHE's options, and made up his mind fast. Within a week of the Listing Site Investigation's release, he decided to risk a major leap from existing precedents. Although no one had accused Wichita of being a polluter, and although the city had not even been listed as a PRP, Cherches proposed that the city take full responsibility for the Gilbert-Mosley cleanup. In doing so, Wichita would attempt to sidestep the time and resources normally spent on Superfund-related litigation, and to create some mechanism to get banks to start lending in the contaminated area again.

The most obvious and immediate barrier to a city-led cleanup was finding an acceptable way to finance it. Cherches was determined that Coleman and other contributors would pay as much as possible for the contamination they had caused. But the city could not count on recouping all cleanup costs from responsible polluters. Some likely contributors were no longer in business, for example, and others lacked the resources to support their share of the cleanup. Moreover, in order to sell the idea to the state and EPA, the city would have to prove it had the funds available to support what could be a 20-year project without relying on uncertain corporate contributions.

---

[3]Marc K. Landy and Mary Hague, "Private Interests and Superfund," *The Public Interest*, No. 108, Summer 1992.

[4]E. Donald Elliott, "Superfund: EPA Success, National Debacle?" *Natural Resources & Environment*, Vol. 6, No. 3, Winter 1992.

Cherches's staff prepared a list of financing alternatives, and the most powerful argument against each, as follows:

- *Establish a special assessment district:* All property owners in the area would be charged an assessment to cover the cost of cleanup. Likely to create an uproar over the inequity of making a large group, comprised mostly of innocent property owners, pay for the pollution of a few.
- *Issue bonds:* Taxes would be raised throughout the city to help pay off the bonds. Could cause a property tax revolt, and would require a change in state statute to allow bonds to be used for ongoing maintenance of the cleanup program.
- *Create a tax increment finance district:* Would dedicate an increment of Gilbert-Mosley property taxes—bolstered by the cleanup—to pay for the program. An untried use of this concept, and, like the bond option, would require a change in state legislation.
- *County pay entire cost, with state assistance:* Based on rationale that the economic health of Wichita is important to the entire county. Would face certain opposition from the county, which believed polluters should pay the tab. The county might seek state reimbursement.
- *Impose a statewide tax:* Would spread the burden to the broadest number of constituents. Certain to provoke strong opposition from a rural state uninterested in solving Wichita's industrial problems.

In addition to the backing of the Wichita City Council, most of these plans would require the approval of the Sedgwick County Council, as well as the Wichita School Board, since their tax bases would be affected.

Even with a financing mechanism in place, though, a city-led plan would face a number of additional obstacles. Politically, the concept probably wouldn't fly unless Coleman and other contributors could be held at least partially accountable. "Some of the very early public response was, 'Why would the city get involved and commit our tax dollars?' " recalled Glaser. "We were thinking of signing on

the dotted line to say we would be responsible for $20 million. Politically and fiscally, that doesn't wash. It's not even reasonable." Unfortunately, if the city wanted to take charge, it would have to make a commitment long before it knew the likelihood of getting major contributors other than Coleman to pay.

Cherches would also have to convince EPA, which had a reputation for being bureaucratic and inflexible, that the city had the resources and the commitment to take on such an unusual arrangement. There was no record of any city ever having stepped in to accept liability for a contamination problem it had not caused.

In addition, unless Wichita could come up with a way to revive lending in the contaminated district, it wouldn't make any difference who was responsible for the cleanup. The central business district could not afford to wait 20 years for life to return to normal.

Finally, a survey of the obstacles made it clear that the ultimate success of the plan would depend on a complex collaboration between multiple, and sometimes opposed, constituencies, including the city manager's office, the city council, the county commission, the school board, lenders, Coleman, KDHE, the state legislature, the governor, and EPA.

KDHE had already warned the city that it would have to report to EPA in January about progress at the Gilbert-Mosley site. Unless a cleanup plan had taken shape, the state would recommend that EPA take over. If Wichita was unable to solve any one of the obstacles it faced, it would have to confront the inevitability of Superfund, with all that could imply for the devastation of the city's core.

Developing the Plan

Wichita City Manager Chris Cherches moved fast to begin consolidating support for a city-led cleanup of the Gilbert-Mosley site. In order to present the plan to the various constituencies that would have to approve it, the city first had to decide how to pay for it. After weighing alternatives, Cherches concluded that creating a tax increment finance (TIF) district would be the most equitable and politically palatable way to raise funds. The city's approach, however, was a novel twist on the traditional TIF concept. Typically, a TIF district is set up in an area slated for redevelopment. After city-backed improvements are in place, the difference between the old, depressed property assessments and the new, higher values that have resulted from the improvements creates an increment that is then used to pay for the revitalization effort.

Wichita, by contrast, proposed what could be called a tax "decrement" plan: as a result of the contamination, the city would devalue all the property in the Gilbert-Mosley area—for example, by the 40 percent that property had dropped at the 29th and Mead contamination site—and then would immediately raise values back to their pre-contamination level, under the argument that the city plan would restore lost value. The difference would create the increment to be set aside each year to finance the cleanup. Although the city could find no examples of TIF being used to support environmental remediation, Glaser felt it was an ideal use of the concept. "This seemed like it really fit what the full intent of TIF was designed to do," he declared.

The city's initial talks with the Kansas Department of Health and Environment (KDHE) about assuming responsibility for Gilbert-Mosley had been encouraging. With the TIF proposal in place, KDHE became openly enthusiastic. Cherches began negotiating a plan for the state to oversee Wichita's cleanup in EPA's stead, thereby avoiding the agency's usual high oversight costs. After presenting the proposed plan to the public, and winning the unanimous approval of the city council, he next approached the local financial community.

Lenders, Cherches soon discovered, made eager allies. After all, they risked not only losing the value of their Gilbert-Mosley investments, but of being held liable for the actual cleanup. They also understood the importance to Wichita's economy—and to their own businesses—of returning real estate activity in the contaminated area to normal. But bankers would not resume lending until they had some sort of legal protection from cleanup liability in place.

The concept that the city and the lenders devised to satisfy this need was deceptively simple. Innocent property owners, including residents, businesses, and banks, could apply to the city for a document called the Certificate and Release for Environmental Conditions. If granted, the document would release the holder from any cleanup liability. With such a release in hand, properties could again be bought and sold without the specter of potential Superfund liability. But while the banking community overall embraced the plan, it would not implement it until the city had received EPA's assurance that it would not take over the site, negoti-

ated firm agreements with KDHE and Coleman, and pushed through the changes in state law necessary to allow tax increment financing to be used for a long-term project.

Final Negotiations

Getting EPA's backing was easier than the city had expected. Cherches proposed that Wichita would follow all the usual EPA steps and requirements in cleaning up Gilbert-Mosley, but with KDHE acting as the primary oversight agency. Throughout the process, the city would report regularly to EPA on its progress. Although the city had expected some opposition, EPA actually had a great deal to gain and very little to lose: If the city succeeded, the agency could declare a victory with minimal expense or effort on its part. Conversely, if the plan failed, there was nothing to keep EPA from stepping in and implementing Superfund. After just one meeting in late November, Morris Kay, director of EPA's four-state Region VII, agreed in principle to support both the city-led plan and the state's offer to oversee the process. Although there was no written agreement guaranteeing that EPA would not intervene, Kay assured the city that as long as it was operating according to agency requirements, it would not intercede.

With EPA's support secure, the city still faced a major legislative challenge. A Kansas state law designed to ensure fiscal responsibility, the Cash Basis and Budget law, would not let local government commit operating revenues beyond one year. Wichita needed an exception to that law, and an amendment to TIF law, in order to be able to commit funds raised from a TIF district to a long-term environmental cleanup. Without the changes, the city would be unable to contract with KDHE to take on and finance what could be a 20-year effort.

Getting legislative approval of the TIF bill promised to be a struggle. The Cash Basis law was, in Cherches's words, a "sacred cow" that the legislature was loathe to touch. In addition, the traditional antagonism that existed between urban Wichita and the largely rural legislature was certain to complicate the bill's chances for passage. The city had to dispel the impression that its plan might be geared in Coleman's favor, a difficult task with the company's liability agreement still in negotiation. Moreover, because Kansas's part-time legislature met only from January through April, the city had a limited window of opportunity to prove the merits of its plan.

Wichita's credibility wasn't helped in March when both the county assessor and the state property valuation director declared unworkable the city's original proposal to establish a tax increment by first lowering and then raising assessed property values. In its place, three Sedgwick County legislators responsible for reviewing the TIF bill worked with the city to craft a new amendment that allowed municipalities in the state that met narrowly defined requirements to earmark 20 percent of a specially created TIF district's base year property taxes, on an annual basis, for environmental cleanups. If the bill passed, Wichita would be able to reserve up to 20 percent of the first year's Gilbert-Mosley property tax revenues to use for groundwater cleanup each year, for the next 20 years.

On March 26, Wichita signed a consent decree with KDHE, spelling out the city's responsibilities, what KDHE's oversight obligations would be, and how the Certificate and Release program would work. But the major obstacle to legislative approval, the Coleman agreement, was not resolved until April 23, slightly more than a week before the legislature adjourned. The agreement divided the contaminated site into three zones: Coleman agreed to pay all cleanup costs for the area where it was the main polluter; it would split costs with the city in a second area where it was a contributor to contamination; and the city would be responsible for cleanup and cost recovery in the final area, where most of the pollution came from other sources. In addition, the camping equipment manufacturer agreed to pay $1 million for the initial Remedial Investigation/Feasibility Study required by EPA.

Although Special Assistant Glaser had expected the Coleman negotiations to be perhaps the biggest barrier to settlement, the manufacturer actually had good cause to settle. The agreement allowed Coleman to convey a responsible civic and environmental image, an important consideration for a maker of outdoor equipment. In addition, if Gilbert-Mosley had become a Superfund site, Coleman would have faced substantially higher costs, and would have been left vulnerable to almost endless third-party lawsuits. In fact, Coleman had already been sued by property owners seeking damages due to contamination-related declines in property values. "I feel we got a pretty good deal from Coleman," said city attorney Thomas Powell. "They needed it as badly as we did."

One week after the Coleman agreement was signed, the Kansas legislature approved the TIF bill, and Cherches began meeting again with the finan-

cial community the next day. On May 14, several major local banks signed an agreement not to refuse to lend on the security of real properties within Gilbert-Mosley if the owner had obtained a Certificate and Release for Environmental Conditions. With the start of the Certificate and Release program on August 2, there was no longer a reason for contamination, alone, to block real estate transactions in the Gilbert-Mosley site.

Epilogue

In August 1992, one year after the Certificate and Release program began, life had begun to return to normal in the Gilbert-Mosley area:

- The city of Wichita had granted more than 800 Certificate and Release forms. Some property owners just outside of the contaminated area had petitioned for inclusion, hoping to receive certificates that would remove all stigma of potential liability from their properties.
- Bank IV, one of Wichita's major lenders, had closed 11 loans in Gilbert-Mosley for a total of $6.4 million.
- Developer David Burk, who received the first Certificate and Release from the city, had wooed back investors to his redevelopment project, and had opened four restaurants and two retail stores in the contaminated area.
- The three plaintiffs in the first court case against Coleman received only $86,000, about one-fifth of what they had requested, after the jury ruled that as a result of the city-led cleanup plan, pollution-caused damage to downtown property values was temporary, not permanent. Thomas Powell, who had left his position as city attorney to enter private practice, appeared as an expert witness on Coleman's behalf to describe how the city plan had restored property values.
- Camp, Dresser & McKee, Inc., the environmental consultant hired by the city, was about to release the results of the Remedial Investigation/Feasibility Study, a site analysis that typically takes as long as five years to complete under Superfund.
- The business community had begun pushing forward on more modest plans for redevelop-

ment. "The contamination is not even something that is widely discussed anymore," declared Mayor Bob Knight, "yet it could have been a total calamity for the city."

Gilbert-Mosley was still a depressed area, as it had been before the contamination was discovered.

But with the city's plan in place, Knight once again had hope that the core downtown area might be rejuvenated. "If people are sufficiently committed to resolving complicated challenges, they can do extraordinary things," he declared. "I believe this is a moment in this community's history when we did something extraordinary."

Chapter 5 Review Questions

1. Why are federalism and intergovernmental relations so critical to effective program performance in the public sector today? What is the difference between federalism and IGR? What were the founding fathers' rationale for establishing U.S. government in this federal manner?

2. What has been the recent practice of intergovernmental relations in the United States according to Laurence J. O'Toole, Jr.? When and why did this IGR pattern emerge?

3. In what ways did the Wichita case study illustrate some of the characteristics and dilemmas of modern intergovernmental relations?

4. Who were the key IGR actors in this case, and how did they "calculate" to secure their own interests? Do you think that they successfully handled and resolved the complex issue? In particular, why was Cherches role so critical?

5. What does the case study say about the role and importance of experts involved in IGR? Who were the experts in this case and how did they derive their professional standards? Is there a problem that their specialized expertise may not always be applied in the public interest? What safeguards are available to ensure that these experts will be guided by the broad public interest?

6. What does the case study say about the significance of political bargaining and coalition-building in IGR and its role in influencing outcomes? Can these political dimensions of IGR be pointed out in Case Study 3, "Dumping $2.6 Million on Bakersfield"?

Key Terms

federalism	Sixteenth Amendment	Tenth Amendment
PIGs	ACIR	policy sectors
intergovernmental relations	project grants	creative federalism
state discretion	marble-cake federalism	unfunded mandates
dual federalism	land grants	vertical functional autocrats
Garcia Decision	general revenue sharing	interdependence
categorical grants	formula grants	complexity
formulas grant	performance standards	intergovernmental bargaining
block grants	crosscutting requirements	Reagan's atttempted IGR
intergovernmental network	The New Federalism	revolution
grants-in-aid		

Suggestions for Further Reading

Some of the best up-to-date sources of information on the changing world of intergovernmental relations can be found in *The National Journal*. Timothy Conlan, *New Federalism: Intergovernmental Reform from Nixon to Reagan* (Washington, D.C.: Brookings, 1998) offers one of the best accounts of IGR during the past three decades and for a fine analysis of the development of American federalism, read Samuel H. Beer, *To Make a Nation: The Rediscovery of American Federalism* (Cambridge, Mass.: Harvard University Press, 1993).

There are also a number of excellent "overviews" available, including Deil S. Wright, *Understanding Intergovernmental Relations,* Fourth Edition (Monterey, Calif.: Brooks/Cole Publishing, 1995); Paul E. Peterson, *What Price Federalism?* (Washington, D.C.: The Brookings Institution, 1995); Robert Stoker, *Reluctant Partners* (Pittsburgh, Pa: Pittsburgh University Press, 1991); and David R. Berman, "Relating to Other Governments," in Charldean Newell, ed., *The Effective Local Government Manager,* Second Edition. (Washington, D.C.: ICMA, 1993), pp. 167–198; and David B. Walker, *The Rebirth of Federalism* (Chatham, N.J.: Chatham House, 1995).

Serious students of IGR also should begin by reading the U.S. Constitution and *The Federalist Papers.* The Kesnbaum Commission Report (June 1955), which contains information still helpful for understanding modern IGR, as well as other basic documents on IGR is contained in Richard J. Stillman, *Basic Documents of American Public Administration Since 1950* (New York: Holmes and Meier, 1982). Laurence J. O'Toole, Jr., ed., *American Intergovernmental Relations,* Third Edition (Washington, D.C.: Congressional Quarterly, 2000); Lewis G. Bender and James A. Stever, *Administering the New Federalism* (Boulder, Colo.: Westview Press, 1986); as well as Deil S. Wright and Harvey L. White, eds., *Federalism and Intergovernmental Relations* (Washington, D.C.: American Society for Public Administration, 1984) offer outstanding collections of current and classic IGR essays. For survey essays on federalism by distinguished scholars in this field, see the entire issue of *The Annals of the American Academy of Political and Social Science* (May 1990), edited by John Kincaid, and entitled "American Federalism: The Third Century." Where we are with the research in this field today is summarized by Vincent L. Marando and Patricia S. Florestano, "Intergovernmental Management: The State of the Discipline," in Naomi B. Lynn and Aaron Wildavsky, eds., *Public Administration: The State of the Discipline* (Chatham, N.J.: Chatham House, 1990).

For an outstanding model of academic research on federalism and IGR, see Martha Derthick *The Influence of Federal Grants* (Cambridge, MA: Harvard University Press, 1970).

CHAPTER 6

Internal Dynamics: The Concept of the Informal Group

F or all of us the feeling of security and certainty derives always from assured membership of a group. If this is lost, no monetary gain, no job guarantee, can be sufficient compensation. Where groups change ceaselessly as jobs and mechanical processes change, the individual inevitably experiences a sense of void, of emptiness. . . .

Elton Mayo

READING 6

Introduction

Public administration was never the primary concern of Elton Mayo and Fritz Roethlisberger. Most of their research efforts centered around the study of business enterprises at the Harvard Business School, yet their impact on general administrative thought has been significant principally because from their investigations developed the *human relations* or *industrial sociological school* in organization theory. This school of thought emphasizes understanding and improving the dynamics of the internal human group within complex organizations; it was both a product of and a reaction to the scientific-management movement of the early part of this century. Frederick W. Taylor, an early founder of scientific management, had stressed that from the rational study of industrial organizations, "principles" of efficient, economical management could be derived.

Similarly, Elton Mayo, Fritz Roethlisberger, and a team of researchers from the Harvard Business School set out in 1927 at Western Electric's Hawthorne Electric Plant in Cicero, Illinois, near Chicago, to measure scientifically the effect of changes in the external environment on workers' output; they studied such matters as more or less lighting, shorter or longer lunch breaks, and increased or decreased hours in the work week. Their goal at first, like the goal of scientific management, was to discover the most efficient way to motivate workers. The Hawthorne Plant manufactured phones and telecommunications equipment for American Telephone and Telegraph (AT&T), employing at the time more than 40,000 workers. The company encouraged the Mayo-Roethlisberger experiments as part of its generally considered progressive management practices (progressive at least for that era).

While following the same methods as Taylor's scientific-management research, the Mayo-Roethlisberger team paradoxically arrived at different conclusions and insights from those of Taylor and his followers. The results of five years of intense study at the Hawthorne Plant revealed that the *primary work group* (that is, the relationships between workers and their supervisors and among workers themselves), had as much if not more impact on productivity as the formal physical surroundings and economic benefits derived from the job. For many, the Hawthorne experiment came "as the great illumination," or as Roethlisberger more modestly described it, "the systematic exploitation of the simple and obvious." It underscored a fundamental truth, obscured for some time by scientific-management theories, namely, that the employees of an organization constituted its basis, and that upon their attitudes, behavior, and morale within their primary groups ultimately depended industrial effectiveness and productivity. As Roethlisberger wrote:

> It is my simple thesis that a human problem requires a human solution. First, we have to learn to recognize a human problem when we see one; and second, upon recognizing it, we have to learn to deal with it as such and not as if it were something else.[1]

The Hawthorne investigators shifted the focus of management studies from simply the external elements of organizations to its internal and nonrational aspects. By interviewing techniques and by close observations of the dynamics of primary groups, that is, interrelations between workers, the investigators sought to understand the social codes and norms of behavior of informal work groups that were rarely displayed on the formal organization chart. "They studied the important social functions these groups perform for their members, the histories of these informal work groups, how they spontaneously appear, how they tend to perpetuate themselves, multiply, and disappear, how they are in constant jeopardy from technical change, and hence how they tend to resist innovation." In essence, like Freud and Jung in clinical psychology, they attempted to rationalize the irrational nature of human beings in the organizational context and find cures for the psychotic disorders of industrial institutions.

The Hawthorne experimenters also challenged the prevailing scientific management view of the individual employee, that is, that the greatest motivating factor for the worker was his or her paycheck. Rather, Roethlisberger argued, "Most of us want the satisfaction that comes from being accepted and recognized as people of worth by our friends and work associates. Money is only a small part of this social recognition. . . . We want the feeling of security that comes not so much from the amount of money we have in the bank as from being an accepted member of a group. A man whose job is without social function is like a man without a country; the activity to which he has to give the major portion of his life is robbed of all human meaning and significance."

After the termination of the Hawthorne Plant experiments, Mayo's writings led to broad speculations about administration and the problems of human society. In these later works, *The Human Problems of an Industrial Civilization* (1933), *The Social Problems of an Industrial Civilization* (1945), and *The Political Problems of Indus-*

[1]Fritz J. Roethlisberger, *Management and Morale* (Cambridge, Mass.: Harvard University Press, 1941), p. 7.

trial Civilization (1947), his central thesis emphasized that social skills have lagged behind technical skills. While the techniques of specialists, including engineers, chemists, and doctors, were important, it was by the leadership of administrators, in particular businesspeople, that human cooperation could be advanced and the problems of organization in society solved. In the deepest sense, Mayo became a social reformer who believed that improving the quality of administrative talent could help to build a better world. In his view, the administrator "becomes the guardian or preserver of the morale through the function of maintaining a condition of equilibrium, which will preserve the social values existing in the cooperative system."

To better understand the following selection by Mayo, it is helpful to know something about his background, which helped to shape the decidedly unique perspective of his writing. Mayo, the senior partner in the Hawthorne research effort, lived from 1880 to 1949 (his assistant, Roethlisberger, lived from 1898 to 1974). Born in Adelaide, Australia, Mayo was the second child in a large, impoverished family of seven. His life was unsettled—while growing up his family moved often, and in trying to find an occupation for himself, he drifted from one job to another. He went from business to publishing, to teaching, and then to medicine, but it was World War I that affected his life the most (as it did the lives of so many of his generation). While working as an interviewer of returning war veterans suffering from shell shock, Mayo learned firsthand about human suffering, dislocation, and tragedy.

Increasingly, thereafter, Mayo was drawn to the study of psychology—particularly the clinical writings of Janet and Freud, as well as the work of social systems theorists like Pareto and Henderson. It was Mayo's unique gift to be able to synthesize the ideas of clinical psychology and develop a grand systems theory into a way that would offer understanding and help for the problems of the worker in the industrial workplace. How were people to deal with and adapt to the traumatic upheavals caused by war, technology, and industrialization in the twentieth century? How could the suffering caused by these massive changes in the human condition be alleviated and possibly cured? How could human life for individuals and groups be improved? Mayo wrestled with these and other major philosophical and social issues for most of his life.

Grants from the Rockefeller and Carnegie Foundations brought Mayo to America in the 1920s, first to the University of Pennsylvania and then later to Harvard University to head the team of researchers at the Hawthorne Plant. There, with his probing mind and inspired personality, along with his emphasis on using rigorous, firsthand field investigations as a way to understand what really was happening inside American industrial life, he was able to give leadership to the overall direction of the Hawthorne experiments. The lasting fame of these experiments in social science and management literature is due in large measure to Mayo. He introduced the modern *team research* concept and indeed inspired other large-scale research efforts such as W. Lloyd Warner's *Yankee City*.

The following selection offers valuable insight into Mayo's views—his unique intuitiveness, his passionate concern for the betterment of human beings, his conviction that close, careful empirical-clinical analysis will yield "the facts" about human problems, and that this analysis can, in turn, lead to resolutions of these problems. Fundamental to all his beliefs is the idea that if only the informal nature of human organizations is recognized and properly dealt with (rather than the scientific, technological, and economic processes), then it is indeed possible to build a better world. This fundamental, reformist conviction spawned much of the human relations literature of post–World War II management thought by writers such as Maslow, Likert, McGregor, Herzberg, and many others who owe a debt to Mayo's writings and the Hawthorne experiments.

Mayo, however, was not without critics: labor unions attacked him for being anti-union, which he denied, and methodologists criticized his work for being unscientific and methodologically unsound, but he never admitted to being a statistician. Some suggest Mayo's values were too "pro-productivity," and not "pro-society" or "pro-human development," to which he would no doubt reply, "I was simply researching industrial productivity, not other factors." And some critics argue that Mayo's emphasis on small, blue-collar unskilled labor groups is outdated in an era of white-collar, educated professionals; but here again, Mayo might respond that he indeed studied a group that was representative of his own era. Furthermore, others would contend that he stressed cooperation and solidarity of the primary work group so much that he failed to appreciate the values of conflict and competition in assuring freedom of workers and progress for the overall organization. Mayo might respond to these criticisms by saying, "I merely reported on what our investigations uncovered at the time."

Most curiously, despite all his work at the Hawthorne Plant, not one of his recommendations was put into practice by the plant's management. Of what importance, then, were Mayo's work and the Hawthorne experiments? Perhaps Mayo's real genius was that he emphatically restated an old truth: human needs, values, and concerns of the basic informal group play a primary role in successful management practices.

As you read this selection, keep the following questions in mind:

Do the informal groups identified by Mayo's experiments in an industrial setting exist in public sector agencies? If so, do they operate in the same way in government as they do in business?

What do you think the similarities, as well as differences, are in the operation of an informal group in the public versus private settings?

Are Mayo's suggestions for dealing with the problems of securing the cooperation of individuals and human groups compatible with the goals and practices of public organizations? Where might there be problems in applying his ideas and techniques?

Referring back to Case Study No. 1, "The Blast in Centralia No. 5," or Case Study No. 3, "Dumping $2.6 Million on Bakersfield," identify the primary groups in these cases. Do Mayo's theories and prescriptions apply to these cases?

Compare Weber's and Mayo's views on the human condition. How do the two theorists compare in their conclusions and prescriptions for solving the bureaucratic problems of modern society? For instance, does Mayo emphasize material motives less than Weber does?

Hawthorne and the Western Electric Company

ELTON MAYO

I shall make no attempt to describe at length that which has been already and fully described. The interested public is well acquainted with *Management and the Worker,* the official account of the whole range of experiments, by my colleagues F. J. Roethlisberger of Harvard University and William J. Dickson of the Western Electric Company. The same public has not yet discovered *The Industrial Worker,*[1] by another colleague, T. North Whitehead. This is unfortunate, for the beginning of an answer to many problems significant for administration in the next decade is recorded in its pages. I refer to the problems involved in the making and adaptive re-making of working teams, the importance of which for collaboration in postwar years is still too little realized. Assuming that readers who wish to do so can consult these books, I have confined my remarks here to some comments upon the general development of the series of experiments.

A highly competent group of Western Electric engineers refused to accept defeat when experiments to demonstrate the effect of illumination on work seemed to lead nowhere. The conditions of scientific experiment had apparently been fulfilled—experimental room, control room; changes introduced one at a time; all other conditions held steady. And the results were perplexing: Roethlisberger gives two instances—lighting improved in the experimental room, production went up; but it rose also in the control room. The opposite of this: lighting diminished from 10 to 3 foot-candles in the experimental room and production again went up; simultaneously in the control room, with illumination constant, production also rose.[2] Many other experiments, and all inconclusive; yet it had

seemed so easy to determine the effect of illumination on work.

In matters of mechanics or chemistry the modern engineer knows how to set about the improvement of process or the redress of error. But the determination of optimum working conditions for the human being is left largely to dogma and tradition, guess, or quasi-philosophical argument. In modern large-scale industry the three persistent problems of management are:

1. The application of science and technical skill to some material good or product.
2. The systematic ordering of operations.
3. The organization of teamwork—that is, of sustained cooperation.

The last must take account of the need for continual reorganization of teamwork as operating conditions are changed in an *adaptive* society.

The first of these holds enormous prestige and interest and is the subject of continuous experiment. The second is well developed in practice. The third, by comparison with the other two, is almost wholly neglected. Yet it remains true that if these three are out of balance, the organization as a whole will not be successful. The first two operate to make an industry *effective,* in Chester Barnard's phrase,[3] the third, to make it *efficient.* For the larger and more complex the institution, the more dependent is it upon the wholehearted cooperation of every member of the group.

This was not altogether the attitude of Mr. G. A. Pennock and his colleagues when they set up the experimental "test room." But the illumination fiasco had made them alert to the need that very careful records should be kept of everything that happened in the room in addition to the obvious engineering and industrial devices.[4] Their observations therefore

From Elton Mayo, *The Social Problems of an Industrial Civilization.* Boston: Division of Research, Harvard Business School, 1945. Reprinted by permission of Harvard Business School Press.

included not only records of industrial and engineering changes but also records of physiological or medical changes, and, in a sense, of social and anthropological. This last took the form of a "log" that gave as full an account as possible of the actual events of every day, a record that proved most useful to Whitehead when he was remeasuring the recording tapes and recalculating the changes in productive output. He was able to relate eccentricities of the output curve to the actual situation at a given time—that is to say, to the events of a specific day or week.

First Phase—The Test Room

The facts are by now well know. Briefly restated, the test room began its inquiry by, first, attempting to secure the active collaboration of the workers. This took some time but was gradually successful, especially after the retirement of the original first and second workers and after the new worker at the second bench had assumed informal leadership of the group. From this point on, the evidence presented by Whitehead or Roethlisberger and Dickson seems to show that the individual workers became a team, wholeheartedly committed to the project. Second, the conditions of work were changed one at a time: rest periods of different numbers and length, shorter working day, shorter working week, food with soup or coffee in the morning break. And the results seemed satisfactory: slowly at first, but later with increasing certainty, the output record (used as an index of well-being) mounted. Simultaneously the workers claimed that they felt less fatigued, felt that they were not making any special effort. Whether these claims were accurate or no, they at least indicated increased contentment with the general situation in the test room by comparison with the department outside. At every point in the program, the workers had been consulted with respect to proposed changes; they had arrived at the point of free expression of ideas and feelings to management. And it had been arranged thus that the twelfth experimental change should be a return to the original

conditions of work—no rest periods, no midmorning lunch, no shortened day or week. It had also been arranged that, after 12 weeks of this, the group should return to the conditions of Period 7, a 15-minute midmorning break with lunch and a 10-minute midafternoon rest. The story is now well known: in Period 12 the daily and weekly output rose to a point higher than at any other time (the hourly rate adjusted itself downward by a small fraction), and in the whole 12 weeks "there was no downward trend." In the following period, the return to the conditions of work as in the seventh experimental change, the output curve soared to even greater heights: this thirteenth period lasted for 31 weeks.

These periods, 12 and 13, made it evident that increments of production could not be related point for point to the experimental changes introduced. Some major change was taking place that was chiefly responsible for the index of improved conditions—the steadily increasing output. Period 12—but for minor qualifications, such as "personal time out"—ignored the nominal return to original conditions of work and the output curve continued its upward passage. Put in other words, there was no actual return to original conditions. This served to bring another fact to the attention of the observers. Periods 7, 10, and 13 had nominally the same working conditions, as above described—15-minute rest and lunch in midmorning, 10-minute rest in the afternoon. But the average weekly output for each worker was:

Period 7—2,500 units

Period 10—2,800 units

Period 13—3,000 units

Periods 3 and 12 resembled each other also in that both required a full day's work without rest periods. But here also the difference of average weekly output for each worker was:

Period 3—less than 2,500 units

Period 12—more than 2,900 units

Here then was a situation comparable perhaps with the illumination experiment, certainly suggestive of the Philadelphia experience where improved conditions for one team of mule spinners were reflected in improved morale not only in the experimental team but in the two other teams who had received no such benefit.

This interesting, and indeed amusing, result has been so often discussed that I need make no mystery of it now. I have often heard my colleague Roethlisberger declare that the major experimental change was introduced when those in charge sought to hold the situation humanly steady (in the interest of critical changes to be introduced) by getting the cooperation of the workers. What actually happened was that six individuals became a team and the team gave itself wholeheartedly and spontaneously to cooperation in the experiment. The consequence was that they felt themselves to be participating freely and without afterthought, and were happy in the knowledge that they were working without coercion from above or limitation from below. They were themselves astonished at the consequence, for they felt that they were working under less pressure than ever before: and in this, their feelings and performance echoed that of the mule spinners.

Here then are two topics which deserve the closest attention of all those engaged in administrative work—the organization of working teams and the free participation of such teams in the task and purpose of the organization as it directly affects them in their daily round.

Second Phase—The Interview Program

But such conclusions were not possible at the time: the major change, the question as to the exact difference between conditions of work in the test room and in the plant departments, remained something of a mystery. Officers of the company determined to "take another look" at departments outside the test room—this, with the idea that something quite

important was there to be observed, something to which the experiment should have made them alert. So the interview program was introduced.

It was speedily discovered that the question-and-answer type of interview was useless in the situation. Workers wished to talk, and to talk freely under the seal of professional confidence (which was never abused) to someone who seemed representative of the company or who seemed, by his very attitude, to carry authority. The experience itself was unusual; there are few people in this world who have had the experience of finding someone intelligent, attentive, and eager to listen without interruption to all that he or she has to say. But to arrive at this point it became necessary to train interviewers how to listen, how to avoid interruption or the giving of advice, how generally to avoid anything that might put an end to free expression in an individual instance. Some approximate rules to guide the interviewer in his work were therefore set down. These were, more or less, as follows:[5]

1. Give your whole attention to the person interviewed, and make it evident that you are doing so.
2. Listen—don't talk.
3. Never argue; never give advice.
4. Listen to:
   (a) What he wants to say.
   (b) What he does not want to say.
   (c) What he cannot say without help.
5. As you listen, plot out tentatively and for subsequent correction the pattern (personal) that is being set before you. To test this, from time to time summarize what has been said and present for comment (e.g., "Is this what you are telling me?"). Always do this with the greatest caution, that is, clarify but do not add or twist.
6. Remember that everything said must be considered a personal confidence and not divulged to anyone. (This does not prevent discussion of a situation between professional colleagues. Nor does it prevent some form of public report when due precaution has been taken.)

It must not be thought that this type of interviewing is easily learned. It is true that some persons, men and women alike, have a natural flair for the work, but, even with them, there tends to be an early period of discouragement, a feeling of futility, through which the experience and coaching of a senior interviewer must carry them. The important rules in the interview (important, that is, for the development of high skill) are two. First, Rule 4 that indicates the need to help the individual interviewed to articulate expression of an idea or attitude that he has not before expressed; and, second, Rule 5 which indicates the need from time to time to summarize what has been said and to present it for comment. Once equipped to do this effectively, interviewers develop very considerable skill. But, let me say again, this skill is not easily acquired. It demands of the interviewer a real capacity to follow the contours of another person's thinking, to understand the meaning for him of what he says.

I do not believe that any member of the research group or its associates had anticipated the immediate response that would be forthcoming to the introduction of such an interview program. Such comments as "This is the best thing the Company has ever done," or "The Company should have done this long ago," were frequently heard. It was as if workers had been awaiting an opportunity for expressing freely and without afterthought their feelings on a great variety of modern situations, not by any means limited to the various departments of the plant. To find an intelligent person who was not only eager to listen but also anxious to help to express ideas and feelings but dimly understood—this, for many thousand persons, was an experience without precedent in the modern world.

In a former statement I named two questions that inevitably presented themselves to the interviewing group in these early stages of the study:

1. Is some experience which might be described as an experience of personal futility a common incident of industrial organization for work?
2. Does life in a modern industrial city, in some unrealized way, predispose workers to obsessive response?[6]

And I said that these two questions "in some form" continued to preoccupy those in charge of the research until the conclusion of the study.[7]

After twelve years of further study (not yet concluded), there are certain developments that demand attention. For example, I had not fully realized in 1932, when the above was written, how profoundly the social structure of civilization has been shaken by scientific, engineering, and industrial development. This radical change—the passage from an established to an adaptive social order—has brought into being a host of new and unanticipated problems for management and for the individual worker. The management problem appears at its acutest in the work of the supervisor. No longer does the supervisor work with a team of persons that he has known for many years or perhaps a lifetime; he is leader of a group of individuals that forms and disappears almost as he watches it. Now it is difficult, if not impossible, to relate oneself to a working group one by one; it is relatively easy to do so if they are already a fully constituted team. A communication from the supervisor, for example, in the latter instance has to be made to one person only with the appropriate instructions; the individual will pass it on and work it out with the team. In the former instance, it has to be repeated to every individual and may often be misunderstood.

But for the individual worker the problem is really much more serious. He has suffered a profound loss of security and certainty in his actual living and in the background of his thinking. For all of us the feeling of security and certainty derives always from assured membership of a group. If this is lost, no monetary gain, no job guarantee, can be sufficient compensation. Where groups change ceaselessly as jobs and mechanical processes change, the individual inevitably experiences a sense of void, of emptiness, where his fathers knew the joy of comradeship and security. And in such a situation, his anxieties—many, no doubt, irrational or ill-founded—increase and he becomes more difficult both to fellow workers and to supervisor. The extreme of this is perhaps rarely encountered as yet, but increasingly we move in this direction as the tempo of industrial change is speeded by scientific and technical discovery.

In the first chapter of this book I have claimed that scientific method has a dual approach—represented in medicine by the clinic and the laboratory. In the clinic one studies the whole situation with two ends in view: first, to develop intimate knowledge of and skill in handling the facts, and, second, on the basis of such a skill to separate those aspects of the situation that skill has shown to be closely related for detailed laboratory study. When a study based upon laboratory method fails, or partially fails, because some essential factor has been unknowingly and arbitrarily excluded, the investigator, if he is wise, returns to clinical study of the entire situation to get some hint as to the nature of the excluded determinant. The members of the research division at Hawthorne, after the twelfth experimental period in the test room, were faced by just such a situation and knew it. The so-called interview program represented for them a return from the laboratory to clinical study. And, as in all clinical study, there was no immediate and welcome revelation of a single discarded determinant: there was rather a slow progress from one observation to another, all of them important—but only gradually building up into a single complex finding. This slow development has been elsewhere described, in *Management and the Worker;* one can however attempt a succinct résumé of the various observations, more or less as they occurred.

Officers of the company had prepared a short statement, a few sentences, to be repeated to the individual interviewed before the conversation began. This statement was designed to assure the worker that nothing he said would be repeated to his supervisors or to any company official outside the interviewing group. In many instances, the worker waved this aside and began to talk freely and at once. What doubts there were seemed to be resident in the interviewers rather than in those interviewed. Many workers, I cannot say the majority for we have no statistics, seemed to have something "on their minds," in ordinary phrase, about which they wished to talk freely to a competent listener. And these topics were by no means confined to matters affecting the company. This was, I think, the first observation that emerged from the mass of interviews reported daily. The research group began to talk about the need for *"emotional release"* and the great advantage that accrued to the individual when he had "talked off" his problem. The topics varied greatly. One worker two years before had been sharply reprimanded by his supervisor for not working as usual: in interview he wished to explain that on the night preceding the day of the incident his wife and child had both died, apparently unexpectedly. At the time he was unable to explain; afterwards he had no opportunity to do so. He told the story dramatically and in great detail; there was no doubt whatever that telling it thus benefited him greatly. But this story naturally was exceptional; more often a worker would speak of his family and domestic situation, of his church, of his relations with other members of the working group—quite usually the topic of which he spoke presented itself to him as a problem difficult for him to resolve. This led to the next successive illumination for the inquiry. It became manifest that, whatever the problem, it was partly, and sometimes wholly, determined by the attitude of the individual worker. And this defect or distortion of attitude was consequent on his past experience or his present situation, or, more usually, on both at once. One woman worker, for example, discovered for herself during an interview that her dislike of a certain supervisor was based upon a fancied resemblance to a detested stepfather. Small wonder that the same supervisor had warned the interviewer that she was "difficult to handle." But the discovery by the worker that her dislike was wholly irrational eased the situation considerably.[8] This type of case led the interviewing group to study carefully each worker's *personal situation* and attitude. These two phrases "emotional release" and "personal situation" became convenient titles for the first phases of observation and seemed to resume for the interviewers the effective work that they were doing.

It was at this point that a change began to show itself in the study and in the conception of the study.

The original interviewers, in these days, after sixteen years of industrial experience, are emphatic on the point that the first cases singled out for report were special cases—individuals—and not representative either of the working group or of the interviews generally. It is estimated that such cases did not number more than an approximate two percent of the twenty thousand persons originally interviewed. Probably this error of emphasis was inevitable and for two reasons: first, the dramatic changes that occur in such instances seemed good evidence of the efficacy of the method, and, second, this type of interviewing had to be insisted upon as *necessary to the training of a skilled interviewer*. This last still holds good; a skilled interviewer must have passed through the stage of careful and observant listening to what an individual says and to all that he says. This stage of an interviewing program closely resembles the therapeutic method and its triumphs are apt to be therapeutic. And I do not believe that the study would have been equipped to advance further if it had failed to observe the great benefit of emotional release and the extent to which every individual's problems are conditioned by his personal history and situation. Indeed, even when one has advanced beyond the merely psychotherapeutic study of individuals to study of industrial groups, one has to beware of distortions similar in kind to those named; one has to know how to deal with such problems. The first phase of the interview program cannot therefore be discarded; it still retains its original importance. But industrial studies must nevertheless move beyond the individual in need of therapy. And this is the more true when the change from established routines to adaptive changes of routine seems generally to carry a consequence of loss of security for many persons.

A change of attitude in the research group came gradually. The close study of individuals continued, but in combination with an equally close study of groups. An early incident did much to set the new pattern for inquiry. One of the earliest ques-

tions proposed before the original test room experiment began was a question as to the fatigue involved in this or that type of work. Later a foreman of high reputation, no doubt with this in mind, came to the research group, now for the most part engaged in interviewing, and asserted that the workers in his department worked hard all day at their machines and must be considerably fatigued by the evening; he wanted an inquiry. Now the interviewers had discovered that this working group claimed a habit of doing most of their work in the morning period and "taking things easy" during the afternoon. The foreman obviously realized nothing of this, and it was therefore fortunate that the two possibilities could be directly tested. The officer in charge of the research made a quiet arrangement with the engineers to measure during a period the amount of electric current used by the group to operate its machines; this quantity indicated the overall amount of work being done. The results of this test wholly supported the statements made by the workers in interview; far more current was used in the morning period than during the afternoon. And the attention of the research group was, by this and other incidents, thus redirected to a fact already known to them, namely, that the working group as a whole actually determined the output of individual workers by reference to a standard, predetermined but never clearly stated, that represented the group conception of a fair day's work. This standard was rarely, if ever, in accord with the standards of the efficiency engineers.

The final experiment, reported under the title of the Bank Wiring Observation Room, was set up to extend and confirm these observations.[9] Simultaneously it was realized that these facts did not in any way imply low working morale as suggested by such phrases as "restriction of output." On the contrary, the failure of free communication between management and workers in modern large-scale industry leads inevitably to the exercise of caution by the working group until such time as it knows clearly the range and meaning of changes imposed from above. The enthusiasm of the efficiency engineer for the organization of operations is excellent; his attempt to resume problems of cooperation under this heading is not. At the moment, he attempts to solve the many human difficulties involved in wholehearted cooperation by formally reorganizing the organization without any reference whatever to workers themselves. His procedure inevitably blocks communication and defeats his own admirable purpose.[10]

This observation, important as it is, was not however the leading point for the interviewers. The existence and influence of the group—those in active daily relationship with one another—became the important fact. The industrial interviewer must learn to distinguish and specify, as he listens to what a worker says, references to "personal" or group situations. More often than not, the special case, the individual who talks himself out of a gross distortion, is a solitary—one who has not "made the team." The usual interview, on the other hand, though not by any means free from distortion, is speaking as much for the working group as for the person. The influence of the communication in the interview, therefore, is not limited to the individual but extends to the group.

Two workers in a large industry were recently offered "upgrading"; to accept would mean leaving their group and taking a job in another department: they refused. Then representatives of the union put some pressure on them, claiming that, if they continued to refuse, the union organizers "might just as well give up" their efforts. With reluctance the workers reversed their decision and accepted the upgrading. Both girls at once needed the attention of an interviewer: they had liked the former group in which they had earned informal membership. Both felt adjustment to a new group and a novel situation as involving effort and private discontent. From both much was learned of the intimate organization and common practices of their groups, and their adjustments to their new groups were eased, thereby effectively helping reconstitute the teamwork in those groups.

In another recent interview a worker of eighteen protested to an interviewer that her mother was continually urging her to ask Mr. X, her supervisor, for a "raise." She had refused, but her loyalty to her mother and the pressure the latter exerted were affecting her work and her relations at work. She talked her situation out with an interviewer, and it became clear that to her a "raise" would mean departure from her daily companions and associates. Although not immediately relevant, it is interesting to note that, after explaining the situation at length to the interviewer, she was able to present her case dispassionately to her mother—without exaggeration or protest. The mother immediately understood and abandoned pressure for advancement, and the worker returned to effective work. This last instance illustrates one way in which the interview clears lines of communication of emotional blockage—within as without the plant. But this is not my immediate topic; my point is rather that the age-old human desire for persistence of human association will seriously complicate the development of an adaptive society if we cannot devise systematic methods of easing individuals from one group of associates into another.

But such an observation was not possible in the earliest inquiry. The important fact brought to the attention of the research division was that the ordinary conception of management-worker relation as existing between company officials, on the one hand, and an unspecified number of individuals, on the other, is utterly mistaken. Management, in any continuously successful plant, is not related to single workers but always to working groups. In every department that continues to operate, the workers have—whether aware of it or not—formed themselves into a group with appropriate customs, duties, routines, even rituals; and management succeeds (or fails) in proportion as it is accepted without reservation by the group as authority and leader. This, for example, occurred in the relay assembly test room at Hawthorne. Management, by consultation with the workers, by clear explanation of the proposed experiments and the reasons for them, by accepting the workers' verdict in special instances, unwittingly scored a success in two most important human matters—the workers became a self-governing team, and a team that cooperated wholeheartedly with management. The test room was responsible for many important findings—rest periods, hours of work, food, and the like: but the most important finding of all was unquestionably in the general area of teamwork and cooperation.

It was at this time that the research division published, for private circulation within the company, a monograph entitled "Complaints and Grievances." Careful description of many varied situations within the interviewers' experience showed that an articulate complaint only rarely, if ever, gave any logical clue to the grievance in which it had origin; this applied at least as strongly to groups as to individuals. Whereas economists and industry generally *tend to concentrate upon the complaint and upon logical inferences from its articulate statement* as an appropriate procedure, the interviewing group had learned almost to ignore, except as symptom, the—sometimes noisy—manifestation of discomfort and to study the situation anew to gain knowledge of its source. Diagnosis rather than argument became the proper method of procedure.

It is possible to quote an illustration from a recently published book, *China Enters the Machine Age.*[11] When industries had to be moved, during this war, from Shanghai and the Chinese coast to Kunming in the interior of China, the actual operation of an industry still depended for the most part on skilled workers who were refugees from Shanghai and elsewhere. These skilled workers knew their importance to the work and gained considerable prestige from it; nevertheless discontent was rife among them. Evidence of this was manifested by the continual, deliberate breaking of crockery in the company mess hall and complaints about the quality of the food provided. Yet this food was much better than could have been obtained outside the plant—especially at the prices charged. And in interview the individual workers admitted freely that the food was good and could not rightly be made the subject of complaint. But the relationship between the skilled workers as a group and the *Chih Yuan*—the executive and supervisory officers—was exceedingly unsatisfactory.

Many of these officers—the *Chih Yuan*—have been trained in the United States—enough at least to set a pattern for the whole group. Now in America we have learned in actual practice to accept the

rabble hypothesis with reservations. But the logical Chinese student of engineering or economics, knowing nothing of these practical reservations, returns to his own country convinced that the workman who is not wholly responsive to the "financial incentive" is a troublemaker and a nuisance. And the Chinese worker lives up to this conviction by breaking plates.[12] Acceptance of the complaint about the food and collective bargaining of a logical type conducted at that level would surely have been useless.

Yet this is what industry, not only in China, does every day, with the high sanction of State authority and the alleged aid of lawyers and economists. In their behavior and their statements, economists indicate that they accept the rabble hypothesis and its dismal corollary of financial incentive as the only effective human motive. They substitute a logical hypothesis of small practical value for the actual facts.

The insight gained by the interviewing group, on the other hand, cannot be described as substituting irrational for rational motive, emotion for logic. On the contrary, it implies a need for competent study of complaints and the grievances that provoke them, a need for knowledge of the actual facts rather than acceptance of an outdated theory. It is amusing that certain industrialists, rigidly disciplined in economic theory, attempt to shrug off the Hawthorne studies as "theoretic." Actually the shoe is on the other foot; Hawthorne has restudied the facts without prejudice, whereas the critics have unquestioningly accepted that theory of man which had its vogue in the nineteenth century and has already outlived its usefulness.

The Hawthorne interview program has moved far since its beginning in 1929. Originally designed to study the comfort of workers in their work as a mass of individuals, it has come to clear specification of the relation of working groups to management as one of the fundamental problems of large-scale industry. It was indeed this study that first enabled us to assert that the third major preoccupation of management must be that of organizing teamwork, that is to say, of developing and sustaining cooperation.

In summary, certain entirely practical discoveries must be enumerated.

First, the early discovery that the interview aids the individual to get rid of useless emotional complications and to state his problem clearly. He is thus enabled to give himself good advice—a procedure far more effective than advice accepted from another. I have already given instances of this in discussing "emotional release" and the influence on individual attitude of personal history and personal situation.

Second, the interview has demonstrated its capacity to aid the individual to associate more easily, more satisfactorily, with other persons—fellow workers or supervisors—with whom he is in daily contact.

Third, the interview not only helps the individual to collaborate better with his own group of workers, it also develops his desire and capacity to work better with management. In this it resembles somewhat the action of the Philadelphia colonel.[13] Someone, the interviewer, representing (for the worker) the plant organization outside his own group, has aided him to work better with his own group. This is the beginning of the necessary double loyalty—to his own group and to the larger organization. It remains only for management to make wise use of this beginning.

Fourth, beyond all this, interviewing possesses immense importance for the training of administrators in the difficult future that faces this continent and the world. It has been said that the interviewer has no authority and takes no action. Action can only be taken by the proper authority and through the formally constituted line of authority. The interviewer, however, contributes much to the facilitation of communication both up and down that line. He does this, first, by clearing away emotional distortion and exaggeration; second, his work manifestly aids to exact and objective statement the grievance that lies beyond the various complaints.

Work of this kind is immensely effective in the development of maturity of attitude and judgment in the intelligent and sensitive young men and women who give time to it. The subordination of oneself, of one's opinions and ideas, of the very human desire to give gratuitous advice, the subordination of all these to an intelligent effort to help another express ideas and feelings that he cannot easily express is, in itself, a most desirable education. As a preparation for the exercise of administrative responsibility, it is better than anything offered in a present university curriculum. It is no doubt necessary to train young men and women to present their knowledge and ideas with lucidity. But, if they are to be administrators, it is far more necessary to train them to listen carefully to what others say. Only he who knows how to help other persons to adequate expression can develop the many qualities demanded by a real maturity of judgment.

Finally, there remains the claim made above that the interview has proved to be the source of information of great objective value to management. The three persistent problems of modern large-scale industry have been stated as:

1. The application of science and technical skill to a material product.
2. The systematization of operations.
3. The organization of sustained cooperation.

When a representative of management claims that interview results are merely personal or subjective—and there are many who still echo this claim—he is actually telling us that he has himself been trained to give all his attention to the first and second problems, technical skill and the systematic ordering of operations; he does not realize that he has also been trained to ignore the third problem completely. For such persons, information on a problem, the existence of which they do not realize, is no information. It is no doubt in consequence of this ignorance or induced blindness that strikes or other difficulties so frequently occur in unexpected places. The interview method is the only method extant[14] that can contribute reasonably accurate information, or indeed any information, as to the extent of the actual cooperation between workers—teamwork—that obtains in a given department, and beyond this, the extent to which this cooperation includes management policy or is wary of it. The Hawthorne inquiry at least specified these most important industrial issues and made some tentative steps toward the development of a method of diagnosis and treatment in particular cases.

Notes

1. Cambridge, Harvard University Press, 1938, 2 vols.
2. *Management and Morale,* pp. 9–10.
3. Op. cit., p. 56.
4. For a full account of the experimental setup, see F. J. Roethlisberger and William J. Dickson, *Management and the Worker,* and T. North Whitehead, *The Industrial Worker,* Vol. 1.
5. For a full discussion of this type of interview, see F. J. Roethlisberger and William J. Dickson, op. cit., Chap. XIII. For a more complete summary and perhaps less technical discussion, see George C. Homans, *Fatigue of Workers* (New York, Reinhold Publishing Corporation, 1941).
6. Elton Mayo, *The Human Problems of an Industrial Civilization* (New York, The Macmillan Company, 1933; reprinted by Division of Research, Harvard Business School, 1946), p. 114.
7. Ibid.
8. F. J. Roethlisberger and William J. Dickson, op. cit., pp. 307–310.
9. F. J. Roethlisberger and William J. Dickson, op. cit., Part IV, pp. 379 ff.
10. For further evidence on this point, see Stanley B. Mathewson, *Restriction of Output among Unorganized Workers,* and also Elton Mayo, *The Human Problems of an Industrial Civilization,* pp. 119–121.
11. Shih Kuo-heng (Cambridge, Harvard University Press, 1944).
12. Ibid., Chap. VIII, pp. 111–127; also Chap. X, pp. 151–153.
13. Chap. III, supra.
14. We realize that there are at present in industry many individuals possessed of high skill in the actual handling of human situations. This skill usually derives from their own experience, is intuitive, and is not easily communicable.

☐ CASE STUDY 6

Introduction

The concept of the informal group provides us with several critical insights into modern organizational life and the need for administrators to be realistic about what can and cannot be achieved, given the sentiments, feelings, values, and outlooks of men and women in any particular work setting. Clearly, as Mayo's essay points out, being realistic about the nature and workings of the human group is paramount in any successful administrative undertaking. Human groups present managers with both potentialities and pitfalls for achieving well-run internal operations. If managers are to lead organizations effectively, human groups need to be recognized, understood and well integrated within their operations.

The following case study "Uniforms in the Closet," by Jennifer Egan, a novelist and journalist, illustrates the importance of considering the human element in the public sector, specifically in this case the treatment of gays in the armed services. The author presents, not the typical case study in this textbook—a story with a clear beginning, middle and end—but rather, anonymous, random interviews with gay marines who tell their own personal stories about their lives, how they work and deal within a professional environment highly hostile to their sexual orientation. The author tries to probe deeply into the realitites of their world—one that is informal, risky, and secretive, and yet is linked together by a special bond, always in dire dread of official exposure. Under the Armed Services 1993 "Don't Ask, Don't Tell" Policy, gays may serve in uniform as long as they refrain from "homosexual acts," and same-sex marriages and they don't tell about their sexual orientation. Commanders are also barred from asking subordinates about or pursuing investigations into sexual orientation without credible evidence. Yet, as this case shows, the relationship between the formal "chain of command" and an informal group, those gays in uniform, is hardly simplified by this policy but is now even more complex and full of paradoxes, with possibly important lessons for all public administrators.

As you read this selection, try to keep in mind what lessons it holds for public administrators based on the following questions:

Why is formal organizational rule-making so difficult, even often at odds with an informal group's needs and concerns?

What specific issues and paradoxes are raised by this case?

Are there options available for the armed services in devising better policies toward gays in uniform? How can gays best respond? What are your own recommended solutions?

Does the foregoing reading by Mayo contain useful ideas for securing worker cooperation with management in achieving organizational goals? Or is it largely irrelevant to coping with the problems presented by this case? If so, why? Or why not?

On the basis of your reading of this case study, can you generalize about the importance of informal groups in the public management processes?

Uniforms in the Closet

JENNIFER EGAN

Before R., a Marine Corps officer, leaves Camp Pendelton, he changes out of the starched camouflage suit that is the everyday uniform of marines into "civvies"—in R.'s case, jeans and a T-shirt. It is normal for a marine to change clothes before leaving the base; by shedding his "cammies," R. leaves behind the obligation to salute other marines in uniform. But for R., the change is also symbolic: as a marine who is gay, he looks forward to the end of each workday as a reprieve from hiding part of himself from everyone around him.

"Uniforms in the Closet," by Jennifer Egan, *New York Times Magazine* (June 28, 1998), pp. 26–31, 48, 56. Reprinted by permission of the author.

Most days, the marines in R.'s battalion are not in the field but at their desks in a modest office building, set amid scrubby Southern California coastland, where images of wives and crinkly faced infants smile from picture frames and computer screens. In R.'s office, the décor is strictly military: photographs of his various units over the 12 years he has been a marine, a picture of the general whom he served as an aide—a demanding and highly prestigious job. (R. has also been a commanding officer, bearing ultimate responsibility for a unit.) R. wishes he could place on his desk a photograph of David, a civilian mechanical engineer and his partner of three years, but a man's picture would almost certainly kindle suspicions. Even a personal telephone call from a man might be considered unusual, so David almost never calls R. at his office, where a single phone line serves dozens of marines.

Yet despite these and a multitude of other precautions, he worries that some men in his unit suspect that he is gay—in part because he is over 30 and unmarried; in part because years of hiding have made him deeply paranoid. "Sometimes I feel like they can look at me and just tell," says R., who would speak with me, and allow me into his life, on condition that I refer to him only by one of his initials. (Other gay military personnel I interviewed for this article similarly requested anonymity.)

Driving from Camp Pendelton into San Diego, 40 miles south, R. grows visibly more relaxed. He has a California tan, deep-set eyes and the sturdy build characteristic of marines, along with a large Marine Corps tattoo—eagle, globe and anchor. A vigorous, sociable man, he is full of plans. After work tomorrow, he will make the two-hour drive north to David's house in Los Angeles, as he does each weekend. On Sunday, they will go to brunch at the home of a gay Marine officer. In a couple of weeks, R. will accompany his battalion to "the desert," Twentynine Palms, a Marine base outside Palm Springs where field training exercises are performed. From there he will head into Palm Springs for the annual White Party, a large all-night gay dance.

This constant switching between mutually exclusive worlds can have some odd, hallucinatory effects, R. says: "Several times I've met someone on base and wondered, Haven't I seen him at a bar? And then I've seen people at bars and thought I recognized them from the base. When I see someone at the mall, I can't remember where I know them from."

R. joined the Marines as a teen-ager and is fiercely loyal to the Corps, particularly to the enlisted men who answer to him—"my marines," he calls them, and adds, "I'm a marine first and gay second." His career has been stellar; he is what is known in the Corps as a "mustang," an enlisted marine who crossed over to become a commissioned officer. "Now that I've been a commanding officer and a general's aide, sky's the limit," he says. Military retirement, which can begin after 20 years, would allow him to draw half his base pay for the rest of his life. But R. plans to leave the Marines at the end of his current commission. The reason is simple. "I'm fed up," he says, "with having to hide."

It has been more than four years since the policy known as "Don't Ask, Don't Tell, Don't Pursue" went into effect. This policy was a compromise eked out among the White House, Congress and the Pentagon after President Clinton's announcement of his intention to lift the ban on homosexuals in the military—a ban that prohibited homosexuals from serving under any circumstances—set off a firestorm of opposition. Under "Don't Ask, Don't Tell," homosexuals (and bisexuals) may serve as long as they tell no one about their sexual orientation, refrain from "homosexual acts" and forgo homosexual marriage. The policy bars the military from questioning service members about their sexual orientation or investigating them without credible information that they have engaged in homosexual conduct. The stated goal of the policy is to allow homosexuals to serve while preserving morale and unit cohesion, which the military believes would be impaired by the presence of openly gay soldiers. But "Don't Ask, Don't Tell" forces a difficult choice upon homosexuals: in order to serve, they must either do without sex, romance and companionship or live uncelibate lives and lie about it—breaking the law and forfeiting their careers if they are caught.

Two months ago, the Pentagon issued figures indicating that the number of homosexuals discharged—997 in 1997—has risen 67 percent since "Don't Ask, Don't Tell" went into effect. Michelle Benecke, co-founder and co-director of Servicemembers Legal Defense Network, a watchdog group that assists military personnel accused under "Don't Ask, Don't Tell," says she believes the rise in discharges indicates that commanders are continuing to seek out homosexuals despite the fact that they are no longer supposed to. "No one has informed commanders of what the new rules are," says Benecke, whose organization has documented 1,379 command violations of the policy in the four years of its existence. "No one has ever told them the intent: to back off."

The Pentagon disagrees, attributing the rise in discharges to an increase in "statement" cases, in which homosexuals—many of them in their first year of service—openly declare that they are gay. But what the military regards as a statement is not always so clear-cut: last November, the Navy tried to discharge a senior chief petty officer named Timothy McVeigh, a nuclear submarine expert who had been in the service for 18 years, on the basis of what it called his homosexual admittance. McVeigh's so-called admittance was an Internet posting with America Online in which he stated, anonymously, that his marital status was "gay"; a Federal judge ruled in January that the military's investigation of McVeigh was in violation of policy and ordered that McVeigh, who has declined to discuss his sexual orientation, be retained. Earlier this month, McVeigh and the Navy reached a settlement under which he will retire this summer with full benefits and receive a payment of $90,000 to cover his legal fees.

During a recent interview, Kenneth H. Bacon, the Pentagon spokesman, told me: "Obviously, there are many people serving in the armed forces who have gay relationships, but they're discreet. They aren't pursued, and they may not even be known about." This suggests a split between the letter and the spirit of "Don't Ask, Don't Tell": the letter says, Don't do it; the spirit says, It's O.K. to do it as long as you are discreet. But this double message leaves homosexuals on queasy middle ground: theoretically, they are allowed to serve, but their private lives are illegal and will cost them their careers—if they get caught. But then, no one is supposed to be trying to catch them. When I raised this notion of the policy's murkiness with Rudy de Leon, Under Secretary of Defense for Personnel and Readiness, he said, "I think we're at the heart of some of the conflicts that are built into the policy, which tries to balance many competing interests."

If, as the Pentagon says, some homosexuals are outing themselves with the knowledge that they will be discharged, it may be that for them, the pressures and risks of serving under "Don't Ask, Don't Tell" are too intense to bear.

R. is part of a sprawling social network of gay marines and sailors, men and women, based in and around San Diego, where the shoreline bristles with dull gray ships and the sky is full of lumbering choppers and S-3's, anti-submarine-warfare planes that honk like gigantic geese as they fly. On this unseasonably cool spring evening, I accompany R. to a 6:30 dinner at the home of a Navy doctor near Hillcrest, a gay neighborhood north of downtown San Diego. The group tonight includes a tank officer who was one of the first to enter Kuwait during the gulf war, where he earned a bronze star; a Navy helicopter pilot, and several noncommissioned officers,

or N.C.O.'s—enlisted men who have worked their way up through the ranks. The off-duty mingling of officers and enlisted people of different ranks is prohibited because of its potential to break down the chain of command, but the fact that gay personnel are forced underground creates a bond among them that transcends military hierarchy. None of these friends work together; they met socially and communicate mostly by E-mail, using a code that eliminates gender-specific pronouns, since the military can monitor any E-mail exchanges that take place on a base. (Most of R.'s friends say they have never met a gay person on duty; even when they suspect that a fellow sailor or marine might be gay, they rarely approach—the risk of being wrong is too great.)

Like a number of his friends, R. joined the military believing he was heterosexual. Reared and educated in a strict Southern Christian community, he was profoundly homophobic. "I would say, 'AIDS is God's judgment on homosexuals'—I really felt that," he says. He was drawn to the Marines by the camaraderie, by the promise of adventure—and also by the largely single-sex environment. "I would think, I'm going to be with all these men—that's kind of exciting," he says. "But I didn't know why I was excited."

Some of R.'s friends, aware of their homosexual inclinations, joined in hopes that the military—the Marines in particular—would "cure" them. "Everybody knows that there are no fags in the Marines," says a former infantryman. Over pizza, R.'s friends talk of other motivations for joining the military, including the desire to get away from home and the hope of proving themselves to a disapproving world. "I'm supposed to be that one guy that can't survive in this environment," says one powerfully built man, an operations officer in the Marine air wing. "I'm the guy that's supposed to be filtered out, the weak one who can't carry the pack."

This officer goes on to tell me that his homosexuality is an open secret. "I know that in my command there are marines who work for me that assume I'm gay," he says. But he is clearly the exception. A logistics officer I'm introduced to at dinner has a dedicated "stunt babe"—a woman who poses as his girlfriend at military events and whose picture he keeps on his desk. The annual Marine Corps Ball, I learn, is the biggest command performance of this sort; R. usually brings a date with whom he has collaborated on a complex romantic history while David stays home, watching TV. It isn't enough to say nothing about your private life; unless you give the appearance of being heterosexual, people will start to wonder—especially now that "Don't Ask, Don't Tell" has alerted them to the fact that there may be homosexuals in their midst.

As a result, R. and his friends monitor themselves obsessively, aware that a single blunder can lead to exposure, humiliation and a discharge they regard as a disgrace—particularly those, like R., whose families don't know they are gay. A strange car in front of your house, clicks on the telephone line, a summons from the commanding officer—in the life of a gay soldier, any one of these can prompt a flicker of anxiety, even all-out panic. "Say you're out with four or five of your friends at a restaurant, and there goes somebody in your department with his wife," says the Navy doctor who is the host of the pizza party. "You know you're nailed."

Even gay nightclubs can be a hazard, although "Don't Ask, Don't Tell" has discouraged the trolling of clubs by investigators, a formerly common practice. One officer says of a popular San Diego club: "Last time I was there on a gay night, I ran into two of my marines, who were there by mistake. They were like, 'Hey, Sir, what're you doing here?'" Another of R.'s friends, P., was an F-18 fighter pilot who dropped bombs on Iraq during the gulf war before leaving active duty three years ago. (He is still with the Marine reserves.) P. was in a long-term relationship with his civilian "roommate" while in the military, but feigned a romance with a lesbian friend for three years to avoid having to go on any more blind dates set up by the Officers' Wives Club. A fair, soft-spoken man who has retained his marine build and haircut, P. says his hardest times were the six-month deployments on aircraft carriers, when he and his partner were rarely able to speak, and when P. rationed the letters he sent home out of fear that too many to the same man would draw attention. The letters his partner sent him were unsigned or signed with a female name, sent without a return address and chary on endearments. (During R.'s ship deployment, he asked his partner to have a woman address his letters.)

Each month, P. recalls, a videotape would arrive on his ship, fashioned by the Officers' Wives Club, filled with greetings from loved ones. "Everybody

else in the squadron's wife or girlfriend would be in the video saying, 'Hey, honey, how're you doing?'" he says. "And you'd be the only one without anything on that tape."

At the end of the deployment, when the ship was within six or seven days of land, senior pilots with wives or fiancées would get to fly the planes ashore early to be with their loved ones. Though P. was always among the most senior, he, being single, had to wait until the ship docked. "You get off, you have this huge welcome-home party and everyone else is there, except yours," he says. "He could be, except you'd have to stand there and shake his hand: *Thanks for coming, buddy.*" And, of course, being met by a man after six months at sea might well arouse suspicions.

Still, in this crowd it is generally felt that gay enlisted people, not officers, have it the worst. The enlisted are a tighter pack, which makes keeping secrets much harder, and the homophobic atmosphere tends to be far more virulent. Twelve of the homosexuals discharged in 1997 were officers; the remaining 985, enlisted people. J., an N.C.O. who says he has witnessed beatings and harassment of those suspected of being gay, told me he would fear for his life if his subordinates were to discover his secret. He socializes in Hillcrest, but tells subordinates that he goes to bars they can't afford: "I'll say: 'Dude, I met this babe last night. We hit it off!' You have to lie. They're like a pack of dogs—if they smell blood, they're going to go after it. You're dealing with kids, 18 or 19, who are trying to prove their manhood." Homosexual jokes and slurs, he adds, are a constant.

So saturated is the Marine Corps with homophobia that some of R.'s friends agree with the Pentagon that they should not be allowed to serve openly, that it would hinder their ability to lead. R. used to feel this way, but like the majority of gay personnel I spoke with, he has come to believe that although President Clinton had good intentions in seeking to change a draconian policy, "Don't Ask, Don't Tell" amounts to a step backward. For one thing, it has turned discrimination against homosexuals—formerly just a military policy—into Federal law. And by forcing homosexuals to remain invisible, R. says, the policy deprives gay military people of the chance to prove themselves and begin to dispel the prejudices against them. "The best way to change people's attitudes is the personal one-on-one relationship," he says, and tells of how a close friend, a heterosexual Marine fighter pilot with whom R. used to trade jokes about homosexuals, has completely revised his views since learning that R. is gay. But under "Don't Ask Don't Tell," R. could be discharged simply for having told his friend that he is homosexual.

"Clinton thought he was doing us this big favor," R. says, "and all he did was build a brick wall around the closet."

Each time J., the N.C.O., recalls one of his fabrications, he begins, "I told a lie," as if to keep straight in his mind what is a lie and what is the truth. Clearly, so much lying troubles him. He shows me the red plastic Core Values card that every marine must carry. "Honor," begins the text, which also includes the words "Integrity," "Responsibility" and "Accountability."

"Look at those and tell me if a marine who lives by that code can be gay in the military and live with himself," J. says. "They encourage integrity, but they expect us to lie."

Yet none of this seems to have blunted J.'s passion for the military. "If I could do it all over again, I would have gone Air Force," he says. (The Air Force and the air wings of the Navy and the Marines are seen as being less intensely homophobic environments.) "But now that I'm a marine, I'm a marine through and through. It's in my blood."

Still, for gay service members, devotion to the military is fraught with the knowledge that it will turn on them instantly if it learns one of the most basic facts about them. Many are haunted by the story of Lieut. Col. Loren S. Loomis of the Army, winner of two bronze stars and a purple heart in Vietnam, whose homosexuality was exposed in a way few could have imagined. After his house near Fort Hood, Tex., caught fire in 1996, the Fire Department, suspecting arson, took a video camera and a videotape from Loomis's home as part of its investigation. The video showed Loomis engaging in gay sex. Although the Fire Department had removed the video without a search warrant or a subpoena, the district attorney's office nevertheless turned it over to the Army. Loomis offered to retire early, but was discharged instead, and thus deprived of his active-duty pension and retirement benefits. Most chillingly to gay service members, his ouster came just five days before his 20-year retirement eligibility would have begun.

"In flight school, in every school I was in," says P., the former F-18 pilot, "I finished first. In every squadron I was in, I was always the No. 1 guy. But no matter how many times you're No. 1, if they find out you're a homo, you're out."

After dinner, I head with R. and some of his friends to Flicks, a gay bar popular with military men and their civilian admirers, known as "chasers," some of whom emulate the distinctive Marine "high and tight" haircut—shaved almost to the scalp around the sides of the head with a flat wedge of hair along the top. Part of the allure of military men is that they're tested regularly for H.I.V. and thus are perceived as "clean."

Andrew Cunanan, who is believed to have murdered Gianni Versace and others, was a chaser, and Flicks was his bar of choice. His bloody rampage across America has fueled the wariness R.'s crowd already says it feels toward civilian homosexuals; at Flicks, he and his friends are a somewhat insular presence, clean-cut and light drinking—most rise at 5:30 A.M. and are in their offices by 6:30 or 7. They talk among themselves or with the other military men they encounter. The night's entertainment is a performance by a former marine, now a stripper and porn star, but that's not why they're there. Military socialization, with its emphasis on patriotism and war, structure and rank, is conservative and unique; it creates a gap between soldiers and civilians that doesn't disappear simply because both are gay. R. and his friends tend to be leery of "nellie," or effeminate, men, though it is a prejudice of which they are somewhat ashamed.

"I know very little about gay culture," R. says. On a gay cruise he and David took recently with some military friends, R. was mystified by a drag spoof of "Whatever Happened to Baby Jane." "The whole place is going wild, and none of us had seen 'Whatever Happened to Baby Jane,' " he says, and admits to finding the hedonism in some pockets of gay culture—the all-night dance parties, for example, which David enjoys—wearying and empty. As for gay advocates in San Francisco and Washington, many of whom are left-leaning and anti-military, R. says: "I don't think they speak for us. I don't think they understand us."

Part of what they don't understand, of course, is what it's like to function in a world where even saying that you are gay is illegal. After the gay cruise, R. says: "When I was going back to work, I actually felt sick, nauseous with dread. I go to bars and these people are able to live without fear. It makes me jealous. It puts a barrier between us."

Yet this barrier leaves R. and his friends in something of a no man's land: socialized by the military but divided from it by sexual orientation; bound to gay culture by definition, yet culturally estranged from it. In a sense, they belong to a group consisting only of one another.

Most of them leave Flicks at 10:30, before the stripper begins performing, and head home to bed.

What R. and his friends hope to ward off through the use of stunt babes, phony photos and other false trappings of heterosexual life are any formal inquiries into their sexuality. Under "Don't Ask, Don't Tell," an inquiry cannot begin without credible information that a person has made a statement of homosexual orientation or engaged in homosexual conduct, but what exactly constitutes "credible information" is up to the commanding officer. (C.O.'s are advised to check with legal counsel before beginning such inquiries.) Sonya Harden, a heterosexual black enlisted woman with the Air Force, was investigated for homosexuality after a former civilian roommate who claimed that Harden owed her money forged letters in Harden's name stating that she was gay and gave them to her commanding officer. Harden's C.O. initiated an inquiry. Such inquiries are often as simple as questioning the service member—or, in the practice, discouraged but still extant, known as witch hunting, pressing the service member for the names of other homosexuals in exchange for leniency. Some inquiries are more complex: in the case of D., a black female marine who was in training for the Military Police, the inquiry included interviews with her parents, her childhood friends and even her prom dates—300 pages of testimony.

After investigating, a commanding officer must decide whether a service member has, in fact, made a statement of homosexuality or engaged in homosexual acts, which current policy defines as any bodily contact that "a reasonable person" would

understand to be for purposes of sexual gratification or an expression of homosexuality—in some cases, as little as a kiss, a hug or hand-holding. If the C.O. determines that a basis for discharge exists, he or she will initiate "separation" proceedings—the administrative process whereby a service member may be prematurely discharged. In the case of D., who had been caught lying on a bed fully clothed with another female trainee, the C.O. read through hundreds of pages of testimony and decided not to seek a discharge. But in Harden's case, the C.O. went ahead with her discharge despite the fact that, by then, her accuser had recanted and had admitted to having forged the incriminating letters.

Service members like Harden who choose to fight their separations must appear before a separation board. Once things have come this far, though, a number of factors weigh heavily against the accused. For one, because a separation hearing is an administrative rather than a criminal proceeding, there are no strict rules of evidence; the Government can present or exclude virtually anything it wants, no matter how it was obtained. (That was why, in Colonel Loomis's case, the videotape could be used against him.) In Harden's case, the Government presented the forged letters—even though the forger herself testified before the board on Harden's behalf—and also chose to exclude a polygraph, which Harden had passed.

Another factor weighing against a service member in a separation hearing is that the members of the typically three-person panel who will determine his or her fate are chosen by—and sometimes answer to—the very commanding officer who is presenting the allegations. Moreover, although the accused is entitled to a military defense lawyer, and by all accounts these lawyers defend their clients assiduously, they are notoriously overworked. Sometimes service members are not provided a lawyer—or even told what they are being charged with—until discharge paperwork is already pending, at which point little can be done to stop it. And most enlisted people cannot afford civilian lawyers.

But perhaps the biggest hurdle facing a service member in a homosexual case is the near impossibility of proving that he or she is unlikely to engage in homosexual acts. "You have to prove that you not only don't have sex, but you have no propensity to," says Beatrice Dohrn, legal director of the Lambda

Legal Defense and Education Fund. "How do you prove that?" With great difficulty, it would seem—even if, like Harden, you are heterosexual. Three former boyfriends testified on her behalf, and Harden gave a sworn statement, but the separation board still ruled against her, and she was discharged in August 1996. "Once somebody says you're gay, you can sleep with a hundred guys, but they're still going to say, 'She's gay,'" Harden says. Harden filed a complaint with the Inspector General of the Air Force, whose job is to investigate alleged command abuses. He ultimately concluded that Harden had been treated fairly without ever interviewing her.

On Harden's discharge form, beside her honorable discharge (in the absence of aggravating circumstances, policy stipulates that the character of a homosexual discharge be commensurate with the character of the person's service) are the words, "Homosexual Acts." She will carry that form with her for the rest of her life, and some employers will want to see it. Even on the so-called short form, there is a code barring reenlistment that many employers recognize. "The humiliation goes on," says Harden, a sad-eyed woman who now works as a police officer in Louisiana. She still wears her Air Force ring.

On a bright, windy spring Friday, R. and I attend the weekly graduation ceremony at the Marine Corps Recruit Depot in San Diego. R. wears his dress-blue trousers, which have a thick red stripe down each side to show that he is an officer; his white "cover," as hats are known in the military; a long-sleeved khaki shirt, and khaki tie. He has misplaced his officer's tie clip; appearing at the graduation without one is out of the question, so we stop to buy another. The marines we pass on our way to the graduation salute R. crisply and say, "Good morning, Sir," as R. returns the salute. He admits to falling naturally into the designated marine walk, swinging his arms so that each hand extends six inches beyond his body and then three inches behind it.

The six graduating platoons, all male (female marines are trained on Parris Island, S.C.), stand perfectly still, occupying a tiny fraction of a runway-size courtyard surrounded by golden California Mission-style buildings. They have just completed three months of famously punishing training—longer than boot camp in the other military services. As the Ma-

rine band begins to play, R. looks at the hundreds of identical-looking soldiers and says: "There's 500 of them. You figure, probably 50 are gay."

During his early years in the Corps, R. had two homosexual experiences, which he viewed as the temptations of Satan. His transformation from rabid homophobe to gay man occurred haltingly over seven confusing years. At times he felt an urge to bond with his enlisted men that led him once to share a hotel room with some of them during a trip in Asia—an act of fraternization and favoritism that he now deplores. "I was in denial," he says. "I told myself I was an officer looking out for my men in a foreign country. Now I see that I was attracted to my men."

It was in 1992 that R.'s perception of himself began to shift. In an officer's meeting, he says: "Somebody told a gay joke, and everyone laughed. Then he said, 'You know, faggots are the last group of people that a marine can joke about without having to worry about offending anyone.' And I said, 'Yeah!' But somewhere in the back of my mind I thought: Good. He can't tell I've had sex with two men."

Several months later, R. admitted to himself that he was homosexual and experienced a tremendous relief, even euphoria, along with a heightened awareness of his actions. "Right after I admitted it, we went to some training in the desert, and they had field showers," he recalls. "It's a room full of 50 naked men. I purposely waited until the very end, when I was the only one there, because I thought, Someday everyone's going to know I was gay, and I don't want anyone saying: 'Oh, I remember. He used to leer at me in the shower.'" To this day, he showers alone whenever possible.

R.'s problems as a gay marine were just beginning. A rumor reached him that after a group sexual experience he was involved in with female prostitutes in the Philippines a year earlier, someone had described him as a guy who was looking a little too closely at other men's anatomy. Desperate to quash the rumor, R. invited a female friend to San Diego to pose as his girlfriend. While at a bar with R., she became interested in one of the straight marines she was supposed to be deceiving. R. made it clear that if she wanted to flirt with the man, she and R. would first have to stage a fight, which they proceeded to do. "We were screaming," he says, "and I went like

I was going to hit her. 'You bitch, you're a slut.' " R. charged out of the bar, passed a couple of hours at a gay bar nearby, then returned to pick up his "girl-friend." By this time, however, the heterosexual ma-rine was bruising for a fight over the way R. had treated the woman, and R. narrowly escaped a punch-out. His life of paranoid dissembling had begun.

When the graduation ends, we drive to Camp Pendelton for lunch. Passing through one of the many military checkpoints in and around San Diego has the quality of falling into a parallel universe; today, near the Staff Noncommissioned Officers' Club, teams of military prisoners in bright orange coveralls are manicuring hedges. As we head inside the dining room, R. is greeted by a leathery man with vivid blue eyes wearing cammies. "How's life on the other side?" the man barks.

I feel R. go tense beside me. "What other side, Sir?" he asks.

"The other side you're on," the man says, and laughs.

While eating his Reuben sandwich, R. mulls over the encounter, trying to recall where he had previ-ously met the man, what he could have meant by "the other side." There are many "sides" in the Ma-rine Corps: officer versus enlisted, ground versus air wing, active duty versus reserves. Most likely, R. muses, the man was alluding to his stint as a gen-eral's aide. But the question lingers: Does he know?

We have arranged to meet M., a gay female friend of R.'s, at lunch. Because she is not in uniform, hav-ing just come from a farewell party, M. is able to join us despite the fact that R. is an officer and she is a staff N.C.O. Still, M. grows anxious at our table; like most military women, she functions in an over-whelmingly male environment where she says that she feels intensely scrutinized. An attractive woman with a small gold cross around her neck, M. has told only one of her heterosexual colleagues, a civilian, that she is gay. "It is relaxing, or easing, to feel like she knows me," M. says.

If male homosexuals feel pressure to invent het-erosexual lives, the pressure on women is exponen-tially greater—they represent 14 percent of the armed forces, yet have accounted for roughly a quar-ter of the homosexuals discharged over the past four years.

Several years ago, M. took a step that is quite common among gay military personnel of both sexes: she got married. In addition to the obvious boon of creating the appearance of heterosexuality, marriage in the military brings myriad financial ben-efits; the most important is a higher Basic Allowance for Quarters when you live off-base—essential for any homosexual who wants a private life, but on an enlisted salary, which begins at $11,113 per year, virtually unaffordable. Marriages of convenience, ei-ther between gay men and women or with foreign-ers seeking American citizenship, are one solution.

M. married a civilian homosexual so that she could live off-base with her partner while securing medical benefits for her "husband," who was her partner's best friend. But guilt over deceiving the Government soon began to gnaw at her. Her rela-tionship foundered; when M. told her partner that she was divorcing the friend, the woman threatened to tell M.'s C.O. that she was gay. Panic-stricken, M. nevertheless held her ground. "I said, 'Go ahead, there are going to be three of us in jail,' " she says. M. proceeded with the divorce, and her partner kept quiet. "I felt haunted by that nightmare for years," she says.

Yet perhaps the biggest problem for gay military women is a problem they share with straight women: they are often deeply resented by their male col-leagues and subordinates, many of whom still feel that women shouldn't be serving at all. Being gay is a vulnerability for women that some male colleagues are only too happy to exploit. The C.O. of one of M.'s friends has threatened to sit outside her house all night to prove that she has female lovers. Often, gay women are reluctant to report sexual harassment for fear of retaliatory investigations into their sexuality. A., an Army officer who has been deployed to both the Persian Gulf and Bosnia, filed a sexual-harassment complaint against a superior who de-manded sexual favors from her. Some months later, an anonymous assertion that she was homosexual appeared in A.'s personnel file, and her security clearance was suspended.

M. has spent more than 10 years in the Corps, but like R., she plans to end her career when her present enlistment is up. "I'm sick of living the lie," she says. "What scares me is that it gets to the point where you don't even notice it. You start to withhold informa-tion that you don't have to. *How was your night? Oh, good.* I'm practicing saying, *We did this and we did that.* Kind of remembering that this is human interaction, and this is O.K."

The military is adamant that it cannot allow homosexuals to serve openly without greatly compromising the readiness and effectiveness of its troops. Military personnel live and work under intimate conditions that would shock most civilians. (On the U.S.S. Constellation, an aircraft carrier I toured, the enlisted men's berthing quarters were crammed with three-tiered bunk beds the size of large dresser drawers.) Unit cohesion is at the heart of a successful fighting force, and Gen. Norman Schwarzkopf and Gen. Colin Powell argued passionately before Congress that openly homosexual men and women would polarize units and destroy that cohesion.

At least some of R.'s gay friends in the military don't dispute this view. "Homophobic people don't want to work with a fag," one officer said. "The group falls apart, we do not fight effectively." And while it is true that many NATO countries allow homosexuals to serve openly in their militaries (as does Israel), anecdotal evidence suggests that most homosexuals in these forces still remain closeted—and must, if they wish to advance in rank.

There is a hesitation to dispute the military's arguments. I, like most Americans, have no idea how wars are fought, and it is easy to underestimate the deep animus toward homosexuals that exists in the armed forces. (General Schwarzkopf, for one, says he believes that allowing homosexuals to serve openly would sharply discourage enlistments.)

Still, several factors complicate this picture. For one, homosexuals have served in the armed forces since the country was founded (even earlier, actually; one of George Washington's generals is said to have been gay), and many have served openly—their units knew of their sexual orientation—without apparent problems. Brig. Gen. Pat Foote, who retired in 1989 after 29 1/2 years in the Army, says, "I don't know many serving officers or N.C.O.'s who have not, in units with which they were affiliated, known that there were men and women other than heterosexuals doing magnificent jobs." Maj. Gen. Vance Coleman, who was wounded in the Korean War and is now retired from the Army, says that he served with homosexuals without incident.

General Coleman, who is black, says that the present-day arguments against allowing homosexuals to serve openly echo prior ones against integrating blacks in the armed forces—including the claims that white soldiers would not follow orders given by black officers and that whites and blacks could not peaceably share a foxhole. When President Truman overrode those arguments in 1948 with an executive order to integrate, military personnel, among others, reacted with horror.

Referring to homosexuals in the military, General Coleman says: "This is a civil rights issue *and* a human rights issue. You're not the same as I am, therefore you're inferior."

Perhaps another factor complicating the military's argument against homosexuals serving openly is that discharges of homosexuals, some suspect, fall during wartime; indeed, revelations of homosexuality during wartime are often received skeptically by the military, as possible ruses to avoid combat, and a person must sometimes furnish sworn statements from sexual partners to be discharged. Though the Pentagon disputes this, General Coleman, among others, says he believes that concern about the presence of homosexuals is a peacetime obsession. "When there's a war, nobody has time to deal with that," he says. "It's about fighting and winning."

Tom Carpenter, a former Marine fighter pilot who met his partner of 20 years, a former naval flight officer, while on active duty in the 70's, says he believes that the military's revulsion from homosexuality is linked to the intense male bonding that has traditionally been a part of military life. Like many historically all-male environments, the military has had its share of homoerotic rituals—most famously the Navy's "Crossing the Line" ceremony ("modified" and "supervised" nowadays, according to the Navy, but said to still occur unmodified on at least some ships). "Crossing the Line" is an initiation for new sailors, or "polliwogs," making their first Equator crossing. Elements of this ritual include the crowning of "King Neptune's queen," played by a young sailor in drag; the whipping and paddling of polliwogs by a gantlet of seasoned sailors, known as "shellbacks," and sometimes simulated fellatio and anal intercourse between shellbacks and polliwogs. At the conclusion, the young initiates strip off their soiled uniforms and pitch them into the sea, then mill about in the nude as proof that they, too, are now shellbacks.

Indeed, by many accounts, what is known as "conditional homosexuality," or homosexual behavior by men who are normally heterosexual, is not uncommon among soldiers during long periods when women are unavailable. Navy phrases like "It ain't queer unless it's tied to the pier" allude to such behaviors. Some married men, it is said, believe that sex with another man does not constitute adultery. There is even a provision in "Don't Ask, Don't Tell" that excuses homosexual conduct if it is aberrant behavior for an individual. Bridget Wilson, a San Diego lawyer who has defended gay military personnel, calls this the queen-for-a-day exception.

Lois Shawver, a clinical psychologist whose book "And the Flag Was Still There" studies attitudes toward homosexuality in the military, says, "The sense of the troops' being demoralized is built on the anxiety that gays are going to stare at them and turn on them sexually." But Shawver's research suggests that this fear is unfounded—that, in fact, homosexuals regulate their behavior even more carefully when they are known to be gay. As for exceptions, military policy and, in some cases, the Uniform Code of Military Justice prohibit displays of physical affection while in uniform, sex in military barracks, sex between people of different ranks and sodomy, which includes oral sex.

"We have within the U.C.M.J. all that we need to deal with people that bring any type of sexual misbehavior to the workplace or the barracks," says General Foote, who recently served as the vice chairman of the Army's Senior Review Panel on Sexual Harassment. "We don't need any more laws."

The next time I see R., a few weeks later, the weather is warmer and El Niño has roused rashes of fluorescent purple flowers along Interstate 5. At the end of his workday, we drive from Camp Pendelton to Hillcrest and meet the tank officer I'd first met at the pizza dinner and his male partner, a naval nurse, in the home they share with a burly chow and a small striped cat.

Over beers, R. recounts a quintessential gay-military snafu that occurred at the Marine officer's brunch he attended a few Sundays back. The officer had invited his straight military friends for brunch on Saturday, his gay friends on Sunday, but one straight Navy pilot got the days confused and arrived with his wife in the midst of the all-male brunch. The host panicked, feigned an emergency and bolted from his own party.

But the heterosexual couple, apparently unfazed, were still there when the shaken host finally returned. According to R., the Marine officer then took his straight friend into a quiet room and said, "There's something I have to tell you"—at which point the guest seized his arm and answered: "Don't worry. I'm on board with the program."

There are people who feel that as a younger generation rises to power within the military, attitudes like that of the Navy pilot will gradually prevail, and that the laws barring open homosexuality will fall away, just as those barring women and blacks eventually did.

But "Don't Ask, Don't Tell" is now Federal law, and laws are not changed easily. So far, the Supreme Court has refused to hear a case challenging it, and three Circuit Courts have upheld the policy. However, the Second Circuit Court, in New York City, recently heard an appeal of a case in which a lower-court judge ruled that "Don't Ask, Don't Tell" violates the constitutional rights of equal protection and free speech. That case, Able v. the United States, may yet reach the Supreme Court, but even then, precedent suggests that the Court may defer to the military.

"If you look at the case in terms of the law and reason, it looks like an overwhelming winner," says Matt Coles, director of the Lesbian and Gay Rights Project of the American Civil Liberties Union, which filed the case jointly with Lambda. "But if you look at it in terms of the courts and the military, it looks like it doesn't have a chance."

The more likely venue for change is Congress, but that, too, seems a long way off. Republicans are virtually unanimous in their opposition to gay rights; so far, even the Employment Non-Discrimination Act, a basic gay rights bill, has failed to pass. Representative Barney Frank (Democrat of Massachusetts), who is openly gay and opposes "Don't Ask, Don't Tell," says that should the Democrats win even a small majority in the House and the Senate in November (no small task), the gay rights bill could eventually pass. However, he holds out little hope for lifting "Don't Ask, Don't Tell" anytime soon.

"The military issue is unfortunately seen as a tougher one," he says. "So you'd need a bigger Democratic majority for that."

Whatever happens, R. will be reading about it in the newspapers, like everyone else; in a few months, he will become a civilian for the first time in his adult life. It won't be an easy transition for him. "It's a way of life," he says of being a marine. "David and I will be walking down the Oceanside Pier, and somebody will see me, and they'll be like, 'Sir, how are you doing?' David's like: 'You're not at work! You're not in uniform! Why are they calling you Sir?' I'm like: 'That's just the way it is. I can't explain it.' "

But R. joined the Marines for the brotherhood, the esprit de corps, and ultimately, his sense of brotherhood has been eroded by the years of hiding. "For the longest time, I felt close to the people," he says. "But more and more, when you hear somebody make an anti-gay comment, that becomes a bookmark in your mind. I can't become close friends with the people I work with. It's definitely made me grow apart from the Marine Corps."

His experience raises the question of whether openly gay soldiers are as great a threat to unit cohesion as closeted homosexuals, whose enforced secrecy gradually distances them from their fellow soldiers. A., the woman who served in the Persian Gulf and in Bosnia, says that as a homosexual "you have this barrier to intimacy with the people you're serving with—and that intimacy is what keeps people alive in hostile situations."

Among the many paradoxes surrounding the issue of homosexuals in the military is this: the fact that R. has thrived in the military—and has the record to prove it—is partly what impels him to move on. "I want to leave in a pristine state," he says. "I'm tired of the looming prospect that tomorrow the whole world could come crashing down."

Chapter 6 Review Questions

1. What is your definition of an informal group in organizations?
2. How are informal groups formed and how do they influence the activities of public organizations?
3. Do informal groups emerge and have an impact on *public* organizations in the same ways as they do upon *business* organizations?
4. In the case, "Uniforms in the Closet," what general lessons did you draw out specifically concerning *administrative* issues involving informal groups and the resolution of these issues?
5. Can you see any evidence of the influence of informal groups in organizations with which you are familiar? If so, how did these groups emerge and in what ways do they affect the policies and activities of those organizations?
6. Based on your personal observations of the workings of informal groups, would you modify the Elton Mayo's concept in any way? For example, could you add more specifics about how to identify informal groups? Measure their strength? Identify their sources of influence on organizations? Reasons for their weakness? Methods for achieving the support of management? Ways of better communication? Means for improving their motivation?

Key Terms

informal group
"great illumination"
social structure

Hawthorne experiments
interview program
scientific-technological change

Suggestions for Further Reading

The best book about the Hawthorne experiments is Fritz Roethlisberger and W.J. Dickson, *Management and the Worker* (Cambridge, Mass.: Harvard University Press, 1939). For a less complicated view, see Fritz Roethlisberger, *Management and Morale* (Cambridge, Mass.: Harvard University Press, 1941). Elton Mayo's broad philosophic interpretations are contained in his "trilogy": *The Human Problems of an Industrial Organization* (New York: Macmillan Co., 1933); *The Social Problems of an Industrial Civilization* (Boston: Graduate School of Business Administration, Harvard University, 1945); and *The Political Problems of an Industrial Civilization* (same publisher, 1947). For an excellent retrospective on Hawthorne, refer to "An Interview with Fritz Roethlisberger," *Organizational Dynamics,* 1 (Autumn 1972), pp. 31–45; "Hawthorne Revisited: The Legend and the Legacy," *Organizational Dynamics,* 4 (Winter 1975), pp. 66–80; and Alfred A. Bolton, ed., "Special Issue: Relay Assembly Testroom Participants Remember: Hawthorne a Half Century Later," *International Journal of Public Administration,* 17, 2 (1994), entire issue.

Two classic interpretations of Hawthorne are George Homans, *The Human Group* (New York: Harcourt, Brace, 1950) and Henry Landsberger, *Hawthorne Revisited* (Ithaca, N.Y.: Cornell University Press, 1958). By contrast, to taste a small sampling of the scholarly arguments over Hawthorne, read Alex Carey, "The Hawthorne Studies: A Radical Criticism," *American Sociological Review,* 32 (June 1967), pp. 403–416; and for a review of small group theory applied to public administration, see Robert T. Golembiewski, "The Small Group and Public Administration," *Public Administration Review,* 19 (Summer 1959), pp. 149–156. For some interesting related perspectives on the psychological dimensions of public management, see Richard L. Schott, "The Psychological Development of Adults: Implications for Public Administration," *Public Administration Review,* 46 (November/December 1986), pp. 657–667; and Larry Hirshhorn, *The Workplace Within: Psychodynamics of Organizational Life* (Cambridge, Mass.: MIT Press, 1991). The legacy of Hawthorne can be found in numerous examples of the prolific postwar authors associated with the Human Relations School of Management, Chris Argyris, Warren Bennis, Frederick Herzberg, Daniel Katz, Robert Kahn, Rensis Likert, Douglas McGregor, Leonard Sayles, William Whyte, and many, many others who owe a tremendous debt to Hawthorne. In turn, their "spinoffs" and "impacts" on public administration have been profound and numerous but largely uncharted by scholars in the field, though for a useful compilation of many of their writings, refer to Frank J. Thompson, ed., *Classics of Public Personnel Policy,* Second Edition (Monterey, Calif.: Brooks/Cole, 1991). Much of the current thinking related to small groups inside organizations today can be found within organizational behavior studies—for example, in journals such as *The International Journal of Organization Theory and Behavior,* or personal and organizational behavior in texts such as Michael L. Vasy et al., *Organizational Behavior and Public Management,* 3d ed. (NY: Marcel Dekker, 1998). To witness the heavy influence of this ongoing emphasis upon developing human resources and potential applied directly to modern public administration and its specific needs for improvment, read the Volcker Commission Report, entitled, "The Report of the National Commission on the Public Service," *Leadership for America: Rebuilding the Public Service* (Lexington, Mass.: Lexington Books, 1990).

CHAPTER 7

Key Decision Makers Inside Public Administration: The Concept of Competing Bureaucratic Subsystems

O ur public bureaucracy is composed of identifiable clusters of individuals who work and act in influential ways inside bureaucracy. Each of these subsystems shapes the broad outcomes of bureaucracy.

Richard J. Stillman II

READING 7

Introduction

Nearly 5 million people work for the federal government, and another roughly 15 million are employed by state and local governments in the United States. They may be highway engineers who maintain or build our roads; police who patrol neighborhoods; public school teachers who educate children; or forest rangers who run the national park system. America's public service is composed of many types of people who perform the vital and varied activities of modern government.

How can we generalize about these public servants? Their characteristics? The roles they play inside bureaucracy? The work they perform? Their influence on the policies and activities of public agencies? Why do *they* so significantly shape "the outcomes" of modern bureaucracy?

In the following selection by the author of this text, drawn from his book *The American Bureaucracy,* he gives us something of "an X-Ray" picture of the inside of modern public bureaucracy. He argues that government is not made up of simply *one* monolithic body of employees but rather distinctive clusters of five varieties of personnel: political appointees, professional careerists, civil servant generalists, unionized workers, and contract employees. The author outlines the attributes of each group, which he labels "bureaucratic subsystems," the roles they play within public agencies, their origins and evolution, sources of recruitment, motivation(s), ladders for promotions, impacts on public policies, and issues or problems confronting each of these bureaucratic subsystems. The writer contends that the types of subsystems that make up the inside of any agency decisively influence the content of its work, direction of its policies, and decisions it makes—or fails to make. "The balance or imbalance of these groups," concludes Stillman, "within any agency is fundamental to its character, policies, and performance."

Rarely does just *one* subsystem comprise any public organization, but rather several of these bureaucratic subsystems are normally found within most modern public bureaucracies. Which one is in charge and how they work out their relationships becomes critical to understanding what happens in public administration. As Stillman writes: "Most bureaucracies in the public sector are, however, dominated not by any one subsystem but by several; indeed, all these subsystems normally are found within their structures. Hence, policy outcomes frequently result from their jockeying for position, influence, and power over public bureaucratic actions. Conflicts between subsystems are common. Sometimes the competition for power and control over the policy-making apparatus can be quite severe and intense."

As you read this selection, you might keep in mind:

Why does the author conclude that contemporary public bureaucracy is *not* composed of only *one* variety of public officials but rather five types? How does this argument compare or contrast with that of Weber in Chapter 2?

According to the author, how did each distinctive subsystem begin, evolve, grow within government, and develop unique value-orientations?

In what ways does each one contribute to influencing decisively the public policy process as well as the implementation of public policy?

How does the size, composition, and relationships of groups in bureaucracy influence its work and "impacts" on society as a whole?

Inside Public Bureaucracy

RICHARD J. STILLMAN II

Once a young aide to President William Howard Taft kept repeating the phrase "machinery of government" while briefing the president. Taft, so the story goes, became exasperated and turned to a friend and whispered, "My God, the man actually *believes* government is a machine!"

Taft had it right. United States government, especially its bureaucracy, is not an automated assembly line, devoid of human beings, lifeless and machinelike. Quite to the contrary, our public bureaucracy is composed of identifiable clusters of individuals who work and act in influential ways inside the bureaucracy. Each of these subsystems shapes the broad outcomes of bureaucratic institutions. Each competes for power and influence over its particular bureaucracy. These human subsystems perform different tasks in government. Through diverse strategies they aim to achieve different goals with different stakes or outcomes for bureaucracy. Each serves vitally important functions within bureaucracy and significantly determines in various ways what bureaucracy does or does not do and how well it performs these functions. The size and influence of each of these human subgroups vary considerably from agency to agency and locale to locale. Yet many public organizations contain several of these subsystems. Some public operations have all five subsystems, which jockey with one another for influence and status.

The boundary between each of the subsystems is not always clear. They tend to overlap with considerable gray areas between them. Subsystems in different agencies do not always exhibit the same exact dimensions, proportions, or precisely similar characteristics. Nor are all five groups necessarily found in every agency. Sometimes only one or two are represented. In other words, these subsystems are fairly open, fluid, and adaptive to differing organizational contexts and situations. They are also fundamentally *human and political, not machinelike in behavior.* Subsystems do have certain important similarities and differences in their roles, values, missions, power, status, functions, activities, and influence within public organizations. This chapter will examine the special characteristics of each subsystem within organizations and particularly how they affect the outputs of every agency from the inside. Brief descriptions of these five subsystems follow.

Political appointees are those individuals who serve without tenure and whose appointments are based often, though not always, upon political ties or party loyalties.

Professional careerists are various groups of personnel with specialized expertise in specific fields. Positions occupied by these groups are usually based on advanced professional training. This subsystem offers lifetime careers and stresses "rank-in-person" rather than "rank-in-job."

The *general civil service* operates under "merit

concepts." Characteristics of this subsystem are tenure, rank in-position, and "classified" hierarchies of positions based upon the amount of tasks and responsibilities.

Unionized workers are blue collar and, increasingly, white collar workers whose employment is based upon negotiated contracts between union representatives and management within the jurisdictions they serve.

Contractual employees are untenured workers whose employment with government is directly or indirectly governed by various contractual agreements negotiated with individuals, private firms, nonprofit organizations, and universities for rendering specific services for a limited or specified time. They are not governed by civil service rules nor do they work under union contracts.

The Political Appointee Subsystem: The Birds of Passage

Most political appointees fill the top-level policy-making posts within federal, state, and local bureaucracies. These men and women serve in government without tenure, holding office at the pleasure of the chief elected official, who hires them, promotes them, or dismisses them. At the federal level, political appointees make up a fairly small group, with only 5,823 out of approximately 3 million federal civilian workers. Federal political appointees are divided into three categories: (1) PASs, or presidential appointments with the consent of the Senate (663); PAs, or presidential appointments not requiring Senate confirmation (1405); and agency appointments, those made by the agency chief (1725). The number of PAS has remained fairly stable over the past two decades (roughly 660), but the number of noncareer SES and schedule C political appointees has grown significantly. The number and categories of political appointees vary considerably in state and local jurisdictions. In some regions where there is no civil service system—particularly rural county governments or the machine-run cities—virtually all government jobs are handed out on the basis of party loyalty or political patronage. Today, however, most cities and states follow the federal pattern in reserving only top-level policy jobs for political appointees, who serve at the pleasure of a governor or mayor. Particularly in "reformed" or "clean" city and state governments, these posts are few and limited to only the very top levels. Colorado, for example, has only two dozen political appointees out of 5,000 manager-level posts. However, in Massachusetts all of the managers' positions in the state, some 3,500 jobs down to the supervisor's level, are considered "policy-making" positions and are available for the governor's appointees. Thus the "range" is quite wide, depending on the influence of "reformism" found within the local/regional politics.

Within federal bureaucracies, in particular, appointees' lack of tenure limits the length of their employment. The average federal political appointee serves only twenty-two months in office. Hugh Heclo has rightly observed that they are "birds of passage"[1] who recognize from the start that they will not be around for very long. The most they can look forward to is a four-year term, and if a president is reelected (and they are lucky) they *might* be reappointed for longer periods—though that is rare. Transience is their only common trademark. Most, therefore, set their sights and adapt their behavior for the short range by recognizing that if they are to accomplish *anything* in their jobs, they must move quickly. Short-term horizons, limited goals, and quick results tend to characterize their actions. This tendency among political appointees also probably characterizes state and local appointees within jurisdictions where there is a competitive party system. But elsewhere, if the top jobs have little or no turnover, political appointees can look forward to longer tenure in office, thus shifting their time horizons to somewhat longer perspectives.

Generally, though, appointees' job uncertainty means that they have to have another position, outside of government, to fall back on in case they fall

out of favor or out of office (a good possibility given the hazards of these untenured posts today). Hence, many political appointees at the federal level are drawn from law firms or are on leave from big businesses, government, or universities. The pool from which they are drawn is thus quite small and tends to be, but is not always, confined to upperclass individuals who can afford a short time away from their regular lines of work. This qualification also tends to drastically limit the social characteristics of political appointees to white, urban, middle-aged males with advanced Ivy League educations and ambitions for high-status careers.[2] While President Jimmy Carter attempted to recruit greater numbers of women and minorities into these posts, the bulk of political appointees even in his administration in the late 1970s, and of Ronald Reagan's in the 1980s, was largely drawn from this very small pool. However, in the 1990s President Bill Clinton drew his top appointees from a wider cross section of Americans. Historically, as law firms, businesses, and universities tended to become more representative, so too the "pool" of political appointees has tended to become more diverse and varied. Political appointees at the state and local levels, particularly as one moves closer to the grass roots, represent much more diversity in talent, training, income, and background. Generally, there is greater heterogeneity and better representation of social groups at lower governmental jurisdictions, though there is by no means a wide popular representation even there.[3]

While there are several prominent examples of political appointees whose faces reappear in government, usually at higher levels of bureaucracy when their party assumes office (George Shultz, James Baker, and Caspar Weinberger crop up repeatedly in Republican administrations, and William Perry and Warren Christopher in Democratic ones), most political appointees have limited backgrounds in government. Very few serve repeated spells in government; few work for more than one administration. Few survive election turnovers in the executive branch. Many simply do not want to stay more than a few years in office, nor can they, because of pressing outside professional or business commitments. Yet most are *drawn from and return to related fields of endeavor.* Western ranchers, businesspersons, and lawyers have tended to occupy the top slots at the Department of the Interior because of their prolonged involvement with western public lands; just as defense contractors, former military officers, and business executives have long been recruited to top political slots at DoD. And most return to these jobs afterwards. Thus different bureaucracies tend to draw their political appointees from different occupational-economic sectors of society as well as from different regions primarily because of these appointees' prior experience with the tasks and activities of the agency. An appropriate "track record" in the policy concerns of the agency, and the correct party identification, and especially policy positions that are in accord with the chief executive's, are important qualifications for such appointments.

Their specific policy roles in bureaucracy can be conceived of as loose-jointed, concentric rings that emanate outward from the office of the elected chief executive—a president, governor, or mayor. The most powerful appointees are those who occupy leadership roles within the major Cabinet-rank departments, sometimes referred to at the federal level as the inner Cabinet. The inner Cabinet is composed of the secretaries of Defense, State, and of the Office of Management and Budget, as well as senior noncareer or career ambassadors to major governments, such as Europe or China. These individuals are responsible for the operations of the largest public agencies (like DoD) and subsequently have powerful policy agenda-setting functions (like OMB). Similarly, inner Cabinets, made up of those closest to the governor or mayor and exercising major policy-organizational tasks, are found at state and local levels as well, though their titles differ. Inner Cabinet members at the federal level are often at the White House with the president or are representing their agencies before Congress. They are responsible for setting—and defending—the major policy priorities of the president and the agency they represent. They also exert the overall leader-

ship within their particular organization, appoint numerous political personnel within the organization, and represent it before the media and special interest groups. Their most important function within government is to translate the campaign platforms and promises of the elected officials into administrative actions of major policy-administrative importance to the chief executive—the president, governor, or mayor. In short, they serve as linchpins between election-night rhetoric and actual institutional performance.

The next ring, or the outer Cabinet, is composed of men and women who see the president (or governor or mayor) less frequently but nevertheless hold Cabinet rank (also normally requiring Senate or legislative confirmation). They are frequently charged with running a major public agency such as the Department of Housing and Urban Development or the Department of Corrections at the state level. They are a rung below the inner Cabinet in *informal* power and status only, for their legal titles and prerogatives are normally much the same as those of their counterparts in the inner Cabinet. Indeed, they may have many of the same responsibilities, such as directing a large department, providing its leadership, setting its policy agenda, defending it before Congress, and so on.

The third level is generally termed the sub-Cabinet. It is composed of deputy secretaries, assistant secretaries, and administrative heads of major non-Cabinet agencies and bureaus. These individuals also occupy important policy-making posts, and sometimes highly sensitive and critical ones, such as that of deputy attorney general in the Department of Justice, who is normally responsible for the daily management of the department's activities, or of the assistant secretary for International Security Affairs in the Department of Defense who is charged with shaping broad strategic policies within DoD. These men and women are generally more specialized in particular fields of expertise than the inner or outer Cabinet members. While they may have had a variety of experiences and backgrounds in government, business, law, or the professions, their training and work experiences tend to be more appropriate to the positions that they occupy. They have also usually had considerable experience handling political issues related to these offices and are expected to take positions on these issues in accordance with the president's overall priorities.

Given the increasing proliferation of special interest groups that watch closely these sub-Cabinet appointments and their pronouncements, key sub-Cabinet officials, at least during the last few years, are often drawn from the ranks of special interest groups and return to these after government service. Democrats tend to draw their appointees from left-leaning policy groups, while Republicans draw theirs from think tanks, legislative staffs, and policy-advocate groups on the right-wing.

Yet some scholars, such as Thomas P. Murphy, Donald E. Nuechterlein, and Ronald Stupak, have argued that the influence of this group of appointees over the policy-making process has declined in recent years, because of its increase in number.[4] Though as a collective group, their prominence and power has on the whole increased in recent years; a modified Gresham's law operates here; that is, increasing numbers of political appointees at this sub-Cabinet level drive down their individual influence over policy decisions. Put simply: a call from an assistant secretary does not mean what it once did.

The fourth group of appointees encompasses a wide variety of advisors to the secretary and directors of agencies and bureaus. Like the previous level of appointees, this level has expanded enormously in the past two decades as secretaries brought in their own people to help run their departments. At the federal level these assorted political appointees do not require Senate confirmation, so for the most part their ranks have grown without legislative oversight and control. Few, however, are active politicians or were closely involved with the election campaign of the chief executive. Most are more directly identified with the professional or policy issues of the agencies where they work. Many have had personal ties or friendships with their immediate supervisors. They are generally reputed to be experts in the field of law, business, or education and may have actually been

drawn from the ranks of the civil service. Some have known or worked with each other before or fought the opposition party together over the very sets of policy issues they are now actively administering and formulating.

Compared with appointees at other levels, these men and women are the most expert and specialized, and they are often more willing to push forward the interests of their particular agencies and resist political intrusions from others. And yet as Frederick Mosher has observed of these appointees: "Some are eminent figures in their fields, often principal representatives and defenders of the services which they superintend. Yet their stance differs from that of the members of the permanent services below them. They *can* be replaced or their situations can be made so uncomfortable as to induce them to resign or at least alter their behavior."[5] Their lack of tenure is the heavy stick that ensures their ultimate responsiveness to higher circles of appointees.

Finally, there is an increasingly large group of individuals in public bureaucracy today who occupy a limbo-land between quasipolitical and nonpolitical territory. Their position at the federal level has been institutionalizd through the creation of the Senior Executive Service (SES) in the 1978 Civil Service Reform Act.

SES developed a new category of upper-level administrators that is formed from supergrade officials in grades GS-16, 17, and 18 and in Executive Ranks IV and V, in which position assignments and pay are determined by political decision makers and yet are also protected by the civil service rules (career officials in SES have the option of retreating to GS-15 grades). The rationale for creating SES came mainly from argument that improved management in government could result from greater mobility of its top executives. Drawn from senior career ranks, it was argued that like in business, the president and top executives should be able to shift senior managers from one post to another more easily than the hide-bound civil service rules allowed prior to 1978. Further, as in the case of business, bonus incentives were provided for rewarding outstanding performances in SES.

On the other hand, unsatisfactory performances could cause removal or replacement in SES. By law, the bulk of these individuals must be drawn from the ranks of the civil service, since only 10 percent of SES members (or 703 of the current 8,130 SES employees) can be political appointees. About 40 percent of SES positions are designated as "career reserved" because of their sensitive positions. The number of SES positions has grown since 1980 but so has the number of noncareer or political-appointee positions.

While the jury is still out on whether or not the introduction of SES has proven successful, it remains a *potentially* important tool for improving federal management and control.

On the state level, twelve states have created SES systems. Four did so prior to the 1978 CSRA: California (1963), Minnesota (1969), Wisconsin (1973), and Oregon (1977). After the creation of the federal level SES, several states adopted their own SES systems shortly afterwards: Connecticut (1979), Florida (1980), Iowa (1980), Michigan (1980), Washington (1980), and Pennsylvania (1981). Both Tennessee and New Jersey passed their SES legislation in 1986, and Massachusetts gave the governor statutory authority to set up a senior career management system, which has not yet been implemented. While the state-level SES systems, like the federal-level one, offer *potentially* enhanced career mobility, managerial control, and leadership flexibility, as Sherwood and Breyer suggest in their evaluation of state-level SES systems: "Little in the twenty-four-year history of executive personnel systems in the states suggests that they have come to occupy a highly significant role in the processes of governance."[6]

Why the disappointing performance of state-level SES systems? According to Deborah D. Roberts, "State SES systems contain too many lofty and contradictory goals that cannot all be satisfied. These contradictions revolve around incentives, membership quandaries, and diversity among the important players." Due to such challenging contradictions, according to Professor Roberts, existing state SES systems "are undergoing painful retrenchment and redirection, and few

states appear willing to adopt new SES initiatives."[7]

To sum up the influence of the political appointee subsystem: First, these individuals occupy the highest, most prominent posts within public organizations. Thus, they serve as linchpins between campaign promises and bureaucratic performance. However, they are characterized overall as a highly diverse, fragmented, and transitory group with little cohesiveness.

Second, their influence within bureaucracy depends upon the policy positions they hold, the length of their government service, their connections with top elected officials, their own personalities, their support from outside groups, the immediate tasks at hand, and whether these lend themselves to imminent solutions. Generally, as one moves up the hierarchy of political officials to the inner Cabinet, these individuals have the most generalized backgrounds, and must deal with the broadest, most critical policy issues. They also exercise the widest, most influential policy roles inside public bureaucracy, if their tenure is long enough and their external support adequate to the performance of the tasks at hand. Here at the top the political winds blow the fiercest; the "turf battles" are the most intense, and the stakes are the highest.

Third, as one moves down the hierarchy of these political officials toward those of quasi-political status, greater degrees of specialization are found as well as more identification with the programmatic goals, tasks, and issues within the agencies they serve. They are less generalist in outlook and more concerned with pushing narrower policy agendas, which often means they are less interested in and responsive to their own chief's re-election priorities.

Fourth, sharp turf fights over policy issues therefore ensue frequently between these various levels of political appointees, largely because of the different perspectives built into their hierarchical roles. Here is where pitched policy battles frequently occur and are resolved. In the pecking order of appointees, those at or near the top push agendas that are broader and more responsive to the chief executive's agenda, while those lower down tend to be more programmatic and responsive to the priorities and issues of the particular agencies in which they work.

Fifth, while the subsystem of political appointees is highly fragmented, these tend to cluster into networks in which those near the top have close personal ties, even long friendships, with the chief elected official (though not necessarily with each other, nor are they necessarily active in his political campaigns). Those on the lower rungs tend to be experts in particular fields and to have personal networks that run downward into the agency and outward into various external support groups associated with an agency's mission.

Sixth, what draws all appointees together and keeps them loyal and responsible, at least to some degree, to the elected official's policy agenda (and makes them a distinct bureaucratic subsystem) is the fact that they can be removed or transferred at any time by a president, governor, or mayor. Fear of losing a job can be a powerful incentive to stay in line with the top-level agenda, or at least to refrain from stating opposing views in public.

However, in this constantly shifting world of personnel and goals, as Norton Long pointed out, determining to whom one is loyal and what one should accomplish become difficult if not impossible tasks. This level in bureaucracy is an ambiguous world in which appearances frequently count more than on-the-job practices. Participants thus spend enormous amounts of time posturing and posing in order to appear to do the correct things for the right people and taking readings and soundings to find information about their own status and about the intentions of others. The closed door, an invitation to the right party, the frequency of meetings with the superior, and the seating arrangement at the conference table often signal more than the untrained eye can perceive or the written document explain. Hard-driving, ambitious men and women, even with considerable experience and exposure, become quickly frustrated and disillusioned with the confusion and pretense inherent in this subsystem, as autobiographies of recent incumbents testify. Policy activity at this level

of bureaucracy is very much like the greased pole competition at the old-fashioned county fair, where few, if any, climb to the top and reach the prize. The way up is slippery, uncertain, and treacherous, often crowded with many other frenzied competitors. There are no sure rules for success. And the prize, once reached, is often temporary, of little value, and hardly worth all that fierce competition and furiously expended energy. Many leave disillusioned and despairing about what they have done or failed to do. Good luck rather than personal skills often decides outcomes.

Seventh, political appointees, despite the highly ambiguous world in which they operate, ultimately are central to the governing processes at all levels of government. They are critical, individually and collectively, in the words of presidential scholar James P. Pfiffner, to assist chief executives in "hitting the ground running." But high job demands, family stress, extensive security checks, comparatively low pay (by contrast to other similarly responsible private-sector jobs), and detailed public and press scrutiny all combine to deter many from seeking such lines of work and to delay appointments. Indeed, President Clinton was slower than his recent predecessors in getting his own policy team in place, leading to criticism of Clinton's capacity to govern effectively.

The Professional Careerist Subsystem: Permanent Clusters of Powerful Experts

Professor Samuel H. Beer has said that U.S. society is governed by "technocratic politics" in which specialists with in-depth training and experience in different fields of government have assumed the duty of charting the course of various public organizations. As Beer argues:

I would remark how rarely additions to the public agenda have been initiated by the demands of voters or the advocacy of pressure groups or the platforms of political parties. On the contrary, in the fields of health, housing, urban renewal, transportation, welfare, education, poverty and energy, it has been in very great measure, people in government service or closely associated with it acting on the basis of their specialties and technical knowledge who first perceived the problem, conceived the program, initially urged it on the President and Congress, went on to help lobby it through to enactment and then saw to its administration.[8]

Some scholars, including Zbigniew Brzezinski, have called the phenomenon "the technetronic age"; Don Price calls it "the scientific estate"; for Daniel Bell it is "the post-industrial age"; for Guy Benveniste, "the politics of expertise."[9] But whatever term is used to describe the role of experts within government, the professional strata, a subsystem below that of political appointees, is now recognized by many scholars as a significant influence over the activities of modern public organizations. As Frederick C. Mosher has perceptively written, "For better or worse—or better and worse—much of government is now in the hands of professionals (including scientists). The choice of these professionals, the determination of their skills and the content of their work are now principally determined not by the general government agencies, but by their own professional elites, professional organizations and the institutions and facilities of higher education. It is unlikely the trend toward professionalization in or outside government will be reversed or even slowed."[10]

Professionalization in government influenced not only the domestic agenda, as Beer suggests, but also how we viewed our broad global responsibilities in the post–World War II era. According to Robert D. Kaplan:

The global responsibilities thrust upon the United States after World War II led to the creation of area experts in government, academia, and think tanks. Their effect on policy and public opinion has been to splinter and compartmentalize what used to be geographic wholes. The academic and policy-making nomenklatura invented a new world based not on real borders so much as on the borders of their knowledge or lack thereof. As someone who has written extensively about Turkey and the Balkans, as well as the Middle East, I have seen how these areas constitute two entirely different subcultures of Washington society and workdom, with little or no cross-fertilization between the two.[11]

The development of professional control over the inner dynamics of U.S. bureaucracy came slowly and in piecemeal fashion, mostly in the twentieth century. Some agencies, such as DoJ, have since their inception been dominated by lawyers, but professionally trained lawyers with LL.B. degrees, steeped in learning, responsive to the American Bar Association's policy concerns. Specialists in highly diverse elements of the law did not appear at DoJ in any sizable numbers until the New Deal in the 1930s. Military officers held the top army posts from the time the War Department was established in 1789, but even throughout most of the nineteenth century officers were poorly trained and politically motivated amateurs with little or no technical competency (except for those trained as engineers at West Point).

The modern generalist-professional cadre of officers did not appear until after 1900, established largely through the reforms of secretary of war Elihu Root, who created the Army General Staff, a unified personnel system, as well as a series of advanced professional educational institutions for military officers. The Rogers Act of 1924 instituted what we now know as the professional foreign service, but the dominance of quality foreign service professionals such as George Kennan and Charles Bohlen throughout key State Department slots did not emerge until after World War II.

Likewise, the professional control of state and local agencies in many regions began at roughly the turn of the century with the formation of small, fledgling professional associations such as the International Association of Chiefs of Police (1893), the International Association of Fire Chiefs (1893), the American Society of Municipal Engineers (1894), the Municipal Finance Officers Association

(1906), the National Recreation Association (1906), the National Association of Public School Business Officials (1910), the National Organization for Public Health Nursing (1912), and the City Managers' Association (1914).

As Robert Wiebe observes of the process of grassroots professionalization in America:

> Social workers . . . acted first to dissociate themselves from philanthropy and establish themselves as a distinct field within the new social sciences. Beginning with local leagues in Boston and New York, they had formed the National Federation of Settlements by 1911 and soon after captured the old National Conference of Charities and Corrections, renaming it the National Conference of Social Work. Also early in the century, they moved from ad hoc classes of special training to complete professional schools within such universities as Chicago and Harvard.[12]

The Federal government also had an important hand in stimulating professionalism at the state and local levels. For example, again in the area of social work, Martha Derthick writes:

> Congress in 1939 gave the Social Security Board authority to set personnel standards, perhaps because it was sympathetic to some degree of professionalism in the performance of public administration (on the assumption that it would lead to "efficiency") if not in the performance of social work. Even before this was done, the Board was demanding—on the basis of its authority to require efficient administration—that state plans include minimum standards for education, training, and experience (for local social workers).[13]

In many respects, at the local level and to a great extent at the federal level as well, professionalism was a means of battling "corruption as well as inefficiency," as Jeremy F. Plant and David S. Arnold point out: "Professionalism had to pervade the entire fabric of modern government," at least in the eyes of reformers who sought better government.[14] But, for the most part, until after World War II these professional groups were weak and ineffective voluntary associations exercising little control over the inner dynamics of local public bureaucracy. The postwar era, however, brought into grass-roots and higher-level government an influx of university-educated specialists with wide assortments of technical competence. The postwar era also brought about a new respect for and demand for these specialists to deal with a myriad of technical tasks from constructing highways, educating children, cleaning air and water, and administering complex regulatory machinery—often spawned by the professionals themselves—for certifying and controlling the application of skills inside and outside government. Today professional public official associations are extensive and varied, exercising hidden yet pervasive influence over government policy through certification, training, setting ethical standards, and playing policy advocacy roles within their specialized fields.

Professionals in government today, however, by no means make up a monolithic group or a homogeneous mass of experts; indeed, they differ considerably from one another. Directly under political appointees, *professional elites* comprise the core group of experts. These are the senior and most prestigious and respected members of the profession. They give not only internal direction to the profession but also to the entire agency by controlling the important positions and advancement to those positions and by setting recruitment and entrance requirements as well as overall personnel policies and priorities for the organization. Rising to these posts is achieved only through long-term career investment in the field, attendance at the "right" schools for basic and advanced training in the field, and advancement through progressive levels of responsibility and prominence in areas closely identified with the central concerns of the agency. Pilots in the air force, line officers in the navy, doctors in the U.S. Public Health Service, foresters in the U.S. Forest Service, senior staff lawyers at DoJ, and top-ranking educators in local school systems or in state departments of education tend to fill the elite slots within their respective agencies.

"Status" at times becomes an obsession with professionals. Knowing where one is or is not or how to advance "in the pecking order" of influence is important to most professionals. The registered nurse is considered an elite within that cluster of professionals. And not only is certification as an RN increasingly important to a nurse's elite status today, further certification within a very narrow specialized field within which she or he works, such as emergency room, orthopedic care, or surgery room practice, is also desirable. The continuous specialization of those who are already specialists within government is staggering.

The elites, in turn, within these various strata of professional clusters, provide the leadership as well as set the work standards, the qualifications for entrance and advancement, and the overall values for the profession. Much of the critical tensions and conflicts between clusters of professional elites are over policy questions and control of turf—between doctors and nurses in hospitals or between air force, army, navy, and marine corps top-ranking officers within DoD. Much of this conflict is hidden from public view. Rarely does it become public, because it can most often be settled between the competing parties or by political superiors. But at times internal dissent can become so strained that work production slows and the mission of the unit becomes jeopardized.

Line professionals, who fall just below the level of the senior elites, actually carry out the day-to-day functions of the public agency. Whereas a few dozen three- and four-star generals compose the army's top professional elite, more than 200,000 army officers from second lieutenants to generals direct much of the real work of the army in a wide variety of combat and noncombat jobs. Some, given their West Point training and combat duties in the infantry, armor, or artillery (combat sections that are considered "ideal" rungs in the ladder to the level of the elite) may become part of the professional elite; others in the line may have neither the interest nor the proper backgrounds to attain

those high level assignments. The line officers are essentially the "doing" and "implementing" functionaries of bureaucracy and are most directly associated with the central missions of an agency.

Staff professionals in public agencies include a wide assortment of specialists and technical assistants who have unique and specialized expertise that may not be directly connected with the central tasks of the agency but are nonetheless critical to carrying out its assigned functions. Today almost every public bureaucracy employs a wide array of these individuals. They assume the critical advisory roles within an agency and in some government offices also frequently assume large and powerful policy roles, even though they are not directly in either the line or the elite ranks. In every federal department, the legal counsels, for example, not only can command high salaries, large staffs, exemptions from civil service hiring rules, and the ear of the top brass in the agency, but also frequently exercise enormous yet quiet influence over central policies of an agency through knowledge and expertise in the law (and often this advice is quite conservative in nature—more "don'ts" than "dos"). The top political and professional cadre yield to such legal policy advice on technical matters because no one else can supply this knowledge (or if the advice is purchased at high cost from outside law firms). One only need attend a city council or county board of supervisors' meeting to watch the frequency with which elected members turn to legal counsel for assistance or to view federal organization charts to discover the strategic positions legal counsels occupy in most departments.

Administrative professionals comprise an assortment of budget officials; program officers; planning personnel; and finance, purchasing, auditing, and supply officials found in every public organization (the G-1 through G-5 jobs in the U.S. military). These men and women are critical to the activities of the agency because they essentially serve as "the directing brain" of the organization ("the directing brain" is Elihu Root's name for this group in his 1902 proposal for the creation of a general staff in the U.S. Army, which was a pattern copied by other public agencies and business corporations). In larger organizations some of these slots are temporarily held by line professionals, but many are filled by permanent careerists from emerging professional groups, such as budgeting, personnel, and purchasing specialists. While these individuals do not as yet rank as full-fledged professionals, they are increasingly taking on all the trappings of professionals, having their own associations, journals, "ideal career tracks," and educational requirements. Some even command higher salaries and status than their professional superiors. Municipal budget officers, for example, today are sometimes paid higher salaries than their bosses, city managers, or chief administrative officers, because of their critical budget and finance expertise in municipal decision-making processes.

In the uncertain environment within which agencies must operate, staff professionals must be adaptive and inventive in coping with the changing needs of their agencies. Much of their work is simply "fire-fighting" in order to maintain their structure amid turbulence, but much also is directed at thinking about the future of the organization, even if this planning is only incrementally achieved through short-term budgets, ad hoc personnel recruitment and selection, and partial programmatic design or redesign.

Finally, *paraprofessionals* make up another group increasingly seen within public agencies. These people receive substantially lower remunerative rewards for their work, although many units of government simply could not perform their assigned tasks without them. Many of these "paras" aspire to becoming full-fledged professionals in the field and use the experience as apprenticeship training. Others see this line of work as a rewarding lifetime career and seek no higher positions. From the standpoint of government, however, these workers are taking on increasing responsibility in various offices because of the rising costs of hiring fully qualified professionals. In other words, using paras is an effective governmental strategy for keeping down rapidly escalating personnel costs. In many cases paras perform the work as well as, if not better than, their highly paid counterparts. In this respect, their primary roles inside public organizations may well be an important economic function.

On the whole, what can be said about the influence of all the professional subsystems upon the activities and outputs of public bureaucratic institutions?

First and foremost, they are essential to the performance of the central missions of virtually every public agency. They define its mission, decide how it should be accomplished and who should accomplish it, as well as when it should be accomplished and where.

Second, by comparison with top-level political appointees, professionals by and large have longevity within agencies, thus giving them an enormous edge in the policy-making processes.

Third, professionals are not a single, unified group. They are part of a well-established pecking order, from elites down to "paras," that is based on education, skills, seniority, levels of responsibility, and general competence and experience. Elites occupy the highest level of policy-making roles; line professionals shape actions mainly through implementation practices; staff professionals fill advisory roles; administrative professionals prepare and plan tasks; and paraprofessionals carry out lower-level and lower-cost work.

Fourth, continuing political strength and popular support of professionals ultimately rest upon their recognized expertise and competence as well as on their ability to exercise these skills in a regular, uniform manner in the public interest. The widespread popularity of city-manager government rests fundamentally on its ability to apply systematic expertise to urban issues at the local level. Since expertise is professionals' stock in trade and is a source of authority and of legitimacy within government, a great deal of their efforts are directed at higher education and improving professionals' reputation for competence and application of knowledge. Professionals look to institutions of higher learning to sustain and enrich their knowledge base through training programs that give the professionals their credentials, and nurture the fundamental ethos and values of the profession. If political appointees draw support from their elected chiefs, professionals in government conversely derive their legitimacy from expertise acquired through higher education. The content and perspectives of these sources of learning influence the long-term priorities and fundamental value of professions. Hence, professions pay enormous attention to the shaping of professional education programs, examinations, accreditation, and licensing processes that help to determine the nature and content of professional work, as well as the knowledge and skill it requires.

Fifth, professionals influence policies not only by contributing a substantial share of the public work force and its top leadership cadre but also by moving upward and outward beyond the contours of their roles within agencies. As noted in the discussion of political appointees, they frequently assume temporary assignments at this level. Similarly, the influence of professionals is moving increasingly outward into legislative staff assignments or related nonprofit or business firms that directly and indirectly influence the course of bureaucratic policies.

Finally, the most serious tensions and conflicts within public organizations are generally hidden from view, since they arise mainly from policy disputes *between* clusters of key professionals and not as much from disputes between professional elites and political superiors. Many top political appointees today look highly professional, indeed *are drawn* from professional cadres, thus the tensions between political appointees and careerists are not as sharp and long-term compared to those *between* professional groups. Fights between the army, navy, and air force over defense appropriations and priorities are a permanent part of the Washington landscape, but it is within these professional service battles that defense policies for DoD develop. Likewise, the typical controversies that occur at the grass roots between police and firefighters over annual budget appropriations, length of work day, and salary increases figure equally prominently in determining the directions of local public safety policies.

The General Civil Service Subsystem: Ladders of Bureaucratic Specialists, Generalists, and Workers

While bits and pieces of the "ideal professional model" are being incorporated gradually into the general civil service, the bulk of government personnel are members of civil service and do not share in the professional model. Civil service is founded on the merit system, whereby positions are assigned on the basis of open, competitive examinations (written and/or oral) and candidates are evaluated and ranked in relationship to particular task requirements of a specific job. Generally, selection is made from among the top three scorers. Unlike the professional subsystem, civil service has no progressive job planning or control by elites but has, rather, a laissez-faire approach in which each individual seeks out and designs his or her own path within the system. Advanced training may or may not be essential. Rank is inherent in the job, not the person. Meeting the specific task requirements of the job is what counts most in landing a slot in civil service. Status, in turn, is derived from the specific job. A GS-9 civil servant, for instance, is a GS-9 because he or she holds that slot. If the employee leaves it, he or she is no longer a GS-9, unlike an air force colonel, who is a colonel wherever he or she serves. In the professional subsystem, conversely, rank inheres in the person, not the job.

The civil service subsystem was grafted onto U.S. bureaucracy somewhat haphazardly almost a century after the creation of the Republic. Even today its "fit" into government seems somewhat awkward and unsure. For the most part, this uncertainty about its place in U.S. public bureaucracy is caused by, as many scholars have noted, the growth of the general civil service out of a reaction to the excesses of the nineteenth-century spoils system, in which employment in public service was based largely, though not entirely, upon party loyalty and political patronage. In other words, it was built on a negative moral reaction to what was perceived as "evil" rather than on a positive and deliberate design.

The story of its growth is long and complex. To sum it up, in the late 1860s and throughout the 1870s a small band of reformers waged aggressive moral and political campaigns on behalf of civil service reform and against incompetence, graft, favoritism, and partisanship within the public service. Merit, they argued, should be the basis of appointment. Substantially modeled on the English civil service system, which had been in operation for nearly a half-century and was adapted to special pragmatic U.S. needs and concerns, the Civil Service Act (Pendleton Act) was enacted in 1883 mainly as a national reaction to the shooting of President James Garfield by a political supporter who had been refused a small patronage post.[15]

Pendleton became the classic model for "good personnel practices" throughout the nation. Extended gradually through executive order to cover increasing percentages of federal workers, it was also copied almost word for word by numerous states and localities. Localities borrowed from it their basic structural arrangements and concepts of merit processes, such as notions of a nonpartisan commission appointed by the chief executive to oversee the system, requirements of open, competitive examinations, probationary period prior to tenure, strict provision against political interference within civil service activities, classification of positions, and equal pay for equal work.

On the state level, New York passed a civil service law the same year as the federal government, and Massachusetts passed one the following year. Much of the civil service movement came in fits and starts. Some states, like Texas, never adopted a civil service system, and others like Virginia, recently abandoned the system entirely. Municipalities likewise moved to developed civil service systems, and most large cities by 1940 had some kind of merit system in place. Counties, though, have remained more backward; relatively few have merit systems in place.

The impetus for adoption of state/local merit systems came from essentially three forces. One was local and state reform groups that saw "merit"

as a method of improving economy and efficiency in government and ridding government of corrupt political machines; another was the federal government, which played a major role in the adoption of grassroots civil service systems. The Social Security Act of 1935 and its 1940 amendments required state and local government employees administering health, welfare, and employment programs funded by the federal government to be covered by merit systems. The Intergovernmental Personnel Act (IPA) of 1970 further spurred local merit system development through its various programs to upgrade public personnel systems and employee skills. Finally, Supreme Court decisions played a major role, especially in limiting patronage systems. In such cases as *Elrod v. Burns* (1976) and *Branti v. Finkel* (1980), the Court struck down patronage practices involving the firing of nonpolicy-making, nonconfidential employees.

The federal civil service work force has stayed fairly constant in size over the past forty years, but the local and state work force has grown, nearly tripling during the same period. In fact, the federal share of the public work force fell from 27.7 percent of the total in 1961 to 16.2 percent in 1992. Also, the distribution of the federal work force shows certain regional biases; a higher percentage (32 percent) is located in the South, compared to 17 percent of the total civilian work force.

Today, 91 percent of the federal civilian work force, or approximately 3 million workers, are covered under civil service personnel rules. While several structural and procedural adaptations over time have been added, such as the Civil Service Reform Act of 1978, its essential concepts of "merit," "open, competitive examinations," and "equal pay for equal work" remain intact. Patricia W. Ingraham and David H. Rosenbloom summed up the current status of "merit" on the federal level: "While there continues to be strong support for the fundamental principles of merit, dissatisfaction with and confusion about the current system is high." They cited the complexity of regulations, the lack of training and trust of agency personnel dealing with civil service provisions, the absence of a clear definition of "merit" or of guidance for achieving a quality work force as critical problems.[16]

Even though a considerable diversity in civil service laws is found across the United States, in those areas of the public service covered by its practices scholars have discovered several common characteristics: First, the U.S. civil servant is largely representative of the general population. Repeated studies have indicated that civil service members—unlike political appointees or upper-level professionals—are broadly reflective of the American people's education, income, social status, age, and geographic backgrounds. Though these representational attributes appear in the aggregate—that is, when the entire public service is viewed statistically—they tend to break down in the various particular units or levels of government. Women are predominant in the bottom ranks as well as in certain fields such as nursing and teaching but are small minorities in police, fire, or other traditionally male occupational roles. Blacks and other minorities have made impressive gains in recent years in all areas of the public service, but the upper ranks still tend to be heavily representative of white males.

Members of the general civil service subsystem generally lack the cohesiveness and unity found among professionals. When asked what she or he does, the typical bureaucrat will say, "I work at the Office of Education" or "I'm with the County Sheriff's Department." Few are likely to see themselves in broader terms and to say, "I'm a bureaucrat" or "I work for the civil service." Whether because of the pejorative connotations attached to government work or the more personal attachment to a particular assigned task, most bureaucrats lack common ties with government as a whole or with the broad *public orientation* of their work. This phenomenon no doubt exists in the private sector as well, where few business people see themselves as dedicated to the free market, but rather perceive themselves as real estate agents, autobody repairmen, or retail sales clerks. Most are like civil servants, who identify with the agency or skill at which they work or with the people with whom

they work. The grand design of the organization or the broad purposes of their occupation generally elude their interests or understanding.

This lack of common ties to the broad aspects and purposes of government may in large part be caused by the general lack of mobility within the civil service. In theory, the civil service subsystem provides for open, competitive exams that permit advancement into every level or part of government (though restricted to particular federal, state, or local jurisdictions). In practice, however, most civil servants spend their working lives within one agency. Eugene B. MacGregor, Jr., who studied the mobility of civil servants at the GS-14 level and above, discovered an average of seventeen to twenty-five years of service in the same agency or department.[17] Civil servants' depth of policy understanding, long-term views of issues, and particular expertise in an agency is therefore unmatched by comparison with those of transitory political appointees, who last in a post a mere twenty-two months at the federal level. Their longevity in an agency, expertise, sheer numbers, and longer time perspectives also make civil servants the core of modern bureaucracy.

So far, this discussion has pointed up several salient features of the civil service subsystem—its representational attributes as a whole, yet its uniquely unrepresentative elements in agencies or levels within the hierarchy: its lack of cohesiveness; its absence of mobility; its emphasis on rank inherent in the job; its diversity of jobs; the long-term career perspectives of its members; and its function as "the reservoir" of government expertise. Given these attributes, it is especially difficult to generalize about its influence on "bureaucratic outputs." As one veteran of government service says, "Civil servants don't really have mutual bonds or ties. There's nothing in particular in common except that these are people who know all the angles about how government works."[18]

Such seasoned cynicism, however, may obscure some of this subsystem's fundamental influences on bureaucratic activities. For one thing, as has already been emphasized, civil servants generally take the longer view of issues, problems, events, and actions, at least by comparison with political appointees (though they share this attribute with professional careerists). Their tenured positions make them somewhat more immune to the need for "quick fixes" or "instant results," compared with their politically driven bosses, who often see no further than the next election. For the most part, permanent bureaucrats realize that much that passes for "instant success" is ephemeral and that any real achievements in government come only in the long haul, after much struggle and persistence. Their view of what constitutes real, enduring change is therefore fundamentally different from the view of political appointees and leads to a much more realistic, conservative approach based upon recognition of the worth of incrementalism; namely that small steps taken over a long period of time will lead to permanent, solid achievements. This strategy of gradualism can be the source of exasperation and deep conflicts between civil servants and endless successions of political appointees, who normally want government to accomplish this or that task immediately, even yesterday. In particular, appointees in recent administrations who are fired up to make speedy changes and who have had little exposure to the realities of government find this philosophy of incrementalism frustrating. It quickly becomes the butt of their jokes about those "damn bureaucrats." These negative references symbolize the radically different time zones within which each subsystem operates. Their different "internal clocks" influence the basically different approaches to handling issues.

Also unlike political appointees, civil servants are restrained by the Hatch Act, and various "little Hatch Acts" that operate on state and local levels, from going public with their political opinions or policy views. Occasionally it may happen that dissent leaks out in the press, but active campaigning is expressly forbidden by law. Hence, civil servants generally must be discreet and work behind the scenes in dealing with the development, formulation, and implementation of policy questions. They realize that a head-on frontal assault on policy issues will only get them into needless politi-

cal controversy. Experience over the years has taught them that those sorts of political firestorms are to be avoided at all costs; they waste time and energy and lead to few tangible results. As a result, on the whole they favor quiet discretion in handling problems.

This cautious attitude comes not merely from pragmatism in effecting programmatic change but also from fear about long-term personal survival. In a world of endlessly shifting political appointees, the civil servant, at least in the top ranks, knows quite well that job security depends on his or her not being too closely allied with any one political party, else he or she become "politically tainted" and shunned by the next group taking office. The desire to stay neutral from the political appointee subsystem and to work quietly from the inside, at least for most top-level civil servants, springs from a very fundamental interest in long-term survival.

Unlike the professional careerist, on the other hand, the general civil servant operates *without* the control of a professional elite and without an extensive mutual support network of peers with status in the subsystem. In the civil service subsystem, every employee charts his or her own way through the bureaucracy. The hazards are many and the minefields often hard to locate. Thus much of their time is spent networking outward and downward into the bureaucracy, building personal bridges and personal friendships inside and outside agencies in order to develop the myriad horizontal and vertical contacts that are necessary for gaining information, accurately assessing the landscape, and making alliances in this hazardous, uncertain, and lonely bureaucratic world.

These clusters of civil servants influence public policies through the social networks they have established over long periods, running in strange and uncharted pathways that run through an agency and outside into other unlikely agencies and even beyond government where information is swapped informally and ideas are traded within social contexts. When presidents complain about government leaking like a sieve, this is why. The informal group, as Elton Mayo and the Hawthorne researchers discovered long ago, operates with a similar potency in government and in business settings, though it is well hidden in the civil service.

What challenges are facing the civil service subsystem as a whole? Three significant task force reports have appeared in recent years examining civil service performance and making numerous recommendations for reform: *Civil Service 2000,*[19] a 1988 study prepared by the Hudson Institute on the federal public service; also at the federal level, *Leadership for America,*[20] a 1989 privately sponsored review, called "The Volcker Commission" in honor of its chair, former Federal Reserve chairman Paul A. Volcker; and at the state and local levels, *Hard Truths/Tough Choices,*[21] a 1993 "Winter Commission" report, named for its chair, former Governor William F. Winter. These studies drew upon some of the most talented expertise from a wide cross section of business, nonprofit, and government to analyze many of the present problems facing America's public service. Collectively, they offered numerous suggestions for improvement. While these reports are too complicated to be summarized in any concise way, overall they found no simple solutions for reforming civil service subsystems, but each one stressed important issues needing attention:

1. *Poor public image:* The Volcker Commission placed the first priority on dealing with the poor public image of the federal civil service. The report repeatedly cited data and examples of the low esteem that Americans had for public service. These negative perceptions led, in the Commission's thinking, to a general distrust of government and to its broader incapacity to function effectively and recruit capable candidates to serve in government. The Commission surveyed, for example, 403 of the "best and brightest" college graduates who accepted employment and found only 16 percent chose positions in government (and half of those who selected public employment were graduates of public administration programs). Big businesses, small businesses, and academic institutions were preferred by a wide margin, leading to the conclusion that "the public service cannot compete for top graduates." Thus, this report laid stress upon targeting the recruitment of a better pool of candidates.

2. *Competence crisis:* Similarly, the Hudson Institute study's key findings and recommendations centered upon the "competency crisis" facing the federal public service. *Civil Service 2000* argued that there was a rising need for "a highly educated-skilled work force," yet attracting these workers in the 1990s "will become much more difficult." Recruitment is a problem, especially in high-wage locales such as New York City and in those top civil service grades, above GS-9 in which "the gap between top federal personnel civil service salaries and comparable private salaries was an average of 24 percent."[11]

3. *Removing barriers to a high performance work force:* On the state and local levels, the Winter Commission Report, by contrast, focused on the problems of "the highly fragmented local structures that impeded executive leadership and performance of the grassroots civil service systems." At the outset of the Winter Report, the priority was seen to:
   Give leaders the authority to act. Put them in charge of lean, responsive agencies. Hire and nurture knowledgeable, motivated employees and give them the freedom to innovate in accomplishing the agencies' missions. Engage citizens in the business of government, while at the same time encouraging them to be partners in problem-solving.

   The report emphasized that achieving such reforms will "hardly be painless or easy. Reforms may require constitutional amendments, new legislations, changes in rules and regulations, and restructuring many agencies and departments. Accomplishment of many of the changes may require political leaders and civic groups to mount aggressive campaigns."

The Unionized Subsystem: Cadres of Workers Inside Bureaucracy

Most texts on government or bureaucracy ignore an important policy-making subsystem of public agencies that over the past three decades has grown rapidly into one of the most potent forces determining the internal directions and external outputs of bureaucracy: namely, unionized public service workers. As David Stanley observes, "A whole new ball game has started since unions in the public sector have begun to operate"[22] Like the aforementioned subsystems, unionization has increasingly gained its own share of power and a role in shaping the inner dynamics of public bureaucracy—that is, its rules, regulations, operating procedures, and structural relationships. Unions also exercise external controls over bureaucratic performance and influence upon society—that is, its productivity, enforcement practices, political relationships, and policy agendas.

The formal institutional structure of public sector collective bargaining is essentially derived from the private sector, and Joel Douglas writes: "The present Public Service Labor Relations (PSLR) . . . legislative and legal framework is based on an adversarial relationship rooted in the National Labor Relations Act (NLRA) and is structured on private sector principles. These include narrow unit determination requirements, bargaining agent election procedures, exclusive union representation, a series of unfair labor and employment practices, and a decentralized bargaining structure. Reliance on the private sector model was successful in developing the (PSLR) legal framework in which employees, subject to restrictions, most notably the anti-strike ban, negotiate with government the terms and conditions of employment. Although the private and public sectors contain many similarities, distinct difference is noted in the public sector, since the government is both employer and regulator at the bargaining table. Other differences include the private sector's reliance on market forces, distributive bargaining and the use of strikes and lockouts."[23]

Much like the professional careerist and civil service subsystems, the union subsystem was not a planned innovation. It just grew inside government, evolving particularly rapidly since the 1960s. As Frederick C. Mosher remarked, "The founders of the civil service did not bargain on collective bargaining."[24] If the Pendleton Act was the landmark piece of legislation creating the civil service, the explosion of union involvement within bureaucracy did not begin in earnest until John F. Kennedy signed Executive Orders 10987 and 10988 in 1962. These two orders for the first time gave unions the right to bargain collectively with federal management representatives on a limited range of items. They stimulated similar measures in numerous states and localities throughout the 1960s and 1970s. And while the unionization movement in government has slowed perceptibly during the 1980s because of cutbacks and the weakening of unions generally, the collective bargaining processes now in place are based largely upon legislation of the 1960s and 1970s and are accepted institutional practices within many jurisdictions throughout the United States.

Though the phenomenon of significant union influence over the activities of public bureaucracy is relatively new, some deep pockets of union activity date from the turn of the century. Indeed, in 1912 the Lloyd-La Follette Act gave federal workers the right to unionize, and for a number of years several large unions represented most of the U.S. postal employees as well as employees in certain fields of civilian defense and in several government corporations such as the Tennessee Valley Authority. States and localities with large urban and industrial populations, which had traditionally strong private sector unions, also saw unionization in limited areas of their public bureaucracies, such as in New York, Michigan, and California. Yet these public service unions were, for the most part, economically weak, poorly organized, and had few legal rights to bargain collectively with representatives from the agency's management.

Why did the 1960s usher in a new era of union influence inside government? The historical reasons are still not clear. Certainly the election of

John F. Kennedy in 1960 was a critical factor. Throughout Kennedy's campaign he pledged union recognition and collective bargaining at the federal level. Shortly after his election, he appointed a task force headed by Arthur Goldberg to make recommendations on how to handle union-management relations within government. In turn, this task force study led to the two executive orders just cited. But other factors were also at work behind the scenes. Statistics show that private sector unionization reached it high point in 1955 with one-fourth of the national work force belonging to unions. This percentage of national union membership has been declining gradually ever since (now standing at 14.2 percent). With the "drying up," so to speak, of the private sector, major union leaders as early as the 1950s recognized that the public service was the last major untapped pool of nonunionized workers, and so they pressed their demands on Kennedy and subsequent administrations for the extension of union rights and prerogatives within this governmental sector. The American Federation of State, County and Municipal Employees (AFSCME) and other groups were instrumental in lobbying state legislatures for the right to organize and bargain collectively with state and local jurisdictions on behalf of public workers. Virtually all states permit some form of collective bargaining, yet today six states prohibit collective bargaining and public employees joining unions, and forbid recognition of unions in government.

Much of the union intrusion into the ranks of bureaucracy resulted from a more tolerant, even perhaps permissive, public attitude toward unions in government. By the 1960s unions were no longer considered entirely "evil" and antithetical to the public interest. No doubt, very real economic forces were at work as well. The promises of higher paychecks, shorter work weeks, and better working conditions lured many government workers, principally blue collar employees but increasing numbers of white collar employees as well, into public service unions. Certainly the postal strike of 1970 and the New York City transit strike of 1966—two early key disputes—stimulated union membership. Finally, union growth was fostered

by legislation such as the Civil Service Reform Act of 1978, which formalized union-management collective bargaining procedures by federal statute. Likewise, on the local level, in New York State, representatives of the Civil Service Employees Association had been meeting with management representatives since the early 1900s, but the Taylor Law was established by statute's formal collective bargaining arrangement for state and union representatives in 1967. In a few states, such as Massachusetts, union membership became a requirement for attaining a public job. In order for workers to have a job and a voice that would represent them at the bargaining table and involve them in the determination of their agency's activities, they joined public employee unions.

Whatever the causes of growth—and there are undoubtedly many—in contrast to the private sector, a sporadic but continuous climb in union strength has been apparent within public organizations. Today 35.9 percent of all federal civilian employees belong to unions (not including the 600,000 postal workers, 90 percent of whom are unionized); 34.3 percent of state and local workers are union members. Levels of unionization, however, range significantly from agency to agency and locale to locale. Thus, in practice the political clout of union members inside bureaucracy varies considerably. The postal service, made up largely of blue collar workers, is almost entirely unionized, whereas the employees of the Federal Reserve Board and the State Department are mainly white collar professionals, largely (though not altogether) untouched by unions. Urban industrial states and large metropolitan communities are heavily unionized, and public unions play major policy-making roles within their various public bureaucracies. On the other hand, rural, poorer, and less-industrialized regions contain fewer union members, who therefore have less policy involvement in their regions of the public sector. Some functional areas, such as education, transportation, and refuse collection, show a much higher level of union activity than other fields.

Today there are three prominent and powerful public service unions (and numerous lesser ones) that speak for many, though certainly not all, public employees: the American Federation of State, County and Municipal Employees, the American Federation of Government Employees (AFGE), and the American Federation of Teachers (AFT). The National Education Association is technically *not* a union but rather a professional association of primary and secondary schoolteachers, yet it looks and acts like a union, often aggressively by representing its rank and file in collective bargaining negotiations in various school districts across the country. NEA became especially active within the Democratic party, substantially assisting President Jimmy Carter's election in 1976 and his bid for re-election in 1980. AFSCME, AFT, and AFGE have grown rapidly in power and prominence within the AFL-CIO labor council over the last decades, extending their activism well beyond traditional union concerns into national political circles of the Democratic party by aiding the party financially as well as through considerable campaign manpower. Public service unions are active at the state and local levels as well, particularly where there are large concentrations of public workers (such as in state or county capitals) and strong Democratic party organizations.

However, the actual conduct of negotiations between unions and management within government—the principal source of union inputs into bureaucracy—remains a highly decentralized process, with local representatives of public employee unions conducting agency-by-agency or local jurisdiction-by-jurisdiction negotiated agreements. In other words, while the public employee unions have grown into the "big three" (or four, depending on how one counts NEA), no one person or group speaks for "the entire management side" of government. Separate bargains must be made with roughly 80,000 governmental jurisdictions in the United States and with many more "suborganizational" units within these separate governments that recognize the union right of negotiation. Not only is the process decentralized, but who actually speaks for the employers or management is also a highly complex and unsettled issue in many areas. Some governments use the civil service as

spokescommission for management (Office of Personnel Management at the federal level); others have teams of top-level executives from *both* legislature and bureaucracy that speak for management. Highly diverse institutional arrangements for representation and the conducting of the actual negotiations are found across the United States, largely because the process still remains somewhat new, experimental, and undeveloped.

Equally unsettled is the scope of the bargaining that is allowed. In most jurisdictions, wages and hours—the two principal bargaining concerns in private industry—are legislatively determined and beyond the scope of public sector negotiations. These negotiations, therefore, mostly center on working conditions, grievance procedures, and other less major subjects. But even here, working conditions, grievance procedures, and "fringes" are often precisely prescribed by legislation, leaving little room for negotiations, even over these seemingly mundane matters. Further, laws on the books often stack the deck in management's favor. For example, according to the 1978 Civil Service Reform Act (CSR), management officials are authorized "to determine the mission, budget, organization, number of employees, and internal security practices of an agency . . . to hire, assign, direct, lay off and retain employees . . . or to suspend, remove, reduce in grade or pay, or take other disciplinary action."[25] In short, the CSR's tilt clearly favors management prerogatives over union rights, although through court decisions and legislative amendments unions have chipped away at these restrictions.

Another important condition of the union subsystem in government is that the actual means for enforcing their views at the bargaining table remain drastically restricted because of the ban on strikes by public employees at every level of government. The basic weapon used by private sector unions to enforce their demands in negotiations is illegal at the federal and many state and local settings. Though thirteen states allow some or all public employees the right to strike. As Theodore Kheel writes, "The strike enables employees through their representatives to participate in the decisions setting wages, hours and working conditions. In the absence of the right to strike, an alternative system of determination is required when negotiating parties reach an impasse."[26] However, no such technique has yet been found for breaking public sector impasses. In reality, however, whether or not public employees are legally permitted to strike, strikes do occur in the public sector; sometimes they are called "the blue flu" or "sick-outs," or they are actual walk-outs. Public unions know very well how to play the inside political game. During negotiations they regularly make "end runs" around management to outside supporters, such as sympathetic legislators on city councils, in state assemblies, or in Congress. These potent friends of public unions frequently enable them to cut deals and achieve their priorities through the back door, thus undercutting management's position or dividing it so badly that its official bargaining position crumbles.

How then can the union subsystem's influence over policy outputs in bureaucracy be summarized vis-à-vis the other previously mentioned bureaucratic subsystems?

The first and perhaps the most significant aspect of union involvement with what happens inside U.S. bureaucracy is its variety. Some unions strive for nothing less than complete control from top to bottom of public bureaucracy. They want the options to select a public agency's top-ranking political cadre; to determine its internal structural arrangements, procedures, and rules as well as its methods of promotion, hiring, and firing; to specify its relations with other external groups; and most of all to call the shots as to what the agency will or will not do for the public. In general, those agencies are characterized by weak political executive oversight, an absence of a controlling professional elite, a strongly unionized rank and file, a degree of institutional autonomy, and traditions of union assertiveness, such as in the federal postal system and in large "weak-mayor" cities such as New York and San Francisco, where public service unions exert powerful long-term influence. At the other extreme, public sector unions are dormant or ineffective in right-to-work states, where public sector unions are outlawed entirely, and in agencies in the tight grip of professionals (strong city manager communities or the military) or under strong, united antiunion political executive leadership. Most situations in which unions operate, though, are at neither extreme, and so unions end up jockeying with other internal bureaucratic subsystems—political appointees, professionals, and civil servants—for varying degrees of autonomy and control over bureaucratic policies and outputs.

Second, the growth and intrusion of unions within bureaucracy have added new levels of complexities and complications to an already complex bureaucratic world. Whether such complexification of government has slowed down its institutional outputs or made it more productive is unclear and unmeasured, but it is apparent in many instances that new personnel and attendant rules and procedures have been added to administer this new subsystem and that relationships between labor and management have therefore become more formal and legalistic.

Third, in cases where the union subsystem has matured fully within public bureaucracies but has not become the dominant subsystem, it has brought with it new bipartisanship management practices. Collective bargaining forces management to sit down at regular intervals with union representatives to discuss grievances, working conditions, and other matters of concern to both parties.

Fourth, in many cases public service unions have won positive reforms that have long been advocated by public administration specialists to enhance, on the whole, the cause of "good government," such as better wages, working conditions, training programs and staffing levels, and organizational reforms promoting institutional productivity.

Finally, the real loser with the advent of public service unions into the internal dynamics of bureaucratic policy making has probably been the underlying philosophy and practices of the century-old civil service subsystem. Concepts such as merit selection, open competitive exams, nonpartisan civil service boards, and "color blind" promotions based upon individual competence have yielded in many areas to union concerns about seniority, "closed shop" union membership, and neutral third-party mediation of disputes by those outside civil service. Indeed, in many instances the old neutral civil service commission has been replaced by highly partisan and political oversight agencies such as the Office of Personnel Management at the federal level. This is not to argue that the civil service subsystem will soon fade into a distant memory and its controlling procedures, rules, and personnel become history. To the contrary, it is alive and well today in many bureaucratic institutions, but it certainly has changed, or given ground to the influx of unionization over the last three decades inside the public service. In several cases as well, due to the fiscal constraints of recent years, we have witnessed considerable union cooperation with civil service managers for the self-interest of each party.[27]

Contract Employment: The Newest, Fastest-Growing Bureaucratic Subsystem

At the federal, state, and local levels, public agencies up to roughly 1950 did most, if not all, of the tasks assigned to them in-house, using their own personnel and resources and the facilities allocated by legislatures and political executives. Hence much of the theory of bureaucracy, as well as the managerial approaches to public enterprise put forward by public administration experts and scholars, were based upon assumptions, increasingly erroneous, that bureaucracies controlled their own operations, did their assigned work inside, with neat, clear lines of managerial control running from top political executives down to the workers who actually carried out the agency's assigned missions.

The reality of internal bureaucratic life today, however, is far different. In the 1990s the federal budget tells another story about how government agencies actually function. Roughly 14 percent of the national budget goes for its own internal personnel services and benefits (excluding pensions). This means that only slightly more than one-eighth of the total federal budget is spent on directing activities that the government performs itself, such as law enforcement, food and drug regulation, forestry service, air traffic control, and so on. However, the category of "other contractual services" indicates the roughly 16 percent of the total annual operating budget is spent for sundry activities performed by others who are contracted to render services from *outside* the federal bureaucracy.

In other words, close to 60 percent of the total obligation for goods and services produced by the federal government is contracted out (excluding funds for grants-in-aid to states and localities, direct transfer payments to individuals, debt servicing, and so on). The percentages run much higher for some agencies, such as NASA and the Department of Energy, which have traditionally contracted out most of their work. The development of most major weapons systems is contracted out to private businesses, as is the construction of large capital projects such as dams, roads, bridges, and sewer systems. Three-fourths of research and development funding at the federal level is contracted out to universities, think tanks, consultants, and private industry.

At the state and local levels there are no comparable figures on the levels of contracting-out by governmental bureaucracy, though they probably mirror the federal pattern, with some communities going to extremes, such as Lakewood, California (originators of the Lakewood Plan), which contracts out all its municipal functions, including police protection. City Hall consists of little more than a city manager and a secretary, who principally act as contract-managers for the city council. While most localities do not go to that extreme degree of contracting for municipal services, most do draw upon private vendors and business enterprises in many ways for the construction of capital projects as well as for a variety of ongoing services, such as data collection, medical facilities, computer services, refuse disposal, as well as for accounting, auditing, and payroll functions. Today, most government agencies house varying mixes of full-time employees and temporary or long-term contract employees working side by side. The regular public employees and contractual employees are often difficult to differentiate from one another.

The story of the rise of contract labor inside bureaucracy is a complicated one. Early in the history of the U.S. government, mail delivery and canal projects were contracted out. However, until 1950 the use and application of contractual arrangements were drastically limited in most public agencies. All this changed, with the hot and cold war demands of the postwar era, when government increasingly needed highly skilled scientific and engineering talent from universities, private enterprises, and consulting firms to conceptualize, build, and implement numerous weapons programs. The Rand Corporation and the National Science Foundation were created by the federal government as outside sources for accomplishing in-house missions of DoD.

The growth of contracting-out for government services since then has been unprecedented in size, scope, and intensity. Government has been driven into contracting willy-nilly in so many fields because it has been asked to perform greater numbers of tasks of ever-greater complexity within shorter time frames, tasks for which it has neither the expertise nor the capacity to acquire it on a short-term basis. At the state and local levels, contractual employment accelerated in the 1970s, 1980s, and 1990s as a device for accomplishing programmatic goals while avoiding rising costs of hiring permanent civil servants (today a permanent civil servant costs government roughly twice the worker's *actual* salary, largely because of "hidden fringes" such as retirement programs and health and other benefit packages). Contracting-out is also a method of doing complex work in which states and localities have little expertise. But it has broad implications.

Some effects on public agencies and their outputs are fairly obvious. First, the growth of the contractual subsystem makes it increasingly hard to tell where government bureaucracy begins and ends. Is the permanent public agency that relies on the expertise of a single outside contractor *really* independent of that outside private enterprise? Or is the private contractor who relies on a public bureaucracy for all or most of his annual income *really* private, and not merely an extension of a public bureaucracy? Increasingly, the worlds separating government agencies and private sector businesses, universities, and consulting firms are dissolving into an area where boundaries overlap or are unclear and difficult to define.

What is clear, however, is that these "outside" groups perform much of the bureaucratic work of government. If their personnel were counted as government employees, the size of government bureaucracy would probably be twice as large as it is. Contracting-out, then, enables politicians to gain services for their constituents *and then* claim that they have "kept the lid on government personnel costs." Such a claim is clearly untrue and leads to further confusion—and deception—about the realities of the size and true nature of government.

Second, some sectors of government have clearly become "captives" of their contractors. The purveyors of many large DoD weapons systems, such as Hughes, Boeing, Rockwell, and McDonald Douglas, not only design and develop these multibillion dollar, multiyear systems but by proposing new weapons systems are also actively involved in establishing DoD and individual service priorities, budget requirements, personnel needs, and even the broad global strategic priorities of U.S. defense policy. And once the weapons are sold, these firms become the sole-source suppliers virtually dictating the costs—often overrun by huge amounts—to the contracting agency. Top executives move back and forth with ease between these firms and top policy-making posts within DoD. Harold Brown (DoD secretary under President Carter), William C. Foster (Brown's research and development specialist), Caspar Weinberger (a former DoD secretary under President Reagan), and John Lehmann (Weinberger's former secretary of the navy), and William J. Perry (President Clinton's secretary of defense) are all products of the contract world surrounding DoD. This is not meant to suggest that these individuals or others who serve "in-and-out" at high DoD policy-making levels have acted unethically or dishonestly; it simply means that their backgrounds and skills are utilized in *both* government and business at various managerial and staff levels and that they therefore significantly influence policies and administration in *both* sectors.

Another effect of the increasing rise and reliance upon the contractual subsystem within public bureaucracy is that there is less and less use for traditional bureaucratic techniques, such as standard in-house top-down rules, for direction and control of personnel and resources. More emphasis is now placed upon contract negotiations, formal agreements, legal sanctions, economic rewards and penalties for inducing compliance by contractors, and auditing and management information systems for "tracking" completion dates. All these procedures are essential for quality control and to make the contractors and subcontractors perform their services according to schedule. Bureaucrats at all levels increasingly are becoming contract managers as opposed to fulfilling their traditional line management roles.

Also, as suggested before, with the growing numbers of public personnel "off the books" because of their nontenured status, the traditional sorts of personnel work rules, personnel oversight controls, and procedures governing employee behavior have diminished in importance. Thus the problems of imposing public accountability on contract workers grow as the numbers of contract agents and subcontractors grow. Proper policy performance and implementation in regard to legality, honesty, competence, correctness of action, and effective completion of projects become increasingly difficult to ensure as the number of private businesses, universities, and others who perform the work of public agencies increases. Recent leaks of highly sensitive national security information by Hughes employees and the massive fraud cases of General Electric subcontractors working on various navy projects illustrate these enormous problems of public accountability and oversight. Indeed, *should* bureaucracy impose its public standards of accountability on such "private" groups and citizens? The difficult and uncharted ethical dimensions of the problems loom large. Finally, as the pressures of the contractual subsystem force new commitments and expenditures of funds years ahead of time, contractual arrangements become legally and politically "untouchable." As many scholars and budget experts now observe, not only is the federal budget out of control but also no one even knows how much is really being spent annually, largely because of the pressures of the growing contractual subsystem. Many contractors simply operate independently of the budget process—off the books and out of sight—developing independent accounting, auditing, and budgeting systems along with separate personnel rules, regulations, and procedures that are well beyond public scrutiny and oversight mechanisms.

Notes

1. Hugh Heclo, *A Government of Strangers* (Washington, DC: Brookings Institution, 1977), p. 103.
2. These characteristics of political appointees have been true for some time. See David T. Stanley, Dean E. Mann, and Jameson W. Doig, *Men Who Govern* (Washington, DC: Brookings Institution, 1967).
3. For data on the backgrounds of city managers that tend to show a high degree of heterogeneity, read Richard J. Stillman II, "Local Public Management in Transition," *The Municipal Year Book 1982* (Washington, DC: International City Management Assoc., 1982), pp. 161–73.
4. Thomas P. Murphy, Donald E. Nuechterlein, and Ronald Stupak, *Inside Bureaucracy: The View from the Assistant Secretary's Desk* (Boulder: Westview Press, 1978).
5. Frederick C. Mosher, *Democracy and the Public Service,* 2d ed. (NY: Oxford University Press, 1982), p. 183.

6. Frank P. Sherwood and L. J. Breyer, "Executive Personnel Systems in States," *Public Administration Review* 47 (Sept./Oct. 1987):410f.

7. Deborah D. Roberts, "The Governor as Leader: Strengthening Public Service Through Executive Leadership," in Frank J. Thompson (ed.), *Revitalizing State and Local Public Service: Strengthening Performance, Accountability, and Citizen Confidence* (San Francisco, CA: Jossey-Bass, 1993), pp. 51–52.

8. See Samuel H. Beer's presidential address before the American Political Science Association, "Federalism, Nationalism and Democracy in America," *American Political Science Review,* 72(1) (March 1978).

9. Zbigniew Brzezinski, *Between Two Ages: America's Role in the Technetronic Era* (New York: Viking, 1970); Don Price, *The Scientific Estate* (Cambridge: Harvard University Press, 1965); Daniel Bell, "Notes on the Post-Industrial Society," *Public Interest,* 6 (Winter 1967): 24–35; and Guy Benveniste, *The Politics of Expertise,* 2d ed. (San Francisco: Jossey-Bass, 1983).

10. Mosher, *Democracy,* p. 142.

11. Robert D. Kaplan, "There Is No 'Middle East,'" *New York Times Magazine,* Feb. 20, 1994, pp. 42–43.

12. Robert Wiebe, *The Search for Order: 1877–1920* (New York: Hill and Wang, 1967), pp. 120–21.

13. Martha Derthick, *The Influence of Federal Grants: Public Assistance in Massachusetts* (Cambridge, MA: Harvard University Press, 1970), p. 159.

14. David S. Arnold and Jeremy F. Plant, *Public Official Associations and State and Local Government: A Bridge across One Hundred Years* (Fairfax, VA: George Mason University Press, 1994), p. 59.

15. The best account of the development of civil service remains Paul P. Van Riper's *History of the United States Civil Service* (Evanston, Ill.: Row Peterson, 1958).

16. Patricia W. Ingraham and Donald F. Kettl, *Agenda for Excellence: Public Service in America* (Chatham, New York: Chatham House, 1993).

17. Eugene B. MacGregor, "Politics and Career Mobility of Civil Servants," *American Political Science Review,* 68 (1974): 24.

18. As cited in Heclo, *Government,* p. 142.

19. The Hudson Institute, *Civil Service 2000* (Washington, DC: U.S. Office of Personnel Management, 1988).

20. Paul A. Volcker, chair, *Leadership for America: Rebuilding the Public Service* (Lexington, MA: Lexington Books, 1990).

21. William A. Winter, chair, *Hard Truths, Tough Choices: Agenda for State and Local Reform,* Winter Commission Report, (San Francisco: Jossey-Bass 1993).

22. David T. Stanley, *Managing Local Government under Union Pressure* (Washington, DC: Brookings Institution, 1972), p. 136.

23. Joel M. Douglas, "Public Sector Collective Bargaining in the 1900s," in Frederick S. Lane (ed.), *Current Issues in Public Administration,* 5th ed. (New York: St. Martin's Press, 1994), p. 261.

24. Frederick C. Mosher, *Democracy and the Public Service* (New York: Oxford University Press, 1968), p. 178.

25. PL 95-45, October 13, 1978, Section 7106.

26. As quoted in Harry H. Wellington and Ralph K. Winter, Jr., *The Union and the Cities* (Washington, DC: Brookings Institution, 1971), p. 30.

27. As Joel M. Douglas concludes, "Bilateralism has replaced unilateralism in the decision-making processes." In Douglas, "Public Sector Collective Bargaining in the 1990s," *op. cit.,* pp. 271–72.

CASE STUDY 7

Introduction

Among the five critical personnel subsystems outlined in the foregoing essay, that of the professional careerist is one of the most influential, for the various reasons outlined by the author. Though they do not operate in a vacuum as a group or as individuals, they do interact with and are surrounded by other personnel subsystems that decisively determine the extent of their influence, the sorts of issues they handle, and what they achieve—or fail to achieve—in their work.

Perhaps the following case, "The Decision to Bomb the Serbs," is the most recent illustration of the enormously vital role that professionals play within modern American government, both in setting policy and in carrying it out. Here we can vividly see how politically elected and appointed officials worked closely with "the pros" from the military, foreign service, and intelligence agencies in defining the policy agenda and its implementation, yet their actions and interrelationships were hardly neat or clear-cut, or at least as neat and clear-cut as the foregoing conceptual essay outlines. Indeed, the complexities and difficulties of these working relationships—especially under such difficult, high-pressure controversies involving war and peace, life and death—are fraught with fundamentally hard value and ethical dilemmas.

A bit of background is useful about the Balkan Region for giving some perspective and understanding about the complicated issues involved with "The Decision to Bomb the Serbs." The Yugoslavian nation was established in 1918, a product of the Versailles Peace Treaty that ended World War I. Thus Yugoslavia was a relatively new nation-state. Prior to 1918 the country had originally been known as the Kingdom of Serbs, Croats, and Slovene—a name symbolizing the deep ethnic divisions of that region that had existed over many centuries. The German occupation of Yugoslavia during World War II only intensified these ethnic rivalries by setting off a brutal civil war, costing 1.75 million lives. Marshall Tito, who became President, established a united Yugoslavia in the immediate postwar era, based on a unique brand of communism—independent of the Soviet Union and without ethnic bias, at least overtly.

After Tito's death in 1980, the nation endured a sharp economic decline that fostered a resumption of ethnic rivalries that some now argue was fanned by the current Serbian President, Slobodan Milosevic, who in 1989 urged the Serbian people to throw off their "inferiority complex" and assume a place as "the big nation in the region." That year saw the first arrests of Albanian Kosovo leaders by Serb officials. As the authority of communism waned, the Yugoslavian nation fell apart, and in the early 1990s six republics—Serbia, Slovenia, Croatia, Bosnia-Herzegovina, Macedonia, and Montenegro, as well as two autonomous provinces, Kosovo and Vojvodina—were established.

While the decade of the 1990s saw numerous complicated political, social, economic, and military issues emerge throughout this region—especially in Croatia and Bosnia—Kosovo, about the size of Connecticut, became the most intensely contested area. The reason: historic ethnic and religious differences. Kosovo is sacred ground to the Christian Serbs, numbering 10.3 million people. It is the site of ancient Orthodox Christian monasteries and a fabled battlefield where Muslim and Christians fought many centuries ago, and it remains deeply revered as a Serbian national landmark. However, 90 percent of Kosovo's two million inhabitants are ethnic Albanian Muslims. In 1989, when Slobodan Milosevic stripped Kosovo of its autonomy and established de facto martial law to underscore Serbia's claim to the province, Kosovo's Albanians organized a resistence movement that remained mostly pacifist until open warfare broke out in 1998. Quickly that movement turned into the Kosovo Liberation Army, an armed guerrilla movement to defend Kosovo's Muslim population with weapons supplied through the mountains on its southwest border from the neighboring independent nation of Albania.

As you read this short case, written by a team of top *New York Times* correspondents, try to focus on the following (issues discussed by the prior conceptual essay:

Who were the key professionals inside the U.S. government that largely shaped decision making concerning Kosovo? Who were the key political appointees involved? Why were some and not others consulted about the decision to bomb the Serbs? Did this affect the choices that were made—namely, by who was included? And by who was excluded?

How did professional and political appointees exercise their influence and ultimately shape the critical choices and methods of implementing those choices? Was it a good team-effort working together with "the pols" and "the pros" in your opinion?

Can you generalize from this case study about the role of professionals versus appointees, their power and influence, and their working relationships within American government today? As well as how in the modern global context, they must work together with other professionals and political appointees to achieve "public purpose"?

"The Decision to Bomb the Serbs"

ELAINE SCIOLINO AND ETHAN BRONNER

On Jan. 19, President Clinton's top aides met in the Situation Room in the White House basement to hear a fateful new plan for an autonomous Kosovo from Madeleine K. Albright, the Secretary of State. NATO, she urged, should use the threat of air strikes on Yugoslavia to force a peace agreement to be monitored by the alliance's ground troops.

The President, who had other matters on his mind, was not there. His lawyers were starting their arguments on the Senate floor against his removal from office. That night he delivered his State of the Union address.

Nearly five thousand miles away, in Belgrade, Gen. Wesley K. Clark, the NATO commander, and Gen. Klaus Naumann, chairman of the NATO military council, were sitting with President Slobodan Milosevic of Yugoslavia. They came brandishing a plastic portfolio of color photographs documenting a

massacre of Albanians three days earlier by Mr. Milosevic's security forces in the Kosovo town of Racak. One picture showed a dead child holding a pacifier.

They also came with threats of NATO air strikes.

This was far from their first encounter with the Serbian leader, but this time, they recalled, they found a newly hardened man with a bunker mentality.

"This was not a massacre," Mr. Milosevic shouted. "This was staged. These people are terrorists."

When General Clark warned him that NATO would "start telling me to move aircraft," Mr. Milosevic was nonplussed by the prospect of bombings. He called the general a war criminal.

Jan. 19 is already seen as a pivotal day in the Clinton Presidency. But it may turn out to be so less for the Senate impeachment hearings and State of the Union address than for the moves toward war over Kosovo.

Kosovo would have presented a daunting foreign

policy challenge even to a President whose powers of persuasion and moral authority had not been damaged by a year of sex scandal and impeachment.

It is unclear whether the President's decisions on Kosovo would have been any different if he had not been distracted by his own political and legal problems. But it is clear that his troubles gave him less maneuvering room to make his decisions, and that diplomacy that came to rely heavily on maximum threats reduced the wiggle room even further. Sharp criticism and questioning of his motives arose each time he did take military action, as with the strikes in December against Iraq when the House was poised to vote on his impeachment. Now, Mr. Clinton is facing mounting criticism for not having acted earlier or more decisively on Kosovo. His critics say that had he done so, Mr. Milosevic would not have been able to move troops and equipment into Kosovo and carry out the massive "ethnic cleansing" of the past four weeks.

As the President viewed the situation, there were only "a bunch of bad options" confronting him, he said earlier this month.

Throughout, the NATO allies hoped, even assumed, that they were dealing with the Milosevic who negotiated the Bosnian peace at Dayton, Ohio, the man who lied and manipulated and ranted in all-night, Scotch-laden negotiations and then cut a deal in the morning when he saw that it was in his interest. Instead they were dealing with the Milosevic of Belgrade, who was willing to employ mass murder to assure his continued dominance of Serbia.

The intelligence assessments presented to Mr. Clinton were also cloudy and included speculation that the Yugoslav leader would back down in the face of air strikes.

One interagency intelligence report in January 1999, for example, concluded that "Milosevic doesn't want a war he can't win."

"After enough of a defense to sustain his honor and assuage his backers he will quickly sue for peace," the assessment went on. Another interagency report in February stated, "He doesn't believe NATO is going to bomb."

Prodded by such assessments and his advisers, the President pressed ahead with a strategy of threats coupled with negotiations, gambling that Mr. Milosevic would back down. These threats quickly became a test of NATO's credibility, with the added onus of the alliance's looming 50th anniversary, which is to be observed next weekend.

Last September, former Senator Bob Dole went to Kosovo to gather facts for an international refugee group of which he is chairman. On his return, he reported his findings to Mr. Clinton. Afterward Mr. Clinton sat with him alone in the Oval Office and asked for his help in lobbying his former Senate colleagues to vote against conviction in the impeachment trial.

In an interview, Mr. Dole said he thought "a lot of attention was diverted" from Yugoslavia and other foreign policy issues by the impeachment. It was "all consuming," he added, and Kosovo "may have been one of the casualties."

Kosovo's Dangers: A Balkan Firestorm That Slowly Spread

From the moment Yugoslavia fell apart in 1991, Kosovo was viewed as a place from which a wider war could erupt. The Bush Administration, which had adopted a hands-off policy on the killings in Croatia and Bosnia, warned Mr. Milosevic on Dec. 29, 1992, that the United States was prepared to take unilateral military action if the Serbs sparked a conflict in Kosovo.

The Clinton Administration reiterated the warning weeks after the inauguration. Three years later, when the Administration convened a peace conference to end the Bosnia war in Dayton, Kosovo was not on the agenda.

"Bosnia was then the emergency, and it had to be stopped," said Richard C. Holbrooke, the American envoy who negotiated the agreement at Dayton, in an interview. "Otherwise there would have been a real risk that Bosnia would merge with Kosovo into a huge firestorm that would destabilize the whole region." Over the next two years, younger, more confrontational ethnic Albanians began to build a ragtag army, supplied with weapons from neighboring Albania and financed largely by the Albanian diaspora in Europe and the United States.

They faced serious obstacles. Mr. Milosevic, who had risen to power on the cause of protecting Kosovo's minority Serbs on the land Serbs prize as their Jerusalem, took away Kosovo's broad autonomy in 1989 and was unlikely to give it back without a fight.

The killing in Kosovo began in earnest in February 1998, when the Serbs retaliated for rebel attacks on policemen with brutal operations of their own in the Drenica area. Members of the Kosovo Liberation Army and their families were slain.

The Administration sent Robert S. Gelbard, its envoy to the region, to confront Mr. Milosevic with horrific photographs of death and mutilation.

A veteran State Department official respected for his tenacity but known for his temper, Mr. Gelbard had experience in Bosnia and Croatia. But he did not have much of a personal relationship with the Serbian leader, whom he castigated in unusually blunt language.

The Drenica killings, Mr. Gelbard felt, were the kind of ruthless act that would further radicalize the restive Albanian population and lead to an explosion that could affect the entire region.

"You have done more than anyone to increase the membership of the K.L.A.," Mr. Gelbard fumed at Mr. Milosevic. "You are acting as if you were their secret membership chairman."

The meeting ended badly, American officials said. Mr. Milosevic was infuriated and would eventually refuse to meet with Mr. Gelbard at all.

The Distractions: Foreign Policy Crisis Comes at a Bad Time

The eruption of violence in Kosovo in early 1998 could not have come at a more inopportune moment for the Clinton Administration.

The President and his aides were consumed by the Lewinsky affair. The Clinton foreign policy team was focused on Presidential visits to China and Africa and on Russia's economic implosion. Legislative electoral politics, especially with an incendiary sex scandal enveloping the White House, was never far from the President's concerns. And Kosovo did not register in any public opinion polls.

One of the President's political advisers said in an interview: "I hardly remember Kosovo in political discussions. It was all impeachment, impeachment, impeachment. There was nothing else."

Nonetheless, the spring of 1998 posed a question: Would the Administration, which had reaffirmed Mr. Bush's Christmas warning, take any action?

Weighing their options, officials said, they quickly ruled out unilateral military strikes, the very

response Mr. Bush had promised. If anything was to be done, it would be in concert with the NATO allies, who along with America had troops on the ground as part of the international force in Bosnia. The United States could not start bombing while its allies were exposed in a neighboring country.

From then on, everything about Kosovo was subject to decisions by an alliance that worked by consensus and was soon to grow from 16 to 19 members.

Senior Administration officials who had lived through the years of delay and inaction in Bosnia believed they had learned a few things about how to deal with Mr. Milosevic. Diplomacy could work, but only if it was linked to the credible threat of force.

Ms. Albright began making the case for military action. At one key meeting in May, Mr. Gelbard argued that the time had come for air strikes.

Officials say Samuel R. Berger, the national security adviser, was opposed. The United States could not threaten without being prepared to follow up with a specific action.

Mr. Gelbard replied that he had already worked out some bombing targets with the NATO commander, General Clark. But Mr. Berger rejected the plan and no one else in the room came to the defense of Mr. Gelbard, who declined to discuss his role, saying only "When I had the lead role on Kosovo issues I had complete support from the President and the Secretary of State."

The Administration then turned to Mr. Holbrooke, who pressed the Albanian political leader, Ibrahim Rugova, to meet with Mr. Milosevic. The payoff for Mr. Rugova was a face-to-face meeting with Mr. Clinton in the Oval Office on May 27, which served only to illustrate the gap between the Americans' public stance and the realities in Kosovo.

In a brief conversation with the President and Vice President Gore, Mr. Rugova warned that without direct American intervention, Kosovo was headed for all-out war. He pleaded for urgent American action and an increased American presence to halt the escalating violence.

"We will not allow another Bosnia to happen in Kosovo," a senior Administration official quoted Mr. Clinton as telling Mr. Rugova. The assurances were largely theoretical. Nothing concrete was promised.

After Mr. Rugova presented the President with a gift of a large piece of quartz mined from Kosovo, Mr.

Clinton spent part of their time together telling him about similar minerals in his home state of Arkansas.

The two men posed for a photo. The meeting received little press coverage.

There was plenty of other news in Washington that spring. The sex-and-lies investigation of Kenneth W. Starr was still preoccupying the White House. There were drawnout court battles between the President's lawyers and Mr. Starr over whether senior Administration aides, a few of whom were involved in foreign policy issues, should be forced to testify before Mr. Starr's grand jury.

In June, with the six-nation Contact Group on the Balkans warning Mr. Milosevic that he could not count on the West's dithering on Kosovo as it had on Bosnia, NATO was ordered to draw up plans for military action. Mr. Milosevic promised concessions.

The Options: From Cruise Missiles To a Force of 200,000

The American strategy seemed to be working.

The situation on the ground, however, was far from stable. The Albanian guerrillas used the early summer to take control of some 40 percent of Kosovo, and Mr. Milosevic responded with a major offensive.

NATO's military planners began weighing their options. These ranged from a limited attack involving only the firing of cruise missiles to a phased air campaign to deployment of peacekeeping troops as part of a negotiated or imposed settlement. The planners also looked at what it would take to invade Yugoslavia. Western officials said the numbers were staggering: as many as 200,000 soldiers would be needed for a ground war.

In the spring and summer of 1992, Serbian forces in Bosnia expelled hundreds of thousands of people from their homes. Seven years later, officials said, no one planned for the tactic that Mr. Milosevic adopted in Kosovo: the expulsion of hundreds of thousands of people from their homes.

"There were a lot of Milosevic watchers who said a few bombs might do it," a senior NATO official said. "What was not assumed, and not postulated, was that he would try to empty the country of its ethnic majority."

NATO officials were wrestling with several legal and political hurdles, officials disclosed. Some NATO members were worried about imposing a peace without the approval of the United Nations Security Council.

Alexander Vershbow, the United States representative to NATO and a former National Security Council aide who had been deeply involved in Bosnia policy, suggested an answer in a classified cable titled "Kosovo: Time for Another Endgame Strategy."

Mr. Vershbow's plan, officials said, arrived with a heavy political price tag: The possible dispatch of NATO soldiers just before a midterm election and in the midst of the impeachment fight.

The cable spelled out a plan to impose a political settlement in Kosovo with the cooperation of the Russians, longtime allies of the Serbs. Moscow and Washington would then go together to the Security Council.

"Kosovo endgame initiative could become a model of NATO-Russian cooperation," Mr. Vershbow wrote. "No kidding."

The proposed deal called for creation of an international protectorate in Kosovo. The settlement would be policed by an international military presence, or ground force. If a peace settlement was negotiated in advance, as many as 30,000 troops might be required to enforce it. But Mr. Vershbow also left open the possibility that NATO might have to impose a settlement without Belgrade's consent, requiring 60,000 troops. To help sell the idea in Congress, Mr. Vershbow said, the American contribution could be limited.

"Sooner or later we are going to face the issue of deploying ground forces in Kosovo," he wrote in his cable. "We have too much at stake in the political stability of the south Balkans to permit the conflict to fester much longer."

The cable landed in Washington on August 7, the day bombs exploded outside the American embassies in Kenya and Tanzania. It was circulated as Mr. Clinton and his aides were preparing for his pivotal appearance before the grand jury investigating the Lewinsky affair and the White House was planning the cruise missile attack against the Sudan and the Afghan bases of Osama bin Laden, the Saudi exile suspected of directing the attacks.

The plan drew some interest among midlevel officials in Washington. Senior officials agreed that it underscored the need to come up with a comprehensive strategy. In the end, nothing came of it.

Mr. Clinton was under attack for his grand jury testimony and faced questions about whether his military moves were motivated by domestic politics.

Jokes about the movie "Wag the Dog" became commonplace. In fact, the President in the movie seeking to distract attention from a sex scandal stages an ersatz conflict in, of all places, Albania.

The Politics: No Will for Troops On Eve of Election

In Washington, impeachment was on Clinton's mind. Returning from a September visit to the region, Bob Dole, the former Senate majority leader, stopped in to see Mr. Clinton and Mr. Berger.

"The President listened carefully," Mr. Dole said in interview. "I don't recall him saying a great deal. He agreed it was terrible. Sandy Berger didn't say much either." Then Mr. Berger left the room. "We discussed impeachment," Mr. Dole said. "This was a critical time in the Monica events."

In fact, Mr. Clinton asked for Mr. Dole's help in securing the 34 Senate votes needed to avoid conviction if the House voted to impeach.

Mid-term elections were also at hand, and the Democrats were perceived to be on the run. Republicans fired another shot across Mr. Clinton's bow, warning against bombing Serbia.

"The Serbians have done what they wanted," Senator Trent Lott, the Majority leader, said in an interview broadcast Oct. 4. "Now they're pulling back and now, only now what appears to be—will be— three weeks before an election, we're going to go in and bomb."

Senate Democrats were warning at the same time that they had little appetite for military involvement in Kosovo of any kind.

Senator Joseph R. Biden, the Democrat of Delaware who favored action on Kosovo, said then that several Democratic colleagues approached him at a party caucus on Oct. 6th and said, "Don't count me in, Joe, don't count me in."

At the White House, the Democrats' leading presidential contender for 2000, Vice President Al Gore, was keeping an eye on his own political future. Officials say he supported air strikes in Kosovo, but was careful to say little in meetings attended by large numbers of officials. His national security adviser,

Leon Fuerth, prodded intelligence officials to scour the files for evidence that might implicate Mr. Milosevic in war crimes.

In October, the President outlined the plan for NATO air strikes in a letter to leading Senators. The attacks, he said, would start out strong and "progressively expand in their scale and scope," especially if Mr. Milosevic and his forces remain in Kosovo.

"There will be no pinprick strikes," the President said in the letter.

NATO had agreed to the approach in a meeting of defense ministers in late September, in Vilamoura, Portugal. At the private meeting, Mr. Cohen challenged his colleagues to embrace a new role for the alliance. If NATO could not muster a threat to Mr. Milosevic under these circumstances, he asked, what was the point of the alliance?

The Defense Secretary's toughened stance was striking. During the Bosnia crisis, Mr. Cohen had assured his congressional colleagues that American troops would be out of the region within 18 months.

There were limits. As Mr. Cohen made clear this week in Congressional testimony, his commitment was to air power, not the deployment of American soldiers on the battlefield. Questioned by the Senate Armed Services Committee as to why the United States did not field a credible ground threat last fall, he replied:

"At that time, you may recall there was great discontent up here on Capitol Hill. If I had come to you at that time and requested authorization to put a ground force in—U.S., unilaterally, acting alone—I can imagine the nature of the questions I would have received. You'd say, 'Well, number one, where are our allies? And number two, who's going to appropriate the money? Number three, how long do you intend to be there? How many? How long? How much? And what's the exit strategy?' "

The Secretary concluded, "And that would have been the extent of the debate and probably would have received an overwhelming rejection from the committee."

The First Deal: Bargain on Monitors Averts an Air Strike

Despite the harsh words and warning to Mr. Milosevic in the fall of 1998, no one, neither in the Administration, nor in NATO, was eager to use force against the Serbs. So the White House turned again to Mr. Holbrooke to broker a deal that would push the issue into the next year.

It was a tall order.

At Dayton, Mr. Holbrooke had softened up Mr. Milosevic for months in advance and sensed the Serbian leader wanted a deal. In Ohio, Mr. Milosevic gave up territory in Bosnia, another country, and ended a war that was costing Belgrade huge sums of money.

Over Kosovo, the American envoy was pushing Mr. Milosevic to loosen his grip on land in his own country, a hallowed battlefield on which Serb soldiers had died trying to repell a Turkish invasion six centuries earlier.

His only inducement was the threat of air strikes.

Mr. Milosevic and Mr. Holbrooke talked for nine days, and when it was over, the Serbian leader had made some concessions, perhaps significant, but which were only loosely outlined.

The Yugoslav leader agreed to withdraw the bulk of his forces from Kosovo. He said he would permit 1,800 unarmed international inspectors to monitor the deal along and would allow overflights by NATO spy planes.

A token number of Yugoslav officers were to be sent to the NATO air base at Vicenza, Italy, with an equally small number of NATO officers stationed inside Serbia's Defense Ministry.

There was a catch. Mr. Milosevic wanted the lifting of the NATO order that gave authority to launch strikes immediately. Mr. Holbrooke made no promises. But he headed to Brussels where he summoned NATO ambassadors to an 11 P.M. meeting to report that a deal was nearly clinched.

The ambassadors voted several hours later to suspend the order, not remove it, angering Mr. Milosevic.

In Belgrade the next day, Mr. Milosevic told Mr. Holbrooke he was enraged that the order was not entirely lifted. "He considered it a declaration of war," said one American involved in the discussions.

President Clinton praised the deal as a triumph of force-backed diplomacy, saying it was the basis for a lasting peace. Mr. Milosevic, he said, has "agreed to internationally supervised democratic elections in Kosovo, substantial self-government and a local police—in short, rights the Kosovars have been de-

manding since Mr. Milosevic stripped their autonomy a decade ago."

Within days, there were strong hints that Mr. Milosevic was not cowed. At a meeting in Belgrade to discuss implementing the agreement, General Clark asked him why the Serbs had not withdrawn from Kosovo some of the security forces covered by the agreement.

"That was not agreed," Mr. Milosevic shot back, according to an American official familiar with the conversation. "You call Holbrooke. He'll tell you what we agreed." "No, I won't do that," replied General Clark, a veteran of hours of negotiations with Mr. Milosevic in Dayton. The general walked to a map to point out the locations of the brigades and battalions he wanted removed.

"We have no extra forces," Mr. Milosevic said. "NATO must do what it must do."

And then General Clark moved bluntly to the alliance's bottom line.

"Mr. President, get real," General Clark replied. "You don't really want to be bombed by NATO."

The Standoff: Deal with Milosevic Is Quickly Unhinged

The October agreement quickly fell apart, and Western officials now acknowledge that the Serbs' preparations for a massive purge of Kosovo were evident in what they did and what they said.

According to NATO officials, the Serbs began infiltrating reinforcements and equipment in violation of the deal. Serb officers bluntly told General Clark in October they were just two weeks away from eliminating the K.L.A.

In January, the commander of the main military unit in Kosovo, Lieut. Gen. Dusan S. Smardzic, told local reporters that they could look forward to a "hot spring" in which the problems in the province would finally be solved.

The Kosovo Albanian rebels were pushing ahead with their own war aims. Sensing that the deal essentially placed the world's most powerful military alliance on their side—despite NATO's continued assurances that it did not want to become the "K.L.A.'s airforce"—the rebels quickly reclaimed territory abandoned by the Serbian forces and mounted a continuous series of small-scale attacks.

American intelligence officials warned Congress that the rebels were buying weapons, improving their training, and were becoming a more formidable force.

The unarmed observers, caught in the middle, could do little. William S. Walker, the American diplomat who headed the observers, was threatened at one point by a belligerent drunken Serb wielding a gun and a hand grenade. Mr. Walker pleaded privately with old friends at the State Department for some security. The State Department was sympathetic but was struggling to cope with the aftermath of the embassy bombings.

American intelligence analysts struggled to read Mr. Milosevic's intentions. Was he playing for time or preparing for war? Were the troop movements in October a prelude to a major offensive in which the population would be displaced so that the Serbs could more easily root out the K.L.A.?

"The October agreement," said a highly classified National Intelligence Estimate dated November 1998, "indicates Milosevic is susceptible to outside pressure." It suggested he "could accept a number of outcomes from autonomy to provisional status, with the final resolution to be determined, as long as he remained the undisputed leader in Belgrade."

Mr. Milosevic, this assessment added, would only accept "new status" for Kosovo "if he thinks he is in danger because the West is threatening to use sustained and decisive military power against his forces."

About the same time, NATO intelligence detected signs of a Serbian military buildup around Kosovo. Western intelligence officials, particularly the Germans, believed that these troops could form the backbone of a military operation to push hundreds of thousands of Albanians out of Kosovo.

Its code name was Potkova—in Serbian, Horseshoe.

American officials agree that Jan. 16 of this year was a turning point. On that day, the bodies of at least 45 peasant farmers and their children were found on hillsides and courtyards in the village of Racak.

Most had been shot at close range in the head or neck by a single bullet, according to American officials. Some had been mutilated.

Witnesses said a small group of hooded men dressed in black and wearing gloves carried out the killings. Mr. Walker arrived on the scene within hours, and accused the Serbian security forces of committing "a crime very much against humanity."

The Serbian Government declared him persona non grata, and fiercely protested its innocence. The massacre galvanized public opinion in the United States and Europe.

Three days after the bodies were discovered, Ms. Albright presented her new plan at the Jan. 19 White House meeting. It again threatened bombing if Mr. Milosevic did not go along with the West. But, for the first time, it demanded that he accept NATO troops in his own country to enforce a deal under which he would withdraw almost all his security forces and grant Kosovo broad autonomy.

Mr. Berger was skeptical. Until then, the goal had been to stick to what came to be known as "October plus," the October agreement reached by Mr. Holbrooke plus some sort of protection for the observers.

Mr. Cohen and Gen. H. Hugh Shelton, Chairman of the Joint Chiefs of Staff, had even more reservations. They had wanted to avoid a troop presence—that would require Americans—at all costs. In the end, the advisers embraced Ms. Albright's approach and sent it to the President, who accepted it.

Two days later, President Clinton was on the phone to British Prime Minister Tony Blair describing the new approach.

The two leaders agreed there were two options: to initiate an immediate bombing campaign in reprisal for Racak, or to fashion a diplomatic solution that included ground troops as peacekeepers in Kosovo, according to a White House aide who listened in on the conversation.

"Blair said that ground troops could not be used to fight a war, but only as part of a political strategy," the official said. "The President said, 'I completely agree with you on that. If we sent in a ground force without some sort of agreement beforehand, sooner or later they're sitting ducks for either side who is willing to provoke something.' "

Mr. Clinton said he would instruct his aides to try to bring Mr. Milosevic and the Kosovo Albanians to the bargaining table. "I will try to get Congress to go along with me," he promised Mr. Blair.

Meanwhile, General Clark and General Naumann were confronting Mr. Milosevic.

The two generals refused food and drink. This was to be a serious negotiating session in which they told Mr. Milosevic he was violating the October agreement.

"We figured we'd starve him out," General Clark told colleagues afterwards.

Mr. Milosevic was, as General Clark told reporters afterwards, "determined to go his own way."

His face red, his voice cracking, the Serb leader said the incident was provocation.

"This was not a massacre!" Mr. Milosevic said, according to a NATO official familiar with the meeting. "It was staged. These people were terrorists. They do these things to people."

Mr. Clark warned that NATO is "going to start telling me to move aircraft" if Serbia did not live up to its agreement.

"You are a war criminal to be threatening Serbia," Mr. Milosevic replied.

Unquestionably, the meeting had gone badly. But General Clark, perhaps because he had lived through the stormy Dayton peace talks, reported to his superiors that he still saw some flexibility.

Two days after General Clark's meeting, two State Department veterans of the Dayton talks, James Pardew and Christopher Hill, delivered a similar message to the Yugoslav President.

This time, Mr. Milosevic said that the massacre was in reality a firefight between Serbian security forces and the rebels. The rebels, he continued, redressed and rearranged the bodies to make them look like peasants and farmers and reshot the bodies through the heads and necks to make it look like a massacre.

Mr. Milosevic's behavior raised a crucial question for Western officials: What were his intentions? Were the troop movements into Kosovo sabre rattling, or preparations for war?

American intelligence agencies, classified reports show, were utterly divided on how to read the Serbian leader.

"Confronted with a take it or leave it deal, Milosevic may opt to risk a NATO bombing campaign rather than surrender control over Kosovo," said one late January report, according to a Government official who has read it. "He may assume he can absorb a limited attack and allies will not support a long campaign."

A week later, the prediction was the opposite.

"Milosevic will seek to give just enough to avoid NATO bombing."

The day the bombing began, March 24, an intelligence report said Mr. Milosevic "would interrupt the offensive and sign the peace plan if he suffers or expects to suffer substantial damage to his armed forces and national level infrastructure from a bombing campaign."

Two days later, the analysts had changed their mind. "Air attacks," they wrote, "will not suffice to shake Milosevic's confidence."

In addition, while it was widely expected that NATO bombing would prompt retaliation against the Kosovo Albanians, officials said there were no predictions that Mr. Milosevic would attempt to empty the province of ethnic Albanians, as he has done.

The Negotiations: Talks at a Castle Set Stage for War

After the Racak massacre in January, some American officials favored air strikes. But there remained the delicate matter of NATO unity.

On January 28, the NATO allies warned that they were ready to use force immediately, and Britain and France said they were prepared to send in ground troops to enforce a peace settlement. Two days later, after United Nations Secretary General Kofi Annan said that the threat of force was justified to get the Serbs to the bargaining table, the allies decided they had justification enough under international law to authorize air strikes against Yugoslavia if it did not agree to negotiate a settlement.

To try to strike that deal, the Europeans wanted a conference that would be their equivalent of Dayton, Ms. Albright said in an interview Friday.

But the gathering at Rambouillet, a former royal hunting lodge near Paris, was no Dayton.

The Americans approached the negotiations hoping to impose a solution on the Serbs and the ethnic Albanians, but that attempt quickly broke down. Mr. Milosevic, who was a central figure at Dayton, didn't even attend the meetings. The Albanians were balky, too, refusing to accept a three-year autonomy deal offered by NATO because it carried no guarantee of eventual independence.

If Dayton was a diplomatic triumph for the Clinton Administration and Mr. Holbrooke, Rambouillet was an embarrassing debacle for Secretary Albright. She told friends it was one of the worst experiences of her career.

With the two-week deadline set for the talks almost expired, Ms. Albright went to Rambouillet and implored the ethnic Albanians to sign on to the deal. Ms. Albright failed to convince the hardliners, the representatives of the Kosovo Liberation Army, who insisted on inserting language that held out promise of a referendum on independence after the three years of autonomy. But they also insisted they needed a two-week pause to sell even that deal to their supporters.

That set the stage for the ultimate failure of diplomacy and the outbreak of war. By refusing to sign the deal, the ethnic Albanians had taken the pressure off the Serbs. "If this fails because both sides say 'No,' there will be no bombing of Serbia," Ms. Albright said on Feb. 21, as the Rambouillet talks wound down.

Mr. Milosevic, for his part, concluded there was not enough incentive for him to deal. Two days after Rambouillet ended, said the European Union envoy to the talks, Wolfgang Petritsch, the Yugoslav President decided he was not going to accept NATO troops—and mustered his own forces and propaganda to prepare for the military showdown.

The standoff over Kosovo was growing more dire as President Clinton's political fortunes were rising and as the crisis drew more of his focus and energy. On February 12, he was acquitted by the Senate. Only a few days later, on a trip to Mexico with Sen. Biden, the President wanted to talk about the Kosovo crisis.

"All the way down on the plane I was reading a book about the Balkans and he saw me reading it," the Delaware Democrat recalled in an interview.

The book was "History of the Balkans," by Barbara Jelavich, published by Cambridge University Press. "And you know how he is," Mr. Biden added. "He asked me to give it to him to read. And I said, 'No, get your own copy.'

And I'll lay odds that he eventually got it and read it.' "

President Clinton believed war could still be averted, though he was prepared to undertake a short burst of bombings, if necessary.

In a meeting with Italy's new Prime Minister, Mas-

simo D'Alema, in the Oval office on March 5, Mr. Clinton said that "Milosevic has accepted almost everything," according to Italian officials in Europe.

Mr. D'Alema, a rough-around-the-edges former Communist, was skeptical. He asked the President what the plan was if there was no deal and NATO air strikes failed to subdue the Serb leader. The result, Mr. D'Alema said, would be 300,000 to 400,000 refugees passing into Albania and crossing the Adriatic into Italy.

"What will happen then?" Mr. D'Alema wanted to know, Italian officials said.

Mr. Clinton looked to Mr. Berger for guidance. NATO will "keep bombing," Mr. Berger replied.

After Rambouillet fell apart, a follow-up conference was called in Paris three weeks later. While the world waited, Mr. Milosevic continued to build up his forces in and around Kosovo.

A defining moment came on March 18 at the International Conference Center on the Avenue Kléber in Paris. To polite applause, four ethnic Albanian delegates signed the peace plan that would give their people broad autonomy for a three-year interim period. The Serbs didn't sign. That paved the way to air strikes.

Even though the United States and its NATO allies were now committed to war, three European Foreign Ministers—Robin Cook of Britain, Hubert Vedrine of France and Joschka Fischer of Germany—began murmuring about making a final appeal to Mr. Milosevic in Belgrade. Ms. Albright persuaded them to allow Mr. Holbrooke to go instead. But even as Mr. Holbrooke was en route to Belgrade, the situation grew more hopeless.

"The racial hatred was unleashed," said one senior Administration official. "Albanians began to kill Serbs; Serbs were shooting up villages."

Mr. Holbrooke has described his last meeting with Mr. Milosevic in Belgrade's Beli Dvor—White House—on March 22 as "unreal." Mr. Milosevic accused the Americans of "sitting at the Albanian side of the table" at Rambouillet.

He insisted that there was no war in Kosovo, just a few terrorists who needed to be rooted out once and for all. Mr. Holbrooke later described parts of his conversation with Mr. Milosevic. "I said to him, 'Look, are you absolutely clear in your own mind what will happen when I get up and walk out of this palace that we're now sitting in?' "

"And he said, 'You're going to bomb us.' "

"And I said, 'That's right.' "

In the end it was Mr. Milosevic who was left to decide whether his country and NATO would go to war. "It was Milosevic who deliberately and consciously chose to trigger the bombing of his own country," Mr. Holbrooke said.

Ms. Albright said that setting up a deal signed by only one side was a crucial step forward. "Signing Rambouillet was crucial in getting the Europeans two things: getting them to agree to the use of force and getting the Albanians on the side of this kind of a settlement."

The Serbs had already begun their offensive, she added, and if the signing had not been forced at that time, "we would be negotiating while they were carrying out their village-a-day-keeps-NATO-away."

At 12:30 in the morning on March 25, just hours after the first bombs fell, the President was wide awake. He had called his key counterparts in NATO and monitored the beginning of the air war that day. His foreign policy team had gone home and there was nothing left to do.

But the President apparently needed to assure and be reassured. So he called his Secretary of State and rousted her out of her bed.

The President said, "We're doing the right thing here," Ms. Albright recalled in an interview. "We've got a long way to go. This is not going to be over quickly and we're all in this. I feel we've explored every option, that we're doing the right thing."

"I feel the same way," the Secretary said she replied. "Nobody should ever think that we had gone into this without our eyes wide open."

Chapter 7 Review Questions

1. What are the five major subsystems in public agencies that decisively influence policy? Briefly describe the characteristics of each one.

2. Where are political appointees situated in the bureaucracy, and what functions do these individuals serve in U.S. government? Who were the political appointees in the case "The Decision to Bomb the Serbs," and what roles did they play? Who were the professionals in the case study, and what role did they play in setting the policy agenda for bombing the Serbs?

3. What are the essential differences between the professional careerists and the political appointees as reflected in the case study? What are the sources of each one's influence and authority? In the case, how were these differences, outlooks, and sources of influence reflected? And why was it critical for them to work together "as a foreign policy team"?

4. Would you consider the professionals in the case to be among the professional elite? Why? Who were they, specifically?

5. Were there conflicts between the foreign policy team and other competing demands on the political leadership? Why was their working relationship influenced by other competing demands on the Presidency and thus, how does timing of issues become so critical to coping with their resolution?

6. What does the case say generally about the ethical dilemmas of modern public professionals in government today? How can and should they behave in relationship to their political superiors? Can you draw out any clear rules of relationship based upon this case study?

Key Terms

political appointees
sub-Cabinet officials
professional careerists
professional elites
SES
"inner" versus "outer" Cabinet
Pendleton Act

GS rating
rank "in person" versus "in job"
Kennedy's Executive Orders
   10988 and 10987
public service unions
contract employment
line versus staff professionals

Suggestions for Further Reading

A number of excellent books deal with the origins, growth, and operations of the five types of bureaucratic subsystems discussed in this chapter. The best account of the rise of the U.S. civil service remains Paul Van Riper's *History of the U.S. Civil Service* (Evanston, Ill.: Row, Peterson, Co., 1958). For accounts of professionalism, read C. L. Gibb, *Hidden Hierarchies* (1966), Don Price, *Scientific Estate* (Cambridge: Harvard University Press, 1965), and Frederick C. Mosher, *Democracy and the Public Service,* Second Edition, (New York: Oxford University Press, 1982). Studies advocating reforms in the civil service systems, such as the Volcker Commission Report, *Leadership for America* (1989), The Hudson Institute, *Civil Service 2000* (1988), and Frank J. Thompson (ed.), *Revitalizing State and Local Government: Strengthening Performance, Accountability, and Citizen Confidence* (1993), as well as several GAO studies such as *The Senior Executive Service* (1988), are some of the best guides to current public personnel practices and problems.

For a thoughtful look at the meaning of "merit" in relation to contemporary civil service, read Patricia W. Ingraham, *The Foundation of Merit* (Baltimore: The Johns Hopkins Press, 1995). For an account of the interplay between political appointees, professionals, and civil servants, read Frank J. Thompson, *Personnel Policy in the City* (Berkeley, Calif.: University of California Press, 1975), and Hugh Heclo, *A Government of Strangers* (Washington, D.C.: The Brookings In-

stitution, 1977). Three books dealing with political appointees include John W. Macy, Bruce Adams, and J. Jackson Walter, eds., *America's Unelected Government: Appointing the President's Team* (Cambridge: Ballinger, 1983), G. Calvin MacKenzie, *The Politics of Presidential Appointments* (New York: Free Press, 1981), and by the same author, *The In and Outers* (Baltimore: Johns Hopkins Press, 1987). Excellent reviews of the impact of the 1978 Civil Service Reform Act are found in Patricia W. Ingraham and David H. Rosenbloom, eds., *The Promise and Paradox of Civil Service Reform* (San Francisco: Jossey-Bass, 1993). For the current operation of SES that was created by CSRA 1978, see OPM, *The Status of the Senior Executive Service* (1991), the Merit Protection Board, *The Senior Executive Service— Views of Former Federal Executives* (1989), Mark W. Huddleton and William A. Boyes, *The Higher Civil Services in the United States* (Pittsburgh: University of Pittsburgh Press, 1995), and the thoughtful essay by Norton Long, "SES and the Public Interest," *Public Administration Review* (May/June 1981). For a helpful overview of key civil service issues, review Patricia W. Ingraham and Don Kettl, *Agenda for Excellence* (Chatham, N.J.: Chatham Press, 1992).

For useful perspectives on professional career systems, see Frederick C. Mosher and Richard J. Stillman II, eds., *Professions in Government* (New Brunswick, N.J.: Transaction Books, 1982). For more recent analyses of professionalism, see James

A. Smith, *The Idea Brokers* (New York: Free Press, 1991), and David S. Arnold and Jeremy F. Plant, *Public Official Associations and State and Local Government: A Bridge Across One Hundred Years* (Fairfax, Va.: George Mason University Press, 1994), and for unions, A. Lawrence Chickering, ed., *Public Employee Unions* (Washington, D.C.: The Brookings Institution, 1977), and David T. Stanley, *Managing Local Government under Union Pressure* (Washington, D.C.: The Brookings Institution, 1972). For more up-to-date studies of where we are today involving the problems of unions and the public service, read Joel M. Douglas's three essays: "Collective Bargaining and Public Sector Supervisors: A Trend Towards Exclusion?" *Public Administration Review* (Nov./Dec. 1987); "State Civil Service and Collective Bargaining Systems in Conflict," *Public Administration Review* (March/April, 1992); and "Public Sector Labor Relations in the 21st Century: New Approaches, New Strategies," in Carolyn C. Ban and N. Riccucci, eds., *Public Personnel Management* (N.Y.: Marcel Dekker, 1991).

Even though the contractual subsystem has emerged as a powerful and significant force within public bureaucracy today, few scholars have examined the subject in much depth. This is both surprising and regrettable, though Clarence H.

Danhof's *Government Contracting and Technological Change* (Washington, D.C.: The Brookings Institution, 1968), although somewhat dated, is still helpful for its history. Various recent books offer useful insights into portions of the contract subsystem: Ruth Hoogland De Hoog, *Partners in Public Service* (New York: SUNY Press, 1986); Don Kettl, *Sharing Power* (Washington, D.C.: The Brookings Institution, 1993); and Susan R. Bernstein, *Managing Contracted Services in a Nonprofit Agency* (Philadelphia, PA: Temple University Press, 1991).

One should not overlook five alternative perspectives for usefully exploring this complex topic: Recent autobiographies, such as Elliot Richardson, *Reflections of a Radical Moderate* (NY: Pantheon Books, 1996); 2) case studies of current policy issues, like Jacob S. Hacker, *The Road to Nowhere* (Princeton: Princeton University Press, 1997); 3) institutional studies, like Paul C. Light, *Monitoring Government* (Washington, DC: Brookings, 1993) or 4) analyses of specific influential groups like Robert Wood, ed. *Remedial Law* (Amherst: University of Massachusetts Press, 1990) and 5) Journals reporting on specific public service groups such as *PM* for city managers or *The Military Review* for army officers.

PART TWO

The Multiple Functions of Public Administrators: Their Major Activities, Responsibilities, and Roles

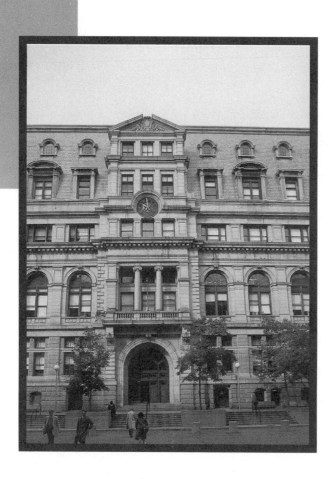

Public administrators must fulfill many functions, often simultaneously. Part Two focuses on several of the important activities performed by public administrators— decision making, administrative communications, management, personnel motivation, budgeting, and implementation. The extent, scope, and capability with which administrators perform these functions vary widely from administrator to administrator, from job to job, and from locale to locale. However, it is safe to say these six functions are considered some of the most critical activities that public administrators must perform if they are to succeed—indeed survive—in their jobs.

As in Part One of this book, in Part Two, chapter by chapter, a single concept is discussed in a reading and its relevance is illustrated in a case study. Although the six major roles of administrators are individually discussed in the following chapters, it should be emphasized that the reality of the administrative processes frequently forces public administrators to assume all these responsibilities at the same time; this makes their work much more complex, less neatly compartmentalized or clear-cut than these individual chapters may suggest. The significant functional concepts discussed in Part Two include:

CHAPTER 8
Decision Making: *The Concept of Incremental Choice* How are decisions made in the public sector and why do public administrators frequently feel as if they are "flying by the seat of their pants"?

CHAPTER 9
Administrative Communications: *The Concept of its Professional Centrality* How does the flow of communications inside and outside organizations influence the way decisions are made and how well (or how poorly) administrators perform their work? And what can be done to improve administrative communication?

CHAPTER 10
Executive Management: *The Concept of Effective Public Organizations* What is a successful management practice for public administrators to adopt? Why is public management often very different from business management?

CHAPTER 11
Public Personnel Motivation: *The Concept of The Public Service Culture* Why is personnel motivation so significant to organizational performance and productivity? How can public administrators most effectively motivate their employees?

CHAPTER 12
Public Budgeting: *The Concept of Budgeting as Political Choice* What is the nature of the budgetary process in government? Why is a knowledge of budgeting so fundamental to administrative survival?

CHAPTER 13
Implementation: *The Concept of an Ambiguity Conflict Model* What is the best way for administrators to get their jobs done in a timely manner, efficiently, correctly, and responsibly? How can one best conceptualize this approach as a model?

CHAPTER **8**

Decision Making: The Concept of Incremental Choice

A *wise policy-maker consequently expects that his policies will achieve only part of what he hopes and at the same time will produce unanticipated consequences he would have preferred to avoid. If he proceeds through a succession of incremental changes, he avoids serious lasting mistakes. . . .*

Charles E. Lindblom

READING 8

Introduction

Few concepts are debated in administration more frequently than decision making—how decisions are made; whom they are made by; why they are decided on in the first place; and what impact they have once the choice is made. Gallons of ink have been spilled in academic journals debating whether decision making is an art or a science, how best to construct a decision-making model, or how to arrive at the most rational (or optimal) choice. One point emerges from these seemingly endless discussions: the process by which individuals and groups determine a correct course of action from various alternatives is one of the central functions of an administrator and thus deserves careful consideration by students of public administration.

What is the decision-making function? On one level, we all use decision making daily in confronting a myriad of personal choices, such as when to get up in the morning and what clothes to wear. On the larger and more complicated level of public administration, however, the decisional process involves vital community or societal choices—where to build a new school, when to negotiate an arms limitation treaty, or how to organize a new federal program for poverty relief. The process of choice runs the length and breadth of public administration and involves 4, 40, 400, or 4,000 steps, depending on the complexity and range of variables presented by the problem at hand.

Charles E. Lindblom (1917–   ), a Yale economist and long-time scholar of public policy issues, offers an important conceptual understanding of governmental decision making in his essay, "The Science of 'Muddling Through.' " Lindblom, unlike most economists, has seriously thought about the relationships between economics and politics for many years, an interest evident in his earliest writings with Robert A. Dahl in *Politics, Economics and Welfare* (1953), as well as in his more recent book,

Politics and Markets (1977). In an effort to realistically analyze the way governmental decisions are made, at the heart of Lindblom's brilliant studies is a model of decision making that he succinctly outlines in the following essay.

Based on earlier writings by Chester Barnard and Herbert Simon, Lindblom's central thesis is that there are two distinct varieties of decision making. One he calls the rational-comprehensive or root method, and the second, the successive limited comparisons or branch method. The first method is found in the classic texts on administration, and the latter is the "real" way decisions are arrived at in government. In the traditional *rational-comprehensive* or *root method* an administrator confronts a given objective, such as reducing poverty by a certain amount. The decision maker, in choosing the best policy to pursue, rationally ranks all the relevant values (or advantages) in attaining this objective, such as improving the health of the poor, reducing crime, improving property values, and eliminating illiteracy. He or she then formulates as many possible alternatives to achieve the stated objective—for example, a guaranteed income plan, direct government subsidies, higher welfare payments, or work-relief programs—and selects from among the options the *best* alternative that serves to maximize the ranked list of values. This approach to decision making is *rational,* because the alternatives and values are logically selected and weighed in relative importance. It is also *comprehensive,* for all the alternatives and values are taken into account by the policy maker.

What *actually* occurs in administrative decision making, argues Lindblom, is quite another process, namely, the *successive limited comparisons* or *branch method.* An objective is established—reducing poverty by a set amount, for example—but in public discussions this objective quickly becomes compromised. It may soon be mixed up with other goals such as educating minority students or providing work relief for the jobless. Administrators tend to overlook or avoid many of the social values that could be derived from their program, concentrating instead on those that they consider immediately relevant. In selecting the appropriate course of action, administrators outline not a broad range of possibilities, but only a few incremental steps that experience tells them are feasible. Furthermore, in practice, policy makers do not rationally select the optimal program that satisfies a clearly delineated list of values. To the contrary, under the successive limited comparisons method, contends Lindblom, public administrators pragmatically select from among the immediate choices at hand the most suitable compromise that satisfies the groups and individuals concerned with the program.

Lindblom sees the first approach, the root method, as wrongly assuming that administrators making decisions have unlimited amounts of time and resources available to them. "It assumes intellectual capacities and sources of information that simply do not exist and it is even more absurd as an approach to policy when the time and money that can be allocated to a policy problem is limited as is always the case." Second, the root method holds that there are always clear-cut values on which all interested parties agree. In fact, argues Lindblom, in a democratic society in which members of Congress, agencies, and interest groups are in continual disagreement over the relative importance of program objectives, policy makers cannot begin to rank explicitly the values derived from any program. There are simply too many groups with too many unknown values. The weight given to their relative importance depends ultimately on personal perspectives. "Even when an administrator resolves to follow his own values as a criterion for decisions, he will often not know how to rank them when they conflict with one another as they usually do." Third, the root method assumes that ends and means in policy choices are distinct, when in fact they are frequently intertwined. Selection of a goal to be accomplished often cannot easily be separated from the means by which it is achieved. For instance, the objective of slum clearance is intrinsically associated with the removal of residents from the neighborhood and the other methods used to achieve the goal, such as the clearing of buildings. Means and ends often become hopelessly confused in public policy choices. Finally, says Lindblom, the choice of a given course of action depends ultimately not on whether it maximizes the intended values (even if the values could be identified and ranked), but rather on whether it serves as a compromise acceptable to all parties concerned. "If agreement directly on policy as a test for the 'best' policy seems a poor substitute for testing the policy against its objectives, it ought to be remembered that objectives themselves have no ultimate validity other than they are agreed upon. . . . Agreement on policy thus becomes the only practicable test of the policy's correctness," argues Lindblom.

Lindblom's view of the reality of administrative decision making contains five characteristics. First, it is *incremental,* for small steps are always taken to achieve objectives, not broad leaps and bounds. Second, it is *noncomprehensive.* In other words, because policy makers' resources are always limited, they cannot take into consideration the full range of policy choices available to them at any given moment, nor can they possibly understand the full effects of their decisions or all of the values derived from any alternative they select. Third, the branch technique of decision making involves *successive comparisons* because policy is never made once and for all, but is made and remade endlessly by small chains of comparisons between narrow choices. Fourth, in practice, decision making *suffices* rather than maximizes from among the available options. "A wise policy maker completely expects that his policies will achieve only part of what he hopes and at the same time will produce unanticipated consequences he would have preferred to avoid." Finally, Lindblom's picture of governmental decision making rests on a *pluralist* conception of the public sector, in which many contending interest groups compete for influence over policy issues, continually forcing the administrator, as the person in the middle, to secure agreement among the competing parties. The political arts of compromise thus become a major part of decision-making methods.

There are two advantages of the branch method, asserts Lindblom. The first is that "if he proceeds through a succession of small incremental changes, the administrator therefore has the advantage of avoiding serious lasting mistakes" as well as permitting easy alterations should the wrong course be pursued. The second benefit of incrementalism is that it fits "hand and glove" with the American political system, which operates chiefly by means of gradual changes, rarely by dramatic shifts in public policies. "Non-incremental policy proposals are therefore typically not only politically irrelevant but also unpredictable in their policy consequences," writes Lindblom. The branch method allows for the art of compromise that American politics demands and produces the gradual changes that American tradition generally favors.

However, from the perspective of the "outside expert" or the academic problem solver, Lindblom points out, this approach seems "unscientific and unsystematic." Indeed, administrators may appear as if they were flying "by the seat of their pants," although in fact the outside theorists do not grasp that administrators are "often practicing a systematic method" of successive limited comparisons. Yet, as Lindblom says, ". . . sometimes decision makers are pursuing neither a theoretical approach nor successive comparisons nor any systematic method."

Lindblom's approach to governmental decision making, which for some may be too descriptive and not sufficiently prescriptive, debunks the classic view of how public choices are made, substituting an incremental model that is peculiarly a product and extension of economic theory of choice (subsequently, much of the language used in decisional theory—words like "optimizing" and "maximizing"—is derived from economics). Kenneth Arrow, Thomas Schelling, Herbert Simon, Edward Banfield, and Robert Dahl are among the major contemporary economists and political scientists who have pioneered the incremental view of decision making in the post–World War II era (refer to the numerous varieties of decision models outlined in the Suggestions for Further Reading at the end of this chapter). Lindblom has fully developed this idea into an elaborate working model in the following article, "The Science of 'Muddling Through.' "

As you read this selection, keep the following questions in mind:

Is Lindblom too pessimistic about the ability of administrators to make profound "big" choices that will significantly alter or reshape their external environment?

What do you see as the benefits and disadvantages of the branch method and are there any remedies for its defects?

How does Lindblom's concept square with any of the previous case studies, such as Case Study 7 The Decision to Bomb the Serbs? Or was it a "root" or "branch" decision?

Does Lindblom's "muddling through" idea primarily apply in normal governmental decisions involving simple issues? How about catastrophes such as in Case Study 1, "The Blast in Centralia No. 5"? What decisional methods might have averted the unfortunate choices made in that case?

Do you agree with Lindblom that "the branch method compared to other decisional models often looks far superior," particularly from the perspective of the practitioner?

The Science of "Muddling Through"

CHARLES E. LINDBLOM

Suppose an administrator is given responsibility for formulating policy with respect to inflation. He

might start by trying to list all related values in order of importance, e.g., full employment, reasonable business profit, protection of small savings, prevention of a stock market crash. Then all possible policy outcomes could be rated as more or less efficient in attaining a maximum of these values. This would of course require a prodigious inquiry into values held by members of society and an equally prodigious set of calculations on how much of each value is equal to how much of each other value. He could then proceed to outline all possible policy alternatives. In a third step, he would undertake systematic comparison of his multitude of alternatives to determine which attains the greatest amount of values.

In comparing policies, he would take advantage of any theory available that generalized about classes of policies. In considering inflation, for example, he would compare all policies in the light of the theory of prices. Since no alternatives are beyond his investigation, he would consider strict central control and the abolition of all prices and markets on the one hand and elimination of all public controls with reliance completely on the free market on the other, both in the light of whatever theoretical generalizations he could find on such hypothetical economies.

Finally, he would try to make the choice that would in fact maximize his values.

An alternative line of attack would be to set as his principal objective, either explicitly or without conscious thought, the relatively simple goal of keeping prices level. This objective might be compromised or complicated by only a few other goals, such as full employment. He would in fact disregard most other social values as beyond his present interest, and he would for the moment not even attempt to rank the few values that he regarded as immediately relevant. Were he pressed, he would quickly admit that he was ignoring many related values and many possible important consequences of his policies.

As a second step, he would outline those relatively few policy alternatives that occurred to him. He would then compare them. In comparing his limited number of alternatives, most of them familiar from past controversies, he would not ordinarily find a body of theory precise enough to carry him through a comparison of their respective consequences. Instead he would rely heavily on the record of past experience with small policy steps to predict the consequences of similar steps extended into the future.

Moreover, he would find that the policy alternatives combined objectives or values in different ways. For example, one policy might offer price level stability at the cost of some risk of unemployment; another might offer less price stability but also less risk of unemployment. Hence, the next step in his approach—the final selection—would combine into one the choice among values and the choice among instruments for reaching values. It would not, as in the first method of policy-making, approximate a more mechanical process of choosing the means that best satisfied goals that were previously clarified and ranked. Because practitioners of the second approach expect to achieve their goals only partially, they would expect to repeat endlessly the sequence just described, as conditions and aspirations changed and as accuracy of prediction improved.

By Root or by Branch

For complex problems, the first of these two approaches is of course impossible. Although such an approach can be described, it cannot be practiced except for relatively simple problems and even then only in a somewhat modified form. It assumes intellectual capacities and sources of information that men simply do not possess, and it is even more absurd as an approach to policy when the time and money that can be allocated to a policy problem is limited, as is always the case. Of particular importance to public administrators is the fact that public agencies are in effect usually instructed not to practice the first method. That is to say, their prescribed functions and constraints—the politically or legally possible—restrict their attention to relatively few values and relatively few alternative policies among the countless alternatives that might be imagined. It is the second method that is practiced.

Curiously, however, the literatures of decision making, policy formulation, planning, and public administration formalize the first approach rather than the second, leaving public administrators who handle complex decisions in the position of practicing what few preach. For emphasis I run some risk of overstatement. True enough, the literature is well aware of limits on man's capacities and of the inevitability that policies will be approached in some such style as the second. But attempts to formalize rational policy formulation—to lay out explicitly the necessary steps in the process—usually describe the first approach and not the second.[1]

The common tendency to describe policy formulation even for complex problems as though it followed the first approach has been strengthened by the attention given to, and successes enjoyed by, operations research, statistical decision theory, and systems analysis. The hallmarks of these procedures, typical of the first approach, are clarity of objective, explicitness of evaluation, a high degree of comprehensiveness of overview, and, wherever possible, quantification of values for mathematical analysis. But these advanced procedures remain largely the appropriate techniques of relatively small-scale problem-solving where the total number of variables to be considered is small and value problems restricted. Charles Hitch, head of the Economics Division of RAND Corporation, one of the leading centers for application of these techniques, has written:

> I would make the empirical generalization from my experience at RAND and elsewhere that operations research is the art of suboptimizing, i.e., of solving some lower-level problems, and that difficulties increase and our special competence diminishes by an order of magnitude with every level of decision making we attempt to ascend. The sort of simple explicit model which operations researchers are so proficient in using can certainly reflect most of the significant factors influencing traffic control on the George Washington Bridge, but the proportion of the relevant reality which we can represent by any such model or models in studying, say, a major foreign-policy decision, appears to be almost trivial.[2]

Accordingly, I propose in this paper to clarify and formalize the second method, much neglected in the literature. This might be described as the method of *successive limited comparisons*. I will contrast it with the first approach, which might be called the rational-comprehensive method.[3] More impressionistically and briefly— and therefore generally used in this article—they could be characterized as the branch method and root method, the former continually building out from the current situation, step-to-step and by small degrees; the latter starting from fundamentals anew each time, building on the past only as experience is embodied in a theory, and always prepared to start completely from the ground up.

Let us put the characteristics of the two methods side by side in simplest terms.

Rational-Comprehensive (Root)

   1a. Clarification of values or objectives distinct from and usually prerequisite to empirical analysis of alternative policies.

   2a. Policy-formulation is therefore approached through means-end analysis: First the ends are isolated, then the means to achieve them are sought.

   3a. The test of a "good" policy is that it can be shown to be the most appropriate means to desired ends.

   4a. Analysis is comprehensive; every important relevant factor is taken into account.

   5a. Theory is often heavily relied upon.

Successive Limited Comparisons (Branch)

   1b. Selection of value goals and empirical analysis of the needed action are not distinct from one another but are closely intertwined.

   2b. Since means and ends are not distinct,

means-end analysis is often inappropriate or limited.

3b. The test of a "good" policy is typically that various analysts find themselves directly agreeing on a policy (without their agreeing that it is the most appropriate means to an agreed objective).

4b. Analysis is drastically limited:

i) Important possible outcomes are neglected.

ii) Important alternative potential policies are neglected.

iii) Important affected values are neglected.

5b. A succession of comparisons greatly reduces or eliminates reliance on theory.

Assuming that the root method is familiar and understandable, we proceed directly to clarification of its alternative by contrast. In explaining the second, we shall be describing how most administrators do in fact approach complex questions, for the root method, the "best" way as a blueprint or model, is in fact not workable for complex policy questions, and administrators are forced to use the method of successive limited comparisons.

Intertwining Evaluation and Empirical Analysis (1b)

The quickest way to understand how values are handled in the method of successive limited comparisons is to see how the root method often breaks down in *its* handling of values or objectives. The idea that values should be clarified, and in advance of the examination of alternative policies, is appealing. But what happens when we attempt it for complex social problems? The first difficulty is that on many critical values or objectives, citizens disagree, congressmen disagree, and public administrators disagree. Even where a fairly specific objective is prescribed for the administrator, there remains considerable room for disagreement on sub-objectives. Consider, for example, the conflict with respect to locating public housing, described in Meyerson and Banfield's study of the Chicago Housing Authority[4]—disagreement which occurred despite the clear objective of providing a certain number of public housing units in the city. Similarly conflicting are objectives in highway location, traffic control, minimum wage administration, development of tourist facilities in national parks, or insect control.

Administrators cannot escape these conflicts by ascertaining the majority's preference, for preferences have not been registered on most issues; indeed, there often *are* no preferences in the absence of public discussion sufficient to bring an issue to the attention of the electorate. Furthermore, there is a question of whether intensity of feeling should be considered as well as the number of persons preferring each alternative. By the impossibility of doing otherwise, administrators often are reduced to deciding policy without clarifying objectives first.

Even when an administrator resolves to follow his own values as a criterion for decisions, he often will not know how to rank them when they conflict with one another, as they usually do. Suppose, for example, that an administrator must relocate tenants living in tenements scheduled for destruction. One objective is to empty the buildings fairly promptly, another is to find suitable accommodation for persons displaced, another is to avoid friction with residents in other areas in which a large influx would be unwelcome, another is to deal with all concerned through persuasion if possible, and so on.

How does one state even to himself the relative importance of these partially conflicting values? A simple ranking of them is not enough; one needs ideally to know how much of one value is worth sacrificing for some of another value. The answer is that typically the administrator chooses—and must choose—directly among policies in which these values are combined in different ways. He cannot first clarify his values and then choose among policies.

A more subtle third point underlies both the first two. Social objectives do not always have the same relative values. One objective may be highly prized in one circumstance, another in another circumstance. If, for example, an administrator values highly both the dispatch with which his agency can carry through its projects *and* good public relations, it matters little which of the two possibly conflicting values he favors in some abstract or general sense. Policy questions arise in forms which put to administrators such a question as: Given the degree to which we are or are not already achieving the values of dispatch and the values of good public relations, is it worth sacrificing a little speed for a happier clientele, or is it better to risk offending the clientele so that we can get on with our work? The answer to such a question varies with circumstances.

The value problem is, as the example shows, always a problem of adjustments at a margin. But there is no practicable way to state marginal objectives or values except in terms of particular policies. That one value is preferred to another in one decision situation does not mean that it will be preferred in another decision situation in which it can be had only at great sacrifice of another value. Attempts to rank or order values in general and abstract terms so that they do not shift from decision to decision end up by ignoring the relevant marginal preferences. The significance of this third point thus goes very far. Even if all administrators had at hand an agreed set of values, objectives, and constraints, and an agreed ranking of these values, objectives, and constraints, their marginal values in actual choice situations would be impossible to formulate.

Unable consequently to formulate the relevant values first and then choose among policies to achieve them, administrators must choose directly among alternative policies that offer different marginal combinations of values. Somewhat paradoxically, the only practicable way to disclose one's relevant marginal values even to oneself is to describe the policy one chooses to achieve them. Except roughly and vaguely, I know of no way to describe—or even to understand—what my relative evaluations are for, say, freedom and security, speed and accuracy in governmental decisions, or low taxes and better schools than to describe my preferences among specific policy choices that might be made between the alternatives in each of the pairs.

In summary, two aspects of the process by which values are actually handled can be distinguished. The first is clear: evaluation and empirical analysis are intertwined; that is, one chooses among values and among policies at one and the same time. Put a little more elaborately, one simultaneously chooses a policy to attain certain objectives and chooses the objectives themselves. The second aspect is related but distinct: the administrator focuses his attention on marginal or incremental values. Whether he is aware of it or not, he does not find general formulations of objectives very helpful and in fact makes specific marginal or incremental comparisons. Two policies, X and Y, confront him. Both promise the same degree of attainment of objectives $a, b, c, d,$ and e. But X promises him somewhat more of f than does Y, while Y promises him somewhat more of g than does X. In choosing between them, he is in fact offered the alternative of a marginal or incremental amount of f at the expense of a marginal or incremental amount of g. The only values that are relevant to his choice are these increments by which the two policies differ; and, when he finally chooses between the two marginal values, he does so by making a choice between policies.[5]

As to whether the attempt to clarify objectives in advance of policy selection is more or less rational than the close intertwining of marginal evaluation and empirical analysis, the principal difference established is that for complex problems the first is impossible and irrelevant, and the second is both possible and relevant. The second is possible because the administrator need not try to analyze any values except the values by which alternative policies differ and need not be concerned with them except as they differ marginally. His need for information on values or objectives is drastically reduced as compared with the root method; and his capacity for grasping, comprehending, and relating values to one another is not strained beyond the breaking point.

Relations Between Means and Ends (2b)

Decision-making is ordinarily formalized as a means-ends relationship: means are conceived to be evaluated and chosen in the light of ends finally selected independently of and prior to the choice of means. This is the means-ends relationship of the root method. But it follows from all that has just been said that such a means-ends relationship is possible only to the extent that values are agreed upon, are reconcilable, and are stable at the margin. Typically, therefore, such a means-ends relationship is absent from the branch method, where means and ends are simultaneously chosen.

Yet any departure from the means-ends relationship of the root method will strike some readers as inconceivable. For it will appear to them that only in such a relationship is it possible to determine whether one policy choice is better or worse than another. How can an administrator know whether he has made a wise or foolish decision if he is without prior values or objectives by which to judge his decisions? The answer to this question calls up the third distinctive difference between root and branch methods: how to decide the best policy.

The Test of "Good" Policy (3b)

In the root method, a decision is "correct," "good," or "rational" if it can be shown to attain some specified objective, where the objective can be specified without simply describing the decision itself. Where objectives are defined only through the marginal or incremental approach to values described above, it is still sometimes possible to test whether a policy does in fact attain the desired objectives; but a precise statement of the objectives takes the form of a description of the policy chosen or some alternative to it. To show that a policy is mistaken one cannot offer an abstract argument that important objectives are not achieved; one must instead argue that another policy is more to be preferred.

So far, the departure from customary ways of looking at problem-solving is not troublesome, for many administrators will be quick to agree that the most effective discussion of the correctness of policy does take the form of comparison with other policies that might have been chosen. But what of the situation in which administrators cannot agree on values or objectives, either abstractly or in marginal terms? What then is the test of "good" policy? For the root method, there is no test. Agreement on objectives failing, there is no standard of "correctness." For the method of successive limited comparisons, the test is agreement on policy itself, which remains possible even when agreement on values is not.

It has been suggested that continuing agreement in Congress on the desirability of extending old age insurance stems from liberal desires to strengthen the welfare programs of the federal government and from conservative desires to reduce union demands for private pension plans. If so, this is an excellent demonstration of the ease with which individuals of different ideologies often can agree on concrete policy. Labor mediators report a similar phenomenon: the contestants cannot agree on criteria for settling their disputes but can agree on specific proposals. Similarly, when one administrator's objective turns out to be another's means, they often can agree on policy.

Agreement on policy thus becomes the only practicable test of the policy's correctness. And for one administrator to seek to win the other over to agreement on ends as well would accomplish nothing and create quite unnecessary controversy.

If agreement directly on policy as a test for "best" policy seems a poor substitute for testing the policy against its objectives, it ought to be remembered that objectives themselves have no ultimate validity other than they are agreed upon. Hence agreement is the test of "best" policy in both methods. But where the root method requires agreement on what elements in the decision constitute objectives and on which of these objectives should be sought, the branch method falls back on agreement wherever it can be found.

In an important sense, therefore, it is not irrational for an administrator to defend a policy as good without being able to specify what it is good for.

Non-Comprehensive Analysis (4b)

Ideally, rational-comprehensive analysis leaves out nothing important. But it is impossible to take everything important into consideration unless "important" is so narrowly defined that analysis is in fact quite limited. Limits on human intellectual capacities and on available information set definite limits to man's capacity to be comprehensive. In actual fact, therefore, no one can practice the rational-comprehensive method for really complex problems, and every administrator faced with a sufficiently complex problem must find ways drastically to simplify.

An administrator assisting in the formulation of agricultural economic policy cannot in the first place be competent on all possible policies. He cannot even comprehend one policy entirely. In planning a soil bank program, he cannot successfully anticipate the impact of higher or lower farm income on, say, urbanization—the possible consequent loosening of family ties, possible consequent eventual need for revisions in social security and further implications for tax problems arising out of new federal responsibilities for social security and municipal responsibilities for urban services. Nor, to follow another line of repercussions, can he work through the soil bank program's effects on prices for agricultural products in foreign markets and consequent implications for foreign relations, including those arising out of economic rivalry between the United States and the U.S.S.R.

In the method of successive limited comparisons, simplification is systematically achieved in two principal ways. First, it is achieved through limitation of policy comparisons to those policies that differ in relatively small degree from policies presently in effect. Such a limitation immediately reduces the number of alternatives to be investigated and also drastically simplifies the character of the investigation of each. For it is not necessary to undertake fundamental inquiry into an alternative and its consequences; it is necessary only to study those respects in which the proposed alternative and its consequences differ from the status quo. The empirical comparison of marginal differences among alternative policies that differ only marginally is, of course, a counterpart to the incremental or marginal comparison of values discussed above.[6]

Relevance as Well as Realism

It is a matter of common observation that in Western democracies public administrators and policy analysts in general do largely limit their analyses to incremental or marginal differences in policies that are chosen to differ only incrementally. They do not do so, however, solely because they desperately need some way to simplify their problems; they also do so in order to be relevant. Democracies change their policies almost entirely through incremental adjustments. Policy does not move in leaps and bounds.

The incremental character of political change in the United States has often been remarked. The two major political parties agree on fundamentals; they offer alternative policies to the voters only on relatively small points of difference. Both parties favor full employment, but they define it somewhat differently; both favor the development of water power resources, but in slightly different ways; and both favor unemployment compensation, but not the same level of benefits. Similarly, shifts of policy within a party take place largely through a series of relatively small changes, as can be seen in their only gradual acceptance of the idea of governmental responsibility for support of the unemployed, a change in party positions beginning in the early 30's and culminating in a sense in the Employment Act of 1946.

Party behavior is in turn rooted in public attitudes, and political theorists cannot conceive of democracy's surviving in the United States in the absence of fundamental agreement on potentially disruptive issues, with consequent limitation of policy debates to relatively small differences in policy.

Since the policies ignored by the administrator are politically impossible and so irrelevant, the simplification of analysis achieved by concentrating on policies that differ only incrementally is not a capricious kind of simplification. In addition, it can be argued that, given the limits on knowledge within which policy-makers are confined, simplifying by limiting the focus to small variations from present policy makes the most of available knowledge. Because policies being considered are like present and past policies, the administrator can obtain information and claim some insight. Nonincremental policy proposals are therefore typically not only politically irrelevant but also unpredictable in their consequences.

The second method of simplification of analysis is the practice of ignoring important possible consequences of possible policies, as well as the values attached to the neglected consequences. If this appears to disclose a shocking shortcoming of successive limited comparisons, it can be replied that, even if the exclusions are random, policies may nevertheless be more intelligently formulated than through futile attempts to achieve a comprehensiveness beyond human capacity. Actually, however, the exclusions, seeming arbitrary or random from one point of view, need be neither.

Achieving a Degree of Comprehensiveness

Suppose that each value neglected by one policy-making agency were a major concern of at least one other agency. In that case, a helpful division of labor would be achieved, and no agency need find its task beyond its capacities. The shortcomings of such a system would be that one agency might destroy a value either before another agency could be activated to safeguard it or in spite of another agency's efforts. But the possibility that important values may be lost is present in any form of organization, even where agencies attempt to comprehend in planning more than is humanly possible.

The virtue of such a hypothetical division of labor is that every important interest or value has its watchdog. And these watchdogs can protect the interests in their jurisdiction in two quite different ways: first, by redressing damages done by other agencies; and, second, by anticipating and heading off injury before it occurs.

In a society like that of the United States in which individuals are free to combine to pursue almost any possible common interest they might have and in which government agencies are sensitive to the pressures of these groups, the system described is approximated. Almost every interest has its watchdog. Without claiming that every interest has a sufficiently powerful watchdog, it can be argued that our system often can assure a more comprehensive regard for the values of the whole society than any attempt at intellectual comprehensiveness.

In the United States, for example, no part of government attempts a comprehensive overview of policy on income distribution. A policy nevertheless evolves, and one responding to a wide variety of interests. A process of mutual adjustment among farm groups, labor unions, municipalities and school boards, tax authorities, and government agencies with responsibilities in the fields of housing, health, highways, national parks, fire, and police accomplishes a distribution of income in which particular income problems neglected at one point in the decision processes become central at another point.

Mutual adjustment is more pervasive than the explicit forms it takes in negotiation between groups; it persists through the mutual impacts of groups upon each other even where they are not in communication. For all the imperfections and latent dangers in this ubiquitous process of mutual adjustment, it will often accomplish an adaptation of policies to a wider range of interests than could be done by one group centrally.

Note, too, how the incremental pattern of policy-making fits with the multiple pressure pattern. For when decisions are only incremental—closely related to known policies, it is easier for one group to anticipate the kind of moves another might make and easier too for it to make correction for injury already accomplished.[7]

Even partisanship and narrowness, to use pejorative terms, will sometimes be assets to rational decision-making, for they can doubly insure that what one agency neglects, another will not; they specialize personnel to distinct points of view. The claim is valid that effective rational coordination of the federal administration, if possible to achieve at all, would require an agreed set of values[8]—if "rational" is defined as the practice of the root method of decision-making. But a high degree of administrative coordination occurs as each agency adjusts its policies to the concerns of the other agencies in the process of fragmented decision-making I have just described.

For all the apparent shortcomings of the incremental approach to policy alternatives with its arbitrary exclusion coupled with fragmentation, when compared to the root method, the branch method often looks far superior. In the root method, the inevitable exclusion of factors is accidental, unsystematic, and not defensible by any argument so far developed, while in the branch method the exclusions are deliberate, systematic, and defensible. Ideally, of course, the root method does not exclude; in practice it must.

Nor does the branch method necessarily neglect long-run considerations and objectives. It is clear that important values must be omitted in considering policy, and sometimes the only way long-run objectives can be given adequate attention is through the neglect of short-run consideration. But the values omitted can be either long-run or short-run.

Succession of Comparisons (5b)

The final distinctive element in the branch method is that the comparisons, together with the policy choice, proceed in a chronological series. Policy is not made once and for all; it is made and remade endlessly. Policy-making is a process of successive approximation to some desired objectives in which what is desired itself continues to change under reconsideration.

Making policy is at best a very rough process.

Neither social scientists, nor politicians, nor public administrators yet know enough about the social world to avoid repeated error in predicting the consequences of policy moves. A wise policy-maker consequently expects that his policies will achieve only part of what he hopes and at the same time will produce unanticipated consequences he would have preferred to avoid. If he proceeds through a *succession* of incremental changes, he avoids serious lasting mistakes in several ways.

In the first place, past sequences of policy steps have given him knowledge about the probable consequences of further similar steps. Second, he need not attempt big jumps toward his goals that would require predictions beyond his or anyone else's knowledge, because he never expects his policy to be a final resolution of a problem. His decision is only one step, one that if successful can quickly be followed by another. Third, he is in effect able to test his previous predictions as he moves on to each further step. Lastly, he often can remedy a past error fairly quickly—more quickly than if policy proceeded through more distinct steps widely spaced in time.

Compare this comparative analysis of incremental changes with the aspiration to employ theory in the root method. Man cannot think without classifying, without subsuming one experience under a more general category of experiences. The attempt to push categorization as far as possible and to find general propositions which can be applied to specific situations is what I refer to with the word "theory." Where root analysis often leans heavily on theory in this sense, the branch method does not.

The assumption of root analysis is that theory is the most systematic and economical way to bring relevant knowledge to bear on a specific problem. Granting the assumption, an unhappy fact is that we do not have adequate theory to apply to problems in any policy area, although theory is more adequate in some areas—monetary policy, for example—than in others. Comparative analysis, as in the branch method, is sometimes a systematic alternative to theory.

Suppose an administrator must choose among a small group of policies that differ only incrementally from each other and from present policy. He might aspire to "understand" each of the alternatives—for example, to know all the consequences of each aspect of each policy. If so, he would indeed require theory. In fact, however, he would usually decide that, *for policy-making purposes,* he need know, as explained above, only the consequences of each of those aspects of the policies in which they differed from one another. For this much more modest aspiration, he requires no theory (although it might be helpful, if available), for he can proceed to isolate probable differences by examining the differences in consequences associated with past differences in policies, a feasible program because he can take his observations from a long sequence of incremental changes.

For example, without a more comprehensive social theory about juvenile delinquency than scholars have yet produced, one cannot possibly understand the ways in which a variety of public policies—say on education, housing, recreation, employment, race relations, and policing—might encourage or discourage delinquency. And one needs such an understanding if he undertakes the comprehensive overview of the problem prescribed in the models of the root method. If, however, one merely wants to mobilize knowledge sufficient to assist in a choice among a small group of similar policies—alternative policies on juvenile court procedures, for example—he can do so by comparative analysis of the results of similar past policy moves.

Theorists and Practitioners

This difference explains—in some cases at least—why the administrator often feels that the outside expert or academic problem-solver is sometimes not helpful and why they in turn often urge more theory on him. And it explains why an administrator often feels more confident when "flying by the seat of his pants" than when following the advice of theorists. Theorists often ask the administrator to go the long way round to the solution of his problems, in effect ask him to follow the best canons of the scientific method, when the administrator knows the best available theory will work less well than more modest incremental comparisons. Theorists do not realize that the administrator is often in fact practicing a systematic method. It would be foolish to push this explanation too far, for sometimes practical decision-makers are pursuing neither a theoretical approach nor successive comparisons, nor any other systematic method.

It may be worth emphasizing that theory is sometimes of extremely limited helpfulness in policy-making for at least two rather different reasons. It is greedy for facts; it can be constructed only through a great collection of observations. And it is typically insufficiently precise for application to a policy process that moves through small changes. In contrast, the comparative method both economizes on the need for facts and directs the analyst's attention to just those facts that are relevant to the fine choices faced by the decision-maker.

With respect to precision of theory, economic theory serves as an example. It predicts that an economy without money or prices would in certain specified ways misallocate resources, but this finding pertains to an alternative far removed from the kind of policies on which administrators need help. On the other hand, it is not precise enough to predict the consequences of policies restricting business mergers, and this is the kind of issue on which the administrators need help. Only in relatively restricted areas does economic theory achieve sufficient precision to go far in resolving policy questions; its helpfulness in policy-making is always so limited that it requires supplementation through comparative analysis.

Successive Comparison as a System

Successive limited comparison is, then, indeed a method or system; it is not a failure of method for which administrators ought to apologize. None the less, its imperfections, which have not been explored in this paper, are many. For example, the method is without a built-in safeguard for all relevant values, and it also may lead the decision-maker to overlook excellent policies for no other reason than that they are not suggested by the chain of successive policy steps leading up to the present. Hence, it ought to be said that under this method, as well as under some of the most sophisticated variants of the root method—operations research, for example—policies will continue to be as foolish as they are wise.

Why then bother to describe the method in all the above detail? Because it is in fact a common method of policy formulation, and is, for complex problems, the principal reliance of administrators as well as of other policy analysts.[9] And because it will be superior to any other decision-making method available for complex problems in many circumstances, certainly superior to a futile attempt at super-human comprehensiveness. The reaction of the public administrator to the exposition of method doubtless will be less a discovery of a new method than a better acquaintance with an old. But by becoming more conscious of their practice of this method, administrators might practice it with more skill and know when to extend or constrict its use. (That they sometimes practice it effectively and sometimes not may explain the extremes of opinion on "muddling through," which is both praised as a highly sophisticated form of problem-solving and denounced as no method at all. For I suspect that in so far as there is a system in what is known as "muddling through," this method is it.)

One of the noteworthy incidental consequences of clarification of the method is the light it throws on the suspicion an administrator sometimes entertains that a consultant or adviser is not speaking relevantly and responsibly when in fact by all ordinary objective evidence he is. The trouble lies in the fact that most of us approach policy problems within a framework given by our view of a chain of successive policy choices made up to the present. One's thinking about appropriate policies with respect, say, to urban traffic control is greatly influenced by one's knowledge of the incremental steps taken up to the present. An administrator enjoys an intimate knowledge of his past sequences

that "outsiders" do not share, and his thinking and that of the "outsider" will consequently be different in ways that may puzzle both. Both may appear to be talking intelligently, yet each may find the other unsatisfactory. The relevance of the policy chain of succession is even more clear when an American tries to discuss, say, antitrust policy with a Swiss, for the chains of policy in the two countries are strikingly different and the two individuals consequently have organized their knowledge in quite different ways.

If this phenomenon is a barrier to communication, an understanding of it promises an enrichment of intellectual interaction in policy formulation. Once the source of difference is understood, it will sometimes be stimulating for an administrator to seek out a policy analyst whose recent experience is with a policy chain different from his own.

This raises again a question only briefly discussed above on the merits of like-mindedness among government administrators. While much of organization theory argues the virtues of common values and agreed organizational objectives, for complex problems in which the root method is inapplicable, agencies will want among their own personnel two types of diversification: administrators whose thinking is organized by reference to policy chains other than those familiar to most members of the organization and, even more commonly, administrators whose professional or personal values or interests create diversity of view (perhaps coming from different specialties, social classes, geographical areas) so that, even within a single agency, decision-making can be fragmented and parts of the agency can serve as watchdogs for other parts.

Notes

1. James G. March and Herbert A. Simon similarly characterized the literature. They also take some important steps, as have Simon's recent articles, to describe a less heroic model of policy-making. See *Organizations* (John Wiley and Sons, 1958), p. 137.
2. "Operations Research and National Planning—A Dissent," 5 *Operations Research*

718 (October, 1957). Hitch's dissent is from particular points made in the article to which his paper is a reply; his claim that operations research is for low-level problems is widely accepted.

For examples of the kind of problems to which operations research is applied, see C. W. Churchman, R. L. Ackoff and E. L. Arnoff, *Introduction to Operations Research* (John Wiley and Sons, 1957); and J. F. McCloskey and J. M. Coppinger (eds.), *Operations Research for Management,* Vol. II, (The Johns Hopkins Press, 1956).

3. I am assuming that administrators often make policy and advise in the making of policy and am treating decision-making and policy-making as synonymous for purposes of this paper.

4. Martin Meyerson and Edward C. Banfield, *Politics, Planning and the Public Interest* (The Free Press, 1955).

5. The line of argument is, of course, an extension of the theory of market choice, especially the theory of consumer choice, to public policy choices.

6. A more precise definition of incremental policies and a discussion of whether a change that appears "small" to one observer might be seen differently by another is to be found in my "Policy Analysis," 48 *American Economic Review* 298 (June, 1958).

7. The link between the practice of the method of successive limited comparisons and mutual adjustment of interests in a highly frag-mented decision-making process adds a new facet to pluralist theories of government and administration.

8. Herbert Simon, Donald W. Smithburg, and Victor A. Thompson, *Public Administration* (Alfred A. Knopf, 1950), p. 434.

9. Elsewhere I have explored this same method of policy formulation as practiced by academic analysts of policy ("Policy Analysis," 48 *American Economic Review* 298 [June, 1958]). Although it has been here presented as a method for public administrators, it is no less necessary to analysts more removed from immediate policy questions, despite their tendencies to describe their own analytical efforts as though they were the rational-comprehensive method with an especially heavy use of theory. Similarly, this same method is inevitably resorted to in personal problem-solving, where means and ends are sometimes impossible to separate, where aspirations or objectives undergo constant development, and where drastic simplification of the complexity of the real world is urgent if problems are to be solved in the time that can be given to them. To an economist accustomed to dealing with the marginal or incremental concept in market processes, the central idea in the method is that both evaluation and empirical analysis are incremental. Accordingly I have referred to the method elsewhere as "the incremental method."

☐ CASE STUDY 8

Introduction

One of the most explosive urban events of recent decades occurred in Philadelphia on May 13, 1985, when the Philadelphia police confronted the black activist cult MOVE. As the introduction to the following case, "The MOVE Disaster," recounts:

After massive gunfire, deluges of water and explosive charges failed to dislodge the group from their fortified row house, police dropped plastic explosives from a helicopter onto a rooftop bunker. The bomb ignited an unexpected fire. Believing they could contain the fire, Police Commissioner Gregore Sambor and Fire Commissioner William Richmond decided to let the bunker burn. They miscalculated badly, and the fire raged out of control. Sweeping through three adjoining blocks, the inferno destroyed 61 homes and left 250 people homeless. Of the occupants of the MOVE house, one adult and one child fled through the flames into police custody. In the ashes were found the bodies of six adults and five children.

What caused this tragedy? Several investigative organizations and other observers attributed much of the blame to ineffective management by the city's mayor, W. Wilson Goode. Ironically, Goode previously had been viewed as a highly successful mayor, not only by those within the city but throughout the nation. This single event severely damaged his reputation as "an effective manager, a rising star in national politics, and a symbol of hope for his city," according to the author, Jack H. Nagel, a professor of political science and public policy and management at the University of Pennsylvania.

In the following case, Nagel focuses on how Goode made his choices related to the MOVE decision and explores the causes of why a previously well-regarded public manager should exhibit such an uncharacteristic breakdown in his performance, bordering on what some viewed as irresponsible behavior. The author first explains the background of MOVE as a controversial activist group within Philadelphia and the two central paradoxes of Mayor Goode's behavior in response to MOVE's actions. Though what makes Nagel's case study especially remarkable and insightful is how the author then goes on to probe beneath the surface of Goode's managerial actions related to MOVE. Nagel analyzes three particular psychological problems that the mayor exhibited and relates these mental difficulties to current theories of the psychology of decision making. From this case, the author generalizes important lessons and implications for government decision-making that relate directly and profoundly to the previous reading by Charles Lindblom.

As you review the following case, try to reflect on:

How did Mayor Goode first decide to respond to MOVE's activities? What misconceptions did Goode implicitly hold about MOVE? What were the sources of these misconceptions, in your view?

Do you agree with the author that these misconceptions were ultimately rooted in the mayor's "unresolved decisional conflicts that impeded responsible and rational handling of the problem"? What were these "three decisional conflicts" according to the author? How does Nagel support his argument by drawing on the theory of decision making developed by Irving Janis and Leon Mann? What are the assumptions of the Janis/Mann thesis?

As opposed to the Lindblom incremental model, does Nagel's story suggest an entirely different understanding of decision making—one rooted in personal values? And what are the implications for public managers and how they can or should improve their own decision-making capacities?

The MOVE Disaster

JACK H. NAGEL

On May 13, 1985, a confrontation between Philadelphia police and a cult called MOVE resulted in one of the most astounding debacles in the history of American municipal government. After massive gunfire, deluges of water, and explosive charges failed to dislodge the group from their fortified row house, police dropped plastic explosives from a helicopter onto a rooftop bunker. The bomb ignited an unexpected fire. Believing they could contain the fire, Police Commissioner Gregore Sambor and Fire Commissioner William Richmond decided to let the bunker burn. They miscalculated badly, and the fire raged out of control. Sweeping through three adjoining blocks, the inferno destroyed 61 homes and left 250 people homeless. Of the occupants of the MOVE house, one adult and one child fled through the flames into police custody. In the ashes were found the bodies of six adults and five children.

The MOVE tragedy severely damaged the reputation of Philadelphia Mayor W. Wilson Goode, who until then had been considered an effective manager, a rising star of national politics, and a symbol of hope for his city. In the aftermath of the disaster, a controversial grand jury decided not to bring criminal charges against the mayor and his chief aides, but condemned them for "morally reprehensible behavior" [Philadelphia Court of Common Pleas, 1988, p. 279]. The Philadelphia Special Investigation Commission (PSIC), appointed by the mayor himself, charged that "the Mayor abdicated his responsibilities as a leader," a condemnation shared by most informed observers.[1] With respect to the twelve values Charles Gilbert [1959] identifies with administrative responsibility, Goode and his key subordinates conspicuously failed to satisfy at least seven—responsiveness, consistency, stability, leadership, competence, efficacy, and prudence.

"The MOVE Disaster," (Originally titled "Psychological Obstacles to Administrative Responsibility: Lessons of the MOVE Disaster"), by Jack H. Nagel, *Journal of Policy Analysis and Management*, Vol. 10, No. 1, pp. 1–23. Copyright © 1991 by John Wiley & Sons, Inc. Reprinted by permission of John Wiley & Sons, Inc.

None of the many commentators ever satisfactorily explained why the previously impressive mayor was so irresponsible in this instance and in particular why his behavior contrasted so sharply with his reputation for hands-on management. Many observers subsequently avoided the incongruity by concluding that Goode had simply been "incompetent" all along. Whereas before MOVE he could do no wrong, after the disaster he seldom got credit for doing anything right. This paper will argue instead that, lamentable though it was, the mayor's performance exemplifies universal tendencies well understood by psychologists of decisionmaking. Analysis of the MOVE case therefore can suggest insights that may enable other administrators to recognize and control situations in which they too might otherwise succumb to irresponsible patterns of action and inaction.

The presentation that follows is organized into five sections: (a) a brief history of MOVE and its conflict with the City of Philadelphia; (b) a description of two central paradoxes in Mayor Goode's response to MOVE; (c) an explanation of both paradoxes using a standard theory about the psychology of decisionmaking; (d) a closer examination of three decisional conflicts that may explain why Goode had such difficulty dealing with this particular problem; and (e) reflections on lessons the MOVE disaster offers for the education of present and future public managers.

MOVE Versus Philadelphia

The origins of MOVE can be traced to the early 1970s in the Powelton Village section of West Philadelphia, near the campuses of Drexel University and the University of Pennsylvania.[2] In this tolerant community, a haven for political and cultural rebels, a charismatic black handyman named Vincent Leaphart developed an anarchistic, back-to-nature philosophy, the main tenets of which were reverence for all animal life, rejection of "the [American] Lifestyle," and absolute refusal to cooperate with "the System." Aided by a white graduate in social work from Penn named Donald Glassey, who transcribed Leaphart's thoughts and taught them in a course at the Community College of Philadelphia, Leaphart attracted a "family" that eventually numbered at least forty members, most but not all of whom were black. At first they called themselves the American Christian Movement for Life, but they later shortened the name to MOVE. Following the example of Leaphart, who now referred to himself as John Africa, all the core members adopted the surname Africa, in honor of the continent where they believed life began.

As they put John Africa's philosophy into practice, MOVE generated frequent tension with landlords and neighbors, who complained about members' grossly unsanitary practices and their harboring of dogs, cats, rats, roaches, and flies. Beyond these spillovers of their peculiar lifestyle, MOVE members courted friction with authorities by confronting "the System" in all its manifestations, from the Philadelphia Zoo to Jimmy Carter. Using bullhorns to demonstrate and disrupt meetings, they perfected a vituperative rhetoric, profane and filled with sexual and racial provocation. When brought to trial, as they were literally hundreds of times, MOVE members acted as their own attorneys and clogged the courts by noncooperative, contemptuous tactics.

During the 1970s, a virtual feud developed between MOVE and the Philadelphia police. The mayor of Philadelphia was then Frank Rizzo, a former police commissioner famous for tough law enforcement. The majority of whites revered Mayor Rizzo's large and aggressive police department as a bulwark against crime and disorder, but political dissidents, blacks, and journalists accused the police of frequent brutality and disregard for civil liberties. As Anderson and Hevenor [1987, p. 11] observe, "MOVE demonstrators were frequently arrested, often harassed, and nearly always regarded with unconcealed disgust and contempt by Philadelphia policemen. With their unwashed, garlic-reeking bodies, dreadlocks, and inpenetrable and obscene harangues, MOVE people were a constant affront to a police force that was (and is) largely white, ethnic . . . and Catholic."[3]

After a melee in March 1976, when MOVE accused the police of causing the death of a MOVE infant, John Africa apparently decided to turn to armed resistance. By this time, core members of MOVE oc-

cupied a house owned by Glassey on North 33rd Street. Using loudspeakers fixed in trees, they frequently harangued their neighbors. Responding to complaints, city officials attempted to investigate code violations but were refused admittance. In September 1975, the city began the protracted process of enforcing the code through the courts. A judgment mandating inspections was obtained in July 1976, whereupon MOVE constructed an eight-foot stockage around their compound. Heeding MOVE warnings that they would "cycle" (kill) their own children before submitting to inspections, the city refrained from enforcing the order. On May 20, 1977, mistakenly anticipating a city attempt to enter the premises, MOVE members brandished guns on the platform of their stockade. Shortly afterwards, Donald Glassey was arrested for filing false information when purchasing firearms. Turning informant to save himself, Glassey helped police seize MOVE guns and explosives at a location elsewhere in Philadelphia.

The stalemate in Powelton continued for nearly a year. On March 1, 1978, the city obtained court permission to blockade the MOVE headquarters for nonpayment of utility bills and refusal to admit inspectors. Police cordoned off a four-block area around the house and shut off gas and water. The siege appeared to have succeeded when intermediaries helped negotiate a settlement that was announced on May 3. MOVE surrendered weapons, allowed officials to inspect the Powelton property, and promised to vacate the house by August 1. In return, the city relaxed its blockade, freed eighteen jailed MOVE members on their own recognizance, and promised to drop all charges once MOVE departed from Powelton.

When August 1 came, MOVE refused to leave, because no one had found a site for relocation they would accept. On August 8, Police Commissioner Joseph O'Neill directed a carefully planned operation to drive the occupants from the house. Announcing each action in advance in order to protect MOVE women and children, whom they regarded as hostages, the police used a bulldozer, ram, and armored truck to breach the walls of the compound. A crane began demolishing the upper stories. Believing that all MOVE weapons had been confiscated in May, authorities were careless about concealing themselves. Suddenly, police saw a gun muzzle protruding from a basement window. After deluge guns flooded the basement, gunfire erupted, killing Officer James Ramp and wounding eight other policemen and firefighters. Following the exchange of shots, police poured in more water and smoke to flush out the occupants. As the MOVE members surrendered, officers beat and kicked Delbert Africa while news photographers recorded the action.

During the next five years, MOVE was visible to most Philadelphians only through a series of trials. In 1980, nine members were sentenced to lengthy prison terms for the murder of Officer Ramp; a tenth followed in 1982. In 1981, three police officers were tried for the beating of Delbert Africa and acquitted.[4] On May 13, 1981, Federal agents arrested John Africa and eight followers in Rochester, New York, where MOVE had owned houses since 1977. (At various times, MOVE also had enclaves in Richmond, Virginia, and Chester, Pennsylvania.) Defending himself and Alphonso Robbins Africa against bombmaking charges, John Africa won acquittal from a jury in Philadelphia in July 1981, after which he dropped out of sight.

As it turned out, the MOVE leader had not gone far. With a group of about a dozen adults and children, he was living in a house owned by his sister, Louise James, at 6221 Osage Avenue in the Cobbs Creek section on the western edge of Philadelphia, three miles from the site of the demolished house in Powelton.

Whereas the 33rd Street house had been a freestanding structure surrounded by a yard and located on a busy street, the new MOVE headquarters was a row house on a narrow, quiet residential street. These physical differences were to prove tactically important during the 1985 confrontation, but events in the two years preceding that catastrophe pivoted around social and political differences between the two neighborhoods. Nonconformist, racially mixed Powelton was a bastion of opposition to Mayor Rizzo. Its residents divided bitterly over whether the cultists or the police were the more distasteful presence in their midst. One can easily imagine Frank Rizzo enjoying some amusement at their discomfort.

In 1980, barred by the City Charter from serving three consecutive terms, Rizzo was succeeded as mayor by the more liberal former Congressman, William J. Green, Jr. Fulfilling a campaign promise to Philadelphia's increasingly powerful black voters, Green appointed W. Wilson Goode as Managing Director, the city's chief appointive official. Goode, a former civil-rights activist, had previously served as executive director of the nonprofit Philadelphia Council for Community Advancement—where he was credited with building more housing than all the city's housing agencies combined [Cohn, 1982, p. 27]—and as chair of the Pennsylvania Public Utilities Commission. As Managing Director, Goode was in charge of ten operating departments, including police and fire. Hard-working, accessible, and highly visible, he soon became hugely popular among blacks and many whites as well. When Green announced in late 1982 that he would not seek a second term, Goode resigned to campaign for the mayoralty. In May 1983, he defeated Frank Rizzo in the Democratic primary, winning the votes of 98% of blacks and 23% of whites. In the November general election, he would face two white opponents.

The Cobbs Creek neighborhood was typical of Wilson Goode's bedrock political base. Its residents, almost all black, were generally stable working- and middle-class families. Most owned their homes and took pride in keeping them pleasant and attractive. By the fall of 1983, MOVE had become an intolerable affliction to this peaceful community. The home of Lloyd and Lucretia Wilson next door was invaded by insects that had spread from 6221. When the Wilsons sought to fumigate, Conrad Africa went berserk. "The bugs are our brothers and sisters. If you exterminate the bugs, you exterminate us," he berated Lloyd Wilson [PSIC, 1985, 10/9 AM, pp. 89–90]. In September 1983, following a dispute over a parking space, a MOVE male struck a neighbor named Butch Marshall to the ground, and three MOVE women bit Marshall on the face, back, and groin. After another assault in October, the neighbors circulated to city authorities a petition that complained about attacks, garbage, rats, a pigeon coop, animals, and MOVE's blocking of a common driveway behind the row.

As the neighbors "were reaching the breaking point," they met with State Representative Peter Truman.[5] Truman implored them not to do anything that would endanger the election of the city's first black mayor. If they would endure a few months longer, he assured them, Goode would solve their problem. Aided by the arrival of cold weather, which lessened health hazards and reduced outdoor interaction with MOVE, the neighbors waited. In November 1983, Goode won a resounding victory with 55% of the vote.

If Goode's triumph held promise of deliverance for the 6200 block, John Africa saw it as a different sort of opportunity, one that would produce intensified torment for the Osage neighbors. Obsessed with freeing his followers from prison, the MOVE leader believed that the mayor had the power to obtain their release and that the residents of Osage Avenue could persuade him to use that power. MOVE therefore embarked upon a campaign of what Goode later would call "psychological warfare" against their neighbors, holding the block "hostage" in order to obtain as ransom the release of their ten convicted comrades. MOVE launched their campaign on Christmas morning, 1983. Beginning near dawn and continuing for eight hours, their rooftop loudspeakers blared an obscene diatribe that denounced the neighbors, the mayor-elect, and the System, and demanded freedom for MOVE prisoners. Eight days later, Wilson Goode became mayor of Philadelphia.

Two Paradoxes

Mayor Goode's response to MOVE's challenge can be characterized by describing two patterns, both of which seem paradoxical. First, for sixteen months he avoided any significant action; but when he finally decided to enforce the law, the city mobilized against MOVE in less than a week and tried to execute a hastily prepared plan in the span of twenty-four hours. Second, although he was widely perceived to be an energetic, detail-oriented administrator, when he decided the city should act against MOVE, Goode had minimal personal involvement in both the planning and the execution of the attack.

Delay Followed by Haste

MOVE's war against the System, by way of their neighbors, continued through 1984 and the spring of 1985. In December 1983, they began fortifying their house by nailing boards across the windows; the ramshackle effect contrasted starkly with the neat white trim and porches of the other houses. In October 1984 they started a rooftop construction that eventually became a bunker made of railroad ties, logs, and steel plates. Similar materials were placed against the interior walls of the house and basement.

In May 1984, a hooded MOVE member brandished a shotgun on the roof, and the cultists began the practice of running across the roofs of the row at night, waking frightened residents. Loudspeaker harangues were conducted daily for six to eight hours through the summer and fall of 1984. In these and other communications, MOVE members threatened the lives of President Reagan, Mayor Goode, judges, and any police officers who might try to enforce the law on Osage Avenue. A favorite tactic was to target a particular neighbor for a day, during which the unfortunate individual would be subjected to personal attacks filled with accusations of homosexuality, child molestation, promiscuity, or sexual inadequacy. As Bennie Swans of the Crisis Intervention Network later commented, "MOVE did not let up on those residents. They simply did not let up" [PSIC, 1985, 10/9 AM, p. 68].

Mayor Goode was aware of most of these developments. On March 9, 1984, Commissioner Sambor briefed him about the deteriorating situation on Osage Avenue. On May 28 and July 4, he met at their request with delegations of residents; they found the mayor knowledgeable about their plight and personally familiar with MOVE members, but unwilling to act. In June 1984, District Attorney Edward Rendell provided Goode with a memo outlining a legal strategy for disarming MOVE and abating the nuisance on Osage Avenue. Goode also received several phone calls from block captain Clifford Bond. On August 9, Lloyd Wilson came to City Hall to complain of an assault he had suffered the day before at the hands of Frank James Africa, while police officers watched from the corner. Goode "whisked" Wilson off to a side office, where he had a lengthy but unproductive conversation with Managing Director Leo Brooks and Commissioner Sambor. Subsequently, Wilson and his family abandoned their home, driven out by vermin, noise, and fear from which their government would not protect them.

During this time, city policy barred operating departments (including Health, Water, Human Services, Streets, and Licenses and Inspections) from carrying out their responsibilities with respect to MOVE, which they were told was "a police matter." For their part, the police maintained surveillance of the 6200 block, but refrained from intervention. They even discouraged state parole officials from serving outstanding fugitive warrants against two residents of the house, Frank James Africa and Larry

Howard [Philadelphia Court of Common Pleas, 1988, p. 26]. In response to the neighbors' entreaties, Goode took only two tangible actions: He extended the hours of nearby city recreation centers so residents' children could escape the loudspeakers, and he arranged psychological counseling to help the children cope with chronic tension.

Five of the MOVE Commission's findings describe and condemn this protracted phase of inaction:

1. Mayor Goode's policy toward MOVE was one of appeasement, non-confrontation, and avoidance.
2. The Managing Director and the city's department heads failed to take any effective action on their own and, in fact, ordered their subordinates to refrain from taking action to deal meaningfully with the problem on Osage Avenue. . . .
3. In the first several months of his administration, the mayor was presented with compelling evidence that his policy of appeasement, non-confrontation, and avoidance was doomed to fail.
4. In the summer of 1984, the mayor was told that the legal basis existed at that time to act against certain MOVE members. Yet, the mayor held back, and continued to follow his policy of avoidance and non-confrontation.
5. From the fall of 1984 to the spring of 1985, the city's policy of appeasement conceded to the residents of 6221 Osage Ave. the continued right to exist above the law. [PSIC, 1986, pp. 11–13]

To this indictment should be added two more charges. First, by tolerating MOVE's abuses, the city government for two years abdicated its most basic responsibilities to the law-abiding residents of Osage Avenue. As Clifford Bond put it, "I was placed in a position of feeling not as a citizen" [PSIC, 1985, 10/9 AM, p. 4]. Second, by giving MOVE time to fortify their house, the policy of nonconfrontation made the task of dislodging the cult immensely more difficult when the mayor finally decided to act.

Sixteen months of delay abruptly gave way to fourteen days of hasty action in the spring of 1985. The shift in policy was precipitated by the neighbors.

Unwilling to accept another summer of stench and harangues, they organized themselves as the United Residents of the 6200 Block of Osage Avenue and held a public protest meeting on April 25, during which several men announced they would respond to MOVE "in kind." At a May 1 press conference, the United Residents expressed their disgust with the city's inaction and requested intervention by Pennsylvania Governor Dick Thornburgh, a Republican. Coupled with new provocations by MOVE, these actions got the attention of the media, and editorialists demanded that the city meet its responsibilities.

On May 3, Mayor Goode convened a high-level meeting at which he asked District Attorney Edward Rendell to establish a legal basis for city action against the occupants of 6221. On May 5 Rendell's staff interviewed Osage residents in order to prepare warrants. At a second high-level meeting on May 7, Goode directed Commissioner Sambor to develop a plan that was to be carried out under the supervision of Managing Director Leo Brooks, a former Army major general.

Having anticipated action, Sambor had set up a planning group a week earlier. Remarkably low in rank for such a major operation, it consisted of three men who had served under Sambor in his previous post as commander of the Police Academy: Lieutenant Frank Powell, head of the Bomb Disposal Unit; Sergeant Albert Revel, a pistol instructor; and Officer Michael Tursi, the Department's top sharpshooter.

On May 9, with Managing Director Brooks at his daughter's graduation in Virginia, Sambor briefed Goode on the plan the three officers had devised. He recommended that warrants be served on Sunday, May 12, which was Mother's Day. Out of concern for the holiday, Goode authorized Sambor to proceed on May 13. On May 11, a judge issued the warrants, and Sambor again briefed Goode. On the afternoon of May 12, police evacuated the neighborhood. Returning from Virginia that evening, Brooks heard on his car radio that the operation he was to head was underway. He arrived in Philadelphia in time to get a quick briefing from Sambor followed by a few hours' sleep.

At 5:35 a.m. on Monday, May 13, Sambor read an ultimatum to MOVE over a bullhorn, demanding that the four MOVE members named on the warrants surrender within fifteen minutes. MOVE used their own loudspeaker to reject the ultimatum in typical style, telling the police that their wives would be collecting insurance and sleeping with black men that night. When the fifteen minutes had expired, authorities directed water, tear gas, and smoke at the house and its roof. According to the police, MOVE responded with gunfire, and officers retaliated massively, firing many thousands of rounds in the next ninety minutes. The debacle was underway.

As the MOVE Commission and the grand jury pointed out, less hurried planning and execution might have prevented numerous errors and oversights. A full list would occupy many pages, so I shall mention just a few of the more egregious consequences of haste:

- Commissioner Sambor and his planners made little attempt to draw on the resources of other agencies, inside or outside the city government; consequently, they failed to consider alternative strategies and deprived themselves of expertise—such as the use of trained hostage negotiators—that might have resulted in better implementation of their plan.
- Goode, Sambor, and Brooks went ahead with the operation even though they knew that the mayor's directive to pick up the MOVE children before the assault had not been implemented. (MOVE adults usually took the children on daily outings to nearby Cobbs Creek Park, and as late as May 12, two of the children were observed outside the house.) Thus they "clearly risked the lives" of six innocent children, five of whom subsequently died in the conflagration [PSIC, 1986, p. 16].
- The quick, secretive, informal planning process deprived the tacticians of crucial knowledge possessed by others in city government, including surveillance officers. As a result, to take just one example, they did not appreciate the extent of the interior fortifications that foiled their initial strategy of attempting to insert tear gas through the walls.
- Contingency plans were not developed; the final, fatal decision to drop the bomb was the result of ill-considered improvisation. After the primary plan failed, officials were apparently determined to occupy the house before dark. When Brooks informed Goode of the

bomb proposal by telephone at 5 p.m., the mayor paused only thirty seconds before approving the idea.
- Insufficient attention was given to communication systems, resulting in slow, incompatible, or nonexistent communication channels between crucial actors—police and the occupants of the MOVE house, police and fire units, the mayor and managing director, and the managing director and police commissioner. Slow communications may have prevented Goode and Brooks from reversing in time Sambor's and Richmond's decision to let the bunker burn.

Arms-Length Action by a Hands-on Mayor

Until May 1985, both as Managing Director and as Mayor, Wilson Goode was perceived by the public as an incredibly hard-working, demanding, detail-oriented manager. Contemporary press descriptions give a vivid sense of his style: "He appears to be everywhere. . . . He annoys a lot of people because he continues to ask questions until he gets an answer that makes sense."[6] "He loves to come down hard on details" [Mallowe, 1980, p. 139]. "His zeal is prodigious, his double-digit days are legend . . ." [Javers, 1983]. "Today, in Philadelphia, in the first year of Wilson Goode's first term of office, there is absolutely no doubt about *who* is in charge" [Mallowe, 1984, p. 168]. Indeed, one of the few criticisms of Goode in this happy period was that he delegated too little: "He seeks near-absolute control over his operating departments" [Cohn, p. 21]. "He has an aversion to delegating authority. He tries to do too much on his own" [Mallowe, 1984, p. 226].

Goode's view of himself corresponded to the public image: "I want to know what the problems are in this city. . . . I can't do that sitting on the 16th floor here, I really can't" [Cohn, 1982, pp. 13]. *"Someone has to be in charge. People through the government must know that the mayor is there giving directions . . ."* [Mallowe, 1984, p. 168]. "I'm a nuts-and-bolts person" [Mallowe, 1980, p. 139]. Perhaps his favorite term was "hands-on."

However, after he authorized an armed confrontation with MOVE, Goode was anything but hands-on. He held only two high-level meetings to plan the operation. The May 7 meeting focused on the legal basis for action, and the May 9 meeting lasted less than thirty minutes. On both occasions, Goode prevented detailed discussion of the police plan. The contrast in styles was pointed out to the MOVE Commission by District Attorney Rendell:

> And I turned to the [Police] Commissioner and I said, "Are you going to use tear gas and water?" And he said yes and started to explain a little bit, and the Mayor said . . . , "Look, I will leave that up to you all. It's your plan and execute it." In other words, he cut off discussion. . . .
>
> And I thought it was somewhat unusual. . . . I had known Wilson for the three years that he was Managing Director. I worked very closely with him . . . , and then while he was Mayor I had significant contact with him. Wilson's management style has always been one where he got involved in all—not in all of the details, but in certainly the significant details. And I thought that was . . . a little out of character. . . . [PSIC, 1985, 10/22 AM, pp. 71–72]

Rendell speculated that Goode wished to avoid leaks, that perhaps he "intended as soon as I walked out of the room to sit down and go over it blow by blow with the Police Commissioner" [PSIC, 1984, 10/22 AM, p. 95]. In fact, Sambor did brief Goode about the plan on May 11, but only because Brooks was out of town—at all other times, including May 13, Goode and Sambor strictly followed the chain of command, communicating with each other only through Brooks. Goode seems not to have been deeply engaged in the May 11 meeting, for he recalled it as occurring over the telephone, whereas Sambor testified in detail that he went to Goode's office. Goode's last briefing was by telephone on the evening of May 12, when Brooks called him to relay the discussion he had just had with the Police Commissioner.

On May 13 itself, Goode heeded the advice of his staff and Brooks by staying away not only from Osage Avenue, but also from Brooks' command post four blocks north at the Walnut Park Plaza, the tallest structure in the area. As the operation began, Goode followed developments together with four black elected officials whom he had invited to his home in Overbrook, about two miles from Osage Avenue. Later, in his office at City Hall, he was understand-

ably preoccupied with MOVE. Although the mayor frequently conferred by phone with Brooks, Goode's distance from the scene and the clumsiness of his communication links prevented him from exercising effective control over the terrible events of that day.

In short, as the MOVE Commission concluded, "The mayor failed to perform his responsibility as the city's chief executive by not actively participating in the preparation, review and oversight of the plan" [PSIC, 1986, p. 16].

Irresponsibility and Decisional Conflict

In 1977, eight years before the MOVE disaster, the psychologists Irving Janis and Leon Mann published a treatise called *Decision Making*.[7] In it, they outlined a model based on psychological conflict that economically explains the two central paradoxes in Wilson Goode's actions, as well as many otherwise puzzling subsidary aspects of his behavior during this tragic episode.

Janis and Mann premise their theory on the idea that decisionmaking is not merely a cool intellectual process but also involves "hot" emotional influences. The need to make a decision is inherently stressful. Although moderate anxiety improves cognitive functioning, excessive stress can severely impair the quality of decision processes. The greatest stress occurs when all known options threaten to impose severe losses, especially if those losses are not merely "utilitarian" but include "highly ego-involving issues," such as severe social disapproval and/or self-disapproval [Janis and Mann, 1977, p. 46].

When a decision maker is faced with an emotionally consequential, no-win choice, how he or she copes with the problem depends crucially on two factors—hope and time. If the decision maker sees realistic hope of finding a solution superior to any of the risky options that are immediately apparent, then that person's efforts are likely to follow the desirable pattern Janis and Mann call *vigilance*, which is close kin to the familiar rational-comprehensive ideal. The vigilant decision maker canvasses a wide set of alternatives; considers the full range of goals and values involved; carefully weighs costs, risks, and benefits; intensively seeks and accurately assimilates new information; reexamines all alternatives before settling on a final choice; makes detailed provisions for implementing the chosen course; and devotes special attention to contingency plans [Janis and Mann, 1977, p. 11].

If, however, a decision maker loses hope of finding an acceptable option, he or she is likely to fall into either of two patterns of seriously defective search and appraisal. The first and more common syndrome, called *defensive avoidance,* typically occurs when there is no overwhelming pressure to change the existing policy even though its consequences are (like those of all other alternatives) highly unfavorable. The chief symptoms of defensive avoidance are procrastination, passing the buck and other ways of denying personal responsibility, and bolstering [Janis, 1989, p. 80]. "Bolstering" is a process of cognitive distortion in which one "spreads" or exaggerates the value of the chosen course compared to alternatives by avoiding exposure to disturbing information, selective attention and recall, wishful thinking, oversimplification, rationalization, and denial.

Defensive avoidance "satisfies a powerful emotional need—to avoid anticipatory fear, shame, and guilt" [Janis and Mann, 1977, p. 85]. Its emotional benefit is a state of "pseudocalm," resulting from the decision maker's suppression of troubling thoughts and avoidance of stimuli that might evoke the painful dilemma.

When external pressures impose a deadline or threaten an imminent disaster if the existing policy is maintained, the state of pseudocalm is shattered and the underlying conflict breaks through to the surface, arousing unbearable emotional stress. In such circumstances, the decision maker is likely to respond with the pattern of behavior Janis and Mann call *hypervigilance.*[8] Responding to "the strong desire to take action in order to alleviate emotional tension," the hypervigilant decision maker "superficially scans the most obvious alternatives open to him . . . , hastily choosing the first one that seems to hold the promise of escaping the worst danger" [Janis and Mann, 1977, pp. 47, 74]. Like defensive avoidance, hypervigilance involves severely defective search and appraisal:

A person in this state experiences so much cognitive constriction and perseveration that his thought processes are disrupted. The person's immediate memory span is reduced and his thinking becomes more simplistic. . . . [T]he person in a state of hypervigilance fails to recognize all the alternatives open to him and fails to use whatever remaining time is available to evaluate adequately those alternatives of which he is aware. He is likely to search frantically for a solution, persevere in his thinking about a limited number of alternatives, and then latch onto a hastily contrived solution that seems to promise immediate relief, often at the cost of considerable postdecisional regret. [Janis and Mann, 1977, p. 51]

An explanation for the first paradox of Wilson Goode's behavior toward MOVE should now be obvious. His delay/haste pattern is a textbook example of defensive avoidance followed by hypervigilance. The two stages are not really paradoxical, because they resulted from the same underlying decisional conflict. As Janis and Mann [1977, p. 66] observe, a "person's defensive avoidance pattern might abruptly change to hypervigilance if he encounters a new, dramatic danger signal." The mobilization of the Osage neighbors signaled to Goode that a continued policy of nonconfrontation would be fraught with new, unacceptable dangers—a certainty of severe political embarrassment and a high probability of unofficial violence against MOVE. The mayor was forced to act, and in his state of hypervigilance, he accepted the first option presented to him—the ill-fated proposal devised by Sambor's planners.

But why was the MOVE problem in particular so difficult for Wilson Goode to handle, when he had been able to deal effectively with many other issues in a distinguished career of public service? Janis and Mann [1977, p. 75] contend that both vigilant and defective patterns of problem solving are within the repertoire of every decision maker. Anyone, they believe, can fluctuate from one pattern to another depending not only on the objective circumstances of action, but also on the relation of those circumstances to personal values and affiliations, which determine whether actions and outcomes will be conducive to self-esteem and social approval for a particular individual. To explain the second paradox, it will therefore be necessary to look more closely at Wilson Goode, as well as at the finer details of his decision processes with respect to MOVE.

The Mayor's Decisional Conflicts

Goode's testimony to the MOVE Commission, coupled with other evidence about his personality and values, suggests that the drama on Osage Avenue aroused within the mayor severe conflicts that he was never able to resolve. Instead, he in effect fled from them, with the result that he virtually abdicated his responsibility as the city's chief administrator.[9] The mayor's conflicts may be summarized as three dilemmas: (1) MOVE's intransigence and irrationality appeared to necessitate the use of force that would almost surely end in bloodshed, but Goode saw himself as a peacemaker and a preserver of life; (2) to enforce the law against MOVE would require the mayor to depend on the Philadelphia Police Department, but the police might well be unreliable, among other reasons because his own relationship with them was uneasy and because many of them hated MOVE; (3) as a black committed to a policy of respecting civil rights, Goode felt dissonance about authorizing official coercion of a black group; but MOVE's bizarre behavior must also have aroused in him anger that he would have difficulty acknowledging, given his religious values and self-image as a controlled person.

Blood on the Hands of a Peacemaker

At first glance, Goode's desire to avoid action against MOVE appears readily understandable. In retrospect, everyone saw Osage Avenue as a no-win situation. If the city refrained from confronting MOVE, the cultists would make life intolerable for their neighbors. If the city attempted to enforce the laws, MOVE would respond violently, producing a high probability of death. District Attorney Rendell described the effect of this realization on the emotions of participants in the crucial meeting:

I have attended a lot of meetings since I have been in public life, but I never ever had attended a meeting that had the impact on me that my meeting on Thursday, May 7, 1985 did, when in fact the plan of action was signed, sealed and delivered; when the arrest warrants and the search warrants were approved, signed by a judge; when we had picked a time and date to act; when we

knew it was going to occur. There was almost a dread in that room so thick that you could have cut it with a knife. Because, understand, every one of us in that room knew that someone—there was an extraordinarily high likelihood that someone was going to die. [PSIC, 1985, 10/22 AM, p. 34]

Nevertheless, to some politicians the MOVE problem might have seemed a golden opportunity. Throughout history, leaders have won popularity by unleashing violence against unpopular enemies, foreign or domestic. By 1985, MOVE had alienated virtually everyone in Philadelphia. Confronting them would have cost Goode little if any support among his black political base, because the neighbors who were pleading for relief were not only black but also representative of his most reliable constituency. MOVE instead offered Goode an excellent chance to broaden his already impressive popularity, because forceful action against them in the name of law and order would have appealed most to those whites who were not yet part of his coalition.

Goode himself noted the political value of decisive leadership. Asked at the MOVE Commission hearings whether his staff's advice that he stay away from the scene of action was "substantive or political or both," he replied:

I thought it was substantive. I don't think that it . . . had anything to do with politics. From my vantage point, both in foresight and hindsight, . . . it is far better for a Mayor to be perceived as being out there on the scene with hands-on than not to be and, therefore, from a political point of view I think I lose points. . . . [PSIC, 1985 10/15 PM, p. 94]

In fact, despite the debacle, polls in the aftermath of May 13 showed strong public support for Goode's decision to act against MOVE. His approval ratings did not drop precipitously until the fall of 1985, when information revealed by the hearings made him appear inept, irresponsible, and evasive [Wilentz, 1985; Stevens, 1985].

True, as 1978 and the aftermath of 1985 showed, the public would be distressed at death to innocent parties—police, firefighters, or MOVE children. Police officers and firefighters do, however, accept mortal risks as part of their jobs; and, forewarned by MOVE's treachery in 1978, they could more carefully protect themselves from gunshots.[10] As for the children, if Goode had insisted on implementation of his explicit order to pick them up before commencing the operation, they probably could have been saved. Thus the people most likely to die in a properly planned and executed operation were MOVE adults. Most Philadelphians perceived them as dangerous, deranged, and incorrigible; their deaths in resisting legitimate authorities would have been mourned by few and welcomed by many.

Although the conclusion of this cold political logic might not have troubled most citizens, it appears to have been unacceptable for Wilson Goode. Perhaps the most revealing moment of his testimony to the MOVE Commission came when he was asked to describe his emotions as his office television showed the fire raging out of control:

> I went through very deep emotions at that time. I cried because I knew at that point that lives would be lost, and I knew that homes would be destroyed and I knew that despite all of our good intentions, that we had . . . an absolute disaster. And I can't explain to you or to anyone the kind of emotions that I went through, because everything about me is about preserving life and to know that any plan that I've had anything to do with would, in fact, bring about the cessation of life, was very tough. [PSIC, 1985, 10/15 PM, p. 95]

There are independent reasons for believing the sincerity of Goode's statement. Widely regarded as a deeply religious man, he has been a devoted and active member of the First Baptist Church of Paschall since 1955, serving during most of this time as a deacon and lay leader of the congregation. Well into adult life, he seriously considered entering the ministry. On his pastor's advice, he prayed for guidance. "I came away feeling strongly that I *was* called," he said later. "But it was a ministry of a different kind, a ministry of public service." An early profiler wrote, "His whole notion of public service is grounded in his faith, and he approaches his work at City Hall with almost an evangelical fervor" [Cohn, 1982, p. 13].

Indeed, most of Goode's career exhibits a marked inclination toward conciliation and peacemaking. As

a community activist in the 1960s and early 1970s, "his low-key manner usually helped keep potentially explosive situations under control" [Cohn, p. 27]. As a politician, he first unified the previously divided black community, then established an effective alliance with white liberals in the Democratic primary, and finally in the 1983 general election, through a series of conciliatory gestures, won the support of Frank Rizzo. Consequently, he carried 27% of the white vote, and Philadelphia during the first year of his term rode a wave of elation, smugly comparing its newfound racial harmony to the bitter divisions in Chicago and other cities. As mayor, many of Goode's early string of triumphs depended on his ability to build consensus and placate opposition. The few criticisms of Goode during this period centered on claims that he was too willing to appease opponents and too reluctant to lead in the absence of consensus. His own view was more positive: "I've had a charmed life as mayor because I've learned the arts of compromise and negotiation" [Wilentz, 1985, p. 22].

A commitment to peacemaking is also consistent with the full pattern of Goode's dealings with MOVE. The disastrously little time and attention he devoted to planning the use of force contrasts strikingly with his extensive involvement in efforts to understand MOVE and to negotiate a solution [Marimow, 1985]. When Managing Director, he met about fifteen times with John Africa's sisters, Louise James and Laverne Sims, both of whom had been involved with MOVE and were also the mothers of MOVE members. "I always had a comfortable relationship with them, when we have shared together, where they have talked with me and I have listened a lot" [PSIC, 1985, 10/15 AM, p. 29]. The open door continued after he became mayor. On July 31, 1984, when city officials were anticipating a confrontation with MOVE on the August 8 anniversary of the Powelton shootout, the two sisters requested a meeting and were given almost instant access. Goode told the MOVE Commission, "I literally jumped at that meeting because for the first time, I thought I had someone that I could talk to that could, in fact, avoid a conflict out there" [PSIC, 1985, 10/15 AM, p. 25]. (Note how the procrastination of defensive avoidance vanishes when hope appears.) As late as May 9, Goode sandwiched in his fateful meeting with Sambor between discussions with community activists, through whom he hoped to arrange a meeting with Gerald Ford Africa:

I then asked them to go back, to indicate to Gerald Ford Africa that I was willing to meet at any point that he decided, that he decided that he wanted to meet. I would come to his house. I would go to a neutral house. . . . I would personally negotiate with him any type of release from the house that they were talking about, any movement they wanted to make at that time. . . . After the optimism on Thursday, about noon, they got back to me the next day and said that there was a 360 degrees turn in the attitude of Gerald Ford Africa when they went back, and that he became profane towards them and said he would not meet with me under any circumstances ever for anything. And it was at this point that that hope which I had of bringing about some negotiation in fact fell through. [PSIC, 1985, 10/15 AM, pp. 62–64]

In directing his personal effort concerning MOVE toward negotiation, Goode was clearly playing to the area where he "felt familiar, resourceful, and competent" [Marimow, 1985]. But such skills had probably developed precisely because they were so consistent with Goode's religious motivation and self-image. In contrast, to be "on the scene with hands-on" in managing a police operation against MOVE would be to risk coming away with blood on his hands—blood that might be politically advantageous but personally intolerable.

Unleashing on Unreliable Force

Thus, when the Osage neighbors precipitated Goode's final stage of hypervigilance, he kept the police operation at arms length, shielding himself from personal responsibility for the onslaught to come by entrusting the planning and execution to the police, whom he described time and again in the hearings as "experts" and "professionals." Goode's seemingly blind trust in his police force prompted this sarcastic interrogation by Commissioner Neil J. Welch, who had once directed the Philadelphia office of the FBI:

Welch: Now, we got a Mayor that's been a Mayor for a year or two and before that he was the Managing Director, and certainly isn't the first time he's seen the Philadelphia Police Department and its personnel perform. . . . [W]hat was your judgment as to

the professional capability, the dependability, the quality and integrity of the Philadelphia Police Department to execute, to draft a plan and to execute it successfully?

Goode: My judgement was that Greg Sambor had the ability within the parameters which I set forth, to go out and to develop a plan. . . . It was my judgment that . . . being the kind of trained professional person and manager he is, that he, in fact, could do that. . . . That when he finished that plan, he was to discuss that with Leo Brooks, who I felt with his 30 years in the armed services, as a Major General, could evaluate appropriately and properly that overall plan. . . . So I left that meeting with full confidence that Greg Sambor and Leo Brooks could, in fact, carry out the assignment given to them.

Welch: Mayor, you displayed great confidence in your Police Department and your Police Commissioner, as you have just outlined. This is the same department that has been or would have been under almost continuous federal investigation, had it not, for a period of some time?

Goode: That's correct. [PSIC, 1985, 10/15 PM, pp. 119–121]

Having had responsibility for the Police Department during most of the past five years, to admit the department's faults would clearly arouse dissonance for Goode; but it is inconceivable that he did not know, at some level, that his police were an unreliable instrument for this task. The Federal investigations to which Welch referred were not only for corruption, but for brutality and civil rights violations; and the mutual hatred between the police and MOVE was obvious, especially after the death of Officer Ramp and the beating of Delbert Africa in 1978.

In his initial attempt to solve the MOVE problem, Goode in fact sought to bypass the Philadelphia police. On May 30, 1984, just two days after his first meeting with a delegation from Osage Avenue, the mayor led ranking city officials to a session with U.S. Attorney Edward Dennis and representatives of the FBI and Secret Service. They rebuffed his argument that MOVE's threats against President Reagan and violations of their neighbors' rights constituted grounds for U.S. intervention. Although consistent with the buck-passing pattern typical of defensive avoidance, Goode's attempt to enlist Federal authorities can also be interpreted as a prudent effort to find an armed force more detached, disciplined, and reliable than his own police.

Worries about controlling the city police were also present, though not emphasized, in the days before the final confrontation. At the May 7 meeting, prompted by Councilman Lucien Blackwell's strong warning about officers who might seek vengeance for 1978, Goode instructed Sambor to "handpick" the men who would serve in the Osage Avenue confrontation. (Sambor later claimed not to have heard such an order and in any case did not implement it. One of the gas-insertion teams included two officers who had been accused of beating Delbert Africa [Anderson and Hevenor, 1987, p. 115].) Goode ultimately admitted to the MOVE Commission that he doubted police fire control so much that he feared their bullets might endanger his own life if he went to the scene:

Commissioner Audrey Bronson: I understand that you felt that your life would have been at risk—by whom?

Goode: Well, I have received a lot of information that simply people said to me, and I will share this candid discussion with you, that I should be careful of, first of all, of people who were MOVE sympathizers in the neighborhood, that with shots going on out there that a shot could easily go awry and hit me, that I should be—I should be—beware of even the potential for police shots going awry on the scene and therefore, there have been, as I was told, instances of the fact that commanders in the Army have, in fact, been mistakenly shot and I should be aware of those kinds of things and the people who talked with me simply persuaded me that, in fact, it would be a risk for me to be in the area. [PSIC, 1985, 11/6 PM, p. 54]

Although not explicit about who were "the people who talked with me," Goode's statement to the Commission is consistent with reports that telephoners purporting to be police officers warned the mayor he might be shot by police if he came to Osage Avenue.

In short, part of Goode's reluctance to act against MOVE must have resulted from doubts, whether conscious or suppressed, that he could sufficiently control the use of force by the police. In the end he made no real attempt to manage the violence he had authorized. Perhaps, as many in Philadelphia believe,

Goode rationally calculated that any such effort might fail and therefore deliberately distanced himself from a potential disaster in order to avoid legal or political responsibility. Such motives cannot be ruled out, but they do not adequately explain the string of cognitive distortions by which the mayor apparently avoided appreciating the reality of what his forces were doing. He told his breakfast guests that police were only firing over the roof of the MOVE house; he interpreted explosions he heard from his home as stun grenades; he thought that the "explosive device" would be placed on MOVE's roof rather than dropped from a helicopter; and he mistook "snow" on his television screen for water from firefighters' squirts [PSIC, 1985, 10/15 AM, pp. 74, 97; 10/15 PM, p. 111; 11/6 AM, p. 111; 10/15 PM, p. 31]. Avowing these beliefs—all unsupported by others' testimony—would hardly help against criminal charges, and they only added to Goode's political vulnerability by subjecting him to ridicule. Such a consistent pattern of misperception seems more suited to deceive on self than to deceive others, and better protection against self-condemnation than against the judgment of courts or voters. It therefore appears likely that deeper sources of ambivalence prevented the mayor from admitting to himself the full import of his decision to unleash official violence against MOVE.

Black Against Black: Identification and Anger

The foregoing analysis is not meant to portray Wilson Goode as a pacifist or as one whose values are entirely antithetical to those of the police. After completing ROTC at Morgan State University, he served in the U.S. Army from 1961 to 1963, rising to the rank of captain and commanding a unit of 223 military policemen. His military experience made a deep impression on Goode. He has said that he learned more about management in the army than he did earning a master's degree in governmental administration at the University of Pennsylvania.[11] As mayor, he has shown a marked penchant for appointing former military officers to high posts—including Leo Brooks, a major general in charge of the Philadelphia Defense Personnel Support Center before Goode persuaded him to become Managing Director, and Gregore Sambor, a veteran and an officer in the reserves.

To Goode, however, the military seems to

represent not so much legitimate violence as it does an organization that develops personal discipline and rewards it, regardless of race—in marked contrast to most of American society in his formative years. Early profiles of Brooks suggest the virtues that Goode most admires:

[A mutual acquaintance described Brooks as] "made out of the same mold as Wilson." Goode and Brooks shared poor childhoods in the South, Army-officer training and strong religious underpinnings. Brooks' father is a Baptist minister . . . Brooks also is a black man who, like his new boss, has achieved success by making hard work his credo. [Cooke and Klibanoff, 1983]

At heart a traditionalist, Brooks believes in the old-fashioned virtues of hard work, self-discipline . . . and taking responsibility for one's own actions. To him, nothing exceeds the importance of family. [Klibanoff, 1984]

To a black man with Wilson Goode's values, MOVE must have aroused deep and intense conflicts.[12] On the one hand, as a former civil rights activist who had himself been twice picked up by police for allegedly creating disturbances [Cohn, 1982, p. 21], Goode must have had some lingering identification with MOVE. In 1978, much of the black and liberal communities had seen the MOVE problem as a racially motivated attack by the Rizzo administration on the rights of a predominantly black group. On one occasion, five thousand demonstrators marched around City Hall to protest the siege in Powelton; their chants linked MOVE with South African blacks as fellow victims of racial oppression. In 1984, U.S. Attorney Dennis, himself black, strongly warned city officials against violating MOVE's civil rights [PSIC, 1985, 10/22 PM, p. 127]. Goode invoked his own concern for minority rights in explaining his reluctance to act:

I think that if I was a different person, that perhaps I may have acted differently back in 1984. But I . . . do not feel that anyone who holds an office ought to use that office to infringe and violate other people's rights in order to achieve the overall good, and I guess I feel that way because I know that for so long in this country that laws

were, in fact, used to deprive blacks and women and Hispanics and others who were different, and therefore, I do not want, as mayor of this city to say to a group: Because you are different, because you don't comply with all the laws, therefore, I have the right, as the mayor, to simply go full speed and trample on you and all your rights. . . . [PSIC, 1985, 10/15 PM, pp. 97–98]

On the other hand, MOVE represented the antithesis of every standard by which Wilson Goode lived. They dwelt in filth; he was always well groomed. They lived communally; he had raised a family. They spewed profanity; he attended church every Sunday. They survived casually; he worked fifteen-hour days. They rejected the system; he aspired to run a major corporation. As they spurned his efforts to negotiate a peaceful solution, as they vilified him and threatened his life, the bizarre cultists must have aroused increasing anger in Goode. The impulse to vent this anger must have been strong, but his religious belief in preserving life and his self-image as a controlled person forbade yielding to it. "I've always felt that I have to be in control of me at all times," he once told an interviewer [Cohn, 1982, p. 27]; and another profiler got "the feeling that the emotion bottled up inside Wilson Goode is always close to eruption. You can see him almost counting to ten, thinking before he responds, calculating each sentence, crafting every phrase, then struggling mightily to reign in what might be rage" [Mallowe, 1984, p. 170].

For a time, the mayor hoped that MOVE itself would assume the moral burden of precipitating violence. After receiving Rendell's memo justifying urgent action in June 1984, Goode delayed until August 8, the anniversary of the Powelton shootout, because reports indicated that MOVE planned a major confrontation with "the System" on that date. At the mayor's direction, the police prepared a plan for capturing the MOVE house,[13] and three hundred officers were assembled near Osage Avenue. Goode's choice of language in describing this incident is revealing:

The August 8th 1984 plan was a reactive plan, was geared to go into effect only if certain types of aggressive behavior, aggressive steps were taken by MOVE members themselves. And therefore when they did not take any aggressive steps, nothing, in fact, was done at that time. [PSIC, 1985, 10/15 PM, p. 59]

The words "aggressive" and "aggression" recur frequently when Goode refers to the initiation of armed confrontation. It appears that he was willing in 1984 to do battle with MOVE, but only if MOVE were the aggressor, if MOVE bore the responsibility of having clearly initiated violence. To let deaths occur (or appear to occur) merely because of noise, stench, code violations, and unpaid utility bills was, to Goode, a morally unbalanced equation.[14]

On August 8, however, MOVE did nothing except take notes about the police preparations. After that day, Goode and other city officials entered a stage of full-blown defensive avoidance that lasted until May 1985. As the MOVE Commission observed about this period. "The policy of appeasement produced a rule of silence in City Hall, where information on the Osage Avenue situation was not disseminated and where city officials knowledgeable about the problems chose not to speak of them" [PSIC, 1986, p. 13]. Goode and his colleagues were thus able to entertain the wishful hope that the Osage Avenue problem "would disappear" by ignoring the readily available knowledge that MOVE members were vigorously and visibly fortifying their compound [PSIC, 1985, 10/15 PM, pp. 76–7]. Goode justified his policy of nonintervention on the grounds that no action should be taken "until such time as we worked out an overall plan that would be comprehensive in nature," but this argument was a rationalization for avoidance, as is shown by the fact that he did absolutely nothing to force the creation of such a plan [PSIC, 1985, 10/15 PM, pp. 75–80]. Indeed, the mayor had no contact with anyone concerning MOVE from August 9 until the end of April 1985 [PSIC, 10/15 AM, p. 40].

Goode's nine months of pseudocalm were then shattered by the United Residents' initiative, which revived what threatened to be an excruciating inner struggle. Rather than endure the tension during a protracted period of careful search and appraisal, the mayor sought to eliminate his conflict quickly by authorizing the police plan. Although he unleashed the violence of the police and perhaps in part vented his own anger through their vengeance, the use of force in this context was so dissonant with his self-image that he could not accept—psychologically at least as much as politically—the ownership that hands-on management would imply.

To shield himself from personal responsibility for violating crucial values, Wilson Goode thus abdicated his responsibility as an administrator. In so doing, he lost his best chance to control and minimize the inevitable violence. Because he was so reluctant to transgress his values, he permitted a series of events that in the end inflicted on them far greater damage than was necessary. The outcome has the irony of genuine tragedy. The preserver of life bore responsibility for eleven deaths; the builder of homes presided as sixty-one burned; the protector of rights permitted grotesquely excessive official violence.

Lessons for Present and Future Managers

Perhaps the only consolation we can take from so awful a disaster is the hope that its lessons will help prevent future catastrophes. Thus the MOVE Commission concluded their report with no fewer than thirty-eight recommendations covering such matters as communication systems, assignment of authority and responsibility, policies for controlling weapons and explosives, strategic planning processes, interdepartmental coordinating groups, and so forth. Though the Commission's proposals may be sensible and worthwhile, from the perspective of the analysis offered in this paper, such advice misses the most fundamental lessons of the MOVE debacle.

Organizational systems, policies, and procedures are ultimately controlled and implemented by human beings. Effective communication will not occur when subordinates believe that their superiors cannot bear to hear the truth. Clear allocation of authority will be wasted on executives who, succumbing to painful quandaries, rationalize evasion of responsibility.

Programs for educating public managers should therefore devote much more attention to the psychology of decisionmaking, with a special focus on its prescriptive implications. For example, Janis [1989, ch. 10] concludes his recent book by suggesting twenty sets of leadership practices that might help policy makers avoid pitfalls that often result in defective decisionmaking. As he observes, most of these recommendations will be costly to leaders and their support staffs in time, effort, and stress. Adjusting curricula to sensitize present and future decision makers to psychological factors will also demand new investments by schools, teachers, and students.

Dramatic examples like the MOVE disaster can help motivate such efforts, but in teaching the case during the past several years, I have found that students adopt their own avoidance strategies. Like the general public, their natural reaction is to debate, as one student put it, "whether moral bankruptcy or simple incompetence best explains this disaster." Whichever verdict is chosen, the effect is to distance oneself from the officials who are blamed for the debacle. The observer in effect is saying, "I would never be so evil, or so uncaring, or so inattentive, or so blundering as to permit such a horror!"

Interpreting the MOVE case in terms of a general theory such as the Janis and Mann conflict model elevates it from an idiosyncratic failure to a universal warning. Students can then move beyond emotional condemnation of a few officials to a sobering recognition of their own vulnerability to similar errors. The generality of the problem can be further emphasized by exploring parallel cases (though few will be so well documented as the MOVE incident). To take several recent examples, the delay/haste pattern appears to fit the British government's treatment of IRA strongholds in Belfast and Derry during the early 1970s, the Chinese government's response to the 1989 student demonstrations in Tienanmen Square, and the U.S. invasion of Panama to overthrow General Manuel Noriega.[15]

Once managers understand the dynamics of defensive avoidance and hypervigilance, what can they do to protect themselves? Because rationalization, denial, selective perception, and wishful thinking are so insidious, no one can be assured of immunity against defective decision processes. For this reason, Janis and Mann [1977, p. 396] recommend embedding preventive strategies in organizational standard operating procedures,[16] because "if the anti-defensive avoidance procedures are not institutionalized but are rather left to the discretion of the leader or the members, they will be more honored in the breach than in the observance."

Nevertheless, it is not unreasonable to hope that individual awareness will also help. Relying on face validity rather than any systematic evidence of effectiveness, I would suggest the following strategy to managers who wish to reduce their vulnerability.

First, learn to recognize the behavioral symptoms of defective decisionmaking. For defensive avoidance, these include procrastinating, buck-passing, and downplaying danger signals. Symptoms of hypervigilance include grabbing the first available alternative, neglecting contingency plans, and believing that action must be taken under extreme time pressure whether or not compelling deadlines exist. Wise managers will not only monitor themselves for these symptoms, but will also encourage trusted advisors to fight the battle for their minds by calling such tendencies to their attention.

Second, when these symptoms are observed, identify the central no-win dilemma or dilemmas.[17] Conflicts that impede effective decisionmaking are not always obvious and will vary from individual to individual. The desire to avoid responsibility and shield oneself from reality behind a screen of cognitive distortions becomes strongest when one's most central values are threatened, so the manager must heed the ancient injunction to "know thyself."

Third, learn to grasp problems firmly even when all options entail distasteful consequences for important values. The example of Wilson Goode shows that cherished virtues, if excessively protected, can be the source of tragic failure. Though vigilant problem solving and decisive management may induce stress, they are usually rewarded—if not with unequivocal triumph, then at least by controlled damage and the respect that strong leaders are accorded. In contrast, the inferno on Osage Avenue should burn into our memories the lesson that however bad available alternatives seem, potential outcomes can be far worse if avoidance and hasty action permit a tough situation to deteriorate into a nightmare.

References

Anderson, John, and Hilary Hevenor (1987), *Burning Down the House: MOVE and the Tragedy of Philadelphia* (New York: W.W. Norton and Co.).

Assefa, Hizkias, and Paul Wahrhaftig (1988), *Extremist Groups and Conflict Resolution: The MOVE Crisis in Philadelphia* (New York: Praeger).

Bowser, Charles W. (1989), *Let the Bunker Burn: The Final Battle with MOVE* (Philadelphia: Camino Books).

Boyette, Michael, with Randi Boyette (1989), *"Let It Burn!" The Philadelphia Tragedy* (Chicago: Contemporary Books).

Cohn, Roger (1982), "Wilson Goode Has Something

to Prove," *Today Magazine, Philadelphia Inquirer* (July 25), pp. 10ff.

Cooke, Russell, and Hank Klibanoff (1983), "Work Is the Credo for New Managing Director," *Philadelphia Inquirer* (November 29), p. 12-A.

George, Alexander L. (1973), "The Case for Multiple Advocacy in Making Foreign Policy," *American Political Science Review* 66, pp. 751–785.

Gilbert, Charles E. (1959), "The Framework of Administrative Responsibility," *Journal of Politics* 21, pp. 373–407.

Goodman, Howard (1989), "Still Haunted by MOVE, Richmond Is Telling His Story," *Philadelphia Inquirer* (May 15), p. B-1.

Janis, Irving L. (1972), *Victims of Groupthink* (Boston: Houghton Mifflin).

Janis, Irving L. (1989), *Crucial Decisions: Leadership in Policymaking and Crisis Management* (New York: The Free Press).

Janis, Irving L., and Leon Mann (1977), *Decision Making: A Psychological Analysis of Conflict, Choice, and Commitment* (New York: The Free Press).

Javers, Ron (1983), "On the Run: Lunch with Wilson Goode," *Philadelphia Magazine* 74 (April), p. 8.

Klibanoff, Hank (1984), "The General," *Philadelphia Inquirer* (May 21), p. 4-B.

Mallowe, Mike (1980), "And Now, the Goode News," *Philadelphia Magazine* 71 (August), pp. 128ff.

Mallowe, Mike (1984), "The No-Frills Mayor," *Philadelphia Magazine* 75 (December), pp. 168ff.

Marimow, William K. (1985), "Two Images of Goode: Activism vs. Delegation," *Philadelphia Inquirer* (October 23), p. 1-A.

Philadelphia Court of Common Pleas (1988), *Report of the County Investigating Grand Jury of May 15, 1986.*

Philadelphia Special Investigation Commission (1985), *Hearings.*

Philadelphia Special Investigation Commission (1986), *Findings, Conclusions, and Recommendations.*

Sharifi, Jahan (1990), Unpublished student paper, University of Pennsylvania.

Stevens, William K. (1985), "Mayor Goode's Once-Solid Path Turns Rocky in Philadelphia," *New York Times* (October 23).

Wilentz, Amy (1985), "Goode's Intentions," *Time* 125 (May 27), p. 22.

Notes

1. PSIC, 1986, Finding 22; see also Findings 3, 15, 17, and 24, which use comparable language. The PSIC is generally known as "the MOVE Commission."

2. This account draws on the following sources, in addition to the author's knowledge as a resident of West Philadelphia during the period described: PSIC [1986], which includes a chronology; Philadelphia Court of Common Pleas [1988], which includes a history of MOVE; Anderson and Hevenor [1987]; Assefa and Wahrhaftig [1988]; Bowser [1989]; and Boyette [1989]. Charles Bowser and Michael Boyette were, respectively, members of the MOVE Commission and the grand jury. The eighteen days of hearings the MOVE Commission conducted in October and November 1985 are my principal source [PSIC, 1985]. Transcripts are available in the Government Publications Department of the Philadelphia Free Library and the Urban Archives Center of Temple University. There is a volume for each day of hearings, with pages numbered separately within each volume for morning and afternoon sessions. I supplemented the transcripts by watching videotapes of key witnesses' testimony. (The hearings were televised live by WHYY-TV, the PBS station in Philadelphia.)

3. See also the testimony of Laverne Sims [PSIC, 1985, 10/10 AM, pp. 65–77].

4. District Attorney Edward Rendell later blamed the acquittal on the invective and curses that Delbert directed at the judge and jury [PSIC, 1985, 10/22 AM, pp. 119–120].

5. PSIC, 1985, 10/8 PM, p. 104. In Philadelphia there are 28 districts for the lower house of the state legislature compared with only 10 councilmanic districts; thus the state representative is often the elected official closest to the people of a neighborhood.

6. Cohn, 1982, p. 27. The second sentence is a quotation from Shirley Hamilton, Goode's chief of staff.

7. Janis is better known among students of politics, policy, and management for his earlier work on "groupthink" [Janis, 1972]. Elements of groupthink can be found in various official groups involved in the MOVE problem, but

the full-blown syndrome does not appear, perhaps because the mayor's interpersonal style inhibited development of the requisite emotional cohesiveness. (Like other cults, MOVE itself exhibited a virulent form of groupthink.) Janis's work on organizational decisions has developed from the specific to the general. In *Decision Making,* he and Mann depict groupthink as a collective version of the broader phenomenon of defensive avoidance, which in turn is part of a "conflict model" based on psychological stress. In his latest book, *Crucial Decisions* [Janis, 1989], the conflict model becomes a component of a still more general "constraints model." The comprehensiveness of the constraints model is a virtue for some purposes, but I believe the paradoxical features of the MOVE case are explained best by the conflict model. Thus my account relies more on *Decision Making* than on *Crucial Decisions.*

8. The choice of words is unfortunate, because the authors use "vigilance" for their ideal problem-solving process; thus, "hypervigilance" suggests too much of a good thing. The hypervigilant actor exhibits too much emotional arousal and too much haste, but no true vigilance.

9. Although based as much as possible on published materials, the analysis that follows is necessarily inferential and speculative.

10. On May 13, only one police officer was struck by a MOVE bullet, and a bulletproof vest saved him from serious harm. A policy of protecting firefighters from possible MOVE gunfire was one reason the fire spread so fast and so far. Having vowed that no firefighter would face gunfire, Fire Commissioner William Richmond deliberately chose to sacrifice property in order to save lives [Goodman, 1989].

11. In a conversation with the author in February 1981.

12. Much the same argument can probably be made for Leo Brooks, which may help explain why he too failed to fulfill his responsibility in the MOVE operation. Despite the advantages of similarity in promoting trust and comfortable personal relations, leaders take a great risk in depending excessively on key subordinates who are too much like themselves.

13. This plan, prepared by Sergeant Herbert Kirk of the Police Academy, was the forerunner of the strategy employed the following May [PSIC, 1985, 10/11 PM].

14. Because some of his radical and civil libertarian supporters, both black and white, might have had the same attitude, Goode's calculation can be seen as both political and moral. As Sharifi [1990] observes, successful political leaders often mirror the potential reactions of key constituencies in their own concerns.

15. I owe these and other suggested parallels to an anonymous reviewer [of this article].

16. An example already well known in the policymaking community is the system of multiple advocacy recommended by Alexander George [1973].

17. One device that might help raise conflicts to consciousness is the decisional balance sheet, a kind of expanded cost-benefit analysis that includes not only utilitarian gains and losses but also the approval and disapproval of reference groups and oneself [Janis and Mann, 1977, ch. 6]. Note that the purpose is to recognize consciously the role of emotional influences, not necessarily to eliminate them.

Chapter 8 Review Questions

1. What are the key differences between the *root* and *branch* methods of decision making? Summarize the advantages and disadvantages of each method.

2. Does the case study, "The MOVE Disaster," exemplify the root or branch method of decision making? Or, another approach? Explain your reasons for your selection by citing examples from the case.

3. How does the case point up the influence of deeply held personal values or "unresolved decision conflicts" in the decisional process? Why did these hidden personal values in this case influence its outcome? In what ways did they impact on the decisional processes?

4. Compare this Case Study 8 involving MOVE with Case Study 4 dealing with the Challenger launch decision. Discuss the major differences in the way these two critical decisions were reached. In particular, consider the number and kinds of people who became involved in the decisional processes, their values, the care and manner by which the options for administrative action were presented and considered, the factors forcing the final decision, and the overall effectiveness of the decisional processes.

5. On the basis of your comparative appraisal of the two cases, can you generalize about how values and proper timing as well as the general political pressures play important roles in the way these or other public decisions are reached?

6. Also on the basis of your comparison of the two cases, why does who gets involved in the decisional process (or who is left out) play such a critical role in the quality and kind of decisions that are made in government?

Key Terms

incremental decision making
root method
branch method
clarification of objectives
intertwining ends and means
successive limited comparisons

rational comprehensive analysis
policy alternatives
maximization of values
empirical analysis
policy outcomes
ranking objectives

Suggestions for Further Reading

Making good, correct, and efficient decisions in the public interest has been a major concern of public administration literature since the early, "conscious" development of the field. In particular, the writings of Frederick Taylor and his followers about scientific management examined methods of rational decision making in organizations at the lower levels of industrial or business hierarchies. However, the post–World War II writings of Herbert Simon, especially his *Administrative Behavior: The Study of Decision Making Processes in Administrative Organization* (New York: Macmillan, 1947), shifted the focus of administrative thinking to *the decision* as the central focus of study and analysis. The enormous impact of this book (for which Simon won the Nobel Prize in

1978), as well as his other writings on public administration, make it worthy of careful attention by students of the field even today. For useful background information on Simon's life and work, read his autobiography, Herbert A. Simon, *Models of My Life* (New York: Basic Books, 1991).

Other important writings on this topic include Charles E. Lindblom, *The Intelligence of Democracy: Decision Making Through Mutual Adjustment* (New York: Free Press, 1965), and his book co-authored with David Braybooke, *A Strategy of Decision* (New York: Free Press, 1963). For criticisms of the Simon-Lindblom incrementalist approach see Yehezkel Dror, "Muddling Through—Science or Inertia?" *Public Administration Review*, 24 (September 1964), pp. 154–157, and Amitai

Etzioni, "Mixed Scanning: A Third Approach to Decision Making," *Public Administration Review,* 27 (December 1967), pp. 385–392. The debate over incrementalism is hardly over, for an entire symposium in the *Public Administration Review,* 39 (November/December 1979) was devoted to its pros and cons. Pay particular attention to the articles by Charles E. Lindblom, "Still Muddling, Not Yet Through" (pp. 511–516); Camille Cates, "Beyond Muddling" (pp. 527–531); and Bruce Adams, "The Limitations of Muddling Through" (pp. 545–552); plus Amitai Eztioni, "Mixed Scanning Revisited," *Public Administration Review,* 46 (January/February 1986), pp. 8–14. By contrast, Aaron Wildavsky, "Toward a Radical Incrementalism," in Alfred DeGrazia, *Congress: The First Branch of Government* (Washington, D.C.: American Enterprise Institute, 1966) pushes the incremental concept about as far as possible; whereas Paul R. Schulman, "Nonincremental Policy Making: Notes Toward an Alternative Paradigm," *American Political Science Review,* 69 (December 1975), presents possibly the most searching critique of the incremental model. James G. March, *A Primer on Decision-Making: How Decisions Happen* (New York: Free Press, 1994), offers a recent restatement of the incremental model as well as Herbert A. Simon, *Models of Bounded Rationality* (Cambridge: MIT Press, 1997).

Since the 1960s numerous decision models other than incrementalism have been proposed with various degrees of success. The most prominent include the *systems model* as represented in Fremont J. Lyden and Ernest G. Miller, eds., *Planning Programming-Budgeting: A Systems Approach to Management* (Chicago: Markham Publishing Co., 1968); *games theory* as outlined in Thomas C. Schelling, *The Strategy of Conflict* (Cambridge, Mass.: Harvard University Press, 1963); the *bureaucratic model* as represented in Graham T. Allison, *Essence of Decision: Explaining the Cuban Missile Crisis* (Boston: Little,

Brown, 1971); *cost-benefit* as found in Edward M. Gramlich, *Benefit-Cost Analysis of Government Programs* (Englewood Cliffs, N.J.: Prentice-Hall, 1981); *personal judgment* approach of Harvey Sherman, *It All Depends* (University, Ala.: University of Alabama Press, 1966); the *policy analysis method* as discussed in William N. Dunn, *Public Policy Analysis: An Introduction* (Englewood Cliffs, N.J.: Prentice-Hall, 1981); For a *chaos paradigm*, see L. Douglas Kiel, *Managing Chaos and Complexity in Government* (San Francisco, Calif.: BASS, 1994); for a *psychological approach*, read Irving Janis and Leon Mann, *Decision-Making: A Psychological Analysis of Conflict, Choce, and Commitment* (New York: Free Press, 1977); and the *garbage can model*, Michael D. Cohen et al., "A Garbage Can Model of Organizational Choice," *Administrative Science Quarterly,* 17 (1972), pp. 1–25. These only scratch the surface of a vast, complex area of decision-making study. You would be well advised to read the current issues of such journals as *Public Administration Review, Administrative Science Quarterly, Journal of Policy Analysis and Management, Public Management,* or *Harvard Business Review* for up-to-date perspectives on decision-making methodology.

For a fine scholarly critique of various decision-making approaches and where we stand today regarding their application to government, read George W. Downs and Patrick D. Larkey, *The Search for Government Efficiency: From Hubris to Helplessness* (New York: Random House, 1986); and for an excellent collection of applied cases involving local decision making, see James M. Banovetz, ed., *Managing Local Government: Cases in Decision Making* 2d ed. (Washington, D.C.: International City Management Assoc., 1998). The recently republished book, Geoffrey Vickers, *The Art of Judgment* (London: Sage, 1995 and first printed in 1965) offers one of the best arguments for practical judgment as the key to effective decision making.

CHAPTER 9

Administrative Communication: The Concept of its Professional Centrality

*P*ublic Administration practitioners and scholars alike have generally failed to give communication the attention and respect it deserves. . . . For communication to reclaim its rightful place at the core of public administration, its rigor, complexity, salience, diversity, and richness need to be rediscovered.

—James L. Garnett

READING 9

Introduction

In arriving at even the most routine policy decisions, the typical public administrator is a prisoner of a seemingly endless communications network that defines the problem at hand and the possible alternatives. Administrators are normally pressed from many sides with informational and data sources flowing into their offices from their superiors, subordinates, other agencies, citizen groups, and the general public. Sometimes the information arrives through routine formal channels; at other times it wells up or trickles down to the administrator via unsolicited routes. Whatever the source, the public decision maker must selectively sort out this information, and, in turn, dispense a substantial quantity of information to people within and outside the organizational structure; this is done by memoranda, reports, conferences, phone conversations, and informal encounters that touch off a new chain of communications and decisions by others. Similar to a telephone switchboard, a policy maker's office acts as a nerve center where the lines of communications cross and are connected and where information is received, processed, stored, assembled, analyzed, and dispensed.

Our conceptual understanding of the importance and complexity of the communications links within public organizations and their critical role in administrative decisions begins to a large extent with the work of Herbert A. Simon (1916–). In collaboration with Donald Smithburg and Victor Thompson, Simon wrote the text *Public Administration* (1950); this work, drawing on Simon's earlier writing, *Administrative Behavior* (1947), for which Simon won the Nobel Prize for economics in 1978, offered one of the first integrated behavioral interpretations of public administration. By introducing ideas from sociology, psychology, and political science, Simon and his associates sought to discover "a realistic behavioral description of the process of administration," emphasizing its informal human dynamics.

At the root of public administration, according to Simon, Smithburg, and Thompson, were continual conflicts among contending groups that resulted from such internal pressures as empire-building tendencies, differing individual backgrounds, and varying group identifications, as well as such external pressures as competing interest groups, members of Congress, and other agency heads struggling for scarce resources and influence. Similar to Norton Long's conception of the political power contest surrounding administrative activities (discussed in Chapter 4), the authors envision administrators as people "in the middle of continual conflict" whose actions and activities demand a considerable effort directed toward conflict resolution and compromise. As they write, "public administrators, and particularly those responsible for directions of unitary organizations, are themselves initiators and transformers of policy, brokers, if you like, who seek to bring about agreement between the program goals of government agencies and the goals and values of groups that possess political power." In short, "the greatest distinction between public administration and other administration is . . . to be found in the political character of public administration."

Decisions within this political setting can never be wholly rational but rather, the authors contend, are of a "bounded rational" nature. Instead of insisting on an "optimal solution," the public policy maker must be satisfied with what is "good enough," or as Lindblom suggests more simply in Chapter 8, must "muddle through." The prime ends of a public administrator's efforts are decisions that are not "maximizing" but "sufficing," that have as their goals not efficiency but achieving agreement, compromise, and ultimately survival.

One of the major vehicles for achieving coordination and compromise, in the view of Simon, Smithburg, and Thompson, is the communications network, which they define as the "process whereby decisional premises are transmitted from one member of an organization to another." The communications network acts principally as an integrating device for bringing together frequently conflicting elements of an organization to secure cooperative group effort. Three steps are involved in the communications process: first, "someone must initiate the communication"; second, "the command must be transmitted from its source to its destination"; and third, "communications must make its impact on the recipient." The information travels in two ways: (1) the formal or planned channels such as memoranda, reports, and written communications; and (2) the unplanned or informal ways such as face-to-face contacts, conferences, or phone calls to friends. Simon, Smithburg, and Thompson place considerable emphasis on the informal lines of communications that many refer to as "the grapevine." "In most organizations, the greater part of the information that is used in decision-making is informally transmitted," they observe.

The central problems in communications are the blockages that occur: "Blockages in the communication system constitute one of the most serious problems in public administration. They may occur in any one of the three steps in the communications process: initiation, transmission, or reception. Those who have information may fail to tell those who need the information as a basis of action; those who should transmit the information may fail to do so; those who receive the information may be unwilling or unable to assimilate it."

Seven critical types of communications blockages in public organizations are enumerated by the authors, the first being, simply, *barriers of language.* Words are frequently misinterpreted or understood differently as messages pass from one individual to another within organizations. Second, *frames of reference* differ so that the perception of information varies among individuals. Personal "mental sets" thus often prevent accurate comprehension of the problem at hand. Third, *status distance* can block communications because as information moves upward or downward through the various hierarchical levels of an organization "a considerable filtering and distorting" occurs. Fourth, *geographical distance* impedes the communications process; a far-flung department with many field offices spread over the nation or the world has great difficulty in ensuring prompt and accurate information exchange among its component units. Fifth, *self-protection* of the individual who reports actions plays a role in the informational links. Often "information that will evoke a favorable reaction will be played up; the mistakes and the fumbles tend to be glossed over." Sometimes the deception is conscious and at other times unconscious, but this activity always serves to distort objective reality. Sixth, *the pressures of work* tend to leave important matters overlooked or unreported. Finally, the *censorship* inherent in many governmental activities such as foreign intelligence or military operations limits the accurate flow of information within many public agencies.

These characteristic psychological and institutional communication blockages, suggest Simon, Smithburg, and Thompson, raise the vital question of "where a particular decision can best be made." Selection of the appropriate place for decision making directly depends on how effectively and easily information can be transmitted from its source to a decisional center, and how effectively and easily the decision can be transmitted from the decision maker to the point where action will occur. For instance, a military hierarchy could grant to individual company commanders the authority for deciding on the use of tactical nuclear weapons. This action would reduce the "time costs" associated with communicating to higher headquarters in the event of possible enemy attack and thus would allow for extreme military flexibility at lower echelons, but "local option" in this case might very well increase other costs, such as the likelihood of a nuclear accident. On the other hand, if authority for using these weapons had to be cleared, say, by the president of the United States and by other major Allied powers, the risk of accident might very well be reduced, but the time costs of gaining consent to use these weapons from many sources might make a decision so cumbersome and lengthy that no opportunity for swift retaliatory response would exist. As Simon, Smithburg, and Thompson point out, "Ease or difficulty of communications may sometimes be a central consideration in determining how far down the administrative line the function of making a particular decision should be located." The authors thus view the communications process not only as determining the outcome of particular decisions but as a prime influence on the structure of decision making within organizations. Extreme decentralization may achieve flexibility and initiative at the local level but may exact costs in terms of uniformity and control of response; vice versa, extreme centralization may produce maximum oversight but may reduce organizational responsiveness. Ultimately, the costs associated with delegating such decisional authority within an organizational hierarchy are always relative and are determined by the values and objectives of the organization.

Simon, Smithburg, and Thompson's ideas on communications are now a half century old and tend to view the topic as akin to "a machine model"—structured, apolitical, and largely functionally oriented. So how is this subject conceptualized today by a modern theorist? The following selection, by Professor James Garnett, chair of the Graduate Department of Public Policy and Administration at Rutgers University at Camden, author of the seminal book *Communicating for Results in Government* (1992), and considered the foremost scholar on this topic, paints a current overview of communication, stressing its professional centrality, ubiquity, *and* complexity for the field.

As you read this selection, keep the following questions in mind:

How does Professor Garnett's contemporary view of communication compare with the foregoing outline of Simon, Smithburg, and Thompson's? What's new in this field, according to Garnett? Reflect on any communications issues that might have been apparent to you in the previous cases, such as "The MOVE Disaster" or "The Last Flight of the Space Shuttle Challenger." Do they square with those outlined by Professor Garnett? Is it possible to trace the internal network of communications in an organization? The external network? What factors create or define the shape of internal *or* external informational network? For example, what impact have computers had in recent years?

Can you draw from this essay generalizations concerning the managing of the communication process as a means for enhancing effectiveness in public organizations? What suggestions does Professor Garnett recommend for managing more effectively?

Consider the following essay in relation to Norton Long's concept of administrative power. How do administrative communication influence issues of policy and power? Specifically, did communication influence the outcomes in the case study in Chapter 3, "Dumping $2.6 Million on Bakersfield"?

Finally, why does Garnett argue that "communication ethics is not an oxymoron"? What does he mean by that comment?

Administrative Communication (Or How to Make All the Rest Work): The Concept of its Professional Centrality

JAMES L. GARNETT

The first executive function is to develop and maintain a system of communication.

—*Chester Barnard,* The Functions of the Executive, *p. 226*

Note: This original essay was prepared especially for the seventh edition by James L. Garnett.

A large part (perhaps all) of an executive's job has to do with giving and re- *ceiving communications. Managers are nerve centers in the organizational communication network. They receive all sorts of memoranda, letters, policy statements, instructions, reports, face-to-face communications and what not. Perhaps nothing is so important to successful administration as successful communication.*

—*Robert S. Lorch,* Public Administration, *p. 174*

Since the time of Lorch's (1978) observation, above, public administrators continue to expend much of their time and effort on those communicative tasks *and* on the growing number and diversity of communications, including e-mail messages, contracts, service agreements, satisfaction surveys, and other forms. The pervasiveness of communication extends beyond the managerial workday. The actual administrative situations depicted by cases in this book testify to the centrality of communication in public service.

- In chapter 1, John Bartlow Martin's classic, vivid case "The Blast in Centralia No. 5: A Mine Disaster No One Stopped," numerous official and unofficial attempts to communicate the danger of Mine No. 5 failed to prompt sufficient action, contributing to the deaths of 111 miners. Leaders and members of UMWA Local 52, safety inspector Scanlon, and others attempting to safeguard mine conditions proved unable to overcome the multiple communication barriers of perception, and hierarchy.
- In chapter 2, George Lardner Jr.'s plaintive account of his daughter's senseless murder by an unstable ex-boyfriend captures repeated occasions where one arm of Boston's criminal justice bureaucracy never received key reports from another arm that might have prevented the shooting. Two official complaints that would have triggered the ex-boyfriend Cartier's arrest and detention were still sitting on a clerk's desk when Kristin was killed.

- In chapter 4, Michael Charles's "The Last Flight of the Spaceshuttle Challenger" forcefully describes a technological breakdown causing the worst space disaster in history, but it also captures a series of communication breakdowns that contributed to this calamity. Such breakdowns occurred within NASA, between NASA and private contractors, among contractors, and within the private bureaucracies of these contractors. This case screams the importance of—and the difficulty of—interorganizational communication, particularly communication across sectors, as do other cases, such as "The MOVE Disaster," in chapter 8.

Not all miscommunication leads to war, deadly explosions, or murder. More commonly, miscommunication has less drastic or immediate consequences but still affects administrative performance and government's ability to serve its citizens. Michael Aron's "Dumping $2.6 Million on Bakersfield (Or How *Not* to Build a Migratory Farm Workers' Clinic)" in chapter 3 vividly demonstrates how miscommunication among ethnic groups, public agencies, professional societies, and other organizations resulted in losses of time, money, goodwill, cooperation, and health care for the intended recipients, people who badly needed adequate care. This is more typical of the effects of communication in public service. As crucial as communication is in life-and-death situations, the larger consequences of miscommunication occur in the countless, daily interactions between public servants and citizens, between public servants and public officials, among public servants, and among the many public, private, and nonprofit actors in the increasingly complex delivery systems that provide public service. The collective consequences of miscommunication in these daily interactions—whether from intent or inadvertence, lack of skill or misuse of skill, overloading or boredom, inadequate technology or technology overkill—take an enormous toll on performance, credibility, trust and on what counts most, citizens' quality of life. Missing welfare checks, foregone medical treatment, cutoff of heat, and extra frustrations over obtaining help are all important to those we are called to serve.

As with the previously mentioned cases and other actual situations, communication is no panacea. Effective communication does not guarantee success, nor does miscommunication guarantee failure. Even if communication had been more prolific and accurate, various Bakersfield organizations had motives for furthering their perceived self-interest that often conflicted with motives and agendas of other organizations. In spite of the weather, strong political, economic, and administrative forces pushed for a Challenger liftoff after previous delays, making it difficult for warning messages to pierce the must-launch-now mindset. So, while communication is hardly a panacea, it does play a crucial role in administrative success or failure. Sound communication contributes to performance and increases the chances for success, and faulty communication contributes to the likelihood of failure. Perhaps what these cases and other slices of real life demonstrate is that communication is an extremely complex process typically undertaken in complicated political, social, economic, and technological contexts. These factors compound the need for communicating with as much knowledge, skill, and effort as possible instead of assuming that because it is so common that communication is so routine. Foltz (1973, 1) sensed this contradiction when he wrote, "Let's get rid of the thought that there's nothing to communicate. Let's recognize that communications is tough, hard, demanding. It's one of the most damned and least understood skills in existence.

It's at the core of every problem facing us as individuals, families, groups, nations." Chester Barnard, one of the seminal writers on administration, also understood the centrality of communication when he emphasized that "developing and maintaining a system of communication" (1938, 226) ranked as the first executive principle.

This chapter aims to raise the salience of communication within Public Administration by emphasizing communication's centrality to almost everything public administrators do. Other aims are to place the various types of public sector communication in context, address some key issues concerning communication, and provide guidance on sound communication practice. Because all the rich cases in this book provide insights about communication, a number of them (along with other events) will be used to illustrate key issues and concepts.

Communication Processes and Players

This section describes key public sector communication processes and roles. These are hardly the only ones, but they are the central ones. Overlap and interaction among these processes and roles is unavoidable—and important. The newsmaking process, although predominantly aimed at external publics, fuels intraorganizational communication within government agencies. While interorganizational communication within the public sector occurs most frequently among service provider organizations, it increasingly involves stakeholder client/customer groups.

Public Officials and the News Media: The Newsmaking Process

The concept of administrative communication typically centers on the newsmaking process. Traditional press relations, now termed *media relations* to reflect the broader efforts to report news through television, radio, the Internet, and other channels, has dominated both the practice and scholarship on government communication—to the detriment of our understanding of other key communication processes. Because of its historically central role, however, newsmaking provides a good point of departure. Most government agencies of any size and financial resources have a staff or person who fields questions from reporters and who proactively attempts to get news coverage (typically favorable) about their agency. Business companies and nonprofit organizations engaged in providing or advocating public services also generally have such a function, whether called public relations, media relations, public information, public affairs, communication, or some other name. In the past, former news reporters or editors typically staffed such units because they knew the newsmaking process and they held strong contacts with fellow reporters and editors. Public information or public affairs specialists disseminated news to newspapers and to radio and television stations by means of news releases, interviews, and news conferences. According to extensive research conducted by Grunig and Grunig (1992), media relations (what they call the *public information model*) is still the predominant model of government (and business) communication, although releases may now be distributed by electronic mail and news conferences be broadcast by satellite.

Several trends have begun to revolutionize the newsmaking process. The public increasingly demands direct communication with public officials rather than have interactions filter through reporters, editors, commentators, and others. Growing audiences for C-SPAN, public radio, and other live, direct broadcasts of agency hearings, legislative debates, and even a presidential impeachment trial attest to this trend. To their credit, many elected and appointed officials have actively pursued more direct contact with constituents rather than rely solely on getting messages conveyed by news sources, however important those sources remain. President Bill Clinton, for one, has shown extraordinary talent at using direct televised presidential addresses and nationally televised "town meetings" to reach citizens in the studio audience and nationwide audiences who witness and identify with this direct interaction. To underscore the constant need to combine communication skill

with ethics, some commentators have observed that part of President Clinton's skill in influencing (and some would say misleading) public opinion about his sexual affairs later aggravated his legal and constitutional problems—and as with his State of the Union address during his trial, helped him survive those challenges. Many federal, state, and local government agencies have increased their direct contact with citizens by using telephone hotlines, interactive cable television, Web sites, neighborhood meetings, and other channels to send information about government policies, programs, and actions and to receive information from citizens about program impact, citizen satisfaction, or consumer preferences.

Even though Osborne and Gabler's influential book *Reinventing Government* said surprisingly little about the role of communication in a more entrepreneurial public sector, its discussion of consumer feedback and the consumer orientation it helped spawn has been another trend that has made governments and others conducting the public's business more attuned to the role as communication *receiver* and less preoccupied with *sending*—traditionally through the news media. Make no mistake: the role of news organizations and their reporters, editors, commentators, and others in the newsmaking process continues to thrive as our individual and professional scholarly fascination with proliferating numbers and formats of news sources will attest. Increasingly, however, public sector actors will pursue the need to diversify their ability to communicate with important stakeholders and other publics.

Just as the demands of citizen consumers have expanded the functions of public sector communication, administrators are increasingly demanding a more managerial focus from their communication function.

Professional Managers and Professional Communicators: The Managerial Communication Process

While all public servants at every level have an essential role as communicators, our specialization-oriented society has singled out some as professional communicators, whether called press secretary, public information officer, public affairs specialist, or some other title. Such specialists, as indicated earlier, have traditionally had backgrounds in journalism and were principally involved in the media-relations role. The first expansion of the communication function involved producing, or helping produce, other forms of information reports, internal and external newsletters, videos, and the like. This required professional communicators to possess a broader set of knowledge and skill but still primarily involved sending information, although to more diverse audiences than news reporters and editors. While savvy officials and administrators appreciated the importance of sound media relations and the broader set of information "products," many public executives and administrators in the last two decades began demanding more of their communication unit. In particular, administrators wanted their communication function to provide help with management tasks and problems. And many professional communicators, wanting to play a more central role, actively sought and prepared for such management-related tasks, including paying attention to what tangible results their efforts were producing. These progressive communication professionals realized that when the communication function in organizations pays no attention to communication effects or to measuring them, it is a "relegated to the status of an output function that executives systematically exclude from decision making and strategic planning" (Broom and Dozier 1983, 5). Best practice communication units in the public sector now provide substantial expertise and support to their organizations and, in turn, need administrative support to be most effective, as Table 9.1 conveys.

The relationship between public administrators and public communicators can be far more productive and satisfying if both regard each other as a professional, see the needs and constraints of the other, and actively work to make the other more effective in serving the public. Even though the relationship with professional communicators is crucial, effective public administrators understand that they are often their organization's most im-

portant communicator and act accordingly. The next two sections examine this role, first with internal and then with external communication.

Public Executives, Administrators, and Employees: The Internal Communication Process

Just as politics is too crucial to administration to be left entirely to politicians, communication is too critical to managerial success to be left solely to the professional communicators. Public executives, first-line supervisors, and all administrators in between must interact daily with managerial superiors, subordinates, peers, staff professionals, and other audiences inside the organization.

Internal communication can be thought of as downward, upward, or lateral. Downward communication has historically received the most emphasis in organization and management theory—and probably also in management practice (Garnett 1997b). Katz and Kahn (1966) identify the functions of downward communication as issuing task directives, giving task-related information, giving feedback on job performance, and conveying an overall sense of mission. Directives and task-related information tend to dominate downward channels in public-sector agencies, leaving performance feedback and mission-related information underused and undervalued. "If this imbalance occurs, public employees can become desensitized to task-related messages and starved for communication about their performance and about agency direction. Imbalance in downward communication often causes other organizational dysfunctions such as depressed morale, preoccupations with routine tasks, and indifference to overall agency performance" (Garnett 1992a, 103). One of the many factors contributing to the MOVE disaster (see Nagel, chapter 8 of this volume) was the lack of downward communication about an overall emergency plan for how each participating department (police, fire, emergency services) fit into the overall plan and feedback on how each phase was progressing. In this case there may not have been enough task-oriented communication

Table 9.1   Mutual Reliance Between Public Administrators and Professional Communicators

Communication Professional Can Help Public Administrators with:

Strategic Planning   In Gathering and organizing information about internal strengths and weaknesses and external opportunities and threats and helping craft a Communication Strategic Plan that supports and helps implement the overall Strategic Plan by identifying key issues, audiences, resource potentials, messages, and outcomes.

Policy and Program Implementation   Assisting with implementation by identifying existing and potential stakeholders for an existing or proposed program or policy, learning stakeholder opinions about such programs or policies, as well as stakeholders' likely response, program or policy revisions, or mutual interests that could facilitate implementation.

Boundary Scanning/Environmental Scanning   Detecting changes in the agency's environment that can affect agency decisions, actions, and results. Training in public opinion and media relations gives many communication professionals the capability to help agencies gather information about trends, actions, perceptions, and so on, beyond their boundaries. Scanning can be done informally through contacts or through systematic surveys, focus groups, interviews, content analyses, and other methods.

Stakeholder Analysis   Regular or special analysis of key agency stakeholders (clients, customers, special interests, other public agencies, and so on) to determine their policy positions, program agendas, organizational strategy, resource needs, posture toward an agency, and specific initiatives.

Issue Marketing   Finding out what clients, constituents, customers, and other key stakeholders regard to be important issues, how they stand on these issues, how likely they are to become actively involved in these issues, and what kinds of messages would best be able to reach them. Issue marketing can also test various stakeholder positions on a predetermined set of issues.

Agenda Setting   Shaping the agency's agenda by discovering what agency stakeholders want to happen and by directly influencing the policy agenda. Communication professionals can utilize opinion research and scanning skills to detect and present stakeholder preferences for the agency's agenda. Communication professionals can also help affect the news media agenda that shapes public and political agendas that, in turn, influence the agency's agenda. This can give an organization more self-control over its policy and management agendas.

Conflict Management/Dispute Resolution   Identifying conflicts or potential conflicts among agencies, stakeholders, interest groups, and others; and helping manage these conflicts constructively by identifying interests and solutions as well as conflicts.

Communication/Information Auditing   Comparing information/communication flows in an agency with actual information/communication needs; assessing the quantity and quality of information; and identifying information overloads, bottlenecks, and gaps.

Outcomes Assessment   Evaluating outcomes—the more fundamental results of policy and programs. Communication professionals can assist in soliciting opinions about customer satisfaction and working with program and policy analysts to craft sound and user-friendly surveys, interviews, focus groups, or other assessment instruments.

Public Administrators Can Help Communicators

See the broader organizational/managerial picture

Stay focused on issues of administrative/performance significance rather than be caught up with brochures, videos, or other "products" of public information

Tap into managerial influence networks so that communicators can get the information and support needed to get the job done

Become involved in the formative stages of a program, project, or issue to facilitate early advice and minimize the need for damage control later

Get the support needed to appropriately evaluate the results of communication

Obtain the training needed to provide broader, more managerial, and strategic capabilities.

either, and upward and lateral communication were also critically deficient.

Upward communication can carry a number of vital messages: feedback on whether downward messages are received, understood, and acted upon; warnings about problems needing attention; intelligence gleaned by subordinates about key stakeholders; soundings about organizational morale and performance. This book is full of cases where inattention to upward messages—both internal and external—lost performance, money, political support, and even lives. As reflected in Case Study 1 in this text, repeated attempts by UMWA Local 52 and Illinois Mine Inspector Driscoll Scanlan to alert state, coal company, union, and other officials of dangerous conditions in Mine No. 5 failed to prompt action. They failed due to economic and political predisposition against their message, and to their inability to convey a greater sense of urgency and to use a broader range of communication channels. The U.S. Department of Health, Education and Welfare was so caught up in issuing directives and instructions for getting the migrant health clinic established in Bakersfield that information about delays and intergroup conflict did not fully register until situations had become more difficult to handle. Research on public-sector communication shows the tendency for upward communication to be distorted or lost because of reluctance to send or receive bad news and the tendency for subordinates to bear self-serving messages up the ranks (Tullock 1965; Downs 1967; Kaufman and Couzens 1973). Garnett (1992a) describes a number of techniques for improving upward communication. Reducing administrative layers that can delay and distort messages might have saved time and lives in situations like the Centralia mine, MOVE, or the Challenger. One of the National Performance Review's justifications for eliminating layers of federal middle management is to make interactions between top and lower organizational levels more direct, efficient, and accurate. Some evidence of this exists (Garnett 1997c), but the full record is still out. By-passing routine channels to get messages more

quickly and directly into the hands of those who need to know can aid upward communication but can also damage accountability and information dissemination if abused. Even though using predetermined codes about weather conditions and parts vulnerability to communicate within NASA and Morton Thiokol could not prevent all miscommunication before the Challenger liftoff, using predetermined codes, signals, language, and other means to make messages more distortion-resistant generally helps.

Important communication within public-sector organizations is increasingly lateral—among organizational peers in the same or different unit. Key functions of lateral communication include task coordination, information sharing, multidisciplinary problem solving, and mutual emotional support. Research summarized in Garnett (1992a) shows that openness, trust, and satisfaction over the level of emotional support relates to the quality of interpersonal communication, especially lateral communication. Because they are shared among status equals, lateral messages tend to be more honest and accurate than are messages up or down the hierarchy. Lateral communication also typically follows *subformal* networks (carrying informal, unofficial messages through formal channels) that tend to be more accurate and honest than *formal* networks that carry official messages through formal channels (Downs 1967). Unlike subformal communication networks used by public servants in their official capacity but not for the official record, *personal* communication networks carry unofficial messages by public servants acting apart from their official capacity. Expressions of personal interest and emotional support are examples of personal communication, as are gossip and rumors. Because rumors are typically conveyed unofficially and laterally, they often are surprisingly accurate. Whether rumors are accurate or misleading, coping with rumors and grapevines is an essential skill for public administrators (Garnett 1992b).

As crucial as it is to organizational health and performance, lateral communication has historically been undervalued, receiving less scholarly attention than have upward, and particularly downward, communication (Garnett 1997b). Research by Walton (1962) showed that interaction among navy engineers and scientists was penalized by superiors who were suspicious of subordinates communicating with each other and who wanted communication to come through them. The increasing need to use multidisciplinary teams to solve increasingly complex public-sector problems and to compensate for reduced staffing heightens the importance of lateral communication. In light of smaller, more professionalized workforces, reduced bureaucratic layering, enhanced communication technologies, heightened attention to assessing performance, and other changes, there are indications of greater attention to upward communication and to downward communication about mission and performance feedback (Garnett 1997c).

Boundary Spanners and External Audiences: The Interorganizational Communication Process

Just when this planet evolved from being primarily dominated by *organizational* dynamics to one characterized by *interorganizational* dynamics is not clear. What *is* clear is that we now live in a world where virtually every policy decision, virtually every business or government transaction, and even virtually every decision about personal lifestyle involves more than one organization or has implications for multiple organizations. Massive public-private partnerships such as space missions like Challenger and emergency responses like MOVE and Waco, or even international, multiorganizational efforts like the Gulf War or intervention in Bosnia, most visibly demonstrate the need for orchestrated cooperation among multiple organizations. But communication between or among public-service providers, regulators, customers, interest groups, or others also characterizes dynamics in more microlevel situations as well. Communication gaps among various parts of

Boston's criminal justice system contributed to Kristen Lardner's murder, for example.

Three factors contribute to the rise of the interorganizational dimension in public management: (1) Economic interdependence, both globally and locally, stimulates interaction among organizations. (2) Issue or policy networks through which political policy decisions are made have tended to become larger and more diverse (see Heclo, in chapter 14 of this volume). The shift from primarily direct government provision of public services to provision by more complex, more diverse networks of public, private, and nonprofit organizations has profound implications for communication as well as governance (Osborne and Gaebler 1992). Since this trend is so powerful and will likely continue, the term *public sector* or *public interest,* rather than *government service,* is used to refer to these diverse networks of service providers. (3) Greater access to information/communication technology and the liberalizing of many political economic, and service institutions have enabled looser coupling among traditional hierarchies and recoupling in various ways, many of them interorganizational.

Because of the enhanced importance of external environments and relationships with stakeholder organizations in the environment that supply resources, purchase services, or monitor behavior, boundary spanning and external communication take on added significance. Boundary spanners are those public executives, communication professionals, or even operating-level employees who systematically or sporadically communicate with their counterparts or with other actors in the external environment and share information and observations both ways. Some boundary spanners, such as community-relations specialists or legislative liaisons, have this assigned role. Others take this on because they recognize its importance. This explains why military base commanders, hospital executives, and city managers, among others, typically maintain active civic and social ties with their communities. Boundary spanning can be informal, relying on the greater accuracy of subformal and lateral communication, or it can be highly formal and systematized, such as with environmental scanning (Garnett 1992a; Harris 1997), issue management (Harris 1997), or regular opinion sampling of stakeholders (Garnett 1992a). Organizations with turbulent environments need effective boundary spanning to learn and adapt.

Interorganizational communication has yet to be explored as much as other facets of public-sector communication, but some salient concepts have emerged (O'Toole 1997). Various interorganizational structures exist, each influencing communication patterns. With a *hierarchical* structure, one agency has authority over others, and channels typically run from that agency to subordinate agencies. The National Institutes of Health reporting to the Office of Secretary of Health and Human Services portrays this structure. A variation of this is the *lead agency* pattern, with a number of agencies reporting to the lead agency for a particular project or assignment. NASA played this role for the Challenger mission. Another variant is the *wheel*, pattern with communication typically flowing to and from one central organization. By having a central clearinghouse for information, coordination can often be achieved without formal authority. In the broken channel structure, "direct links exist among some agencies, but no agency is linked directly to all others with control over the others (Garnett, 1992a. 162).

Public administrators who discover they need to communicate externally within a broken channel pattern need to make extra effort to identify and compensate for the gaps that exist. Understanding the particular dynamics of the other interorganizational patterns is also helpful. For example, O'Toole (1997 p. 64) has observed that "those [organizations] located most centrally in the structure of interdependence also sit at the nexus of more interaction and communication links. A unit's location within an organizational structure can thus determine information flows and information can be a source of power." In general, communicating with people in a different organization from our own requires greater planning and effort. Communication preferences of the intended audience, the organizational culture they work in, the management system and routines into which your message will enter, and other factors are likely to be less familiar than for internal interaction and will require more analysis and planning (Garnett 1992a).

Crucial Issues in Public Sector Communication

Understanding public-sector communication involves more than knowing the players and processes. A number of issues overlap or even transcend players and processes. Addressing all salient issues in an overview chapter like this one is impossible. However, we can address several of the most crucial communication issues facing public administrators at the dawn of the twenty-first century.

Gaining and Maintaining Credibility with Citizens: Conventional Government Communication Is Likely to Fail!

In another work (Garnett 1997a), I pose *The Credibility Conundrum* that: *"at a time when government communication most needs credibility to help restore public confidence, it has the least"*. According to the National Commission on Civic Renewal (1998 29), 77 percent of Americans in 1964 trusted their national government to do the right thing usually or most of the time, but only 37 percent held that opinion in 1994. In 1999, immediately after the United States Senate acquitted President Clinton of charges of perjury and obstruction of justice, public trust in government had been further damaged in the United States. Don Eberly, Director of the Civil Society Project that monitors and promotes citizen participation in governance assessed that "this scandal will rank with Vietnam and Watergate as a source of lasting scars. . . . It will strengthen the cancers that are already rampant in our body politic. Trust in our national institutions has almost evaporated" (Polman 1999, A1). Thus, at a time when government credibility is most needed to break the cycle of distrust, its lack becomes a barrier to improving trust. Campaigns to restore public confidence through media blitzes face difficulties, because media institutions themselves face a credibility crisis and because many citizens have become skeptical of government public relations. The *Propaganda Paradox* (Garnett 1997a, 8) holds that *"the more zealous government's efforts to persuade citizens, the less they are persuaded."* Related to the *Credibility Conundrum,* this paradox reflects historic skepticism in many nations that governments are communicating honestly and openly (Heise 1985; Garnett 1992a; Carnevale 1995). Whether they regard government communication as propaganda, public relations, or "spin doctoring," citizens have become conditioned to expect the "spin" from their governments and to consciously or subconsciously discount these messages through counterbias (Downs 1967; Garnett 1992a).

Another reason for what Heise (1985) calls "the confidence gap" between government and the governed arises because governments have traditionally employed communication practices that have been either unilateral or, if bilateral, more oriented to government's sending messages than to receiving them. Historically, government communication in the United States (and in other developed and developing nations) tends to fit three of Grunig and Hunt's (1984) stages of public relations. The first stage, the press agentry/publicity model, was practiced to promote early celebrities such as Andrew Jackson, Buffalo Bill, P.T. Barnum, and the like. This model is characterized by unabashed, one-sided promotion of a person, product, or cause and can still be found in electoral campaigns and promotions of star athletes and entertainers. At the turn of the 20th century, according to Grunig and Hunt (1984) and Grunig and Grunig (1992, 288) ". . . a second model of public relations, the public information model, developed as a reaction to

attacks on large corporations and government agencies by muckraking journalists. Leaders of these organizations realized they needed more than the propaganda of press agents to counter the attacks on them in the media. Instead, they hired their own journalists as public relations practitioners to write 'press handouts' explaining their actions. Although practitioners of the public information model generally chose to write only good things about their organizations, the information they did report generally was truthful and accurate."

Both the press-agentry and public information models constitute basically one-way sending to publics, primarily through the news media. Behavioral and social science knowledge that exploded during and after World War I enabled the use of what Grunig and Grunig (1992) typed the two-way asymmetrical model. In this model, information was sought as well as sent to external publics, but the emphasis was clearly on getting publics to accept government's or other sender's position by using scientific theories that enabled persuasion, propaganda, and the "engineering of consent" (Grunig and Grunig 1992, 288). This model, what Garnett (1997a) calls the public affairs model, is more proactive in outreach but still treats publics more as audiences to be enlightened and convinced than partners to be involved. This model too has widespread use in governments worldwide.

According to a growing body of scholarship, these traditional models of public relations that have relied on sending messages and manipulating consent have generally been unsuccessful in both promoting the organizational agenda and in promoting a broader sense of the public interest (Grunig 1997). Such research includes that on the U.S. Nuclear Regulatory Commission (Childers 1989), higher education (Kelly 1989), various government organizations (Heise 1985; Garnett 1992a), and a wide range of business, nonprofit, and government organizations (Grunig and Grunig 1992; Grunig 1997). The general sense of such research is that basically one-way "tell and sell" approaches fail to improve the image of those organizations that use them either in terms of media coverage or direct stakeholder perception. Thus these approaches tend to fail in achieving the very purpose for which they were designed: influencing public opinion, not to mention achieving more fundamental aims of improving public-sector performance.

Four reasons exist for the general failure of these basically unilateral communication approaches: First, the track record of most governments, (and businesses) for generally communicating messages favorable to them and playing down or ignoring unfavorable messages has conditioned citizens to reject or discount what they regard as the same old propaganda (Heise 1985).

Second, Government's publics, usually without thinking about it, reflect a general finding of communication research that shows people, especially more educated people, tend to reject messages they perceive to be extreme or implausible (Zimbardo, Ebbeson, and Maslach 1977; Garnett 1989). People therefore tend to be suspicious of one-sided arguments or claims they think are beyond the realm of plausibility. "When government communications convey the message that 'no problem exists' or 'everything is under control,' such skewed messages tend to trigger cynicism and counterbias" (Garnett 1997a, 8). Governments serious about improving their public image concentrate on improving their performance, product, and responsiveness, not on preoccupation with spin-doctoring their image. Well-regarded governments recognize the difference between marketing and promotion. *Promotion* concentrates on getting people to like the existing product. *Marketing* attempts to discover what product people want, what features it should have, and how to get people to use that product. Without improving product and performance the best-conceived promotions have a "tough sell."

Third, often lacking true reciprocity in communicating with their governments to voice their preferences or to raise questions, many citizens have taken the most cautious course or the only course open to them—disbelieving the government's mes-

sage or discounting it. And fourth, in an era of "-call-in" or "talk-back" radio, interactive television, and interactive computer communication, where citizens are accustomed to taking an active role, many resent the passive role relegated to them by basically one-way communication from government and other public-sector organizations that maintain a press agentry or public information model. Despite the demonstrated lack of effectiveness of the public information and press agentry models, they are the most numerous public relations models applied in government (Grunig 1997).

If these predominantly one-way "tell and sell" approaches to communicating tend to fail, particularly in the long run, what does work? Part of the answer comes from research on the effectiveness of the various communication models and part from examples of new approaches for facilitating involvement. "The fourth model, the 'two-way symmetrical,' describes a model of public relations that is based on research and that uses communication to manage conflict and improve understanding with strategic publics. Because the two-way symmetrical model bases public relations on negotiation and compromise, it does not force the organization to choose whether it is right on particular issues. Rather, two-way symmetrical public relations allows the question of what is right to be settled by negotiation, since nearly every side to a conflict—such as nuclear power, abortion, or gun control—believes its position to be right" (Grunig 1997, 264). "The IABC [International Association of Business Communicators] research provided strong evidence that excellent public relations departments use the two-way symmetrical model and that as a result they more often meet the objectives of their communication and make the organization more effective" (Grunig 1997, 265). The IABC research program that studied a number of government as well as business organizations found that in actuality effective public relations departments use both the two-way symmetrical (what I call the communication model) and the two-way asymmetrical (public affairs) model to negotiate with stakeholders or to persuade them, as appropriate.

One example of the two-way symmetrical communication model at work involves the highly controversial issue of cleaning up nuclear waste. Fernald, Ohio, near Cincinnati, is the site of a former nuclear weapons uranium refinery now operated by the U.S. Department of Energy. In an effort to improve public participation in making decisions about nuclear cleanup at environmental Superfund sites like Fernald, the Department of Energy created advisory boards for each major nuclear waste site. These boards were comprised of public officials, environmentalists, neighbors of the nuclear site, local activists, health professionals, businesspeople, academics, labor representatives, and as non voting members, representatives of DOE and federal and state environmental protection agencies. Basic options for these advisory boards were to reject any local disposal of nuclear waste (not-in-my-backyard [NIMBY] response), "accepting its political, technical and financial costs; it could accept on-site disposal of all contaminated soil, and lose the use of some land while incurring some local political fallout; or it could find an acceptable middle ground, avoiding or minimizing the worst drawbacks to either extreme" (Applegate and Sarno 1996, 1).

The last course of action was pursued and involved extensive two-way give-and-take negotiation among those represented. A game simulation was created to help participants, both experts and novices, see the trade-offs involved in various removal or cleanup alternatives (Applegate and Sarno 1997). This facilitated communication and decision making. The consensus reached provided for cleanup in less than half the time originally projected and at a savings of over $2 billion.

The chief lessons here are that instead of ignoring the problem and complaints about it or relying on persuading citizens that no problem existed or that they could learn to live with it, the government actively involved citizens in a mutual process of communicating and problem solving. This involved more risk in some ways, because the government had to be willing to also be persuaded by the arguments of others, making the necessary adjustments in policy or practice. But it was a more productive and more ethical process, because it avoided unilaterally trying to pass off ideological or technical positions onto citizens. The government in this case started with the assumption that the public had a right to know and to be heard. This attitude was reflected in the wide range of communication mechanisms established, including regular public meetings, educational programs, direct contacts with key stakeholders, a liaison program, and an extensive public reading room, among others (Applegate and Sarno 1997). This genuine spirit of reciprocity and partnership and the extra communication effort involved has resulted in improved performance (quicker cleanup at lower cost) and a deeper sense of mutual trust and credibility.

This approach to communicating and problem solving is also practiced in many other contexts. "In Santa Monica, California, the Public Electronic Network, . . . a pioneering community network set up by the city, has allowed city residents from all walks of life to share ideas, debate issues, and seek common solutions to local problems. In an effort to address Santa Monica's growing problems with homelessness, homeowners and homeless people who logged on from public terminals joined with city council members and other city staff in an electronic discussion that led directly to the creation of a new program that provided public services that the homeless needed and that homeowners could support (*Communication as Engagement,* prologue). Such efforts at two-way communication that attempt to negotiate meaning rather than solely transmit it will become more common in the next century if public administrators and communication professionals can rise to the challenge of changing their perspective and practice. Another example of the government recognizing that the receiving, listening role is at least as important as the sending role is the U.S. Internal Revenue Service's use of in-person and electronic forums to get feedback from taxpayers. This parallels efforts made by many governments and other public service organizations at all levels to tap citizen/customer feedback using multiple channels, a practice discussed in the next section.

Linking Diverse Audiences Using Diverse Media: Making the Most of Cyberspace and the Coffee Klatch

We tend to think of communication/information technologies as high-tech (computer communication, satellite television, remote-sensing systems, and the like). Technology, broadly defined as a means to achieving an end, can also be low-tech (for example, drama, flyer distribution, and neighborhood coffee klatches). The challenges for public administrators include being knowledgeable about the communication technologies range (both high-tech and low-tech) currently available, as well as about emerging technologies. Knowing the current range of communication technologies helps administrators and professional communicators use appropriate media to reach particular target audiences. Public officials in Los Angeles were able to address a number of social and legal issues relevant to their Spanish-speaking citizens by incorporating these issues into plots for a popular soap opera, "Cancion de la Raza." Public administrators also need to know what technologies are emerging or are likely to emerge, so that they don't fall behind the technology curve. Some populations in India, for example, have no reliable telephone service but can be reached by satellite television. This is only one example of communication technologies leap-frogging a generation or more.

In making decisions about which technologies to utilize, the inherent strengths and weaknesses of various media need to be considered along with the compensating advantages of using multiple media (Garnett 1996). Oral messages typically are more vulnerable to misinterpretation than are written messages. Renovations of the U.S. Air Traffic Control System scheduled for 2000 include installing the capability for using e-mail to communicate between airport control towers and airplane cockpits. The Federal Aviation Administration expects that adding the capability to report or verify flight instructions in writing to replace or supplement current voice communication will reduce misinterpretations that cause airplane accidents. In the Centralia mine case, the overreliance on written reports and letters (a slower, less dramatic medium) lowered the chances of miners and mine inspectors to vividly convey mine dangers. Likewise, in chapter 12, Tom Mills's case "County Prison Overtime," Donald Dexter's insistence on sending memos to the Director of Corrections instead of talking directly with him left a permanent, sharable record that escalated this issue and made it harder to resolve. A multiple-media strategy involving radio, newspapers, rallies, and other media might have conveyed the miners' message more vividly and forcefully, while a less formal, more negotiable message would have better served Finance Director Dexter.

Reaching hard-to-reach audiences is another issue that deserves—and is getting more—attention. For the 2000 census, the U.S. Bureau of the Census is making efforts on an unprecedented scale to identify and reach stakeholder groups and audiences that are historically underrepresented in census counts (such as urban Hispanic Americans) and other hard-to-reach groups more recently identified (such as survivalist communes). Bureau communication specialists and consultants have been traveling to target areas, finding group members knowledgeable about the communication behaviors and preferences of that group, and obtaining and following their advice about how best to reach that audience. This constitutes one of the largest efforts at targeted, communication strategic planning (Garnett 1992a) ever practiced by the United States Government.

Radio is another medium that governments, public interest groups, and others have used effectively to air emergency warnings and information and to engage citizens in dialogue through call-in interactive radio and through regular broadcasts from officials. Savvy public officials know which radio stations Spanish-speaking, Hebrew-speaking, sports-minded, or other kinds of groups would likely listen to in their geographic area and can utilize these stations to listen to and talk to such target audiences. Today, however, through the technology of Internet radio, the number and range of stations that citizens can tune in to are multiplying rapidly. Most standard computers today can be used to tune in to stations in all parts of the United States, Canada, Europe, Asia, Australia, and other continents, typically for free at this stage (Ahrens 1999). This allows Hebrew-speaking stakeholder groups in Los Angeles, for example, to access radio programs in New York or even Jerusalem, thus diversifying the news, cultural programming, and other programming they get. It has also become cheaper and easier for citizens to start their own station by means of computer, further multiplying and diversifying the messages and agendas carried by radio. Public-sector officials will need to become aware of changing radio-use patterns of key stakeholder groups in their regions and communicate accordingly.

Access constitutes another critical issue for determining appropriate communication technologies. The widespread availability of public information on government World Wide Web sites has increased access for numerous organizations and individuals, making it easier, cheaper, and faster to acquire information or to do business with government. Despite the creation of Internet labs in many public libraries and public schools, access to this communications technology is limited by factors such as geography, income, and educational level. Public librarians in Muncie, Indiana thought that people in the library's service area needed the access that their bookmobiles provided, but a higher-tech version. They therefore added seven computer terminals and converted a bookmobile into a CyberMobile that travels throughout their district, including rural areas, so that citizens had access and instruction for using the Internet. Efforts such as these hardly guarantee access to communication technologies, but they help. Utilizing a number of various communication technologies—low-tech as well as high-tech—for both sending and receiving increases the likelihood of access with various publics.

When utilizing communication technologies, public administrators also need to recognize the ways that people obtain and process information. Because of their potential for richness and interest, stories have always been an integral means to transmit values and heritage in a society. Thinking perhaps that stories were more trivial and subjective than survey results or other forms of information, governments and other public-sector actors have only rarely used the potential of stories to convey or receive messages on many levels. Because stories have the capability of capturing the emotional as well as the informational level, stories typically are often superior in terms of message impact, retention, and motivating people. Preachers recognize this when they include stories in sermons. Parents tell children about their own childhood in order to teach lessons but also to establish emotional bonds. "The potential power of stories as communication forms will increasingly be rediscovered. Sagas, legends, proverbs, myths, folklore, and other types of the story form have influenced values and behavior regarding government and administration. The influence of stories and folklore can be positive, as with attempts to help families understand policy changes affecting them in rural areas (Thompson 1982), or invidious, as with Nazi uses of legend to stir nationalism and feelings of racial superiority (Lixfeld 1994)" (Garnett 1997c, 756).

Part of the impact of the excellence movement (Peters and Waterman 1982) and reinvention movement (Osborne and Gaebler 1992) is that their lessons of best practice are conveyed by stories about actual companies, government organizations, and people—and that they are told in a more compelling way than dry case accounts. Reports of the National Performance Review are full of stories of reinvention successes, often told by actual managers or stakeholders themselves, and increasingly by means of the more visual media of video or CD Rom. In the rush toward high-tech, stories, drama, poetry, humor, and other creative forms can provide the "high-touch" that is equally necessary (Holzer 1997; Lundberg 1997).

The power of thinking and communicating spatially is also becoming better understood. Every Thursday morning Philadelphia Police Chief John Timony hosts a meeting of top brass and district commanders. The first part of the meeting consists of using Geographic Information Systems crime-mapping to view the types of crime that have occurred by location. Patterns of crime can then be detected that would go unnoticed with a less visual analysis. District commanders are then grilled about how their forces will respond to these crime patterns. The power of crime mapping has been given substantial credit for reducing crime in Philadelphia and in New York City, where Chief Timony learned the technique. Creative use of the many technologies for communicating, including simulations and electronic networks described earlier, deserves greater attention among public administrators.

The Concept of Communication Ethics Is Not an Oxymoron

An earlier discussion (Garnett 1992a) maintained that ethical communication requires the qualities of *accuracy, usefulness, openness,* and *fairness.* Violations of communication ethics tend to damage individual or collective credibility and produce other destructive consequences. Disinformation (deliberate distortion) in relations between Iraq and the United States contributed to misunderstanding and ultimately to war. If information is deliberately or inadvertently inaccurate, negotiations or other relations become problematic, because the parties cannot depend on that information for basing their actions. *Usefulness* in communicating means avoiding bombarding stakeholders with messages they cannot use because of faulty content or inappropriate medium. It also means supplying stakeholders with information they need for acting responsibly, whether as citizens or as public servants. Case Study 2 in this text, "How Kristin Died," for example, involved too many instances of her friends or public servants failing, because of inertia or not wanting to become involved, to relate information that might have made a difference. Too often, actors in this tragedy lament, "If only I had known." A decided challenge in today's public service (with an increasing number and complexity of issues and more numerous and more diverse sets of stakeholders) is to provide sufficient useful information while avoiding overload. In a classic research study on administrative feedback between federal agency headquarters and field offices, Kaufman and Couzens (1973) discovered that employees rarely think they have too much information to do their jobs properly. Even

with the prodigious information technologies available today, we tend to err on the side of disseminating too little information. If public administrators fail to supply others with adequate information for acting competently, then ethically they share responsibility for performance failures.

Another quality of ethical communicating is *responsiveness.* Stakeholders have a right to know that their messages will be acted on responsibly and responsively. This means, among other things, making sure that those public servants who are complained about are not the primary or only ones to respond to complaints. In Case Study 1 in this book, "The Blast in Centralia No. 5," Local 52 was unable to effectively bypass the formal chain of command within the governor's office to get Governor Green's attention. Staff member Chapman short-circuited the miners' Save Our Lives letter by routing it to the Department of Mines and Minerals for reply even though that department's inaction was the chief object of the miners' complaints. This pattern of bureaucratic pigeon-holing is still common. Where feasible, more independent, neutral parties should also be involved in investigating complaints and responding to them. The widespread use of centrally staffed complaint hotlines; ombudsmen, public advocates, or system navigators; inspectors general and other mechanisms, often with response tracking and deadlines for responding, has helped to improve responsiveness in many jurisdictions.

• • •

A related ethical issue that deserves far more attention than could be devoted here is groupthink, "a mode of thinking that people engage in when they are deeply involved in a cohesive in-group, when the members' strivings for unanimity override their motivation to realistically appraise alternative courses of action" (Janis 1972, as cited in 't Hart and Kroon 1997, 104). The irony with groupthink is that the characteristics of good groups or teams—loyalty, camaraderie, homogeneity of purpose and training, strong unimpartial leadership, and group cohesion—can discourage independent thinking and promote groupthink to avoid conflict. External pressure to decide, whether real or perceived, also increases the tendency for group-think. The strong sense within NASA and Morton Thiokol that Challenger, as reflected in Case Study 4, "The Last Flight of Space Shuttle Challenger," had to be launched "this time" to avoid further economic and political costs of delay muted isolated cautions about weather hazards. Some experts might even suggest that because the Challenger episode involved multiple organizations and multiple teams, it is a less obvious example of "group-think," perhaps more of *"systemthink."* According to Nagel (in chapter 8 of this volume) and Vizzard (in Case Study 9 of this volume), failure to seek and factor in opposing views and insufficient objections to ill-conceived operational "plans" in the MOVE and Waco confrontations contributed to those situations getting out of control. To avoid groupthink and its dangers public executives and administrators need to learn to recognize its symptoms and correct them, or better yet, build mechanisms for accountability, impartial leadership, links to sound information, vigilance over process, heterogeneity of membership, and other factors that minimize groupthink. Groupthink does not always result in policy fiascoes, and policy fiascoes can occur for other reasons ('t Hart and Kroon 1997), but certainly groupthink should be discouraged in most cases. To knowingly foster conditions that tend to produce faulty decision making would be irresponsible and unethical.

Raising the Salience of Communication in Public Administration

For reasons discussed here and elsewhere (Garnett 1997a, b), public administration practitioners and scholars alike have generally failed to recognize the centrality of communication in their profession and to give communication attention. Administrative communication that was mostly "tell and sell" was often manipulative and rarely linked to organizational performance and, thus, did not deserve much attention or respect. In the realm of public administration scholarship, administrative communication, after being more valued in

the heyday of the field (Garnett 1997b), has too often been perceived as "soft" or "too applied." Ironically, these are labels the field of public administration itself has fought to overcome. For communication to reclaim its rightful place at the core of public administration, its rigor, complexity, salience, diversity, richness, and, above all, centrality, will need to be rediscovered.

References

Ahrens, F. 1999. The Radio Waves of the Future: Internet Stations Give Listeners a New Way to Tune In. *Washington Post* online edition, 21 January.

Applegate, J. S., and D. J. Sarno. 1996. "Coping with Complex Facts and Multiple Parties in Public Disputes." *Consensus: Helping Public Officials Resolve Stubborn Policy Disputes* 21 (July): MIT-Harvard Public Disputes Program.

———. 1997. "FUTURESITE: An Environmental Remediation Game-Simulation." *Simulation & Gaming* 28, (1):13–27.

Barnard, C. I. 1938. *The Functions of the Executive.* Cambridge, Mass: Harvard University Press.

Broom, G. M., and D. M. Dozier. 1983. "An Overview: Evaluation Research in Public Relations." *Public Relations Quarterly* 28 (3): 5–8.

Carnevale, D. G. 1995. *Trustworthy Government: Leadership and Management Strategies for Building Trust and High Performance.* San Francisco: Jossey-Bass.

Childers, L. 1989. "Credibility of Public Relations at the NRC." Pp. 97–114 in Public Relations Research *Annual,* ed. J. E. Grunig, and L. A. Grunig. Vol. 1.

Downs, A. 1967. *Inside Bureaucracy.* Boston: Little, Brown.

Foltz, R. G. 1973. *Management by Communication.* Philadelphia: Thomas Nelson and Sons.

Garnett, J. L. 1989. "Effective Communication." In *Handbook of Public Administration,* ed. J. L. Perry. 554-558 San Francisco: Jossey-Bass.

———. 1992a. *Communicating for Results in Government: A Strategic Approach for Public Managers.* San Francisco: Jossey-Bass.

————. 1992b. "Coping with Rumors and Grapevines: Practical Lessons for Public Personnel Administration." *Review of Public Personnel Administration* 12 (3): 42–49.

————. 1996. "Communicating Effectively." In *Handbook of Public Administration,* 2d ed., ed. J. L. Perry. 665-681 San Francisco: Jossey-Bass.

————. 1997a. "Administrative Communication: Domain, Threats, and Legitimacy." In *Handbook of Administrative Communication,* ed. J. L. Garnett, and A. Kouzmin. 1-20 New York: Marcel Dekker.

————. 1997b. "Trends and Gaps in the Treatment of Communication in Organization and Management Theory." In *Handbook of Administrative Communication,* ed. J. L. Garnett, and A. Kouzmin. 21-60 New York: Marcel Dekker.

————. 1997c. "Epilog: Directions and Agendas for Administrative Communication." In *Handbook of Administrative Communication,* ed. J. L. Garnett, and A. Kouzmin. 747-770 New York: Marcel Dekker.

Grunig, J. E. 1997. "Public Relations Management in Business and Government." In *Handbook of Administrative Communication,* ed. J. L. Garnett, and A. Kouzmin. 241-283 New York: Marcel Dekker.

Grunig, J. E., and L. A. Grunig. 1992. "Models of Public Relations and Communication." In *Excellence in Public Relations and Communication Management,* ed. J. E. Grunig. Hillsdale, IL: Lawrence Erlbaum Associates.

Grunig, J. E., and T. Hunt. 1984. *Managing Public Relations.* New York: Holt, Rinehart & Winston.

Harris, Richard. 1997. "Boundary Spanners, Legitimacy, and Corporate Communications." In *Handbook of Administrative Communication,* ed. Garnett, J. L. and Kouzmin, A. 309-328 New York: Marcel Dekker.

't Hart, Paul, and Marceline Kroon. 1997. "Groupthink in Government: Pathologies of Small-Group Decision Making." In Garnett, J. L. and Kouzmin, A. (eds.), *Handbook of Administrative Communication.* 101-139 New York: Marcel Dekker.

Heise, A. 1985. "Toward Closing the Confidence Gap: An Alternative Approach to Communication Between Public and Government." *Public Administration Quarterly* (Summer): 196–217.

Holzer, M. 1997. "Communicating Through Forms." In *Handbook of Administrative Communication,* ed. J. L. Garnett, and A. Kouzmin. 203-225 New York: Marcel Dekker

Katz, D., and R. L. Kahn. 1966. *The Social Psychology of Organizations.* New York: John Wiley & Sons.

Kaufman, H., with M. Couzens. 1973. *Administrative Feedback: Monitoring Subordinates Behavior.* Washington, D.C.: The Brookings Institution.

Kelly, K. S. 1989. Shifting the Public Relations Paradigm: A Theory of Donor Relations Developed Through a Critical Analysis of Fund Raising and its Effect on Organizational Autonomy. Ph.D. diss., University of Maryland, College Park.

Lorch, R. S. 1978. *Public Administration.* St. Paul: West.

Lundberg, E. 1997. "Communicating Through Humor in the Workplace: Looking for Laughs in All the Work Places." In *Handbook of Administrative Communication,* ed. Garnett, J. L., and A. Kouzmin. 227-240 New York: Marcel Dekker.

National Commission on Civic Renewal. 1998. *A Nation of Spectators: How Civic Disengagement Weakens America and What We Can Do About It.* College Park, Md.: The National Commission on Civic Renewal.

Osborne, D., and T. Gøebler. 1992. *Reinventing Government: How the Entrepreneurial Spirit is Transforming the Public Sector from Schoolhouse to Statehouse, City Hall to the Pentagon.* Reading, Mass.: Addison-Wesley.

O'Toole, L. 1997. "Interorganizational Communication: Opportunities and Challenges for Public Administration." In *Handbook of Administrative Communication,* ed. Garnett, J. L., and A. Kouzmin. New York: Marcel Dekker.

Peters, T., and A. Waterman. 1982. *In Search of Excellence.* New York: Warner Books.

Polman, D. 1999. Echoes of Scandal May Go Past 2000. *The Philadelphia Inquirer,* 14 February.

Tullock, G. 1965. *The Politics of Bureaucracy,* Washington, D.C.: Public Affairs Press.

Walton, E. 1962. A Magnetic Theory of Organizational Communication. China Lake, California. U.S. Naval Ordnance Test Station.

Zimbardo, P. G., E. B., Ebbesen, and C. Maslach. 1977. *Influencing Attitudes and Changing Behavior.* Reading, Mass.: Addison-Wesley.

Acknowledgment

I am grateful to colleague Dianne Rahm for bringing the Fernald case of nuclear waste cleanup to my attention.

☐ CASE STUDY 9

Introduction

As Dr. Garnett's essay stresses, for public administrators today, internal and external communications are central to influencing their work, both in terms of helping to set the agenda for what they do and then decisively shaping public opinion about how well or poorly they perform their roles. External media such as radio, TV and newspaper coverage, its volume and content, as well as various "internal players," help to create the issues public agencies address, how they perform or fail to perform their tasks, and then largely determine public perceptions of what they accomplish. In our modern communications-drenched environment, communications, its success or failure, may well be the most important factor shaping public program today.

Few instances of communications influence on public officials in recent years were more pronounced than what happened in the federal assault on the Branch Davidian compound. On February 28, 1993, near Waco, Texas, four agents from the Treasury Department's Bureau of Alcohol, Tobacco, and Firearms (ATF) were killed, and more than twenty other agents were wounded when David Koresh and members of his religious cult, the Branch Davidian, ambushed a force of seventy-six ATF agents. The agents were attempting to execute a search and issue arrest warrants at the Branch Davidian compound. Tipped off that the agents were coming, Koresh and more than one hundred followers waited inside the compound and opened fire using assault weapons even before the agents reached the door. The gunfire continued until the Davidians agreed to a cease-fire, but the ensuing standoff lasted fifty-one days, ending on April 19, when the entire compound erupted in a fire that had been set by cult members after the Federal Bureau of Investigation (FBI) used tear gas to force the occupants to leave. The fire destroyed the compound, and more than seventy residents died, many from gunshot wounds apparently inflicted by their fellow cult members.

The Branch Davidian movement was started by a number of Seventh Day Adventists, who believed strongly in the biblical prophecies of the book of Revelation. David Koresh, then named Vernon Wayne Howell, took over the leadership of the cult in 1987. The members became extremely devoted to Koresh, and many believed that he was "The Lamb of God." ATF involvement with the cult began in June, 1992, when its Special Agent Davy Aguilera started an investigation of the Davidians on suspicion of their purchasing illegal firearms.

Over the course of events that led to ATF's raid on the cult, in retrospect, the agency made several mistakes, such as in the planning for the assault, in their flawed decision-making process that approved this raid and the ineffective oversight exhibited by Treasury officials. However, communications was a central problem throughout this ATF operation.

The following case, "Waco," by William J. Vizzard, a former career ATF official and now professor of Criminal Justice at California State University, Sacramento, thoughtfully explores ATF's raid on the Branch Dividian compound. Note that throughout all phases of ATF's planning, decision making, and execution, communications played the central role in shaping what happened at Waco and thus relates directly to Dr. Garnett's foregoing thesis.

As you read this piece, look specifically at how communications decisively influenced events:

> In what various ways did the communication process specifically shape the development of ATF's strategy at Waco?

> ATF assumed that a show of force by distinctively uniformed agents would communicate authority and legitimacy. How did the *perception* of that communication by the Davidians and critics like Henry Hyde differ from the *intended* communication?

> ATF agents communicated information regarding a variety of perceived violations of law to the U.S. Attorney and others. What did they intend to communicate with this information, and how was it received by critics and members of the congressional committee?

> ATF agents planning the raid failed to discuss options for response to massive armed resistance with their headquarters. What did this lack of communication communicate?

> How did the style of management exercised by the ATF Associate Director, Dan Hartnett, influence communications?

> Was communication influenced by receivers' selection of what they wanted to hear? Give examples.

> How did the nature of the events surrounding the raid itself distort communications?

> Whenever the meaning of a communication was ambiguous—for example, when the Davidians knew that the ATF agents were coming—how did preconceived assumptions influence their interpretation?

> Where did the media influence this case? Cite specific examples.

Waco

WILLIAM J. VIZZARD

On the morning of February 28, 1993, near Waco, Texas, ATF agents attempted to serve a search warrant on Mount Carmel, a compound housing the religious sect commonly referred to as Branch Davidians, and an arrest warrant on the sect's leader, Vernon Wayne Howell. The attempt resulted in a gun battle in which four agents and six Davidians died and twenty-eight agents and four Davidians, including leader David Koresh, received injuries. Forced to withdraw and leave the compound in the hands of the Davidians, ATF surrendered primary control of the scene to the FBI within days and withdrew to a supporting role. The subsequent fifty-one-day standoff ended on April 19, 1993, when agents of the Federal Bureau of Investigation's Hostage Rescue Team injected tear gas into the compound and the occupants responded by initiating multiple fires. The fires and self-inflicted gunshot wounds resulted in the death of over seventy occupants, including a number of children. Both the Departments of Justice and the Treasury conducted extensive investigations, as did the Texas Rangers, who were requested to conduct the investigation of the shootings by the United States Attorney's Office to avoid a conflict of interest. A subsequent trial in United States District Court resulted in the conviction of several Davidian survivors on weapons and manslaughter charges but acquittal on murder and murder conspiracy charges.

To date, three congressional hearings have been conducted on the raid and siege. The most extensive of these, by a joint House of Representatives subcommittee, extended over nine days during the summer of 1995. These later hearings were believed to have resulted, at least partially, from pressure from the NRA and others opposed to ATF and gun laws. The Treasury report determined that there had been significant errors in the command and control of the

ATF raid and that some managers had attempted to distort the fact that an undercover agent had warned that secrecy had been compromised but that the raid commanders still had proceeded with the raid. This was particularly critical because the tactics employed were dependent upon surprise. As a result, two ATF managers were dismissed, and the director, associate director of law enforcement, and deputy associate director of law enforcement all retired prematurely under pressure. The administration moved Secret Service Director John Magaw to the position of ATF director, which apparently served the dual purpose of placing a high-profile director in charge of a beleaguered ATF and removing from a sensitive post, with access to White House activity, a person closely associated with former president Bush.

Background

The community of Mount Carmel was originally established by Victor Houteff and a small group of followers who left the Seventh Day Adventist Church. Although the group remained isolated from much of the larger society and focused their attentions on preparing for the imminent second coming of Christ, it was neither militant nor armed. Upon Houteff's death, the group divided between followers of Houteff's widow, Florence, and those who accepted the leadership of another member, Ben Roden, who referred to his followers as The Branch. After Florence Houteff's 1959 prediction of the slaughter and resurrection of all the believers failed to materialize, many of her followers drifted away and Roden's faction predominated. After Roden's death in 1978, his widow, Lois, assumed leadership of the group.

In 1981, Vernon Wayne Howell, a twenty-two-year-old high school dropout and sometimes rock musician, came to live at Mount Carmel. Howell came to exercise substantial influence on Lois Roden and was engaging in a sexual relationship with the seventy-one-year-old Roden by 1982. A contest for control of the group developed between Howell and George Roden, Lois's son, and in 1984 Howell left Mount Carmel with a group of followers. Lois Roden died in 1986, and in 1987 Howell and a group of armed followers fought a gun battle with Roden for control of the Mount Carmel compound. Although Howell and the seven who accompanied him on the raid were charged with felony assault, Roden made a very poor victim and witness and the jury failed to reach a verdict on Howell and found the others not guilty. Howell and his followers obtained control of the property by paying back taxes, and Roden was later placed in a mental institution.

For nine years, Howell, now known as David Koresh, functioned as the unquestioned spiritual leader and absolute potentate of the community at Mount Carmel, as well as among followers elsewhere. During this time, Howell-Koresh decreed celibacy for all the male residents and claimed all the female residents as his wives, in some cases engaging in sexual intercourse with girls as young as ten. Koresh also acquired numerous firearms in preparation for a prophesied coming conflagration and rejected the jurisdiction of secular government and law over his actions.

In May 1992 local authorities requested assistance from ATF in investigating the activities of Koresh and residents of the compound relating to the production of explosives and illegal firearms. The subsequent investigation established probable cause that members were making and possessing unregistered NFA firearms, specifically machine guns and hand grenades, in the compound. The investigation also revealed allegations of child abuse, child sexual molestation, and holding persons against their will, as well as indications that the Davidians might resist lawful authority by force.

ATF's investigation included the infiltration of an undercover agent into the compound and the establishment of an observation post that could watch the compound. Operating on the belief that they could overwhelm the Davidians with a show of force and the use of surprise, ATF developed a plan to serve search and arrest warrants on the compound. On February 28, 1993, a force of seventy-six ATF agents dressed in dark blue utility uniforms and protective vests, distinctively marked with large gold badges and the letters *ATF,* moved to the scene hidden in two large cattle trailers pulled by pickups. As the agents burst from the trailers and raced for the

front door and rear windows, they were met with automatic weapons fire and grenades. After an extended gunfight between the agents, who were pinned down in a hopeless position, and the occupants, a cease-fire was negotiated by telephone and the agents withdrew with their dead and wounded. Before the day ended, Treasury officials had decided to surrender control of the scene to the FBI to avoid any future allegations of bias by ATF and to capitalize on the resources of the HRT. The weeks and months following the Waco incident proved the most trying in ATF history. Every aspect of the operation proved controversial, and the initial ATF decision to make a dynamic entry and the FBI decision to use tear gas to attempt to precipitate a surrender proved the most controversial issues. To understand how and why Waco occurred requires that the events be viewed not through the benefit of hindsight but with an understanding of ATF history, culture, structure, and experience.

The Decision

Given both the physical risk to agents and the potential political risk to the organization, why did ATF proceed with the raid on Mount Carmel? The organization had historically displayed an aversion to risk consistent with its precarious political position. No bold new leaders had assumed control. The political environment had not undergone significant change. What then explains ATF's actions? Viewed in the context of organizational routines formed by structure, culture, environment, and task and as a series of interrelated but distinct decisions by individuals within ATF, the raid becomes understandable, though not essentially defensible. Although the personality and nature of key actors also played a critical role in the Waco decisions, the factors of structure, culture, environment, and task had influenced both the placement and outlook of these key actors.

The process began as a routine investigation after a referral of information and request for assistance made to the Austin ATF office by the McLenan County Sheriff's Department, regarding shipments of explosives components, inert grenade hulls, firearms parts, and large quantities of firearms to a location called the Mag Bag, a small building near the Davidian compound used by the Davidians. Subsequent investigation by Special Agent David Aguilera revealed that the Davidians were ordering numerous kits of replacement parts for M-16 machine guns. Represented as repair parts for legally registered machine guns, these kits have primarily been used to convert semi-automatic AR-15 rifles to fully automatic M-16 machine guns. The Davidians also had obtained explosive components and grenade hulls that could serve as components to manufacture grenades. Agents coupled the orders with statements from former members and reports of machine gun fire from the compound to establish the probable cause required to obtain a search warrant to examine the compound for machine guns, grenades, and evidence of their manufacture.

With some exceptions these constituted routine events for ATF agents. An information referral and request for assistance from a local law enforcement agency precipitated an investigation by ATF agents that revealed probable violations under ATF jurisdiction. In addition, the investigation revealed evidence of probable child abuse and sexual abuse of minors by David Koresh. The United States Attorney's Office concurred with the evaluation of the probable cause and the need to proceed with federal action. This satisfied the usual standard for further ATF action. The normal questions asked of an agent were: Is there evidence of a crime? Is the crime within ATF's jurisdiction? Do the actions justify prosecution? And does the United States attorney concur? ATF's standard for prosecution had long required more than just a violation of law to generate enforcement action. Even before the passage of the GCA, the official orders had recognized something called a "nonwillful violation." Cases that did not involve convicted felons, large-scale commercial violations, or other crimes were not to be pursued unless the violator had been previously warned and persisted. This standard applied only to firearms violations and not to alcohol violations. Although the official policy of not prosecuting isolated firearms violations ceased after 1968, it remained as an unofficial standard.

Much has been made by some critics, particularly in academia, of law enforcement's efforts to portray the Davidians as engaged in child molestation and abuse, when these were not the crimes charged in the warrants. ATF actions were rooted in years of experience and conditioning. Critics have repeatedly attacked the agency for not pursuing real criminals

and for using the gun laws to harass innocent citizens. Congressional investigations have repeatedly focused on this issue and United States attorneys have used other criminal activity as a key element for deciding which firearms violators to prosecute. Both the press and the public have displayed far more support for pursuit of firearms violations when the violator has been perceived as a criminal. ATF has interpreted these events as evidence that the importance of a firearms violation is largely dependent on the other criminal activities of the violator. Prosecution of firearms violations become important when directed at a person or persons whose activities are otherwise objectionable or dangerous. Thus illegal possession of a machine gun is of little consequence unless the possessor is a criminal or otherwise demonized. Likewise, illegal sales of firearms are of little consequence unless the purchasers are criminals or other violent persons. This constitutes a far different standard than the one applied to drug laws, but it is similar to the attitude toward gambling and liquor laws.

As a result of these experiences, ATF has focused as much on who violated the law as what law they violated. It has become both a formal and informal component of the investigative routine to consider this issue. Thus, the attention agents gave to information that Koresh molested young children, had been involved in a past violent confrontation, held people against their will, and talked of future violent confrontations was consistent with normal working routine that evolved from past experience. Virtually any police agency would have focused on the same information in evaluating the public safety aspects of the case. ATF agents did not see themselves as gun regulators, whose job was to stop Koresh from obtaining machine guns. They saw themselves as protectors of public safety, whose job was to investigate Koresh and bring to light all his crimes. The firearms jurisdiction was their legal justification for doing so. Federal agencies, particularly the FBI, have followed this same practice for years and been afforded widespread acclaim. The very nature of federal laws that utilized the marginal interstate nexus to allow federal jurisdiction over hate crimes, kidnapping, carjacking, gun possession, and bombing reveal that Congress has assumed this to be a legitimate federal role since the passage of the Mann Act at the beginning of the century.

The symbolic and political importance of

additional criminal acts was apparent in the 1995 House hearings on Waco. Widely assumed to be engineered by the Republicans to embarrass the administration and pacify the NRA, the hearings quickly changed course with the testimony of Kiri Jewel, who described her rape by Koresh when she was ten years of age. As it became apparent that parents routinely allowed their children to be sexually assaulted by Koresh, both Koresh and the parents lost status as victims. Soon Republicans found it necessary to begin every session with the caveat that they did not seek to support Koresh or attack law enforcement, and the political dynamic of the hearing changed direction.

Thus for ATF, the decision to investigate Koresh reflected the application of organizational routine in a classic sense. This investigation was exactly what the agency existed to do. Had the investigation revealed no criminal activity, other than firearms violations, and no evidence of a threat to public safety, the decision would have been far more problematical, and management might have forced the agents to back away from a law enforcement approach. The decision to use a search warrant flowed directly from the decision to pursue a criminal investigation. Prosecution required seizure of the evidence, in this case the converted firearms and grenades. In addition, the arrest of Koresh and service of a search warrant very likely would aid in revealing other crimes on the premises. Because firearms are difficult to hide or destroy quickly and are routinely retained for very long periods of time, search warrants have proven a very effective tool for obtaining evidence in firearms investigations. The tendency to retain firearms has resulted in ATF being able to obtain warrants and seize evidence using probable cause that would be considered stale in other types of cases.

Why the Raid?

The raid on the Branch Davidian compound by a large number of uniformed, armed agents shocked a significant portion of the public. Their reaction is typified by Representative Henry Hyde, Republican chairman of the House Judiciary Committee. During the 1995 hearings, Representative Hyde repeatedly expressed shock that seventy-five armed agents

wearing helmets and ski masks attacked the compound. Even after being repeatedly told that there were no ski masks and that the agents were uniformed for identification and wore helmets for protection, Hyde seemed unable to comprehend any possible justification for what he apparently viewed as an armed attack on a religious community. ATF agents and other law enforcement officers across the country found Hyde's response as bewildering as Hyde found the raid procedures.

For veterans of the wars on crime and drugs and for those who live in the neighborhoods where these wars are waged, the scene was unusual only in its scope. Similar scenes, in fact, appeared regularly on the local news in urban areas across the country. ATF had consistently received congressional and administration support for similar actions during the implementation of the ACES and the ACES II, both of which received extensive favorable coverage in the Washington media. What, then, prompted the strong reaction to ATF's tactics at Waco from individuals and organizations who had paid little heed to similar actions by ATF and numerous other agencies in the war on drugs? The differences in reaction apparently derived from three separate causes. For the NRA and its followers, the use of coercive force to enforce firearms laws lacked legitimacy because the firearms laws lacked legitimacy. In addition, criticism of the raid and increased fear of ATF served their political agenda. For a portion of the population who saw the raid as a conflict between the power of the secular state and unpopular religious views, the raid was an unacceptable repression of religion. Finally, civil libertarians, typified by the American Civil Liberties Union, and radical libertarians, such as militia members, objected to virtually all uses of coercive force by the government. Representative Hyde appears to represent this final view, which recoils when confronted with the unmasked use of force, except in narrowly construed circumstances of self-defense. U.S. culture has displayed a dichotomous pattern with regard to use of coercive force by government. In general, government authority and coercive means of enforcing it have been distrusted, yet this pattern has reversed when the subjects of the action are perceived as evil or alien.

The agents investigating the case invoked organizational routine and proceeded to obtain a search warrant. Their actions constituted standard practice given the existence of probable cause of a crime under their jurisdiction, related criminal activity, interest from the United States attorney, and the need for physical evidence to establish proof of a crime. Although the involvement of a religious sect distinguished this case from others, the investigation had followed familiar patterns that invoked familiar technology and routines. The next phase of the investigation also involved familiar technology and routines, but the magnitude of the operation exceeded anything ATF had previously undertaken. . . . The organizational failure began as a failure of management to comprehend the implications of this change in magnitude, thus management made only incremental adjustments to adapt.

The evolving nature of ATF's mission and task environment combined with promotion patterns to produce a top level of management with little or no applicable experience for overseeing the Waco operation. Aggravated by the common bureaucratic pattern of assigning authority based on position rather than experience, knowledge, or skill, this lack of managerial experience resulted in a severe lack of overall command and control. Conversely, the Special Response Team commanders, who were experienced supervisors with extensive experience in police and military tactical operations, enjoyed substantial credibility. The result was an operation in which the operational level was far more qualified than the management level. This was not unusual in ATF and normally would have had only limited implications. In this case, however, command and control capacity was necessary, particularly in assuring that intelligence was gathered, analyzed, dispersed, and utilized. The entire Department of the Treasury report is critical of command and control, with particular emphasis on poor intelligence support.

Functions such as intelligence, operational security, and overall command and control had not been well developed in ATF because normal ATF operations could not justify the expenditure of resources for training specialists. Therefore, managers had very little opportunity to develop command and control skills. These are essentially military concepts, although law enforcement, firefighting, and civil defense require command and control in circumstances such as riots and natural disasters. Maintenance of command and control capabilities requires an organization to either engage actual experience

or practice under realistic simulation utilizing all the organizational components. The military maintains these skills at substantial cost in training and simulation, but law enforcement historically does not. For instance, the Los Angeles Police Department's failure to respond effectively and rapidly to the 1993 riots reflected a failure in command and control. Law enforcement agencies commit virtually all their resources to routine daily operations. Budgets have not allowed for the overstaffing necessary to conduct large-scale tactical training operations or maintain reserve forces for emergencies. At the federal level, only the FBI maintains a full-time tactical team with full logistical support. Even that team, which represents less than 1 percent of the FBI's agent staffing, did not exist prior to the mid-1980s.

Many of the problems might still have been avoided if ATF managers had been innovative thinkers who recognized the potential risks, asked hypothetical questions, or invoked different paradigms. This was not the case. ATF law enforcement had cultivated managers and staff for their loyalty and dependability, not for their innovation and intellect. Associate Director Daniel Hartnett was well known throughout the agency as a person uncomfortable with change and dissent. He did not seek out alternate points of view nor cultivate hypothetical discussions. The operational plan for the raid, for instance, was not reviewed or critiqued by ATF's Headquarters Enforcement Staff. Although they were briefed by the Houston SAC and others regarding the investigation, the raid briefing was given to only Hartnett and Conroy. Higgins, who had come up through the regulatory side of ATF, had no expertise or background in tactical operations. This, no doubt, reinforced his tendency to delegate operations to those who, in his mind, had the expertise.

In spite of the fact that the operation appeared on the surface to be similar to past ATF operations, it was not. Excepting the Marion and CSA cases, this situation was not like anything ever faced by ATF. It was, in fact, more dangerous than any operation conducted by a law enforcement agency in the history of the United States. The level of danger was not fully evident to the Special Response Team (SRT) supervisors who planned the raid, utilizing intelligence information that was not properly collected, analyzed, or disseminated. The planners never accepted the worst-case scenario, that is, that the occupants would resist en masse, using firearms.

The Decision to Use Dynamic Entry

Critics of ATF and the Waco raid have repeatedly characterized it as some sort of poorly planned publicity stunt directed by ATF management for the purpose of enhancing the agency's image. This characterization reflects a misunderstanding of both ATF's structure and procedures. ATF's management has never successfully controlled the field activities of its law enforcement personnel. ATF's law enforcement component displays the combined traits of what James Q. Wilson calls craft and coping organizations. These organizations are characterized by very limited management control of operators. Although headquarters originated the concept for some projects, such as Project CUE and the ACES, individual agents always initiate the actual investigations. ATF management has attempted to capitalize on visible activity, as has the management of most agencies.

In the case of Waco, much of the criticism has focused on the actions of Sharon Wheeler, the public information officer for the Dallas Division. Wheeler has stated that she was directed by Dallas SAC Ted Royster to obtain weekend contact telephone numbers for Dallas television news organizations. Wheeler told the contacts at the stations that she wanted the numbers because something important might be happening in the area over the weekend. This evidenced an effort by Royster to capitalize on an expected success at Waco to obtain favorable publicity, not a headquarters-directed plan to concoct the Waco raid for publicity.

Ironically, the Waco operation did turn into the biggest press event in ATF's history. The disastrous mistakes in planning, command and control, intelligence, and postraid response resulted in the press quickly dubbing the operation as the "bungled Waco raid." A combination of sloppy research and outright fabrication have received wider acceptance than otherwise might have been the case had the mainstream press not laid the groundwork through the repetition of stories characterizing the raid as bungled, without more detailed explanation.

The attempts to characterize Waco as the bungling of an incompetent agency, or worse, as a deliberately illegal attack on peaceful citizens, serve only to conceal the very serious issues raised by the events. The command and control and intelligence failures that plagued this operation would very likely reoccur in most law enforcement agencies, given a similar problem. Although extensive planning and preparation had preceded the raid, a close examination of the planning process reveals a very fundamental dilemma. Even with adequate intelligence, planning, and command and control, there may be no legally and socially acceptable means of dealing with situations like those confronted at Mount Carmel. A review of the testimony given at the 1995 House hearings reveals a curious pattern. Numerous witnesses are critical of ATF's choice of tactics, but no alternative that allowed for all known difficulties was offered. Each alternative had its own potential risks, and calculating the risk level requires substantial speculation. Although a siege-and-wait option appears to be favored by agencies after Waco, this strategy forfeits all initiative to the violators, establishes a precedent of rewarding the threat of forceful resistance, creates immense costs, and risks mass suicide.

Once the probable cause for a warrant had been developed and the decision made that no other course was available, the issue was how the warrant should be served. Two other options were available to ATF, although both so violated the values and routines of the field agents that top-level management would have had to invoke them. ATF could have ignored the violations, and taken no action. This could have been done by simply closing the case and ignoring the evidence of violations or by making the very questionable assumption that Koresh had not intentionally violated the law and by negotiating a voluntary surrender of the firearms. ATF has done both in the past when political risk appeared unacceptable. None of the factors that would support such approaches were present, however. Koresh appeared to constitute a potential threat to public safety and to be engaged in other criminal activity, precluding the argument that the violations were innocent mistakes by a law-abiding citizen. The magnitude and nature of the violations also invalidated such an interpretation. The United States attorney showed interest in the case, thus depriving ATF of any justification for dropping it due to lack of prosecutive potential. Finally, the referral of the case to local authorities would have been difficult, given the earlier request by those authorities for ATF assistance. Had ATF failed to take any action and had

Koresh and his followers taken some violent action similar to the Jonestown massacre or the Tokyo subway gassings, the agency would likely have been the focus of intense criticism from many of its current critics.

A far more professionally and politically prudent approach would have been to request the FBI HRT to effect the service of the warrant. The HRT was clearly the most highly trained and best-equipped law enforcement tactical group in the United States. Although the operation might well have been beyond their capabilities and likewise ended in disaster, ATF would have been politically buffered. Although this would have been a politically shrewd move, and the FBI hardly could have avoided accepting the challenge, it would have met a firestorm of resistance within ATF. At both the management and operational levels, ATF had spent twenty years attempting to differentiate itself from the FBI. Even when ATF actions were critical to an investigation, joint participation with the FBI assured that ATF would be relegated to a minor role in the eyes of the press and public. ATF Special Response Teams had been created largely to preclude the need to turn to the FBI. There is no indication in the official record or in any informal discussion that this alternative was ever considered, though it might have been the best option for ATF.

Four SRT team leaders, each with substantial tactical experience, planned the raid. The planners had information from local officials, former Davidians, neighbors, and an ongoing undercover operation. ATF had placed several agents, posing as students enrolled in a nearby technical college, in a house adjacent to the compound. One of the agents, Robert Rodriguez, had established contact with Koresh. This residence provided a surveillance post to observe the compound but afforded the agents a view of only one entrance.

The planners considered three options: a siege, the arrest of Koresh away from the compound combined with a raid or siege, and a dynamic entry. Initially favored, the siege option faced the problems of a lack of cover for agents and the presence of .50-caliber weapons. The range of these weapons required a parameter beyond ATF's capabilities. The most influential of the raid planners, William Buford, shifted from a position favoring a siege to one advocating dynamic entry. Buford stated that he changed his position primarily in response to information from former Davidians that convinced him the group might engage in mass suicide and that adequate supplies existed on the compound to hold out for at least three months and likely longer. The planners also believed that a siege would result in the destruction of most of the evidence, nullifying the purpose of the search. Finally, the planners faced the possibility an assault might still be necessary if a siege failed, albeit against a far more prepared target.

Based on information that the men in the group usually worked outside during the day in a large excavation, referred to as "the pit," and that weapons were locked in an arms room, a dynamic entry became the favored option. This is not surprising in light of the fact that SRTs were created primarily to engage in dynamic entry. Originally designated "entry control teams," their primary role consisted of making initial entries on arrest and search warrants. Dynamic entry constituted their core technology, their reason for being. Team members had experienced great success with this methodology as had members of tactical teams across the country.

Unfortunately, the decision was predicated on faulty information. Apparently, the men did not work in the pit regularly, and the arms were sometimes distributed and stored in the members' rooms. Numerous other intelligence oversights occurred, thus providing an inadequate and undependable information basis for planning the operation. Planners did not seriously prepare for the contingency that the women might forcefully resist. The plan also lacked adequate checks to assure that no changes had taken place. Finally, no contingency plan was developed to extract the agents and secure the compound if there was an ambush. In retrospect, it appears clear that in spite of the awareness of the large number of weapons and the apocalyptic rhetoric of Koresh, the planners just did not contemplate that they would face armed resistance by a significant number of occupants. The Treasury report attributes this to an assumption that the ATF presence would intimidate the Davidians.

The truth is likely even more complex. Although the planners accepted the concept of risk as an abstract reality, they had never observed or experienced such massive armed resistance in a domestic law enforcement setting. It was simply not an internalized reality. Similar assumptions had cost the lives of two FBI agents in Miami several years before.

Similar inability to foresee risk appears in international relations, despite the availability of extensive intelligence and large planning staffs. To explain the inability to comprehend such risks is to explain why the United States was surprised at Pearl Harbor, the Soviets by the Nazi invasion, or the United Nations Forces by the intervention of the Chinese in Korea. To some extent, the operation of a civil law enforcement function requires the assumption that citizens will rationally respond to authority and submit. Without such an assumption, police would routinely have to strike first.

An effort to enlist the aid of the Texas Department of Protective and Regulatory Services to lure Koresh out of the compound failed when managers at that agency refused cooperation. Having been advised by former members and the case worker from Protective and Regulatory Services that Koresh seldom left the compound, and having failed to confirm his departure through surveillance from the undercover residence near the compound, the planners concluded that arresting Koresh away from the compound was not practical. This conclusion now appears to have been reached prematurely without adequate intelligence collection and analysis. Although the planners may have reached their conclusions prematurely, their decision may not have been incorrect. Subsequent reports that Koresh left the compound on several occasions do not essentially imply he could have been arrested away from the compound. Arresting a potentially violent person away from a fortified stronghold and weapons is clearly a desirable tactic. Use of this strategy requires some predictability in the subject's departure, however. Random occasional forays present planners with the need to keep an arrest team on constant alert without being detected. Because the search warrant service would have to be coordinated with the arrest, this team would also have to be ready to act on a moment's notice. A mistake in the identity of the individual leaving the compound would have compromised the entire operation, as would detection of the arrest or search teams by the press or others.

The Plan

Convinced that no alternative means allowed the entry team to avoid or easily overcome resistance,

the planners turned to the technology most familiar to them, dynamic entry. Once committed to this option, they followed a common pattern by both attempting to perfect the plan and ignoring its most troubling potential weaknesses. The failure to plan for contingencies, such as the evacuation of the raiding party in the case of an ambush, likely reflects the fact that admitting such contingencies would have undermined support for the plan. Such a contingency was beyond ATF's ability to respond to, both practically and politically. For instance, providing for intense covering fire or aggressive use of armor to allow a withdrawal would have raised questions that could not have been answered. To plan for such contingencies would have constituted an admission that the operation presented a higher risk than ATF management would have accepted. Combined with weak management oversight and poor intelligence, the tendency to avoid facing worst-case scenarios resulted in underestimating the downside risks of the raid plan. In spite of the tactical competency of the planners, intense preparation for the raid, and dedicated personnel, the raid turned into a disaster for ATF.

The final plan was to serve the arrest and search warrants at 10:00 A.M. on Monday, March 1, 1993. The planners expected that most of the men would be working outside in the construction area known as the pit, thus separated from the women and children, and more importantly from the weapons. The plan called for the use of three SRT teams, from Houston, Dallas, and New Orleans, to make the entry along with additional agents, who would function as arrest teams. In all, the raiding party would number seventy-five agents. Although the special agents in charge from each of the three field divisions would be present, the Houston SAC would exercise overall command, since Waco was in the Houston District. Although a veteran agent and former police officer, Houston SAC Philip Chojnacki had no special expertise or training in tactical operations. He delegated planning oversight to his assistant special agent in charge (ASAC), Charles Sarabyn. As the supervisor of the SRT, Sarabyn had received SRT training but was relatively young and had only limited tactical experience. As had been the ATF pattern, position and not specific knowledge or background drove the selection of key personnel, a practice that received harsh criticism by the Treasury review.

Raid planners made advance arrangements for a

command post and a separate assembly point for the agents, both several miles from the compound. New Orleans ASAC Jim Cavanaugh was assigned to the undercover house for the purpose of exercising overall command there. The plan also called for advance placement of several forward observer, or sniper, teams on two sides of the compound. All the agents involved were required to wear blue tactical uniforms with badges and the letters *ATF* in gold clearly visible on them. Each agent would also wear a bullet-resistant vest and helmet. A small number of agents were assigned to carry AR-15 rifles, and several others would carry MP-5 carbines or submachine guns. Only the AR-15 rifles assigned to the forward observers had the capacity to effectively penetrate walls. The MP-5s and the pistols carried by all agents utilized a low-velocity, 9-mm cartridge and were useful only in a direct confrontation and not for returning fire against barricaded opponents. The arms allocated reflected the planners' assumption that agents would make entry quickly and face risk only from isolated individuals inside the compound.

Assigned to secure the arms room, the New Orleans SRT would first have to scale the roof and enter the second story through the windows. The primary entry team, consisting of agents from the Houston and Dallas SRTs, would sprint for the front door, announce their identity and purpose, and make entry. Other teams were designated to control the men in the pit and control the dogs. In the service of any search warrant, officers must first locate and control all the occupants to assure the safety of the officers and occupants and prevent the destruction of evidence. This is normally accomplished by sweeping the premises quickly, searching, disarming, and moving all occupants to a central location. Although occupants may leave, officers have authority to control any who do not. The search of Mount Carmel did not differ from other warrants in this regard, except that clearing a complex of this size and locating and controlling approximately a hundred people presented tactical problems exponentially more difficult than those normally encountered when clearing a house or apartment.

Planners made extensive preparations for emergency medical care of any injured persons. Agents designated and trained as emergency medical technicians received additional training from Army Special Forces medics, and emergency supplies were stockpiled. In addition, ATF arranged to have ambulances available on standby for the morning of the raid, a preparation that would contribute to the ultimate disaster. After assembling in Waco, the entire raid team engaged in a series of rehearsals at the army's urban warfare training facilities at nearby Fort Hood, Texas. Army Special Forces advisers critiqued and advised the rehearsals and made suggestions for improvements.

The Execution

One of the agents residing in the residence near the compound, Robert Rodriguez, had established contact with Koresh. Rodriguez went to the compound regularly and talked with Koresh about religion and biblical teaching, and they sometimes went shooting together. As the raid became more imminent, the undercover agent's role was transformed from investigation to collection of tactical intelligence. Ultimately, Rodriguez played a critical role, not only in the investigation but also in the aftermath that shook ATF to its roots.

Although the raid was originally scheduled for Monday, March 1, 1993, external events accelerated the date. The local Waco newspaper, the *Tribune-Herald,* had been pursuing a story on Koresh and the Davidians since the spring of 1992. In October 1992, a reporter contacted the office of the United States attorney for information on Koresh, and the United States attorney informed ATF of the request. Subsequently, ATF and the United States Attorney's Office received information that the paper had prepared a feature story titled "The Sinful Messiah" for publication. The story included much of the information that had been gathered during the ATF investigation including allegations of child molestation and abuse and information regarding acquisition of firearms. On February 1, 1993, ASAC Sarabyn and Group Supervisor Earl Dunagan met with the managing editor of the paper and requested a delay in the publication of the article, offering "front-row seats" to the paper in any upcoming law enforcement action. ATF representatives continued to meet with the paper in efforts to secure a delay in the publication of the article on the assumption that its publication would alert Koresh and heighten security at the compound. In so doing they compromised operational security, although this may have been worth the risk if they had been successful.

As the raid date approached, ATF personnel became convinced that the "Sinful Messiah" article would be published on Sunday, February 28. In fact, the article was scheduled for Saturday, February 27. Special Agent in Charge Chojnacki pushed his tactical commander, Sarabyn, to move the raid up to Saturday; however, Sarabyn indicated that Sunday was the earliest possible date. The date of the raid could not easily be altered. Almost a hundred agents had to be brought to Waco, equipped, briefed, and rehearsed. Once set in motion, the mechanics of the operation largely dictated the timeline. Thus, through a series of unfortunate circumstances, the agents would arrive the day after Koresh became agitated and alarmed by an article that accused him of criminal activity and implied strong law enforcement interest in his activities. The efforts to serve the warrant before the publication of the story resulted in scheduling for the day on which Koresh would be most focused on and agitated by the article.

While the teams assembled and prepared for the operation, ATF headquarters notified the office of the assistant secretary of the treasury for enforcement of the pending operation in a one-page memorandum. The notification arrived at Treasury on the afternoon of Friday, February 26, 1993. On the same date, ATF was notified by the *Tribune-Herald* that the "Sinful Messiah" story would run the next day. Events were beginning to move beyond the capacity of the ATF managers to evaluate and respond to them.

After receiving notification on Friday afternoon, Acting Assistant Secretary John Simpson contacted Director Higgins and notified him that ATF should not go forward with the operation at this time. Higgins subsequently recontacted Simpson after conferring with Associate Director Hartnett, who, in turn, conferred with Chojnacki. Higgins provided additional information on the raid and assured Simpson that the plan would allow ATF to avoid the danger of the Davidians' weaponry and protect the children present. Higgins also assured Simpson that the undercover agent, Rodriguez, would reenter the compound before the raid and assure that no preparations were being made by the Davidians to resist ATF.

Unknown to Higgins and others in ATF, who were focused on making last-minute preparations and satisfying Treasury concerns, an even more critical element in the unfolding events had already taken place. Word of the pending action by ATF had leaked from the newspaper to a local television news reporter. Another employee of television station KWTX had determined from a friend, who was employed as a dispatcher by a Waco ambulance service, that ATF had requested that ambulances be placed on standby for Sunday morning. On Saturday the newspaper article appeared and local attention was specifically focused on the Branch Davidians and any potential law enforcement action. By piecing together their knowledge of an ongoing ATF investigation with the request for ambulances, the local television news staff and newspaper reporters had both concluded that some sort of action was scheduled for Sunday.

All components for a disaster were now on an intersecting course. Momentum had taken over the ATF operation, which could not be delayed, only canceled. Local news staffs had correctly concluded the location and approximate time for ATF activity. Publication of an article accusing Koresh of crimes and implying imminent law enforcement action had raised awareness and suspicion at the compound to a peak. And finally, ATF had divided its command structure across several layers, with no single person in a position to exercise overall control. Worse yet, it appears that at least some in that chain of command conceptually focused solely on overt preparations by the Davidians as the criteria for aborting the operation, while others believed that any compromise of the element of surprise would precipitate an abort order. This resulted in a fragmentation in command without even those involved fully comprehending that this had occurred. Any decision to abort was made even more difficult by the lack of any alternative options and by the fact that those actively involved in and overwhelmed by the operational details were the only ones who were positioned to make the final call. The pending disaster resulted as much from faulty structure and planning as any error in execution of the operation. An operation of this magnitude has immense inertia. To terminate such an operation requires organizational and moral authority, self-confidence, reliable information, courage, and detachment. Although key participants collectively possessed these elements, they were not concentrated in a single individual.

Saturday, February 27, 1993

On Saturday, February 27, 1993, the final elements of the raiding party came together in the Waco area with intensive activity, including establishing a command post at the Texas State Technical College campus, housing personnel in over 150 motel rooms, and moving ATF bomb trucks and National Guard helicopters into the area. Although ATF made an effort to maintain operational security, the sheer size of the operation rendered this effort largely ineffectual.

On Saturday morning, Rodriguez attended a worship service at the compound and reported that Koresh preached about the "Sinful Messiah" article and told his followers that "they" were coming after him. He did not specify who "they" were, but told the followers to remain calm and do what he had told them to do. What actions might be taken by Koresh were not clear to Rodriguez. That afternoon Rodriguez met with SAC Chojnacki and reported this information. Chojnacki's specific questions related to preparations for combat by the Davidians, and Rodriguez reported that he had seen none. The role of analyzing intelligence was clearly being commingled with command. The planners lost much of the value of their inside source by focusing exclusively on overt preparations by the Davidians for armed resistance as indicators of danger. Rodriguez returned to the compound at 5:00 P.M. and remained until midnight. Assistant Special Agent in Charge Sarabyn instructed Rodriguez to return to the compound the next morning to make a final check on conditions and to exit the compound by 9:15 A.M. Rodriguez, concerned for his own safety, reluctantly agreed to return but expressed concern that his actions were likely to arouse suspicion and that he might have difficulty exiting on time.

Sunday, February 28, 1993

At 5:00 A.M. seventy-six agents consisting of the three SRT teams and the supporting entry teams assembled at Fort Hood. They then traveled by vehicle to the designated assembly point, the Bellmead Civic Center. The large collection of agents, dressed in distinct blue uniforms with *ATF* in large letters on the front and back, and the numerous vehicles created a very conspicuous scene. At 8:00 A.M., Sarabyn briefed the raid personnel inside the center. Three Texas

National Guard helicopters arrived at the Texas State Technical College, and Division Chief Andy Vita opened a command center at ATF headquarters in Washington. Concurrent with the last-minute ATF preparations, news personnel from both the *Tribune-Herald* and KWTX Television, who had collectively analyzed their information to conclude activity was likely on Sunday, set out for the compound. Amazingly, no evidence has emerged from either the Treasury review or the subsequent congressional hearings that the extensive movement of agents compromised the operation. This was most likely the result of accident than any action by ATF, as the size of the operation made it impossible to conceal.

If fortune favored ATF on the one hand, it revoked the favor with the other. ATF had arranged for police to isolate the compound with roadblocks immediately before the raid on Sunday morning. The decision to hold off the roadblocks until the last minute to avoid attracting attention allowed the reporters, who started early in the morning, to move very close to the compound before the roadblocks were established. At least one Texas Department of Public Safety officer and agents in the undercover house became aware of the reporters' presence. Although the agents relayed the reporters' presence to ASAC Cavanaugh, who was in command at the undercover house, no procedures existed to process and utilize this information. KWTX cameraman Jim Peeler became lost. Although he requested directions from his office by cellular telephone, he was still unable to find the compound. He encountered David Jones, a rural mail carrier in a vehicle bearing a "U.S. Mail" sign, and asked for directions to the compound. Unknown to Peeler, Jones was a Davidian follower. During the ensuing conversation Peeler advised that some type of law enforcement action might be taking place there that morning and that there could be shooting. Jones drove directly to the compound to report the information.

At 8:00 A.M. on February 28, Rodriguez again went to the compound. Koresh invited him to join a Bible study session with Koresh and two other Davidians. Shortly after David Jones drove to the compound, his father, Perry Jones, called Koresh out of the Bible study group for a telephone call. Koresh initially ignored the request. Perry Jones then told him that the call was from England and Koresh left the room to take the call. When Koresh returned, he appeared agitated, had trouble holding the Bible, and could not talk. When Rodriguez asked him what was wrong, Koresh responded that "neither the ATF nor the National Guard will ever get me." He then walked to the window, looked out, and stated, "They're coming, Robert. The time has come." He repeated, "They're coming, Robert, they're coming." Rodriguez became alarmed for his own safety, noting that other Davidians had entered the room, effectively cutting him off from the door. He made an excuse that he had a breakfast appointment and left, driving directly to the undercover house near the compound.

Warning Ignored

Rodriguez immediately reported the events at the compound to Cavanaugh at the undercover house, who instructed Rodriguez to call Sarabyn. Sarabyn asked a series of questions relating to the presence of weapons and specific preparations from a prepared list, to which Rodriguez responded in the negative. Sarabyn then asked what the people in the compound were doing when Rodriguez left, and Rodriguez responded that they were praying. Sarabyn and Cavanaugh discussed the situation at the compound, and Cavanaugh advised that he could see no overt signs of preparation there. Sarabyn then went to the tarmac where Dallas special agent in charge Ted Royster and Chojnacki were preparing to board National Guard helicopters. Over the noise of the helicopters, which were warming up, Sarabyn and Chojnacki held an impromptu conference that would decide the fate of agents and Davidians alike.

The exact content of the discussion remains in contention. Sarabyn and Chojnacki were subsequently dismissed from ATF employment over their actions and Royster was transferred to a far less important and desirable assignment. Regardless of the exact words, the general focus can be reconstructed from events, statements, and the subsequent testimony of the participants. The discussion apparently focused on specific preparations for resistance by the Davidians and not on loss of the element of surprise. No doubt, momentum played a significant role, as did the fractured command structure, lack of pre-planning for this specific contingency, the physical location of the discussion, haste, and some breakdown in communication as information was passed from Rodriguez to Sarabyn to Chojnacki. Regardless of the relative importance attributed to specific causes, this constituted the most critical moment of organizational and individual failure. Although circumstances and command structure contributed significantly to their mistake, the failure of Chojnacki and Sarabyn to cancel the raid at this moment constituted the most grievous error in the entire chain of events leading to the disaster at Waco.

Chojnacki returned to the command post and called the ATF headquarters communication center. He notified them that Rodriguez was out and that the raid was going forward. He then returned to the helicopters and both he and Royster departed. Sarabyn left for the staging area where he told agents that Koresh was aware ATF and the National Guard were coming and that they had to hurry. Rodriguez subsequently arrived at the command post, but Sarabyn had already left for the staging area. Rodriguez testified at the House hearings that he was emotionally distraught and shocked that the raid had not been aborted. What seemed clear to Rodriguez and to most that have examined the events subsequently was apparently not clear to Chojnacki and Sarabyn. They somehow focused exclusively on what actions Koresh took in response to his discovery of the pending raid. Others, including Rodriguez, understood the discovery alone was the critical piece of information.

At about 9:25 A.M., the raid team left the staging area, concealed in two large cattle trailers towed by pickups, a familiar sight in rural Texas. Sarabyn rode in the cab of the first truck and maintained constant contact with Cavanaugh at the safe house, who reported no signs of unusual activity at that location. Ironically, the raid likely would have been canceled if even a couple of armed sentries had been observed. However, the possibility of an ambush seems to have been outside the parameters considered by the raid commanders.

Prior to the arrival of the two trailers, the plan called for the helicopters to create a diversion. However, the helicopters arrived concurrently with the trailers. When the helicopters were about 350 meters from the compound they began receiving fire from the compound and turned away. They landed in a nearby field and conducted an inspection that revealed two of the aircraft had been hit. It has been alleged by some that the helicopters fired on the compound. These were not attack helicopters. Thus they carried no armament other than the 9-mm pistols carried by the agents. These weapons would have been highly ineffectual against a structure at any range and virtually useless firing from a moving helicopter at 350 meters. The rotor noise from the helicopters would have masked the sound from small-caliber weapons, making it virtually impossible for compound residents to hear gunfire from the helicopters. Aimed rifle fire from the ground, however, would have posed a threat to the aircraft.

The two trucks and trailers carrying the ATF agents pulled up along the southwest side of the compound. The first vehicle carried the Dallas agents, who were assigned the front door, and a portion of the Houston agents, who were assigned the pit area. The second vehicle carried the rest of the Houston agents and the New Orleans agents, who were assigned to move around the northeast side of the compound, scale the roof, and secure the arms room on the second floor. The first agents out of the vehicles were equipped with fire extinguishers to repel dogs, a common raid practice. As agents raced toward the front door, Koresh stepped outside and shouted, "What's going on here?" The agents, who were wearing helmets and distinct blue uniforms with badges and the letters *ATF* on the chest, responded by identifying themselves and shouting, "Freeze and get down." Koresh stepped back inside and closed the doors. Immediately thereafter, gunfire erupted through the front door, wounding one agent. Cavanaugh later testified before the House Joint Subcommittee that the fire from inside was so intense that the door appeared to bulge out. The agents dispersed for any cover they could find as they were subjected to attack by automatic weapons fire and hand grenades.

The New Orleans SRT moved around the east side of the building and scaled the roof using a ladder. Seven agents climbed to the roof while an eighth provided cover from the ground. Kenny King, Conway LeBleu, Todd McKeehan, and David Millen went to the northwest pitch, where they came under heavy fire. McKeehan and LeBleu were killed outright, and King was shot six times. Badly wounded, King rolled off the roof into a courtyard, where he would remain for almost two hours, undetected by the Davidians. Millen retreated over the ridge of the roof to the southeast pitch and joined agents Jordan, Buford, and Constantino, who had made entry through a window into what had been identified as the arms room. Millen positioned himself at the window. The Davidians fired through the walls and floor

of the room with automatic weapons, wounding Buford three times and Jordan twice. The bullets fired through the interior walls of the room exited the exterior wall near Millen, who also was being subjected to automatic weapons fire through the roof from below. The combined fire forced him to retreat to the ground. This sequence of events was captured by television news footage, as was Jordan's earlier entry into the window. The wounded agents escaped back out through the window and dropped to the ground. Remaining behind to cover the exit of the wounded agents, Constantino was confronted by a male subject with an assault rifle, who entered the room immediately after the two agents escaped. Constantino fired and the subject fell. Constantino then jumped through the window, striking his head as he did. He subsequently fell from the roof and was severely injured in the fall. Both Constantino and Buford were pulled to safety by other agents. Although it has received little attention in the aftermath of Waco, ATF agents performed repeated acts of courage in rescuing and treating injured comrades while under fire, returning fire in a disciplined manner while in exposed and vulnerable positions, and retrieving wounded and dead agents under the guns of the Davidians. Although television and movies often portray police performing heroically under fire, few actually experience exposure to gunfire and very few encounter sustained fire. The performance of the agents is even more commendable if one understands that they were not trained nor prepared for such eventualities. Their experience was more akin to Normandy or Iwo Jima than to policing.

The agents huddled behind any available cover outside the compound and returned fire as best they could, although their weapons were poorly suited to the task. The forward observers, or snipers, kept up a steady fire against the windows. Although they were firing from far greater distance and had a slower rate of fire, their superior weapons actually posed the greatest threat to the Davidians. Close observation of the films of the events reveals that the Davidians utilized their volume of fire rather than exercising fire discipline. This likely resulted from a lack of training and experience combined with the ATF return fire. Had the Davidians engaged in effective target identification and produced disciplined, aimed fire, ATF casualties would have been catastrophic. As it was, fifteen of the agents on the ground suffered gunshot wounds, of whom two, Steven Willis and Robert

Williams, died. In addition, seven agents were wounded by grenade fragments, and several others received substantial injuries.

Cease-Fire

At 9:48 A.M., within a minute of the raid's onset, the McLennan County Sheriff's Department received a 911 call from Wayne Martin, a resident at the compound. Although the deputy could hear gunfire, he could not get Martin to talk with him, and after fourteen minutes, someone at the compound hung up the phone. The Sheriff's Department called back, using the number that appeared automatically on their screen, and reestablished contact with the compound but was unable to reach their liaison officer at the ATF command post, whose radio had been turned off. For almost two hours, periodic contact was made between various compound occupants and the Sheriff's Department and ATF. It was during one of these calls that Koresh stated that they were under attack and demanded that everyone get off the property.

Eventually, Cavanaugh established communication with Steve Schneider and negotiated a cease-fire. No formal hierarchy designated positions for members, but Schneider functioned as a key assistant and spokesman for Koresh. Once both sides stopped shooting, negotiations continued over removal of the dead and wounded and withdrawal of the agents from their locations immediately around the compound. Schneider initially demanded immediate withdrawal, but Cavanaugh refused to do so until the dead and wounded were removed. Eventually, Schneider agreed to allow the seriously wounded King to be removed by four agents, who retrieved him from the rear courtyard utilizing a ladder as an improvised stretcher. A few minutes later, Schneider agreed to allow the removal of the remaining dead and injured agents, and there was a general withdrawal by ATF.

Because there were no contingency plans for the events that occurred, there were no plans for controlling the scene in the aftermath. The perimeter around the compound was not secured. This was a direct result of several factors, including a combination of command breakdown, inadequate procedures, and efforts by the ATF management structure to direct events from Washington. Local and state officers responded to the scene by closing all roads, but

the Davidians could have walked away en masse. ATF agents did intercept Davidians attempting to enter the compound in two instances. In one instance, a group of Davidians attempting to make their way from a shop away from the main compound engaged in a gunfight with agents, and one Davidian was killed. Although individual agents did seek out and perform necessary tasks, the command structure essentially ceased to function.

Although ATF management quickly dispatched three additional SRTs to Waco, a request for the FBI HRT was made immediately after the cease-fire. ATF, Treasury and the FBI reached agreement that ATF would relinquish control of the scene to the FBI if the HRT was deployed. Ironically, a request for the HRT to serve the warrant might have spared ATF much of the political attack that subsequently was directed toward it. The HRT would have faced the same logistical problems encountered by ATF, and the results might have proved equally disastrous. The FBI, however, would have been far better positioned to weather the political and media storm. The FBI enjoyed a large reservoir of public recognition and support and lacked a well-organized opposition devoted to attacking their every action. It would, therefore, have offered a far less inviting target for ridicule by the media or politicians. Turning to the FBI after the disaster, on the other hand, simply reinforced public perceptions of ATF incompetence among the media, politicians, and the public.

By March 2, 1993, the FBI had assumed operational control of the Waco scene. Cavanaugh, who continued negotiations after the withdrawal, continued his role as negotiator under FBI direction and succeeded in obtaining the release of some of the children in the compound. Although ATF management's initial concern focused on the injured and dead agents, their attention soon turned to determining what went wrong and ultimately to providing a public explanation.

Retrospective*

On April 19, 1993, the FBI attempted to end the nearly two-month-long standoff with the Branch Da-

Note: This "retrospective" was written especially for the 7th edition of this text by William J. Vizzard.

vidians that began with the ATF raid. As FBI armored vehicles battered the buildings and inserted tear gas, the occupants refused repeated requests to surrender. Ultimately, they engaged in a mass suicide by means of firearms and fire. This suicide by fire on live television assured that the events at Waco would remain a media focus for some time. Three years later, April 19, 1995, Timothy McVeigh, a young former soldier and opponent of government and gun laws, bombed the federal building in Oklahoma City, killing 168 people in apparent retaliation for the deaths in Waco. In an ironic twist, a newly elected conservative majority in Congress responded to the Oklahoma City bombing with an investigation of Waco.

For ATF, the problems of Waco did not end with the transfer of the scene to the FBI. ATF Associate Director Dan Hartnett continued to appear in press conferences for several days with the FBI on-scene commander. During these appearances, Hartnett continued to deny that ATF had any advance warning of the dangers waiting for them within the Davidian compound. Although the Texas Rangers conducted the criminal investigation of the events surrounding the raid at the request of the Department of Justice to avoid any taint of bias by ATF or the FBI, ATF initiated its own internal shooting review. This review quickly revealed that the raid commanders had become aware that David Koresh knew of the pending raid and that the commanders chose not to call the raid off. When Hartnett was advised of this information, he immediately contacted the Special Agent in Charge in Houston and was assured that the raid leaders did not have adequate reason to call off the raid. Hartnett continued to inform Director Steve Higgins that this was the case and ordered all personnel to so inform the press.

Outraged agents quickly "blew the lid off" the official ATF version. As press accounts emerged, Higgins finally realized that he had not been served well by his deputy, but it was too late. The Secretary of the Treasury ordered an extensive investigation that ultimately resulted in Higgins, Hartnett and Hartnett's deputy accepting early retirement. Houston Special Agent in Charge Chojnacki and Assistant Special Agent in Charge Sarabyn were both dismissed, although both eventually were reinstated to non–law enforcement positions on appeal.

Hartnett's intense agency loyalty and conservative nature had served both himself and the agency poorly. Higgins's openness and trust in Hartnett had done the same. At a moment when brutal honesty and self-examination might have allowed managers to quickly respond to a disastrous situation, managers had chosen to believe what was comfortable. ATF's lack of experience with high-profile events no doubt exacerbated the situation. In retrospect, managers should have assumed that reporters would ferret out any negative information and that self-serving assertions by on-scene managers would not give an adequate picture of events.

Information played a critical role in every phase of the Waco tragedy. ATF's inability to process and analyze the intelligence data and the failure to convey data to top management set up the circumstances. The misperception of the potential for a large-scale violent confrontation, based on past experience, moved agents one step closer. The misinterpretation of information during tactical planning put lives directly at risk. The leakage of information from ATF and the careless dispersal of information by members of the press created the immediate circumstances for the ambush. The failure to comprehend and heed the last-minute warnings from the undercover agent robbed the managers of their last opportunity to avoid disaster. Once disaster struck, the courageous and artful negotiation by agent Cavanaugh saved numerous lives of both agents and children in the compound.

In the aftermath, the attempt to manage information and the failure to seek out or accept unfavorable information resulted in key ATF managers losing their jobs and the agency being held up to additional ridicule. Waco would become a symbol for anti-government activists, gun control opponents, law enforcement critics, and religious scholars. The true nature of events was largely lost in the battle to control Waco, the symbol. For the media, the word "botched" would become the standard modifier when referring to the Waco raid and would be used by many writers with no independent knowledge of any of the events of February 1993. Few who referred to Waco would understand that it was primarily about organizational routines, information management, and the inability of managers to conceptualize in alternative ways to what they had routinely done before.

Chapter 9 Review Questions

1. According to James Garnett, why do public administrators need to keep in mind the centrality communications? How does one find out about the key players and processes influencing communications both inside and outside an organization and learn to deal with them effectively? Do you concur with Garnett's thesis about the professional centrality of information networks? Why or why not?

2. What problems of communications are illustrated in the Waco case? Which were the most important ones in creating the dilemmas that ATF officials faced.

3. What types of communications issues discussed in the Garnett reading are illustrated in the Waco case? How would Garnett advise ATF to deal with those issues?

4. What does the case study tell us especially about the communications between headquarters and the field, as well as between the media and public agencies today? Any enduring lessons for public administrators?

5. How do communications systems make or break an administrator's ability to control and direct the policies of his or her organization? As an administrator, what techniques would you utilize to ensure that the information you receive is accurate, timely, and *not* distorted by preconceived personal or institutional biases? Explain for example, how you would insure a subordinate like Dan Hartnett, ATF associate director, was only giving fair information.

6. Can you generalize about the ethical dilemmas created by communications processes for those who work for a public organization, especially for those who value truthfulness and open communications in performing their work? What risks are apparent within the organization when people are not able to communicate *everything* or are not *told* everything necessary to perform their work? Can you identify your own ethical standards concerning communications in a public agency?

Key Terms

internal versus external communications processes

communications players

government communication

newsmaking process

managerial communication process

interorganizational communications

the credibility conundrum

the propaganda paradox

"tell and sell" communications methods

the two-way symmetrical model

ethical communication

Suggestions for Further Reading

The importance placed on communications processes in shaping governmental and organizational decisions was largely the result of several seminal works. These writings of the following key theorists should be studied with some care: Chester Barnard, *The Functions of the Executive* (Cambridge, Mass.: Harvard University Press, 1938); Herbert Simon, *Administrative Behavior: A*

Study of Decision-Making Processes in Administrative Organization 4th ed. (New York: Free Press 1997); Karl W. Deutsch, *The Nerves of Government* (New York: Free Press, 1950); Norbert Weiner, *Cybernetics: Or Control and Communication in the Animal and the Machine* (New York: John Wiley & Sons, 1948). For a useful study of Herbert Simon and his contributions not only to this area but the entire field of public administration, see the whole issue *Public Administration Quarterly* (Fall 1988), especially the opening interview with Simon. One should also read Simon's autobiography, *Models of My Life* (New York: Basic Books, 1991). For an evaluation of Barnard's contributions, see the entire issue of Jack Rabin and Thomas Vocino, eds., "Special Issue: Papers in Honor of Chester I. Barnard," *International Journal of Public Administration,* 17 (1994) as well as William G. Scott, *Chester I Barnard and the Guardians of the Managerial State* (Lawrence, KS: University Press of Kansas, 1994). Harlan Cleveland, *The Knowledge Executive: Leadership in an Information Society* (New York: E. P. Dutton, 1985), presents a lively study of this topic from a leadership perspective.

For more pragmatic works on the subject, review Herbert Kaufman in collaboration with Michael Couzens, *Administrative Feedback: Monitoring Subordinates' Behavior* (Washington, D.C.: The Brookings Institution, 1973); Hindy Schachter, *Public Agency Communication* (Chicago: Nelson-Hall, 1983); and D. Graber, *Public Sector Communications* (Washington, D.C.: CQ Press, 1992). The best practical textbooks on this topic are David S. Arnold, Christine S. Becker, and Elizabeth K. Kellar, *Effective Communication: Getting the Message Across* (Washington, D.C.: International City Management Association, 1983); James L. Garnett, *Communicating for Results in Government: A Strategic Approach for Public Managers* (San Francisco, Calif.: Jossey-Bass, 1992); and P. V. Lewis, *Organizational Communications: The Essence of Effective Management,* Third Edition. (New York: Wiley, 1987).

General handbooks provide useful overviews of this topic. See C. C. Arnold and J. W. Bowers, eds., *Handbook of Rhetorical and Communication Theory* (Needham Heights, Mass.: Allyn & Bacon, 1984); C. R. Berger and S. H. Chafee, eds., *Handbook of Communication Science* (Newbury Park, Calif.: Sage, 1987); and James L. Garnett and Alexander Kauzmir, ed., *Handbook of Administrative Communication* (New York: Marcel Dekker, 1997).

The crisis of war can illuminate problems of administrative communications with unusual clarity. For some excellent examples, see Gordon W. Prange, *At Dawn We Slept: The Untold Story of Pearl Harbor* (New York: McGraw-Hill, 1981); E. B. Potter, *Battle for Leyte Gulf: Command and Communications* (Syracuse, N.Y.: Inter-University Case No. 126); John W. Spanier, *The Truman-MacArthur Controversy and the Korean War* (Cambridge, Mass.: Harvard University Press, 1959); Sam Adams, "Vietnam Cover-up: Playing War with Numbers," *Harper's Magazine* (May 1975); Deborah Shapley, *Promise and Power: The Life and Times of Robert McNamara* (Boston: Little, Brown, 1993); and from the Gulf War, in Bob Woodward, *The Commanders* (New York: Simon and Schuster, 1991). Perhaps the best of such military studies remaining, however, Douglas S. Freeman, *Lee's Lieutenants,* 3 volumes (NY: Scribner's, 1944) and John Keegan, *The Face of Battle* (NY: Viking, 1976).

CHAPTER 10

Executive Management: The Concept of Effective Public Organizations

The discussion here . . . can proceed using a relatively straightforward definition of agency effectiveness: the agency preforms well in discharging the administration and operational functions pursuant to the mission. It achieves the mission as conceived by the organization and its stakeholders or pursues achievement of it in an evidently successful way.

—Hal G. Rainey and Paula Steinbauer

Introduction

Writings on public management are a comparatively new phenomena; in fact, they are peculiarly products of this century because large-scale formal organizations, both public and private, are modern in origin and existence. Humanity's dependence on massive organizations that span the continent and the globe is therefore recent; hence, the comprehensive, detailed analysis of these institutions is also new to scholarly interest. The flood of modern literature analyzing the nature, behavior, and ideal methods for constructing viable human institutions and internal personal relationships has been prompted in part by the need to establish and construct these organizations in ways that effectively cope with problems of the present age.

One critical dilemma in studying modern organizations and their management lies in the proper theoretical perspective. As Dwight Waldo reminds us, studying organization is akin to the fable of the blind men and the elephant. "Each of the blind men . . . touched with his hands a different part of the elephant, and as a result there was among them a radical difference of opinion as to the nature of the beast."[1]

A principal cause of the considerable divergence of opinion about organizations thus stems from the specialized vantage points from which observers come to examine human institutions. The economist has a different view than the philosopher, so also the insider versus the outsider and the worker versus the manager. These ideas are not right or wrong; rather, a number of approaches exist for reaching the truth about

---

[1]Dwight Waldo, *Ideas and Issues in Public Administration* (New York: McGraw-Hill, 1953), p. 64.

complex formal organizations. In studying organizations, material that is valid or useful to one individual may not seem so to another.

For one reason or another, very often *one* theoretical perspective in America tends to dominate our understanding of what constitutes good or appropriate public sector organizational practices, namely business perspectives. Not infrequently do we read about political candidates or their appointees promising, "I can make government more businesslike!" or citing as their reason for holding high public office "a successful track-record as a manager in private enterprise." Editorial writers, civic association speakers, and media pundits often echo these refrains in favor of applying entrepreneurial talent to public enterprises. Popular opinion generally supports the viewpoint that if only public administrators would simply manage their affairs like business, government—and maybe even the entire country—would run a lot better.

The tendency to identify good management in government with good business management is common even in serious public administration literature. Indeed, discussions of business management methods dominated much of the early development of the conscious study of public administration at the beginning of the twentieth century. Frederick W. Taylor and his business-oriented scientific management concepts served as the core of much of the field of public administration prior to World War II. The Brownlow Committee Report (1937), which some scholars believe was the highwater mark of the influence of public administration thinking on government, largely mirrored the business organization practices of the day. In many respects, this strong influence of business practices on government continues today through application of private sector techniques as performance budgets, cost-benefit analysis, cost-accounting procedures, performance appraisals, management by objective, zero-based budgeting, and so on. Indeed, you only need to think about the names of major governmental processes and institutions to appreciate the enormous influence of what Waldo calls "our business civilization"—via government corporations, city managers, efficiency ratings, contracting out for services, chief administrative officers, and county executives.

At the conceptual root of making government run more like a business is a belief in the "Three *E*'s," or the values of efficiency, economy, and effectiveness. "If only government could be more efficient, economical, and effective, our worries would be over!" So the popular view goes. During the last decade or so, thanks to the "reinventing government" movement, which drew heavily on the writings of business guru Peter Drucker whose writings focus on effective business managers, the third *E,* effectiveness, emerged prominently and pervasively throughout the public sector as an important, if not *the* important value for managers to strive toward. Yet, despite the recent renewed enthusiasm on both scholarly and popular levels to "reinvent government" in order to run it more effectively just like business, the fundamental issue remains unanswered: What is an effective government enterprise? What does the term mean and how is it practiced by public managers? How can it be applied to the public sector? What are its theoretical elements and their implications for government executives? What are its utility and its limitations?

In the following essay, "Galloping Elephants," Professor Hal G. Rainey, a distinguished scholar in the field of public management, and his doctoral student Paula Steinbauer, both currently at the University of Georgia, thoughtfully examine the considerable evidence surrounding the contemporary literature and research on effective government organizations. Their goal, as they indicate at the outset, is to develop the elements of a conceptual framework, or a theory, to explain public agency effectiveness. The authors begin by citing examples of government effectiveness that stand in stark contrast to popular notions about its incompetence and wastefulness. Drawing on current scholarships, the authors next create a list of propositions about effective public agencies. What they discover from the available research is a conceptual framework that includes the following basic components: supportive behaviors from external stakeholders, such as political authorities; agency autonomy in refining and implementing its mission; high mission "valence" or an attractive mission; a strong, mission-oriented culture; and certain leadership behaviors. Combined, these factors enhance several forms of motivation for people in any agency—task motivation, mission motivation, and public service motivation—that can be linked together to promote effective public agency management.

Note how the authors at the beginning of their article define *effectiveness* as: "whether the agency does well that which it is supposed to do, whether people in the agency work hard and well, whether the actions and procedures of the agency and its members are well suited to achieving its mission, and whether the agency actually achieves its mission."

As you review this thought-provoking article that maps out the vast intellectual landscape of current research on this subject in a readable and concise way, you might think about the following issues:

> Do you concur with how the authors define *effectiveness,* which serves as the basis for their argument? Is it a workable and useful definition? Are there any elements you would add—or delete?

> How does the authors' understanding of effective public agencies relate to other values that are so basic to government, such as economy, efficiency, rule of law, and equity? Can such values be related to or included easily within the "effectiveness" framework, or are they fundamentally different? Why or why not?

> On a practical level, based upon your own experiences and readings, do the authors' arguments make good sense for public managers and supervisors to pay attention to as well as practice? If so, how? Or if not, why not?

Galloping El   of a Theory of Effect

PAULA STEINBAUER

*A corollary of this
common claim: t
ganizations cann
erate as efficient
(Simon 1998, 11)*

The elephant ser
symbol of a large, c
Yet an elephant ca
means thick-skinne
tivity in acts of alt
those that are instir
mals. Government o
have virtually an a
some, bungling enti
very well. Impugne
they also commonl
sponsiveness to the needs of clients and others
(e.g., Goodsell 1994; Gore 1995, 49). This article
develops and advances concepts and propositions,
summarized in Exhibit 10.1, about why government
agencies perform well, when they do. In its
present form, this set of propositions will evoke
comparisons to the parable of the blind men trying
to describe the elephant, because the propositions
need much more articulation, justification, and

itions among them. They do,
nd develop some fundamental
it provides the basic incentive
nance of government agencies,
onomic markets for their out-
public service motivation or a
ve the mission of the agency, or
ask-related incentives such as
tasks themselves, or is it pay
The propositions hold that all
vation contribute to the perfor-
e agencies, especially when
ncy see them as linked together.
lso hold that characteristics of
ght and political influence on the
effectiveness, as do character-
's mission, culture, leadership,
these factors in turn enhance the
three forms of motivation just mentioned.

This article develops such propositions as a step
toward development of a theory of effective government agencies on the argument that we need
more theoretical development of that topic.[1] That
public and academic discourse on bureaucracy
tends to be negative will be considered here to be
obvious and will not be elaborated, even though this
mostly negative orientation involves many important issues and nuances. Much of the literature treats
the government bureaucracy as a social problem
and liability, rather than as an asset. Many authors
focus on the problem that public bureaucracies are
too bureaucratic, with too much hierarchy, too little innovativeness and energy, too much red tape,
too much spending, too little efficiency, too little responsiveness to almost everyone and everything
outside their boundaries and most of what is inside
them, too much of a lot of other bad things, and too

[1]Wolf (1993) tests seven theories of bureaucratic effectiveness
and argues that we do not need new theories, we need tests of
existing theory. The propositions and discussion in this article
draw on Wolf's analysis as valuable, but also proceed on the
argument that such theories as we have need much more articulation.

little of a lot of other good things (e.g., Barton 1980; A. Downs 1967; Niskanen 1971; Warwick 1975).[2] If this list seems long, it is rather brief compared to Caiden's (1991) listing of 175 bureaucratic pathologies (cited in Bozeman forthcoming).[3]

On the other hand, all along in academic and public discussion of the government bureaucracy, one can detect more ambivalence than rigid antipathy, even in predominantly negative treatments. Recently, too, more and more authors defend the public bureaucracy or debunk stereotypes and negative allegations about it (e.g., G.W. Downs and Larkey 1986; Goodsell 1994; Milward and Rainey 1983; Stillman 1996; Wamsley et al. 1990), while others describe and analyze excellent leadership and management in government agencies (Ban 1995; Barzelay 1992; Behn 1991; Cohen and Eimicke 1995; Cooper and Wright 1992; Denhardt 1993; Doig and Hargrove 1987; Hargrove and Glidewell 1990; Holzer and Callahan 1998; Osborne and Gaebler 1992; Riccucci 1995; Thompson and Jones 1994). Recent empirical research further undercuts some academic assertions about public bureaucracies, indicating that they are not as evasive of external control and oversight as is often alleged (Rubin 1985; Wood and Waterman 1994) and that people in them show more effort and motivation, and less shirking and slacking, than sometimes is alleged (Brehm and Gates 1997; H.G. Rainey 1983). Recent research also shows evidence of the historical inaccuracy of some current reformers' depictions of public bureaucracies as traditionally hidebound hierarchies that resisted innovation and entrepreneurial behaviors; rather, the evidence indicates frequent instances of entrepreneurial, innovative, and generally effective performance (Wolf 1997).

[2]This observation overstates the case in an effort at lively discourse. In fairness one should acknowledge that the references cited provide a more balanced and subtle analysis than depicted in this sentence.

[3]While not necessarily negative in its assessment of bureaucratic performance, much of the academic literature on public bureaucracy concentrates on the problem of bureaucratic power, whether there is too much of it, and how it can be controlled (see Hill 1991 and 1992; Durant 1992), rather than on when and why it performs effectively.

Examples of Agency Effectiveness

In addition, numerous specific examples of agency accomplishments provide evidence that government agencies often carry out their tasks and missions very competently. About the Social Security Administration (SSA), for example, one can point out the following:

• The agency operates the social security program efficiently in an administrative sense. An economist discussing reforms of the system in 1998 pointed out that one reason to save the system is that it is very efficient, with administrative costs running at 0.8 percent of benefits (Eisner 1998). This is lower than comparable figures for private annuity companies, even considering that they must pay taxes and provide payouts to shareholders. The figure for SSA represents increased efficiency over the last decade. A Roper survey in the early 1980s asked a representative sample of Americans to estimate the percent of each dollar in the Social Security program that goes to administrative expenses. The median estimate was fifty dollars out of every one hundred. The actual figure at that time was $1.30 out of every one hundred.
• The efficiency gain reflects ongoing efforts to control costs. During the 1980s, SSA carried out Project 17,000, which reduced employment in the agency by 17,000 employees.
• Outside Kansas City, large caves have been developed as industrial storage facilities, and one can drive underground on roads that run through the caves, accompanied by large trucks that deliver and receive materials at the storage facilities. The SSA Public Service Center (PSC) in Kansas City operates a file storage facility in one of these caves, containing millions of file folders. SSA employees work in this facility, communicating

information from the files to other employees in the PSC offices downtown, who need information from the files to process client claims and requests. The PSC operates this storage facility to hold down costs. It is much less expensive to store the files in this remote site than to store them in office space in downtown Kansas City.

- SSA has proficiently advanced the computerization of claims processing, with computers now performing many of the functions that employees once performed.

- In 1995, the rankings of a major national survey of customer satisfaction with telephone service found that the SSA ranked number one in the nation. Others high in the ratings included Southwest Airlines; L.L. Bean; Nordstrom; Xerox; Disney; Saturn; Federal Express; and AT&T Universal Credit. Mutual fund companies ranked 8th, and variable annuity providers ranked 11th; these rankings are noteworthy because these companies provide services roughly similar to those of the Social Security Administration (Gore 1995, 49–51).

- In the 1970s, SSA reorganized the structure for claims processing in their large public service centers (Rainey and Rainey 1986). To solve a problem of excessive delays in processing the claims, SSA created work modules of about forty people each, that included all the specialists necessary to process a claim from beginning to end. The work modules were essentially teams that worked on a particular set of cases—much like having work teams build automobiles rather than manufacturing them on assembly lines. The change to these modules was painful, difficult, innovative, well-led, well-managed, and very successful. This provides an excellent example of effective leadership of major organizational change (H.G. Rainey 1997, 344–48).

Significantly, one can also point to an example about a very distinct agency, the U.S. Department of Defense. In the Gulf War, the military performed so well in certain ways that one could call the results virtually miraculous. In the years after Vietnam, authors made national reputations and became talk show celebrities by criticizing the poor management and leadership of the U.S. military. Whether or not one approved of the Gulf War, and in spite of many controversies and criticisms related to it, the success in actually carrying out the operations (including related functions such as logistic support) was so evident, with such a low number of casualties on the part of the U.S. and allied forces, that it has to be striking to anyone at all familiar with military operations.

One can point to other examples as well—such as the Centers for Disease Control—that typically receive favorable assessments of their general performance and professionalism, and still others such as those described by authors cited in this article (e.g., Denhardt 1993; Holzer and Callahan 1998; Wolf 1993 and 1997). Gold (1982), for example, identifies as well-managed, successful organizations the U.S. Forest Service, the U.S. Customs Service, the U.S. Passport Office, and the governments of Sunnyvale, California, and Charlotte, North Carolina. Wolf (1997) identifies the Bureau of Standards in the Commerce Department between 1917 and 1924 as the agency most highly rated for effectiveness in his large sample of agencies, thus suggesting that effective public agencies have been around for a long time. Significantly, also, Osborne and Gaebler's (1992) very influential proposals for reforms of public management draw almost exclusively on examples of practices that already exist in governmental organizations. The examples illustrate the point that in spite of immensely complex issues over what performance means and how one assesses it, public agencies often perform very well.

Mixed Results of Privatization

Another indication of effective performance by public agencies comes from the limited success of privatization initiatives. Assessments of the privatization of public services generally tend to report savings that result from privatization, but the results also show a mixed pattern with many instances where no savings were achieved, and with few findings of the very large savings projected by some proponents of privatization. The more carefully designed the study, the smaller the reported savings (e.g., Gill and Rainey 1997). Similarly, evaluation of the privatization of state-owned enterprises is much more complicated than its aggressive proponents have projected (Durant, Legge, and Moussios 1998). These limited successes of privatization support Simon's assertion, quoted at the beginning of this article, that public organizations can and often do perform as well as private firms.

Lowery (1997), among others, helps to explain why one should expect mixed results from certain types of privatization when he analyzes quasi market failures, such as the failure of a market to develop for the contract (i.e., there may be little competition for the contract). As Lowery points out, the aggressive proponents of privatization implicitly rely on the dubious assumption that the bureaucrats who could not manage effectively before contracting-out suddenly become transformed into highly efficient and effective managers of the development and monitoring of contracts. The mixed results suggest that the success of privatization initiatives depends heavily on sound management by government employees, and they return us to the questions: When and how do government agencies and the people in them perform well? Why would bureaucrats who otherwise have weak incentives for efficiency, or who otherwise face dysfunctional incentives and information patterns, be motivated to have a successful contracting process?

Power Sharing and the Hollow State

In addition, the extension of privatization arrangements, and the increasingly *networked* or *hollow*

state character of many public programs, strains the depiction of the public bureaucracy as a centralized, retentive, monolithic entity. If so centralized and retentive, why has the bureaucracy allowed all this privatization, and how could it remain so centralized and retentive if it is sharing power with so many entities (Kettl 1993; Milward, Provan, and Else 1993)? These developments, then, indicate the need to rethink the more negative depictions of public bureaucracy and to consider theories that explain effective government agencies.

Business Blunders and Generic Theories of Management

Business firms produce abundant examples of waste, inefficiency, blundering, and fraud, even in the most reputable and admired firms. This raises the issue of whether market exposure actually causes business firms to perform more effectively than nonmarket government agencies. A rich tradition in organization and management theory involves a generic perspective on those topics. This tradition is the idea that distinctions between public and private, and for-profit and nonprofit organizations amount to stereotypes and oversimplifications (H.G. Rainey 1997, 55ff). Many scholars who study organizations emphasize the commonalities among organizations, especially among those that purportedly differ by location in the public and private sectors. Simon (1998, 11), in the assertion mentioned above and quoted at the outset, provides an example of this perspective. Significantly, in relation to the later sections of this article, he attributes the prospects for effective public organizations to, among other factors, the presence of dedicated public servants who are motivated not by narrow economic self-interest but by organizational loyalty and identification (and by implication, an ideal of public service). Simon also argues that effective public administration is essential to democracy. He thus quite dramatically implies the need to seek explanations and theories of effective government organizations.

Models of Excellence in Government Organizations

To develop a theory of effective government agencies, one obviously has to decide how to proceed. Lowery (1997), while not directly pursuing models of effective agencies, suggests employing concepts and methods from economics-based and public choice theory to analyze some of the over-simplifications of those same approaches. His analysis of quasi market failures develops useful concepts for elaborating that discussion. The approach in this article, however, focuses more on government agencies and their general effectiveness, and it draws more on case studies and empirical research in public administration and public bureaucracy as well as concepts from organization and management theory. The propositions advanced later will draw on conclusions from many of the authors on successful leadership and management who are cited above. Some of those authors concentrate on one part of the elephant such as leadership, mission, or culture, and some draw only implicit conclusions about linkages to organizational effectiveness. The full group of references is not easily summarized here.

One subset of the references, however, includes efforts to characterize government agencies that perform efficiently. These profiles represent efforts to develop models of excellent organizations and to specify their attributes. Exhibit 10.2 summarizes some of these profiles. An elaborate review and critique of these efforts is beyond the scope of this article, but the row headings on the left of the exhibit indicate common topics in the profiles, including aspects of the agency mission and public orientation (including public service), leadership and primary means of managing employees, and task design and work environment. Especially as summarized in the exhibit, in ways that cannot do full justice to the analyses, the profiles need much more specification and articulation to move in the

direction of a theory. Yet some of their implications are clear, and they show up in the propositions in Exhibit 10.1 and in the discussion of them that follows.

Also of significance are some omissions in the implicit models in Exhibit 10.2. (In the parlance of organizational effectiveness researchers, they mostly represent *internal process models*.) Additional factors receive emphasis in other research on agency effectiveness. Wolf (1993) analyzed forty-four case studies of federal agencies to construct measures of the agencies' characteristics and their relationships to the organization's effectiveness. As do most of the profiles in Exhibit 10.2, his findings indicated the importance of leadership and sense of mission. In addition, however, he found important a variable representing political autonomy (that included *universal political support* and/or freedom from direction by political authorities). This variable indicates the importance of relations with oversight authorities and other external stakeholders, a topic that receives little or no emphasis in the profiles in Exhibit 10.2. It also suggests the need for a supportive and delegative role by those authorities that allows the agency reasonable autonomy to develop and pursue its mission (cf. Wilson 1989; Meier 1993a).

Propositions and a Framework

As we indicated earlier, Exhibit 10.1 states propositions about effective agencies that draw on the references just cited and on additional references and examples that are described below. Figure 10.1 provides a diagram that suggests a framework linking these propositions and their component concepts. While Exhibit 10.1 does not clearly posit all the relationships, it bears the implication that all the components in Exhibit 10.1 should be positively related in the more effective agencies. Also, in Figure 10.1 and in the discussion to follow, some of the relationships are hypothesized so clearly that they have sharp and challenging implications for research, theory, and practice.

Exhibit 10.1   Propositions About Effective Public Agencies

Public agencies are more likely to perform effectively when there are higher levels of the following conditions.

Relations with oversight authorities (legislative, executive, judicial) that are:
• Attentive to agency mission accomplishment
• Supportive
• Delegative

Relations with other stakeholders characterized by:
• Favorable public opinion and general public support
• Multiple, influential, mobilizable constituent and client groups
• Effective relations with partners and suppliers
    • Effective management of contracting and contractors
    • Effective utilization of technology and other resources
    • Effective negotiation of networks

Autonomy in operationalization and pursuit of agency mission, but not extremely high levels of autonomy (a curvilinear relationship between autonomy and agency effectiveness)

Mission valence (the attractiveness of the mission):
• Difficult but feasible
• Reasonably clear and understandable
• Worthy/worthwhile/legitimate
• Interesting/exciting
• Important/influential
• Distinctive

Strong organizational culture, linked to mission

Leadership characterized by:
• Stability (a curvilinear relationship between leadership stability and agency effectiveness)
• Multiplicity—a cadre of leaders, teams of leaders at multiple levels
• Commitment to mission
• Effective goal setting in relation to task and mission accomplishment
• Effective coping with political and administrative constraints

Task design characterized by:
• Intrinsic motivation (interest, growth, responsibility, service, and mission accomplishment)
• Extrinsic rewards (pay, benefits, promotions, working conditions)

Utilization of technology

Development of human resources:
• Effective recruitment, selection, placement, training, and development
• Values and preferences among recruits and members that support task and mission motivation

Professionalism among members:
• Special knowledge and skills related to task and mission accomplishment
• Commitment to task and mission accomplishment

Motivation among members:
• Public service motivation
• Mission motivation
• Task motivation

The Meaning of Effectiveness

In the literature on organization theory, the topic of organizational effectiveness is complex and inconclusive in certain ways, and it involves an unresolved diversity of models, including goal models, internal process models, stakeholder models, resource dependence models, participant satisfaction models, and competing values models (Daft 1998, ch. 2; H.G. Rainey 1997, ch. 6). The discussion here cannot resolve these variations, but it can proceed using a relatively straightforward definition of agency effectiveness: The agency performs well in discharging the administrative and operational functions pursuant to the mission. It achieves the mission as conceived by the organization and its stakeholders, or pursues achievement of it in an evidently successful way. While it skirts some of the controversies over the concept of organizational performance, this approach to effectiveness bears similarities to conceptions some researchers and authors use (Collins and Porras 1994; Gold 1982; Peters and Waterman 1982; Wolf 1997).

This concept of effectiveness refers to whether the agency does well that which it is supposed to do, whether people in the agency work hard and well, whether the actions and procedures of the agency and its members are well suited to achieving its mission, and whether the agency actually achieves its mission. Does it produce the actions and outputs pursuant to the mission or the institutional mandate (Osborne and Gaebler 1992, 351; Wolf 1997), and does it appear to contribute to outcomes indicated by the mission? Did the U.S. military win the Gulf War, does the CDC reduce health risks, and does the Social Security Administration pay benefits expeditiously, accurately, and appropriately, and do all these results come in significant part from the activities of the agencies and their members? As additional examples, the Coast Guard has stated as one of its central goals the reduction of accidental deaths and injuries from maritime casualties (U.S. Coast Guard 1996). The National Highway Traffic Safety Administration (1996) includes in its mission the goals of saving lives, preventing injuries, and reducing traffic-related health care problems. Evidence that the agencies' operations have contributed substantially to the achievement of these goals provides evidence of agency effectiveness.

This concept of effectiveness concerns the organization's administrative and operational effectiveness, and not necessarily the effectiveness of the general policy design in which the agency operates. For example, the Social Security Administration may operate the Old Age and Survivors Insurance program very effectively, in the sense that claimants' benefits are expeditiously and accurately authorized, calculated, and paid in ways that provide income security for the clients. The program, however, still may need reform through some form of privatization or some other adjustment because of the fiscal and financial implications of the benefits and benefit schedules that Congress mandated for the program. As another example, the U.S. military performed well in the Gulf War, but critics can dispute or lament the policy decision to proceed with military force. In addition, declaring that the Forest Service is an effective organization does not resolve controversies over the use of public forests for timbering by private firms.

Numerous other conceptual and methodological complexities can be discussed at length. The most important objective of this article, however, is to advance concepts and generalizations useful to theorizing about agency performance, so it is best simply to move to the propositions themselves.

Relations with Stakeholders

The propositions use the term *stakeholders* from the organization theory literature to refer to persons, groups, and institutions that have an interest in the activities and outcomes of the organization sufficient to draw their participation and attention to the agency. Oversight authorities such as legislative, executive, and judicial authorities are one obvious component of this part of the framework.

Exhibit 10.2   Characteristics of High Performance Government Agencies

	Gold (1982)	**STEP (1985)**	**Wilson (1989)**
Mission/public orientation	Emphasize clear mission and objectives	Closer contact with customers to better understand their needs	Mission is clear and reflects a widely shared and warmly endorsed organizational culture
			External political support
Leadership/ managing employees	Employees take pride in the organization and its product	Increased discretionary authority for managers and employees for greater control over accountability	Executives command loyalty, define and instill a clear sense of mission, attract talented workers, and make exacting demands of subordinates
	Focus on treating employees fairly and respectfully through honest and open communication	Increased employee participation taps their knowledge, skills, and commitment	Leaders make peer expectations serve the organization
	Emphasize delegation of responsibility and authority as widely as possible		Maximize discretionary authority for operators
	Management aims at challenging and encouraging people		Executive takes resposibility for organizational maintenance
	Management emphasizes innovative ways of managing		Bottom-up implementation perspective
Task design/ work environment	Places great value on the people in the organization	Partnerships to allow the sharing of knowledge, expertise, and other resources	Clearly defined goals
	Job tasks and goals are clear	State-of-the-art productivity improvement techniques	Widespread agreement on how critical tasks are performed
		Improved work measurements to provide a base for planning and implementing service improvements and worker evaluation	Agency autonomy to develop operational goals from which tasks are designed
			Ability to control or keep contextual goals in proper perspective.

Note: Portions of this exhibit are adapted from Rainey (1997, 359) and from Hale (1996, 139), with portions using Hale's terminology and summary.

Other stakeholders, such as constituent and client groups, the general public, and various partners and suppliers such as contractors, exert less legally formal influences on government agencies.

Effective agencies will have oversight authori- *ties that are supportive, delegative, and attentive to agency mission accomplishment.* The authorities will devote attention to the agency, in a demanding way that emphasizes effective performance. Yet the authorities also will tend to be supportive

Denhardt (1993)	Alliance (1994)	Hale (1996)	Holzer and Callahan (1998)
Dedication to public service and understanding public intent Serving the public, which represents democratic values	Mission clarity and understanding Maintain open and productive communication among stakeholders	Focused mission that is clarified and communicated to organization members	Customer focused Build partnerships with public and private organizations and citizens
Leader demonstrates commitment to mission Manager builds sense of community in organization Manager clearly articulates values Managers insist on high ethical standards Empowered and shared leadership Employees accept responsibility and performance accountability	Empowered employees Organizations allocate resources for continual learning Employees accept accountability to achieve results with rewards and consequences Motivate and inspire people to succeed	Enabling leadership that emphasizes learning, communication, flexibility, sharing, and vision development	Manage for quality using long-term strategic planning with support from top leadership Develop human resources and empower employees through team building, systematic training, recognition, and balancing employee and organizational needs
Pragmatic incrementalism (change in natural, appropriate) Approach to change is creative and humane Commitment to values	Defined outcomes and focus on results (performance measures) Institute new work processes as necessary Flexible, adjust nimbly to new conditions Competitive in terms of performance Restructure work processes to meet customer needs	Emphasize learning and carefully support learning, risk taking, training, communication, and work measurement Nurturing-community culture that is supportive and emphasizes teamwork, participation, flexible authority, and effective reward and recognition	Adapt technologies that include open access to data, automation for productivity, cost-effective applications, and cross-cutting techniques that deliver on public demands Measure for performance by establishing goals and measuring results, justifying and allocating as necessary resource requirements, and developing organizational improvement strategies

in the sense of providing resources and authorization necessary to support good performance. They will be delegative in that they will refrain from micromanagement and extensive intervention in decisions about the management of the agency.

As an example of these conditions of oversight, one can point to the response of congressional leaders such as Wilbur Mills when the Social Security Administration was having serious problems with backlogs in claims processing during the 1970s.

Figure 10.1   Characteristics of Effective Government Agencies

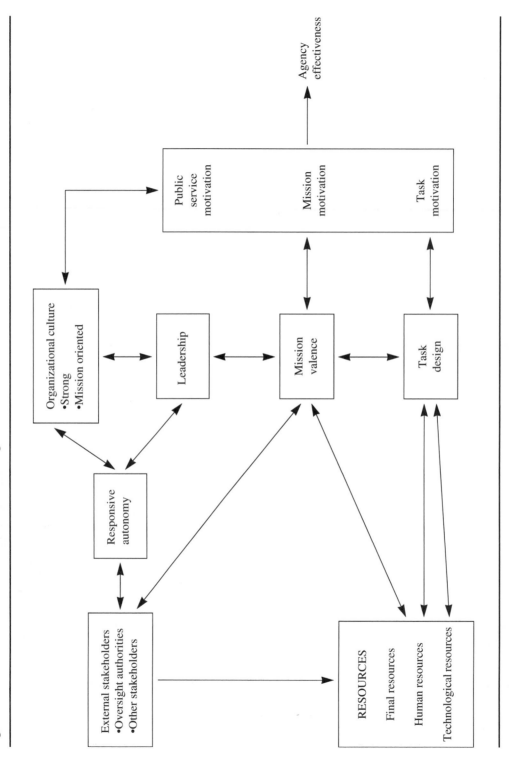

Congress had expanded the types of coverage and benefits of the social security program, and the population of entitled persons had grown rapidly. Decisions about claims became more complicated, more varied, and simply more voluminous. More claims took longer to process, and citizens complained to their congressmen about delays in receiving a response about their claims and inquiries. To oversimplify for brevity, Mills and other congressional leaders essentially told Commissioner Robert Ball to fix the problem and accepted Ball's assurances that such efforts were underway. SSA actually took some time to adopt reforms, while devoting considerable attention to diagnosis and planning. The ultimate solution, which involved reorganizing the major payment centers (public service centers) into work modules where teams worked together to process claims, proved highly successful. While demanding a solution, congressional leaders delegated the selection and management of the solution to the agency's leaders. By contrast, in more recent years observers have expressed concern that rapid turnover in the top executives at SSA, due to efforts by presidential administrations to increase their control over the agency, has damaged effective management within the agency (Rainey and Rainey 1986; U.S. GAO 1986). As a roughly similar example, the highly effective Gulf War operations were conducted relatively autonomously by commanders there, without extensive control or intervention from Washington. As an example of the failure of oversight officials to focus on mission accomplishment, the Federal Emergency Management Agency (FEMA) had a reputation for weak performance at one point, frequently attributed to oversight officials' use of the agency as a haven for political cronies.

Other Stakeholders

Summarizing research on the influence of interest groups on public bureaucracies, Meier (1993a) concludes that *an agency is better able to obtain resources and autonomy of operations when it has interest groups that, in addition to being attentive and interested, are geographically dispersed, diverse along various dimensions (such as demographic makeup), mobilizable, and multiple.* That is, an agency loses autonomy if it is captured by an interest group, and it gains autonomy and influence if it has supporters that are diverse but mobilizable. The agency can play different groups off against each other but, as is elaborately discussed in the literature on public bureaucracy and public management, it usually needs the support of interest groups to gain resources. In addition, as is implied in the discussion of issue networks, policy subsystems, and subgovernments, other actors, such as experts, play a part in this process.

Agencies will also tend to be more effective when they have favorable public support. This includes generally favorable public opinion and media coverage.

More effective agencies also will manage well their relations with allies and partners (Holzer and Callahan 1998) *such as contractors and other public, private, and nonprofit entities with which they interact in carrying out their work.* For example, a growing literature now details the requirements for the effective management of contracts and privatization initiatives (e.g., Globerman and Vining 1996; Donahue 1990; Gill and Rainey 1997; Kettl 1993; Lowery 1997; H.G. Rainey 1997; Rehfuss 1989) as well as the effective management of networks of actors and organizations more generally (Provan and Milward 1995; O'Toole 1997). Agencies that have in place systems that meet these requirements should more effectively manage such relations and thereby enhance their own effectiveness.

Autonomy

Government agencies will be more effective when they have higher levels of autonomy in relation to external stakeholders, but not extremely high levels of autonomy. (The relationship between autonomy and effectiveness is curvilinear.)

When oversight authorities are supportive and

delegative, as we have described above, they grant autonomy to the agency. Autonomy to manage its mission and tasks tends to enhance an agency's performance of the mission and tasks. Yet the following discussion of organizational culture describes examples of agencies that became too insular. The SSA example above illustrate the responsiveness of the agency and its leaders to the demands of stakeholders. An effective agency's autonomy does not imply extreme isolation from communication and exchange with external stakeholders; it should be conceived as a responsive autonomy. Wolf (1998) concludes from his data that agency leaders earn grants of autonomy from oversight officials through skillful management of relations with external stakeholders.

Mission Valence

The higher the mission valence of the government agency, the more effectively the agency will perform. The concept of mission valence draws on the concept of *valence* from the expectancy theory of work motivation. Formulations of that theory use the concept of valence from chemistry (the positive or negative charges of atomic particles) to refer to the positive or negative attractiveness of an outcome of behavior—to how good or bad, attractive or unattractive, a person considers an outcome to be (H.G. Rainey 1997, 229–32). An agency's mission can be attractive or abhorrent (e.g., combat, war) to individuals. The more engaging, attractive, and worthwhile the mission is to people, the more the agency will be able to attract support from those people, to attract some of them to join the agency, and to motivate them to perform well in the agency (depending on some other conditions we will discuss).

The external stakeholders and the members of the organization interactively establish the organization's mission. The mission is the general social contribution and purpose of the agency and its related general goals. The military services must defend the nation, be prepared for combat

engagements and, when necessary, to win them. The Social Security Administration provides income security for retired persons and their survivors. The Centers for Disease Control must defend the populace against diseases and other dangers to health. Any organization has a mission, in this general sense, whether or not the organization has joined the herd of organizations issuing mission statements. The mission has higher valence when it has higher levels of the dimensions listed in Exhibit 10.1 (cf. Behn 1991, 67–69; Di-Iulio 1994; Hargrove and Glidewell 1990; Wilson 1989).

Organizational Culture

Effective government agencies have a strong organizational culture, effectively linked to mission accomplishment.

Organizational culture is probably the most overused and loosely used term in contemporary management discourse. Journalists regularly use it to interpret developments in business firms and other organizations. In any brainstorming or planning session of government employees that is concerned with organizational improvement, leadership, or related matters, participants will repeatedly refer to the need to change the cultures of agencies. These casual uses of the term typically refer to a subdimension of culture, such as employees' attitudes toward risk taking, but their common usage suggests the need for a concept such as culture. Scholars, of course, have devoted much attention to culture and regularly assert its importance to organizational analysis (Schein 1992; Trice and Beyer 1993), including the analysis of government agencies (Wilson 1989; H.G. Rainey 1997, 273–81).

Culture refers to patterns of shared meaning in organizations, including shared values and beliefs about appropriate behaviors and actions. It also refers to such matters as the nature of the organization and its relation to other entities or to the basis for authority in the organization. Culture can be manifest in, and influenced by, symbols, ceremonies, statements, and actions of leaders. The proposition above asserts that a strong organizational culture will be related positively to agency effectiveness when the culture is effectively linked to mission accomplishment. The literature now contains numerous examples of strong or salient cultures in agencies that promote the agencies' effectiveness in accomplishing their missions and the roles of leaders in shaping such cultures (e.g., Doig and Hargrove 1987; Lewis 1980 and 1987; Maynard-Moody, Stull, and Mitchell 1986; Mashaw 1983, 216; Meier 1993a; Rainey 1997, 273–81; Wilson 1989). In addition, authors suggest guidelines for leaders in their efforts to influence and develop culture (Schein 1992; Trice and Beyer 1993; Yukl 1998).

Like other propositions advanced here, this proposition about strong agency culture runs into complexities and potential controversy, since a strong culture could make an agency impervious to external oversight and control, resistant to innovation, or otherwise poorly adapted to imperatives of its environment. Examples of such a problem include Hoover and the FBI, and the case of a public health agency in Kansas that became so focused on professional autonomy that the legislature ultimately intervened to assert authority over the agency (Maynard-Moody et al. 1986). Strong culture does not need to imply insularity or arrogance. Values strongly espoused in a strong culture can include adaptiveness, surveillance of the environment, and responsiveness. The two examples above can be interpreted as illustrations of ineffective linkages to agency mission that in the long run damaged the agencies' effectiveness.

Leadership

The more effective the leadership of the agency, the more effective the agency. More effective leadership is characterized by more stability, multiplicity, commitment to mission, effective goal setting, and effective administrative and political coping.

Scholars regularly cite leadership as an essential element in the success of public agencies. Leadership has long been treated as an important determinant of an agency's power and influence (Meier 1993a, 75–77; Rourke 1984). More recently, numerous authors describe and analyze effective, innovative, and exemplary leaders in government agencies (Behn 1991; Cooper and Wright 1992; Doig and Hargrove 1987; Hargrove and Glidewell 1990; Riccucci 1995; Terry 1995). As we noted earlier, Wolf (1993) reports empirical evidence of a significant role of leadership in achieving agency effectiveness. Holzer and Callahan (1998, 160) report results of a survey of winners of an award for exemplary state and local public service initiatives, in which the respondents rate the support of top agency executives as the most important factor in the success of agency innovations.

Like most fundamental topics in the social sciences, the topic of leadership is vast, richly elaborated, and inconclusive (Yukl 1998). Enough listings of desirable leadership skills and qualities could be gathered to build another great pyramid. They vary widely, and none of them can claim conclusive validation. One could choose any of a number of such listings, but one can reasonably choose, as a general conception of leadership skills for government agencies, the *Executive Core Competencies* of the Senior Executive Service (U.S. OPM 1998). The competencies include the following: leading change (including leadership competencies of creativity and innovation and service motivation, among others); leading people (e.g., conflict management, team building); results driven [sic] (e.g., accountability, customer service); business acumen (financial, human resources, and technology management); and building coalitions and communication (e.g., interpersonal skills, partnering, political savvy). From many sources in the leadership literature, one can add that leaders need a basic motivation for the role, along with a drive to take responsibility, to lead others, and to make a difference.

In addition to such general conceptions,

however, the subdimensions of leadership cited in the proposition above and in Exhibit 10.1 seem particularly important to leadership in government agencies. First, scholars and experts emphasize the problems that result from rapid turnover of top executives in public agencies (e.g., Warwick 1975; Heclo 1978; U.S. GAO 1986). Conversely, various researchers have reported an apparent linkage between stable, long-term leadership—often from career civil servants—and effective performance of public agencies (Behn 1991; DiIulio 1994; Doig and Hargrove 1987; G.W. Rainey 1990; Rainey and Rainey 1986; Riccucci 1995). Excessive stability of leadership can build a harmful insularity, of course, and there are also important examples of generalist leaders such as Eliot Richardson who earned reputations as excellent government executives through a variety of relatively short-term posts in different agencies. Riccucci (1995) provides additional examples of effective leaders without long-term governmental experience. Leadership stability, then, needs to be considered in association with other dimensions in Exhibit 10.1, which hypothesizes a curvilinear relationship between leadership stability and agency effectiveness.

Shared leadership, for example, can make a short-term leader more influential on agency effectiveness. The literature on management in both the public and private sectors increasingly emphasizes the importance of sharing leadership roles among teams or cadres of leaders, as well as the empowerment of individuals to assume roles in the leadership of various parts of the work (e.g., Behn 1991; Denhardt 1993; Huber and Glick 1993; Sims and Lorenzi 1992; Terry 1995, ch. 4). As an example of a skillful approach to shared leadership, one can cite James Webb's creation of a leadership triad at NASA and his emphasis on maximal leadership continuity in the agency (Lambright 1987). Although he did not possess scientific skills, he established a strong relationship with assistant administrators who did have those skills, and he thereby enhanced his own legitimacy, and more importantly the quality and legitimacy of the decisions of the leadership team. Somewhat similarly, Nancy Hanks, as the early and influential chair of

the National Endowment for the Arts, empowered her deputy chairman to serve as the chief spokesperson for the agency, to complement her own abilities and her preference for working in small, informal settings (Wyszomirski 1987). Such skillful exercises in empowerment and team leadership can help even short-term political appointees to ensure that their influences on the agency endure (Ingraham 1988).

The problem of turnover at the top of many agencies also makes a strong commitment to an agency's mission an important aspect of leadership. The most effective agency executives, such as Robert Ball, Hyman Rickover, Nancy Hanks, James Webb, and Gifford Pinchot, all embody such a commitment. Analysts of their careers conclude that they displayed a desire to "make a difference" (Doig and Hargrove 1987, 11) coupled with an ability to see new possibilities, which led them to focus on the agency and its mission as an avenue for exerting influence on the development and pursuit of new possibilities.

The most frequently repeated observation about the distinctive characteristics of public agencies concerns the vagueness, multiplicity, and mutual conflict among agency goals. Therefore, skillful leadership through mission development and through goal setting in relation to the mission contribute significantly to agency effectiveness. The literature now offers numerous examples of such leadership practices (e.g., Behn 1991; Denhardt 1993; Riccucci 1995; Wilson 1989).

Finally, it seems to be obvious that leaders of effective public agencies will display skills in coping with the political and administrative pressures and constraints of their roles. Yet the importance of this dimension of leadership is reflected in frequent expressions of concern that these constraints penalize effective leadership and make it scarce in public agencies (e.g., National Academy of Public Administration 1986; Thompson 1993, 18–22). Significantly, accounts of the most influential and innovative agency leaders emphasize their ability to turn into opportunities the constraints that supposedly impede many executives and to cope with the pressures and complexities of their roles (Ban

1995; Doig and Hargrove 1987; Hargrove and Glidewell 1990; Lewis 1980 and 1987; Riccucci 1995).

Task Design

The more the task design in the agency provides extrinsic and intrinsic rewards to individuals and groups, the more effective the agency.

In addition to the general mission, there are more specific characteristics of the work people do, and in the framework these are included in a broad conception of *task*. Included in this conception of task are those factors associated with an individual's relatively specific ongoing activities that provide extrinsic and intrinsic rewards for work. Organizational behavior researchers commonly define extrinsic rewards as those mediated externally to the individual and provided by the organization, such as pay, promotion, and physical conditions of work. Intrinsic rewards are mediated internally to the individual and include psychological rewards such as interest in the work, enjoyment of the work, a sense of growth and development, and a sense of worthwhile accomplishment. Organizational psychologists have developed measures of the motivating potential of jobs, which assess the degree to which the job provides autonomy, task significance, task identity, feedback from the work, and skill variety. These factors tend to increase intrinsic work motivation (Hackman and Oldham 1980). This conception of task design is intended to include conditions mentioned in the profiles of excellent public organizations described in earlier sections, such as whether the members are empowered, whether they are organized into teams and have a teamwork orientation, and whether decisions are participative.

Included in this conception of task and task design are extrinsic rewards associated with the more specific, day to day work of the individual, such as those that are mentioned above. These rewards will also depend, of course, on organizational structures and policies such as human resource management/personnel policies.

The distinction between task and mission is useful in analyzing whether they are two distinct sources of incentive and motivation in government agencies that are separable but that need to be linked together. For example, consider a professor who is excited about her work for the day. How much is she motivated by the overall mission or general societal contribution of the university, and how much by the intrinsic rewards from her enjoyment of the more specific activities of teaching and research? A NASA employee may enjoy his job designing and implementing training procedures for space shuttle astronauts. How much additional motivation does he derive from the overall mission of advancing space exploration and travel?

Utilization of Technology and Development of Human Resources

Exhibit 10.1 hypothesizes that utilization of technology and development of human resources relate to agency effectiveness, because Holzer and Callahan (1998) emphasize the importance of these processes in innovative government agencies and because of the obvious importance of such processes in building the internal capacity of an agency. Holzer and Callahan provide elaboration on effective utilization of technology and human resources; other examples and case studies abound. SSA, for example, has used computerization to improve markedly the efficiency and accuracy of case processing. Herbert Kaufman's classic study, *The Forest Ranger,* provides case illustrations of the effective development of human resources.

Professionalism

Various authors attribute agency effectiveness to professionalism among the members of the agency (Brehm and Gates 1997; Wilson 1989; Wolf 1993 and 1998). Authors in public administration have analyzed professionalism in that field, and an elaborate literature examines the topic of professionalism in sociology and organization theory. This latter material develops the concept more elaborately than do some of the authors who write about professionalism in public agencies. For example, sociologists define professions as occupations with the following characteristics: they apply advance skills based on theoretical knowledge; they require advanced training; they require testing of competence through examinations and other means; they are organized into professional associations; they emphasize adherence to a code of conduct; they espouse altruistic service. Members of such professionalized occupations tend to have values and beliefs that accord with the occupational characteristics, such as belief in collegial maintenance of standards among professionals, identification with other professionals, and commitment to professional norms. Authors on professionalism in public agencies tend to define it less elaborately—as involving specialized skills that require advanced education or training, membership in professional groups outside the agency (Wilson 1989), or simply a commitment to professional norms of performance and behavior and to do the work right and well (Brehm and Gates 1997).

Professionalism can enhance an agency's performance by increasing its autonomy, due to the social status and intellectual authority and independence of professionals in the agency (Wolf 1998). In addition, professional norms and technical training provide incentives and guidelines for individuals in the agencies (Wilson 1989; Brehm and Gates 1997).

Motivation

Effective government agencies have high levels of motivation among their members, including high levels of public service motivation, mission motivation, and task motivation.

The preceding propositions lead to this one. The framework and propositions generally assert the important role of motivation that stimulates effort and effective behaviors among people in the organization. The proposition refers to all of the several forms of motivation to emphasize the important questions: Can we actually conceive and validate these three separate forms? Is there a general motive to serve the public? Is it stimulated in government agencies, stimulated to higher levels in some than others, and in turn translated into motivation, effort, and effective behavior?

Public Service Motivation

Public service motivation can be defined as a general altruistic motivation to serve the interests of a community of people, a state, a nation, or humankind. Major social scientists recently have referred to evolutionary developments that have fostered in human beings motives and attitudes conducive to communal and collective behaviors, including trust, reciprocity, and identification with organizations (Ostrom 1998; Simon 1998). Since animals display altruistic behaviors, behaviors that involve self-sacrifice on the part of their groups, these motives should be considered fundamental in humans as well, and in some persons as strong as the more extrinsic motives for money or other material gain. Such forms of motivation have been part of human discourse since classic times, when, for example, Athenians pledged to leave their city better than they found it.

A form of public service motivation has been part of discourse in public administration for a long time. Frederickson and Hart (1985), for example, discuss a "patriotism of benevolence" that involves benevolent impulses and behaviors toward a broad community. They define it as an affection for all people in the nation and a devotion to defending their basic rights, as granted by enabling documents such as the Constitution. Frederickson (1997) treats such a motive, and associated ethical and equitable behaviors, as a central theme in public administration.

Interestingly, however, this topic has attracted not nearly as much systematic research as one might have expected. Various surveys have found that government executives and managers tend to express a motive to serve the public or society in a worthwhile way (e.g., Sikula 1973). Kilpatrick, Cummings, and Jennings (1964) found that federal executives, scientists, and engineers gave higher ratings than did their counterparts in business to work-related values such as the importance of doing your best, even if you dislike your work, the importance of doing work that is worthwhile to society, and the importance of helping others. H.G. Rainey (1983) found that state agency managers rated the "opportunity to engage in meaningful public service" as a more important work reward than did managers in large business firms. Among the very large sample of executives and managers in the *Federal Employee Attitude Surveys,* high percentages of the respondents who enter the federal government rate public service and having an impact on public affairs as the most important reasons to enter federal service; very low percentages of these groups rate salary and job security as important attractions (Crewson 1995, 94). Analyzing other large social surveys such as the *General Social Survey,* Crewson (1997) also finds that public sector respondents, as compared to private sector respondents, place a higher value on work that is useful to society and that helps others. These results and other findings within such surveys suggest the form that general service motives in government may take—placing a high value on work that helps others and benefits society as a whole, on a degree of self-sacrifice, and on responsibility and integrity. Public managers often mention such motives (Hartman and Weber 1980; Lasko 1980; Kelman 1989; Sandeep 1989).

Seeking to refine the conception of public service motives, Perry and Wise (1990) suggest that public service motives can fall into three categories: *instrumental motives,* including participation in policy formulation, commitment to a public program because of personal identification, and advocacy for a special or private interest; *norm-based motives,* including a desire to serve the public interest, loyalty to duty and to government, and social equity; and *affective motives,* including commitment to a program based on a conviction about its social importance and the patriotism of benevolence (Frederickson and Hart 1985; Frederickson 1997).

Perry (1996a and 1997) provides more recent evidence of the dimensions of a general public service motive and ways to assess it. He analyzed survey questionnaire responses from about four hundred people, including managers and employees in various government and business organizations, and graduate and undergraduate students. He developed scales for four dimensions of public service motivation: attraction to public policy making, commitment to the public interest and civic duty, compassion, and self-sacrifice. He found higher levels of some of these factors associated with religious involvement and family background.

These findings and those cited above show that public service motivation is a complex concept that deserves more attention. The evidence, however, strongly supports the existence of a general form of public service motivation that tends to be more prevalent among government employees than private sector employees. The evidence also suggests that this form of motivation involves a general motive to provide significant service that benefits the community, the public, or society in dutiful, compassionate, and self-sacrificing ways.

Mission Motivation

The above proposition about motivation also holds that high levels of mission motivation contribute significantly to the effectiveness of public agencies. Why coin a term such as *mission motivation* and propose it as a new concept? Wilson (1989) describes the existence of a *sense of mission* in such agencies as the Army Corps of Engineers and the Forestry Service. Various authors describe how leaders develop a sense of mission for their agencies and inculcate it into the culture of the agency through goal setting, symbolic actions, and other techniques (e.g., Behn 1991; Cooper 1987; Denhardt 1993). The proposition about mission motivation asserts that members have perceptions of the mission of the agency and may be highly motivated to contribute to the achievement of the mission. When so motivated, an individual will extend effort and seek to perform well in ways that he or she perceives to be related to accomplishing the mission.[4]

This pattern of motivation differs from public service motivation, although the propositions and framework assert that they have a strong relation to each other in effective agencies. While public service motivation focuses on altruistic service that benefits a community or a larger population, mission motivation has as its target or objective the mission of the agency. For example, this distinction raises the issue of how much of a person's motivation is accounted for by a sense that her actions contribute to a general public service, and how much is accounted for by this sense of mission? When a tank commander in the Desert Storm operation works hard to contribute to an effective combat initiative by his unit, how much is he motivated by a perception or belief that he is contributing a valuable service to the nation or to humankind, and how much by a perception or belief that his actions contribute to the mission of winning combat engagements in defense of the nation? How much is a module manager in a public service center of the Social Security Administration motivated by a belief that her actions contribute to something worthwhile and important to the nation as a whole, and how much is motivated by a belief that sound management of her module will contribute to the mission of providing income security for the retired people who have earned it through their contributions to the program?

An earlier section introduced the concept of mission valence because of its relevance to the role of mission motivation. A mission can have a high valence for an individual and attract that person to an agency. Members of NASA, for example, observe that many people came to NASA and remained there because of interest in and excitement about the mission of space exploration, when they could have worked in the private sector for higher pay. Motivation in organizations always involves at least two general steps—first, joining and stay-ing; second, working hard and well. One can take the first step without taking the second (March and Simon 1958). High levels of mission valence will tend to attract certain individuals who will self-select into the organization on the basis of the valence of the mission for them, but then their levels of mission motivation will further depend on their perceptions about the linkage of their work to the mission. Buchanan (1974 and 1975) some years ago reported evidence that idealistic people may enter the public service and later become discouraged because they cannot see the linkage of their work activities to their ideals. Through leadership practices such as those described earlier, the agency must sharpen and make salient the relations of individuals' work to the mission. In turn, the perceived linkage of the mission to public service values can enhance both mission valence and mission motivation, such that in the government agencies that perform the best, members will show both high levels of mission motivation and high levels of public service motivation and will feel that the mission of the agency contributes to general worthwhile public service.

Task Motivation

The distinction made earlier in this article between the general concept of task motivation and the concepts of public service motivation and mission motivation serves a purpose of distinguishing among patterns of motivation. Returning to the example of the highly motivated professor, consider how much of that person's motivation might derive from a sense of contributing a valuable public service; how much from a sense of contributing to the university's mission of advancing teaching, research, and public service; and how much from enjoyment of the specific work itself? Other examples of the task motivation at issue here include a NASA employee who finds it fun and exciting to develop and implement safety and emergency drills for training astronauts. Also, a district office manager for the Social Security Administration enjoys the tasks of managing the of-

---

[4]A reason to use a term such as *mission motivation* is that it implies a different concept from a sense of mission. It includes not just the perception of a mission but the extension of effort toward achieving it.

fice, supervising personnel, and engaging in public relations activities such as appearing on a local radio show to answer questions about the social security programs.

These examples illustrate the broad concept of task motivation advanced here. They reflect the influence of the relatively specific and immediate extrinsic and intrinsic rewards available through the person's role in the organization, as described earlier in the discussion of task design. These factors can be independent of, or weakly related to, public service motivation and mission motivation. For example, agency employees may express high levels of motivation in spite of low levels of some of these rewards, such as favorable physical surroundings at work. Ultimately, however, the framework and the proposals hold that agency effectiveness will be highest where organizational design, task design, leadership, and other factors produce desirable levels of extrinsic and intrinsic rewards through tasks and where members of the agency perceive that task activities and accomplishments contribute to mission accomplishment, which in turn contributes to the provision of a worthwhile and valuable public service.

Ultimately, too, the propositions and framework hypothesize that the several forms of motivation play a significant role in determining agency effectiveness, as do the other factors such as leadership and culture. These actually posit very debatable and researchable concepts and relations that might be opposed by other interpretations. For example, one might argue that external forces, such as technological and economic factors, drive the performance of public agencies by providing new technologies and human and financial resources, such that the espoused motives of bureaucrats and the dramaturgy of leadership provide merely a superficial, self-justificatory labeling for developments that are essentially out of the control of the people in the organizations. Such alternative interpretations, along with the general importance of the performance of government agencies, provide all the more reason to continue to develop theories to explain their performance.

Direction for Further Development and the Problem of Parsimony

The concepts and relations in the propositions advanced here need more development in a variety of ways. In particular, however, many related concepts and topics that are not discussed here need further consideration in relation to the propositions and agency effectiveness. These include typologies of agencies and differences by type of agency; organizational socialization processes; organizational commitment or identification; performance measures and their availability and adequacy; and numerous others.

The lengthy list of variables in Exhibit 10.1 raises the question of whether the list can and should be pared down to a more parsimonious set. In a sense, the set of variables is not so vast if one conceives it as basis for a LISREL analysis or a similar analysis that would treat the subdimensions under the more general variables as indicators of the more general variable that would factor together in measures of it. As a hypothetical statement about the most important variables, however, based on the literature reviewed and cited in this article, one can posit that the variables for the following concepts will emerge as the most important: relations with external authorities and stakeholders, autonomy, leadership, professionalism, and motivation among members.

A Symbiosis of Freedom?

As we noted earlier, Simon (1998) emphasizes the essential role of effective public administration in maintaining the strength of democracy. Other social scientists have remarked on the interesting tendency of democratic systems to coincide with free market systems, and conservative economists often have mentioned the need for an effective, albeit limited, government in a prosperous economy. Analysis of effective government agencies should be part of a new dialogue on the role of government and public administration (e.g., Durant 1998) that recognizes that effective organizations in business, government, and the nonprofit sector benefit each other. Pursuit of systematic explanations and theories about effective government agencies should continue as part of the effort to enhance these mutual benefits.

References

Ban, C. 1995. *How Do Public Managers Manage?* San Francisco: Jossey-Bass.

Barton, A.H. 1980. "A Diagnosis of Bureaucratic Maladies." In *Making Bureaucracies Work,* C. H. Weiss and A. H. Barton. eds. Thousand Oaks, Calif.: Sage.

Barzelay, M. 1992. *Breaking Through Bureaucracy.* Berkeley: University of California Press.

Behn, R.D. 1991. *Leadership Counts.* Cambridge, Mass.: Harvard University Press.

Bozeman, B. *Bureaucracy and Red Tape.* Upper Saddle River, N.J.: Prentice-Hall. Forthcoming.

Brehm, J., and Gates, S. 1997. *Working, Shirking, and Sabotage: Bureaucratic Response to a Democratic Public.* Ann Arbor: University of Michigan Press.

Buchanan, B. 1974. "Government Managers, Business Executives, and Organizational Commitment." *Public Administration Review* 35: 339–47.

———. 1975. "Red Tape and the Service Ethic: Some Unexpected Differences Between Public and Private Managers." *Administration and Society* 6:423–38.

Caiden, G. 1991. "What Really Is Public Maladministration?" *Public Administration Review* 51:6:486–93.

Cohen, S., and W. Eimicke. 1995. *The New Effective Public Manager.* San Francisco: Jossey-Bass.

Collins, J.C., and J.I. Porras. 1994. *Built to Last: Successful Habits of Visionary Companies.* New York: Harper Business.

Cooper, J.M. 1987. "Gifford Pinchot Creates a Forest Service." In Doig and Hargrove, eds., 63–95.

Cooper, T.L., and N.D. Wright. 1992. *Exemplary Public Administrators.* San Francisco: Jossey-Bass.

Crewson, P.E. 1995. "A Comparative Analysis of Public and Private Sector Entrant Quality." *American Journal of Political Science* 39:628–39.

———. 1997. "Public-Service Motivation: Building Empirical Evidence of Incidence and Effect." *Journal of Public Administration Research and Theory* 7:4:499–518.

Daft, R.L. 1998. *Organization Theory and Design,* 6th ed. Cincinnati, Ohio: South-Western College Publishing.

Denhardt, R.B. 1993. *The Pursuit of Significance.* Belmont, Calif.: Wadsworth.

DiIulio, J.D. 1994. "Principled Agents: The Cultural Bases of Behavior in a Federal Government Bureaucracy." *Journal of Public Administration Research and Theory* 4:3:277–318.

Doig, J.W., and E.C. Hargrove. eds. 1987. *Leadership and Innovation: A Biographical Perspective on Entrepreneurs in Government.* Baltimore: Johns Hopkins University Press.

Donahue, J.D. 1990. *The Privatization Decision.* New York: Basic Books.

Downs, A. 1967. *Inside Bureaucracy.* Boston: Little, Brown.

Downs, G.W., and P. Larkey. 1986. *The Search for Government Efficiency: From Hubris to Helplessness.* New York: Random House.

Durant, R.F. 1992. *The Administrative Presidency Revisited: Public Lands, the BLM, and the Reagan Revolution.* Albany: State University of New York Press.

———. 1998. "Agenda Setting, the 'Third Wave,' and the Administrative State." *Administration & Society* 30:211–47.

Durant, R.F., J.S. Legge, and A. Moussios. 1998. "People, Profits, and Service Delivery: Lessons from the Privatization of British Telecom." *American Journal of Political Science* 42:1:97–117.

Eisner, R. 1998. "Cut Social Security? No, Expand It." *Wall Street Journal,* 16 Dec., p. 22.

Frederickson, H.G. 1997. *The Spirit of Public Administration.* San Francisco: Jossey-Bass.

Frederickson, H.G., and D.K. Hart. 1985. "The Public Service and the Patriotism of Benevolence." *Public Administration Review* 45:547–53.

Gill, J., and H.G. Rainey. 1997. "The Relationship Between Privatization and Public Management in Georgia State Government." Paper presented at the Southeastern Conference on Public Administration, Knoxville, Tenn., Sept. 25.

Globerman, S., and A.R. Vining. 1996. "A Framework for Evaluating the Government Contracting-Out Decision with an Application to Information Technology." *Public Administration Review* 56:6:577–86.

Gold, K.A. 1982. "Managing for Success: A Comparison of the Public and Private Sectors." *Public Administration Review* 42:568–75.

Goodsell, C. 1994. *The Case for Bureaucracy,* 3d ed. Chatham, N.J.: Chatham House.

Gore, A. 1993. *From Red Tape to Results: Creating a Government That Works Better and Costs Less. Report of the National Performance Review.* Washington, D.C.: U.S. Government Printing Office.

———. 1995. *Common Sense Government: Works Better and Costs Less. Third Report of the National Performance Review.* Washington, D.C.: U.S. Government Printing Office.

Hackman, J.R., and G.R. Oldham. 1980. *Work Redesign.* Reading, Mass.: Addison-Wesley.

Hale, S.J. 1996. "Achieving High Performance in Public Organizations." In *Handbook of Public Administration,* J. L. Perry, ed. 151–66. San Francisco: Jossey-Bass.

Hargrove, E.C., and J.C. Glidewell, eds. 1990. *Impossible Jobs in Public Management.* Lawrence: University Press of Kansas.

Hartman, R., and A. Weber. 1980. *The Rewards of Public Service.* Washington, D.C.: Brookings.

Heclo, H. 1978. "Issue Networks and the Executive Establishment." In A. King, ed. *The New American Political System.* Washington, D.C.: American Enterprise Institute.

Hill, L.B. 1991. "Who Governs the American Administrative State? A Bureaucratic-Centered Image of Governance." *Journal of Public Administration Research and Theory* 1:3:261–94.

———1992. "Introduction: Public Bureaucracy and the American State," and "Taking Bureaucracy Seriously." In *The State of Public Bureaucracy,* Larry B. Hill, ed. 1–57. Amronk, N.Y.: Sharpe.

Holzer, M., and K. Callahan. 1998. *Government at Work: Best Practices and Model Programs.* Thousand Oaks, Calif.: Sage.

Huber, G.P., and W.H. Glick, eds. 1993. *Organizational Change and Redesign.* New York: Oxford University Press.

Ingraham, P.W. 1998. "Transition and Policy Change in Washington." *Public Productivity Review* 12:61–72.

Kelman, S. 1989. "The Making of Government Good Guys." *New York Times,* 2 July, business section, 1.

Kettl, D.F. 1993. *Sharing Power.* Washington, D.C.: Brookings.

Kilpatrick, F.P., M.C. Cummings and M.K. Jennings. 1964. *The Image of the Federal Service.* Washington, D.C.: Brookings.

Lambright, W.H. 1987. "James Webb and the Uses of Administrative Power." In Doig and Hargrove, eds. 174–203.

Lasko, W. 1980. "Executive Accountability: Will SES Make a Difference?" *Bureaucrat* 9:6–7.

Lewis, E.B. 1980. *Public Entrepreneurship.* Bloomington: Indiana University Press.

———. 1987. "Admiral Hyman Rickover: Technological Entrepreneurship in the U.S. Navy." In Doig and Hargrove, eds.

Lowery, D. 1997. "Consumer Sovereignty and Quasimarket Failure." Department of Political Science, University of North Carolina at Chapel Hill.

March, J.G., and H. A. Simon 1958. *Organizations.* New York: Wiley.

Mashaw, J.L. 1983. *Bureaucratic Justice.* New Haven, Conn.: Yale University Press.

Maynard-Moody, S., D.D. Stull, and J. Mitchell. 1986. "Reorganization as Status Drama: Building, Maintaining, and Displacing Dominant

Subcultures." *Public Administration Review* 46:301–10.

Meier, K.J. 1993a. *Politics and the Bureaucracy.* Pacific Grove, Calif.: Brooks/Cole.

———. 1993b. "Representative Bureaucracy: A Theoretical and Empirical Exposition." In James L. Perry, ed. *Research in Public Administration,* vol. 2, 1–36. Greenwich, Conn.: JAI Press.

Milward, H.B., K.G. Provan, and B.A. Else. 1993. "What Does the 'Hollow State' Look Like?" In B. Bozeman, ed. *Public Management: State of the Art,* 309–22. San Francisco: Jossey-Bass.

Milward, H.B., and H.G. Rainey. 1983. "Don't Blame the Bureaucracy." *Journal of Public Policy* 3:149–68.

National Academy of Public Administration. 1986. *Revitalizing Federal Management.* Washington, D.C.: National Academy of Public Administration.

National Highway Traffic Safety Administration. 1996. *The National Highway Traffic Safety Administration Case Study: Strategic Planning and Performance Measurement.* Washington, D.C.: National Highway Traffic Safety Administration.

Niskanen, W.A. 1971. *Bureaucracy and Representative Government.* Chicago: Aldine.

Osborne, D., and T. Gaebler. 1992. *Reinventing Government.* Reading, Mass.: Addison-Wesley.

Ostrom, E. 1998. "A Behavioral Approach to the Rational Choice Theory of Collective Action." *American Political Science Review* 92:1:1–22.

O'Toole, L.J. 1997. "Treating Networks Seriously: Practical and Research-Based Agendas in Public Administration." *Public Administration Review* 57:1:45–52.

Perry, J.L. 1996a. "Measuring Public Service Motivation: An Assessment of Construct Reliability and Validity." *Journal of Public Administration Research and Theory* 6:5–24.

———. 1996b. *Handbook of Public Administration,* 2d ed. San Francisco: Jossey-Bass.

———. 1997. "Antecedents of Public Service Motivation." *Journal of Public Administration Research and Theory* 7:2:181–98.

Perry, J.L., and L.R. Wise. 1990. "The Motivational Bases of Public Service." *Public Administration Review* 50:367–73.

Peters, T.J., and R.H. Waterman. 1982. *In Search of Excellence: Lessons from America's Best-Run Companies.* New York: Harper & Row.

Provan, K.G., and H.B. Milward. 1995. "A Preliminary Theory of Interorganizational Network Effectiveness: A Comparative Study of Four Community Mental Health Systems." *Administrative Science Quarterly* 40:1–33.

Rainey, G.W. 1990. "Implementation and Managerial Creativity: A Study of the Development of Client-Centered Units in Human Service Programs." In D.J. Palumbo and D.J. Calista, eds. *Implementation and the Policy Process.* New York: Greenwood.

Rainey, G.W., and H.G. Rainey. 1986. "Breaching the Hierarchical Imperative: The Modularization of the Social Security Claims Process." In D.J. Calista, ed. *Bureaucratic and Governmental Reform.* JAI Research Annual in Public Policy Analysis and Management. Greenwich, Conn.: JAI Press.

Rainey, H.G. 1983. "Public Agencies and Private Firms: Incentive Structures, Goals, and Individual Roles." *Administration and Society* 15:207–42.

———. 1997. *Understanding and Managing Public Organizations,* 2d ed. San Francisco: Jossey-Bass.

Rehfuss, J. 1989. *The Job of the Public Manager.* Homewood, Ill.: Dorsey.

Riccucci, N.M. 1995. *Unsung Heroes: Federal Executives Making a Difference.* Washington, D.C.: Georgetown University Press.

Rourke, F.E. 1984. *Bureaucracy, Politics, and Public Policy.* Boston: Little, Brown.

Rubin, I.S. 1985. *Shrinking the Federal Government: The Effect of Cutbacks on Five Federal Agencies.* New York: Longman.

Sandeep, P. 1989. "Why Government Can't Always Get the Best." *Government Executive* (March): 64.

Schein, E.H. 1992. *Organizational Culture and*

Leadership: A Dynamic View. San Francisco: Jossey-Bass.

Sikula, A.F. 1973. "The Values and Value Systems of Governmental Executives." *Public Personnel Management* 2:16–22.

Simon, H.A. 1998. "Why Public Administration?" *Journal of Public Administration Research and Theory* 8:1:1–12.

Sims, H.P., and P. Lorenzi. 1992. *The New Leadership Paradigm.* Newbury Park, Calif.: Sage.

Stillman, R. 1996. *The American Bureaucracy,* 2d ed. Chicago: Nelson-Hall.

Terry, L.D. 1995. *Leadership of Public Bureaucracies: The Administrator as Conservator.* Thousand Oaks, California: Sage.

Thompson, F.J., ed. 1993. *Revitalizing State and Local Public Service.* San Francisco: Jossey-Bass.

Thompson, F., and L.R. Jones. 1994. *Reinventing the Pentagon.* San Francisco: Jossey-Bass.

Trice, H.M., and J. M. Beyer. 1993. *The Cultures of Work Organizations.* Englewood Cliffs, N.J.: Prentice-Hall.

U.S. Coast Guard. 1996. *Using Outcome Information to Redirect Programs: A Case Study of the Coast Guard's Pilot Project under the Government Performance and Results Act.* Washington, D.C.: American Society for Public Administration.

U.S. General Accounting Office (GAO). 1986. *Social Security: Actions and Plans to Reduce Agency Staff.* GAO/HRD-86-76BR. Washington, D.C.: U.S. General Accounting Office.

U.S. Office of Personnel Management (OPM). 1998. *OPM Message to the Senior Executive Service.* Washington, D.C.: U.S. Office of Personnel Management (winter):SES-98-02.

Wamsley, G.L. et al. 1990. *Refounding Public Administration.* Newbury Park, Calif.: Sage.

Warwick, D.P. 1975. *A Theory of Public Bureaucracy.* Cambridge, Mass.: Harvard University Press.

Wilson, J.Q. 1989. *Bureaucracy.* New York: Basic Books.

Wolf, P.J. 1993. "A Case Survey of Bureaucratic Effectiveness in U.S. Cabinet Agencies: Preliminary Results." *Journal of Public Administration Research and Theory* 3:2:161–81.

———. 1997. "Why Must We Reinvent the Federal Government? Putting Historical Developmental Claims to the Test." *Journal of Public Administration Research and Theory* 7:3:353–88.

———. 1998. "Explaining Political Autonomy in U.S. Federal Agencies: The Relative Importance of Leadership, Professionalism, and Specialization." Paper presented at the annual meeting of the American Political Science Association, Boston, Sept. 3–6.

Wood, B.D., and R. W. Waterman. 1994. *Bureaucratic Dynamics.* Boulder, Colo.: Westview.

Wyszomirski, M.J. 1987. "The Politics of Art: Nancy Hanks and the National Endowment for the Arts." In Doig and Hargrove, eds., 207–45.

Yukl, G. 1998. *Leadership in Organizations.* Upper Saddle River, N.J.: Prentice-Hall.

☐ CASE STUDY **10**

Introduction

From the standpoint of modern public managers, the demands of running government organizations are heavy, complicated, *and* certainly not as neat, tidy, or simple as many management theorists suggest or have us believe. Indeed today the reality of much of government sector activities is accomplished in partnership with a maze of for-profit, non-profit, and other government entities. There is little left today of "solo in-house" public management enterprise. To do the public's work requires instead that chief executives manage numerous complicated systems, involving multiple organizations often crossing national borders, even spanning the globe, relying upon sophisticated technologies and professional expertise to make them operate, as well as on numerous other organizations for support to achieve their mission(s).

The following case, "The Lessons of Valujet 592," ably demonstrates that very point, namely, the complexities of modern management systems and, even with the best management practices, why they can sometimes fail, with disastrous consequences.

The author, William Langewiesche, himself a commercial pilot, got to the recovery site nineteen hours after the well-publicized crash of Valujet 592, which killed all aboard, 110 people, on May 11, 1996. He carefully recounts what happened and thoughtfully probes its causes. Beyond the immediate fire in the cargo-hold resulting from an accidentally triggered oxy-generating canister onboard Flight 592, the author reveals a highly complex managerial system set up to prevent such accidents, but through a series of mistakes the system failed to function properly.

As you read the following story, try to reflect on:

What were the sequence of failures in the management system that led to the crash of Valujet 592? Where did the FAA regulatory management system break down, and why?

Why does the author argue the ValuJet case "represents a nearly perfect system accident"?

How does this case compare with "The Blast in Centralia?" Were the same "system failures" readily apparent there as well?

Do you agree with the author that in complex systems like this one, some accidents are "normal" and bound to occur *and* that trying to prevent them *all* could even make operations more dangerous? Upon what theory and assumptions does Langewiesche base his thesis?

Does this case ultimately support the effectiveness thesis of the previous essay, namely, that elements of effectiveness are identifiable and, if attended to properly by government managers, can prevent such tragedies from occurring? If so, explain what a public manager at the FAA *should* have done to have prevented this crash. Or do you concur with the author of this case study that indeed there are real limits on details that any public manager reasonably can or should pay attention to? And so, accidents like this one are bound to occur periodically?

Finally, how did what the author calls "engineer speak" contribute to the accident, and what can be done about it?

The Lessons of ValuJet 592

WILLIAM LANGEWIESCHE

On a muggy May afternoon in 1996 an emergency dispatcher in southern Florida got a call from a man

William Langewiesche, "The Lessons of ValuJet 592," as appeared in *The Atlantic Monthly* (March 1998), pp. 81–98. Reprinted with permission.

on a cellular phone. The caller said, "Yes. I am fishing at Everglades Holiday Park, and a large jet aircraft has just crashed out here. Large. Like airliner-size."

The dispatcher said, "Wait a minute. Everglades Park?"

"Everglades Holiday Park, along canal L-sixty-seven. You need to get your choppers in the air. I'm a pilot. I have a GPS. I'll give you coordinates."

"Okay, sir. What kind of plane did you say? Is it a large plane?"

"A large aircraft similar to a seven-twenty-seven or a umm . . . I can't think of it."

This lapse was unimportant. The caller was a born accident observer—a computer engineer and a private pilot with pride in his technical competence and a passion for detail. His name was Walton Little. When he first saw the airplane, it was banked steeply to the right and flying low, just above the swamp. Later he filed an official report, in which he stated,

There was no smoke, no strange engine noise, no debris in the air, no dangling materials or control surfaces, no apparent deformation of the airframe, and no areas that appeared to have missing panels or surfaces. . . . Sunlight was shining on the aircraft, and some surfaces were more reflective and some less reflective. I saw a difference in reflection of the wing skin in the area where I would expect the ailerons to be, as though they were not neutral. In particular, the lower (outboard) portion of the right wing appeared less reflective as though the aileron was deflected upward.

Nearby fishermen ducked into their boat for cover—but not Walton Little, who stood on his deck, facing "about 115 degrees," and watched the airplane hit the water. The shock wave passed through his body.

I was in disbelief that the crash had occurred. I stood there for just a moment to consider that it really did happen. I was already thinking that I needed to get my cellular phone out of the storage compartment and call 911, but I wanted to assure myself of what I was doing because it is against the law to make false calls to 911.

He called within a minute. After telling the dispatcher about the crash and reading off his latitude and longitude, he said, "I'm in a bass boat on the canal. I thought it was an aircraft from an air show or something, and . . ."

The dispatcher interrupted. "What did you . . . Did you see flames and stuff come up, sir?"

"I heard the impact, and I saw dirt and mud fly in the air. The plane was sideways before it went out of my sight on the horizon about a mile from me."

"Yes, sir. Okay. You said it looked like a seven-twenty-seven that went down?"

"Uh, it's that type aircraft. It has twin engines in the rear. It is larger than an executive jet, like a Lear-jet."

"Yes, sir."

"It's much bigger than that. I won't tell you it's a seven-twenty-seven, but it's that type aircraft. No engines on the wing, two engines in the rear. I do not see any smoke, but I saw a tremendous cloud of mud and dirt go into the sky when it hit."

"Okay, sir."

"It was white with blue trim."

"White with blue trim, sir?"

"It will not be in one piece."

Walton Little was right. The airplane was a twin-engine DC-9 painted the colors of ValuJet, an aggressive young discount airline based in Atlanta. When it hit the Everglades, it was banked vertically to the right and pointed nearly straight down. The airplane did not sink mysteriously into the swamp, as reports later suggested, but shattered as it hit the surface with the furious force of a fast dive.

By the time Walton Little felt the shock wave, everyone aboard was dead—two pilots, three flight attendants, and 105 passengers. Their remains lay in a shallow, watery crater filled with liquid mud and grass. All that marked the surface was a fractured engine, a few dead fish, some jet fuel, and a scattering of personal papers, clothes, and twisted pieces of aluminum—the stuff of tragedy. During those first few days some officials worried aloud about the accident's effect on nature, but the swamp was not so fragile as that, and quickly resumed its usual life. The families of those who died have proved less resilient. Most will feel the poison forever.

For the rest of us, though, the accident should be finished business. The official investigation is over, a "cause" has been found, contributing factors have been acknowledged, and the Federal Aviation Administration has written new regulations. Editorialists have expressed their outrage, and individuals have been held responsible. After a long suspension ValuJet has returned to the air with a renewed commitment to safety. Other airlines, too, have promised to be more careful. And even the FAA has gone through a housecleaning. So by conventional standards the reaction to the tragedy has been admirable.

And yes, we know anyway that flying is almost always safe. After years as a working pilot, I have a poetic idea of why: airplanes are fundamentally at home in the sky. Certainly my own experience is that passengers do not need to cower around the exit rows, or carry emergency "smoke hoods," or fear bad weather, or worry about some impending collapse of airline safety. Those are ideas promoted by aviation illiterates—overly cautious people who can always find an audience, and who would smother us in their fear of violent death. The public has the sense in the long run to ignore them. Nonetheless, the ValuJet accident continues to raise troubling questions—no longer about what happened but about why it happened, and what is to keep something similar from happening in the future. As these questions lead into the complicated and human core of flight safety, they become increasingly difficult to answer.

Consider, for simplicity, that there are three kinds of airplane accidents. The most common ones might be called "procedural." They are those old-fashioned accidents that result from single obvious mistakes, that can immediately be understood in simple terms, and that have simple resolutions. To avoid such accidents pilots must not fly into violent thunderstorms, or take off with ice on their wings, or descend prematurely, or let fear or boredom gain the upper hand. Mechanics, ramp agents, and air-traffic controllers must observe equally simple rules. As practitioners, we have together learned many painful lessons.

The second kind of accident could be called "engineered." It consists of those surprising materials failures that should have been predicted by designers or discovered by test pilots but were not. Such failures at first defy understanding, but ultimately they yield to examination and result in tangible solutions. An American Eagle ATR turboprop dives into a frozen field in Roselawn, Indiana, because its de-icing boots did not protect its wings from freezing rain—and as a result new boots are designed, and the entire testing process undergoes review. A USAir Boeing 737 crashes near Pittsburgh because of a rare hard-over rudder movement—and as a result a redesigned rudder-control mechanism will be installed on the whole fleet. A TWA Boeing 747 blows apart off New York because, whatever the source of ignition, its nearly empty center tank contained an explosive mixture of fuel and air—and as a result explosive mixtures may in the future be avoided.

Such tragic failures seem all too familiar, but in fact they are rare, and they will grow rarer still as aeronautical engineering improves. One can regret the lives lost and deplore the slowness with which officials respond, but in the long run there is reason to be optimistic. The Wright brothers were products of the Enlightenment. Our science will prevail.

The ValuJet accident is different. I would argue that it represents the third and most elusive kind of disaster, a "system accident," which may lie beyond the reach of conventional solution, and which a small group of thinkers, inspired by the Yale sociologist Charles Perrow, has been exploring elsewhere—for example, in power generation, chemical manufacturing, nuclear-weapons control, and space flight. Perrow has coined the more loaded term "normal accident" for such disasters, because he believes that they are normal for our time. His point is that these accidents are science's illegitimate children, bastards born of the confusion that lies within the complex organizations with which we manage our dangerous technologies. Perrow is not an expert on commercial flying, but his thinking applies to it nonetheless. In this case the organization includes not only ValuJet, the archetype of new-style airlines, but also the contractors that serve it and the government entities that, despite economic deregulation, are expected to oversee it. Taken as a whole, the airline system is complex indeed.

Keep in mind that it is also competitive, and that if one of its purposes is to make money, the other is to move the public through thin air cheaply and at high speed. Safety is never first, and it never will be, but for obvious reasons it is a necessary part of the venture. Risk is a part too, but on the everyday level of practical compromises and small decisions—the building blocks of this ambitious enterprise—the view of risk is usually obscured. The people involved do not consciously trade safety for money or convenience, but they inevitably make a lot of bad little choices. They get away with those choices because, as Perrow says, Murphy's Law is wrong—what *can* go wrong usually goes *right*. But then one day a few of the bad little choices come together, and circumstances take an airplane down. Who, then, is really to blame?

We can find fault among those directly involved—and we probably need to. But if our purpose is to attack the roots of such an accident, we may find them so entwined with the system that they are impossible to extract without toppling the whole structure. In the case of ValuJet the study of system accidents presents us with the possibility that we have come to depend on flight, that unless we are willing to end our affordable airline system as we know it, we cannot stop the occasional sacrifice. Beyond the questions of blame, it requires us to consider that our solutions, by adding to the complexity and obscurity of the airline business, may actually increase the risk of accidents. System-accident thinking does not demand that we accept our fate without a struggle, but it serves as an important caution.

Smoke in the Cockpit

The distinction among procedural, engineered, and system accidents is of course not absolute. Most accidents are a bit of each. And even in the most extreme cases of system failure the post-crash investigation must work its way forward conventionally, usefully identifying those problems that can be fixed, before the remaining questions begin to force a still-deeper examination. That was certainly the way with ValuJet Flight 592.

It was headed from Miami to Atlanta, flown by Captain Candalyn Kubeck, age thirty-five, and her copilot Richard Hazen, age fifty-two. They represented a new kind of commercial pilot, experienced not only in the cockpit but in the rough-and-tumble of the deregulated airline industry, where both had held a number of low-paid flying jobs before settling on ValuJet. It would have been no shock to them that ValuJet pilots were non-unionized, or that the company required them to pay for their own training. With 9,000 flight hours behind her, more than 2,000 of them in a DC-9, Kubeck earned what the free market said she was worth—about $43,000 a year, plus bonuses. Hazen, formerly in the Air Force and with similar experience, earned a bit more than half as much.

Pilots were not the only low-paid employees at ValuJet—flight attendants, ramp agents, and mechanics made a lot less there than they would have at a more traditional airline. So much work was farmed out to temporary employees and independent contractors that ValuJet was sometimes called a "virtual airline." FAA regulators had begun to worry that the company was moving too fast, and not keeping up with its paperwork, but there was no evidence that the people involved were inadequate. Many of the pilots were refugees from the labor wars at the old Eastern Airlines, and they were generally as competent and experienced as their higher-paid friends at United, American, and Delta. ValuJet was helping the entire industry to understand just how far cost-cutting could be pushed. Its flights were cheap and full, and its stock was strong on Wall Street.

But six minutes out of Miami, while climbing northwest through 11,000 feet, Richard Hazen radioed, "Ah, five-ninety-two needs an immediate return to Miami." In the deliberate calm of pilot talk this was strong language. The time was thirty-one seconds after 2:10 P.M., and the sun was shining. Something had gone wrong with the airplane.

The radar controller at Miami Departure answered immediately. Using ValuJet's radio name "Critter" (for the company's cartoonish logo—a smiling airplane), he gave the flight clearance to turn initially toward the west, away from Miami and conflicting traffic flows, and to begin a descent to the airport. "Critter five-ninety-two, ah roger, turn left heading two-seven-zero, descend and maintain seven thousand."

Hazen said, "Two-seven-zero, seven thousand, five-ninety-two."

The controller was Jesse Fisher, age thirty-six, a seven-year veteran, who had twice handled the successful return of an airliner that had lost cabin pressurization. He had worked the night before, and had gone home, fed his cat, and slept well. He felt alert and rested. He said, "What kind of problem are you having?"

Hazen said, "Ah, smoke in the cockpit. Smoke in the cabin." His tone was urgent.

Fisher kept his own tone flat. He said, "Roger." Over his shoulder he called, "I need a supervisor here!"

The supervisor plugged in beside him. On Fisher's radar screen Flight 592 appeared as a little oval and an associated group of numbers, including a readout of its altitude. Fisher noticed that the airplane had not yet started to turn. He gave the pilots another heading, farther to the left, and cleared them down to 5,000 feet.

Aboard the airplane Hazen acknowledged the new heading but misheard the altitude assignment. It didn't matter. Flight 592 was burning, and the situation in the cockpit was rapidly getting out of hand.

One minute into the emergency the pilots were still tracking away from Miami, and had not begun their return. Hazen said, "Critter five-ninety-two, we need the, ah, closest airport available."

The transmission was garbled or blocked, or Fisher was distracted by competing voices within the radar room. For whatever reason, he did not hear Hazen's request. When investigators later asked him if in retrospect he would have done anything differently, he admitted that he kept asking himself the same question. Even without hearing Hazen's request he might have suggested some slightly closer airport. But given that the flight's position was only twenty-five miles to the northwest, Miami still seemed like the best choice, because of the emergency equipment there. In any case "Miami" was the request he *had* heard, and he intended to deliver it.

To Hazen he said, "Critter five-ninety-two, they're gonna be standing, standing by for you." He meant the crash crews at Miami. "You can plan Runway One-two. When able, direct to Dolphin now."

Hazen said, ". . . need radar vectors." His transmission was garbled by loud background noises. Fisher thought he sounded "shaky."

Fisher answered, "Critter five-ninety-two, turn left heading one-four-zero."

Hazen said, "One-four-zero." It was his last coherent response.

The flight had only now begun to move through a gradual left turn. Fisher watched the target on his screen as it tracked through the heading changes: the turn tightened and then slowed again. With each sweep of the radar beam the altitude readouts showed a gradual descent—8,800, 8,500, 8,100. Two minutes into the crisis Fisher said, "Critter five-ninety-two, keep the turn around, heading ah one-two-zero."

Flight 592 may have tried to respond—someone keyed a microphone without talking.

Fisher said, "Critter five-ninety-two, contact Miami Approach on—correction, no, you just keep on my frequency."

Two and a half minutes had gone by. It was 2:13 P.M. The airplane was passing through 7,500 feet when suddenly it tightened the left turn and entered a steep dive. Fisher's radar showed the turn and an altitude readout of XXX—code for such a rapid altitude change that the computer cannot keep up. Investigators later calculated that the airplane rolled to a sixty-degree left bank and dove 6,400 feet in thirty-two seconds. During that loss of control Fisher radioed mechanically, "Critter five-ninety-two, you can, ah, turn left, heading one-zero-zero, and join the Runway One-two localizer at Miami." He also radioed, "Critter five-ninety-two, descend and maintain three thousand."

Then the incredible happened. The airplane rolled wings-level again and pulled sharply out of its dive. It is highly unlikely that the airplane would have done this on its own. It is possible that the autopilot kicked in, or that one of the pilots, having been incapacitated by smoke or defeated by melting control cables, somehow momentarily regained control. Fisher watched the radar target straighten toward the southeast, and again read out a nearly level altitude—now, however, merely a thousand feet. The airplane's speed was almost 500 miles an hour.

The frequency crackled with another unintelligible transmission. Shocked into the realization that the airplane would be unable to make Miami, Fisher said, "Critter five-ninety-two, Opa-Locka Airport's about ah twelve o'clock at fifteen miles."

Walton Little, in his bass boat, spotted the airplane then, as it rolled steeply to the right. The radar, too, noticed that last quick turn toward the south, just before the final nose-over. On the next sweep of the radar the flight's data block went into "coast" on Fisher's screen, indicating that contact had been lost. The supervisor marked the spot electronically and launched rescue procedures.

Fisher continued to work the other airplanes in his sector. Five minutes after the impact another low-paid pilot, this one for American Eagle, radioed, "Ah, how did Critter make out?" Fisher didn't answer.

The Recovery Operation

It was known from the start that fire took the airplane down. The federal investigation began within hours, with the arrival that evening of a National Transportation Safety Board team from Washington. The investigators set up shop in an airport hotel, which they began to refer to as the "command post." The language is important. As we will see, similar forms of linguistic stiffness, specifically engineerspeak, ultimately proved to have been involved in the downing of Flight 592—and this is a factor that the NTSB investigators, because of their own verbal awkwardness, have been unable quite to recognize.

It is not reasonable to blame them for this, though. The NTSB is a technical agency, staffed by technicians, which occupies a central position in the stilted world of aviation. Its job is to examine important accidents and to issue nonbinding safety recommendations—opinions, really—to industry and government. Because the investigators have no regulatory authority and must rely on persuasion to influence events, it may at times be necessary for them to use official-sounding language. Even among its opponents, who often feel that its recommendations are impractical, the NTSB has a reputation for technical competence. The NTSB is a piece of engineering done right. In a world built on compromise, it manages to play the old-fashioned, unambiguous role of the public's defender.

The press plays a more difficult role, though one equally important to the public's safety. It has a classically symbiotic relationship with the NTSB, relying on the investigators for information while providing them with their only effective voice. Nonetheless, in the time of crisis immediately after an accident, a tension exists between the two. Working under pressure to get the story out, reporters resent the caution of the investigators and their reluctance to speculate anonymously. Working under pressure to get the story right, investigators, for their part, resent the reporters' incessant demands during the difficult first days of an accident probe—the recovery of human remains and airplane parts. By the time I got to Miami, nineteen hours after Flight 592 hit the swamp, the two camps had assumed their habitual positions and were passing each other warily in the hotel lobby.

Twenty miles to the northwest, deep in the Everglades, the recovery operation was already under way. The NTSB had set up a staging area—a "forward ops base," one official called it—beside the Tamiami Trail, a two-lane highway that traverses the watery grasslands of southern Florida. Within two days this staging area blossomed into a chaotic encampment of excited officials—local, state, and federal—with their tents and air-conditioned trailers, their helicopters, their cars and flashing lights. I quit counting the agencies. The NTSB had politely excluded most of them from the actual accident site, which lay seven miles north, along a narrow levee road.

The press was excluded even from the staging area, but was provided with two news conferences a day, during which investigators cautiously doled out tidbits of information. One NTSB official said to me, "We've got to feed them or we'll lose control." But the reporters were well behaved, and if anything a bit overcivilized. Near the staging area they settled into their own little town of television trucks, tents, and lawn chairs. The location gave them good Everglades backdrops and shots of alligators swimming by; the viewing public could not have guessed that they stood so far from the action. They acted impatient, but in truth this was not a bad assignment; at its peak their little town boasted pay phones and pizza delivery.

Maybe it was because of my obvious lack of deadline that the investigators made an exception in my case. They slipped me into the front seat of a Florida Game and Fish helicopter whose pilot, in a fraternal gesture, invited me to take the controls for the run out to the crash site. From the staging area we skimmed north across the swamped grasslands, loosely following the levee road, before swinging wide to circle over the impact zone—a new pond defined by a ring of turned mud and surrounded by a larger area of grass and water and accident debris. Searchers in white protective suits waded side by side through the muck, piling pieces of people and airplane into flat-bottomed boats. It was hot and unpleasant work performed in a contained little hell, a place that one investigator later described to me as reeking of fuel, earth, and rotting flesh—the special smell of an airplane accident. We descended onto the levee, about 300 yards away from the crash site, where an American flag and a few tents and trucks constituted the recovery base.

The mood there was quiet and purposeful, with no sign among the workers of the emotional trauma that officials had been worriedly predicting since the operation began. The workers on break sat in the shade of an awning, sipping cold drinks and chatting. They were policemen and firemen, not heroes but straightforward guys accustomed to confronting death. Not knowing who I was, they spoke to me frankly about the gruesome details of their work, and made indelicate jokes, but they seemed more worried about dehydration than about "taking the job home" or losing sleep. I relaxed in their company, relieved to have escaped for a while the expectation of grief.

It was, of course, a somber place to be. Human remains lay bagged in a refrigerated truck for later transport to the morgue. A decontamination crew washed down torn and twisted pieces of airplane, none longer than several feet. Investigators tagged the most promising wreckage, to be trucked immediately to a hangar at an outlying Miami airport, where specialists could study it. Farther down the levee I came upon a soiled photograph of a young woman with a small-town face and a head of teased hair. A white-suited crew arrived on an airboat and clambered up the embankment to be washed down. Another crew set off. A boatload of muddy wreckage arrived. The next day the families of the dead came on buses, and laid flowers and cried. Pieces of the airplane kept being hauled up for nearly another month.

Much was made of this recovery, which—prior to the offshore retrieval of TWA's Flight 800—the NTSB called the most challenging in its history. It is true that the swamp made the search slow and difficult, and that the violence of the impact meant that meticulous work was required to reconstruct the critical forward cargo hold. However, it is also true that the physical part of the investigation served to confirm what a look at a shipping ticket had already suggested—that ValuJet Flight 592 burned and crashed not because the airplane failed but, in large part, because the airline did.

To me as a pilot, the most impressive aspect of the investigation was the speed with which it worked through the false pursuit of an electrical fire—an explanation supported by my own experiences in flight, and all the more plausible here because the ValuJet DC-9 was old and had experienced a variety of electrical failures earlier the same day, including a tripped circuit breaker that had resisted the attentions of a mechanic in Atlanta, and then mysteriously had fixed itself. I was impressed also by the instincts of the reporters, who for all their technical ignorance seized on the news that Flight 592 had been loaded with a potentially dangerous cargo of chemical oxygen generators—more than a hundred little firebombs that could have caused this accident, and that indeed did.

Flight 592 crashed on a Saturday afternoon. By Sunday the recovery teams were pulling up scorched and soot-stained pieces. On Monday a searcher happened to step on the flight-data recorder, one of two required black boxes meant to help with accident investigations. The NTSB took the recorder to its Washington laboratory and found that a blip in the flight data six minutes after Flight 592's takeoff seemed to

indicate a momentary rise in air pressure. Immediately afterward the recorder began to fail intermittently, apparently because of electrical-power interruptions. On Tuesday night, at a press conference at the hotel, Robert Francis, the vice-chairman of the NTSB and the senior official on the scene, announced in a monotone, "There could have been an explosion." A hazardous-materials team would be joining the investigation. The investigation was focusing on the airplane's forward cargo hold, which was located just below and behind the cockpit, and was unequipped with fire detection and extinguishing systems. Routine paperwork indicated that the Miami ground crew had loaded the hold with homeward-bound ValuJet "company material," a witch's brew of three tires—at least two of them mounted—and five cardboard boxes of old oxygen generators.

Inferno in the Air

Oxygen generators are safety devices. They are small steel canisters mounted in airplane ceilings and seat-backs and linked to the flimsy oxygen masks that dangle in front of passengers when a cabin loses pressurization. To activate oxygen flow the passenger pulls a lanyard, which slides a retaining pin from a spring-loaded hammer, which falls on a minute explosive charge, which sparks a chemical reaction that liberates the oxygen within the sodium-chlorate core. This reaction produces heat, which may cause the surface temperature of the canister to rise to 500° Fahrenheit if the canister is mounted correctly in a ventilated bracket, and much higher if it is sealed in a box with other canisters, which may themselves be heating up. If there is a good source of fuel nearby, such as tires and cardboard boxes, the presence of pure oxygen will cause the canisters to burn ferociously. Was there an explosion on Flight 592? Perhaps. But in any event the airplane was blowtorched into the ground.

It is ironic that the airplane's own emergency-oxygen system was different—a set of simple oxygen tanks, similar to those used in hospitals, that do not emit heat during use. The oxygen generators in Flight 592's forward cargo hold came from three MD-80s, a more modern kind of twin jet, which ValuJet had recently bought and was having refurbished at a hangar across the airport in Miami. As was its practice for most maintenance, ValuJet had hired an outside company to do the job—in this case a large firm called SabreTech, owned by Sabreliner, of St. Louis, and licensed by the FAA to perform the often critical work. SabreTech, in turn, hired contract mechanics from other companies on an as-needed basis. It later turned out that three-fourths of the people on the project were just such temporary outsiders. The vulnerability of American wageworkers could be sensed in their testimony after the accident. They inhabited a world of boss men and sudden firings, with few protections or guarantees for the future. As the ValuJet deadline approached, they worked in shifts, day and night, and sometimes through the weekend as well. It was their contribution to our cheap flying.

We will never know everyone at fault in this story. ValuJet gave the order to replace oxygen generators on the MD-80s, most of which had come to the end of their licensed lifetimes. It provided SabreTech with explicit removal procedures and general warnings about the dangers of fire. Over several weeks SabreTech workers extracted the generators and taped or cut off their lanyards before stacking most of them in five cardboard boxes that happened to be lying around the hangar. Apparently they believed that securing the lanyards would keep the generators from being fired inadvertently. What they did not do was place the required plastic safety caps over the firing pins—a precaution spelled out on the second line of ValuJet's written work order. The problem for SabreTech was that no one had such caps, or cared much about finding them. Ultimately the caps were forgotten or ignored. At the end of the job, in the rush to complete batches of paperwork on all three MD-80s, two mechanics routinely "pencil-whipped" the problem by signing off on the safety-cap line as well as on the others, certifying that the work had been done. SabreTech inspectors and supervisors signed off on the work too, apparently without giving the caps much thought.

The timing is not clear. For weeks the five boxes stood on a parts rack beside the airplanes. Eventually mechanics lugged them over to SabreTech's shipping-and-receiving department, where they sat on the floor in the area designated for ValuJet property. A few days before the accident a SabreTech manager told the shipping clerk to clean up the area and get all the boxes off the floor in preparation for an upcoming inspection by Continental Airlines, a potential customer. The boxes were unmarked, and the manager did not care what was in them.

The shipping clerk then did what shipping clerks do, and prepared to send the oxygen generators home to ValuJet headquarters, in Atlanta. He redistributed them equally among the five boxes, laying the canisters horizontally end to end, and packing bubble wrap on top. After sealing the boxes he applied address labels and ValuJet company-material stickers, and wrote "aircraft parts." As part of the load he included two large main tires and a smaller nose tire—at least two of which were mounted on wheels. The next day he asked a co-worker, the receiving clerk, to make out a shipping ticket, and to write "oxygen canisters—empty" on it. The receiving clerk wrote "Oxy Canisters" and then put "Empty" between quotation marks, as if he did not believe it. He also listed the tires.

The cargo stood for another day or two, until May 11, when the SabreTech driver had time to deliver the boxes across the airport to Flight 592. There the ValuJet ramp agent accepted the material, though federal regulations forbade him to, even if the generators were empty, since canisters that have been discharged contain a toxic residue, and ValuJet was not licensed to carry any such officially designated hazardous materials. He discussed the cargo's weight with the copilot, Richard Hazen, who also should have known better. Together they decided to place the load in the forward hold, where ValuJet workers laid one of the big main tires flat, placed the nose tire at the center of it, and stacked the five boxes on top of it around the outer edge, in a loose ring. They leaned the other main tire against a bulkhead. It was an unstable arrangement. No one knows exactly what happened then, but it seems likely that the first oxygen generator ignited during the loading or during taxiing or on takeoff, as the airplane climbed skyward.

Two weeks later and halfway through the recovery of the scorched and shattered parts a worker finally found the airplane's cockpit voice recorder, the second black box sought by the investigators. It had recorded normal sounds and conversation up to the moment—six minutes after takeoff—when the flight-data recorder indicated a pulse of high pressure. The pulse may have been one of the tires exploding. In the cockpit it sounded like a chirp and a simultaneous beep on the public-address system. The captain, Candalyn Kubeck, asked, "What was that?"

Hazen said, "I don't know." They scanned the airplane's instruments and found sudden indications of electrical failure. It was not the cause but a symptom of the inferno in the hold—the wires and electrical panels were probably melting and burning along with other, more crucial parts of the airplane—but the pilots' first thought was that the airplane was merely up to its circuit-breaking tricks again. The recording here is garbled. Kubeck seems to have asked, "About to lose a bus?" Then, more clearly, she said, "We've got some electrical problem."

Hazen said, "Yeah. That battery charger's kickin' in. Oooh, we gotta . . ."

"We're losing everything," Kubeck said. "We need, we need to go back to Miami."

Twenty seconds had passed since the strange chirp in the cockpit. A total electrical failure, though serious, was not in those sunny conditions a life-threatening emergency. But suddenly there was incoherent shouting from the passenger cabin, and women and men screaming, "Fire!" The shouting continued for thirteen seconds and then subsided.

Kubeck said, "To Miami," and Hazen put in the call to Jesse Fisher, the air-traffic controller. When Fisher asked, "What kind of problem are you having?" Kubeck answered, off-radio, "Fire," and Hazen transmitted his urgent "Smoke in the cockpit. Smoke in the cabin."

Investigators now presume that the smoke was black and thick, and perhaps poisonous. The recorder picked up the sound of the cockpit door opening, and the voice of the chief flight attendant, who said, "Okay, we need oxygen. We can't get oxygen back there." Did she mean that the airplane's cabin masks had not dropped, or that they had dropped but were not working? If the smoke was poisonous, the masks might not have helped much, since by design they mix cabin air into the oxygen flow. The pilots were equipped with better, isolating-type masks and with goggles, but may not have had time to put them on. Only a minute had passed since the first strange chirp. Now the voice recorder captured the sound of renewed shouting from the cabin. In the cockpit the flight attendant said, "Completely on fire."

The recording was of little use to the NTSB's technical investigation, but because it showed that the passengers had died in agony, it added emotional weight to a political reaction that was already spreading beyond the details of the accident and that had begun to call the entire airline industry into question. The public, it seemed, would not be placated this time by standard reassurances and the discovery of a culprit or two. The press and the NTSB had put aside their on-site antagonism and had joined forces in a natural coalition with Congress. The questioning was motivated not by an immediate fear of unsafe skies (despite the warnings of Mary Schiavo, a federal whistle-blower who claimed special insight) but rather by a more nuanced suspicion that competition in the open sky had gone too far, and that the FAA, the agency charged with protecting the flying public, had fallen into the hands of industry insiders.

The Hunt for Blame

The FAA's administrator then was a onetime airline boss named David Hinson—the sort of glib and self-assured executive who does well in closed circles of like-minded men. Now, however, he would have to address a diverse and skeptical audience. The day after the ValuJet accident he had flown to Miami and made the incredible assertion that ValuJet was a safe airline—when for 110 people lying dead in a nearby swamp it very obviously was not. He also said, "I would fly on it," as if he believed that he had to reassure a nation of children. It was an insulting performance, and it was taken as evidence of the FAA's isolation and of its betrayal of the public's trust.

After a good night's sleep Hinson might have tried to repair the damage. Instead he appeared two days later at a Senate hearing in Washington sounding like an unrepentant Prussian: "We have a very professional, highly dedicated, organized, and efficient inspector work force that do their job day in and day out. And when we say an airline is safe to fly, it is safe to fly. There is no gray area."

His colleagues must have winced. Aviation safety is nothing but a gray area, and the regulation of it is an indirect process of negotiation and maneuver. Consider the size of the airline business, the scale of the sky, and the loneliness of an airplane in flight. The FAA can affect safety by establishing standards and enforcing them through inspections and paperwork, but it cannot throw the switches or turn the wrenches, or in this case supervise the disposal of old oxygen generators. Safety is ultimately in the hands of the operators, the mechanics and pilots and their managers, because it involves a blizzard of small judgments. Hinson might have admitted this reality to the American public, which is certainly capable of understanding such subtleties, but instead, inexplicably, he chose to link the FAA's reputation to that of ValuJet. This placed the agency in an impossible position. Whether for incompetence or for cronyism, the FAA would now inevitably be blamed.

Within days it came out that certain inspectors at the FAA had been worried about ValuJet for some time and had described their concerns in their reports. Their consensus was that the airline was expanding too fast (from two to fifty-two airplanes over its two-and-a-half-year life) and that it had neither the procedures nor the people in place to maintain standards of safety. The FAA tried to keep pace, but because of its other commitments—including countering the threat of terrorism—it could assign only three inspectors to the airline. At the time of the accident they had run 1,471 routine checks on the operation and made two additional eleven-day inspections, in 1994 and 1995. This level of scrutiny was about normal. But by early 1996 concern had grown within the FAA about the disproportionate number of infractions committed by ValuJet and the string of small bang-ups it had had. The agency began to move more aggressively. An aircraft-maintenance group found such serious problems in both the FAA's surveillance and the airline's operations that it wrote an internal report recommending that ValuJet be "recertified" immediately—meaning that it be grounded and started all over again. The report was apparently sent to Washington, where for reasons that remain unexplained it lay buried until after the accident. Meanwhile, on February 22, 1996, headquarters launched a 120-day "special emphasis" inspection, a preliminary report on which was issued after the first week. This suggested a wide range of problems. The special-emphasis inspection was ongoing when, on May 11, Flight 592 went down.

As this record of official concern emerged, the question changed from why Hinson had insisted on calling ValuJet "safe" after the accident to why he had not shut down the airline before the accident. Trapped by his own simplistic formulations, he could provide no convincing answer. The press and Congress were sharply critical. The FAA launched an exhaustive thirty-day review of ValuJet, perhaps the

most concentrated airline inspection in history, assigning sixty inspectors to perform in one month the equivalent of four years' work. Lewis Jordan, a founder and the president of ValuJet, complained that Hinson was, in effect, conducting a witch hunt that no airline could withstand. Jordan had been trying shamelessly to shift the blame for the deaths onto his own contractor, SabreTech, and he received little sympathy now. No one was surprised when ValuJet was grounded indefinitely five weeks after the accident.

Here now was proof that the FAA had earlier neglected its duties. The agency's chief regulator, Anthony Broderick, was the first to lose his job. Broderick was an expert technocrat, disliked by safety crusaders because of his conservative approach to instituting and applying regulations, and respected by aviation insiders for the same reason. Hinson let him take the fall: Broderick was a man of integrity and would accept responsibility for the FAA's poor performance. But if Hinson thought that he himself could escape with this sacrifice, he was wrong. Broderick's airline friends now joined the critics in disgust. Hinson announced his upcoming resignation.

In a sense, the system worked. The tragedy did have some positive consequences—primarily because the NTSB did an even better job than usual, not only pinpointing the source and history of the fire but also recognizing some of its larger implications. With a well-timed series of press feedings and public hearings the accident team kept the difficult organizational issues alive and managed to stretch the soul-searching through the end of the year and beyond. By shaking up the FAA, the team reminded the agency of its mandate to oversee the safety of the airlines—perhaps prodding the FAA into a renewed commitment to inspections and a resolution to hold airlines responsible for their actions and for the performance of outside shops.

For the airlines, the investigation served as a necessary reminder of the possible consequences of cost-cutting and complacency. Among airline executives smart enough to notice, it may also have served as a warning about the public's growing distrust of their motives and about widespread anger with the whole industry—anger that may have as much to do with the way passengers are handled as with their fears of dying. However one wants to read it, the ValuJet turmoil marked the limits of the public's tolerance. The airlines were cowed, and they submitted eagerly to the banning of oxygen generators as cargo on passenger flights. They then rushed ahead of the FAA with a $400 million promise (not yet fulfilled) to install fire detectors and extinguishers in all cargo holds. The desire to find hidden hazards runs up against the practical difficulties of inspecting cargo. Nonetheless, ground crews can be counted on for a while to watch what they load into airplanes and what they take out and throw away.

And the guilty companies? They lost money and were sued, of course. After firing the two mechanics who had falsely signed the work orders, SabreTech tried to put its house in order. Nonetheless, its customers fled and did not return. The Miami operation shrank from 650 to 135 employees, and in January of 1997 was forced to close its doors. Soon afterward, as the result of a two-month FAA investigation, SabreTech's new Orlando facility was forced to close as well. ValuJet survived its grounding, and under intense FAA scrutiny returned to the sky later in 1996, with a reduced and standardized fleet of DC-9s; it ultimately changed its name to AirTran. For a while it was probably the safest airline in the country. What, then, explains the feeling, particular to this case, that so little has in reality been achieved?

A "Normal Accident"

Pilots are safety practitioners, steeped in a can-do attitude toward survival and confident in their own skills. We tend to think that man-made accidents must lie within human control. This idea has been encouraged to some extent by the work of a group of Berkeley professors—notably the political scientist Todd La Porte—who study "high-reliability organizations," meaning those with good track records at handling apparently hazardous technologies: aircraft carriers, air-traffic-control centers, certain power companies. They believe that organizations can learn from past mistakes and can tailor themselves to achieve new objectives, and that if the right, albeit difficult, steps are taken, many accidents can be avoided.

Charles Perrow's thinking is more difficult for pilots like me to accept. Perrow came unintentionally to his theory about normal accidents after studying the failings of large organizations. His point is not

that some technologies are riskier than others, which is obvious, but that the control and operation of some of the riskiest technologies require organizations so complex that serious failures are virtually guaranteed to occur. Those failures will occasionally combine in unforeseeable ways, and if they induce further failures in an operating environment of tightly interrelated processes, the failures will spin out of control, defeating all interventions. The resulting accidents are inevitable, Perrow asserts, because they emerge from the venture itself. You cannot eliminate one without killing the other.

Perrow's seminal book *Normal Accidents: Living With High-Risk Technologies* (1984) is an unusual work—a hodgepodge of storytelling and exhortation, out of which this new way of thinking has risen. His central device is an organizational chart on which to plot the likelihood of serious system accidents. He does not append numerical values to the chart but uses a set of general risk indicators. In one quadrant stand the processes—like those of most manufacturing—that are simple, slow, linear, and visible, and in which the operators experience failures as isolated and containable events. In the opposite one stand the opaque and tangled processes characterized by a combination of what Perrow calls "interactive complexity" and "tight coupling." By "interactive complexity" he means not simply that there are many elements involved but that those elements are linked in multiple and often unpredictable ways. The failure of one part—whether material, psychological, or organizational—may coincide with the failure of an entirely different part, and this unforeseeable combination will cause the failure of other parts, and so on. If the system is large, the possible combinations of failures are practically infinite. Such unravelings seem to have an intelligence of their own: they expose hidden connections, neutralize redundancies, bypass "firewalls," and exploit chance circumstances that no engineer could have planned for. When the operating system is inherently quick and inflexible (like a chemical process, an automated response to missile attack, or a jet airliner in flight), the cascading failures can accelerate out of control, confounding the human operators and denying them a chance to jury-rig a recovery. That lack of slack is Perrow's tight coupling. Then the only difference between a harmless accident and a human tragedy may be a question, as in chemical plants, of which way the wind blows.

I ran across this thinking by chance, a year before the ValuJet crash, when I picked up a copy of Scott D. Sagan's book *The Limits of Safety: Organizations, Accidents, and Nuclear Weapons* (1993). Sagan, a Stanford political scientist who is a generation younger than Perrow, is the most persuasive of Perrow's interpreters, and with *The Limits of Safety* he has solidified system-accident thinking, focusing it more clearly than Perrow was able to. *The Limits of Safety* starts by placing high-reliability and normal-accident theories in opposition and then tests them against a laboriously researched and previously secret history of failures within U.S. nuclear-weapons programs. The test is a transparent artifice, but it serves to define the two theories. Sagan's obvious bias does not diminish his work.

Strategic nuclear weapons pose an especially difficult problem for system-accident thinking, for two reasons: first, there has never been an accidental nuclear detonation, let alone an accidental nuclear war; and second, if a real possibility of such an apocalyptic failure exists, it threatens the very logic of nuclear deterrence—the expectation of rational behavior on which we continue to base our arsenals. Once again the pursuit of system accidents leads to uncomfortable ends. Sagan is not a man to advocate disarmament, and he shies away from doing so in his book, observing realistically that nuclear weapons are here to stay. Nonetheless, once he has defined "accidents" as less than nuclear explosions (as false warnings, near launches, and other unanticipated breakdowns in this ultimate "high-reliability" system), Sagan discovers a pattern of accidents, some of which were contained only by chance. The reader is hardly surprised when Sagan concludes that such accidents are inevitable.

The book interested me not because of the accidents themselves but because of their pattern, which seemed strangely familiar. Though the pattern represented possibilities that I as a pilot had categorically rejected, this new perspective required me to face the unpredictable side of my own experience with the sky. I had to admit that some of my friends had died in crazy and unlucky ways, that some flights had gone uncontrollably wrong, and that perhaps not even the pilots were to blame. What is more, I had to admit that no matter how carefully I checked my own airplanes, and how cautiously I flew them, the same could happen to me.

That is where we stand now as a society with ValuJet Flight 592, and it may explain our continuing discomfort with the accident. The ValuJet case represents a nearly perfect system accident. It arose from a process that fits most of Perrow's technical requirements of unpredictability and interactive complexity and some of those of tight coupling. More important, it fits the most basic definitions of an accident caused by the very functioning of the system or industry within which it occurred. Flight 592 burned because of its cargo of oxygen generators, yes, but more fundamentally because of a tangle of confusions that will take such entirely different from next time. It is frustrating to fight such a thing, and wrongdoing is difficult to assign.

ValuJet's Pretend Reality

Take, for example, the case of the two SabreTech mechanics who helped to remove the oxygen canisters from the ValuJet MD-80s, ignored the written work orders to install safety caps, stacked the dangerous canisters improperly in cardboard boxes, and finished by falsely signing off on the job. They will probably suffer for the rest of their lives for their negligence, as perhaps they should. But here is what really happened: Nearly 600 people logged time working on the three ValuJet airplanes in SabreTech's Miami hangar, and of them seventy-two logged 910 hours over several weeks for replacing oxygen generators, in most cases because they had "expired"—reached the end of their approved lives. According to ValuJet work card No. 0069, which was supplied to investigators, the second step of the seven-step removal process was *If generator has not been expended, install shipping cap on firing pin.*

This required a gang of hard-pressed mechanics to draw a verbal distinction between canisters that *were* "expired," meaning most of the ones they were removing, and canisters that were *not* "expended," meaning many of the same ones, loaded and ready to fire, on which they were expected to put nonexistent caps. Also involved were canisters that were expired and expended, and others that were not expired but were expended. And then, of course, there was the set of new replacement canisters, which were both unexpended and unexpired. If this seems confusing, do not waste your time trying to figure it out—the SabreTech mechanics did not, nor should they have been expected to. The NTSB suggested that one problem at SabreTech's Miami facility may have been the presence of Spanish-speaking immigrants on the work force, but quite obviously the language problem lay on the other side—with ValuJet and the English-speaking engineers, literalists, who wrote the orders and technical manuals as if they were writing to themselves. The real problem, in other words, was engineerspeak.

Before the accident the worry was not about old parts but about new ones—the safe refurbishing of the MD-80s in time to meet the ValuJet deadline. The mechanics quickly removed the oxygen canisters from their brackets and wired green tags to most of them. The green tags meant "repairable," which these canisters were not. It is not clear how many of the seventy-two workers were aware that these canisters couldn't be used again, since the replacement of oxygen generators is a rare operation, though of the people questioned after the accident most claimed to have known at least why the canisters had to be removed. But here, too, there is evidence of confusion. After the accident two tagged canisters were found still lying in the SabreTech hangar. On one of the tags, under "Reason for Removal," someone had written, "out of date." On the other tag someone had written, "generators have been fired."

Yes, a mechanic might have found his way past the ValuJet work card and into the huge MD-80 maintenance manual, to chapter 35-22-01, within which line "h" would have instructed him to "store or dispose of oxygen generator." By diligently pursuing his options, the mechanic could have found his way to a different part of the manual and learned that "all serviceable and unserviceable (unexpended) oxygen generators (canisters) are to be stored in an area that ensures that each unit is not exposed to high temperatures or possible damage." By pondering the implications of the parentheses he might have deduced that the "unexpended" canisters were also "unserviceable" canisters and that because he had no shipping cap, he should perhaps take such canisters to a safe area and "initiate" them, according to the procedures described in section 2.D. To initiate an oxygen generator is of course to fire it off, triggering the chemical reaction that produces oxygen and leaves a mildly toxic residue within the canister, which is then classified as hazardous waste. Sec-

tion 2.D contains the admonition "An expended oxygen generator (canister) contains both barium oxide and asbestos fibers and must be disposed of in accordance with local regulatory compliances and using authorized procedures." No wonder the mechanics stuck the old generators in boxes.

The supervisors and inspectors failed miserably here, though after the accident they proved clever at ducking responsibility. At the least they should have supplied the required safety caps and verified that those caps were being used. If they had—despite all the other errors that were made—Flight 592 would not have burned. For larger reasons, too, their failure is an essential part of this story. It represents not the avarice of profit takers but rather something more insidious—the sort of collective relaxation of technical standards that the Boston College sociologist Diane Vaughan has called "the normalization of deviance," and that she believes existed at NASA in the years leading up to the 1986 explosion of the space shuttle *Challenger*. The leaking O-rings that caused the catastrophic blow-by of rocket fuel were a well-known design weakness, and had been the subject of worried memos and conferences up to the eve of the launch. Vaughan's book *The Challenger Launch Decision* (1996) is a 575-page exercise in system-accident thinking. After a long immersion in NASA's technical culture, Vaughan concludes that the O-ring worries were put aside in part because the agency had gotten away with launching the O-rings before. As Perrow has argued, what can go wrong usually goes right—and then people draw the wrong conclusions. In a general way this is what happened at SabreTech. Some mechanics now claim to have expressed their concerns about the safety caps, but if they did, they were not heard. The operation had grown used to taking shortcuts.

But let us be honest—mechanics who are too careful will never get the job done. The airline system as it stands today requires people, in flight or on the ground, to compromise, to make choices, and sometimes even to gamble. The SabreTech crews went astray—but not far astray—by allowing themselves quite naturally not to worry about discarded parts. A fire hazard? Sure. The mechanics taped off the lanyards and may have shoved the canisters a little farther away from the airplanes they were working on. The canisters had no warnings about heat on them and none of the standard hazardous-materials placards. It probably would not have mattered anyway, because the work area was crowded with placards and officially designated hazardous materials, and people had learned not to take them too seriously. Out of curiosity a few of the mechanics fired off some canisters and listened to the oxygen come out—it went *pssst*. No one seems to have considered the possibility that the canisters might accidentally be shipped. The mechanics did finally carry the five cardboard boxes over to the shipping department, but only because that was where ValuJet property was stored—an arrangement that itself made sense.

When the shipping clerk got to work the next morning, he found the boxes without explanation on the floor of the ValuJet area. The boxes were innocent-looking, and he left them alone until he was told to tidy up. Sending them to Atlanta seemed like the best way to do that. He had shipped off "company material" before without ValuJet's specific approval, and he had heard no complaints. He knew he was dealing with oxygen canisters, but apparently did not understand the difference between oxygen storage tanks and generators designed to fire off. When he prepared the boxes for shipping, he noticed the green "repairable" tags mistakenly placed on the canisters by the mechanics, and misunderstood them to signify "unserviceable" or "out of service," as he variably said after the accident. He also drew the unpredictable conclusion that the canisters were therefore empty. He asked the receiving clerk to fill out a shipping ticket. The receiving clerk did as he was asked, listing the tires and canisters, and put quotation marks around the word "Empty." Later, when asked why, he replied, "No reason. I always put like, when I put my check, I put 'Carlos' in quotations. No reason I put that." The reason was that it was his habit. On the shipping ticket he also put "5 boxes" between quotation marks.

But a day or so later, over by Flight 592, the ValuJet ramp agent who signed for the cargo didn't care about such subtleties. ValuJet was not authorized to carry hazardous cargoes of any sort, and it seems obvious now that a shipping ticket listing tires on wheel assemblies and oxygen canisters (whether or not they were empty) should have aroused the ramp agent's suspicions. No one would have complained had he opened the boxes, or summarily rejected the load. There was no hazardous-materials paperwork associated with it, but he had been formally trained in the recognition of unmarked hazards. His ValuJet station-operations manual specifically warned, "Cargo may be declared under a general description that may have hazards which are not apparent, that the shipper may not be aware of this. You must be conscious of the fact that these items have caused serious incidents, and in fact, endangered the safety of the aircraft and personnel involved." It also said,

> Your responsibility in recognizing hazardous materials is dependent on your ability to: 1. Be Alert! 2. Take the time to ask questions! 3. Look for labels! . . . Ramp agents should be alert whenever handling luggage or boxes. Any item that might be considered hazardous should be brought to the attention of your supervisor or pilot, and brought to the immediate attention of Flight Control and, if required, the FAA. REMEMBER: SAFETY OF PASSENGERS AND FELLOW EMPLOYEES DEPENDS ON YOU!

It is possible that the ramp agent was lulled by the company-material labels. Would the SabreTech workers ship hazardous cargo without letting him know? His conversation with the copilot, Richard Hazen, about the weight of the load may have lulled him as well. Hazen, too, had been formally trained to spot hazardous materials, and he would have understood better than the ramp agent the dangerous nature of oxygen canisters, but he said nothing. It was a routine moment in a routine day. The morning's pesky electrical problems had perhaps been resolved. The crew was calmly and rationally preparing the airplane for the next flight, a procedure that had always worked for them before. As a result the passengers' last line of defense folded. They were unlucky, and the system killed them.

Giving Up on a Zero-Accident Future

What are we to make of this tangle of circumstance and error? One suspicion is that its causes may lie in the market forces of a deregulated airline industry, and that in order to keep such catastrophes from happening in the future we might need to consider the possibility of re-regulation—a return to the old system of limited competition, union work forces, higher salaries, and expensive tickets. There are calls now for just that. The improvement in safety would come from slowing things down, and allowing a few anointed airlines the leisure to discover their mistakes and act on them. The effects on society, however, would be costly and anti-egalitarian—a return to a constricted system that many fewer people could afford to use. Moreover, technical trends would argue against it. Despite the obvious chaos of the business and the apparent frequency of airline accidents, air travel has become safer under deregulation. Reductions in "procedural" and "engineered" accidents have more than compensated for any increase in system accidents—which in any case must have occurred in the past as well.

The other way to regulate the airline industry is not economic but operational—detailed governmental oversight of all the technical aspects of flight. This is an approach we have taken since the birth of the airlines, in the 1920s, and it is what we expect of the FAA today. Strictly applied standards are all the more important in a free market, in which unchecked competition would eventually require airlines to cut costs to the point of operating unsafely, until accidents forced them out of business one by one. A company should not overload its airplanes or fly them with worn-out parts, but it also cannot compete effectively against other companies that do. Day to day, airline executives may resent the intrusion of government, but in their more reflective moments they must also realize that they need this regulation in order to survive. The friendship that has grown up between the two sides—between the regulators and the regulated—is an expression of this fact, which no amount of self-reform at the FAA can change. When after the ValuJet crash David Hinson, of the FAA, reacted to accusations of cronyism by going to Congress and humbly requesting that his agency's "dual mandate" be eliminated, so that it would no longer be required by law to promote the airlines, he and Congress (which did as he requested) were engaged in a particularly hollow form of political theater.

The FAA's critics had real points to make. The agency had become too worried about the reactions of its allies in the airline industry, and it needed to try harder to enforce existing regulations. Perhaps it needed even to write some new regulations. Like NASA before the *Challenger* accident, the FAA needed to listen to the opinions and worries of its own lower-level employees. But there are limits to all this, too. When, at a post-crash press conference in Miami, a

reporter asked Robert Francis, of the NTSB, "Shouldn't the government protect us against this kind of thing?" the best answer would have been "It cannot, and never will."

The truth helps, because in our frustration with such system accidents we may be tempted to invent solutions that, by adding to the obscurity and complexity of the system, may aggravate just those characteristics that led to the accidents in the first place. This argument for a theoretical point of *diminishing* safety is a central part of Perrow's thinking, and it seems to be borne out in practice. In his exploration of the North American early-warning system Sagan found that the failures of safety devices and backup systems gave the most dangerous false indications of missile attack—the kind that could have triggered a response. The radiation accidents at Chernobyl and Three Mile Island were both induced by failures in the safety systems. Remember also that the ValuJet oxygen generators were safety devices, that they were backup systems, and that they were removed from the MD-80s because of regulations limiting their useful lives. This is not an argument against such devices but a reminder that elaboration comes at a price.

Human reactions add to the problem. Administrators can think up impressive chains of command and control, and impose complex double checks and procedures on an operating system, and they can load the structure with redundancies, but on the receiving end there comes a point—in the privacy of a hangar or a cockpit—beyond which people rebel. These rebellions are now common throughout the airline business—and, indeed, throughout society. They result in unpredictable and arbitrary actions, all the more so because in the modern, insecure workplace they remain undeclared. The one thing that always gets done is the required paperwork.

Paperwork is a necessary and inevitable part of the system, but it, too, introduces dangers. The problem is not just the burden that it places on practical operations but also the deception that it breeds. The two unfortunate mechanics who signed off on the nonexistent safety caps just happened to be the slowest to slip away when the supervisors needed signatures. The other mechanics almost certainly would have signed too, as did the inspectors. Their good old-fashioned pencil-whipping is perhaps the most widespread form of Vaughan's "normalization of deviance." The falsification they committed was part of a larger deception—the creation of an entire pretend reality that includes unworkable chains of command, unlearnable training programs, unreadable manuals, and the fiction of regulations, checks, and controls. Such pretend realities extend even into the most self-consciously progressive large organizations, with their attempts to formalize informality, to deregulate the workplace, to share profits and responsibilities, to respect the integrity and initiative of the individual. The systems work in principle, and usually in practice as well, but the two may have little to do with each other. Paperwork floats free of the ground and obscures the murky workplaces where, in the confusion of real life, system accidents are born.

It would be wrong to conclude that we should join the alarmists in their prophesies of doom. Flying will remain safe, and for conventional reasons, including the admirable reaction we have seen to the ValuJet crash. But it should also be clear that there are structural limits to flight safety, and that any dream of a zero-accident future is probably about as realistic as the old ValuJet promise to put safety first. If that is true, we had better get used to it. Conventional accidents—those I call procedural or engineered—will submit to our solutions, but as air travel continues to expand, we can expect capricious system accidents to blossom. Understanding why might keep us from making the system even more complex, and therefore perhaps more dangerous, too.

Chapter 10 Review Questions

1. Briefly, what arguments do Rainey and Steinbauer put forward to develop a concept of effective government performance? In your view, do they make their case? Why or why not?

2. Despite their thesis, there is a repeated public demand—evidenced in the popular press and in political campaigns—that government is ineffective, inefficient, and uneconomical, and thus needs to become more businesslike. In your opinion, what are the sources and causes of this repeated public outcry? According to the authors, why is it an inaccurate perception? Or why is it only partly correct?

3. From your own experiences, how best can or should citizens become informed about the realities of government performance? And support its improvement?

4. If you were charged with constructing a better FAA management system that would prevent such problems as the ValuJet disaster from recurring in the future, what would you recommend? Or, as the author of the ValuJet case argues, do we simply have to learn to live with the eventualities of such disasters and preventing all these from occurring is impossible, even counterproductive?

5. Does the case "The Lessons of ValuJet 592" ultimately support or contradict the Rainey and Steinhauer argument? Does the case offer a different, even a more convincing model?

6. What is meant by Diane Vaughan's phrase "the normalization of deviance" (as cited in this case)? How can organizations guard against that from happening?

Key Terms

oversight authorities
stakeholders

intrinsic motivation
extrinsic rewards

autonomy
mission valence
mission-oriented culture
task motivation
mission motivation
public service motivation
task design

agency effectiveness
privatization
the hollow state
generic theories of management
empower leadership
work environment
professionalism

Suggestions for Further Reading

Much of the earliest literature on management in this century focused on the role of line managers in business, for example, Henri Fayol, *General and Industrial Management,* translated by Constance Storrs (London: Pitman, 1949); or Frederick W. Taylor, *Scientific Management* (New York: Harper & Row, 1911). Their emphasis on the values of efficiency, rationality, and clear lines of hierarchy was carried over into the public sector by such authors as Henry Bruere, W. F. Willoughby, Frederick Cleveland, Luther Gulick, and others, who pioneered the development of management techniques in the public sector prior to World War II. For a good collection of the works of these writers, see Frederick C. Mosher, *Basic Literature of American Public Administration, 1787–1950* (New York: Holmes and Meier, 1981); and for several excellent summary essays on the lives of key management theorists, read Brian R. Fry, *Mastering Public Administration* (Chatham, N.J.: Chatham House, 1989).

A book that should be read in its entirety is Chester I. Barnard, *The Functions of the Executive* (Cambridge, Mass.: Harvard University Press, 1938), because Barnard stands in marked contrast to the pre–World War II scientific management theorists and because he made an enormous impact on other postwar writers like Herbert Simon, writers who decisively reshaped our whole view of this field. William B. Wolf, *The Basic Barnard* (Ithaca, N.Y.: Institute of Labor Relations, Cornell University, 1974) offers the best available commentary on Barnard's life and work. A good summary of the work of another important figure, Henry Mintzberg, can be found in Henry

Mintzberg, *Mintzberg on Management: Inside Our Strange World of Organizations* (New York: Free Press, 1989).

Postwar management thought is aptly described by Harold Koontz as "the management theory jungle," i.e., it is divided into multiple schools and perspectives. To sample some of these diverse points of view, read C. West Churchman, *The Systems Approach* (New York: Dell Publishing, 1968), or Bertram M. Gross, *The Managing of Organizations* (New York: Free Press, 1964), for the *systems approach;* read Harry Levinson, *The Exceptional Executive: A Psychological Conception* (Cambridge, Mass.: Harvard University Press, 1968), or Rensis Likert, *The Human Organization: Its Management and Value* (New York: McGraw-Hill, 1967), for the *human behavioral school;* refer to the several hundred cases available through the Harvard Business School that were instrumental in pioneering the methodology of the *case method;* for the *policy emphasis,* see Paul Appleby, *Policy and Administration* (University, Ala.: University of Alabama Press, 1949); and the *decision school* of management is well represented in books by Charles E. Lindblom and Herbert A. Simon, (discussed in Chapters 8 and 9).

Where are we today in public management thought? Again, no consensus prevails as described in the excellent overview essay by Hal G. Rainey, "Public Management: Recent Developments and Current Prospects," in Naomi B. Lynn and Aaron Wildavsky, eds., *Public Administration: The State of the Discipline* (Chatham, N.J.: Chatham House, 1990). One is also encouraged to consult an excellent review essay on where we stand today in this field, Eugene B. McGregor Jr., "Public Management", *JPAM*, 16, no. 1, 153–61 (1997). The older schools are still very influential, but unquestionably economic pressures have brought about a new outpouring of ideas on efficiency and cutback management, which are reflected in various "how to" *practical efficiency-oriented managerial writings*. For the best and largest current collection of these writings that apply to local government, contact the International City/County Management Association, Washington, D.C. There are numerous, more specialized books that focus also on peculiar management problems associated with various levels of government as well as on many specialized policy fields like defense, law enforcement, health care, and others. Though today the *effective leadership trait* perspective is especially popular, as reflected by John W. Gardner, *On Leadership* (New York: Free Press, 1990); and Jameson W. Doig and Erwin C. Hargrove, eds., *Leadership and Innovation: Entrepreneurs in Government* (Baltimore: Johns Hopkins University Press, 1990).

For two excellent textbooks that provide an up-to-date realistic picture of the recent problems and prospects in public management, see Hal G. Rainey, *Understanding and Managing Public Organizations,* 2nd ed., (San Francisco: Jossey-Bass, 1997); and Charldian Newell, ed., *The Effective Local Government Manager,* 2nd ed. (Washington, D.C.: ICMA, 1993). For two useful readers on this topic, refer to J. Steven Ott et al., eds. *Public Management* (Chicago: Nelson-Hall, 1991); and Patricia W. Ingraham et al., eds. *New Paradigms for Government* (San Francisco: Jossey-Bass, 1994). Many outstanding cases on public management can be obtained through the case program, John F. Kennedy School of Government, Harvard University, 79 JFK Street, Cambridge, Massachusetts 02138, and for the best case collection related to local government management, see James M. Banovetz, ed. *Local Government: Cases in Decision Making* 2d ed. (Washington, D.C.: ICMA, 1998). And for "best practice and model program" cases, see Marc Holzer and Kathe Callahan, *Government at Work* (Thousand Oaks, CA: SAGE, 1997).

In the 1990s, public management practices have been dominated by the "reinventing government movement" and so the two critical works that are "must" reading on this topic are David Osborne and Ted Gaebler, *Reinventing Government* (Reading, Mass.: Addison-Wesley, 1992); and Vice President Al Gore, *Creating a Government That Works Better and Costs Less* (Washington, D.C.: USGPO, 1993). For a current critical appraisal of the application of reinventing ideas to federal government, see Donald F. Kettl and John J. DiIulio, Jr., eds. *Inside the Reinvention Machine* (Washington, D.C.: The Brookings Institution, 1995). Some of the best treatments in the 1990s of key public management issues by leading scholars include: Mark H. Moore, *Creating Public Value* (Cambridge: Harvard University Press, 1995); Paul C. Light, *Thickening Government* (Washington D.C.: The Brookings Institution, 1995); Donald F. Kettl, *Sharing Power* (Washington D.C.: The Brookings Institution, 1993); Norma Riccucci *Unsung Heroes* (Washington, D.C.: Georgetown University Press, 1995); and Laurence E. Lynn, Jr., *Public Management As Art, Science, and Profession* (Chatham, N.J.: Chatham Publishers, 1996). For current managerial research studies, several excellent journals and worth sampling such as the *Harvard Business Review, Public Administration Review, Governing* and the *Journal of Public Administration Research and Theory.*

CHAPTER 11

Public Personnel Motivation: The Concept of the Public Service Culture

. . . *We* *must wonder why the nurturing of a public service culture has received so little attention in government organizations, society, or the research community. Public service motives are the underpinnings for the uniqueness that defines the public service culture. They provide the basis for activities that educate and empower the citizens as members of a democratic state. They are the platform from which public servants bring values and engagement to their work. They fortify public servants to overcome self-serving interests, moral inertia, and risk avoidance.*

—*Lois Recascino Wise*

READING 11

Introduction

The emphasis on contemporary research in personnel motivation has resulted in an impressive subfield of public administration that deals with the many ramifications of the individual in public organizations. Today, most scholars and practitioners of public administration are aware that the handling of personnel motivational issues can be one critical key to the successful management of any public agency.

Chapter 6 explored how our important understanding of the role of the informal group within organizations began. Though concerned primarily with business organizations, Elton Mayo's discoveries in the field of human relations at Western Electric in the 1920s expanded the traditional theories of public administration by showing how critical an impact the human group had on the management process.

However, early researchers in the personnel field tended to accept the basic goals of increased efficiency in organizational activities and actually sought ways by which management could obtain greater productivity from workers. Initially, monotony, alienation, and worker fatigue frequently were problems focused upon in personnel studies. These studies often recommended a restructuring of the formal or procedural aspects of the institution to achieve greater or improved efficiency.

The second-generation personnel specialists like Chris Argyris, Warren Bennis, Rensis Likert, and Douglas McGregor have continued to stress the significance of the problems of the individual in organizations, but frequently with less concern about organizational performance and more careful attention toward helping to achieve worker satisfaction and personal growth on the job. Such writers de-emphasized traditional administrative goals such as efficiency and, instead, stressed support of individual values and a humanistic environment within organizations.

In the following essay, "The Public Service Culture," written especially for this text, Lois Recascino Wise, who is an internationally respected professor specializing in human resource management at the School of Public and Environmental Affairs at Indiana University, offers a unique assessment of the current state of motivational research as it pertains to the public service. She begins her essay with a review of the current research literature in this field, but as Dr. Wise suggests, her aim more involves conceptualizing and "enriching understanding of the construct of public service motives, the process of public service motivation, and its implications for democratic governance." Her argument is premised on the assumption that "a public service motive is a type of human need," that is "stronger for some people than others." Professor Wise defines "public motives" as "the process that causes individuals to perform acts that contribute to the public good as a way of satisfying their personal needs." Substantively, such motives entail "affective, norm-based and rational attributes" that the author discusses in some depth. Not everyone in government, of course, is disposed toward public service motivations, nor are they necessarily absent in other organizations, even in McDonalds, argues Dr. Wise. She says, however, that "public service motivation is more prevalent in government than in business or industry" because of "the nature and mission (of) government organizations."

Above all, Dr. Wise believes, "Public service motives are significant because they provide a value basis for governance," especially in three ways, by (1) fostering "citizenry educated in the issues and processes of government"; (2) incorporating values, and not merely facts or analytical techniques, into administrative decision-making; and (3) encouraging commitment and responsibility for the work of government and its consequences. Professor Wise concludes by suggesting that public managers should make a conscious effort to develop a culture of public service throughout the workplace, for "if managers do nothing to promote and reward people who display public service motives, we should not expect those motives to be important in the organizations they lead."

Briefly, a word about Dr. Wise's academic background. Her research interests center on the broad areas of employment and management, with special focus on the public sector, especially civil service systems, administrative reforms, attitudes toward change and innovation, performance motivation in the public and private sectors, and systems for distributing organizational rewards and determining status in the bureaucracy. Dr. Wise teaches primarily in the areas of public management and human resource management, and her works have appeared in the major scholarly and professional journals. She is the author of *Labor Market Policies and Employment Policies in the United States* and is one of the most respected international scholars in this field of study. Dr. Wise serves as a consultant to public- and private-sector organizations in the United States and Europe and was recently awarded one of the highest prizes in Sweden for her research contributions to that nation's public administration development.

As you review her thoughtful exploratory essay on the "state of the art" of this subject, you might consider the following questions:

How does Dr. Wise define the term "public service motivation"?

Where does the author argue that most of our understanding of personnel motivation derives from?

Do you agree with her fundamental idea that public service motivation is more prevalent in government?

What does the author mean by the terms "rational," "norm-based," and "affective"? How do these concepts shape public service motivation?

How can "the public service culture" concept specifically help practicing public administrators in motivating their employees? Is it a pragmatic *and* valid conceptual framework, in your view, that can apply to all levels of public service—local, state, and federal? If so, explain how you would use her concept to motivate employees in the public sector.

The Public Service Culture

LOIS RECASCINO WISE

In 1961 President Kennedy issued the challenge "Ask not what your country can do for you but what you can do for your country." The call inspired a generation of Americans to government service. Thousands joined the newly created Peace Corps and its domestic counterpart, Volunteers in Service to America, but interest in working for the state overall was also high during the 1960s and 1970s. This was a generation that not only believed it could make the world a better place to live but also believed that it had a responsibility to shoulder the burden. In those days, college graduates who chose their first full-time job based on the size of the salary offered were seen as odd and were perhaps even stigmatized by their peers (Orloff 1978; Johnson and Prieve 1975).

Times have changed. In response to flight from government by officials who converted their

knowledge into private sector expertise for higher pay, President Bush asserted, "Government should be an opportunity for public service, not private gain" (Waldman 1989: 16). More recent evidence suggests that high pay lures graduates from programs in public affairs into private sector consulting (Barrett and Greene 1998). Graduates are more likely to look with a jaundiced eye at the notion of employment as a form of personal sacrifice. At the same time, public management practices seem to be increasingly grounded in the assumption that monetary rewards, rather than purposive or social rewards, are the principal incentives for organizational membership and job performance among government employees. We can see this underlying belief in the use of special salary allowances for recruiting certain occupational groups, for example, and in continuing efforts to find an effective way to link performance to pay.

It was in this context that at the beginning of the

"The Public Service Culture," by Lois Recascino Wise. This essay was written especially for this volume.

1990s Perry and Wise (1990) called for a renewed interest in studying and testing the propositions of public service motivation. Drawing on previous research, including work focused on voluntary organizations (Knoke and Wright-Isak 1982), they attempted to identify a theoretical framework for public service motivation. They identified three categories of public service motives and put forward a set of research propositions about the process of public service motivation. They called for research examining the behavioral implications of those propositions, for research developing new methods to operationalize and measure public service motivation, and for research that would refine the theoretical framework and research hypotheses pertaining to the motivational bases of public service.

Over the last two decades, using various definitions of the construct, a number of researchers have examined public service motivation. These empirical studies can be mainly placed in two different categories. The first set focuses on finding evidence of whether or not a public service motivation exists (Rainey 1982; 1976; 1991; Crewson 1995; 1997; Jurkewicz et al. 1998; Gabris and Simo 1995; Brewer 1998; Vinzant 1998). The second set attempts to develop more sophisticated measurements for operationalizing the public service motivation construct (Perry 1996; Perry 1997). Research is still limited, however, regarding the development of a theoretical framework for how public service motives affect behavior or for exploring the implications of public service motivation for bureaucratic outputs.

The contributions that contemporary studies have made to our ability to measure and compile evidence of public service motivation, however, are not the focus of this essay. Our interest lies more in elaborating and enriching understanding of the construct of public service motives, the process of public service motivation, and its implications for democratic governance. To this end the essay turns to a discussion of public service motives and the operating conditions of public service motivation. It then considers the linkages and tensions between public service motives and attributes of bureaucracy in a democracy. Some

management implications for developing a public service work culture are discussed in the conclusions.

What Do We Know?

In this section we review literature regarding public service motivation and address four key questions. The first asks what public service motives are, and the second, what the operating conditions of public service motivation are. Under the second question we consider whether public service motives are constant and exclusive to the public sector. The third question pertains to whether public service motivation is more prevalent in the public sector, and the fourth seeks to explore the significance of public service motives.

What Are Public Service Motives?

A public service motive is a type of human need. The desire to fulfill human needs influences behavior. People have many different competing needs. Both theorists and empirical researchers have attempted to define human need structures and explain the way they affect behavior in various situations, including the workplace. Not all motives for work are identified by these content theories of human needs (Georgiou 1973; Perrow 1978). None of these theories, for example, identifies human spiritual needs as having implications for work motivation, but there are many people whose spiritual needs are so strong that they choose a career in a church, synagogue, or other religious organization. By the same token, individuals may have such strong needs to perform acts of public service and to contribute to the advancement of the quality of life in society that they may choose a career of public service. Like spiritual needs, public service motives will be stronger for some people than they are for others.

Behavior that contributes to the public good fulfills a human need among those with public service needs or motives. We believe that these motives are primarily addressed in the public sector because government work focuses on public service, because it is in the interest of public sector organizations to promote and cultivate these values and motives, and because the public sector is larger than the nonprofit sector. This is not to say that everyone working in the public sector is predisposed to public service motives, nor is it to say that people who are stimulated by public service motives do not have other needs that are responsive to the incentives that their organizations offer. In the same way, people working for the church, temple, or mosque are not motivated by their spiritual needs alone.

Public service motivation pertains to the process that causes individuals to perform acts that contribute to the public good as a way of satisfying their personal needs. Acts rooted in the desire to fulfill a public service need can involve the decision to pursue public administration as a field of study, and the decision to join an organization that provides opportunities to fulfill public service needs, as well as the performance of a set of responsibilities and tasks related to one's status as an employee or volunteer in an organization. As a form of intrinsic motivation, the potential gain from public service motivation is a function of how individuals expect to feel as a consequence of performing acts of public service.

Based on previous theoretical work, Perry and Wise (1990) organized public service motives into three broad categories. These are affective, norm-based, and rational motives. The same act can be motivated by various public service needs. For example, one individual may join the military service based on a love of country, while another joins because of a sense of duty and responsibility.

Normative orientations are based on social values and norms of what is proper and appropriate and include a desire to serve the public interest; to fulfill a sense of duty to the community; and to express a unique sense of loyalty to the government (Downs 1967; Karl 1979; Buchanan 1975; Knoke and Wright-Isak 1982). Frederickson (1970) argues that the pursuit of social equity is a primary obligation of public servants.

Affective motives are rooted in an individual's emotions. Affective motives would include a deep belief in the importance of a particular program to society. Gulick referred to this sort of commitment as anchored in a nobility of the great objectives of public service (Blumberg 1981), distinguishing it from public service acts based on a personal identification with a public program. For example, person A is motivated to join public service to advance the goals of the War on Poverty because she experienced poverty and deprivation as a child. Person B is motivated to join the War on Poverty because he abhors starvation in a rich society. Person A's behavior is rooted in rational motives while Person B's behavior is affective. An affective love of nature and a desire to protect the environment draws individuals into public sector employment. Frederickson and Hart (1985) contend that a primary motive for public servants is a patriotism of benevolence, which they define as an encompassing love of and desire to protect the people within a political jurisdiction. This love of humanity provides opportunities for moral heroism and personal sacrifice for others.

Perry and Wise (1990) include rational motives as a basis for public service behavior. The underlying premise is that individual choice among a set of possible alternatives is motivated by an assessment of the potential utility maximization from each option. Rational motives would include a desire to represent some special interest and a personal identification with a program or policy goal, as well as desires for personal gain and personal need fulfillment (Downs 1967). The opportunity to participate in policy formulation or program implementation may be anchored in needs for power, esteem from others, and self-esteem. According to Rawls (1971:84), public service enables individuals to experience ". . . the realization of self which comes from a skillful and devoted exercise of social duties."

This third category of public service motives is not universally accepted. Some argue that public service can be rooted only in prosocial behavior (Rainey 1982). According to this school of thought, rational, self-serving motives by definition are not public service motives regardless of the social or public good they produce. We take the perspective here that human beings are complex and contradictory and indeed may embark on public service careers or perform acts of significant public service primarily based on their own human needs and self-interest. These motives may mature and develop into normative or affective bases for behavior. If this is so, then how members of a society prioritize their needs and interests becomes increasingly important for the furtherance of the public good.

What Are the Operating Conditions of Public Service Motivation?

Are Public Service Motives Constant?

Human behavior is based on a mix of motives, and motives vary over time in their salience to single individuals and to society as a whole. By extension, the motives for public service employment should vary among countries and geographic regions and also among units of government that have separate purposes and client groups. Not only can individuals switch among the categories of public service motives that they identify as important, but individuals may also turn away from these motives altogether as their needs are fulfilled, as their beliefs are proven wrong, or as other needs become more dominant (Homans 1961; Clark and Wilson 1961; Opsahl and Dunnette 1970; Deci and Ryan 1987). If the underlying assumptions for management practice and administrative policy in an organization change, we should expect shifts in the priority attached to different motivational bases for work (March and Simon 1958).

Individuals with public service motives are not by definition devoid of other motives and human needs. Concerns for basic human needs may be central for a Peace Corps worker in a primitive setting. Worries about job security may preoccupy public service–oriented workers during a reduction in force. Concerns for personal safety and career advancement are also important motivators for individuals dedicated to law enforcement, for example. In the same vein, persons pursuing religious careers have needs for personal development and growth that motivate their job-related behavior.

Contextual factors may also be significant in explaining trends in public sector employment. For example, the availability of government jobs affects the likelihood that a particular individual will find employment in the public sector regardless of the strength of her public service needs. If government jobs are clustered in some distant central location, such as a capital city, or if government imposes a hiring freeze, individuals will turn to other sectors. When government organizations undergo a reduction in force or pay cuts, human needs for job security and monetary reward may gain importance over public service motives for incumbent employees. If bureaucratic red tape prevents action or change for the public good, the strength of public service motivation among individuals will be negatively affected (Buchanan 1975). The perception that effort exerted to create change inside the bureaucracy amounts to "pushing Jell-O" reduces the likelihood that individuals will be motivated to participate in innovation and reform activities in the future. The rational person acts under the belief that effort produces some result. When environmental forces inhibit goal achievement, motivation is reduced (Luthans and Kreitner 1975; Pfeffner and Salancik 1978).

Situational factors play a role in explaining when public service motives surface and dominate individual behavior and when behavior occurs as a consequence of other motives. Public service motives may be dominant, for example, when an individual embarks on a career or makes similar life choices. Public service motives may dominate in certain situational contexts on the job that trigger deeply held values and beliefs and call for acts of moral heroism. For example, Brewer (1998) reports that fraud and abuse account for whistle-blowing behavior among individuals with public service motives. Public service motives may anchor individual discretion and judgment and decisions to depart from established practice. The strength of public service motives may give individuals the courage to resist organizational norms and peer pressure that are in conflict with the way they interpret the public good. These tensions between self-serving interests and interests that serve the public good may occur in the daily performance of their work. They may develop into a habitual behavior in which public servants increasingly lean toward the end of the continuum that represents their own interests rather than the end that represents the public good (Gawthrop 1998b: 134).

As Gawthrop (1998b: 139) notes:

Public managers must recover the truly authentic and creative freedom to decide what they should do ethically in resolving the daily conflicts and challenges that confront them. Until they are capable of freeing themselves from the bondage of habit, any attempt to define professional behavior as truly ethical is an exercise in futility that can only result in a pathetic self-deception. The habits of the self-serving good allow public servants to pursue procedural quasi-ethical life. The net result, to paraphrase H. Richard Niebuhr, is a government of persons without fault, operating in a society without judgment, through the ministrations of a Constitution without purpose.

Are Public Service Motives Exclusive to the Public Sector?

We know by deduction that that public service motives cannot be found exclusively in the public sector. There is no mechanism to test and sort individuals in the labor market to identify and steer those with certain motives into one sector or another. Many people do not consciously choose a sector of employment and may not be fully aware of their own motives for joining a particular organization (Oldham 1976; Orloff 1978; Soelberg 1967; Wanous 1972; 1979; 1980). Individuals in the labor market rely on imperfect information and assumptions about employers in choosing organizations. Public sector employers may send conflicting signals to potential employees by emphasizing high pay and monetary benefits in their recruitment programs, thereby attracting and recruiting individuals whose motives for work are met by monetary rewards rather than the intrinsic returns from acts of public service. By the same token, we know that individuals with strong spiritual motives for work can fulfill these needs in other sectors. A priest or rabbi, for example, can work in the military as a chaplain. A deeply religious person can find rewarding secular employment in health care, counseling, or the arts, for example.

Another reason that public service motives cannot be exclusive to the public sector is that boundaries between sectors of employment are vague and organizational purposes and tasks overlap between sectors. The health care industry in the United States, for example, is found in the public, private, and nonprofit sectors. The opportunity to serve the public interest or to advance the public good is not exclusively limited to public sector employment. This is not to say that there are not unique motives that pertain to public service, but rather to acknowledge that public service can occur in many forums. Many corporations have public policy programs. An individual working for the McDonalds Corporation, for example, could fulfill strong affective needs for public service by being involved in the Ronald McDonald House Program.

Is Public Service Motivation More Prevalent in the Public Sector?

If public service motives are not exclusively found in the public sector, is public service motivation prevalent in government organizations (Brewer 1998)? The question has two meanings. One is whether public service motivation is more prevalent than other types of motivation in government. To grant this premise, we would have to assume that public service motives are so strong that they always dominate human needs for growth, social contact, and physical and security-related needs, for example. Those public servants that Downs (1967) refers to as zealots may meet this assumption, but it does not seem a reasonable expectation for most.

The other interpretation is whether public service motivation is *more prevalent* in government than it is in other sectors of employment. There is a logic for thinking that public service motivation is less prevalent in business and industry, as Brewer (1998) demonstrates. One reason would be that by the nature of their mission and purpose, government organizations overall provide more opportunities for individuals to fulfill public service needs and thus would attract more of those individuals who prioritize their public service motives than would business or industry. Further, if government employers value public service motivation, then it should be expected that the work culture in public sector organizations cultivates and reinforces public service motives more than organizations in business or industry, as some research suggests (Romzek 1990).

If we posit that public service motivation is more prevalent in government than in business or industry, we acknowledge that systemic and organizational factors contribute to an organization's value orientation, and in turn, that public organizations must have separate value orientations. Consequently, the extent to which agencies or firms are able to recruit people with public service motives and are able to maintain and strengthen those human needs should also vary. We should also expect variations within organizations in the extent to which public service motivation accounts for behavior. Individuals will adapt to the operating incentive structure (Deci 1975; Wanous 1972; Clary and Miller 1986). For different reasons, certain branches or divisions might be less likely to recruit or nurture public service motives. Individuals working in certain occupational groups or professional areas may be more or less likely to be motivated by public service needs than others. Vinzant (1998), for example, contend that public service motivation enables protective services workers to cope with the particularly difficult stresses of their occupation.

In defining public service motivation, we have given examples of various categories of public service motives, identified factors in the public service motivation process, and identified some contextual factors important in the process of public service motivation. Public service motives are at the root of the behaviors and actions taken to achieve outcomes that serve the public good. The performance of public service acts and the attainment of public good outcomes are both dependent upon the strength and nature of an individual's public service motives and needs. But the public service motivation process is affected by individual and contextual factors, as motivation theories indicate. For example, an individual may have a strong desire to work for the state but believe that some personal attribute or characteristic makes such employment unlikely. The expectancy theory of motivation would posit that such an individual would have low motivation to apply for a government job, despite the high value she or he attaches to it as a vehicle of public service. Recruitment agents of the state could reinforce or counter the belief of low probability. The mission, policies, administrative structure, and culture of organizations can promote or dampen an individual's belief that the workplace provides an opportunity to fulfill public service needs. At the same time, an individual might think that even if the public service act were performed, factors affecting political, economic, or social capital would make goal achievement unlikely, and this in turn can reduce the amount of motivation an individual would have. These expectations might vary at times, depending on factors such as leadership support or available resources.

Of What Significance Are Public Service Motives?

If public service motives can exist in any sector and may appear in varying degrees of strength within public organizations, what significance does the construct have for public administration or more generally for the advancement of democratic and social values? Public service motives are significant because they provide a value basis for governance.

In developing the notion of the human side of public administration, Gawthrop (1998a) argues that members of the public service must act from a personal commitment to a public problem and an allegiance to the community. Public service motives anchor bureaucratic behavior and action, a connection that becomes increasingly significant as prevailing ideas about the role and status of public servants are rejected, and calls for responsibility, courage, flexibility, and proactive behavior are continually heard. Three ideas are central to these writings. These are the responsibility for educating the public in democratic issues and processes, the importance of individual values in administrative life, and the responsibility for engaging the citizenry in the administrative process.

Education

An important output of bureaucracy is a citizenry educated in the issues and processes of government (Gaus 1947; Gawthrop 1998a). Gaus (1947) sees education as a way of enhancing human growth and the value of human worth. Gawthrop (1998a) describes the responsibility for educating the citizenry as rooted in affective motives and based on a love of humanity. Education of the citizenry contributes to the bureaucracy's responsibility for engaging the public in the democratic and administrative process and achievement of an enriched sense of community. Education empowers the citizenry. It balances bureaucratic values and engagement as inputs in the administrative process because an educated citizenry is an empowered partner in governance.

Educating the public is in tension with both the tenets of efficiency and professionalism. The norm of professionalism means that individuals should use their professional expertise to make the best

judgment based on the facts of the case (Mosher 1978). The tenet of efficiency means that tasks should be performed with the least use of resources and in the least amount of time. Educating the public would slow down the process, increase costs related to educational activities themselves, and occupy greater numbers of public servants in the education process itself.

Values

Gawthrop (1998a) contends that there is an integral relationship between administration and democratic values. In arguing for the appropriateness of values in public administration, he contends that an emphasis on facts and evidence in decision making does not mean that values must be excluded from the equation. Both facts and values contribute to solutions of public administration questions, but the public servant must weigh the consequences of both in making a decision. Frederickson (1971) also makes a strong case for incorporating values into public administration when he asserts "Administrators are not neutral, they should be committed to both good management and social equity as values. . . ." If we are concerned about justice and equity in the outcomes of government, value judgments are an integral part of the administrative process.

Shared values may be the cornerstone of a cohesive public organization (Meier 1997: 73, 74). To the extent that shared values facilitate achieving a common goal among members of an organization, they may be associated with greater commitment to organizational purposes, and consequently to higher levels of motivation and performance related to achieving those goals (Meier 1997). Individuals with congruent values are more able to anticipate each other's actions and are more likely to have the same assessments regarding which workplace behavior is important (Schein 1985; Kluckhohn 1951). Empirical studies show that especially when an individual public servant's values are like those held by the work group or organization, personal values are more likely to be reflected in decisions involving discretion (Meier 1997:74). But at the same time, shared values may limit the range of problem solutions considered and may function as a form of peer pressure. The strength of individual public service motives may counter the possibility of "group think" and other conformist behavior when they challenge the public interest.

In direct conflict with the notion of introducing individual values to administrative behavior is the prevailing administrative norm of neutrality. The norm of neutrality means that bureaucrats should remain emotionally disaffected by the problems they face and detached from the clients they serve. Thompson (1985) captures the kernel of the neutrality ethic:

> The use of discretion . . . can never be the occasion for applying any moral principles other than those implicit in the orders and policies of the superiors to whom one is responsible in the organization. The ethic of neutrality portrays the ideal administrator as a completely reliable instrument of the goals of the organization, never injecting personal values into the process of furthering these goals.

Many years ago Herbert Simon (1945: 2) posited and Blau's (1955: 30) pioneering work demonstrated that even lower-level public servants make discretionary decisions that modify public policy outcomes and have significant consequences for agency clientele—for example, in determining eligibility for benefits or opportunities for employment. Neiderhoffer (1967: 10) similarly found that police officers may decide if and how the law should be applied. These decisions may be turning points in the lives of young offenders, for example. Some research suggests that police discretion is bounded by organizational norms and values (Jones 1977: 300–301; 200). Vinzant (1998) argue that public servants who clearly articulate value conflicts in their work demonstrate higher job satisfaction and greater motivation even in a highly stressful work situation.

Engagement

A concern for engagement focuses on securing greater personal involvement from public servants for their work and its consequences. Many scholars think that bureaucrats mainly try to limit their responsibility and risk in discretionary situations and that this behavior reduces the quality of government outputs for target citizens and undermines an organization's ability to achieve its primary mission (Jones 1977: 301; Blau 1955: 50).

Engagement means that public servants should not take a passive role in the policy implementation process, for example, but should be fully engaged in the event and able to identify pitfalls and problems that can undermine program success. In defining the philosophy of a New Public Administration, Frederickson (1971), for example, calls for public servants to become engaged in change. New Public Administration means "changing those policies and structures that inhibit social equity."

Engagement also means that public servants should ". . . think of what ought to be done instead of merely doing that which must be done" (Gawthrop 1998a). They cannot seek refuge within the boundaries of their job description and assigned responsibilities when presented with professional dilemmas. Gawthrop (1998a) submits that both moral inertia and unimaginative performance on the part of public servants are unacceptable. In this sense, the demand for engagement challenges the morality of rule-following behavior. A religious leader may perform the forms and rituals of the sacrament without engaging an internal spiritual emotion that creates an affective bond with the congregation. Similarly, a bureaucrat may go through the routines and motions of a job following the forms and rules prescribed but never engaging an affective emotion for the citizen clients he or she is positioned to serve, or in turn, feeling any concern for the outcome of their interaction.

The call for greater engagement is similar to what Carnevale (1995: 38) calls "working beyond contract." Working beyond contract means that job performance includes moral involvement, innovative behavior, spontaneity, and prosocial behavior. Working beyond contract means doing more than meeting minimum job performance standards or even meeting satisfactory standards. Similarly, Wise (1999) describes as outmoded the notion that a civil servant's tasks and responsibilities can be defined and contained in a box, arguing that civil servants must step outside the box and anticipate the work that needs to be done, contributing their creativity and problem-solving ability to the organization.

This call for engagement is in tension with what Thompson (1985) refers to as the tenet of structure. That is the notion that a person's position and status in an organization determines his or her responsibility.

> The ethic of structure asserts that, even if administrators may have some scope for independent moral judgment, they cannot be held morally responsible for most of the decisions and policies of government. Their personal moral responsibility extends only to the specific duties of their own office for which they are legally liable.

This means that the policies of an organization can be morally wrong, but individual employees can be held harmless if they perform the duties and routines of their jobs and follow existing rules and regulations. Such thinking inhibits democratic accountability (Thompson 1985). Public servants must assume the moral responsibility for their work. By engaging in questions of public administration, we require public servants to accept accountability for the full consequences of public administration activities. Good intention does not absolve public servants of responsibility for their actions; administrators must demonstrate that they were fully engaged in the issue and that they attempted to foresee possible negative consequences (Thompson 1985). Individuals need to bring imagination and creativity to their work (Gawthrop 1998a).

Conclusions

Public service motives have the potential for advancing the democratic state, but they also are at the heart of a fundamental tension with key tenets of administrative behavior. These ideas run counter to a large body of work and thinking in public administration that rests on a different set of notions about what should be prioritized in bureaucratic conduct. If "good" public administration means rule-based, efficient, economical, and professional management, then it is incompatible with an emphasis on values, education, and engagement. Efficiency, for example, is clearly at odds with the slow task of engaging and educating the citizenry so that people can participate in the administrative process. Similarly, if professional management means reliance on expert advice and knowledge, it too is at odds with education and engagement. Likewise, rule-following behavior is in tension with the tenets of moral responsibility and individual courage. It may fail to deliver socially equitable public outcomes and may cloak acts of moral cowardice.

Public service motivation does not occur in a vacuum. We have argued that contextual factors related to individual actors, situations, events, and the organizations in which behavior occurs influence the strength of public service motivation. This means that to some significant degree both organizations and societies can enhance or reduce the prevalence of public service motivation, and in turn, the performance of acts that serve the public good and represent the public interest.

Organizational policies and practices may account for variations within the public sector in the strength of public service motives. If managers do nothing to promote and reward people who display public service motives, we should not expect those motives to be important in the organizations they lead. Without evidence that the administrative policies and management practices of a particular organization reward and promote public service motivation, we can not expect to find public service the motivational basis for behavior.

Steven Kelman (1987: 94) remarked that "if the norm of public spirit dies, our society would look bleaker and our lives as individuals would be more impoverished." In that spirit we must wonder why the nurturing of a public service culture has received so little attention in government organizations, society, or the research community. Public service motives are the underpinning for the uniqueness that defines the public service culture. They provide the basis for activities that educate and empower the citizens as members of a democratic state. They are the platform from which public servants bring values and engagement to their work. They fortify public servants to overcome self-serving interests, moral inertia, and risk avoidance. They anchor acts of judgment and discretion in a concern for the common good. It is for these reasons that public service motives are significant.

References

Adler, N. J. 1997. *International Dimensions of Organizational Behavior.* 3d ed. Cincinnati, Ohio: South Western College Publishing.

Barnard, C. I. 1938. *The Functions of the Executive.* Cambridge: Harvard University.

Barrett, K., and R. Greene. 1998. "A Managerial Brain Drain." *Governing* 11:(November): 72.

Blau, P. M. 1955. *The Dynamics of Bureaucracy.* New York: John Wiley & Sons.

Blumberg, S. K. 1981. "Seven Decades of Public Administration: A Tribute to Luther Gulick." *Public Administration Review* 41:(2):245–248.

Brewer, G. 1998. "Whistleblowers in the Federal Civil Service: New Evidence of the Public Service Ethic." *Journal of Public Administration Research and Theory* 8:(3):413–430.

Buchanan, B. 1975. "Red Tape and the Service Ethic." *Administration and Society* 6:(4): 423–44.

Carnevale, D. G. 1995. *Trustworthy Government.* San Francisco: Jossey-Bass.

Clark, P. B., and J. Q. Wilson. 1961. "Incentive Systems: A Theory of Organizations." *Administrative Science Quarterly* 6:129–165.

Clary, E.G., and J. Miller. 1986. "Socialization and Situational Influences on Sustained Altruism." *Child Development* 57:1358–69.

Crewson, P. E. 1995. The Public Service Ethic. Ph.D. diss., American University, Washington, D.C.

———. 1997. "Public Service Motivation: Building Empirical Evidence of Incidence and Effect." *Journal of Public Administration Research and Theory* 7:(4):499–519.

Deci, E. 1975. *Intrinsic Motivation.* New York: Plenum Press.

Deci, E., and R. M. Ryan. 1987. "The Support of Autonomy and the Control of Behavior." *Journal of Personality and Social Psychology* 53:1024–37.

Downs, A. 1967. *Inside Democracy.* Boston: Little, Brown.

Frederickson, H. G. 1970. *Toward a New Public Administration.* Scranton, Penn.: Chandler.

Frederickson, H. G., and D. K. Hart. 1985. "The Public Service and Patriotism of Benevolence." *Public Administration Review* 45:(5):547–53.

Gabris, G. T., and G. Simo. 1995. "Public Sector Motivation as an Independent Variable Affecting Career Decisions." *Public Personnel Management* 24:(1):33–51.

Gaus, J. 1947. *Reflections on Public Administration.* Tuscaloosa, Ala: University of Alabama Press.

Gawthrop, L. C. 1998a. "The Human Side of Public Administration." *PS Politics and Society* 31:4 (December): 763–769. (See also www.apsanet.org/PS/dec98)

———. 1998b. *Public Service and Democracy: Ethical Imperatives of the 21st Century.* New York: Chatham House.

Georgiou, P. 1973. "The Goal-Paradigm and Notes towards a Counter Paradigm." *Administrative Science Quarterly* 18:291–340.

Hofstede, G. 1980. *Culture's Consequences: International Differences in Work-Related Values.* London: Sage.

Homans, G. 1961. *Social Behavior: Its Elementary Forms.* New York: Harcourt, Brace.

Hyneman. 1950. *Bureaucracy in a Democracy.* New York: Harper & Brothers.

Johnson, A.C., and E.A. Prieve. 1975. "Changing Perspectives of College Students toward Salary Offers." *Personnel Journal* 54:156–161.

Jones, B. D. 1977. "Distributional Considerations in Models of Government Services Provision." *Urban Affairs Quarterly* 12:291–312.

Jurkiewicz, C. L., T. K. Massey, and R. G. Brown. 1998. "Motivation in Organizations." *Public Productivity and Management Review* 21:(3)230–250.

Karl, B. D. 1979. "Louis Brownlow." *Public Administration Review* 39, (6):511–516.

Kelman, S. 1987. "Public Choice and the Public Spirit." *The Public Interest* 87 (Spring):80–94.

Kluckhohn, C. 1951. "Values and Value-Orientations in the Theory of Action." in *Toward a General Theory of Action,* ed. T. Parsons, and E. Schils. Cambridge, Mass.: Harvard University Press.

Knoke, D., and C. Wright-Isak. 1982. "Individual Motives and Organizational Incentive Systems." *Research in the Sociology of Organizations* 1:209–254.

Luthans, F., and R. Kreitner. 1975. *Organizational Behavior Modification.* Glenview, Ill.: Scott, Foresman.

Macy, J. W. Jr., 1971. *Public Service: The Human Side of Government.* New York: Harper & Row.

March, J. G., and H. Simon. 1958. *Organizations.* New York: John Wiley & Sons.

Meier, K. J. 1992. *Politics and the Bureaucracy: Policy Making in the Fourth Branch of Government.* 3d ed. Pacific Grove, Calif.: Brooks/Cole.

———. 1997. "Bureaucracy and Democracy: The Case for More Bureaucracy and Less Democracy." *Public Administration Review* 57:(3):193–199

Mosher, F. C. 1978. "Professions in the Public Service." *Public Administration Review* 368:144–50.

Neiderhoffer, A. 1967. *Behind the Blue Shield.* Garden City, N.Y.: Anchor Books.

Oldham, G. 1976. "Organizational Choice and Some Correlates of Individuals' Expectancies." *Decision Sciences* 7:873–884.

Opsahl, R.L., and M.D. Dunnette. 1970. "The Role of Financial Compensation in Industrial Motivation." In *Management and Motivation,* ed. V. H. Vroom and E. L. Deci. PP. 127–159. New York: Penguin Books.

Orloff, J. K. 1978. "Public or Private Sector Bound?" *Civil Service Journal* 19:14–17.

Perrow, C. 1978. "Demystifying Organizations." PP. 105–120 in *The Management of Human Services Organizations,* ed. E. Hansfield and R. Saari. New York: Columbia University Press.

Perry, J. L. 1996. "Measuring Public Service Motivation: An Assessment of Construct Reliability and Validity." *Journal of Public Administration Research and Theory* 6:(1):5–22.

———. 1997. "Antecedents of Public Service Motivation." *Journal of Public Administration Research and Theory* 7:(2):181–97.

Perry, J. L., and L. R. Wise. 1990. "The Motivational Bases of Public Service." *Public Administration Review* 50:(3):367–73.

Pfeffner, J., and G. R. Salancik. 1978. *The External Control of Organizations: A Resource Dependence Perspective.* New York: Harper & Row.

Rainey, H. 1976. "Perceptions of Incentives in Business and Government." *Public Administration Review* 36:233–244.

———. 1982. "Reward Preferences among Public and Private Managers: In Search of the Service Ethic." *American Review of Public Administration* 50:(3):374–82.

———. 1991. *Understanding and Managing Public Organizations.* San Francisco: Jossey-Bass.

Rawls, J. 1971. *A Theory of Justice.* Cambridge, Mass.: Belknap Press.

Romzek, B. 1990. "Employee Investment and Commitment." *Public Administration Review* 50 (May/June): 374–382.

Schein, E. H. 1985. *Organizational Culture and Leadership.* San Francisco: Jossey-Bass.

Simon, H. 1945. *Administrative Behavior.* New York: Free Press.

Soelberg, P.O. 1967. "Unprogrammed Decision Making." *Industrial Management Review* 8: 19–29.

Thompson, D. F. 1985. "The Possibility of Administrative Ethics." *Public Administration Review* 45:5:555–61.

Vinzant, J.C. 1998. "Where Values Collide: Motivation and Role Conflict in Child and Adult Protective Services." *American Review of Public Administration* 28:4:347–366.

Waldman, S. 1989. The Revolving Door. *Newsweek,* 6 February.

Wamsley, G. L. et al. 1990. *Refounding Public Administration.* Newbury Park, Calif.: Sage.

Wanous, J. 1972. "Occupational Preferences." *Journal of Applied Psychology* 56:152–55.

———. 1976. "Organizational Entry: From Naïve Expectations to Realistic Beliefs." *Journal of Applied Psychology* 61:22–29.

———. 1979. T. Keon and J. C. Latack. *Choosing an Organization.* Lansing, Mich.: Dept. of Management, Michigan State University.

———. 1980. *Organizational Entry.* Reading, Mass.: Addison-Wesley.

Wise, L. R. 1999. "Job Evaluation: White Elephant on the Path to Reform." *Review of Public Administration Research.* In press.

☐ CASE STUDY **11**

Introduction

Late in May 1996, Admiral Jeremy Boorda, The Chief of Naval Operations (CNO), the Navy's top commander, faced, as usual, a busy afternoon schedule—a meeting with the Deputy Secretary of Defense at 1:15 P.M., a meeting with President Clinton at the White House at 3:30 P.M., and sandwiched in between, an interview with two *Newsweek* reporters. Boorda had planned to eat lunch at his desk at the Pentagon. When his meal arrived, however, Boorda said to his aide that he needed to run home to his CNO residence at the Washington, D.C. Naval Yards, fifteen minutes away, and that he would be back in time for the *Newsweek* interview. He asked the Vice-CNO to take his place at the 1:15 P.M. meeting. When Boorda went home, he typed two notes. One was a love letter to his wife, Bettie, and the other, a message of faith in the Navy and in public service to "my sailors." Then he went to the far corner of his backyard garden and put a barrel of .38 calibre pistol to his chest and pulled the trigger.

Why did the Navy's top leader, one highly praised as a "people person" and said to be a CNO most in touch with the common sailor's concerns, suddenly commit suicide?

The following story by Peter J. Boyer, a *New Yorker* staff writer, thoughtfully probes Boorda's background, his career, and the events leading up to his death. What emerges from this insightful essay is a rare insider look at personal motives within the public service, and how complex and difficult they are to comprehend, not to mention how powerful they are in shaping government organizations and the lives—or deaths—of those serving within them.

As you read this case, try to think about how it relates to Professor Lois Wise's foregoing essay:

What factors motivated Admiral Boorda to drop out of high school and enlist in the Navy at age 16 as a sailor and then turn into a workaholic throughout his career that led to the Navy's highest position? Was it due to "public service motives"? Or, what?

How would you characterize the traditional Navy culture that Admiral Stanley Arthur represented? Its ideals? Model career? Values? In your view, can this "old Navy" culture be equated with the "public service culture" that Dr. Wise envisions?

Why was Boorda considered an "outsider" or a "mustang" and yet selected in 1994 as CNO? What characterized his views of "public service" as opposed to those of "old Navy"? Or, for that matter, what the author characterized as the new "culture wars"?

What flaws in Boorda's decision making became apparent after he became CNO? Were his motives "flawed," or simply not in line with the "old Navy" culture? What in retrospect should Boorda have done to better accommodate these traditional values and outlooks—or would "compromise" have been impossible?

Do you think that the concept of a "public service culture," advanced by Professor Wise, has any relevance to this case? Or at least, would it have some promise in application to improving the Navy's overall organizational effectiveness? If so, how specifically?

Admiral Boorda's War

PETER J. BOYER

The suicide of Admiral Jeremy Michael Boorda, the Chief of Naval Operations, brought new anguish to the sea service, but also a small, muted hope: Might the death of the Navy's top uniformed officer finally conclude the Tailhook trauma? In the nearly five years since the incident, in which drunken aviators ritually molested as many as several dozen women at an annual convention in Las Vegas, there had come a series of investigations, judicial proceedings, corrective policies, and scuttled careers. To some people, such as Senator John McCain, of Arizona, it had begun to seem that the price the Navy paid for Tailhook was a state of perpetual penance. McCain, the son and grandson of admirals and himself a much decorated naval aviator, had been among the first to condemn the 1991 Tailhook rampage: he wrote to the Secretary of Defense and the chairman of the Joint Chiefs of Staff and angrily demanded an

investigation. Now he says, "Something that should have been, at maximum, a six-month kind of story has turned into a five-year story. At some point, even if the Navy screwed it up, we have to say, 'O.K., this episode is closed.' We've got to have closure on it. And possibly the tragedy of Boorda's death brought some closure to it."

The connection between Boorda's death and Tailhook may not be immediately apparent, but within the Navy the last five years has been like a new epoch—the Tailhook Age. The event is felt as a catastrophe, not only because of the shame of the incident itself but because of the moment it represents: a time of uncertain purpose, unwelcome change, and rampant scandal. Old hands measure it against Pearl Harbor in its devastating effect on the Navy: the laxity and inattention that left the American fleet vulnerable in 1941 cost a single admiral his job; so far, the careers of fourteen admirals and nearly three hundred naval aviators have been ended or damaged by Tailhook. The scandal became the divide between the old Navy, flawed but secure in its verities, and the new, conceived in the heat of the nation's culture wars. "What you've got in the Navy is a culture cracking," Colorado's Representative Pat Schroeder, a member of the House Armed Services Committee, says, without discernible remorse. Tailhook brought women in combat; mandatory career-long sensitivity training; and politicians into the Navy's sacred promotion process. It also, in April, 1994, brought Mike Boorda into the Navy's highest job.

In an ordinary time, Admiral Boorda would not have been an obvious choice for Chief of Naval Operations. He was not a heroic figure: he did not serve in one of the Navy's glamour arenas—aviation and submarines—and he had never been fired upon in combat (a rite whose value, events would show, Boorda knew only too well). He was a Jew, and Jews are rare in the Navy's upper rungs; he was not an Annapolis man (as all his predecessors had been); and he was a former seaman (as none of his predecessors had been), who rose through the ranks. Even his physical aspect—he stood only five feet four—helped convey an image of the quintessential bureaucrat, which, as the former Chief of Naval Personnel, he was. But the old ideal of a military leader bore the Tailhook taint, and was precisely what was being rejected. In that sense, Boorda was perfectly suited to the moment: he was smart, was politically attuned, and had a reputation as a "people person," a "Call me Mike" kind of guy. Another principal candidate for the job of C.N.O., Admiral Charles Larson, was an esteemed warrior—an aviator and a submariner—and an Annapolis man. President Clinton chose the people person.

Boorda's sympathetic communion with the men and women of the Navy was not a political contrivance. He was someone who had seen the Navy from the bottom up as well as from the top down. He knew the coarse-denim sociology of the fo'c'sle, where the Navy was something to run away to, or from. Boorda had done both. He was the middle child of three, born, in 1939, to Herman and Gertrude Boorda, in South Bend, Indiana. Theirs was a life that Boorda used to describe only vaguely, saying that his home was unhappy enough to prompt him to drop out of school when he was sixteen and to lie about his age and join the Navy.

Both of his parents were children of Jewish corner-store merchants—on his father's side, immigrants from Lithuania and the Ukraine—who had settled in South Bend. But Herman and Trudy, as Mike's mother was called, never really settled anywhere. When Mike was still in the crib, the family moved to Chicago, where Herman ran a clothing store. It was a brief stay. Sybil Nahrgang, Mike's older sister by four years, says that one of her earliest memories was of her father suddenly breaking down in tears one night. "I didn't know what was the matter," she says. "I suppose I just thought it was overwork."

The family moved on to Madison, Wisconsin, and Great Falls, Montana, but always returned to South Bend. In 1943, Herman was called into the Navy. When the war ended, in 1945, he returned to South Bend, and the family enjoyed a period of relative stability. The Boordas had a third child, Tim; they moved into a home of their own; and, for the first time, the older children were able to remain in one set of schools. Trudy was a forceful woman, and Herman, though of a softer nature, and given to quoting Shakespeare and the Bible, was prone to dark, disconnected moods. There were arguments, and gradually the semblance of a balanced home began to tilt. Then, as Mike entered adolescence and Sybil was finishing high school, their father's condition was diagnosed as paranoid schizophrenia. "Looking back, I think that all the different times that he changed jobs it was probably the same illness," Sybil says. She remembers her father going to the local hospital for outpatient treatment; she later learned it was electroshock therapy, and says that he would come home dazed, recognizing only his wife and his daughter.

One day in the winter of 1953, when Mike was thirteen and Sybil was a senior in high school, Herman Boorda came undone. He and Trudy were out in the family's green Oldsmobile 88, Trudy behind the wheel and Herman in the front passenger seat. As they crossed the rickety bridge over the St. Joseph River, Herman suddenly said that he needed to get some cigarettes. He opened the door of the moving car, stepped to the edge of the bridge, and jumped. The suicide attempt did not succeed. Herman was fished out of the water and rushed to the hospital, and there he was kept under police guard. "I'll always remember seeing those clothes in the basement afterward," Sybil says.

Trudy Boorda did not dwell on her husband's

breakdown. She explained to the children that their father was ill, and carried on, taking a job in a department store. Three months after the incident at the bridge, Herman Boorda came home from the psychiatric ward of the veterans' hospital in Fort Wayne, in time for his daughter's high-school graduation. But soon Herman and Trudy decided they could not stay in South Bend. "He did not think people would ever forget," Sybil says of the suicide attempt, "and I'm sure a lot of my mother's family never did forget."

After graduation, Sybil took a room at the South Bend Y.W.C.A., and Trudy and Herman moved the boys to Momence, Illinois, a tiny farm town, where the Boordas opened a clothing store. Mike, in high school by then, had friends and played ball for the school, and didn't talk much about his home life. As time went on, Sybil says, "My mother and father got angrier and angrier with each other. I would listen to my mom talk about my dad, and I wasn't supposed to bring his name up. And I imagine Mike went through this, too. And then I would listen to my dad talk about my mom, and I wasn't supposed to bring her up. And I would listen to each talk about how rotten they'd each been." Mike lost interest in school, took to drinking beer and goofing off, and, in 1956, in the middle of his junior year, quit school and joined the Navy.

Seven years later, Herman Boorda and his wife divorced, an event that was followed by another breakdown. Trudy, who got custody of Tim, moved to California and remarried there. Herman sold the store, moved into a trailer, and went to work at the post office. He had little contact with Trudy or Tim and only sporadic contact with Sybil, from whom he periodically declared an estrangement. Sybil stayed in touch with her mother, but she knows very little of Tim, who became a teacher in Berkeley. Somehow, Mike sustained a relationship with them all. After Herman developed cancer, Mike had him admitted to the Soldiers' and Airmen's Home in Washington, and when the old man died, last year, Mike made all the arrangements. He was the only member of his family who attended the funeral.

When Boorda quit school, at sixteen, he didn't necessarily have the Navy in mind. His sister says that their parents were furious at his quitting and later told her that they not only endorsed his decision to join the Navy but drove him to the recruiting station and

watched as he signed the enlistment papers that lied about his age. "They thought he'd be home in two weeks," Sybil says.

At first, Boorda hated boot camp, in Illinois, and when his parents visited him he sat in their car and nearly cried. "This is awful," he wrote in a letter to his sister. Even after he made it through boot camp, he still had his doubts about the Navy. At one point, he went AWOL, and nearly got kicked out. Soon, though, he found himself comforted by the Navy's order and discipline. He told a group of recruits in 1989 that "the Navy filled in some of the things that had been missing in my life."

The Navy sent Boorda to a training center in Norman, Oklahoma, and there he fell in love with a seventeen-year-old named Bettie Moran. All the parents objected to the romance, because of the couple's youth and different faiths—she was a Christian—but Mike and Bettie married anyway. Within the year, they became parents. Tragically, their baby, David, was born with only one eye and was otherwise malformed. The doctor who delivered him told the young father that his child was afflicted with a rare disorder called Goltz syndrome and would require repeated surgery but might never see and would always be severely disabled. The doctor advised the Boordas to place the child in a facility that could care for children like David, but Mike and Bettie refused to institutionalize him, and insisted on caring for him themselves. By his fourth birthday, David had undergone seventeen surgeries. For the rest of Boorda's life, David, who is legally blind, occupied the central place in his world away from work: Boorda didn't play golf, he didn't hunt and fish—he helped attend to David. One of Boorda's favorite pastimes was enjoying Redskins broadcasts with him.

David's birth and its consequences had a focussing effect on the young Boorda's view of the Navy, both as an institution that took care of its own, including his son, and as an avenue for his own ambitions. He and Bettie had three more children—two boys and a girl, all healthy—and at work Boorda became a model can-do sailor. He could type like a demon, and that skill got him a job in personnel. He worked ferociously hard and showed initiative, and in 1962 he was chosen for the officer corps. Not many of his fellow Navy officers knew that Boorda was Jewish, which might suggest that he had obscured his heritage as a price for advancement. But

Boorda's religion was not central to his identity; he had married a Christian, and when Bettie said that she wanted to rear their children in her faith Mike acceded to her wish. The far greater challenge to Boorda's ambitions was his entry into the officer class—through Officer Candidate School, the lowest portal to an officer's commission. The sea service has always been a classist enterprise, dating back to the British Navy, where the captain of a ship was the complete sovereign and his officers were captains-in-waiting. The world and warfare changed, but neither the British nor the American Navy ever fully shed the élitist image of its white-glove officer class. To this day, up-from-the-ranks American Navy officers like Boorda are called "mustangs," as distinct from creatures of pure breeding. The favored career tracks are those that begin at Annapolis—or, at least, in some university's R.O.T.C. program. Boorda, though, was a high-school dropout.

He compensated by assuming a brutal workload, which included obtaining a college degree in 1971. Sybil says, "He was a workaholic even when he was a young lieutenant, which isn't as healthy as it sounds sometimes. It's a form of escape." Perhaps, but, if so, Boorda was determined to escape upward. That was not made easier by the fact that his branch of the Navy, once he became an officer, was surface warfare—meaning deployment on destroyers, battleships, cruisers, and the like. Of the Navy's war units, the surface guys had the least chance to achieve glory. While submariners got to sneak up on Soviet subs all over the globe and Navy aviators were among the first into every sort of American skirmish, the surface Navy hadn't had a starring role since the Pacific campaign ended in 1945. Boorda did two tours of duty in Vietnam, including one aboard the destroyer U.S.S. Craig, on which he was the enthusiastic weapons officer who directed several coastal barrages. But no one ever fired back. At the end of the cruise, only one of the ship's officers, the captain, received the coveted bronze "V" for his ribbon, signifying the valor of combat service.

In 1977, Commander Boorda was posted to the Pentagon as an assistant in the Naval Secretariat dealing with manpower and the reserves. Any officer assigned to duty in Washington must develop at least a tolerance for politics, and successful ones develop actual skill at it. Boorda developed a passion. His first Washington tour lasted four years, and then he was sent out to command a destroyer. But in

1983, by now a captain, he was back on the Potomac; by December of 1984, he had reached a new peak, as executive assistant to Admiral James Watkins, Chief of Naval Operations. In January, 1985, he became a rear admiral.

Boorda used these opportunities to expand his political network. When John Lehman became the Navy Secretary, in 1981, he kept Boorda on as the de-facto Assistant Secretary for several months while waiting for his political appointee to be confirmed. Lehman remembers, "He had an agenda—good ideas that were his ideas on how to fix things. And that's when we put a lot of these programs in—special sea pay, bonuses. We had re-up bonuses, and aviator bonuses, and we put in the family-service centers on the bases, so that the moms could go there to get some help to get the washing machine fixed. Just good, common-sense ideas. That was always his strength."

In 1988, Boorda began his tour as Chief of Naval Personnel. Admiral Stanley Arthur, who came to play a key role in the major drama of Boorda's tenure as C.N.O., was one of those officers who tolerated, rather than embraced, the political aspect of a Washington job, and he marvelled at Boorda's fascination with the town. "It was like a flame to him—he loved it," Arthur says. "I always felt, Just keep it at arm's length. You had an appreciation of it, but don't use it, don't play it, don't get into it. So I always put it out here and watched it very carefully and looked for opportunities when I thought it was the right kind of time to do good things for the Navy. I was very careful. But Mike loved to get right to the flame, just as fast as he could."

Tailhook might have been a short-term story, limited in its effect, as John McCain suggests it should have been, except for the accident of its historic timing. The 1991 Tailhook convention occurred on the weekend of September 5th through 8th. Two days later, the Senate Judiciary Committee began hearings on the Supreme Court nomination of Judge Clarence Thomas. The hearings mutated into a series of accusations and denials of sexual harassment, acted out by Thomas, Anita Hill, and fourteen white male United States senators. It was the time of Long Dong Silver, and of the cry "Men just don't get it." Thomas won confirmation, but Hill and her supporters won the culture war. It would soon be the Year of the

Woman—the perfect moment for critics of the military's handling of women's issues to make political gains.

Less than a week after Thomas was sworn in, news of the Tailhook melee broke in the national press. The early stories were sketchy but revolting: a group of drunken aviators had forced women through a clothes-tearing, flesh-grabbing gantlet at a convention attended by senior Navy staff. The official description of Tailhook as an annual aviation "symposium" now seemed laughable, but that was its original purpose, and it was the one time in the year when the most junior officer could directly question the most senior admiral. Over the years, the symposium had become an excuse for partying, and the ever-heightening level of debauchery had occurred with at least the winking acquiescence of the Navy brass—a vestigial nod to the timeless tradition of sailors bingeing on shore. There was also a degree of acquiescence among some of the women who attended Tailhook; in fact, several female naval officers were active participants in the events. Many women who made a career as Navy aviators, though they were not allowed in combat, had become part of the swaggering subculture—a group whose death-defying daily routine set them apart within the Navy. They talked tough and weren't prissy about sex, and one would occasionally show her spirit by grabbing a male colleague's crotch and shouting, "Package check!"

Roxanne Baxter became a Navy flier twenty years ago, and recognized from the start that the aviators' subculture could not be defeated by the women joining its ranks, only emulated. "I bought into it, too," she says. "What I was supposed to be like, everything." Baxter participated in her share of boys'-club rowdiness. "One of the things I learned when I came into the Navy is that they didn't expect you to cry as a naval officer. The ideal naval officer was a man. You had to be like a man. And that was the message that a lot of women got." But Baxter came to believe that she was betraying herself by mimicking the men, and after experiencing incidents of Tailhook abuse she spoke out about the assaults, and she believes that her career suffered for it. She is now out of the Navy (she is married to a former naval aviator) and is studying to be a family therapist. "I don't think the culture has changed to accommodate the women," she says. "You lose something of yourself. I've ex-

perienced that. You give up some of the values that you have."

On the Saturday night at Tailhook '91, Lieutenant Paula Coughlin, a helicopter pilot and a rear admiral's aide, found herself trapped in the gantlet. The next morning, when she complained to her boss that she'd been "practically gang-banged," he did not immediately request a formal investigation. But Coughlin was persistent. Within a month, she was giving off-the-record interviews to the San Diego *Union-Tribune,* and by summer she had appeared on Peter Jennings's "World News Tonight." This was followed by an invitation to the Bush White House.

Amid the Tailhook controversy, the issue of women in combat was finally, and quietly, resolved. Pat Schroeder had long used her seat on the House Armed Services Committee to advocate repeal of the law excluding women from combat. She also believed, along with the committee's chairman (and future Clinton Defense Secretary), Les Aspin, that until women were allowed into every military job they couldn't hope for career parity or equal respect. The principal argument against women in combat was also the oldest one—the assumption that Americans could not tolerate the prospect of their daughters, sisters, and mothers returning from war in body bags. There were also some legitimate operational issues, which pertained especially to the Navy: grouping hundreds of post-adolescent men and women together in a crowded metal container and sending them off to sea for six months seemed unlikely to work out in a way that advanced the idea of gender neutrality.

The Gulf War provided a vivid example of the potential problems of a gender-integrated fleet. The Acadia—a tender, which supplied and repaired destroyers but was not technically a combat vessel—was one of the first Navy ships to deploy women. When the ship left its home port of San Diego for the Middle East, three hundred and sixty women constituted about a quarter of the crew; by the time it returned, ten per cent of those women had been evacuated because of pregnancy. The ship, which became known as the Love Boat, supplied Schroeder's opponents with an argument against the women-in-combat idea, and through most of 1991 a victory for Schroeder's side was anything but certain. After the Hill-Thomas experience, though, there was little enthusiasm in Congress for another gender battle; Schroeder had slipped a provision repealing the combat ban into a military-budget-authorization bill, and in November it passed easily.

Tailhook became a self-perpetuating nightmare for the Navy: it stretched out over months and then years. The Navy Inspector General's investigation, released in April of 1992, revealed sordid details, such as a leg-shaving booth (where a male lieutenant would give women a high shave and "make them see God") and the "belly shot" ritual (in which alcohol was lapped up from women's navels); those revelations brought further outrage, and a demand for additional investigations. The Department of Defense began a two-tiered set of inquiries in August, 1992, probing the Tailhook involvement of both junior and senior officers.

The Navy's top leaders had initially responded with a coverup, then hastily capitulated to political pressure. The political and military heads—Secretary of the Navy H. Lawrence Garrett III and Admiral Frank Kelso—had both been at Tailhook. In the damage-control scramble after the first Navy investigation, early in October, Kelso and other top Navy leaders echoed the outrage expressed in Congress and the press, and vowed to take steps to eliminate sexism in the forces. Sensitivity training was ordered, and Kelso abruptly became an ardent supporter of the idea of women in combat. He and his Pentagon staff ordered that women combat pilots be aboard the aircraft carriers Eisenhower and Abraham Lincoln on their next deployments. That meant rushing women to the head of the training line, which not only caused resentment among the men who were pushed aside but made clear to the women's commanding officers that their success was an imperative.

Then, in October, 1994, one of these women, Kara Hultgreen, crashed and died while attempting to land her F-14 Tomcat on the Lincoln, off the California coast. The Navy pulled the wreckage from the ocean floor and examined it for possible malfunction. In a subsequent press conference, the Navy issued a report saying that Lieutenant Hultgreen's crash had been caused by engine failure. She was buried at Arlington National Cemetery, in a ceremony befitting a pioneer aviator: it was attended by top Pentagon brass and the Secretary of the Navy. "As C.N.O., I must have attended five hundred fu-

nerals at Arlington," the former Chief of Naval Operations Thomas Moorer said recently, "and I never saw a Secretary of the Navy at one of them." Within weeks, an internal report on the Hultgreen crash, which was intended to instruct fliers on safety, revealed that the Navy investigation had found pilot error to be the cause; Hultgreen's left engine did probably quit, but partly because she stalled it out with an improper approach and then failed to respond to a "wave-off" instruction, which might have saved her life. No one considered her anything less than a brave and competent pilot, but many Navy people questioned whether she had been ready for an F-14. In any case, the Navy's disingenuousness in handling her death only fed the growing resentment and cynicism among male aviators.

None of this, in the end, saved Admiral Kelso or Secretary Garrett. Kelso retired early; Garrett resigned. Kelso's departing words, two full years after Tailhook, were "I think this is the end of Tailhook," but he was so strongly identified with the scandal that his retirement became the subject of another bitter Senate fight. Schroeder, who had led a march of congresswomen to the Senate in a much noted demand for justice during the Clarence Thomas hearings, staged another march across the Hill to protest Kelso's retirement at full rank; they wanted Kelso stripped of two of his four stars. They lost that fight, but the debate kept Tailhook in the news.

The Navy leadership became increasingly desperate to placate its critics. When Garrett resigned, his temporary replacement ordered a one-day Navy-wide stand-down—meaning that all operations stopped—to "contemplate the problem of sexual harassment." Two weeks later, the new Navy Secretary, Sean O'Keefe (who had never served in the military), put the top brass on notice, firing two admirals, one of whom, a popular aviator, had allowed his men to issue a newsletter that contained a sexist joke comparing women with beer. "I need to emphasize a very important message," O'Keefe declared at a jammed news conference. "We 'get it.' "

The mechanism most responsible for keeping Tailhook alive has been the so-called "certification" process of the Senate Armed Services Committee. Military critics had long accused the committee of being a functional auxiliary of the armed forces, and in 1992, under pressure from women's-rights activists, the committee, then headed by Sam Nunn, of Georgia, determined to show its independence. The committee put a freeze on the promotions of five thousand officers in connection with Tailhook, and ordered the Navy to compile a confidential list of the men who were implicated in Tailhook wrongdoing, so that their promotions could be given special Senate scrutiny. This "flagging" of personnel files established a new, and most unwelcome, precedent of political involvement in naval promotions at all levels of the officer corps.

The Senate had always exercised its constitutional right of advice and consent on Presidential appointments, but in military promotions (which are also technically Presidential appointments) individual Senate attention has traditionally been limited to only the highest echelon. The Tailhook-flagging process meant that the Senate was also involved in the promotions of commanders and captains, who had already met the test of the Navy Secretary's selection boards. Now Senate staffers were debating a candidate's fitness for promotion based partly on Tailhook criteria: Was witnessing a striptease performance a disqualifying malfeasance? Being "implicated" in Tailhook often meant, too, that an officer was merely the subject of a rumor or an unsubstantiated accusation that the investigation had produced. The Department of Defense regularly granted immunity to junior officers in the hope of ensnaring their squadron commanders, who thus became permanently "implicated" even if they were subsequently cleared of wrongdoing. At least one officer was "implicated" and punished despite his insistence that he wasn't even at Tailhook, a claim that was later verified. The Navy imposed a policy requiring that any Navy officer anywhere in the world who came up for promotion had to sign a piece of paper after checking "yes" or "no" to the questions "Were you at Tailhook '91?" and "Was anybody in your command at Tailhook '91?" If the answer to either question was "yes," the candidate's promotion was set aside for special consideration.

Among aviators, the effort to address the offenses at Tailhook began to feel like a political vendetta (Witchhook, they called it), and, as morale declined, an increasing number of aviators decided to quit, and went off to the airlines. Among some of the younger officers, who watched with dismay as the senior leadership seemed willing to embrace any new compromise, officers above the rank of commander were referred to as "the dark side."

At Boorda's confirmation hearing, in April of 1994, Senator Nunn posed a long list of problems awaiting the new Navy chief, and Tailhook topped the list. Strom Thurmond, the committee's ranking Republican, asked Boorda how he had responded to the Tailhook scandal. Boorda confidently replied that there was no women's-issue problem in his command, the Bureau of Naval Personnel, and he claimed credit for having instigated the Tailhook investigations. He said that Paula Coughlin was a roommate of one of his staffers, and that when he heard her story "I brought the Lieutenant to work directly for me, because I wanted to get her out of a bad situation and make sure she could feel comfortable." Boorda relished the exercise of beneficent intervention. After becoming the C.N.O., he made a point of going out to the fleet, meeting the sailors, and fixing their personal problems with a simple command. If a sailor with marital difficulties wanted a shortened tour, Boorda would respond, "Done! Next?" If he bent a rule or interrupted the usual chain of command, so be it; and the sailors loved him. The press and the politicians loved him, too—a fact that may have obscured a considerable unease felt by those in the Old Guard who feared that he was being too enthusiastic in changing the Navy's culture, and not enthusiastic enough in defending it. In the opinion of many Navy defenders, Tailhook was a leadership failure that should have been addressed immediately, cleanly, and firmly.

James Webb, who was Navy Secretary during the Reagan Administration and had been a highly decorated marine in the Vietnam War, believed that in the public debate the Navy's top leaders should have separated Tailhook from the Navy culture—should have cut Tailhook off, and killed it—and then defended the culture. Webb, a member of the Naval Academy's class of 1968, is a best-selling novelist, a journalist, and the most forcefully articulate defender of the Navy culture, so discredited since Tailhook. As such, he became an important voice in what might be described as a kind of post-Tailhook resistance movement. It is more a resistance view, really, shared by a significant (though unmeasurable) group of Navy people, ranging from former admirals to Annapolis plebes, and expressed in opinion articles, public speeches, and private conversation.

A few days after the 1996 Olympics ended, Webb sat in his living room talking about Kerri Strug, the American gymnast whose injured-ankle performance had made her a national hero. He referred to a young man, John Paul Bobo, who had been a soldier in Vietnam. "He won the Medal of Honor because he got his leg blown off and he stuck his stump into the ground and fought until he died," Webb said. "You know, *that's* a hero. And this country, the majority of it, can't even relate to that anymore. Doesn't even comprehend what it takes to do it. It's lost not only its respect but its ability to form a respect for it."

Webb lives on the Virginia side of the Potomac, in a high-rise that overlooks the Iwo Jima memorial. He is never very distant from the warrior ideal, or from the complicated transformation that that ideal has undergone in his generation. Webb believes that there is a fundamental schism between our nation's military culture and its civilian society—a society that has mostly never served. In that gap, there grew a misunderstanding of the warrior class, and eventually a devaluation of it, which allowed people unfriendly toward the military ethos to seize upon Tailhook and exploit it politically. In the process, the Tailhook incident came to be allowed to stand for the entire Navy culture.

The defenders of the warrior ideal believe that the Navy has been as sorely dishonored by a weak, acquiescent leadership after Tailhook as it was by the incident itself. In 1988, as Secretary of the Navy, James Webb fought against a proposed fleet reduction by laying his job on the line, and when he lost the political argument, he resigned. Such an act of honor and sacrifice, Webb now says, is what the Navy has to have from its leaders before Tailhook can end. "There should have been a point where the senior leadership said, 'This is beyond the authority of the Congress. We will not go along with it. Find somebody else to go along with it,' " he says. "The great leaders in the American military have always done that."

The selection of Boorda as the new Chief of Naval Operations did not necessarily ease the qualms of the Navy's Old Guard. Everyone knew why President Clinton had chosen Boorda. As the former Navy Secretary John Lehman, a steadfast traditionalist, puts it, "Mike's strength as C.N.O. was letting everybody know that there was somebody there looking after their welfare. He was picked because he was committed to removing the last vestiges of discrimination against women, and Tailhook, and so forth." Few doubted that Boorda could help to quiet the critics in Congress and the press. What the institution wanted to know was how stoutly Boorda would defend the Navy. Would he put an end to Witchhook?

From the viewpoint of the Old Guard, Boorda set out to resolve one politically explosive case—involving, as it happened, Stan Arthur—in exactly the wrong way. Boorda himself later said that his handling of the Arthur case was the worst mistake of his career. Few disagreed.

Admiral Arthur, who, as Vice-Chief of Naval Operations, was the second-highest-ranking officer in the sea service, was the epitome of the Navy's heroic ideal. He was a big man with a jovial nature (Dancing Bear was one of his flight handles), a beloved figure in the Navy, who also enjoyed an outsized measure of respect. Other admirals most often describe him simply as "a great war fighter." As an aviator during the Vietnam War, he flew more than five hundred missions, earning the Distinguished Flying Cross eleven times; during Desert Storm, he commanded America's naval forces in the Persian Gulf. Arthur was one of the Navy's prized officers, and in April of 1994 he was rewarded, when President Clinton selected him to be commander-in-chief of all American forces in the Pacific. Arthur was particularly well suited to the job: a Pacific sailor during most of his career, he had spent the year following the Gulf War attending to American interests on the Pacific Rim as commander of the Seventh Fleet, and building along the way personal relationships with military people and heads of state from Manila to Bangkok to Tokyo.

But Arthur's nomination to the Pacific post was sidetracked at the end of April. A year earlier, a constituent of Minnesota's Senator David Durenberger, a Navy lieutenant named Rebecca Hansen, had complained that she had been unfairly washed out of flight school in retaliation for filing a sexual-harassment complaint. The judgment that Hansen was unqualified for wings had then been reviewed by her commanding officer, a Navy review board, and the Inspectors General of the Navy and the Department of Defense. Hansen persisted in her protest, and earlier in April Arthur himself, the Navy's top aviator, intervened. He reviewed Hansen's flight records, met with her, and then confirmed the decision to drop her from flight training. But Hansen still did not accept the decision, and neither did Durenberger, and Arthur's pending appointment provided him with a convenient means of protracting the fight. On April 28th, five days after Boorda became C.N.O., Durenberger, invoking senatorial prerogative, asked that a "hold" be placed on Arthur's appointment.

One day in 1981, an English class at Harvard High School, in Harvard, Illinois, was asked by the teacher to describe the meaning of the word "conflict." There was a pause as the students considered the word, and then one student said, "Rebecca Hansen is a conflict."

"Oh," the teacher replied. "That's very good."

That story was told the summer of 1996 by Rebecca's mother, Kay Hansen, in an attempt to convey that her daughter's life had always been unusually prone to drama. Both women were sitting at a kitchen table at a friend's house in a suburb of St. Paul, where they now live. Rebecca seemed younger than her thirty years. Both she and her mother bubbled with good-natured Midwestern enthusiasm. Kay Hansen was quite young when she married Rebecca's father, whom she divorced when Rebecca was a toddler. Mother and daughter developed an intensely close relationship—that of fierce allies in a world whose forces sometimes seemed aligned against them. Kay said that Rebecca had always been a fighter, and that "when she commits to do something, she really is not going to stop short of doing it, no matter what price has to be paid."

Kay's second husband, who adopted Rebecca, is an executive with *Farm Journal,* which allowed the family to pick a home town in the Chicago region. The Hansens chose Harvard, a small farm community in northeastern Illinois, because they sought the tranquil, nurturing benefits of the small-town ideal. Things did not work out according to plan, however. The Hansens never quite fitted into the community, and, somehow, Rebecca became the focus of their difficulty. "I had some problems in Harvard," Rebecca said. "And I had some notoriety in Harvard,

too." Rebecca was athletic and attractive, and she got along well with the boys but never found a place among the girls. "I was really hated," she recalled. "It was really traumatic. . . . I joined the basketball team, and they made fun of me. The ringleader made fun of me about how I walked. . . . They made fun of the shorts that I wore: 'Oh, your shorts are so short that your mother has to sew your underwear in them.' " Kay Hansen believed that the other girls were just jealous of her daughter ("There were a lot of big, moosy girls, who walked with their feet two feet apart"), but the antagonisms grew beyond the usual high-school social friction and turned into a conflict that consumed the whole school—indeed, the entire community. Robert Iftner, the principal of Harvard High for twenty years, who is now retired, responded to the mention of Hansen's name with a long, bitter laugh. "Oh, I remember Becky," he said. "She asked for the problems she got, and I don't give a damn what the Hansens say."

Rebecca's difficulties culminated during homecoming week in her sophomore year. As Rebecca told it, the students were gathered at the school one night for the usual decorating and pep rituals when a gang of older girls suddenly seized her. There was a tradition of seniors putting a younger student on the water fountain and getting her pants wet, and the group of girls had chosen Rebecca. In this case, the prank was unsuccessful. A brawl ensued that ended only when Rebecca, as she put it, gave "an uppercut to the stomach" of one of the assailants and managed to get away.

The Hansens did not see the incident as a mere prank; they sued the school district, and also the families of the other girls. That didn't make things easier at school, and the tension got so bad, Rebecca recalled, that she became reluctant to use the bathroom at school. She was allowed to attend the homecoming game, but a police officer was assigned to accompany her. Finally, Rebecca's parents pulled her out of school and paid fees to the school district in the next town, Woodstock, so that Rebecca could finish high school there.

Rebecca graduated in 1984 and went off to Iowa State University, where she received a partial scholarship to join the school's cross-country and track team. She had always had big dreams—she once wanted to be an astronaut—and at Iowa State her plan was to get a degree in aeronautical engineering. However, she switched to journalism before graduation, and briefly worked as a TV sports-caster—a career that ended after a dispute with her boss. After moving back home with her parents, in the St. Paul suburb, she worked for a temp service, then in a clothing store, and then as a flight-attendant trainee at Continental Airlines. One day in 1991, while she was at home reading the want ads, she called out to her mother. "Get this one," Rebecca said, reading an ad that had caught her eye. "The Navy is looking for women pilots."

Hansen, who had become a born-again Christian in her late teens, prayed about joining the Navy and sought guidance from a book of devotions. "It has a list of things, like loyalty and faithfulness, submission to authority, leadership, honor," she recalled recently. "It was like the words were coming out at me—that in service I would really learn leadership and honor and integrity and selflessness and submission to authority." She took some tests at a naval recruiting station and was accepted into the Navy's Aviation Officer Candidate School. Kay recalls, "The day she was sworn in, the recruiter said, 'Psychologically, believe me, they've never had anybody like you down there.' "

Basic training for officers, in Pensacola, Florida, was not easy for Hansen. "Some of the guys acted like they were better than the women," she said, and she came to believe that, as one of only seven women (the number eventually shrank to two) in her class of twenty-seven, she was singled out. "I would say it was sexual harassment, really—being told that the shorts I was wearing were too short. You wear shorts and a T-shirt. Men made a big thing about my shorts. My shorts were no different from anybody else's shorts. So they made me wear long pants." She flunked two of the most important courses at Pensacola—navigation and engineering—and had to attend an extra week's classes before passing. But in July, 1991, she received her commission and became an ensign in the Navy.

Hansen was assigned to flight training at the naval air station in Corpus Christi, Texas, and she reported there in August, 1991, just a few weeks before the Tailhook convention. The course of her long, bitter fight with the Navy paralleled, and reflected, the events at Tailhook and their aftermath. Not long after she arrived for flight training, Hansen recalled, she was subjected to verbal abuse amounting to sexual harassment from one of her flight instructors, a lieutenant named Larry Meyer. In June, 1992, after being

sent into the next phase of helicopter training, she filed a formal harassment complaint against Meyer. She cited his behavior during one flight as the most egregious example of his abuse. When, in the preflight check, she had noted that a friction-control knob was stuck, Meyer said, "Isn't that just like a woman to complain about the friction?" Later, during the flight, Meyer suggested that Hansen try contact lenses, on the ground that she would "look really good with blue eyes." He also advised her to dye her hair auburn, and, Hansen complained, "he told me that I should wear either a black or pink bikini bathing suit, but that I should avoid wearing an orange bikini because that would not look very attractive on me." After the flight, Meyer summoned Hansen by saying, "Come on, wench." A few days later, Hansen said, Meyer approached her from behind and grabbed her hair and joked to a group of nearby students, "This is the way I like to control my women."

It didn't help Meyer's case that he was his unit's human-relations officer, charged with guarding against sexual harassment. He protested that he had meant no offense by his remarks—that they had been intended only as friendly banter, and that he would have stopped if Hansen had ever indicated offense. The Navy removed him from his human-relations duty and punished him for making inappropriate remarks—actions that became part of his record. He thought that his career had been unfairly damaged by Hansen, who he believed wanted to rationalize her poor flight performances, and he left the Navy the following year. Hansen believed that the Navy had whitewashed the matter by failing to punish Meyer for harassment and allowing him to leave the service on his own timetable.

By far the most significant development in the case, however, had occurred ten days after Meyer received his punishment. Grousing about the case in the Officers' Club, Meyer had complained that Hansen was "a shitty stick" (a bad pilot) and that he had "buddies just waiting to fly with her." These remarks were reported, and became the basis for Hansen's argument that everything that happened to her afterward was retribution for filing a harassment complaint.

Hansen's progress in helicopter-flight training was problematic. In preflight briefings, one of her instructors noted, "she consistently tensed up, both physically and mentally, when directly questioned on discussion items. Her whole body would tense and she would have difficulty answering or would blurt out related information, but not what was asked." The instructor said that he considered Hansen's case a personal challenge, and determined to improve her training work and get her through that phase, but, when he talked to her about it, "I sensed a great amount of pent-up hostility, though outwardly she was subdued," he wrote. "She had misinterpreted everything I had ever said and now turned everything around into an argument suiting her purposes. . . . Though she would not acknowledge her weak performance, she blamed me, weather, Christmas leave . . . for anything that I as a flight instructor perceived as a problem."

That was the consistent view of Hansen's instructors, and in March, 1993, she was "attrited"— washed out—from aviation training. She appealed the decision, and a review concluded, "Hansen presents a neat, well groomed and professional military appearance. She has no academic problems, is motivated to continue flight training, and is well prepared for her briefs. However, she seems paranoid. She perceives everyone is out to get her, refusing to accept responsibility for her poor performance, which has been well documented from [Officer Candidate School] to present. . . . She evidently does not take constructive criticism well. . . . The squadron does not feel she can successfully complete the program or be an asset to the fleet. They have recommended attrition. I concur."

In the pre-Tailhook era, Hansen would have been discharged, and both she and the Navy would have moved on. But Hansen did not accept the Navy's decision to wash her out. She argued that she was being retaliated against, thereby launching a Navy investigation, and when its results confirmed her washout she dismissed them as further evidence of retaliation. Meanwhile, Hansen's mother, who had been keeping track of her problematic Navy career, wrote to the Minnesota congressional delegation, and found a key ally on the staff of Senator Durenberger (whose career, coincidentally, was about to come to a close as a result of a series of financial scandals). One of Durenberger's caseworkers, Anne Crowther, had taken an interest in the post-Tailhook political fight over the Navy, and she now focussed on the Hansen case with zeal. She still says of it, "It is a mission to me."

Crowther and Kay Hansen worked together preparing Rebecca's case, and Durenberger's staff wrote the Navy several letters over Durenberger's name, with the aim of getting the service to show that Hansen's washout was the product of retaliation. A senator's involvement at just that time, in the post-Tailhook heat of 1993 and 1994, was a mighty sword for Hansen, and her relatively low-level case became a consuming priority for Navy officials.

Stan Arthur found himself—and his own career—ensnared in the Hansen dispute when Navy Secretary John Dalton, who had been appointed in August of 1993, asked for his help. "I stepped into that one as a favor to the Secretary," Arthur says. "She was just going to file charges and countercharges and countercharges . . . endless." Arthur seemed just the right man for Dalton to turn to. He was old Navy, but he had also had a direct hand in bringing women into naval aviation and, eventually, into combat planes. A peerless flier himself, Arthur saw aviation talent as one of God's mysterious gifts—"monkey skills," he called it—that are distributed indiscriminately on a gender-neutral basis. He also had a particular expertise in evaluating a flight student's training progress, having served as a senior member of the review board charged with taking away pilots' wings. Arthur figured that he could bring authority to the review of the Hansen case, and that his decision would stand. "I may have been overly confident in that regard," he says now, deadpanning the understatement.

After Arthur reviewed Hansen's training records, he was surprised that her complaint had got as far as it had. "What I saw was the most dangerous of all individuals that we would try to get through flight training," he says. "Most of her flights were extended, because she started out and had terrible tendencies at the start, they would work on them, and by the end of the flight they would get to a satisfactory level and she would get the marginal grades associated with that. Come right back, the next flight, and the same tendencies were there at the start. In other words, there was no learning curve, where each day you develop a bigger base of capabilities. This is the most dangerous of all tendencies, because, basically, people will give you credit for learning, and then somebody is going to make a mistake, thinking you have learned this technique, and then you're off on your own someday and you didn't learn it at all."

Arthur met with Durenberger and his staff before beginning his evaluation, and with Hansen as well, and he conveyed his conclusions to them afterward. He told Hansen he believed that, if anything, the Navy had misled her by not discharging her after she failed the two courses in Officer Candidate School. He said the record showed him that the Navy seemed to have done everything it could to help her succeed.

But Arthur's decision did nothing to sway Hansen and her champions. The Durenberger staff posed a series of questions to Arthur about just how carefully he had reviewed her case. To Arthur's mind, the questions were merely a way of sticking it to the Navy. The staffers would ask a question, and he would answer it, drawing from his reading of the reviews, and his answer would prompt more questions: What facts were considered? What people did he talk with? Arthur, an old-Navy man of honor, thought it was enough that he, the Navy's top aviator and the Vice-Chief of Naval Operations, had personally reviewed her flight records and found the attrition warranted. The Senator's chief staffer, Rick Evans, believed that Arthur was probably right about Hansen, but this wasn't a moment for taking the Navy's word for anything. Evans says, "The concern . . . particularly regarding the Navy, with its history of being dominated by men, was: Did he reach that conclusion because that's what guys do, they all protect each other?" In the spring of 1994, Durenberger said that he would lift his hold on Arthur's nomination to take over the Pacific command only when his questions were satisfactorily answered. Durenberger now says that his questions were eventually answered, but too late for Stan Arthur.

Hansen began to receive sympathetic coverage in the press ("Perhaps the only way women can make their point is to take a few admirals down with the ship," a column in *Time* concluded that August), and the Navy saw its control over the case pass into the hands of Congress. In late 1993, the Minnesota congressional delegation had got the Navy to transfer Hansen to a base in Minnesota, because she was uncomfortable in Florida. ("I wasn't eating or sleeping, I was feeling very threatened. . . . I was being followed, people were showing up at my house. And I was isolated, too; I think they do that on purpose.")

From her parents' house, she was constantly on the phone with one Pentagon staffer or another, as the Navy became ever more desperate to resolve the case.

It was all exhausting for Hansen, and she developed mononucleosis. After her recovery, she decided to take a vacation. Her lawyer, provided by the Navy, advised against it; the Navy wanted her to meet with her superiors in Florida. In February, however, she went on a ski holiday in Vail, Colorado. On her first day on the slopes, she fell and seriously hurt her knee. When the Navy made her take a bus to receive treatment at a military facility, it became another cause of grievance.

In May, an Assistant Secretary of the Navy, Frederick Pang, asked her lawyer what it would take to get her to accept her attrition. Hansen and her team met with Pang without success. Then another meeting was arranged, this time between Hansen and Navy Secretary Dalton. Hansen had read statements that Dalton made when he came into the job after Tailhook, in which he said, in effect, that the Navy "gets it," and she thought it entirely possible that he might say yes when she told him she wanted to work for him in the Secretariat itself, helping to shape the Navy's policy on women's issues. Dalton offered her only the change to be a naval flight officer—a "back seater," who handles radar and so on—and Hansen was deeply disappointed. "When I found out the way Secretary Dalton was, it was really hard," she says. "It was, like, here's the man at the very top and he doesn't care. He cares more about his suntan and his bank account than he does about the Navy and what's really going on. He seemed completely uninterested."

In June, Hansen prepared for a second meeting with Pang. She and her mother sat in a Denny's restaurant in Minneapolis and drew up a list of demands that might warrant her ending her fight. These included a written apology from Dalton, the excision of all negative evaluations from her record, return to flight school, time off to attend law school, time and money for civilian flight training, promotion, and, when she finished law school, a service job dealing with women's issues. On being asked now whether she thought those requests were realistic, Hansen says, "It was realistic in what happened, and how they had screwed up, and these were the closest thing to trying to make amends." When her lawyer found out about the list, he strongly disagreed with her tactics; Rick Evans says that he would have advised against her presenting this wish list. But Hansen went ahead, and, accompanied by Crowther, presented her list to Pang. He did not accede to her demands.

Mike Boorda stepped into the Hansen case when he stepped into the job as C.N.O. The very forces that had helped bring Boorda to the top job in the Navy now presented him with his first challenge—resolving a sexual-harassment controversy. Boorda agreed with Arthur's disposition of the Hansen case, but he knew that if he fought for Arthur that would once again put the Navy—now his Navy—on the wrong side of a splashy harassment dispute. Boorda finessed a solution.

He met with Arthur, who badly wanted the Pacific job, though it was not his style to appear eager. "I'm not going to be railroaded out of town on this deal, I'm going to fight it," Arthur told his new boss, but he added that he didn't want to be the cause of anything that might hurt the Navy. The Pacific post had always been a Navy job, but technically it could be filled by someone from another of the armed services. Arthur said he wouldn't want the Navy to lose the billet because of him.

"No, no, you can't quit on me," Boorda replied. "You've gotta hang in." But Arthur had given Boorda an opening. "This will be O.K.," Boorda said. "Let me do some work on it." What Boorda proceeded to do, apparently, was maneuver Stan Arthur out of the picture. On the Hill, Sam Nunn assured Boorda that he could get Arthur confirmed, but that doing it might take time. Boorda played up the delay to Arthur, who knew that the other services were already suggesting candidates for the job. Arthur wondered whether General John Shalikashvili, the chairman of the Joint Chiefs of Staff, would be willing to hold the Pacific job open until Arthur's confirmation. Boorda said he would measure the General's mood, and a few days later he gave Arthur bad news. Arthur recalls, "He called me in and said, 'I just talked to Shali, and this isn't going to work.' I said, 'I'll have my letter in in the morning' "—asking for retirement.

Boorda had made his decision: there would be no fight for Stan Arthur. But, technically, it wasn't Bo-

orda's nomination to pull: Arthur had been appointed by President Clinton, and it was up to Clinton's Secretary of the Navy, Dalton, to withdraw Arthur's name. Dalton strongly believed that Arthur was the right person for the position, but Boorda gave him the impression that Arthur might not have the stomach for a political fight—an impression that Dalton has come to suspect was the product of some Boorda spin. "Had I had this to do over again," Dalton says now, "I would have called Stan Arthur into my office personally, and discussed with him his feeling about his fighting this battle with the Senate, and how he personally felt, rather than just taking Admiral Boorda's report to me about it. Admiral Boorda had worked for me as C.N.O. at that time for about a month, and I hadn't learned how to interpret how he did business and how he communicated."

On Friday, June 24th, the Navy issued a statement announcing that Arthur's nomination would be withdrawn, and that Arthur would retire from the Navy. That news by itself was more than enough to excite antipathy toward Boorda. Retired Rear Admiral Clarence (Mark) Hill, for one, expresses such a feeling. "No. 1, we all knew Mike Boorda was not a warrior," Hill has since said of the Old Guard's reaction to the scuttling of Arthur's nomination. "It was such a traumatic thing for the Navy in general—how could they take it out on a guy who'd proved himself in so many different ways?" And what Boorda did next may have put the damage he had suffered in the Arthur episode beyond repair.

That day, Boorda took a Navy plane to Chicago to visit recruits. It was a big moment for him, not only because he delighted in meeting with the fresh-faced kids but because his destination was the Great Lakes Naval Training Center, his own first stop in the Navy. But, while Boorda was en route, his office heard some disturbing news: among those sailors waiting at Great Lakes to meet the new C.N.O. was Lieutenant (j.g.) Rebecca Hansen.

Hansen had virtually given up her hope of becoming a Navy flier, but when she learned that Boorda was about to visit Great Lakes, she spoke to Anne Crowther, and was told that Durenberger's staff would try to arrange a meeting for Hansen with the C.N.O. Upon hearing of this, members of Boorda's staff called his plane to warn him. But Boorda nevertheless agreed to meet with Hansen. After all, he had responded to Tailhook by bringing Paula

Coughlin onto his staff, so perhaps a meeting with Hansen could finally end this nettlesome problem.

After Boorda's meeting with the sailors, Hansen was summoned into her commander's office, and there she was granted a private session with the Chief of Naval Operations. This was not a usual procedure, as Hansen herself recognized. "It was bizarre," she says. "And you know what he said to me? He goes, 'Yeah, we don't always talk about you. Sometimes we talk about North Korea and stuff like that.' "

According to Hansen, Boorda first scolded her for disputing the Navy's contention that Larry Meyer had been properly dealt with. Then he ordered his aide out of the room, and gave Hansen a lesson in the Boorda style.

"It started out with him saying, several times, 'I like you a lot,' " Hansen recalls. "And then he goes, 'You know what I like to do with people I like a lot? I like to bring 'em in close.' And, because of my experience of Navy men acting very weird, I thought he was going to say something about giving him a hug, or something. And then he said, 'I like to bring them into the family.' As he went on to explain, it became evident that people at the Pentagon were family. I didn't understand at first."

Then Boorda offered Hansen a job: he told her that he wanted her to come to Washington and work for him at the Pentagon. "He said he wanted me to report directly to him," Hansen says, "because he needed to have somebody tell him the truth."

Boorda assured Hansen that they were on the same side, and he asked her if she thought she could work for him. She said yes; the meeting ended happily; and it seemed that the Rebecca Hansen case had finally been resolved.

By the time Boorda returned to Washington, though, he had apparently begun to have second thoughts. Back at the Pentagon, he went directly to Stan Arthur. "He came back," Arthur recalls, "and he says, 'I just did something really dumb. I've gotta tell you so you don't hear it from somebody else. I saw Rebecca.' "

"Yeah, that's why we called the airplane—because we knew she would be there," Arthur replied.

"I told her that I would do anything—I would give her any other opportunity in the Navy she wanted, not to go back to flight training," Boorda said. "You name it, you've got it, and you can come back to Washington and work for me.' "

Arthur was nonplussed, and furious. Not only had Boorda acquiesced (at the least) in the undoing of Arthur's career but he had, in one impulsive meeting, effectively reversed the unanimous view of the long review chain that Arthur had endorsed. The Secretary of the Navy had already decided to sign Hansen's discharge papers, and now Boorda was bringing her to the Pentagon. "I almost walked away from him on that episode," Arthur says. "I thought it really pulled the rug right out from under me, and that really made me feel bad."

But Arthur decided not to make an issue of it. "I chalked it up to another one of those Boorda things," he says. "I thought, Ah, well, this is vintage Boorda, you know? 'There's never a problem I can't fix, just let me.' He just fell into that damned trap again."

In the eyes of the institution, Boorda had just traded Stan Arthur for Rebecca Hansen, sacrificing the Navy ideal for the perfect symbol of the Navy's post-Tailhook torment. "That curdled the milk, particularly with the retired guys," John Lehman says. "I don't think Mike ever got over that. Even though he admitted it was wrong, he could sense that the old four-stars that used to call him weren't calling him anymore. And I think he really felt that he had lost the allegiance of the system."

Boorda apologized to Arthur personally, and acknowledged his mistake publicly, but the Arthur furor had a lasting effect, both on the way Boorda was perceived through the rest of his tenure and on the institution. On a practical level, Navy leaders began to worry about "the Arthur factor." If a four-star could lose his promotion because he'd backed his subordinates' judgment on a politically sensitive case, how would that affect such judgments in the future? Who would flunk the next Rebecca Hansen? Who would support such a decision? On a personal level, Boorda lost a measure of good will, a kind of regard peculiar to the military culture.

Boorda took some stinging rebukes in a series of opinion pieces, including a *Times* Op-Ed piece in which James Webb wrote that the Arthur decision raised "serious questions about Admiral Boorda's fitness to be Chief of Naval Operations." Elaine Donnelly, a conservative military advocate, accused Boorda of being whipsawed by feminists.

Because the Arthur case was Boorda's first

important decision as C.N.O., it became the unintended motif of his tenure—the defining fact, which colored everything else. It began to seem that Boorda couldn't escape the criticism even when he was among friends. Retired Admiral Lee Baggett, a courtly Mississippian, who was a Boorda admirer, tells a story about a dinner party held by a group of admirals, retired and active, in San Diego, at which Boorda was a guest. There was a discernible edge to the evening, and Baggett decided to address the issue straight. "I'm disappointed in you," Baggett told the younger man, admiral to admiral. Boorda brushed Baggett's criticism aside, but the issue hung over the evening, and at the end, after Boorda had given a little pep talk and asked for questions, the wife of one of the senior aviators spoke out. "Admiral Boorda, why aren't you supporting Stan Arthur?" she asked. It was a harsh rebuke, coming from an officer's wife, and Boorda could only answer, "Well, we just don't want to get into a confrontation over this issue. I've inherited all these problems, and I'm playing the cards I was dealt."

In August, 1995, the *Proceedings* of the Naval Institute published a bitter satire of the new, politically correct Navy, written by the former Navy officer Larry Di Rita, which captured the subversive mood of the Navy's traditionalist resistance. The satire presents the weary reflections of Captain Will Keith, a decidedly old-Navy officer who is trapped aboard the U.S.S. Boorda sometime in the multicultural, environmentally sensitive, smoke-free future. The ship is conducting "rain forest preservation research" under the command of a Bangladeshi commodore, as part of a United Nations task force. Training operations have to be postponed because of a "Diversity Stand-Down," ordered by the C.N.O.—who is now called the "Chief of Maritime Services" because the President has been convinced by the U.N. that "Chief of Naval Operations" sounds too warlike. Keith, drawing on a cigar (although he knows he shouldn't smoke, because his cabin is on the same ventilation system as that of the crew nursery), slips into a reverie about Tailhook and its aftermath, and the case of Stan Arthur:

> The whole thing had a perverse logic. That this wartime leader should be lost because of "insensitivity" reflected a turning point for the Navy that had started somewhere between the deserts of the Middle East and the deserts of Nevada. Anyway,

the lesson was clear to mid-grade officers like Keith: if flag officers could watch Arthur go down with nary a whimper, what could a lieutenant commander with kids and a mortgage hope to achieve by speaking out?

Eventually, the widespread criticism became naked ridicule. In the spring of 1996, the *Navy Times* published a letter from a Navy officer who called on Boorda to resign, writing, "Adm. Mike Boorda has not only lost the respect of his admirals. [Rather,] every officer from four star to the newest midshipman at the academy has no respect for the man at the top of their organization. . . . Behind his back, admirals often refer to the C.N.O. as 'Little Mikey Boorda.' "

It fell to James Webb to give a unifying context to the gathering discontents—all the floating anxieties and resentments. In a speech in April to the annual conference of the Naval Institute, at Annapolis, Webb summoned the ghosts of the Navy's great men, invoking the creed that guided them and their service: "Where principle is involved, be deaf to expediency." The Navy's current leaders, Webb made clear, had inverted that creed, sacrificing principle for the sake of their own careers. Webb did not mention Admiral Boorda by name, but no one who heard his speech missed the reference. He pleaded the case for Stan Arthur ("One of the finest candidates for commander-in-chief of the Pacific in recent times [was] ordered into early retirement by the Chief of Naval Operations. Who expressed their outrage? Who fought this?") and for Admiral Jack Snyder, an esteemed fighter pilot who had been Paula Coughlin's commanding officer and was reassigned after Tailhook. Webb went on to denounce the "permanent stigma and the destruction of the careers" of a "whole generation of officers" by the political response to Tailhook, and asked, "What admiral has had the courage to risk his own career by putting his stars on the table and defending the integrity of the process and of his people?" He concluded his speech with a challenge: "If the Navy is to regain its soul and its respect, the answer lies in the right kind of leaders. Leaders who understand that the seemingly arcane concepts of tradition, loyalty, discipline and moral courage have carried the Navy through cyclical turbulence in peace and war. . . . It is time to give the Navy back to such leaders." The midshipmen gave Webb a standing ovation—one that the Pentagon could not fail to notice.

If Mike Boorda believed he needed to redeem himself after the Arthur debacle, he had no shortage of opportunity. The ongoing Tailhook purge provided a vast supply of perceived outrages, the most notable of which was the case of a forty-four-year-old commander named Robert Elmer Stumpf.

Stumpf was something close to the Navy's posterboy ideal—handsome, smart, a brilliant fighter pilot, an unquestioned war hero. In the Gulf War, he was one of the earliest pilots over Baghdad during the first night of the war, flying his F-18 Hornet through heavy anti-aircraft fire to take out Saddam Hussein's radar installations; he flew twenty-two combat missions in all, earning a Distinguished Flying Cross, among other citations for valor. After the war, Stumpf was chosen as commander of the élite Blue Angels squadron, the Navy's demonstration flight team that performs in air shows around the world, and in that role he became the first American to fly a fighter over Moscow since the Second World War. In 1994, he was recommended for command of a carrier air wing which required a promotion to the rank of captain. A promotion board put his name on a list of nominees for captain's rank, and the list was approved by Secretary Dalton and by the Secretary of Defense.

Stumpf's promotion was routinely approved by the Senate that May, along with the promotions of more than a hundred others. But before it took effect the Navy discovered a problem: Stumpf had not been "flagged," though he had been sent to Tailhook in 1991 to receive an award for his fighter squadron as Best in the Navy. The evening after receiving the award, he attended a party organized by his men to celebrate their recent "wetting down"—Navy talk for promotion. For entertainment, they had provided a pair of exotic dancers who danced nude, and one of the women then performed fellatio on one of the men. The Navy Court of Inquiry had subsequently investigated the case, had determined in September of 1993 that Stumpf was not in the room at the time the sex act occurred, and had given him full acquittal. But the important senators on the Senate Armed Services Committee were angry when, in June of 1994, the matter was belatedly brought to their attention. The committee requested that no action be taken on Stumpf's promotion until Dalton provided details of the aviator's Tailhook involvement. It was the month of the Arthur decision, and both Boorda and Secretary Dalton wanted to avoid another cause célèbre; Dalton interviewed Stumpf, reviewed his case, and recommended his promotion to the committee—to no avail.

Stumpf thus became another test case for Boorda, who was caught once again between two imperatives. He could not make an appearance or give a speech without someone's asking him if he would support Stumpf. Boorda sought the counsel of retired Admiral Thomas Moorer, one of his predecessors as C.N.O. and one of the giants cited by James Webb in his Annapolis speech. Moorer gave Boorda some pointed advice: "I told him that people in aviation and the military are very upset about what they just call 'Washington.' I said, 'You've got to face up to the fact that you are viewed as being part of Washington.'" But the Armed Services Committee held its ground.

Then, this year, the Navy's promotion board once again selected Stumpf for promotion to captain, clearly challenging Boorda to make a Webb-style, stars-on-the-table gesture. According to Stumpf and his supporters, Boorda decided to make just such a gesture. He met privately with Stumpf, and told him, "I believe that you should be a captain, and I'll support you," and at a conference attended by dozens of admirals and aviators he was reported to have raised his hand and vowed a fight to the finish for Stumpf, even if it cost him his job as C.N.O. "There's absolutely no question in my mind that he was going to apply full pressure to get Stumpf promoted," Moorer says. On Friday, May 10th, at the Naval Aviation Museum, in Pensacola, Boorda, speaking to a Navy crowd, was once again pressed on the Stumpf issue, and once again he pledged his support. It seemed that at last, by taking a firm stand, he might begin to earn back the respect of the Navy's warriors. But then another crisis arose—one that was both personally and professionally threatening to Boorda, and promised another series of public disclosures that would embarrass the Navy.

It was discovered that Boorda had worn two combat "V"s—the tiny bronze pins signifying the valor of combat service. Medals and ribbons are the military culture's private language: they tell other military people where you've been, whether you risked your life, who you are. At some point after Boorda reached the rank of admiral, in 1985, he acquired the pins (which can be bought at a military exchange), and attached them to his ribbons. Some of Boorda's fellow-officers knew that he had been on two cruises off the coast of Vietnam, but very few knew that he had not been awarded those "V"s.

Of all the traumas that Boorda had experienced up to this point, perhaps none could have been more damaging than this discovery. It did not merely promise another political fight. It was not simply rooted in the question of personal honor. Rather, it entailed honor of a particular sort—a warrior's valor. Boorda, a C.N.O. who had never seen battle, must have felt especially vulnerable on this point, and he had known for some time that it might become an issue. A year earlier, he had been informed that Roger Charles, an Annapolis graduate and a former Marine lieutenant colonel, who was known to many Washington journalists as a military watchdog, had filed a Freedom of Information Act request for paperwork on Admiral Boorda's medals. Boorda, as a former Chief of Naval Personnel, must have known that he was not entitled to wear the "V"s. Nevertheless, on learning of Charles's inquiry he had a Navy lawyer research the question for him, going back to the Vietnam tour aboard the Craig. The lawyer told Boorda that he should not be wearing the "V"s. Boorda took them off, and waited. Weeks passed, and then months, and nothing happened.

But one morning in May, as Boorda was finishing a meeting with Admiral Skip Bowman, the head of Navy personnel, on the subject of admirals' misconduct, Rear Admiral Kendell Pease, the Navy's top spokesman, came in to say that two Newsweek reporters were coming to talk about the decorations. Charles had discovered that there was no authorization for Boorda to wear them, Pease said. Charles, after calling an office specializing in the awarding of medals and decorations, and being told that the right to wear a combat "V" had to be specifically enunciated in the award citation, had pursued the matter further and then gone to Newsweek with the story. Boorda was momentarily shaken. "What should we do?" he asked Pease. Then, according to Pease, Boorda answered his own question: "We'll just tell the truth."

Boorda had a full schedule that afternoon—a meeting with the Deputy Secretary of Defense at one-fifteen, and a meeting with President Clinton at

the White House at three-thirty, and, now, the Newsweek interview, which he had just squeezed in before the White House meeting—so he had planned to eat lunch in his office. The meal had already arrived, but Boorda said he wanted to run home—the C.N.O. residence was at the Washington Naval Yard, just fifteen minutes away—and would be back in time for the Newsweek session, and that his Vice-C.N.O. could take his place at the one-fifteen meeting. He ordered his car, and joked with Pease. He'd always told people that someday, when he left the Navy, he was going to open a hardware store somewhere, and work normal hours. "Well, Pease," he said, "I may be opening that hardware store sooner than I thought." He then told his aide that he would drive himself home, and asked the aide to send his driver to the C.N.O. residence. He got in his car, a Navy Lincoln, and drove off.

At home, Boorda typed two notes, one to his wife and one that was meant to be shared with "my sailors." The note to Bettie, according to people familiar with it, was a message of love and regret. The other note was a message of faith in the sailors and the service. He explained that the business with the decorations was an honest mistake, but that the media would leap at it and the inevitable controversy would only add to the Navy's miseries. (Neither of the notes has been publicly released.) Boorda had a gun at home—a .38-calibre pistol lent him by his son-in-law for personal protection, because the Navy Yard is in a relatively rough neighborhood. After finishing the notes, Boorda carried the gun to a far corner of the garden, put the barrel to his chest, near his heart, and pulled the trigger.

Boorda's death did not end the Navy's culture war. After Arthur's nomination for the Pacific job was withdrawn, President Clinton nominated Vice-Admiral Richard Macke for the job, and his nomination was quickly approved by the Senate. But Macke's tenure was brief. Unlike Arthur, who had seemed ideally suited to the Pacific post—because he knew the people and he knew the cultures—Macke was relatively unseasoned. After three American sailors were arrested and tried for raping a twelve-year-old Japanese girl in Okinawa, in September of 1995—an episode that greatly strained U.S.-Japanese relations—Macke commented that the sailors should have hired a prostitute. He was out of the job by the end of that day, on orders from the White House.

Commander Bob Stumpf's second promotion to captain was never considered by the Senate. Navy Secretary John Dalton, on being informed that there would be more questions about Tailhook, ordered yet another investigation into Stumpf's involvement. After two and a half hours of interrogation, Stumpf concluded that the purpose of the new investigation was not to clear him but to validate his promotion denial, and he quit the session. He will leave the Navy.

Rebecca Hansen had never gone to work for Admiral Boorda. She left the Navy at the end of October, 1995—having been classified as disabled because of her skiing injury. She plans to attend law school. . . .

Shortly after Boorda's death, President Clinton nominated Admiral Jay Johnson, the Vice-Chief of Naval Operations, to become his successor. Johnson, an aviator, had been at Tailhook. Word went around the Navy that if he was confirmed he intended to stand up and draw the line—insist that the certification process end. He has not done that, and he probably won't, for, at his confirmation hearing before the Senate Armed Services Committee in the summer of 1996, he said he believes that flagging should continue until all the officers on the certification list have been through the Tailhook promotion "scrub" at least once. Johnson did, however, give an indication of what sort of C.N.O. he means to be. "I'm Mike Boorda-trained, and I'm intensely proud of it," he told the committee. When he was asked by Chairman Strom Thurmond what his top priorities would be if he was confirmed, he replied, "Mr. Chairman, the No. 1 priority will be people. It is people, it will continue to be people." The Senate approved his appointment.

Any political mystery invites speculation—none more than a suicide—and Boorda's death seemed to demand interpretation. Hillary Clinton, herself besieged by the Whitewater and Travelgate controversies, perhaps heard in Boorda's death an echo of her friend Vince Foster's suicide, and concluded that Boorda might have fallen victim to "the relentless and unforgiving glare that people who live in public life are subjected to." John Lehman, voicing the Old Guard view, suggested that Boorda was driven to his death by the political-correctness zealots still hounding the Navy after Tailhook. Charles Gittins,

Bob Stumpf's attorney, believes that Boorda was driven to despair by Navy Secretary Dalton's ordering another investigation of the Stumpf case. "I can't prove it, but he didn't shoot himself over the combat 'V's," Gittins says.

But the former C.N.O. Thomas Moorer, the old warrior and a friend of Boorda's, was inclined to let Boorda speak for himself on the matter. After all, the fact that Boorda had troubled to adorn himself with the insignia of valor is the most compelling evidence of their worth, and his reference in his suicide note to the embarrassment he feared for the Navy is a measure of the weight he attached to the discovery. Moorer said recently that Boorda knew that many people believed he had betrayed the Navy culture, "and that is one of the factors, I think, that led to his shooting himself." He went on to explain, "When he found out that *Newsweek* was going to go after him with a full-court press, he was concerned that that would be interpreted as a failure on his part, a weakness in the area of honor—that he'd be seen to have done something that was unbefitting a C.N.O. And he thought he'd put a stop to that . . . by just disappearing from the scene."

The keepers of the flame had demanded that someone in the leadership finally make a stand, perform some gesture of personal sacrifice and honor. One of the oldest chapters in the warrior-culture script, reaching back in history beyond the samurai to the ancients, is that of the honorable death. Mike Boorda, a bridging figure between a culture of absolutes and one of compromise, chose as his final gesture an absolute act—one that was unambiguously clear. He died a warrior's death.

Author's Retrospective

On June 25, 1998, Navy Secretary John Dalton put a letter into Admiral Boorda's personnel file from Admiral Elmo Zumwalt Jr., the Chief of Naval Operations during the Vietnam War, that stated it was "appropriate and proper" for Boorda to have attached the small, bronze combat Vs to the ribbons on his uniform. The Navy also modified Boorda's records to list the Vs among his other decorations. Thus the Navy quietly recognized that he was entitled to wear the decoration, yet it stopped short of what Zumwalt sought—namely, unambiguous public recognition that Boorda violated no regulations.

Zumwalt said in an interview that Dalton's action was a "posthumous validation of Admiral Boorda's right to have worn the Vs based on instructions given by me when I was Chief of Naval Operations. My interpretation is that retroactively he has been authorized to wear the Vs."

Chapter 11 Review Questions

1. In your own words, can you describe the Wise concept of "public service culture"? What does the author mean by that term? What assumptions about human nature does her motivational concept rest on? Do you believe these are valid assumptions?
2. Why does Wise argue that public service motivation is found more often in government than business or elsewhere? Do you agree or disagree? Why or why not?
3. Regarding the foregoing case study, "Admiral Booda's War," describe the various cross-pressures and multiple responsibilities that Boorda, as C.N.O., faced. Why do these persisting cross-pressures and responsibilities make it so difficult, if not impossible, to frame or understand what can be a clear, consistent motivational system for top public officials like Boorda?
4. Are public sector motives rooted in rational, norm-based, affective categories, as Wise's essay theorizes? Why or why not?
5. Given the difficult realities of the contemporary working environment of public administration today, how would you develop and implement an effective "public service culture" for a government agency? Assess some of the strengths and weaknesses of this system that you envisioned, as well as the difficulties and issues establishing it.
6. Select any one of the prior cases in this text and examine carefully the motivations of one or a few of the public officials in this case. How do these motives compare and contrast with those discussed in Case 11—are they the same or fundamentally different and explain why?

Key Terms

public service motives
public service culture
rational motives
norm-based motives
affective motives
normative orientation

rule-following behavior
self-interested motives
normative values
engagement
professional management

Suggestions for Further Reading

Public personnel administration is a field of enormous complexity, specialization, and rapid change, and, therefore, looking at several basic introductory texts is necessary for a good overview: N. Joseph Cayer, *Public Personnel Administration in the U.S.,* Third Edition (New York: St. Martin's,

1995); Dennis Dresang, *Public Personel Management and Public Policy*, Third Edition (Reading, Mass.: Addison-Wesley, 1999); Steven W. Hays and Richard C. Kearney, *Public Personnel Administration,* Third Edition (Englewood Cliffs, N.J.: Prentice-Hall, 1994); Lloyd G. Nigro and Felix A. Nigro, *The New Public Personnel Administration,* Fourth Edition (Itasca, Ill.: F. E. Peacock Publishers, Inc., 1995); Carolyn Ban, *Public Personnel Management*, Second Edition (New York: Longman, 1997); Donald Klinger and John Nalbandian, *Public Personnel Management,* Fourth Edition (Englewood Cliffs, N.J.: Prentice-Hall, 1993); and Dennis D. Riley, *Public Personnel Administration* (New York: Harper Collins, 1997). To supplement these introductions, students should further examine the basic *framing* documents of public personnel, such as the Civil Service Act of 1883, the Hatch Act, the Civil Service Reform Act of 1978, as well as several others contained in Frederick C. Mosher, ed., *Basic Documents of American Public Administration: 1776–1950* (New York: Holmes and Meier, 1976), and Richard J. Stillman II, ed., *Basic Documents of American Public Administration: Since 1950* (New York: Holmes and Meier, 1982).

For the best history of the American civil service system, see Paul Van Riper, *History of U.S. Civil Service* (New York: Harper & Row, 1958). For an insightful view of personnel practices at the local level, read Frank J. Thompson, *Personnel Policy in the City: The Politics of Jobs in Oakland* (Berkeley, Calif.: University of California Press, 1975); and for a view of its operation at the federal level, see Frederick C. Mosher, *Democracy and the Public Service,* Second Edition (New York: Oxford University Press, 1982); Patricia W. Ingraham, *The Foundation of Merit: Service in American Democracy* (Baltimore, Md.: Johns Hopkins Press, 1995); or Hugh Heclo, *A Government of Strangers: Executive Politics in Washington* (Washington, D.C.: The Brookings Institution, 1977). Articles contained in the "clas-

sics" series on personnel give readers a useful overview of the scope, diversity, and complexity of this field, especially in Frank J. Thompson, ed., *Classics of Public Personnel Policy,* Second Edition (Monterey, Calif.: Brooks/Cole, 1990), as well as a more contemporary set of readings in Patricia W. Ingraham and Barbara Romzek, eds., *Rethinking Public Personnel Systems* (San Francisco: Jossey-Bass, 1994), Jack Rabin, et al. (eds.) *Handbook of Public Personnel Administration* (New York: Marcel Dekker, 1995), and part 6 of James L. Perry, *Handbook of Public Administration*, Second Edition (San Francisco: Jossey-Bass, 1996). "Further Readings" in section 9 of this text offers useful additional references. Excellent sources for further readings on personnel motivation are also found in chapters 6 and 7 in Hal G. Rainey, *Understanding and Managing Public Organizations*, Second Edition (San Fancisco: Jossey-Bass, 1996).

For a comprehensive look that explains the state-of-the-art of public personnel labor relations see Richard C. Kearney, *Labor Relations in the Public Sector,* Second Edition (New York: Marcel Dekker, 1992); and Jack Rabin et al., eds., *Handbook of Public Sector Labor Relations* (New York: Marcel Dekker, 1994).

Reading the Volcker Commission Report for a federal review of this topic, *Leadership for America* (Lexington, Mass.: Lexington Books, 1990), or for the local level, Frank J. Thompson, ed., *Revitalizing State and Local Government* (San Francisco: Jossey-Bass, 1993) can provide numerous useful ideas for improving public service motivation throughout government. Norma M. Riccucci's *Unsung Heroes* (Washington, D.C.: Georgetown University Press, 1995) offers good examples of what motivates outstanding federal executives.

One would also do well to skim current issues of *Public Administration Review, Harvard Business Review, Public Personnel Management, The Bureaucrat,* and *Public Management* for recent and fast-changing trends in the field of personnel.

CHAPTER 12

Public Budgeting: The Concept of Budgeting as Political Choice

The essence of budgeting is that it allocates scarce resources and hence implies choice between potential objects of expenditure. Budgeting implies balance and it requires some kind of decision-making process.

Irene S. Rubin

READING 12

Introduction

Budgets serve many important functions in government. In one sense, budgets are contracts annually agreed on by the executive and legislative branches that allow executive agencies and departments to raise and spend public funds in specified ways for the coming fiscal year (normally running in state and local governments from July 1 to June 30; changed at the federal level by the Congressional Budget Act of 1974 to end on September 30 and to begin October 1 each year). A budget imposes a mutual set of legal obligations between the elected and appointed officers of public organizations with regard to taxation and expenditure policies. A budget is, therefore, a legal contract that provides a vehicle for fiscal controls over subordinate units of government by the politically elected representatives of the people.

Budgets have other purposes as well: they can be planning devices used to translate presently scarce fiscal and human resources in the public sector into future governmental goals and programs. In this respect, budgets are vital instruments for directing what tasks government will perform and how human talent in society and public monies will be used.

In addition, budgets are forces for internal coordination and efficiency in public administration. Budget formulations annually impose choices concerning how public programs should be undertaken, interrelated, and measured in terms of their value, effectiveness, and worth to the general public. Related to the concept of budgets as a coordinating device is the idea that budgets are economic documents. In this role federal budgets are tools of fiscal policy, for they stimulate or slow down national economic growth through increased or decreased taxation or revenue expenditures.

Finally, budgets can also be viewed as political documents, reflecting through the allocation of funds the ultimate desires, interests, and power of various groups within the body politic as expressed by elected legislative bodies. In setting up an annual budget, various political participants engage in log rolling, compromises, and bargains to create a document that by and large mirrors the current priorities of the locality, state, or nation. The quality and quantity of government that the citizenry desires and will support at any given time is expressed by the budget.

Our conceptual understanding of these roles of the budget in modern government is comparatively new, being chiefly a twentieth-century phenomenon. In large part, our instituting formal budget documents began in the Progressive Era, when public budgets were developed as vehicles for governmental reform to produce improved economy and efficiency in the public sector and as instruments for imposing greater control over public spending. Many of these ideas and concepts were borrowed from the experience and practices of business management.

Although there remains a strong emphasis on the earlier notions of budgets as vehicles for imposing control, economy, and efficiency in government, a prominent current view of the role of budgets—and a perspective frequently held by political scientists, budgeting specialists, and public administration practitioners—is a political one: budgets are principally governed by considerations of compromise, strategy, and bargaining. Irene S. Rubin, a political scientist and prominent authority on public budgeting at Northern Illinois University, presents the political view of budget making in the opening chapter of her book *The Politics of Public Budgeting*. Rubin envisions government budgets as "not merely technical managerial documents" but rather "they are also intrinsically and irreducibly political." Her thesis is that although public budgets share many features of budgeting in general such as presenting choices over possible expenditures and problems of balancing revenues with expenditures, they differ in fundamental ways. The open environments within which budgets are developed, the variety of actors involved, the constraints imposed as well as the emphasis on public accountability, give budgets special and distinctive features in the public sector. These aspects add complexity and unique dilemmas to their formulation, operation, and conceptualization.

Professor Rubin's essay at the outset defines "what is budgeting" and the distinctive features of government budgets. From a local case of budget making in Dekalb, Illinois, she underscores the critical political dynamics of public budgeting processes and the variety of participants that are involved, even within the local setting. The elements of budgetary politics concern, in her view, "separate but linked" decision clusters, specifically five clusters dealing with the revenue process (How much income will be available and from where?); budget process (How to make the budget choices?); expenditure process (Which programs will get what?); the balance cluster (How revenues and expenditures will be balanced?); and budget implementation issues (How the budget will be put into operation?). Her essay concludes with an important distinction between understanding "macrobudgeting," or top-down budget viewpoints, versus "microbudgeting," which focuses on the specific actors and their strategies in putting together budgets.

As you read the following selection, keep in mind such questions as:

Why does Rubin stress throughout her writing the political over the technical or managerial aspects of public budgeting?

What differences are apparent from her perspective between government and business budget-making? Do you agree with her conclusions about these fundamental differences?

How do "macro" and "micro" points of view of budgets differ and yet why are *both* essential for a complete understanding of the budgetary process? What are the advantages and disadvantages of both ways of conceptualizing budgets? Do these perspectives on budgets relate to any of our earlier readings such as Charles Lindblom's "incremental decision-making model"?

Why does Rubin focus on understanding modern budgetary processes as "separate but linked decision clusters"? What are the major clusters of issues apparent in each?

The Politics of Public Budgets

IRENE S. RUBIN

Public budgets describe what governments do by listing how governments spend money. A budget links tasks to be performed with the amount of resources necessary to accomplish those tasks, ensuring that money will be available to wage war, provide housing, or maintain streets. Budgets limit expenditures to the revenues available, to ensure balance and prevent overspending. Most of the work in drawing up a budget is technical, estimating how much it will cost to feed a thousand shut-ins with a Meals on Wheels program or how much revenue will be produced from a 1 percent tax on retail sales. But public budgets are not merely technical managerial documents; they are also intrinsically and irreducibly political.

- Budgets reflect choices about what government will and will not do. They reflect general public consensus about what kinds of services governments should provide and what citizens are entitled to as members of society. Should government provide services that the private sector could provide, such as water, electricity, transportation, and housing? Do all citizens have a guarantee of health care, regardless of ability to pay? Are all insured against hunger? Are they entitled to some kind of housing?

- Budgets reflect priorities—between police and flood control, day care and defense, the Northeast and the Southwest. The budget process mediates between groups and individuals who want different things from government and determines who gets what. These decisions may influence whether the poor get job training or the police get riot training, both as a response to an increased number of unemployed.

- Budgets reflect the relative proportion of decisions made for local and constituency pur-

"The Politics of Public Budgets" from *The Politics of Public Budgeting* by Irene B. Rubin (Chatham, N.J.: Chatham House Publishers, 1990), pp. 1–28. Reprinted by permission.

poses, and for efficiency, effectiveness, and broader public goals. Budgets reflect the degree of importance legislators put on satisfying their constituents and the legislators' willingness to listen to interest-group demands. For example, the Defense Department may decide to spend more money to keep a military base open because the local economy depends on it and to spend less money to improve combat readiness.

- Budgets provide a powerful tool of accountability to citizens who want to know how the government is spending their money and if government has generally followed their preferences. Budgeting links citizen preferences and governmental outcomes.

- Budgets reflect citizens' preferences for different forms of taxation and different levels of taxation, as well as the ability of specific groups of taxpayers to shift tax burdens to others. The budget reflects the degree to which the government redistributes wealth upward or downward through the tax system.

- At the national level, the budget influences the economy, so fiscal policy affects the level of employment—how many people are out of work at any time.

- Budgets reflect the relative power of different individuals and organizations to influence budget outcomes. Budgetary decision making provides a picture of the relative power of budget actors within and between branches of government, as well as the importance of citizens in general and specific interest groups.

In all these ways, public budgeting is political. But budgeting is not typical of other political processes and hence one example among many. It is both an important and a unique arena of politics. It is important because of the specific policy issues reflected in the budget: the scope of government, the distribution of wealth, the openness of government to interest groups, and the accountability of government to the public at large. It is unique because these decisions have to take place in the context of budgeting, with its need for balance, its openness to the environment, and its requirements for timely decisions so that government can carry on without interruption.

Public budgets clearly have political implications, but what does it mean to say that key political decisions are made in the context of budgeting? The answer has several parts. First, what is budgeting? Second, what is public budgeting, as opposed to individual or family budgeting or the budgeting of private organizations? Third, what does *political* mean in the context of public budgeting?

What Is Budgeting?

The essence of budgeting is that it allocates scarce resources and hence implies choice between potential objects of expenditure. Budgeting implies balance, and it requires some kind of decision-making process.

Making Budgetary Choices

All budgeting, whether public or private, individual or organizational, involves choices between possible expenditures. Since no one has unlimited resources, people budget all the time. A young child makes a budget (a plan for spending, balancing revenues and expenditures) when she decides to spend money on a marshmallow rabbit rather than a chocolate one, assuming she has money enough for only one rabbit. The air force may choose between two different airplanes to replace current bombers. These examples illustrate the simplest form of budgeting because they involve only one actor, one resource, one time, and two straightforward and comparable choices.

Normally, budgeting does not take place by comparing only two reasonably similar items. There may be a nearly unlimited number of choices. Budgeting usually limits the options to consider by grouping together similar things that can be reasonably compared. When I go to the supermarket, I do not compare all the possible things I could buy, not only because I cannot absorb that number of comparisons, but because the comparisons would be meaningless and a waste of time. I do not go to the supermarket and decide to get either a turkey or a bottle of soda pop. I compare main dishes with main dishes, beverages with beverages, desserts with desserts. Then I have a common denominator for comparison. For example, I may look at the main course and ask about the amount of protein for the dollar. I may compare the desserts in terms of the amount of cholesterol or the calories.

There is a tendency, then, to make comparisons within categories where the comparison is meaningful. This is as true for governmental budgeting as it is for shoppers. For example, weapons might be compared with weapons or automobiles with automobiles. They could be compared in terms of speed, reliability, availability of spare parts, and so on, and the one that did the most of what you wanted it to do at the least cost would be the best choice. As long as there is agreement on the goals to be achieved, the choice should be straightforward.

Sometimes, budgeting requires comparison of different, and seemingly incomparable things. If I do not have enough money to buy a whole balanced meal, I may have to make choices between main dishes and desserts. How do I compare the satisfaction of a sweet tooth to the nourishment of a turkey? Or, in the public sector, how do I compare the benefits of providing shelters for the homeless with buying more helicopters for the navy? I may then move to more general comparisons, such as how clearly were the requests made and the benefits spelled out; who got the benefits last time and whose turn is it this time; are there any specific contingencies that make one choice more likely than the other? For example, will we be embarrassed to show our treatment of the homeless in front of a visiting dignitary? Or, are disarmament negotiations coming up in which we need to display strength or make a symbolic gesture of restraint? Comparing dissimilar items may require a list of priorities. It may be possible to do two or more important things if they are sequenced properly.

Budgeting often allocates money, but it can allocate any scarce resource, for example, time. A student may choose between studying for an exam or playing softball and drinking beer afterward. In this example, it is time that is at a premium, not money. Or it could be medical skills that are in short supply, or expensive equipment, or apartment space, or water.

Government programs often involve a choice of resources and sometimes involve combinations of resources, each of which has different characteristics. For example, some federal farm programs involve direct cash payments plus loans at below-market interest rates, and welfare programs often involve dollar payments plus food stamps, which allow recipients to pay less for food. Federal budgets often assign agencies money, personnel, and sometimes borrowing authority, three different kinds of resources.

Balancing and Borrowing

Budgets have to balance. A plan for expenditures that pays no attention to ensuring that revenues cover expenditures is not a budget. That may sound odd in view of huge federal deficits, but a budget may technically be balanced by borrowing. Balance means only that outgo is matched or exceeded by income. The borrowing, of course, has to be paid off. Borrowing means spending more now and paying more in the future in order to maintain balance. It is a balance over time.

To illustrate the nature of budget balance, consider me as shopper again. Suppose I spend all my weekly shopping money before I buy my dessert. I have the option of treating my dollar limit as if it were more flexible, by adding the dimension of time. I can buy the dessert and everything else in the basket, going over my budget, and then eat less at the end of the month. Or I can pay the bill with a credit card, assuming I will have more money in the future with which to pay off the bill when it comes due. The possibility of borrowing against the future is part of most budget choices.

Process

Budgeting cannot proceed without some kind of decision process. Even in the simplest cases of budgeting, there has to be some limit set to spending, some order of decision making, some way to structure comparisons among alternatives, and some way to compare choices. Budget processes also regulate the flow of decisions so they are made in a timely manner.

Back to my shopping example: If I shop for the main course first, and spend more money than I intended on it because I found some fresh fish, there will be less money left for purchasing the dessert. Hence, unless I set a firm limit on the amount of money to spend for each segment of the meal, the order in which I do the purchasing counts. Of course, if I get to the end of my shopping and do not have enough money left for dessert, I can put back some of the items already in the cart and squeeze out enough money for dessert.

Governmental budgeting is also concerned with procedures for managing tradeoffs between large categories of spending. Budgeters may determine the relative importance of each category first, attaching a dollar level in proportion to the assigned importance, or they may allow purchasing in each area to go on independently, later reworking the choices until the balance between the parts is acceptable.

The order of decisions is important in another sense. I can determine how much money I am likely to have first and then set that as an absolute limit on expenditures, or I can determine what I must have, what I wish to have, and what I need to set aside for emergencies and then go out and try to find enough money to cover some or all of those expenditures. Especially in emergencies, such as accidents or other health emergencies, people are likely to obligate the money first and worry about where it will come from later. Governmental budgeting, too, may concentrate first on revenues and later on expenditures, or first on expenditures and later on income. Like individuals or families, during emergencies such as floods or hurricanes or wars, governments will commit the expenditures first and worry about where the money will come from later.

Governmental Budgeting

Public budgeting shares the characteristics of budgeting in general but differs from household and business budgeting in some key ways. First, in public budgeting, there are always people and organizations with different perspectives and different goals trying to get what they want out of the budget. In individual budgets, there may be only one person involved; and in family and business budgets, there may be only a limited number of actors and they may have similar views of what they want to achieve through the budget.

Second, public budgets are more open to the environment than budgets of families or businesses are. Not only are public budgets open to the economy but also to other levels of government, to citizens, to interest groups, to the press, and to politicians.

Third, budgets form a crucial link between citizen taxpayers and government officials. The document itself may be a key form of accountability. This function does not apply to businesses, families, or individuals.

Fourth, public budgeting is characterized by a variety of constraints, legal limits, perceived limits imposed by public opinion, rules and regulations about how to carry out the budget, and many more. Public budgeting is far more constrained in this sense than budgets of individuals or businesses.

Public budgeting has five particular characteristics that differentiate it from other kinds of budgeting. First, public budgeting is characterized by a variety of budgetary actors who often have different priorities and different levels of power over budget outcomes. These actors have to be regulated and orchestrated by the budget process. Second, in government there is a distinction between those who pay taxes and those who decide how money will be spent—the citizens and the elected politicians. Public officials can force citizens to pay taxes for expenditures they do not want, but citizens can vote politicians out of office. Third, the budget document is important as a means of public accountability. Fourth, public budgets are very vulnerable to the environment—to the economy, to changes in public opinion, to elections, to local contingencies such as natural disasters like floods, or political disasters such as the police bombing of MOVE headquarters in Philadelphia, which burned down part of a neighborhood. Fifth, public budgets are incredibly constrained. Although there is a built-in necessity to make budgets adaptable to contingencies, there are many elements of public budgets that are beyond the immediate control of those who draw up budgets.

A Variety of Actors

The first characteristic of public budgeting was the variety of actors involved in the budget and their frequently clashing motivations and goals. On a regular basis, bureau chiefs, executive budget officers, and chief executives are involved in the budget process, as are legislators, both on committees and as a whole group. Interest groups may be involved at intervals, sometimes for relatively long stretches of time, sometimes briefly. Sometimes citizens play a direct or indirect role in the budget process. Courts may play a role in budgets at any level of government at unpredictable intervals. When they do play a role in budgetary decisions, what are these actors trying to achieve?

Bureau Chiefs. Many students of budgeting assume that agency heads always want to expand their agencies, that their demands are almost limitless, and that it is up to other budget actors to curtail and limit their demands. The reasons given for that desire for expansion include prestige, more subordinates, more space, larger desks, more secretaries, and not incidentally, more salary. The argument presumes that agency heads judge their bureaucratic skills in terms of the satisfaction of their budget requests. Successful bureaucrats bring back the budget. Agency expansion is the measure of success.

Recent research has suggested that while some bureaucrats may be motivated by salaries, many feel that one of their major rewards is the opportunity to do good for people—to house the homeless, feed the hungry, find jobs for the unemployed, and send out checks to the disabled.[1] For these bureaucrats, efforts to expand agency budgets are the result of their belief in the programs they work for.

Recent research has also suggested that the bureaucracy has become more professional, which introduces the possibility of another motivation, the desire to do a good job, to do it right, to put in the best machinery that exists or build the biggest, toughest engineering project or the most complicated weapons.

The generalization that bureaucrats always press for budget increases appears to be too strong. Some agencies are much more aggressive in pushing for growth than others. Some are downright moribund. Sometimes agency heads refuse to expand when given the opportunity,[2] suggesting there are some countervailing values to growth. One of these countervailing values is agency autonomy. Administrators may prefer to maintain autonomy rather than increase the budget if it comes down to a choice between the two. A second countervailing value to growth is professionalism, the desire to get the job done, and do it quickly and right. Administrators generally prefer to hire employees who have the ability to get the job done, plus a little, spare amount of intelligence, motivation, and energy just in case they need to get some extra work done or do it fast in response to a political request.[3] Administrators may refuse to add employees if the proposed employees do not add to the agency's capacity to get things done.

A third countervailing value is program loyalty. Expansion may be seen as undesirable if the new mission swamps the existing mission, if it appears contradictory to the existing mission, or if the program requires more money to carry out than is provided, forcing the agency to spend money designated for existing programs on new ones or do a poor job.

A fourth countervailing value is belief in the chain of command. Many, if not all, bureaucrats believe that their role is to carry out the policies of the chief executive and the legislature. If those policies mean cutting back budgets, agency heads cut back the agencies. Agency heads may be appointed precisely because they are willing to make cuts in their agencies.[4]

Bureaucrats, then, do not always try to expand their agencies' budgets. They have other, competing goals, which sometimes dominate. Also, their achievements can be measured by other than expanded budgets. They may go for some specific items in the budget without raising totals, or may try for changes in the wording of legislation. They may strive to get a statutory basis for the agency and security of funding. They may take as a goal providing more efficient and effective service, rather than expanded or more expensive service.

The Executive Budget Office. The traditional role of the budget office has been to scrutinize requests coming up from the agencies, to find waste and eliminate it, and to discourage most requests for new money. The executive budget office has been perceived as the naysayer, the protector of the public purse. Most staff members in the budget office are very conscious of the need to balance the budget, to avoid deficits, and to manage cash flow so that there is money on hand to pay bills. Hence they tend to be skeptical of requests for new money.

In recent years, however, there has been a change in the role of budget office. At the national level under President Ronald Reagan, budgeting became much more top-down, with the director of the Office of Management and Budget (OMB) proposing specific cuts and negotiating them directly with Congress, without much scrutiny of requests coming up from departments or bureaus. OMB became more involved in trying to accomplish the policy goals of the President through the budget.[5] At state levels too, there has been an evolution of budget staff from more technical to more political and more policy-related goals. When the governor is looking for new spending proposals these may come from his budget office.

Chief Executive Officers. The role of chief executive officers (the mayor or city manager, the governor, the President) is highly variable, and hence these executives' goals in the budget process cannot be predicted without knowledge of the individuals. Some chief executives have been expansive, proposing new programs; others have been economy minded, cutting back proposals generated by the legislatures. Some have been efficiency oriented, reorganizing staffs and trying to maintain service levels without increases in taxes or expenditures.

Legislators. Legislators have sometimes been described as always trying to increase expenditures.[6] Their motivation is viewed as getting reelected, which depends on their ability to provide constituents services and deliver "pork"—jobs and capital projects—to their districts. Norms of reciprocity magnify the effects of these spending demands because legislators are reluctant to cut others' pork lest their own be cut in return. At the city level, a council member described this norm of reciprocity, "There is an unwritten rule that if something is in a councilman's district, we'll go along and scratch each other's back."[7]

For some legislators, however, getting reelected is not a high priority. They view elected office as a service they perform for the community rather than a career, and while they may be responsive to constituents' needs, they are simply not motivated to start new projects or give public employees a raise in order to get reelected. Also, some legislators feel secure about the possibility of reelection, and hence have no urgent need to deliver pork in order to increase their chances of reelections.[8]

Even assuming the motivation to get reelected, holding down taxes may be as important to reelection as spending on programs and projects. The consequence of tax reduction is usually curtailed expenditures. Legislators are bound to try to balance the budget, which puts some constraints on the desire to spend.

The tendency to provide pork is real, but there are counterbalancing factors. Some legislators are more immune to pressures from constituents because they are secure electorally, and legislators can organize themselves in such a way as to insulate themselves somewhat from these pressures. They can, for example, select more electorally secure representatives for key positions on appropriations committees; they can separate committees that deal extensively with interest groups from those that deal with expenditures; they can set up buffer groups to deal with interest groups; they can structure the budget process so that revenue limits precede and guide spending proposals.

Moreover, legislators have interests other than providing pork. Some legislators are deeply concerned about solving social problems, designing and funding defense and foreign aid systems, and monitoring the executive branch. The proportion of federal budget spent on pork-type projects has declined in recent years, despite reforms in Congress that decentralized control and allowed pressure for pork to increase.[9] "Congressmen are not single-minded seekers of local benefits, struggling feverishly to win every last dollar for their districts. However important the quest for local benefits may be, it is always tempered by other competing concerns."[10] The pull for local benefits depends on the program. Some, like water projects, are oriented to local payoffs; others, like entitlements programs for large numbers of people, are not. Programs with local pull account for smaller and smaller proportions of the budget[11] and the trend has accelerated since 1978.[12]

Interest Groups. Interest groups, too, have often been singled out as the driving force behind budget increases. They are said to want more benefits for their members and to be undeterred by concerns for overall budget balance or the negative effects of tax increases. Moreover, their power has been depicted as great. Well-funded interest groups reportedly wine and dine legislators and provide campaign funding for candidates who agree with their positions.

There is some truth to this picture, but it is over-simplified. Interest groups have other policy goals besides budget levels. In fact, most probably deal with the budget only when a crisis occurs, such as a threat to funding levels. Because they can be counted on to come to the defense of a threatened program, they reduce the flexibility of budget decision makers, who find it difficult to cut programs with strong interest-group backing. But many areas of the budget do not have strong interest-group backing. For example, foreign aid programs have few domestic constituencies. Agencies may even have negative constituencies, that is, interest groups that want to reduce their funding and terminate their programs. The American Medical Association sought for years to eliminate the Health Planning Program.

Often when there are interest groups, there are many rather than one, and these interest groups may have conflicting styles or conflicting goals, canceling one another out or absorbing energy in battles among themselves. A coalition of interest groups representing broad geographic areas and a variety of constituencies is likely to be more effective at lobbying.

Hence coalitions may form, but individual members of the coalition may not go along with measures supported by others, so the range of items lobbied for as a unified group may be narrow. Extensive negotiations and continual efforts are required to get two or more independent groups together for a lobbying effort, and the arrangement can then fall apart. In short, interest groups are often interested in maintaining their autonomy.

Individuals. Individuals seldom have a direct role in the budget process, as they did in the DeKalb case, but they often have an indirect role. They may vote on referenda to limit revenues, forbid some forms of taxation, or require budgetary balance. They voice their opinions also in public opinion polls, and more informally by calling or writing their elected representatives and giving their opinions. Their knowledge of the budget is not usually detailed, but their feelings about the acceptability of taxation are an important part of the constraints of public budgeting. Their preferences for less visible taxes and for taxes earmarked for specific approved expenditures have been an important factor in public budgeting.

The Courts. Another budget actor that plays an intermittent role in determining expenditures is the courts.[13] The courts get involved when other actors, often interest groups, bring a case against the government. Suits that affect the budget may involve service levels or the legality of particular forms of taxation. If a particular tax is judged unconstitutional, the result is usually lost revenues. If there are suits concerning levels of service, governments may be forced to spend more money on that service. There can also be damage suits against governments that affect expenditures. These suits are usually settled without regard to the government agencies' ability to pay. The result may be forced cuts in other areas of the budget, tax increases, or even bankruptcy. When the courts get involved, they may determine budget priorities. They introduce a kind of rigidity into the budget that says do this, or pay this, first.

Typical areas in which courts have gotten involved and mandated expenditures for state and local governments are prison overcrowding (declared cruel and unusual punishment) and deinstitutionalization of mentally ill and mentally handicapped patients. In each case, the rights of the institutionalized population required more services or more space, often involving expenditures of additional funds. From the perspective of the courts, the priority of rights outweighs immediate concerns for budget balances, autonomy of governmental units, and local priorities.

Power Differentials. These various actors not only have different and potentially clashing budgetary goals, but they typically have different levels of power. Thus, at times, the budget office may completely dominate the agencies; at times, the Congress may differ from the President on budgetary policy and pass its own preferences. The courts may preempt the decision making of the executive and the legislature. Some particular interest groups may always be able to get tax breaks for themselves.

The combination of different preferences and different levels of power has to be orchestrated by the budget process in such a way that agreement is reached, and the players stay in the game, continuing to abide by the rules. If some actors feel too powerless over the budget, they may cease to participate or become obstructionist, blocking any agreements or imposing rigid, nonnegotiable solutions. Why participate in negotiations and discussions if the decision will go against you regardless of what you do? If some actors lose on important issues, they may try to influence budget implementation to favor themselves. Or the actors with less budget power may try to change the budget process so that they have a better chance of influencing the outcomes.

The Separation of Payer and Decider

The second feature of public budgeting is that decisions about how money will be spent are made not by those providing the money but by their representatives. The payers and the deciders are two distinct groups. The payers are not given a choice about whether they want to pay or how much they want to pay. The power of the state may force them to pay. They may protest if they do not like how their money is being spent, and elect new representatives. They cannot, generally, take their money and do something else with it.

The distinction between the payers and the deciders leads to two crucial characteristics of public budgeting: public *accountability* and political *acceptability*. *Accountability* means to make sure that every penny of public money is spent as agreed, and to report accurately to the public on how money was spent. *Acceptability* means that public officials who make budget decisions are constrained by what the public wants. Sometimes they will do precisely what they think the public wants, even if the results are inefficient or inequitable, and sometimes they will present the budget so that it will be accepted by the public, even if they have not precisely followed public will. This effort may involve persuasion or deception.

Since public demands may not be clearly expressed, and since different segments of the public may make different and competing demands, and since public officials themselves may have priorities, officials may not be able or willing to be bound tightly to public opinion. Nevertheless, if politicians knowingly make decisions that differ from what the public wants, there is pressure to present the budget in a way that makes it appear acceptable. That pressure creates a tension between accountability, which requires nearly complete openness, and acceptability, which sometimes involves hiding or distorting information or presenting it in an unclear fashion.

The Budget Document and Accountability

Because of the separation of payer and decider, the budget document itself becomes an important means of public accountability. How did the public's representatives actually decide to spend taxpayer money? Did they waste it? Did they spend it on defense or police or on social services? The streets are in terrible shape—how much money did they spend on street repair? Citizens do not typically watch the decision making, but they and the press have access to the budget document and can look for the answers. They can hold the government accountable through the budget, to see that what officials promised them was actually delivered.

But budgets do not always present a complete and accurate picture. One example of how budgets can lose information happened recently in a state university. A university president decided to expand the big-time sports program, in an environment of overall financial scarcity. While some faculty members undoubtedly favored the action, many would have opposed it if they had been asked. The president did not ask their opinions, however; instead, the full costs of the program were disguised to make the budget appear acceptable. Because of progressive underestimates of

costs in the sports program, some pundits labeled the sports program the case of the disappearing budget.

To obscure the real costs, the president broke up the costs for the program and scattered them among different portions of the budget. To complicate the picture further, he drew on different pockets of revenue, including student athletic fees, bond revenues, and voluntary donations. When asked, he said money going to the athletic programs was earmarked and could not be spent on other programs, so that professors trying to get more money to teach history or biology would look elsewhere than to sports. The amount of money showing as costs in the athletic program remained constant every year, although the program costs were expanding. Fearing conflict and disapproval, the president hid the costs in the budget.

The more complicated the budget, the more different activities and accounts, the greater the discretion of the administrators. As one university president offered, "Not a day goes by when we do not wish we had a more complex budget." The complexity allows for choice of where to report expenditures, and which revenues to use, to highlight some expenditures and gloss over others.

It would be misleading to suggest that the tension between accountability and acceptability always leads to more distortion or more secrecy. Sometimes the balance tends toward more accountability and budgets become clearer and more representative of true costs. The federal budget, for example, has moved toward clearer and more comprehensive portraits of public expenditures in recent years. But the tension is always present, and each budget represents some degree of selectivity about what it will present and how. The art of selective revelation is part of public budgeting.

Openness to the Environment

Public budgets are open to the environment. The environment for budgeting includes a number of different factors including the over-all level of resources available (the amount of taxable wealth, the existing tax structure, current economic conditions); the degree of certainty of revenues; and a variety of emergencies such as very heavy snow-fall, tornadoes, wars, bridge collapses, droughts, chemical explosions, and water pollution. The environment also includes rigidities resulting from earlier decisions, which may now be embodied in law. For example, rapid inflation in housing prices in California resulted in a citizen referendum to protect themselves from rapidly rising property taxes. The result of the referendum was incorporated in the state constitution, limiting the taxing options of local government. Constitutional restrictions to maintain a balanced budget or limit expenditures or put a ceiling on borrowing operate in a similar manner. Prior borrowing creates a legal obligation for future budgets, an obligation that may press other possible expenditures out of consideration or require higher levels of taxation. The environment in this sense may frame policy issues and limit alternatives. Public opinion is also part of the budgetary environment, and the perception of change in public opinion will be reflected in changing budgets.

The intergovernmental system is also a key part of the environment for budget actors. The legal sources of revenues, limits on borrowing, strings attached to grants, and mandated costs are but a few of the budgetary implications of the intergovernmental system. The requirement that some grants be spent on particular items or that a recipient match expenditures on grants may result in a pattern of spending different from what the state or local government would have preferred.

Budget Constraints

Openness to the environment creates the need for budgets to be flexible. Public officials have to be able to adapt quickly, reallocating funds to meet emergencies, spending more now and making up the difference later, cutting back expenditures during the year to meet sudden declines in revenues or increases in expenditures. But the same openness to the environment that creates the need for flexibility may simultaneously subject budgeting to numerous constraints.

For example, in California, a statewide referendum limited the rate of growth of local assessments, restraining the growth of property tax revenues. Federal grants provide budgetary constraints when they can be spent only on particular programs. The courts may create budgetary constraints by declaring programs inadequate or taxes illegal. Legal obligations to repay debt and maintain public businesses separate from the rest of the budget also create constraints.

The need for flexibility and the number of budgetary constraints contest with one another, creating patterns typical of public budgeting. For example, local officials may press for home rule, which gives more independence and autonomy to local governments to manage their own affairs and adapt to changing conditions. But state officials may erode home rule through continually mandating local costs. State universities may try to squirrel away contingency funds outside those appropriated by the legislature so that they can respond to emergencies; the legislature may then try to appropriate and hence control this new local source of revenues.

The Meaning of Politics in Public Budgeting

Public budgets have a number of special characteristics. These characteristics suggest some of the ways that the budget is political. Political is a word that covers a number of meanings, even when narrowed to the context of budgetary decision making. The purpose of this book is to clarify the meaning of politics in the context of budgeting by sorting out some key meanings and showing how these meanings apply to different parts of budgetary decision making.

Concepts of Politics in the Budget

The literature suggests at least five major ways of viewing politics in the budget: reformism, incrementalist bargaining, interest group determinism, process, and policy making.

- The first is a reform orientation, which argues that politics and budgeting are or should be antithetical, that budgeting should be primarily or exclusively technical, and that comparison between items should be technical and efficiency based. Politics in the sense of the opinions and priorities of elected officials and interest groups is an unwanted intrusion that reduces efficiency and makes decision making less rational. The politics of reform involves a clash of views between professional staff and elected officials over the boundary between technical budget decisions and properly political ones.

- The second perspective is the incrementalist view, which sees budgeting as negotiations among a group of routine actors, bureaucrats, budget officers, chief executives, and legislators, who meet each year and bargain to resolution. To the extent that interest groups are included at all in this view, they are conceived of in the pluralist model. The process is open, anyone can play and win, and the overall outcome is good; conflict is held down because everyone wins something and no one wins too much.

- The third view is that interest groups are dominant actors in the budget process. In its extreme form this argument posits that richer and more powerful interest groups determine the budget. Some interests are represented by interest groups and others are not, or are represented by weaker interest groups; the outcome does not approximate democracy. There may be big winners and big losers in this model. Conflict is more extensive than in the incrementalist model. This view of politics in budgeting raises the questions whether these interest groups represent narrow or broad coalitions, or possibly even class interest. To what extent do these interest groups represent oil or banking or the homeless, and to what extent do they represent business and labor more broadly?

- The fourth view of politics in the budget is

that the budget process itself is the center and focus of budget politics. Those with particular budget goals try to change the budget process to favor their goals. Branches of government struggle with one another over budgetary power through the budget process; the budget process becomes the means of achieving or denying separation and balance between the branches of government. The degree of examination of budget requests, and the degree to which review is technical or political, cursory or detailed, is regulated by the budget process. The ability of interest groups to influence the budget, the role of the public in budget decisions, the openness of budget decision making—all these are part of the politics of process. In this view of politics, the individual actors and their strategies and goals may or may not be important, depending on the role assigned to individual actors in the budget process, and depending on whether the external environment allows any flexibility.

- The fifth view is that the politics of budgeting centers in policy debates, including debates about the role of the budget. Spending levels, taxing policies, and willingness to borrow to sustain spending during recessions are all major policy issues that have to be resolved one way or another during budget deliberations. Budgets may reflect a policy of moderating economic cycles or they may express a policy of allowing the economy to run its course. Each is a policy. Similarly, budgets must allocate funding to particular programs, and in the course of doing so, decide priorities for federal, state, and local governments. This view of politics in the budget emphasizes tradeoffs, especially those that occur between major areas of the budget, such as social services and defense or police. This view also emphasizes the role of the budget office in making policy and the format of the budget in encouraging comparisons between programs.

These five views of politics have been developed over time, and like an ancient document, the messages have been written over one another. Surely they are not all equally true, and certainly they often contradict each other. Parts of each may still be true, and they may be true of different parts of budgetary decision making, or true of budgetary decision making at different times or at different levels of government.

Budgetary Decision Making

The focus . . . is to explore the kind of politics that occurs in budgetary decision making. What is budgetary decision making like? We have already discovered that public budgeting is open to environmental changes and deals with policy conflicts. Policy conflicts can delay particular decisions or prevent them from being made at all; other budget decisions must be independent enough to be made without the missing pieces. They can be corrected later when missing pieces fall into place. Environmental emergencies can reorder priorities and alter targets that have already been determined. As a result, public budgeting must be segmental and interruptible. The need for segmentation and interruptibility is satisfied by dividing budgeting into separate but linked decision clusters: revenues, process, expenditures, balance, and implementation.

Decision making in each cluster proceeds somewhat independently while referring to decisions made in the other clusters, or in anticipation of decisions likely to be made in other clusters. These decision clusters are ultimately interdependent, but do not occur in a fixed sequence. The decision one needs to have in one decision cluster may not be made by another decision cluster in time to use. Then one may guess, or use an old figure, and then change when the new figure is determined. Sometimes decision-making cycles between estimates of revenues, estimates of expenditures, new estimates of revenues and new estimates of expenditures, in an iterative process.

The Revenue Cluster

Revenue decisions include technical estimates of how much income will be available for the following year, assuming no change in the tax structures, and policy decisions about changes in the level or type of taxation. Will taxes be raised or lowered? Will tax breaks be granted, and if so, to whom, for what purpose? Which tax sources will be emphasized, and which deemphasized, with what effect on regions, and economic classes, or on age groups? How visible will the tax burden be? Interest groups are intensely involved in the revenue cluster. The revenue cluster emphasizes the scarcity of resources that is an essential element in budgeting and illustrates the tension between accountability and acceptability that is a characteristic of public budgets. Revenues are also extremely sensitive to the environment because changes in the economy influence revenue levels and because the perception of public opinion influences the public officials' willingness to increase taxes.

The Budget Process

The process cluster concerns how to make budget decisions. Who should participate in the budget deliberations? Should the agency heads have power independent of the central budget office? How influential should interest groups be? How much power should the legislature have? How should the work be divided, and when should particular decisions be made? Normally the legislature takes a key role in establishing budget process, although the chief executive may propose desired changes. Interest groups play a minor role, if any role at all. The politics of process may revolve around individuals or groups trying to maximize their power through rearranging the budget process. This jockeying for power rises to importance when the competing parties represent the executive and legislative branches and involve the definition of the separation and balance between the branches of government. The politics of process may revolve around the policy issues of the level of spending and the ability of government to balance its budget.

The Expenditure Cluster

The expenditure cluster involves some technical estimates of likely expenditures, such as for grants that are dependent on formulas and benefit programs whose costs depend on the level of unemployment. But many expenditure decisions are policy relevant—which programs will be funded at what level, who will benefit from public programs and who will not, where and how cuts will be made, and whose interests will be protected. Agency heads are more involved in these decisions than in taxation or process decisions, and interest groups are also often active. This portion of the budget emphasizes the element of choice between items of expenditures in the definition of budgeting and illustrates the nature of the constraints on choices that is characteristic of public budgeting in particular.

The Balance Cluster

The balance cluster concerns the basic budgetary question whether the budget has to be balanced each year with each year's revenues, or whether borrowing is allowed to balance the budget, and if so, how much, for how long, and for what purposes. The politics of balance deals with questions whether balance should be achieved by increasing revenues, decreasing expenditures, or both, and hence reflects policies about the desirable scope of government. Sometimes the politics of balance emphasizes definitions, as the group in power seeks to make its deficits look smaller by defining them away. The balance cluster also deals with questions of how deficits should be eliminated once they occur and their amounts are pinned down. At the national level, because deficits may be incurred during recessions in an effort to help the economy recover, the ability to run a deficit is linked to policies favoring or opposing the role of the budget in controlling the economy and, in particular, the use of the budget to moderate unemployment. These issues—whether budgets should balance, the

proper scope of government and level of taxation, and the role of government in moderating unemployment—are issues that the general public cares about. Citizens may participate in this decision cluster through referenda and opinion polls; broad groups of taxpayers and interest-group coalitions representing broad segments of society may be involved in lobbying on this issue. Political parties may even include their policies toward deficits in their election platforms.

Budget Implementation

Finally, there is a cluster of decisions around budget implementation. How close should actual expenditures be to the ones planned in the budget? How can one justify variation from the budget plan? Can the budget be remade after it is approved, during the budget year? The key issues here revolve around the need to implement decisions exactly as made and the need to make changes during the year because of changes in the environment. The potential conflict is usually resolved by treating implementation as technical rather than policy related. Executive branch staff play the major role in implementation, with much smaller and more occasional roles for the legislature. Interest groups play virtually no role in implementation. The allowance of technical changes does open the door to policy changes during the year, but these are normally carefully monitored and may cause open conflict when they occur.

Microbudgeting and Macrobudgeting

The five clusters of decision making outline the nature of the decisions actually being made, but tell little about how and why the decisions are made. On the one hand there are a number of budget actors, who all have individual motivations, who strategize to get what they want from the budget. The focus on the actors and their strategies is called *microbudgeting*. But the actors do not simply bargain with one another or with whomever they meet in the corridor. The actors are assigned budget roles by the budget process, the issues they examine are often framed by the budget process, and the timing and coordination of their decisions are often regulated by the budget process. The budget actors are not totally free to come to budget agreements in any way they choose. Individual actors are bound by environmental constraints. There are choices they are not free to make because they are against the law, or because the courts decree it, or because previous decision makers have bound their hands. The total amount of revenue available is a kind of constraint, as is popular demand for some programs and popular dislike of others. Budgetary decision making has to account not just for budgetary actors but also for budget processes and the environment. This more top-down and systemic perspective on budgeting is called *macrobudgeting*. Contemporary budgeting gives more emphasis to macrobudgeting than exclusively to microbudgeting.

One way of viewing the determinants of budgetary outcomes is as a casual model, depicted in Figure 12.1. In this schema, the environment, budget processes, and individuals' strategies all affect outcomes.

The environment influences budgetary outcomes directly and indirectly, through process and through individual strategies. The environment influences outcomes directly, without going through either budget process or individual strategies, when it imposes emergencies that reorder priorities. Thus a war or a natural disaster preempts normal budgetary decision making.

The environment influences the budget process in several ways. The level of resources available—both the actual level of wealth and the willingness of the citizens to pay their taxes—influences the degree of centralization of budgeting. When resources are especially scarce and there is apparent

need to either cutback according to a given set of policies or make each dollar count toward specific economic goals, there is no room for bottom-up demands that result in compromises and a little bit of gain for everyone regardless of need. When resources are abundant, a more decentralized model of process may hold, with less emphasis on comparing policies and less competition between supporters of different policies.

The environment may influence the format of budget as well as the degree of centralization of decision making. When revenues are growing, there may be more emphasis on planning and on linking the budget to future community goals, to stimulate public demands for new spending. When there is little new money, the idea of planning may seem superfluous. Changing direction, or setting new goals, may seem impossible in the face of declining revenues that make current goals difficult to sustain.

Environment in the sense of the results of prior decisions may also influence process. If there is a huge accumulation of debt and little apparent way to control it, or if the budget has been growing very rapidly for reasons other than war, there may be attempts to change the budget process in an effort to control spending and debt. In contrast, if the environment suggests the need for additional spending, and the current budget process is delivering very slow growth, the process may be changed to make spending decisions quicker and easier.

The level of certainty of funding influences strategies as well. If whatever an agency was promised may never arrive, agency heads are likely to engage in continuous lobbying for their money, and continual rebudgeting internally every time circumstances change. Long-term or future agreements will be perceived as worthless; the possibility of toning down conflict by stretching out budget allocation times will disappear. Attention will focus on what is available now, and going after whatever it is, whether it is what you want or not, because what you really want may never show up and hence is not worth waiting for.

The intergovernmental grant structure is part of the environment that may influence strategies. Because some grant money may seem free, state and

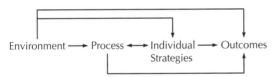

Figure 12.1   Decision making: Environment, process, and strategies

local governments may focus their energies on getting grants instead of raising local revenues. Or they may seek to decrease the amount of match required for a grant or increase their authority over how the money can be spent. Intergovernmental grants may make some expenditures relatively cheap, and some cutbacks relatively expensive, and hence frame constraints and choices for state and local budget officials.

The legal environment also influences strategies. For example, if public school teachers want tax raises to fund education and there is a provision in the state constitution forbidding income taxes, the teachers must either campaign for a constitutional revision (a time consuming and difficult task) or support a tax they know to be more burdensome to the poor. Thus the environment frames choices and influences strategies.

In Figure 12.1, the budget process influences strategies directly, and to a lesser extent, outcomes directly. But there is a double-headed arrow on the linkage between budget processes and strategies, suggesting that individuals' strategies also influence budget processes.

Budget processes influence strategies in some fairly obvious ways. If the budget structure allows for lengthy detailed budget hearings, open to the public and interest groups, at which decisions are often made, then various actors are likely to concentrate their efforts on making a good impression at these hearings. If the chief executive prepares the budget, which is subject to only superficial scrutiny and pro forma hearings before being approved by the legislature, anyone who wants to influence the budget—including the legislators themselves—must make their opinions heard earlier in the process, before the final executive proposal is put together. Informal discussion with department heads, or even telephone calls to the budget office, may be the route to influence. If the budget is made two or three times, with only the last one effective, then strategies may be to play out the first time or two with grandstanding—extreme positions to attract media attention—and more detailed and moderate positions later when the final decisions are made. The budget process orders the decisions in such a way that some of them are critical and determine or influence those that come afterward. Budget strategies naturally gravitate to those key decisions no matter where they are located.

When budget outcomes contradict some group's preference, the group may try to change the budget process to help it get the outcomes it prefers. When coalitions of the dissatisfied can agree on particular changes, fairly substantial changes in process may result. A change in process will bring about a change in outcome if the change in process shifts power from one group of individuals who want to accomplish one goal to another group with different goals.

The final link in the figure is between the strategies of budget actors and outcomes. The effect of different strategies on the outcomes is hard to gauge. It seems obvious, however, that strategies that ignore the process or the environment are doomed to failure. Budget actors have to figure out where the flexibility is before they can influence how that flexibility will be used. Strategies that try to bypass superiors or fool legislators generally do not work; strategies that involve careful documentation of need and appear to save money are generally more successful.

Summary and Conclusions

Public budgeting shares the characteristics of all budgeting. It makes choices between possible expenditures, it has to balance, and it has a decision-making process. But public budgeting has a number of additional features peculiar to itself, such as its openness to the environment; the variety of actors involved in budgeting, all of whom come to it with different goals; the separation of taxpayers from budget decision makers; the use of the budget document as a means of public accountability; and the numerous constraints typical of public budgeting.

Public budgeting is both technical and political. Politics takes on some special meanings in the context of budgetary decision making. Budgetary decision making must be flexible, adaptive, and interruptible, which leads to a structure of five semi-independent strands of decision making, revenues, process, expenditures, balance, and implementation. Each such strand generates its own political characteristics.

Budget outcomes are not solely the result of budget actors negotiating with one another in a free-for-all; outcomes depend on the environment, and on the budget process as well as individual strategies. Individual strategies have to be framed in a broader context than simply perceived self-interest.

Budgeting is not well described as an annual process with little change from year to year. Budgetary decision making changes over time: interest group power waxes and wanes, competition in the budget increases and decreases, and the budget process itself varies over time. Changes in process take place in response to individuals, committees, and branches of government jockeying for power; in response to changes in the environment from rich to lean, or vice versa; in response to changes in the power of interest groups; and in response to scandals or excesses of various kinds.

Notes

1. Patricia Ingraham and Charles Barilleaux, "Motivating Government Managers for Retrenchment: Some Possible Lessons from the Senior Executive Service," *Public Administration Review* 43, no. 3 (1983): 393–402. They cite the Office of Personnel Management Federal Employee Attitude Surveys of 1979 and 1980, extracting responses from those in the Senior Executive Service, the upper ranks of the civil service and appointed administrators. In 1979, 99 percent of the senior executives said that they considered accomplishing something worthwhile was very important; 97 percent said the same in 1980. By contrast, in response to the question "How much would you be motivated by a cash award," only 45 percent said either to a great extent or a very great extent.

2. Twelve percent of LeLoup and Moreland's

Department of Agriculture requests between 1946 and 1971 were for decreases. See Lance LeLoup, *Budgetary Politics,* 3d ed. (Brunswick, Ohio: King's Court, 1986), 83. For a more recent case study of an agency requesting decreases, see the case study of the Office of Personnel Management, in Irene Rubin, *Shrinking the Federal Government* (White Plains: Longman, 1985). See Irene Rubin, *Running in the Red: The Political Dynamics of Urban Fiscal Stress* (Albany: State University of New York Press, 1982) for an example of a department refusing additional employees.

3. For a good discussion of this phenomenon, see Frank Thompson, *The Politics of Personnel in the City* (Berkeley: University of California Press, 1975).

4. See Rubin, *Shrinking the Federal Government,* for examples during the Reagan administration.

5. U.S. Senate, Committee on Governmental Affairs, *Office of Management and Budget: Evolving Roles and Future Issues,* Committee Print 99–134, 99th Cong., 2d sess., prepared by the Congressional Research Service of the Library of Congress, February 1986.

6. See, for example, Kenneth Shepsle and Barry Weingast, "Legislative Politics and Budget Outcomes," in *Federal Budget Policy in the 1980s,* Gregory Mills and John Palmer, eds. (Washington, D.C.: Urban Institute Press, 1984), 343–367.

7. Rubin, *Running in the Red,* 56.

8. For a vivid account of the relationship between pork-barrel spending and building political coalitions, see Martin Shefter, "New York City's Fiscal Crisis: The Politics of Inflation and Retrenchment," *Public Interest* 48 (Summer 1977): 99–127.

9. See John Ellwood, "Comments," in Mills and Palmer, *Federal Budget Policy in the 1980s,* 368–378.

10. Douglas Arnold, "The Local Roots of Domestic Policy," in *The New Congress,*

Thomas Mann and Norman Ornstein, eds. (Washington, D.C.: American Enterprise Institute, 1981), 252, quoted by Ellwood, in Mills and Palmer.

11. Arnold, "Local Roots," 282.
12. Ellwood, in Mills and Palmer, 370.

13. Linda Harriman and Jeffrey Straussman, "Do Judges Determine Budget Decisions? Federal Court Decisions in Prison Reform and State Spending for Corrections," *Public Administration Review* 43, no. 4 (1983): 343–351.

☐ CASE STUDY 12

Introduction

Perhaps nothing is more vital to our understanding of public administration than how monies are budgeted to achieve public purposes. This subject, many believe, directly and decisively influences what policies are pursued and how management of public programs is achieved. For some, budgets in reality are what public administration is all about, namely the translation of public purposes into practical actions through the raising and expenditures of government monies. Rubin's foregoing essay therefore offers several stimulating insights into this critical process. It especially shows why this subject should not be viewed as merely a dry, technical document but as something that affects the central fabric of modern democratic society and the choices it faces.

Let's next turn to an actual example of what Rubin's selection addressed by studying the following case, "County Prison Overtime." This case study concerns a dispute over the amount and use of funds for the payment of overtime in a county correctional facility. At first glance, this may seem like a mundane and uninteresting problem. A county budget office staff prods an operating department to cooperate in a cost containment program to reduce the overall level of county spending (seemingly a trivial management task). But this routine administrative matter about overtime pay, which starts out as a simple exchange of memos, turns into an acrimonious confrontation between staff and line personnel and soon involves the county manager, the county board, and other local interests. County administrator George Truly finds himself in the middle of a battle over what Rubin called, "budget implementation decisions" that have important consequences for his workforce and the community at large.

As you read this case, you might reflect on the following points:

What was the basic nature of county government, its structure, workforce, and the politics of the whole community that contributed to the problems raised in this case?

Why is the case about what Rubin refers to in her essay as "budget implementation decisions"? What clusters of issues are involved?

How were these problems first raised in the case and what specific questions did the county administrator, George Truly, confront?

Can you outline the data, methods of analysis, understanding of the community, budgetary policies, and particular sensitivity of people that Truly required to make his decision? What alternatives were presented? Do you think he resolved the issue fairly, creatively, and effectively? Why or why not?

County Prison Overtime

TOM MILLS

Background

Franklin County is a suburban/rural county located in one of the Mid-Atlantic states; it adjoins a large eastern city. Franklin County has a land area of 650 square miles; a population of approximately 500,000; and 45 local governments that consist of boroughs, villages, and townships. The local governments have their own police forces but lack secure holding facilities for defendants arrested and bound over by local magistrates for trial in the county courts.

The county provides all criminal justice system services from the county courthouse located in Franklinville, the county seat. On a tract of county-owned land just outside of Franklinville, the county operates two detention facilities: a small medium-security facility for juveniles and a large, modern medium-security facility for both male and female adult detainees. The latter facility, called the county prison, has a capacity of approximately 340 inmates and is maintained and operated by a staff of 181 employees.

Franklin County's chief lawmaking and administrative authority is the elected county commission, which is vested with both executive and legislative powers. Voters also elect a number of administrative officers—including the sheriff, the controller, and the district attorney—and the judges of the county court, called the supreme court of common pleas.

The county commission consists of three members elected countywide for four-year terms. The county code requires that one of the three commissioners be a member of the opposing, or minority, party. The county is predominantly Republican, and members of that party regularly control the countywide elective offices. The county commission, perhaps owing to its higher visibility, has occasionally been controlled by a Democratic majority.

"County Prison Overtime," by Tom Mills from *Managing Local Government: Cases in Decision Making*, James M. Banovetz, ed. (1990). Reprinted with permission of the International City/County Management Association, 777 North Capitol Street, NE, Suite 500, Washington, D.C. 20002. All rights reserved.

The county commissioners appoint a county administrator, all nonelected department heads, and the members of most county boards and commissions. The day-to-day operation of the county is the responsibility of the county administrator, who is a professional local government manager recruited and appointed on the basis of technical competence. The county boasts a commitment to professionalism. The county administrator recruits and hires his or her own staff and has been responsible for securing the appointments of the finance director, the personnel director, and the director of purchasing.

The county code constrains the county commissioners' powers of appointment in some instances. The power to appoint the director of the department of corrections, who oversees both the county prison and the juvenile rehabilitation center, is vested in a prison board. The prison board is composed of the president judge of the supreme court of common pleas or that judge's designee, the district attorney, the sheriff, the controller, and the three county commissioners. Five of the seven members of the board were Republicans at the time this case begins.

The Case

In the previous election, the Democratic party had won the majority of seats on the county commission by taking what proved to be the more popular position on a critical environmental issue. In hopes of reelection, the Democratic commissioners instituted a cost containment program that, if successful, would enable them to complete their term without raising taxes. The commissioners issued a directive to all department heads instructing them to implement economies wherever possible. The county administrator, George Truly, was given the principal responsibility for implementing the cost containment program. He, in turn, had charged the finance director, Donald Dexter, with much of the operating responsibility for the program.

After monitoring the expenditures of the county

prison, Dexter was convinced that overtime expenditures were out of control. He had met on several occasions with Charles Goodheart, the director of corrections, and had called him almost weekly in an effort to reduce overtime costs. In Dexter's view, those contacts had been of little value, since overtime expenditures continued at what he regarded as an excessive rate. Somewhat reluctantly, he decided to go "on record." He dictated what was to be the first in a series of memorandums.

March 12
TO: Charles R. Goodheart, Director of
          Corrections
FROM: Donald D. Dexter, Finance Director
SUBJECT: Excessive Prison Overtime

Pursuant to the county commissioners' directive of January 8 establishing the cost containment program, my staff and I have been closely monitoring the overtime expenditures incurred in the operation of the county prison. We have had several meetings and numerous telephone conversations regarding this matter with both you and your key staff members—all to no avail. Overtime expenditures have continued to rise and might well exceed the budget allocation. This I find to be particularly distressing, since we had every hope that this was one area of your operation in which we could effect significant savings.

I would greatly appreciate it if you would provide me, at your first opportunity, with a detailed justification for the current rate of overtime usage and your plans to keep such expenditures to an absolute minimum.

cc: George S. Truly, County Administrator
      Frank Friendly, Personnel Director

Before sending this memorandum, Dexter had given the action considerable thought and had concluded that, even if the memorandum was a bit strong, it was warranted in this case.

In the weeks that followed, Dexter continued to scrutinize the prison payroll records but did not observe any reduction in the use of overtime. He was about to schedule yet another meeting with Goodheart when he received the following memorandum.

April 5
TO: Donald D. Dexter, Finance Director
FROM: Charles R. Goodheart, Director of
          Corrections
SUBJECT: Response to Your Request for
          Information Regarding Overtime
          Expenditures

You indicated in your memorandum of March 12 that you felt we were utilizing an excessive amount of overtime. I welcome the opportunity to explain what might appear to be excessive overtime usage, but which really is no more than prudent prison management.

You will recall that during the budget hearings last year, I shared with you information on overtime usage in the four surrounding counties. Each of these counties has a comparable prison system, and, as I noted then, each uses more overtime than we do.

You must remember that I requested $434,400 as an overtime allocation for the current fiscal year (including holiday overtime). The overtime figure that was allocated to this department was substantially less. When budget allocations were announced, there was no explanation for the reduced overtime figure other than a general statement—which certainly is appropriate for you as finance director to make—that times were difficult, money was tight, and every effort must be made to curtail unnecessary expenditures. Although I accept these comments in the spirit in which they were made, I still am held responsible and accountable to the prison board for operating a safe and secure correctional institution. Prisons are potentially very dangerous, and that danger can be averted only by keeping staffing levels at safe and realistic levels.

As we both know, there are many justifiable causes for overtime usage in a prison setting. In the following paragraphs I'll attempt to identify the major causes.

Turnover During last year and continuing into this year, we have experienced high levels of turnover among our correctional officers. When staff members leave we are required to fill their posts, which we do through the use of overtime. The problem continues during recruitment for replacements and during the three-week training course to which all recruits are sent. When you add the two-to-four-week delay in filling positions to the three-week training period, you can readily see that a considerable amount of overtime might be involved. Turnover is perhaps our most critical problem. Previously I sent you a detailed commentary on our turnover experience. Over the past several years, I have told everyone willing to listen that there is a strong relationship between turnover in a correctional institution and overtime expenditures.

First of all, entry-level correctional officers are poorly paid, and, as I've told the county commissioners at every budget hearing, that is certainly true in our case. Second, this is a very difficult profession, and prison personnel are continually required to work at very high stress levels. Finally, we enjoy very little public esteem, and the working conditions can on occasion be very unpleasant. Small wonder that there is high turnover not only in our prisons but in prisons all across this country. When a staff member leaves, the need to fill the post continues. Unless the prison board tells me that it does not want me to fill vacant posts, I will continue to do so, and I have no choice but to use overtime.

Hospital watches   Whenever an inmate requires inpatient treatment in a local hospital, I must provide the necessary security. Recently, two inmates were hospitalized. For each day of hospitalization, we provided two correctional officers per shift, three shifts per day, for a total of forty-eight hours of coverage. As you can see, the time mounts up rapidly. We have no fat in our shift complements; therefore, when a need like this arises, it must be covered with overtime.

Emergency situations   Whenever there is reason to believe that inmates might be planning an action that could endanger the security of the institution, I adopt an emergency plan that puts all supervisors on twelve-hour shifts. I do not place this institution on an emergency footing for any trivial or illusory cause. Those instances in which I have used emergency overtime have been fully justified, and I stand by my actions.

Sick leave   Our sick leave usage compares favorably with that of other county departments that enjoy less trying working conditions. Still, when a correctional officer calls in sick, his or her position must be filled, and it is usually filled by the use of overtime. We can't call in a replace-

ment on one hour's notice on the person's day off, upset his or her family life, and worsen a bad morale situation simply to cover an eight-hour shift. We feel that the use of overtime in these situations is the most sensible solution.

Workers' compensation   I have frequently remarked on this problem in the past. Today we are filling two posts that are vacant as a result of workers' compensation claims against the county. When an employee is injured on the job and a doctor certifies that he or she may not work, I have no choice but to utilize overtime to fill the post. I simply don't have any slack resources that would permit me to do otherwise.

Reserve duty   Under the laws of this state, all staff members who are members of bona fide military reserve units are authorized to take fifteen days of paid military leave annually. When they depart for their military training, their posts remain, and we are responsible for filling them. The problem is exacerbated by the tendency of both military leave and vacations to cluster in the summer months. Another aspect of military reserve duty also generates overtime. Our correctional officers are scheduled around the clock and frequently are scheduled to work on a weekend when they are expected to attend reserve drills. Under the policy adopted by the county commissioners, the reservists may take "no-pay" time and fulfill their reserve obligations. While the county saves their straight-time pay, I am forced to use overtime to fill their posts.

Vacations   We do make a concerted effort to schedule vacations so as not to result in overtime expenditures. Unfortunately, as a direct result of our lean staffing, on occasion we must resort to overtime to permit our correctional officers to enjoy the vacations they have earned.

Training programs   Compared to the standard advocated by national authorities, our training efforts are extremely modest. We provide equal employment opportunity training, particularly with respect to our female correctional officers, and some supervisory training. In addition, we provide training in interpersonal communication skills—training I regard as essential in an institution such as ours. Since our shift schedules contain no fat, personnel must be brought in for training on their days off, which, of course, results in overtime.

The major causes of our overtime expenditures are as noted above. I have brought these problems and their causes to the attention of the county commissioners at every budget hearing over the past nine years. Our staff utilization records and overtime documentation are available to anyone who wishes to review them. We have nothing to hide.

I don't mean to be flippant or discourteous, but frankly I'm no wizard. I cannot operate this institution without a reasonable overtime allocation any more than the Jews of antiquity could make bricks without straw. For you to insist that I do so strikes me as being every bit as unreasonable as was the order of the Pharaoh's overseer.

If you can provide specific suggestions regarding policies or methodologies that you feel will assist in overtime reduction without compromising safe and efficient operation of this institution, please be assured that we will be happy to work with you in implementing them. We are open to any thoughtful and constructive recommendations that you or your staff may have. In the meantime, you might consider funding a comprehensive study of our staffing needs, including the need for overtime, by a nationally recognized group specializing in the field of corrections.

cc: Members of the County Prison Board
     George S. Truly, County Administrator
     Frank Friendly, Personnel Director

Dexter read the memorandum twice, his feelings alternating between anger and frustration. He regarded Goodheart highly, knowing him to be a caring individual and a respected corrections professional. "But clearly," thought Dexter, "He's no administrator. I asked him for a detailed justification of his use of overtime and his plans to keep those expenditures to a minimum, and what did he do? He offered me a lesson in biblical history and tried to put the monkey on my back with that bit about 'any thoughtful and constructive recommendations' I might have—baloney!" Dexter noted that Goodheart had twice mentioned his accountability to the county prison board and had been ingracious enough to copy the prison board members on the memorandum. "That," thought Dexter sourly, "is just

a brazen example of saber rattling. Maybe he thinks that if he can broaden the controversy by bringing in the prison board, he can get me off his case. Not likely!" Still angry, he spun in his chair, picked up the mike of his recording machine, and dictated his reply.

Meanwhile, Jim Kirby, chair of the county commission, was enjoying his new role. He was no stranger to county government; he had been the minority commissioner for eight years under Republican administrations; but that, he felt, was essentially a "naysayer" role. Now, as chairman in a Democratic administration, he was in a position to take the lead on policy decisions, and he was enjoying it. He had founded a very successful business in the county and had called the shots there for more than thirty years. Although Kirby had often mused that government and business were much more different than alike—at least on paper—he relished his leadership role in the county.

Kirby prided himself on his capacity for work and made every effort to keep on top of things. He regretted that he had not read Goodheart's memorandum of April 5 before attending the monthly prison board meeting. He hated to be blindsided! The presiding judge of common pleas court, Harvey Strickland, who was also president of the prison board, had shown Kirby his copy of the memorandum as well as a copy of Dexter's memorandum of March 12, which had prompted Goodheart's reply. Strickland had been his usual amiable self, but Kirby knew from long experience that with him, you worried not about what he said but about what he left unsaid. The fact that Strickland had brought the memorandums with him to the meeting and his oblique references to "those in this life who are penny-wise and pound-foolish" convinced Kirby that trouble was brewing.

As soon as Kirby got back to his office, he called George Truly, the county administrator, and asked him to stop by. Truly was the perfect balance to Kirby. Kirby was "born to lead"—an activist by nature, full of ideas and restless energy and impatient with detail. Truly, on the other hand, was a "doer." A professional administrator with substantial background in local government, he disliked the publicity and pressure of policy leadership, preferring instead the satisfaction that came from making policies work and seeing that services were delivered. The two men understood each other and had developed an effective working relationship. Neither one worried about the line between policy and administration; each one understood the overlap between the two activities and freely advised the other about county problems.

As Truly walked through the doorway, Kirby asked him, "Are you familiar with Don Dexter's memo of March 12 and Charlie Goodheart's reply?"

Truly said that he was and that he had already spoken to Dexter about them but that he had been too late.

"What do you mean, too late?" Kirby asked. "This thing looks to me like it can still be salvaged."

"Then," Truly replied, "I guess you haven't seen Don's memorandum of April 7."

April 7
TO: Charles R. Goodheart, Director of
           Corrections
FROM: Donald D. Dexter, Finance Director
SUBJECT: Your Evasive Memorandum of April 5

In a sincere effort to implement the county commissioners' directive establishing a countywide cost containment program, I wrote to you on March 12. In my memorandum I asked you to provide me with a detailed justification for the current rate of overtime usage and your plans to keep such expenditures to an absolute minimum.

In reply, you gave me three pages of generalities and gratuitous comments. You're the prison expert, not me. If I had any good ideas on how you could run your operation more efficiently or economically, you can be sure I'd offer them. But as I see it, that's your job, not mine. My job is to see to the financial well-being of this county, and I can't do my job if I don't get cooperation. That's all I'm asking for—your cooperation in achieving the goals set for all of us by the county commissioners. Your knowledge of the Old Testament is doubtless better than mine, but I do know that the Pharaoh didn't pay overtime. As far as I am concerned, you can have all the straw you want, but cut down on the overtime.

cc: George S. Truly, County Administrator
      Frank Friendly, Personnel Director

The Decision Problem

After Kirby had finished reading Dexter's memo of April 7, he sighed wearily, laid it aside, looked up at Truly, and said, "I see what you mean. Any suggestions?"

Truly was a career administrator who had spent twenty-two years in a series of increasingly demanding city management jobs before being recruited by Kirby to serve as Franklin County administrator. He had been given carte blanche in the recruitment of his administrative staff, and he had picked, among others, Don Dexter. Dexter was extremely bright; he had been the controller for a large manufacturing firm in the county—quite an accomplishment for a man who was not yet thirty. "But," Truly reflected, "he's never swum in political waters before, and there's no question that he's in over his head."

As the two men reviewed the situation, they tried to define the problem specifically, to identify possible courses of action, and to anticipate the probable outcomes of those alternatives.

It was evident that whatever they did, they had to do it quickly. Strickland could not yet have seen Dexter's memorandum of April 7. If he had, he would have had it with him at the meeting, and he would not have been so affable.

The cost containment program was important to Kirby and the other Democrat on the county commission. It was probably their best hope of reelection. If they exempted the county prison from the program for fear of what the prison board might do, the program could be weakened throughout the county. After all, why should the other departments conform if the prison wasn't expected to do its part?

Under the county code, the prison board, not the county commission, was responsible for approving all prison-related expenditures. The board, with its Republican majority, could give Goodheart a blank check if they wanted to, and the commissioners would be able to do nothing about it. "Well not exactly 'nothing,' " groused Kirby. "We could direct the county solicitor to sue the prison board, but since the president of the board is also the presiding judge, that's more of a theoretical than a practical remedy."

In fact, it was much more likely that the prison board would wind up suing the county commissioners. If the board alleged that an imminent threat to public safety was created by the refusal of the commissioners and their agents to fund the county prison adequately, it could bring an action *in mandamus.* In that event, the prison board would not be likely to limit the action to the question of prison overtime but would, in all likelihood, open a Pandora's box of problems. Goodheart had documented many of these problems in his memorandum of April 5, and that memo would probably be Exhibit A at a trial. Issues most likely to be litigated included the needs for adequate prison staffing levels, proactive strategies to combat the high rate of turnover, and higher salaries for correctional officers.

Kirby knew that if political warfare broke out, the Republicans would move quickly to seize the high ground. They would allege that the Democrats were jeopardizing the safety and tranquility of the community for the sake of a few paltry dollars. Kirby was too old a hand to suppose that arguments of efficiency and economy would carry any weight with the public in such a debate—especially if people were convinced that they were going to be murdered in their beds.

Since all the elected officials in the county were Republicans with the exception of Kirby and the other Democratic commissioner, they could really make things untenable. So far, the elected officials had been cooperating in the cost containment program. If, however, they chose to support the prison board in a confrontation with the commission, the cost containment program would be thoroughly scuttled.

"Don Dexter really put us in a box," remarked Kirby.

"Yes, but he's young and bright; he won't make the same mistake again," replied Truly.

"If the presiding judge gets him in his sights, he won't have the opportunity," observed Kirby solemnly.

"Funny thing," Kirby continued, "Don was right; that memorandum from Charlie was evasive, but Don should have known better than to say so. More than that, he shouldn't have written at all. In a situation like that, you go to see the guy. Writing is a very incomplete, very limited way to communicate. It's a lot easier to talk tough to your dictating machine than to an adversary. My rules have always been, never write a letter if you can avoid it, and never throw one away."

After almost an hour of discussion, the two men

had identified five alternative approaches to the problem. Unfortunately, none of them were without risk.

1. Exempt the prison from the cost containment program. Under this alternative, Kirby would contact Strickland informally and intimate that the commission would not be unduly concerned if the prison did not achieve its cost containment objectives. The justification offered would be that as a public safety and law enforcement agency, the prison ought not be held to the same standard of cost reduction as other agencies, lest public safety suffer. The main problem with this approach was that party loyalty was paramount in this county, and Strickland was certain to share this information with the other elected officials, especially the district attorney and the sheriff, who headed justice system agencies. Once the commissioners had yielded on the prison, it would be difficult for them to hold the line on other justice system agencies, and the cost containment program would be seriously jeopardized. The result could be that the majority commissioners would be branded as weak men of little resolve, and that could have serious spillover effects in other areas.

2. Fund an in-depth study of the prison by a nationally recognized group specializing in corrections. Since this was a solution proposed by the director of corrections, it would most likely gain the acceptance of the prison board. Apart from the cost of such a study, which could be considerable, its recommendations were not likely to be favorable to the county administration. Through long experience, Kirby and Truly had come to believe that special interest groups of whatever ilk rarely supported anything antithetical to their special interest. Worse yet, a comprehensive study might only document and verify the types of complaints that the director of corrections had been making for years. It was one thing to ignore his complaints; it would be something quite different were the county administration to ignore the studied recommendations of nationally recognized experts.

3. Conduct an in-house study of the need for

prison overtime. This alternative appeared to have a good deal to recommend it. The county had a small management analysis team that reported directly to the county administrator. The supervisor of the team was a thoroughly honest and objective career professional who had been a founding member of the Association of Management Analysts in State and Local Government (MASLIG) and was well respected both within the county and beyond its borders. The problem, of course, was one of credibility. Despite his excellent reputation, his objectivity might be questioned in the partisan political climate that prevailed in Franklin County. Moreover, the prison board might refuse to approve such a study. A study could be undertaken without the prison board's concurrence, as a prerogative of the majority commissioners, but in that event, the prison board might view the study as flawed.

4. Attempt to find an "honest broker" to conduct a study of prison overtime. "Honest" in this context meant someone who would be considered honest in the eyes of the prison board—someone they would perceive as having no ax to grind. Ideally, this person should already work for the county and be known by, and enjoy the confidence of, the prison board. But who? The downside of this alternative, assuming that such a person could be found, was that the "honest broker" might not be all that honest. Should such a person be selected with the prison board's concurrence, that person might very well take the prison board's side, to the considerable embarrassment of the county administration.

5. Invite Strickland to undertake the overtime study with members of his staff. The court's administrative staff included several career professionals in court administration who were graduates of the Institute for Court Management. They were undoubtedly capable of conducting the study, and Strickland and the prison board, which he clearly dominated, would certainly find them acceptable. The question, again, was one of objectivity. Truly favored this alternative, arguing that if, as he believed, they were really professionals, they would be objective. Kirby's response was insightful: "I don't recall book and verse, but somewhere in the scripture it is written, 'Whose bread I eat, his song I sing,' and those fellows eat court bread."

What really was needed was a dispassionate review of prison overtime usage, the development of sound recommendations that would reduce overtime expenses without endangering the public, and an appraisal of the adequacy of the current budgetary allocation for prison overtime. This last point was particularly important. Goodheart continually reminded the prison board that his overtime request had been cut arbitrarily by the finance department without consultation or even explanation. True, there were other important questions that the study could appropriately consider, such as the adequacy of entry-level salaries for correctional officers and the appropriateness of current staffing levels. But solutions to both of these problems would be likely to cost the county more money. Given a choice, Kirby would prefer to postpone consideration of all problems that might result in increased cost to the county until after the next election.

Fortunately, the collective bargaining agreement with the local union that represented the correctional officers was due to expire in September. The study would certainly be completed well before then, and any recommendations requiring work-rule changes could be negotiated as part of the contract settlement.

Kirby turned to Truly and said, "George, give this some thought—and quickly! See what you can come up with."

Truly knew he had to work fast to answer two questions: (1) Which of the alternatives should be recommended? and (2) If a study were to be undertaken, what kind of person should be given the assignment?

The Aftermath

Truly's recommendation was a combination of alternatives 3, 4, and 5. He saw no reason to exempt the prison from measures that applied to all other parts of the county government, and he believed that the only way to obtain data for an objective approach to the issue was to commission a study, preferably by an "honest broker." After considering and rejecting several possibilities, Truly recommended that a study be conducted by a team to be headed by Geraldine Eager, administrative assistant to the minority commissioner. Eager was the daughter of the county chair of the Republican party. All of the Republican majority members of the prison board had known her since she was an infant, and all were beholden to her father. Eager had just completed her work for an M.P.A. degree and was looking forward to a career as a professional local government manager. She had interned in Truly's office, and he had established a mentoring relationship with her. She was relatively inexperienced, but that problem could be overcome by having the county's management analysis staff assist her in the study.

Kirby suggested the arrangement to minority commissioner Joe Finley, Eager's boss. He felt reasonably certain that Finley would jump at the idea. Kirby knew that Finley had promised Eager's father to give Eager responsible work and that Finley had thus far been unable to deliver on that promise. Kirby also knew from his own experience that in the commission form of government, minority commissioners, themselves, have little challenging and responsible work to do.

Finley agreed to propose the arrangement to the prison board. The board concurred in the study plan, imposing the condition at Strickland's suggestion that a member of the court administrative staff be on the study team.

The study team reviewed finance department and prison budget files, central payroll records, prison overtime expenditure reports, staffing plans, and shift staffing schedules. By using several different methods of calculating overtime budget estimates, the team determined that a reasonable overtime budget request from the prison would have ranged between $294,200 and $348,600, well below the $434,400

requested by the prison but in line with the finance department's allocation of $319,000.

The study team also found that the prison's estimate of overtime needed for holidays had been overstated by nearly $100,000 and that overtime costs had been inflated because higher-paid employees were working appreciably more overtime than their lower-paid co-workers. Finally, the study team found that 12.5 percent of all nonholiday overtime was occasioned by turnover, thus supporting Goodheart's contention that turnover was a serious problem.

In discussing possible solutions, the team came up with the concept of a correctional officer pool. Under this plan, twenty more correctional officers than were authorized in the budget would be recruited and sent to the three-week training program. On completing their training, they would be placed in a pool from which permanent appointments would be made as vacancies occurred. In the meantime, they would be on call to cover overtime assignments, but at a straight-time rate. In effect, until they achieved their permanent appointments, they would be per diem employees. The start-up costs of the pool were estimated at $16,152, and approval by the collective bargaining agent for the correctional officers was required, since this was a fundamental change in work rules.

The politics of the study worked out as well as the analysis did. The prison board accepted the study and endorsed the the pool concept, which was subsequently implemented. Kirby gave the prison board credit for the $50,000 in annual overtime savings realized by the pool arrangement. Potentially embarrassing aspects of the study were downplayed from the outset. The $100,000 overstatement of holiday overtime requirements was shrugged off by Goodheart with the quip that since he was sure that Dexter was going to cut his overtime request, it was just good budgetary strategy to build in a safety margin. This time, Dexter did not dispute his explanation.

Chapter 12 Review Questions

1. Why does Irene Rubin at the outset argue that "public budgets are not merely technical managerial documents; they are also intrinsically and irreducibly political"? Do you agree or disagree based on your reading of the case "County Prison Overtime"?

2. In two or three sentences, summarize how Rubin defines "a public budget." How does it differ from the budget of a private firm?

3. Why does Rubin stress that the chief tension in public budgeting is between public accountability and public acceptability? What does she mean by those terms? Was that tension illustrated in the case study, "County Prison Overtime?"

4. Who are the major participants that Rubin believes are most involved in the public budgetary processes? What are they trying to achieve? Who was involved in the "County Prison Overtime" case and what were the positions they took as well as the strategies they used to achieve their goals?

5. List the five basic "budgetary decision-making clusters" that Rubin's essay outlines. Who are the key actors involved in each cluster? The special pattern of politics in each cluster? Did "County Prison Overtime" represent any one cluster? Does it "fit" Rubin's "cluster model" and if so, why? Or, why not?

6. What are the essential differences between microbudgeting and macrobudgeting according to Rubin? Why is it important to distinguish between the two? Did the case, "County Prison Overtime," represent either or both?

Key Terms

bureau chiefs

chief executive officers

power differentials

separation of payer and decider

open environment

budget constraints

reform orientation

incrementalist view

revenue cluster

expenditure cluster

balance cluster

budget implementation

microbudgeting

macrobudgeting

legal environment

intergovernmental grant structure

individual strategies

budget outcomes

fiscal year

policy choices

Suggestions for Further Reading

An excellent way to increase your understanding of budgets is to obtain a current city, county, state, or federal budget (usually the summary document provides all the important information) and read it carefully. Most summaries are written so that the layperson can understand their major contents and proposals. Also, now that public budgets are frequently the subjects of front-page headlines, read the major news coverage devoted to them, particularly in leading newspapers like the *New York Times, Washington Post, Christian Science Monitor, Los Angeles Times, St. Louis Post Dispatch,* and *Wall Street Journal* as well as in news magazines like *Time, The Economist,* and *Newsweek.* The best up-to-date, scholarly survey of budgetary subjects is found in a thoughtfully edited journal, *Public Budgeting and Finance.* Each issue contains insightful articles by some of the leading experts in the field. Also do not neglect studying current issues of the *Public Administration Review* or *Governing,* as well as the annual volumes of *Setting National Priorities* published by the Brookings Institution in Washington, D.C.

Although they become dated quickly, introductory texts also offer a useful overview. For the best recent ones, see Robert D. Lee, Jr., and Ronald W.

Johnson, *Public Budgeting Systems,* 6th ed. (Gaithesburg: Aspen Publishing, 1998); Donald Axelrod, *Budgeting for Modern Government,* 2d ed. (New York: St. Martin's Press, 1995); Irene S. Rubin, *The Politics of Public Budgeting* (Chatham, N.J.: Chatham House, 1990); Albert C. Hyde, *Government Budgeting: Theory, Process, Politics,* 2d ed. (Pacific Grove, Calif.: Brooks/Cole, 1992); Don A. Cozzetto, Mary G. Kweit, and Robert W. Kweit, *Public Budgeting* (New York: Longman, 1995); John L. Mikeskill, *Fiscal Administration* (Pacific Grove, Calif.: Brooks/Cole, 1995); and James J. Gosling, *Budgetary Politics in American Government,* 2d ed. (New York: Gasland, 1997). For an outstanding historic collection of several of the best essays written on public budgeting, see Allen Schick, *Perspectives on Budgeting,* Revised Edition (Washington, D.C.: American Society for Public Administration, 1987). A handy, free guidebook that explains the difficult and arcane jargon of budgeting is *A Glossary of Terms Used in the Federal Budget Process* (Washington, D.C.: General Accounting Office, 1977). For a useful handbook of synthesizing our knowledge on various aspects of budgeting, see Allen Schick, *The Capacity to Budget* (Washington, D.C.: Urban Institute, 1990).

Undoubtedly, a profound impact on federal budgetary practices was made by the enactment of the 1974 Congressional Budget Reform Act, which is examined in several scholarly books, including Allen Schick, *Congress and Money* (Washington, D.C.: The Urban Institute, 1980); Dennis S. Ippolito, *Congressional Spending* (Ithaca, N.Y.: Cornell University Press, 1981); Lance T. LeLoup, *The Fiscal Congress* (Westport, Conn.: Greenwood Press, 1980); Rudolph G. Penner, ed., *The Congressional Budget Process After Five Years* (Washington, D.C.: American Enterprise Institute, 1981); and James P. Pfiffner, *The President, the Budget, and Congress* (Boulder, Colo.: Westview Press, 1979). For two thoughtful case studies of federal budgetary politics, read Paul Light, *Artful Work: The Politics of Social Security Reform* (New York: Random House, 1985); and Irene S. Rubin,

Shrinking the Federal Government (New York: Longman, 1985); and for an excellent look at where we are with the application of various budgetary systems, see George W. Downs and Patrick D. Larkey, *The Search for Government Efficiency* (New York: Random House, 1986), especially Chapters 4 and 5; and Roy T. Meyers, *Strategic Budgeting* (Ann Arbor: University of Michigan Press, 1997); as well as two insightful essays in the *Public Administration Review* 44 (March/April 1984): Hardy Wickwar, "Budgets One and Many," pp. 99–102, and Naomi Caiden, "The New Rules of the Federal Budget Game," pp. 109–117.

For practical, "how-to" books on budgeting, refer to Edward A. Leham, *Simplified Government Budgeting* (Chicago, Ill.: Municipal Finance Officers Association, 1981); Richard J. Stillman II, *Results-oriented Budgeting for Local Public Managers* (Columbia, S.C.: Institute of Governmental Research, University of South Carolina, 1982); Garasimos A. Gianakis and Clifford P. McCue, *Local Government Budgeting: A Managerial Approach*, (Westport, Conn.: Praeger, 1999); and Dall W. Forsythe, *Memos to the Governor* (Washington, D.C.: Georgetown, 1997). Part five of James L. Perry, ed., *Handbook of Public Administration*, 2d ed. (San Francisco: Jossey-Bass, 1996), offers several applied essays on public budgeting.

A remarkable inside look at modern federal budgeting is William Greider, *The Education of David Stockman and Other Americans* (New York: Dutton, 1981). Also read David Stockman's autobiography, *The Triumph of Politics: The Inside Story of the Reagan Revolution* (New York: Harper & Row, 1986).

Finally, three recently published handbooks by Marcel Dekker are also worth consulting: *Handbook of Public Finance*, (NY: 1998) edited by Fred Thompson and Mark T. Green; *Handbook of Debt Management*, (NY: 1996) edited by Gerald J. Miller, and *Public Budgeting and Finance*, 4th ed., (NY: 1999) by Robert T. Golembiewski and Jack Rabin.

CHAPTER 13

Implementation: The Concept of an Ambiguity-Conflict Model

As implementation research evolved, two schools of thought developed as to the most effective method for studying and describing implementation: top-down and bottom-up. Top-down theorists see policy designers as central actors and concentrate their attention on factors that can be manipulated at the central level. Bottom-up theorists emphasize target groups and service deliverers, arguing policy really is made at the local level. Most reviewers now agree that some convergence of these two perspectives . . . is necessary for the field to develop.

Richard E. Matland

READING 13

Introduction

From the very beginning of its conscious development as a field of study, public administration has stressed the importance of "good," "correct," "timely," and "efficient" execution of public objectives. Sound implementation was and perhaps still is "the bottom line" of what the administrative enterprise is all about. As Woodrow Wilson wrote in "The Study of Administration," the first American essay on public administration in 1887, "The broad plans of government action are not administration; the detailed execution of such plans is administration."[1]

Although "detailed execution" may well have always been the central preoccupation of public administrators, the last two decades have witnessed an impressive emergence and growth of scholarship directed specifically at exploring this subject. Indeed, by the 1980s implementation scholarship had become a distinct and separate subfield of public administration, political science, and policy studies. Implementation scholarship now boasts its own considerable array of professional journals and dedicated scholars, as well as sizable conferences oriented toward discussing various intellectual viewpoints and new methodologies related to this subject.

Much of the original impetus to develop a conscious subfield of study concerning

---

[1]Woodrow Wilson, "The Study of Administration," *Political Science Quarterly,* 2 (June 1887), p. 197.

implementation came from what many perceived as the apparent failure of the Great Society Programs. In the mid-1960s President Lyndon B. Johnson succeeded in pushing through Congress in a relatively short period a vast range of new types of social programs designed to alleviate major social problems (such as hunger, delinquency, poverty, unemployment, racial discrimination, and urban decay) as well as other prominent social concerns of the day and aimed at building "The Great Society." As Robert T. Nakamura and Frank Smallwood write, "It was not long before disillusionment began to set in as it became apparent that it might be easier to 'legitimize' social policy by passing ambiguous legislation than to carry out such policy by means of effective program implementation."[2]

By the late 1960s and early 1970s students of public affairs began questioning the value of passing so many laws creating new social programs without paying adequate attention to whether these laws were effectively implemented or carried out at all. Theodore Lowi, in his *The End of Liberalism* (1969), popularized this attack on the broad expansion of governmental activities, which, he argued, had eroded clear standards for administrative accountability and consequently had led to a crisis of public authority over the role and purposes of government in society. As public programs grew into more and more abstract and complex activities, according to Lowi, "it became more difficult to set precise legislative guidelines for execution of public policy."[3] It also opened up government programs to chaotic pluralistic competition. Lowi termed this phenomenon *interest group liberalism.* His solution was to return to a more simplified structure in which Congress and the president make precise laws and the courts formulate strict judicial standards to guide administrative actions, thereby reducing administrative discretion to a minimum. Hence, implementation would become little if any problem for administrators because their choices would be restricted and their direction from policy makers would be well defined and specific.

Meanwhile, other scholars were by then also busily pointing out that the Great Society Programs were not working as planned. Several case studies appeared at this time making much the same point—namely, that the Great Society Social Programs, for various reasons, were not or could not be effectively implemented—such as Martha Derthick's *New Towns In-Town*[4] and Daniel P. Moynihan's *Maximum Feasible Misunderstanding.*[5] Jeffrey Pressman and Aaron Wildavsky's *Implementation* (1973)[6] especially sparked much of the serious academic interest in this topic. Pressman and Wildavsky wrote what was essentially a case study of the Economic Development Administration's effort in the late 1960s to provide jobs for the "hard-core" unemployed in Oakland, California. Their case turned out to be a study in how not to get things done in government. At the end of their book they offered a prescriptive list of warnings about what should *not* be done to accomplish public policy objectives: "Implementation should not be divorced from policy"; "Designers of policy [should] consider

[2]Robert T. Nakamura and Frank Smallwood, *The Politics of Policy Implementation* (New York: St. Martin's Press, 1980), p. 11.

[3]Theodore J. Lowi, *The End of Liberalism* (New York: W. W. Norton, 1969), p. 127.

[4]Martha Derthick, *New Towns In-Town* (Washington, D.C.: Urban Institute, 1972).

[5]Daniel P. Moynihan, *Maximum Feasible Misunderstanding* (New York: Free Press, 1970).

[6]Jeffrey L. Pressman and Aaron B. Wildavsky, *Implementation* (Berkeley: University of California Press, 1973).

the direct means for achieving their ends"; "Continuity of leadership is important"; "Simplicity in policies is much to be desired"; and so on.

After the appearance of the Pressman and Wildavsky book, Edwin C. Hargrove of the Urban Institute called implementation "the missing link" in social theory, and soon an impressive array of new methodological approaches began to search for "the missing link."[7] Several of the more prominent implementation theories that have been put forward during the past three decades include the following:

Implementation as a linear process: Donald S. Van Meter and Carl E. Van Horn, in an essay entitled "The Policy Implementation Process: A Conceptual Framework," which appeared in *Administration and Society* (1975), argue that implementation involves a linear process composed of six variables that link policy with performance: standards and objectives; resources; interorganizational communications and enforcement activities; characteristics of the implementing agencies; economic, social, and political conditions; and the disposition of the implementers.[8] Presumably relationships or changes in any one of these inputs ultimately, according to the authors, can influence the successful performance of the policy objectives.

Implementation as politics of mutual adaptation: In a study of several federal programs by Milbrey McLaughlin in 1975 for the Rand Corporation, the writer concludes, "The amount of interest, commitment and support evidenced by the principal actors had a major influence on the prospects for success."[9] In other words, the political support from the top, according to McLaughlin, was the key to success or failure of program implementation.

Implementation as gamesmanship: Eugene Bardach's *Implementation Game* (1977), as the book's title indicates, sees the subject essentially as a "game," "where bargaining, persuasion, and maneuvering under conditions of uncertainty occur"[10] to exercise control of outcomes. For Bardach, implementation therefore involves all the arts of gamesmanship: learning the rules of the game, devising tactics and strategy, controlling the flow of communications, and dealing with crises and uncertain situations as they arise.

Implementation as conditions for effectively accomplishing objectives: Paul Sabatier and Daniel Mazmanian in "The Conditions of Effective Implementation: A Guide to Accomplishing Policy Objectives" (1979)[11] attempt to forecast what conditions promote or prevent policy implementation. They argue that the likelihood of implementation is enhanced by the existence of a favorable or "optimal" set of conditions. Conversely, in their view, implementation is impeded or altogether prevented when some or all of these conditions do not exist. Much of their

---

[7]Edwin C. Hargrove, *The Missing Link* (Washington, D.C.: Urban Institute, 1975).

[8]Donald S. Van Meter and Carl E. Van Horn, "The Policy Implementation Process: A Conceptual Framework," *Administration and Society,* 6, no. 4 (February 1975), p. 449.

[9]Milbrey McLaughlin, "Implementation as Mutual Adaptation," in Walter Williams and Richard Elmore (eds.), *Social Program Implementation* (New York: Academic Press, 1976), pp. 167–180.

[10]Eugene Bardach, *The Implementation Game* (Cambridge, Mass.: M.I.T. Press, 1977), p. 56.

[11]Paul Sabatier and Daniel Mazmanian, "The Conditions of Effective Implementation: A Guide to Accomplishing Policy Objectives," *Policy Analysis,* 5, no. 4 (Fall 1979), pp. 481–504.

essay is devoted to elaborating on the five conditions they consider necessary "that can go a long way toward assuring effective policy implementation if they are met."

Implementation as a circular policy leadership process: By comparison, Robert T. Nakamura and Frank Smallwood perceive implementation as a circular process intricately involved within the entire public policy-making process. In their book *The Politics of Policy Implementation* (1980), the authors argue, "Implementation is but one part of this [policy] process and is inextricably related to, and interdependent with, the other parts."[12] For Nakamura and Smallwood the critical element linking implementation to the rest of the policy process is leadership, which, in their words, is necessary "to coordinate activities in all three environments" (policy formulation, implementation, and evaluation) to achieve program goals.

Implementation as contingency theory: Ernest R. Alexander, by contrast, in "From Idea to Action," in *Administration and Society* (1985), develops a contingency model of policy implementation.[13] He views implementation as a complex "continuing interactive process," one that involves interactions with the environment, stimulus, policy, programs, and outcomes—all very much depending on the specific content, elements, and timing of these interactions.

Implementation as case analysis: As with the Pressman and Wildavsky book, case studies of a single implementation situation remain a popular approach to understanding this subject. They seek to draw specific "lessons" about right—or wrong—approaches to accomplishing public policies within a specialized policy field. Charles S. Bullock III and Charles M. Lamb's *Implementation of Civil Rights Policy* (1986) presents a highly sophisticated case analysis of this sort.[14] It analyzes in depth five cases in the civil rights field and draws conclusions about the significance of ten specific variables involving the effective implementation of civil rights policies. The authors conclude that five variables in particular are critical for successful policy implementation: federal involvement, specific agency standards, agency commitment, support from superiors, and favorable cost/benefit ratios.

Today the debate among scholars continues over what constitutes the appropriate conceptual framework to best comprehend the implementation of public policy. It remains hardly a settled matter, with theories and counter-theories being put forward at a brisk pace. Certainly, as yet, scholars have not agreed on any *one* model to explain public implementation processes or how models work in government. Nevertheless, it would be worthwhile to look closely at one of the more recent approaches to this topic to help clarify and understand this topic more thoroughly. The following current conceptual framework is presented by Richard E. Matland of the University of Houston. The author begins with "a dragnet review" of the vast implementation literature over the past three decades. He synthesizes and reconceptualizes the previous studies into two major

---

[12]Nakamura and Smallwood, *The Politics of Policy Implementation,* p. 21.

[13]Ernest R. Alexander, "From Idea to Action: Notes for a Contingency Theory of the Policy Implementation Process," *Administration and Society,* 16, no. 4 (February 1985), pp. 403–425.

[14]Charles S. Bullock III and Charles M. Lamb, *Implementation of Civil Rights Policy* (Monterey, Calif.: Brooks/Cole Publishing, 1986).

schools that he terms "top-down" and "bottom-up" approaches. His new model attempts to reconcile both approaches by offering another conceptual framework, one that builds upon prior thinking, or what he refers to as "The Ambiguity-Conflict Model." The author describes carefully how he develops his model, which essentially sees implementation processes, their success or failure, as dependent upon the degree of a policy's ambiguity as well as upon its degree of inherent conflict. His thinking leads, in turn, to four pardigms that he discusses in some detail as a way to clarify our contemporary understanding of implementation processes.

As you read this selection, keep the following questions in mind:

What assumptions does the author make in building his conceptual model of ambiguity-conflict for implementation? Did he assume, for example, that implementation activities take place in an open, democratic, and pluralistic society? One governed by laws? Or what? How do such assumptions shape the concept he puts forward?

What implications does this model have for practicing public administrators? Can they use it successfully to predict when conditions are "ripe" for implementing programs or *how* to implement programs? Indeed, how does Matland define "successful implementation"? Do you concur with him?

Is the author optimistic about the possibilities of predicting conditions to allow for successful implementation of public policies? Explain the "pros/cons" of his ambiguity/conflict model as a predictor of success.

Would this model have proved useful for the policy makers and administrators designing a program in any of the previous case studies you have read in this text, such as "Dumping $2.6 Million on Bakersfield"? If so, how? Or, why not?

Synthesizing the Implementation Literature: The Ambiguity-Conflict Model of Policy Implementation

RICHARD E. MATLAND

Several recent articles and books have reviewed the policy implementation literature, summarizing what has been learned and identifying obstacles standing in the way of further knowledge (O'Toole

Reprinted by permission of Transaction Publishers. "Synthesizing the Implementation Literature: The Ambiguity-Conflict Model of Policy Implementation," by Richard E. Matland. *Journal of Public Administration Research and Theory,* Part V (April 1995). Copyright © 1995 by Transaction Publishers; all rights reserved.

1986; Sabatier 1986; McLaughlin 1987; Van Horn 1987; Goggin et al. 1990). The extent of agreement is surprising; most of these authors paint a similar picture of past work and suggest similar paths for future work. These reviews emphasize the need for closure and coherence in our theoretical models. Perhaps most telling is O'Toole's (1986) review of more than one hundred implementation studies, in which he finds these studies referring to over three hundred key variables. A literature with three hundred critical variables doesn't need more variables: It needs *structure*.

As implementation research evolved, two schools of thought developed as to the most effective method for studying and describing implementation: top-down and bottom-up. Top-down theorists see policy designers as the central actors and concentrate their attention on factors that can be manipulated at the central level. Bottom-up theorists emphasize target groups and service deliverers, arguing policy really is made at the local level. Most reviewers now agree that some convergence of these two perspectives, tying the macrolevel variables of the top-down models to the microlevel variables "bottom-uppers" consider, is necessary for the field to develop. This article reviews the two major implementation schools and previous attempts to synthesize the literature. The ambiguity-conflict model then is presented as an alternative model for reconciling the existing findings on implementation.

Top-down, Bottom-up, and Attempts to Combine Them

Top-down Models

Top-down models (Van Meter and Van Horn 1975; Mazmanian and Sabatier 1981; 1983; 1989) see implementation as concern with the degree to which the actions of implementing officials and target groups coincide with the goals embodied in an authoritative decision. Mazmanian and Sabatier (1983, 20) define implementation as "The carrying out of a basic policy decision, usually incorporated in a statute but which can also take the form of important executive orders or court decisions . . ." The starting point is the authoritative decision; as the name implies, centrally located actors are seen as most relevant to producing the desired effects.

In the most fully developed top-down model, Mazmanian and Sabatier (1989) present three general sets of factors (tractability of the problem, ability of statute to structure implementation, and nonstatutory variables affecting implementation) which they argue determine the probability of suc-

cessful implementation. These factors then are developed into a set of sixteen independent variables that are hypothesized to influence goal compliance. The complexity of their model points to one of the more striking problems and recurrent criticisms of implementation research—the lack of parsimony.

Top-downers have exhibited a strong desire to develop generalizable policy advice. This requires finding consistent, recognizable patterns in behavior across different policy areas. Belief that such patterns exist and the desire to give advice has given the top-down view a highly prescriptive bent and has led to a concentration on variables that can be manipulated at the central level. Common top-down advice is: Make policy goals clear and consistent (Van Meter and Van Horn 1975; Mazmanian and Sabatier 1983); minimize the number of actors (Pressman and Wildavsky 1973); limit the extent of change necessary (Van Meter and Van Horn 1975; Mazmanian and Sabatier 1983); and place implementation responsibility in an agency sympathetic with the policy's goals (Van Meter and Van Horn 1975; Sabatier 1986).

Top-downers meet three sets of criticisms. First, top-down models take the statutory language as their starting point. This fails to consider the significance of actions taken earlier in the policy-making process. Winter (1985 and 1986) notes that many implementation barriers are found in the initial stages of the policy-making process and to understand policy implementation these processes must be studied carefully. Nakamura and Smallwood (1980) argue that the policy-formation process gives implementers important cues about intensity of demands, and about the size, stability, and degree of consensus among those pushing for change. An analysis that takes policy as given and does not consider its past history might miss vital connections. By concentrating on the statutory language, top-downers may fail to consider broader public objectives. O'Toole (1989) argues that a top-down analysis of wastewater treatment would find that privately managed facilities are superior because they are built more quickly, they are less expensive to build, and they provide approximately the same quality of waste treatment as publicly owned facilities. When broader issues such as affirmative action, compliance with Davis-Bacon labor laws, use and development of innovative technology, and local government autonomy and accountability are considered, publicly owned and operated facilities score much higher.

Second, top-downers have been accused of seeing implementation as a purely administrative process and either ignoring the political aspects or trying to eliminate them (Berman 1978; Hoppe, van de Graaf, and van Dijk 1985; Baier, March, and Saetren 1986). For example, the call for clear, explicit, and consistent goals contradicts much of what is known about how legislation is passed. Passage of legislation often requires ambiguous language and contradictory goals to hold together a passing coalition. The top-down emphasis on clarity, rule promulgation, and monitoring brings to mind the Weberian bureaucrat making independent decisions based on merit and technical criteria, free from political influence. It is, however, rarely possible to separate politics from administration. Attempts to insulate an inherently political subject matter from politics do not necessarily lead to apolitical actions. They instead may lead directly to policy failure.

Finally, top-down models have been criticized for their exclusive emphasis on the statute framers as key actors. This criticism has two primary variants. One argues from a normative perspective that local service deliverers have expertise and knowledge of the true problems; therefore, they are in a better position to propose purposeful policy. Top-down models, however, see local actors as impediments to successful implementation, agents whose shirking behavior needs to be controlled. The second variant argues from a positive perspective that discretion for street-level bureaucrats is inevitably so great that it is simply unrealistic to expect policy designers to be able to control the actions of these agents. That service deliverers ultimately determine policy is a major tenet of bottom-up models.

Bottom-up Models

Bottom-uppers, such as Berman (1978 and 1980); Hjern and Porter (1981); Hjern (1982); Hjern and Hull (1982); Hull and Hjern (1987); and Lipsky

(1978) argue that a more realistic understanding of implementation can be gained by looking at a policy from the view of the target population and the service deliverers. Policy implementation occurs on two levels (Berman 1978). At the macroimplementation level, centrally located actors devise a government program; at the microimplementation level, local organizations react to the macrolevel plans, develop their own programs, and implement them. Berman argues that most implementation problems stem from the interaction of a policy with the microlevel institutional setting. Central planners only indirectly can influence microlevel factors. Therefore, there is wide variation in how the same national policy is implemented at the local level. Contextual factors within the implementing environment can completely dominate rules created at the top of the implementing pyramid, and policy designers will be unable to control the process. Under these conditions, according to the bottom-uppers, if local level implementers are not given the freedom to adapt the program to local conditions, it is likely to fail (Palumbo, Maynard-Moody, and Wright 1984).

Bottom-uppers argue that the goals, strategies, activities, and contacts of the actors involved in the microimplementation process must be understood in order to understand implementation. It is at the microlevel that policy directly affects people. The influence of policy on the action of street-level bureaucrats must be evaluated in order to predict that policy's effect (Weatherley and Lipsky 1977). Because implementation arises from the interaction of policy and setting, it is unrealistic to expect the development of a simple or single theory of implementation that is "context free" (Maynard-Moody, Musheno, and Palumbo 1990).

The most extensive empirical work within the bottom-up tradition has been that of Benny Hjern (1982) and his colleagues (Hjern and Hull 1985; Hull and Hjern 1987). Hjern's strategy is to study a policy problem, asking microlevel actors about their goals, activities, problems, and contacts. This technique enables Hjern to map a network that identifies the relevant implementation structure for a specific policy at the local, regional, and national levels, and allows him to evaluate the significance of government programs vis-à-vis other influences such as markets. It also enables him to see strategic coalitions as well as unintended effects of policy and the dynamic nature of policy implementation. Hjern finds that central initiatives are poorly adapted to local conditions. Program success depends in large part on the skills of individuals in the local implementation structure who can adapt policy to local conditions; it depends only to a limited degree on central activities.

While top-downers have a strong desire to present prescriptive advice, bottom-uppers have placed more emphasis on describing what factors have caused difficulty in reaching stated goals. The strongly inductive nature of this research combined with results finding most of the relevant factors varying from site to site has led to few explicit policy recommendations. The primary policy recommendation from researchers within this tradition is for a flexible strategy that allows for adaptation to local difficulties and contextual factors (Maynard-Moody, Musheno, and Palumbo 1990). Some researchers have suggested that policy changes should be consonant with the values of implementing agents (Berman 1978).

Two criticisms of bottom-up models appear with some consistency—one normative, one methodological. The normative criticism is that, in a democratic system, policy control should be exercised by actors whose power derives from their accountability to sovereign voters through their elected representatives. The authority of local service deliverers does not derive from this base of power. Decentralization should occur within a context of central control. Street-level bureaucrats *do* have great discretion in their interactions with clients. To proceed from this fact to theorize that because such flexibility exists it should serve as the basis for designing policy, however, is to turn the role of theory on its head (Linder and Peters 1987). It effectively equates description with prescription. Flexibility and autonomy might be appropriate when the goals of the policy formulators and implementers are the same, but if they differ greatly, flexibility and autonomy may lead to policies which result in lower performance on official goals. Classic organizational theory is rife with ex-

amples of agents subordinating the goals of their principals and concentrating on their own subgoals (March and Simon 1958; Merton 1957; Michels 1949; Selznick 1949).

The second criticism is that the bottom-up methodology overemphasizes the level of local autonomy. Hjern's methodology relies on perceptions; therefore, indirect effects and the effects actors are unconscious of are not registered. Variations in actions can be explained largely by local level differences, yet all actions may fall within a limited range where the borders are set by centrally determined policy. While central actors do not act in detail or intervene in specific cases, they can structure the goals and strategies of those participants who are active. The institutional structure, the available resources, and the access to an implementing arena may be determined centrally and substantially can affect policy outcomes. Sabatier (1986) notes that a bottom-up analysis of environmental regulations in the United States would find that central government authorities play only a limited role. Most suits are brought by environmental interest organizations on behalf of individuals. Yet the decision to give individuals standing and the right to sue for collective damages under class-action suits is a crucial factor that was decided by policy designers when they framed the policy. By giving these actors access, the central policy designers structured the actions that occurred later.

Combinations of the Two Perspectives: Previous Attempts

Limited number of attempts have been made to combine these two major perspectives and other perspectives on implementation. One group of researchers has proposed different ways of combining the two formats within the same model and another group has searched for conditions under which one approach is more appropriate than the other.

Elmore's concept of forward and backward mapping (1982 and 1985) is an early attempt to combine top-down and bottom-up perspectives. Elmore argues that policy designers should choose policy instruments based on the incentive structure of target groups. Forward mapping consists of stating precise policy objectives, elaborating detailed means-ends schemes, and specifying explicit outcome criteria by which to judge policy at each stage. Backward mapping consists of stating precisely the behavior to be changed at the lowest level, describing a set of operations that can insure the change, and repeating the procedure upwards by steps until the central level is reached. By using backward mapping, policy designers may find more appropriate tools than those initially chosen. This process insures consideration of the microimplementers' and target groups' interpretations of the policy problem and possible solutions.

Elmore's approach is a useful suggestion for policy designers; micro implementers' and target groups' views must be considered in planning an implementation strategy. On the other hand, it is not a theoretical model in the traditional sense. Sellitz, Wrightsman, and Cook (1976, 16) define theory as a "set of concepts plus the interrelationships that are assumed to exist among those concepts." The consequences that logically follow from the relationships posed in the theory should be testable hypotheses. Elmore's model has no predictions as to generalized behavior. No specific interrelationships are hypothesized; effectively there are no hypotheses to test. As a tool, Elmore's discussion is useful; as a theory, however, it lacks explanatory power.

Sabatier (1986; 1988; 1991; Sabatier and Pelkey 1987) has moved away from the top-down perspective, which he helped develop, and toward a combined perspective. He now argues that policy needs to be analyzed in cycles of more than ten years. The longer time allows for an opportunity to consider policy learning, a concept emphasized by Sabatier. Policies operate within parameters most easily identified by using a top-down approach. These parameters include socioeconomic conditions, legal instruments, and the basic government structure. These remain relatively stable over long periods of time. Within this structure, however, substantial actions occur. Sabatier argues that advocacy coalitions should be the main unit of analysis in the study of these actions. Advocacy coalitions are groups of policy advocates from differing organizations, both public and private, who share the same set of beliefs and goals.

These groups attempt to have their views of policy problems, solutions, and legitimate actors accepted. Sabatier urges the use of Hjern's networking methodology to develop a mapping of these advocacy coalitions.

Sabatier's proposal represents a legitimate method for studying public policy. When examining a broad policy area over a long period of time, however, the question of whether this is actually studying implementation becomes a relevant concern. Sabatier's definition of implementation does not appear to be about the same process. A policy field followed over many years can change so radically that it bears little resemblance to its initial form. If implementation research is to retain a meaningful definition, it should be tied to a specific policy rather than to all actions in a policy field.

Goggin et al. (1990) present a communications model of intergovernmental policy implementation that sees state implementers at the nexus of a series of communication channels. They describe three clusters of variables that affect state implementation: inducements and constraints from the top (the federal level), inducements and constraints from the bottom (state and local levels), and state-specific factors defined as decisional outcomes and state capacity. Elements of the two major models are considered by including signals from both the top and the bottom. The communication model also emphasizes that signals are perceived differently, distortions occur, and contextual conditions can affect the interpretation of signals.

Some authors prefer to discuss when a model is appropriately applied rather than to try to build a combined model. Dunshire (1978) and Saetren (1983) argue that the two perspectives should apply to different times in the implementation process. Top-down perspectives are more appropriate in the early planning stages, but a bottom-up view is more appropriate in later evaluation stages.

Berman (1980) argues that an implementation plan should be developed using either the top-down or bottom-up approach depending on a set of parameters that describes the policy context. He argues that these situational parameters are dimensions that the implementation designer cannot influence. They include scope of change, validity of technology, goal conflict, institutional setting, and environmental stability. Berman suggests that when change is incremental, technology is certain, environment is stable, goal conflict is low, and institutional setting is tightly coupled, an implementation plan should follow the tenets of the top-down model. He convincingly argues that when a viable solution already exists, efforts should be concentrated on making sure that solution is used. Therefore a top-down strategy is appropriate. Berman suggests further that major policy changes involving uncertain technology— with goal conflicts and an unstable and loosely coupled environment—should be built around a bottom-up framework. This argument is less convincing. Part of the confusion lies in the distinction between a descriptive and a prescriptive model. It virtually is certain that when major policy changes are implemented where technology is uncertain and goal conflict high, bargaining *necessarily* occurs and adjustments are made. As a description of the process, many factors emphasized in bottom-up models are relevant. A prescription that suggests these conditions should lead to the delegation of autonomy to microlevel implementers, however, makes implementation feasibility the sole criterion on which to evaluate implementation plans. Linder and Peters (1987) argue that while feasibility is an important consideration, other political, economic, or ethical criteria may lead to a desire for a more centrally directed policy. For example, instituting or expanding civil rights to a new sector of the populace is a policy that probably exhibits most of the conditions in which Berman recommends a bottom-up strategy. Nevertheless, a policy with strong central steering may be preferred as the most effective way to assure actions consistent with policy objectives. Berman argues that choosing a top-down strategy can lead to resistance, disregard, and pro forma compliance. Such dangers certainly do exist. Choosing a bottom-up strategy, however, may lead to cooptation and pursuit of individual goals that run contrary to the policy objectives, and these are often more objectionable.

In synthesizing the two implementation models

I have chosen to develop a model that explains when the two approaches are most appropriate rather than to develop a model that combines both simultaneously. I believe this is the most fruitful approach to synthesis for both theoreticians and practitioners. Until now, implementation studies have tended to present long lists of variables that may affect implementation. The conditions under which these variables are important and the reasons we should expect them to be important and the reasons we should expect them to be important have been ignored to a large degree or have been treated superficially. This has given us a field overflowing with diagrams and flow charts with a prodigious number of variables. Synthesis that merely combines ten variables considered by the top-downers with ten variables considered by the bottom-uppers, without exploring the theoretical relationship between them, is likely to exacerbate the problem. I have chosen, therefore, to concentrate on a more limited set of variables and to explore their theoretical implications more fully.

Structuring implementation research and bringing some closure to the topic is likely to be even more important for policy designers. While many factors may be relevant and more accurate decisions could be made if all factors were considered, even readily available information isn't considered when decisions are made (Feldman and March 1981). Therefore, while it is proper to remind policy designers to consider all relevant factors, a much greater service is rendered if policy designers are given an adequate description of the implementation process that directs them to the variables of greatest importance and to the factors on which to focus their scarce resources should their search processes be limited, as they inevitably are.

What Is Successful Implementation?

Before turning to model exposition, a proper definition of *successful implementation* should be discussed. Policy can be defined as the programmatic activities formulated in response to an authoritative decision. These activities are the policy designer's plans for carrying out the wishes expressed by a legitimating organization, be it a legislature, a judicial agent, or an executive body. The pivotal question is whether attention should be focused on fidelity to the designer's plan or on the general consequences of the implementation actions when determining success? Disagreements between top-down and bottom-up theorists have at their very base disagreements over this question. Top-down theorists desire to measure success in terms of specific outcomes tied directly to the statutes that are the source of a program. Bottom-up theorists prefer a much broader evaluation, in which a program leading to "positive effects" can be labeled a success (Palumbo, Maynard-Moody, and Wright 1984).

The failure to specify what is meant by *successful implementation* causes considerable confusion. Ingram and Schneider (1990) note several plausible definitions of successful implementation. Among these are: agencies comply with the directives of the statues; agencies are held accountable for reaching specific indicators of success; goals of the statute are achieved; local goals are achieved, or there is an improvement in the political climate around the program. In determining which of these definitions is appropriate, the decision hinges on whether the statutory designer's values should be accorded a normative value greater than those of other actors, especially local actors. If the policy designers' desires do have a superior value, then the bottom-uppers' measure of success is inappropriate. This assertion is grounded in democratic theory. Statutory designers derive their power by being elected or by receiving a mandate from duly elected officials. This mandate can be revoked through electoral disapproval by sovereign voters. The street-level bureaucrat has no such base of power. Clearly, discretionary power exists at the local level, but this power is based on the inability to control actions. Street-level bureaucrats do have legitimate claims to power based on their expertise, but this power claim does not have the same moral

quality as claims based on powers bestowed by a sovereign citizenry. It is therefore legitimate to measure implementation success in terms of its ability to execute faithfully the goals and means present in the statutory mandate.

This proposal quickly runs into difficulties, however, when specific policies are considered. Statutory mandates often are exceedingly vague. They do not incorporate specific goals and they fail to provide reasonable yardsticks with which to measure policy results. Broader evaluation standards need to be used when significant ambiguity exists regarding the specific goals of a policy. These can range over a broad set of plausible measures. For example, efficiency gains and economic growth may be used in one case, whereas enhanced support of the political system may be valid in another. Increased understanding and alleviation of local problems are two measures of success that frequently are likely to be relevant.

To recapitulate, when policy goals explicitly have been stated, then, based on democratic theory, the statutory designers' values have a superior value. In such instances the correct standard of implementation success is loyalty to the prescribed goals. When a policy does not have explicitly stated goals, the choice of a standard becomes more difficult, and more general societal norms and values come into play.

A Comprehensive Model of Implementation: Theoretical Bases

In reviewing the implementation literature it becomes apparent that top-downers and bottom-uppers choose to study different types of policies. Top-downers tend to choose relatively clear policies. Bottom-uppers study policies with greater uncertainty inherent in the policy. Because so many of the studies are single case studies, few consider how implementation varies when a different type of policy is considered. Building a more effective model of implementation requires a much more careful evaluation of a policy's characteristics. The ambiguity/conflict model presented below is a contingency model that attempts to provide this more comprehensive and coherent basis for understanding implementation.

Four implementation perspectives are developed in the ambiguity/conflict model, based on a policy's ambiguity and conflict level. Organizational theorists and decision-making scholars have invested substantial effort in showing how conflict and ambiguity affect decision making. The ambiguity/conflict model draws extensively on that work. Through analysis of a policy's level of ambiguity and conflict this model provides an analytical tool for identifying which of several differing models in the literature best describes the implementation process. Before considering the four perspectives individually, the attributes by which policies are to be differentiated—ambiguity and conflict—need to be described thoroughly.

Policy Conflict

Conflict plays a central role in distinguishing between decision-making models; it is just as relevant when distinguishing between descriptions of the implementation process. Both rational and bureaucratic politics models of decision making assume that individual actors are rationally self-interested. They differ, however, on the degree of goal congruence that exists. Rational models assume goals are agreed upon and therefore one can maximize individual or social welfare functions, subject to a set of situational constraints. The problem is defined as finding the one best way to attain an agreed-upon goal (Luce and Raiffa 1957; Raiffa 1970; Lave and March 1975). Bureaucratic politics models (Allison 1971; Halperin 1974), on the other hand, posit that a utility function cannot be written, because there is no agreed-upon set of goals. While the rational model defines decision making so that conflict does not exist, the bureaucratic politics model makes conflict its primary emphasis. When conflict exists actions change and actors resort to bargaining mechanisms such as side payments, log rolling, and oversight to reach agreements and hold coalitions together. Coercive methods of insuring compliance are used. Actions tend to be the results of a long bargaining process. The bargaining process does not lead to an agreement on goals, rather it focuses entirely on reaching an agreement on actions (means). Often the process culminates in no action, because actors are unable to reach agreement.

For conflict to exist there must be an interdependence of actors, an incompatibility of objectives, and a perceived zero-sum element to the interactions (Dahrendorf 1958). Policy conflict will exist when more than one organization sees a policy as directly relevant to its interests and when the organizations have incongruous views. Such differences can arise regarding either the professed goals of a policy or the programmatic activities that are planned to carry out a policy. Disputes over policy means can develop over jurisdictional issues or over the substance of the proposed means for reaching the goals. For example, pollution reduction may be an agreed-upon goal. Nevertheless, an engineer, an economist, and a lawyer may prefer very different means to carry out the agreed-upon policy. The intensity of conflict increases with an increase in incompatibility of concerns, and with an increase in the perceived stakes for each actor. The more important a decision is, the more aggressive behavior will be.

Many top-down authors have treated conflict as an endogenous variable that policy designers can influence and should minimize. Virtually all have emphasized the importance of delegating policy to a sympathetic agency. Placing a policy in an agency where it conflicts with existing policies and goals leads to few resources, little support, and almost certain failure. Top-downers also recommend scaling back a project to engender less opposition and limit interdependence. The hope is that by decreasing the conflict level the implementation process will move toward the rational decision-making model and away from the bureaucratic politics model. While top-downers have seen conflict as manipulable, bottom-uppers have argued that the policy's conflict level is not manipulable and is given, because of subject matter (Berman 1980).

Certain types of conflict are manipulable. It is

possible to make policies more palatable by limiting the changes they bring about, by means such as hold-harmless clauses, or by providing remunerative incentives for essential actors to join. On the other hand, there are clear limits to this. Some policies are inevitably controversial and it is not possible to adjust them to avoid conflict. Often a conflict is based on an incompatibility of values and it is not possible to placate the involved parties by providing resources or other side payments. The level of policy conflict has a number of important effects. Policy conflict directly affects the ease of access to the implementation process. At low levels of conflict access is relatively easy; at high levels of conflict barriers to entry are higher. Intensity also rises with conflict levels. The types of conflict resolution mechanisms also change: analytical methods such as persuasion or problem solving are most common at low levels of conflict and bargaining and coercion are most common at high levels of conflict.

Policy Ambiguity

Policy ambiguity in implementation arises from a number of sources but can be characterized broadly as falling into two categories: ambiguity of goals and ambiguity of means. In top-down models goal clarity is an important independent variable that directly affects policy success. Goal ambiguity is seen as leading to misunderstanding and uncertainty and therefore often is culpable in implementation failure. The position of top-downers is quite explicit—policies should be pushed in the direction of greater goal clarity.

This recommendation fails to consider the dysfunctional effects of clarity and the positive effects of ambiguity. In designing a policy, goal conflict and ambiguity often are negatively correlated. One of the ways to limit conflict is through ambiguity. The clearer goals are the more likely they are to lead to conflict. In a study of personnel information policy in the United States and the United Kingdom, Regan (1984) argues that considering implementation in the policy formulation phase led to the sacrifice of programmatic goals. As the policy became more explicit, existing actors be-

came aware of threats to their turf and acted to limit the scope and range of proposed policy changes to maintain existing patterns of bureaucratic power and structure. Under other conditions, ambiguity is often a prerequisite for getting new policies passed at the legitimation stage. Many legislative compromises depend on language sufficiently ambiguous that diverse actors can interpret the same act in different ways. This is a natural and inevitable result of the working of political process (Berman 1978; Baier, March, and Saetren 1986).

Ambiguity is not limited to goals; it also affects policy means. Ambiguity of means appears in many ways, perhaps most obviously in cases where the technology needed to reach a policy's goals does not exist. Policy means also are ambiguous when there are uncertainties about what roles various organizations are to play in the implementation process, or when a complex environment makes it difficult to know which tools to use, how to use them, and what the effects of their use will be.

There have been calls to avoid ambiguity in policy means by limiting policy to those areas with an understanding of how actions occur and those areas with known instrumental means to attain desired goals. If actions were thus limited, however, many important but difficult questions would remain unanswered. As Tukey (1962) has noted, "Far better an approximate answer to the *right* question, which is often very vague, than an exact answer to the wrong question, which can always be made precise." Finding an answer often requires a learning and experimenting process. The implementation process not only provides an opportunity to learn new methods, it also provides an opportunity to reach new goals (Offerdal 1984). Offerdal suggests implementation should be a phase where principles and visions as well as technological knowledge are tested.

While several top-down models recommend eliminating ambiguity, it is unclear whether policy ambiguity can be manipulated easily when designing policy. At times, ambiguity more appropriately is seen as a fixed parameter. Even when it is not completely fixed, it is likely to be resistant to substantial movement. This may be due to a fragile political coalition, but it also may be due to poor understanding of a problem. Especially when prescribing means, policy designers rightly may believe they lack the technical knowledge to produce a programmed implementation package.

Leaving aside the normative aspect of whether ambiguous policies should be enacted, it is sufficient to note that such policies *are* enacted. Politicians react to demand for action by producing action. They do not pause to consider the feasibility of policy implementation (Jones 1975). The system routinely produces policies with ambiguous goals and exceedingly ambiguous means (Lowi 1979). It is therefore reasonable to expect that public policy will have a wide range of ambiguity.

The degree of ambiguity inherent in a policy directly affects the implementation process in significant ways. It influences the ability of superiors to monitor activities, the likelihood that the policy is uniformly understood across the many implementation sites, the probability that local contextual factors play a significant role, and the degree to which relevant actors vary sharply across implementation sites.

A Comprehensive Implementation Model: Exposition of the Four Perspectives

In reviewing proposals for remedying implementation failure O'Toole (1986) found that the literature makes contradictory recommendations. I believe this occurs because the underlying antecedent characteristics of a policy are analyzed insufficiently. The factors that help implement policy under one set of conditions exacerbate already existing problems under another. Previous theoretical work has failed to identify the conditions under which policy recommendations will be effective. The conflict-ambiguity matrix presented in Exhibit 13.1 is an initial step toward sorting out various useful recommendations in the literature.

Each box in Exhibit 13.1 presents the type of

Exhibit 13.1   Ambiguity-Conflict Matrix: Policy Implementation Processes

	CONFLICT	
	Low	**High**
AMBIGUITY **Low**	*Administrative Implementation* Resources Example: Smallpox eradication	*Political Implementation* Power Example: Busing
High	*Experimental Implementation* Contextual Conditions Example: Headstart	*Symbolic Implementation* Coalition Strength Example: Community action agencies

implementation process, the central principle determining outcomes for this type of implementation, and an example of a policy that fits this category. The four cells in the conflict-ambiguity matrix are reviewed below. The following aspects are discussed for each perspective: the central principle describing the factor expected to have the greatest influence on the implementation outcome; a description of the implementation process with special emphasis on the implications of policy ambiguity and conflict; a discussion of the expected pitfalls; and the appropriateness of top-down or bottom-up approaches as a description of the process.

Administrative Implementation: Low Policy Ambiguity and Low Policy Conflict

In decision-making theory, choice opportunities where ambiguity and conflict are low provide the prerequisite conditions for a rational decision-making process. Goals are given and a technology (means) for solving the existing problem is known. Simon (1960) called decisions of this type "programmed decisions." The central principle in administrative implementation is *outcomes are determined by resources.* The desired outcome is virtually assured, given that *sufficient resources* are appropriated for the program.

The implementation process can be compared to a machine. At the top of the machine is a central authority. This authority has information, resources, and sanction capabilities to help enact the desired policy. Information flows from the top down. Implementation is ordered in a hierarchical manner with each underlying link receiving orders from the level above. The policy is spelled out explicitly at each level, and at each link in the chain actors have a clear idea of their responsibilities and tasks. The paradigm invoked is Weberian bureaucrats loyally carrying out their appointed duties.

Low levels of ambiguity mean it is clear which actors are to be active in implementation. As the actors are stable over time, they develop standard operating procedures to expedite their work. The transparency of the technology makes clear which resources are required, and resource procurement is built into the implementation process. The system therefore is relatively closed to outside influence. The isolation from environmental factors, along with the programmed nature of policy, results in relatively uniform outcomes at the microlevel across many settings.

Etzioni (1961) describes three types of mechanisms for gaining compliance from an actor: normative, coercive, and remunerative. A normative mechanism induces compliance through reference to a mutually held goal or to the legitimacy of the person requesting action (for example, a superior in a hierarchy). A coercive mechanism threatens sanctions for failing to comply with a request for action. A remunerative mechanism includes sufficient incentives, often additional resources, to make the desired course of action attractive to the agent. For administrative implementation, where levels of conflict are low, normative compliance mechanisms are generally sufficient. The orders given are perceived as legitimate, and there is little controversy that might lead to subversion. Re-

munerative mechanisms may be used, especially for pulling in outside resources, but most actions are induced through normative mechanisms. In those few cases where coercive mechanisms are needed, they can be expected to be effective since means are clear and easily monitored.

Since a technology for dealing with the problem exists, implementation activities are concerned primarily with getting the technology in place and functioning. They often consist of a set of rules that structures discretion so as to insure the preferred outcomes. Implementation failure occurs because of technical problems: the machine sputters. Problems occur because of misunderstanding, poor coordination, insufficient resources, insufficient time to use the correct technology, or lack of an effective monitoring strategy to control and sanction deviant behavior.

As messages pass through a communication network, they tend to get distorted. Even when the message appears clear to the sender, it may fail to be comprehended fully due to cognitive limitations of the receiver. In addition, cognitive dissonance may lead to selective perception. Pressman and Wildavsky (1973) calculate the probability of successful implementation as less than 50 percent if an order is followed with 90 percent accuracy after going through six hierarchical levels. If orders are comprehended with less than 90 percent accuracy, the probability of success will fall even faster.

This description of the implementation process closely parallels those found in traditional top-down approaches. Top-down models are descended from old public administration models, and the Wilsonian tradition, which defined administration as separate from politics, is effective in these cases. When a policy is characterized by a high degree of consensus and the means for reaching the policy goal are known, the implementation process becomes dominated by technocratic questions of compliance and follow-up. An example of such a policy is the World Health Organization's (WHO) program to eliminate smallpox. The means—mass vaccination and quarantine—and goals—eradication of smallpox—were clear. As the program developed, standard operating procedures were established to decrease discretion and increase efficiency. Success was determined largely by the level of resources available and the efficiency of the program developed to implement the policy. The difference between WHO's program to eradicate smallpox and the U.S. program to contain tuberculosis show strikingly the crucial role that resources play for administrative policies. In the case of smallpox, there were sufficient resources to continue active implementation until the disease was eliminated completely. In the case of tuberculosis, existing policy led to a decreasing number of cases and appeared to have effective control over tuberculosis into the early 1980s. At that time federal funding was cut off. The consequence of that action has been both a resurgence of tuberculosis in the 1990s and the appearance of a drug-resistant strain of tuberculosis.

Kelman (1984) describes how he developed an implementation plan for the Emergency Energy Assistance program. This program was to take effect in case of a new energy crisis. The policy theory was to allow market prices on energy, tax the windfall profits of energy companies, and recycle the money back to citizens via an emergency energy rebate. The rebate portion of the program was both clear and nonconflictual, and therefore it fit the administrative implementation paradigm. Nevertheless, difficulties existed with implementation. This program required substantial new capacity; virtually all adult citizens in the United States would need to be identified and to have checks mailed to them, all in a short time. There were many obstacles: finding an agency with the expertise and capacity to process tremendous numbers of cases quickly (i.e., a problem of sufficient resources); combining several different lists to develop one complete list of eligible recipients (coordination problems); and providing citizens access throughout the country to file complaints in case of oversight (resource problems). Kelman, using the implementation literature as a guide, revised the initial plans, which called for state agencies to provide lists of recipients. Noting the great difficulties involved in getting 150 different agencies to provide data on short notice, he devised a plan that gave full responsibility to the Internal Revenue Service (IRS) and based the identification

of recipients on IRS records. Placing the primary responsibility for the program with the IRS helped to minimize possible coordination problems and enabled policy designers to take advantage of IRS's capacity to train large numbers of employees quickly. IRS also had the necessary expertise to quickly process applications and to deal with consumer complaints. According to Kelman, IRS support was relatively easy to enlist because of its loyalty to the congressional mandate, a promise of resources, and an opportunity for the IRS to improve its image by giving people money rather than taking money away from them. Kelman's discussion is instructive: it indicates that the problems that arise under conditions of low ambiguity and low conflict are primarily technical, and it shows that, even for policies with low levels of conflict and ambiguity, an implementation plan can require substantial effort.

Political Implementation: Low Policy Ambiguity and High Policy Conflict

Low ambiguity and high conflict are typical of political models of decision making (Allison 1971; Halperin 1974; Elmore 1978). Actors have clearly defined goals, but dissension occurs because these clearly defined goals are incompatible. Equally conflictual battles can occur over means. It is often precisely in the designing of the implementation policy that conflicts develop and vigorous battles erupt. The central principle in political implementation is that *implementation outcomes are decided by power.* In some cases one actor or a coalition of actors have sufficient power to force their will on other participants. In other cases actors resort to bargaining to reach an agreement.

For policies of this type, compliance is not automatically forthcoming. While there is an explicit policy, essential resources are controlled by skeptical actors outside the implementing organization or by actors actively opposed to the proposed policy. Often both conditions exist. Such a system is more open to influences from the environment than from administrative implementation. The implementation program consists of securing the compliance of actors whose resources are vital to policy success and ensuring that the process is not thwarted by opponents of the policy. Since some of the actors whose cooperation is required may disagree with the policy goals, successful implementation depends on either having sufficient power to force one's will on the other participants or having sufficient resources to be able to bargain an agreement on means. Coercive and remunerative mechanisms will predominate.

Coercive mechanisms are most effective when the desired outcomes are easily monitored and the coercing principal controls a resource essential to the agent. This point is made convincingly by Durant (1984) in his study of two controversies involving the Tennessee Valley Authority (TVA) and the Environmental Protection Agency (EPA). He found that where the sanctions available to the EPA threatened the central mission of the TVA, compliance was quickly forthcoming. In the case where the controversy did not threaten the central mission of the TVA and the sanctions seemed less onerous, several years were spent arguing and litigating before the TVA finally complied.

The greater the implementer's authority to require agent action, the more likely it is that agents will comply with the principal's requests. Agents, however, often are not in a direct line relationship with the implementer, and coercive mechanisms fail to bring about compliance. Many actors have independent bases of power and can refuse to participate without having their own missions threatened. Even where there are relatively strong sanction opportunities (such as federal grants to states and local entities) states and municipalities exhibit a surprising degree of independence (Ingram 1977). Under these conditions, activities are directed toward reaching a negotiated agreement on actions. Agreement on goals is unnecessary, agreement on actions is sufficient. Many bargaining techniques commonly found in the legislative forum reappear. Disputes are resolved through side payments, logrolling, oversight, or ambiguity. Questions that cannot be resolved can be buried in ambiguous text and left for later resolution.

The opposing sides of a policy question previously may have done battle at the policy adoption stage. The shift of forum, however, can result in a

change in the balance of power. A legislative coalition often consists of actors whose support is fleeting. Supporters agree to vote for a policy on the basis of logrolling, in response to political pressure, or simply because it appears to be a sensible policy. Many of these supporters have little interest in the implementation stage. Even among those with an active interest the rewards from oversight are limited and likely to lead to only sporadic activities (Mayhew 1974; Ogul 1976). This venue shift can result in the nonimplementation of policy. This view is borne out by the regulation literature, which finds industries more successful at influencing the implementation phase than the legislative phase of policy (Stigler 1971; Joskow and Noll 1985).

The description of the policy process proposed by the newer top-down models comes closest to capturing the essence of the implementation process under these conditions. The traditional public administration models and the earliest top-down models took an administrative view of what is essentially a political problem; they failed to identify the sources of implementation barriers. The more sophisticated top-down models, which were developed partially in response to the failings of standard public administration teachings, emphasize political factors. Among the political factors built into Mazmanian and Sabatier's model (1989) are general public support, support from upper-level political leaders, resources and support from relevant constituency groups, and the commitment of implementing officials.

The bottom-up argument, that policies are decided at the microlevel, fails because it does not take account of the considerable forces and power that can be brought to bear upon an issue when it is unambiguously and explicitly formulated. School integration through busing is an example of a highly contentious yet unambiguous issue implemented by central authorities, with local officials looking on with little power to halt actions. While local authorities may disagree, sometimes vehemently, with the means that are used, the central authorities (i.e., the courts) have sufficient power to force their plan on the other participants. Low ambiguity insures that monitoring of compliance is relatively easy; attempts at subversion are likely to be caught and swiftly punished.

Experimental Implementation: High Policy Ambiguity and Low Policy Conflict

If a policy exhibits a high level of ambiguity and low level of conflict, outcomes will depend largely on which actors are active and most involved. The central principle driving this type of implementation is that ***contextual conditions dominate the process.*** Outcomes depend heavily on the resources and actors present in the microimplementing environment. These are likely to vary strongly from site to site, therefore broad variations in outcomes will occur. In decision-making terms, this type of implementation condition closely parallels a "garbage can" process with streams of actors, problems, solutions, and choice opportunities combining to produce outcomes that are hard to predict. The conditions that are required for a choice opportunity to develop into a garbage can are problematic preferences (ambiguous goals); uncertain technology (no predefined correct behavior); and fluid participation (actors vary over time) (Cohen, March, and Olsen 1972; March and Olsen 1976 and 1986). By definition, experimental implementation defines cases where preferences are problematic and technology is uncertain. The crucial element is: Which participants are active and what is their intensity of participation? Participants' level of activity in a choice situation depends on the intensity of their feelings, the number of other demands on their time, their physical proximity to the place where decisions are made, and a host of other variables.

As a result of policy ambiguity, the implemented program differs from site to site. The constellation of actors participating, the pressures on the actors, the perceptions of what the policy is, the available resources, and possible programmatic activities vary widely across policy settings. The lack of conflict is likely to open the arena for a large number of actors to participate and to provide those who have intense interests, or substantial slack re-

sources, with an opportunity to mold policy significantly. The opportunities are excellent for bureaucratic entrepreneurs to create policies to deal with local needs.

This process is more open to environmental influences than are other forms of implementation. Program mutations arise as different organizations implement different policies in different environments. These mutations can be seen as natural experiments, and it is important for policy designers to actively use them to enhance their knowledge of change processes within the policy area, with a strong emphasis on formative evaluations (Mohr 1988). For policies that have clear goals, it is possible to carry out and use summative evaluations that explicitly state whether the policy has reached its appointed goal. For policies with unclear goals, it is far more useful to use formative evaluations that describe the process and describe the way outcomes are arrived at without an explicit stamp of approval or disapproval.

Policies where both goals and means are unclear naturally fall into the category of experimental implementation. In addition, policies with clear and widely supported goals but with unclear means of implementation take on experimental characteristics. For many policies the goals are agreed upon and known, yet the means of reaching these goals is unknown. Implementing policies of this type can be technology-forcing and can lead to the development of entirely new capabilities. Nakamura and Smallwood (1980) point to the Clean Air Act of 1970 as a prime example of a case where the technology did not exist before the policy was passed; it developed quickly in response to the Act. Biomedical research is another example where technology doesn't exist but policy is widely supported. On the other hand, ambiguous policies can breed limited accountability and can lead to the creation of minifiefdoms with leaders pursuing their own interests. These may have little, if any, connection to the public interest.

The emphasis on seeing each iteration of a policy as an experiment is important when one evaluates possible pitfalls to the implementation process. More important than a *successful* outcome is one that produces learning. Policies operate in areas where there is insufficient knowledge to institute programmed implementation or of how elements in the policy environment are causally connected. Ambiguity should be seen as an opportunity to learn both new means and new goals. Two pitfalls must be avoided. First, the process should not be forced into an artificially constrained form. Programs demanding conformity are likely to meet with superficial compliance efforts from local implementers. In addition, demanding uniformity when processes are poorly understood robs us of vital information and limits the street-level bureaucrats' use of their knowledge as a resource. Since uniformity is to be discouraged, development of effective compliance monitoring mechanisms is of limited relevance. Second, the process requires a conscious realization that learning is the goal. If there are fifty sites with fifty differing results, but the information is neither gathered nor compared, then learning is likely to occur in a random pattern. Evaluation and feedback are vital components of effective learning.

The bottom-up description of the policy implementation process is superior to the top-down in describing conditions in this category. The emphasis on the opportunities available to local-level actors appears most appropriate. Tolerance for ambiguity is much greater in bottom-up than in top-down models. The top-down models emphasize command, control, and uniformity and fail to take into account the diversity inherent in much implementation that occurs.

Headstart is an excellent example of experimental implementation. It officially was approved in March 1965 and was to begin in the summer of 1965. The Office of Economic Opportunity (OEO) had barely three months to prepare, far too short a time to develop any type of comprehensive plan. The central administration had only the most general notion of what the goals of a preschool program for disadvantaged children should be. At the same time, Sargent Shriver III, the director of the OEO, had a serious problem in that he was unable to spend all of his budget. These factors combined to produce a situation in which virtually all pro-

posals for summer school programs were approved. There was a cornucopia of proposals, and Headstart meant many different things for its first several iterations. Over time, as information was gathered, the program became more structured, but at the start few attempts were made to steer it from the top. The meaning of Headstart in those early stages was dependent almost exclusively on which actors were involved at the microlevel and what resources they had at their disposal.

Symbolic Implementation: High Policy Ambiguity and High Policy Conflict

It may seem implausible that a policy can have high levels of ambiguity and yet be conflictual. As was noted earlier, many scholars suggest making a policy more ambiguous to diminish conflict. Nevertheless, policies do exist that appropriately are characterized as having both high levels of ambiguity and high levels of conflict. Policies that invoke highly salient symbols often produce high levels of conflict even when the policy is vague. Symbolic policies play an important role in confirming new goals, in reaffirming a commitment to old goals, or in emphasizing important values and principles (Olsen 1970). The high level of conflict is important, because it structures the way resolutions are developed. The high level of ambiguity results in outcomes that vary across sites. The central principle is that local level *coalitional strength* determines the outcome. The policy course is determined by the coalition of actors at the local level who control the available resources.

For policy with only a referential goal, differing perspectives will develop as to how to translate the abstract goal into instrumental actions. The inherent ambiguity leads to a proliferation of interpretations. Competition ensues over the correct "vision." Actors see their interests tied to a specific policy definition, and therefore similar competing coalitions are likely to form at differing sites. The strength of these actors will vary across the possible sites. Contextual conditions at the local level affect outcomes through their effect on coalition strength. Variations in coalition strength and dominant coalition make-up manifest themselves in differing programs in different localities. Outcomes are bounded and less differentiated than for cases of experimental implementation, because opposition coalitions are able to put effective limits on policy even when they cannot determine its content. Nevertheless, substantial variation is expected, with coalition strength at the local level being of central importance in determining the policy outcome.

Professions are likely to play an especially important role for symbolic policies. Professional training provides a strong set of norms as to legitimate activities and effective problem-solving actions. When faced with a vague referential goal and an ambiguous program of action, actors with professional training are likely to step in quickly with proposals grounded in their professions. Professions with competing claims over an area and different standard programs for attacking problems often form the core of competing coalitions. For example, a youth employment program may have an official goal of improving opportunities for disadvantaged youths. This policy has a referential goal that may include any of the following subgoals: decreased crime, increased educational opportunities, increased income, and provision of on-the-job training. Among actors with different training, there are substantially different proposals for implementing this policy. Their implementation battles are likely to be long and bitter.

Policies aimed at redistributing power or goods are perhaps the most obvious examples of programs that fall under this category. Policy goals often provide little information to a policy designer about how to proceed, yet the symbols are sufficient to create significant opposition before any plans are promulgated. The Community Action Agencies (CAA) established as part of the War on Poverty are a prime example of a symbolic policy. The stated goal of the CAA was to facilitate local citizenry empowerment. What this meant was unclear to virtually all participants. Despite great ambiguity, the CAA generated considerable controversy and animosity, often precisely because the policy was ambiguous and there was a fear of what the policy implied for existing relationships.

Symbolic implementation policies are conflict-ual, therefore they exhibit similarities to political implementation. Actors are intensely involved, and disagreements are resolved through coercion or bargaining; problem solving or persuasion are used to a limited degree only. Any actor's influence is tied to the strength of the coalition of which she is part. Symbolic implementation *differs* from political implementation in that coalitional strength at the microlevel, not at the macrolevel, determines the implementation outcome. This difference occurs because of a high ambiguity level. When a policy has a referent goal and ambiguous means it is solidly in the symbolic quadrant. As the ambiguity level decreases the policy moves upward, toward the political implementation quadrant. A decrease in ambiguity, either through explicit goals or a crystallization of discussion around a limited number of possible means, would provide central level actors an increased opportunity to assert some control and influence. When the policy is very clear, the macrolevel actors are able to exert considerable control, and this becomes a case of political implementation.

When dealing with cases of symbolic implementation, identifying the competing factions at the local level, along with the microlevel contextual factors that affect the strengths of the competing factions, is central to accurate explanations of policy outcomes. Neither the top-down nor bottom-up models appear entirely appropriate in describing the implementation process when there is substantial conflict and an ambiguous policy. The macroimplementers who are so prominent in the top-down models see their powers diminish. Policy ambiguity makes it difficult for the macroimplementers to monitor activities, and it is much more difficult to structure actions at the local level. Nevertheless, centrally located actors do constitute an important influence through provision of resources and incentives and through focusing attention on an issue area. Because of the higher level of conflict, the process is likely to be highly political, but it will be dominated by local actors. The bottom-uppers are correct in that the local actors are paramount, but their models do not emphasize the strongly political nature of the interactions.

Conclusion

I noted at the outset that the implementation literature suffers from a lack of theoretical structure. By drawing on the organizational theory literature, considering how ambiguity and conflict affect policy implementation, and combining these factors into the ambiguity/conflict model, this article provides a more theoretically grounded approach to implementation. By studying a policy's level of conflict and ambiguity, testable predictions can be made as to how the implementation process will unfold.

Traditional top-down models, based on the public administration tradition, present an accurate description of the implementation process when policy is clear and conflict is low. The recommendations found in this literature provide a useful set of heuristics in promulgating an implementation plan. Because there is a clear policy, macroimplementation planners wield considerable influence. Bottom-up models provide an accurate description of the implementation process when policy is ambiguous and conflict is low. The expectation is that conditions at the microimplementation level dominate and should be encouraged to vary. Under conditions identified as political implementation, where conflict is high and ambiguity is low, the newer top-down models—which emphasize the importance of structuring access and providing resources with a conscious concern for the heavily politicized atmosphere that attends such policies—provide an important starting point. When there is substantial conflict and an ambiguous policy, both models have some relevancy. Microlevel actors dominate the process, but actions are highly political as emphasized by top-down models.

One implicit concern underlying this model is that ambiguity should not be seen as a flaw in a policy. Despite its being blamed often for implementation failure, ambiguity can be useful. Ambiguity can ease agreement both at the legitimation and the formulation stage. It provides an opportunity to learn new methods, technologies, and goals. Widespread variation provides an abundance of knowledge which should be actively nurtured. Ambiguity should be viewed neither as an evil nor as a good.

It should be seen as a characteristic of a policy, without imbuing it with any normative value.

Finally, while I have argued that under certain conditions it is most appropriate to hold either a top-down or a bottom-up perspective, it is important to recognize that both schools contain kernels of truth relevant in any implementation situation. For example, central authorities inevitably influence policy implementation through decisions on funding and jurisdiction, even when policies are vague and conflict is low. It is also clear that policies are almost never self-executing. A microimplementation process occurs, even for purely technical questions with all the characteristics of administrative implementation. This model provides a description for the policy designer pondering where the most important problems are likely to lie. For the researcher it provides a map to those elements expected to most greatly influence policy outcomes.

References

Allison, Graham.
1971 *Essence of Decision: Explaining the Cuban Missile Crisis.* Boston, Mass.: Little, Brown.

Baier, Vicki; March, J.G.; and Saetren, H.
1986 "Implementation and Ambiguity." *Scandinavian Journal of Management Studies* 2:197–212.

Berman, Paul.
1978 "The Study of Macro- and Micro-Implementation." *Public Policy* 26:2:157–84.

1980 "Thinking about Programmed and Adaptive Implementation: Matching Strategies to Situations." In H. Ingram and D. Mann, eds. *Why Policies Succeed or Fail.* Beverly Hills, Calif.: Sage.

Cohen, Michael D.; March, James; and Olsen, Johan P.
1972 "A Garbage Can Model of Organizational Choice." *Administrative Science Quarterly* 17: 1–25.

Dahrendorf, Ralf.
1958 "Towards a Theory of Social Conflict." *Journal of Conflict Resolution* 2:2:170–83.

Dunshire, Andrew.
1978 *Implementation in a Bureaucracy.* Oxford: Martin Robertson.

Durant, Robert F.
1984 "EPA, TVA and Pollution Control: Implications for a Theory of Regulatory Policy Implementation." *Public Administration Review* 44:3:305–15.

Edelman, Murray S.
1964 *The Symbolic Use of Politics.* Champaign: University of Illinois Press.
1977 *Political Language: Words That Succeed and Policies That Fail.* New York: Academic Press.

Elmore, Richard F.
1978 "Organizational Models of Social Program Implementation." *Public Policy* 26:2: 185–226.
1982 "Backward Mapping: Implementation Research and Policy Decisions." In Walter L. Williams, ed. *Studying Implementation: Methodological and Administrative Issues.* Chatham, N.J.: Chatham Publishing.
1985 "Forward and Backward Mapping." In K. Hanf and T. Toonen, eds. *Policy Implementation in Federal and Unitary Systems.* Derdrecht: Martinus Nijhoff.

Etzioni, Amitai.
1961 *Complex Organizations: A Sociological Reader.* New York: Holt, Rinehart, and Winston.

Feldman, Martha S., and March, James G.
1981 "Information in Organizations as Signal and Symbols." *Administrative Science Quarterly* 26:171–86.

Goggin, Malcolm L.; Bowman, Ann; Lester, James P.; and O'Toole, Laurence J., Jr.
1990 *Implementation Theory and Practice: Toward a Third Generation.* Glenview, Ill.: Scott, Foresman/Little, Brown.

Gormley, William T., Jr.
1986 "Regulatory Issue Networks in a Federal System." *Polity* 17:2:595–620.

Halperin, Morten H.
1974 *Bureaucratic Politics and Foreign Policy.* Washington, D.C.: Brookings.

Hjern, Benny.
1982 "Implementation Research—The Link Gone Missing." *Journal of Public Policy* 2:3:301–08.

Hjern, Benny, and Hull, Chris.
1982 "Implementation Research as Empirical Constitutionalism." *European Journal of Political Research* 10:2:105–16.
1985 "Small Firm Employment Creation: An Assistance Structure Explanation." In K. Hanf and T. Toonen, eds. *Policy Implementation in Federal and Unitary Systems.* Dordrecht: Martinus Nijhoff.

Hjern, Benny, and Porter, David.
1981 "Implementation Structures: A New Unit of Administrative Analysis." *Organization Studies* 2:211–27.

Hoppe, Robert; van de Graaf, Henk; and van Dijk, Asje.
1985 "Implementation as Design Problem: Problem Tractability, Policy Theory, and Feasibility Testing." Paper presented at meeting of the International Political Science Association, Paris, July.

Hull, Chris, and Hjern, Benny.
1987 *Helping Small Firms Grow: An Implementation Approach.* London: Croom Helm.

Ingram, Helen.
1977 "Policy Implementation through Bargaining: Federal Grants in Aid." *Public Policy* 25:4:499–526.

Ingram, Helen, and Schneider, Anne.
1990 "Improving Implementation Through Framing Smarter Statutes." *Journal of Public Policy* 10:1:67–88.

Jones, Charles.
1975 *Clean Air: The Politics and Unpolitics of Air Pollution Control.* Pittsburgh: University of Pittsburgh Press.

Joskow, Paul L., and Noll, Roger C.
1985 "Regulation in Theory and Practice: An Overview." In G. Fromm, ed. *Studies in Public Regulation.* Cambridge, Mass.: MIT Press.

Kelman, Steven.
1984 "Using Implementation Research to Solve

Implementation Problems: The Case of Energy Emergency Assistance." *Journal of Policy Analysis and Management* 4:1:75–91.

Lave, Charles A., and March, James G.
1975 *An Introduction to Models in the Social Sciences.* New York: Harper & Row.

Linder, Stephen H., and Peters, B. Guy.
1987 "A Design Perspective on Policy Implementation: The Fallacies of Misplaced Prescription." *Policy Studies Review* 6:3:459–75.

Lipsky, Michael.
1978 "Standing the Study of Policy Implementation on Its Head." In Walter D. Burnham and Martha Weinberg, eds. *American Politics and Public Policy.* Cambridge, Mass.: MIT Press.

Lowi, Theodore J.
1979 *The End of Liberalism.* New York: Norton.

Luce, Duncan R., and Raiffa, Howard.
1957 *Games and Decisions.* New York: Wiley.

McLaughlin, Milbrey Wallin.
1987 "Learning From Experience: Lessons From Policy Implementation." *Educational Evaluation and Policy Analysis* 9:2:171–78.

March, James G., and Olsen, Johan P.
1976 *Ambiguity and Choice in Organizations.* Oslo: Universitetsforlaget.
1986 "Garbage Can Models of Decision Making in Organizations." In James G. March and Roger Weissinger-Baylon, eds. *Ambiguity and Command: Organizational Perspectives on Military Decision Making.* Cambridge, Mass.: Ballinger.

March, James G., and Simon, Herbert A.
1958 *Organizations.* New York: Wiley.

Mayhew, David R.
1974 *Congress: The Electoral Connection.* New Haven, Conn.: Yale University Press.

Maynard-Moody, Steven; Musheno, Michael; and Palumbo, Dennis.
1990 "Street-wise Social Policy: Resolving the Dilemma of Street-Level Influence and Successful Implementation." *Western Political Quarterly* 43:4:833–48.

Mazmanian, Daniel, and Sabatier, Paul A.
1983 *Implementation and Public Policy.* Glenview, Ill.: Scott, Foresman.

1989 *Implementation and Public Policy.* rev. ed. Latham, Md.: University Press of America.

Mazmanian, Daniel, and Sabatier, Paul A., eds.
1981 *Effective Policy Implementation.* Lexington, Mass.: Lexington Books.

Merton, Robert K.
1957 *Social Theory and Social Structure,* 2d ed. Glencoe, Ill.: Free Press.

Michels, Robert.
1949 *Political Parties.* Glencoe, Ill.: Free Press.

Mohr, Lawrence B.
1988 *Impact Analysis for Program Evaluation.* Chicago: Dorsey.

Nakamura, Robert T., and Smallwood, Frank.
1980 *The Politics of Policy Implementation.* New York: St. Martin's.

Offerdal, Audun.
1984 "Implementation and Politics, or: Whether It Is a Success or a Failure." (in Norwegian) *Statsviteren,* Nr. 2–3).

Ogul, Morris S.
1976 *Congress Oversees The Executive.* Pittsburgh: University of Pittsburgh Press.

Olsen, Johan P.
1970 "Local Budgeting—Decision-Making or Ritual Act?" *Scandinavian Political Studies* 5:85–118.

O'Toole, Laurence, Jr.
1986 "Policy Recommendations for Multi-Actor Implementation: An Assessment of the Field." *Journal of Public Policy* 6:2:181–210.
1989 "Goal Multiplicity in the Implementation Setting: Subtle Impacts and The Case of Waste-water Treatment Privatization." *Policy Studies Journal* 18:1:1–20.

Palumbo, Dennis J.; Maynard-Moody, Steven; and Wright, Paula.
1984 "Measuring Degrees of Successful Implementation." *Evaluation Review* 8:1:45–74.

Pressman, Jeffrey, and Wildavsky, Aaron.
1973 *Implementation.* Berkeley: University of California Press.

Raiffa, Howard.
1970 *Decision Analysis.* Reading, Mass.: Addison-Wesley.

Regan, Priscilla M.
1984 "Personal Information Policies in the United States and Britain: The Dilemma of Implementation Considerations." *Journal of Public Policy* 4:1:19–38.

Sabatier, Paul A.
1986 "Top-Down and Bottom-Up Approaches to Implementation Research: A Critical Analysis and Suggested Synthesis." *Journal of Public Policy* 6:1:21–48.

1988 "An Advocacy Coalition Framework of Policy Change and the Role of Policy-Oriented Learning Therein." *Policy Sciences* 21:3:129–68.

1991 "Towards Better Theories of the Policy Process." *PS: Political Science and Politics* 24:2:147–56.

Sabatier, Paul A., and Pelkey, Neil.
1987 "Incorporating Multiple Actors and Guidance Instruments into Models of Regulatory Policymaking: An Advocacy Coalition Framework." *Administration and Society* 19:2:236–63.

Saetren, Harald.
1983 *The Implementation of Public Policy.* (in Norwegian) Oslo: Universitetsforlaget.

Sellite, Claire; Wrightsman, Lawrence S.; and Cook, Stuart W.
1990 *Research Methods in Social Relations.* 3d ed. New York: Holt, Rinehart, and Winston.

Selznick, Philip.
1949 *TVA and the Grassroots.* Berkeley: University of California Press.

Simon, Herbert A.
1960 *The New Science of Management Decision.* New York: Harper.

Stigler, George.
1971 "The Economics of Regulation." *Bell Journal of Regulation* 2:3–21.

Tukey, John.
1962 "The Future of Data Analysis." *Annals of Mathematical Statistics* 33:1:13–14.

Van Horn, Carl E.
1987 "Applied Implementation Research." Paper presented at Midwest Political Science Association Meeting, Chicago.

Van Meter, Donald S., and Van Horn, Carl E.
1975 "The Policy Implementation Process: A Conceptual Framework." *Administration and Society* 6:4:445–88.

Weatherley, Richard, and Lipsky, Michael.
1977 "Street-Level Bureaucrats and Institutional Innovation: Implementing Special Education Reform." *Harvard Educational Review* 47:170–96.

Winter, Soeren.
1985 "Implementation Barriers." (in Danish) *Politica* 17:4:467–87.

1986 "How Policy-Making Affects Implementation: The Decentralization of the Danish Disablement Pension Administration." *Scandinavian Political Studies* 9:4:361–85.

☐ CASE STUDY 13

Introduction

As the foregoing essay by Richard E. Matland indicates, serious scholars are spilling a lot of ink over the problems of public sector implementation. Theories about bureaucratic implementation, as a consequence, now abound in books and journals. But from the standpoint of the practicing public administrator on the firing line, how does a new program get developed, find support, and ultimately become implemented? How are governmental objectives achieved in practice? What are successful methods used for implementation and what are the real-life problems administrators encounter in the implementation process? Does the theory of successful implementation "square" with its actual practice from the standpoint of the flesh-and-blood public administrator?

The following is an award-winning case for Innovations in American Government. "The Political Paradox of Rationing: The Case of the Oregon Health Plan," co-authored by Theodore Marmor, a professor of public policy specializing in health care at Yale's School of Management; Lawrence Jacobs, an associate political science professor at the University of Minnesota; and Jonathan Oberlander, an assistant professor of social medicine at the University of North Carolina, Chapel Hill's School of Medicine. In essence, they tell a success story of a remarkable *and* radical implementation of a statewide health care reform plan in Oregon, including how and why it was implemented and continues to remain popular, even though its rationale sounds draconian—that is, prioritized health care funding based upon systematic ranking of medical services rendered to the public. Ironically, as the authors point out, its appeal was largely technocratic, in that it "promised to develop a rational, scientific instrument—'a list'—to prioritize resources." But in fact, "systematic rationing simply has not arrived in Oregon" by means of cost-benefit analysis or any other rational methods for sorting out priority heath care needs, as opposed to less urgent medical requirements. Rather, the plan's successful implementation and contined expansion, as well as statewide public support derives from political rather than technical factors—hence the authors' title, "The Political Paradox of Rationing."

As you study this case, think about the following issues:

Why did Oregon first develop this innovative experiment in health care? What was its basic "new" approach?

What were the chief rationale(s) used to support this reform project and in what ways did it actually gain support?

What prompted its extension and forged the sources of its continued popularity?

Did the Oregon plan's implementation "square" with the ideas about implementation in the foregoing reading by Richard E. Matland? If not, on the basis of this case, how would you amend his model? Or, is Matland's model adequate as is? And if so, why?

The Political Paradox of Rationing: The Case of the Oregon Health Plan

LAWRENCE R. JACOBS
THEODORE MARMOR
JONATHAN OBERLANDER

The Oregon Health Plan has been widely heralded as an important innovation in medical care policy.

"The Political Paradox of Rationing: The Case of the Oregon Health Plan," by Lawrence R. Jacobs, Theodore Marmor, and Jonathan Oberlander," from May 1998 Innovations in American Government Taubman Center for State and Local Government, J.F.K. School of Government, Harvard University.

Throughout the past decade, Oregon's pioneering model of prioritizing funding for health care through systematic ranking of services has drawn national and international attention. Indeed, the Oregon story has seemed so compelling, and is by now so familiar, that it has attained, as Rudolf Klein recently noted, "nearly mythical status" in the health policy community.[1]

Oregon's claim to fame is its apparent willingness to confront head-on the hard choices, ethical dilemmas, and unavoidable trade-offs raised by the inflationary and technological pressures of modern medicine. In particular, the state sought to expand access to health insurance for uninsured Oregonians through unusual means. The price for expanded coverage was to be paid by rationing medical care services provided to the state's low-income Medicaid population. The rationing of services ostensibly rested on a complex technical analysis, underpinned by the emergent tools of cost-benefit analysis, as well as on an elaborate process of public participation in policymaking decisions. The Oregon approach represented a striking contrast to both the well-established practice of implicitly rationing medical care in the United States for the uninsured, and to the less visible resource allocation decisions made by health policymakers and professionals in other countries. Oregon's innovation, then, was its commitment to a process of explicit rationing informed by science and democracy.

However, from the beginning, the Oregon Health Plan (OHP) has ignited substantial controversy. What appeared as brave innovation to some analysts was viewed instead by others as dangerous and morally dubious experimentation. Positions on the Oregon Plan—whether pro or con—were formed early-on, during the heated debate over its enactment in the late 1980s. For most health policy observers, those positions still define today their understanding of rationing in Oregon.

That is unfortunate because, as we argue here, it turns out that the operation of the OHP has in several crucial respects very little to do with the debate over its enactment. The worst fears of Oregon's critics and the tough choices promised by its advocates have both failed to materialize. In this paper, we focus on the implementation and operation of medical care rationing in Oregon. Our purpose is to re-evaluate its status as a health policy innovation and analyze the heretofore overlooked political dynamics of the OHP. We argue that the Oregon plan does indeed represent a significant innovation in American health policy, but that the nature of its innovation has been widely misinterpreted.

The case proceeds in three sections. First, we review the original debate over rationing in Oregon and summarize how the operation of the OHP has defied expectations. Next, we explore how the politics of rationing has unfolded in Oregon from enactment to implementation of the OHP. Finally, we consider the character of Oregon's innovation and the lessons it holds more broadly for health care reform. Our analysis is based predominantly on field research in Oregon, including interviews with numerous government officials and participants in health care policy in the state, and other primary-source evidence such as state documents.

The Oregon Surprise

During the 1980s, Medicaid spending increased dramatically and the program consumed a growing share of state budgets. In response, many states lowered eligibility standards for Medicaid to an income level well below the federal poverty line (FPL) and cut coverage for optional enrollee categories, such as the medically needy. By the end of the decade, the health insurance program for poor Americans covered only 42% of the poor; in order to qualify for Medicaid, AFDC recipients typically needed to live on incomes only 50% of the FPL. In addition, those who were not "categorically eligible," such as low-income men and women without children, were excluded from Medicaid in most states. Eroding access to Medicaid added to the growing ranks of America's uninsured.

Oregon's reformers promised an alternative to the practice of denying coverage to the insufficiently poor. At a time when most states were ratcheting down income eligibility for medical assistance, Oregon proposed to extend Medicaid coverage to *all* persons living below the poverty line, regardless of traditional eligibility categories. Indeed, Oregon's ultimate aim was universal coverage; the expansion of Medicaid was to be followed by an employer mandate to cover all of Oregon's workers and their families. However, it was the state's proposed financing mechanism for Medicaid expansion that drew national attention. Put simply, Oregon intended to add more people to Medicaid by covering fewer services. Expanded coverage for the poor would be made affordable by offering recipients "a basic set of health benefits more limited than those currently offered by Medicaid . . . " Services would be explicitly prioritized according to their medical benefit and contribution to population health. The state legislature could not respond to funding short-falls, as it had done in the past and as was common practice in other states, by cutting eligibility for Medicaid. Instead, they would have to reduce program coverage of services according to guidelines established in the prioritization process. In other words, expanded access to health insurance for the poor was to be purchased by rationing medical care (though advocates preferred the less incendiary language of "prioritization and resource allocation."

In its requests for waivers from the Federal Government's Health Care Financing Administration (HCFA), Oregon argued its plan "would make the rationing of care—a phenomenon that already exists—more explicit and reasoned." The aim was to use the prioritization process to allocate money for Medicaid-covered services in a more sensible, systematic, and utilitarian manner—benefiting the greatest number of recipients possible within limited resources—than existing program policies and federal regulations allowed. Systematic prioritization would allow the state to identify less valuable and effective services where funding could be cut, thereby making coverage expansions affordable. Yet, in the eyes of the plan's advocates, rationing meant not simply limiting services, but also rationalizing health priorities.

Oregon's plan for rationing rested on an elaborate technical analysis that merged cost-benefit analysis and medical outcomes research with public preferences. A Health Services Commission was given the job of scientifically compiling clinical information from physicians, treatment cost and benefit data, and community values from the public in order to reduce over 10,000 services to a prioritized list that ranked 709 condition and treatment pairs. The Legislature's decision on how much to fund Medicaid literally "drew a line" in this list, with beneficiaries provided all services above the line and denied all services below it. Advocates of Oregon's Plan, such as senior administrator Jean Thorne, trumpeted the state's "painful and explicit choices" as necessary to "allow government to buy more health for the health care dollar."[2] Oregon justified its process to HCFA as "recognizing that society cannot afford to pay for everything that is medically possible."[3]

The OHP's case for denying coverage to low ranked services for Medicaid recipients touched off a firestorm of protest from outside the state. External critics assailed the plan as unfair for singling out the poor and, especially, women and children for rationing. Services for the most vulnerable would be cut, it was charged, while the benefits enjoyed by those more able to absorb reductions would be left intact. Sara Rosenbaum, an advocate for the Children's Defense Fund, alleged that the "Oregon Plan is not an experiment that can be justified legally, scientifically, programmatically, or ethically"; it is "only one more in a long series of proposals to reduce benefits to the very poor."[4] Critics' fears that the State was unjustly singling out the poor for rationing were fueled by reports that low-income Oregonians were underrepresented among attendees at community meetings to discuss the priorities of the OHP.[5]

Critics maintained that the OHP's promise to ration care was not only unfair, but also unnecessary. Eliminating administrative waste, squeezing drug companies and providers, and spending more represented, it was claimed, proven alternatives. Brookings Institution economist Joshua Weiner argued, for instance, that it was "troubling to ration medically effective procedures before we have truly exhausted other routes to cost containment."[6] Finally, the critics of the OHP criticized the methodology of Oregon's rationing plan. The attempt to conflate thousands of complex diagnoses and treatment scenarios into 709 homogenous categories appeared to defy human and organizational ability—and common sense. Even proponents of the inevitability of rationing, such as Henry Aaron, contended that the OHP was problematic. Oregon's approach of covering all services above and no services below the line regardless of an individual patient's medical condition or treatment prognosis meant that "patients who stood to benefit greatly were denied care, while others, who benefited slightly, received it."[7] The OHP confirmed, in the eyes of outside critics, the worst dangers of administrative science. Moral and professional judgment would be replaced by the detached logic of cost-benefit analysis and a flawed methodology.[8]

For many observers, this initial debate still defines, depending on one's perspective, either the serious limitations or courageous virtue of the OHP. Missed in the decade since controversy first enveloped the Oregon Plan is how the Plan has actually operated. The reality is that developments during the implementation of the OHP have been nearly opposite to what was feared by critics and hoped for by advocates.

The Myths and Reality of the Oregon Health Plan

Critics and defenders of the OHP from outside Oregon would both be surprised—as we were—by 4 developments during its operation. These developments reveal a persistent large gap between external understandings of the OHP and understandings of the plan within the state.

The Rationing That Never Was

The OHP has not funded expansion of Medicaid—as its initial rhetoric promised—by rationing services in order to generate savings. The process of setting priorities and drawing a "line," which attracted external attention, was never implemented as a formulaic mechanism for denying previously available care and cutting costs.

Some savings have been realized by limiting services and using managed care. But the Legislature has largely financed both the expansion of eligibility to Medicaid and the provision of subsidies to those above the poverty line through increased expenditures from general revenues and the imposition of a tobacco tax. In 1993, the initial expansion of Medicaid coverage was funded primarily through a 17% increase in state general funds, and a 10 cent cigarette tax. To a lesser extent, the OHP was also funded by pushing more Medicaid recipients into managed care plans. Eighty-seven percent of all Medicaid recipients are in managed care plans now as compared with 33% before enactment of the OHP. The increased reliance on managed care is estimated by administrators to account for 6% of savings off the total costs of the program.

In striking contrast to their initial claim that Medicaid expansion would be funded through "prioritization," OHP administrators estimate that the prioritized list has saved the state only 2% on total costs for the program over its first 5 years of operation. The failure to cut costs through "prioritization" as initially promised by reformers resulted from the rules imposed by the Federal government and HCFA, as well as the political dynamics within the state, which we discuss later. During the budget crisis in 1996, for instance, HCFA pared back the State's attempt to reduce the number of covered benefits, though it did fully approve Oregon's reduction the previous year.

Far from representing a radical new step towards systematic rationing of medical care, the OHP has been funded the old-fashioned and familiar way: raising revenues and contracting with managed care plans. Oregon, no doubt, was well positioned to use these familiar approaches because of its growing economy and its comparatively low level of expenditures on Medicaid—prior to the enactment of the OHP, Oregon ranked 46th among all states in spending on Medicaid as a proportion of the state budget.

Not only has rationing failed to produce significant cuts in services, but the process of drawing up the "list" actually generated, in many respects, a more generous package of benefits than what Medicaid or even the private sector had offered prior to the OHP's implementation: coverage for mental health, preventive, and dental services exceed the state average. Mental health services, for instance, which government and private insurers have resisted covering, are not only included but are subject to no limitations on the duration of care. HIV carriers—an especially expensive, vulnerable, and stigmatized set of patients—have found that legislators are unwilling to cut off their coverage, which extends far beyond basic services.[9] Despite the fears of national critics, the prioritization process did not produce a significant cost containment mechanism. Indeed, the list has ultimately functioned much more as a mechanism for defining a benefits package than as a rationing device.

In a further departure from the paradigm of strict rationing, doctors, hospitals, and private insurance companies delivering health services to OHP beneficiaries have not consistently "rationed" care, as anticipated in the original presentation of the Oregon reform. Doctors and hospitals regularly provide (and insurers pay for) services "below the line" that they consider appropriate or medically necessary.[10] One major health plan contracting with the state found that 5% of its total claims for OHP were actually "below the line." Below-the-line treatment is in fact inevitable. Many OHP patients are diagnosed not with one condition on the list, but with comorbidities that are difficult to treat separately. In addition, all diagnostic services are above the line and are often required to diagnose conditions that are not covered by the list. The bottom line is that the OHP's "list" has not been strictly enforced by medical providers, nor is it possible to do so.

The limited implementation of prioritization and external misunderstandings about what has transpired in Oregon is sharply illustrated by the case of transplantations. The OHP caught national attention in 1987 when the media zeroed-in on the death of a seven-year-old boy with leukemia—Coby Howard—who had been denied a bone marrow transplant. The Howard case seemed to confirm fears that rationing in Oregon would literally kill patients who were denied high-cost, low-benefit services.[11] Indeed, some transplants are an understandable target for rationing because they may require extremely high expenditures for a small number of individuals and deliver uncertain benefits. In fact, the main proponent of the OHP—Governor John Kitzhaber—targeted cuts in transplants during the initial debate as a means to generate the savings to expand access. Oregon, he argued, should "save as many people as we can, because we can't save them all."[12]

The rhetoric about rationing transplants during the debate over the enactment of the Oregon plan, however, stands in stark contrast to the reality during the operation of OHP. Coverage of transplants is now more generous under the OHP than under the previous Oregon Medicaid system or many commercial plans. In part, the expanded coverage resulted from new federal guidelines in the 1988 catastrophic health insurance legislation which required states to cover transplants for children. Yet the OHP exceeds the new federal requirements. The state voluntarily expanded coverage of transplants from children (as mandated by the federal government) to adults for a number of conditions, including bone marrow, heart, and lung transplants. Moreover, in contrast to the initial rhetoric, the state's internal process for ranking health services has consistently ranked transplants high on the list.

Expanding Access

The advocates of the OHP promised from the outset to expand access to Medicaid to all the poor; this was the payoff from what they preferred to call prioritization. The OHP has more than delivered. Oregon's Medicaid program now covers all residents who are below the poverty line. The number of beneficiaries has increased by almost 50%, with 320,000 new beneficiaries covered over the plan's first 4 years.

Although national attention has focused on Oregon's reform of Medicaid, its reformers actually aimed for the broader objective of universal access. Reformers proposed to cut the number of uninsured by pursuing a "pincer movement" that combined expansion of Medicaid with a range of policies to help those above the poverty line—instituting an employer-mandate, establishing insurance pools for high risk groups, reforming insurance practices to allow portability and prohibit exclusions based on pre-existing conditions, and offering subsidies to individuals above the poverty line to purchase commercial health insurance.[13]

Reforms on behalf of Oregonians above the poverty line have produced significant but mixed results. Oregon's effort to implement an employer mandate was blocked by opposition from segments of the business community and federal inaction on granting the necessary federal exemption from the Employee Retirement Income Security Act (ERISA). On the other hand, the State did establish insurance pools for small businesses and high risk groups that now include 40,000 individuals, as well as insurance reforms that offer protections for individuals and small groups. Moreover, recent legislation in July 1997 further expanded eligibility of Medicaid above the poverty line. An estimated 20,000 new beneficiaries will be added to OHP by covering children through age 12 and pregnant women up to 170% of the federal poverty line. The 1997 reforms also created the Family Health Insurance Assistance Program (FHIAP), which will offer a voucher subsidy to help low and moderate income families who do not presently qualify for OHP to purchase insurance. The FHIAP is expected to reduce the uninsured population in Oregon by an additional 20,000 persons.

Perhaps most striking, the proportion of employers providing health insurance in the state has apparently *increased* since the introduction of the OHP despite the failure of the employer mandate. This development is particularly surprising given current concerns about expanded public coverage "crowding out" privately sponsored insurance. Although economic growth and competition for workers has created pressure to offer attractive benefits, the OHP may well have contributed—as some of its supporters in the state believe—to changing the dynamics of private insurance coverage in the state. The debate over universal coverage and fully insuring the poor, it is argued, raised expectations within the state and generated pressure on private employers to provide workers with health insurance, producing a novel "crowding in" effect.[14]

In any case, the impact of the OHP on access is clear: since the plan was implemented in 1994, the number of uninsured Oregonians has fallen dramatically. In 1993, 17% of Oregonians lacked insurance; the proportion dropped to 11% in 1996. (The national uninsurance rate was 15% in 1996.) The patterns for children and dependents are even more striking. The percentage of Oregonian children without health insurance fell from 21% in 1990 to 8% in 1996 (nationally it rose from 14% to 15% during that period).

The story of expanding access in Oregon is not over. The latest round of reforms in July 1997 are expected to reduce the number of uninsured from 11% in 1996 to 9% of the population. The proportion of children without insurance is expected to drop from 8% in 1996 to 5%, or even lower when taking into account the new federal monies from the recently enacted Kiddiecare legislation. And state reformers are planning additional changes that will further cut the ranks of the uninsured.

The Absence of Administrative Science

Oregon has not implemented the scientific form of rationing it promised. Resource allocation decisions in the state have remained political and subjective.

The limited influence of administrative science on the operation of the OHP is illustrated by how the prioritization list is revised. Originally, planners envisioned that medical treatments would be moved up or down (or in the case of new procedures, onto) the list based on new information that could be incorporated into a cost-benefit formula that would yield the precise quantitative value of medical procedures. Social science and objective methodologies, not political pressures or arbitrary considerations, would determine the state's health spending priorities.

But, in practice this technocratic vision has failed. Adjustments to the list have consistently been determined not by scientific formula, but "by hand" on the basis of subjective judgments by the Health Services Commission. The subjective process that compromised the original prioritization methodology of 1991 became necessary because of Federal requirements and opposition within Oregon over the rankings in the initial list. In fact, an analysis by the Office of Technology Assessment (OTA) found that quantitative cost-benefit data, when compared to the considerable influence of subjective judgments by the Health Service Commissioners, had "surprisingly little effect" on the ordering of health services in the list. Once the original methodology was com-

promised and a list of medical treatments had been altered to reflect political pressures and subjective judgments, it was simply impossible to modify future versions of the list on a formulaic basis. Scientific rationing has not, in fact, been implemented in Oregon.

Growing Political Support

Critics of the OHP predicted that the plan would be swept away (or at least stalled) by a tidal wave of opposition within the state.[15] After all, health care reform efforts in Massachusetts, Vermont, Kentucky, Washington and elsewhere have collapsed. The added burden in Oregon of an untested rationing plan only seemed to increase the odds against the program's survival. Denying services, it was reasoned, could only spark anger and counter-mobilization by advocates of the poor and other vulnerable populations, as well as by providers who resent the interference in their clinical judgment. Commentators warned that adoption of the OHP would touch off explosive media stories of deserving patients going without care and an unraveling of support by legislators.

The predictions of imminent doom have turned out, however, to be unfounded. The OHP has become what some observers inside the state term the "third rail" of state politics.[16] By the time its founding legislation was passed in 1989, the OHP was supported by the general public, the Oregon Medical Association, large business organizations, and the AFL-CIO. And members of the Oregon House and Senate gave the legislation nearly unanimously support. The continuing support of the general public is reflected in the 54-46% vote in favor of a 1994 referendum (despite intense tobacco industry opposition and the conservative electoral tidal wave that year) to impose a 30 cent cigarette tax to finance the OHP.

Advocacy groups for the aged and disabled have been converted from skeptics to supporters. Their initial fears that the OHP would systematically deny necessary medical services to vulnerable populations were calmed, replaced by an appreciation that the OHP offers better benefits (especially for mental illness and disability) than many private insurers. The same advocates who once denounced the OHP now support expanding the program to encompass more of the state's population and their constituents.

Nearly ten years after authorizing the program, the legislature continues to reward the OHP with new infusions of funds. Attempts to divert funds from the cigarette tax earmarked for the program in 1994 were defeated, and the expansion of coverage has consistently won broad, bipartisan majorities. Politicians from both parties frequently claim credit for the success of the OHP. And the program emerged relatively unscathed from a 1995 state budget crisis, which did result in the imposition of an assets test, a slight reduction in benefits, and a sliding-scale premium for those eligible for the OHP as a result of the Medicaid demonstration.

Ironically, the Oregon plan, which began under a cloud of controversy and predictions of its imminent demise, has proven far more politically durable than health reform efforts by other states that were heralded as promising alternative routes to change.

The Political Sources of Oregon's Surprise

Most national observers of the OHP have missed the story of its increased political support, its generous benefits, and the absence of systematic rationing.[17] In part, national observers have misjudged the Oregon case because of the initial rationing rhetoric used by OHP advocates. Reformers now concede that they misleadingly hailed the scientific grounding of rationing, repeatedly compromised what was presented as a scientific process, and oversold the extent to which services would be cut. But these facts about the OHP are only reluctantly (and quietly) acknowledged by program architects, and therefore have not reached outside observers whose impressions of the Oregon plan were seared by the original rationing rhetoric.

Yet the main reason the Oregon story has been misread is that many analysts have overlooked, or misunderstood, the political dynamics of rationing in Oregon. As we have argued, rationing has not functioned as a technical administrative instrument for reallocating resources. But the focus on the technical dimension of rationing has obscured its political value; namely, the extent to which the *rhetoric and process* of rationing (as opposed to its application) have been crucial to reformer's efforts to mobilize support for health care reform in the state.

Motivation: Mobilizing Support in an Inhospitable Environment

The policy entrepreneurs who formulated and promoted the OHP shared an unwavering devotion to expanding health insurance, a commitment that would sustain them through a decade or more of setbacks and harsh external criticism. Their motto was, "we keep coming back."[18] Establishing a process of scientific prioritization that would aggressively limit services was never the ultimate objective of Oregon's reformers; it was pragmatically latched onto as the means to widen access.

Oregon's policy entrepreneurs possessed a talent for interacting with a multiplicity of players and for adjusting to changes in their political environment in order to pursue their long-term goal of expanded access. John Kitzhaber, who led the reform effort and is currently Governor, combined policy awareness based on his experience as a doctor and state legislator with rhetorical skills to seize the bully pulpit and a long-term commitment to fighting for health reform. Others committed to reform (within government and outside of it) possessed a similar blend of policy expertise and broad political experience in working with legislators and the executive branch.

From the beginning, reformers drew on these political skills in tailoring their policy proposals to what they saw as significant political obstacles, though they failed to appreciate just how daunting they would be. The political situation during the second half of the 1980s was hardly propitious for would-be health reformers. Republicans hostile to government activism had controlled the White House for three consecutive terms and were a significant influence in Oregon's government—they controlled the governor's seat during 1981–85 and had cut Democratic majorities in the State House to razor thin margins.

Reformers designed their proposal on the premise that they needed bipartisan support to carry the OHP through the natural vagaries of electoral politics. Indeed, the 1994 election that elevated Newt Gingrich to Speaker of the House also lifted Republicans into control of the Oregon legislature. Reformers also worried about state business interests. They hoped to win the backing of larger businesses or at least neutralize them, while tempering the damage from the expected opposition of smaller firms.

In short, the motivation for the OHP was not a

technocratic vision based on administrative science, but rather a commitment to expanding access that was informed by a realistic assessment of the obvious political barriers to reform.

The Political Strategy of Oregon's Policy Entrepreneurs

Oregon's health leaders designed their political strategy to mitigate the anticipated resistance and to mobilize the state's potentially fractious political community behind a broad vision of health reform. They latched onto the language and procedures of administrative science and rationing as the centerpiece of a strategy to build and "manage political momentum."[19] Their strategy had four components.

Capitalize on Oregon's Participatory Culture

The first was to capitalize on Oregon's participatory culture. As noted earlier, the prioritized list was to be informed by public input on basic values solicited through professionally conducted town hall meetings and public opinion surveys. These meetings, and the activities of the Health Services Commission, attracted sustained media coverage and public attention.

While external critics focused intently on the final list produced by the Commission's process of prioritization and its alleged shortcomings and inconsistencies, Oregonians championed the process that produced it. Within the State's culture, the process of prioritizing health services was viewed as a welcomed continuation of Oregon's participatory tradition. Land use planning and other policy discussions in Oregon have long used community involvement and corporatist bargaining through commissions to bring together government, businesses, and citizens.[20]

The state's participatory culture offered reformers a political opportunity. After all, the OHP could have been designed in a closed room by a handful of experts. Instead, policy entrepreneurs methodically designed a process that sought out the attention of everyday Oregonians and sparked a very public debate across the state. Reformers appeared to have solicited public participation as a part of a genuine effort to incorporate the public's "substantive input on the relative importance of health care services."[21] But, they also recognized the political benefits of public input.

Oregon's reformers (and their external critics[22]) appreciated the technical limitations of obtaining a representative measure of public preferences.[23] They hoped that soliciting some kind of public input would induce "public buy-in" into the OHP and a sense that it was "their" process.[24]

Reformers welcomed public input partly to avert two potentially damaging reactions by Oregonians against helping the uninsured. First, they worried about a welfare backlash. Proposing to expand benefits to poor residents ran the real risk of alienating Oregonians.[25] It was precisely this fear of the politically damaging consequences of targeting the uninsured that prompted President Clinton to frame his health reform plan as offering "security for all." The second fear of reformers was that rampant public distrust of government would produce apathy, disinterest, and suspicion toward any government intervention. Pursuing reform without public input, OHP advocates believed, would set the process up to fail.

Setting up a process that invited public input and made explicit health care choices in public forums was a carefully designed tactic, its advocates explained, to "break out of the alienation from government" and avert a welfare backlash.[26] Indeed, OHP administrators look back and credit public participation and the prioritization process for restoring some confidence in Oregon government and creating a level of "trust" and a "reservoir of good will."[27] As one administrator explained to us, "the public input process was effective at building . . . consensus . . . precisely because [policy makers] said that [the public's] input was being taken seriously and reflected in policy decisions."[28]

The focus of national critics on the design of the public forums and their skewed representation misses their political significance. Their primary value was not in precisely representing or measuring public attitudes, but in building public support for controversial reform. By contrast, the Clinton administration's closed health reform process in 1993 invited mistrust and fueled damaging speculation about secret deals.

Establish Political Accountability The second strategy was to transform the legislative politics that had previously dominated health policy. In particular, reformers organized the process of prioritization

to change the "political paradigm" and make legislators politically accountable for explicit decisions to cut benefits. Although the ostensible purpose of the scientific prioritization process was to cut unnecessary services, the architects of the OHP viewed it as a political mechanism to "put legislators on the hook and force them to make the commitment to expanding access."[29] They astutely calculated that the process of explicitly discussing reductions in services would be politically difficult and would in fact pressure legislators to expand access without significantly reducing covered services.[30]

Following the script of reformers, independent actuaries estimate the cost of each treatment ranked by the Health Services Commission and present the Legislature with the list carrying a price tag assigned to each of the ranked services. Legislators then must decided how much of the list Oregon can afford. "The idea," a longtime administrator explained, is to replace "quiet decisions" over cutting the number of people eligible for Medicaid with "very public decisions to change the benefit package according to very explicit guidelines."[31] Governor Kitzhaber put it plainly: "Let legislators make explicit decisions so that they can be held accountable for them."[32]

The result has been to put legislators in the position of reaching decisions on funding which have direct and visible cause-and-effect consequences for reducing (or expanding) the number of services offered. Under the OHP, withholding treatment for specific services is easily traceable to a specific legislator's decision not to provide funding. Legislators are put in the politically uncomfortable position of facing voters' scrutiny over very "public" and explicit decisions to deny specific health services to program beneficiaries. Legislators in both political parties face the clear prospect that their constituents may recoil at cuts in actual medical care and punish them in the next election.

Paradoxically, then, the use of rationing rhetoric has made actual rationing of medical care for poor Oregonians *less*, not more likely, just as reformers intended.

Define the Target Population Expansively The
third strategy was to define their target population expansively to encompass a broad rather than restricted set of recipients. National observers have been riveted to Oregon's changes in Medicaid, but

the State's reformers persistently presented their proposals within Oregon as encompassing a population broader than Medicaid recipients. Their specific proposals for employer mandate, insurance pools, and private insurance reforms were all aimed at dispelling the perception that health reform was a poor people's program, which would give "handouts" to a stigmatized target population.[33]

In addition to proposing programs that would reach beyond the poor, reformers also explicitly presented their elaborate and quite public process of prioritization as an effort to define the care of the entire population. Participants in its design were warned against singling out the Medicaid population.[34] "The concept of the OHP," one long time OHP administrator emphasized, rested on "making the prioritized benefit package the floor for all Oregonians' coverage, not just Medicaid."[35]

Mobilize Providers and Interest Groups Reformers also used the process of prioritization to transcend formal boundaries between government and private individuals and groups in order to organize continuous negotiations among doctors, hospitals, insurance companies, employers, and labor. The prioritization process, one administrator explained, "provided a nexus for the discussions about how limited resources would be allocated" and kept the different stakeholders "directly engaged" for a protracted period.[36]

Hospitals supported reform from the start as a means to reduce the financial drain of handling uncompensated care and inappropriate visits to the emergency room. More telling, though, is the conversion of physicians from initial skeptics to loyal supporters. According to administrators, doctors "didn't particularly take to the idea of public input about what is important in health and health care" but were persuaded of its political importance as a tactic to induce Oregonians' support in a period when the public was in no mood to defer to experts.[37] Physicians had a second concern: the "absence of sound, scientific, longitudinal studies" on the costs and benefits of health services prevented the Health Services Commission from devising a list based on objective as opposed to subjective evaluations. But, physicians working on the Commission and reformers—led by fellow physician Kitzhaber—persuaded doctors that they would continue in reality to make "medical decisions every day based on their best clinical judgment."[38] Indeed, after the implementation of the OHP, physicians continued to exercise their judgment, providing services that were at times not covered by the list. Physician support for OHP was also cultivated by a promise that Oregon would provide generous payments for covered services. That promise has held; Oregon's capitation payments for OHP enrollees are comparatively high.[39] After physicians' reservations were addressed, they rallied behind the OHP's goal of expanding access to the uninsured and funding more of the cost of treating Medicaid patients.

The importance of the prioritization process for organizing ongoing bargaining was especially important in managing political relations with business representatives. Large and small business were divided over the OHP reforms and the employer mandate. Although small business were steadfast opponents, larger businesses favored the reforms because it would compel small firms to contribute to their employees' health costs and thereby reduce the costs that were shifted to large employers. Although large business initially backed employer mandate, the election of a Republican State Legislature in 1994, vociferous small business opposition, and the near certainty that the Gingrich-controlled Congress would not grant an exemption from ERISA weakened their support for the employer mandate. The result—as some reformers anticipated—was that the employer mandate was stripped from the OHP reforms in 1995. The prioritization process, though, kept big business "engaged" in the coalition that supported the OHP as a whole even as some of its components—like the employer mandate—became targets of vocal opposition and were dropped.

Conclusion

Intended and Unanticipated Consequences

The Oregon Health Plan that has operated since 1994 bears little resemblance to the program that was envisioned by both promoters and critics during the national debate over its adoption. The political strategies of reformers have been crucial in shaping the Oregon surprise. Reformers used the

rhetoric and process of rationing to mobilize public support, involve health care providers and other social interests in the process, and establish a new mechanism for political accountability. Ultimately, this helped maintain a broad political coalition that has paradoxically made it harder for politicians to ration medical care and easier to raise funds for the state's poor.

Much of what has happened in Oregon, then, was intended but not well understood outside the state. Still, political strategy alone cannot explain the surprising outcome in Oregon. Unanticipated developments and fortuitous conditions have also played a critical role in the development of the OHP.

Clearly, Oregon's reformers never fully controlled or anticipated their destiny. They were blindsided by unexpected political troubles such as the protracted battle for a Medicaid waiver and the chorus of national criticism. Ironically, the same political strategies and processes that were crafted to produce consensus in the state produced controversy outside of it. These unanticipated developments had important feedback effects on the formulation of the OHP. For instance, the national outcry over the Howard case and the initial list intensified HCFA's scrutiny and constrained the State's ability to place services such as transplants lower on the list and to cut funding for other services. Similarly, federal opposition to the plan helped erode the scientific foundation of the prioritization process and guarantee that subsequent reordering of the list could not be done on a formulaic basis.

Oregon's health reformers also benefited from several favorable contingencies that raised the probability of success but could not have been predicted. The OHP has been implemented during a period when the state economy prospered, health care inflation moderated, and its most prominent sponsor was elected governor. Absent these favorable conditions, the state may have been forced to make harder choices about spending priorities and the OHP may have confronted stronger pressures for strict rationing.

Oregon's Innovation

The appeal of the Oregon plan was largely technocratic. The state promised to develop a rational, scientific instrument—"the list"—to prioritize resources. The reputed technical power of this administrative instrument has drawn many visitors to Oregon eager to learn its precise formulas and gain a new tool to negotiate the technological and financial dilemmas of modern medicine. Yet, the technical power of this innovation has proven to be largely an illusion.

Systematic rationing simply has not arrived in Oregon. Based on the rather small and relatively medically insignificant set of services now excluded from the OHP (as well as its generous benefit package), observers will be hard pressed to discover evidence in Oregon of the "tough decisions" reformers promised. Nor has the OHP operated as an objective, scientific vessel of resource prioritization, as the process of updating the list by hand has vividly demonstrated. Reformers have, in fact, repeatedly compromised the much-heralded scientific rigor of their prioritization process for political gain.

In short, the actual implementation of rationing in Oregon has failed to demonstrate the successful application of quantitative cost-benefit analysis to health care resource allocation. Instead, the OHP's operation confirms the prediction of the Office of Technology Assessment that Oregon's "outcome and cost-effectiveness data . . . are inadequate for use as the building blocks of a ranking system for all services."[40]

The innovation in Oregon, then, is political rather than technical. State reformers used the rhetoric and process of prioritization and rationing to build a durable political coalition in favor of expanded access for the poor. Remarkably, Oregon has used a discourse—rationing—thought to be dangerous to the uninsured in a successful effort to help them. Oregon's reformers developed a coherent political strategy for navigating a political environment hostile to social reform.

Oregon's experience potentially offers a powerful political reason for reconsidering the traditional reticence of reformers to discuss rationing openly. In Oregon, the rhetoric of rationing pulled into the open the decisions that privately occur every day and that deny services to uninsured or underinsured Americans. The OHP points to an unanticipated political benefit of rationing rhetoric: it reconfigures debate toward openly acknowledging as a society what health services Americans—even the politically eviscerated poor—should receive or go without, and puts politicians in the vulnerable position of pulling the plug on particular health services. Paradoxically,

a process that is ostensibly aimed at saying no may force the voters and politicians—as it did in Oregon—to recoil in horror and say yes.

Whether Oregon's innovation can or should be borrowed by others remains, however, in serious doubt. Explicit discussion of which services to include or exclude has been avoided by reformers because it will almost surely elicit substantial controversy and opposition, as it did with the OHP. Public forums and deliberative democracy also presents vexing ethical problems regarding how to protect the needs of patients who are small in number and politically and economically vulnerable.

Most crucially, however, Oregon offered a unique setting for the rationing process to flourish: an unwavering commitment to expanding access, a culture of citizen participation, a relatively liberal ideological environment, the sustained commitment of a political sponsor (Governor Kitzhaber), as well as a strong economy and moderate health care inflation. In the absence these favorable conditions, the rationing process could produce quite different (and for the uninsured, harmful) results in other states or at the national level.

In the end, what has been widely regarded outside of Oregon as innovative—a scientific approach to confronting the hard choices raised by health care rationing—has not been the significant innovation. And the real innovation in Oregon—the political strategy of using rationing rhetoric—has been overlooked. The real foundation of the Oregon Health Plan is not science, but politics.

Notes

1. Rudolf Klein, Patricia Day, and Sharon Redmayne, *Managing Scarcity* (Philadelphia: Open University Press, 1996), p. 108.
2. Sara Rosenbaum, "Poor Women, Poor Children, Poor Policy: The Oregon Medicaid Experiment," in *Rationing America's Medical Care: The Oregon Plan and Beyond* ed. by Martin Strosberg, Joshua Wiener, Robert Baker, and I. Alan Fein (Washington, DC: The Brookings Institution, 1992), 27.
3. "The Oregon Medicaid Demonstration: Waiver Cost Estimate." Prepared for HCFA

and submitted by the Office of Medical Assistance Programs, Oregon Department of Human Resources, April 15, 1991, p. ES3.

4. Sara Rosenbaum, "Poor Women, Poor Children, Poor Policy: The Oregon Medicaid Experiment," in *Rationing America's Medical Care: The Oregon Plan and Beyond* ed. by Martin Strosberg, Joshua Wiener, Robert Baker, and I. Alan Fein (Washington, DC: The Brookings Institution, 1992), 103–4.

5. Office of Technology Assessment. "Evaluation of the Oregon Medicaid Proposal." (Washington, DC: US government Printing Office, 1992), pp. 76–77.

6. "Rationing in America," *Rationing America's Medical Care: The Oregon Plan and Beyond* ed. by Martin Strosberg, Joshua Wiener and Robert Baker (Washington, DC: The Brookings Institution, 1992), p. 20.

7. *Rationing America's Medical Care: The Oregon Plan and Beyond* ed. by Martin Strosberg, Joshua Wiener and Robert Baker (Washington, DC: The Brookings Institution, 1992), p. 110.

8. Lawrence Brown, "The National Politics of Oregon's Rationing Plan," *Health Affairs,* Summer 1991; Michael Garland, Harvey Levit and Bob DiPrete, "Letter: Policy Analysis or Polemic on Oregon's Rationing Plan?" and Lawrence Brown, "Letter: Settling the Score on Oregon," *Health Affairs,* Winter 1991; Daniel Fox and Howard Leichter, "The Ups and Downs of Oregon's Rationing Plan," *Health Affairs,* Summer 1993; *Rationing America's Medical Care: The Oregon Plan and Beyond* ed. by Martin Strosberg, Joshua Wiener and Robert Baker (Washington, DC: The Brookings Institution, 1992).

9. Richard Conviser, Margaret Retondo, and Mark O. Loveless, "Predicting the Effect of the Oregon Health Plan on Medicaid Coverage for Outpatients with HIV," *American Journal of Public Health,* December 1994, p. 1996; Richard Conviser, Margaret Retondo, and Mark O. Loveless, "Universal Health Coverage, Rationing, and HIV Care; Lessons from the Oregon Health Plan Medicaid Reform," *AIDS and Public Policy Journal,* Summer 1995.

10. Interview with Hersh Crawford, Director, Office of Medical Assistance Programs, June 1996 and May 1997; Interview with Annie Mockabee, Representative of Blue Cross/Blue Shield, June 1996 and May 1997.

11. The controversy over the case of Coby Howard continues to dominate national understanding of the OHP. The facts of this particular case appear to be much more complex than initially reported in the national media: Howard's condition was not treatable and he died before the OHP was implemented.

12. Kitzhaber quoted in Daniel Fox and Howard Leichter, "Rationing Care in Oregon: The New Accountability," *Health Affairs* Summer 1991, p. 15.

13. Interview with Vicki Gates, administrator, Oregon Health Plan Administrator's Office, June 1996; Interview with Mark Gibson, Governor's Policy Advisor on Health Care, Human Services, and Labor June 96.

14. Interview with Crawford.

15. Fox and Leichter, "The Ups and Downs of Oregon's Rationing Plan"; Brown, "The National Politics of Oregon's Rationing Plan."

16. Interview with Crawford.

17. Thomas Bodenheimer is a notable exception. Thomas Bodenheimer, "The Oregon Health Plan—Lessons for the Nation," *The New England Journal of Medicine,* August 28.

18. Interview with D'Anne Gilmore, Deputy Administrator, Health Plan's Administrator's office, May 1997; Interview with Michael J. Garland, President, Oregon Health Decisions, June 1996 and May 1997.

19. Interview with Gates.

20. The connection between aspirations of participatory democracy and the development of public administration in the Oregon Health Plan reflects a recurrent theme in American politics. These dynamics are described by James A. Morone in *The Democratic Wish* (New York Basic 1990).

21. Personal Correspondence with Bob Diprete, January 2, 1998.

22. Brown, "The National Politics of Oregon's Rationing Plan"; Brown, "Letter: Settling the Score on Oregon," *Health Affairs;* Fox and Leichter, "The Ups and Downs of Oregon's Rationing Plan."

23. Norman Daniels in *Rationing America's Medical Care: The Oregon Plan and Beyond* ed. by Martin Strosberg, Joshua Wiener and Robert Baker (Washington, DC: The Brookings Institution, 1992); Fox and Leichter, "The Ups and Downs of Oregon's Rationing Plan," p. 70.

24. Interview with Garland; Interview with Gilmore; Interview with Human Services officials.

25. Interview with Garland; Interview with Gilmore.

26. Interview with Gibson; Interview with Kitzhaber.

27. Interview with Garland; Interview with Gilmore; Interview with Human Services officials.

28. Letter from Bob DiPrete, Director of Oregon Health Council, to Lawrence Jacobs, February 11, 1998.

29. Interview with Crawford; Interview with Gates.

30. Interview with Kitzhaber.

31. Interview with Bob DiPrete.

32. Maggie Mahar, "Memo to Hillary: Here's How to Cure What Ails Our Health Care System," *Barron's,* March 1, 1993.

33. Interview with Gates; Interview with Gibson.

34. Interview with Garland; Interview with Crawford.

35. Interview with DiPrete.

36. Ibid.

37. Interview with Garland, June 1996; Interview with Crawford, May 1997.

38. Ibid.

39. Bodenheimer, "The Oregon Health Plan—Lessons for the Nation."

40. Office of Technology Assessment. "Evaluation of the Oregon Medicaid Proposal." (Washington, DC: US Government Printing Office, 1992), p. 21.

Chapter 13 Review Questions

1. How do you define the word "implementation"? In what ways does "implementation" differ from "management" or "administration"? What are the similarities and differences among these terms?

2. Can you outline how the concept of implementation draws on other ideas concerning decision making, communications, politics, budgeting, intergovernmental relations, public professional expertise, and the general environment that have been discussed earlier in this text? How does the concept of implementation both use and build on these other concepts?

3. Why has implementation become such a major concern for students and practitioners of public administration and public policy in recent decades? What was responsible for its development as a recent focus of scholarly research? Do you think there is a valid need for studying implementation in the public sector and, if so, why?

4. What are the essential elements of the implementation model that Richard T. Matland proposes? How did he develop his "new" model? What are its basic assumptions and utility for practicing public administrators? Can you define in your own words its basic processes? Is it applicable to all situations, such as in foreign affairs? Or, just within America? Do you see any limitations to this model?

5. From your reading of this case, "The Case of the Oregon Health Plan," what part of the four cell matrix of Matland's model would you categorize it, and best describe what allows for its effective program implementation. Did Matland's model, in your view, adequately address these political factors for success?

6. Consider the key policy-makers in the case study and evaluate why they were successful at implementing this program. By what standards, according to Matland, can we judge "success" of program implementation? In your opinion, what was the *most critical* ingredient for making the program implementation successful? Did the Oregon case exemplify "success" in your opinion?

Key Terms

top-down approaches
policy conflict
target population
statutory language
key actors
conflicting policy priorities
veto points
policy feedback

bottoms-up approaches
policy ambiguity
prescriptive policy advice
descriptive causal factors
street-level bureaucrats
fixers
performance evaluation
constituency intervention points

Suggestions for Further Reading

The book that started much of the contemporary theorizing about this subject is now in its second edition and is still well worth reading, Jeffrey L. Pressman and Aaron B. Wildavsky, *Implementation,* Second Edition (Berkeley, Calif.: University of California Press, 1978) as well as several of the case studies that criticized the implementation of Great Society programs and also stimulated early research in this field, especially Martha Derthick, *New Towns In-Town* (Washington, D.C.: Urban Institute, 1972); Daniel P. Moynihan, *Maximum Feasible Misunderstanding* (New York: Free Press, 1969); Stephan K. Bailey and Edith K. Mosher, *ESEA: The Office of Education Administers a Law* (Syracuse: Syracuse University Press, 1968) as well as Beryl A. Radin, *Implementation, Change and the Federal Bureaucracy* (New York: Teachers College Press, 1977).

Serious students of implementation theory should review carefully the major conceptual approaches cited in the introduction to this chapter as well as other important contributions, such as Martin Rein and Francine F. Rabinovitz, "Implementation: A Theoretical Perspective," in Walter D. Burnham and Martha W. Weinberg, eds., *Ameri-*

can Politics and Public Policy (Cambridge, Mass.: MIT Press, 1978); and also in the same book, Michael M. Lipsky, "Implementation on Its Head"; Carl E. Van Horn, *Policy Implementation in the Federal System* (Lexington, Mass.: Lexington Books, 1979); A. Dunsire, *Implementation in Bureaucracy* (New York: St. Martin's Press, 1979); Walter Williams, *The Implementation Perspective* (Berkeley, Calif.: University of California Press, 1980); J. S. Larson, *Why Government Programs Fail* (1980); Helen M. Ingram and Dean E. Mann, eds., *Why Policies Succeed or Fail* (Los Angeles: Sage, 1980); R. D. Behn, "Why Murphy Was Right," *Policy Analysis* (Summer 1980); G. C. Edwards, *Implementing Public Policy* (Washington, D.C.: Congressional Quarterly Press, 1980); Susan Barrett and Colin Fudge, eds., *Policy and Action: Essays on Implementation of Public Policy* (London: Methuen, Inc., 1981); Dennis J. Palumbo and Marvin A. Harder, eds., *Implementing Public Policy* (Lexington, Mass.: Lexington Books, 1981); Daniel A. Mazmanian and Paul A. Sabatier, eds., *Effective Public Policy Implementation* (Lexington, Mass.: Lexington Books, 1982); B. Hjern and D. O. Porter, "Implementation Structure," *Organ-*

ization Studies (1981); Randall B. Ripley and Grace A. Franklin, *Bureaucracy and Policy Implementation* (Homewood, Ill.: Dorsey Press, 1982); Walter William et al., *Studying Implementation: Methodological and Administrative Issues* (Chatham, N.J.: Chatham House, 1982); and B. Hjern and C. Hull, eds., "Implementation Beyond Hierarchy," Special Issue, *European Journal of Political Research.* For a helpful reader, see George C. Edwards III, ed., *Public Policy Implementation* (Greenwich, Conn.: JAI Press, 1989). For two reviews of techniques, strategies, and directions for further research, read David L. Weimer, "The Current Data of Design Craft: Borrowing, Tinkering and Problem Solving," *Public Administration Review,* 53 (March/April 1993), pp. 110–120, as well as Helen Ingram, "Imple-

mentation: A Review and Suggested Framework," Naomi B. Lynn and Aaron Wildavsky, eds., *Public Administration: The State of the Discipline* (Chatham, N.J.: Chatham House, 1990).

Three important book-length, scholarly implementation studies are Lester M. Salamon, ed., *Beyond Privatization: The Tools of Government Action* (Washington, D.C.: The Urban Institute, 1989; Malcolm L. Goggin, Ann O'M. Bowman, James P. Lester, and Laurence J. O'Toole, Jr., *Implementation Theory and Practice: Toward a Third Generation* (Glenview, Ill.: Scott, Foresman and Co., 1990); see especially its excellent bibliography, as well as Robert Stoker, *Reluctant Partners* (Pittsburgh: University of Pittsburgh Press, 1991).

PART THREE

Enduring and Unresolved Relationships: Central Value Questions, Issues, and Dilemmas of Contemporary Public Administration

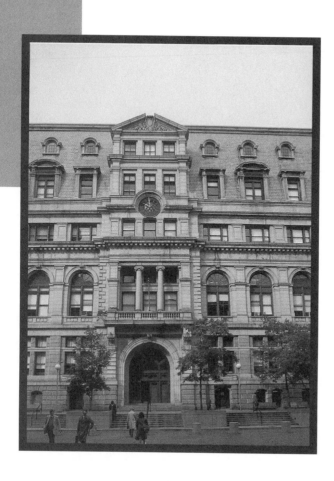

Part Three focuses on three key persistent and pressing relationships in the field of public administration today: the problems of political-administrative relationships; the bureaucracy and the public interest; and ethics and the public service. All of these relational issues are new in the sense that they have come to the forefront of recent discussions and controversies in public administration. Yet, these issues have certainly been part of the problems and perplexities of public administration since its inception as an identifiable field of study after the turn of the twentieth century. Indeed, the topics of political-administrative relationships, the problems of ethics, and relationships between bureaucracy and the public interest were central themes of the writings of many early administrative theorists, such as Woodrow Wilson, Frederick Taylor, Luther Gulick, Louis Brownlow, and Leonard White. No doubt one could even trace the origins of these topics back to the classic writings of Plato, Aristotle, Moses, and Pericles. But for a variety of reasons, we are witnessing the reemergence of these older issues as very real dilemmas for public administrators today. Readings and cases in Part Three therefore address these critical issues:

CHAPTER 14
The Relationship Between Politics and Administration: *The Concept of Issue Networks* What are the current trends and practices in political oversight and control of administration? What are the implications for public administration and the governance of America?

CHAPTER 15
The Relationship Between Bureaucracy and the Public Interest: *The Concept of Public Sector Deregulation* What is the "public interest"? Is there such a thing that can serve as a guide to public administrators' work? How can it be applied as a meaningful concept to influence the direction and activities of government bureaucracies?

CHAPTER 16
The Relationship Between Ethics and Public Administration: *The Concept of Competing Ethical Obligations* How are ethical choices involved in contemporary decisions facing public servants? What is an appropriate conceptual model for understanding how ethics influence public administrators' choices? How can these choices be made in a more responsible manner?

CHAPTER 14

The Relationship Between Politics and Administration: The Concept of Issue Networks

T
he iron triangle concept is not so much wrong as it is disastrously incom-
plete. And the conventional view is especially inappropriate for under-
standing changes in politics and administration during recent years. . . . Looking
for the closed triangles of control, we tend to miss the fairly open networks of
people that increasingly impinge upon government.

Hugh Heclo

READING 14

Introduction

Perhaps no issue has been more controversial or more discussed in public administration since its inception as a self-conscious field of study than the appropriate relationship between the politically elected representatives of the legislature and the
permanent bureaucracy of the executive branch. Indeed, as was pointed out in Chapter 1, the first essay on the subject of public administration written in the United States,
"The Study of Administration," prepared by a young political scientist named
Woodrow Wilson in 1887, essentially wrestled with the problem of the proper relationship between these two spheres of government: politics and administration.[1] Wilson wrote his essay at a time when civil service reform had recently been instituted
in the federal government (the Pendleton Act had been passed in 1883). Wilson sought
to encourage the development of the newly established merit system and the emergence of a field of academic study—public administration—because in his words, "It
is getting to be harder to run a constitution than to frame one." The new complexities
of government—both in terms of widening popular participation of the citizenry in
democratic government and the rising technological problems of organizing public
programs—created, in Wilson's view, the urgent need for developing effective administrative services free from congressional "meddling."

[1]Woodrow Wilson, "The Study of Administration," *Political Science Quarterly,* 2 (June 1887), pp. 197–222.
Reprinted with permission from *Political Science Quarterly.*

Generally, the drift—both in terms of intellectual thought and institutional reform in the United States during the century after Wilson's writing—until the 1970s was toward a realization of the Wilsonian argument in favor of greater administrative independence from legislative oversight. War, international involvements, economic crises, and a host of other influences (including public administration theorists) supported the claims for administrative independence from detailed legislative control. In particular, as political scientist Allen Schick notes, three factors led to congressional acquiescence. The first factor was the massive growth in the size of government. "Big government weakened the ability of Congress to govern by controlling the details and it vested administration with more details over which to govern. In the face of bigness Congress could master the small things only by losing sight of the important issues." This was bolstered by the message of public administration theorists "that a legislature should not trespass on administrative matters inevitably registered on Congressional thinking about its appropriate role, especially because the theme was so attractively laced with the promise of order and efficiency in the public service and carried the warning that legislative intrusion would be injurious to good government."[2]

Nonpartisanship in foreign affairs also played a powerful role in checking congressional intrusion in executive affairs by conveying "the assurance that unchecked executive power would be applied benevolently in the national interest of the United States." Pluralism, a third factor in fostering congressional retreat, according to Schick, furthered administrative independence by the convincing certainty that wider administrative discretion over executive agencies would be in fact used "to provide benefits to powerful interests in society to the benefit of everyone."

In retrospect, perhaps these assumptions were naive, but they were generally accepted as truths until the early 1970s. Suddenly the abuses of Watergate, the disastrous consequences of Vietnam, the failure of numerous Great Society social programs, combined with an unusually high turnover of congressional seats, brought about a dramatic revival of congressional interest in the problems of Congress' control over executive activities. A variety of new laws were enacted to achieve more control: for example, widening the requirement of Senate approval of presidential appointees to executive offices; creation of the Congressional Budget Office to act as a legislative fiscal watchdog; the passage of the Freedom of Information Act to provide Congress and the general public with greater access to executive activities; and the War Powers Resolution, which restricted presidential initiative in foreign military involvements.

Concomitant with the rise of congressional oversight in the 1960s and 1970s, it became fashionable to argue that governmental policies emerged from *iron triangles*—three-way interactions involving elected members of Congress, particularly key committee and subcommittee chairpersons; career bureaucrats, particularly agency heads or senior staffers; and special interest lobbies, particularly powerful lobbies in specialized fields such as health, welfare, education, and defense. From this closed triad of interests, so the theory goes, governmental policies emerge by means of members of Congress writing and passing favorable legislation, bureaucrats implementing these

---

[2]Allen Schick, "Congress and the 'Details' of Administration," *Public Administration Review,* 36 (September/October 1976), pp. 516–528.

congressional mandates in return for bigger budgets, and special-interest groups backing (with re-election monies and other support) the helpful members of Congress: in all, a tidy and closed relationship.

Is this how the political-administrative relationships in government actually work today? In the following essay, Hugh Heclo (1944–   ), currently distinguished Robinson University professor at George Mason University, takes issue with the iron triangle conception of modern political-administrative relationships. He emphasizes, "The iron triangle concept is not so much wrong as it is disastrously incomplete." "Unfortunately," writes Heclo, "our standard political conceptions of power and control are not very well suited to the loose-jointed play of influence that is emerging in political administration. We tend to look for one group exerting dominance over another, for subgovernments that are strongly insulated from other outside forces in the environment, for policies that get 'produced' by a few 'makers.' " Instead, says Heclo, in "looking for the few who are powerful, we tend to overlook the many whose webs of influence provoke and guide the exercise of power. These webs, or what I will call 'issue networks,' are particularly relevant to the highly intricate and confusing welfare policies that have been undertaken in recent years."

Note that in Heclo's view of the *issue networks,* unlike the iron triangle concept, which assumed a small identifiable circle of participants, the participants are largely shifting, fluid, and anonymous. In fact, he writes, "it is almost impossible to say where a network leaves off and its environment begins." Whereas iron triangles are seen as relatively stable groups that coalesce around narrow policy issues, Heclo's issue networks are dispersed and numerous players move in and out of the transitory networks, without anyone being clearly in control over programs or policies. Although the "iron triangles at their roots had economic gain as an interest of all parties concerned," Heclo believes "any direct material interest is often secondary to intellectual or emotional commitment involving issue networks." Passion, ideas, and moral dedication replace, to a significant degree, material and economic gain from policy involvement.

The profound influence of the rise of these issue networks on government is manifold, Heclo thinks, especially in adding new layers of complexity to government. First, networks keep issues, potentially simple to solve, complex instead, primarily to gain power and influence by virtue of their own specialized expertise. Second, rather than fostering knowledge and consensus, issue networks push for argument, division, and contention to "maintain the purity of their viewpoints," which in turn sustain support from their natural but narrow public constituencies. Third, issue networks spawn true believers who become zealots for narrow interests rather than seekers of broad mandates of consensus, support, and confidence for public programs. Finally, rather than pushing for closure of debate, issue networks thrive by keeping arguments boiling and disagreements brewing. They survive by talking, debating, and arguing the alternatives, and not by finding common grounds for agreement and getting down to making things happen.

As you read this selection, keep the following questions in mind:

How does Heclo's issue network concept differ from the notion of iron triangles as the basis for political-administrative relationships?

What examples does Heclo give to support his new conceptualization of this relationship?

Do you find his arguments reasonable and correct on the basis of your experience or your reading of the case studies in this text?

What impact does the rise of issue networks have on democratic government in general and public administration in particular?

What new roles must public administrators assume, given the growth of issue networks today? Specifically, in your opinion, how can an administrator prepare or be trained for assuming these new roles?

Issue Networks and the Executive Establishment

HUGH HECLO

The connection between politics and administration arouses remarkably little interest in the United States. The presidency is considered more glamorous, Congress more intriguing, elections more exciting, and interest groups more troublesome. General levels of public interest can be gauged by the burst of indifference that usually greets the announcement of a new President's cabinet or rumors of a political appointee's resignation. Unless there is some White House "tie-in" or scandal (preferably both), news stories about presidential appointments are usually treated by the media as routine filler material.

This lack of interest in political administration is rarely found in other democratic countries, and it has not always prevailed in the United States. In most nations the ups and downs of political executives are taken as vital signs of the health of a government, indeed of its survival. In the United States, the nineteenth-century turmoil over one type of connection between politics and administra-

"Issue Networks and the Executive Establishment" by Hugh Heclo from *The Political System,* edited by Anthony King, 1978, pp. 87–124. Reprinted with permission of The American Enterprise Institute for Public Policy Research, Washington, D.C.

tration—party spoils—frequently overwhelmed any notion of presidential leadership. Anyone reading the history of those troubled decades is likely to be struck by the way in which political administration in Washington registered many of the deeper strains in American society at large. It is a curious switch that appointments to the bureaucracy should loom so large in the history of the nineteenth century, when the federal government did little, and be so completely discounted in the twentieth century, when government tries to do so much.

Political administration in Washington continues to register strains in American politics and society, although in ways more subtle than the nineteenth-century spoils scramble between Federalists and Democrats, Pro- and Anti-tariff forces, Nationalists and States-Righters, and so on. Unlike many other countries, the United States has never created a high level, government-wide civil service. Neither has it been favored with a political structure that automatically produces a stock of experienced political manpower for top executive positions in government.[1] How then does political administration in Washington work? More to the point, how might the expanding role of government be changing the connection between administration and politics?

Received opinion on this subject suggests that we already know the answers. Control is said to be vested in an informal but enduring series of "iron triangles" linking executive bureaus, congressional committees, and interest group clienteles with a stake in particular programs. A President or presidential appointee may occasionally try to muscle in, but few people doubt the capacity of these governments to thwart outsiders in the long run.

Based largely on early studies of agricultural, water, and public works policies, the iron triangle concept is not so much wrong as it is disastrously incomplete.[2] And the conventional view is especially inappropriate for understanding changes in politics and administration during recent years. Preoccupied with trying to find the few truly powerful actors, observers tend to overlook the power and influence that arise out of the configurations through which leading policy makers move and do business with each other. Looking for the closed triangles of control, we tend to miss the fairly open networks of people that increasingly impinge upon government.

To do justice to the subject would require a major study of the Washington community and the combined inspiration of a Leonard White and a James Young. Tolerating a fair bit of injustice, one can sketch a few of the factors that seem to be at work. The first is growth in the sheer mass of government activity and associated expectations. The second is the peculiar, loose-jointed play of influence that is accompanying this growth. Related to these two is the third: the layering and specialization that have overtaken the government work force, not least the political leadership of the bureaucracy.

All of this vastly complicates the job of presidential appointees both in controlling their own actions and in managing the bureaucracy. But there is much more at stake than the troubles faced by people in government. There is the deeper problem of connecting what politicians, officials, and their fellow travelers are doing in Washington with what the public at large can understand and accept. It is

on this point that political administration registers some of the larger strains of American politics and society, much as it did in the nineteenth century. For what it shows is a dissolving of organized politics and a politicizing of organizational life throughout the nation. . . .

Unfortunately, our standard political conceptions of power and control are not very well suited to the loose-jointed play of influence that is emerging in political administration. We tend to look for one group exerting dominance over another, for subgovernments that are strongly insulated from other outside forces in the environment, for policies that get "produced" by a few "makers." Seeing former government officials opening law firms or joining a new trade association, we naturally think of ways in which they are trying to conquer and control particular pieces of government machinery.

Obviously questions of power are still important. But for a host of policy initiatives undertaken in the last twenty years it is all but impossible to identify clearly who the dominant actors are. Who is controlling those actions that go to make up our national policy on abortions, or on income redistribution, or consumer protection, or energy? Looking for the few who are powerful, we tend to overlook the many whose webs of influence provoke and guide the exercise of power. These webs, or what I will call "issue networks," are particularly relevant to the highly intricate and confusing welfare policies that have been undertaken in recent years.

The notion of iron triangles and subgovernments presumes small circles of participants who have succeeded in becoming largely autonomous. Issue networks, on the other hand, comprise a large number of participants with quite variable degrees of mutual commitment or of dependence on others in their environment; in fact it is almost impossible to say where a network leaves off and its environment begins. Iron triangles and subgovernments suggest a stable set of participants coalesced to control fairly narrow public programs which are in the direct economic interest of each party to the alliance. Issue networks are almost the reverse image in each respect. Participants move in and out of the networks constantly. Rather than groups united in dominance over a program, no one, as far as one can tell, is in control of the policies and issues. Any direct material interest is often secondary to intellectual or emotional commitment. Network members reinforce each other's sense of issues as their interests, rather than (as standard political or economic models would have it) interests defining positions on issues.

Issue networks operate at many levels, from the vocal minority who turn up at local planning commission hearings to the renowned professor who is quietly telephoned by the White House to give a quick "reading" on some participant or policy. The price of buying into one or another issue network is watching, reading, talking about, and trying to act on particular policy problems. Powerful interest groups can be found represented in networks but so too can individuals in or out of government who have a reputation for being knowledgeable. Particular professions may be prominent, but the true experts in the networks are those who are issue-skilled (that is, well informed about the ins and outs of a particular policy debate) regardless of formal professional training. More than mere technical experts, network people are policy activists who know each other through the issues. Those who emerge to positions of wider leadership are policy politicians—experts in using experts, victuallers of knowledge in a world hungry for right decisions.

In the old days—when the primary problem of government was assumed to be doing what was right, rather than knowing what was right—policy knowledge could be contained in the slim adages of public administration. Public executives, it was thought, needed to know how to execute. They needed power commensurate with their responsibility. Nowadays, of course, political administrators do not execute but are involved in making highly important decisions on society's behalf, and they must mobilize policy intermediaries to deliver the goods. Knowing what is right becomes crucial, and since no one knows that for sure, going through the process of dealing with those who are

judged knowledgeable (or at least continuously concerned) becomes even more crucial. Instead of power commensurate with responsibility, issue networks seek influence commensurate with their understanding of the various, complex social choices being made. Of course some participants would like nothing better than complete power over the issues in question. Others seem to want little more than the security that comes with being well informed. As the executive of one new group moving to Washington put it, "We didn't come here to change the world; we came to minimize our surprises."[3]

Whatever the participants' motivation, it is the issue network that ties together what would otherwise be the contradictory tendencies of, on the one hand, more widespread organizational participation in public policy and, on the other, more narrow technocratic specialization in complex modern policies. Such networks need to be distinguished from three other more familiar terms used in connection with political administration. An issue network is a shared-knowledge group having to do with some aspect (or, as defined by the network, some problem) of public policy. It is therefore more well-defined than, first, a shared-attention group or "public"; those in the networks are likely to have a common base of information and understanding of how one knows about policy and identifies its problems. But knowledge does not necessarily produce agreement. Issue networks may or may not, therefore, be mobilized into, second, a shared-action group (creating a coalition) or, third, a shared-belief group (becoming a conventional interest organization). Increasingly, it is through networks of people who regard each other as knowledgeable, or at least as needing to be answered, that public policy issues tend to be refined, evidence debated, and alternative options worked out—though rarely in any controlled, well-organized way.

What does an issue network look like? It is difficult to say precisely, for at any given time only one part of a network may be active and through time the various connections may intensify or fade among the policy intermediaries and the executive and congressional bureaucracies. For example, there is no single health policy network but various sets of people knowledgeable and concerned about cost-control mechanisms, insurance techniques, nutritional programs, prepaid plans, and so on. At one time, those expert in designing a nationwide insurance system may seem to be operating in relative isolation, until it becomes clear that previous efforts to control costs have already created precedents that have to be accommodated in any new system, or that the issue of federal funding for abortions has laid land mines in the path of any workable plan.

The debate on energy policy is rich in examples of the kaleidoscopic interaction of changing issue networks. The Carter administration's initial proposal was worked out among experts who were closely tied in to conservation-minded networks. Soon it became clear that those concerned with macroeconomic policies had been largely bypassed in the planning, and last-minute amendments were made in the proposal presented to Congress, a fact that was not lost on the networks of leading economists and economic correspondents. Once congressional consideration began, it quickly became evident that attempts to define the energy debate in terms of a classic confrontation between big oil companies and consumer interests were doomed. More and more policy watchers joined in the debate, bringing to it their own concerns and analyses: tax reformers, nuclear power specialists, civil rights groups interested in more jobs; the list soon grew beyond the wildest dreams of the original energy policy planners. The problem, it became clear, was that no one could quickly turn the many networks of knowledgeable people into a shared-action coalition, much less into a single, shared-attitude group believing it faced the moral equivalent of war. Or, if it was a war, it was a Vietnam-type quagmire.

It would be foolish to suggest that the clouds of issue networks that have accompanied expanding national policies are set to replace the more familiar politics of subgovernments in Washington. What they are doing is to overlay the once stable political reference points with new forces that com-

plicate calculations, decrease predictability, and impose considerable strains on those charged with government leadership. The overlay of networks and issue politics not only confronts but also seeps down into the formerly well-established politics of particular policies and programs. Social security, which for a generation had been quietly managed by a small circle of insiders, becomes controversial and politicized. The Army Corps of Engineers, once the picturebook example of control by subgovernments, is dragged into the brawl on environmental politics. The once quiet "traffic safety establishment" finds its own safety permanently endangered by the consumer movement. Confrontation between networks and iron triangles in the Social and Rehabilitation Service, the disintegration of the mighty politics of the Public Health Service and its corps—the list could be extended into a chronicle of American national government during the last generation. The point is that a somewhat new and difficult dynamic is being played out in the world of politics and administration. It is not what has been feared for so long: that technocrats and other people in white coats will expropriate the policy process. If there is to be any expropriation, it is likely to be by the policy activists, those who care deeply about a set of issues and are determined to shape the fabric of public policy accordingly. . . .

The Executive Leadership Problem

Washington has always relied on informal means of producing political leaders in government. This is no less true now than in the days when party spoils ruled presidential appointments. It is the informal mechanisms that have changed. No doubt some of the increasing emphasis on educational credentials, professional specialization, and technical facility merely reflects changes in society at large. But it is also important to recognize that government activity has itself been changing the informal mechanisms that produce political administrators. Accumulating policy commitments have become crucial forces affecting the kind of executive leadership that emerges. E. E. Schattschneider put it better when he observed that "new policies create new politics."[4]

For many years now the list of issues on the public agenda has grown more dense as new policy concerns have been added and few dropped. Administratively, this has proliferated the number of policy intermediaries. Politically, it has mobilized more and more groups of people who feel they have a stake, a determined stake, in this or that issue of public policy. These changes are in turn encouraging further specialization of the government's work force and bureaucratic layering in its political leadership. However, the term "political" needs to be used carefully. Modern officials responsible for making the connection between politics and administration bear little resemblance to the party politicians who once filled patronage jobs. Rather, today's political executive is likely to be a person knowledgeable about the substance of particular issues and adept at moving among the networks of people who are intensely concerned about them.

What are the implications for American government and politics? The verdict cannot be one-sided, if only because political management of the bureaucracy serves a number of diverse purposes. At least three important advantages can be found in the emerging system.

First, the reliance on issue networks and policy politicians is obviously consistent with some of the larger changes in society. Ordinary voters are apparently less constrained by party identification and more attracted to an issue-based style of politics. Party organizations are said to have fallen into a state of decay and to have become less capable of supplying enough highly qualified executive manpower. If government is committed to intervening in more complex, specialized areas, it is useful to draw upon the experts and policy specialists for the public management of these programs. Moreover, the congruence between an executive leadership and an electorate that are both uninterested in party politics may help stabilize a rapidly changing society. Since no one really knows how to solve the policy puzzles, policy politicians have the important quality of being disposable without any serious political ramifications (unless of course there are major symbolic implications, as in President Nixon's firing of Attorney General Elliot Richardson).

Within government, the operation of issue networks may have a second advantage in that they link Congress and the executive branch in ways that political parties no longer can. For many years, reformers have sought to revive the idea of party discipline as a means of spanning the distance between the two branches and turning their natural competition to useful purposes. But as the troubled dealings of recent Democratic Presidents with their majorities in Congress have indicated, political parties tend to be a weak bridge.

Meanwhile, the linkages of technocracy between the branches are indeliberately growing. The congressional bureaucracy that has blossomed in Washington during the last generation is in many ways like the political bureaucracy in the executive branch. In general, the new breed of congressional staffer is not a legislative crony or beneficiary of patronage favors. Personal loyalty to the congressman is still paramount, but the new-style legislative bureaucrat is likely to be someone skilled in dealing with certain complex policy issues, possibly with credentials as a policy analyst, but certainly an expert in using other experts and their networks.

None of this means an absence of conflict between President and Congress. Policy technicians in the two branches are still working for different sets of clients with different interests. The point is that the growth of specialized policy networks tends to perform the same useful services that it was once hoped a disciplined national party system would perform. Sharing policy knowledge, the networks provide a minimum common framework for political debate and decision in the two branches. For example, on energy policy, regardless of one's position on gas deregulation or incentives to producers, the policy technocracy has established a common language for discussing the issues, a shared grammar for identifying the major points of contention, a mutually familiar rhetoric of argumentation. Whether in Congress or the executive branch or somewhere outside, the "movers and shakers" in energy policy (as in health insurance, welfare reform, strategic arms limitation, occupational safety, and a host of other policy areas) tend to share an analytic repertoire for coping with the issues. Like experienced party politicians of earlier times, policy politicians in the knowledge networks may not agree; but they understand each other's way of looking at the world and arguing about policy choices.

A third advantage is the increased maneuvering room offered to political executives by the loose-jointed play of influence. If appointees were ambassadors from clearly defined interest groups and professions, or if policy were monopolized in iron triangles, then the chances for executive leadership in the bureaucracy would be small. In fact, however, the proliferation of administrative middlemen and networks of policy watchers offers new strategic resources for public managers. These are mainly opportunities to split and recombine the many sources of support and opposition that exist on policy issues. Of course, there are limits on how far a political executive can go in shopping for a constituency, but the general tendency over time has been to extend those limits. A secretary of labor will obviously pay close attention to what the AFL-CIO has to say, but there are many other voices to hear, not only in the union movement but also minority groups interested in jobs, state and local officials administering the department's programs, consumer groups worried about wage-push inflation, employees faced with unsafe working conditions, and so on. By the same token, former Secretary of Transportation William Coleman found new room for maneuver on the problem of landings by supersonic planes when he opened up the setpiece debate between pro- and anti-Concorde groups to a wider play of influence through public hearings. Clearly the richness of issue politics demands a high degree of skill to contain expectations and manage the natural dissatisfaction that comes from courting some groups rather than

others. But at least it is a game that can be affected by skill, rather than one that is predetermined by immutable forces.

These three advantages are substantial. But before we embrace the rule of policy politicians and their networks, it is worth considering the threats they pose for American government. Issue networks may be good at influencing policy, but can they govern? Should they?

The first and foremost problem is the old one of democratic legitimacy. Weaknesses in executive leadership below the level of the President have never really been due to interest groups, party politics, or Congress. The primary problem has always been the lack of any democratically based power. Political executives get their popular mandate to do anything in the bureaucracy secondhand, from either an elected chief executive or Congress. The emerging system of political technocrats makes this democratic weakness much more severe. The more closely political administrators become identified with the various specialized policy networks, the farther they become separated from the ordinary citizen. Political executives can maneuver among the already mobilized issue networks and may occasionally do a little mobilizing of their own. But this is not the same thing as creating a broad base of public understanding and support for national policies. The typical presidential appointee will travel to any number of conferences, make speeches to the membership of one association after another, but almost never will he or she have to see or listen to an ordinary member of the public. The trouble is that only a small minority of citizens, even of those who are seriously attentive to public affairs, are likely to be mobilized in the various networks.[5] Those who are not policy activists depend on the ability of government institutions to act on their behalf.

If the problem were merely an information gap between policy experts and the bulk of the population, then more communication might help. Yet instead of garnering support for policy choices, more communication from the issue networks tends to produce an "everything causes cancer" syndrome among ordinary citizens. Policy forensics among the networks yield more experts making more sophisticated claims and counterclaims to the point that the nonspecialist becomes inclined to concede everything and believe nothing that he hears. The ongoing debates on energy policy, health crises, or arms limitation are rich in examples of public skepticism about what "they," the abstruse policy experts, are doing and saying. While the highly knowledgeable have been playing a larger role in government, the proportion of the general public concluding that those running the government don't seem to know what they are doing has risen rather steadily.[6] Likewise, the more government has tried to help, the more feelings of public helplessness have grown.

No doubt many factors and events are linked to these changing public attitudes. The point is that the increasing prominence of issue networks is bound to aggravate problems of legitimacy and public disenchantment. Policy activists have little desire to recognize an unpleasant fact: that their influential systems for knowledgeable policy making tend to make democratic politics more difficult. There are at least four reasons.

Complexity

Democratic political competition is based on the idea of trying to simplify complexity into a few, broadly intelligible choices. The various issue networks, on the other hand, have a stake in searching out complexity in what might seem simple. Those who deal with particular policy issues over the years recognize that policy objectives are usually vague and results difficult to measure. Actions relevant to one policy goal can frequently be shown to be inconsistent with others. To gain a reputation as a knowledgeable participant, one must juggle all of these complexities and demand that other technocrats in the issue networks do the same.

Consensus

A major aim in democratic politics is, after open argument, to arrive at some workable consensus of

views. Whether by trading off one issue against another or by combining related issues, the goal is agreement. Policy activists may commend this democratic purpose in theory, but what their issue networks actually provide is a way of processing dissension. The aim is good policy—the right outcome on the issue. Since what that means is disputable among knowledgeable people, the desire for agreement must often take second place to one's understanding of the issue. Trade-offs or combinations—say, right-to-life groups with nuclear-arms-control people; environmentalists and consumerists; civil liberties groups and anti-gun controllers—represent a kind of impurity for many of the newly proliferating groups. In general there are few imperatives pushing for political consensus among the issue networks and many rewards for those who become practiced in the techniques of informed skepticism about different positions.

Confidence

Democratic politics presumes a kind of psychological asymmetry between leaders and followers. Those competing for leadership positions are expected to be sure of themselves and of what is to be done, while those led are expected to have a certain amount of detachment and dubiety in choosing how to give their consent to be governed. Politicians are supposed to take credit for successes, to avoid any appearance of failure, and to fix blame clearly on their opponents; voters weight these claims and come to tentative judgments, pending the next competition among the leaders.

The emerging policy networks tend to reverse the situation. Activists mobilized around the policy issues are the true believers. To survive, the newer breed of leaders, or policy politicians, must become well versed in the complex, highly disputed substance of the issues. A certain tentativeness comes naturally as ostensible leaders try to spread themselves across the issues. Taking credit shows a lack of understanding of how intricate policies work and may antagonize those who really have been zealously pushing the issue. Spreading blame threatens others in the established networks and may raise expectations that new leadership can guarantee a better policy result. Vagueness about what is to be done allows policy problems to be dealt with as they develop and in accord with the intensity of opinion among policy specialists at that time. None of this is likely to warm the average citizen's confidence in his leaders. The new breed of policy politicians are cool precisely because the issue networks are hot.

Closure

Part of the genius of democratic politics is its ability to find a nonviolent decision-rule (by voting) for ending debate in favor of action. All the incentives in the policy technocracy work against such decisive closure. New studies and findings can always be brought to bear. The biggest rewards in these highly intellectual groups go to those who successfully challenge accepted wisdom. The networks thrive by continuously weighing alternative courses of action on particular policies, not by suspending disbelief and accepting that something must be done.

For all of these reasons, what is good for policy making (in the sense of involving well-informed people and rigorous analysts) may be bad for democratic politics. The emerging policy technocracy tends, as Henry Aaron has said of social science research, to "corrode any simple faiths around which political coalitions ordinarily are built."[7] Should we be content with simple faiths? Perhaps not; but the great danger is that the emerging world of issue politics and policy experts will turn John Stuart Mill's argument about the connection between liberty and popular government on its head. More informed argument about policy choices may produce more incomprehensibility. More policy intermediaries may widen participation among activists but deepen suspicions among unorganized nonspecialists. There may be more group involvement and less democratic legitimacy, more knowledge and more Know-Nothingism. Activists are likely to remain unsatisfied with, and nonactivists uncommitted to, what government is doing. Superficially this canceling of forces might

seem to assure a conservative tilt away from new, expansionary government policies. However, in terms of undermining a democratic identification of ordinary citizens with their government, the tendencies are profoundly radical.

A second difficulty with the issue networks is the problem that they create for the President as ostensible chief of the executive establishment. The emerging policy technocracy puts presidential appointees outside of the chief executive's reach in a way that narrowly focused iron triangles rarely can. At the end of the day, constituents of these triangles can at least be bought off by giving them some of the material advantages that they crave. But for issue activists it is likely to be a question of policy choices that are right or wrong. In this situation, more analysis and staff expertise—far from helping—may only hinder the President in playing an independent political leadership role. The influence of the policy technicians and their networks permeates everything the White House may want to do. Without their expertise there are no option papers, no detailed data and elaborate assessments to stand up against the onslaught of the issue experts in Congress and outside. Of course a President can replace a political executive, but that is probably merely to substitute one incumbent of the relevant policy network for another.

It is, therefore, no accident that President Carter found himself with a cabinet almost none of whom were either his longstanding political backers or leaders of his party. Few if any of his personal retinue could have passed through the reputational screens of the networks to be named, for example, a secretary of labor or defense. Moreover, anyone known to be close to the President and placed in an operating position in the bureaucracy puts himself, and through him the President, in an extremely vulnerable position. Of the three cabinet members who were President Carter's own men, one, Andrew Young, was under extreme pressure to resign in the first several months. Another Carter associate, Bert Lance, was successfully forced to resign after six months, and the third, Griffin Bell, was given particularly tough treatment during his confirmation hearings and was being pressured to resign after only a year in office. The emerging system of political administration tends to produce executive arrangements in which the President's power stakes are on the line almost everywhere in terms of policy, whereas almost nowhere is anyone on the line for him personally.

Where does all this leave the President as a politician and as an executive of executives? In an impossible position. The problem of connecting politics and administration currently places any President in a classic no-win predicament. If he attempts to use personal loyalists as agency and department heads, he will be accused of politicizing the bureaucracy and will most likely put his executives in an untenable position for dealing with their organizations and the related networks. If he tries to create a countervailing source of policy expertise at the center, he will be accused of aggrandizing the Imperial Presidency and may hopelessly bureaucratize the White House's operations. If he relies on some benighted idea of collective cabinet government and on departmental executives for leadership in the bureaucracy (as Carter did in his first term), then the President does more than risk abdicating his own leadership responsibilities as the only elected executive in the national government; he is bound to become a creature of the issue networks and the policy specialists. It would be pleasant to think that there is a neat way out of this trilemma, but there is not.

Finally, there are disturbing questions surrounding the accountability of a political technocracy. The real problem is not that policy specialists specialize but that, by the nature of public office, they must generalize. Whatever an influential political executive does is done with all the collective authority of government and in the name of the public at large. It is not difficult to imagine situations in which policies make excellent sense within the cloisters of the expert issue watchers and yet are nonsense or worse seen from the viewpoint of ordinary people, the kinds of people political executives rarely meet. Since political executives themselves never need to pass muster with the electorate, the main source of democratic accountability must lie with the President and Congress. Given

the President's problems and Congress's own burgeoning bureaucracy of policy specialists, the prospects for a democratically responsible executive establishment are poor at best.

Perhaps we need not worry. A case could be made that all we are seeing is a temporary commotion stirred up by a generation of reformist policies. In time the policy process may reenter a period of detumescence as the new groups and networks subside into the familiar triangulations of power.

However, a stronger case can be made that the changes will endure. In the first place, sufficient policy-making forces have now converged in Washington that it is unlikely that we will see a return to the familiar cycle of federal quiescence and policy experimentation by state governments. The central government, surrounded by networks of policy specialists, probably now has the capacity for taking continual policy initiatives. In the second place, there seems to be no way of braking, much less reversing, policy expectations generated by the compensatory mentality. To cut back on commitments undertaken in the last generation would itself be a major act of redistribution and could be expected to yield even more turmoil in the policy process. Once it becomes accepted that relative rather than absolute deprivation is what matters, the crusaders can always be counted upon to be in business.

A third reason why our politics and administration may never be the same lies in the very fact that so many policies have already been accumulated. Having to make policy in an environment already crowded with public commitments and programs increases the odds of multiple, indirect impacts of one policy on another, of one perspective set in tension with another, of one group and then another being mobilized. This sort of complexity and unpredictability creates a hostile setting for any return to traditional interest group politics.

Imagine trying to govern in a situation where the short-term political resources you need are stacked around a changing series of discrete issues, and where people overseeing these issues have nothing to prevent their pressing claims beyond any resources that they can offer in return. Imagine too that the more they do so, the more you lose understanding and support from public backers who have the long-term resources that you need. Whipsawed between cynics and true believers, policy would always tend to evolve to levels of insolubility. It is not easy for a society to politicize itself and at the same time depoliticize government leadership. But we in the United States may be managing to do just this.

Notes

1. Hugh Heclo, *A Government of Strangers: Executive Politics in Washington* (Washington, D.C.: Brookings Institution, 1977).

2. Perhaps the most widely cited interpretations are J. Leiper Freeman, *The Political Process* (New York: Random House, 1965); and Douglass Cater, *Power in Washington* (New York: Vintage, 1964)

3. Steven V. Roberts, "Trade Associations Flocking to Capital as U.S. Role Rises," *New York Times,* March 4, 1978, p. 44.

4. E. E. Schattschneider, *Politics, Pressures and the Tariff* (Hamden: Archon, 1963), p. 288 (originally published 1935).

5. An interesting recent case study showing the complexity of trying to generalize about who is "mobilizable" is James N. Rosenau, *Citizenship Between Elections* (New York: The Free Press, 1974).

6. Since 1964 the Institute for Social Research at the University of Michigan has asked the question, "Do you feel that almost all of the people running the government are smart people, or do you think that quite a few of them don't seem to know what they are doing?" The proportions choosing the latter view have been 28 percent (1964), 38 percent (1968), 45 percent (1970), 42 percent (1972), 47 percent (1974), and 52 percent (1976). For similar findings on public feelings of lack of control over the policy process, see U.S. Congress, Senate, Subcommittee on Intergovernmental Relations of the Committee on Government Operations, *Confidence and Concern: Citizens View American Government,* committee print, 93d Cong., 1st sess., 1973, pt. 1, p. 30. For a more complete discussion of recent trends see the two articles by Arthur H. Miller and Jack Citrin in the *American Political Science Review* (September 1974).

7. Henry J. Aaron, *Politics and the Professors* (Washington, D.C.: Brookings Institution, 1978), p. 159.

☐ CASE STUDY 14

Introduction

Professor Heclo in the foregoing reading advances an important conceptualization, or rather reconceptualization, of political-administrative relationships, which some scholars suggest are central to the problems confronting modern public administration. However, from the standpoint of the practitioner of public administration, what skills and attributes are most critical for individuals working within high-level policy making arenas? What characteristics are evident in those civil servants who perform well in top political-administrative positions? Are there special human abilities to be found in public officials who effectively do their jobs where politics and administration intersect?

The following case study is from a recent book, *The Politics of Fat,* by Laura Sims, Professor of Human Nutrition at the University of Maryland, College Park and a former administrator of the U.S. Department of Agriculture's Human Nutrition Information Service. Her case recounts how the half-century-old National School Lunch Program, which had as its original goal to feed malnourished school children while supporting farmers, was transformed in the 1990s into a new kind of program promoting sound nutrition for youth. By exploring the process of this program's "reinvention," Dr. Sims affords us a rare insider glimpse behind the scenes, showing how various health and consumer advocates came into play to support this change, along with those who wanted to keep the program running the way it was originally set up, especially the American School Food Service Association and other local school administration groups. The author calls these groups "advocacy coalitions," which is different terminology but means much the same thing that Hugh Heclo refers to in the foregoing essay on "issue networks." Dr. Sims not only gives excellent insights into how these networks actually operate within this particular policy arena, but also emphasizes the central role of a "policy entrepreneur," Ellen Haas, the USDA's Undersecretary for Food, Nutrition, and Consumer Services, as well as the broader changing external political environment for creating this new agenda issue, building support for its adoption, and making the policy change ultimately happen.

As you read "Reinventing School Lunch," try to think about:

Who was specifically involved, pro *and* con, within this issue network? And why?

What most influenced the policy reform—the political strength of its advocates? Weakness of the opposition? The effective leadership of Ellen Haas? The broad changes in the external political environment? Or what?

After carefully studying this case, do you think that it supports Heclo's thesis, or not, concerning the way that public policy is developed within American Government today?

Reinventing School Lunch: Transforming a Food Policy into a Nutrition Policy

LAURA S. SIMS

The largest and the oldest of all child nutrition and food assistance programs is the National School Lunch Program, permanently authorized in 1946 through the National School Lunch Act and created by Congress as "a measure of national security, to safeguard the health and well-being of the Nation's children and to encourage the domestic consumption of nutritious agricultural commodities and other food." That same premise—feeding schoolchildren while supporting agriculture—remains a grounding principle for the National School Lunch Program today but also has served as the basis for rancorous disputes and conflicting policies regarding its operation.

Administered at the federal level by the U.S. Department of Agriculture's (USDA's) Food and Consumer Service (FCS) (formerly named the Food and Nutrition Service [FNS]), the National School Lunch Program is administered at the state level by the state department of education and usually at the local

"Reinventing School Lunch: Transforming a Food Policy into a Nutrition Policy," by Laura S. Sims from *The Politics of Fat: Food and Nutrition Policy in America* (Armonk, NY: M. E. Sharpe, 1998) pp. 67–89. Reprinted by permission of M. E. Sharpe.

level by the school district administration. All public schools are automatically eligible to participate in the program, and it is voluntary in private schools. Almost all public schools (99 percent) and the majority of private schools (83 percent) in the nation do participate in the National School Lunch Program—over 93,000 schools in fiscal year 1996, according to the USDA.

Even though the NSLP is available to about 92 percent of all students, only 56 percent actually participate, and participation is much greater in elementary schools than in secondary schools. In 1992, 25 million children participated in the NSLP each day, at a cost to the government of $4.1 billion.

Schools that elect to participate in the NSLP get both federal cash subsidies and donated agricultural commodities from the USDA for each meal served. The NSLP currently operates as an "entitlement," meaning that federal funds must be provided to all schools that apply and meet the program's eligibility criteria. A three-tiered reimbursement system is used to calculate benefits the school district receives, as follows: children from households with incomes at or below 130 percent of poverty receive free meals; those between 130 percent and 185 percent of poverty receive reduced-price meals; and those above 185 percent of poverty pay for a "full-price" meal. Federal subsidies to each school district are based on the number of children from each of the above groups (even those who are paying full price) who participate in the school feeding program. In 1993, free, reduced-price, and full-price meal subsidies to school districts were $1.695, $1.295, and $0.1625, respectively. Average full prices for lunches ranged from $1.11 in elementary schools to $1.22 in middle and high schools. Severe-need schools (defined as those providing at least 40 percent free meals, with higher costs than the regular rate) are eligible to receive additional assistance of $0.02 per meal served. Current estimates show that over half of all participating children receive either free or reduced-price lunches.

The original 1946 legislation that created the National School Lunch Program set the standard for the kinds of foods that were to be offered to schoolchildren participating in the program. Until recently, these requirements were based on a standard "meal pattern" for all school lunches. The traditional school lunch, offered to children for half a century, was required to include the following foods:

1/2 pint fluid milk

2 ounces protein (meat, fish, 2 eggs, 4 tablespoons peanut butter, or 1 cup dry beans or peas)

3/4-cup serving consisting of two or more vegetables or fruits or both (juice can meet half of this requirement)

8 servings of bread, pasta, or grain per week

This meal pattern reflects a goal that, over the period of one week, children will receive at least one-third of the recommended dietary allowances (RDA) (a standard set to meet the amounts of nutrients needed by groups of healthy people) for basic nutrients, such as protein, vitamins, and minerals. USDA studies show that low-income children depend upon the NSLP to provide up to one-third to one-half of their total daily nutrient intake.

Policy Issues at Work in the National School Lunch Program

When the National School Lunch Program was established in the mid-1940s, the dietary concerns were not the same as they are today. Formulators of that original bill were worried about nutrient deficiencies and making sure that young people received *enough* food to be well nourished. Today, however, concerns are in the opposite direction: obesity among schoolchildren has reached an all-time high. The Dietary Guidelines for Americans, a document first released by both the U.S. Departments of Agriculture and Health and Human Services in 1980, serves as the basis for all nutrition policy. The third edition of that document (published in 1990) was the first to quantify the recommendation for dietary fat; its text suggested that healthy people (over the age of 2) should consume no more than 30 percent of their calories as fat. As explained in more depth later, studies had indicated that school lunches were failing to meet this criterion. Thus, a policy dilemma arises when a major USDA program—such as the NSLP—is not following policy guidelines issued by the same federal department!

Another major policy issue emanates from the initial two-pronged policy objectives for the National School Lunch Program—providing nutritious lunches for children while at the same time providing a ready outlet for agricultural commodities. Can the USDA be friend to both farmer and health professional? Can a food program also be a nutrition and health program? (Those who answer in the affirmative cite the phenomenal success of the "WIC" Program [the Supplemental Nutrition Program for Women, Infants, and Children], where targeted supplemental food has been shown to produce documented health benefits.)

This policy dilemma is captured directly in the controversy over using agricultural commodities in the National School Lunch Program. Those who favor their use cite economic reasons—that it is simply good business not to be wasteful but to use any surplus foods to feed hungry children. (In fact, according to one USDA estimate, if donated food commodities had not been used in 1987, the costs of the NSLP would have been $880 million higher than its actual cash costs.) Those who oppose the use of commodity products in school meals cite the fact that a number of these products (notably, processed cheese, peanut butter, processed meat, and the like) provide higher levels of dietary fat, cholesterol, sugar, and sodium than are suitable for children.

To receive federal benefits for running the National School Lunch Program, the school district agrees to abide by the rules and follow the requirements for participation. This means that in order to accept cash subsidies to run the NSLP, the school district must also agree to accept various donated agricultural commodities, the value of which is estimated to be between 15 percent to 20 percent of the cash outlay for the NSLP. Both "entitlement commodities," valued at about 14 cents a meal, and "bonus" commodities are available to school food service managers. These donated foods are essentially "free" to the school food authority; the other 80 percent of the food must be purchased locally. Therein lies the dilemma—local school food service managers often feel that if they choose not to accept the donated commodities, they run the risk of pricing themselves out of an ability to provide free and reduced-price lunches to the children who need them.

Recognizing that some products are especially high in fat (and particularly saturated fat), the USDA has recently made a concerted effort to cut back on the amount of dietary fat in surplus commodities donated to schools. Low-fat beef patties are a good ex-

ample of this initiative. In the early 1990s (the first years these alternative low-fat products were offered), they made up only 5 percent of the total ground beef used in the program. School lunch managers, already operating under tight financial constraints and recognizing that children will eat only those foods with which they are familiar, are reluctant to use the new lower-fat products for fear of operating at a deficit. This aspect of running the NSLP was dramatically captured in the title of an article that appeared in the *Washington Post*, "Dissing the Salmon: Schools Can't Sell USDA's Delicacies," which described a situation in which the USDA had been able to purchase millions of pounds of flaked salmon and over a million pounds of frozen asparagus for distribution to schools, only to learn that the children refused to eat the food!

Advocacy Coalitions at Work in the National School Lunch Program

The policy subsystems at work in the National School Lunch Program are vast. The web of interest groups, consumer advocacy groups, and professional associations interested in the National School Lunch Program is as complex as it is dedicated. Those systems starting with the legislative and regulatory aspects of the program as well as those dealing with the implementation of the NSLP span the range from those who produce, process, and deliver the food to school administrators and school food service personnel, to cafeteria workers who prepare and serve the food, to advocacy groups and professional organizations that are interested in the delivery of government-sponsored food assistance programs, to parents and caregivers, and finally to the children who actually participate in the program. With a program that has existed for fifty years and is so prominently remembered by most adults in this country, it is no surprise that an entire industry has built up over the years to lobby for and to implement the NSLP.

The variety and array of agencies, legislative committees, media, interest groups, consumer advocacy groups, and professional associations that have built up around the issue of the National School Lunch Program are vast indeed. In the executive branch of government, the U.S. Department of Agriculture has had primary responsibility for the administration of this program since its creation in 1946. More recently, the School Lunch Program has been given a more prominent role as a key domestic policy area by the White House—i.e., the Executive Office of the President—both in welfare reform and in agriculture policy.

Within the Congress, two major types of committees exist that influence both the reauthorization of the program and its operation: the authorizing committees and the appropriations committees. The authorizing committee responsible for the NSLP in the House of Representatives was the Education and Labor Committee, reconfigured and renamed for the 104th Congress as the Economic and Educational Opportunities Committee. In addition, the House Committee on Agriculture—with its Subcommittee on Departmental Operations, Nutrition, and Foreign Agriculture—has played a key role in oversight of the operation of the NSLP. In the Senate, the Agriculture, Nutrition, and Forestry Committee has retained authorizing responsibility for the National School Lunch Program. Appropriations committees in each house of Congress—the Agriculture Appropriations Subcommittee in the House and the Agriculture, Rural Development, and Related Agencies Appropriations Subcommittee in the Senate—have final authority to approve the amount of money appropriated for the operation of the program. Thus, while an "education" committee in the House authorizes the program, an "agriculture" subcommittee actually approves the funding.

In November 1994, Republicans assumed control of both houses of Congress after a hiatus of forty years. The committee structure and leadership changed dramatically, resulting in changing roles and responsibilities for numerous legislators. A number of Republican legislators found themselves cast in the role of downsizing or even eliminating those very programs of which they were once personally very supportive. One example of this dilemma was William F. Goodling (R-Pennsylvania), whose personal story was chronicled in a detailed *Washington Post* article. Representative Goodling, chairman of the House Economic and Educational Opportunities Committee, was quoted as saying, "I have long defended some of these programs, especially the school lunch program. But, that doesn't mean that school lunch or any of the other food and nutrition programs

cannot be improved. And we are under the mandate from the Republican Caucus and in the Contract with America, to make some changes." Other GOP members in the House publicly described their ideological dilemma—while they remained supportive of nutrition programs, they were committed to giving state governments greater flexibility and less paperwork in the administration of the programs.

A vast network of groups in the private sector exists to actively influence the operation of the NSLP. A group's interest in the program stems primarily from the base concern of the organization. If an organization mainly represents food or agricultural commodity interests, it will be far more concerned about commodity specifications, cost considerations, transportation, food storage and safety issues, and other matters related to the food offered to children in schools. These organizations range from agriculture production groups such as the Farmers Union to commodity-specific organizations, such as the National Cattlemen's Beef Association, the National Dairy Council, the United Fresh Fruit and Vegetable Association, and the National Wholesale Grocers' Association.

If the organization represents health and nutrition professionals, it will more likely be concerned with issues such as the nutritional quality of the meals served, whether the children are learning good nutritional and health practices, and personnel issues such as whether credentialed professionals are providing the needed services. Professional associations—such as the American Dietetic Association (ADA) (with nearly 70,000 members), the American Public Health Association (APHA), and smaller groups of professionals such as the Society for Nutrition Education (SNE) and the National Association of State Nutrition Education and Training Program Coordinators (NASNET)—are active in monitoring changes to the NSLP. Most active, however, in representing its members' vested interests regarding the administration of the NSLP is the American School Food Service Association (ASFSA), which has over 65,000 members.

Large organizations with specific targeted purposes such as the ASFSA have the resources to mount effective lobbying efforts, being able both to operate at the "grassroots" level and to hire well-trained, well-connected lobbyists in Washington. In this regard, the ASFSA has long retained the services of a well-known lobbyist in Washington circles, Marshall

Matz, a lawyer who boasts a long record of key bipartisan accomplishments with various food and nutrition programs. In addition, the ASFSA has a "government relations" manager on its own staff to organize and coordinate the organization's lobbying efforts (incidentally, the person who most recently held this position was a key staff member for a member of Congress who was on the NSLP authorizing committee). The approaches and effectiveness of the American School Food Service Association's lobbying efforts as the organization has sought to influence key regulatory and legislative changes proposed for the National School Lunch Program are key to this case study.

Consumer advocacy organizations certainly are concerned about many similar issues, but their focus is usually on the recipients of program services—that is, whether entitled children are receiving access to the program and whether the program is meeting the needs of poor and disadvantaged groups. Other consumer groups have focused on the internal, "qualitative" aspects of the menus served in the NSLP, concerned primarily with the nutritional value of the food served. An example of the first type of organization is the Food Research and Action Center (FRAC), which has focused its efforts on the "access" issue for low-income children, while groups such as Public Voice for Food and Health Policy and the Center for Science in the Public Interest (CSPI) have mounted an extensive effort (primarily via the media) to inform the public about the nutritional quality of the meals offered in the School Lunch Program.

A number of coalitions has also been formed whose activities focus on the NSLP. The Child Nutrition Forum, organized and administered by the FRAC, consists of a number of child advocacy organizations, public interest groups, and professional associations; its focus is to bring these various groups together to draw legislative and media attention to access issues involving participation of low-income children in child nutrition programs, including school lunch, school breakfast, and other child care feeding programs. A more recently formed, but short-lived, coalition was Advocates for Better Children's Diets (A-B-C-D). Included among its members were many of the same organizations that are in the Child Nutrition Forum, but the group also included trade associations, such as the American Soy Association. Those unfamiliar with this issue may question why such a group would want to be involved in a coalition that seeks to influence the operation of the School Lunch Program. Texturized vegetable protein (made from soy) is a key ingredient of ground beef patties served to schoolchildren as one measure to reduce the dietary fat in the School Lunch Program. Therefore, this product can be promoted in efforts to improve the "quality" (i.e., reduce the fat content) of the school lunch meals.

Specialized media also play a role in the web of groups that comprise the School Lunch Program's policy subsystem by informing both the internal and external groups about the activities going on in Washington related to the program. For example, the American School Food Service Association publishes two periodicals, the *School Lunch Journal* and the *School Food Service Research Review.* Published twice annually, the latter publication, which is designed primarily for the academic reader, contains articles that feature evaluation and research conducted on the School Lunch Program. Coalitions and advocacy groups also use publications as a means of disseminating their message and often develop "media kits" to inform the public via the print and visual media.

Documenting the Need for Policy Changes in the National School Lunch Program

A substantive factual research base is often required to define the nature of policy changes that may be needed. Older program evaluation reports, authorized and funded by the USDA, had focused on the nutritional content of the school meals but had limited their analysis to those nutrients identified in the original 1946 legislation. Times were much different at the close of World War II, and the goals of the School Lunch Program were aimed primarily at assuring that undernourished children would receive adequate food with sufficient calories, vitamins, and minerals. Using data from the Survey of Food Consumption in Low-Income Households, 1977–78, researchers in the early 1980s gave high grades to the NSLP. Students participating in the School Lunch Program had higher nutrient intakes than nonparticipants, especially for protein and most vitamins and minerals, but not for calories, iron, magnesium, and vitamin B-6.

Using data collected between 1979 and 1983, the USDA's Food and Nutrition Service, under contract with the System Development Corporation in Santa Monica, California, conducted the National Evaluation of School Nutrition Programs. The study concluded that children who participated in the School Lunch Program received more of almost all nutrients examined than nonparticipants. The positive impact of school lunch on energy intakes as well as vitamins A and B-6 were noted, although the program did not improve children's intakes of iron and vitamin C. It must be noted that these evaluations focused mainly on assessing calories, vitamins, and minerals, according to the criterion for meeting one-third of the RDA for those nutrients as specified in the 1946 legislation that established the program.

What was needed, of course, was a current analysis of the nutritional content of school meals reflective of the macronutrient content, such as fat. No longer were micronutrients, such as most vitamins and minerals, of major health concern, and the older evaluations did not provide much usable data on those nutrients shown to be associated with the development of debilitating chronic diseases, such as fat, cholesterol, and sodium. In the late 1980s and early 1990s, the only data available on the fat content of school lunches were those collected by consumer advocacy organizations as a result of conducting their own surveys. The Center for Science in the Public Interest in its "White Paper on School Lunch Nutrition" showcased the results of its analyses of lunches from three school programs. In two of the programs, they found an average of 42 percent of calories from fat, and lunches from the third program contained 41 percent of calories from fat when whole milk was served and 35 percent when skim milk was served.

Another organization that was prominent in showcasing problems with the National School Lunch Program was Public Voice for Food and Health Policy, founded by Ellen Haas in 1983. In 1988, after reviewing menus from fifty school districts nationwide, Public Voice asserted that "many schools have pumped their menus with high-fat commodities contributed from farm surpluses, such as butter, cheese, eggs, and processed foods—[thus] cutting food costs but also cutting dietary value." At a press conference, Ellen Haas publicly went on record as suggesting that "the program is run more as an agricultural support program than a nutritional program."

These first efforts to publicly expose the types of meals fed to schoolchildren as part of the National School Lunch Program were followed by a series of four reports issued by Public Voice—"What's for Lunch? A Progress Report on Reducing Fat in the School Lunch Program," in 1989; "What's for Lunch? II: A 1990 Survey of Options in the School Lunch Program"; "Heading for a Health Crisis: Eating Patterns of America's School Children," in 1991; and "Agriculture First: Nutrition, Commodities and the National School Lunch Program," in 1992. Most of these reports carried a common theme—that USDA administrators were placing higher priority on distributing agricultural commodities than on providing nutritious school lunches. Recommendations were usually targeted both to Congress to reform dairy policies and to the USDA to reform its commodity distribution practices to encourage the purchase of lower-fat dairy, meat, and poultry products and to expand the availability of fresh fruits and vegetables. The 1991 report, in particular, was notable because it was followed by a response from then USDA Secretary Edward Madigan, who publicly "pledged to take steps to reduce the fat content of meals provided by the National School Lunch Program, [thus] bringing their nutritive content into compliance with federal dietary guidelines by 1994."

The data needed to reform the National School Lunch Program were actually collected as part of a study initiated during the George Bush administration by former USDA Secretary Madigan, who was also personally committed to improving the nutritional quality of the meals served in the School Lunch Program. This study, the School Nutrition Dietary Assessment Study, was conducted by Mathematica Policy Research, under contract with the USDA's Food and Nutrition Service. The study collected meal information from a nationally representative sample of 545 schools and 3,350 students in May 1992. A most significant finding was that for the first time, the amount of dietary fat in school lunches was documented, and the results showed just how different the amounts of macronutrients were in school lunches compared to the amounts recommended in the Dietary Guidelines. School lunches provided much more dietary fat (38 percent, compared to the Dietary Guidelines' recommendation of 30 percent), saturated fat (15 percent, compared to 10 percent), and sodium (1,479 mg, compared to 800 mg). Further, less than 5 percent of the 515 schools sampled offered school lunches that were close to the Dietary Guidelines' recommendation for fat. On the positive side, however, school lunches were providing one-third or more of the daily recommended dietary allowances for calories; protein; vitamins A, C, and B-6; and the minerals iron, zinc, and calcium. Thus, this study confirmed what many health professionals and nutritionists had long suspected—the NSLP does a good job of providing at least one-third of the RDA for many nutrients, but the meals contained far too much fat, saturated fat, cholesterol, and sodium.

One of the concerns reported was that those schools that offered low-fat (32 percent or less of calories) meals showed a 6 percent lower participation rate than other schools. The report noted, however, that NSLP participation rates in schools offering meals that were in the range of 32 to 35 percent of calories from fat were similar to participation rates in schools where the average meal's fat content was 35 percent or higher. According to the authors of the report, "these findings suggest that schools can make some modifications to reduce the fat content of lunches without adversely affecting participation; if, however, the fat content is reduced to levels below 32 percent of calories, participation falls substantially."

Regulatory and Legislative Reform Efforts

In most traditional analyses, regulatory actions follow legislative changes. However, in the case of reform of the National School Lunch Program, this sequence of policy changes did not apply. The NSLP was permanently authorized, but related programs that were carried under the same legislation were due to expire in 1994. Thus, congressional action was needed to reauthorize these programs, and Congress used this forum as a vehicle to make changes in the NSLP as well. The changes proposed to the NSLP—both legislative and regulatory—will be discussed in chronological sequence in this section of the case study. (To highlight these various policy activities, accounts of the legislative endeavors will be in *italics,* while those initiatives taking place in the regulatory arena will be in "regular" font.)

Building on her success as a consumer activist and media specialist and fresh from her appointment as the USDA's assistant secretary (later, the position

was elevated to the title of undersecretary) for Food, Nutrition, and Consumer Services, Ellen Haas decided to take her school lunch reform message directly to both the public and to the health professionals and consumer advocates who had supported her activities in the past. The School Nutrition Dietary Assessment Study had provided ample evidence for the kind of reforms in the quality of the school meals that she had long envisioned. This report, released in October 1993, was the first study of the school meals program in ten years and provided important documentation of the nutritional performance of the program. Disturbing—but a clear mandate for Haas—was the finding that virtually none of the schools offered meals that conformed to the Dietary Guidelines recommendations. The study had shown that school lunches exceeded dietary guidelines for fat by 25 percent, saturated fat by 50 percent, and sodium by nearly 100 percent. The report also stated that children who ate school lunch consumed significantly higher amounts of calories from fat than children who got their lunch elsewhere. Especially troubling was the finding that nearly half of the more than 25 million school meals served were to needy students, for whom this may be their only nourishing meal of the day.

This message was taken to the public in a series of public hearings focusing on "Nutrition Objectives for School Meals." These regional hearings were held in four cities—Atlanta; Los Angeles; Flint, Michigan; and Washington, D.C.—in late fall 1993. Originally announced in the *Federal Register* (58 FR 47853 September 13, 1993), the hearings were staged "to provide an opportunity for public dialogue before policy changes are proposed for the National School Lunch Program." The response exceeded everyone's expectations. There were 350 witnesses at the four hearings—including children, parents, teachers, nutritionists and dietitians, school food service personnel, farmers, physicians, the food industry, and community leaders—and 2,500 additional comments were filed afterward by the public. Over 90 percent of these comments supported changes in the National School Lunch Program and applauded the USDA's efforts to improve the nutritional quality of the meals served. In addition to these "public" hearings, Haas provided a forum for interested professionals by meeting regularly with a small group of representatives from consumer, health, and professional groups. In addition, she was a popular "keynote" speaker at meetings of these professional and consumer groups. She continued to court the media, especially those reporters with whom she had developed friendships from her days at Public Voice—Marian Burros from the *New York Times* and Laura Shapiro of *Newsweek.* Clearly, the objective of "creating a positive political climate" for reform of the National School Lunch Program had been initiated.

On November 2, 1993, Senator Patrick Leahy (D-Vermont), chair of the Senate Agriculture, Nutrition, and Forestry Committee, introduced S. 1614, the Better Nutrition and Health for Children Act. Designed to add health-promotion aspects to current child nutrition programs that were up for congressional reauthorization in 1994, the bill was designed to improve child nutrition programs by making school meals conform to the Dietary Guidelines. It also provided for increased funding for nutrition education and increased access to meals for children during the summer.

Representative Kildee (D-Michigan) introduced a related bill in the House (H.R. 8) on January 5, 1993, and it was referred to the House Committee on Education and Labor (the name of the committee before it was changed by the 104th Congress). Hearings were held before the Subcommittee on Elementary, Secondary, and Vocational Education on April 12 and 14, 1994, some sixteen months after the bill was introduced. The bill, known at this point as the Healthy Meals for Healthy Americans Act of 1994, received voice vote approval on May 18, 1994, from the full House Education and Labor Committee.

During markup of the bill, several amendments were approved by voice vote, including one proposed by Representative George Miller (D-California) that would permit some schools to drop whole milk from their menus if it accounted for less than 1 percent of the total milk consumed at the school in the previous year. Miller's amendment initially was opposed by Representative Steven Gunderson (R-Wisconsin), whose dairy state had long supported the School Lunch Program's requirement that schools must offer whole milk along with other types. Gunderson offered a substitute that would have allowed milk purchases to be based on a survey of students' preferences. He later withdrew his amendment, saying that he thought the Miller amendment would have little effect in most school districts.

The action line of the story now shifts back to the regulatory arena. Following on the heels of the widely publicized School Nutrition Dietary Assessment Study and personal stories gleaned from hearings and reported in popular media stories, the USDA's Ellen Haas clearly had the tools she required—along with a formidable arsenal of departmental regulatory tools and legislative connections—to bring about changes to the National School Lunch Program. The approach used in making the announcement was Haas's trademark press announcement plus public relations effort, tied this time to regulatory reform.

On June 8, 1994, then Secretary of Agriculture Mike Espy and Undersecretary Ellen Haas announced the USDA's School Meals Initiative for Healthy Children. In regulatory parlance, these changes were formulated as "proposed rules," a form of enforceable policy initiated by the executive branch that does not require congressional action. The complete text of the preamble and proposed rules appeared in the June 10, 1994, edition of the *Federal Register,* allowing for a ninety-day comment period, ending on September 8, 1994.

The USDA's School Meals Initiative for Healthy Children was based on four strategies to update and improve the quality of school meals:

1. *Eating for health:* Using the power of regulatory reform to ensure that school meals would meet standards for fat and saturated fat content as well as for key nutrients and calories, thus meeting the 1990 Dietary Guidelines for Americans' recommendations
2. *Making food choices:* Launching a nutrition education initiative for children as well as working with professional chefs and other members of the food and agricultural community to offer training and technical assistance to local meal providers
3. *Maximizing resources:* Improving the nutritional profile of commodities by putting nutrition labels on commodities, working more closely with federal partners at the Department of Health and Human Services (DHHS) and the Department of Education (DOE), as well as establishing links to local farmers to enhance access to locally grown commodities
4. *Managing for the future:* Streamlining administration of the NSLP by using technology, reducing paperwork and procedures, and emphasizing flexibility

In order to ensure that schools met the Dietary Guidelines recommendations, a new plan was designed to replace the "meal pattern" system, which school lunch directors had followed since 1946 (i.e., planning meals by incorporating a USDA-specified number of servings of certain foods, such as meat/meat alternative, fruit and/or vegetables, bread, and milk), and use instead a "flexible system of menu planning" called "nutrient standard menu planning" or NuMenus. The USDA-proposed rule mandated that schools use a "nutrient standard" to ensure that the meals offered to children complied with the Dietary Guidelines. The plan required school food services to determine the nutritional content of the school meals by using a computer analysis program, or alternatively, schools could use an "assisted" version of the nutrient analysis by receiving help from outside groups, like state agencies or consultants.

The American School Food Service Association, the major professional organization concerned with the administration of school lunch programs, initially applauded the USDA (at least in public statements) for the "high priority [it] has given to the National School Lunch . . . program" and for giving the 92,000 schools participating in the program four years to comply with the regulations. But its campaign to overturn the regulations was just beginning. ASFSA members complained about the "paperwork burden" associated with compliance, the cost of the new foods in the program, and the level of technical competence required to use computers to determine the nutrient content of school meals. So the association took its cause—and its lobbyist—instead to the Congress, where program reauthorization debates were in progress.

On July 19, 1994, the House passed H.R. 8, and on August 25, 1994, the Senate passed S. 1614 by voice vote. Although the two bills had similar goals, a House-Senate conference committee was needed to work out differences between the measures. The amended legislation was finally approved by the House on October 5 by voice vote and agreed to by the Senate on October 6, 1994. The resulting bill, the Healthy Meals for Healthy Americans Act, was signed into law by President Bill Clinton on November 2, 1994, as Public Law 103-448.

The final legislation reauthorized child nutrition programs as expected but also contained some important policy changes. The USDA's proposed regulations had called for schools to adopt a "nutrient standard menu-planning" system by 1996, a method *that would use computers to track the nutrient content of a meal offered in the School Lunch Program. This measure, in particular, was quite unpopular with many school food service directors, who voiced their opposition through the ASFSA's lobbying efforts. In response to this pressure, Congress offered a loophole—the final legislation included language that gave schools an additional option of using a "food-based menu-planning" system, which would allow school lunch directors to meet the Dietary Guidelines in their menus by tracking foods rather than nutrients—the way they were used to doing it.*

After years of debate, Congress also settled the issue of whether schools must offer students whole milk as one of their beverage options. Nutritionists have long argued that the requirement adds unnecessary fat to children's diets. But under a carefully crafted provision in the law, the whole-milk requirement was replaced with language that requires schools to "offer students a variety of fluid milk [whole, chocolate, 1 percent, etc.] consistent with prior year preferences." In other words, if students didn't drink whole milk one year, it didn't have to be served the next. To placate the dairy lobby, which strenuously fought the removal of the whole-milk language, the bill required the USDA to provide schools with an amount of low-fat cheese that is the "milkfat equivalent" of the "lost" whole milk.

The final bill also excluded a provision in the House version that would have required the USDA to engage in a formal process known as "negotiated rule making," making it mandatory that the agency meet with interest groups before it issued certain proposed regulations. This provision was sought by groups such as the American School Food Service Association that strenuously opposed the USDA's June 1994 proposed regulations and wished to be able to change any contentious language before such regulations were issued. (Those close to the situation felt that "neg-reg," as it is colloquially called, is just a way of letting a special-interest group write the regulations it wants to implement.)

The chapter on regulatory reform was not closed until June 13, 1995, when the *final* rule on the Schools Meals Initiative for Healthy Children was published as 7CFR Parts 210 and 220, "Child Nutrition Programs: School Meal Initiatives for Healthy Children; Final Rule." The USDA called this final rule "the most comprehensive and integrated reform of school meals in the 50 year history of these programs." (Much more than just new rules for menu planning, the School Meals Initiative included support for innovative nutrition education, improved opportunities for technical assistance and training for school lunch personnel, and reformulation of donated commodities.) The USDA's final rule was similar to that which the department had proposed a year earlier, except that it included a new menu-planning approach: a food-based menu plan, which, while reminiscent of the plan currently in use, suggested alternatives for reducing the fat content of the meal by adding foods such as grains, fruits, and vegetables. Thus, the final rules accepted three-menu planning approaches—the nutrient-based, the assisted nutrient-based, and the newly added food-based.

In addition to these regulatory changes, the USDA initiated "Team Nutrition," a nationwide integrated program designed to help implement the School Meals Initiative for Healthy Children. The mission of Team Nutrition was "to improve the health and education of children by creating innovative public and private partnerships that promote food choices for a healthful diet through the media, school, families and the community."

The Team Nutrition initiative was announced publicly on June 12, 1995, at a media extravaganza attended by first lady Hillary Rodham Clinton and USDA Secretary Dan Glickman. In addition to the regulatory changes previously discussed, Team Nutrition included several other initiatives—a nutrition education initiative designed to motivate children to make food choices for a healthy diet; a training and technical assistance initiative to provide support to school food service personnel; and changes to reduce the fat content of agricultural commodities used in the NSLP.

Nutrition Education

This initiative clearly has received the lion's share of public attention and resources. Moving away from the "typical" sources of nutrition education materials and techniques, USDA Undersecretary Ellen Haas clearly wanted something different and reached out to popular media channels. In less than two years, partnership agreements were reached with the Walt Disney Company to use two characters, "Timon" and "Pumbaa," from its movie *The Lion King* as "spokestoons" to promote the importance of a healthy diet to children; with Scholastic,

Inc., to develop nutrition education materials for use in schools; with the national PTA organization for distribution of materials promoting parent involvement in the effort; with the USDA's Cooperative State Research, Education, and Extension Service to develop and distribute a community action kit; and with the California Department of Education to serve as models and evaluation projects for Team Nutrition's community-based nutrition promotion efforts.

Technical Assistance and Training

The technical assistance component of Team Nutrition has included the development of "tasty, low-fat, low-cost" recipes with chefs working with local school food service directors (another source of great consternation for the ASFSA); the development of a training plan and standards; the participation of volunteer chefs at local school cafeterias; as well as the development of a national nutrient database and software to implement the NuMenus system in schools.

Commodity Improvement

As described earlier in this case study, the use of donated commodities has long been a source of frustration for those seeking to reduce the dietary fat content of School Lunch Program menus. One direct way of reducing the fat content of school lunches is to change the nature of the agricultural commodities offered free to school lunch administrators or to offer more "low-fat" commodities.

Staff at the USDA's Food and Consumer Service unit work with staff at other USDA agencies, the Agricultural Marketing Service (AMS) and the Farm Service Agency (FSA), in developing the specifications for commodities that are used in the NSLP. The AMS handles "Group A Commodities," such as livestock, poultry, dairy, and fruits and vegetables; while the FSA has its own dairy division and a domestic program that handles grains, peanuts, and other miscellaneous items. Unlike menu standards for the NSLP, commodity specifications are not published in the *Federal Register* or codified in the *Code of Federal Regulations* (CFR). Rather, they are distributed to the industries that bid to supply these foods. When specifications are developed, the requesting organization—in this case, the FCS—works with the AMS and the food industry to develop them. Issues that are considered in developing these specifications include technical feasibility of supplying the products, flavor and acceptability, body and texture, color, and nutrient quality.

To support the USDA's School Meals Initiative for Healthy Children and meet the concerns about agricultural commodities in the NSLP, the USDA established the Commodities Improvement Council in May 1994, early in the process of school lunch reform. Composed of USDA undersecretaries of Food, Nutrition, and Consumer Services and Farm and Foreign Agriculture Services and the assistant secretary for Marketing and Regulatory Programs, the council was charged with developing policy for improving the nutritional profile of USDA commodity offerings while maintaining the department's support for domestic agriculture markets.

The council established a Tri-Agency Task Force to conduct a comprehensive review of the specifications for all commodity products. The charge to the task force was to identify commodities that could be improved by modifying their fat, sodium, or sugar levels while making sure that the products were acceptable to schoolchildren. As a result of this review, more than two-thirds of the 142 distributed commodities (such as fruits, vegetables, grain products, and most unprocessed poultry products such as turkey and chicken) were excluded from further modification because they are typically purchased in their simplest, most natural or unprocessed form. Of the remaining 46 commodities considered for improvement, the council approved half for modification. Meat, cheese, and peanut butter were among the products targeted for fat reduction from their current levels. Canned meat will be reduced from 22–25 percent fat to 19–22 percent, fresh ground beef and pork from 20–21 percent to 17–18 percent fat content, and frozen ground beef and pork from 17–19 percent to 15–17 percent fat content. The task force also recommended that the USDA work with the food industry to develop some new products, including "lite" butter, low-fat macaroni and cheese, meatless spaghetti sauce, reduced-fat cheese, boneless turkey ham, and prune puree (to be used as a fat substitute).

In addition to these low- or reduced-fat products, the USDA is also seeking to provide schools with additional quantities of fruits, vegetables, and grain products that contain virtually no fat. It is also pilot-testing a program in which fresh produce is purchased for the USDA by the Department of Defense and delivered directly to schools. While the American School Food Service Association supported the commodity initiative, many school food service directors were skeptical of its effect, questioning whether children would accept the taste of reduced-fat, -sugar, and -sodium products.

The legislative story had not ended, however. Shortly after the final rules for the School Meals Initiative for Healthy Children were announced by the USDA, Representative William Goodling (R-Pennsylvania) introduced H.R. 2066, the Healthy Meals for Children Act. On July 19, 1995, the proposed bill was referred to the House Committee on Economic and Educational Opportunities, and on August 4, 1995, it was referred to the Subcommittee on Early Childhood, Youth, and Families. After languishing in legislative limbo for nine months, the bill was discharged from subcommittee action by the full committee on May 1, 1996, and on the same day, the committee considered H.R. 2066, amended it in markup, and passed it by voice vote, ordering it to be reported. After being reported to the House (as amended) by the full committee on May 7, it was called up by the House under suspension of the rules on May 14 and passed by voice vote. For many who were not following these developments closely, the bill is quite innocuous. It simply "amend[s] the National School Lunch Act to provide greater flexibility to schools to meet the Dietary Guidelines for Americans under the school lunch and school breakfast programs, as amended."

On March 14, 1996, Senator Thad Cochran (R-Mississippi) introduced a similar bill (S. 1613) into the Senate. Described by Senator Cochran as "virtually the same as H.R. 2066," the bill passed the Senate on May 16, 1996, without amendment by unanimous consent. The bill, which passed by voice vote in both houses, met with bipartisan support in Congress.

Critics of the bill had argued that its wording was too vague and did not provide for accountability for schools to follow nutrient-based standards in the NSLP. Before the bill was signed by President Clinton, an important clause was added at the "eleventh hour" to alleviate administration concerns. (A spokesperson for the ASFSA said that the decision apparently came directly from the Office of Management and Budget [OMB] in the White House, with Agriculture Secretary Dan Glickman's support.)

The OMB's suggested amendment gave the secretary of agriculture the final decision-making authority to determine whether submitted menu plans met the nutrient standards for the NSLP; the official wording of the legislation now reads that schools can use any method "within guidelines established by the Secretary." On May 29, 1996, President Clinton signed into law the enrolled version of the bill, which became Public Law 104–149.

Looking Back . . .

Why was such legislation needed when new regulations governing the implementation of the NSLP had just been promulgated? Several reasons may be offered. The first has to do with the larger political environment under which changes to the NSLP were made. The 104th Congress, which took office in January 1995, had originally attempted to "block-grant" the School Lunch Program as one of its first actions in the Contract with America legislative proposals. The rationale was to improve decision making and implementation at the local level and decrease the level of federal involvement. After vigorous lobbying by the ASFSA and others, the NSLP was not included in any "block-grant" legislation. However, it was appealing to Republicans to offer a bill later that appeared to decrease the level of federal involvement in the School Lunch Program.

Legislation that permits "maximum flexibility" in planning school lunch menus certainly sounds as though it would decrease federal involvement in how the program would be operated at the local level. As Representative William Goodling was quoted as saying, "The bottom line is that the basic responsibility for developing reasonable approaches to meeting the dietary guidelines is with the school food authorities, with Federal guidance and oversight, but not a panoply of prescriptive rules or preset options."

Democrats and Republicans alike say this episode vividly "illustrates how a well-meaning federal agency carrying out a long-overdue change in nutritional standards barged into an area where local school districts know best." Even the *Congressional Record* contains the following statement: "We are moving this bipartisan legislation because the USDA Food and Consumer Service under the direction of Ellen Haas is out of control. In the name of advancing good nutrition for children, the USDA is burying our schools in bureaucratic paperwork and regulatory micromanagement."

The bill was backed by an intense lobbying effort by the American School Food Service Association, which used all its power—strong, effective lobbying coupled with an intensive grassroots letter-writing campaign from its 65,000 members—to ensure passage of the bill. It also enlisted the support of the American Association of School Administrators, the National School Boards Association, and the Association of School Business Officials by publishing estimates of increased costs associated with implementing the USDA regulations and by raising fears of increased "Washington involvement" in local affairs. Former House Speaker Tip O'Neill's maxim that "all politics is local" certainly held true in this case.

A second reason for the legislative activity is that school food service officials were quite unhappy with the new USDA regulations; in fact, after the proposed rules were announced in June 1994, the USDA received over 14,000 comments, 12,000 of those reportedly coming from disgruntled ASFSA members. Feeling that their comments had not been attended to in writing the regulations, fearing increased costs associated with implementing the new regulations, and desiring more flexibility in implementing them, the group sought the only way to offset regulations to which it was opposed—new legislation. This new act allowed school food service authorities to use "any reasonable approach" to meet the Dietary Guidelines for Americans under the National School Lunch Act. (Presumably this language also permits the very same meal pattern that the USDA, in the School Nutrition Dietary Assessment Study, had found to be high in fat and saturated fat, and had found not to meet Dietary Guidelines recommendations.) Further, the bill states, "The Secretary [of the USDA] may not *require* a school to conduct or use a nutrient analysis to meet the requirements," the clause to which school food service managers were most opposed.

While the USDA and the ASFSA membership share many common goals and say they have never disagreed on the ultimate outcome of improving the nutritional quality of the NSLP, the "devil," as they say, "is in the details." The USDA regulations can specify the nutrient standards on which the NSLP is based, but the overriding legislation now stipulates how and when those nutrient standards can be met. The USDA's goals of having school meals meet the recommendations of the 1990 Dietary Guidelines for Americans can be met mainly by serving more grains and breads in school lunches and increasing the amount of fruits and vegetables offered, options that school food service managers maintain are too expensive. Further, in order to ensure that these requirements were met, the USDA wanted school food service administrators to keep track of the nutrient content of school meals by using computer-based nutrient analyses. School food service administrators balked, much preferring to continue using their current system and not wanting to implement new technology that was highly dependent on computers and personnel trained to use them.

The third, and perhaps most telling, reason is the "feud" that developed between Ellen Haas and the American School Food Service Association, the primary professional organization supporting the lobbying effort behind the National School Lunch Program. Appointed as USDA assistant secretary in 1993 (over one of ASFSA's former presidents), Ellen Haas had one of the most powerful jobs in the federal bureaucracy and control over nearly 60 percent of the entire USDA budget (roughly $40 billion), the third largest nondefense department in the federal government.

During her professional rise in visibility and influence from local consumer activist to prominence at the national level, Ellen Haas became known as a clear, strong voice for consumers. She developed an enviable record of being able to court the media, policy makers, and "regular citizens advocates" with equal fervor and convince them of the validity of her views. In her role as executive director and founder of the consumer advocacy and research group Public Voice for Food and Health Policy, Haas demonstrated an ability to strongly and ardently advocate for changes in the quality of the foods served in the School Lunch Program. Since 1990, the series of reports issued by Public Voice had publicly—and personally—identified her with concerns about the quality of the food served in the School Lunch Program and had pitted her against the program's most powerful political ally, the American School Food Service Association. Now as the bureaucrat "in charge" of this vast and important program, how could she bring about the various changes that she had so long and so staunchly advocated?

The American Food Service Association was already piqued by the Haas appointment. Then, as one of her first public acts as assistant secretary at the USDA, the ASFSA was the target of criticism for participation figures in the NSLP and for the nutritional quality of the meals served to schoolchildren, criticisms it felt were unfair and undeserved. In announcing what needed to be done to improve school meals, the ASFSA felt Haas had overlooked the "good news" in the School Nutrition Dietary Assessment Study—that NSLP meals offered more than the recommended amounts of protein and selected vitamins and minerals, and that a statistically significant proportion of the schools surveyed were already meeting the Dietary Guidelines using the current meal plan.

Further insult came when the NSLP came under attack by the legislative proposals of the 104th Congress to block-grant the program. Many closely associated with the process felt that Haas had not been a true "advocate" for the NSLP when her personal dynamism and contacts were most needed on Capitol Hill. They felt she had taken personal ownership of the Team Nutrition project to such a degree that she had no time or interest in working with them to fend off the block-grant proposals.

The disaffection between the USDA's undersecretary and the primary professional organization for school food service managers was clearly a public embarrassment for the Clinton administration. The AFSFA accused Haas of writing "heavy-handed" regulations by proposing that criminal penalties would be imposed if school food service personnel refused to change the meal patterns that did not meet the Dietary Guidelines. Former officers of the ASFSA publicly criticized Haas's administration of the NSLP, saying, "Ever since Haas started in the administration, the Under Secretary has discredited the school lunch program . . . she has humiliated [school food service] people . . . maligned and discredited them."

The "feud" between Haas and the ASFSA has manifested itself in a variety of rather subtle, but devastatingly personal ways; she was snubbed as a speaker at the ASFSA's annual meeting, a veritable "command performance" for the USDA undersecretary with responsibility for the NSLP. And when it came to Team Nutrition, the school food service group felt it had been insulted and bypassed. She was accused of snubbing old-timers at the ASFSA by bringing in executive chefs from high-class restaurants to "show them how to cook," and rather than reinforcing the efforts of local "experts," they felt that educational efforts had been turned over to Disney "spokestoons" and outside consultants. The relationship was never "healthy"—for either the undersecretary or the ASFSA—and probably irreparably harmed the effort to reform the NSLP.

Analysis and Comment

Reform of the National School Lunch Program is a perfect example of the importance of the agenda-setting stage of the policy-making process. The reauthorization of the National School Lunch Program was due in 1994. This action was usually pro forma; no one seriously challenged the existence of the program after fifty years, and serious modifications to the content of the program were felt to be within the realm of USDA bureaucrats. Therefore, any major changes to the program would need to take place in the regulatory arena.

Nutrition and health professionals had clamored for change in the nutritional standards of the NSLP for years. All knew perfectly well that while school meals were meeting the recommended amounts of vitamins, minerals, and protein, they provided too much fat, saturated fat, sodium, and cholesterol. It took the power of a USDA-financed study, the School Nutrition Dietary Assessment Study, to bring this to the attention of policy makers who were in a position to remedy the problem.

The other key to putting reform of the NSLP on the public agenda was the appointment in 1993 of Ellen Haas as assistant secretary of Food, Nutrition, and Consumer Services. She served as a "policy entrepreneur" in this matter. Without her energy and attention focused on the matter of the *quality* of school meals offered to children in the NSLP, any reform efforts would certainly have been much milder and less riveting. In bringing the matter to the attention of professionals and the public (who usually are only mildly interested, at best, in these issues), the results might have been more successful in the long run and certainly would have exacted less personal cost to Haas.

Chapter 14 Review Questions

1. How does Heclo conceptualize the current relationship between politics and administration? What are the basic elements of his *issue network* idea and how does the idea differ from the *iron triangle* notion of political-administrative relations?

2. Heclo primarily applied the issue network notion to the federal level of government. Is it possible to apply it to state and local levels as well? Describe why or why not.

3. In what ways does the issue network concept pose serious dilemmas for democratic government in general and public administration in particular? Does the case offer "answers" to this issue?

4. What implications does the issue network theory hold for the practical functions and training of public administrators? Does it essentially alter the types of jobs, tasks, and roles they perform? Think about what the case study tells us about preparing students for these kinds of jobs.

5. Did you find this issue network concept evident in the "Reinventing School Lunch" case study? If so, in what ways? If not, how would you conceptualize the political-administrative relationships as reflected in the case study?

6. On the basis of your analysis of the foregoing reading and case study, what general recommendations would you make to improve the relationships between administration and politics in America? Be sure to think carefully about the *value implications* of any new reform measures you may advocate.

Key Terms

politics-administration dichotomy
issue networks
proliferation of interests
think tanks
technopols
trade and professional associations
public policy processes

iron triangles
policy makers
issue specialization
issue watchers
single-issue organizations
presidential appointees
professional-bureaucratic complex

Suggestions for Further Reading

You would do well to compare and contrast Heclo's ideas with those of earlier theorists who argued for a clearer, more distinct separation of politics and administration (what is termed the political-administrative dichotomy), especially Woodrow Wilson, "The Study of Administration," *Political Science Quarterly,* 2 (June 1887), pp. 197–222; Frank J. Goodnow, *Politics and Administration* (New York: Macmillan, 1900); or the later writers who discovered the interest groups involved with administrative processes and gave roots to the iron triangle concept, particularly Paul H. Appleby, *Policy and Administration* (University, Ala.: University of Alabama Press, 1949); E. Pendleton Herring, *Public Administration and the Public Interest* (New York: Russell and Russell, 1936); and David B. Truman, *The Governmental Process* (New York: Alfred A. Knopf, 1951).

Of course, because of the sheer size, complexity, and power of American government, more complicated political-administrative relationships have arisen in the last three decades, described by several astute observers, including Hugh Heclo, *A Government of Strangers: Executive Politics in Washington* (Washington, D.C.: The Brookings Institution, 1977); Don K. Price, *The Scientific Estate* (Cambridge, Mass.: Harvard University Press, 1965); Frederick C. Mosher, *Democracy and the Public Service,* 2d ed. (New York: Oxford University Press, 1982); Christopher H. Foreman, Jr., *Signals from the Hill* (New Haven, Conn.: Yale University Press, 1988); Emmette S. Redford, *Democracy in the Administrative State* (New York: Oxford University Press, 1969); Francis E. Rourke, *Bureaucracy, Politics and Public Policy,* 3d ed. (Boston: Little, Brown, 1984); Harold Seidman and Robert Gilmour, *Politics, Position and Power,* 5th ed. (New York: Oxford University Press, 1986); Lawrence C. Dodd and Richard L. Schott, *Congress and the Administrative State* (New York: John Wiley & Sons, 1979); Louis Fisher, *The Politics of Shared Power: Congress and the Executive* (Washington, D.C.: Congressional Quarterly Press, 1981); and Herbert Kaufman, *The Administrative Behavior of Federal Bureau Chiefs* (Washington, D.C.: The Brookings Institution, 1981).

The *National Journal, Governing,* and *Congressional Quarterly* provide timely insiders' views of this topic. You should give particular attention to the writers who discuss the changes in the 1990s that have decisively altered political-administrative relationships: see David M. Ricci, *The Transformation of American Politics* (New Haven, Conn.: Yale University Press, 1993); Donald F. Kettl, *Sharing Power* (Washington, D.C.: The Brookings Institution, 1993); James Q. Wilson, *Bureaucracy* (New York: Basic Books, 1989); Paul C. Light, *Thickening Government* (Washington, D.C.: The Brookings Institution, 1995); and James H. Svara, *Official Leadership in the City* (New York: Oxford University Press, 1990).

The federal health care reform attempts in the 1990s point out well the influence of issue networks, and the two best books so far on this topic are Jacob S. Hacker, *The Road to Nowhere* (Princeton, N.J.: Princeton University Press, 1997) and Mark E. Rushefsky and Kant Patel, *Politics Power and Policy Making* (Armonk, N.Y.: M. E. Sharpe, 1998). For where we are today with issue network theory, see Lawrence J. O'Toole Jr., "Treating Networks Seriously," *Public Administration Review* 57 (Jan./Feb.); pp. 45–52; and R.A.W. Rhodes, *Understanding Governance* (Buckingham, U.K.: Open University Press, 1997).

CHAPTER 15

The Relationship Between Bureaucracy and the Public Interest: The Concept of Public Sector Deregulation

To do better, we have to deregulate the government. If deregulation of a market makes sense because it liberates the entrepreneurial energies of its members, then it is possible that deregulating the public sector may also help energize it.

James Q. Wilson

READING 15

Introduction

Since the advent of public administration as an identifiable field, considerable scholarly debate has ensued over the question of public interest. Is there such a thing? How can it serve to guide the work of practicing public administrators? From where does the concept of public interest derive? How can it be applied as a meaningful concept in public agencies to influence the direction of administrative decisions?

Thoughtful administrative theorists have wrestled with these questions throughout the twentieth century but have arrived at very different "answers." Much of the dialogue on this subject turns ultimately on what "image" or "identity" theorists support for the field or how they define its substance and boundaries as an academic and applied field of practice. Three major perspectives have been put forward by scholars.

First, there are those administrative scientists who identify public administration essentially as a "tool" or "technique" in order to produce this or that most "efficient," "economical," or "effective" result. These writers tend to be highly positivist and rational in their thinking about the field. They view the emergence of "the public interest" from the application of the "right value-free tool of analysis" that will automatically achieve "correct results" for the general welfare. Writings by Frederick Taylor, the father of scientific management, or Herbert Simon, one of the founders of the behavioral movement within contemporary administrative sciences, advance such points of view. Listen to Herbert Simon's perspective on this topic:

The theory of administration is concerned with how an organization should be constructed and operated in order to accomplish its work efficiently. A fundamental principle of administration, which follows almost immediately from the rational character of "good" administration, is that among several alternatives involving the same expenditure, the one should always be selected which leads to the greatest accomplishment of administrative objectives; and among several alternatives that lead to the same accomplishment the one should be selected which involves the least expenditure.[1]

By contrast to this "rational machine model," whereby administrators become like "cogs" or "robots," the field of public administration is seen by other writers as central to the governance of America's constitutional democracy. They give public administrators key, creative leadership role(s) in promoting "the public interest." There is a long tradition of reformist literature in the field, dating from Woodrow Wilson's classic 1887 essay (refer to Chapter 1), which advance this viewpoint, namely that public administration is essential in order "to run the constitution." By placing public administration at the center of constitutional governance, administrative discretion and influence are enhanced, and "the public interest" consequently becomes equated with trained, enlightened public administration that advances broad community interests through the wise application of expertise and problem-solving skills. Influential authors such as Paul Appleby, Norton Long, Emmette Redford, and Merle Fainsod have advocated this perspective, but perhaps Carl Friedrich most forcefully articulated it:

> A modern administrator is in many cases dealing with problems so novel and complex that they call for the highest creative ability. This need for creative solutions effectively focuses attention upon the need for action. The pious formulas about the will of the people are all very well, but when it comes to these issues of social maladjustment, the popular will has little content. . . .
>
> . . . Throughout the length and breadth of our technical civilization there is arising a type of responsibility on the part of the permanent administrator, the man who is called upon to seek and find the creative solutions for our crying technical needs, which cannot be effectively enforced except by fellow-technicians who are capable of judging his policy in terms of the scientific knowledge bearing upon it.[2]

If Friedrich's view sees "good government" derived from the professionalism, expertise, training, ethical standards as well as the creativity of the public service, a third set of influential writers such as Arthur Bentley, David Truman, and Robert Dahl view the "public interest" as mainly the product of the pulling and hauling of various group interests in society. For these political scientists, there is no such "absolute" as "the public interest," but rather "it" is merely a "process" or the resultant of the contest among special interests as codified in law, rules, and informal agreements. Public administrators thus become much less important figures in shaping "the public interest." Among group theorists' writings, public administrators are viewed as "people-in-the-middle" for resolving competing interests or as catalysts through which varied interests are transmuted and represented. David Truman describes the administrator's mediatory role as follows:

The administrator is called upon to resolve the difficulties that were too thorny for the legislature to solve, and he must do so in face of the very forces that were acting in the legislature, though their relative strength may have changed. Note that it is not the ambiguities in the law that make difficult the question of what groups shall have privileged access to an administrator. Almost all legislative declarations are ambiguous in part. It is rather the causes of the ambiguity that make the difference. If the administrator holds out for an interpretation of these controverted ambiguous provisions that is not in itself a compromise, he invites the affected groups either to denounce his "dictatorial" methods and his "unscrupulous assumption of powers not granted to him" or to expose his "sell-out" of the "public interest."[3]

In the following selection from his recent book, *Bureaucracy,* James Q. Wilson, (1930–) the James Collins Professor of Management Emeritus at the University of California, Los Angeles, and 1990 recipient of the James Madison Award of the American Political Science Association, examines this subject in light of the operations of public agencies in the late 20th century. His book drew upon a wide range of contemporary studies of the U.S. Army, FBI, DEA, CIA, Social Security, and other public entities and tried to provide a comprehensive analysis, as the book's subtitle suggests, of "what government agencies do and why they do it." In his last chapter, Wilson offers his appraisal of how public agencies can be made more responsible and responsive to "the public interest." While he does not define what the "public interest" is, Wilson begins by making the assumption that "the daily incentives operating in the political work encourage a very different course of action" by bureaucrats which often is contradictory to achievement of their own "public purposes." In other words, the incentive structures within which bureaucrats must operate often confounds or prevents attainment of "the public interest." Wilson outlines why this happens and what, in his view, can be done about it. His reforms are modest, but they are argued compellingly.

As you read Wilson's essay, you should think about:

What assumptions does he make about the nature of public administration which in turn shape his understanding about "what is the public interest"?

How do you evaluate his proposed reforms? Their pluses? Negatives?

In what ways does Wilson's thinking compare and contrast with the three historic perspectives on the public interest and public administration which were outlined in this introduction? Does Wilson offer us a fourth alternative model? Since most of Wilson's argument is derived from federal examples, do his ideas also apply to state/local levels?

Notes

1. Herbert A. Simon, *Administrative Behavior: A Study of Decision-Making Processes in Administrative Organization* (New York: Free Press, 1947), p. 38.
2. Carl J. Friedrich, "Public Policy and the Nature of Administrative Responsibility," in Friedrich and Mason, eds., *Public Policy* (Cambridge: Harvard University Press, 1940), p. 12.
3. David B. Truman, *The Governmental Process* (New York: Alfred A. Knopf, 1951), p. 443.

Bureaucracy and the Public Interest

JAMES Q. WILSON

The German army beat the French army in 1940; the Texas prisons for many years did a better job than did the Michigan prisons; Carver High School in Atlanta became a better school under Norris Hogans. These successes were the result of skilled executives who correctly identified the critical tasks of their organizations, distributed authority in a way appropriate to those tasks, infused their subordinates with a sense of mission, and acquired sufficient autonomy to permit them to get on with the job. The critical tasks were different in each case, and so the organizations differed in culture and patterns of authority, but all three were alike in one sense: incentives, culture, and authority were combined in a way that suited the task at hand. . . . [But,] the daily incentives operating in the political world encourage a very different course of action.

Armies

Though the leadership and initiative of field officers and noncoms is of critical importance, the Pentagon is filled with generals who want to control combat from headquarters or from helicopters, using radios to gather information and computers to process it. Though the skill of the infantryman almost always has been a key to military success, the U.S. Army traditionally has put its best people in specialized units (intelligence, engineering, communications), leaving the leftovers for the infantry.[1] Though it has fought wars since 1945 everywhere except in Europe, the army continues

to devote most of its planning to big-tank battles on the West German plains.

Prisons

. . . Many observers gave the most favorable attention to prison executives who seemed to voice the best intentions (rehabilitation, prisoner self-governance) rather than the best accomplishments (safe, decent facilities).

Schools

Especially in big cities, many administrators keep principals weak and teachers busy filling out reports, all with an eye toward minimizing complaints from parents, auditors, interest groups, and the press. Teachers individually grumble that they are treated as robots instead of professionals, but collectively they usually oppose any steps—vouchers, merit pay, open enrollment, strengthened principals—that in fact have given teachers a larger role in designing curricula and managing their classrooms. . . . politically, extra resources . . . go to all schools "equally" rather than disproportionately to those schools that were improving the most.

These generals, wardens, administrators, and teachers have not been behaving irrationally; rather, they have been responding to the incentives and constraints that they encounter on a daily basis. Those incentives include the need to manage situations over which they have little control on the basis of a poorly defined or nonexistent sense of mission and in the face of a complex array of constraints that seems always to grow, never to shrink. Outside groups—elected offi-

Source: "Bureaucracy and the Public Interest" from *Bureaucracy: What Government Agencies Do & Why They Do It* by James Q. Wilson. Copyright © 1989 by BasicBooks, Inc. Reprinted by permission of BasicBooks, a member of Perseus Books, L.L.C.

cials, interest groups, professional associations, the media—demand a voice in the running of these agencies and make that demand effective by imposing rules on the agencies and demanding that all these rules be enforced all of the time. Moreover, habitual patterns of action—the lessons of the past, the memories of earlier struggles, the expectations of one's co-workers—narrow the area within which new courses of action are sought.

Bureaucrats often complain of "legislative micromanagement," and indeed it exists. . . . with respect to the armed forces, there has been a dramatic increase in the number of hearings, reports, investigations, statutory amendments, and budgetary adjustments with which the Pentagon must deal.[2] But there also has been a sharp increase in presidential micromanagement. Herbert Kaufman notes that for a half century or more the White House has feared agency independence more than agency paralysis, and so it has multiplied the number of presidential staffers, central management offices, and requirements for higher-level reviews. Once you start along the path of congressional or White House control, the process acquires a momentum of its own. "As more constraints are imposed, rigidities fixing agencies in their established ways intensify. As a result, complaints that they do not respond to controls also intensify. Further controls, checkpoints, and clearances are therefore introduced."[3] Much the same story can be told with respect to the growing involvement of the courts in agency affairs.

With some conspicuous exceptions the result of this process has been to deflect the attention of agency executives away from how the tasks of their agencies get defined and toward the constraints that must be observed no matter what the tasks may be. Who then decides what tasks shall be performed? In a production agency with observable outputs and routinized work processes, the answer is relatively simple: The laws and regulations that created the agency also define its job. But in procedural, coping, and craft agencies, the answer seems to be nobody in particular and everybody in general. The operating-level workers de-

fine the tasks, occasionally by design, as in those cases where operator ideology makes a difference, but more commonly by accident, as in those instances where prior experiences, professional norms, situational and technological imperatives, and peer-group expectations shape the nature of the work.

From time to time a gifted executive appears at a politically propitious time and makes things happen differently. He or she creates a new institution that acquires a, distinctive competence, a strong sense of mission, and an ability to achieve socially valued goals. The Army Corps of Engineers, the Social Security Administration, the Marine Corps, the Forest Service, the FBI: For many years after they were created, and in many instances still today, these agencies, along with a few others that could be mentioned, were a kind of elite service that stood as a living refutation of the proposition that "all bureaucrats are dim-witted paper-shufflers." And these are only the federal examples; at the local level one can find many school systems and police departments that have acquired a praiseworthy organizational character.

But one must ask whether today one could create from scratch the Marine Corps, or the FBI, or the Forest Service; possibly, but probably not. Who would dare suggest that a new agency come into being with its own personnel system (and thus with fewer opportunities for civil servants to get tenure), with a single dominant mission (and thus with little organizational deference to the myriad other goals outsiders would want it to serve), and with an arduous training regime designed to instill *esprit de corps* (and thus with less regard for those niceties and conveniences that sedentary people believe to be important)? Or how optimistic should we be that today we could organize a Social Security Administration in a way that would bring to Washington men and women of exceptional talent? Might not many of those people decide today that they do not want to risk running afoul of the conflict-of-interest laws, that they have no stomach for close media and congressional scrutiny, and that they would not accept the federal pay levels pegged to the salaries of members of Congress fearful of raising their own compensation?

It would be a folly of historical romanticism to imagine that great agencies were created in a golden age that is destined never to return, but it would be shortsighted to deny that we have paid a price for having emphasized rules and constraints to the neglect of tasks and mission. At the end of her careful review of the problems the SSA has had in managing disability insurance and supplemental security income, Martha Derthick makes the same point this way: "If the agencies repeatedly fall short, one ought at least to consider the possibility that there is a systematic mismatch between what they are instructed to do and their capacity to do it."[4] In recent years, when Congress has been creating new programs and modifying old ones at a dizzying rate, often on the basis of perfunctory hearings (or, as with the Senate's consideration of the 1988 drug bill, no hearings at all), a government agency capable of responding adequately to these endless changes would have to be versatile and adaptable, "capable of devising new routines or altering old ones very quickly." These qualities, she concludes, "are rarely found in large formal organizations."[5] I would only add that government agencies are far less flexible than formal organizations generally.

Things are not made much better by our national tendency to engage in bureaucrat-bashing. One has to have some perspective on this. It is true that bureaucracies prefer the present to the future, the known to the unknown, and the dominant mission to rival missions; many agencies in fact are skeptical of things that were "NIH"—Not Invented Here. Every social grouping, whether a neighborhood, a nation, or an organization, acquires a culture; changing that culture is like moving a cemetery: it is always difficult and some believe it is sacrilegious. It is also true, as many conservatives argue, that the government tries to do things that it is incapable of doing well, just as it is true, as many liberals allege, that the government in fact does many things well enough. As Charles Wolf has argued, both markets and governments have

their imperfections; many things we might want to do collectively require us to choose between unsatisfactory alternatives.[6]

A Few Modest Suggestions That May Make a Small Difference

To do better we have to deregulate the government.* If deregulation of a market makes sense because it liberates the entrepreneurial energies of its members, then it is possible that deregulating the public sector also may help energize it. The difference, of course, is that both the price system and the profit motive provide a discipline in markets that is absent in non-markets. Whether any useful substitutes for this discipline can be found for public-sector workers is not clear, though I will offer some suggestions. But even if we cannot expect the same results from deregulation in the two sectors we can agree at a minimum that detailed regulation, even of public employees, rarely is compatible with energy, pride in workmanship, and the exercise of initiative. The best evidence for this proposition, if any is needed, is that most people do not like working in an environment in which every action is second-guessed, every initiative viewed with suspicion, and every controversial decision denounced as malfeasance.

James Colvard, for many years a senior civilian manager in the navy, suggests that the government needs to emulate methods that work in the better parts of the private sector: "a bias toward action, small staffs, and a high level of delegation which is based on trust."[7] A panel of the National Academy of Public Administration (NAPA), consisting of sixteen senior government executives holding the rank of assistant secretary, issued a report making the same point:

*I first saw this phrase in an essay by Constance Horner, then director of the federal Office of Personnel Management: "Beyond Mr. Gradgrind: The Case for Deregulating the Public Sector," *Policy Review* 44 (Spring 1988): 34–38. It also appears in Gary C. Bryner, *Bureaucratic Discretion* (New York: Pergamon Press, 1987), 215.

Over many years, government has become entwined in elaborate management control systems and the accretion of progressively more detailed administrative procedures. This development has not produced superior management. Instead, it has produced managerial overburden. . . . Procedures overwhelm substance. Organizations become discredited, along with their employees. . . . The critical elements of leadership in management appear to wither in the face of a preoccupation with process. The tools are endlessly "perfected"; the manager who is expected to use these tools believes himself to be ignored. . . . Management systems are not management. . . . The attitude of those who design and administer the rules . . . must be reoriented from a "control mentality" to one of "how can I help get the mission of this agency accomplished."[8]

But how can government "delegate" and "trust" and still maintain accountability? If it is a mistake to foster an ethos that encourages every bureaucrat to "go by the book," is it not an equally serious problem to allow zealots to engage in "mission madness," charging off to implement their private versions of some ambiguous public goal? (Steven Emerson has written a useful account of mission madness in some highly secret military intelligence and covert-action agencies.[9]) Given everything we know about the bureaucratic desire for autonomy and the political rewards of rule making, is there any reason to suppose that anybody will find it in his or her interest to abandon the "control mentality" and adopt the "mission accomplishment" mentality?

Possibly not. But it may be worth thinking about what a modestly deregulated government might look like. It might look as it once did, when some of the better federal agencies were created. At the time the Corps of Engineers, the Forest Service, and the FBI were founded much of the federal government was awash in political patronage, petty cabals, and episodic corruption. Organizing an elite service in those days may have been easier than doing so today, when the problems are less patronage and corruption than they are officiousness and complexity. But the keys to organizational success have not changed. The agencies were started by strong leaders who were able to command personal loyalty, define and instill a clear and powerful sense of mission, attract talented workers who believed they were joining something special, and make exacting demands on subordinates.

Today there is not much chance to create a new agency; almost every agency one can imagine already has been created. Even so, the lessons one learns from changing agencies confirm what can be inferred from studying their founding.

First: Executives should understand the culture of their organizations—that is, what their subordinates believe constitute the core tasks of the agency—and the strengths and limitations of that culture. If members widely share and warmly endorse that culture the agency has a sense of mission. This permits the executive to economize on scarce incentives (people want to do certain tasks even when there are no special rewards for doing it); to state general objectives confident that subordinates will understand the appropriate ways of achieving them; and to delegate responsibility knowing that lower-level decisions probably will conform to higher-level expectations.

A good executive realizes that workers can make subtle, precise, and realistic judgments, but only if those judgments refer to a related, coherent set of behaviors. People cannot easily keep in mind many quite different things or strike reasonable balances among competing tasks. People want to know what is expected of them; they do not want to be told, in answer to this question, that "on the one hand this, but on the other hand that."

In defining a core mission and sorting out tasks that either fit or do not fit with this mission, executives must be aware of their many rivals for the right to define it. Operators with professional backgrounds will bring to the agency their skills but also their biases: Lawyers, economists, and engineers see the world in very different ways. You cannot hire them as if they were tools that in your skilled hands will perform exactly the task you set for them. Black and Decker may make tools like that, but Harvard and MIT do not. Worker peer groups also set expectations to which operators conform, especially when the operators work in a threatening, unpredictable, or confrontational environment. You may design the ideal patrol officer or schoolteacher, but unless you understand the demands made by the street and the classroom, your design will remain an artistic expression destined for the walls of some organizational museum.

These advantages of infusing an agency with a sense of mission are purchased at a price. An agency with a strong mission will give perfunctory attention, if any at all, to tasks that are not central to that mission. Diplomats in the State Department will have little interest in embassy security; intelligence officers in the CIA will not worry as much as they should about counterintelligence; narcotics agents in the DEA will minimize the importance of improper prescriptions written by physicians; power engineers in the TVA will not think as hard about environmental protection or conservation as about maximizing the efficiency of generating units; fighter pilots in the USAF will look at air transport as a homely stepchild; and navy admirals who earned their flag serving on aircraft carriers will not press zealously to expand the role of minesweepers.

If the organization must perform a diverse set of tasks, those tasks that are not part of the core mission will need special protection. This requires giving autonomy to the subordinate tasks subunit (for example, by providing for them a special organizational niche) and creating a career track so that talented people performing non-mission tasks can rise to high rank in the agency. No single organization, however, can perform well a wide variety of tasks; inevitably some will be neglected. In this case, the wise executive will arrange to devolve the slighted tasks onto another agency, or to a wholly new organization created for the purpose. Running multitask conglomerates is as risky in the public as in the private sector. There are limits to the number of different jobs managers can manage. Moreover, conglomerate agencies rarely can de-

velop a sense of mission; the cost of trying to do everything is that few things are done well. The turf-conscious executive who stoutly refuses to surrender any tasks, no matter how neglected, to another agency is courting disaster; in time the failure of his or her agency to perform some orphan task will lead to a political or organizational crisis. Long ago the State Department should have got out of the business of building embassies. Diplomats are good at many things, but supervising carpenters and plumbers is not one of them. Let agencies whose mission is construction—the Army Corps of Engineers or the navy's Seabees—build buildings.

Second: Negotiate with one's political superiors to get some agreement as to which are the *essential* constraints that must be observed by your agency and which the marginal constraints. This, frankly, may be impossible. The decentralization of authority in Congress (and in some state legislatures) and the unreliability of most expressions of presidential or gubernatorial backing are such that in most cases you will discover, by experience if not by precept, that all constraints are essential all of the time. But perhaps with effort some maneuvering room may be won. A few agencies obtained the right to use more flexible, less cumbersome personnel systems modeled on the China Lake experiment, and Congress has the power to broaden those opportunities. Perhaps some enlightened member of Congress will be able to get statutory authority for the equivalent of China Lake with respect to procurement regulations. An executive is well advised to spend time showing that member how to do it.

Third: Match the distribution of authority and the control over resources to the tasks your organization is performing. In general, authority should be placed at the lowest level at which all essential elements of information are available. Bureaucracies will differ greatly in what level that may be. At one extreme are agencies such as the Internal Revenue Service or maximum-security prisons, in which uniformity of treatment and precision of control are so important as to make it necessary for there to be exacting, centrally determined rules for most tasks. At the other extreme are public schools, police departments, and armies, organizations in which operational uncertainties are so great that discretion must be given to (or if not given will be taken by) lower-level workers.

A good place in which to think through these matters is the area of weapons procurement. The overcentralization of design control is one of the many criticisms of such procurement on which all commentators seem agreed. Buying a new aircraft may be likened to remodeling one's home: You never know how much it will cost until you are done; you quickly find out that changing your mind midway through the work costs a lot of money; and you soon realize that decisions have to be made by people on the spot who can look at the pipes, wires, and joists. The Pentagon procures aircraft as if none of its members had ever built or remodeled a house. It does so because both it and its legislative superiors refuse to allow authority to flow down to the point where decisions rationally can be made.

The same analysis can be applied to public schools. As John Chubb and Terry Moe have shown, public and private schools differ in the locus of effective control.[10] At least in big cities, decisions in private schools that are made by headmasters or in Catholic schools that are made by small archdiocesan staffs are made in public schools by massive, cumbersome headquarters bureaucracies. Of course, there are perfectly understandable political reasons for this difference, but not very many good reasons for it. Many sympathetic critics of the public schools believe that the single most useful organizational change that could be made would be to have educational management decisions—on personnel, scheduling, and instructional matters—made at the school level.[11]

Fourth: Judge organizations by results. This [essay] has made it clear that what constitutes a valued result in government usually is a matter of dispute. But even when fairly clear performance standards exist, legislatures and executives often ignore them with unhappy results. William E. Turcotte compared how two state governments oversaw their state liquor monopolies. The state that applied clear standards to its liquor bureaucrats produced significantly more profit and lower ad-

ministrative costs than did the state with unclear or conflicting standards.[12]

Even when results are hard to assess more can be done than is often the case. If someone set out to evaluate the output of a private school, hospital, or security service, he or she would have at least as much trouble as would someone trying to measure the output of a public school, hospital, or police department. Governments are not the only institutions with ambiguous products.

There are two ways to cope with the problem in government. One is to supply the service or product in a marketlike environment. Shift the burden of evaluation off the shoulders of professional evaluators and onto the shoulders of clients and customers, and let the latter vote with their feet. The "client" in these cases can be individual citizens or government agencies; what is important is that the client be able to choose from among rival suppliers.

But some public services cannot be supplied, or are never going to be supplied, by a market. We can imagine allowing parents to choose among schools, but we cannot imagine letting them choose (at least for most purposes) among police departments or armies. In that case one should adopt the second way of evaluating a public service: carry out a demonstration project or conduct a field experiment. (I will use the two ideas interchangeably, though some scholars distinguish between them.[13]) An experiment is a planned alteration in a state of affairs designed to measure the effect of the intervention. It involves asking the question, "if I change X, what will happen to Y, having first made certain that everything else stays the same?" It sounds easy, but it is not.

A good experiment (bad ones are worse than no experiment at all) requires that one do the following: First, identify a course of action to be tested; call it the treatment. A "treatment" can be a police tactic, a school curriculum, or a welfare program. Second, decide what impact the treatment is intended to have; call this the outcome. The outcome can be a crime rate, an achievement score, a work effort, a housing condition, or an income level. Third, give the treatment to one group (the experimental group) and withhold it from another (the control group). A group might be a police precinct, a class of students, the tenants in a housing project, or people who meet some eligibility requirement (say, having low incomes). It is quite important how the membership in these groups is determined. It should be done randomly; that is, all eligible precincts, schools, tenants, or people should be randomly sorted into experimental and control groups. Random assignment means that all the characteristics of the members of the experimental and control groups are likely to be identical. Fourth, assess the condition of each group before and after the treatment. The first assessment describes the baseline condition, the second the outcome condition. This outcome assessment should continue for some time after the end of the treatment, because experience has shown that many treatments seem to have a short-term effect that quickly disappears. Fifth, make certain that the evaluation is done by people other than those providing the treatment. People like to believe that their efforts are worthwhile, so much so that perhaps unwittingly they will gather data in ways that make it look like the treatment worked even when it did not.*

The object of all this is to find out what works. Using this method we have discovered that tripling the number of patrol cars on a beat does not lower the crime rate; that foot patrol reduces the fear of crime but not (ordinarily) its incidence; and that arresting spouse-beaters reduces (for a while) future assaults more than does counseling the assaulters.[14] We have learned that giving people an income supplement (akin to the negative income tax) reduces work effort and in some cases encourages families to break up.[15] We have learned that giving special

job training and support to welfare mothers, ex-offenders, and school drop-outs produces sizable gains in the employment records of the welfare recipients but no gain for the ex-offenders and school drop-outs.[16] We have learned that a housing allowance program increases the welfare of poor families even though it does not improve the stock of housing.[17] We have learned that more flexible pay and classification systems greatly benefit the managers of navy research centers and improve the work atmosphere at the centers.[18]

There also have been many failed or flawed management experiments. In the 1930s, Herbert Simon carried out what may have been the first serious such experiment when he tried to find out how to improve the performance of welfare workers in the California State Relief Administration. Though elegantly designed, the experimental changes proved so controversial and the political environment of the agency so unstable that it is not clear that any useful inferences can be drawn from the project.[19] The attempt to evaluate educational vouchers at Alum Rock was undercut by the political need to restrict participation by private schools. There are countless other "studies" that are evaluations in name only; in reality they are self-congratulatory conclusions written by program administrators. The administrative world is a political world, not a scientific laboratory, and evaluators of administration must come to terms with that fact. Often there are no mutually acceptable terms. But where reasonable terms can be struck, it is possible to learn more than untutored experience can tell us about what works.

Such dry and dusty research projects probably seem thin fare to people who want Big Answers to Big Questions such as "How can we curb rampant bureaucracy?" or "How can we unleash the creative talents of our dedicated public servants?" But public management is not an arena in which to find Big Answers; it is a world of settled institutions designed to allow imperfect people to use flawed procedures to cope with insoluble problems.

The fifth and final bit of advice flows directly from the limits on judging agencies by their results. All organizations seek the stability and comfort

---

*Matters are, of course, a bit more complicated than this summary might suggest. There is a small library of books on evaluative research that go into these matters in more detail; a good place to begin is Richard P. Nathan, *Social Science in Government* (New York: Basic Books, 1988). On the political aspects of evaluation, see Henry J. Aaron, *Politics and the Professors* (Washington, D.C.: The Brookings Institution, 1978). On the technical side see Thomas D. Cook and Donald T. Campbell, *Quasi-Experimentation* (Chicago: Rand McNally, 1979). There is even a journal, *Evaluation Review*, specializing in these issues.

that comes from relying on standard operating procedures—"SOPs." When results are unknown or equivocal, bureaus will have no incentive to alter those SOPs so as better to achieve their goals, only an incentive to modify them to conform to externally imposed constraints. The SOPs will represent an internally defined equilibrium that reconciles the situational imperatives, professional norms, bureaucratic ideologies, peer-group expectations, and (if present) leadership demands unique to that agency. The only way to minimize the adverse effect of allowing human affairs to be managed by organizations driven by their autonomous SOPs is to keep the number, size, and authority of such organizations as small as possible. If none of the four preceding bits of advice work, the reader must confront the realization that there are no solutions for the bureaucracy problem that are not also "solutions" to the government problem. More precisely: All complex organizations display bureaucratic problems of confusion, red tape, and the avoidance of responsibility. Those problems are much greater in government bureaucracies because government itself is the institutionalization of confusion (arising out of the need to moderate competing demands); of red tape (arising out of the need to satisfy demands that cannot be moderated); and of avoided responsibility (arising out of the desire to retain power by minimizing criticism).

In short, you can have less bureaucracy only if you have less government. Many, if not most, of the difficulties we experience in dealing with government agencies arise from the agencies being part of a fragmented and open political system. If an agency is to have a sense of mission, if constraints are to be minimized, if authority is to be decentralized, if officials are to be judged on the basis of the outputs they produce rather than the inputs they consume, then legislators, judges, and lobbyists will have to act against their own interests. They will have to say "no" to influential constituents, forgo the opportunity to expand their own influence, and take seriously the task of judging the organizational feasibility as well as the political popularity of a proposed new program. It is hard to imagine this happening, partly because politicians and judges have no incentive to make it happen and partly because there are certain tasks a democratic government must undertake even if they cannot be performed efficiently. The greatest mistake citizens can make when they complain of "the bureaucracy" is to suppose that their frustrations arise simply out of management problems; they do not—they arise out of governance problems.

Bureaucracy and the American Regime

The central feature of the American constitutional system—the separation of powers—exacerbates many of these problems. The governments of the United States were not designed to be efficient or powerful, but to be tolerable and malleable. Those who devised these arrangements always assumed that the federal government would exercise few and limited powers. As long as that assumption was correct (which it was for a century and a half) the quality of public administration was not a serious problem except in the minds of those reformers (Woodrow Wilson was probably the first) who desired to rationalize government in order to rationalize society. The founders knew that the separation of powers would make it so difficult to start a new program or to create a new agency that it was hardly necessary to think about how those agencies would be administered. As a result, the Constitution is virtually silent on what kind of administration we should have. At least until the Civil War thrust the problem on us, scarcely anyone in the country would have known what you were talking about if you spoke of the "problem of administration."

Matters were very different in much of Europe. Kings and princes long had ruled; when their authority was captured by parliaments, the tradition of ruling was already well established. From the first the ministers of the parliamentary regimes thought about the problems of administration because in those countries there was something to administer. The centralization of executive authority in the hands of a prime minister and the exclusion (by and large) of parliament from much say in executive affairs facilitated the process of controlling the administrative agencies and bending them to some central will. The constitutions of many European states easily could have been written by a school of management.

Today, the United States at every level has big and active governments. Some people worry that a constitutional system well-designed to preserve liberty when governments were small is poorly designed to implement policy now that governments are large. The contrast between how the United States and the nations of Western Europe manage environmental and industrial regulation is illuminating: Here the separation of powers insures, if not causes, clumsy and adversarial regulation; there the unification of powers permits, if not causes, smooth and consensual regulation.

I am not convinced that the choice is that simple, however. It would take another book to judge the advantages and disadvantages of the separation of powers. The balance sheet on both sides of the ledger would contain many more entries than those that derive from a discussion of public administration. But even confining our attention to administration, there is more to be said for the American system than many of its critics admit.

America has a paradoxical bureaucracy unlike that found in almost any other advanced nation. The paradox is the existence in one set of institutions of two qualities ordinarily quite separate: the multiplication of rules and the opportunity for access. We have a system laden with rules; elsewhere that is a sure sign that the bureaucracy is aloof from the people, distant from their concerns, and preoccupied with the power and privileges of the bureaucrats—an elaborate, grinding machine that can crush the spirit of any who dare oppose it. We also have a system suffused with participation: advisory boards, citizen groups, neighborhood councils, congressional investigators, crusading journalists, and lawyers serving writs; elsewhere this popular involvement would be taken as evidence that the administrative system is no system at all, but a bungling, jerry-built contraption wallowing in inefficiency and shot through with corruption and favoritism.

That these two traits, rules and openness, could coexist would have astonished Max Weber and continues to astonish (or elude) many contemporary students of the subject. Public bureaucracy in this country is neither as rational and predictable as Weber hoped nor as crushing and mechanistic as he feared. It is rule-bound without being overpowering, participatory without being corrupt. This paradox exists partly because of the character and mores of the American people: They are too informal, spontaneous, and other-directed to be either neutral arbiters or passionless Gradgrinds. And partly it exists because of the nature of the regime: Our constitutional system, and above all the exceptional power enjoyed by the legislative branch, makes it impossible for us to have anything like a government by appointed experts but easy for individual citizens to obtain redress from the abuses of power. Anyone who wishes it otherwise would have to produce a wholly different regime, and curing the mischiefs of bureaucracy seems an inadequate reason for that. Parliamentary regimes that supply more consistent direction to their bureaucracies also supply more bureaucracy to their citizens. The fragmented American regime may produce chaotic government, but the coherent European regimes produce bigger governments.

In the meantime we live in a country that despite its baffling array of rules and regulations and the insatiable desire of some people to use government to rationalize society still makes it possible to get drinkable water instantly, put through a telephone call in seconds, deliver a letter in a day, and obtain a passport in a week. Our Social Security checks arrive on time. Some state prisons, and most of the federal ones, are reasonably decent and humane institutions. The great majority of Americans, cursing all the while, pay their taxes. One can stand on the deck of an aircraft carrier during night flight operations and watch two thousand nineteen-year-old boys faultlessly operate one of the most complex organizational systems ever created. There are not many places where all this happens. It is astonishing it can be made to happen at all.

Notes

1. Arthur T. Hadley, *The Straw Giant* (New York: Random House, 1986), 53–57, 249–52.
2. CSIS, *U.S. Defense Acquisition: A Process in Trouble* (Washington, D.C.: Center for Strategic and International Studies, March 1987), 13–16.
3. Herbert Kaufman, *The Administrative Behavior of Federal Bureau Chiefs* (Washington, D.C.: The Brookings Institution, 1981), 192.
4. Martha Derthick, *Agency Under Stress: The Social Security Administration and American Government* (Washington, D.C.: Brookings Institution, forthcoming).
5. Ibid., chap. 3.
6. Charles Wolf, Jr., *Markets or Governments: Choosing Between Imperfect Alternatives* (Cambridge, Mass.: MIT Press, 1988).
7. James Colvard, "Procurement: What Price Mistrust?" *Government Executive* (March 1985): 21.
8. NAPA, *Revitalizing Federal Management: Managers and Their Overburdened Systems* (Washington, D.C.: National Academy of Public Administration, November 1983), vii, viii, 8.
9. Steven Emerson, *Secret Warriors* (New York: G. P. Putnam's Sons, 1988).
10. John E. Chubb and Terry M. Moe, "Politics, Markets, and the Organization of Schools," *American Political Science Review* 82 (1988): 1065–87.
11. Chester E. Finn, Jr., "Decentralize, Deregulate, Empower," *Policy Review* (Summer 1986): 60; Edward A. Wynne, *A Year in the Life of a School* (forthcoming).
12. William E. Turcotte, "Control Systems, Performance, and Satisfaction in Two State Agencies," *Administrative Science Quarterly* 19 (1974): 60–73.
13. Richard P. Nathan, *Social Science in Government: Uses and Misuses* (New York: Basic Books, 1988), chap. 3.
14. These projects were all done by the Police Foundation and are described in James Q. Wilson, *Thinking About Crime,* rev. ed. (New York: Basic Books, 1983).
15. See Joseph A. Pechman and P. Michael Timpane, eds., *Work Incentives and Income Guarantees* (Washington, D.C.: Brookings Institution, 1975); and R. Thayne Robson, ed., *Employment and Training R&D* (Kalamazoo, Mich.: Upjohn Institute for Employment Research, 1984).
16. Nathan, *Social Science,* chap. 5; and Manpower Demonstration Research Corporation, *Summary and Findings of the National Supported Work Demonstration* (Cambridge, Mass.: Ballinger, 1980).
17. See studies cited in chap. 19.
18. See references to China Lake research cited in chap. 8.
19. Clarence E. Ridley and Herbert A. Simon, *Measuring Municipal Activities* (Chicago: International City Managers' Association, 1938).

☐ CASE STUDY 15

Introduction

On December 6, 1994, Orange County, California, having 2.3 million residents, was forced to file for bankruptcy under Chapter 9 of the Bankruptcy Code. The move came after Robert Citron, the Country Treasurer, admitted that Orange County's $7.7 billion investment pool that he managed on behalf of 187 local communities and agencies in the County had lost $1.5 billion since January 1, 1994.

Ironically, Orange County has one of the richest per-capita incomes among American counties, and Mr. Citron's 17-year career was nationally recognized as having one of the best municipal fund management records. Indeed, only a few months before, both Standard and Poor's and Moody's Bond Rating Services had assigned their highest short-term bond ratings to Orange County's last big issuance of $110 million debt.

Then suddenly on December 6, when Orange County failed to come up with the cash plus collateral it owed of $1.25 billion, CS First Boston—one of several Wall Street firms that had lent the county cash to buy bonds—quickly seized $2 billion of securities it had been holding as collateral and dumped them on the market at a significant loss to the county. The rise in interest rates since Spring 1994 had shrunk the county's liquid assets from $2.2 billion to $350 million, or a mere fraction of what they owed creditors in December. When word went out about the county's insolvency, there was soon "a run on" the county's remaining cash reserves and the county had no recourse other than to seek bankruptcy protection from its creditors.

However, Orange County came close to preventing its historic insolvency from occurring. The following *Wall Street Journal* article by staff writer Laura Jereski recounts the remarkable eleventh-hour attempt to save the county's investment fund from default. It is a tale of secret codes and of all-night frantic efforts set amid a siege mentality and an odd kind of governmental arrangement—the sort of stuff of spy novels, not municipal administration. Through the hard work of the assistant county treasurer, Matthew Raabe, his staff, lawyers, and investment bankers, "a rescue package" was designed to "save the County fund." However, the arcane structure and rules of operation imposed severe—and ultimately fatal—restrictions upon the county commissioners in dealing effectively *and* quickly with the fiscal nightmare.

As you read this relatively brief, though fascinating, case, reflect upon what it says in relationship to Wilson's foregoing essay:

How did the Orange County "incentive structures" inhibit the commissioners from preventing the default?

Why were these structures created in the first place?

What would you recommend to reform the governmental structures so as to permit the county managers "to manage" future crises such as these more effectively *and* quickly? (You might think about some of Wilson's recommendations.) Where else in other case studies within this book might Wilson's prescriptions for reform work effectively? Or, not?

But No Cigar: How a Rescue Mission Failed, Just Barely, in Orange County

LAURA JERESKI

Early in the morning of Dec. 6, just hours before Or-

ange County's final financial collapse, local officials came within a penstroke of preventing the largest municipal bankruptcy in U.S. history.

A rescue mission, operating in secret in New York and Santa Ana, had hammered out a plan to restructure the county's toppling investment fund and avoid default. Time was critical. The fund was hemorrhaging cash, with losses at $1.5 billion and mounting. To avoid tipping off financial markets about any plans, the team coded its cellular-phone messages: Orange County was "Oscar."

After four days of round-the-clock meetings, the rescue team of county finance officials, consultants and Wall Street experts was within sight of its goal. To prevent a messy and costly liquidation of the fund's $20 billion portfolio, one of four big investment banks would be chosen to restructure the fund's debts and stop further losses. All that was needed was a green light from the county government.

A Beleaguered Board

That wasn't going to be easy, however. Unlike many jurisdictions, Orange County had no chief executive to whom the rescue team could turn. Instead, crucial decisions rested with a board of five elected supervisors—a former policeman, a social worker, a former business-school professor and two career politicians near retirement.

Despite a population of 2.6 million and one of the highest per-capita incomes in the nation, the county retains a system of government devised in simpler times, the 1870s. Its government is "clearly a 19th-century artifact struggling to cope with the emerging 21st century," says Peter Detwiler, staff director to the California Senate local-government committee.

The five individuals are isolated by laws inhibiting them from meeting freely, without 24 hours' public notice. In contrast to practices elsewhere, they can't override these "sunshine" laws even in emergencies. To keep informed, the supervisors were forced to rely heavily on an outside law firm whose own interests, in part, diverged from theirs, say people involved in the county's debacle. Burdened by conflicting advice, the supervisors ultimately left the county's fate to market forces.

Asking for Their Money

Not until mid-November, in fact, when those market forces began squeezing the fund, did the supervisors first realize the depth of their problem. Sensing trouble, the fund's participants—more than 180 local governmental bodies—started clamoring for their money. "We were told there was a liquidity prob-

lem," recalls Supervisor Roger Stanton, the former professor.

Through its bond counsel at LeBoeuf, Lamb, Greene & MacRae, a New York law firm, the county hired Capital Market Risk Advisors (CMRA), a New York consulting firm, last month to do some sleuthing in the portfolio. At that point, the county simply wanted to find out what the portfolio contained.

What CMRA found was far worse than anyone imagined. For years, the fund's manager, County Treasurer Robert L. Citron, had been chalking up high yields by borrowing heavily from Wall Street brokers to buy even more bonds. That worked fine when interest rates were falling, but when rates turned back up this year, losses mounted. Instead of calling it quits, Mr. Citron doubled up.

Demands for Collateral

As the portfolio's value continued to slide, the lenders demanded that he put up more collateral. Those demands drained the fund of almost $900 million by Dec. 1, leaving it with only $350 million of quickly available money—just a fraction of what was needed to meet additional collateral payments of $1.25 billion falling due the following Tuesday, Dec. 6.

Before the county officials could fully come to grips with the CMRA analysis, word of the fund's difficulties was spreading fast. So, the county called a news conference on Dec. 1 to announce a $1.5 billion "paper loss," roughly 20% of the value of the fund's principal.

The news conference was a grueling public debut for Matthew Raabe, the county's assistant treasurer. Mr. Citron, who was soon to be forced out of office, sat despondently in the background while Mr. Raabe explained the situation and fielded questions.

The earnest 38-year-old accountant had been Mr. Citron's deputy since 1987. But stepping into his boss's shoes would be problematical. Despite Mr. Raabe's years in the treasurer's office, he had made none of the critical investment decisions, according to colleagues and reports by the county auditor, Steven Lewis.

At first, Mr. Raabe's lack of knowledge of the fund's investments made it hard for him to understand how bleak the situation really was, his colleagues and outside consultants say. In a telephone conference call that Friday morning with Moody's

Investors Service, Mr. Raabe couldn't answer some basic questions. For example, he said he didn't know how $900 million in cash had left the fund in six weeks, say several participants in the call, or about the fund's huge unhedged holdings of "inverse floaters," volatile bonds that dropped sharply in value as interest rates rose. Mr. Raabe's attorney declined to make him available for comment.

The CMRA consultants, by contrast, recognized all the markings of impending financial collapse. The disclosure of Orange County's loss meant the county's once-accommodating brokers would quit bankrolling the tottering fund. In particular, Tuesday's $1.25 billion collateral payment loomed with chilling urgency.

If the fund couldn't meet that commitment, its lenders probably would seize its collateral and dump it to recover their money. Those fire sales could rack up big additional losses for the fund. And the fund's participants would undoubtedly step up demands for their money.

Reversing the fund's existing losses was out of the question, of course. But raising much-needed cash would give the fund some breathing room to reorganize its finances and head off bankruptcy. The potential long-term costs of bankruptcy were considerable. As New York City's brush with insolvency in the 1970s showed, the bond market can be very unforgiving. For a multibillion-dollar bond issuer such as Orange County, the lasting drag on its financing costs would be immense.

Exploring the Options

On Friday, the CMRA consultants contacted every Wall Street firm that had avoided doing business with Mr. Citron to explore the fund's options and negotiate a workout. Four stepped up: J.P. Morgan & Co., Goldman, Sachs & Co., Salomon Inc. and Swiss Bank Corp. They were coded as "Joe," "Golf," "Sierra" and "White Cross."

At 8 o'clock Saturday morning, CMRA and TSA Capital Management, a bond firm specializing in exotic securities, met with bankers in a suite at the Regency Hotel in New York. They shuffled half-hour spots to accommodate the christening of one banker's child. By the time the Goldman bankers left, shouldering tuxedos on the way to their annual dinner, about 100 experts were filtering through the fund's financial data.

None of the firms was told which others had been consulted. J.P. Morgan was so anxious to prevent word from seeping out to its trading desks that it rewired conference rooms for computers to quarantine its Orange County experts.

Meanwhile, in Santa Ana, the task of coordinating the county's rescue had fallen to Mr. Raabe. He and three other members of the county staff set up a "war room" on the third floor of the Orange County Hall of Administration, an ultramodern inverted pyramid of white stone in the city's civic center. They spent all Saturday on the phone with the consultants in New York, racing in turn to retrieve trading records and other statistics on the portfolio from the treasury building 50 yards away.

A Ray of Hope

On Saturday night, over dinner at a local grill, Mr. Raabe told other members of the county's staff and two lawyers from LeBoeuf Lamb that he expected to be able to present some possible solutions to board members the following day.

That same night, the LeBoeuf Lamb lawyers called the Securities and Exchange Commission, trying to throw the fund on its mercy and pleading that the agency ask for appointment of a receiver, according to SEC officials and a LeBoeuf Lamb lawyer. However, the supervisors say they weren't told until the next day.

But "the only basis to intervene would have been to allege that there was a fraud, that it was continuing and that there was going to be imminent damage to the public interest," William McLucas, the SEC's chief of enforcement, says now. Only if those conditions were met could the SEC ask a federal court for permission to appoint a receiver.

The LeBoeuf Lamb attorneys may have had reasons of their own for this bold initiative. The fund's dire condition posed a knotty problem: Just a few months before, the law firm had cleared a $600 million county bond issue whose proceeds went into the investment fund. The offering documents, registered at the SEC, disclosed none of the fund's burgeoning problems and, indeed, cited its good track record. The fund's imminent collapse could make the firm vulnerable to bondholder lawsuits.

"The point here was to salvage the situation. We went to the SEC for the county and the bondholders," says Taylor Briggs, a LeBoeuf Lamb partner. Mr.

Briggs denies that there could be any conflict between the interests of the bondholders seeking payment from Orange County and those of the cash-strapped county itself or between the county and the law firm. "At the time that we were advising the county, our interests were not adverse to the county," he says. Indeed, not until Orange County filed for bankruptcy on Dec. 6 did LeBoeuf Lamb concede that the firm would face a conflict if it continued to represent the county.

Bankruptcy Specialist Consulted

As the lawyers talked over the weekend with the SEC, they also began consulting with Carl Eklund, their bankruptcy specialist in Denver, Mr. Eklund says.

Back in New York, J.P. Morgan offered the best hope to avert bankruptcy. The two sides set up a meeting for 4 a.m. Sunday to nail down details. In a boardroom at Morgan's headquarters in a deserted Lower Manhattan, the consultants met with some 18 investment bankers, many in business suits despite the odd hour.

The Morgan bankers proposed to take the fund's nearly $5 billion face value of unencumbered holdings off the county's hands. Those assets mainly consisted of risky derivative securities, whose market value had been hammered by rising short-term rates to less than $4.5 billion.

J.P. Morgan agreed to stand by to purchase the fund's bonds as its cash needs required, up to a total outlay of $4.4 billion. Assuming the market didn't move against the bank, Morgan stood to make up to $100 million, says a person familiar with the bid. Armed with this commitment, the consultants dashed to make a 6:50 a.m. flight to Orange County.

Early Sunday afternoon, Supervisor William Steiner was watching a Los Angeles Rams game when he got a call. Could he immediately go to his office for an important briefing, a staffer asked.

He and the other supervisors rushed to the Hall of Administration for a 1 p.m. meeting with members of Mr. Raabe's team and Terry Andrus, the county counsel, who represents the board of supervisors. The supervisors had to wait alone in their office suites while staffers ran from office to office to brief each in turn.

There was a lot of news, all of it bad.

Mr. Stanton and other supervisors recall being told at those meetings that the SEC, which had begun an investigation of the fund, might freeze the assets. Moreover, the SEC probably would sue Mr. Citron for fraud. And "in a general sense," says Supervisor Stanton, "we were told there was an attempt to get cooperation from Wall Street firms."

A 'Stunned' Supervisor

Supervisor Steiner, who headed a home for abused children until he was appointed to the board by California Gov. Pete Wilson last year, felt broadsided. "We were stunned" by the news, he recalls.

But because of the sunshine laws, it was illegal for the supervisors to confer that day. "This is the most inefficient form of government you can imagine," says Supervisor Gaddi Vasquez, the former cop. To satisfy the sunshine law, the board couldn't meet before midafternoon Monday, at the earliest. The delay, Mr. Andrus says, "turned out to be a definite impediment to effective decision-making."

Monday morning, without telling Mr. Raabe and the county staff, Mr. Andrus began consulting with LeBoeuf Lamb's Mr. Eklund about the county's filing for bankruptcy, Mr. Eklund recalls.

At a closed-door session of the board on Monday afternoon, the conflicting agendas of the county staff and the board's advisers at last collided. In a letter to the board the following day, Mr. Raabe summarized what took place: Mr. Raabe presented the details of the Wall Street workout plan. He explained that at least one firm stood ready to make a bid for the entire portfolio. (Indeed, J.P. Morgan had already begun pricing the bonds in the market.)

The main snag, Mr. Raabe wrote, was that he wasn't empowered to hire a fiduciary to oversee the sell-off. As he explained, no investment bank would risk bidding for the portfolio without a fiduciary on hand to ensure proper pricing.

At the Monday meeting, the county staff, which works directly for the supervisors, seconded Mr. Raabe's recommendation that a fiduciary be hired. Unexpectedly, however, LeBoeuf Lamb objected, throwing the meeting into disarray.

According to Supervisor Stanton, the lawyers still hoped to get the SEC to take over the fund. So, anything that side-stepped the possibility of fraud—as the Wall Street plan did—might threaten the lawyers' own hopes of SEC intervention.

Wall Street Plan Blocked

In the meeting, the LeBoeuf Lamb lawyers, joined by Mr. Andrus, the county counsel, blocked the Wall Street plan by throwing up two legal hurdles. First, they argued the fund's legal status was so unclear that they couldn't say who actually owned the assets. What's more, Mr. Andrus balked at indemnifying the fiduciary against any lawsuits that might arise over the sale of the portfolio.

Faced with conflicting advice, the supervisors adjourned. After they left, the lawyers continued bickering with the staff long into the night, staff members say.

At 2:45 a.m., at Mr. Andrus's suggestion, the staff dispatched police cars to rouse the supervisors to reconsider the issue. Mr. Raabe "was frantic," Supervisor Steiner says. The staff "had a siege mentality." Again, discussions with the supervisors took place one on one.

As Mr. Steiner recalls, "We were told that potentially the entire pool would melt down, with a loss far in excess of $1.5 billion, and there was J.P. Morgan poised" to buy the portfolio. Mr. Stanton recalls that bankruptcy and bringing in the SEC "were the two options, the two viable options." He stresses

that "no other recommendation was presented to us."

However, Mr. Raabe made a last desperate plea for the plan. "I implore you to consider the devastating outcome if this request is not approved," he wrote in his summary, noting on the document the hour: 3 o'clock on Tuesday morning.

The board and its lawyers turned him down. "We were under incredible pressure to make a decision for the other investors" in the fund, Mr. Steiner says. "They would never forgive us."

Later Tuesday, unable to meet its collateral demands, the county and its fund sought refuge in bankruptcy court. At that point, LeBoeuf Lamb, admitting a conflict of interest, turned the case over to bankruptcy specialists at Stutman, Treister & Glatt, a Los Angeles law firm.

On Tuesday and Wednesday, the fund's lenders rushed to unload some $11.4 billion of its bonds. Late Wednesday, the county hired Salomon Brothers—one of the Wall Street white knights, which had been prepared to buy $1.5 billion of bonds from the county just the day before—to auction off the fund's remaining assets. Already, the fund's losses exceed $2 billion, while the yoke of bankruptcy court will hamper Orange County for years to come.

Epilogue*

ALAN SALTZSTEIN

Today Orange County is no longer in bankruptcy and most of its residents enjoy the fruits of a strong economy and a strategic location within the greater Los Angeles urban area. The public sector shares in this prosperity; its employees are creatively planning for the new millennium. Bankruptcy, however, left many scars personally on the participants, created a debt that will affect county taxpayers for many years, and set back regional cooperation between governments significantly. Recovery required severely cutting services and laying off many employees. Without the burden of

debt payments that will continue well into the twenty-first century, one can imagine benefits from other public improvements or lower taxes. Thus there are lessons for all to learn from this unfortunate chain of events. This addendum will summarize the aftermath of the bankruptcy, speculate as to why it occurred, and in conclusion offer some lessons for the public administration community.

The Aftermath of the Bankruptcy

Ms. Jereski's writing leaves us as the county declares bankruptcy. Immediately there was much

*This epilogue was written especially for the seventh edition of this text by Professor Alan Saltzstein, California State University, Fullerton.

disbelief. The bankruptcy of so large a government in such a prosperous setting run by accomplished elected and appointed officials seemed beyond belief. Understandably, much public outrage followed. The impact spread beyond the confines of county government, since many school districts, special districts, and civil governments throughout the state had invested in the fund (all Orange County school districts were required to place their money in the county fund). A grand jury investigation and legal indictments followed. Alternative structures of government were proposed. In sum, it was a period of extreme political and governmental chaos.

Major organizational changes followed. County Treasurer Bob Citron resigned his position shortly after the bankruptcy. A former state official was appointed by the court to oversee the county's finances and propose a financial recovery plan. Restructuring required sizable budgetary reductions and the securing of new debt instruments to spread out the debt. The board of supervisors then hired a corporate expert, William Popejoy, as the Chief Administrative Officer (CAO) with significantly expanded powers.

Popejoy implemented impressive downsizing of the county operation. Services were cut back and the workforce decreased by more that 12 percent (Wilgoren 1995). Service charges, one of the few revenue sources at the discretion of the supervisors expanded. He also worked to secure agreements among the fund participants to set priorities for paying the contributors. Since, of course, much money had been lost, participants had to agree to accept less than they had contributed, and of course they lost projected interest payments. Agreement on these decisions required months of conflictual negotiations between city, county, and school officials.

Major jolts to a political system frequently are the impetus for organizational changes. A charter commission proposed a more unified and centralized organization for the county that would have made the treasurer appointed by the board of supervisors, and created a stronger CAO position. A referendum increasing the sales tax was proposed

to pay off the bankruptcy debt and restore the county's credit rating. Voters, however, were in no mood to accept the judgement of political leaders, and defeated both of these measures soundly.

The grand jury testimony led to criminal indictments of several of the central players. Citron was indicted and ultimately pleaded guilty to six felony counts. He was sentenced to a year in prison and fined $100,000. Frail in health and over 70 years old, he served an eight-month probated sentence. Ronald Rubino, the Chief Budget Officer of the county was accused of aiding Citron in concealing the financial plight of the county from the supervisors. His trial ended in a hung jury. Ultimately, Rubino pleaded guilty to a much-reduced charge, requiring him to perform one hundred hours of community service. Mathew Raabe, the hero of Ms. Jereski's article, was convicted of diverting funds illegally and sentenced to three years in prison, the only significant prison time served by bankruptcy participants.

Civil actions were also filed against two members of the board of supervisors for "failing to safeguard the financial health of the county." A state appeals court eventually dismissed these charges. A charge of willful misconduct was also made against the elected auditor-controller. The state attorney general also dismissed this charge (Baldasarre 1998, 176).

By 1999 all of the major players in these events had left the scene. The last member of the board of supervisors to serve during the bankruptcy ended his term in 1998. A new treasurer was appointed following Citron's resignation and elected to the position in 1995. Popejoy resigned as CAO following the defeat of the charter amendment and the tax increase. His replacement serves as CAO but with reduced powers. Thus the structure and operation of the county remains very similar to that before the bankruptcy. The board of supervisors and the separately elected treasurer continue as the central financial players in county government.

Much of the pain of these events is behind the county as well. A strengthened economy has restored much of the lost revenue, and Orange County bonds are again well received on Wall

Street. Slowly the conflict among participants declined as new resources eased some of the pain.

Why Did It Happen?

Preventing the repetition of the Orange County bankruptcy requires an understanding of why it happened. Unfortunately, we have several theories but no definitive explanation for these events. Four explanations are commonly cited.

1. It Was Citron's Fault

Bob Citron is an unusual man; he appears to be at least two very different people. First, there is the quiet, soft-spoken grandfather, over his head in the high financial circles he was placed in. He was appointed to the treasurer's position in 1970, when little discretion was given to the position. At the time, funds had to be held in safe liquid assets and there was a great deal of state supervision. He lacked a college degree and had little financial experience other than his years as a treasurer's assistant.

Financial concerns of the county treasurer changed, however, as local governments looked to investments as a source of income rather than to liquidity. Citron was then asked to do things he really was not competent to do. Thus perhaps he was easy prey for the "slick traders" of Wall Street.

At his trial, Citron complemented this impression by arguing that his mental facilities had declined in recent years. Senility had set in, impairing his judgment and leading him to accept advice without evaluation. It was also reported that he regularly relied on an astrologer for financial advice (Recard 1998).

The other side of Citron is evident on the wall of his office, cluttered with awards and honors from the financial and public administration communities. The Orange County American Society for Public Administration Chapter awarded him its "Public Official of the Year" award six months prior to the bankruptcy. Supervisors and county administrators regularly praised him as a financial ge-

nius. One Supervisor said to me a few months before the bankruptcy, "I don't understand how he does it, but the man is an absolute genius." Other governments and private individuals had so much confidence in Citron that they voluntarily invested their funds with the county. Judges often required that settlements be placed in the fund to ensure a good, safe return. He influenced the writing of state legislation that granted treasurers expanded authority to invest. Nationally, he was considered tops in his field. Senile, perhaps, but to paraphrase what Lincoln said of Grant, the supervisors wished all their employees were so senile.

2. It Was the Broker's Fault

When counties became more interested in the financial return of their holdings and state laws permitted more diverse investment opportunities, financial advisors and Wall Street firms became important players in local finance. A government as large as Orange County was a plum contract for a trading house—enough to make the careers of several individual traders. Orange County, through Bob Citron, was a regular customer of several brokerage firms and financial advisers.

Are these advisers responsible for bad advice, when public funds are involved? County officials thought so and proceeded to sue several brokerage firms. Many of these suits led, collectively, to settlements that are among the largest received in the public sector. Over $700 million of the $1.6 billion dollars lost has in fact been recovered through several court actions and mediated agreements. The success of these efforts suggests that the legal system finds fault in the advice given to Mr. Citron.

3. Governmental Structure Is at Fault

Authority in Orange County is divided between supervisors elected in large districts and several separately elected officials including the county treasurer. The CAO was nominally responsible for budget preparation, though in fact the supervisors and their staffs and other elected department heads like the sheriff were strong players in the decisions. Consequently, few speak for the concerns of the county as a whole. "I am the CAO of my district," one supervisor stated to me when discussing why a strong CAO was not necessary.

Investment decisions were considered the prerogative of the treasurer in Citron's day, and influence by the supervisors was resisted. To many, he guarded this authority carefully and often imperially. Current supervisor Jim Silva recalls his first conversation with Citron while he was running for office prior to the bankruptcy. "I asked him about the investment pool, and he basically says he's doing a good job. He has a very good track record, and if I didn't believe him that I could read his press clippings. And he turned around and walked away from me" (Baldassare 1998, p. 49). Supervisors claimed that, when they asked Citron for information about investment policies he refused to give it, stating that he was responsible only to the voters.

Thus, to many, the Orange County system was one of divided authority without central responsibility. Supervisors tend to focus on the concerns of their districts while centrally elected officials concentrate on their functional responsibilities only. Would a strong CAO whose job would include the treasury as well as expenditures place investment policy within a broader context? While the experience of governments and the writings of many of the stalwarts in the public administration field would say yes, the voters and many key decision-makers apparently disagreed when they soundly rejected the charter amendment.

4. Environmental Demands, Voter Mistrust, and Wishful Thinking

The last reason looks more broadly at social, economic, and political changes in the Orange County environment. Ms. Jereski points out that Orange County has one of the highest per-capita incomes of any county in the nation. Aggregate figures, while accurate, mask underlying problems of a large share of the population. The county's needy population expanded significantly from 1980 to 1990. Immigration from Latin America and Asia

increased, leaving the county with the sixth-largest Latino and fourth-largest Asian population in the country (Baldasarre 1998). By 1990, 27 percent of the population was foreign born and 26 percent had no health insurance (Phillips 1997, p. 3).

Counties in California are responsible for most of the costs associated with poverty; welfare, public health, homelessness. Thus these programs required higher budgets as the poverty population increased. The county is also the main provider of jails and is the police force in unincorporated areas. Demands for jail space and more sheriffs increased as crime increased in the late 1980s and early 1990s.

Politically, the county remained conservative, and its middle-class residents, facing some of the highest housing prices in the nation, were very sensitive to increases in taxes. Orange County voters had strongly supported the property-tax cut of Proposition 13 in 1978 and subsequent tax cutting measures.

State support of local governments had also declined during this time period as a consequence of various initiatives that earmarked money to various concerns and a faltering economy that generated less state revenue. Several unincorporated areas of south Orange County incorporated as cities during the late 1980s, leaving the county with a smaller revenue base.

County board members faced an impossible problem. Demands for services had increased significantly, and in many cases the county was required to serve the poor population at rates determined by other governments. Resources had declined, and there was no reason to expect them to increase. Decision makers were limited in their search for new revenues and were opposed to increasing general taxes.

Bob Citron's pool of money and the magical returns he seemed to be able to produce became, perhaps, a solution to this awful conundrum. Perhaps he really was a wizard, thought the board of supervisors. Each year the portion of the county's income derived from investments increased. It was estimated at 35 percent of the total county income in the year of the bankruptcy. Hindsight tells us that no government ever gets nearly that kind of income from investments, but to the board members, perhaps Citron could for just one more year.

Lessons for Public Administrators

Can we absolve public administrators of any responsibility for the financial default of Orange County? Maybe an apparently competent elected official lost his mind? Or was just an easy mark for "slick bond traders" Perhaps it was caused by a governmental structure that failed to provide central direction to the decision-making process? Or possibly high demands for services and declining resources gave the decision makers no choice but to gamble on risky investments?

The setting of Orange County in the early 1990s made it difficult to warn the policy makers that bankruptcy might occur. Yet some did see the problem. John Moorloch, the present treasurer, campaigned for Citron's job in the spring of 1995 by raising concerns over the treasurer's investments, but few listened. Citron received the endorsement of most elected officials and won the election handily. Internally, some undoubtedly raised questions, but few concerns were voiced even when projected income from investments reached 35 percent of the budget.

This story is a classic case of short-term thinking driving out the necessity for long-range planning. Questions about Citron's investment policies could be raised only by those less dependent on immediate rewards or political benefits. It is surely difficult for most elected officials who must worry about the public's immediate reaction to do so. Public administrators, on the other hand, who are less governed by the day-to-day reaction of the electorate, should be the first to register concerns for the general health of their organization over the long-haul.

Orange County needed whistle-blowers who were willing to inform elected officials and the public of the risk associated with Citron's decisions. To protect employees from recriminations, policies ought to be framed to encourage employees to come forth freely, and superiors must be willing to listen to grievances.

A skepticism of authority on the part of all the parties is a final lesson of the Orange County bankruptcy. Errors were clearly made by those who had strong support from the public and political leaders. Major interest groups, the press, and leaders of other governments who invested in the county fund raised few concerns about treasury management. Everybody, within the system failed to remain alert to the potential for error even among those we trust.

References

Baldassare, M. 1998. *When Government Fails: The Orange County Bankruptcy.* Berkeley: University of California Press.

Phillips, E. G. 1997. "Ensuring the Safety Net: Where Do We Stand and Where Do We Go From Here." Costa Mesa, Calif.: Partnership for Responsible Public Policy, Mimeo.

Recard, E. S. 1988. Citron Says 'Cognitive Defects' Led to His Risky Investments. *Los Angeles Times* 23 July.

Wilgoren, J. (1995). "O.C. Services Sliced About 50%, Work Force 13% in New Budget." *Los Angeles Times* 31 March.

Chapter 15 Review Questions

1. Sum up in a few sentences James Q. Wilson's approach to improving bureaucratic responsiveness to the public interest. How does his perspective compare and contrast to the three approaches outlined in the introduction to this chapter?
2. What are some of the basic unstated assumptions about public bureaucracy and public interest implicit in Wilson's argument? Are these assumptions valid in your view?

3. In the Orange County case study, list the central problems that you found led to the county filing Chapter 9 bankruptcy. Do they agree with those cited by Dr. Saltzstein's epilogue?

4. Given your list, what specific recommendations by James Q. Wilson might prevent this problem from reoccurring in the future? Or, are Wilson's ideas not applicable? If not, why? Or, if so, why?

5. Would you propose any reforms for securing "the public interest", other than those outlined by Wilson? And if so, explain your reasons?

6. What might be some of the difficulties in implementing your proposed reforms (Think of what happened to the reforms attempted by Orange County as outlined by Dr. Saltstein)?

Key Terms

deregulate government
culture of the organization
control mentality
mission accomplishment
balancing distribution of
    authority with program tasks
overcentralization of control

judging agencies by results
separation of powers
paradoxical bureaucracy
legislative micromanagement
presidential micromanagement
turf-conscious administrator

Suggestions for Further Reading

The proper role of government in serving the public interest is one that has been considered and debated for decades. Certainly with the founding of the United States, one need only turn to the Federalist papers to read about the concerns for the role of government. Specifically, "Publius" [James Madison], *The Federalist* No. 10," (New York Packet, November 23, 1787) serves as a starting point for understanding the interests and intensity of the citizen's desires for assuring a "public voice" in government matters. Readings that continue this debate concerning government's relationship with the public can be found in John Stuart Mill's *On Liberty* (London: J.W. Parker and Son, 1859) and *Consideration on Representative Government* (London: Parker, Son and Bourn, 1861) and Georg Wilhelm Friedrich Hegel, *The Philosophy of Right* (Berlin: In der Kicolaischen Buchhandlung, 1821). For a good introductory discussion of democratic administration, one should read Paul H. Appleby's

Big Democracy (New York: Alfred A. Knopf, 1945), as well as *Policy and Administration* (University: University of Alabama Press, 1949) and *Morality and Administration in Democratic Government* (Baton Rouge: LSU Press, 1952). Appleby clearly is one of the most influential American authors on the subject of administrative democracy. For further interpretations of his essays, a helpful compilation is included in Roscoe C. Martin's, ed., *Public Administration and Democracy: Essays in Honor of Paul H. Appleby* (Syracuse, N.Y.: Syracuse University Press, 1965).

The discussion involving bureaucracy and the public interest is further outlined when one explores the literature on political bureaucracy. For an overview of the requirements for serving the public interest from a bureaucratic standpoint, one should read Lewis C. Mainzer, *Political Bureaucracy* (Glenview, Ill.: Scott, Foresman and Co., 1973), and Peter Woll, *American Bureaucracy*

(New York: W. W. Norton and Co., 1963). Additionally, for several essays in defense of the "administrative machinery's" ability to respond to the public interest, see Norton Long, *The Polity* (Chicago: Rand McNally and Co., 1962). On the other hand, Peter Blau, *The Dynamics of Bureaucracy* (Chicago: University of Chicago Press, 1955), argues that bureaucracy and democracy are incompatible and are incapable of successfully coexisting.

Another level of discussion on bureaucracy and the public interest can be found within debates over representative bureaucracy. Much of this literature argues for its importance as a democratic ideal. Steven G. Koven's chapter, "The Bureaucratic-Democratic Conundrum: A Contemporary Inquiry into the Labyrinth," in *Handbook of Bureaucracy,* Ali Farazmand, ed. (New York: Marcel Dekker, Inc., 1994), pp. 79–96; and Brian J. Cook, "The Representative Function of Bureaucracy: Public Administration in Constitutive Perspective," *Administration & Society,* 23, 4 (February 1992), pp. 403–429, provide a valuable "first-look" at the significance of representative bureaucracy. Further, Charles M. Wiltse, "The Representative Function of Bureaucracy," *American Political Science Review,* 35 (June 1941), pp. 510–516 should be reviewed for discussion on bureaucracy's role in assisting Congress in fulfilling its constitutional obligation of providing representation. Students of public administration should also be familiar with Norton E. Long, "Bureaucracy and Constitutionalism," *American Political Science Review,* 46 (September 1952), pp. 808–818, and Charles Merriam, *Political Power* (New York: McGraw-Hill, 1934). A more recent theoretical exploration is offered by Samuel P. Krislov, *Representative Bureaucracy* (Englewood Cliffs, N.J.: Prentice-Hall, 1974), and Harry Kranz, *The Participatory Bureaucracy* (Lexington, Mass.: Lexington Books, 1976). Further readings should include Morris Janowitz, Deil Wright, and William Delany, *Public Administration and the Public—Perspectives Toward Government in a Metropolitan Community,* no. 36 in University of Michigan, Michigan Governmental Studies (Ann Arbor: Bureau of Government, Institute of Government Administration, University of Michigan, 1958).

The challenge to representative bureaucracy, in practice involves how to hold it institutionally accountable to the public. And so Bernard Rosen's *Holding Government Bureaucracies Accountable,* 3d ed., (New York: Praeger Publishers, 1999) offers a basic overview of these accountability techniques. The difficulties in doing so, however, are defined in M. Shamsul Haque's chapter, "The Emerging Challenges to Bureaucratic Accountability: A Critical Perspective," in *The Handbook of Bureaucracy,* Ali Farazmand, ed. (New York: Marcel Dekker, 1994), pp. 265–286.

Further, J. Donald Kingsley, *Representative Bureaucracy: An Interpretation of the British Civil Service* (Yellow Springs, Ohio: Antioch Press, 1944), introduced representative bureaucracy as class and racial issue. One should, as counterpoint to this book also examine the role of public personnel in a democratic regime, and thus read Frederick C. Mosher's *Democracy and the Public Service* (New York: Oxford University Press, 1968). More specifically, it would be helpful to examine the public administrator as a link with the public interest. Peter deLeon calls for "participatory policy analysis" in "The Democratization of the Policy Sciences," *Public Administration Review,* 52, 2 (March/April 1992), pp. 125–129. Other excellent readings include Richard C. Box, "The Administrator as Trustee of the Public Interest: Normative Ideals and Daily Practice," *Administration & Society,* 24, 3 (November 1992), pp. 323–345; John Clayton Thomas, "Public Involvement and Governmental Effectiveness: A Decision-Making Model for Public Managers," *Administration & Society,* 24, 4 (February 1993), pp. 444–469, and Philip Selznick, *TVA and the Grass Roots* (New York: Harper & Row, 1949). Norton E. Long provides a standard for evaluating the outcomes, management structures, and processes, programs, and policies in "Conceptual Notes on the Public Interest for Public Administration and Policy Analysts," *Administration & Society,* 22, 2 (August 1990), pp. 170–181. Finally, the argument that public administration is the "mechanism" whereby decisions are made in compatibility with the basic tenets of democracy is found in Emmette S. Redford, *Democracy in the Administrative State* (New York: Oxford University Press, 1969).

"The public" is defined in numerous ways: first, the so-called "active citizen" is often characterized as being on the receiving end of public goods. For a useful essay on the active citizenship, read Camilla Stivers, "The Public Agency as Policy: Active Citizenship in the Administrative State," *Administration & Society,* 22, 1 (May 1990), pp. 86–105, and also worthwhile is Norton E. Long's "Seeking the Polity's Bottom Line: A Conceptual Note," *Administration & Society,* 24, 2 (August 1992), pp. 107–114. One of the most famous evaluations of how the public interest is defined at the local level as an interplay of pluralist forces is Robert A. Dahl's *Who Governs? Democracy and Power in an American City* (New Haven: Yale University Press, 1961).

No discussion is complete without examining the role of public interest groups in the American bureaucratic regime. A "must-read" on this topic is E. Pendleton Herring, *Group Representation before Congress* (Baltimore: Johns Hopkins Press, 1929) and his *Public Administration and the Public Interest* (New York: McGraw Hill, 1936). Others worth scanning include Allan J. Cigler and Burdett A. Loomis, eds., *Interest Group Politics* (Washington, D.C.: Congressional Quarterly Press, 1983); V.O. Key, Jr., *Politics, Parties, and Pressure Groups* (New York: Thomas Y. Crowell Co., 1942); and David B. Truman, *The Governmental Process* (New York: Alfred A. Knopf, 1951). For the best book outlining the problems associated with pressure groups, read Theodore

Lowi's *The End of Liberalism* (New York: W. W. Norton and Co., 1969); yet, by contrast an examination of the usefulness of special interests to the public good can be found in Grant McConnell's *Private Power and American Democracy* (New York: Alfred A. Knopf, 1966).

Public opinion is also another important aspect for shaping the public's interest. For a discussion on public opinion and the means for directing it toward advancing the public interest read Harold D. Lasswell, *Democracy Through Public Opinion* (Menasha, Wisconsin: George Banta Publishing Co., 1941). Other books include: V. O. Key, Jr., *Public Opinion and American Democracy* (New York: Alfred A. Knopf, 1961); Water Lippmann, *Public Opinion* (New York: Harcourt, Brace, and Co., 1922); Angus Campbell, Philip E. Converse, Warren E. Miller, and Donald Stokes, *The American Voter* (New York: John Wiley and Sons, 1960).

The 1990s books addressing important aspects of "bureaucracy/public interest" interrelationships include: Richard C. Box, *Citizen Governance* (Thousand Oaks, Calif.: Sage, 1998); Peter deLeon, *Democracy and the Political Sciences* (New York: Suny Press, 1997); Louis C. Gawthrope, *Public Service and Democracy* (Chatham, N.J.: Chatham House, 1998; Patricia W. Ingraham, *The Foundation of Merit: Public Service in American Democracy* (Baltimore, Md.: Johns Hopkins, 1995); Peter A. Lawler, et al. (eds.), *Active Duty* (Landam, Md.: Roman and Littlefield, 1998); William D. Richardson, *Democracy, Bureaucracy and Character* (Lawrence, KS: Kan., 1997); and Gary C. Wamsley, et al. (eds.) *Refounding Democractic Public Administration* (Thousand Oaks, Calif.: Sage, 1996).

CHAPTER 16

The Relationship Between Ethics and Public Administration: The Concept of Competing Ethical Obligations

The twentieth century has hardly been distinguished either by its observance of agreed moral codes or by its concentration on ethical inquiry. On the contrary, it has been distinguished by a "decay" of traditional moral codes, a widespread feeling that morality is "relative" if not utterly meaningless, and a disposition to regard ethical inquiry as frivolous, irrelevant. These currents of thought and feeling have been associated with a "falling away" from religious belief and a concomitant rise of "belief" in science and its philosophical—or anti-philosophical—aura.

Dwight Waldo

READING 16

Introduction

Leading thinkers in public administration long ago recognized that the critical issues of government ultimately involved moral choices. The definitive policy decisions made by public officials often have at their base conflicting ethical issues, such as whether to give precedence to the public interest or to the narrower demands of profession, department, bureau, or clientele. The ambivalent position in which public officials often find themselves has led some sensitive administrative theorists like Chester Barnard to say that the chief qualification of an executive is the ability to resolve these competing ethical codes—legal, technical, personal, professional, and organizational codes. In Barnard's view, the strength and quality of an administrator lies in his or her capacity to deal effectively with the moral complexities of organizations without being broken by the imposed problems of choice: ". . . neither men of weak responsibility nor those of limited capability," writes Barnard, "can endure or carry the burden of many simultaneous obligations of different types. If they are 'overloaded' either ability, responsibility, or morality or all three will be destroyed. Conversely, a condition of complex morality, great activity, and high responsibility cannot endure without commensurate ability."[1]

For Paul Appleby, another administrative theorist, the institutional arrangements in government provide the most effective safeguards for ensuring ethical administrative behavior. Appleby, in his book *Morality and Administration in Democratic Government,*[2] contends, however, that the traditional constitutional arrangements, such as checks and balances, federalism, or the Bill of Rights, do not supply this protection against immorality. Rather, two institutional safeguards are the best guarantees of administrative morality: (1) the ballot box and (2) hierarchy. By means of the *ballot box* the electorate judges direct the performance of government at periodic intervals. Through *hierarchy* important decisions are forced upward in the administrative structure where they can receive broader, less technical, and more political review. Appleby equates the application of broad, disinterested, and political judgment with responsible and ethical administration.

In another selection written as a memorial essay to Appleby, "Ethics and the Public Service," Stephen K. Bailey draws on Appleby's writings to develop some further insights into the essential qualities of moral behavior in the public service. At the core of Bailey's essay is his emphasis on three moral qualities in public administration: "optimism, courage, and fairness tempered by charity." Optimism, in the author's view, is the ability of a public servant to deal with morally ambiguous situations confidently and purposefully. Courage is the capacity to decide and act in the face of situations when inaction, indecision, or agreement with the popular trend would provide the easy solution. Fairness tempered by charity allows for the maintenance of standards of justice in decisions affecting the public interest.[3]

Bailey emphasizes the high ethical content of most important public questions. He points out how the varied complexities of public service add enormous complications to moral behavior so that the resolution of public issues can never be black or white. The "best solution," writes Bailey, "rarely is without its costs. . . . And one mark of moral maturity is in the appreciation of the inevitability of untoward and often malignant effects of benign moral choices." A strain of pessimism appears in Bailey's writing, for he observes that public policies rarely lead to a total victory for the "right" and a total defeat for the "wrong." Indeed, policy solutions themselves often create new policy problems.

Is ethical conduct in the public service the result of Barnard's thesis of an administrator's creative ability to resolve "competing ethical codes"? Or, Appleby's "institutional safeguards"? Or, Bailey's essential "moral qualities"?

In the following selection by Dwight Waldo, "Public Administration and Ethics," the author attempts to "map" the difficult and complicated terrain of the relationship between public administration and ethics. As Waldo asserts at the beginning: ". . . moral or

---

[1]Chester I. Barnard, *The Functions of the Executive* (Cambridge, Mass.: Harvard University Press, 1938), p. 272.

[2]Paul H. Appleby, *Morality and Administration in Democratic Government* (Baton Rouge, La.: Louisiana State University Press, 1952).

[3]Stephen K. Baily, "Ethics and the Public Service," in Roscoe C. Martin, ed., *Public Administration and Democracy* (Syracuse, N.Y.: Syracuse University Press, 1965).

ethical behavior in public administration is a complicated matter, indeed *chaotic.*" In order to elaborate on the reasons for this current complexity, he proceeds to sketch briefly the historical backdrop of how the distinction between "public" and "private" morality evolved and the relationship between "the state and higher law." Here we are treated to a concise 2000-year overview of political theories that brought us to our present twenty-first century dilemmas. He thus provides us with a thoughtful intellectual background for comprehending our contemporary confused scene. Waldo then develops further perspectives on the present by what he calls "a map—of sorts" or an outline "of the sources and types of ethical obligations to which the public administrator is expected to respond." He identifies a dozen ethical obligations, ranging from the broadest "Obligations to the Constitution" and "To Religion and to God" to the narrowest, "To Self" and "To Family and Friends." He defends this "mapping project" in the subsequent sections on "A Need for Maps" and "A Need for Navigation Instruments" because "If we are going to talk about ethics in public life, it would be useful to know what we are talking about." In the end, Waldo offers no easy answers but rather concludes with six thought-provoking "observations and reflections" on this topic concerning "some of the matters that would be worthy of attention in a more serious and systematic way."

A word about Dwight Waldo (1913–   ): This selection you are about to read came from one of his eleven out-of-course lectures that he delivered before he retired as the Albert Schweitzer Distinguished Service Professor from the Maxwell School of Citizenship and Public Affairs, Syracuse University. Together these lectures were published as a book, *The Enterprise of Public Administration: A Summary View,* in which Waldo attempted to sum up his four decades of involvement both as a practitioner and as an academic within the field. Waldo served in the Bureau of the Budget during World War II, as director of the Institute of Governmental Studies at the University of California at Berkeley in the 1950s, as editor-in-chief of the *Public Administration Review* for twelve years in the 1960s and 1970s, and as president of the National Association of Schools of Public Affairs and Administration in the 1970s. However, he made his lasting mark on the field by his seminal writings, such as *The Administrative State, The Study of Public Administration, Perspectives on Administration, The Novelist on Organization and Administration,* and many others. Waldo's contributions were deemed so important to the advancement of the field by his peers that the American Society for Public Administration named its annual prize for lifetime academic achievement, The Dwight Waldo Award.

When you read his essay, you will no doubt gain an appreciation of why Waldo's contributions are regarded so highly by administrative scholars. Few others write with such stylistic grace, raise such profound questions, and provide the historical context to present-day issues in public administration. In particular, try to think about these questions as you read the essay:

Why does Waldo argue we need "maps" and "navigation instruments" to guide us through this subject? What does he mean by those terms and do you concur with his rationale for advancing this thesis?

Do you agree with his list of twelve "ethical obligations"? Would you add or delete any on his list?

Why does he contend that "the twentieth century has hardly been distinguished either by its observance on agreed moral codes or by its concentration on ethical inquiry"? The sources for this decay of morality?

From your reading of Waldo, what practical advice does his essay offer the public administrator on-the-firing-line in sorting out the ethical dilemmas that he or she faces?

Public Administration and Ethics: A Prologue to a Preface

DWIGHT WALDO

"No process has been discovered by which promotion to a position of public responsibility will do away with a man's interest in his own welfare, his partialities, race, and prejudices."—James Harvey Robinson

"You are welcome to my house; you are welcome to my heart . . . my personal feelings have nothing to do with the present case. . . . As George Washington, I would do anything in my power for you. As President, I can do nothing."—George Washington, to a friend seeking an appointment

"There is not a moral vice which cannot be made into relative good by context. There is not a moral virtue which cannot in peculiar circumstances have patently evil results."—Stephen Bailey

"The big organization dehumanizes the individual by turning him into a functionary. In doing so it makes everything possible by creating a new kind of man, one who is morally unbounded in his role as func-

tionary. . . . His ethic is the ethic of the good soldier: take the order, do the job, do it the best way you know how, because that is your honor, your virtue, your pride-in-work."—F. William Howton

"It seems to be inevitable that the struggle to maintain cooperation among men should destroy some men morally as battle destroys some men physically."—Chester Barnard

"The raising of moral considerations in any discussion on organizations usually causes discomfort. . . . Nonetheless, if morality is about what is right and wrong, then behavior in organizations is largely determined by such considerations."—David Bradley and Roy Wilkie

"The first duty of a civil servant is to give his undivided allegiance to the State at all times and on all occasions when the State has a claim on his service."—Board of Inquiry, United Kingdom, 1928

The subtitle of this presentation and the several heterogeneous epigraphs are directed toward emphasizing the central theme of this presentation, namely, that moral or ethical* behavior in public administration is a complicated matter, indeed, *chaotic.* While some facets of the matter have been treated with insight and clarity, nothing in the way of a comprehensive and systematic treatise exists—or if so I am unaware of it.[1] This situation may not reflect just accident or lack of interest. What may be reflected is the fact that a systematic treatise is impossible, given the scope, complexity, and intractability of the material from which it would have to be constructed and given an inability to find acceptable or defensible foundations of ideas and beliefs on which it could be grounded.

In this discussion I hope to indicate some of the subjects that might be given attention in a systematic treatise. I appreciate that even this hope may represent pretentiousness.

Public Morality and Private Morality

An appropriate beginning is to note a distinction between public and private morality and the possibility of a conflict between them.[2] This is a very elementary distinction, but much evidence indicates that it is little understood. As presented in the media, including the columns of the pundits, morality in public office is a simple matter of obeying the law, being honest, and telling the truth. *Not so.*

Public morality concerns decisions made and action taken directed toward the good of a collectivity which is seen or conceptualized as "the public," that is, as an entity or group larger than immediate social groups such as family and clan. Conventionally, "the public" in the modern West is equated with "the nation," or "the country." Thus when decisions are made and actions taken vis-à-vis other nations or countries a public interest is presumed to be in view. Similarly, when the decision or action is directed inward toward the affairs of the nation-state, a public or general interest is presumed to come before private or group interests.

In either case a decision or action justified as moral because it is judged to be in the interest of the public may be immoral from the standpoint of all, or nearly all, interpretations of moral behavior for individuals. The most common example is killing. When done by an individual it is, commonly, the crime of homicide. When done in warfare or law enforcement on behalf of the public it is an act of duty and honor, perhaps of heroism—presuming the "correct" circumstances. All important governments have committed what would be "sins" if done by individuals, what would be "crimes" if done under their own laws by individuals acting privately.

Those in government who decide and act on behalf of the public will from time to time, of *necessity* as I see it, be lying, stealing, cheating, killing. What must be faced is that all decision and action in the public interest is inevitably morally complex, and that the price of any good characteristically entails some bad. Usually the bad is not as simple and stark as the terms just listed signify; but sometimes it *is,* and honesty and insight on our part can begin with so acknowledging.

Ironically, the concept of "the public" is regarded, and I believe properly, as a good and even precious thing. It is a heritage from Greek and Roman antiquity. Its projection, elaboration, nurture, and defense are generally represented as the work of inspired thinkers, virtuous statesmen, and brave warriors. How can this be, when sins and crimes are committed in the name of the public? The answer is twofold. First, my favorite question: Compared to what? Assuming government is desirable, or at least inevitable, what legitimating concept is better? At least the idea of government in the name of a public advances that enterprise beyond purely personal and often tyrannical rule. Second, once in motion, so to speak, the concept of the public becomes invested with, a shelter for, and even a source of, goods that we identify with words such as citizenship, security, justice, and liberty.

---

*Strictly speaking, *moral* signifies right behavior in an immediate and customary sense; *ethical* signifies right behavior as examined and reflected upon. But no warranty is given that this distinction is always made in what follows.

The State and Higher Law

To see the matter of public and private morality in perspective it is necessary to understand the complicated relationship of both moralities to the concept of *higher law*. The concept of higher law, simply put for our purposes, holds that there is a source and measure of rightness that is above and beyond both individual and government. In our own history it is represented prominently in the justification of the Revolution against the government of George III, and it inspired the Declaration of Independence.

The classical Greek philosophers, from whom much of our tradition of political thought derives, sought a moral unity. Are the good man and the good citizen the same? Both Plato and Aristotle answered the question affirmatively, though Plato more certainly than Aristotle. In the comparatively simple world of the city-state this answer could be made plausible, given the Greek conviction of superiority and the elitist nature of citizenship: the polity creates citizens in its admirable image and is thus the source of man's morality; there can be no legitimate appeal from what it holds to be right.

But as Sophocles' *Antigone* signifies, the idea of a higher law—in this case the laws of Zeus as against those of the king, Creon—existed even in Athens. During the Hellenistic period, after the decline of the city-state, the idea of a natural law above and beyond the mundane world was elaborated, especially by the Stoics. A sense of personhood apart from the polity, and of the essential equality of humans *as* humans was developing, and this was accompanied by a growing belief that right and wrong rested on foundations beyond the polity. As Sabine put it in his history of political theory; "Men were slowly making souls for themselves." With Christianity these ideas were of course broadened and deepened. The idea of God's law, or natural law—and characteristically the two became conflated—was to become a powerful force in relation to both private and public morality.

For more than a millennium after the fall of Rome, during a period in which government all but disappeared in the West, the relationship of the two powers, the sacred and the secular—for most purposes to be equated with Church and secular authority—was at the center of political philosophy and political controversy; but the theoretical and logical supremacy of the higher law was seldom questioned. With the emergence of the modern state a new era opened. The authority of a state, even a secular state, to determine right and wrong for its citizens was powerfully asserted by political theorists, notably Machiavelli and Hobbes. On the other hand, the long era of higher-law thinking had left an indelible imprint on thought and attitude. That there is something to which one's conscience gives access and which provides guidance on right and wrong remains a strong feeling even among those who regard themselves as completely secular.

The discussion of higher law has indicated that the initial duality of public morality and private morality was simplistic. There *is* an important, and insufficiently appreciated, distinction between the two, as I hope was demonstrated. But two important matters are now apparent. One is that higher law does not equate with or relate only to private morality as against public. Its sanction can be claimed by the polity if the polity represents the sacred as well as the secular, that is, if there is no separation of church and state—or perhaps even if there is.

The other matter is that the public-private distinction is but one example, albeit a crucial one for our purposes, of a class of relationships that can be designated *collectivity-person*. The biological person is of course distinguishable from any collectivity: nation, party, union, family, whatever. But whether the person can have or should have moral standing apart from the collectivities that have created him and given him meaning is a large part of what ethics is about; for all collectivities of any durability and significance will claim, explicitly or implicitly, to be the source of moral authority. While the state may well, and in some cases inevitably will, claim moral supremacy, the individual will have to weigh its claims against his or her interpretations of competing claims of other collectivities *and* the claims of higher law and "conscience."

Plainly, the ethical landscape is becoming very cluttered and complex. More to this shortly. But first a few words on *reason of state.* Reason of state is public morality at its extreme reach. Plainly put, it is conduct that violates all or nearly all standards of right conduct for individuals; this in the interests of the creating, preserving, or enhancing state power, and rationalized by "the ends justify the means" logic. A few years ago I had occasion to review the literature on this subject in Political Science in the United States. Significantly, what I found was very little, and this mostly by émigré scholars. Unbelievably, there is no entry for this important subject in the seventeen-volume *International Encyclopedia of the Social Sciences,* even though it was planned and executed during the moral-ethical hurricane of the Vietnam War. A number of historical factors, beyond exploring here, have led us to gloss over and even deny the complexities and contradictions that exist when public and private morality conflict, as inevitably they sometimes will.

A Map—of Sorts

A few years ago, attempting to address the subject "Ethical Obligations and the Public Service," I made a rough sketch of the ethical obligations of the public administrator as seen from one point of view. Later, this sketch was somewhat elaborated and refined in collaboration with Patrick Hennigan in a yet unpublished essay. It will serve present purposes to indicate the nature of this endeavor.

The sketch, or "map," as we called it, is of ethical obligations of the public administrator with special reference to the United States. The perspective taken is that of the *sources* and *types* of ethical obligations to which the public administrator is expected to respond. We identify a dozen, but as we indicate, the list is capable of indefinite expansion and does not lend itself to logical ordering.

FIRST. OBLIGATION TO THE CONSTITUTION.

This is a legal obligation of course, but it is also a source of ethical obligations, which may be symbolized and solemnized by an oath to uphold and

defend the Constitution. The upholding of regime and of regime values is a normal source of public-service obligation, and the Constitution is the foundation of regime and of regime values for the United States. But note: not an unambiguous foundation. A great deal of our history, including a civil war, can be written in terms of different interpretations of the Constitution.

SECOND. OBLIGATION TO LAW.

Laws made under the Constitution are a source not just of legal obligation but also of ethical obligations, as public-service codes of ethics normally underscore. Note again the ambiguities and puzzles. What if the law is unclear? What if laws conflict? What if a law seems unconstitutional, or violates a tenet of higher law? What is the ethical status of regulations made under the law?

THIRD. OBLIGATION TO NATION OR COUNTRY.

By most interpretations, a nation or country or people is separable from regime, and plainly this sense of identity with a nation, country, or people creates ethical obligations. Indeed, in many situations the obligation to country—Fatherland, Motherland, Homeland, however it may be put— overrides the obligation to regime. Lincoln, justifying his actions in 1864: "Was it possible to lose the nation, and yet preserve the constitution?"

FOURTH. OBLIGATION TO DEMOCRACY.

As indicated in previous discussions, this is separable from obligation to Constitution, granted that the relationship is complicated and arguable. Whatever the intent of the Framers—and I do not expect agreement on that, ever—democracy happened: it came to be accepted as an ideology or ethic and as a set of practices that somewhat overlie and somewhat intertwine with the Constitution. The emotional and intellectual acceptance of democracy creates obligations that are acknowledged and usually felt by the public administrator. But again, note the ambiguities: Is the will of the people *always* and *only* expressed in law? If in other ways, how? And how legitimated? Is the *will* of the people, however expressed, to be put ahead of the *welfare* of the people as seen by a public official with information not available to the people?

FIFTH. OBLIGATION TO ORGANIZATIONAL-BUREAUCRATIC NORMS.

These may be logically divided between those that are *generic* and those that are *specific*. The generic obligations are deeply rooted, perhaps in human nature, certainly in history and culture. They are associated with such terms as loyalty, duty, and order, as well as, perhaps, productivity, economy, efficiency. Specific obligations will depend upon circumstance: the function, the clientele, the technology.

SIXTH. OBLIGATION TO PROFESSION AND PROFESSIONALISM.

The disagreements among sociologists as to what precisely *profession* entails may be disregarded here. All would agree that a profession, indeed a well-developed occupation, has an ethos that acts to shape the values and behavior of members. This ethos concerns actions pertaining to fellow professionals, clients, patients, employers, and perhaps humanity in general. We have become much more aware of the strength and effects of professional values and behavior in public administration since the publication of Frederick Mosher's *Democracy and the Public Service*.

SEVENTH. OBLIGATION TO FAMILY AND FRIENDS.

Obligation to family is bedrock in most if not all morality. But in countries shaped by the Western political tradition it is formally accepted that *in principle* obligation to country and/or regime as well as to the public is higher than that to family. While the newspaper on almost any day will indi-

cate that the principle is often breached, we are very clear and insistent on the *principle,* and on the whole we believe that the principle prevails. But in countries in which the concept of public is recent and inchoate and in which family or other social group remains the center of loyalty and values, the principle is breached massively, so much so that the creation of an effective government may be impossible.

Friendship is less than family, but shares with it the immediate, personal bond; and friendship as well as family is honored in moral tradition. To indicate the ethical problems that may arise from this source one has only to set forth a name: Bert Lance.

EIGHTH. OBLIGATION TO SELF.

Yes, to self: this is a respectable part of our moral tradition, best epitomized in the Shakespearean "This above all, to thine own self be true." Selfishness and egocentrism are by general agreement bad. The argument for *self* is that self-regard is the basis for other-regard, that proper conduct toward others, doing one's duty, must be based on personal strength and integrity. But, granting the principle, how does one draw the line in practice between proper self-regard and a public interest?

NINTH. OBLIGATION TO MIDDLE-RANGE COLLECTIVITIES.

In view here is a large and heterogeneous lot: party, class, race, union, church, interest group, and others. That these are capable of creating obligations felt as moral is quite clear, and that these obligations are carried into public administration is also quite clear. When, and how, is it proper for such obligations to affect administrative behavior, to influence public decisions?

TENTH. OBLIGATION TO THE PUBLIC INTEREST OR GENERAL WELFARE.

This obligation is related to Constitution, to nation, to democracy. But it is analytically distinct. It is often explicitly embodied in law, but also has something of a separate existence. The concept is notoriously difficult to operationalize, and has been repeatedly subject to critical demolition. But presumably anyone in public administration must take it seriously, if only as a myth that must be honored in certain procedural and symbolic ways.

ELEVENTH. OBLIGATION TO HUMANITY OR THE WORLD.

It is an old idea, and perhaps despite all a growing idea, that an obligation is owed to humanity in general, to the world as a total entity, to the future as the symbol and summation of all that can be hoped. All "higher" religions trend in this direction, however vaguely and imperfectly. It is certainly an ingredient in various forms of one-world consciousness, and it figures prominently in the environmental ethic and in ecological politics.

TWELFTH. OBLIGATION TO RELIGION, OR TO GOD.

Immediately one must ask, are these two things or the same thing? The answer is not simple. But that obligations are seen as imposed by religion or God is not doubted even by atheists. One could quickly point to areas of public administration in which these felt obligations are at the center of "what's happening"—or possibly not happening.

A Need for Maps

Obviously, this listing of sources and types of ethical obligations involved in public administration is rough. The number, twelve, is plainly arbitrary. Perhaps some of the items were wrongly included, or should be combined. Perhaps some should be further divided and refined. Certainly other items might be included: *science,* for example, since science is interpreted not just to require a set of proper procedures but to be an ethos with accompanying ethical imperatives. As we know, *face-to-face groups* develop their own norms and powerfully influence behavior, but were not even mentioned. And what of *conscience*? Is it to be regarded as only a passive transmitter of signals or as in part at least an autonomous source of moral conduct?

You will have noticed that I did not attempt to order the twelve types of obligations, that is, list them in order of importance or ethical imperative. This was neither an oversight nor—I believe—a lack of intelligence on my part, but rather reflected the untidiness of the ethical universe. Perhaps the list included incommensurables. In any event, we lack the agreed beliefs which would enable us to construct an order of priority, one to twelve, with the higher obligation always superior to the lower.

How are we to proceed? How can we achieve enough clarity so that we can at least discuss our differences with minimum confusion, the least heat and the most light? My own view is that a desirable, perhaps necessary, preliminary activity is to construct more and better maps of the realm we propose to understand. Granted that this expectation may reflect only the habits of academia; professors are prone to extensive preparation for intellectual journeys never undertaken. But I do not see how we can move beyond a confused disagreement until there is more agreement on what we are talking about.

If I am essentially correct, then what would be useful would be a serious and sizable mapmaking program. We need various types of maps, analogous to maps that show physical features, climatic factors, demographic data, economic activity, and so forth. We need maps of differing scale, some indicating the main features of a large part of the organizational world, some detailing particular levels, functions, and activities. Despite common elements, presumably—no, certainly—the ethical problems of a legislator are significantly different from those of a military officer, those of a regulatory commissioner different from those of a police chief, those of a first-line supervisor from those of a department head.

Simply put: If we are going to talk about ethics in public life it would be useful to know what we are talking about.

A Need for Navigation Instruments

The metaphor of maps may not have been the most apt, but I now use one that may be less felicitous, that of navigation instruments. But at least the second metaphor is complementary: given maps, how do we navigate? How do we find our way through what the maps show us? Let me indicate the nature of some navigation equipment that would be of use.

First, it would be useful to have an instrument to guide us through the historical dimensions of our ethical problems in public administration. Above all, it would be useful to have an explication of the implications and consequences of the disjunction, noted in earlier discussions, between the rise of political self-awareness and the rise of administrative self-awareness. Both as a part of that inquiry and independently, what do we know about the rise and growth of administrative morality, of notions of stewardship, duty and obligations, reciprocal or unilateral? With respect to estate management, which has been so large a part of administrative history, have rules of proper conduct been widely divergent, or has the nature of the function disposed toward uniformity? Since estate management has been centrally involved in royal governance, from Sumer to the Sun King—and beyond—what effect has this had on bureaucratic morality? Perhaps it is worth more than mere mention that *estate* and *state* are cognates, both derived from the Latin *stare:* "to be *or* stand"; the essential notion in both cases is of substance, firmness, an organizing center.

Second, it would be useful to have instruments provided by the social sciences or derived from a survey of them. Immediately, we face the fact indicated in the epigraph from Bradley and Wilkie at the head of this chapter: "The raising of moral considerations in any discussion on organizations usually causes discomfort." In addressing organizational behavior as in contemporary social science generally, ethics is not just a neglected interest, it is a rejected interest. I shall return to this point; but what I have in mind presently need not cause serious discomfort, though it no doubt would strike many as a peculiar interest and a waste of energy. What I have in view is not an addressing of ethical issues as such, but rather a survey to determine what the several social sciences have to say about ethical matters, either directly or indirectly. For

example, are ethical issues present in disguise—morality pretending to be science? We can see that the *yes* answer has often been true in the past, and not a few claim it is true now. What would the most honest, nonideological view reveal? Aside from this question, do the paradigms and tools of the several social sciences offer any handles for ethical inquiry?

Political Science, presumably, would be most centrally involved. And that brings me, inevitably, back to the theme of disjunction: what are the consequences for both Political Science and Public Administration, more broadly, *politics* and *administration,* of the fact that politics reached self-awareness in classical Greece and administration not until the late nineteenth century—this despite the fact that, even (especially?) in small and simple polities, politics and administration were inevitably intermingled.

The other social sciences, even Anthropology, need also to be surveyed. "Even Anthropology?"—an argument could be made that its determined lack of normativeness plus its comparativeness make it particularly germane. Sociology—beginning with its ancestry in Montesquieu and others, and certainly decisively in Comte, Spencer, Durkheim, Weber, Parsons, and other major figures—is rich with relevant material; whether in spite of or because of its scientific stance is hard to say. And Economics? One should not, of course, be put off with its scientific aura and impressive technical apparatus. Adam Smith, in his own view and that of his contemporaries, was a moral philosopher; and Irving Kristol has recently reminded us that Smith's *An Inquiry into the Nature and Causes of the Wealth of Nations* was not intended as a defense of the *morality* of free enterprise. Economics, both in what it attends to and in what it refuses to attend to, in the behavior it licenses and in the behavior it forbids, is very central to any inquiry into ethical conduct in administration: As a random illustration, the recent realization that noxious waste chemicals simply have been dumped in tens of thousands of locations. What sins are committed in the name of externalities and exogenous variables?

Third, ethics as a self-aware enterprise, together

with the philosophic matrices from which differing ethical theories are derived, needs to be searched and ordered for the purposes of ethical analysis and judgment in public administration. It may be thought peculiar, to say the least of it, that only well into this discussion ethical theory as such is brought to the fore. But as I view the matter it deserves no high priority. For ethics has little attended to proper behavior in large-scale organization. Its central interests have been elsewhere, tending to oscillate between the probing of traditional relationships such as those of family and friendships and rather abstract and bloodless general principles of conduct. While there is to be sure a great deal in the literature that is relevant, its relevance becomes clear only by extrapolation and application.

Fourth, religion also needs to be surveyed with the object of determining what instruments of navigation it can provide. For our purposes attention should be centered on the Judeo-Christian stream of religious thought and practice, but all major religions should be included. Among the many subjects on which I am not expert are theology and religious history. However, it takes only a little knowledge and understanding to appreciate three things. The first is that theology as such, like ethics to which it is linked in many ways, has attended very little to proper conduct in formal organizations, at least those not religious. Second, as with ethics, there is in theology a great deal that can be made relevant by extrapolation and application. In fact, the writings of Reinhold Niebuhr moved vigorously in this direction; and perhaps I do less than justice to others of whose work I may be unaware. Third, the history and effect of religious institutions and the second, third and X-order effects of religious thought and practice are of so great import for organizational life that one could devote a career to the matter without doing more than explore a few areas. The point is made simply by referring to the work under the heading of Protestant Ethic.

The Pyramid Puzzle

Not surprisingly, many of the most interesting and significant questions concerning administration and ethics concern the theory and practice of hierarchy. Some of these questions are generic, in the sense that they apply to business and nonprofit private organizations as well as to public administration. But some have a special relevance to public administration, as they concern governmental institutions and political ideology. It will be instructive to focus briefly on this pyramid puzzle in the public context.

Central, at least to my own interest, is the fact that hierarchy is represented both as a force for morality and a source of immorality. Both cases are familiar to us, though perhaps not in the context of ethics.

The affirmative case has it that hierarchy is a force that works both for the soft values of democracy and the hard values of effectiveness, efficiency, and economy; indeed, that the achievement of the soft and hard values is complementary, not two things but a single thing. This is a central theme of old-line Public Administration, and the reasoning and conclusions are familiar: Democracy is, realistically, achievable only if power is concentrated so that it can be held accountable, and this is possible only through hierarchy. Otherwise, responsibility bleeds into the social surround. The devices for focusing citizen attention so that it could be made effective—devices such as the short ballot and party reform—were part of the old-line package. Responsibility was viewed as owed upward, subordinate to superordinate, to the top of the pyramid, then bridged over by the electoral principle to the people. Authority was viewed as moving the other direction, upward from the people through their elected representative, then bridged over to the top of the pyramid and descending, echelon by echelon, to every officer and employee.

That this way of viewing things has considerable logic and force strikes me as self-evident. It is plausibly, though hardly unarguably, based on Constitution and history, and can be bolstered with much evidence. It can be, and has been, buttressed by arguments from foreign experience and from business practice. Able and honorable persons have supported the main tenets of the argument. Thus Paul Appleby in his *Morality and Administration in Democratic Government:*[3] The hierarchical principle forwards effective government, but above all it is necessary to democratic government, insuring through its operation the triumph of the general interest over special interests. Thus Marver Bernstein in "Ethics in Government: The Problems in Perspective,"[4] arguing that serious ethical irregularities as well as inefficiencies are all but assured through the absence of hierarchical control in the arrangements for some regulatory agencies, which create conflicts of interest or in effect make the regulatory agencies captives of the interests to be regulated. Thus Victor Thompson in his *Without Sympathy or Enthusiasm: The Problem of Administrative Compassion,*[5] where he argues that the prescriptions for participation equal an invitation for the unauthorized to steal the "tool" of administration from its "owners," the public.

The case against hierarchy in turn has considerable logic and force. It also has roots in Constitution and history, and can be bolstered with much evidence. In this case persons who are able and honorable have stressed the contradictions involved in using hierarchy as a means of promoting democracy, the limitations of hierarchy as a means of achieving effectiveness and efficiency, and its complicity in forwarding immorality. Thus Vincent Ostrom in this *The Intellectual Crisis in American Public Administration,*[6] arguing the spuriousness of the case for centralization, and the greater democracy achievable by organizing public administration into smaller units more in accord with "consumer" will and control. Thus the advocates of a New Public Administration,[7] who take social equity as guiding principle and seek to achieve it "proactively," through client-oriented and client-involving devices. Thus F. William Howton—quoted in one of the epigraphs[8]—who speaks for many who believe that hierarchy with its accustomed corollaries creates deformed humans with deadened consciences. Thus Frederick Thayer in his *An End to Hierarchy! An End to Competition!*[9] who finds hierarchy implicated in immorality as well as promoting inefficiency, and necessarily to be abolished if there is to be a tolerable future—indeed, perhaps, a *future.*

My aim is not to weigh the arguments, much less render a verdict, but rather to emphasize the tangle of ethical problems in and related to the principle and practice of hierarchy; this by way of illustrating the central position of ethical concerns in our professional business—whether or not we care to attend to them *as* ethical questions. But before passing on, let me pose one question that many would regard as the paramount one: What difference does democracy make with respect to the morality of actions taken by government? Rousseau, if I understand him correctly, argued that while the people can be *mistaken,* they cannot be *wrong.* Two examples to ponder, the first from history, the second hypothetical. (1) If the bombing of Haiphong was "immoral," was the firebombing of Hamburg and Dresden—which was massively greater—also immoral? If not, why not? (2) If the Holocaust had been carried out under a democratic government rather than a dictatorship, would an Eichmann have been any more or less immoral? In reflecting on this, bear in mind Herman Finer's notable essay on "Administrative Responsibility in Government,"[10] in which he holds with regard to the public servant: "The first commandment is subservience."

Observations and Reflections

The spirit and nature of this discussion was indicated by the [essay] subtitle, A Prologue to a Preface. At most I can hope to point to some of the matters that would be worthy of attention in a more serious and systematic inquiry. In conclusion, the following further observations and reflections. I shall proceed discontinuously, serially.

FIRST

The twentieth century has hardly been distinguished either by its observance of agreed moral codes or by its concentration on ethical inquiry. On the contrary, it has been distinguished by a "decay" of traditional moral codes, a widespread feeling that morality is "relative" if not utterly meaningless, and a disposition to regard ethical inquiry as frivolous, irrelevant. These currents of thought and feeling have been associated with a "falling away" from religious belief and a concomitant rise of "belief" in science and its philosophical—or anti-philosophical—aura.

These developments have coincided with the Organizational Revolution: an unprecedented increase in the variety, number, size, and power of organizations, at the center of which is government, public administration. It has coincided also, and relatedly, with the arrival of administrative self-awareness, with a new type of "scientific" interest in administrative study and a resulting increase in administrative technology.

So we confront this historical situation: Just at the time the organizational world is thickening and thus the need for ethical guidance increasing, not only does old morality erode but no serious effort is made to create new codes of conduct appropriate to the new situation; and the scientific mentality that is largely responsible for the Organizational Revolution simultaneously makes it difficult to take ethical matters seriously.

SECOND

In no country does the level of conscious ethical conduct in government reach the level of complex reality, but the United States may have one problem to an unusual degree. It has often been observed that Americans tend to view morality very heavily if not exclusively in sexual and pecuniary terms: in the public area, Elizabeth Rays on payrolls and Tongsun Parks passing envelopes of currency behind closed doors.

As I see it, a concern for *public* morality must indeed include a concern with the ordinary garden varieties of sexual and pecuniary misconduct within or affecting public life; we would have to be ignorant of history and oblivious to contemporary political life to think otherwise. However, as even my few shallow probes indicate, the matter of ethically proper conduct reaches far, far beyond the popular images of sex and money. It presents problems of conduct for which traditional morality, growing in and shaped to simpler times, provides little guidance. Or worse, it provides *misguidance*.

THIRD

Some of the better writings bearing on our subject emphasize the prevalence, perhaps even the necessity, of "moral ambiguity" in organizational life. Thus Stephen Bailey in his "Ethics and the Public Service";[11] I refer back to the epigraph from this essay emphasizing the "contextuality" of good and evil. Thus Melville Dalton in his *Men Who Manage,*[12] who concluded that persons from a middle-class background are more likely to become successful managers than persons from a working-class background, not because of superior ability or technical skill but because of a socialization that better prepares them to cope with moral ambiguity.

If we cannot *clarify* the ethics of the organizational world, perhaps it will help if we can advance *understanding* of the complexity and confusion. If ambiguity cannot be eliminated, then a "tolerance for ambiguity" becomes an essential operating skill. A *moral* quality as well as an operating skill? I shall not try to answer that.

FOURTH

The following seems to be true, almost axiomatically: Moral complexity increases as memberships in organizations increase; persons in formal organizations in addition to traditional/nonformal organizations face greater moral complexity than those only in the latter; those in formal *public* organizations face more moral complexity than those in nonpublic organizations; and moral complexity increases as responsibilities in an administrative hierarchy increase.

If this is a correct view, then high-placed administrators (managers, executives) in public organizations are at the very center of ethical complexity. In this connection I refer you to the probing of morality in relation to administration in Chester Barnard's *The Functions of the Executive*[13]—from which comes the epigraph at the head of this chapter. *The Functions* is of course widely and correctly viewed as a seminal work. But it is a commentary on the interests of the past generation that this discussion of morality has been generally ignored.

Barnard believed that "moral creativeness" was an essential executive function. As the quoted sentence indicates, he believed also that the burden assumed could lead to moral breakdown. In a similar vein Stephen Bailey, in the essay cited in observation Third above, uses the metaphor "above the timber line" to signify the severe moral climate in which the high executive must operate and the dangers to which he is exposed.

FIFTH

We have recently seen, and we presently see, the growth of a gray area, an area in which any clear distinction between the categories of *public* and *private* disappears, disappears in a complex and subtle blending of new organizational modes and legal arrangements. In this gray area, hierarchy is diminished, but does not disappear; new lateral and diagonal relationships grow up and operate along with it, making it formally and operationally difficult to answer the question: Who's in charge here?

As I view it, our ethical problems are compounded in this growing gray world. Who will be responsible for what to whom? In what will duty consist and by what can honesty be judged? One view is that, with hierarchy relaxed and freedom increased, the way is open for the development of authentic *personal* morality. Harlan Cleveland seeks a solution in the hope and prescription that managers in the "horizontal"[14] world that is emerging will regard themselves as "public managers"—because in fact they will be. I confess that on most days I find it hard to share either of these two varieties of optimism.

SIXTH

As the epigraph from David Bradley and Roy Wilkie indicates, "the raising of moral considerations" in the study of organizations has not been popular. Indeed, the chapter on Morality and Organizations in their *The Concept of Organization*[15] is, to my knowledge, without a parallel in the scores of general treatments of organizational behavior or theory.

A number of factors, some pertaining to American public affairs and without need of mention, and some pertaining to the general climate of our intellectual life that are beyond explicating here, suggest that there may be a change in the situation, that we will begin to address seriously the ethical dimensions of our organizational world—here I allow myself a bit of optimism. This may be best done—perhaps it can be done only—by working from the empirical base legitimated in recent social science. It might begin, for example, with map-making, along the lines suggested earlier. Later, just possibly, we may be able to address the ethical as such.

One point of view has it that ethical inquiry is dangerous. Samuel Butler put it this way: "The foundations of morality are like all other foundations: if you dig too much about them, the superstructure will come tumbling down." But in our case, the digging has been done; the superstructure is already down. But then, the old superstructure was not to our purpose anyway. Perhaps on a new foundation we can use some of the fallen materials to build a superstructure that *is* to our purpose?

Notes

1. Certainly Robert T. Golembiewski's *Men, Management, and Morality: Towards a New Organizational Ethic* (New York: 1965) is an able and useful work, and I do not wish to demean it. But the picture in my mind is of a work even broader in scope, one taking into account developments of the past decade. Neither do I mean to slight the useful work of Wayne A. R. Leys, done when ethics was *really* unfashionable: *Ethics and Social Policy* (New York: 1946), and *Ethics for Policy Decisions: The Art of Asking Deliberative Questions* (New York: 1952).

2. The analysis set forth in this section is a brief version of that in my "Reflections on Public Morality" (*6 Administration and Society* [November 1974], pp. 267–282).

3. Paul Appleby, *Morality and Administra-*

tion in Democratic Government (Baton Rouge, La.: 1952).

4. Marver Bernstein, "Ethics in Government: The Problems in Perspective" (*61 National Civic Review* [July 1972], pp. 341–347).

5. Victor Thompson, *Without Sympathy or Enthusiasm: The Problem of Administrative Compassion* (University, Ala.: 1975).

6. Vincent Ostrom, *The Intellectual Crisis in American Public Administration* (University, Ala.: 1973).

7. See the symposium, H. George Frederickson, ed., "Social Equity and Public Administration" (*34 Public Administration Review* [January/February 1974], pp. 1–51).

8. F. William Howton, *Functionaries* (Chicago: 1969).

9. Frederick C. Thayer, *An End to Hierarchy! An End to Competition! Organizing the Politics and Economics of Survival* (New York: 1973).

10. Herman Finer, "Administrative Responsibility in Democratic Government" (*1 Public Administration Review* [Summer 1941], pp. 335–350).

11. Stephen Bailey, "Ethics and the Public Service" (*23 Public Administration Review* [December 1964], pp. 234–243).

12. Melville Dalton, *Men Who Manage* (New York: 1959).

13. Chester Barnard, *The Functions of the Executive* (Cambridge, Mass.: 1947). See especially Chapter 17, The Nature of Executive Responsibility.

14. Harlan Cleveland, *The Future Executive: A Guide for Tomorrow's Managers* (New York: 1972).

15. David Bradley and Roy Wilkie, *The Concept of Organization: An Introduction to Organizations* (Glasgow: 1974).

⬜ CASE STUDY 16

Introduction

Dwight Waldo's foregoing essay treated readers to a broad-brush overview of the modern complicated ethical terrain confronting public administrators. Rather than *one* code, he "maps" a dozen (or more) competing ethical obligations to which administrators must be loyal. How in fact does an administrator choose among these codes and decide which one or several to adhere to? How do administrators juggle these competing demands? Prioritize them? Decide which one or several that they owe their ultimate allegiance to? Especially when "the answers" are not clear-cut, nor even the "questions," as is true in many difficult administrative problems?

In the following interesting case study by Professor Douglas F. Morgan of Portland State University, we can see in a concrete way why ethical dilemmas of modern public administration are so complicated just as Waldo's essay outlined in theory. The case recounts the moral quandary posed for public librarians because of vocal complaints from patrons over the circulation of a book, Madonna's *Sex*. Professor Morgan outlines how the controversy began and describes the three different kinds of responses to this issue made by libraries across America. He stresses how the librarians' professional association, the American Library Association, especially its Office of Intellectual Freedom, played a critical role shaping the choices made by individual libraries. As he concludes:

The Madonna controversy provides us with an important lesson to ponder about the problem of administrative role ambiguity. This problem cannot be solved without some way of ordering the multiplicity of claims that are made upon our career public servants. Librarians in the Madonna case and in other censorship efforts have been largely successful in undertaking this ordering process. They have done so by relying on a strong professional ethos, an organizational standard bearer to help educate its members into first principles, and concrete administrative strategies for translating first principles into plans of action.

As you review this case study, consider some of these questions:

Why is it difficult for librarians to develop clear-cut policies for dealing with the circulation of books like Madonna's *Sex*?

What were the three varieties of administrative responses libraries around the United States used in handling this issue? Their criteria for dealing with it and your evaluation of the applied administrative criteria?

How did the official librarian professional association, the ALA, help individual libraries sort out their choices? Why were professional standards so influential in this case?

Which of Waldo's ethical codes were used to resolve this problem? Does Waldo's point about the emphasis upon "sex" and "money" in ethical considerations in the public sector, particularly in America, have relevance to this case study? And if so, why do both topics tend to stir up intense controversies?

Madonna's *Sex*

DOUGLAS F. MORGAN

"Some are born great; some achieve greatness; some have greatness thrust upon them." It is in this way that librarians have become a censor of literature. . . . Books that distinctly commend what is wrong, that teach how to sin and how pleasant sin is, sometimes with and sometimes without the added sauce of impropriety, are increasingly popular, tempting the author to imitate them, the publishers to produce, the bookseller to exploit. Thank Heaven they do not tempt the librarian *(quoted in ALA, Manual, p. xvi).*

—*Arthur E. Bostwick, ALA President, 1908*

"Madonna's *Sex*" by Douglas F. Morgan from *Administrative Theory & Praxis*, 15 (2), 1993. Copyright © 1993 by Public Administration Theory Network (PAT-Net). Reprinted by permission.

Susan Miller was completing the final routines of the day at the library circulation desk when she was suddenly confronted by an angry father accompanied by his 14-year old son who had just picked up a book held on reserve in his name.

"What's going on here?", the patron asked as he thrust the book into the face of the librarian. "Don't you restrict things like this from circulating to minors? Why is this kind of book even in the library in the first place? It clearly is unfit reading!"

This is not what you needed to hear at this time of day. As the Head of Public Services, two of your clerks failed to appear for work because of icy road conditions. That did not seem to stop the hoards of school children who flocked to the library to pass the time of day. As a result of having to work without a rest-break checking out books all day at the circulation desk, you will have to spend the evening completing your budget request for the next fiscal year in order to meet the 8:00 AM deadline set by your Library Director.

As a children's librarian by training, you deeply resent all of the endless administrative work that takes you away from what you most enjoy and have been best prepared to carry out—selecting and recommending good literature to children and their parents. Increasingly, you've been having second thoughts about whether you are really cut out for your current environment. There is just too much time spent on keeping track of clerical routines, doing budget preparation, undertaking personnel evaluations, and responding to patrons' complaints. As you fantasized about what it might be like to work in a larger library system where you could make more use of the professional knowledge and skills for which you have been trained, you are suddenly jolted out of your fantasizing by a distraught parent who insists that you, not he, should make the choices about what is suitable reading for his son.

You notice that the book is a copy of Madonna's *Sex*, a series of personal poses taken by a well-known photographer who erotically captures the pop star's sexual fantasies. The photo album has been on the *New York Times* best seller list for the past four weeks and there is a backlog of 57 reserve requests. You've dealt with this kind of situation before, so you politely give the Library's standardized response:

"We encourage parents to help their children select material that is appropriate to their interests and level of reading skill. Could I help you find a more suitable book?" "That's not the point. The public tax dollars should not be used to support this kind of material. It contains graphic pornographic illustrations and encourages a lifestyle that is socially devastating. Moreover, you have a special responsibility to protect our young people from getting access to this kind of material at the taxpayer's expense."

As the line of patrons waiting to check out books begins to build, you see that your efforts are not going to prevail. So you resort to another technique that has usually worked in the past. You ask the angry patron to formally file his objections on a special complaint form the library has prepared for this purpose.

That did not end the matter. The following week the Director of the Library hands you the completed complaint form from Charles Jones, the angry father who had confronted you about Madonna's *Sex*. The Director requests you to draft a reply that can be sent out under the Library Director's signature.

As you think about what to do, all kinds of questions begin to run into a swirling eddy in your mind. Is the complaint from Jones a part of an organized campaign within the community to determine what the library purchases? Does the new Director wish to have such complaints handled the same way they have been handled in the past? How should the occasion be used to edify two new members of the Board that have recently been appointed? Is it really time to move, even though not a particularly good time in terms of the economy and your personal family situation?

You go to your file drawer and pull out a copy of the last letter the former director sent to an angry patron under similar circumstances. What should you do?

Administrative Fantasies and Role Ambiguity

Sue Miller's moral dilemma is fertile ground for those concerned with the ethical basis of administrative discretion. The practical consequences of deciding whether to purchase a book like Madonna's *Sex* and how to make it available to patrons provides a pedagogically rich opportunity to explore the meaning of integrity (Benjamin, 1990; Dobel, 1990), and the conflict among personal, professional, and organizational claims. For some library employees Madonna's *Sex* presented them with the moral dilemma of facilitating the circulation of material they found personally objectionable. Some even requested alterations in their work assignments, using as leverage the employer's legal requirement to make "reasonable accommodations". These circumstances provide rich fodder to explore questions of prudence, integrity, compromise, exit, voice, and loyalty. In short, they provide an opportunity to examine the appropriate substantive standards that ought to guide the exercise of administrative discretion. However, in this [essay] I am primarily interested in using the Madonna controversy to explore the institutional conditions (both organizational and professional) necessary to translate principles of right action into effective administrative practice. For the remainder of this [essay], I will assume that the professional librarian is not in doubt about the professional moral standards (hereafter referred to as stewardship principles) that ought to guide the exercise of her discretion and that these standards are not in conflict with her personal ethical beliefs.

Even when a career administrator is confident about the "right thing to do", frequently there is a large abyss between the cup of stewardship belief and the lip of institutional action. For example, under the circumstances described above, libraries and their administrative agents have a variety of options that may be equally consistent with stewardship principles. Some may use the controversy to avoid organizational risk, to temporize and forestall, or to shift decision making responsibility somewhere else in the administrative and political process. Others may choose to mobilize constituency support, or to redefine the universe of moral discourse, or to educate and edify citizens within the community. Choices about which of these courses of action best reflect the responsible exercise of one's stewardship obligations greatly depend on the influence of mediating organizational and professional conditions.

Much of the recent literature on administrative ethics agrees on the need to ground the exercise of bureaucratic discretion on some larger stewardship principles (Kass, 1990; Rohr, 1986, 1989; Morgan and Kass, 1991; Spicer & Terry, 1993; Stivers, 1993). While helping to clarify the content and locus of stewardship obligation, this literature does not help us understand the social, organizational, and professional mediating processes that enable these principles to be translated into effective action. On the other hand, those who have shed light on the conditions for effective moral action within social and organizational settings, tend to leave career administrators at sea about the higher stewardship obligations these conditions are intended to serve (Hummel, 1987; McGregor, 1967; Likert, 1961; Weisband & Frank, 1975). The role of librarians in the Madonna controversy allows us to explore this linkage between stewardship principles and the mediating conditions for effective moral practice.

There are at least three reasons why librarians and local public libraries are particularly useful in exploring the linkage between principles of "right

thinking" and the conditions for "right action." First, libraries, along with schools, reflect as well as shape the social construction of meaning within local communities. Second, professional librarians participate in this process of "making social meaning" with the kind of formal professional training that does not differ in significant respects from that received by most public sector career administrators. Finally, both librarians and libraries are greatly influenced by the American Library Association's growing role in shaping the meaning of censorship controversies in cases like Madonna's *Sex*.

Local libraries, especially in smaller communities, are about as close as we get today to the politics of the Greek agora. They are the chief organizational venues for reading programs, communal forums, and cultural activities that foster a commonly shared sense of community. They occupy a morally tender place in the soul of a community and depend on the financial sustenance of local citizens to keep them in operation. It is not surprising, then, that they occasionally become the lightening rod within local communities for differences of opinion about the meaning of democratic governance.

Over the last several years local differences of opinion over what books libraries should purchase and to whom they should be made available have dramatically increased. From September 1, 1990 through April 15, 1993, the Office of Intellectual Freedom of the American Library Association received 1,577 reports of challenges to library materials. In the 1991 calendar year there were 512 reported cases. This grew to 653 cases in calendar year 1992, a 28% increase. In the first four months of 1993, there were 253 reported cases (ALA, Office of Intellectual Freedom, May 1990). If that pace continues throughout 1993, reported challenges will have doubled within the past two years. How much of this increase is a result of increased reporting and how much from increases in attempts to censor is impossible to determine. However, library professionals agree that attempts by community groups to censor the purchase and dissemination of local library materials have sharply increased in recent years.

Since libraries are expected to reflect the needs of their citizens and protect the right of access to ideas for all users, they cannot easily hide from disgruntled patrons who do not like the books they purchase. Since a library cannot remain a library without purchasing books, and since no library has unlimited financial resources to purchase everything that is published, choices have to be made. Why shouldn't community acceptability be a key book selection standard, especially when the majority of the community foots the bill? The answer is not so easy and so obvious as is reflected in the responses of libraries in the Madonna controversy. Institutional responses to complaints about the acquisition of *Sex* have ranged all the way from not purchasing the book, to removing it once purchased, to vigorously defending the purchase in the face of protracted public opposition, to making alterations in priorities (if not policies) in order to enable parents to have more control over what their children read.

A second reason the controversy over Madonna's *Sex* is so interesting to students of administrative discretion is that librarians are like most trained professionals. They graduate from professional school, having spent more time learning the techniques and skills of good librarianship than acquiring a clear understanding of the ends these skills are intended to serve. Like most career bureaucrats, they arrive at positions of discretionary administrative authority without much prior training and education about their larger leadership role within and to the local communities they serve. But by virtue of living within a local glass house, in the words of Alan Bostwick, they have the opportunity for greatness to be "thrust upon them". In fact, they frequently are unable to avoid this opportunity.

Finally, professional librarians carry out their work under the guiding mantle of the First Amendment, the principles of which are reflected in a Library Bill of Rights which simultaneously opposes censorship and aggressively promotes the acquisition and dissemination of materials that provide "for the interest, information, and enlightenment of all people of the community the library serves" (ALA, Manual, p. 3). Taken literally, these words seem to make even a smidgen of community interest sufficient justification for the purchase, display, and dissemination of library resources, however unpopular they may be. Yet local libraries, like schools, are political entities controlled and funded by officials who are selected with an expectation that they will be responsive to the will of the community. This expectation has taken on greater poignancy in recent years as taxpayers have be-

come ever more vigilant in guarding their tax dollars. A group of citizens who threaten to withhold its support in the next levy election until Madonna's *Sex* or some other objectionable material is removed from the Library has to be taken seriously! In doing so, there are at least two questions of interest to students of administrative discretion. What influence does a professional association standard like the Library Bill of Rights have on shaping the universe of local moral discourse? Second, what lessons can be learned from this controversy about rendering various notions of "constitutional stewardship" useful practical guides to the exercise of administrative discretion?

Madonna's *Sex:* Patterns of Administrative Response

The controversy began on October 21, 1992 when Madonna's much publicized *Sex* was released for sale. The book was a mylar-wrapped, spiral-bound series of photographs portraying the sexual fantasies of the exhibitionist pop star in revealing and erotic poses. Advance reviews of the book were nonexistent, since no pre-publication copies were released. With a hefty price tag of $49.95 and a fragile binding, librarians were compelled to decide whether or not to purchase the book based on the publicity surrounding it and/or patron requests. In many places, such requests were extremely large, as tends to be the case with most highly publicized best sellers. But in the case of *Sex,* more often than not requests for the book were accompanied by an equal number of requests to remove or restrict it (ALA Newsletter, Jan. 1993, p. 1). The administrative dilemma this presented for local librarians was nicely summarized by Judith Krug, Director of the ALA, Office of Intellectual Freedom. If libraries refused to buy the book, it would appear to be censorship, since there was surely patron demand; if they bought a lot of copies for circulation, however, these might be stolen or damaged. Many libraries chose to buy just one or two copies to keep on reserve, but this often sparked as much opposition and criticism as if the library had purchased dozens of copies to satisfy demand (ALA Newsletter, Jan. 1993, p. 1). Libraries responded to this dilemma with three different patterns of administrative action.

1. "Just Say No" or Emptio Interuptus

Ironically, Madonna's home town of Rochester Hills, Michigan, was one of the cities where the decision not to purchase *Sex* did not raise a controversy. "We don't see it as an essential purchase," said public library director Christine Hage, "and because of the cost we wouldn't just buy it without the interest. We meet public demand; if the public is curious, this is a good use of public money. I guess the public isn't interested" (*American Libraries*, December, 1992).

But what should a library director do when confronted with a large public demand for the book? To what extent should demand be tempered by considerations of whether a book passes some kind of cost-benefit or good buy test, an external consensus about quality, or the appropriateness of the content for the collection? Typical of many library directors facing these kind of questions, Ralph Edwards, Director of the Phoenix public library waited until reviews of the book began to appear and then decided the book wasn't worth buying. "If you've read the reviews, you know they're all bad. We decided it didn't have sufficient artistic quality or content quality to make it worth spending $50 a shot on" (*Phoenix Gazette*, October 29, 1993). In Scottsdale, Arizona, library director Linda Saferite concluded that the spiral binding would not survive repeated circulations (*Scottsdale Progress*, October 30, 1992). In Glendale, Arizona, library director Rodeane Widom reported that she didn't have the budget to spend on a photo book whose photographer "is not anyone who was given any real acclaim" (*Arizona Republic*, October 29, 1993).

In Mesa, Arizona the book provoked substantial controversy after library director Vince Anderson revealed that he had placed an order for it. After receiving hundreds of complaints about the decision, the library director canceled the order at the request of Mesa Mayor Willie Wong. The mayor reported that when he got up October 27th and saw a newspaper story about the library purchase, he thought, "My career is over. I'm dead meat. I had to take the community into consideration, although I'm a strong supporter of the First Amendment. My feeling is that the community is not in support of Madonna's book. So I canceled the order." Asked why he did not refer the book to the review committee, Wong said, "I'm not really sure how we purchase books. All I know

is this particular book is very controversial" (*Mesa Tribune*, October 27, 28, 1992).

The chair of the Mesa Library Advisory Board, Fred Missel, complained "that a precedent has been set regarding censorship and the library. . . . I will abide by [Wong's] decision, but there is a broader issue at work here. I'm concerned that the process of the community evaluating itself had been taken away" (*Mesa Tribune*, October 29, 1992).

In Colorado Springs, Colorado, after three days of answering over 400 angry telephone calls, Pikes Peak Library officials decided to cancel the library's order for the Madonna book. Many callers threatened to vote against a November 3rd bond issue that would raise $8 million for physical improvements at a library branch. Following its normal protocol the library had ordered the book after four patrons requested it. After the order was placed, an additional 73 patrons requested the book before the order was canceled.

Library director Bernie Margolis said that officials didn't buckle under to pressure from "any narrowly focused perspective", but he did acknowledge that the scores of irate callers influenced the decision. "Certainly," he said, "the calls help us gauge the importance of the items to the community." Margolis claimed that the bond issue was not a factor in the decision. "I think we would have sacrificed the winning of a bond issue to stand up for the First Amendment," he said. "In my personal view, this book is not worth fighting for. I believe, personally, that it's pornography." Margolis said the book was rejected because it did not meet the library's purchasing criteria (*Colorado Springs Gazette-Telegraph*, October 20, 21, 23, 1992). The library bond issue did not pass.

2. Making Madonna's *Sex* Safe

Some libraries were willing to permit Madonna's *Sex* to enter the library doors, but not to allow its easy exit. Some of the justification for restricted access was based on the fragile quality of the book's binding and some was based on the appropriateness of the contents for minors. Most libraries restrict circulation of various materials, including reference books, expensive art portfolios, and similar items that are expensive and/or have heavy short-term demand. However, restricted access, as opposed to noncirculation, is undertaken less frequently, usually because of the need to pass First Amendment tests.

The controversy over restricted access was especially heated in Houston and Austin, Texas. In Houston, a group called Citizens Against Pornography (CAP) began to mobilize when it became known that the library had ordered four copies of the controversial book for its main branch, using an anonymous donation. Two copies of the book were to be shelved in the Fine Arts section and available for circulation. The other two copies were to be shelved in the reference section for library use only. Citing a 1978 City Council Resolution on community standards, CAP President, Geneva Kirk Brooks called on Mayor Bob Lanier to halt the purchase. The group also called for the resignation of Library Director, David Henington. "Some of the worst pornography is in our libraries and schools," Brooks declared.

On November 24 Brooks led about a dozen people to a City Council meeting where they angrily called on lawmakers to remove the book or face recall. "If some slut performed the same acts on the streets of Houston, she'd be arrested, so why should we let Madonna perform the same vulgarity on the shelves of our public library?" asked one of the participants. Another observed that "the likes of Thomas Jefferson, James Madison, et al. never in their wildest imaginations envisioned a foul-mouthed, trashy woman masturbating with a crucifix," and concluded by calling on the city's vice squad to shut the library down (*Houston Chronicle*, November 11, 25, 27, 1992).

As the demonstrators cajoled the council, a review of the book by a special library committee was already underway, following receipt of a formal request to reconsider it. On December 2, the committee decided and Library Director Henington agreed to restrict in-library access to adults only (*Houston Chronicle*, December 2, 1992).

In Austin, library officials were compelled to restrict access to *Sex* after Travis County Attorney Ken Oden issued an opinion declaring that it was illegal for minors to see the book. Prior to this opinion the Austin libraries had added *Sex* to their collections on November 12. Library Director, Brenda Branch had decided to limit access to Madonna's *Sex* by keeping copies behind the circulation desk and requiring reviewers to present a photo identification listing their address in order to prevent theft or damage to the book. Her decision drew protests from the community, including Mayor Bruce Todd, who said he objected to minors having access to the book "be-cause these types of publications exploit women." The next day, Library Director Branch changed her opinion, saying the library would review its open access policy with respect to Madonna's work. That review was rendered moot by County Attorney Oden's opinion.

Oden issued an opinion on the legality of circulating Madonna's *Sex* to minors after Austin police vice officers asked whether the book could be classified as pornography. Oden responded to the police request with an official opinion, declaring that "in our community this publication is legal for adults, but it is not legal for sale, distribution or display to children unless the child is accompanied by a consenting parent or guardian. . . . There is really no distinction between public libraries or private businesses. The government has no greater right to sell, display or distribute this material than private businesses have. . . . We would prosecute any public or private organization which chose after notice of the grand jury ruling to continue to provide the publication to children." (*Austin American-Statesman*, November 26, December 1, 1992).

In Ingham County, Michigan, restricted access has been raised to a highly developed administrative art. Parents can fill out a form requesting specific titles or subjects that are approved for their children. If staff are in doubt, they must call the parent and receive explicit permission for the material to be checked out. These forms must be filed in each of the system's five separate branches and renewed each year.

3. Unrestricted Access: Madonna's *Sex* May Be Had for the Price of a Library Card

Many libraries throughout the United States relied on their existing selection policies and principles of unrestricted access to purchase Madonna's *Sex* and circulate it to anyone with a library card. Some of these libraries have faced spirited challenges from angry patrons. One of the most extreme attacks occurred in Monroe County, Michigan. In the face of angry citizens demanding the removal of Madonna's *Sex* after it had been ordered and placed on unrestricted access, the Monroe County Library Board voted to retain the Madonna book, supporting unrestricted access. Both the library Director, Gordon Conable, and the Library Board Chair, Judith See, were asked to resign and received threatening and harassing phone calls both at their homes and places of work from angry members of the community. There were even terrorist threats to the library, which resulted in evacuation and temporary closure (Office of Intellectual Freedom, "Memorandum," March 1993).

One of the more bizarre twists on the Monroe County tale is that the Board Chair, Judith See, an employee of the Agricultural Extension Service and a program director of local 4-H programs, was pressured by her employer/supervisor to submit her resignation as Board Chair. After doing so, pressure was exerted by high level sources within national Republican Party circles on local county board commissioners to refuse to accept Judith See's resignation. They did so and Judith See continued as Board Chair. But there is an uneasy peace in Monroe County. The elected District Attorney has threatened to issue an opinion similar to the one prepared by the County Prosecutor in Austin, Texas, which classifies Madonna's *Sex* as pornographic, thus making it illegal to disseminate to minors under 18 without explicit parental consent ("Interview with Gordon Conable", Director, Monroe County Library, April 2, 1993).

Impact of ALA's Office of Intellectual Freedom

When faced with the extreme attacks and hard-ball political pressures described in the above section, library directors and their Boards turned to lawyers for official legal opinions. Most of these opinions indicated that Madonna's *Sex* did not meet the constitutional standard of obscenity for minors. However, these opinions did not necessarily improve the librarian's ability to carry on a dialogue with angry members of the community, or for that matter, stand tall in the face of strident community opposition. Of greater assistance in this regard was the American Library Association's Office of Intellectual Freedom.

Throughout the Madonna controversy, the Office of Intellectual Freedom provided its local members with information, guidance, and, most important of all, an ethical compass from which to take and keep their bearing. Through a variety of communication sources the American Library Association and its affiliated offices have constantly re-

minded its members that their primary mission is to promote and defend intellectual freedom against all forms of censorship.

Compared to most other public professions, this stewardship responsibility is well-developed and reasonably well defined. While the profession's basic reference source recognizes that the philosophy of intellectual freedom is too young to be rooted in tradition, . . . it has gained recognition as the substance of the total philosophy shaping library service in the United States. . . . From the standpoint of intellectual freedom, the library's role in our society is not based on the principle of majority rule, but on the principle embodied in the First Amendment, that minority points of view have a right to be heard, no matter how unpopular with or even detested by the majority. (American Library Association, Intellectual Freedom Manual, xxxv, 12, hereafter cited as Manual).

This commitment to intellectual freedom is reflected in the Library Bill of Rights first adopted in 1939 and an Intellectual Freedom Committee (IFC) created in 1940 to recommend policies to safeguard these rights.

Library Bill of Rights

The Library Bill of Rights consists of the following six provisions:

1. Books and other library resources should be provided for interest, information, and enlightenment of all people of the community the library serves. Materials should not be excluded because of origin, background, or views of those contributing to their creation.
2. Libraries should provide materials and information presenting all points of view on current and historical issues. Materials should not be proscribed or removed because of partisan or doctrinal disapproval.
3. Libraries should challenge censorship in the fulfillment of their responsibility to provide information and enlightenment.
4. Libraries should cooperate with all persons and groups concerned with resisting abridgment of free expression and free access to ideas.
5. A person's right to use a library should not be denied or abridged because of origin, age, background, or views.

6. Libraries which make exhibit spaces and meeting rooms available to the public they serve should make such facilities available on an equitable basis, regardless of the beliefs or affiliations of individuals or groups requesting their use.

The Bill of Rights is accompanied by more than 125 pages of interpretive guidelines governing the application of the rights under varying circumstances. These include placing the responsibility on parents for controlling access to materials by minors; opposing labeling or expurgation of library materials; preventing restrictions on access which may place a heavy burden on the homeless, the elderly, the physically handicapped, and other classes with special needs; protecting patron's rights of privacy over law enforcement needs, unless accompanied by a court order; etc.

Taken together the Library Bill of Rights and Interpretative Guidelines promote an absolutist interpretation, or what the *Manual* characterizes as a "purist approach" (xviii), to a reading of the First Amendment to the Constitution. The justification for this interpretation is based on the First Amendment language which states that "Congress shall make no law . . . abridging freedom of speech, or of the press." The *Manual* concedes that there are exceptions to this "purist approach," such as fighting words, obscenity, etc. but the ALA takes the position that the courts and not libraries or their agents should assume responsibility for making these exceptions (Manual, p. 61 ff.).

Office of Intellectual Freedom

What intellectual freedom means in practice is not left to the unguided discretion of individual librarians. In 1967 an Office of Intellectual Freedom (OIF) was established to serve as the educational arm of the IFC. The Office of Intellectual Freedom bears responsibility for educating librarians and the general public on the importance of intellectual freedom, using ALA policies as a guide. The OIF has become a powerful organizational force in cultivating national conformity among librarians to the tenants of intellectual freedom.

The philosophy of the *Office of Intellectual Freedom* is based on the premise that if librarians are to appreciate the importance of intellectual freedom

they must first understand the concept as it relates to the individual, the institution, and the functioning of society. Believing that with understanding comes the ability to teach others, OIF maintains a broad program of information publications, projects, and services (Manual, pp. xxii–xxiii).

The OIF publishes a bimonthly *Newsletter on Intellectual Freedom* and a monthly *OIF Memorandum*. In addition, the office prepares special materials, including the *Banned Books Week Resource Kit; The Bill of Rights Bicentennial: A Resource Book*, prepared for use during the 1991 bicentennial celebration of the Bill of Rights; issue-oriented monographs such as *Censorship and Selection: Issues and Answers for Schools;* and *Confidentiality in Libraries: An Intellectual Freedom Modular Education Program*. Each year the OIF publishes a list of books that have been challenged or banned from public and school libraries through local community action. In addition to preparing publications, the OIF consults with librarians confronting potential or actual censorship activities.

Within the scope of this study, it has not been possible to determine the causal significance of the various OIF activities mentioned above in socializing members of the library profession into the meaning of stewardship. For example, at an individual level it would be interesting to examine the impact of the OIF on both the form and substance of the decisions made by individual librarians during the Madonna controversy. At institutional level it would be interesting to examine the number of successful censorship efforts in relationship to the number of library boards that have explicitly adopted the Library Bill of Rights as official board policy. However, there is one measure of impact that is worth mentioning and about which we have some empirical evidence.

According to the Office of Intellectual Freedom, development of a materials selection policy is one of the central factors in helping to fend off censorship attempts by members of the local community. While "[t]he primary purpose of a materials selection or collection development program is to promote the development of a collection based on institutional goals and user needs . . . , the secondary purpose is service in defending the principles of intellectual freedom (ALA, Manual, 207)." In a recent examination of seven variables affecting successful censorship attempts of local school boards, Dianne McAfee concluded that the use of a materials selection policy "is found most consistently to predict retention" (Hopkins, 1993, p. 66). In another report of these findings, Hopkins recommended what the Office of Intellectual Freedom has been advising library selection specialists for years: "have a board approved materials selection policy which is followed when a challenge occurs; seek support when material is challenged; and before material is reviewed, be sure to have the complaint submitted in writing (ALA, *Newsletter*, January, 1992, pp 1, 20)."

There are several characteristics of a materials selection policy which strengthen a librarian's ability to fend off censorship attempts. First, the development of the policy and frequent re-examination of what it means provides an opportunity for the organization to educate both its employees and new board members as to the nature of the institution's larger stewardship obligations. This can be especially important for library board members who may be indirectly appointed to their positions, with little prior experience or instruction in the exercise of governmental authority. Second, a concrete selection policy enables abstract principles of stewardship to be institutionalized into the day-to-day routines of the organization, thereby facilitating the transformation of abstract principles into tradition. Third, when disputed cases arise, a materials selection policy helps to structure the universe of discourse away from what is offensive to a particular patron to the contributions of the selection policy to the good of the larger community.

Through its various publications, model policies, and legal support, the Office of Intellectual Freedom has provided those exercising administrative discretion with a mediating institutional structure for defining the meaning of stewardship by linking library policy with constitutional principles. Without this institutional linkage . . . the core philosophy of intellectual freedom could [not] have developed over the past 40 years into the rooted tradition it presently enjoys in the library profession.

Conclusion

The Madonna controversy provides us with an important lesson to ponder about the problem of administrative role ambiguity. This problem cannot be solved without some way of ordering the multiplicity of claims that are made upon our career public servants. Librarians in the Madonna case and in other censorship efforts have been largely successful in undertaking this ordering process. They have done so by relying on a strong professional ethos, an organizational standard bearer to help educate its members into first principles, and concrete administrative strategies for translating first principles into plans of action. The chief lesson we can learn from the Madonna controversy is the need to go beyond our concern for defining the proper catechism for administrative practice and pay equal attention to the mediating social, organizational, and professional structures that transform this catechism into meaningful moral action.

Endnotes

1. Without abandoning responsibility for sins of omission and commission, I wish to especially thank Candace Morgan, Deputy Director, Community Library Services, Fort Vancouver Regional Library, and Chair of the ALA Intellectual Freedom Committee, for her thoughtful comments and corrections of factually inaccurate representations.
2. "Madonna Book Found Legal by Illinois Attorney General", Library Hotline, American Library Association, vol. 22:2. (May 24, 1993).

References

American Library Association, Office of Intellectual Freedom, *Intellectual Freedom Manual,* 4th Edition (Chicago, 1992), p. xvi.

American Library Association, Office of Intellectual Freedom, *Newsletter on Intellectual Freedom,* published bimonthly.

American Library Association, Office of Intellectual Freedom, *Memorandum,* published monthly.

Dobel, J. P. (1990). "Integrity in the public service," *Public Administration Review,* 50(May/June), 354–364.

Hopkins, D. M. (1993). "A conceptual model of factors influencing the outcome of challenges to library materials in secondary school settings." *Library Quarterly,* 63(1), 40–72.

Hummel, R. P. (1987). *The Bureaucratic Experience.* (2d ed.) New York: St. Martin's Press.

Kass, H. D. (1990). "Stewardship as a fundamental element in images of public administration." In H. D. Kass and B. L. Catron (Eds.), *Images and Identities in Public Administration.* Newbury Park, CA: Sage.

Likert, R. (1961). *New Patterns of Management.* New York: Harper.

McGregor, D. (1967). *The Professional Manager.* New York: McGraw Hill.

Martin, B. (1990). *Splitting the Difference: Compromise and Integrity in Ethics and Politics.* Lawrence, KS: University of Kansas Press.

Morgan, C. (1990). "Whose on first?", *ALKI.* Washington State Library Association: 6: 86.

Morgan, D. & Kass, H. D. (1991). "Legitimizing administrative discretion through constitutional stewardship." In J. S. Bowman (Ed.), *Ethical Frontiers in Public Management.* San Francisco: Jossey-Bass Publishers.

Morgan, D. (1990). "Administrative phronesis: discretion and the problem of administrative legitimacy in our constitutional system." In H. D. Kass and B. L. Catron, ed., *Images and Identities in Public Administration.* Newbury Park, CA: Sage.

Morgan, D. (1993). The public interest. In T. Cooper (Ed.), *Handbook of Public Administration,* 125–146, New York: Marcel Dekker.

Rohr, J. (1986). *To Run a Constitution: The Legitimacy of the Administrative State.* Lawrence, KS: University of Kansas Press.

Rohr, J. (1989). *Ethics for Bureaucrats: An Essay on Law and Values.* (2nd, ed.), New York: Marcel Dekker.

Spicer, M. W. & Terry, L. D. (1993). "Legitimacy, history, and logic: public administration and the constitution." *Public Administration Review,* (May/June), 239–246.

Stiver, C. (1991). *Gender Images in Public Administration: Legitimacy and the Administrative State.* Newbury Park, CA: Sage.

Weisband, E., & Frank, T. M. (1975). *Resignation in Protest: Political and Ethical Choices Between Loyalty to Team and Loyalty to Conscience in American Public Life.* New York: Grossman.

Wildavsky, A. (1984). *The Politics of the Budgetary Process.* 4th ed. Boston, MA: Little Brown.

Author's Epilogue

While the Madonna's *Sex* controversy is no longer in the headlines, librarians throughout American still wrestle with the question of what to do with explicit materials. Recently the controversy has only intensified further by the use of computers that permit access to the Internet, which contains what many patrons view as pornographic materials. How, where, and when should such Web porn and smut be filtered out? And by whom and for whom? Today, software filters are available to block out such obscenities, however, even the best and most expensive filters also block legitimate information protected by the First Amendment of the U.S. Constitution. To complicate this issue, in 1998 the U.S. Supreme Court struck down two major provisions of the 1997 Federal Communications Decency Act (CDA) that were intended to protect minors from "indecent and patently offensive" communications on the Internet. In its ruling, the high court argued that "in order to deny minors access to potentially harmful speech, the CDA effectively suppresses a large amount of speech that adults have a constitutional right to receive and to address one another." The court's opinion concluded: "The interest in encouraging freedom of expression in a democratic society outweighs any theoretical but unproven benefit of censorship."

Chapter 16 Review Questions

1. In brief, can you concisely sum up the advice about ethical behavior in the public office suggested by Waldo's essay? How do his views on the subject differ from those of Chester Barnard, Stephen Bailey, or Paul Appleby, to which the introduction of this chapter refers? Whose approach to ethics in government do you find the more persuasive? Explain your answer.
2. What factors caused Madonna's *Sex* to pose a difficult ethical dilemma for librarians? How did they deal with these problems? What norms or values most influenced their actions? Which factors were the *most* influential in shaping these values and why? Were their choices fundamentally moral and ethical in your opinion? Why or why not?
3. On the basis of your reading of the case study, would you add any points to Waldo's essay regarding other obligations as well as criteria or standards for deciding upon "proper" moral behavior by public officials?
4. Why do issues that arise in government always contain at least some degree of ethical or moral choice? In your opinion, are similar moral choices apparent in decision making in the private sector?
5. Some observers argue that it is impossible to teach individuals who are preparing for public service careers to be moral and ethical—in other words, family background, religion, personal attitudes, and upbringing have more to do with a person's ethical orientation than does formal educational training. Do you agree? Or, are there ways formal classroom training can inculcate ethical behavior in those persons who may someday fill government posts?
6. Compare and contrast Case Study 1, "The Blast in Centralia No. 5," with Case Study 16 from the standpoint of their ethical lessons for public administrators. Can you extract from the two cases a specific list of important lessons for practicing public administrators?

Key Terms

public versus private morality
higher law
ethical obligations
moral complexity

reason of state
the pyramid puzzle
metaphor of maps
ethical theory

Suggestions for Further Reading

Despite the enormous concern expressed about this topic in recent years, perhaps the most sensitive treatments remain those by earlier theorists: Chester Barnard, *The Functions of the Executive* (Cambridge, Mass.: Harvard University Press, 1938)—especially Chapter 17; Paul H. Appleby, *Morality and Administration in Democratic Government* (Baton Rouge, La.: Louisiana State University Press, 1952); and Frederick C. Mosher, *Democracy and the Public Service,* Second Edition (New York: Oxford University Press, 1982)—especially Chapter 8.

The classic scholarly debate over this subject (though it is couched in terms of responsibility instead of ethics) is between Carl J. Friedrich, "Public Policy and the Nature of Administrative Responsibility," *Public Policy*, 1 (Cambridge, Mass.: Harvard University Press, 1940), pp. 3–24; and Herman Finer, "Administrative Responsibility in Democratic Government," *Public Administration Review*, 1 (Summer 1941), pp. 335–350. Along with the Friedrich-Finer arguments, which remain highly germane even today, you should also read John M. Gaus, "The Responsibility of Public Administration," in Leonard D. White, *The Frontiers of Public Administration* (Chicago: University of Chicago Press, 1936), pp. 26–44, as well as Arthur A. Maass and Laurence I. Radway, "Gauging Administrative Responsibility," *Public Administration Review*, 9 (Summer 1949), pp. 182–192.

For more recent writings that have addressed this subject with varying degrees of success or failure, see John Rohr, *Ethics for Bureaucrats*, 2d ed. (New York: Marcel Dekker, 1988); Sissela E. Bok, *Lying* (New York: Random House, 1979), and *Secrets* (New York: Pantheon, 1983); John P. Burke, *Bureaucratic Responsibility* (Baltimore: The Johns Hopkins Press, 1986). Terry L. Cooper, *An Ethic of Citizenship for Public Administration* (Englewood Cliffs, N.J.: Prentice Hall, 1991); William L. Richter et al., *Combating Corruption/Encouraging Ethics: A Sourcebook for Public Service* (Washington: D.C.: American Society for Public Administration, 1990); Terry L. Cooper, *The Responsible Administrator: An Approach to Ethics for the Administrative Role*, 3rd ed. (San Francisco: Jossey-Bass, 1990); Gerald M. Pops and Thomas J. Paulak, *The Case for Justice* (San Francisco: Jossey-Bass, 1991); David H. Rosenbloom and James D. Carroll, eds., *Towards Constitutional Competence: A Casebook for Public Administrators* (Englewood Cliffs, N.J.: Prentice Hall, 1990); Kathryn G. Denhardt, *The Ethics of Public Service: Resolving Moral Dilemmas in Public Organizations* (New York: Greenwood, 1988); James Q. Wilson, *The Moral Sense* (New York: Free Press, 1993); and Louis C. Gawthrop, *Public Service and Democracy: Ethical Imperatives for the 21st century* (Chatham, N.J.: Chatham House, 1999).

In addition, there are several excellent essays, such as Mark T. Lilla, "Ethos, 'Ethics' and Public Service," *The Public Interest*, 63 (Spring 1981), pp. 3–17, or, in the same issue, Thomas C. Schelling, "Economic Reasoning and the Ethics of Policy," pp. 37–61. For other essays, see York Wilbern, "Types and Levels of Public Morality," *Public Administration Review*, 44 (March/April 1984), pp. 102–108; Barbara S. Romzek and Melvin J. Dubnik, "Accountability in the Public Sector: Lessons from the Challenger Tragedy," *Public Administration Review*, 47 (May/June 1987), pp. 227–238; Terry L. Cooper, "Hierarchy, Virtue, and the Practice of Public Administration: A Perspective for Normative Ethics" *Public Administration Review*, 47 (July/August, 1987), pp. 320–328; Dennis F. Thompson, "The Possibility of Administrative Ethics," *Public Administration Review*, 45 (September/October 1985), pp. 555–561; James S. Bowman, "Ethics in Government, A National Survey of Public Administration," *Public Administration Review*, 50 (May/June 1990), pp. 345–353; J. Patrick Dobel, "Integrity in the Public Service," *Public Administration Review*, 50 (May/June 1990) pp. 354–366; Lloyd G. Nigro and William D. Richardson, "Between Citizen and Administration: Administrative Ethics and *PAR*," *Public Administration Review*, 50 (November/December 1990), pp. 623–635; Richard T. Green, "Character Ethics and Public Administration," *International Journal of Public Administration*, 17 (1994), pp. 2137–2164; Debra Stewart, "Theoretical Foundations of Ethics in Public Administration: Approaches to Understanding Moral Action," *Administration and Society*, 23 (November 1991), pp. 357–373; Philip H. Jos and Samuel M. Hines, Jr., "Care, Justice and Public Administration," *Administration and Society*, 25 (November 1993), pp. 373–392; Lewis Mainzer, "Vulgar Ethics for Public Administration," *Administration and Society*, 23 (May 1991), pp. 3–28; Louis C. Gawthrop, "The Ethical Foundations of American Public Administration," *International Journal of Public Administration*, 16 (1993), pp. 139–163; Dennis

Wittmer, "Ethical Sensitivity and Managerial Decision-Making: An Experiment," *Journal of Public Administration Research and Theory,* 2 (1992), pp. 443–462; Frank Marini, "The Use of Literature in the Exploration of Public Administration Ethics: The Example of Antigone," *Public Administration Review,* 52 (September/October 1992), pp. 420–426; as well as the entire issue of *The Annals* (January 1995) devoted to essays on "Ethics in American Public Service." For an unusual counterargument that ethical conduct is a result of our biological make-up and thus there is little we can do about it, see Edward O. Wilson, "The Biological Basis of Morality," *The Atlantic Monthly* 281, No. 4 (April, 1998), pp. 53–70.

Any in-depth review of this subject should include study of the Ethics in Government Act of 1978, as well as the enabling legislation and debates over such seminal oversight mechanisms as the War Powers Resolution of 1973, Freedom of Information Act 1967 (with 1974 amendments), Privacy Act (1974), the Inspector General's Office (1976), and the various ombudsman offices instituted within state and local governments. For many of these recent documents, see Richard J. Stillman II, ed., *Basic Documents of American Public Administration Since 1950* (New York: Holmes and Meier, 1982). Additionally, one should not overlook various professional association codes of conduct for their membership, such as the Code of Ethics of the American Society for Public Administration in *Applying Standards And Ethics in the 21st Century,* 4th ed., (Washington, D.C., ASPA, 1998).

For useful, up-to-date essays concerning ethics education, read James Bowman and Donald Menzel (eds.), *Teaching Ethics and Values in Public Administration Programs* (New York: Suny Press, 1998).

Also, it is helpful to consider five routes for studying this topic. First, many novels focus on the role of ethics in public life. For an excellent discussion of how they contribute to our understanding of the subject, see Dwight Waldo, *The Novelist on Organization and Administration: An Inquiry into the Relationship Between Two Worlds* (Berkeley, Calif.: Institute of Governmental Studies, June 1968), or Marc Holzer, Kenneth Morris, and William Ludwin, *Literature in Bureaucracy* (Wayne, N.J.: Avery Publishing, 1979). Second, autobiographies of distinguished public servants are worth reading, such as Elliot Richardson, *Reflections of a Radical Moderate,* (NY: Pantheon Books, 1996). Third, insightful films on important leadership issues are also very helpful. For the application of films to study these issues, see Hartwick Classic Leadership Cases, available from Hartwick Humanities in Management Institute, Hartwick College, Oneonta, New York 13820. Fourth, the new journal, *Public Integrity,* which began with the Winter 1999 issue, contains numerous, thoughtful essays, commentaries, reports, and book reviews on contemporary public ethics. Finally, biographers remain rich sources for ethical insight, for example, see Gary Willis, *Certain Trumpets* (NY: Simon & Schuster, 1994)

Index

Aaron, Henry J., 454, 456n, 482n
ACIR, 143
Ackoff, R. L., 236n
Adler, N. J., 351n
Administrative Behavior: A Study of Decision-Making Process in Administrative Organization (Simon), 22, 257
Administrative communication, 257–295
  access to communication, 273
  areas of usage, 264–265
  communication blockages, 259
  communication processes/players, 262–268
  communication technologies, 272–274
  credibility conundrum, 268–269
  crucial issues, 268–274
  downward communication, 265–266
  ethics, 274–275
  groupthink, 274–275
  internal communication process, 265–267
  interorganizational communication process, 267–268
  lateral communication, 266–267
  managerial communication process, 263–265
  newsmaking process, 262–263
  one-way tell and sell approaches, 269–270
  propaganda paradox, 269
  reaching hard-to-reach audiences, 272–273
  responsiveness, 274
  spatial thinking/communication, 273–274
  stories, 273
  two-way symmetrical model, 270–271
  upward communication, 266
  usefulness, 274
Administrative decision making. *See* Decision making
Administrative ecology, 80–82
Administrative implementation, 416–418
Administrative power, 101–124
Administrative professionals, 192
Administrative rationality, 104–107

"Administrative Responsibility in Government" (Finer), 509
Administrator, 474–475
"Admiral Boorda's War" (Boyer), 354
Advisory Commission on Intergovernmental Relations (ACIR), 143
AFDC, 142
Affective motives, 315, 344
Agency autonomy, 309–310, 380
Agency effectiveness, 300–301. *See also* Executive management
Agenda setting, 264
Ahrens, F., 273, 275n
Aid to Families with Dependent Children (AFDC), 142
Alexander, Ernest R., 406
Allison, Graham, 414, 418, 423n
Altshuler, Alan, 147n
Ambiguity-conflict model, 414–422
"American Bureaucracy, The" (Stillman), 182
Anti-statism, 16
Antigone (Sophocles), 503
Anton, Timothy, 146n
Appleby, Paul H., 22, 102, 474, 499, 508, 511n
Applegate, J. S., 271, 275n
Argyris, Chris, 340
Aristotelian analysis of constitutions, 106
Aristotle, 503
Armed forces
  gay marines, 169–180
  suicide of Admiral Boorda, 353–372
Armies, 476
Army Corps of Engineers, 450, 477
Arnoff, E. L., 236n
Arnold, David S., 191, 206n
Arnold, Douglas, 391n
Aron, Michael, 88, 261
Arrow, Kenneth, 225
Autonomy, 309–310, 380
Avoided responsibility, 483

Bacher, Robert N., 26
Backward mapping, 411
Baier, Vicki, 409, 415, 423n
Bailey, Stephen K., 499, 501, 510, 511, 512n

Baker, James, 185
Bakuninism, 61
Balance cluster, 388
Balance of power, 108
Ball, Robert, 309, 312
Ballot box, 499
Ban, C., 300, 318n
Banfield, Edward C., 225, 228, 236n
Bank Wiring Observation Room, 165
Banovetz, James M., 393n
Bardach, Eugene, 405
Bargaining, 138–139
Barilleaux, Charles, 391n
Barnard, Chester I., 21, 105, 160, 223, 260, 262, 275n, 351n, 498, 501, 511, 512n
Barnum, P. T., 269
Barrett, K., 342, 351n
Barriers to language, 259
Barton, A. H., 300, 318n
Barzelay, M., 300, 318n
Beard, Charles A., 83, 87n
Beck, M., 122n
Beer, Samuel H., 189, 190, 206n
Behn, R. D., 300, 310–312, 315, 318n
Bell, Daniel, 190, 206n
Bell, Griffin, 454
Bell, T. E., 122n
Bendix, Reinhard, 51, 53
Bennis, Warren, 340
Bentley, Arthur, 474
Benveniste, Guy, 190, 206n
Berman, Paul, 409–412, 414, 415, 423n
Bernstein, Marver, 509, 512n
Bews, J. W., 82, 87n
Beyer, J. M., 310, 311, 321n
Beyond Privatization (Salamon), 27
"Blast in Centralia No. 5: A Mine Disaster No One Stopped" (Martin), 31
Blau, Peter M., 53n, 349, 351n
Block grants, 133, 140–141
Blue flu, 202
Blumberg, S. K., 344, 351n
Bluntschli, 10
Bohlen, Charles, 190
Boorda, Jeremy, 353–372
Bottom-up models, 409–410
Boundary scanning, 264

Boundary spanning, 267–268
Bounded rationality, 258
Bowman, Ann, 424n
Boyer, Peter J., 354
Bozeman, B., 300, 318n, 320n
Bradley, David, 501, 507, 511, 512n
Branch Davidians, 277–293
Branch method, 223–224, 226–228, 234–235
Branti v. Finkel, 195
Brehm, J., 300, 313, 314, 318n
Brewer, G., 343, 345–347, 351n
Breyer, L. J., 188, 206n
Brody, M., 122n
Bronner, Ethan, 208
Broom, G. M., 264, 275n
Brown, Harold, 204
Brown, R. G., 352n
Brownlow Committee Report, 297
Bryner, Gary C., 478n
Brzezinski, Zbigniew, 190, 206n
Buchanan, B., 316, 318n, 344, 345, 351n
Budget constraints, 385
Budget document, 384
Budget implementation, 388
Budgets. *See* Public budgeting
Buffalo Bill, 269
Bullock, Charles S., III, 406
Bureau chiefs, 380
Bureaucracy, 50–79
  characteristics, 54–55
  economic/social consequences, 62–63
  executive establishment, and, 444–472
  officials, 55–59
  permanent character of, 60–62
  power of, 63
  public interest, and, 473–497
  technical advantages, 59–60
  Weber, 50–63
Bureaucracy (Wilson), 475
Bureaucratic hierarchy, 52, 54
Bureaucratic power, 63
Bureaucratic rules, 52, 60
Bureaucratic subsystems, 182–219
  contractual employees, 202–204
  general civil service, 194–198
  political appointees, 184–189
  professional careerists, 189–194
  unionized workers, 199–202
Burnham, Walter D., 425n
Bush, George, 142, 342

Business blunders, 302. *See also*
  ValuJet airline disaster
"But No Cigar: How a Rescue Mission Failed, Just Barely, in Orange County" (Jereski), 486
Butler, Samuel, 511

CAA, 422
Cabinet-rank departments, 186
Caesarism, 58
Caiden, G., 300, 318n
Calculable rules, 60
Calista, D. J., 320n
Callahan, K., 300, 301, 307, 309, 311, 313, 319n
Campbell, Donald T., 482n
Carnevale, D. G., 269, 275n, 349, 351n
Carr, Adrian, 53n
Carter, Jimmy, 23, 140, 185, 201, 204, 450, 454, 455
Case studies
  Admiral Boorda's War, 354
  Blast in Centralia No. 5: A Mine Disaster No One Stopped, 31
  But No Cigar: How a Rescue Mission Failed, Just Barely, in Orange County, 486
  County Prison Overtime, 393
  Decision to Bomb the Serbs, 208
  Dumping $2.6 Million on Bakersfield (Or How Not to Build a Migratory Farm Workers' Clinic), 88
  How Kristin Died, 64
  Last Flight of Space Shuttle Challenger, 110
  Lessons of ValuJet 592, 322
  Madonna's *Sex*, 512
  MOVE Disaster, 238
  Political Paradox of Rationing: The Case of the Oregon Health Plan, 427
  Reinventing School Lunch: Transforming a Food Policy into a Nutrition Policy, 457
  Uniforms in the Closet, 170
  Waco, 279
  Wichita Confronts Contamination, 147
Catastrophe, 86
Categorical grants, 133–134
Catron, B. L., 522n
Catron, Byard L., 26, 29n
Censorship, 259. *See also*
  Madonna's *Sex*

Centralia mine disaster, 30–45
Chain of command, 380
Challenger shuttle disaster, 109–122, 275
Charismatic authority, 51
Charles, Michael T., 110, 261
Chief executive officers, 381
Childers, L., 269, 275n
China Enters the Machine Age, 167
China Lake experiment, 480
Chrislip, David, 26
Christopher, Warren, 185
Chubb, John E., 481, 485n
Churchman, C. W., 236n
Citrin, Jack, 456n
Civil Service Reform Act of 1978, 195, 200–201
Civil service subsystem, 194–198
Civil Service 2000, 198
Clark, P. B., 345, 351n
Clary, E. G., 347, 351n
Cleveland, Harlan, 511, 512n
Clinica Sierra Vista, 94–97
Clinton, Bill, 25, 142–144, 185, 189, 204, 263, 268
Cohen, Michael D., 420, 423n
Cohnen, S., 300, 318n
Coleman, William, 452
Collective bargaining, 202
Collectivity-person, 503
Collins, J. C., 305, 318n
Colvard, James, 478, 485n
Communicating for Results in Government (Garnett), 260
Communication. *See* Administrative communication
Communication ethics, 274–275
Communication/information auditing, 265
Communications blockages, 259
Communications model of intergovernmental policy implementation, 411
Communitarians, 26
Community action agencies (CAA), 422
Community Health Clinic Act (Weedpatch, California), 96
Comparative analysis of incremental changes, 233
Complexity, 138–139, 143, 453
Comte, Auguste, 507
Concept of Organization, The (Bradley/Wilkie), 511

"Conditions of Effective Implementation: A Guide to Accomplishing Policy Objectives, The" (Sabatier/Mazmanian), 405
Confederation, 129
Confidence gap, 269
Conflict management, 265
Confusion, 483
Consensus, 453
Contamination (hazardous chemicals), 146–154
Contract with America, 142–143
Contractual employees, 202–204
Control mentality, 479
Cook, Stuart W., 411, 426n
Cook, Thomas D., 482n
Cooper, J. M., 315, 318n
Cooper, T. L., 311, 318n
Cooperation, 130–132
Coppinger, J. M,, 236n
Countervailing values to growth, 380–381
Counties, 128
County health officer, 126
County Prison Overtime (Mills), 393
Courage, 499
Couzens, M., 266, 274, 276n
Creative federalism, 135–138
Credibility conundrum, 268–269
Crewson, P. E., 315, 318n, 343, 351n
Crime mapping, 273–274
Culture, 310. *See also* Motivation, Public service culture
Cummings, M. C., 315, 319n

Daft, R. L., 305, 318n
Dahl, Robert A., 21, 22, 29n, 222, 225, 474
Dahrendorf, Ralf, 414, 423n
Dalton, Melville, 510, 512n
Deci, E. L., 345, 347, 351n, 352n
Decision making, 222–256
    bargaining, 138
    budgets, and, 387–388
    good policy, test of, 230
    intertwining evaluation/empirical analysis, 228–229
    means-end relationship, 230
    non-comprehensive analysis, 231–233
    rational-comprehensive (root) method, 223–224, 226–228
    succession of comparisons, 233–234

successive limited comparisons (branch) method, 223–224, 226–228, 234–235
    theorists/practitioners, 234
Decision to Bomb the Serbs (Sciolino/Bronner), 208
Democracy and the Public Service (Mosher), 505
Democratic administrative paradigm, 23
Democratic idealism, 22–25, 28
Denhardt, Robert B., 3, 301, 307, 312, 315, 318n
Derby, P., 121n
Deregulation of public sector, 473–497
Derthick, Martha, 27, 191, 206n, 404, 478, 485n
Dexter, Donald, 272
Diamant, Alfred, 53n
Diamond, Martin, 145n
Dickson, William J., 160, 161, 169n
DiIulio, J. D., 310, 312, 318n
Dimock, Gladys, 2
Dimock, Marshall E., 2, 82n
Directing brain, 192
Dispute resolution, 265
Dobel, J. P., 521n
Doig, Jameson W., 205n, 300, 311–313, 318n, 319n, 321n
Don't Ask, Don't Tell policy, 170
Donahue, J. D., 309, 318n
Douglas, Joel M., 199, 206n
Downs, A., 266, 269, 275n, 300, 318n, 344, 347, 351n
Downs, G. W., 300, 318n
Downward communication, 265–266
Dozier, D. M., 264, 275n
Drucker, Peter, 297
Dual federalism, 130, 145
Dubnick, Melvin J., 2, 122n
"Dumping $2.6 Million on Bakersfield (Or How Not to Build a Migratory Farm Workers' Clinic)" (Aron), 88
Dunnette, M. D., 345, 352n
Dunshire, Andrew, 411, 424n
Durant, Robert F., 27, 30o, 302n, 318n, 419, 424n
Durkheim, Emile, 507
Dwight Waldo Award, 500

Ebbesen, E. B., 270, 277n
Eberly, Don, 268

Ecology of public administration, 80–100
Edelman, Murray S., 424n
Educating the public, 348
Effectiveness, 304–308. *See also* Executive management
Egan, Jennifer, 170
Eimicke, W., 300, 318n
Eisenhower, Dwight D., 135
Eisner, R., 300, 318n
Elazar, Daniel J., 145n
Elephant, 299
Ellwood, John, 391n
Elmore, Richard F., 410, 411, 418, 424n
Elrod v. Burns, 195
Else, B. A., 302, 320n
Emergency energy assistance program, 418
Emerson, Steven, 479, 485n
Emotional release, 164
Empirical analysis, 228–229
End of Liberalism, The (Lowi), 404
End to Hierarchy! an End to Competition, An (Thayer), 509
Engagement, 349–350
Enterprise of Public Administration: A Summary View, The (Waldo), 500
Environmental scanning, 264
Esch, K., 122n
Ethics, 498–525
    communication, 274–275
    higher law, 503–504
    map of ethical obligations, 504–506
    need for maps, 506
    need for navigation instruments, 506–508
    observations/reflections, 509–511
    public vs. private morality, 502
    pyramid puzzle, 508–509
"Ethics and the Public Service" (Bailey), 499, 510
"Ethics in Government: The Problems in Perspective" (Bernstein), 509
Etzioni, Amatai, 26, 417, 424n
Excellence movement, 273
Executive budget office, 381
Executive management, 296–339
    autonomy, 309–310
    effectiveness, 304–308
    examples of agency effectiveness, 300–301

leadership, 310–312
mission motivation, 315–316
mission valence, 310
organizational culture, 310–311
privatization, 301–302
professionalism, 313–314
public service motivation,
314–315
stakeholders, and, 305–309
task design, 313
task motivation, 316–317
Executive Order 10987, 199
Executive Order 10988, 199
Expenditure cluster, 388
Experiment, 481–482
Experimental implementation,
420–421
External communication, 267–268

Fainsod, Merle, 474
Fairness tempered by charity, 499
Farazmand, Ali, 53n
"Fear of Bureaucracy: A Raging
Pandemic" (Kaufman), 23
Federal financial aid, 131–134, 142
Federalism, 128
Feldman, Martha S., 412, 424n
Fesler, James W., 3, 21, 22, 29n
Finer, Herman, 22, 509, 512n
Finn, Chester E., Jr., 485n
Fiscal year, 374
Fischhoff, B., 121n
Follett, Mary Parker, 21
Foltz, R. G., 262, 275n
Ford, Gerald, 139
Forest Ranger, The (Kaufman), 313
Formal communication networks,
266
Formula grants, 134
Forward mapping, 410
Foster, William C., 204
Fox, Douglas, 2
Frames of reference, 259
Frank, T. M., 522n
Frederickson, H. George, 314, 315,
318n, 344, 348, 349, 351n, 512n
Freeman, J. Leiper, 456n
Freud, Sigmund, 157, 158
Friedrich, Carl J., 22, 50, 474, 475n
"From Idea to Action" (Alexander),
406
Fromm, G., 424n
Functions of the Executive, The
(Barnard), 510
Furniss, Norman, 146n

Gabris, G. T., 343, 351n
Gaebler, Ted, 25, 29n, 263, 267, 273,
276n, 300, 301, 305, 320n
Galston, William, 26
Garnett, James L., 195, 257, 260,
265–270, 272–274, 275n, 276n
Gates, S., 300, 313, 314, 318n
Gaus, John M., 80–82, 348, 351n
Gawthrop, Louis C., 27, 346,
348–350, 351n
Gay marines, 169–180
Geddes, Sir Patrick, 83
General civil service subsystem,
194–198
General revenue sharing, 133,
139–140
Generalist leaders, 312
Generalist-professional cadre of offi-
cers, 190
Geographical distance, 259
George III, 125, 503
Georgiou, P., 343, 351n
Gerth, Hans H., 54n
Gilbert-Mosley area (contamination),
146–154
Gill, J., 302, 309, 319n
Glick, W. H., 312, 319n
Glidewell, J. C., 300, 310, 311, 313,
319n
Globerman, S., 309, 319n
Goggin, Malcolm L., 407, 411,
424n
Gold, K. A., 301, 305–306, 319n
Goldberg, Arthur, 200
Goldman, Deborah D., 3
Golembiewski, Robert T., 511n
Good government, 474
Good management. *See* Executive
management
Goodnow, Frank J., 19, 29n
Goodsell, Charles T., 26, 299, 300,
319n
Gordon, George J., 3
Gore, Albert, Jr., 143, 299, 301,
319n
Gormley, William T., Jr., 424n
Gouldner, A., 122n
Government communication. *See*
Administrative communication
Governmental budgeting, 379–380.
See also Public budgeting
Governmental decision making. *See*
Decision making
Graham, Cole Blease, Jr., 2
Grant-in-aid, 132

Grants
block, 133, 140–141
budgets, and, 389–390
categorical, 133–134
formula, 134
land, 131
project, 134
Great Society Programs, 404
Greene, R., 342, 351n
Grodzin, Morton, 126, 146n
Groupthink, 274–275
Grunig, J. E., 269, 270, 275n, 276n
Grunig, L. A., 263, 269, 275n, 276n
Gulick, Luther, 20, 29n, 344

Hackman, J. R., 313, 319n
Hadley, Arthur T., 485n
Hager, M., 122n
Hale, S. J., 306n, 307n, 319n
Halperin, Morten H., 414, 418, 424n
Hamilton, Alexander, 5, 17, 29n, 108
Hanf, K., 424n
Hanks, Nancy, 312
Hansfield, E., 352n
Hard Truths/Tough Choices, 198
Hargrove, Edwin C., 300, 310–313,
318n, 319n, 321n, 405
Harriman, Linda, 392n
Harris, Richard, 268, 276n
Hart, D. K., 314, 315, 319n, 344,
351n
Hart, Paul T., 110n
Hartman, R., 315, 319n
Hartz, Louis, 17, 29n
Hatch Act, 197
Hawthorne experiments, 156–169
Hays, Steven W., 2
Hazardous chemical contamination,
146–154
Headstart, 421
Heady, Ferrel, 53n
Health care reform plan (Oregon),
427–439
Heclo, Hugh, 185, 205n, 206n, 267,
312, 319n, 444, 446, 447, 456n
Hegel, Georg, 7
Heise, A., 269, 270, 276n
Hennigan, Patrick, 504
Herrington, E. Pendleton, 102, 105
Herzberg, F., 159
Hierarchical structure, 268
Higher law, 503
Hill, Larry B., 300n, 319n
Hitch, Charles, 227
Hjern, Benny, 409, 410, 424n

Hobbes, Thomas, 18, 503
Hofstede, G., 351n
Hogans, Norris, 476
Hollow state, 302
Holmes, Justice, 87n
Holzer, M., 276n, 273, 300, 301,
    307, 309, 311, 313, 319n
Homans, George C., 169n, 345, 352n
Hopkins, D. M., 521n
Hoppe, Robert, 409, 424n
Horner, Constance, 478n
"How Kristin Died" (Lardner), 64
Howton, F. William, 501, 509, 512n
Huber, G. P., 312, 319n
Hull, Chris, 409, 424n
*Human Problems of an Industrial
    Civilization, The* (Mayo), 157
Human relations, 156
Hummel, R. P., 522n
Hunt, T., 269, 276n
Huntington, S. P., 29n

Ideal-types, 51
IGR. *See* Intergovernmental relations
    (IGR)
*Images and Identities in Public Ad-
    ministration* (Kass/Catron), 26
Implementation. *See* Policy imple-
    mentation
Implementation (Pressman/Wil-
    davsky), 404
Implementation Game (Bardach), 405
*Implementation of Civil Rights Pol-
    icy* (Bullock/Lamb), 406
Incremental decision making, 225.
    See also Decision making
Industrial sociological school, 156
Industrial Worker, The (Whitehead),
    160
Informal group, 156–181
Ingraham, Patricia W., 195, 206n,
    312, 319n, 391n
Ingram, Helen, 413, 419, 423, 424n
Inner Cabinet, 186
*Inquiry into the Nature and Causes
    of the Wealth of Nations, An*
    (Smith), 507
Instrumental motives, 315
*Intellectual Crisis in American Ad-
    ministration, The* (Ostrom), 23,
    509
Interdependence, 138–139, 143
Interest group liberalism, 404
Interest groups. *See* Public interest
    groups (PIGs)

Intergovernment assistance,
    131–134, 142
Intergovernment grant structure,
    390–391
Intergovernment relations (IGR),
    125–155
  bargaining, 138–139
  Carter, 140
  complexity, 138–139, 143
  cooperation, 130–132
  creative federalism, 135–138
  defined, 128
  dual federalism, 130, 145
  federal financial aid, 131–134, 142
  federalism, contrasted, 128
  interdependence, 138–139, 143
  New Deal, 134–135
  Nixon, 139–140
  Reagan, 141
  reform/simplification, 141,
    143–144
Intergovernmental activism,
    136–137
Intergovernmental bargaining,
    138–139
Intergovernmental cooperation,
    130–132
Intergovernmental Personnel Act
    (IPA) of 1970, 195
Internal communication process,
    265–267
Internal process models, 303
Interorganizational communication
    process, 267–268
Interpretivists, 26
Interview program (Hawthorne ex-
    periments), 162–169
*Introduction to the Study of Public
    Administration* (White), 18, 20
Iron triangles, 445–446, 448
Issue marketing, 264
Issue networks, 446–456. *See also*
    Political-administration rela-
    tionship

Jackson, Andrew, 269
Jacobs, Lawrence R., 427
Janis, I. L., 122n, 274
Jarman, Alan, 122n
Jay, John, 5, 17, 29n
Jefferson, Thomas, 17, 108
Jennings, M. K., 315, 319n
Jereski, Laura, 486
Johnson, A. C., 342, 352n
Johnson, Lyndon B., 135, 137, 404

Johnson, William C., 3
Joint stock companies, 130
Jones, B. D., 349, 352n
Jones, Charles, 416, 424n
Jones, L. R., 300, 321n
Joskow, Paul L., 419, 424n
Jun, Jong S., 2
Jung, Carl, 157
Jurkiewicz, C. L., 343, 352n

Kahn, R. L., 265, 276n
Kaplan, Robert D., 190, 206n
Karl, B. D., 20, 29n, 344, 352n
Kass, H. D., 522n
Kass, Henry D., 26, 29n
Katz, D., 265, 276n
Kaufman, Herbert, 23, 29n, 274,
    276n, 313, 477, 485n
Kauzmin, Alexander, 53n
Keeney, R., 121n
Kelly, K. S., 269, 276n
Kelman, Steven, 315, 319n, 351,
    352n, 418, 424n
Kennan, George, 190
Kennedy, John F., 23, 199, 200, 342
Keon, T., 353n
Kettl, Donald F., 3, 27, 206n, 302,
    309, 319n
Kheel, Theodore, 201
Killing, 502
Kilpatrick, F. P., 315, 319n
King, Anthony, 319n, 447n
King, Martin Luther, Jr., 23
Kluckhohn, C., 348, 352n
Knoke, D., 343, 344, 352n
Kosovo, 207–217
Kouzmin, Alexander, 122n, 276n
Kreitner, R., 345, 352n
Kristol, Irving, 507
Kroon, Marceline, 274, 275, 276n
Krosenberg, Philip S., 26

La Rochefoucauld, 102, 108
*Labor Market Policies and Employ-
    ment Policies in the United
    States* (Wise), 341
Lamb, Charles M., 406
Lambrwright, W. H., 312, 319n
Lance, Bert, 454
Land grant, 131
Lane, Frederick S., 206n
Langewiesche, William, 322
Lardner, George, Jr., 64, 261
Lardner, Kristen, 267
Larkey, P., 300, 318n

Lasko, W., 315, 319n
"Last Flight of Space Shuttle Challenger" (Charles), 110
Latack, J. C., 353n
Lateral communication, 266–267
Lave, Charles A., 414, 425n
Lead agency pattern, 268
Leadership, 310–312
Leadership for America, 198
Legal-rational authority, 51
Legge, J. S., 302, 318n
Legislators, 381–382
Lehmann, John, 204
Leivesley, Robert, 53n
LeLoup, Lance, 391n
"Lessons of ValuJet 529" (Langewiesche), 322
Lester, James P., 424n
Levine, Charles H., 2
Lewis, E. B., 311, 313, 319n
Leys, Wayne A. R., 511n
Libraries (censorship—Madonna's *Sex*), 512–522
Lichtenstein, S., 121n
Light, Paul, 27
Likert, Rensis, 159, 340, 522n
Lilienthal, David, 83
Lindblom, Charles E., 222–225
Linder, Stephen H., 410, 412, 425n
Line professionals, 192
Lipsky, Michael, 409, 425n, 426n
Little Hatch Acts, 197
Lloyd-La Follette Act, 199
Local governments, 128–129
Locke, John, 17
Long, Norton E., 22, 101–103, 189, 258, 474
Lorch, Robert S., 261, 276
Lorenzi, P., 312, 321n
Lowery, D., 302, 303, 309, 319n
Lowi, Theodore J., 404, 416, 425n
Luce, Duncan R., 414, 425n
Lundberg, E., 273, 276n
Luthans, F., 345, 352n

MacGregor, Eugene B., Jr., 196, 206n
Machiavelli, Niccolo, 18, 102, 108, 503
Macrobudgeting, 389
Macy, J. W., Jr., 352n
Madison, James, 5, 17, 29n, 102, 106, 129, 145n
"Madonna's *Sex*" (Morgan), 512
Management and the Worker (Roethlisberger/Dickson), 160, 164

Management experiments, 482
Management issues. *See* Executive management
Managerial communication process, 263–265
Mandates, 139, 142–143
Mann, Dean E., 205n, 423n
Mann, L., 122n
Mann, Thomas, 392n
Marble-cake federalism, 134
March, James G., 235n, 316, 319n, 345, 352n, 409, 410, 412, 414, 415, 420, 423n, 424n, 425n
Marini, F., 29n
Marketing, 270
Marmor, Theodore, 427
Martin, B., 522n
Martin, John Bartlow, 31, 261
Martin, Roscoe C., 499n
Mashaw, J. L., 311, 319n
Maslach, C., 270, 277n
Maslow, Abraham, 159
Massey, T. K., 352n
Mathewson, Stanley B., 169n
Matland, Richard E., 403, 406, 407
Maximum Feasible Misunderstanding (Moynihan), 404
Mayhew, David R., 419, 425n
Maynard-Moody, Steven, 311, 319n, 409, 410, 413, 425n
Mayo, Elton, 21, 156–160, 169n, 197, 340
Mazmanian, Daniel, 405, 408, 419, 425n
McCloskey, J. F., 236n
McConnell, M., 121n, 122n
McGregor, Douglas, 159, 340, 522n
McLaughlin, Milbrey, 405, 407, 425n
Means-end relationship, 230
Media relations, 262–263
Meier, K. J., 303, 309, 311, 320n, 348, 349, 352n
Men Who Manage (Dalton), 510
Merovingian, 108
Merton, Robert K., 410, 425n
Meyer, Marshall W., 53n
Meyerson, Martin, 228, 236n
Michels, Robert, 410, 425n
Microbudgeting, 388
Migratory farm workers' clinic, 88–96
Milakovitch, Michael E., 3
Mill, John Stuart, 454
Miller, Arthur H., 456n

Miller, J., 347, 351n
Milliken, F. J., 122n
Mills, C. Wright, 54n
Mills, Gregory, 391n
Mills, Tom, 272, 393
Mills, Wilbur, 307, 309
Milward, H. B., 300, 302, 309, 320n
Mine disaster (Centralia, Illinois), 30–45
Minnowbrook Conference, 23
Mission accomplishment mentality, 479
Mission motivation, 315–316
Mission valence, 310
Mitchell, J., 311, 319n
Moe, Terry M., 481, 485n
Mohr, Lawrence B., 420, 425n
Monied economy, 52
Montesquieu, Charles de Secondat, Baron de, 507
Moral choices. *See* Ethics
Morality and Administration in Democratic Government (Appleby), 499, 508
Morgan, C., 522n
Morgan, Douglas F., 513, 522n
Mosher, Frederick C., 4, 19, 22, 29n, 187, 190, 199, 205n, 206n, 348, 352n, 505
Motivation
    mission, 315–316
    public service. *See* Public service motivation
    task, 316–317
Moussios, A., 302, 318n
"MOVE Disaster" (Nagel), 238
Moynihan, Daniel P., 404
Muddling through, 235
Municipalities, 128–129
Murphy, Thomas P., 187, 205n
Musheno, Michael, 409, 410, 425n

Nagel, Jack H., 238, 265, 275
Nakamura, Robert T., 404, 406, 408, 420, 425n
Nathan, Richard P., 482n, 485n
National performance review (NPR), 143
National school lunch program, 457–470
Neiderhoffer, A., 349, 352n
Neutrality, 349
New bureaucratic analysis, 27
New Deal, 134–135
New federalism, 139–140

New realism, 102
New Towns In-Town (Derthick), 404
Newland, C. A., 20, 29n
Newsmaking process, 262–263
Niebuhr, H. Richard, 346
Niebuhr, Reinhold, 11, 508
Nigro, Felix A., 2, 22
Nigro, Lloyd G., 2
Niskanen, W. A., 300, 320n
Nixon, Richard, 139–141, 151
Noll, Roger C., 419, 424n
Non-comprehensive analysis,
    231–233
Norm-based motives, 315, 344
Norm of neutrality, 349
Normative orientations, 344
NPR, 143
Nuechterlein, Donald E., 187, 205n

O'Toole, Laurence J., Jr., 125–127,
    268, 276n, 309, 320n, 407, 408,
    416, 424n, 425n
Objective expert, 60
Offerdal, Audun, 415, 425n
Officials, 55–59
Ogul, Morris, 419, 425n
Oldham, G. R., 313, 319n, 346, 352n
Olsen, Johan P., 420, 421, 425n
Opsahl, R. L., 345, 352n
Optimism, 499
Orange County bankruptcy, 485–494
Oregon Health Plan, 427–439
Organizational culture, 310–311. *See
    also* Motivation, Public service
    culture
Orloff, J. K., 342, 346, 352n
Ornstein, Norman, 392n
Osborne, David, 25, 29n, 263, 267,
    273, 276n, 300, 301, 305, 320n
Ostrom, E., 314, 320n
Ostrom, Vincent, 23, 24, 29n, 509,
    512n
Our business civilization, 297
Outcomes assessment, 265
Outer Cabinet, 186
Oversight authorities, 305–307
Overtime (county prisons), 392–400

Pachyderm, 299
Palmer, John, 391n
Palumbo, Dennis J., 320n, 409, 410,
    413, 425n
*Papers on the Science of Administra-
    tion, The* (Gulick), 20
Paradoxical bureaucracy, 484

Paraprofessionals, 193
Park, Tongsun, 510
Parker, Robert S., 4
Parsons, T., 352n, 507
Pechman, Joseph A., 485n
Pelkey, Neil, 411, 426n
Pendleton Act, 195
Pennock, G. A., 160
Perrow, C., 121n, 343, 352n
Perry, James L., 275n, 276n, 315,
    319n, 320n, 343, 344, 352n
Perry, William J., 185, 204
Personal communication networks,
    266
Personal Responsibility and Work
    Opportunity Reconciliation Act,
    142
Personnel subsystems. *See* Bureau-
    cratic subsystems
Peters, B. Guy, 2, 410, 412, 425n
Peters, T. J., 273, 276n, 305, 320n
Pfiffner, James P., 22, 27, 189, 345,
    352n
Physical technology, 85
PIGs. *See* Public interest groups
    (PIGs)
Pinchot, Gifford, 312
Plant, Jeremy F., 191, 206n
Plato, 503
Policy and program implementation,
    264
Policy implementation, 403–441
    administrative implementation,
        416–418
    ambiguity-conflict model,
        414–422
    bottom-up models, 409–410
    budgets, 388
    combined top-down-bottom-up
        perspective, 411–412
    communications model, 411
    experimental implementation,
        420–421
    forward/backward mapping,
        410–411
    implementation theories, 405–406
    political implementation, 418–420
    successful implementation,
        412–413
    symbolic implementation,
        421–422
    top-down models, 408–409
"Policy Implementation Process: A
    Conceptual Framework, The"
    (Van Meter/Van Horn), 405

Political-administration relationship,
    444–472
    advantages of issue networks,
        451–452
    closure, 454
    complexity, 453
    confidence, 453–454
    consensus, 453
    iron triangles, 445–446, 448
    issue networks, 448–456
    problems/weaknesses of issue net-
        works, 452, 454
Political appointee subsystem,
    184–189
Political implementation, 418–420
"Political Paradox of Rationing: The
    Case of Oregon Health Plan"
    (Jacobs/Marmor/Oberlander),
    427
*Political Problems of Industrial Civi-
    lization, The* (Mayo), 157
Politics and Administration (Good-
    now), 19
Politics and Markets (Dahl), 223
Politics of expertise, 190
*Politics of Policy Implementation,
    The* (Nakamura/Smallwood),
    406
Politics of Public Budgeting, The
    (Rubin), 375
Politics, Economics and Welfare
    (Dahl), 222
Politics-administration dichotomy, 5
Pollock, Sir Frederick, 87n
Polman, D., 269, 276n
Pork, 381
Porras, J. I., 305, 318n
Porter, David, 409, 424n
POSDCORB orthodoxy, 20–21, 28
Posner, Paul, 143
Post-industrial age, 190
Power
    administrative, 101–124
    bureaucracy, and, 63
Power and Administration (Long),
    101–102
Press agentry/publicity model, 269
Pressman, Jeffrey, 146, 404–406,
    408, 417, 425n
Pressures of work, 259
Price, Don, 22, 190, 206n
Prieve, E. A., 342, 352n
*Principles of Scientific Management,
    The* (Taylor), 19
Prisons, 476

Privatization, 301–302
Process cluster, 387
Professional careerist subsystem,
    189–194
Professional elites, 191–192
Professional public official associa-
    tions, 190–191
Professionalism, 313–314, 380
Program loyalty, 380
Progressive Era, 131
Project grants, 134
Promotion, 270
Propaganda paradox, 269
*Protestant Ethic and the Spirit of
    Capitalism, The* (Weber), 51
Provan, K. G., 302, 309, 320n
PSLR legal framework, 199
Public administration
    definitions, 1–4
    eras, 20–28
Public Administration (Simon), 257
Public budgeting, 374–402
    acceptability, 383–384
    accountability, 383–384
    balance cluster, 388
    balancing/borrowing, 378–379
    budget document, 384
    budget process, and, 390
    bureau chiefs, and, 380–381
    business budgeting, contrasted,
        379
    characteristics, 379–380
    chief executive officers, and, 381
    constraints, 385
    courts, and, 383
    decision making, 387–388
    dynamic nature of, 391
    environment, and, 389
    executive budget office, and, 381
    expenditure cluster, 388
    flexibility, 385
    implementation, 388
    individual strategies, and, 390
    individuals, and, 382–383
    interest groups, and, 382, 386
    intergovernmental grant structure,
        and, 390–391
    legal environment, and, 390
    legislators, and, 381–382
    microbudgeting vs. macrobudget-
        ing, 388–389
    openness to environment, 384–385
    politics, 385–387
    power differentials, 383
    process cluster, 387

revenue cluster, 387
    selective revelation, 384
    separation of payer/decider,
        383–384
Public choice, 23
Public information model, 263, 269
Public interest, 267
Public interest and bureaucracy,
    473–497
Public interest groups (PIGs)
    activities, 137
    budgetary constraint, and, 144
    budgetary process, and, 382, 386
    creative federalism, 136
    State and Local Fiscal Assistance
        Act, 140
    TANF, 143
Public morality, 502
Public sector, 267
Public sector deregulation, 473–497
Public service culture, 342–351
Public service labor relations
    (PSLR), 199
Public service motivation, 314–315,
    340–373
    affective motives, 344
    contextual factors, 345
    defined, 344
    educating the public, 348
    engagement, 349–350
    exclusivity to public sector, 346
    norm-based motives, 344
    prevalence in public sector,
        346–347
    rational motives, 344
    situational factors, 345
    values, 348–349
Pyramid puzzle, 508–509

Raadschelders, J. C. N., 19, 29n
Rahm, Dianne, 277n
Raiffa, Howard, 414, 425n
Rainey, G. W., 301, 309, 312, 320n
Rainey, Hal G., 27, 296, 297, 299,
    300–302, 305, 306, 309–312,
    315, 319n, 320n, 343, 345, 352n
Rank-in-job, 184
Rank-in-person, 184
Rank-in-position, 184
Rational-comprehensive (root)
    method, 223–224, 226–228
Rational machine model, 474
Rational motives, 344
Rawls, J., 344, 352n
Rays, Elizabeth, 510

Reagan, Ronald, 23, 128, 140–142,
    145, 185, 204, 381
Reason of state, 504
Red tape, 139, 483
Redford, Emmette, 474
Reflections on Public Administration
    (Gaus), 80–81
*Refounding Democratic Public Ad-
    ministration* (VPI refounders),
    26
Refounding movement, 25–28
Refounding Public Administration
    (VPI refounders), 26
Regan, Priscilla, 415, 426n
Rehfuss, J., 320n
Reinventing Government
    (Osborne/Gaebler), 25, 263
"Reinventing School Lunch: Trans-
    forming a Food Policy into a
    Nutrition Policy" (Sims), 457
Reinvention movement, 273
Reinventors, 25
Relationships
    bureaucracy-public interest,
        473–497
    political-administration, 444–472
Revenue cluster, 387
Revenue sharing, 133, 139–140
Riccucci, N. M., 300, 311–313, 320n
Richardson, Elliot, 312, 451
Rickover, Hyman, 312
Ridley, Clarence E., 485n
Riggs, Fred, 82
Roberts, Deborah D., 188, 206n
Roberts, Steven V., 456n
Robinson, James Harvey, 501
Robson, R. Thayne, 485n
Roethlisberger, Fritz J., 21, 156–162,
    169n
Rogers Act of 1924, 190
Rohr, J., 522n
Romzek, Barbara S., 2, 122n, 347,
    352n
Roosevelt, Franklin D., 106, 134
Root method, 223–224, 226–228
Root, Elihu, 190, 192
Rosegrant, Susan, 147
Rosenau, James N., 456n
Rosenbloom, David H., 3, 195
Rosenthal, Uriel, 110
Rossiter, Clinton, 145n
Rourke, F. E., 311, 320n
Rousseau, Jean Jacques, 509
Rubin, Irene S., 300, 320n, 374–376,
    391n

Rule-following behavior, 350
Rutgers, M. R., 19, 29n
Ryan, R. M., 345, 351n

Saari, R., 352n
Sabatier, Paul A., 405, 407, 408, 410, 411, 419, 425n, 426n
Sabine, 503
Saetren, Harald, 409, 411, 415, 423n, 426n
Saint Simon, Duc de, 102, 108
Salamon, Lester M., 27, 29n
Salanick, G. R., 345, 352n
Saltzstein, Alan, 490
Sandeep, P., 315, 320n
Sanitarian, 126
Sarno, D. J., 271, 275n
Schattschneider, E. E., 451, 456n
Schein, E. H., 310, 311, 320n, 348, 353n
Schelling, Thomas, 225
Schick, Alan, 445
Schils, E., 352n
Schneider, Anne, 413, 424n
School districts, 129
School lunch program, 457–470
Schools, 476, 481
Schwarz, John E., 146n
"Science of Public Administration: Three Problems" (Dahl), 21
Scientific-technological change, 163
Sciolino, Elaine, 208
Self-protection, 259
Self-serving motives, 345
Sellite, Claire, 426n
Selznick, Philip, 26, 410, 426n
Senior executive service (SES), 187–188
Sense of mission, 315
Separation of powers, 484
SES systems, 187–188
Sex (Madonna), 512–522
Shared leadership, 312
Shared values, 348–349
Shefter, Martin, 391n
Shepsle, Kenneth, 391n
Sherwood, Frank P., 188, 206n
Shih Kuo-heng, 169n
Shriver, Sargent, III, 421
Shultz, George, 185
Sick-outs, 202
Sikula, A. F., 315, 321n
Simo, G., 343, 351n
Simon, H. A., 22, 30n, 102, 105, 223, 225, 235n, 236n, 257–260,

299, 302, 314, 316, 317, 319, 321n, 345, 349, 352n, 353, 410, 416, 425n, 426n, 475n, 482, 484
Sims, H. P., 312, 321n
Sims, Laura S., 457
Sixteen Amendment, 131
Skocpol, Theda, 18, 30n
Skopcol, S., 30n
Skowronek, S., 18, 30n
Small eradication, 417–418
Smallwood, Frank, 404, 408, 420, 425n
Smith, Adam, 18, 108, 507
Smith, Alfred E., 86
Smithburg, Donald W., 236n, 257–260
Social Problems of an Industrial Civilization, The (Mayo), 157
Social science heterodoxy, 21–22, 28
Social structure, 163
Social technology, 83
Soelberg, P. O., 346, 353n
Sophocles, 503
SOPs, 483
Spatial thinking/communication, 273–274
Special districts, 129
Spencer, Herbert, 507
Spicer, M. W., 522n
Staff professionals, 192
Stakeholder analysis, 264
Stakeholders, 305–306
Stalking, 63–77
Standard operating procedures (SOPs), 483
Stanley, David T., 199, 205n, 206n
Starbuck, W. H., 122n
Starling, Grover, 3
State and Local Fiscal Assistance Act, 139–140
State SES systems, 188
Statism, 16
Status distance, 259
Stein, Harold, 3, 4n
Steinbauer, Paula, 296, 297, 299
Stephen, L., 121n
Stigler, George, 419, 426n
Stillman, Richard J., II, 17, 182, 183, 205n, 300, 321n
Stiver, C., 522n
Stokes, Sybil L., 53n
Stories, 273
Strategic planning, 264
Straussman, Jeffrey, 392n
Strikes, 202

"Study of Administration, The" (Wilson), 6, 403, 444
Stull, D. D., 311, 319n
Stupak, Ronald, 187, 205n
Sub-Cabinet officials, 186–187
Subformal communication networks, 266
Subnational governments, 144
Subsystems. *See* Bureaucratic subsystems
Successful implementation, 412–413
Successions of comparisons, 233–234
Successive limited comparisons (branch) method, 223–224, 226–228, 234–235
Sufficing, 258
Suicide of Admiral Boorda, 353–372
Symbolic implementation, 421–422
Systemthink, 275

t'Hart, Paul, 274, 275, 276n
Taft, William Howard, 183
TANF, 142–143
Task design, 313
Task motivation, 316–317
Taylor Law, 200
Taylor, Frederick W., 19, 30n, 156, 157, 297, 473
Tead, Ordway, 21
Team research, 158
Technetronic age, 190
Technocratic politics, 189
Tell and sell communication approaches, 269–270
Temporary Assistance to Needy Families (TANF), 142–143
Tenth Amendment, 130
Tenure in office, 58
Terry, L. D., 311, 321n, 522n
Thayer, Frederick C., 509, 512n
Thiokol, Morton, 266, 275
Thompson, D. F., 349, 350, 353n
Thompson, Frank J., 2, 206n, 300, 312, 321n, 391n
Thompson, Victor A., 236n, 257–260, 273, 509, 512n
Three Es, 297
Tilton, Timothy, 146n
Timony, John, 273
Timpane, P. Michael, 485n
Tools-makers, 26–27
Toonen, T., 424n
Top-down models, 408–409
Townships, 129

Traditional authority, 51
Trice, H. M., 310, 311, 321n
Truman, David B., 474, 475n
Tuberculosis containment, 418
Tukey, John, 415, 426n
Tullock, G., 266, 277n
Turcotte, William E., 481, 485n
Turner, Frederick Jackson, 81, 87n
Two-way asymmetrical model,
    270–271

UMRA, 142–143
Unfunded mandates, 139, 142–143
Unfunded Mandates Reform Act
    (UMRA), 142–143
"Uniforms in the Closet" (Egan), 170
Unionized subsystem, 199–202
United States v. Lopez, 144
Upward communication, 266

Values, 348–349
ValuJet airline disaster, 321–337
van de Graaf, Henk, 409, 424n
van Dijk, Asje, 409, 424n
Van Horn, Carl E., 405, 407, 408,
    426n
Van Meter, Donald S., 405, 408,
    426n
Van Riper, Paul P., 206n
Vaughan, Diane, 122
Vertical functional autocracies, 138
Vining, A. R., 309, 319n
Vinzant, J. C., 343, 347, 349, 353n
Vizzard, William J., 275, 279
Volcker, Paul A., 198, 206n
Volcker Commission, 198
VPI refounders, 26
Vroom, V. H., 352n

"Waco" (Vizzard), 279
Waldman, S., 342, 353n

Waldo, Dwight, 4, 17n, 22, 296,
    498–501
Waldo, O., 30n
Walker, David B., 146n
Walton, E., 267, 277n
Wamsley, Gary L., 26, 30n, 300,
    312n, 353n
Wanous, J., 346, 347, 353n
Warner, W. Lloyd, 158
Warwick, D. P., 300, 312, 321n
Washington, George, 501
Waterman, A., 273, 276n
Waterman, R. H., 320n
Waterman, R. W., 300, 321n
Wealth of Nations (Smith), 507
Weatherley, Richard, 409, 426n
Webb, James, 312
Weber, A., 315, 319n
Weber, Max, 50–54, 484, 507
Weinberg, Martha, 425n
Weinberger, Caspar, 185, 204
Weingast, Barry, 391n
Weisband, E., 522n
Weiss, C. H., 318n
Weissenger-Baylon, Roger, 425n
Wellington, Harry H., 206n
Western Electric Company
    (Hawthorne experiments),
    160–169
Wheel pattern, 268
White, Leonard, 18, 20, 22, 30n,
    82n, 448
Whitehead, T. North, 160, 161,
    169n
"Wichita Confronts Contamination"
    (Rosegrant), 147
Wiebe, Robert, 19, 30n, 191, 206n
Wildavsky, Aaron, 404–406, 408,
    417, 425n, 522n
Wilkie, Roy, 501, 507, 511, 512n
Williams, Walter L., 305, 424n

Willoughby, W. W., 21
Wilson, James Q., 27, 303, 306, 310,
    312–315, 321n, 345, 351n, 473,
    475, 485n
Wilson, Woodrow, 1, 4–6, 18, 27,
    30n, 403, 444, 445, 474, 483
Winter Commission Report, 198
Winter, Ralph K., Jr., 206n
Winter, Soeren, 408, 426n
Winter, William A., 206n
Winter, William F., 198
Wise, Lois Recascino, 27, 315, 320,
    340–344, 350, 352n, 353n
Wishes and ideas, 85
*Without Sympathy or Enthusiasm:
    The Problem of Administrative
    Compassion* (Thompson),
    509
Wolf, Charles, Jr., 478, 485n
Wolf, James T., 26
Wolf, P. J., 299n, 300, 301, 303, 305,
    310, 311, 313, 314, 321n
Women seeking protection,
    63–77
Wood, B. D., 321n
Wright, Deil S., 146n
Wright, N. D., 311, 318n
Wright, Paula, 409, 413, 425n
Wright-Isak, C., 343, 344, 352n
Wrightsman, Lawrence S., 411,
    426n
Wynne, Edward A., 485n
Wyszomirski, M. J., 312, 321n

Yankee City (Warner), 158
Young, Andrew, 454
Young, James, 448
Yugoslavia, 207–217
Yukl, G., 311, 321n

Zimbardo, P. G., 270, 277n